Woody Allen

Also by Patrick McGilligan

AS AUTHOR

Funny Man: Mel Brooks
Young Orson: The Years of Luck and Genius on the Path to Citizen Kane
Nicholas Ray: The Glorious Failure of an American Director
Oscar Micheaux: The Great and Only
Alfred Hitchcock: A Life in Darkness and Light
Clint: The Life and Legend
Fritz Lang: The Nature of the Beast
Jack's Life: A Biography of Jack Nicholson
George Cukor: A Double Life
Robert Altman: Jumping Off the Cliff
Cagney: The Actor as Auteur

AS EDITOR

Tender Comrades: A Backstory of the Hollywood Blacklist (with Paul Buhle)
Film Crazy: Interviews with Hollywood Legends
Still Film Crazy After All These Years: Collected Interviews
Six Screenplays by Robert Riskin
Backstory: Interviews with Screenwriters of Hollywood's Golden Age
Backstory 2: Screenwriters of the 1940s and 1950s
Backstory 3: Interviews with Screenwriters of the 1960s
Backstory 4: Screenwriters of the 1970s and 1980s
Backstory 5: Interviews with Screenwriters of the 1990s

Woody Allen

A Travesty of a Mockery of a Sham

Patrick McGilligan

HARPER

An Imprint of HarperCollins*Publishers*

 For information, address HarperCollins Publishers, 195 Broadway, New York, NY 10007.

HarperCollins books may be purchased for educational, business, or sales promotional use. For information, please email the Special Markets Department at SPsales@harpercollins.com.

FIRST EDITION

Designed by Bonni Leon-Berman

Library of Congress Cataloging-in-Publication Data has been applied for.

ISBN 978-0-06-294133-6

24 25 26 27 28 LBC 5 4 3 2 1

For Walter Bernstein and Martin Ritt,
who are sorely missed

Everyone has three lives: a public life,
a private life, and a secret life.

—Gabriel García Márquez

Contents

Fanfare

2025

Death Defying Act

Woody Allen wakes up early in the morning after a bad night's sleep, as usual, and fumbling with the thick, dark-frame glasses that are his signature look, he glances in the mirror and what does he see? A stooped, partly deaf old man with once carrot-colored hair now snow white and raggedy, with watery brown eyes—one eye drooping—but otherwise recognizable as himself, and he doesn't look so bad for age eighty-nine going on ninety.

We know that face, and probably the clothes he will select to wear today, from stage and screen, television and films, dating back to the time in the early 1960s when Allen rose to fame as one of America's funniest and most influential comedians and, later, arguably just as hilarious and even more influential as a singular filmmaker whose work set the standard for quality, range, and depth, whose insistence on his individuality and independence defied the realities of the American cinema, and whose example inspired many in his wake.

He probably will have the same breakfast he enjoyed as a boy—cereal with banana slices, counting the slices—skim the New York Times, *where the name Woody Allen can no longer be mentioned with impunity, much less any frequency; and then he will likely spend most of the morning doing some writing on scripts—a play, a film. Allen will take pills and do his exercises, including working out on the treadmill, as recommended by his doctors. After a light lunch he may go for a walk through his beloved Central Park with his wife of twenty-five-plus years, Soon-Yi Previn, the daughter of the actress Mia Farrow, who starred in a few of the most acclaimed Woody Allen pictures. He will practice his clarinet for an hour or so in the afternoon, maybe give an interview or two to foreign journalists by telephone or Zoom. He and Soon-Yi have two daughters, both college graduates with good careers, who may join the couple for dinner. Friends from the old days also may drop by. After dinner the world-famous man may watch a little sports on television before going to bed early, so he can sleep badly and rise early anew and the next day do more of what he likes doing best—write and write.*

One reality Woody Allen has been defying for a long while now is death. Not that Death: not the Dark Everlasting that haunts his movies, usually humorously, most recently in his penultimate film to date, Rifkin's Festival, *in which Death plays a mean game of chess. No—the living death of being declared an "unperson" by the Woke Generation, the most militant of whose representatives do not care if the entertainer has ever been charged or convicted of a crime, but they believe he molested his seven-year-old daughter in 1992, among the many other negative things about him they believe. These true believers have tried to blackball his films, pressure other celebrities into denouncing him, destroy his ability to direct more movies—"cancel" him as a person. However, in this crusade his enemies have not been entirely successful, because even* Rifkin's Festival, *after modest foreign success, sneaked into some twenty-six US theaters in 2022, which is more than the blacklisted Hollywood Reds could have hoped to achieve at the height of McCarthyism in the 1950s. And Allen's golden oldies continue to play on television and on the Internet, and they are embedded in the DNA of our popular culture regardless of the opprobrium heaped on his name.*

But what's in a name? Who is the real Woody Allen? Are there still vestiges in the man of Allan Stewart Konigsberg, once a surprisingly normal, mischievous, wisecracking boy? In what ways is the adult version, the comedian and filmmaker who enjoyed decades of success and popularity before self-destructing, an amalgam of truth and fiction? The answer reveals much about show business, the mercurial nature of fame and public favor, and the inevitable consequences of leading a fluid double life.

As this is being written, the fiftieth film directed by Woody Allen, which he made in Paris entirely in the French language in the autumn of 2022, has been completed and released. Fifty films—a higher number counting telefilms and movies in which he merely acted—as writer, director, or star is a remarkable output over seven decades of work, a formidable statistic even before you get to the box office and accolades and awards that don't come as often anymore, not that he has ever cared. Coup de chance, *the Paris film, might be a clinker, as some critics said. Or, according to others, it might be sharp-minded and entertaining, if not the masterpiece he would tell you has always eluded him. Still, Allen would give away any or all of his record number of Writers Guild awards or Oscars, he often said in interviews, for just one more day of life.*

Oh, that other death? The real death—the last day of his life—is coming. Perhaps the comedian and filmmaker's death will finally assuage his enemies, who want him shunned, condemned, vilified, hounded to the grave. His father lived until one hundred. His mother also made it nearly to her centenary. So when Allen, a man who has always lived by the clock, rises early tomorrow, he will be keenly aware of the most important clock of all ticking. . . .

This is his story.

I

Easy Writer

Chapter 1

1935

Prep Day

Birth, a Misspent Boyhood, Easy Writing, and Gags for Sale

Death worried him as a little boy, and from boyhood he was inclined to joke about things that worried him. Death worried Diane Keaton too, among many things they had in common, and decades later Woody Allen tried to reassure her. Death is probably like what happens after the injection for a colonoscopy, Allen told the actress. Death is a dark, peaceful sleep. So don't worry, Keaton—he called her Keaton—death is pretty much like a colonoscopy. The problem is, he added, waggling his eyebrows à la Groucho Marx, life is like the prep day.

Prep day for Allan Stewart Konigsberg began on December 1, 1935. The baby was not named Woody Allen, because that creature was concocted over time in his imagination, a fabrication that shape-shifted with the years. Some found the Woody Allen creature funny, entertaining, or artistic, while others, even early in his career, discerned a Frankenstein monster. Yet in many ways, growing up, the short, scrawny boy with an unruly thatch of orange-red hair was typical as well as precocious, and no soothsayer could have predicted he would grow into one of the most peculiar animals in the human zoo, or that he was headed for a public burning after a spectacular rise to fortune and celebrity—and an even more precipitous and spectacularly unexpected fall.

"I'm complicated," the film-crazy, lovelorn Allan Felix says in *Play It Again, Sam*. Allen wrote himself into the lead character he was playing with his own birth name: Allan. He went so far as to describe the character in the text as "a short man with red hair and glasses." Repeatedly, he declared in interviews: "I am him." He'd keep that idea fluid—how similar he was to his characters in films—but inarguably, Woody Allen née Allan Stewart Konigsberg *is* complicated, contradictory in ways, a weave of personal and professional ironies and paradoxes. The boy version was also more complicated than any surface impression, and from minute one of his prep day the complicated nature of the boy began to compound curiously as he grew.

In 1935, the year of his first prep day, Ernest Hemingway was writing *To Have and Have Not* in the Bahamas. Jazzman Sidney Bechet was running a tailor shop in Harlem to make ends meet. Gertrude Stein visited the US for the first time in decades, sipped tea with Eleanor Roosevelt in the White House, met with Charles Chaplin in Hollywood, and returned to Paris. The fast-rising comic Bob Hope made his network radio debut. Babe Ruth played his last game for the Boston Braves (he wears a Yankees uniform in *Zelig*, however). *Top Hat* with Fred Astaire and Ginger Rogers and music by Irving Berlin ranked number two at the box office and was Oscar-nominated for Best Picture. Ingmar Bergman, in his late teens, was spending his summers in Germany, where he attended a Nazi rally in Weimar and fell under the spell of the "unbelievably charismatic" Adolf Hitler, for a while becoming an avid supporter of *der Führer*. The Reichstag enacted the Nuremberg Laws against Jews.

WOODY ALLEN'S PARENTS, Mr. and Mrs. Konigsberg, were "characters," and they recur as characters in much of his work. Even after their boy became a world-renowned comedian, writer, actor, and director making his own movies, his parents were inclined to wish aloud that he had entered a more solid if not stolid profession. Maybe he should have become a pharmacist. They boasted colorful traits and idiosyncrasies, and in his stand-up act, short stories, plays, and films, their son would poke unflagging fun at—to the point of ridiculing—their foibles.

Martin Konigsberg was his father. His mother was Nettie Cherry. They married in June 1930, and within five years Nettie delivered their firstborn, who was probably underweight. (The birth certificate has never been made public.) Sunday, December 1, 1935, was his official birth date, although

Allen claimed in his autobiography he was actually born on November 30, "and my parents pushed the date so I could start off on day one."

Both parents were immigrants. Isaac Konigsberg, Martin's father, came from Russia at the turn of the century, and after marrying Janette, also a Russian national ("she was fleeing Russian pogroms and he compulsory military service"), Isaac pursued the American dream. He rose up before World War I to own a string of taxis and movie palaces including the Midwood Theater, where his grandson would grow up expending his youth "in flight from reality," in his words. Isaac kept a box at the Metropolitan Opera and sailed to Europe for the horse races. He fathered three boys and favored the oldest, Martin, born in 1900, even arranging for Martin to serve as a mascot for the Brooklyn Dodgers. "No high school, the Navy at sixteen, on a firing squad in France when they killed an American sailor for raping a local girl," Allen later recalled of his father. "A medal-winning marksman, always loved pulling a trigger." Martin survived the war, once swimming miles to shore after his boat was shelled; and drove a Kissel Roadster, a lavish gift from his father, around postwar Europe.

Isaac Konigsberg suffered his first financial reversal in the 1919 recession, and after the Wall Street crash almost ten years on he was reduced to getting by as a butter-and-egg man in a Greenwich Village market in lower Manhattan. Martin was the chief salesman and candler—a candlelight method of nurturing the viability of eggs as they incubated.

Nettie Cherry's father, Leon, meanwhile emigrated from Vienna at age twenty-six in 1891, married Sarah Hoff and, by 1908, the year of Nettie's birth, owned a luncheonette near their Lower East Side abode, where his wife helped with the cooking and customers. Nettie was one of five sisters, the youngest of seven Cherry children. By 1930, by which time the Cherrys had moved from Manhattan to the Bronx, a temporary stop for the family before they landed in Brooklyn, Nettie, in her early twenties, had begun to keep accounts for another merchant in the Greenwich Village market. She struck up a friendship with Isaac Konigsberg, whom she saw as a kind, older, cultivated gentleman. Isaac saw her as a match for Martin.

Accounts have described Martin Konigsberg as a hail-fellow-well-met type who physically resembled the Hollywood tough guy George Raft. Thirty years of age when he married Nettie, Martin inherited a high-roller swagger from his father and was always generous with money to the point of profligacy. Although steeped in butter and eggs until he was forty, at which time Isaac retired, Martin must have been hardworking, if occupationally peripatetic, since the jobs he held over time included pool-hall manager, bartender, taxi driver, bookmaker, gem engraver, and waiting tables at Sammy's Bowery Follies, a lower Manhattan saloon and cabaret known, half-ironically to swells, as the "Stork Club of the Bowery." Allan's father mixed with the constabulary through a relative who made police badges, and mingled with equal affability with organized crime, running summer bets to the Saratoga Race Course for Brooklyn waterfront mobster Albert Anastasia.

Nettie, her son would say uncharitably in interviews, had a beaky nose and resembled the Marx brother with the moustache and cigar. The parents in *Take the Money and Run* wear Groucho masks. A sympathetic female biographer studied Nettie's wedding portrait and found the twenty-one-year-old bride to be "an attractive young woman, a spunky, tart-tongued redhead." Bookkeeping, which was Nettie's lifelong occupation, provided a good foothold and reliable income for high-school-educated women before technology simplified accounting.

During Allan's toddler years the Konigsbergs lived within the Flatbush neighborhood of Brooklyn, moving several times. Often, the family resided in the upper stories of houses where they pooled the rent with Nettie's older sister—the sister closest in age—Celia, a stenographer; and her husband, Joe Cohen, an electrical parts contractor, who brought fish home for dinner from angler friends in Sheepshead Bay. (Celia, Ceil or Cecilia—Cecilia is the name of Mia Farrow's character in *The Purple Rose of Cairo*—are names that recur in Woody Allen films.) At times the Konigsbergs lived with other cousins, aunts, uncles, and vague kin "running in and out of rooms," including German-speaking relatives fleeing from Hitler's Third Reich. Extended families sharing close quarters were common in Flatbush. Though Martin still worked for his father, Isaac, he splurged on dinner and dance dates with Nettie at the Tavern on the Green in Central Park when it opened in 1934.

Baby Allan happened to be born in the Bronx because the family thought there were better hospitals in that borough, and when the family required a doctor, they visited a Park Avenue physician in Manhattan. Although the Konigsbergs never owned a house, and they were "lower-lower-middle-class," in their son's words, Flatbush was a comfortable district, "one of

Brooklyn's most desirable residential neighborhoods" according to 1939's Federal Writers' Project *WPA Guide to New York City*. Much of the time the family was nestled within Midwood, south of Flatbush, which was predominantly middle-class and mostly Jewish—primarily Orthodox, like the Konigsbergs, or Hasidic. Allen recalled the main commercial drag, Avenue J in Midwood, as "a paradise" of candy and toy stores, delicatessens, bakeries, butcher shops, Chinese restaurants, poolrooms, and motion picture theaters. The residential streets were lined with trees. The big houses had porches, front lawns, backyards.

Martin was a mensch ("a sweet guy, warmer, more demonstrably affectionate" than Nettie, Allen would recall) who worked his odd jobs, religiously played the numbers, and tithed to his son, bringing home from F.A.O. Schwarz a cowboy costume with six-shooters for Allan when he was ten years old and, later, when the youth was in high school, routinely leaving a fiver for the teenager on his night table. ("The other kids I knew were getting fifty cents or maybe one dollar" allowances.) Extra money trickled in from cousins, uncles, and all those aunts ("I was the cynosure of my mother's five sisters, the only male child, the darling of these sweet yentas"), supplying endless pocket change for recreation. The boy's playthings included a Lionel chemistry set—another of his father's F.A.O. Schwarz purchases—which Allan used to dye his mother's fur coat, an incident re-created in *Radio Days*. As a teenager he owned his own typewriter and several musical instruments. The family boasted an excellent radio and an early television set. When Nettie went back to work, she hired babysitters and a weekly cleaning woman. Growing up, the boy was more pampered than deprived.

COMING FROM AN observant background, Nettie kept a kosher kitchen, celebrated seders, and served her big weekly supper on the Sabbath, inviting neighbors and relatives. Claiming indifference and atheism, Martin preferred to skip Yom Kippur and other ceremonies religious, opting for Chinese takeout. Starting at age five Allan began attending a weekly Hebrew school, where he learned to read and write in the Semitic language of the Jewish people. But Irish and Italian Catholic families dominated blocks of Midwood, and Nettie was broad-minded enough to send her boy to an interfaith camp one summer, where, as Woody Allen liked to joke in one of his later stand-up routines, "I was sadistically beaten up by boys of all races and creeds."

At the time of the 1940 census the Konigsbergs and Cohens (then childless) shared a six-room flat on the upper floor of a two-story brick rowhouse at 968 East Fourteenth Street near Avenue J in Midwood, a half mile from Public School 99 on East Tenth, where Martin Konigsberg had attended elementary school. The farsighted Nettie submitted her son to an IQ test and enrolled the boy in a "special school for sharp kids" at Hunter College, but "the long train ride every day from Brooklyn into Manhattan was too grueling for my mother or my aunt, who alternated taking me on the subway." Following in his father's footsteps, Allan entered PS 99 in the fall of 1940.

In many later interviews he recalled that around this time in his life—kindergarten, or first grade—he began to view the world as a coffin half-empty, lying in wait for him. Life would inevitably consist of disappointment, troubles, death. Hitherto "a nice, sweet, cheerful boy," in his words, Allan underwent a psychological metamorphosis, feeling burdened by "an intense sense of failure," a "genetic dissatisfaction" with himself and existence in general, a pervasive pessimism and melancholy. He suffered bouts of depression.

The anxiety and foreboding that became a hallmark of his comedy may have been seeded by an early incident in his childhood. In the American Masters documentary about Woody Allen's life and career, first shown on television in 2011, the famous man was still talking about the mother's helper who one day stared malevolently down at her ward as he cooed in a cradle. Swaddling him too tightly in a blanket, the nanny purred she could smother him if she wished and stick his body in the trash. (Still, he could joke about it: "The world would have been poorer a number of great one-liners.") When he started at PS 99 Nettie returned to full-time bookkeeping for a florist, and Martin worked nights. Daily care was handed over to minders, relatives, and teachers.

His mother was never forgiven. Nor was the school. While some people ranked PS 99 among Brooklyn's exceptional primary schools, the little boy underwent his banishment from home with resentment. Decades later, any mention of PS 99 stirred egregious memories. Woody Allen recalled the PS 99 teachers as "backward and anti-Semitic . . . stupid and mean . . . unpleasant people." Or: "Mean-looking, sorry, sad, and bitter."

Indeed, some of the teachers may have been stupid or worse, but they did not appreciate Woody Allen's anti-nostalgia. An early biographer spoke to several PS 99 educators from the school of that era, and one said the Konigsberg boy was a nonentity, whom she had discussed "with other teachers and none of us can call him to mind." No one disputes that the young nonentity seemed born to write, however. He wrote easily and fast, he wrote exceptionally well, and rarest of all he enjoyed the writing. He achieved an epiphany in third grade when during "library period" he was dispatched to select a book from the school library, practicing the newly learned Dewey decimal system. Plucking *Six Plays by Kaufman and Hart* from the shelf ("the smallest book I could find in the stacks"), he began to read something called *You Can't Take It with You*, whose title "drew my attention simply because that was the phrase used by my father to defend the inevitable results of his numbers habit." As he turned the pages of this stage play by George S. Kaufman and Moss Hart, the first script he had ever heard of much less read, the description of the setting made him chuckle: "The home of Martin Vanderhof—just around the corner from Columbia University, but don't go looking for it." Turning the pages, the third-grader read on, "a life-changing experience. Not only was the play truly funny and imaginative, but the agglomeration of hilarious oddballs cohabiting in surreal chaos was enormously warming and magical."

Although some time would pass before he developed true writerly ambitions, the play's "delightful cartoon lunacy never left my system." The boy easily wrote in a similar vein. "Although I never laughed out loud then, I was a funny kid," he recalled. "My viewpoint was funny, and I said funny things." He channeled his gift into class assignments, unsettling teachers when, at age twelve, for example, the adolescent expounded on "How I Spent My Summer Vacation" by describing a pretty girl at the beach as someone with whom he could imagine having "a child by a future marriage."

He freely admitted keeping a low profile in PS 99, although sitting in class was "never a pleasurable experience. It was a spectacular treat to be sick because you could avoid school." Encouraged by Nettie, he joined the Cub Scouts. "I hated it," Allen wrote in his memoir. "I never learned even the most basic scouting skills like reading a compass." He took jabs at Cub and Boy Scouts in his stand-up comedy act and in many later movies, but the Scouts didn't torture him for very long, and they were usually mild-mannered jokes.

The boy made friends, yet then as later he wasn't an easy mixer like his father. His aloofness was rooted defensively first at home, then at school. His ability to socially integrate was not helped by the fact that the Konigsberg family kept trailing after relatives into new homes and neighborhoods, living for one idyllic summer in Long Beach in Nassau County about nineteen miles east of Brooklyn, a beach city nestled on a barrier island between the Reynolds Channel and the Atlantic Ocean. The Konigsbergs lived close to the Atlantic boardwalk and lingered in Long Beach past August. Allan was briefly enrolled in a new school. "I remember going to school barefoot, walking on the beach," recalled the future forsworn enemy of sun and sand. "I liked it a lot." The Long Beach school was better than PS 99, he also said later, because "the kids were dumber."

Then the Konigsbergs followed the Cohens to Port Chester, a village fifty miles north across Long Island Sound, where the family lived for another spell before returning to Brooklyn. Once again, the family showed up in Midwood, this time cohabiting with Nettie's oldest sibling, Sadie, whose family included husband Joe Wishnick, a garment factory worker, and their two daughters—Rita and Phyllis—both older than their boy cousin.

The Wishnick girls loomed as role models for the latest addition to the Konigsberg family: baby Ellen, called Letty, her middle name, who was born on the very same day as her older brother—December 1—in 1943. Eight-year-old Allan, now displaced as an only child, could have nursed a grudge, but according to all accounts he hoisted his maverick flag and doted on baby sister Letty from first sight. His fondness for New Year's Eve, which came one month after their joint birthday, probably originated from that year, when an aunt awakened him for the rare family celebration at midnight—as 1943 became 1944—which also happens in *Radio Days*.

The Konigsbergs shared the American popular fascination with crime and criminals. The only real book lying around their house, Woody Allen recalled in later interviews, was a well-thumbed edition of *The Gangs of New York*, a nonfiction history of the underworld by Herbert Asbury, first published in 1927. "I knew gangsters like most boys knew ball players," Allen said. The Konigsbergs returned to Midwood in time for the boy to hear reports of the execution of Murder Inc. racketeer Louis Buchalter, commonly known as Lepke, which were broadcast on the radio in March 1944.

A few years later came his thirteenth birthday and bar mitzvah. From Sammy's Bowery Follies Martin inveigled the variety singer Mabel Sidney, a tubby belter of schmaltzy standards—a precursor of Lou Canova, the lounge lizard of *Broadway Danny Rose*—to entertain friends and family. Yet the highlight of the occasion was the newly bar mitzvahed teenager mimicking Al Jolson crooning "Swanee" from *The Jolson Story*, a recent biopic of Al Jolson starring Larry Parks. This blackface performance was a curious rite of passage for many boys at bar mitzvahs dating as far back as the Jewish Jolson's popularization of the song in *The Jazz Singer*, the first "talkie" in 1927. However, the movie the boy was really thinking of at his bar mitzvah, Woody Allen said years later, was the "B" film noir he had seen the day before: *Canon City*, about a penitentiary breakout.

With the family back in Midwood, the boy was also back in the bosom of the dread PS 99, from which Allan Konigsberg escaped by graduating from eighth grade in June 1949. He scribbled, in the autograph book of classmate Richard Soreff, the first surviving example of his incipient genius: "Roses are red / Violets are blue / Alan Ladd is handsome / So what!"

If the teenager nursed antipathies that would harden into adult phobias, quite apart from his aversion to dying, by the time he entered high school the youth also had mapped out a quadrant of enthusiasms that would give him pleasure over the course of his long life. He was already deeply in love with movies and almost as much with sports, magic, and jazz, especially the New Orleans variant.

IN 2014, OVER lunch one day on the set of *Irrational Man*, Allen and his sister, Letty, reminisced about their youth and their mother Nettie's cooking. Every day Nettie brought home "half a cake" from their favorite bakery, Ebinger's, encouraging Allen's lifelong sweet tooth. "By Letty's account," according to Allen's authorized biographer Eric Lax, "she [Nettie] was a good if predictable cook: Monday fish; Tuesday lamb chops; Wednesday steak; Thursday liver; Friday candles were lit for a Shabbat dinner with chicken but no prayers. There were always extra people that night, making perhaps a dozen in all around the table. The housekeeper who came on Fridays would answer the phone, 'You coming tonight? Just tell me your name.' Saturday leftovers; Sunday Chinese."

The names and faces around the family table rotated constantly as the Konigsbergs moved between houses, and whenever they changed their address Allan had to make corresponding personal adjustments to new synagogues, schools, playgrounds, relatives, and friends. "When I think about it, it's so clear why I'm so neurotic and I've had such a neurotic life," Woody Allen reflected years later. "Think of the number of times I changed school and moved around, having to get acclimated to new friends and new schools and liking it or hating it—usually hating it."

Movies were comfort food. Their fictional universe, their alternate realities, fueled his dreams. In those days it seemed as though there were an endless number of movie houses in Flatbush, including the Midwood Theater, near the Konigsbergs. Once in flush times owned by his grandfather Isaac Konigsberg, the Midwood was still a picture palace of sumptuous design with hundreds of seats and smartly dressed ushers.

His much-maligned mother took her son to his first motion pictures, including *Snow White and the Seven Dwarfs*. Three-year-old Allan broke from his seat and dashed up the aisle trying to touch the flickering images. Two years later, she held his hand at *Pinocchio*. When she took him to Tyrone Power's swashbuckler *The Black Swan* in 1942, the six-year-old had a fleeting notion—"Hey, I could make movies like this!"—which he just as quickly forgot. The same year, Nettie brought him to *The Road to Morocco* with Bob Hope and Bing Crosby, and immediately he became the world's most fanatical Hope fan, realizing "from that moment on exactly what I wanted to do with my life." Only the Marx Brothers rivaled his devotion to Hope. While their careers were winding down by the 1940s, the anarchic Marx Brothers comedies were often revived in Brooklyn theaters. The acerbic, womanizing heels he'd play in Woody Allen films were akin to Bob Hope and Groucho.

According to Lax, as a boy Allan did not enjoy the "good love picture" his mother sometimes picked out, "so if only for reduced common interest he attended just a handful of movies with her, almost all before Letty was born, and fewer with his father." Among these, one of the last was *The White Cliffs of Dover* in 1944, with Nettie yanking Allan up the aisle at the end complaining, "Why can't you be more like Roddy McDowall?"

Her son was hypnotized by moving pictures and fascinated by how they were created. One day, heading home after a movie, eight-year-old Allan rummaged through alley garbage cans and found discarded 35mm snippets of *Four Jills in a Jeep*, a musical reenactment of Hollywood stars putting on shows for overseas GIs. The boy endlessly pored over the few frames he managed to salvage, holding the celluloid strips of comedian Phil Silvers and "Brazilian Bombshell" Carmen Miranda up to the light. These were precious keepsakes.

On Sundays his father, Martin Konigsberg, was more likely to take his son to war pictures, sports "biopics," or Westerns—genres Woody Allen would assiduously avoid in his later filmmaking career. "Personally," he said later, "I've never cared greatly for Westerns except for *Shane* which, for me, is a masterpiece." Together father and son went to see *Beau Geste* with Gary Cooper, *Salute to the Marines* with Wallace Beery, Cecil B. DeMille's *The Story of Dr. Wassell* also with Coop, *The Babe Ruth Story* starring William Bendix, and *City of Bad Men*, a shoot-'em-up with a side plot involving a Gentleman Jim Corbett boxing match.

Martin's greatest contribution to his cultural education was sweeping the boy off to Manhattan for his sixth birthday. Allan was bowled over by Times Square with its infinity of theaters and shops packed into a wedge stretching for blocks. He returned with his father to Times Square on many future Sundays. A different area of Manhattan, the Upper East Side, would become another lodestar in his teenage years, after Allan began to add Fred Astaire, MGM musicals, and champagne comedies to his growingly sophisticated moviegoing diet. He yearned for those Upper East Side penthouses with elegantly dressed ladies walking around and uttering bons mots. His "biggest regret" in life was that "my parents didn't live in Manhattan," he said ruefully decades later.

Intrepidly, by age ten, he regularly hopped the subway to Times Square, seeing all the pictures on offer, but he also stood first in line most Saturdays for the noon opening of the Midwood, where he'd spend all day watching the double or triple features. The boy schemed to win the audience contests for a tiddlywinks game. While watching movies, he gorged on Raisinets, Milk Duds, Chuckles, or Jujubes, sweet-tooth snacks for which the adult Woody Allen never lost his taste; he was known to bring malteds to his sets and offer Snickers bars from his pocket to journalists during an interview. For a "timid" and "withdrawn" boy, as his father later described him, who often stayed in his bedroom doing secret things behind a closed door, movie theaters were the home away from home—the interior home of his imagination—walled off from the real world.

"You would see pirates and you would be on the sea," the grown comedian and film director would gush when reminiscing, "and then you would be in a penthouse in Manhattan with beautiful people. The next day you'd go to another house, and you'd be in a battle with the Nazis and in the second feature you'd be together with the Marx Brothers. It was just a total, total joy, the greatest kind of tranquilizer and embalmment."

Poring through newspaper listings, Allan discovered a Flatbush theater with a regular lineup of low-budget, lowbrow, often knockabout farces that were distinctly less classy but more rousing than the champagne comedies. There the double and triple features were interspersed with live vaudeville acts ("a singer, a tap dancer, acrobats, another singer, a comedian") and accompanied by full orchestras. The aging vaudevillians could be counted on for the corniest of gags, the wackiest impressions of movie stars. The low-class variety revues were another form of bliss. On ticket stubs and candy wrappers Allan wrote down the funniest jokes of the vaudevillians, which he'd test at school when called upon, doing his essays, or bantering with friends.

"I WAS A loner from an early time," Woody Allen said in later interviews. But the amount of time he boasted about spending alone in his room at home, even eating his meals apart from his family, as he always insisted, must be balanced by the many friends, relatives, and activities that accrued to the packed résumé of his youth. The loner had many good influences that were like a Greek chorus, always hovering behind him, whispering and nudging.

A family acquaintance gift-wrapped the E-Z Deluxe Magic Set for his tenth birthday, and for his thirteenth and bar mitzvah a relative gave him *Illustrated Magic* by Ottokar Fischer, an early picture-guide to magic tricks, first published in Austria in 1929. "This book," he said later, "with its photos of exciting equipment, Chinese boxes, a vanishing bird cage, billiard balls and silks, a guillotine, and myriad other paraphernalia, whetted an interest in me that grew into an obsession." Using such tools, behind the closed door of his bedroom, he learned to shuffle cards and disappear coins. Like-minded friends accompanied his endless forays to the Circle Magic Shop, tucked into a Times Square arcade, where he could buy magic supplies and handbooks.

Although his official biographer would state Woody Allen "generally avoids encountering heroes of his even when they're alive," the opposite would seem to be the case, and heroes began to cross his path, early on, materializing next to him as easily as they do in *Zelig*. One day, playing hooky from high school, Allan and a friend spotted comedian Milton Berle at the Circle Magic Shop. At the time Berle was a television celebrity, the host of NBC's number-one-rated *Texaco Star Theater*, but that did not deter Allan from approaching the star, sticking out his hand, and introducing himself: "Henny Youngman." Berle didn't blink. "Red Skelton," the comic replied.

When Allan told Berle he was something of a magician, Berle said if the youth could demonstrate the traditional one-hand cut, maybe he'd find a spot for him on his prime-time show. Allan brought out a deck of cards and attempted the sleight of hand, which he had practiced for hours at home alone in the hushed sanctuary of his room. Nervously, however, the youth bungled the simple trick. Berle took the cards, executing the classic move faultlessly. "That's OK," Berle sympathized before leaving, "I don't usually work with kids."

For a while Allan fantasized about growing up to become a professional magician. As a teenager he gave backyard shows and even staged his act at the East Midwood Jewish Center, with his sister, Letty, as his assistant, staring up at him worshipfully. Not only did he become adept at manipulating cards, coins, and scarves, friends say the youth was also a convincing "mentalist" with extrasensory powers. Twice the wannabe auditioned for *The Magic Clown*, a Sunday-morning fifteen-minute "fill-in" television series of games, songs, and magic tricks produced by NBC and sponsored by Bonomo Turkish Taffy. The series starred the "magic clown" Zovello with young talent plucked from the audience. Quite apart from any mistakes or clumsiness, Eric Lax reported, Allan's straight-from-the-kit act was too canned and grown-up for the show's preteen fans.

WOODY ALLEN'S LOVE of sports was also deeply embedded in boyhood and became another lifetime outlet for his energy. Not all sports: not ice hockey, not swimming or bicycling. He liked to walk everywhere, loathed bikes.

He was surprisingly athletic, despite his puny look. As a teenager Allan Konigsberg even tried boxing and later claimed he could have competed in his weight division in the Golden Gloves—"I had a vicious right upper cut"—if his parents had not vetoed it. He kept up with this cherished sport as a fan, and when Joe Louis fought Jersey Joe Walcott in December 1947, twelve-year-old Allan was among the gathering that watched the heavyweight bout on a neighbor's newfangled TV set. Years later down the road, himself a celebrity, the comedian and filmmaker could be spotted ringside at major fights in New York and Las Vegas.

He was fleet of foot and took a few medals in junior high track races, winning prizes like the hundred-yard-dash pin his character dangles before a failed date in *Play It Again, Sam*. He ran the ball as a halfback in neighborhood football until he fell to arguing with an opponent over the rules and ended up in the hospital with a flattened nose. He enjoyed schoolyard basketball and had "a good shot." (His enthusiasm for tennis would come later.)

Baseball was his most beloved sport. His father later insisted (despite countervailing theories) that the "Woody" nickname came from the regulation wooden bat the youth brought to neighborhood pickup games. Second base was his position; he and Mickey Rose—taller, muscular, handsome with tawny hair, his divorced mother an ex–chorus girl—bonded in high school art classes but their friendship was truly cemented when Rose played third base with Allan on second for the Police Athletic League's 70th Precinct team. Another pal, Jerry Epstein, played first, so it was three friends—Epstein to Konigsberg to Rose—for the triple play.

Accounts differ as to his actual prowess. "I was a terrific hitter," Woody Allen himself boasted, "always the lead-off" and "one of the first people picked." But Epstein thought Allan was just OK at baseball and better in track. "An excellent player who hit countless homers," official biographer Lax wrote, flattering his subject. The youth was also an exceptional fielder, Lax added, "in the manner of [Hall of Fame second baseman] Nellie Fox," who spent the greater percentage of his 1947–65 career with the Chicago White Sox, and who, in another similarity to Allan, was also a southpaw.

True to his iconoclastic nature, Allan was alone among his gang of friends in rooting *not* for the Brooklyn Dodgers—the home team, playing in nearby Ebbets Field, and the team for which his father had once served as mascot—but for the New York Giants, their deadly rivals from the Polo Grounds in Manhattan. Allan used to roller-skate to Ebbets ("I was a fast skater") when the Dodgers played the Giants, and beg for autographs from the stars. Dodgers shortstop "Arky Vaughan once kicked me when I asked for an autograph," he recalled.

Every Giants and Dodgers fan remembered where they were on the day Giants third baseman Bobby Thomson hit a home run off Dodgers right-hander Ralph Branca at the Polo Grounds in the ninth inning of the third game of the October 1951 playoffs, winning the National League pennant. Fifteen-year-old Allan was plying one of his many after-school jobs as a delivery boy for a Wall Street stationery firm. He stood "near a newsstand at a corner. Must have been a hundred people around me listening to the radio, and when [Thomson] hit it, we just exploded. We went crazy. That was the single greatest moment probably in sports in my lifetime."

Also, by 1951, his sophomore year in high school, Allan had been serendipitously introduced to jazz in the form of Sidney Bechet, whose concert from Paris on Saturday morning's *Ted Husing's Bandstand* was tape-recorded off the radio by pal Jerry Epstein. The frenzied music of the New Orleans–born saxophonist, clarinetist, and composer spoke to the teenager in ways he never stopped rhapsodizing about. Allan became hooked on Bechet, an expatriate who lived and died in Paris. He also became hooked on a romantic vision of Paris.

He and kindred jazz-crazy friends sought out rare recordings and frequented music shops and passed around LPs of Bechet, Jelly Roll Morton, Bunk Johnson, George Lewis, and Louis Armstrong. Another one of Allan's prized possessions was a top-quality Victrola. "While all the other kids were submerged in pop commercial music of the day, Patti Page, Frankie Laine, the Four Aces," he'd recall, "we sat at our record players playing jazz music, hour after hour." He and his friends frequented Childs Paramount, a cavernous jazz club under the Paramount Theater in Times Square. Allan took piano lessons and briefly tried the soprano sax. Eventually he settled on the clarinet, which Bechet had pioneered for jazz solos. The very first clarinet the teenager bought—conforming to the B-flat Boehm system—he'd treasure among his belongings for decades.

Enterprising to a fault, Allan observed Gene Sedric playing the saxophone and clarinet in Conrad Janis's jazz combo at Childs, then looked up Sedric in the telephone book and phoned his Harlem residence, asking Sedric if he gave lessons. The musician, who'd famously toured with Fats Waller, said it would cost the young caller a couple of dollars per session, and a short time later Sedric began regular subway rides to Midwood for clarinet tutorials. "He would just sit in the living room with me, and play something and say, 'Now you do it now.' And gradually I learned." Nettie, omnipresent, made sandwiches for Sedric.

Allan's love of sports was typically all-American. His love of jazz was less common for a teenager. The typical and the uncommon mingled in his personality. Among the many things Allan tinkered with privately in his bedroom, increasingly as a teenager he took out his clarinet and practiced—happily—for hours and hours. He never did learn to read music. He always played by ear and practiced by blowing notes along with his favorite recordings. He never claimed he got good; he was more likely to say the daily practice maintained a certain level of badness. Still, playing the clarinet remained forever among his few unalloyed pleasures.

MIDWOOD HIGH SCHOOL was among the finest Brooklyn secondary schools. The school was located on Bedford Avenue across from Brooklyn College about a mile and a half northeast of where the Konigsbergs lived, roughly from 1946 to 1952, at 1144 East Fifteenth, halfway between K and L. Students could select a general, commercial, or academic curriculum. Over seven hundred freshmen entered ninth grade in the fall of 1949.

Physically, Allan Konigsberg stood out for his pint size—he'd peak around 5 feet, 6 inches as a senior*—his wiry frame and long face topped by an unruly carrottop. Yet he tried for invisibility. School was "joyless," he always said: he hated the regimentation, the morning rituals (the "bullshit prayer" and Pledge of Allegiance), the peer pressures. His parents made him take the academic curriculum, but he evinced little enthusiasm. He may have been a budding writer, but he was not a bookworm. He pored over the sports pages, always lingering over the boxing prose of columnist Jimmy Cannon, and riffled Donald Duck, Bugs Bunny, and other comic books.

* His Selective Service System Registration Card, dated at age eighteen on December 15, 1953, says 5 feet, 6 inches.

Hard-boiled Mickey Spillane and humorist Max Shulman were among the few fictioneers he read.

He neglected the higher literature you might think would stimulate a prospective artist. "There was an awful lot he didn't like at school," recalled Mickey Rose. "Shakespeare, for instance. I remember he couldn't stand [Shakespeare]; or maybe he didn't understand him, then. I know he hated having to learn the plays." The teenager viewed most homework as "sleazy projects," and he "never, ever" completed the dull take-home assignments. After-school clubs and organized pastimes were likewise not for him. "He didn't take part in anything," said Jack Victor, another friend. "But he was terribly funny, and his close circle of friends knew it."

Midwood sponsored an annual variety show that was the highlight of his freshman year. The professional comic Morty Gunty emceed the revue and introduced the student talent. Allan, sitting in the audience and chuckling at Gunty's patter, was struck by another one of those sudden brain waves: Hey, maybe he could be a funnyman one day. He already had plenty of scribbled jokes and jotted-down ideas on scraps of paper, matchbook covers, ticket stubs, and "the torn-up inside of the Good & Plenty boxes." He wrote such notes to himself in soda shops, watching movies in theaters, at home in his room, anywhere the jokes and ideas popped into his head. It was a lifelong habit that never lapsed. Gunty went away after the talent show, but Woody Allen remembered the comic when casting the deli guys sitting around and telling tales in *Broadway Danny Rose*.

Allan thought he might test his comedy wings for another school talent show. He rehearsed a spiel that relied heavily on his impersonations of Peter Lorre, Clark Gable, and James Cagney. However, Jerry Epstein performed his audition before Allan, and his ease and confidence threw his classmate. Epstein's jokes were neither stale, nor cribbed. Thanks to his older brother Sandy, who emceed Dickinson College shows and behaved like a professional, Jerry had crafted a smooth routine, with "opening remarks, funny one-liners, material about war movies and gangster films." That is when he and Jerry became inseparable. Jerry's brother pitched in to teach Allan "a number of bits and gags" and Sandy was "a very big early influence on me."

Not that Allan Konigsberg had trouble being funny. Really, he couldn't stop himself. Apart from making wisecracks with friends and in the classroom, however, at Midwood High School his comedy was expressed mainly in writing. He wrote amusing English essays, drawing on his bottomless wellspring of humor. He developed tricks he'd carry over into filmmaking. One day back at PS 99 he'd referenced "Freud, the id, and the libido" in a school essay, even though he hardly knew "what I was talking about." From that point on the youth cultivated an "odd flair" for seizing on what he liked to call jots of superficial knowledge and turning these brief references into riffs that "make the reader or audience think I know much more than I do." Rain (Juliette Lewis) in *Husbands and Wives* boasts of the same knack from her girlhood, and Rain remembers having written a "whole story set in Paris" when she was ten, but "I'd never been there—it's a trick." "There was never a week when the composition I wrote was not the one that was read to class," Allen later averred.

His mother facilitated the purchase of a German-made Olympia Deluxe portable typewriter. Transferring ideas from brain to paper is the basic hurdle for writers, but it was never a problem for Woody Allen. "I just sit down at the typewriter and think funny," he told his high school newspaper in 1953. He kept the Olympia in working order and showed it off in the 2011 American Masters documentary about his life. "It cost me $40. . . . I think the guy told me it would be around long after my death, and I've typed everything that I've ever written—every script, every *New Yorker* piece, everything I've ever done—on this typewriter."

Very often, especially with the onset of puberty, his funniest essays revolved suggestively around cute girls. The teachers squirmed at lines like "She had an hourglass figure, and I'd like to play in the sand." Nettie became a familiar figure at Midwood High, summoned to the principal's office to defend her wayward son. "He's always flirting with girls," one teacher complained. That was true: "I've thought about sex since my first intimation of consciousness," he admitted. Perhaps he needed a psychiatrist, another teacher suggested.

Among the student body the teenager had a whispered, half-derisive nickname: Red. But "Red" was never teased or bullied, Allen later insisted, because he was not any kind of loser. He'd fight back, even if he sometimes did it by shrugging off the insults. "I am surprised at how Woody has downplayed the impact of Nazism on our youth," Alan Lapidus, editor of the Midwood High School student newspaper, said later. "We were bullied—not just because of the normal course of schoolyard bullying, but because we were Jewish."

Allan could deftly parry the verbal bullies. His humor and sangfroid stumped them. "Woody would get a little local harassment because he wasn't part of the crowd and he didn't join in things," explained Rose. On one occasion Rose accused a classmate of filching his favorite fountain pen, which was conspicuously protruding from the suspect's shirt pocket. "Yeah, so what!" barked the young tough. Allan quickly handed the bully Rose's packet of companion writing utensils, saying, "Hey, you may as well have the pencils too because it would be a shame to break up the set!" It was the perfect, cowardly, Bob Hope–ish rejoinder, Rose thought.

His circle of friends was a tight one, and they would stand by him for the rest of his life, giving interviews to journalists and biographers, almost uniformly affectionate and admiring of Woody Allen. Although many of his friends entered white-collar professions—doctors, scientists, professors—they saw Allan as "the most popular of their group," said Rose. "We all knew Woody was going to be famous one day," recalled Jack Victor. His friends called him Al, or Allan. His parents never stopped calling him "Allan."

After hours, the gang ate burgers at White Castle, played board games, cast their lines for sunfish at Prospect Park Lake (Allan Konigsberg could tie flies with the best). To really fit into his circle the teenagers had to share most or all of their leader's enthusiasms: sports, magic, jazz, movies. When Allan planned a trip to Childs, the gang followed. When he skipped school, one or more friends tagged along. The subway, which cost only a nickel, whisked them to Times Square. They would haunt the pool halls and Skee Ball parlors, stop in the Automat for cherry pie and coffee, buy a newspaper and pass the sports pages around until the doors opened for the first showing at the Paramount or Roxy. Hubert's Museum, with many flea-circus oddities, was in an arcade basement. "I saw a hermaphrodite at Hubert's," Allen recalled. "It lifted its skirt up and you could see what it had."

The friends began to roam beyond Times Square, discovering the Museum of Modern Art, where Allan was exposed for the first time to Matisse, Chagall, Kirchner, Emil Nolde and Karl Schmidt-Rottluff, *Guernica*, Jackson Pollock, Max Beckmann triptychs, and Louise Nevelson's sculptures. They would eat lunch in the museum cafeteria and catch the afternoon screening of a vintage Hollywood movie, or a subtitled foreign film.

If Allan was keen on a personality—the gauche Frenchman Jacques

Tati, the wacky Englishman Terry-Thomas, or the nimble Alec Guinness, "a great, great actor, no question about it," Allen thought, "the like of Olivier or Gielgud"—they would all go and check out the star's latest picture. Dramas too: When *Gone with the Wind* was reissued, "because he was the dominant person in our crowd, we all saw it every day that week, twice each day, ten times altogether," recalled Jack Victor. The screen adaptation of Tennessee Williams's *A Streetcar Named Desire*—with what Allen described as the "thrill capacity" of Marlon Brando—was a life-changing experience. When, that year, José Ferrer surpassed Brando to win the Oscar for Best Actor for his performance in *Cyrano de Bergerac*, the prize-giving marked the beginning of his lifelong contempt for film awards. "I was just an adolescent at the time," Allen said later, "but I could see something was wrong."

He was profoundly influenced by the pictures he saw in the years overlapping high school and graduation. *Born Yesterday*, written by Garson Kanin, was "the best comedy play in America," Allen often said, although he had not enjoyed the original Broadway production in 1946; what he saw was the Hollywood movie directed by George Cukor in 1950, starring William Holden, Broderick Crawford, and Judy Holliday. Holliday won the Academy Award for her lead role of Billie Dawn, which she had created on the stage. The story revolved around Billie, the dumb-blonde mistress of a crude and corrupt junk dealer, who falls for the investigative journalist who has taken her under his wing. Everyone discovers Billie is smarter than she looks, and tables are turned. *Born Yesterday* spoke to Allen at an impressionable age. He'd borrow the relationship between a homely, overbearing older man and his younger, birdbrained show business mistress for several key films.

Even as a youth, Allan loved musicals, and the "best" list he later ticked off for Stig Björkman began with his moviegoing in the 1940s and stretched into the late heyday of the Hollywood musical in the 1950s: *Meet Me in St. Louis*, *On the Town*, *Singin' in the Rain* ("the best musical in my opinion"), *The Band Wagon*, and the Paris-based *Gigi* ("a lovely musical, very sophisticated"). *An American in Paris* and *Guys and Dolls*, he told Björkman, "are good, but not great." *My Fair Lady* was a special case: George Bernard Shaw's *Pygmalion* was a half-comedy, half-drama that bewitched Allen almost as much as *Born Yesterday*—being pretty much a twist on the same kind of lopsided age-gender relationship. Allen had a soft spot for the 1964

George Cukor movie, he liked most Cukor films, but a movie could never be as great as *Pygmalion* or *My Fair Lady* alive onstage.

The best musicals were in color. The earlier black-and-white ones were "charming little relics" uplifted by Fred Astaire and their song-and-dance numbers, but otherwise "nothing," Allen told Björkman. "All of the ones I have mentioned have good books, and that's an important thing for me. And the musical numbers and the lyrics, whether they are original, as in *My Fair Lady* or *Gigi*, or classical songs like in *Singin' in the Rain*. The choreography works from start to finish. They're exciting and they move you and you are involved in the story. And it's funny when it's supposed to be funny, and charming when it's supposed to be charming."

OVER TIME MICKEY Rose proved his most literate, show-business-minded friend. Physically, he and Allan were Mutt and Jeff, but they bonded over their mutual reverence for the playwright George S. Kaufman, whom they glimpsed as a panelist on game shows in the early 1950s. Allan noticed when "his wonderful sour puss began showing up on television," partly because Kaufman was "homely but sharp as a matzoh—a combination I could identify with because I was homely and longed to be sharp." He never forgot how, once at Christmastime, Kaufman "scandalized the prissy multitudes by daring" to proclaim, "Let's make this one program on which no one sings 'Silent Night.'" "You just had to love a guy like that," Woody Allen, a Christmas-hater, reminisced fifty years later. The teenager began to copy Kaufman mannerisms, including the playwright's affected two-finger salute. "When I found out Kaufman's mother's name was Nettie, same as my mother's," Allen wrote in *Apropos of Nothing*, "it erased all my scientific skepticism, and I felt there was some karma we shared."

Males dominated his circle, and there is contradictory testimony about how many girls truly belonged to the group, or which of them stirred Allan's most pathetic desires. For a while during high school the teenager shared a bedroom with his cousin Rita Wishnick, who was five years older. The close cousins liked to play cards while listening for hours to the radio. "I knew all the popular music," Allen would recall. "In those days, the radio was on from the minute you woke up till you went to sleep." Rita, who brought her younger cousin along on movie outings with older friends, decorated her walls with Hollywood pinups. She also had a collection of movie-star costume books that kept the two busy "cutting out paper dolls and dressing Deanna Durbin cutouts." ("Joan Crawford cut-out books" would be mentioned in *Midnight in Paris*.) Allan began to acquire a sophistication about the feminine wardrobe that would prove a boon to his filmmaking aesthetic, even though Woody Allen himself, in his comedic persona and in real life, was better known for the fashion sense of a schnook.

Cohabiting with an older girl during high school years "might in some cases be a source of physical embarrassment and sexual curiosity," Eric Lax wrote, but "it was never awkward with them, Woody says, because she was a very close cousin and anything like that would have been unthinkable." In his memoir Allen fondly recalled Rita as blonde, zaftig, "with a slight limp" from a brush with polio. No hint of any infatuation.

Some disagree. "She was very beautiful, and Woody had a crush on her," said Jack Victor. "He would talk quite explicitly about his sexual appetite in relation to the opposite sex. But then at that age you tend to be ravenous about girls so there wasn't much wrong or unusual with that. I think we all had crushes on our cousins then!"

All the boys were girl crazy, but Allan was the "king of turndowns," recalled Mickey Rose, a "terribly shy, introverted guy who hated studying and was very precocious yet unsuccessful with women, full of longings and fantasies and unusually powerful sex drives, yet hard up for girls." Still, Allan was able to notch his quota of "dates," sometimes donning a trench coat and dangling a cigarette "to look like Bogart," as friend Elliot Mills recalled. Another time he wore "white buckskin [shoes] which were the rage at the time," Rose said, and as happens somewhat differently in *Take the Money and Run*, the movie they would later write together, "some of the local toughs came by and made fun of the shoes and they would scuff one, so Woody would scuff the other."

Among the few girls who hung around with them was Bryna Goldstein. Allan doted on Bryna, telephoned her daily, wrote her flirtatious and amusing missives. Ringing her doorbell, he'd wait forever on her Avenue K stoop, between Ninth and Tenth, until she came home. They'd hang out in her basement until past midnight, chatting, which was a specialty of his—endless talking, earnest listening. When Bryna suffered a leg injury and had to convalesce at home with a plaster cast on her leg, Allan visited her with elaborately prepared jokes or stories. When her leg cast was removed, he presented Bryna with a front-page facsimile he had ordered up in Times Square, with a headline extolling her gams: "Bryna Goldstein, Cast Removed, Dietrich Faints."

The obstacles to their courtship included Bryna's mother, Sadie, who privately found Allan "one of the ugliest kids you ever saw." The short, ugly kid must have known or at least suspected these indignities, absorbing the hurt into his psychology. He'd repeatedly write dialogue for characters he would play in films, referencing himself as short, ugly, and inept with girls. Some of the crueler critics echoed him. Peter Conrad in the *Observer* complained about the "wizened dwarf," the "stooped and balding, perpetual adolescent" who beds the teenage Tracy (Mariel Hemingway) in *Manhattan*. John Simon, critiquing *Stardust Memories*, described the film director Allen portrays in the picture as "small, Jewish, and ugly, like Woody." Stanley Kauffmann told Marion Meade, "Watching him kiss a girl—any girl—made me want to look the other way."

The short, ugly kid won Mrs. Goldstein over, however, by always being "up to something funny. He was a sweet guy." Regardless, "My mother threw Woody out of the house every night of the week for four years," recalled Bryna. "He was the last person on earth she wanted me to be with." At best, she was probably an almost-girlfriend. "All we were interested in at the time was six-foot-tall boys," Bryna said, "who we thought of as men—with square chins and fabulous physiques." She wasn't mentioned in his autobiography.

ALLAN KONIGSBERG WAS "raised in a bubble," he said later, cocooned in "a large, loving, extended family who were all nice to me." The only not-nice person in the bubble? His mother, the dominant woman in his life.

Nettie did everything possible to curtail her son's chronic hooky-playing, but the teenager would dine for breakfast on the leftover chocolate cake she had brought home, wash it down with a glass of milk while his parents were still asleep, and take off for his high school day—not! Rather, he would head for Times Square, clutching his coins and newspaper listings. Nettie was desperate to bolster her boy's inferior grades, which did not reflect the high marks he always got on IQ tests, and the potential she believed was inside him. Nettie tried to police his constant mischief-making. Her boy had a smart-aleck mouth, but he would deliver his most brutal wisecracks with such deadpan innocence—the blank, enigmatic look French author Thierry de Navacelle later described as his "Zelig face"—it made people wonder if the boy really meant it. Or was he kidding?

His laissez-faire father, Martin, faded into the background during his high school years. "I loved him more," Allen wrote of his father in his autobiography, even though Nettie was "a much better parent." Gone at night for work, Martin "always toted a gun," his son insisted in interviews, whether from World War I habit, police, or criminal contacts. Afternoons, his father would slump on the couch in front of black-and-white Westerns on TV. He'd slip cash to Allan whenever his gang of friends floated through the living room. A fastidious and snappy dresser, Martin changed clothes several times daily, one of his many idiosyncrasies.

The serious child-rearing was left to Nettie, who arrived home with a bouquet of roses left over from the florist shop where she worked. Many characters in Woody Allen films—Allen in real life too—visited flower shops and ordered roses for lovers. But as with the white roses for Geraldine Page in *Interiors*, the daily, "single white rose" the over-the-hill nightclub singer sends to his mistress in *Broadway Danny Rose*, or the white roses offered up by the ophthalmologist to his paramour in *Crimes and Misdemeanors*, flowers could be futile gestures. Nettie worried about her loner son who broke rules and norms. His chums tended to support his view that Mrs. Konigsberg was "a cartoon character," in Elliot Mills's words, "on the verge of hysteria most of the time. She was always in absolute panic—I mean the house was in a constant state of panic, and Woody used to drive her into even greater fits of hysteria." Mickey Rose said: "A typical nagging kind of mother." Jack Victor agreed: "Extremely naggy [but] she wasn't nefarious. . . . We were far more afraid of other mothers than Woody's."

Inarguably her nagging was resented even when her son provoked it. No matter how hard he tried to block out her voice, however, she stamped him with her maxims. "Aim high!" was one of Nettie's sayings. Another was "Don't waste time!" Woody Allen learned not to waste time—he fiendishly organized his time—and he always did try to aim higher. "Beyond any shadow of a doubt," Mills reflected, "it was a strange family situation with this marriage which inexplicably survived and all these relatives coming in and out of the household. But I think [Woody] paints the family situation darker than it is. I never got the impression that he was unhappy. It was an incredibly funny household. His mother was unconsciously funny, his father was naturally a very funny man, and his sister Letty was just as funny as Woody—in exactly the same way."

Nettie and her acid-tongued son engaged in ferocious verbal fisticuffs. "When she had cataracts and a patch over one eye," remembered Jack Victor, "[Woody] said, 'Shut up, Mom, or I'll blind the other eye.'" Mickey Rose recalled likewise: "He would say she looked like Groucho Marx and then instead of being insulted or taking umbrage she would say: 'Well, so what? He's a handsome man!' And so Woody would say, 'But Ma, you're a woman,' and we would fall about but she didn't have a clue what we were laughing at."

According to Jack Freed, a next-door neighbor and friend, when the nagging didn't work Nettie's "hot temper" took over and Allan's mother "was always taking a whack at him." But "he never cried," recalled Freed. "He had an amazing ability to restrain his emotions." Years later, Woody Allen filmed interviews with his mother and Mia Farrow's mother, actress Maureen O'Sullivan, for a planned documentary, provisionally titled "Two Mothers," contrasting the lives of the disparate matriarchs. "I remember you would hit me every day when I was a child," Allen reminded Nettie, with the cameras rolling. "You were always slapping me."

Nettie's usual stoicism wavered. "You were an active child, you spoke young," she defended herself. "You were very bright, and you ran and jumped. I didn't know how to handle that type of child. You were too active and too much of a child for me. I wasn't that good to you because I was very strict, which I regret. Because if I hadn't been that strict, you might have been a more, a not so impatient . . . you might have been a—what should I say? Not better. You're a good person. But, uh, maybe softer, maybe *warmer*. That's the word I want to use. . . . But it was hard for me to handle you. I was much sweeter to Letty than I was to you."

Often in interviews Allen painted his parents as an ordinary drab couple trapped in a loveless marriage. "A typical Jewish neighborhood cliché," he'd say unsympathetically, or "Silly people in a grotesque way." He'd denigrate the carefree Martin Konigsberg: "He never let a thought enter his head." He etched this portrait of his kvetch of a mother: "She gets up in the morning. . . . She works in a little flower shop downtown, she rides the subway home, and she makes dinner. Beyond that she is not too interested in too many things."

The father characters in his later films were often henpecked, the mothers overbearing scolds. Not in any of his films did Woody Allen evince interest in the daily struggles of parenting, much less the inner lives of his own mother and father, their achievements, largely on his own behalf. The mother caricatures in *Radio Days* and in his "Oedipus Wrecks" segment of *New York Stories*—the giant supernatural nag floating over Manhattan—were flecked with uproarious moments exaggerated from his own upbringing. But the parent caricatures were much like the jots of sophistication in all his writing, shrewdly devised and incorporated, highly entertaining, but also intentionally fictionalized and superficial—real-life jots that hinted at soul-baring, while cleverly drawing a line, as he always insisted, between his comedy and the more painful aspects of his life story.

IN THE WEEKS leading up to the start of his senior year in high school, Allan hung out with Bryna Goldstein at her family's summer house in Long Beach. What he was going to do after graduation weighed on him. Late that spring, "Allan Konigsberg" had seen his first byline on "a terse description of a simple card trick," as it was later described, in "Towns' Teen Topics," part of Glen E. Towns's featured column in *Genii: The Conjuror's Magazine*. The trick involved identifying a card randomly chosen by an audience member, which depended upon "a fake deck of all-alike cards" and a seemingly guileless assistant—sister Letty—or what in magic circles is known as a "stooge." "The use of a stooge," the teenager explained, "is a most controversial subject. There are stooge haters and stooge users. Some of the great magicians of our times have used stooges. I suppose, if the effect warrants, the stooge is just as permissible as apparatus. There are those who will disagree."

He spent the early part of the summer as a camp counselor with his friend and fellow tent supervisor Jerry Epstein, but "eventually he got fired," according to Epstein, because sixteen-year-old Allan was supposed to linger over lunches with campers in the mess hall, but after eating his meals he simply got up and left. Allan cajoled his mother into a different rural experience, taking him and Letty to Accord, New York, a Rondout Valley hamlet one hundred miles upstate in the Catskills, where using show business trade papers and East Midwood Jewish Center connections, he'd laboriously contrived a tryout as a magician at Weinstein's Majestic Bungalow Colony.

While Nettie and Letty sunbathed at a nearby vacation retreat, Allan took the stage at the Majestic Bungalow Colony. He demonstrated the dove pan trick, passe-passe bottles, and rope stunts. He conscripted a pretty young vacationer as his assistant, closer to his own age than Letty, conjuring this assistant again in the flashback of his boyhood magic act in *Stardust Memories.* The teenage magician was "very different from any kid I had ever known," recalled the assistant, Marion Drayson, "quiet, gentle, smart, and very funny in a strange kind of way. . . . As performance time grew near, I grew increasingly nervous. He soothed my stage fright, calmed my fears, and convinced me that there was no way he could possibly go on without me as his assistant."

When his magic act did not go over like gangbusters, the Konigsbergs returned to Brooklyn. Up to this time, Allan had nursed pipe dreams of a future as a magician. In the summer of 1952, his ambitions pivoted. "You should write some of your gags down," a friend suggested after hearing the insults the teenager hurled at the screen one afternoon as they watched a movie. "They're funny." A bell went off in his head. It was "a casual remark, but through the noise of the Flatbush streets, I heard it," Allen recalled. "Why don't you show your wisecracks to Phil Wasserman?" Nettie suggested (pausing "in her daily ritual of slapping my face on spec"). A vague relative, Wasserman was a publicist at Reach, McClinton & Co., a national advertising firm headquartered in Manhattan. Allan wrote a few jokes down; Wasserman read them and said they were pretty good. His vague relative advised the teenager to send his one-liners to newspaper columnists, a phenomenon of the era, particularly in New York, where many columnists toiled at upward of a dozen metropolitan papers.

Preparing carefully typed postcards for the columnists, the teenager decided "Allan Stewart Konigsberg" was unwieldy and too obviously Jewish for someone already, as a youth, diffident about his family and his religion. Plus, his real name would attract unwanted attention at Midwood High School. He needed a pen name, something catchy and Anglicized. "It was an ongoing discussion for months," remembered Elliot Mills. "We'd be walking along Avenue K to play stickball in the [PS] 99 schoolyard, talking about what would sound best. Early on he decided to use his first name as his last name. The problem was the new first name. 'Miles' was a candidate but not a strong one. It dropped out of contention fast when 'Woody' came up."

Some friends say the nom de plume was originally "Heywood." According to this theory, "Heywood" was borrowed from the name of the younger brother of a cute girl they all knew. Another friend said it was "the name of the pet dog" of the cute girl. Either way, "Heywood" would be reported as his first name in early articles and books about Woody Allen stretching into the 1960s. He'd introduce himself as "Master Heywood Allen" when performing stand-up, and "Heywood Productions" was the designated name of his early business entities.

The "Woody" was also slippery. The first articles and books about him considered the possibility that the comedian's first name was inspired by famous Woodys, such as jazz clarinetist and big-band leader Woody Herman, left-wing folk singer Woody Guthrie, or even Woody Woodpecker, a cartoon bird with a similarly long, angular face topped by orange-red hair. "The truth is, it was arbitrary," Allen wrote in *Apropos of Nothing.* "It was short, went with Allen, and had a light, vaguely comic touch, as opposed to, say, Zoltan or Ludvicio."

"Enclosed are some gags for your consideration and sent exclusively to you," the sixteen-year-old pecked out on his Olympia at the end of the summer of 1952, sending the first batch of his waggery to Nick Kenny, a well-known seven-day-a-week man, whose "Nick Kenny Speaking" appeared in the *New York Daily Mirror.* The postcards with jokes included were signed "Woody Allen"—his first declaration of independence.

Kenny published his first jokes without attribution, but the postcards kept coming. On November 10, 1952, the newcomer made his authorial debut under the concluding "Knick Knacks!!!" section of Kenny's column: "I don't have to do this for a living. . . . I can always go back to my old job . . . putting pontoons on floating crap games—Woody Allen." A few days later, this specimen followed: "She was so ugly she wore her hair in a ponytail . . . to swat the flies off her face—Woody Allen." Then another: "This ugly girl had a mink coat on," said Woody Allen, "but the only trouble was that she wasn't wearing it . . . she was growing it."

Allen, in his memoir, warned readers that his early newspaper jokes were "not the equal of Voltaire or La Rochefoucauld. They were girlfriend and mother-in-law jokes, parking space jokes, income tax jokes, with maybe an occasional topical one." To this list could be added many jokes that derided "ugly girls," a tradition among comics of the era. Other celebrities made similar jokes; Warren Beatty, for example: "Charity is taking an ugly girl to lunch." Maybe it was the natural extension of ridiculing Nettie's looks, or a kind of projection. Allen's second wife, actress Louise Lasser, recalled, "He was always very hard on ugly people. I don't know why, but he was."

"Hey, you're in Nick Kenny's column," a friend phoned to tell him. Woody Allen jokes surfaced in a few more Nick Kenny columns, and suddenly, it seemed, he was a hot commodity. His gags began appearing in Hy Gardner's column in the *New York Herald Tribune*, Bob Sylvester's in the *Daily News*, Frank Farrell's in the *New York World–Telegram*, Leonard Lyons's and—more important to Allen's future—Earl Wilson's in the *Post*.

Kenny's *Daily Mirror* was a Hearst tabloid with headlines feasting on bloody crimes and sex scandals: "Plant Woman Cops in Tubes to Trap Rapists!" A local colorist, Kenny was beloved for his regular itemization of hospitalizations, urging people to write and cheer up the sick folk, and for his aphorisms and light verse, which ranged from sentimental ("dog spelled backward is God") to prayerful or patriotic. A rabid backer of Joseph McCarthy, Kenny routinely wrote poems praising the Wisconsin senator's anticommunist crusade.

"Nick Kenny's column was soppy and square," Allen recalled. "Earl Wilson was the voice of Broadway." His Kenny clippings allowed him to trade up, and Allen began to mail his postcards and gags exclusively to Wilson, whose "It Happened Last Night" column originated in the larger-circulation, more decorous *Post*, but also was nationally syndicated to hundreds of newspaper and radio subscribers. Wilson focused on Broadway and Hollywood, prided himself on scoops, got interviews with major stars. Also, Wilson paid hard cash—as much as 75 cents per contribution—while Kenny did not. Wilson unveiled his first signed Woody Allen joke in late November: It teased the US Office of Price Stabilization, a federal agency tasked with controlling prices during the Korean War: "Woody Allen figured out what O.P.S. prices are—Over People's Salaries."

Several more jokes, less topical, more typical, ran in December, but the interesting thing Wilson did was begin to transform "Woody Allen" from a byline into a personality, linking him with a "fictitious show girl character" named "Taffy Tuttle," who routinely made "stupid remarks" in his column.

"Taffy Tuttle told Woody Allen that her new dress was custom-made—but the designer must have had some strange customs." And: "Taffy Tuttle complained to Woody Allen: 'The motor in my car is so bad, the car runs better without it.' "

His jokes began to appear "in a fairly consistent manner" in Wilson's column, two or three a month by early 1953. The high schooler even took pride of place in the widely read "Earl's Pearls" sign-off: "Woody Allen boasts that he just made a fortune—he was downtown auctioning off his parking space. . . . That's Earl, brother."

IN THE MEANTIME, the senior classman was trying to keep his head down at Midwood High School. His nom de plume had been concocted partly to help him avoid the curious glances, stares, and interrogatories of classmates who might recognize the byline of Allan Konigsberg. A friend tipped off the school newspaper, the *Midwood Argus*, where his only previous mention—"Never play cards with Konigsberg"—alluded to his magic and poker-playing skills. "I was shocked," Alan Lapidus, the *Argus* student editor, recalled thinking, when informed of the true identity of "Woody Allen." "Nobody had given a second thought to this little schlemiel."

Lapidus quickly assigned an interview with the "carrot-topped senior" who had carved "quite a name for himself as a gag writer." According to the *Argus* profile, "Woody Allen" had already submitted humorous sketches to representatives of Bob Hope, Bob and Ray—a comedy team said to rank among his radio-listening favorites—and the up-and-coming stand-up comic Larry Storch. The *Argus* said Allan/Woody also was a piano player, tap dancer (he had taken lessons), and magician. No mention was made of the clarinet.

The *Argus* feature stirred a flurry of excitement at Midwood HS. Jack Victor, who was the sports editor of the school paper, talked the faculty adviser into giving Allan/Woody a sports columnist audition. The adviser was a female teacher. "While talking with him [Allen]," according to Eric Lax, "for some reason she began to finger his shirt, which he did not like. So, he fingered her blouse. Whereupon she threw him out of the office."

Allan/Woody was soon trumpeted as a sketch writer for the senior class revue, but the annual show did not eventuate that year. Regardless, now he was Woody Allen. Writer. And when Morris Purcell asked his social studies class about their vocational plans after graduation, one senior's hand shot up. Allan/Woody said he was going be a sanitation worker because then "I'd earn money and still have all the time I need to write, and review plays and operas." Like a lot of things that guy said, Purcell didn't know if he was kidding.

He was barely noted in his 1953 yearbook, the *Epilog*, which carried no mention of "Woody Allen" and, in fact, misspelled his birth name as "Alan Konigsberg." The *Epilog* did not record a single extracurricular activity for the senior who had spent four years trying to blend into the wallpaper. Allen said later he had few pleasant memories of high school, with one exception being the senior class spring trip to Washington, DC. The high school students spent a "very quiet and peaceful" overnight at a Catholic monastery where, not for the last time, he found himself fascinated and/or beguiled by the beliefs and rituals of the Roman Catholic Church. "There were very few people there," Allen recalled. "Just the thought that the monks would wake up in the morning and they would tread those paths, and they were not afraid of dying, and they didn't want anything—I loved that. It was a stoic life. They had no great desires. They just tread, and sat, and thought, and prayed."

He had learned "nothing of value" at Midwood High School, he often said later, and his movies would mostly skip that part of his life story too, except for flashbacks, distorted for laughs, which reflected the boyhood of his characters—rarely the high school years—or made wisecracks about his youth, right down to *To Rome with Love* in 2012, his last appearance to date in a Woody Allen picture, where he boasts of flunking high school Spanish.

WHEN THE NEWLY christened Woody Allen graduated in June 1953, Dwight Eisenhower was the US president. The Rosenbergs were executed as spies on June 19. The gypsy jazz guitarist Django Reinhardt died in May, and playwright Eugene O'Neill, another one of Allen's artistic gods, passed away in November. The Minneapolis Lakers won the NBA championship four games to one over the New York Knicks. Arthur Miller's *The Crucible*, which dramatized the Salem witch trials, earned the Tony for Best Play of the Year.

However, Midwood High School was already in his rearview mirror by the time Woody Allen marched to the strains of "Pomp and Circumstance." He was slogging away at a new job—not sanitation worker—writing one-liners and squibs for the celebrity and corporate clients of David O. Alber Associates, a public relations agency that had been a New York fixture since 1929. For weeks, after he finished his day's regimen of high school classes, Allen rode the subway to Alber's offices at East Fifty-Third near Madison Avenue, clocking in for three hours alongside a half dozen other scribes. He'd always arrive with a head start, having scribbled jokes on the train.

How he got the job happened like this, as Earl Wilson might say. Wilson's legman Martin Burden ran into Alber's vice president Gene Shefrin at singer Peggy Lee's March opening at La Vie en Rose on the Upper East Side. Alber was looking to bulk up his writing staff. Burden recommended the Brooklyn kid who had been submitting good bits to "Earl's Pearls." Alber telephoned Wilson and asked, "Who the hell is this Woody Allen?" Frankly, Wilson replied, he couldn't say. They had never met. "I was too busy to see Woody," Wilson recalled. Alber got a phone number and called. Alber was surprised to learn Allen was still in high school, but the $20 to $25 Alber offered him as a daily rate was better than what the teenager had been getting for delivering "meat for a butcher shop and dry-cleaning for a tailor," which amounted to "thirty-five cents an hour plus tips." Allen said he could show up every day after 1 p.m. when his classes were done. Hmm, OK, said Alber.

Alber Associates handled publicity for a broad range of radio and television programs and entertainment personalities as well as many corporations, including the toy and game manufacturer Parker Brothers and the soap, shampoo, and Crisco giant Procter & Gamble. Alber's guiding tenet was that "comprehensive press coverage was of immense importance" to any person or business's success. To make sure his clients got that important coverage, Alber kept their names in the public eye with quips and anecdotes his agency streamed to newspaper, magazine, wire service, and broadcast columnists. The one-liners, supposedly straight from the lips of dance maestro Arthur Murray, bandleader Guy Lombardo, or songwriter Sammy Kaye, were ghosted by Alber's staff.

Fellow Alber's writers Don Garrett and Mike Merrick were several years older than Allen, who was still exclaiming "Wow!" and "Gee!" when they met him. They had lengthier résumés. Garrett had toiled for the television station WPIX in New York, and Merrick boasted an advertising degree and some stand-up comedy experience in college. They befriended the young hire, hung out with him, helped to groom him in flackery.

They and the other Alber's writers "had heard so much about me and followed my jokes in the paper," Allen recalled. "I was this young prodigy, like Willie Mays." The prodigy went hitless in his initial at-bats, however, because his gags were old-fashioned: "dumb women, husbands with nagging wives, or necking in the parking lot," according to Eric Lax. "Read the front pages of the newspaper [for inspiration]!" Shefrin urged Allen. The teenager insisted he *did* read the front pages, though headline humor would never be his forte.

"Nobody ever said, 'This kid is going to be a genius,' " recalled Merrick, who in those days wore thick black-frame eyewear and a silver bracelet. Merrick looked and acted like "a real Broadway guy," Allen thought, and indeed after years of press agentry Merrick proved out as the producer of *Camelot* and other Broadway hits. Late in 1953, around the time of his eighteenth birthday, Allen went to an eye doctor and learned that he was nearsighted. It was Merrick who helped his youthful colleague pick out some big, black-frame glasses that were similar to his own, which completed the skinny, red-haired kid's slightly dazed, cerebral look. Allen would wear those glasses for the rest of his life, and in interviews he often said it was the glasses that allowed people to mistake him for an intellectual. He'd evoke the horror of Snellen eye charts in several films, including, humorously, in the final credits of *What's Up, Tiger Lily?* And, tellingly, in *Crimes and Misdemeanors*.

The teenage staff writer "was overwhelmingly likeable," Merrick remembered. "He was personable, he was sweet, he was curious, and we thought he was a character in a positive sense. He was the antithesis of a smart-ass. He would come in completely unassuming and never make any noise and knock out these original, funny lines for, say, Sammy Kaye. We'd read them and say, 'Sammy Kaye should be so clever.' "

Over the summer of 1953 Allen gradually found his footing in the job. His jokes began to click with Shefrin and Alber and, increasingly, various public personalities and companies benefited from his unsigned contributions. Earning a salary for writing was "like being paid to play baseball, or something," Allen recalled. He'd write fifty jokes and one-liners a day, "always five to a page, ten pages," and sometimes in other ways he'd sneak into public view, because Alber's was known to pose its famous clients playing Monopoly, for example; with Allen, glimpsed from behind as the opposing player, the agency got paid double by the celebrity and Parker Brothers.

His byline continued to make spot appearances in "Earl's Pearls," building on the public persona of Woody Allen. Earl Wilson and Alber's opened doors. The agency had a direct line to Bob Hope, and Allen sent a few pages of his comedy to Hope's manager. Nothing but an encouraging letter and future connection came of it. His phone rang with referrals: Sol Leon, a William Morris agent who liaised with Alber's, sent him to meet with the homespun humorist Herb Shriner, who hosted CBS's prime-time game show *Two for the Money*. Allen began writing stuff for Shriner, "a very fine comedian in the rural Will Rogers style but better," in his words, working closely with head writer Roy Kammerman, a television veteran twenty years older than him.

Word spread about the kid from Brooklyn with an inexhaustible supply of energy and jokes. He never said no to additional work for hire. He always found time for more work. The writing came so easy for him.

ANOTHER REVELATION, THAT first summer after high school, was seeing the film *Summer with Monika*, directed by someone with the strange-sounding name of Ingmar Bergman. OK, Allen and Mickey Rose later admitted, they went to see the subtitled Swedish opus after reading about sexy actress Harriet Andersson's nude scenes. They admitted enjoying the nudity, but they were really knocked out by the film's style and subject matter, which was different than anything they had seen, "more mature than the American cinema," in Allen's words, serious thematic ideas rendered in a "poetic style." Bergman swiftly became their favorite foreign director, and Allen and his friends also began paying attention to other European filmmakers, especially the Italian neorealists, some of whom—like Federico Fellini—were blazing paths into more personal and autobiographical cinema.

Serendipity struck in the form of his jazz idol Sidney Bechet, who was making a whirlwind American tour, with appearances at the Bandbox, a club near Birdland, followed by nights at Childs, Jimmy Ryan's, and one week at the Apollo in Harlem. Allen went to hear Bechet twice, the second time "the most fulfilling artistic experience of my life," he later told Ralph J. Gleason. "He was a startling musician, his ferociousness was incredible. I was struck by the intensity of his playing." The Brooklyn youth, who had made nice with Milton Berle in a Times Square magic shop, was drawn to meet another hero. He went up to Bechet and shook his hand.

In the fall he could only keep afternoon hours at Alber's, because Nettie insisted her son pursue a higher education. Reluctantly he enrolled in morning classes at New York University, commuting by subway from where the Konigsberg family, and a fresh array of relatives, now lived on the ground floor of an apartment building at Fifteenth and K in Midwood, to the NYU campus near Washington Square Park in lower Manhattan. While conforming to the college preparatory curriculum at Midwood High School, he had performed poorly in science, math, and Spanish, yet miraculously his borderline grade average of 72 got him into NYU. With a distinctly superior academic record, Mickey Rose also enrolled at NYU and in the fall the frosh friends tramped off to college. Allen signed up for the minimum load of three courses: English, Introductory Spanish, Film Studies.

Again, however, he proved a middling pupil. Allen missed lectures, and even in the film courses he was taking with Rose he would show up for the screenings but skip the rest of the class "fifty percent of the time." Every morning he'd jump on the subway with honorable intentions, only to find himself zooming past the NYU stop until he landed in Times Square, where he'd browse the shops and wait for the theaters to open. Sometimes he was joined by a comely NYU senior, who thought the hooky-playing freshman was charming and amusing. The coed lived near Alber's office, and she'd drop him off in the afternoons for his joke-writing chores.

His NYU English professor gave him an F on his maiden essay, in which Allen tried to ape the light satire of Max Shulman, catching hell for it because the teacher was outraged by such bald imitation. The professor wrote in the margins, "Son, you need a lesson in rudimentary manners. You are a callow adolescent and are not a diamond in the rough." Barely lasting the semester, Allen received poor marks in English; Introductory Spanish, which he was repeating after low grades in high school; and even Film Studies. "I never actually failed a college course," he later said in an interview. "It was always a very indefinite D."

Summoned before NYU deans, the callow adolescent was told he couldn't be readmitted in the fall without taking remedial summer courses. One administrator warned him to get psychiatric help. Instead, to "keep my mother from opening her wrists," as he liked to say, Allen enrolled in a nighttime filmmaking seminar at the City College of New York, which would earn transferable credits, but the CCNY experience was "a total disaster," he recalled, "a dreadful film course compared to NYU's." So he reenrolled in Film Studies and English at NYU in the summer of 1954, hoping to erase his previous grades. His classmates thought his parody of Ernest Hemingway's "The Killers" was pure gold, but the professor who read it aloud to everyone thought it was more like brass leaf. Once again Allen failed English, this time dropping out of college forever. "I did not like elementary school or high school," Allen said later, "and I liked college the least of the three."

Then and later—for the rest of his life—Allen preferred personal tutorials where he didn't have to mingle with too many students: ballet, cooking, philosophy, French. He and Mickey Rose, who'd persevere at NYU, attaining a communications degree after four years, splurged on acting lessons in a West Side brownstone. They looked around for someone to instruct them in the art and techniques of photography. Allen signed up for Hungarian émigré Lajos Egri's playwriting seminar, which was taught to small groups of aspirants out of Egri's Columbus Circle offices. Allen felt attuned to Egri's character-driven approach and later praised *The Art of Dramatic Writing*, Egri's 1942 how-to, as "the most stimulating and best book on the subject ever written."

Acting, playwriting, photography—these were some of the light bulbs flashing on and off in his head—and one night Allen even attempted his first stand-up comedy for the Young Israel Social Club in the basement of the East Midwood Jewish Center, his family's Conservative synagogue on Ocean Avenue. Allen didn't need much persuading from the emcee of the weekly talent show who, knowing of Allen's day job and his reputation as a funny guy, put him on the calendar. Mike Merrick rehearsed Allen, supplying him with a binder of his old college routines. The performance included jokes about cowboys and miracle horses and noncompliant girls. In his biography of Allen, Eric Lax gave this prime example: "I'm coming home with a girl on a date and six blocks from the house, she gets her key out. (Big laugh from the audience.) Now I take her to the steps, and I put my arms around her fast and she says, 'No, no, don't. I'll hate myself in the morning.' So, I said, 'Sleep late.' "

His act went over surprisingly well. "I was as natural on the stage at that age as I ever would be, as I ever got in my life," Allen recalled. "It was an instinct, it was easy for me." Of course, his high school buddies, many but not all of them Jewish, packed the club audience. They already thought Woody Allen was the funniest guy in Brooklyn. Most were in college now, but everyone still congregated nights and weekends.

THE FRIENDS FORMED a fooling-around jazz band with Jack Victor on kazoo, Jerry Epstein on bass, Elliot Mills and Mickey Rose alternating on drums, and led by Allen as their clarinetist. Other friends with other instruments, some of which Martin Konigsberg supplied "with their serial numbers filed off," in Mills's words, joined intermittently. But if the band wanted to play a date at the East Midwood Jewish Center in the summer of 1954, they required a pianist. Somebody knew Harlene Susan Rosen, who had just finished her junior year at James Madison High School in Sheepshead Bay, a Brooklyn neighborhood that abutted the Atlantic Ocean.

"Kind of tall and nice-figured with dark hair," as Allen recalled, Harlene was an introspective beauty with an almond complexion and dark eyes. Mickey Rose remembered, speaking to Francine du Plessix Gray, that Harlene had "very big breasts." Fifteen or sixteen years old at the time, the pianist was "soft, nice," in Jack Victor's words. "She was quiet and all that, but you couldn't push her around." Allen felt an instant attraction. "She was pretty, she was bright, she came from a good family who had a lovely house and a boat, and she played classical music and took acting lessons," he recalled. "In short, she was much too good for me."

In shifting aggregations, the amateur musicians began rehearsing more regularly, often repairing to the huge basement of the Rosen home. Harlene's parents were younger and more prosperous than the Konigsbergs. Harlene's father owned a children's shoe store, and he had played the trumpet professionally before marrying Rosen's mother, who'd been a singer. Her father dusted off his horn, occasionally jamming with the youngsters.

Allen began escorting Harlene privately to "very romantic, sophisticated places. Off-Broadway shows, Birdland to see Miles Davis and John Coltrane. Candlelight restaurants in Manhattan," in his words. "I held my own as a charmer and lover with the exception of when her family took me out for a day on their boat." He got horribly seasick and "vowed never" to ride in a boat again "and didn't until over a decade later." One of their first dates took them to the studio where Herb Shriner's show was being broadcast, with Allen hoping to impress Harlene with jokes he had written for the host. They stood in a long line with other ticket hopefuls, until Shriner's manager, who knew Allen, spotted the couple and herded them backstage to the VIP room.

Allen gave numerous interviews over the years in which he generalized about the type of women he was attracted to physically in his youthful days. Some interviews were tongue-in-cheek, but some sounded truthful. Early on, Allen confessed, he was turned on by the "Jules Feiffer type of girl": the artistic and cerebral, droll, witty type that congregated in Greenwich Village. Harlene, even as a teenager, was that type: a brainy artiste.

"I had to read to survive with the women that I coveted," Allen explained in one interview, linking the brainy girls to his hunger for self-improvement. "All I knew about was baseball," he said. "I used to take them out and they'd say, 'Where I'd really like to go tonight is to hear Andrés Segovia.' And I'd say, 'Who?' Or they'd say, 'Did you read this Faulkner novel?' And I'd say, 'I read comic books. I've never read a book in my life.' "

There was little disguising the fact that he was a college dropout. One girl whom he dated asked Allen if he'd take her to the film *O. Henry's Full House*. "The only O. Henry I knew was a candy bar." To "keep pace" with the brainy beauties he was meeting as a young joke-writer—girls like Harlene—Allen transformed himself into a lifelong autodidact. "The things those women read and liked," Allen told Eric Lax, "led them inevitably to Nietzsche and Trotsky and Beethoven, and I had to struggle to stay alive in that company."

He began to supplement his reading: adding humorists James Thurber and S. J. Perelman to Max Shulman, switching from Mickey Spillane to William Faulkner, F. Scott Fitzgerald, Ernest Hemingway, and Herman Melville. He started to read the heavyweights: Thomas Mann, Kafka, Camus, Flaubert, Stendhal, Turgenev, Tolstoy, Dostoyevsky—"A full meal with vitamins and wheat germ added," as his character describes the latter Russian novelist in *Husbands and Wives*. Poetry also: Allen learned, to his surprise, he liked poetry, with Emily Dickinson and Rainer Maria Rilke among the favorites he'd quote in future Woody Allen pictures.

Still, he always read "indiscriminately and there remained great gaps in my knowledge," Allen admitted. He never turned the pages of *Ulysses*, *Don Quixote*, *Lolita*, *Catch-22*, *1984*; "no Virginia Woolf, no E. M. Forster, no D. H. Lawrence. Nothing by the Brontes or Dickens." However, he kept a must-read list of authors and books and ticked them off throughout his life, reading widely and, amazedly, "I found I liked what I read."

He always held it against his parents that they had never taken him, as a boy, to a museum, a symphony, or a Broadway play. The theater would become another devotion, and in time an avocation. He branched out from his early appreciation of George S. Kaufman to devouring the published scripts of other playwrights and seeing everything that opened on Broadway and every single off-Broadway play and nearly every off-off-Broadway play. (In his memoir he mentions a *Macbeth* performed by Thai puppets.) He had a passion for the hit musicals. Ever since responding to the screen adaptation of *A Streetcar Named Desire*, he was avid about Tennessee Williams. Now he caught up with and was humbled by Eugene O'Neill, Arthur Miller, Ibsen, and Chekhov, whose plays Allen read and saw performed for the first time in the early 1950s. Those playwrights wrote tragedies that revolved around deeply flawed characters, "lost souls," and Allen learned that he identified with the lost souls and solemn works, which he often preferred to laugh-out-loud comedies. He felt the first tug away from mere joke-writing.

ALLEN HAD ENJOYED "a great high" from the audience at the Young Israel Social Club laughing at his fledgling stand-up routine. But Mike Merrick cautioned him: "It's a tough life. You've got to want it more than anything else." For the time being Allen didn't know if he wanted it. He felt "drawn more to writing. I liked the anonymity." However, "my goal subtly shifted." Allen would continue working at Alber Associates, and he'd also write for other entertainers as word spread about abilities, but "perhaps I should write deeper things" in the future, he thought.

His time at Alber's was well spent professionally. Allen once estimated he wrote some twenty thousand jokes for the agency, and thousands more while moonlighting during the nearly two and a half years he spent in public relations. While Dave Alber often rejected the jokes of his that were, in his opinion, the most irreverent and cutting-edge, the agency proved his first crucible of learning on the job, and it was a badge of pride on his CV. Moreover, Alber's gave him financial independence from his parents while he was still a teenager. "Their combined salaries would be maybe less than a hundred dollars a week combined. Immediately I was making close to $200 a week." After adding in his sideline writing, he more than tripled their income. Allen splurged to the tune of $600 for a 1951 Plymouth convertible for driving Harlene around, which occasioned various near-death accidents that made him wonder if automobiles, any more than boats, were his thing.

During the summer of 1955, another guy who lived in Midwood knocked on the Konigsberg family door, having heard of the "neighborhood wunderkind," in Allen's words. Formerly with the William Morris Agency, Harvey Meltzer was a freelance talent representative. Meltzer told Allen he had the "inside track" on the National Broadcasting Company's Comedy Development Program for "promising beginners," which the television network had announced, with fanfare, in May. This pilot program would train young writers for network shows. If Meltzer got Allen a slot, would the wunderkind sign a seven-year contract with him? Yes!

Told NBC required writing samples, Allen scribbled several legal-pad pages' worth of jokes and one-liners and mailed them to Tad Danielewski, an acting teacher working for NBC who was helping to vet the young candidates. "A lot were wife jokes," Danielewski recalled. "Even so, I was conquered immediately."

While still on Alber's payroll Allen spent much of August under Danielewski's tutelage, collaborating with Paul W. Keyes, another prospect for the program who was ten years older than Allen and a World War II veteran; Keyes had written for the long-running syndicated Hearst radio show *Front Page Drama*. Together they developed a "rough and unpolished working script," a forty-page tryout for the program titled "Mama Mia." If NBC liked "Mama Mia," the network might develop the script to launch the zany, multitalented actress-singer Kaye Ballard into a half-hour comedy series, with Danielewski as director and producer. This was the first known scriptwriting by nineteen-year-old Woody Allen, and it was sophisticated in form and content, consisting of a dual monologue between Ballard playing herself and also Ballard as her grandmother Nana—a kind of "Oedipus Wrecks" Italian Catholic smothering grandmother. The camera would jump between the two characters as they shared the monologue, using "live" as well as taped footage. "The last roll we propose to film," Danielewski explained to higher-ups in a memo, "so that the sketch would run through cutting from film to 'live.' Miss Ballard's make-up would all be on the obvious side as that of an old Italian lady."

By dint of age and experience, Keyes was the lead writer and more in charge of the continuity. Allen pitched his jokes. The dual monologues were heavily flavored with ethnic Italian Catholic humor. Many of the jokes were hokey, like Ballard's gibe about a wealthy family, unlike her own, for whom "money not only grows on trees, but they grow it in their window boxes. These people are around money so much they all have green sunburns!" Although NBC hemmed and hawed about a Kaye Ballard series, Danielewski liked the "Mama Mia" draft, and Allen passed the tryout. Both he and Keyes were signed for the Comedy Development Program.

Simultaneously, in late summer Allen was called in by Gene Shefrin to be told Alber Associates was cutting payroll. Shefrin gave the Brooklyn kid a bonus and laid him off. Sheepishly, after accepting the bonus, Allen told Alber he'd been on the verge of quitting. He'd just taken a position with NBC. The name "Woody Allen" appeared for the first time in the show business trade paper *Variety* a week or two later, on September 14, 1955. The "gag writer" had "resigned from the Dave Alber flackery," according to the item, and joined NBC "as a staff comedy writer"—a slight exaggeration of the reality. As his celebrity magnified over time, *Variety* would spin his name into *Variety*ese, and all Hollywood would come to know him as "the Woodman."

Chapter 2

1955

The Woodman Cometh

In Which the Neophyte Writer Gets Married and Reaches the Top of the Hack Heap

The Comedy Development Program, which had percolated at NBC for months before Allen heard of it, was envisioned as a kind of college of comedy, with seasoned professionals teaching auspicious newcomers the fundamentals of joke- and sketch-writing for network variety and situation comedy series. The old pros would seed the next generation of laughmakers, helping to reinvigorate doddering shows and spawn new ones.

The first four recruits came from "universities, colleges, NBC Radio and TV affiliates, little theaters, dramatic schools, as well as periodicals," according to network publicity. They were Woody Allen, who came from none of these places; Paul Keyes, Allen's "Mama Mia" collaborator, who had been a broadcast writer for several years; Harvey Miller, a former social director of a Catskills hotel; and Paul Pumpian, a University of North Carolina theater graduate who was recommended by his professor. Pumpian was twenty-six years old and Miller was a year older than Allen, who was the youngest with the least amount of professional background.

Young Allen's crucial development from a neophyte TV writer to a knock-kneed stand-up comic with a zany, neurotic persona would begin here, with friends and mentors, false starts as well as breakthroughs, and most importantly, his single-minded ambition propelling him, over the next five eventful years, into the national limelight.

By August the four "promising beginners" were sharing temporary workspace at the Forrest Hotel on Broadway and Forty-Ninth. They all underwent tryouts similar to "Mama Mia" before being offered six-month contracts starting October 1, with pickup options into 1956. Despite the fact Kaye Ballard's TV series never got off the ground, network official Tad Danielewski saw Allen as a unique talent. "Woody's material was different when it was not constricted by the personality of a great performer," he recalled. "I thought it showed originality."

Until now Allen had never seen a multiyear agreement in physical form. His signature was urgently required on two: the NBC contract, and Harvey Meltzer's seven-year personal management pact. Allen decided he needed the advice of an older, wiser eminence in the field, and again he found one with his mother Nettie's assistance.

Abe Burrows was Allen's "distant cousin by marriage," as Burrows later traced their familial relationship, because Burrows's father's sister's husband "had a sister named Nettie." New York born and bred, Burrows had been cutting a wide swath in the entertainment industry. A former radio comedy writer, Hollywood scenarist, and nightclub satirist, he had gravitated to Broadway and, as cowriter of the *Guys and Dolls* libretto, in 1951, he hit the mother lode of success. Ten years later Burrows had another hit musical—*How to Succeed in Business without Really Trying*—for which he would share a Pulitzer Prize with collaborators. The forty-four-year-old playwright was old enough to be Allen's father and, unlike Martin Konigsberg, he knew from show business.

Family overtures elicited Burrows's address, and Nettie pushed her son to visit the famous distant cousin's luxury apartment building at West Eighty-First and Central Park West in the fall of 1955. Allen carried with him samples of his joke-writing along with his three-page, seven-year, tentative agreement with Meltzer—as yet unsigned. There was an extra blank space at the bottom of this document and also on his NBC contract for the co-signature of "Mrs. Nettie Konigsberg," because Woody Allen, "a wispy little fellow, very innocent-looking, but [with] an interesting gleam in his eyes," as Burrows recalled from their first meeting, was still only nineteen.

Burrows invited his young relation upstairs. The playwright was bald, bespectacled, with a tic of blinking behind his shell-rimmed glasses. He was known to speak hoarsely with language "something like a mug," recalled

Broadway colleague Adolph Green, but always with "a great intellect and frame of reference." Allen handed over the Meltzer contract, then "asked me if I would like to see some of his work," Burrows remembered. Two pages of about thirty jokes. Furiously blinking, Burrows peered at the unwanted offering. "It can be very painful to read a bunch of jokes by a new, inexperienced comedy writer, but in this case, I had no choice," the playwright recalled. "I politely started to read them and wow! His stuff was dazzling."

Burrows called to his wife in another room, saying his young visitor had written a batch of terrific jokes, "none of which I could ever have thought of," in Burrows's words. The setups and punch lines "seemed to come from a different world" other than traditional comedy setups. One of the jokes, Burrows recalled, revolved around the young man trying to take a quiet bath in his tub at home, with his mother always walking in on him whenever she felt like it and sinking his toy boats. (An early example of a favorite joke Allen adapted into other contexts, he'd bring the joke into his later stand-up act with a fresh bête noire—his first wife.)

Burrows asked Allen if he had ambitions beyond television. "You should think of the theater," he counseled. Knowing the Comedy Development Program was going to send him to Hollywood, Allen said movies were another possibility. "A screenwriter is nothing, just an anonymous name whose work is butchered!" Burrows countered sharply. "All the screenwriters in California would love to get a play on Broadway." Allen politely agreed with his famous distant cousin, as he often agreed with advice, face-to-face, before going away to think things over.

Won over by his newfound relative, Burrows said he would write letters recommending Allen to comedian Sid Caesar; television writer Nat Hiken, creator of the *Phil Silvers Show*, a.k.a. *Sergeant Bilko*; and broadcast personality Peter Lind Hayes. He promised to scrutinize the Meltzer contract and report back.

The Meltzer contract worried him, Allen told Burrows. He had given his word to sign with Meltzer if NBC hired him, but it was "a much-too-piggish agreement," as Allen reiterated in his memoir. The contract stipulated Meltzer would receive 15 percent of Allen's initial gross weekly salary from NBC up to a ceiling of $200 weekly. If Allen's pay rose above $200, Meltzer claimed 20 percent until his salary reached $500 weekly; and if his salary rose above $500 weekly, Meltzer took 25 to 30 percent of the aggregate. The contract was nonexclusive, applying only to Allen's work for NBC, but "in the event a contract is entered into for my services with an employer other than NBC and if an agent has secured such contract for me," according to one lawyerly clause, "it is mutually understood and agreed that your compensation to be received hereunder shall be reduced by five per cent (5%), in the event agent receives ten per cent (10%) commission."

After scratching his head over the nuances of the Meltzer document, Burrows returned it to Allen by mail, having perused the language "very carefully." He told Allen he agreed "it is a very annoying contract, as you say, and I am almost certain that eventually something can be done about it." However, Burrows was a practical-minded fellow with a reputation for taking anonymous fix-it jobs on stage and screen scripts; and he didn't count pennies. He advised his young cousin to sign the Meltzer contract, keep in mind his long-term goal of writing a Broadway play, meanwhile see all the stage plays he could, learning from the good and bad plays both, and focus on honing his craft in the NBC writing program. Burrows would stay in touch as a pen pal.

"You should put [the contract] out of your mind and just concentrate on your work," Burrows urged. "At the moment this is just a problem of money, and oddly enough I think that's the least important problem for a writer." Allen duly signed the personal management contract, feeling temporarily stuck with Meltzer.

ALLEN, PAUL PUMPIAN, and Harvey Miller formed a Three Musketeers for lunches at a nearby Chinese restaurant. His father's favorite ethnic food, Chinese food was Allen's go-to cuisine in life and often in his films. Fellow writer Pumpian recalled Allen as "a funny little guy, shy," who muttered funny little things as they traversed the hotel's corridors. An example: "There's something sexy about a hotel corridor!" As much as Allen had blossomed since high school, he still had—always would have—room to grow with gaps of knowledge and blind spots. Not only the youngest of the trio, he was also the most "naïve," Pumpian recalled. One day the three were strolling toward their Chinese lunch when someone mentioned Tennessee Williams. Allen jumped in, fervently praising Williams and *A Streetcar Named Desire*—influences that would shadow a number of his later films.

"He's gay, you know?" Miller remarked, stopping Allen dead in his tracks. Allen looked stricken. "I put my arm around him," Pumpian recalled. " 'That's the way I felt about Randolph Scott,' I told him."

By the end of October there were six or eight rookies in the burgeoning writing program. The NBC strategy of bringing the novices together with established writers and comics, as well as interesting up-and-comers, gave the young writers the opportunity to try their jokes on a variety of funnymen. "Young comics would show up and show us their stuff," Allen recollected, "and we'd pick ones to write for, thus presumably developing writers and comedians. Mostly, we saw stiffs." But the aspiring comedy writers also met with a few non-stiffs like Don Adams and Jonathan Winters, who were just starting to break out in their respective comedy careers, although the rule of thumb was that the "real talent," i.e., those guys, "needed little or no help from us."

The apprentices were advised to use their off-hours constructively as well, and Les Colodny, a former agent for William Morris who was helping to supervise the Comedy Development Program, told Allen he should go see Mort Sahl and NBC would "pay the tab." The network was high on the digressive monologist, who had been booked into the Blue Angel, a chic East Side cabaret on Fifty-Fifth between Lexington and Third, in mid-October. Sahl had made his first New York appearance in 1954, but he wasn't on Allen's radar at that time.

Sahl stood onstage and read from the daily newspaper while commenting acerbically on the headlines and news. Free-associative, whimsical as well as topical, he was a departure from the old school of comedy and a shock of the future in the stand-up world. Allen was "blown away" by Sahl. While Allen himself would rarely broach news or politics in his later routines, he recognized Sahl had "revolutionized the medium" of joke-telling. "Ugly girls" and "Take my wife—please!" one-liners belonged to a dying tradition. Sahl pointed the way toward more personal, political, and philosophical types of humor. "I loved everything he did, every word out of his mouth," Allen remembered. "There was nothing that he ever did or said, every inflection, every joke, every nuance, that I didn't think was brilliant. I mean, I just thought he was the greatest thing I ever saw."

Allen felt another one of those twinges: Maybe he should try for a career as a stand-up comedian, after all. Allen went backstage to meet Sahl, and from that day forward he made a supreme effort to forge a friendship with his comedy idol. Allen's warmth was not always reciprocated by Sahl, and the oft-prickly monologist was known to throw verbal punches at his young admirer. Allen represented "the degeneration of the Jew as a social force," Sahl wrote acidly in his memoir. But Allen never lost his reverence for Sahl as an innovator.

The young writers didn't get much material on the air. "I wrote one single joke for Don Adams," Allen wryly recalled. But as usual, Allen found other spot work. Although Sid Caesar and Nat Hiken replied noncommittally to Abe Burrows's recommendation, Peter Lind Hayes, who appeared on several radio and TV shows, often with his wife, Mary Healy, met with Allen and wrote out a fifty-dollar check for a batch of jokes. "Peter has since told me that the check was never cashed," Burrows wrote in his memoir. "Woody framed it."

The fall of 1955 was their trial period, and around Thanksgiving NBC rewarded a handful of the cadets, Allen included, by picking up their options and giving them plane tickets to Hollywood. The group would leave in early 1956 to help buoy the new *NBC Comedy Hour*, the midseason replacement for the *Colgate Comedy Hour*, which had started out shakily. Coinciding with another milestone, his twentieth birthday, Allen announced his engagement to Harlene Rosen, who'd just graduated from high school with plans to enter Manhattan's Hunter College in the spring or fall. Over the past months the couple had grown more romantically, if still chastely, entwined. Marriage seemed the obvious next step for them. "We were kids," Allen remembered. "There was nothing else to do. We had seen all the movies and shows, hit the museums, played miniature golf, sat over cappuccino at Orsini's, and spent a day at Fire Island." The young comedy writer wanted to cement his relationship with Harlene before his West Coast departure date.

The Konigsbergs hosted an awkward celebratory dinner, with Allen showing off his purchase of an expensive engagement ring for Rosen. Things turned sour, however, when Nettie began kvetching about immature people getting married and Allen's dim horizons as a writer. Allen stalked out of his Flatbush home, never again to reside with his parents, which was part of the appeal of getting married anyway, he said later.

Another occasion for champagne toasts took place on the Sheepshead

Bay lawn of the Rosens, but that party also curdled when Harlene's mother, Judith, voiced displeasure over the impulsive engagement, unloading on Allen's manager Harvey Meltzer, who was among the well-wishers. "There was great trepidation in her mind about her daughter marrying someone she regarded as a schmuck," recalled Meltzer. "Judith was very anxious for me to intervene, but I told her it was none of my business. I was his manager, not his mother."

Among his family, Allen's distant cousin Abe Burrows was perhaps most supportive, sending a humorous congratulatory note to the young man and his betrothed: "I hope you have told her how horrible the life of a comedy writer's fiancée can be. There is only one thing worse and that is the life of a comedy writer's wife." When Allen, along with a half dozen of his fellow pacesetters, flew to Los Angeles in the middle of January, it was with the understanding that he would make Harlene a comedy writer's wife as soon as possible.

One of the last things Allen did before getting on the plane was to catch Kaye Ballard's new act at the popular Greenwich Village club the Bon Soir. Ballard had been booked ahead as a guest star on the *NBC Comedy Hour*. Apart from Allen, the other youngish writers onboard included original recruits Paul Keyes and Harvey Miller, along with Phil Green, Bruce Howard, and Bernie Ilson, with Lois Balk the only woman in the group. On the same flight were two of Allen's favorite radio comics: Bob and Ray—Bob Elliott and Ray Goulding—who were also slated to appear on the *NBC Comedy Hour*. "Discerning members of the Bob and Ray cognoscenti," wrote David Pollock in his Bob and Ray biography, "have long delighted in pointing out that two of the team's charter cast members [in radio sketches], Fielding Lovely and Mug Melisch, had their distinctive names lovingly combined in Woody's 1971 film *Bananas*, in the person of his own character, 'Fielding Melisch.'"*

WHEN, IN JANUARY 1956, Allen's flight landed in California, Dwight Eisenhower—Ike, as he was commonly known—was recovering from a heart attack and had not yet decided whether to campaign for a second term

* It is differently spelled "Fielding Mellish" in most synopses of the film.

as president. Articles in the Hollywood trade papers contrasted the sagging output and fortunes of the major motion picture studios with the boom in television programming and revenue. On winter days in Los Angeles, a heavy blanket of smog—a low cloud chilling the air—hung in the morning sky until the sun burned it off.

Allen and the other newbies were put up in monthlies with bar and kitchen at the Hollywood Hawaiian Hotel at the corner of Yucca and Grace, a half mile from the theater at Hollywood and Vine where the *NBC Comedy Hour* was rehearsed and broadcast. The fresh arrivals were matched with old-timers, and Allen was assigned to share a suite with Milt Rosen, "an older, portly comedy writer," a World War II veteran. "A horror worse than an aviation disaster," Allen recalled. "Not only would I be sharing a bathroom . . . the bed was a double bed."

In his Woody Allen biography John Baxter wrote that someone, upon meeting him—probably his roommate—asked the twenty-year-old what his ambitions were in Hollywood, and he replied, "To host the Oscars and write for Bob Hope." Allen also said something else: "His first words were, 'Tennessee Williams is the greatest writer who ever lived,' " Rosen remembered, "then he went out and bought a pair of shoes for six cents and almost immediately he had blisters." Rosen, who turned out to be a perfectly nice guy, smart and funny, offered to buy Allen another pair of shoes that fit better. "No, I bought them, and I have to wear them," Allen replied. Keeping to a budget, even if it meant spending stingily on himself, was already an ideology with him.

Although he and Rosen shared living space, Allen's true mentor was Danny Simon, another old pro hired to teach the ins and outs of script work for television and hone the sketches, monologue material, and blackouts of the neophytes before passing their stuff along to *NBC Comedy Hour* staff producers. The *Comedy Hour* aired on Sunday nights opposite the wildly popular *Ed Sullivan Show*. Many top comedians performed on the *Comedy Hour* during its brief run—besides Kaye Ballard and Bob and Ray, Mort Sahl and Jonathan Winters also stopped by. But the early January premiere had drawn lackluster reviews and ratings hadn't improved. "Ed Sullivan can continue to relax," said *Variety*. The outlook for the show depended, in part, on the youngbloods.

In his late forties, Danny was the older, more extroverted brother of Neil

"Doc" Simon, both of them alumni of Sid Caesar's acclaimed early 1950s variety show—*Your Show of Shows*—which was another NBC series. The Simons had written as a team, with Danny known as "The Shouter" and Neil "The Whisperer," and Danny was later acknowledged by his brother to be, early on, the senior partner, Doc's mentor too. In all there were five professionals receiving NBC salaries to shepherd the younger generation from New York. Simon was the highest profile and highest paid among them; he earned a $1,100 weekly retainer, while Allen and the other recruits without portfolio saw their contracts renewed at the Writers Guild minimum of $161 weekly.

Danny was "a very compulsive guy who fought with every partner he worked with after Doc," in Allen's words, but he and Allen hit it off as fellow New Yorkers who felt displaced on the West Coast. Things in Hollywood seemed to happen in maddeningly slow motion, and it was "too easy to slip into a lax stupidity from all the sun and pools and pseudo artists who lay around on payrolls earning small fortunes because their brother-in-laws hold company stock," in Allen's words. He spent "a lot of time" with Danny Simon, Allen wrote Abe Burrows, describing Simon as "a good friend" who was teaching him "the principles of good sketch construction."

Danny drilled Allen on how to use gags to build characterization. He preached discipline, daily writing, multiple drafts, and endless revisions. Danny was always the "pacer," and the shouter. Allen was the "sitter," or typist—also true for the rest of his career—and more of a whisperer. Mentoring him, Danny exuberantly voiced the lines and performed the scenes as he paced, and his young disciple learned the value of trying the same. Danny spewed dictums. "Great straight lines make great punch lines" was one admonition. "Never have the character say something that wasn't perfectly natural," Allen recalled Danny saying, "just to get to a great punch line I had waiting." Be prepared to throw out your best joke if it hampered the narrative drive.

Sometimes, when Allen proposed an idea, Danny would fix him with a blank look and demand to know, "And then what?"—meaning, what happens next in the story? Rather than dream up fantastical premises or funny bits that led down rabbit holes, Allen had to think ahead with plausible plotting. "Always begin at the beginning and go right to the end of the sketch" was another of Danny's precepts, and "never write a scene out of sequence, never write when you're not feeling well because the material will reflect the lack of energy and health." (Still, there were other schools of thought. "Bullshit," another Sid Caesar writer, Larry Gelbart, was known to say, "the true test of a comedy writer is to be funny when you're hung over and your wife just left you.")

As Allen learned the rudiments, he realized "I was theoretically [moving] a step up from writing jokes. And sketches are theoretically a prelude to writing for the theater, because at least you get your feet wet writing for actors." He always credited Danny Simon with teaching him the basics of script construction during this formative Hollywood sojourn, and above all "one of the many things he instilled in me, because *he* had it," Allen said, "was an unyielding self-confidence, an unyielding sense in your own convictions, and I've never lost it."

MEANWHILE, THE *NBC Comedy Hour* went steadily downhill. The East Coast contingent couldn't reverse the slide; for one thing, the younger writers competed among themselves and they also competed with the professional staff. Nobody could figure out how to salvage the program. None of Allen's sketches made it on the air, he wrote glumly to Abe Burrows. Burrows had watched the *Comedy Hour* "once or twice briefly," the playwright wrote back, "and from what I have seen of it, you should be very happy that your stuff isn't on it. The show is unbelievably bad." Writing to a Brooklyn friend, however, Allen claimed ownership of "the sketch on Sunday, the 12th [February]—the beach sketch," adding the sketch was "Danny Simon's and mine. . . . Mostly his."

Right away, as was his wont, Allen pursued other opportunities. He reached out to Bob Hope's manager, Jimmy Saphier, whom he knew from Alber Associates, and managed to wangle a meeting with Hope. Allen found that, in person, the great Hope—one of the comedians he admired above all—was unpretentious and likeable. "He has that certain small-town idiom in his speech," Allen wrote to a friend, "and when someone mentioned a fact to him, he said (with his grin and in wonderment), 'No kidding, is that the awful truth?' "

Hope offered Allen a "spec" assignment for his next TV special, a skit that would pair the comedian with Kathryn Grayson, which Allen might craft "in my spare time in the hopes that I may work myself into something worthwhile," he explained in a letter. NBC was also Hope's home network, and if Allen wrote any jokes or sketches used by Hope—or any other NBC show—he'd get bonused above his weekly salary.

As February sped by, without any of his jokes or sketches making it on the air, however, Allen took Burrows's suggestion and began toying with a "play outline." "I can agree with him [Burrows]," he wrote a friend, "about why the stage, with its lack of censorship, its intelligence and depth is the only medium to wind up in."

March arrived with the *NBC Comedy Hour* on its last legs. Allen wrote Burrows he was considering resigning and returning to New York to focus on the stage play he was writing. Burrows sympathized with his young cousin, recalling his own frustrating first gig in Hollywood, the radio show *Texaco Star Theater* in 1939, also "full of competition and backbiting and unhappiness." Still, Burrows urged patience. Allen shouldn't rush to abandon his first good job in show business nor, as yet, the medium of television. "You can learn a lot from the steady grind of that crazy business. Certainly, it forces a man to write something every day."

This was Danny Simon's bottom line too: Write something every day, he advocated, so Allen did: jokes, sketches, scenes for a play, notes for other future projects. Allen continued to esteem Danny, who "has worked many patient hours with me, outlining proper construction for sketches," while always expressing "the highest confidence in all the material of mine." When NBC official Les Colodny flew to Hollywood to assess the writing program's efficacy, Danny gave Allen his highest praise: "Les, I think the kid is my next brother!"

The thirty-seven-year-old Simon treated Allen like a kid brother, even though Danny was almost old enough to be his father. Danny was so gung-ho about him, Allen wrote Burrows, he'd been invited to be his writing partner at Camp Tamiment over the summer of 1956. Tamiment was a breeding ground for talent located one hundred miles northwest of Brooklyn in Pennsylvania's Pocono Mountains. The Simon brothers had launched their careers at the fabled Tamiment Playhouse. That summer Danny was planning to direct some playhouse shows, as part of his long-range goal of becoming a Broadway director. He and Allen could collaborate on Tamiment scripts—just as Danny and his brother, Neil, used to do—and Danny would stage the shows they wrote. After the summer Simon would be a "wonderful contact" for Allen in New York. Simon was "in line for some top shows and each day he asks me if I'm interested in writing for them under him," Allen reported. "He feels the experience of writing under such a good writer-director arrangement, plus the experience of seeing my material played each week, plus the material I will accumulate for Broadway sales will make the summer a big boon to me. . . . I'm not sure as to whether I should and I'm wondering if it's as good as it sounds."

No, it wasn't as good as it sounded, Burrows thought, quickly writing back to say he didn't know Danny Simon personally, but he knew him by reputation as a writer left behind by his brother, Neil, who was proving to be the superior talent. Danny was good at playing the wise owl but what he badly needed was another kid brother, or junior partner, to prop him up. "Never tie yourself to someone because he is a 'wonderful contact,'" Burrows advised. "First of all, a writer who can turn out comedy material doesn't need contacts. Secondly, people who are good contacts are only as good as their contacts. . . . I would only stay with this guy if I really enjoyed working with him as a collaborator." As for Tamiment, Burrows added, "I would only do this if I thought I would enjoy it. . . . I don't know exactly why Danny Simon is going to Tamiment unless it's for a summer vacation."

Mulling over their correspondence, Allen decided the playwright was right. One thing for sure, Allen didn't want to role-play as someone's kid brother. Reflected glory was never for him; in his long career Woody Allen would take on few collaborators, steer clear of adaptations, even at times downplay obvious influences on his films. Burrows's avuncular tone, his creed of working hard and learning in the moment, his farsighted vision of a playwriting career for his relative, these resonated with the budding comedy writer. Allen's next letter to New York reflected his changed views. "I don't enjoy working with him [Simon] and never did," Allen wrote Burrows, "but he had much to teach me and the weeks of painstaking work with him were worth it. He's a good craftsman. After lots of good advice, I doubt if I will spend the whole summer with him in Tamiment.'

NEVER MIND THE smog, way back in the mid-1950s Allen experienced the world of Southern California as "monotonously sunny," with Hollywood "pastel and Oz-like," a place like a "rural village that would bore you stiff in no time." Long before *Annie Hall*, he was complaining about the weather and empty sidewalks and weird social mores. In a letter to Jack Victor back home he wrote: "It's an honor system town with few traffic lights, and there's nobody at the newsstands on the corners, as they depend on you to pay for your paper and stop for pedestrians."

While the other promising young comedy writers spent their sunshine-filled free time lolling around the Hawaiian Hotel swimming pool, Allen holed up in the shadows of his room, writing, reading, and practicing his clarinet to jazz LPs on the record player he had lugged to California. He devoted several weeks to D. H. Lawrence and the collected plays of Ibsen and O'Neill. Recommending *Desire Under the Elms*, *Dynamo*, and *The Hairy Ape* to his Brooklyn friend Jack Victor, Allen said O'Neill's plays captured "the mood of the kind of thing that I'm interested in writing. You'll notice that my ideas, although lacking in craft and a coherent point of view, lean always to what I can only call a poetic mood built from existential horror, insanity, and death."

He introduced the habit of taking a break from work in the afternoons and embarking on long walks in his ill-fitting shoes. He did some sightseeing and gawking and spotted the occasional celebrity. "Yesterday on the street I passed [Asian character actor] Richard Loo," Allen joked in a letter. He dined like royalty at the Brown Derby. He saw the latest movies in Art Deco theaters on Hollywood Boulevard and "flipped" over the screen version of Tennessee Williams's *The Rose Tattoo*, Allen wrote friends, marveling at the performance of Anna Magnani; and he also loved the Shakespeare adaptation *Richard III*, or "Dick the III" as he dubbed it, directed by and starring Laurence Olivier. He was proud his Brooklyn pen pals also preferred the art cinema. "Nobody here of all the so-called 'artistes' mentioned anything [about arty films] but you did in your letter," he wrote Victor, "and it was so refreshing to know you still have close friends who are moved by something that really tries."

At night he ventured out with friends from the Comedy Development Program, trying to pick up girls. He failed miserably at this goal. Many of the other writers boasted wives or girlfriends. Allen was still a clueless virgin. The older writers ribbed the twenty-year-old, wondering if he was familiar with the disparate erogenous zones and orifices of the female body.

Back in Brooklyn, when discussing his engagement to Harlene Rosen with Elliot Mills, Mills had to describe the wonderful world of clitorises by drawing one in the dirt of Wingate Field. Danny Simon offered to set Allen up with a hooker whose prowl included the Hawaiian. "Oh, wow!" exclaimed Allen, reaching for his wallet with a poker face. "Do you think she'll take a traveler's check?"

This hooker was "never engaged," according to official biographer Eric Lax, but perhaps it happened like that awkward, prolonged scene in Allen's 2016 film, *Café Society*, set in Golden Age Hollywood, where Allen alter ego Jesse Eisenberg balks at consummating his arranged tryst with first-time call girl Anna Camp. Other biographers believe Allen had a longtime fascination with call girls, which began with virginity, loneliness, and the leisure time and money he had to burn in Hollywood in 1956.

Over time call girls and prostitutes became a fixture of his short stories (e.g., "The Whore of Mensa") and movies, with their appearances mounting in frequency after his 1992 bust-up with Farrow. "They are tremendous people, very strong symbols of our society," Allen once explained, "a little like the Mafiosi and gangsters of [the films of Francis] Coppola or [Steven] Spielberg. Dostoyevsky depicted them in his novels, Fellini in his films. They are the women who add color to life but who are always considered, here [in the US], as less than nothing, destined to be punished by humiliation or death."* In his work, however, Allen always treated prostitutes comically if sympathetically, while Fellini, for example, painted a tragical portrait of Cabiria.

In truth, Allen pined for Harlene. As would happen other times in his life when he was besotted, Allen telephoned or wrote to his fiancée every day, several times a day. "Five letters a day," recalled Hawaiian Hotel roommate Milt Rosen, "each twenty-five pages long." By March Allen had developed an itch that had to be scratched. It was time for him and Harlene to get married. A phone call summoned her to Hollywood.

Although Allen, in interviews, always emphasized his early-in-life

---

* Often Allen spoke more reflectively to French interviewers. He addressed the question of the many prostitutes in his films seriously, again mentioning Dostoyevsky, when interviewed by Michel Ciment and Frank Garbarz for *Positif* in 1998. "Prostitutes are interesting characters from a dramatic point of view, insofar as they are genuinely maladjusted socially and live on the margin of society," Allen explained. "They've always interested artists. From Dostoyevsky to Lautrec, because they're highly colorful characters who evolve in a dangerous environment, one charged with a permanent sexual tension. They're excellent nourishers of artistic creation."

disillusionment with the Jewish religion and culture, the Allen-Rosen nuptials, on March 15, 1956, took place in the living room of an Orthodox rabbi handpicked by the husband-to-be. Morris Kaplan presided over the nearby Congregation Knesseth Israel, which had just opened on Vermont Avenue after a building campaign led by comedian Red Skelton. "A nod to her parents," Allen insisted in his autobiography, although the Rosens and Konigsbergs were absent from the occasion. Other comedy writers served as witnesses and congratulants. Rabbi Kaplan may or may not have privately counseled the unsophisticated twosome about intercourse, as Allen later jokingly told friends at Tamiment. "Mount her like a young bull!" the rabbi supposedly exhorted the sexually inexperienced groom.

Allen was twenty; precocious Harlene was just seventeen. According to Lax, comedy-writing colleagues Danny Simon and Milt Rosen "short-sheeted their bed" after the wedding ceremony, so the two had to flee to another motel for their first night together. Rosen moved out of their abode at the Hawaiian, and the new Mrs. Allen moved in with her husband. Harlene's mother, Judith, arrived belatedly and checked in to her own quarters at the Hawaiian for a few weeks. Her grudging attitude added to the natural strain between the couple.

The newlyweds squabbled. The young comedy writer anxious about his future now had a missus who padded around his sacred workspace. Said lady "walks five paces behind me at all times," Allen wrote half in jest to neighborhood buddies. "Harlene flew out and we got married," he matter-of-factly reported to Abe Burrows after tying the knot. Yet to Brooklyn peers, Allen jokingly confided he was "seized with a selfish horror," realizing he was now a certified hubby. His teenage wife was not much of a cook either. Chicken was her best recipe, he reported, but everything she cooked tasted like chicken, even the coffee she brewed. The sex was better: "I'm happy as a husband except for the time spent out of bed." Still, you could never tell if the kid was kidding.

Harlene's mother departed, and the newly marrieds found their own rhythm. Allen focused on writing. Harlene painted. Appraising her artwork, he conceded she was rather gifted. His wife looked good with her clothes off too, which is why he snapped Polaroids of her in the buff, a common enough pastime among young lovers. The same divertissement decades later, with college-age Soon-Yi Previn, triggered his bitter split from Farrow and raised puritanical eyebrows across America. Sharing Harlene's nudies with a Brooklyn pal when he returned to New York was perhaps not as common a practice. His wife walked in on the sneak peek, interrupting the chuckling friends, and Allen "turned several shades of red." But the snapshots "weren't lewd in any way, just naked," the friend recalled.

No matter how much time he spent targeting skits or jokes for NBC shows—all in vain—or working on his embryonic stage play, the couple had happy off-hours. Mr. and Mrs. Woody Allen filled their playtime with walks and moviegoing and stopping in record stores to listen to and buy LPs. They made their own vinyl discs in the pay booths—dueting on recorders—riffing on tunes by George Gershwin and Cole Porter they both loved.

BY MAY IT was clear the network was going to cancel the *NBC Comedy Hour*, and it was just as clear the Comedy Development Program was on the chopping block. To keep NBC's college of comedy alive during the upcoming summer months of tryout and substitute fill-in shows would entail inordinate effort and expense.

Allen's jokes and sketches had "impressed" everyone regardless, he wrote Abe Burrows. As the *Comedy Hour* faltered, he shifted entirely to "spec" possibilities for other NBC programs. He pitched bits to his old Circle Magic Shop confrere Milton Berle, now headlining *The Milton Berle Show*; Dave Garroway, anchoring the *Today* show; and Steve Allen, host of *The Tonight Show*. His offerings were either rejected, or heavily reworked. The NBC producers preferred "outdated vaudeville pieces," Allen complained to Burrows. The silver lining was the "back-log of quality material" he was building up and storing for the future. He threw nothing away, and for the rest of his career he would pluck jokes, sketches, and ideas from his bottomless back-log.

NBC made a stab at collecting the unsold best of the Comedy Development Program into "an intimate television revue," a summer replacement series that would showcase the writers' unsold skits and their joke-telling and performance skills. But after a hasty and disorganized dress rehearsal, which impressed no one, the quixotic notion was abandoned. The onrush of conflicting summer commitments, added to network scheduling and budget problems, proved insurmountable. The network circulated a memo lauding the program as a wonderful experiment before shutting it down permanently and recommending the demobilized writers repair to some safe outpost like Camp Tamiment for the summer, where they might continue to learn and grow.

Like Allen, many of the college-of-comedy writers who first went to Hollywood in 1956 forged strong careers. Harvey Miller, for example, earned numerous television credits before producing and writing films including *Private Benjamin*, for which his co-script was Oscar-nominated. Paul Pumpian wrote top NBC comedy specials. The fourth writer in the original quartet, Paul Keyes, served as an Emmy-winning writer and producer of *Rowan & Martin's Laugh-In*. Yet it always stuck in Allen's craw that Keyes, his collaborator on "Mama Mia," went on to stage White House entertainments for President Richard Nixon. "The creepiest of the group wound up writing 'warmth lines' for Richard Nixon's speeches," Allen wrote in *Apropos of Nothing*.

In late May, thanks to Danny Simon, NBC threw Allen a lifeline. Looking ahead to the fall, the network hired Allen to craft "outlines" for a situation comedy series called *Stanley*, which was being planned for live broadcast from New York. The new television series was the brainchild of producer Max Liebman, the legendary mastermind of *Your Show of Shows*, who was part of the Tamiment genealogy—he had run the playhouse in the 1930s and '40s. The TV series would star comedian Buddy Hackett as the title character—a harried hotel clerk. Danny had decided to forgo his Tamiment summer for the better-paying job of script consultant on the series. His brother, Neil, was busy writing the pilot episode. The *Stanley* contract put Allen in the august company of the Simon brothers and Max Liebman, and it gave him job security with a raise in weekly salary to $1,000.

He and Harlene packed their duds and embarked on a delayed honeymoon in Las Vegas. The Andrews Sisters and Brooklyn funnyman Alan King were appearing at the Flamingo. Nat King Cole shared the stage at the Sands with the young comics Rowan and Martin. Husband and wife both—Allen considered himself something of a card shark—indulged in a bit of gambling. They had planned to visit New Orleans, where Allen wanted to track down jazz clarinetist George Lewis, before they ran out of playtime. Work beckoned Allen in New York.

RETURNING TO NEW YORK in midsummer, Allen had gained a wife and made strides in his craft. He also had acquired a lifelong antipathy to California and the commercial exigencies of television. He intended to channel his NBC earnings into a higher goal: finishing his first stage play. Not once, in all his letters from Hollywood, did Allen voice any ambition to break into motion pictures, even if he still regularly lost himself at the movies.

He and Harlene briefly moved into her family's Brooklyn home until they found an apartment on the Upper East Side of Manhattan at Park Avenue and Sixty-First. It was not the setting for a penthouse champagne comedy, however: The apartment was a "very small" single-room flat in a multidwelling brownstone, boasting a sofa bed, a kitchen table with chairs, a television set, several lamps, and "a stand with a large tape recorder." Allen worked on his typewriter at the kitchen table; between jokes for hire and ideas for *Stanley*, he puttered on his play.

He and Harlene resumed an active nightlife, attending all the mainstream Broadway shows as well as off-Broadway, avant-garde dance recitals, poetry readings, art gallery exhibits. *My Fair Lady* was the uncontested smash success of 1956. The young man who was sifting through mentors and father figures in his professional career was captivated by the musical adaptation of *Pygmalion*, with arrogant phonetics professor Henry Higgins molding the young cockney Eliza Doolittle. In his filmmaking years he'd endlessly rework *Pygmalion* themes.

Habitually in the afternoons Allen still took walks, contriving to stroll nearby on Sixty-Second Street, imagining the famous people creatively collaborating inside George S. Kaufman's mansion, planning their next Broadway triumph. He read all he could about the playwright and admired his 24-7 work ethic: all day, every day, Sundays and holidays too. Kaufman could work "at home or late in hotel rooms under pressure and do the hard labor, the tedious, glamourless structuring and rewriting and merciless cutting that is crucial" to breathing life into a script. Kaufman ruthlessly cut his favorite jokes if necessary. "Make it shorter" was a Kaufman rule. Musing about Kaufman inspired Allen. "Feeling invigorated, I'd scoot back in my single room and with a burst of renewed creativity, turn out five brilliant pages." One day, though, spoilsport Harlene told him Kaufman lived on Sixty-Third Street, in fact, and Allen had been drawing brain waves "from the wrong house on the wrong block."

Cooped up in crowded space, the young-marrieds squabbled anew as September dawned. "I was moody, unhappy, nasty to her very nice parents," Allen remembered. "I couldn't stand my wife's friends. I got on her nerves with my constant, sullen unhappiness. I began getting nauseated often, usually in the dead of night." It was a good thing Rosen immersed herself in undergraduate life at nearby Hunter College, where she started out with plans to major in painting and philosophy. "I walked her to school every morning before digging into work," Allen said. "I was so glad when she was gone because there was not a single thing we could agree on."

The *Stanley* job did little to lighten his disposition. Amid organizing his new household, Allen reported to Max Liebman at offices in the City Center theater building one block south of Carnegie Hall. The producer's desk was filled with plaques and awards. "Gee, Max, I didn't know you played tennis!" Allen cracked. In those days the young comedy writer was known for his wiseacre greetings and parting shots, but Liebman, who liked to enjoin his staff to "Make me laugh!" did not laugh at that first Woody Allen joke, nor at many that followed. Another Jewish Brooklynite by way of Vienna, Liebman had started in vaudeville as a sketch writer, then made his reputation before World War II as the maestro of Tamiment Playhouse revues that launched entertainers such as Imogene Coca and Danny Kaye. His big discovery was Sid Caesar, who had never made the Tamiment scene; Liebman met Caesar during wartime, put him in military revues, and placed the talented unknown under personal contract. Liebman had steered *Your Show of Shows* to glory before NBC separated the producer and star in 1954, giving independence to Caesar with special projects for Liebman to produce for the network.

However, *Stanley* evolved into a mess to rival the *NBC Comedy Hour*. A brash, mugging monologist, Buddy Hackett needed bolstering in the situation comedy format, and Carol Burnett, a young, gifted nonesuch who had blossomed at Tamiment, was rushed in after the premiere to liven up the show as Hackett's "love interest." Liebman and Hackett clashed over script ideas, and in mid-October the show was abruptly reinvented as "a variety layout, sans any plot or story lines, with new writers," according to *Variety*. Then, one week later, the reinvention was reversed, and *Stanley* became a new, improved sitcom with ever-mutating story elements.

Liebman liked to encourage volatile story conferences, where the writers were known to shout over one another. Allen was spookily reserved. "We didn't converse at all," the producer recalled. "I began to wonder if he was dumb." Hackett saw Allen likewise: "He was a very timid kid who didn't say much." According to Liebman, "Woody would listen, nod, then go away that night and come in next day with reams of paper. I got the impression he'd been working half the night. But it wasn't right. It wasn't what I wanted for the show."

Be that as it may, Liebman's métier was variety programming, and the producer was at sea with a conventional situation comedy that required narrative continuity. The producer was "too strong a personality and too wrong-headed" about his ideas, Allen thought. *Stanley* lasted half the season before, in December, NBC summarily axed the show. Not for the last time did Allen feel he had eclipsed his own personality by writing to satisfy the fixed persona of someone else. The problem wasn't just Hackett's persona; it was the power the star wielded over the script. Characters' names were important to Allen, for example, and he tried to come up with unusual names, often drawing on variations of close friends and family. But Hackett had even fiddled with the characters' names in the *Stanley* scripts. He "rubs them out and puts his own family names in," Allen griped to a Brooklyn friend.

Allen managed to last the run, however, and he shared the credit for writing two episodes. There was no pressing financial crisis. Danny Simon, who was liaising with story editors on multiple television series, kept in contact with his protégé from phone booths, always "very secretive," in Allen's words, offering "a great thing for you to work on. I can't get much money, but I can get you a tiny bit." Allen also raked in some extra money writing jokes for numerous "anonymous nightclub comics, who had no personality and never would have."

Suddenly, he found himself with abundant free time. Allen told counterculture journalist Paul Krassner that was one reason to undergo psychoanalysis: to "kill time." Being able to afford the fees of psychiatric sessions was another reason Allen gave, in interviews, for why, turning twenty-one in 1956, he made his first afternoon appointment with Dr. Peter Blos, a German-born American expert on the effects of childhood and adolescence on psychological development. "I was not happy," Allen wrote in his memoir. "I was gloomy, fearful, angry, and don't ask me why." He looked forward to talking his life over with his therapist so much he found a different analyst for some other afternoons.

Parental conflicts, coping with marriage and his vexatious wife, emotional intimacy, lack of creative fulfillment—above all, the meaningless of life—these were the general fodder for his sessions. Although Allen was a high-functioning personality, his many neuroses and fears suggested "a touch of Asperger's," which Gatsby, his alter ego played by Timothée Chalamet, proudly admits to exhibiting in *A Rainy Day in New York*, Allen's 2019 film. Allen had a number of phobias he'd never shed. He was only comfortable around closest friends.

In years to come Allen steadfastly dodged the details about what precisely ailed or bothered him. "I was very unhappy," he told *Seventeen* in 1968. "No particular reason, just a feeling I couldn't shake, but it was a terrible, terrifying feeling to have." Every therapy session was basically the same. "In, whine for fifty minutes, out again. Dull, dull, dull." Allen often said his analysts never volunteered solutions. They just listened.

Yet the therapists served at least one valuable function. They would inspire and enrich the numerous psychiatrist characters that, over time, loomed large in Woody Allen films. Dream sequences and excursions into the minds of the characters Allen played would become an expected hallmark of his work. Not only therapists; over time Allen saw a wide array of physicians—dentists, surgeons, other specialists—and doctors would crop up regularly in his stories and scripts. After "actress" and "interior designer," "doctor" was the most frequent profession of supporting characters in his films. He himself often played a writer struggling with his anxieties.

Allen's fictional therapists were versatile, listening to their patients in his comedies as well as his dramas; sometimes they were sage-like presences, other times they were inscrutable or unwise. The movie therapists might be crucial to the plot, or they might be of minor importance to the goings-on. Either way, the movie therapists never seriously explored what Allen himself discussed with their real-life counterparts behind closed doors.

••

AROUND THIS TIME the twenty-one-year-old received his military draft notice. "I quickly contacted every physician I knew," Allen recalled, "and begged for notes, claiming I was physically handicapped." He trundled off to be examined, armed with medical excuses and psychiatrists' letters. The army doctor surprised him, he later joked, by asking him to hold out his hand, peering at his fingernails, and stamping him 4-F. "Rejected by the army because I was a nail-biter." Probably the true reason was another physical or psychological disability, and he was indeed rejected. But the full explanation for his 4-F status remains one of Allen's well-kept secrets.

The summer of 1957 stretched ahead. Tamiment, Tamiment, Tamiment: That was a refrain Allen had heard from Danny Simon, various NBC officials, and—straight from the horse's mouth—Max Liebman. When, regardless of his mounting viability and income as a writer, he applied to spend July and August at the famous summer resort in the Pocono Mountains near Stroudsburg, Pennsylvania, it was not because he relished the country life, sunbathing, or golf. It was because Camp Tamiment staged weekly musical shows with Actors' Equity professionals in a 1,200-seat playhouse for guests and area audiences; and Tamiment would give Allen the opportunity he desired, above all, to see his sketches performed from beginning to end, purely as he wrote them.

Allen's NBC credentials were good enough for Monroe B. Hack, known as Moe Hack, a backstage jack-of-all-trades who had taken the baton from Liebman and run the Tamiment Playhouse since the early 1950s. The short, stocky, bald, cigar-smoking Hack was not any kind of writer, but he prided himself on the stable of writers he collected every summer to anchor the playhouse entertainments: six to nine sketch writers, composers and lyricists, and a special ballet composer to work with the camp choreographer, most of them New York professionals on warm-weather hiatus. Tamiment was "a true writer's theater," according to Martha Schmoyer LoMonaco in her authoritative book *Every Week, a Broadway Revue: The Tamiment Playhouse, 1921–1960.*

When Allen asked Hack for a job for his wife, Harlene, Hack made Harlene his secretary and typist of the playhouse scripts. Allen's $150 weekly came with room and board, but for his first Tamiment summer Mr. and Mrs. Woody Allen eschewed the usual cabin in the woods and sheltered in a nearby boardinghouse.

With a huge dining room and vast dance hall jutting above a lake, a Broadway-size auditorium, tennis courts, and golf course, Camp Tamiment—the "South Wind" of Herman Wouk's novel *Marjorie Morningstar*, published in 1955—originated in the early twenties as a socialist campground with politically themed entertainments. Liebman swept away the left-wing politics in the late 1930s, championing musical revues with song, dance, and artistic interludes. Hack had continued to modify the template. On an impressive budget of a reputed $100,000 weekly he produced Saturday night musicales that wove the skits, songs, and dance numbers into a unified theme—what were dubbed "mini-musicals." The Saturday night shows were repeated on Sundays for new camp attendees, and on Sundays Hack presided over a meeting of the writers to plan the next week's show.

The mini-musicals were calculated to run no longer than an hour and fifteen minutes, without intermission, and each writer was expected to produce at least two skits weekly, about ten minutes long, plus other contributions. Hack was the ultimate arbiter. Everyone recalls him as a good guy, if a screamer. When Hack rejected any one of Allen's ideas, the writer seemed to have dozens more in his quiver, and Allen was *fast*. "When he typed," said playhouse actor Len Maxwell, "it sounded like a buzz saw because he was that fast a typist."

Everyone had a favorite among Allen's Tamiment sketches. There was the one about the Cape Canaveral rocket that has gone wildly astray and is heading straight toward New York City. There was a skit about a warden's daughter eloping over the prison walls with an escaping felon. (That skit would make a later cameo appearance in *Take the Money and Run*.) There was the one about the family of a playwright attending the premiere of his bleak tragedy, which mercilessly lampoons their own reality. In four chairs facing the Tamiment audience sat the mother, two aunts, and in later summer repeats, Allen himself appearing as the playwright.

Not all the sketches and Saturday night shows were indelible triumphs; there were many glitches and failures, and sometimes the audience sat on their hands. But failures were to be expected and savored almost as much as the grueling weekly pace, which was comparable to "live" television. The freedom to fall on your face was part of the Tamiment philosophy, and Allen absorbed two beliefs into his evolving professional creed: Expedience was a virtue. And as a writer one had the absolute right—perhaps the duty—to gamble and fail.

What artists and entertainers treasured about Tamiment beyond the playhouse productions was the feeling of "a very close-knit family," in the words of composer Jerry Bock, a summer camp veteran. Everyone recalled Allen as a shy but friendly member of the close summer family. With sticks of spearmint gum to offset his nervousness, or so people assumed, he adjusted surprisingly well to rusticity, albeit regularly phoning his Upper East Side analyst. Although he avoided the lake, he played baseball with the busboys. Every day he practiced his clarinet and occasionally sat in with the house band. Sometimes he and Harlene played duets on their recorders on the porch of the main building. Afternoons he'd sprawl in a straw chair on the porch, reading a fat book. "People joked that the books were marriage manuals," said Mary Rodgers, then a Tamiment composer.

Martin and Nettie Konigsberg visited during that first summer, and people liked Allen's parents. Hack thought they were "a very nice couple." Allen's father brought medals he had engraved for the camp contests.

"Mrs. Woody" is how company members fondly referred to Harlene, and perhaps camp life—every day round-the-clock work, with pleasant distractions—eased the fault lines in their marriage. Black was the color Harlene usually wore. And although Mr. and Mrs. Woody appeared to be sweetly devoted to each other, Paula Cohen, Moe Hack's daughter, who helped manage the camp, thought Allen's wife served as "a substitute for Woody's mother. She gave him constant bolstering, which he needed a lot of." Actress Jane Connell said the husband and wife were "more like little kids, brother and sister," with Harlene evoking "Olive Oyl in the comics." Quiet and shy like Allen, Harlene "didn't show her feelings," said Hack, but was "cool and capable."

Professional directors staged the weeklies, and Hack told Allen he could direct his own sketches if he returned next summer. Allen "never felt that I was getting the sketches mounted exactly the way he wanted," Hack recalled. The directing offer was "inducement enough" for Allen. Mr. and Mrs. Woody agreed to return.

ALLEN WOULD STRENUOUSLY avoid television situation comedies for sixty years after *Stanley*. He despised most television and sitcoms, even though later in his career he often cast actors in his movies who had broken out in popular TV series. Still, his reputation for availability and quickness—so deft he'd come up with jokes on the phone—continued to grow, adding to his revenue stream, which frequently involved anonymous work for television shows. Danny Simon continued to phone with fix-it jobs. Allen also wrote on demand for nightclub comics and for "various hosts" of *The Tonight Show* and *The Ed Sullivan Show* who needed booster shots; and he even wrote uncredited material for Paul Winchell's ventriloquist dummies Jerry Mahoney and Knucklehead Smiff. Realizing he still had a lot to learn about sketch writing, he tabled the idea of an O'Neill-type drama. Nowadays he jotted ideas for a stage comedy. Yet he spent most of his writing time on skits and jokes, partly because the construction and continuity of a full play remained daunting.

After the summer, he and Harlene moved into a larger, two-and-a-half room apartment in a brownstone on East Seventy-Eighth off Fifth. Allen continued to pay Harlene's college tuition and expenses, along with tutors and private seminars for both of them in literature and philosophy, "beginning with the pre-Socratics," as Eric Lax itemized, "then moving through Plato, Aristotle, Dante, Thomas More and up to James Joyce." The young marrieds haunted museums and art galleries, stage and movie theaters, jazz clubs and cabarets. At home they listened together to classical and jazz recordings, and on occasion dueted on their musical instruments of choice. With Mickey Rose and his wife-to-be Judy Wolf—a Hunter College classmate of Harlene's—the couple attended Madison Square Garden hockey games, with everyone rooting for the hometown New York Rangers. (Allen would reference his rare enthusiasm for the city's professional ice hockey team, which share their arena with his beloved New York Knicks, at the beginning of his 1993 film *Manhattan Murder Mystery*.)

Their awkward domesticity was something about which Allen could—and did—make jokes. Not quite out of her teens, Harlene remained a lousy cook. "Elliot Mills remembered a dinner of boiled beef hearts and overcooked string beans [at their place]," Marion Meade wrote, "as the worst meal he had ever eaten." Len Maxwell recalled another supper with the couple: steak and peas, with the peas straight from the can, cold.

THE SUMMER OF 1958 was destined to be remembered as the "pinnacle year" of the Tamiment Playhouse, according to Martha Schmoyer

LoMonaco. The camp would close permanently in 1960. This was the second time around for Mr. and Mrs. Woody, and this time they joined the company in accepting a cabin in the woods. Again, Allen's sketches delighted everyone, so much so they began to be repeated as audience favorites. *Opening Night* was brought back from the previous summer, and *Psychological Warfare*—with a troop of soldiers drilling for a psychological assault—was performed several times over the summer, and then several times more during the summer of 1959. "Hit them in the ego! . . . Hit them in the id! . . . Hit them in their inferiority complexes, and if that doesn't work, hit them below the belt and we'll go back to the old way!"

Another of Allen's prized sketches, *Son of the Cupcake*, involved a giant chocolate cake gone amok and wreaking havoc on panicked crowds in the manner of *War of the Worlds*, the famous *Mercury Theater* radio broadcast of a space invasion, presided over by Orson Welles in 1938. Later, people realized *Son of the Cupcake* was the forerunner of the humongous breast on a rampage that Allen depicts in *Everything You Always Wanted to Know About Sex** as well as cousin to the volcano eruption of an instant chocolate pudding in *Sleeper*.

For the first time Allen directed some of his sketches. "The directing was purely out of self-preservation," he insisted later, "and was not the fulfillment of some longtime desire to direct." Even as a first-time director, however, Allen manifested certain idiosyncrasies. At Tamiment the parts were often tailored to the strengths of individual performers, but the directors usually made an effort to allot the roles as democratically as possible. After casting and handing out his script pages—typed by Harlene in her capacity as camp secretary—Allen would talk to the performers about the setup of a sketch and spell out the mechanics of the action, while encouraging the cast to tinker with his dialogue, or tweak his ideas for the staging. One time, actor Len Maxwell made so many changes to his script Allen insisted Maxwell share the writing credit for that week's Saturday night show. When Maxwell's name was accidentally omitted, Allen and Harlene handwrote his name into all of the flyers. Allen's faith in the actors was such that he sometimes would absent himself from the run-throughs, waiting until Saturday's dress rehearsal before observing how the skits had evolved, and then delivering his notes.

Tamiment colleagues unfailingly remember Allen as a mild-mannered fellow, always "extremely helpful [to others] in the most unselfish way," in the words of Christopher Hewett, a stage director on the staff. Allen would build lasting friendships among the summer company, including a close bond with another writer, "the odd and brilliant" David Panich, "whom I owe much to," along with tall, burly Maxwell, the actor for whom Allen wrote the kookiest parts in his sketches. It was already becoming the case that he worked best with empathetic friends. Maxwell could be "brilliant" in sketches, according to Hewett, "but only under Woody's direction."

"I've never been a country person," Allen reflected later, "so that part [of Tamiment] didn't move me that much. It was the creative atmosphere I liked. I sort of got a kick out of the fact that we'd be in those crude little bungalows that shared a bathroom with an adjacent bungalow. Musicians practicing their instruments during the day, songwriters pounding out songs. David Panich and myself would be wandering around thinking of blackout lines and punch lines. . . . [Tamiment] had a really George S. Kaufman–esque *Stage Door*-feeling."

Another performer Allen rewarded with substantial parts, that second summer, was Milt Kamen, who when not performing at Tamiment was a stand-up comic with a nightclub act that satirized movie reviews. Kamen also happened to be a lighting double for Sid Caesar on his various television series. Sid Caesar, Sid Caesar, Sid Caesar: that was another mantra Allen had been listening to for a few years, starting with Abe Burrows's letter to Caesar on his behalf in 1955. Danny Simon had told many anecdotes about the agonies and ecstasies of writing for Caesar. Allen had gotten a writing feeler from Caesar's show the past spring, but it led nowhere.

Caesar was in the market for writers for his new series in the fall of 1958, Kamen told Allen. After having a showdown with NBC, which had canceled *Sid Caesar Invites You* in the spring, Caesar was returning to the airwaves on ABC, revamping his weekly variety format as intermittently scheduled and variously themed specials. Kamen brought Allen to Caesar's first story conference as the Tamiment summer ended. Kamen grandly announced: "I've got the young Larry Gelbart with me!" "Hey, I thought *I* was the young Larry Gelbart!" objected a voice in the room, the one and same Gelbart—a doyen of Caesar's writing stable.

Allen thought "Young" Gelbart—age thirty—"seemed so fragile, so unformed, a tadpole in horn-rims" at first glance. "Then he started pitching jokes. Magically, he became instantly handsome, growing a foot taller with each fresh and funny punch line. This frog was a prince of comedy." Privately, Allen was feeling "scared," he confessed later, to find himself suddenly in the midst of important, established writers. Several times he took bathroom breaks. "I'd run into the bathroom," he said, "and just breathe and relax for a minute or two." By day's end, despite a sotto voce style that raised the eyebrows of Caesar and the others, he had passed the test.

"I'm hired?" Allen wondered as he and Gelbart stepped into the elevator heading down after the long day. "If you'll work for the minimum," Gelbart joked. Only twenty-two, the young scribe had reached the mountaintop, joining Sid Caesar's writers' room, the most celebrated comedy staff in television history. "Writing for Caesar was the highest thing you could aspire to, at least as a TV comedy writer," Allen recalled.

Among the scribblers dashing in and out of Caesar's madcap story conferences—some just dropping by, others getting paid—were Danny and Neil Simon and a pair of Mels: longtime head writer Mel Tolkin and enfant terrible Mel Brooks. Sometimes Caesar's story conferences seemed "a mass of hostilities and jealousies," Allen recalled. The others warned him about Brooks, who was known to leap up on desks, hurl epithets, and shout his punch lines the loudest. But Brooks, who could be a contrarian, behaved as nicely and sweetly as possible to the youthful comedy writer, making a point of passing the torch and referring to Allen as "The Kid," Brooks's own former sobriquet, dating back to the early 1950s when Brooks had been the nipper in the room. "We'd walk home together every night," Allen remembered. "He regaled me with his romantic adventures, and I marveled at how such a small Jew could mesmerize one magnificent woman after another."

They never lost that camaraderie. For a brief time in the early 1970s every American movie critic compared them—Woody Allen and Mel Brooks—both Jewish Brooklynites, one headquartered in New York, the other anchored in Hollywood, busy making their dissimilar hit comedies. Allen did not embrace all of Brooks's shtick, but he was known to chuckle throughout his movies, which for him was saying a lot. What Allen really admired was the ebullience and confidence of Brooks. Allen's pictures were shot through with anxiety and angst. "I think he gets more joy out of it [making his films] than I do," Allen once said. "He's joyful and I'm depressive. His films are quite funny, in an affirmative, kidding-around, joyful sense." On the rare occasions they crossed paths—by chance on a New York street or at a Hollywood party—Brooks always made him smile.

There was song and dance with burlesques of other TV shows and movies in the first Sid Caesar special, which aired in late October. The sketches satirized the overheated drama of *Playhouse 90* and the corny hipness of *American Bandstand* with, in the case of the latter, the rock group the Sisters Karamazov straight out of Allen's Russian-lit funny bag. Caesar's luster had begun to dim, but *Variety* praised the premiere, making note of the "good scripting," with Gelbart and Allen the only names credited. The premiere and next several Sid Caesar specials featured Art Carney as the second banana, vocalist Jo Stafford, and actress Shirley MacLaine, who repeated as a guest during the season. Allen's passing acquaintance with MacLaine would bear fruit in the future.

Gelbart, Allen's writing partner, was no shouter like Brooks. Dapper and witty, he blended with Allen like a smoothie. The quirks and peccadilloes of the young comedy writer amused the veteran to no end. On one occasion, Caesar chauffeured the two writers to his Long Island retreat, where "in predictably unpredictable Caesarean fashion" the boss announced their story conference would convene in his steam room. "Woody wouldn't hear of it," recalled Gelbart. "When Sid and I entered the sauna, Woody stayed outside, refusing to get undressed, saying he couldn't be funny naked." Allen would channel this awkward incident into the hysterical scene in *What's New Pussycat?* in which—inexplicably fully clothed—he and Peter O'Toole indulge in a steam bath.

One advantage of writing for Caesar was that no joke was too far out. When NBC took over the ABC series for the second half of the season, Caesar presided over an *At the Movies* special that was like an encyclopedic parody of every worst Hollywood cliché—one of Allen's strengths. Caesar sent up Valentino, Cagney, drive-ins, musicals. This time Gelbart was absent from the credits, and it was Woody Allen and the two Mels.

Caesar was the gold standard for TV writers—partly because he paid gold. Allen's paycheck rose to $1,700 weekly. But Caesar could also be mercurial, and he was notorious for his rants. All the material had to be tailored to his whims, and Caesar was always the last writer—embroidering everything he did. Too often this made for ragged sketches. As *Variety* noted, "[The] writers' major trouble is exiting a skit on the same high note it began, before it starts to run down." Writers, plural: It was always "group writing" for Caesar.

Still, it was quality writing for a quality show. Sylvania honored Gelbart and Allen with an excellence award for the fall premiere, and that episode was also Emmy-nominated for "Best Writing of a Single Musical or Variety Program." In the first week of May 1959 Allen wrestled himself into a tuxedo and plunged into a taxicab heading for the Writers Guild awards banquet at Toots Shor's. "I went up to the door," Allen recalled, "and I couldn't go in, and I never did go in. I went home, and I felt so relieved." One of his psychological bugbears was an "entering phobia," meaning a profound unease about entering any thronged party, or occasion. Having little to do with the fact he and Gelbart lost in their category to Bud Yorkin and Herbert Baker, who collaborated on *An Evening with Fred Astaire*, Allen's ambivalence about awards deepened after that night.

EVEN THOUGH *AT THE MOVIES* was taped before a large, responsive audience at the Ziegfeld Theater, ABC added a laugh track—which was a growing television trend. The writers were annoyed. Sponsors also nipped at their heels. In the *American Bandstand* parody for the premiere, for example, the Gelbart-Allen script had the Dick Clark–type emcee (Art Carney) praising teens "for coming here instead of doing your homework," adding, "[now] here's a record I get an awful lot for playing!" Chevrolet objected. "We can't offend teenagers," the reps explained. "I guess because they steal a lot of Chevys," Gelbart cracked. The offending joke had to be cut. Another time Chevrolet insisted upon deleting an establishing shot of Manhattan because, gazing at the footage, attentive viewers might spot their dread rival automobile manufacturer's eponymous Chrysler Building.

At the Tamiment Playhouse there were no laugh tracks, corporate sponsors, or high salaries. With Sid Caesar and an Emmy-nom in his cap, Allen returned for his third summer in 1959. Moe Hack had said he was a contender to write the summer finale, a "book musical" that was longer than the usual Saturday mini-musical, with more of a story, or "book." New York talent agents made annual pilgrimages to Tamiment to watch the season-ending "book musical." The shining example of a Tamiment "book musical" was the past summer's version of Hans

Christian Andersen's fairy tale *The Princess and the Pea*, which had been written by playhouse staff writers Marshall Barer, Mary Rodgers, and Jay Thompson. The summer-ender had evolved into the successful Broadway musical *Once Upon a Mattress*, which opened in May 1959 and catapulted Carol Burnett to stardom.

With this hope in mind, Allen set up a pre-summer meeting with Barer and Dean Fuller, another Tamiment veteran who had contributed to *Once Upon a Mattress*. Allen was "brilliant and just a delightful person," Barer thought, but their "obviously nervous" junior colleague hemmed and hawed, gradually building up to the concept he was pitching for the "book musical": a comic adaptation of Mary Shelley's *Frankenstein*. This concept, which anticipated Mel Brooks and *Young Frankenstein* by more than a decade, struck Barer and Fuller as "terribly corny, unworkable." When the pair overpolitely rejected his pitch, they instantly realized how much they had "hurt" Allen. "He was trembling; he was so eager for us to understand it and accept it, and we didn't."

Allen took disappointments stoically, however. His last summer at Tamiment passed without him writing the wishful *Frankenstein* musical, but also without any apparent bitterness. He directed the season's first big revue, *Bag of Tricks*, presented to audiences on the July Fourth weekend, and he wrote all the skits, save one. Dorothy Loudon was the soloist on songs by Barer and Rodgers and the future *Cabaret* lyricist Fred Ebb.

His third and last Tamiment summer might best be remembered for his *acting* onstage, for Allen had also begun to play small parts he crafted for himself. He had gotten his feet wet the previous summer—by chance, Allen always claimed—when the company sat around one day listening to him read out one of his skits. After he wondered aloud who might play a certain comedic role, someone said, "Woody, do it yourself! You can perform it better than anyone here." He had a sheepish "Me, onstage?" reaction but agreed to give it a try.

Allen always performed his Tamiment roles "in a most, most innocuous way," he insisted in his oral history with Martha Schmoyer LoMonaco. "I had no desire at that point in my life, at all, to be on the stage in any way." Yet as camp playbills attest, Allen was an onstage fixture all July and August. "Not everyone thought he came across well," playhouse director Christopher Hewett recollected. "The trouble was he had such a quiet voice. We had to mike him up a lot and this wasn't always easy. It got in the way of the action."

If the Tamiment company noticed anything different about Woody Allen in the summer of 1959, it was not any air of superiority he might have gained from his illustrious stint with Sid Caesar. It may have been that the gulf between him and Mrs. Woody appeared to be widening. Harlene spent her days typing in the office, and most of the rest of the time she hid out alone in their bungalow. "Well, I've got to go back to the cabin and do the husband bit," Allen would announce with a risqué inflection as he departed story conferences and rehearsals. "On reflection, I guess she just didn't like show business," recollected Bob Dishy, a Tamiment actor and Brooklynite who'd later stay in touch with the couple in New York. "Woody's concentration [on show business] was intense."

When Mr. and Mrs. Woody said goodbye at the end of August, Allen let Moe Hack and others know he would not be returning to Camp Tamiment in 1960. Summer stock seduced many people in show business who loved the annual retreat to camps for its respite and feeling of family, but the sunshiney life was not for him. In the long run the communal creativity was no more appealing than group writing. Still, Allen had absorbed many positive influences. He liked the regimentation of Tamiment: the daily work and weekly performances, every hour of every day blocked out with writing sessions, production planning, staging, and run-throughs—with downtime built in for creative replenishment. This was his kind of grind and discipline, every day, seven days a week, hard work and constant rethinking and rewriting, with the aim of mounting the best possible show.

FELLOW SID CAESAR alumnus Larry Gelbart had become the head writer for Pat Boone, and after the summer Gelbart paved the way for Allen to join him in writing the Christian pop singer's 1959–60 television specials, which were also being underwritten by Chevrolet. Allen got along surprisingly well with the low-key, clean-cut Boone, who was just one year older than him. Boone warmly recalled standing in the hallway with Allen while the young comedy writer, "in his agitated, insistent way," pitched his far-out bits and jokes. "I'd slide down the wall laughing and sit on the floor at the audacity" of his ideas. Boone surrendered. "I did some Woody Allen jokes that originated in his fervid brain." Among the highlights of the *Pat Boone–Chevy Showroom* fall premiere was a zany Gelbart-Allen satire of TV quiz shows—again biting the hand that fed him.

Boone's specials boasted unusual guest stars, and one day Allen ticked off another idol when Sugar Ray Robinson stepped into the elevator with him to ride up to an upper floor of the ABC building. Both men felt uncomfortable in elevators because both suffered from claustrophobia. Allen listened politely as the boxer told him opera was his true passion; after retirement, Robinson said, he was going to surprise everyone when he revealed his singing prowess. Later, hearing Boone and Robinson's duet on the telecast, Allen knew that ambition was deluded. But Robinson, the greatest fighter of his era, stayed on his list of sports heroes.

What Allen really fixated on, in the fall of 1959, was parlaying his Tamiment Playhouse sketches into a Broadway "non-book" musical. Allen's best playlets had been earmarked for a revue called *From A to Z*, which had English actress Hermione Gingold onboard as its nominal star. The music would come from ex-Tamiment composers Jerry Herman, Mary Rodgers, Marshall Barer, and Fred Ebb. The cast and crew would feature Tamiment performers and backstage personnel, including director Christopher Hewett, who had staged many of the Saturday night entertainments. The producers of *From A to Z* were a wealthy Texas married couple.

In late October Allen signed a contract making him the show's lead writer. He was expected to contribute five sketches, with at least four recycled from the Tamiment playhouse: *Psychological Warfare* ("Hit 'em in the ego!"); *Report to America* (the Cape Canaveral sketch); *Surprise Party* (two men at a party where all the women eerily resemble Groucho Marx); and *Opening Night* (the one with the playwright's family aghast at the bleak drama about their lives). Allen also agreed to write an additional number of new sketches to be made "exclusive" to the projected musical. As well as his signing payment of $1,000, and $125 per sketch for additional new material, Allen was guaranteed a 50 percent share of the 2 percent gross of monies that were set aside as a pool for all the writers. Only four other sketches and two monologues were planned, initially.

For Allen, who dreamed of writing a Broadway musical, this was a chance at the brass ring. Over the next months, while writing for Pat Boone, Allen revised and emendated the Tamiment sketches for *From A to Z*. He wrote new monologues and skits, closely liaising with Hewett, dashing off connecting bits on demand.

It was the problem of all such revues to organize the disparate musical numbers and comedy sketches, juggling their tone and sequence, while balancing the supporting cast and chorus with the stage time allotted to the main stars. Partly to accommodate Gingold, skits and songs were constantly being added or dropped throughout rehearsals. The writing and rewriting were never-ending. After the first of the year Allen "made himself available for the entire out-of-town run" of *From A to Z*, according to production records, traveling to the New Haven tryout performances to assess the previews and make fast changes, even though Allen "stood to lose a tidy sum of income that he could earn" in New York, in the words of Harvey Meltzer, who was still acting as his manager. Allen had made "this sacrifice because he knows that in order to make the necessary changes in his sketches, to polish them, in addition to doing the extra work that was requested of him and which he has consented to do without immediate compensation, he must be with the company at all times."

Even as the show began to founder Allen stayed loyal and tireless. His number of sketches fell to three after New Haven critics singled out certain skits as merely "fair." When *From A to Z* staggered into the Plymouth Theater in late April, the New York reviewers were even less kind. Hewett felt obliged to excise *Surprise Party* from the running order, which left only *Psychological Warfare* and a short new blackout called *Hit Parade*—a spoof with beatnik lovers listening to a funereal "Dolan Timmus" recording—as written by Woody Allen.

Allen's deal was ironclad, giving him 50 percent of the writers' 2 percent of the gross for the seven sketches initially mandated in his agreement. The producers pleaded with him to accept a pro-rated amount, since his final percentage constituted "ten percent of the total sketches and fifty percent of the total blackouts," according to production records. Not now or ever did Allen overly care about the money; he cared about the work. And typically, feeling responsible when producers lost money, Allen readily consented to the voluntary slash in his share. The ink was scarcely dry on his revised contract, however, before *From A to Z* closed on May 7. Allen framed the poster for the show and for years it was the one constant, wherever he moved, hanging on a wall.

••

FROM A TO Z's failure was disheartening. Allen would never face an emptier summer. He still wrote remunerative pieces for stand-up comics and TV shows, but all this, by now, he had decided was "hack work." This was "a hard time for Woody," according to Bob Dishy, a Tamiment alumnus among the *A to Z* cast.

He finally broke with Harvey Meltzer. Allen had felt compelled to sign with Meltzer as a lowly recruit for NBC's Comedy Development Program in 1955, but "the more I earned, the higher Harvey's cut was," Allen recalled, whereas other agents and managers took the same percentage or less when their client's income surged. Meltzer was a small-timer. Allen wanted aggressive representation, jobs with more prestige. He was "always unhappy, because he never thought he had got as far as he deserved to get," Meltzer said later.

Allen flirted with representatives of the William Morris Agency, which sent its young talent to Camp Tamiment for summer seasoning and always scouted the major playhouse shows. Yet the most powerful agents never returned his phone calls. So when *From A to Z* came along, Allen briefly turned to Bill Keenan, who specialized in writers and television for General Artists Corporation, an international booking organization with New York headquarters. Meltzer had cosigned the initial *From A to Z* contract in late 1959, but by the time the revue opened on Broadway Allen had severed ties with Meltzer. It was Keenan negotiating the revised clauses.

A more personal nagging issue was the deteriorating state of his marriage, which also seemed like a multiyear contract about to expire. What Allen cared most about in life, it was clear by now, was his writing, his clarinet-playing, and his relaxation rituals of long walks, moviegoing, museum visits, jazz clubs, and sports events. His regimen nowadays included afternoon forays to the Metropolitan Museum with friend Len Maxwell, where Allen's custom was to systematically absorb the exhibits, rationing his tours to one hour daily. Harlene, now twenty-one, a junior focusing on philosophy and German at Hunter College, had gravitated to more of a beatnik lifestyle. She possessed the beatnik look—sans makeup—and was more wont to spend her spare time in Greenwich Village rather than hanging around the Upper East Side, which had become Allen's comfort zone. Their bickering and friction had lessened, but the couple was obviously drifting apart. "[Harlene] tried hard to please, and she dabbled at a variety of artistic and intellectual pursuits," said mutual friend Jack Victor. "It wasn't quite working out, and people could tell because they never seemed very happy with one another."

Self-improvement was still a shared passion. Allen continued to shadow Harlene's college courses, reading the assigned books and jotting down lists of unfamiliar words to improve his vocabulary. Tutors visited them in their home. But Allen did not warm to Harlene's friends, their collegiate interests, or their beatnik jabber.

Allen was the breadwinner of the household, paying the rent and monthlies on their apartment. But there were times—as happened with *From A to Z*, when great expectations did not add up to the actual income—when Harlene took part-time jobs. The couple's growing domestic crisis was temporarily forestalled by the sudden flurry of work that landed on Allen's doorstep at the end of the long, empty summer of 1960.

Once again, Larry Gelbart rode to the rescue with another television variety special, this one revolving around themes of romance. Lavishly budgeted by *General Electric Theater*, the Sunday-night show, called *Hooray for Love*, starred Art Carney with Tony Randall, Janis Paige, and Jane Powell. Gelbart and Allen reestablished their rapport, and Gelbart recalled inviting Mr. and Mrs. Woody to his upstate farm for a "working weekend." The couple detrained, revealing Allen in a "three-piece suit (at least), button-down shirt and black tie," evoking "a rabbi in mid-elopement," with Harlene, "his bride and widow all in one" in a "black dress, a veiled hat, and elbow-length gloves." All the writing got done, if mainly indoors, because Allen "never went near, let alone into the swimming pool," and he bemoaned the noisy birds and swarming mosquitoes.

Once again, Gelbart and Allen blended their skills, crafting sketches that evinced a new parity in their collaboration. Two skits were especially Woody Allen–ish: a lurid send-up of Tennessee Williams and a burlesque of Ingmar Bergman's recent masterpiece *Wild Strawberries*. The latter presaged *What's Up, Tiger Lily?* with Art Carney speaking Swedish gibberish over absurdist subtitles.

The producer of *Hooray for Love* was David Susskind, who was just coming into his own as a talk-show host and purveyor of wide-ranging television, stage, and film fare. A button-down man who took himself seriously, Susskind had a fondness for comics and comedy writers, and he bonded with Allen. Susskind said maybe they should get together as partners on a comedy project. Allen said he would try to think of something.

Meanwhile Allen continued to ghost for nightclub comedians and talk-show hosts, among them Garry Moore, who had a weekly one-hour variety show, for which Neil Simon served as head writer. Allen's ambivalence about writing for comics and television worsened, however, even as the jobs paid better. Ironically, that was Harlene's insistent theme. Her husband had the capacity to be a brilliant writer, she told friends, but he was "cheapening his gifts," writing for the boob tube. Too often, Allen felt the same way.

THE EVIDENCE SUGGESTS Allen didn't finish many of the stage plays he started, leading up to 1960, certainly not any Eugene O'Neill–type drama. The only complete unproduced script in his archives, overlapping the 1950s and '60s, is "They Laughed at Fulton," which involved a press agent's stunt of running a supersmart computer for president. The script, touched-up over the years, boasted quips about Nietzsche, Sartre, John Dillinger, Willie Mays, and *Cleopatra*. An "open audition" for the computer's first lady was among its highlights. Cole Porter's "Just One of Those Things" is one stipulated song. Allen would bring that favorite composer back for many films and the song itself twenty years later in *Stardust Memories*. There are elements of *Bananas* and *Sleeper* in "They Laughed at Fulton," and the concept was unabashedly silly, laugh after laugh. But it was all jokes, all dialogue; the antic comedy overwhelmed the story, and the talky scenes did not add up.

As he approached his twenty-fifth birthday Woody Allen felt in the grip of a professional identity crisis. Was he a jokesmith for hire, a contractor for television comedy, a possible future Broadway playwright, or director? Or what? He discovered the answer not from a psychiatrist but from two strangers he met who changed his life.

On their museum excursions his friend Len Maxwell had been singing the praises of the personal management team of Jack Rollins and Charles H. Joffe. Allen was anxious about a long-term replacement for Harvey Meltzer, and in mid-1960 he went looking for the two men in a basement club at the Hotel Duane, where the personal managers were watching the act of their clients, the comedians Mike Nichols and Elaine May. In his stammering way

Allen asked if "we could conceivably be interested in him as a writer" for the Nichols and May act, according to Rollins. Rollins and Joffe demurred. Nichols and May wrote their own material, and they improvised as they performed, Rollins told Allen. The comedy writer went away disappointed.

A few months later, Allen showed up again at the West Fifty-Seventh Street offices of Rollins and Joffe, this time asking if the partners would consider taking him on as a client. He said the personal management team could arrange "his affairs in a conventional fashion," Rollins recalled, "to better his career as a TV writer." No, they told Allen, their office did not represent pure writers. Rollins-Joffe handled performing artists. Well, Allen muttered, he had thought about maybe working up a little stand-up comedy act based on his own jokes.

"Ever since I saw Mort Sahl, I harbored a gnawing urge to be a comedian," Allen explained. Rollins asked, "Doing what kind of stuff? Like Sahl . . . ?" Allen replied: "Well, I've been toying with this notion: that the *New York Times* is the only paper with no comic strip, and what if they had one, and it was like Superman but, when he changed his clothes, he changed into a Wall Street broker. . . ." Rollins and Joffe exchanged a look.

Brooklyn-born, college-educated, a World War II veteran twenty years older than Allen, Rollins was the rumpled senior partner with a round face, dark pouched eyes, oiled hair, and a cigar that seemed omnipresent, rotating in his mouth. He was a mournful old lefty who, in younger days as a William Morris agent, was notorious for his zealous promotion of lost causes and eccentric comics. Thwarted in his ambitions to become a stage producer, Rollins hung up his shingle as a personal manager in the early 1950s and was soon joined by Joffe, another scion of Brooklyn. A Syracuse University journalism graduate, Joffe had clocked time booking nightclubs and as a Music Corporation of America (MCA) agent. Rollins was the wise old guru, the foreseer and true believer of the duo. Joffe was the wisecracking, zestful, ebullient partner, but also the brutal dealmaker. (Later, another Rollins-Joffe client, Robin Williams, would dub Joffe "the Beast.") United Artists studio executive Steven Bach was not the only person acquainted with Rollins and Joffe to detect a "Mutt 'n' Jeff quality" to the pair, differences that hinted, Bach wrote, at "a vaudeville team called Manic 'n' Depressive."

Among their earliest clients was the progressive calypso and folk singer Harry Belafonte, who had Hollywood acting ambitions. When Belafonte rose to stardom, he left Rollins and Joffe, causing an everlasting bitterness. The Rollins-Joffe team had settled into nurturing improvisational comedy acts such as Nichols and May and nonpareils like Len Maxwell and Tom Poston. They were a proud mom-and-pop operation compared to the giants of the business—William Morris or MCA—and worked differently from the giants. They didn't simply answer the telephone and write contracts. They guided unique personalities toward individual goals and handcrafted careers intended to fulfill their clients artistically as well as financially. Over time Rollins-Joffe would come to be regarded as hallowed figures, personal managers par excellence, especially for comedians.

Trying to convince the two men of his talent and potential, Allen auditioned for the management duo by reading aloud from a portfolio of his jokes, monologues, and sketches. "He'd be dead serious when he read a sketch of his," Rollins remembered, "but it hit us funny. He didn't know why we were laughing. He'd give a what's-so-funny look. Very removed he was. Quiet and shy. And the whole thing struck us funny."

Rollins wouldn't let go of the notion of Allen as a stand-up comic. He said Rollins-Joffe would consider representing Allen only if he'd undergo a trial period as a comedian, performing his own jokes before audiences. Allen acted "surprised, if not a little shocked" at the suggestion, according to Rollins. The writer said no, went away, then to their amusement he returned a third time. There was "an indefinable thing about him," Rollins recalled. "He'd waltz in with that bony nose and serious mien and we'd break up and laugh."

Although shy and deadly serious even when reading out his jokes ("The shyest man I've ever met," said Rollins), both partners thought Allen was "incredibly funny." Talking things over with the comedy writer, discussing his ideas and enthusiasms—talking about the plays and movies they had all seen—the managers had one of those epiphanies that made their reputation as show business savants. "He [Allen] displayed the talents of a director," said Rollins. "He'd see things and say why something was handled right or wrong." Allen had the potential to become "a triple threat"—a Jewish Orson Welles—a "writer, director, actor," all rolled into one.

As a first step, Rollins and Joffe insisted, Allen had to try stand-up comedy. Their flattering vision of his grand future won him over. If he had been faking his reluctance, it was his greatest performance. "OK, I'd like to try it," Allen finally agreed, "but you guys had better be ready to catch me when I fail." That was as much a watershed as changing his name from Allan Stuart Konigsberg. Indeed, that day marked the rebirth of Woody Allen. It was agreed that Rollins and Joffe would take 15 percent of his income, but only ever 15 percent. "We shook hands, never signing any papers, and remained together till [Jack] died at a hundred," Allen recalled.

EVERYTHING MOVED VERY quickly after that. Allen worked up a monologue and practiced privately for Jack Rollins, his wife Jane, and Charles Joffe. "Everyone (except me)," Allen recalled in his memoir, "thought I was a natural comedian." He made his stand-up debut even as *Hooray for Love*, the television special starring Art Carney, was being taped for broadcast. Laugh-getter Shelley Berman was the headliner at the Blue Angel, New York's preeminent showcase for comedy and music, when the club reopened in the fall of 1960. One night late in September Berman left the stage after his set with these words: "Here is a young television writer who is going to perform his own material. Would you please welcome a very funny man . . . Woody Allen!"

Earlier in the week Rollins had brought Allen to meet the Blue Angel proprietors, Herbert Jacobi and Max Gordon, who together ran the nightclub. Gordon, who also operated the influential Village Vanguard jazz club in Greenwich Village, recalled Rollins introducing "a kid with glasses and uncombed hair," who was "sitting at a table. The kid got up as Jack introduced us. He was a short, frightened kid with a weak handshake." Addressing Gordon, Rollins pointed to Allen's shoes. "You see," Rollins explained, "he walks all over New York with his toes sticking out of his shoes, while the guys he's writing for are driving their Cadillacs!" Rollins then spoke directly to "the kid," whose demeanor was placid. "Haven't I told this to you a hundred times? If only you'd get up and do the material yourself, you could be rich. Instead of which, you are the schlep walking around town like a tramp. And they make it good on your stuff!" Puffing on a cigar, Gordon silently observed this odd interaction. "The kid was sitting there drinking it all in as if his father was talking to him," Gordon recalled. "Honest to God he didn't show anything. Not even anger. He just looked up like somebody told him he was a great writer, and would he autograph one of their books!"

Although skeptical, Gordon trusted Rollins, a shrewd man who'd "done us quite a few good turns, bringing us people like Harry Belafonte and Mike [Nichols] and Elaine [May]." Also, Rollins was "crazy about Woody to the point where nothing would stop him persevering" anyway. Gordon said "the kid" could go onstage after Shelley Berman on the weekend.

A red carpet guided patrons into the Blue Angel, whose small but elegant stage at the front of a long, narrow back room was lit by a spotlight. "A mass of terrors," in his words, Allen, tightly wrapped in a monkey suit, his hair stiffly groomed, shuffled on stage, clutching the microphone stand like the hand brake on a car careening downhill, and executed his first professional—albeit unpaid—comedy routine. "The laughter came back so strong" at the beginning of the night that "Jack Rollins told me I went right into my shell." The first part of the show went best. "Laughter and applause," Allen remembered, and "the next day offers came in."

Larry Gelbart sat among the crowd. He was one of many who had been tipped off by Allen, or by the Rollins-Joffe publicist. Gelbart thought Allen's jokes were amusing but his somewhat shambling conversational style evoked "Elaine May in drag." Allen's imitation of May was "by design," Gelbart later wrote. "Woody often said how much he admired her delivery. Her influence was evident in his timing and his inflections."

After the performance Gelbart went backstage. A critic for a New York daily had occupied the dressing room "moments earlier to type his review of Woody's act and had thrown the carbon paper into the wastebasket." As was much the case throughout his career, Woody was drawn to the crumpled review with equal parts curiosity and contempt. "Reading it," Gelbart said, "Woody was crushed. The critic had characterized him as an intellectual Menasha Skulnick, an actor-comedian of the period famous for his thick Yiddish accent, but certainly not for his intellect. Woody had worked so hard to come off as hip and sophisticated (which he was), and here he was being compared to a shticky immigrant comic (which he definitely was not)."

In a ritual he'd repeat "many times over the next few years," in Allen's words, Rollins also rambled backstage with a list of criticisms and suggestions. The jokes had been pretty good, Rollins said, but it wasn't enough to tell good jokes. The audience had to get to know and like him as a personality. "If they connect with you, they will like your jokes," Rollins explained. "If they don't, the best gags in the world won't get you there."

Allen had to build his own characterization through jokes, craft more of a persona. He had to become the one and only Woody Allen, not—like that first night onstage—a composite of other comedic personalities. To become the one and only, he had to start over in small clubs, Rollins said, until he developed his persona to the point of forgetting he was onstage. Allen "balked at every sensible and correct thing," Rollins recalled, but Rollins "was patient and insistent and said if I just shut up and did what he told me and then looked up in two years, we could reassess and see who was right."

JACK ROLLINS PREVAILED upon Jan Wallman, owner of a small club on Grove Street in Greenwich Village called the Duplex, which included an upstairs cabaret that served as a launchpad for comics and musicians. With no salary or advertising, Allen was penciled in for one or two sets nightly, six late nights a week at Upstairs-at-the-Duplex. He'd spend long, excruciating nights there in the closing months of 1960. "At eleven at night, I'd get in a cab in the freezing cold and go down there and perform for nothing for five or six people," he remembered. "A godforsaken, mostly empty club at 1 a.m. and then nobody would laugh. . . . I wanted to die."

Rollins or Joffe or both were always in the sparse audience, loudly laughing and cheering Allen on, then after the performance steering him to an all-night deli and delivering their notes about what should be cut or fixed. They criticized him freely while bolstering his confidence. For a long time, they were the only people who thought Allen had any future in stand-up comedy. "To start with," Rollins said, "he was terrible. He was *terrible*. Perhaps the worst comedian you've ever seen." Allen's blank Zelig face was accompanied by a blank Zelig style of delivery. All the drama was psychological: Allen wrestling with the microphone—the mike stand and long cord—whipping the cord around himself like a spinning top until he was nearly strangling himself. He'd pace back and forth like a caged canary rather than meet people's eyes, rushing through memorized jokes in a low monotone. If patrons heckled, Allen would glare at them stonily; or sometimes he'd heckle back.

"He would recite his stuff like a child doing show-and-tell," Rollins recalled. "It was mechanical, lifeless, bloodless, monotonous."

"He was arrogant and hostile," said Joffe. "If the audience didn't get it, he had no patience."

"He didn't know anything about pacing his material or stopping for laughter," added Rollins.

"You do lines that only dogs can hear!" Joffe would complain, meaning Allen's comedy was aimed at too high and esoteric a frequency. Allen muttered exclamations like "Bird lives!" that Joffe said had to be weeded out. Maybe some people in the audience at Upstairs-at-the-Duplex would get his side-of-the-mouth references to bebop saxophonist Charlie Parker, who had died in 1955, but not everyone would. Rollins and Joffe had bigger eyes and a broader popularity in mind for the future of Woody Allen.

For months he felt like a miserable failure on- and offstage. Before every performance Allen could be overheard talking to himself as he paced the dressing room. "I hope they like me. . . . I hope they like me. . . ." He'd vomit before shows, sometimes afterward too. All day he worried about the upcoming nightly performance. "It was unspeakably agonizing," recalled Allen. "I didn't know what I was doing. I would shake and tremble, thinking about standing up that night before people and trying to be funny." Often, said Howard Storm, another Rollins-Joffe comic appearing at Upstairs-at-the-Duplex, "Charlie and Jack would just push him on the stage."

The six-nights-a-week trial run didn't do much for Allen's deteriorating marriage either. One time Allen arrived back home in the wee hours after another dispiriting performance at Upstairs-at-the-Duplex, accompanied by Rollins and his wife Jane, who'd sat up with him afterward at the Stage Deli, critiquing and reassuring the would-be comedian. Mrs. Woody wheeled on Rollins. "What are you doing to my husband?" Harlene hissed. "He's a man who's a brilliant writer and you want to turn him into a cheap comic!"

More than once Allen waved the white flag. "Do you fellas really think I should continue?" he'd ask them plaintively. His personal managers, not yet earning a dime for their efforts, stood by him. His act was gradually improving, they said. They had faith in his prospects. "I make a very good living as a writer," Allen would argue, "and I'm making nothing here. Does that make sense?" Rollins always replied, "To us, it makes sense."

Finally, one time Allen said he couldn't do it anymore. "If it's too difficult," Rollins said softly, "you certainly should not continue." Allen went away, and in the predawn phoned Joffe, closer to him in age than Rollins and from the same part of Brooklyn. "In business he is Woody's brother to

Rollins's father," wrote Eric Lax. He and Joffe talked. The next day Allen showed up at the office. "I'll give it six more months," he said.

FRIENDS FROM TELEVISION and Tamiment and New York show business checked him out at Upstairs-at-the-Duplex as word-of-mouth spread. Mel Brooks dropped by, guffawing. One night Bob Dishy from Tamiment brought a date, an aspiring actress named Louise Lasser, three years younger than Allen and, he couldn't help but notice, "a knockout." She had long strawberry-blonde hair with bangs and a ponytail, blue eyes, and a toothy smile.

Lasser lived with her affluent parents in an elegant Fifth Avenue duplex between Seventy-Third and Seventy-Fourth, near Allen and Harlene's apartment, and she invited the couple to her family's New Year's Eve party. Her father was J. K. Lasser, well known as the author of income tax guides for Americans. Her mother was an interior decorator. The Lassers were a progressive family—Pete Seeger had visited her summer camps when she was a girl—and Louise enjoyed the best education money could buy at the Ethical Culture Fieldston School in Manhattan and then Brandeis University, before dropping out in her senior year to pursue acting and singing.

Allen and Harlene were barely on speaking terms by now, but New Year's Eve was one holiday Allen liked to celebrate. The couple attended the Lasser party and began to socialize with Louise. Allen and Harlene had been discussing a separation, but they were delaying the inevitable until spring, when they planned a trip to Washington, DC, "away from the tensions and familiar routines of Manhattan." Vacationing in the nation's capital, the couple would visit the monuments and statues and museums, dine out at the most elegant restaurants, and "among the unspeakable beauty of the cherry blossom trees, we fought," Allen later wrote.

Back in New York in April, sitting alone at his typewriter with Harlene in classes, Allen thought about Louise Lasser. She was smart, effortlessly funny, and a looker into the bargain. "She had a chesty voice, and carnal promise oozed out of every pore," Allen recalled. Her upper-class Upper East Side upbringing was the pedigree Allen had coveted since Brooklyn boyhood. "While I was growing up on linoleum eating Del Monte string beans out of a can," Allen said, "she was knocking off escargot on Fifth

Avenue, where a liveried doorman would get a cab for her so she could speed off to the theater and after to Gambelli's restaurant."

On impulse he phoned the well-heeled charmer and asked if she wanted to stroll with him through Central Park and maybe stop and browse LPs at the Jazz Record Center. Sure, Lasser answered, "and with that one word my life made a seismic shift, although I didn't realize it." The two walked through the park, he bought a Billie Holiday recording for Lasser, and the blissed-out Allen arranged to meet her again the next day. That night, performing at Upstairs-at-the-Duplex and talking the show over afterward with Jack Rollins at the Stage Deli, all Allen could think about was Lasser, whom he planned to take to the Belmont racetrack in the afternoon.

On their second "date" Allen went further—holding her hand, giving her a kiss, sharing a bottle of Bordeaux, taking Lasser for a romantic horse-and-carriage ride around Central Park. "There is some talk of my marital status," Allen recalled, "but I assure her quite truthfully that we married too young and while my wife is lovely and brilliant, we are both on the verge of ending it." So close was the verge, in Allen's retelling, that he arrived back at his current domicile sporting a wine-black tongue, where Mrs. Woody suspiciously awaited. Harlene eyed her husband. "I want to talk to you," she said. "I want to discuss how we'd do it if we broke up."

His extramarital affair had begun, even as his separation and divorce were a fait accompli. Allen drew many life lessons from the failure of his first marriage, but perhaps as much as anything the experience exerted an obvious creative impact. A surprising number of Woody Allen pictures would be galvanized by fissures in romantic relationships. His fictional marriages are often fragile or doomed, and the married men in his films are destined to flirt and stray. Affairs are depicted as natural disasters. "I am ready for this dismantling," Allen wrote in his memoir, "having fortuitously stumbled upon the neurotic's philosopher's stone, the overlapping relationship."

THE TRICK IN honing his stand-up act was to embrace his calling and become another person altogether onstage. As Jack Rollins urged, Allen began to go out onstage with more enthusiasm, meeting the audience halfway with warmth. Warmth was the hardest thing. By degrees, his act became less traditional, no longer one joke after another, but a fiction with his Jewish identity and preoccupation with women integral to the comedy. His act was never very sexually explicit, but a little sexual innuendo broke ground in stand-up comedy, and his intimacies moved audiences. His monologue developed into a soliloquy, with himself the antihero of a digressive series of life-story anecdotes that touched as well as tickled his audiences. He presented himself as a brainy, neurotic Jewish bumbler, a physical coward, a loser with women. This persona was a laugh-making guise, and even more so, as his act—and he personally—matured. In time his persona evolved to become more enigmatic and complex, yet the fiction mixed with shards of autobiography was always its special alchemy.

"The character was really assigned to me by my audience," he said later. "They laughed more at certain things. Naturally I used more of those things. And the critics helped assign me a character, too. They would write about me and also write about me as a certain type. So, I put more material into the act that would fit the type."

By late January, Allen was ready for another stab at the Blue Angel, where he had only mixed success four months before. Owner Herbert Jacobi liked Allen and was amenable, but co-owner Max Gordon was not enthusiastic. Jack Rollins tried talking Gordon into an extended booking over several weeks. "Salary doesn't matter. Pay Woody what you like," Rollins told Gordon. Gordon was unmoved. "Look," Rollins added, spreading his hands, "if he loses money for you, I'll pay his salary myself." Gordon took that with a grain of salt, but he carved out a block of time for Allen, not as any kind of headliner, but sharing a bill with other talent.

With Rollins and Joffe came the services of their hardworking publicity agent, Richard O'Brien, whom Rollins always referred to as "the greatest publicist in the world." It helped that O'Brien believed in Allen almost as much as Rollins and Joffe. The publicist wrote comedy material on the side, including jokes for Allen, "only on the understanding that I never claim them as my own." O'Brien fed the buzz, and he would handle Allen's publicity for the next two decades. Among the people O'Brien tipped off about Allen's return to the Blue Angel was Dick Cavett, a young talent coordinator for *The Jack Paar Show*—a.k.a. *Tonight Starring Jack Paar*. Like many people in this chapter of Allen's life story, Cavett was also a Rollins-Joffe client.

Witty and literate, Cavett was from Baptist stock before turning agnostic. The twenty-four-year-old hailed from Nebraska, probably a commonwealth

Allen never visited. At this time Cavett was an aspiring actor and/or comic, although he'd later find his niche befriending celebrities and interviewing them on television. Cavett came to the Blue Angel already pre-dazzled by Allen's résumé, especially his Sid Caesar credits. "I had the feeling this was someone I would like to get to know, even though I had never seen him nor met him." He was not disappointed. "His opening jokes were marvelous. They showed complex intelligence and genuine wit. . . . This high level [was] sustained throughout his act, instead of the intermittent gems of good but lesser comics. Yet about a third of the way through the audience began to murmur and talk. Woody plowed on, his face largely concealed by the mike, and ended, more by excusing himself than finishing, and left the stage to polite applause."

After Allen finished his performance, the folk-singing Clancy Brothers took the stage and Cavett wended backstage, sought Allen out, "and we sat down in the pink light of one of the lounge booths of the Angel, hit it off immediately, and talked until it was time for his late show, then went to his apartment and talked some more." Ever since that first night, they remained "close friends," said Cavett. "We look different and have vastly contrasting social and ethnic backgrounds, but we have the same reactions to and estimates of a lot of things, which make us simpatico despite the miles between Brooklyn and Nebraska, geographically and otherwise. We both dug the Hope-Crosby road pictures as kids, appreciated comedy at an early age, had a serious side that made us seem a little odd to our friends in school, and tend to be amused by the same things."

Allen's stand-up style had progressed since his Blue Angel tryout. Now, rather than imitating Elaine May, he sometimes took on the mannerisms of another idol: Mort Sahl. One reviewer dubbed him "Son of Sahl," and temporarily the label stuck. "I was such a great fan of Mort Sahl's," Allen later admitted, "that . . . his delivery crept into me." Some in the audience thought Allen was very funny and much improved, regardless. Some didn't. "The [Blue Angel] audience was too dumb to realize what they were getting," Cavett thought.

Rollins sat up front every night, and every night after the show the manager raced backstage to Allen's dressing room. "You're doing terrific, you hear? Terrific!" He exhorted Max Gordon: "Tell Woody he's terrific!" Once a doubter, Gordon began to develop an appreciation for the neurotic comedian. Allen took "a lot of punishment," Gordon recalled. "Only the real highbrow people, the sophisticated few, enjoyed and understood his low-key delivery and style. What I call the 'schlemiel approach.' For the rest he was nothing."

Cavett became a repeat visitor to the Blue Angel, and he brought samples of Allen's comedy back to Jack Paar, trying to coax Paar into booking Allen as a guest on his nationally broadcast late-night talk show on NBC. Allen was a hard sell with Paar, however, and it took several months for Cavett to convince the host, by which time Allen had long since wrapped up his Blue Angel stint and returned to Upstairs-at-the-Duplex and other small Greenwich Village havens that paid little or no money to mostly young and unknown talent.

Finally, "Jack read some of his jokes and agreed to have him on," recalled *Tonight* director Hal Gurnee. "Jack didn't understand Woody's humor because it was so different and edgier than his own," said Garry Marshall, who was on Paar's writing staff at the time. In his half-hearted way, Paar "killed the introduction" to the new comic, according to Gurnee. Allen stepped out to audience silence. "Really good jokes," Gurnee recalled, but "no reaction at all." One bit was about an island nation "where sex was fine and very open and progressive," Allen recalled, "but food was a dirty subject. . . . Little strange guys run up to you on the street, saying, 'Hey, buddy, how'd you like to get a rye bread?' and 'I can get you a picture of a grilled cheese sandwich.' . . ."

At rehearsal, Paar's staff lapped it up. But watching Allen before the cameras, Paar got steamed. "What was all that about?!" he demanded afterward, scolding Allen for being "too intellectual." Paar cut Allen's routine, which had been scheduled to close the show. It was a humiliation because Allen's parents were guests in the audience. (Nettie didn't laugh either.) The too-intellectual Allen would also be snipped from his second and third *Jack Paar* appearances later in the year. Paar "was vile to me until I made it," Allen later wrote.

Still, Cavett proved a good friend, consoling Allen by saying he'd keep trying to get him on the show. And publicist O'Brien turned the humiliation into a gambit. Allen's new handouts admitted his *Tonight* appearance was "too intellectual." Allen added an enterprising joke to his act, noting he was "above Paar for Jack."

Chapter 3

1961

The Big Noise

Standing-Up, Falling-Down Funny—Wives Trade Places—and the Rising Star with a Loser Persona Reaps Wild

Allen's stand-up skills were still shaky, but as his confidence grew to match his literary talents, a curious divergence widened between his private and public selves. As Allen solidified his Everyman image as a cowardly nebbish, unlucky in love, the very self-assurance that underlay this persona also provided him with an offscreen life that was its complete opposite. Fame brought wealth and women.

The long-range goal of Jack Rollins and Charles Joffe was to turn Allen into a household name. To that end, through ties with International Talent Associates, which booked acts nationally, the management team pushed Allen to branch out beyond New York and take his stand-up comedy to other major US cities. By mid-1961, they thought the comedian was sufficiently primed for his first engagement outside Manhattan. Somewhat doubtfully, in July, Allen packed his bags for Saint Louis, Missouri, and two weeks at the Crystal Palace cabaret theater, "one of the hippest in the Midwest," according to the *New York Times*. Rollins-Joffe clients Mike Nichols and Elaine May had preceded him at the Crystal, which was located in Saint Louis's Gaslight Square entertainment district. Allen was booked as the headliner of two variety shows nightly, Mondays through Thursdays, with three performances on Fridays and Saturdays. He, along with several music acts, including jazz singer Irene Kral and a six-piece Afro-Cuban band, were billed as the "Stars of Tomorrow," with Allen's flyers hailing "a comedy writer turned performer in the tradition of Mort Sahl and Sid Caesar. His material is a wry mixture of sociological and cultural analysis of the ordinary happenings of today's average personality."

Established as a showcase for experimental theater, jazz, and blues, the Crystal Palace seated three hundred and took its name from its floor-to-ceiling stained-glass murals. Allen instantly felt like a fish out of water in the heartland. His confidence sagged; his comedy relapsed. "I hope they like me. . . . I hope they like me. . . ." Allen was again overheard muttering in his dressing room before each show. "They didn't," noted Crystal Palace owner Jay Landesman. After each performance "he'd make a long-distance call to his psychiatrist to get him out of this desperate situation. By the end of the first week his phone bill was larger than his salary."

Allen's act had begun to focus "on his being the world's biggest loser in relationships," Landesman said, with anecdotes about unattainable Greenwich Village girls and jokes that skewered the Boy Scouts ("I got out of the Boy Scouts on a Section 8"). "He was the most nervous performer I had ever seen, but also the funniest," recalled Landesman. "The audience didn't throw things, but they found his delivery understated."

A miserable Allen took Landesman aside. "I can't seem to find myself," he confided. "Does it look like I'm coming over as your average neurotic boy next door? It's all a mistake. I wish I'd never left New York."

The staff tried boosting Allen's spirits by stocking his dressing room with "New York–style pastrami sandwiches," and Landesman offered "the use of our family analyst." But the fish out of water "refused to enjoy himself," Landesman said. "On a really bad night when he felt his performance had made the world forget about sunrise, he would call both his analyst and his girlfriend, begging either or both of them to come out to Saint Louis to save him from committing suicide onstage. I encouraged him to develop the suicide line in his act."

The first week proved such a catastrophe from Allen's point of view, he didn't feel right about accepting his fee. "Keep it," Allen told Landesman apologetically. "I'll do better next week, but I think I'm hopeless as a comic. Give the check to the Afro-Cuban band. They were a lot better." Landesman pointed out the money might come in handy to defray his long-distance phone expenses. "I suppose you're right," Allen conceded, pocketing his check. "I'm ashamed of myself for not being able to hold out against the phone company."

Rushing off to phone New York again, this time he talked his girlfriend "into coming out [to Saint Louis] to watch his slow death," recalled Landesman. "Her presence required twice as many phone calls to his therapist." His finances were aggravated by the fact Allen didn't care for the way the shower was set up in his hotel room. He was finicky about shower heads, water pressure, and bathroom drains. He wasn't shy about letting the world know about his shower phobias. "I hate my shower," he told the *New York Times* in 1963. "It hates me, too, but I hated it first." According to Eric Lax, several times a week Allen walked to a nearby Howard Johnson's motel to "rent a room, have a long and vigorous wash, then check out." "It took my whole salary," Allen recalled.

He found allies wherever he went, however, including the eccentric Saint Louis artist Ernest Trova, who had a studio in Gaslight Square and was a mainstay at the Crystal Palace. In the fall Allen would attend Trova's inaugural exhibition of "Falling Man" paintings at the Pace Gallery in Manhattan, where Trova's works sold out to museums. Later, in sculptures, Trova's armless, faceless human figures became icons of Pop Art.

After his two weeks at the Crystal Palace Allen scurried back to New York with his tail between his legs. Next time Allen went out on the road, Rollins vowed, either he or Joffe would accompany the anxious-nervous comedian. Allen would not perform outside New York for another two years, and with the exception of Chicago he'd skip the Midwest for most of the rest of his stand-up career—and as a location for Woody Allen films too.

THE "GIRLFRIEND" HE phoned from Saint Louis was, of course, Louise Lasser, whom Allen had begun to rendezvous with furtively even before he and his wife separated on a trial basis early in 1961. His slow-motion romance with Lasser had turned carnal just before he departed for the Crystal Palace. Allen had moved out of the Upper East Side apartment he shared with Harlene, promising to stick by his wife financially until she graduated from Hunter College. The nearby flat he rented for the summer was "a very romantic apartment with a fireplace in the bathroom, not that I ever used it." He recalled the place fondly because he and Lasser "began a love affair" there, and he "first realized what love was and what it felt like and finally I got what they mean, the poets, the lyricists." He could pinpoint the date, because he never forgot Ernest Hemingway committed suicide on July 2, 1961, the day after their first lovemaking. "I called Louise, or she called me to commiserate," he said.

Along with charm and intelligence, Lasser was "very sexy," Allen later wrote, and she had the curious impulse to engage in sex almost anywhere, anytime, any old place, just like the character Lasser would play in one segment of *Everything You Always Wanted to Know About Sex**. In *Apropos of Nothing* Allen said on one occasion the couple sat down to dine at a Midtown New York restaurant. While awaiting their "succulent" appetizer of smoked salmon, all of a sudden Lasser jumped up and declared, "I feel like making love!" Allen claimed he was all but dragged outside and "pushed into what is a dark, secluded outdoor spot in midtown Manhattan. All around us, traffic and pedestrians barely out of sight. Finally, lust trumps lox and I succumb."

Just as happened in Saint Louis, Lasser showed up at Allen's gigs with more enthusiasm for his stand-up career than Harlene ever evinced. Over the summer the lovers grew closer. In the ceremonial practice he repeated with many women over the years, Allen took Lasser to his favorite movie theaters, museums, restaurants, nightclubs, and small shops. They would go for "long walks in the [Central] Park," Lasser said, "and talk about art and philosophy and life. . . . I had a cultural upbringing, and he learned a lot of that from me."

The crown of her cultural upbringing was her family's "beautifully decorated Fifth Avenue duplex," with tasteful decor and furnishings that would be replicated in many Woody Allen films to come. "The furniture, some of which was designed by the mother," as Allen described the Lasser residence, "is sleek with every lamp, ashtray, chair, and table, understated and tasteful, arranged with a gentle simplicity. The colors are muted pastels, soft blues and grays, there is much cherrywood. Everything is in place and looks perfect to the eye."

On the surface Lasser looked as "perfect to the eye" as her family abode, but by the end of summer Allen had learned that beneath her girl-next-door looks, her pleasantly distracted air, and kooky sense of humor, the aspiring actress was a genuinely troubled person. She had "a sort of Judy

Garland–ish appeal to her," observed Allen's friend Jack Victor, after meeting Lasser at Upstairs-at-the-Duplex. Allen thought his girlfriend had left Brandeis for artistic pursuits. Now Lasser revealed she had taken a leave of absence owing to "psychological problems." She suffered mood swings, and some days just couldn't get out of bed. Perhaps it was an inherited gene: Lasser's mother, the interior decorator with everything in place, was chronically depressed, suicidal. None of this mattered to him at first. Allen was madly in love, and "I never felt like this about anyone before."

RETURNING TO NEW YORK from Saint Louis, Allen needed walking-around money, so with trepidation he agreed to a day job on the writing staff of the weekly, hour-long, Tuesday night *The Garry Moore Show.* Not a singer or comedian, Moore had been a popular all-purpose host on radio before shifting to television. Another Sid Caesar alumnus, Neil Simon, had just left his post as head writer of Moore's prime-time series, and Simon told Allen working for the eponymous star of the show was easy and not soul-destroying. The past season, while on the job, Simon had finished *Come Blow Your Horn*, his first Broadway play. Allen could ply his stand-up trade at night. It was part of the attraction that he'd be writing sketches, for Moore's 1961–62 season, to revolve around Carol Burnett, the onetime Camp Tamiment multitalent whose star had continued to ascend after her Tony-nominated lead in *Once Upon a Mattress.*

Suddenly, however, Allen's precious mornings were filled with script meetings, and in the afternoons he was stuck cranking out comedy lame enough to please Moore. His weekly $1,700 was a godsend, but Allen felt more conflicted than ever about small-screen money. Moore claimed a large staff of writers, and once again the job was basically group writing for someone else's fixed persona. The writers were sometimes thrown on camera performing silly sketches, with Moore coaxing Allen into singing "Little Sir Echo" with a dog. Allen didn't mind the on-camera foolery, having done as much at Tamiment. But he began arriving late, leaving early.

"Woody always had a wisecrack" at the Friday morning read-alouds, recalled writer Coleman Jacoby. "After one reading, he got up and in his best George S. Kaufman voice said, 'Well, boys, I might as well tell you. I'm not putting any money on this one.' And then he snapped off Kaufman's trademark two-finger salute. Guys were furious." Not Jacoby and his fellow staff writer Carroll Moore, however, who "laughed like hell." Allen felt as if he was under a microscope, and everyone knew what he was really focused on was his stand-up.

They were constantly reminded of his rising status as a "new comedian," because Allen began popping up on television shows other than Garry Moore's. Dick Cavett, still a talent coordinator for Jack Paar, had spun his wheels trying to finagle another—undeleted—appearance for Allen on Paar's nighttime gabfest, but it was the Rollins-Joffe team who arranged Allen's true broadcast debut on *P.M. East* in late August, shortly after his return from Saint Louis. A syndicated variety and talk show sponsored by Westinghouse, cohosted by Mike Wallace and Joyce Davidson, *P.M. East* aired on a dozen or so stations, including New York's Channel 5 on weeknights from 11 p.m. to midnight, which was then followed by a West Coast half hour, *P.M. West*. Although its run was brief—Wallace's departure killed the series after a year—*P.M. East* specialized in up-and-coming New Yorkers and nominally competed with *The Jack Paar Show*. Allen shared his *P.M. East* debut with jazz singer Carol Sloane and blues guitarist Casey Anderson, and the comedian would return to *P.M. East* several times in the months ahead, sometimes on the same show as meteoric newcomer Barbra Streisand, who held the record for *P.M.* appearances—fourteen.

Allen's act was still raw and evolving. He told a whopper about police surrounding his apartment because of an overdue library book, and another yarn about a neighbor in his building who, resisting a robbery, took "a tremendous shot across the frontal lobe" and now sat on his bed smiling and was "not as perceptive as the average tree stump." (This corollary to his "ugly girl" jokes took a while to go the way of all sophomoric comedy; even Ike/Allen in *Manhattan* worries about being struck by lightning during a storm in Central Park and turning "into one of those guys who sell comic books outside Bloomingdales.") In *P.M. East* days Allen closed his act with: "I have a message in my work. . . . You should love your neighbor and lay off fatty foods."

Co-anchor Davidson was dating producer David Susskind—later they would marry—and even though Susskind had no formal function on *P.M. East* he was fussing around behind the scenes. Susskind remembered the writer turned comedian fondly from *Hooray for Love*, the Susskind-produced special Allen cowrote with Larry Gelbart in 1960. Susskind was blossoming as host of the syndicated *Open End* talk-show series where, discoursing interminably and with perfect alliteration, he presided over expert panels on "serious" topics. Susskind elevated Allen to *Open End* visibility in December 1961. The experts debating facets of comedy included prominent funnymen Mickey Rooney, Jack Carter, Johnny Carson—who had not yet taken over *The Tonight Show*; he was still hosting daytime variety and game shows—and last-billed, Woody Allen.

An eleventh-hour substitute for Mort Sahl, Allen was so eager for the golden opportunity to appear on *Open End* he told Rollins-Joffe press agent Richard O'Brien that he'd type out his own résumé and publicity:

> *Born and raised in Brooklyn.*
> *Ejected from NYU as poor student in his freshman year.*
> *Writing professionally while still in high school.*
> *Successful at anything I set out to do, charming, witty, raconteur, sportsman, lover, spoiler of women, and all 'round good egg. Best remembered for his invention of the steam engine. Died mad in debtors' prison.*

ALLEN WENT OVER well on *P.M. East* and *Open End* while ruffling the feathers of Garry Moore. Allen told fellow scribe Garry Marshall the real reason the TV host got fed up with him was because the boss liked to be chummy with his staff, and to that end Moore presided over Sunday afternoon barbecues, inviting everyone to his home. Allen spurned the invitations. Shortly after the new year, Moore let Allen go for "nonfeasance." Goodbye to $1,700 weekly. Over the years Allen offered different explanations for what went wrong. "I'd hand in sketches," he told *Newsweek* a short while later, "and they'd say: 'We don't want to mention Khrushchev's name because he's the leader of the slave world.' They preferred to do sketches where Carol Burnett falls down." Allen was hardly known for his Khrushchev jokes, however, and later he admitted, "I didn't blame them. I hated that job. It was too much like school. You were supposed to show up every morning, and I didn't."

Although Jack Rollins and Charles Joffe were still earning little or nothing for their services, things started to perk up in early 1962, the pivotal year in Allen's stand-up career. For one thing, not long after Moore fired him, the *New York Times* noticed the new comic for the first time. Allen was not appearing at a nightclub, or on a TV show. It was March 1962 at the 92nd Street Y on the Upper East Side. Amid a roster of entertainers and musicians that included the Bill Evans Trio and Herbie Mann's Afro-Jazz Sextet, "a relatively unknown comedian," in the words of music critic John S. Wilson, "walked off with the honors." Resembling "a somewhat unkempt Wally Cox," Allen proved "a monologist in the Mort Sahl style who ranges over almost every area except politics." Allen riffed on jazz, Dylan Thomas, "an impoverished off-Broadway company that was so short of actors it tried to do *Faust* without Mephistopheles," and the difficulties of filing for divorce in New York: "The Ten Commandments say 'Thou shalt not commit adultery,' but New York State says you have to."

"Allen's quiet, underplayed style enabled him to get laughs with what might otherwise have been little more than casual remarks. But his steady rapport with the audience served to emphasize the rather awkward position in which some jazz groups—even nominally good ones—can find themselves in a concert hall."

If anything, Allen's pending divorce contributed to the positive momentum. As much as he was a fabulist, the adultery jokes at the 92nd Street Y were an early example of his penchant for sneaking his real-life woes into his comedy. By March, Harlene had found a lawyer to handle her side of the dissolution. Accounts vary as to the details: Eric Lax says Allen "moved out [of the couple's apartment] in the spring of 1961, about a year after she graduated from Hunter College," with Allen still supporting her costs. In her biography, Marion Meade narrows the time differently: "Harlene would not actually graduate until June 1962, finally getting her degree after six years because periodic shortages of money had forced her to drop out for some semesters and work."

As indicated by his 92nd Street Y clipping, Allen was still not well known in New York, nor was he earning big bucks for telling jokes—the Y show was a benefit. His dates were scattered at Greenwich Village clubs like the Bon Soir, the Bitter End, and the Village Gate. He still wrote for other comics, and over the summer he launched into writing the one thing he said he'd never write: a "spec" television sitcom for David Susskind.

Not until November in the pivotal year of 1962 would the real floodgates open up for him, thanks to another effusive review in the *New York Times*. The Bitter End had booked Allen for an extended engagement, and Arthur Gelb's rave for his act sent his stock soaring. Allen's jokes about flunking out of NYU, the girlfriend whose favorite pastime was "listening to Marcel Marceau LPs," and his lopsided encounters with Boy Scouts and bullies were "wildly amusing," Gelb wrote in the *Times*. The "slight, bespectacled, unhappy-looking" comedian possessed "a carefully cultivated nebbish quality," evoking "a Chaplinesque victim with an S. J. Perelman sense of the bizarre and a Mort Sahl delivery (despite the fact he steers clear of topical material)."

Harlene could have read this November 21, 1962, *Times* accolade, published just before Allen's twenty-seventh birthday, while sunning herself in Chihuahua, Mexico, where she had flown for a quickie divorce. Their lawyers had finally worked out an agreement between the couple, sundering their marriage of seven years. Allen "promised to pay a lump sum of $1,750, followed by an extremely modest $75 a week in alimony for the rest of her life, or until she remarried," according to Marion Meade's book, which is sympathetic to Harlene. "Should he be continuously employed with a running contract, the sum would be increased to $125 [weekly]." The settlement, which coincided with his Bitter End gig and the laudatory *Times* notice, amounted to "peanuts" for Harlene, friend Jack Victor thought. Allen's alimony payments proved "erratic" anyway, wrote Meade.

CHET HUNTLEY AND David Brinkley read out Arthur Gelb's *Times* review on their nightly NBC newscast, which was another marker on the road to Allen becoming a household name. The phone rang off the hook for reservations at the Bitter End, lines formed around the block, and his performances sold out. Turning twenty-seven, Allen concluded his triumphant Bitter End run in December. Meanwhile, he had been a busy beaver in daylight hours, polishing the pilot script for his projected television situation comedy series, *The Laughmakers*. Daniel Melnick, the ABC executive who worked closely with David Susskind and Susskind's staff producer, Robert Alan Aurthur, believed in its potential, although the premise was decidedly offbeat for the network.

Allen's script followed an avant-garde improvisational troupe performing in a Village club called the Freudian Slip. Some of the characters' names, like Tad and Danny, were nods to Allen's mentors (Danielewski and Simon), and dialogue references to Nietzsche, Schopenhauer, Shelley, and Bartok, as well as a joke about someone's mother overdosing on mah-jongg tiles, would resurface in later Woody Allen films. Dixieland jazz played under the opening credits. The improv bits flowed from Allen's Tamiment past (soldiers fighting psychological warfare) toward his moviemaking future (takeoffs on stickups that anticipated *Take the Money and Run*).

The director of record for the pilot episode was Joshua Shelley, a formerly blacklisted actor who later emoted in the cast of *The Front*, which starred Allen. One of the behind-the-camera assistants was Ulu Grosbard, who'd later direct Allen's play *The Floating Light Bulb* on Broadway. Allen sat in on all the auditions and casting, observing and saying little, while guiding the selection of Louise Sorel and Paul Hampton as the leads of the prospective sitcom, and doling out lesser parts to a cast of then unknowns including Alan Alda with a Beatles hairdo, the pre–*Bonnie and Clyde* Michael J. Pollard, and of course Allen's aspiring actress–girlfriend Louise Lasser. Allen hovered on the set, during the rehearsals, staging, and photography too.

His script blended the sitcom format with that of a variety show, breaking up the narrative with the improv troupe's skits and songs. The main story revolved around the romance between Sorel and Hampton, who are members of the troupe. But the loose-knit ensemble approach made for a weak continuity. Susskind brought in a shrewd editor, Ralph Rosenblum, who'd edited his pilot for the hit dramatic series *East Side, West Side*, but ABC decided *The Laughmakers* took too many risks, and the network passed. "The network didn't get it," recalled Sorel. "It was ahead of its time." The Woody Allen sitcom was meant to cap the pivotal year. Instead, the show went on the shelf. Typically, Allen shrugged off the defeat. Over time, he'd make it on the averages.

NINETEEN SIXTY-THREE WOULD be his breakthrough year, or the year of "the big noise," as Allen liked to say. His niche turned out to be not the Upper East Side, where he lived, but Greenwich Village, the setting of *The Laughmakers*. The Village clubs that took him to heart were all within a short walk: the sophisticated Bon Soir on West Eighth; the dark, smoky Bitter End, a folk music coffeehouse, on Bleecker; and the Village Gate, the largest of the three at the corner of Bleecker and Thompson. Village audiences were more sympathetic to the rough edges and patchwork persona that alienated some critics who first caught Allen's comedy at the Blue Angel. ("If Woody Allen could get rid of a few of his unnecessary Mort Sahl gestures he would be an authentic original comic talent," Jack O'Brian had written in the *New York Journal–American*.) In the historically rebellious, nonconformist Village, everyone was undergoing an identity crisis. Allen's perpetual identity crisis was the subtext of his comedy, and the "serious, intelligent" Village people (his words) got his vibe. The hip and bohemian flocked to see him. "Anxiety was the juice that electrified him," wrote critic Vivian Gornick, "that set him going and kept him running. And thousands of us drank in his anxiety like adrenaline, because it was the same for us. Half in the culture, half out, we too were anxious." Ironically, even as he'd nightly taxi downtown from upper Manhattan, Allen became the embodiment of the antibourgeois Village scene, where authenticity counted for everything.

By early 1963 Allen had found his groove, taking his time with his monologue, interacting more with audiences. "I didn't understand the concept of the performer," Allen later reflected. "I thought, having been a writer all my life, that it's just the material they're responding to. I felt if I came out on the stage and read the material, they would laugh if the material was funny. . . . Jack Rollins explained to me that it's the *man* that's funny. . . . So I had to get less literary in my performance. You have to come out and say hello and talk to them and relate to them and hook them in—and if they like you, they find your stories funny, they go with you. That took me a while to realize. It's experience."

Rather than telling jokes in a straight-ahead monotone, he now crafted pauses and rubbed his eyes while stalling a punch line. He mugged and gulped. He incorporated the expected cord-twisting and writhing. Rather than piling up the laughs as quickly as possible, "I began to get comedy ideas that could only be expressed in [longer] monologues." Engaging more with some members of the audience helped control heckling while also allowing him to improvise, which he was good at—making for a more spontaneous-seeming Woody Allen. Shouted question: "Do girls laugh at you on dates?" Answer: "Only in the last twenty minutes."

His early fans at the Bitter End, Arthur Gelb wrote, had enjoyed the privilege of watching "a rising young comedian develop into an established young comic." Even so, not everyone got him, not then and not later, either. In a continued effort to win over the William Morris Agency, for example, Jack Rollins brought Abe Lastfogel, the head of the all-powerful agency, to see Allen at a Village date in late 1962. "Too Greenwich Village, too Jewish, too corduroy," sniffed Lastfogel, which was, oddly, exactly what Allen was doing right.

On the heels of Gelb's review in the *Times*, Rollins-Joffe announced Allen's first national tour—actually, his first dates outside of New York since the Crystal Palace washout in Saint Louis. Although he'd skip most of flyover country then and later, Rollins-Joffe arranged bookings for him at the hungry i in San Francisco, the Crescendo in Los Angeles, and Mister Kelly's in Chicago. Charles Joffe would go along as his security blanket.

In early March Allen made his first trip to San Fran, where he shared the bill at the hungry i, the fabled North Beach basement venue, with the folk group the Highwaymen, whose number-one hit was "Michael, Row the Boat Ashore." Allen had stiff local competition from Lenny Bruce, who was holding forth at the Off Broadway on Kearney Street. (Allen never missed an opportunity to say he didn't cotton to the political satire or profane style of Bruce.) Moreover, San Francisco was not Greenwich Village, and the City by the Bay was as yet unprepared for the New York Jewish neurotic nebbish "who twists and squirms while he talks in a manner reminiscent of a spider climbing a web," as Ralph J. Gleason wrote somewhat pityingly in the *Chronicle*.

"Midway through his opening performance, pale and trembling," recalled house pianist Don Asher, "he turned from the audience, bent his elbows on the piano, and sunk his face in his hands." Chronicling Allen's early career, comedy historian Kliph Nesteroff said Allen outright "bombed" at the hungry i, which was certainly the case at the performance where he became so annoyed with the restive crowd he turned toward the back wall and rushed through his jokes to the end without making further eye contact. Some patrons demanded their money back; the management dressed Allen down. He wrote Dick Cavett: "A fast note to explode the myth of the hungry i. The allegedly hip audiences that nurtured Sahl, Berman, Nichols and May have vanished and gone over the horizon. I can't see any difference between this and a Lions Club audience in the Midwest."

Now and forever, Allen and Joffe enjoyed hanging out on the road, and

Joffe still gave notes for improvement after Allen's performances. Allen traveled with his record player and Bunk Johnson LPs, and daily practiced his clarinet. He patronized the nearby City Lights bookstore, perusing the poetry volumes between sets. As the winds of change blew in San Francisco, perhaps his worst offense was that his act "eschews politics," as Gleason noted, never, unlike every other laugh-monger playing the hungry i, so much as mentioning President Kennedy, pro or con. Allen, defensively in his memoir, pointed out he had stood "on street corners handing out flyers" supporting JFK's opponent Adlai Stevenson in the New York primary.

Another thing Allen did in San Francisco was to take lunches with hungry i stage manager Alvah Bessie, who was famously one of the Hollywood Ten, the screenwriters, directors, and producers imprisoned in 1951 after refusing to cooperate with the House Committee on Un-American Activities (HUAC) investigating communist subversion of the film industry. Bessie was loquacious, and Allen listened respectfully as Bessie reminisced about fighting the Loyalists in Spain, spending time in jail for his beliefs, scrounging for a living as a blacklisted writer, and drawing humble wages for backstage work at the hungry i. Allen took a few pointers about American history and politics from Bessie, and the blacklist would evolve as a leitmotif in his later films—worse, later, blacklisting became a grim reality in his life after his career was derailed and poisoned by unproven child-abuse allegations. Returning with the stage manager to the hungry i after one lunch, Allen was impressed when a man jumped out of a car and shouted "a cheerful hello" to Bessie. Recognizing a former comrade who had given the kind of "friendly" HUAC testimony that enabled the blacklist, Bessie shouted back—"How dare you say hello, after all the things you said about me?!"—then rushed up and punched the man in the nose.

AFTER HIS DIVORCE, the imp was out of the bottle with Allen and women. He had not been catnip to girls in high school, nor a ladies' man as a young comedy writer. But his new Woody Allen persona—brainy, goofy, self-deprecating—enhanced his sex appeal. He had to adjust to the fact his persona made him suddenly attractive to some women. Dedicated to making up for lost time and his conventional sexual past, Allen was in no hurry to get married again after splitting up with Harlene. Indeed, Allen was rarely in a hurry for any reason. Personally, and professionally, his speed was methodical. Louise Lasser was still his girlfriend, but their romance blew hot and cold, and Lasser was mentally unstable, chronically depressed. He dubbed her "The Wild Mouse," and later said their eight-year relationship as an intermittent couple was a wild ride in which he rode in the sidecar of her cyclical highs and lows: her binge dieting, drug-taking—"Recreational and medicinal" drugs including grass, uppers, amyl nitrate, Quaaludes, according to Allen—and periodic hospital stays. Even her sexual friskiness had its downside. Lasser was "supersonically promiscuous," in Allen's words. (He'd turn this, in his comedy and films, into the recurrent phrase that a certain type of sexy woman was "polymorphously perverse.") Although Lasser tried making "a real effort to be the perfect girlfriend," as Allen wrote in his memoir, "she never met a mattress she didn't like and had a cottontail's libido." He stoically endured her flings with other men, the same way he accepted his professional setbacks. Through it all, it was hard for him not to love her. Lasser remained adorable, Allen wrote a half century later, "full of sharp insights, always funny."

His relationship with Lasser would soldier on, but "unsteadily," as Jack O'Brian, who had the inside track via Richard O'Brien, noted in his *New York Journal–American* column. Their spells of togetherness were interrupted by "a temperamental tizzy or two" from his mood-swinging girlfriend. The aspiring singer-actress was at her best when her time was constructively occupied, and in 1962–63 Lasser made career strides. She caught the eye of critics as Barbra Streisand's understudy in *I Can Get It for You Wholesale* on Broadway, and drew positive notices, in the first half of 1963, mixing songs with comedy at the Bon Soir and Bitter End.

During one "off" period, Allen chatted up an aspiring fashion designer who waited on tables at the Cafe Wha? basement space on MacDougal Street, where he had performed early in his stand-up career. Another nobody, Bob Dylan, was famously introduced to New York on a Cafe Wha? open-mike night in January 1961. Allen's cautious approach did not work miracles on the pretty waitress pursued by many men, whose name was Vicky Tiel. "This was the sexual revolution," Tiel recalled. "Everybody slept with everybody. Except Woody." The two "dated" but "he wouldn't even kiss me because he was too timid." Tiel would elude Allen in the Village and, later, in Paris.

Allen had better luck with Judy Henske, a 6 foot, 1 inch thunderbolt that struck him in April 1963, upon his return from the hungry i. An unmistakably tall string bean, a banjo-playing and husky-voiced songstress from Chippewa Falls, Wisconsin, Henske was fortuitously booked on the same Village Gate bill. Soon to earn the Village sobriquet of "Queen of the Beatniks," Henske had Louise Brooks bangs and a Bessie Smith wail. She stomped her foot on the floor so hard the floorboards shook when she played her banjo and sang. Henske also interjected "pseudo-folk explanations of her songs that are [as] psychotic as they are funny—and they are funny," in the words of *Billboard*. Since starting her career in the early 1960s Henske had opened for Lenny Bruce, recorded with Kingston Trio founder Dave Guard and his Whiskeyhill Singers, and chorused with other voice artists on "Nine Hundred Miles" and "The Ox Driver" for the *How the West Was Won* soundtrack.

Jac Holzman had just signed Henske to his hipper-than-thou Elektra Records, and her self-titled first album, *Judy Henske*, would be released during her Village Gate stand with Allen. Allen's own first comedy recording was still one year away. "She stood apart from anyone else around, anywhere," Elektra founder Holzman recalled. "There was no pretense about Judy Henske. She was totally authentic and herself." Allen, who was totally *himself*, loved Henske's Storyville murder ballads, blues laments, and whorehouse songs such as those—in fact, some of the exact same songs—that found their way onto the soundtrack of *Blue Jasmine*.

Physically and in other ways, they were the least likely romantic couple. Yet almost from the moment the two met there was electricity in the air, and Henske fast became known around the Village as "Woody's girlfriend." Lasser was relegated to the background for most of 1963. Never before had Allen wooed a Catholic girl, nor had Henske dated a Jew. "He was fascinated by how different I was," Henske recalled. "I was fascinated by how different he was. We were exotic to each other. We were interested in each other. We liked each other. In a way he was so much more square than I was, but in a way, he was so much hipper than me."

They never performed together onstage. Henske opened separately for Allen, with bebop trumpeter Clark Terry also on the bill. The show drew crowds at the Village Gate for six weeks. Allen was still "very, very nervous onstage," Henske recalled. His nervousness was still part genuine torment as well as part a quirk adopted for his act and his persona. One night another young comic, Bill Cosby, who was rocketing to stardom around the corner at the Bitter End, entered the stage door as Allen edged onto the runway of the main room at the Gate, to see what all the fuss was about. As Allen launched his routine, Cosby placed a chair in one corner of the stage and sat down, arms folded, glaring at his stand-up rival. Although Cosby's stage persona was avuncular, his physical presence was scary. Cosby told Henske he thought Allen had "carloads of material and no stage presence." But Cosby was "just trying to teach Woody not to be afraid," Henske recalled. Like Abe Lastfogel, Cosby didn't quite get Woody Allen, and that night Allen seemed even more rattled than usual.

In time, Allen and Cosby became friendly. They would meet up between shows—when Allen appeared at the Gate and Cosby was at the Bitter End, or vice versa—and take healthy walks around the block between sets, talking, laughing, then heading back for the next show, meeting again later before the third show for more circling. When Allen later substituted for Johnny Carson on *The Tonight Show*, Cosby was his first guest.

After they finished their several nightly shows, Allen and Henske would head to bars or late-night cafés and yak, yak, yak. Both were indefatigable talkers and tireless listeners. They explored each other's religious upbringings. Henske was in the process of leaving behind a lifetime of Catholicism: grade school and high school in northern Wisconsin, then Rosary College in Illinois, which was run by Dominican nuns; after being thrown out of Rosary for flunking theology, she'd gone to finish up at the University of Wisconsin in Madison.

Allen was still weaning himself from his boyhood religious indoctrination. He had evolved from a first marriage presided over by a rabbi to feeling deeply conflicted about his Jewish background, especially since he had embraced the consummate Jewish trade of joke-telling with an onstage persona hinging on his Jewish heritage. At restaurants they would discuss shellfish, which Allen associated with his subversive father, who used to sneak him off to Lundy's in Brooklyn to pig out on "clams, oysters, and shellfish." If lobster was on the menu, which appealed to a Catholic native of northern Wisconsin, Allen, adopting a sorrowful mien, hilariously invoked Jewish dietary laws forbidding him to eat creatures that crawled upon the earth or the ocean floor.

Together in the afternoons they roamed the Village, turning up in odd places. Henske had a friend named Terry Gilliam—the future filmmaker—who in those days was an assistant to comic artist and editor Harvey Kurtzman, who'd abandoned *Mad* magazine for the satirical *Help!*. Many celebrities contributed to *Help!*, and Gilliam asked Henske if she'd pose for a *Help! fumetti*, or photo story. She brought along Woody Allen, who spent the day emoting in a *fumetti* called "The Unmentionables," a gangster parody spoofing *The Untouchables* by Gilliam and Chuck Alverson, who would later work on *Brazil* and *Jabberwocky*. Playing the evil mastermind "Mr. Big," Allen sports a straw hat and boulevardier moustache, and *The Unmentionables* marked his first appearance, in any story, on the streets of a faux Paris. "*Fumetti* were the perfect training ground for would-be filmmakers," Gilliam recalled. "You were framing shots and bringing storyboards to life."

Even lovestruck, Allen was organized. He elaborately staged his courtship with Henske, surprising her by renting an immaculate red-and-white convertible and chauffeuring her into the countryside one sunny day for their first tryst. "Yes, he can drive!" recalled Henske. "He was a good driver"—although this would be one of Henske's or anyone's last glimpses of him behind the wheel. The day after their country idyll Allen sent her a Western Union telegram: "You were fabulous last night!" signed "Lon Chaney, Man of a Thousand Faces."

Henske enjoyed Allen's overboard enthusiasms about simple things like names. He collected names, wrote the bizarre ones down. Later, playing Chicago, he made a friend named Minnow Moskowitz, who trailed after him and sometimes showed up in New York. They shot pool together. Moskowitz wanted to be a writer, or comedian. A sketchy-looking guy, Moskowitz rarely uttered a word, however, and his ominous silences evoked, Allen liked to say, a mysterious gangster. Allen would point to him and say, Look at that guy, *Minnow Moskowitz*, savoring the name on his lips. Moskowitz had a brother everyone called "Fishy"—even better.

The daughter of a physician, Henske boasted a keen intellect, and she was insatiable for knowledge. Once, knowing "she'd read anything that came her way," Allen gave Henske the joke gift of "the most un-romantic book I could find," he told Eric Lax, which was "something like 'Pennsylvania Real Estate Laws.'" Actually, the gift was a "Rock-Hound's Field Guide," according to Henske, which she did find hilariously unromantic and proceeded to devour cover to cover, eventually becoming a lifelong amateur geologist and rock collector.

Some nights the couple crashed at Allen's Upper East Side apartment—now, post-Harlene, a different address off Park Avenue—which reflected his bachelor disorder and financial growing pains. The impersonal furniture and plethora of mirrors seemed to have been collected from a hotel auction. He had expensive window sheers that opened to a grand view of the cityscape. Allen liked to gaze at the stars and sky from a huge telescope on a tripod, a prize possession. He also owned a humongous dictionary that rested on a wooden catafalque. Allen and Henske were both fascinated by mentalism, and one time the couple, amorously entwined on the couch, tried turning the pages of the dictionary telepathically. But the pages did not move.

ALLEN MADE A heralded return to the Blue Angel in the late spring, with singer-pianist Bobby Short as the opening act. Celebrities streamed to the Upper East Side nightspot, albeit some—like Paddy Chayefsky, Frank Loesser, Billy Rose, Harpo Marx, and the Broadway producer Max Gordon—coming primarily for the popular singer-pianist, then staying for Woody Allen. Luck—what Allen always touted as the most important thing in life—and the Rollins-Joffe publicity machine was with him. Shirley MacLaine arrived arm in arm with photographer Sam Shaw. Both wept from laughter. MacLaine told her brother, actor Warren Beatty; and film producer Charles K. Feldman, to hurry over and catch Allen's act. Beatty and Feldman laughed hardest at the jokes about sex and psychiatry, which happened to be the subject of a film project they were trying to conjure into existence. Jack Rollins and Charles Joffe tipped Allen off that something was up, and the next day at a movie matinee with Bob Dishy, Allen couldn't sit still and enjoy himself because he was waiting to hear.

Feldman was the suave embodiment of an agent turned producer, so much so people liked to describe him as "a more intelligent Clark Gable." Yet his matinee-idol looks were deceptive. Part of Feldman's charm was that he looked like Gable while behaving like the worst sort of vulgar Hollywood producer. Feldman had pioneered the "packaging" of films when he was a high-octane agent, and now he worked much the same way when producing movies.* Feldman was in the market for a writer for a movie for which he had a star, a title, and little in the way of a viable script. "What's new pussycat?" was how the handsome Romeo Beatty answered the telephone—it was his tease line for picking up women. Rollins-Joffe asked for $35,000 for Allen to write a script for *What's New Pussycat?*, which was less money, according to all accounts, than Feldman had been willing to pay. Allen was tasked with writing the best possible lead role for Beatty, but he could also create a supporting role for his own acting debut. The story, in preexisting script drafts, concerned the priapic editor of a fashion magazine who, surrounded by luscious models, can't be faithful to the fiancée he loves. He must undergo therapy for his debilitating Don Juan–ism. "Write something where we all go to Paris and chase girls," Feldman told Allen.

No problema. Allen said yes with his poker face, not appreciating how much this manna from hell was going to revolutionize his life. "I didn't have breathtaking interest in the project because I thought it was never going to happen," Allen recalled. "I thought it was just a lot of big talk." Feldman followed Allen from the Blue Angel to the Bitter End, coming "night after night" to the club, whispering big-screen ideas in his ear. "He'd hang out with me between shows, and on the street afterwards." Allen met with Beatty at Hotel Delmonico, where the Beatles had stayed in 1964, with the star opening the door in a white terrycloth bathrobe before phoning a restaurant for reservations: "Hi, I'm calling for Warren Beatty"—a trick Allen took under advisement.

"The kid's a genius," Feldman told fellow producer Robert Evans. "We went to Danny's Hideaway for a steak last night. I laughed so hard I couldn't eat." Allen agreed to burrow through the previous script drafts and weed out the dross. He'd take phone calls and meetups with Feldman and Beatty over the summer ahead. Although his schedule was increasingly busy with stand-up comedy shows, he'd find time to jot notes and jokes and write the proverbial fresh draft before reporting to Feldman and Beatty on the West Coast in the fall.

* "Packaging" was and is a "package deal" organized by an agency and offered to a producer, usually consisting of a completed screenplay with commitments from potential stars and/or a "name" director, all represented by the one and same agency.

IN JULY, WITH Charles Joffe once more as his travel companion, Allen resumed his select national tour, playing at the outdoor Carter Barron Amphitheater in Washington, DC, and for the first time at Mister Kelly's in Chicago. In the American capital he opened for the Kingston Trio, and the *Washington Post* urged people to "come early if you don't want to miss a very funny cerebral-type comedian named Woody Allen." Friend Jack Victor came from Brooklyn to see the show, and afterward, on a whim, he and Allen consulted an astrologer.

In Chicago after DC, Allen shared the stage with jazz vocalist Nancy Wilson at the low-ceilinged Mister Kelly's, an intimate supper club on North Rush. Wilson's label was Capitol Records, and the local promotion man, hosting the press and paying bar tabs, was John Doumanian. Doumanian and his wife, Jean, came to every one of the shows at Mister Kelly's, and they forged a friendship with the comedian which, especially in the case of Jean Doumanian, was destined to grow long and complicated. Born Jean Karabas in Chicago, the same year as Allen, her Greek parents owned a diner. She married and became the buyer for a local boutique. Jean boasted the willowy figure and chic wardrobe of a model. With her ebony hair and preference for black couture she might be said to evoke an elegant Midwest version of Harlene Rosen.

Allen, Joffe, and the Doumanians got to know one another better after his Mister Kelly's performances at a nearby late-night coffee shop. Allen expressed curiosity about the latest dance crazes, and Jean, a balletomane in high school days, hooked him up with a Chicago instructor to give him some tips about the Swim and the Monkey. Jean harbored a curiosity about everything pertaining to show business and comedy. "It was tough to make her laugh, though," wrote Marion Meade. "Instead, she would say, 'That is *soo* funny.'"

Allen lingered in the Chicago area. At the behest of Rollins-Joffe—it was part of their national household-name strategy that he should do everything expected of a visiting celebrity—he even appeared at an August United Charities benefit held at a hot-dog parlor. He liked big, noisy, sprawling Chicago, the Midwest metropolis that most resembled New York, and Chicago liked him too. The *Chicago Tribune* wrote: "Best new acts of the year: Female—Barbra Streisand, at Mister Kelly's; Male—Woody Allen, at Mister Kelly's."

Departing Chicago at the end of August, Allen did something he didn't publicize. When playing DC, he had read newspaper stories filled with apprehension about the upcoming March on Washington to be led by Dr. Martin Luther King Jr. While his comedy eschewed politics, increasingly offstage Allen aligned himself with left-liberal causes. On his way back to New York he made a point of passing through DC and mingling with the quarter-million other anonymous participants of the historic civil rights demonstration, hearing the Reverend King intone the historic words: "I have a dream. . . ." The famous people who also marched included Sidney Poitier, Paul Newman, Charlton Heston, Burt Lancaster, Sammy Davis Jr., and Marlon Brando. Among the folk singers entertaining the crowds were Bob Dylan, Joan Baez, and Peter, Paul, and Mary. All Allen did was hoist a premade equal-rights sign that was handed to him and stand, Zelig-like, amid the sea of people. "I doubt if I was noticed," he later told Paul Krassner. Woody Allen was not yet that kind of supercelebrity.

NINETEEN SIXTY-THREE WAS also the year Allen got to know Marshall Brickman. The comedian often appeared onstage with folk singers, and at the Bitter End he alternated with the Tarriers, a long-standing musical unit that had topped the charts in 1956 with a variation of Harry Belafonte's hit "The Banana Boat Song." Like Belafonte, members of the Tarriers were Rollins-Joffe clients. The folk music group underwent constant personnel shifts, and in 1962 the new banjo player was Brickman, a twenty-three-year-old who also played fiddle and bass. Born in Brazil to American parents, Brickman had been raised in a literate, left-wing household, and educated at the University of Wisconsin in Madison. Tall, short-haired, bespectacled, so nondescript he evoked "an ophthalmologist from Minnesota," as the *New York Times* later described him, the banjoist was versatile musically but a sucker for New Orleans jazz. He was also a budding writer. Brickman handled the dry, witty introductions to the Tarriers songs, which had audiences in stitches before the first musical notes were sounded.

When they first met in late 1962, Allen and Brickman merely nodded and smiled at each other, passing backstage at the Bitter End. "His material was not going over well—he was talking about things he said to his psychoanalyst," remembered Brickman. "But I could understand him, and he was just stunning." Allen's comedy was still formative at that time—a pastiche of Tamiment bits and borrowings from other comedians. "He did premise stuff," Brickman said. "What if Russia launched a missile and it was coming toward New York and Khrushchev had to call Mayor Lindsay?"* He then did a phone bit like Bob Newhart. . . ."

Later, at other clubs, the two started talking and couldn't stop. Both were shy, effete, defensive personalities, preoccupied with "the fact that you're going to die, loneliness, alienation, disappointment, not being able to get to sleep," in Brickman's words. The deep kinship they felt for each other made them sort of brothers under the skin with "such similar inflections, in fact," as a *New York Times* journalist later observed. "An eavesdropper might wonder if the two of them are really just a single schizophrenic talking to himself."

One tip his cousin Abe Burrows had given Allen was to take regular breaks from writing and seek inspiration during long walks, as the playwright Robert Sherwood used to do, "writing ideas in his mind and speaking the lines as they came to him," in the words of Eric Lax. Brickman also liked long walks, so he and Allen began to join together for afternoon sojourns through Central Park, swapping jokes and stories, stopping to buy an ice cream cone and sit on a favorite park bench and people-watch. Knowing of their friendship, Charles Joffe suggested Brickman might write some stuff for Allen's act. "I would back into premises and ideas logically," explained Brickman. "He had a way, an instinct, of jumping to some absurd place. One day we were walking down the street and there was a guy coming toward us, a fashion designer. I said, 'Isn't that [well-known New York haberdasher] Roland Meledandri?' 'He looks terrible,' Woody said, 'he's just gone through a very bad divorce.' I said, 'Didn't he used to have a mustache?' Woody said, 'His wife sued for the whole face, but settled for the mustache.' It just came out of him. That would happen a lot."

As he gravitated increasingly to writing, Brickman worked for *Candid Camera*, *The Tonight Show*, and *The Dick Cavett Show* and other shows where Allen made frequent appearances. Brickman and Mickey Rose both contributed bits to Allen's stand-up comedy. Brickman's walks with Allen

* This was Allen's old Tamiment sketch recycled and always updated with the current mayor's name. Be that as it may, in 1963 Robert F. Wagner was mayor of New York City, not John Lindsay.

would continue for five decades, and he'd become his close collaborator on future screenplays many believe rank among the filmmaker's finest.

BRIEFLY, IN THE fall of 1963, Allen returned to the Blue Angel, where he had been introduced as a "new act" only two years before. Then he shuttled from the Blue Angel back to the Bitter End. He had shed the obvious Elaine May, Mort Sahl, and Bob Newhart mannerisms. His public identity, with all its tics, traits, and enigmatic teases, had solidified. Audiences came to his shows expecting to see him—Woody Allen—a persona cobbled together out of autobiography, observation, craft, appropriations from other performers, and long-standing comedy traditions.

In accordance with the Rollins-Joffe master plan, in the fall of 1963 Allen also accepted a recurring slot on a most unlikely television show that would transport him into Middle America's living room on Sunday nights. Someone on the staff of *Candid Camera*, the successful series hosted by genial Allen Funt, scouted Allen's nightclub act and approached the comic to write sketches and perform them for the long-running broadcast series, in which ordinary Americans were trapped on video in elaborately contrived embarrassing situations.

The hokey *Candid Camera* was among "the degrading things I had to do when I started," Allen told Eric Lax, rolling his eyes, though years later he had to admit he still felt "irresistibly drawn" to the show's fake-vérité concept. The mock-reality approach had a lot in common with certain skits he'd written for the Tamiment Playhouse and, moreover, with similarly faked interviews and newsreels in subsequent Woody Allen movies. In one *Candid Camera* skit Allen played an airport "greeter," in top hat and tails, for a nonexistent civic organization, and in another, a manic bookstore salesman compulsively revealing the endings of great novels. "Woody was funny in everything he did for us," Funt recalled. "His best piece involved dictating a love letter to a stenographer. Of course, it was a completely ridiculous love letter," with utterances like "I must have you!"—while the stenographer, an unwitting victim of the filmed prank, blinking in disbelief, stifled her laughter.

The hip, Village-y side of Allen was also on display on TV in the fall. He became the token comedian for the second season of *Hootenanny*, which aired on Saturday nights on ABC, hosted by Jack Linkletter, who made Allen Funt seem groovy. *Hootenanny* was a folk-singing series that encompassed everyone from the Clancy Brothers to the New Christy Minstrels, not to mention the Tarriers with banjo-playing Marshall Brickman. Well, not quite everyone: In fact, the more activist folk musicians, including Joan Baez, Ramblin' Jack Elliott, and others, organized a boycott of *Hootenanny* after the series declined to make room for Pete Seeger, an elder statesman of the folkie movement, who had been blacklisted for his left-wing activities in the 1950s. That didn't seem to bother Allen, whose *Hootenanny* stints were mostly excerpted from his nightclub act—still resolutely apolitical—including riffs on the Swedish cinema and his errant college days. Between gigs in New York, Allen flew to "live" *Hootenanny* tapings at universities in Boston, Pittsburgh, and Arizona.

He could be spotted on syndicated daytime programming as well: *The Steve Allen Show* and *The Merv Griffin Show* and mundane game shows like *Password*. Following Jack Paar's departure from *The Tonight Show*, Allen appeared on the late-night talk show several times with Griffin guest-hosting. And before flying to the West Coast in November he taped his first *Tonight Show* with Johnny Carson, who had met him on David Susskind's *Open End* in 1961. Curiously, even as Allen often told interviewers that television was "idiot stuff, designed by idiots for idiots," he was on his way to becoming virtually ubiquitous on the small screen.

HE WAS A relentless traveling man by now, but his early November visit to Hollywood was the first time he had been in the television and motion picture capital since 1956. He checked into Gene Autry's Continental Hotel on Sunset Boulevard across the street from the Crescendo jazz club, where there was an upstairs room, called the Interlude, for stand-up comedy. Unfortunately, his Los Angeles comedy debut was another debacle. Stone—if not stoned—faces greeted him at some Interlude performances, including the one where an exasperated Allen told the audience they were prime candidates for the *Guinness Book of World Records*' "worst crowd ever."

Dick Cavett had moved to Los Angeles, where he had a job writing for *The Jerry Lewis Show*, which was on ABC. Cavett introduced Allen to Lewis, whom Allen admired more as a film director than for his "infantile" brand of humor. The two funnymen enthused over each other and spoke about collaborating on something of mutual interest someday. Cavett took Allen to lunch with his friend Groucho Marx, and Allen was thrilled "to meet the great comedian whose voice made everything he said sound funny, but I also felt sad thinking Groucho was exactly like any number of Jewish uncles or relatives I had who cracked jokes or teased at a family wedding or bar mitzvah." (Unlike his relatives, however, Groucho's "funny remarks took a quantum leap into comedy genius.") Imbued with nostalgia for Hollywood's Golden Age, Allen and Cavett drove around Beverly Hills with a "Map of the Stars," tracked down Jack Benny's address, and stood reverently outside W. C. Fields's onetime mansion residence, where they "gazed longingly at it as the sun set and fantasized being invited in by the late host himself for a game of billiards and some essence of grape," as Cavett recalled.

Warren Beatty was in and out of town. The star was known for playing hard to get. Most of the time, for script conferences, Allen got producer Charles K. Feldman instead. Allen's new draft of the *What's New Pussycat?* script had "a million great jokes" in it, Allen thought. He had shaped the lead, the lecherous fashion magazine editor, for Beatty, while crafting a key supporting role for the psychiatrist who is treating Beatty's Don Juan–ism. The therapist, who suffers penis envy over Beatty, is unhappily married to a Valkyrie. Allen thought Groucho Marx might play the therapist. He built up another role for himself as Beatty's pal, a doofus as hapless with ladies as the other is adroit—going so far as to create a special moment for his character at La Closerie des Lilas on the Left Bank, a café Ernest Hemingway frequented during his *Moveable Feast* period.

Allen unveiled his work in progress to Feldman by reading aloud from the script he had "typed on Corrasable Bond," performing the scenes as he turned the pages. The producer's "old school" reaction was disappointing. "I had named the lead female character Becky, a Jewish name," Allen recalled. "He didn't like it. And when she met the lead male, who was supposed to be Warren, she had confident dialogue, she would say, 'Well, you know, I'm gorgeous and great-looking.' Charlie couldn't countenance that because it was immodest and against the cliché of what the heroine would say. He regarded me as a quote-unquote beatnik."

Allen dutifully agreed to go back to the well. Just as the budding scenarist was getting down to work on revisions on the morning of November 22,

1963, a chambermaid knocked on the door of his room at the Gene Autry Hotel and told him President John F. Kennedy had been assassinated in Dallas, Texas. Allen turned on his hotel television set and watched as the news was being reported, "thought about it for a minute, then finished my bowl of Cheerios, went to my typewriter, and got to work," as he recalled in *Apropos of Nothing*.

Mort Sahl had arrived in Los Angeles for a Democratic Party fundraiser that had to be canceled because of the Dallas tragedy. Sahl and Cavett joined Allen in his hotel room to commiserate. Allen was due to take the stage at the Interlude later that night. "All of them [were] wisecracking that nobody was going to show up" for Allen's act, Marion Meade narrated, "but then nobody had showed up before the assassination either."

Regardless, this calamity—the death of a president he "never mentions" in his act, according to all his early clippings—accelerated Allen's political awakening. He had grown up and cracked wise inside a vacuum where politics rarely penetrated, and his stand-up comedy would stay, by and large, apolitical. But reality had pierced this particular zone of isolation in which he preferred to exist. Sahl, Allen's idol, would become fanatical on the subject of the assassination, sacrificing career momentum. What mysterious forces formed the conspiracy behind JFK's death? What were the political consequences for the nation? What should ordinary citizens do? Allen was hardly as consumed by Kennedy's death as Sahl was, although Alvy Singer in *Annie Hall* is, and there was a good joke in Allen's later repertoire about moving the Warren Commission Report over to the fiction section if he ever came across it in a bookstore. Regardless, Allen too became interested in assassination conspiracy theories and later supported Mark Lane's Citizens' Committee of Inquiry to the tune of $50,000. Influenced by the crusading folkies that surrounded him in the 1960s, and by his many progressive friends and acquaintances—Rollins and Joffe, Marshall Brickman, Mort Sahl, Alvah Bessie—after the assassination Allen became increasingly committed to benefit appearances and donations to support Democratic Party issues.

BACK IN NEW YORK, Allen made club and television appearances while reworking *What's New Pussycat?* He turned up in episodes of the US version of the British satirical series *That Was the Week That Was.* He quickly became a favorite of Johnny Carson's and a regular on *The Tonight Show,* which was still based in New York. Richard O'Brien handled the growing press interest. *Newsweek* and *Time* interviewed Allen. At the end of 1963, *Playboy* profiled the "Mirthful Masochist" for the nudie magazine's tenth-anniversary holiday issue. Hugh Hefner was an early Allen enthusiast, and later *Playboy* gave him his first prose platform.

Among other things, Allen's long stay in California spelled the end of his romance—if you called it a romance, which they didn't—with Judy Henske. They were never going to last as strange bedfellows. Neither had any illusions about their relationship. They were such different people. Both were locked into careers with separate lifestyles that would never be compatible. Henske was devoted to music, making records, touring and singing in concerts. Allen was a comic ultimately headed for Broadway and, it was dawning on him, movies. Even when Allen was home in New York, he stayed compulsively busy. Work ate up most of his time.

By the time Allen left for Hollywood the couple had all but broken up. Sometime in the second half of 1963, Henske found herself spending more and more time with Jerry Yester, a southern folkie and multi-instrumentalist who had started out with the New Christy Minstrels before joining the Modern Folk Quartet. Henske fell in love with Yester, and Allen circled back to Louise Lasser, sipping champagne with her and Johnny Carson on New Year's Eve on *The Tonight Show* and pointedly referring to her as his girlfriend.

Nevertheless, Henske was on the same bill as Allen when he returned to Mister Kelly's in Chicago in early March 1964. This was Henske's first time at Mister Kelly's. Allen still suffered from acute nervousness, she recalled. He still had bad nights. At one show—seven on the weekends with the last at 2 a.m.—Mister Kelly's was crowded with National Asphalt Convention delegates, who were dining on surf and turf and salad with Green Goddess dressing. Henske could smell the lobster and Green Goddess upstairs in the dressing room. When Allen took the stage, the delegates raucously drowned him out. Charles Joffe came pounding upstairs to the dressing room, hysterically shouting, "Pandemonium! Pandemonium!" Someone asked him what was happening. "Woody is lying under the piano in a fetal position whispering into the microphone!" exclaimed Joffe.

Chicago was the midwestern crossroads of show business, and Warren Beatty happened to be in the Windy City at the same time, making *Mickey One* with director Arthur Penn. Beatty phoned Allen at the Ambassador, where he was staying, and insisted the comedian move over to his hotel, the new Astor Tower—a glassy rectilinear building on Astor Street that had been designed by the modernist Bertrand Goldberg, with Art Nouveau decor and room service from a basement bistro modeled after Maxim's in Paris. Allen did as Beatty suggested, and then he checked into the Astor whenever he was in Chicago for years ahead. During the daytime he wrote in his suite, finishing a new draft of *What's New Pussycat?* and getting a good start on what would become *Don't Drink the Water*—his first Broadway play. At night, he told tall tales at Mister Kelly's.

Many celebrities passed through Chicago—Arthur Godfrey, Angie Dickinson, and Alan King were ringside guests during his three weeks at Mister Kelly's—and, prefiguring *Broadway Danny Rose*, Allen took lox and bagels at Eli's Stage Deli with fellow stand-ups Henny Youngman, Jackie Gayle, and Don Adams.

Burning the midnight oil was not really Allen's reputation, yet he kept up a "strong night life" in his younger days and after his Chicago performances he socialized with John and Jean Doumanian and a widening circle of friends who called the city home. "After my late show at Mister Kelly's, they'd take me out for ribs someplace, and we'd go to someone's house, and wind up at [Playboy founder Hugh] Hefner's mansion at two o'clock in the morning. I'd play pool and sit around there with other show business people 'til four." One time, interviewed by columnist Irv Kupcinet for his local television broadcast, the round-the-clock man fell asleep on air. "I sort of closed my eyes," Allen recalled sheepishly. "I guess I was tired from the night life."

Through Rollins-Joffe, Louise Lasser arranged a booking in Chicago for March and April. She'd sing at the Happy Medium cabaret, located near Mister Kelly's on Rush Street. Lasser moved in with Allen at the Astor, passing Henske like a ship in the night. One Sunday, Henske slipped away from Chicago to marry Jerry Yester on the East Coast, returning early the next week, after the briefest of honeymoons, to resume at Mister Kelly's.

It was at Mister Kelly's one night in the spring that Allen recorded his first album for Colpix Records, the recording division of Columbia Pictures. His performances were uneven, the crowd reaction mixed, with several good jokes that didn't land right each time. Allen was not satisfied with the recording until the thirty-fifth attempt late in his run. There would be scant editing, and the LP was his full set "live." Its release was planned for late June, just before Allen was scheduled to take over *The Tonight Show* for a week. Both milestones were timed to compensate for his absence from clubs and TV for months after he left to make *What's New Pussycat?* in Europe.

Allen's nightclub salary had risen to $1,000 weekly. He was also getting paid for spot appearances on an increasing number of TV programs. He had raked in the dough for writing *Pussycat?* and would be earning an additional high fee for acting in the movie. He still earned as much as an extra $1,500 weekly for supplying nameless comics "with a five-minute bit" here and there. Nowadays Rollins and Joffe were getting their percentages. And when playing poker with Joffe and friends, Allen made more money, often winning the pot. One fine day in Chicago Allen went shopping at the Richard Feigen Gallery and bought a Giacometti.

On another fine day in Chicago, he announced his engagement to Lasser, although the comedian left the city before his fiancée could finish her stand at the Happy Medium to keep a two-week commitment at the Shadows, a Georgetown cabaret in Washington, DC. Then, after the DC stint, Allen returned for one last hurrah at the Village Gate on a bill with Judy Henske and her new husband, Jerry Yester, and the Modern Folk Quartet. Allen would make Henske one of his musical guests the next month when he took over *The Tonight Show*. Another of his *Tonight* guests was Lasser. Allen probably saw Henske for the last time that summer of 1964. The folk-blues artist was spiraling down a different road in life. "Judy Henske is one of the few people I lost touch with that I wish I had touch with," Allen told official biographer Eric Lax wistfully, twenty-five years later, when standing outside the Bleecker Street Cinema during a pause in the filming of *Crimes and Misdemeanors*.

OFTEN, IN THIS phase of his busy, hectic career—and most other times—Allen seemed to be perpetually standing in the crowded elevator of a towering skyscraper, rising and descending continuously as he stepped out to keep appointments on different floors, one after the other. Whether performing comedy or, later, making films, Allen kept up an exacting schedule of work and travel. The common thread in all his activity was writing. He was eternally writing. Writing jokes, ideas, scenes on scraps of paper. Writing on planes, in cars, even when riding in elevators. Other writers suffered the occasional block, or took weekends off at the beach. Allen wrote and wrote, squeezing in a miraculous amount of professional activity and, always, set-aside playtime.

For a while it seemed as though US president Lyndon Baines Johnson (a.k.a. LBJ) was a passenger in Allen's elevator to success and renown. Following the Kennedy assassination in 1963, Allen became an avid Johnson backer, and on May 26, 1964, he served as a celebrity emcee at a fundraising gala for the president in Washington, DC. Two days later he did similar duty at the "Salute to President Johnson" extravaganza held at Madison Square Garden, which drew over seventeen thousand people and raised $1.5 million for the Democratic Party. Allen along with most of the guest stars had been corralled by Arthur B. Krim, a former entertainment lawyer who was the head of United Artists, the studio behind *What's New Pussycat?* An influential party fundraiser, Krim found Allen funny and cultivated him as a friend and as a political donor. After the extravaganza, LBJ mingled with VIPs and celebrities, including Allen, at Krim's Upper East Side residence, which was coincidentally near Allen's.

After the Madison Square Garden event, President Johnson invited Allen to a state dinner paying tribute to the president of Costa Rica at the White House on the Fourth of July weekend, attended by many celebrities including evangelist Billy Graham, composer Richard Rodgers, and entertainer Jimmy Durante. In a rented tux and shoes, Allen showed off his dance lessons, indulging in a "brisk foxtrot" with the president's wife, Lady Bird Johnson, who got a kick out of the milquetoast comedian. When speaking to LBJ, Allen fumbled for small talk. ("Why am I such a wallflower?" the comedian lamented to a columnist.) His "ugly girl" comedy streak surfaced in private cracks to friends: the president's daughters were "two of the ugliest sisters" he'd ever seen.

When he returned from DC, the *New York Times* reported another professional benchmark: The "nightclub and television comedian" was making progress on an "untitled" stage play, which concerned "the adventures of a New Jersey family abroad." Allen's first play would be ready for Broadway by "next season," with Max Gordon producing. Not the Village Vanguard's

Max Gordon—this one was a friend of the Marx Brothers, whose stage hits included the Garson Kanin comedy *Born Yesterday*, beloved by Allen. Gordon's last Broadway show had been *The Solid Gold Cadillac* in 1955, but the producer had seen and enjoyed Allen's nightclub act at the Blue Angel and then warmed to him in person in the Rollins-Joffe office. "Only the first act is finished," according to the *Times*, but Allen and Gordon had shaken hands on it.

By day, that summer in New York, Allen huddled with Clive Donner, the British New Wave director whose low-budget black comedy *Nothing But the Best* had impressed *What's New Pussycat?* producer Charles K. Feldman. Donner was now in charge of *Pussycat?* Meeting to discuss the screenplay with the Englishman, Allen congenially worked through the never-ending revisions. "Though he [Allen] would occasionally, at some of my jokes, give me a *look*," Donner recalled wryly. They were still tailoring the lead for Warren Beatty.

That left his nights free in July, and while Johnny Carson kept a booking in Las Vegas, Allen clocked in as the one-week substitute host of *The Tonight Show.* Carson was by now an unabashed fan, and Allen had already appeared on the late-night talk show nine or ten times, so he knew "all the cues and format," he told journalists. An amateur magician and musician like Allen—in Carson's case, a drummer—the *Tonight* host found the nebbish comedian the easiest of guests. Dick Cavett, who later made his longtime friend a frequent guest on his own eponymous talk show, said much the same thing about Allen: Cavett would spot Allen in the wings, about to come onstage, and his grinning would start because he always knew there was going to be fun ahead.

In the afternoons before the nightly tapings Allen seemed surprisingly relaxed, sitting for interviews, and insisting "I don't have the faintest idea what I'm going to say" when the show went "live" at 11:30 p.m. Eastern time. An established motif in his interviews nowadays was the banality of the small screen. "I hate to say it, but most television is degrading," Allen said, as he got ready to go on air. "It's junk. But I say this as a spectator, not a performer. I'm not above performing on it." Regardless, he was collecting $2,400 for the week.

Allen's guests over the five nights reflected his up-to-the-minute enthusiasms in comedy and music: the comics included Bill Cosby, Godfrey

Cambridge, Allan Sherman. Count Basie was among the musicians. The old acquaintances stopping by included Danny Meehan, a hoofer and singer who appeared in nightclubs with Allen, comedian Will Jordan, and past and present paramours Judy Henske and Louise Lasser. Allen's loose stance paid off, and his seeming spontaneity in front of an audience—more spontaneous if the audience of millions was invisible—had grown into a forte. One critic wrote: "Carson had better hurry back from Vegas."

At the end of the week of hosting *The Tonight Show*, Allen posed for *Life* and *Esquire* spreads and chatted on Mimi Benzell's New York lunchtime radio show about his future. The small club dates were going to evanesce, he told the broadcaster. He was gravitating to mammoth auditoriums. In August, for example, he'd appear at the Forest Hills Tennis Stadium in New York, sharing the stage with Count Basie and Trini Lopez, and shortly before leaving for Europe he was going to headline a similar arena at Red Rocks Park in Colorado. Benzell stole a glance at Allen's daybook planner, raising an eyebrow. It was like a grid with all the blocks of time—every day, all day—blacked out with appointments, meetings, interviews, stand-up shows, travel.

ACCOMPANIED BY THE faithful Charles Joffe, Allen flew overseas in early August, landing in London, where his first comedy recording, which introduced him to the British market, had just been released to generally favorable comment. In the US, *Woody Allen* had peaked at number sixty-three on the *Billboard* chart of Top LPs, although it floated around in the top one hundred for a few months. The actual unit figures and income derived from the recording were disheartening in the US, however, Allen always said—and that is supported by the letters he wrote privately to publicist Richard O'Brien. Allen bemoaned that "my sales have been awful." Adding to his disgruntlement, the company had misspelled his name on the spine of the LP: WODDY ALLEN.

Allen had written the *What's New Pussycat?* script with Paris in mind, but producer Charles K. Feldman maddeningly refused to commit to a location, saying they might be shooting scenes in London or Rome, depending on the financial exigencies. Checking into the Dorchester Hotel, Allen and Joffe had little time for sightseeing before Clive Donner whisked them off to the South of France, the Hotel du Cap on the Riviera, where Feldman was encamped in luxury and presiding over preproduction plans. Feldman had a surprise: Warren Beatty was no longer the star of *Pussycat?* Although Beatty thought Allen had written "the funniest script I ever read," the leading man wanted to cast one of his inamoratas, Leslie Caron, among his lovers in the picture, while Feldman outvoted him with another French actress, Capucine, the producer's own former mistress. Beatty dropped out, and Peter O'Toole, hot off his Best Actor Oscar nomination for *Lawrence of Arabia*, dropped into the starring role of the fashion magazine ladies' man. What's more, Groucho Marx had fallen out of favor as the psychiatrist character with a bad marriage who is on the prowl for a mistress of his own. Feldman had shown script pages to Peter Sellers, who agreed to his first acting job since a series of heart attacks, in April 1964, forced him out of Billy Wilder's *Kiss Me, Stupid*.

All this worried Allen, who foresaw his work as expendable. Feldman told the comedian to relax, get a little sun, go for a swim—with sunshine and swimming high on Allen's list of unfavorite things. Instead, Allen gambled at night in the casinos. With O'Toole and Sellers, two box office names, *Pussycat?* began "growing and growing," in Donner's words—the rewrites, the budget, the advance hoopla. Feldman and Donner sat around the pool debating sexy actresses. "I hate her, she's got a big ass!" Feldman would say when Donner mentioned an available party. "But she *acts* well, Charlie. . . ." Donner tried coaxing. They agreed on Romy Schneider for O'Toole's sweet fiancée; Paula Prentiss as the pill-popping American who writes poetry about peaceful coexistence and better housing ("A fabulous and beautiful comedienne," Allen wrote in his memoir, "I should say he [Feldman] interviewed her at my begging"); and voluptuous James Bond girl Ursula Andress as the beauty who drops into O'Toole's lap from a parachute. (Allen would remember that happy contrivance and bring it back for *Mighty Aphrodite*.) Capucine, as predetermined, was the nymphomaniac open to a threesome.

Off they all traipsed, first to the Hotel Excelsior in Rome, where Feldman hoped to drum up some money from investors and conduct a little casting and perhaps shoot some exteriors—although Allen kept reminding him *Pussycat?* was set in Paris. The producer banished Allen and Joffe to a week of frivolity and girl-chasing in Florence. Apart from his frustrations with Feldman, this interlude was the beginning of Allen's lifelong love affair with Italy, but his time in Rome ended on a sad note when news arrived from America that Harpo Marx had died, age seventy-five, in a Hollywood hospital. Producer Max Gordon had introduced the blond-wigged Marx brother to Allen after a Blue Angel show. Allen wrote Groucho a letter of heartfelt condolences.

At last Feldman surrendered to the inevitability of Paris. Everyone repaired to the French capital for three months of exteriors and indoor filming at the Billancourt Studios in Boulogne. Among the minor pleasures of the last decision-making was the casting of Eddra Gale, a Czech-American who lived in Paris, as the harpy wife of Peter Sellers. Gale had been memorable as the slutty La Saraghina in Federico Fellini's *8½*, and now she joined a picture already sprinkled by Allen with many sly Fellini-isms, manifestly so in O'Toole's fevered dream—like Marcello Mastroianni's—where O'Toole is swarmed and taunted by his many girlfriends, wives, and passing fancies.

Allen found it difficult to relate to the great Sellers, whom he had admired since youth. Sellers had started out his career as the lowliest comedian in a troupe before proving himself a brilliant chameleon in British and Hollywood movies. When Allen met Sellers for the first time in the lobby of the Hotel George V, where both were lodged, however, the two men "eyed one another carefully," as Allen noted in a diary concocted as publicity for *What's New Pussycat?* The awkwardness and tension between them were exacerbated by the fact the two performers uncannily resembled each other, which more than a few people noticed. "I think he senses in me a threat to his current position as cinema's leading funnyman," Allen wrote. "I tried to make him feel at ease."

Not to happen: According to actress Sian Phillips, who was married to Peter O'Toole at the time, both Sellers and O'Toole were decidedly "not nice" to the American comedian and scenarist of *Pussycat?* during the filming. Sellers's biographer, Ed Sikov, said the two bigger names "rudely belittled" Allen, pulling rank and taking over his script to embellish their own scenes, inflating their speeches, improvising dialogue they thought funnier than what Allen had written, and devising jokes and bits on the fly. "They would say, 'That scene between you and Peter Sellers, or you [Allen] and Peter O'Toole, we're going to let the two Peters do it,'" Allen recalled.

Allen swiftly understood who was destined to be the odd man out.

Although he had written his own role as a showcase for his talents—during the revisions, shamelessly expanding his scenes—he was left with few moments to shine. Among the few was an exchange he jotted in Paris, after he and Charles Joffe paid a visit to Le Crazy Horse Saloon, a cabaret combining magic and variety acts with striptease artists. He gave Victor Shakapopulis, his oddly named character, the profession of "wardrobe man" for the revue, inspiring the most Woody Allen–ish line in *Pussycat?* Victor/Woody tells Michael James (O'Toole) he is gainfully employed, assisting the Crazy Horse striptease ladies with dressing and undressing for twenty francs weekly. "That's not much money," Michael notes sympathetically. "Yes," deadpans Victor, "but it's all I can afford."

It was all the more demeaning when the two Peters demanded Allen revise their revisions. "They used to give me rewrites," Allen recalled in one interview, "and I used to run home and do them, really, in five minutes; this is no exaggeration, a half hour at most. I typed the first thing that came to mind, then I'd bluff and say, 'Yes, I'm sweating over it and I'll have it for you in three more days.' And then I'd give it to them." Behind Allen's back, however, Feldman allowed the two higher-paid stars to tinker and worse. Joffe accused Feldman of "crucifying" Allen, and there came a rare moment, after Allen sat through the rushes one day, when the comedian told Feldman to go fuck himself. Still, the expletive rolled off Feldman's back. Nothing could dampen the producer's enthusiasm for Allen, whose contract he tore up and reconfigured to add three more movies. Joffe told Allen to take a deep breath and think about the money and the once-in-a-lifetime chance.

Paris offered pleasant distractions. His presence on the set was not always required—or desired. Allen continued with the French language tutorials he'd initiated in Los Angeles and made a point of visiting "every museum and cathedral" in the guidebooks. One day he brushed past Brigitte Bardot when heading into a movie theater: "Black stockings, blonde braids. What a face!" Another time he crossed paths with Samuel Beckett at a sidewalk café; there is a photograph of the memorable encounter in Eric Lax's first book about Allen. He could boast of dining with Jack Lemmon, Orson Welles, and the Burtons—Richard and Elizabeth Taylor—who were in Paris around the same time making *The Sandpiper.* One night he brought Julie Christie with him to listen to Claude Luter, "a boyhood idol," a clarinetist and saxophonist who had performed with Sidney Bechet. (Bechet had passed away in 1959.) "I go to see him [Luter] constantly where he plays at a joint called the Slow Club," Allen wrote O'Brien. He gave interviews, and posed for photographs with Luter, and, another time, with the Crazy Horse erotic dancers for a "What's Nude Pussycat?" layout earmarked for a future *Playboy*.

Because of a lifelong love-hate relationship with steaks he dined monotonously on Dover sole at a chic restaurant near his hotel. Feldman kept his room stocked with Hershey bars, which were among the confections Allen liked close at hand when at work; malted milk shakes were another. He toiled scrupulously on *Don't Drink the Water*—the Broadway play he was writing for producer Max Gordon—and kept up with his reading: Saul Bellow's National Book Award–winning *Herzog*, which concerned a Jewish academic's midlife crisis, and Richard Ellmann's masterly James Joyce biography. Every day without fail Allen practiced his clarinet.

His typewriter had broken, and it was not easy to get the machine fixed in Paris. It typed only in CAPS. Corresponding with Gordon, Allen kept the producer apprised of his forward progress on *Water*, and by October he was deep into the second act. The plot concerned an obstreperous Newark, New Jersey, wedding caterer and his family, the Hollanders, who are mistaken for American espionage agents while taking a vacation behind the Iron Curtain. The Hollanders take refuge in a US embassy, where the ambassador's bumbling son—filling in for his father, who is off "concluding an oil deal with the Sultan"—tries to cope with the international crisis caused by the spy misunderstanding. The young diplomat develops a crush on the caterer's beautiful twentysomething daughter. The supporting characters include a priest who has been hiding out in the embassy for six years and who has used the time to practice elaborate magic tricks that, when performed, go spectacularly awry.

Allen did not want to show "progress" to Gordon until he had completed the two-act play. When writing a script, he believed in starting on the first blank page and writing through to the end, before criticisms and changes. He did write now, and sometimes later as a filmmaker, with possible casting in mind. *Don't Drink the Water* aimed for a broad appeal akin to Neil Simon's *Come Blow Your Horn*, Allen wrote Gordon. Allen thought Lou Jacobi, who had been extremely good in *Horn*, would be right for the lead in *Water.* If not Jacobi, then maybe someone like Zero Mostel, who was "overrated but still funny." Betty Walker, who'd impressed Allen in Paddy Chayefsky's *Middle of the Night*—play and film—"Might be very good" as Jacobi's wife.

Allen said he wanted "clearly Semitic" accents and cadences from the actors playing the Hollanders, but "I hope the central family is not coming out too Jewish, although I feel they are," in his words. Jewish but not "too Jewish" was also a balance he tried to strike in his comedy act and later Woody Allen pictures. There was no mention in their correspondence of Allen infusing the Hollander family with traits culled from his own parents and relatives, which Allen later said, in publicity interviews, informed his writing of *Water.* And there would be no mention at all of the family being Jewish in the published version of the stage script, which explains only, upon their entrance in act one, that the wedding caterer, Mr. Hollander, is "a typical tourist, complete with loud, short-sleeved shirt worn outside his pants. . . . The Hollanders are a family from Newark, on vacation."

Gordon should treat the script, when it arrived on his desk, as simply a working draft, Allen advised the producer. In early November Jack Rollins flew to Paris to meet with Allen and talk over contracts and scheduling for 1965. But he also came to read *Water* before Gordon did and make suggestions for revisions.

Hollywood studios were now interested in Allen for other movies, Rollins reported. The many offers to sift through and the explosion of interest in Allen meant there was a logjam of scheduling ahead, and they needed to hire a personal secretary for the writer-comedian. Rollins recommended a former actress named Norma Lee Clark from Jefferson, Missouri, who would assist the agency in reading his mail, screening communications, and organizing his chockablock calendar. Clark, who was a romance novelist on the side, would work out of the Rollins-Joffe offices for the next thirty-five years, speaking with Allen daily by phone. "I don't think Woody has ever asked me a personal question," Allen's secretary informed the *New York Times* some fifteen years later, in 1980. "He doesn't encourage intimacy. My only problem with him has been trying to keep the relationship impersonal, since I have a real mothering instinct. But the reverse is true, too. He's very easy and undemanding as a boss. He has never done anything mean or malicious or unkind, and I've never seen him lose his temper, though," Clark added as an afterthought, "sometimes I think it would be good if he did."

After reading the "rough first copy" of *Don't Drink the Water*, Rollins gave useful notes. Rollins was "greatly enthused" about the draft, Allen wrote Gordon, but he was now embarking on a vigorous revision. When, later, Gordon received the script, the producer turned the draft over to his preferred director, Robert B. Sinclair, at one time George S. Kaufman's assistant. He and Sinclair would continue to liaise with Allen about the script and casting. The "next season" announcement had been wildly optimistic. *Don't Drink the Water* would take almost two years to jell.

EARLY ON DURING the filming of *What's New Pussycat?* Allen renewed his once-upon-a-time flirtation with Vicky Tiel, the erstwhile waitress from Cafe Wha?, now more gainfully employed as an assistant to costumer Gladys de Segonzac. Allen vied romantically for Tiel, who already knew him as "the antithesis of a seducer," with none other than director Clive Donner. There were no hostilities between the writer and the director of *What's New Pussycat?* however. On the occasion of Tiel's twenty-first birthday in October, the company threw a "Vicky" contest in which the rivals agreed to compete for her love favors. Each would buy her a gift, the cast and crew would vote for the best gift, and the winner would "get to sleep with me that night," Tiel recalled, adding, "This was not just for fun but also for a commitment."

Donner presented Tiel with a supersize box of Godiva chocolates. Allen went shopping and found a giant pinball machine and hired two guys to haul it up five flights to Tiel's rented flat, shared with another costumer. The giant pinball machine easily won the cast and crew vote, and Allen claimed the right to bed the birthday girl. "Victorious Woody, ever the director, gave me very specific instructions," Tiel said. "He did not want to sleep with me that night but planned it for the next so he could 'set the stage.' I was to arrive at the Hotel George V at precisely eight o'clock. I was then directed to go into the bathroom, take a long shower with the door open, come out nude, and walk to the bed. He promised he would also be nude—and erect—under the sheets."

Alas for Allen, the very next day Tiel was having lunch with Ursula

Andress and Paula Prentiss in the Billancourt Studios commissary when the assistant costumer spotted "the most virile man I had yet to see in Paris" push through the swinging doors in the company of Elizabeth Taylor and Richard Burton. Makeup man Ron Berkeley couldn't help but notice Tiel as well—she was wearing a "see-through lace jumpsuit"—and promptly asked for her telephone number. Berkeley phoned a few hours later, asking Tiel out for a drink, then kissed her passionately when she opened the door for their drink date and whisked her off to bed for hours. Tiel woke up with a start. "Oh my God, Woody!" She spied Allen the next morning and "I could tell he was very upset with me." Tiel explained she "fell in love yesterday at lunch with a guy I met and am going to marry." Allen gave her "that trademark woebegone look," asking piteously, "At lunch?" Tiel and Berkeley did get married, yet somehow—back in New York and over the years—Tiel also managed to stay friends with Allen.

MOST DAYS IN Paris Allen telephoned his "on and off" girlfriend Louise Lasser, who had remained in New York. He spent an inordinate amount of time on the phone on most days, calling friends and associates, but he missed Lasser. One day Lasser surprised him with news. "We're chatting and in the middle of the conversation she says, 'The leaves are starting to turn. You'd love them. You love fall colors. And what else?—Oh, my mother committed suicide,' " as Allen recalled. The conversation was "odd," Allen wrote in *Apropos of Nothing*, and "all I can say is the whole deal resembles no known social interaction I recognize from Avenue J in Brooklyn."

Paula Lasser had tried to kill herself on several previous occasions before storing up her prescription pills and overdosing in late September 1964. One of those earlier times, after coming out of a coma in the hospital, she asked how she was still alive and was told her daughter, Louise, had rushed in to save her. "I'll never forgive her," Paula said. Divorce from Louise's father had stoked Paula's despondency. While Blanche DuBois from *A Streetcar Named Desire* was the fountainhead of the privileged, wounded women in *Interiors* and *Blue Jasmine*—the bleakest of Woody Allen films—Louise Lasser's mother was their real-life correlative.

Consoling Lasser, Allen urged her to come to Paris and stay with him at the Hotel George V. Arriving, she moved into his suite. Allen spoke with

Clive Donner and arranged for an unbilled cameo for his girlfriend in a scene where she plays a neurotic housewife who massages Peter Sellers's back during group therapy.

Not long after, Allen made one last appearance on behalf of the Democratic Party and the presidential campaign of Lyndon Baines Johnson, who was running for his first full term. The US national election loomed in November. Among the "Artists and Writers for Johnson" congregating at the Eiffel Tower for a "Sky High for L.B.J." fundraiser were Josephine Baker, Memphis Slim, Jean Seberg, Paul Newman, Joanne Woodward, and Woody Allen. "I opened by saying, 'Good evening, ladies and gentlemen, this is my first tower,'" he wrote Richard O'Brien. "I'm one of the few comics who can look at that structure in a movie and say, 'I played that room.'"

While in Paris, he celebrated his twenty-ninth birthday and the new year of 1965. The gray weather was just the kind he liked. Both the *What's New Pussycat?* filming and the *Don't Drink the Water* stage play he had been working on feverishly were finished by the time he flew to Washington, DC, in mid-January for the inaugural ball and gala. As one of the celebrity emcees—others included Johnny Carson and Mike Nichols and Elaine May—Allen endured hours of rehearsal at the National Guard Armory. The greenroom was enlivened by the presence of Alfred Hitchcock, another emcee. It was the one and only time Allen met the master of suspense, whose movies he admired, although they weren't his usual cup of tea. "He was charming and funny," Allen recalled. "What were they talking about?" the *Washington Post* asked rhetorically, answering: "Movies." Was Allen taking notes for *Match Point*?

Onstage at the gala, celebrating President Johnson's oath of office, Allen regaled the crowd with his comedy, with some of the routines newly hatched from Paris. The first lady found herself smiling and chuckling. "Woody Allen, that forlorn, undernourished little comedian," Lady Bird Johnson recorded in her audio diary, offered "about five minutes of jokes that I found hilarious, and I am no lover of comedy on the stage. He looks like you want to give him a blood transfusion. . . ." Lady Bird laughed especially hard at his extended bit about a man who shoots a moose, straps him onto the roof of his car, and then takes the moose to a party.

Onetime collaborator Larry Gelbart, who had last seen Allen's stand-up act at his Blue Angel debut in 1960, was among the crowd of people at the thronged event, and he recognized a new man. "His transformation was total," said Gelbart. Allen had "become a performer who exuded confidence and authority, doing joke after joke. . . . Absolutely stunning material, material that showcased his gift for defying and deflating that which disturbs him most: life, sex, no sex, not enough sex, too much sex, and of course, that old standby, death."

Flying home to New York, Allen was astonished to read Hearst columnist Dorothy Kilgallen, on the front page of the *New York Journal–American*, singling him and Johnny Carson out as "COMICS IN BAD TASTE AT INAUGURAL." Kilgallen had found his DC routine objectionable, particularly the surrealistic moose tale that Lady Bird Johnson had found so hilarious. In the moose bit Allen notes that the New York Athletic Club was "restricted" (i.e., no Jews). Though "not as offensive as Carson," Kilgallen wrote, Allen "did pretty well . . . [electing] in the guise of comedy to make heavy points of prejudice deserving of a far more serious setting—and far more serious treatment." Jack Paar and now Dorothy Kilgallen, with many others to come: For all the progress he had made toward becoming a household name, for many Americans Woody Allen would always be a cultural outlier. The appreciative audience for his comedy was mysterious and unpredictable, and in this instance included a delighted first lady. The humorless and puritanical often took umbrage at his jokes.

II

Mr. Everything

Chapter 4

1965
The First Golden Age

Hollywood, Broadway, Las Vegas, and Beyond . . .

Early in the new year, Allen shook up his therapy regimen, switching, after eight years with Dr. Peter Blos, his first psychiatrist, to Dr. Lou Linn, whose practice was also located on the Upper East Side. There was no big reason for the move, he insisted in interviews, no dramatic spike in his needs or problems: simply, time for a change in doctors. He joked about it, with the jokes revealing little. He met with Dr. Linn "twice a week in a face-to-face situation. He was quite brilliant, but I easily outfoxed him and remained safely uncured."

Perhaps it was the pressure-cooker year that stretched ahead of him, personally and professionally. Eight months had passed since, in Chicago in the spring of 1964, Allen had announced his engagement to Louise Lasser. While he and Lasser had returned to cohabiting, their relationship was still "on again, off again," and Allen didn't really know if he wanted to marry his longtime girlfriend—or break up with her. Lasser was never more vulnerable than in the months following her mother's suicide. There were advantages to Allen's incessant work and travel. He could endlessly delay domestic crises, and any decisions he might have to make.

Anticipation for *What's New Pussycat?* fueled his burgeoning celebrity. The forthcoming screen comedy was "already, before a foot of film has been edited, a guaranteed blockbuster, the big comedy picture of 1965," the London *Observer* predicted. Allen was in demand for television, and the

Rollins-Joffe team had him slotted for the January premiere of the new variety show *Hullabaloo*. His live shows continued to balloon in size, and his return to stand-up came in February at the Café Crystal of the Diplomat Hotel in Hollywood, Florida, between Miami and Fort Lauderdale.

There were pluses and minuses to the higher-bracketed stand-up gigs. His income rose steeply—his price was now a reported $9,000 weekly base, with a percentage of the gross—as more tickets were sold. "I like a big room better than a small room," Allen explained half-jokingly to the *New York Times*, "because I can be more nervous, and the audience doesn't see it." Unavoidably, though, there was a physical and psychological disconnect to the bigger venues. Reviewing Allen's performance in Florida, his first show in months, *Variety* pointedly noted the Café Crystal was "a difficult room for an artist to establish rapport, with an audience. It is a vast, dark cavern with a stage at the far end. . . . Only those in front can get the benefit of facial expression."

Over the next half of the decade, he'd complete his transition to motion pictures, but those first efforts would teach a few hard lessons. Mainly, that he needed to gain independence from small-minded studio heads and ignore the opinions of critics. Yet even as his professional accomplishments and pressures mounted, he held at arm's length his personal problems—however useful for comedy riffs—a feat all the trickier as his success mounted.

Nineteen sixty-five was the year Allen definitively left the Village behind in favor of luxury hotels and huge auditoriums such as the Basin Street East in the Shelton Towers, the Royal Box at the Americana, and the Playboy Club—all in Manhattan. In Los Angeles, he played the six-thousand-seat Greek Theatre. The intimate clubs remained the best for trying out new comedy material, however, and consequently Allen would sneak back to the Bitter End now and then, unadvertised, unpaid. Also, for the time being, he kept a few smaller oases on his itinerary like the Shadows in Washington, DC, Mister Kelly's in Chicago, and the hungry i in San Francisco.

While only a modest success commercially, Allen's first comedy recording drew a Grammy nomination from admiring peers in the Recording Academy. *Woody Allen* lost to another debut LP: *Bill Cosby Is a Very Funny Fellow . . . Right!* Colpix wanted a second Woody Allen album as soon as possible, and Allen was under pressure to recharge old routines that were already familiar to the public. *Woody Allen, Volume 2* was recorded at the

Shadows in the spring. One new piece, "European Trip," reimagined his ill-fated dalliance with Vicky Tiel.

He had worked hard to win over reviewers and audiences outside New York, and nowadays his fans showed up expecting the Woody Allen persona and wanting to hear familiar riffs they knew from TV or his first Colpix LP. He "scampered through the aisle," the once skeptical Ralph J. Gleason reported when Allen returned triumphantly to the hungry i, "hopped up onstage and grabbed the microphone and was funny before he opened his mouth. From then on, he couldn't do anything wrong. The audience broke up on cue every time."

He opened a run in Chicago in June 1965, just before *What's New Pussycat?* opened in theaters. He felt at home, almost ebullient, headlining at Mister Kelly's. He even played his clarinet publicly, for the first time, at the Velvet Swing on nearby Walton, sitting in with local banjoist Eddy Davis's Dixieland jazz band.

It hardly mattered that many—not all—reviewers found *Pussycat?* to be a silly, strained, and not very titillating sex farce. Some sequences, like the Mack Sennett–style go-kart climax, were devoid of any Woody Allen touches. In a few other scenes, however, his sidesplitting jokes stuck out like arrows in a corpse. The manic energy of Peter O'Toole, Peter Sellers, and the sexy actresses tipped the balance for audiences. With the help of a catchy Burt Bacharach–Hal David title song, which Tom Jones caterwauled up the pop charts, *Pussycat?* struck a wacky chord with young moviegoers in a fast-changing America and became the box office crowd-puller of the summer, eventually grossing over $18 million worldwide—a record for a comedy of the era.

Allen emoted and gesticulated in only a handful of scenes, the best of which saw him flirting foolishly with Romy Schneider. For him, at least, the movie successfully transmitted his guise as a cerebral shlub—heretofore known only to nightclub and television audiences in the US—to the greater worldwide market. It was understandable he was embarrassed by his prominent credit as the movie's sole scenarist, especially when critics who didn't like the picture tended to fault his script. The worst notices, seizing on his name, singled him out. "No one in his right mind could have written this script," Bosley Crowther wrote in the *New York Times*. Judith Crist in the *New York Herald Tribune* bemoaned the "tediously plodding plot and stale comedy routines."

Allen drew several lessons from his first outing as a screenwriter and thespian. First, he often said, he himself could have made a better movie, except his version wouldn't have made as much money. In fact, he vowed never to write another film script without having more control over the result. Not that he himself ever saw *What's New Pussycat?* He didn't care to relive the experience. "All it could do is bother me," he told interviewers.

And he learned from the reviews to ignore critics as much as possible. "I hate all critics," he went on record saying in 1969. "To me, they only serve a destructive function." At the same time, however, critics' brickbats gnawed at him, even if Allen insisted they did not. Rollins-Joffe publicist Richard O'Brien sent friendly notes around to the major critics Allen habitually read, including Crist at the *Tribune* and Whitney Bolton at the *Morning Telegraph*, asking if they would care to read his *Pussycat?* screenplay and decide for themselves if his plot plodded, or were his pages funnier than the half-baked movie? Bolton interviewed Allen and assured readers: "What is on the screen is not what emerged from his typewriter." A copy was messengered to Crist, and Allen followed up with a dinner invitation. This was the beginning of a friendship of the sort he formed with many film critics over the years, those whose writings he respected and whose favorable verdicts he sought. Allen and Crist would continue to socialize in years to come; he'd send her advance copies of scripts, and invite the prominent critic to early screenings. All of which would lead to *Stardust Memories* fifteen years later.

"I was a paid hack," Allen told populist broadcaster Studs Terkel, who interviewed him for his radio program between sets at Mister Kelly's, even as Chicagoans flocked to see *What's New Pussycat?* "They paid me a lot of money and they said, 'We'll let you get into the film business if you write one film and write it the way we want it.' Even though it came out to be a funny film, I think, it's not the kind of film I would do had I total command." Allen said he'd have "much more control over" the new script he was writing for himself—this time as star—as part of the new three-picture contract he had with *Pussycat?* producer Charles K. Feldman.

Tape-recording the interview for later airing, Terkel introduced Allen to his listeners as "a comic Job," likening him to the biblical prophet, a virtuous man upon whose head Satan, with God's permission, rains down a series of disasters. Job struggles to survive and to understand God. Terkel also described Allen as already "a celebrated figure" in American society.

His comparison of Allen to Job showed how the comedian had begun to be regarded by his more Village-y fans as a man whose humor could be interpreted as a kind of common-man wisdom.

Asked if fame and affluence had affected him, Allen replied with a fast no. "You fail with a better class of women." Although for the first time, the comedian admitted, he had been chauffeured around in a limousine in Paris. "I couldn't relate to the chauffeur," Allen added. "Same problems—just expressed with richer people."

Who are you really? Terkel asked earnestly. Are you the person we get to know onstage?

"I am shy and awkward offstage and onstage," Allen replied. "The truth is everything I do [onstage] is highly exaggerated . . . a cartoon." He worked very hard at crafting the persona he presented onstage, Allen told Terkel. "I put very little premium on [improvisation]," he explained. "I've figured out my stories, I've figured out how I'm going to tell them, and I try to pack them with as many laughs as I can—and that's it."

Allen was inclined, he said in the interview, to divide comedians into two categories. One type is "acted upon constantly," and the other is "the personality who aggresses in a situation." Personally, Allen preferred the aggressor comedians, reprobates like W. C. Fields and the Marx Brothers, but "I enter more like Robert Benchley would and something falls on me." Terkel brought up the name of another nonaggressor: Charles Chaplin. What did Allen think about Chaplin? Wasn't Allen's persona a "little man" akin to Chaplin's?

Over time Allen would express mixed feelings about Chaplin. "I'm not Chaplinesque," he'd inform many interviewers, including JoAnne Stang for his first *New York Times* profile in 1963. He praised a few of Chaplin's classic comedies while others (*The Circus*) he claimed he had never seen. More than once he knocked *The Great Dictator* as a timely comedy that wasn't very funny. Chaplin tended to irk him as a comparison. Chaplin was too heartwarming. "It's unfortunate that I don't like Chaplin that much," Allen told Terkel backstage in Chicago. "I think that he's a bore, he's pretentious. Some of his work is superb . . . but I don't put any premium on making the audience cry. . . . The best of the Marx Brothers wipes out Chaplin."

What kind of films, Terkel asked, would Allen create if he had the same kind of power as Chaplin, as a combined writer, director, and star? Well, he would not make films "geared toward a moron level," Allen mused. "A heavyweight comedy," he ventured. "I would do comedies that are more adult . . . certainly [more adult] than Jerry Lewis."

Interviews were de rigueur for publicity, and Allen had a professional grounding in—and professional need for—press coverage. A mountain of interviews would pile up in the years ahead. Over time Allen would answer tens of thousands of interview questions, treating most people who politely phoned him up, or sent him a letter, with the same civility he reserved for major byliners. Future publishers would issue several entire books of lengthy interviews with him, including one from Eric Lax, distinct from his other books about Allen.

Inevitably, there would be many examples of discrepancies and contradictory statements in the collected interviews. He'd refuse to admit the obvious—certain cinematic influences on his pictures, for example, which were often indebted to other people's movies he admired. He was prone to sweeping statements that were one "tell"—the "never, evers" that rolled off his tongue and were hyperbole. This was perhaps not that unusual for a celebrity who spoke on the record so often, and for whom the instinct for privacy warred with his candid impulses.

When another interviewer, Paul Krassner, turned on his tape recorder for *The Realist*, shortly before *Pussycat?*'s release, his subject surprised him by leaning back and lighting a cigarette. "Hey, I thought you didn't smoke," said Krassner, who had done his homework and read the clippings. "I *didn't* smoke," Allen explained. "Well, I originally did smoke, when I was young. And then I began to see where it was going to be trouble for me. . . . I stopped smoking. And then, I didn't smoke for years. And the day the surgeon general's report came out that you could die from smoking [in 1964] I started smoking again. Not consciously for that reason. Just, I felt all of a sudden, a tremendous urge to have a cigarette that day. And I haven't stopped smoking since then."

As other interviewers discovered by chance, Allen also smoked the occasional cigar.

Much of what Allen told Krassner and Terkel in the summer of 1965, when he finally became the household name Rollins-Joffe had predicted for him, would be echoed if not repeated verbatim down the years.

••

DESPITE HIS QUALMS, Allen's maiden foray into motion pictures was undoubtedly "a huge plus for me," he later reflected. *What's New Pussycat?* "was the big launching pad. Suddenly, I could command huge figures. . . . For all the things I disliked about it, the movie had a certain vitality that people all over the world responded to."

Charles K. Feldman had coaxed Allen into a three-picture contract with the promise he could direct one of the three. The script Allen mentioned to Studs Terkel, the one over which he intended to exert "more control," was a collaboration with high school friend Mickey Rose. Initially, their story was going to be embedded in Allen's profession, dealing "with the life and development of a comedian who is a criminal and who ingeniously keeps committing major crimes, being apprehended and then escaping the arm of the law." It was called, in embryo, "I'll Take the Money and Run," with a lead character named "Woody Allen." Their script progress was interrupted, however, by a more pressing item in Feldman's deal with Allen, *Casino Royale*, a James Bond spoof—with Allen onboard as an actor only—which was going to be shot in London in early 1966.

Partly for the money and because he had the time—it was still a few months before the London shoot—Allen took a side job redubbing a Japanese action-comedy into an exploitation spoof for the American "youth market." Actually, it was two films from the *International Secret Police* series starring Tatsuya Mihashi.

The producer of the project was Henry G. Saperstein, a onetime merchandiser for Elvis Presley and Lassie, who'd bailed out the floundering United Productions of America animation company in 1960 and rode a wave of success selling Mr. Magoo, Gerald McBoing Boing, and Dick Tracy cartoons to television. Saperstein also had licensed the Japanese Godzilla monster for the US market as part of an ongoing business relationship with Toho Studio, which produced the *Godzilla* horror pictures and the *International Secret Police* action-comedy series.

Saperstein had offered the redubbed spoof first to Lenny Bruce, but Bruce declined when Saperstein told him he couldn't use four-letter words. Okay, Saperstein said, "Who's a clean you?" Bruce mentioned Woody Allen, who was already on Saperstein's radar. Saperstein had chased Allen to Paris in late 1964 to discuss the possibility of him doing a movie based on *Catch a Falling Spy*, Nathaniel Benchley's comic novel about Cold War espionage, with Allen adapting and starring. But Allen's contract with Feldman didn't permit him to write or star in another picture without the producer's permission. No matter, now Saperstein had this other idea: redubbing the *International Secret Police* series into an English language comedy. On paper, it looked rinky-dink to Feldman and Allen, who signed with Saperstein for $66,000. It was easy money from the comedian's point of view, and American International Pictures, Hollywood's low-budget, youth-oriented studio, jumped in with a chunk of money to cofinance and distribute the picture. The title, *What's Up, Tiger Lily?*—twitting *What's New Pussycat?*—was Saperstein's. Allen hated it, but Saperstein was the boss.

Approaching the idea as a lark, in the late summer Allen took a suite at the nearby Stanhope Hotel on Fifth Avenue in his neighborhood, convened a group of close friends, and watched and rewatched the *International Secret Police* series. They stole a few moments from *Kayaku no taru* or *Keg of Gunpowder*, a 1964 release, while primarily drawing from *Kagi no kagi* or *Key of Keys*, the 1965 action-comedy directed by Senkichi Taniguchi. Allen was abetted by Mickey Rose, Louise Lasser, Frank Buxton, and Len Maxwell from Tamiment days, and someone the credits list as Bryna Wilson, who was likely his old high school flame. All day long they spitballed gags and bad puns for group consensus. "The jokes came machine-gun style," Saperstein recalled. "A character would walk through a door and Woody would say, 'I need a door joke,' and they would fire off about two hundred door jokes." Said Maxwell: "How I knew things were funny: Woody would roar." This was a form of "group writing"—with friends, and Allen in command—he enjoyed.

Allen and the others concocted a ludicrous plot that entailed secret agents and criminals vying for a stolen recipe for the world's greatest egg salad—"So good you could plotz." Allen would give the lead Asian tough guy (Mihashi) a Brooklyn moniker—Phil, with the last name Moskowitz—like his friend Minnow. He kept most of the sexy scenes with exotic dancers and scantily clad women, renaming two of the femme fatales Teri and Suki Yaki, and larded the script with absurd one-liners and movie-star imitations that sent up Peter Lorre, James Cagney, W. C. Fields, and Nelson Eddy. (A clubgoer in one scene, watching a stripper strut her stuff, remarks: "Isn't she fantastic! She was even better in *The Sound of Music*!") There would be Jewish mothers and dying Japanese villains crying out for their rabbi. Allen and friends gleefully broke all the usual fourth-wall rules. When the reel abruptly snaps, leaving the screen dark, the audience is momentarily transported into the projectionist's booth, where Allen and his girlfriend (Lasser) are etched in silhouette—kissing and necking.

The group also voiced many of the parts. Taking over a studio, Allen and his cohorts, with a few hired players, dubbed the oft-nonsensical, colloquial English into Japanese mouths. Also going behind the camera for the first time, Allen shot an extended sequence sparring with an interviewer—a narrative device, like the announcers he'd incorporate into future Woody Allen pictures, which helped disguise the ramshackle continuity. After a brief introduction to the movie, Allen parries the dumb questions that follow. Interviewer: "Can you give us a brief rundown of what's gone on so far?" Allen, after a pause: "No." He also staged the faux end-credits with Mort Sahl's wife, China Lee, steamily disrobing as Allen sprawls blithely behind her on a couch, crunching on an apple. Viewers are distracted by the eye chart rolling up over one half of the screen. Allen stops her at black lingerie. "I promised I'd put her in the film," is his last line, "somewhere."

He and Lasser sprinkled in some weekend breaks in East Hampton, visiting Charles Joffe's beach home, with Allen complaining about the sun, sand, and flies. Working in tandem on *What's Up, Tiger Lily?*, sharing laughs, he and his girlfriend were never closer. Allen was reminded why he loved Lasser. Perhaps their relationship was truly cemented, in the fall, when Lasser read the humorous essay Allen had been writing for *Playboy* and told him the piece was too good for the men's nudie magazine. He should try for the *New Yorker*.

Considering his later acclaim as a writer of films with complex roles for women, it is easy to forget how closely associated with *Playboy* Allen was early in his career. He had already penned droll pieces for *Playboy* that anticipated his later, better-known writing, such as "My War with the Machines" from the January 1965 issue, in which the narrator engages in a "very Hemingway"–like fight with a television set and endures anti-Semitic remarks from an elevator. The *New Yorker* had a venerable tradition of short comic pieces, or "casuals"—"A word they invented," according to Allen, "in the tradition of Benchley or Perelman," two of his literary heroes. Allen preferred his phrase: "little souffles." He could only dream of the *New Yorker*, yet Allen took Lasser's advice, submitted to the higher-brow magazine, and was happily surprised when his piece was accepted—provided he'd meet a few editor's criticisms and made changes, including to his ending. He did so gladly.

ALLEN WAS HYPERACTIVE in the fall of 1965: dubbing and filming for *What's Up, Tiger Lily?*, reworking the script of *Don't Drink the Water*, and revising his first "little souffle" for the *New Yorker*. He also kept stand-up dates at the Concord Resort Hotel in the Catskills and the Americana in New York while courting college students at Franklin & Marshall College in Lancaster, Pennsylvania, and Indiana University in Bloomington. On television he showed up on the most middlebrow of programs. Donning top hat and tails for *The Perry Como Show* he gave his best imitation of Fred Astaire in a lavish dance number—although, as *Variety* noted pointedly, "a song and dance man, Allen is not." Broadway producer Max Gordon's whispers into Ed Sullivan's ear helped bring Allen onto Sullivan's top-rated Sunday-night show for the first time. During the afternoon run-through in October 1965 Allen ran through a mock-up of his routine for the benefit of lighting and camera movement. For the actual taping, however, he let loose with his "real material," which included an hysterical bit about a sexually unfulfilled wife who invests in "orgasmic insurance." The straitlaced Sullivan burst into his dressing room after the taping, denouncing Allen's indelicate comedy, and told him "attitudes like yours are why kids are burning their draft cards." Allen sat in his chair, "shocked, thinking, Should I tell this guy to fuck off and leave?" Instead, more his style, Allen bit his tongue. After all, the Rollins-Joffe plan was to conquer the middle part of America too. He agreed to delete the "orgasmic insurance" and other risqué jokes from the later broadcast. "From that day on I had no better ally in show business," Allen recalled. "Ed plugged him" in his syndicated newspaper column, James Maguire wrote in his Sullivan biography, and booked him "for three additional appearances."

The auspicious new year of 1966 was tolled, on January 25, with his first publication in the *New Yorker*. Allen's debut in the magazine came in the form of "The Gossage-Vardebedian Papers," a parody of a chess match by correspondence, which unfolds as a smackdown by two venomous grandmasters. Allen took chess lessons, he was an avid player, and chess had already reared its head in his script for *What's Up Pussycat?*, where Victor Shakapopulis (Allen) is a chess-cheater. Chess would loom in numerous future Woody Allen films, most notably in *Whatever Works*, where Larry David is a brutal taskmaster to kids learning the game.

Then two weeks later, on February 7, Allen and Louise Lasser slipped away from their final obligations on *What's Up, Tiger Lily?* for a hastily arranged wedding. Lasser and her "shrink" had discussed her erratic and turbulent relationship with the comedian, Allen later wrote, "and the notion arose that maybe the act of marrying, the commitment, would put a totally different and more solid cast on the relationship. We were both willing to give it a try." Lasser's father and his second wife were about to embark on a vacation trip around the world, according to accounts, and the bride-to-be wanted to catch them before their departure and have them present for the auspicious occasion.

The press was not forewarned, but Richard O'Brien teased out the details to pet journalists, including Jack O'Brian of the *New York Journal-American* and columnist Earl Wilson. Allen, "with his great hero's heart, gave Louise the afternoon off [from *What's Up, Tiger Lily?*] to get a wedding dress," O'Brian reported. Eschewing the "traditional virginal white" she'd wear in *Bananas*, the bride opted for "a beige wool tailored dress, beige textured stockings, beige shoes." The man of the hour threw on a natty sports jacket and bought a $1.98 ring in Times Square. The nuptials were preceded by what Allen would describe in *Take the Money and Run* as "a deeply moving blood test," required by law to rule out venereal disease. Allen fainted, Lasser insisted.

Imagine a nice Jewish boy getting married twice without inviting his parents, because that is how it went down this time too. "Up to a few minutes before the ceremony Woody's parents hadn't even been apprised," O'Brian reported. According to columnists, the wedding took place at the Lasser family's East Side home; according to Allen's memoir, the couple pledged their troth in an upstairs suite at the Americana Hotel, where he was scheduled to appear at the Royal Box. Either way, Mickey and Judy Rose and Chicago friend Jean Doumanian, who had relocated to New York, were among the last-minute guests rounded up. New York State Supreme Court justice George Postel, a Lasser family friend, presided. Judge Postel had not heard of "the famous Woody Allen," and proved it by referring to the groom as "Woody Herman" during the vow exchange.

That same night Allen took the stage at the Royal Box, performed his appointed two sets, then hosted a small wedding party in a suite after hours, inviting a few show business and Brooklyn pals. A honeymoon was never to be. For one thing, Allen was too busy: along with nightlies at the Royal Box, he had joined in a Gene Kelly television tribute to New York City, and he was still writing and planning "I'll Take the Money and Run," which was intended to follow *Casino Royale*. Allen had spoken to Jerry Lewis, who was open to directing.

Two weeks later, Allen flew to England for *Casino Royale*, leaving his bride behind to prepare their move to a new townhouse address on East Seventy-Ninth. Acting lessons and rehearsals for a new nightclub act with comedian Vaughn Meader would occupy Lasser while Allen was away. Although the second Mrs. Woody visited London, and Allen flew home at least once—for another East Hampton weekend with Charles Joffe—Allen would be on call in London for months. "I guess it was not a good sign for our marriage," he said later.

WHAT'S NEW PUSSYCAT? was disciplined artistry compared to *Casino Royale*, which Charles K. Feldman trumpeted as a "James Bond extravaganza." Before all was said and done, five directors shared credit for the extravaganza, including the dab hand of John Huston, who handled the scenes in which he acted. Three writers other than Ian Fleming saw their names on the screen, and another seven or eight, including Allen, chipped in.

In this spoof gone wild of Fleming's secret agent novels, David Niven had been cast as 007. The story had 007 plucked from retirement after the death of M to lead a unit of ultrasecret agents, male and female, all code-named "James Bond" in order to deceive and defeat the megacriminal SMERSH organization. The mercurial Peter Sellers and the wondrously sculpted Ursula Andress were among the holdovers from *Pussycat?* And they were joined by a hot and cold smorgasbord of international stars including Orson Welles, Deborah Kerr, William Holden, Charles Boyer, George Raft, and Jean-Paul Belmondo. Allen was playing the part of "Little Jimmy Bond," nephew of the bona-fide 007, whom the plot reveals as "the master heavy," in the words of the *New York Times*. "Little Jimmy Bond" has been scheming to double-cross his uncle and rule the world.

Casino Royale was "a silly picture, with a lot of money wasted," Allen said later. But as his private correspondence confirms, he felt that way at the time too. "The film stinks as does my role," he wrote publicist Richard O'Brien. Hired principally to act, Allen was "of course doing a bit of writing on the script," the *New York Times* reported. The "bit of writing" was just "a few ad-lib jokes to my own part," Allen told O'Brien. He met with Val Guest, the director of his few scenes, in his Saint John's Wood home. The two got along, although Allen believed Feldman would cut anything he wrote that was good. "This murderer! This murderer!" Allen would moan. "I said, 'Don't worry about it, we'll put it back on the floor [while filming],'" recalled Guest, "and we did."

The film's stars, along with Allen and Charles Joffe, who was in and out of London during the months of filming, were quartered at the Dorchester. The photography took place largely at Shepperton Studios, but ground on over the summer. Allen really had very little to do. Characteristically, he made excellent use of his idle time, however, writing as well as keeping in the public eye. Early in the filming he dashed off his second "little souffle" for the *New Yorker*—an attack on mimes called "A Little Louder, Please"—and by summer's end he'd written his third—"Yes, But Can the Steam Engine Do This?," a disquisition on the glorious history of the sandwich.

His early pieces would remind longtime *New Yorker* readers of the humorists who had preceded him in the "casuals" tradition. His writing seemed "dangerously derivative," Allen admitted. Editor Roger Angell cautioned Allen, "We already have one Perelman. We don't need another." At the same time, from the very first his pieces flaunted his distinct ideas and preoccupations. "A Little Louder, Please," for example, was spiced with Krafft-Ebing, Boy Scouts, James Joyce, and mention of the Coney Island roller coaster. Although usually written in a humble vernacular, his *New Yorker* pieces were dotted with oddball names, false facts, and made-up history, and sometimes they were so funny they were "too funny," according to Angell, who now and then trimmed a few laugh lines. Allen always deferred to the editing. "Mr. Shawn is delighted," Angell informed Allen when accepting his short pieces, meaning William Shawn, the hallowed senior editor of the magazine.

Every year for the next decade the *New Yorker* would publish two or three Woody Allen contributions, which began to skew more toward Benchley after getting "Sid's [Perelman] mannerisms out of his system," in Angell's words. Allen's antecedents were integrated into his own individual style. In time he'd augment his "little souffles" in the *New Yorker* with many other forays into print, "more than fifty comic pieces" between 1966 and 1980 in Eric Lax's estimate. Twenty-eight appeared in the *New Yorker*, and the rest—some initially rejected by Angell—turned up in small corners such as the *Kenyon Review*, the *New Republic*, the *Evergreen Review*, et al.

Many future Woody Allen pictures would evince seedings and throwaways from these "little souffles," some of which were like drafts of bigger ideas. "How I Became a Comedian," for example, was a first-person reminiscence Allen spun originally for the *Chicago Daily News* in 1968. This "casual," a spoof of Ernest Hemingway's *A Moveable Feast*, took place in the 1920s and revolved around an American hanging out in Paris with Ernest Hemingway and Gertrude Stein. "We laughed a lot and had fun and then we put on some boxing gloves and [Hemingway] broke my nose," the American narrates. He pays visits to Picasso, Man Ray, and Salvador Dalí; he consoles F. Scott Fitzgerald over the impossible Zelda. More or less the same happens, under different circumstances forty years later, to the American played by Owen Wilson in Allen's late-career romantic comedy *Midnight in Paris*.

Writing short pieces was not very profitable financially, compared to writing stage plays or motion pictures. "We probably paid him a thousand dollars" for "The Gossage-Vardebedian Papers," Angell recalled. But Allen's facility for prose deepened his writing reputation. The *New Yorker* pieces drew praise from other authors, and dinner party invitations began to arrive from George Plimpton, Arthur Miller, and Norman Mailer. "The Kugelmass Episode," from the May 2, 1977, *New Yorker*, won the annual O. Henry prize for Best Short Story of the Year. Latin American masters of surrealism read his "little souffles" and recognized Allen as a compatriot. Carlos Fuentes hailed Allen as "Pirandellian." Gabriel García Márquez corresponded with him and was photographed with the writing comedian. In time there would be enough "little souffles" for several book collections, with the first three—*Getting Even*, *Without Feathers*, *Side Effects*—becoming instant bestsellers.

WHILE IN LONDON, Allen also labored on the final polish of *Don't Drink the Water* for Broadway and a new producer, David Merrick. Max Gordon had developed cold feet and backed out of his planned comeback. Merrick took over as *Don't Drink the Water* inched toward its fall opening. Allen stayed loyal to Robert B. Sinclair, Gordon's original choice for director, who was still attached to the project, but Merrick was to Broadway what producer Charles K. Feldman was to Hollywood—a bossy boss—and Allen, in London, lagged behind some decisions. Merrick threw his weight behind casting Vivian Vance from *I Love Lucy* as Mrs. Hollander, a part Allen had envisioned for a Jewish actress. Learning to negotiate his power as a playwright, Allen had to absorb the blow.

London nights were recreational—it was the swinging London of the midsixties—and Allen swung. He gambled until dawn with heavyweights in a private room at the Pair of Shoes casino. "I was having a wonderful time playing twenty-four-hour poker games," he recalled, "because *The Dirty Dozen* was also being made in town, and Lee Marvin, Telly Savalas, and Charles Bronson were here for it." Allen steered his five-figure winnings into London souvenirs: a tailor-made corduroy suit; stacks of vintage jazz recordings he scrounged in small shops; and expensive English antiques and art he would bring back to decorate his new home on East Seventy-Ninth.

If you had to be stuck somewhere for months, at least London was "tops in music, fashion, and film," as Allen recalled. When, in free time, he wasn't card-sharking, he haunted discotheques, restaurants, and the watering holes of folk whose fame dwarfed his. "The Beatles were in town, so I would run into them frequently."

His relationship with his wife—"Open" before their marriage—was now wide open. Louise Lasser saw his absence from New York as "a golden opportunity for her to run amuck with other men," according to Allen. After he "got wind of what was going on I must say I didn't resist the many delectable temptations" in London.

Lasser flew to London and into her husband's arms in mid-March, just in time for him to be presented to Queen Elizabeth at the benefit Royal Command Performance of *Born Free*, whose producer, Sam Jaffe, was once Feldman's talent agency partner. In tailcoat and tie, Allen stood in a receiving line of *Born Free*, among *Casino Royale* cast members and stray celebrities, sandwiched between Raquel Welch and Ursula Andress. "How do you do? Do you enjoy your power?" Allen asked the queen, or so Eric Lax reported. Lasser said the comedian behaved himself, "was too nervous to say anything clever," and she and her husband sneaked out early to go back to the Dorchester, where they shed their formalwear and felt "very high," in her words, "just to be free."

When Lasser returned to New York, Allen plunged into professional overdrive. He posed for Smirnoff advertisements, even though he was a man who drank sparsely. He'd massage that contradiction into his stand-up act, explaining, re: Smirnoff, that his phone rang one day and he innocently picked up the receiver. "How would you like to be this year's vodka man?" asked a voice. "No, I'm an artist," Allen replied. "I do not do commercials. I don't pander. I don't drink vodka. And if I did, I wouldn't drink your vodka." "Too bad," harrumphed the caller, "it pays fifty thousand dollars." A pause. "Hold on, I'll put Mr. Allen on the phone." For his do-re-mi he shared a Smirnoff vodka mule with Monique Van Vooren, a bosomy, Belgian-born ex–beauty queen known for small acting parts. Two additional Smirnoff full-pagers followed, and after that, Allen also posed for advertisements as a most unlikely sexy pitchman for Foster Grant clip-ons. He generously bestowed himself on British television too, appearing on *Chelsea at Nine*, *The Eamonn Andrews Show*, and a Dusty Springfield special. Willing to try anything for laughs, Allen went so far as to box a kangaroo on the short-lived *Hippodrome*, a vaudeville-style revue that originated in the UK. The kangaroo won.

Many nights found Allen wandering around Playboy executive Victor Lownes's pleasure dome in Knightsbridge, which was akin to "a mini–Hefner mansion," in Allen's words. "In addition to some very beautiful women, you'd find all the movie guys in town there—Warren Beatty, Roman Polanski, Michael Caine, Terence Stamp, Albert Finney." Lownes liked Allen, laughed at his jokes, and made the American comic the "guest attraction" of the Park Lane Playboy Club's opening bash in London in July. "We had a great time, and everybody came," Allen recalled, "Julie Christie, Ursula Andress, Margot Fonteyn, Rudolf Nureyev, Peter Cook, and Dudley Moore."

Done with London—the filming and night life—Allen was back in New York by late September to start out-of-town tryouts for *Don't Drink the Water*. Soon after he left London, producer Charles K. Feldman announced a new fifteen-picture pact with United Artists, which was set to launch with Woody Allen's "I'll Take the Money and Run." "Mr. Everything," as *Variety* dubbed Allen, would write, direct, and star in the Feldman comedy to be "shot entirely in Chicago," probably in black and white on a $600,000 to $700,000 budget, "next spring."

THE LONDON SUMMER of money from *Casino Royale*, gambling, television, and advertising jobs helped offset the expense of his newly renovated East Seventy-Ninth Street duplex. The design of the apartment was overseen by Olga San Giuliano, a decorator for the rich and famous whose interiors were regularly featured in *Architectural Digest*, a magazine Allen read devoutly, soaking up tips about decor and furnishings. The elegant interiors of the homes and apartments in many Woody Allen films were often juxtaposed with the disordered lives of their inhabitants.

One room was paneled in wood; another was silk-covered. Installed in the library was a vintage billiards table replete with regulation pool-hall lighting. "It took up so much of the room that a short cue was needed to make shots from one side," reported Eric Lax. "I am a surprisingly bad player for someone who owns a table," Allen enjoyed telling journalists. "I may be the worst owner-player." Allen liked to roam small shops for "preposterously expensive" things to fill the rooms, such as Queen Anne chairs, quill pens, or music boxes. He wrote characters for himself to play who gave similar music boxes as tokens of affection: Diane Keaton gets one in *Play It Again, Sam*, as does Juliette Lewis in *Husbands and Wives*. "I like to wake up in the morning," he said, "and be surrounded by good things, shiny objects, attractive women and expensive artifacts."

His growing art collection now included an Emil Nolde watercolor, a Kokoschka ink drawing, a Matisse, two lithographs, an oil by Gloria Vanderbilt, and the Chicago Giacometti. Allen briefly fancied himself a painter, took a few lessons and tried his hand at abstracts, apologetically showing the indistinct results to journalists who visited. Yet for all that—the English antiques, a Tiffany lamp, an Aubusson rug, endless books and LPs, magic accessories and personal mementos on the shelves—most people thought the huge new place was "sparsely furnished," in the words of one visitor, "with a few expensive pieces, the ceiling pierced with pin-spots, to illuminate pictures, but there were no pictures on the wall." The paintings rested on floors and leaned against walls. Louise Lasser turned every room into

"Hiroshima," Allen wrote in *Apropos of Nothing.* His wife was the messy opposite of her mother's "compulsive neatness." And Allen was a man always heading out the door.

HE WASN'T AT home much of the time in the fall because he had responsibilities in Philadelphia and Boston where *Don't Drink the Water* was being tested on audiences. The early signs were ominous for Allen's first stage comedy, which nearly every critic saw as weakly constructed and lacking originality and depth. "A howl as a gag-writer," *Variety* wrote of Allen, not unsympathetically, reviewing one preview, but "dubious as a playwright." David Merrick turned out to be the usual producer's blend of God and the devil—his "presence in the room," Allen wrote in *Apropos of Nothing*, "was always accompanied by the smell of burning sulfur." They were compatible, watching sports on television, but at work the producer was demanding, often clashing with Allen and Robert B. Sinclair, the director of *Water*, insisting he knew better what stage audiences found funny. Merrick certainly knew better than Sinclair, who in Philadelphia, the first tryout stop, was fired for a musty approach.

Allen briefly took over the directing reins, spending most of his time working with a boyish actor playing the role that had been tagged for Allen in the show's earliest publicity—that of the novice diplomat Axel, son of the absent ambassador, who must babysit the rambunctious New Jersey family that seeks refuge in the American embassy. Twenty-seven-year-old Anthony Roberts had auditioned several times for the role of Axel. Although Allen played in a poker circle with his father, Ken Roberts, a New York broadcaster, Allen resisted Merrick's enthusiasm for the son until the producer insisted that he go see Roberts in the lead he'd taken over from Robert Redford in Neil Simon's long-running *Barefoot in the Park*. After attending the show, Allen was persuaded. Visiting his dressing room after the performance, Allen told Roberts the role of Axel was his. "You're wonderful in this show [*Barefoot*]," Allen said. "Why are you such a terrible auditioner?"

It was the beginning of a long, beautiful friendship between Allen and Roberts, who was four years younger. During the Philadelphia rehearsals, Allen repeatedly tried to demonstrate a pratfall for Roberts. The actor just couldn't bring it off, and Allen had to change the blocking to lose the pratfall. "He [Allen] is as artful at that sort of physical comedy as Charlie Chaplin," Roberts marveled, speaking to Eric Lax. In Boston, veteran Broadway director Stanley Prager took over, bringing a fresh energy, confidence, and easygoing humor to the task that allowed Allen to concentrate on the script problems, and problems there were. Traveling with his trusty typewriter, Allen seemed to thrive in the pressure cooker, reworking scenes in his hotel room late at night after previews and run-throughs, even while running a cold and fever. He told interviewers he had initially modeled the Hollanders after the Konigsbergs. "I wanted to show what my family would do if they were caught in a country behind the Iron Curtain and had to take refuge in an American embassy." But autobiographical writing was not his bag, and the rewrites, sharpening stage business and feeble jokes, further reduced the comparison.

And there were other problems. On the road the cast changed "oftener than the Mets line-up," as Cecil Smith chronicled in the *Los Angeles Times*. One major change was the departure of Vivian Vance, the Ethel Mertz of *I Love Lucy*, who had been playing the wife of the New Jersey caterer, acted by Lou Jacobi (Allen's first choice). "Her part had never emerged from Woody's typewriter with any dimensions," Smith reported, "save being a straight woman" for the "immensely funny" Jacobi. Vance herself wanted out. Allen thought Vance was a "pill" and never liked her for the job anyway. She didn't evoke his mother in the least, whereas the actress who joined the cast in Boston—Kay Medford, a brassy New Yorker, albeit Irish American—did.

After two months of personnel changes, rewrites, and so-so previews, *Don't Drink the Water* opened at the Morosco Theatre on November 17, 1966. A journalist who followed Allen around for the Broadway premiere reported that before the curtain went up the playwright visited backstage and chatted genially with everyone, wishing them good luck. Then he vanished with Mickey Rose, skipping the actual performance for billiards at nearby McGirr's. After shooting pool the friends supped humbly at an Automat—macaroni and pumpkin pie. From the first, Allen hated to sit through the openings of his plays or movies, dreading the audience reaction and the reviews.

The New York critics applauded the talented cast and laugh-out-loud dialogue but found "nothing sturdy" to admire in the scaffolding of the play, in the words of Walter Kerr in the *New York Times*. "Little more than a succession of jokes," seconded *Variety*, which noted, however, that while the reviews were "mixed," *Water* was "a very funny show and a real crowd-pleaser." The crowd-pleaser would run until April 1968, nearly six hundred performances. Merrick swiftly auctioned off the screen rights to producer Joseph E. Levine, with Jack Rollins (uncredited) and Charles Joffe (credited) attached as coproducers to watch over Allen's best interests, technically the first of the dozens of Woody Allen pictures for which they served a supervisory function.

Waiting for the stage play to close its run, the screen adaptation of *Don't Drink the Water* did not materialize in theaters until November 1969, however. Allen was briefly touted to direct the movie, although another item in the trade papers said he was again tempted to play Axel, the role he almost played on Broadway. Ted Bessell, another Rollins-Joffe client, ended up as Axel rather than Anthony Roberts. Allen, under the pseudonym "R. S. Allen," and Marshall Brickman (uncredited) tweaked the stage script for the movie, but their tweaking was no great improvement. When Joseph E. Levine insisted on casting the Irish Catholic Jackie Gleason in the lead Allen originally fashioned for Lou Jacobi, all the once-intended Jewishness of the property was opaqued. "I adored him [Gleason]," Allen said later. "He's a genius. But he's the wrong guy." Memorable as Sid Caesar's pipsqueak foil on television, Howard Morris—who had directed a few big-screen comedies—was also the wrong guy. "A truly dreadful film," was Allen's appraisal in *Apropos of Nothing*. But to be fair, Allen admitted, *Don't Drink the Water* was "a real terrible play . . . just a group of a million gags all strung together."

THE SAME MONTH *Don't Drink the Water* opened on Broadway, *What's Up, Tiger Lily?* was released in the US, attracting surprisingly fervent reviews. The redubbed Japanese comedy was "the kind of project I would normally deplore," Andrew Sarris wrote in the *Village Voice*, but also "one of the funniest movies of the year." Moreover, the one-of-a-kind movie performed robustly at the box office, especially in varsity towns, where *Tiger Lily?* became a perennial rerun, with college students chanting along with Phil Moskowitz's attack mantra: "Saracen pig! Spartan dog! Turkish taffy!"

Although every bit as rickety as *Water, Tiger Lily?* was night and day from the old-fashioned play and by far the funnier, more innovative, and Woody Allen–ish work.

Allen made a few publicity appearances on behalf of *What's Up, Tiger Lily?*, but he hated the final emendations ordered up by producer Henry G. Saperstein, which included footage of the mellow rock-and-rollers the Lovin' Spoonful, whose "Summer in the City" had serendipitously risen to number one on the charts in August. The Spoonful played music at intervals to stretch the movie's short length to eighty minutes. Allen considered suing Saperstein, but instead filed papers against MGM/Kama Sutra for exploiting his animated likeness on the cover of the LP: *The Lovin' Spoonful: Woody Allen's What's Up, Tiger Lily?** The soundtrack did not enjoy the same success as "Summer in the City," and Allen made a point of avoiding commercial rock-and-roll in future Woody Allen films. While many of his fans love *What's Up, Tiger Lily?*, Allen never lost the sour taste and rarely ducked the chance to disavow the redubbed Japanese action-comedy as "a nice idea that, in my opinion, didn't come off."

There was no question, however, that Allen was batting two for two in 1966, with a Broadway hit and a big-screen nonpareil. "I guess this *has* been a good year," Allen told a columnist. And as the good and busy year edged to a close—the year of his marriage to Louise Lasser, his authorial debut in the *New Yorker*, his *Casino Royale* summer in London, the popular success of *Don't Drink the Water* and the curveball success of *What's Up, Tiger Lily?*—Mr. and Mrs. Woody planned a New Year's Eve and housewarming party. About 150 people were invited, but more than five hundred showed up at their new digs. Lasser vetoed her husband's suggestion of "topless waitresses," Earl Wilson wrote, but "seventy-five percent of the gals wore mini-skirts" to go along with the discotheque theme. Not Tom Poston, who sported "mini-pants," nor stuffy David Merrick in a tux.

The attendees bopped and weaved to 45s preloaded into Allen's Wurlitzer jukebox. The writer-comedian asked guests to introduce themselves into a newfangled video camera hooked up to a taping machine and operated by "an Oriental from Sony," in Allen's words. "Woody later played the tapes back for his own amusement," according to one account, "but never

* Jerry Yester, now married to Judy Henske, was not yet in the mellow-rock Lovin' Spoonful. He joined the band in 1967.

used the recorder again." Early in the evening, Allen ran out of his free supply of Smirnoff and had to send out for more. Later, his wife became overwhelmed by the maelstrom and burst into tears, so the couple sneaked outside, where they sat on the curb, sipping soda pop.

ON THE PAPER anniversary of their marriage Lasser gave her husband the gift of a framed letter, which she had ferreted out of a London memorabilia shop. The letter from Sir Arthur Conan Doyle, the creator of Sherlock Holmes, made mention of the famous magician Harry Houdini. The anniversary gift was framed on the wall of their master bedroom, one of the more finished rooms in the penthouse, whose interiors were still indeterminate.

Casino Royale—a weird blip in Allen's career—became available to moviegoers in April. Producer Charles K. Feldman's secret-agent "extravaganza" proved the least popular and successful James Bond film of all time. "I was in the picture for three minutes," Allen said later. "It was an unredeeming, moronic enterprise."

"Little Jimmy Bond" could be seen to better effect in clubs and on television. In fact, in the first half of 1967, Allen seemed omnipresent on TV channels. When guest-starring on *Our Place*, a summer substitute for *The Smothers Brothers Comedy Hour*, the reviews foreshadowed later complaints about his filmmaking prolificacy. "He's getting very close to the overexposing point," *Variety* noted. "The strain has been showing."

For a few months, while he waited for the go-ahead on "I'll Take the Money and Run," Allen toyed with an offer from MGM. The studio wanted him to turn Richard Powell's novel *Don Quixote, U.S.A.*, into a movie, with "Mr. Everything" writing, directing, and starring. Cy Howard, a Bob Hope writer, was producer of the enterprise, and Charles K. Feldman, who had fallen ill, temporized over how much Allen could be involved. Allen and pal Mickey Rose—whose day job, nowadays, was writing for *The Tonight Show*, where Rose worked alongside Marshall Brickman, tightening Johnny Carson's monologues—turned the pages of Powell's novel, whose story concerned an idealistic Peace Corps volunteer who is thrust into the political turmoil of a banana republic. The two longtime friends produced a draft script, called "El Weirdo," which took so many liberties with the novel it was no longer the book MGM had optioned. Regardless, the idea progressed to the stage where MGM announced a May 1967 start date in Mexico, with Robert Morse starring instead of Allen. Feldman finally put his foot down, MGM lost interest, and the ephemeral idea went away—though not forever.

"I'll Take the Money and Run" returned to the fore. Only now, the Allen–Mickey Rose script was called *Take the Money and Run*. It was no longer about a comedian turned gangster; it was the story of the exploits of a bumbling, lowlife criminal. Allen's fascination with the exploits of criminals and gangsters dated from his boyhood, and from the once upon a time when he had fancied himself a light-fingered shoplifter and card sharp. Allen had family connections to mobsters through his father, who'd once been employed by crime lord Albert Anastasia; and even as he and Rose polished the script there were newspaper headlines about Harold "Kayo" Konigsberg, a Mafia enforcer, whom the FBI attempted to link to Anastasia and involvement in the killing of an informant, whose tip had led to the arrest of bank robber Willie Sutton. According to one friend, the dead informant was Allen's "distant cousin," and probably Kayo Konigsberg, a man with the same surname as you know who, was also remotely related.

The lead character that had been crafted as Allen's first starring role was now an inept bank robber named—not "Woody Allen"—Virgil Starkwell. The Allen-Rose script had evolved into a mock documentary, or "mockumentary," with announcers and filmed interviews framing Starkwell's saga. Allen had a fondness for newsreels and documentaries, and the mockumentary format was useful for storytelling purposes as well as papering over continuity gaps. As was true of a surprising number of his films, *Take the Money and Run* had antecedents in a Tamiment Playhouse sketch called "The Hold Up," which dated back to his first Tamiment summer.

He and Rose found ways to make visual the kind of jokes familiar from his monologues: the boyhood flashbacks, the first of many in Woody Allen pictures; the puns translated into sight gags; nods to and snipes at other movies. Rose "had no discipline, but a lunatic sense of humor, totally original," Allen said in his memoir.

Allen always wrote the first drafts, when working with collaborators: Rose, and later Brickman, and later still, Douglas McGrath. "Final decisions," according to Eric Lax, "were Woody's, as was the final draft." For at least the first decade of his moviemaking, there was another ritual: Jack

Rollins and Charles Joffe would read every Woody Allen script and give their criticisms before the start of filming. However, his management team was welcomed to Allen's apartment only "one at a time," according to Lax, for individual readings, so the two men could not be influenced by each other and could not band together to win arguments against Allen. As often as not they espoused disparate views anyway, allowing Allen to pick and choose from their suggestions.

Once the script was in shape, Allen dithered about who should direct the movie. For most of 1966—the columns made frequent note of it—Jerry Lewis had been penciled in. Lewis knows how to *cinematically* tell a joke, Allen told interviewers. After meeting with Lewis on a trip to the West Coast, however, Allen had second thoughts. Lewis said he and his regular collaborator Bill Richmond would probably rewrite the Allen-Rose script as a matter of policy. Then when Allen said he wanted the picture shot inexpensively, inside of eight weeks, photographing scenes in black and white to simulate newsreel à la the "News on the March" from *Citizen Kane*, Lewis didn't like what he was hearing. Lewis said he'd rather shoot the picture in color. "Woody," Lewis said finally, "I spend twenty-eight weeks in prep. Shooting in eight weeks? We're talking thirty-six weeks. . . . Why don't you do it yourself?" It didn't help their prospective alliance that Allen gave so many interviews deriding Lewis's adolescent comedy. "He debauches himself," Allen bluntly told Studs Terkel.

It was almost a relief when United Artists, which was producing the picture under its pact with Charles K. Feldman, vetoed Lewis. Briefly, Allen courted Val Guest because he had enjoyed working with Guest on *Casino Royale*. But piqued by the *Don Quixote, U.S.A.* trial balloon, Allen surrendered to the growing itch he couldn't deny. He was probably the best interpreter of his own comedy. He would direct *Take the Money and Run*.

The qualms and delays could also be chalked up to the growing medical problems of Feldman, the producer who had promised "Mr. Everything" absolute control of *Take the Money and Run*. By late 1967, Feldman was locked in a death struggle with cancer, and his illness made UA hesitate about moving ahead with Allen as director. Feldman died in May 1968. ("A hands-on producer" was Allen's eulogy in his memoir, "a weird combination of risk-taking and also a hack.") Without Feldman, UA didn't feel confident in Allen and, adding insult to injury, the studio said if it agreed to bankroll the screen comedy, the budget had to be kept below $750,000. All along Allen had planned on a low ceiling, but UA's hesitation and cost-consciousness were slaps in the face. Rollins and Joffe went shopping for another studio willing to gamble on a first-time filmmaker.

TAKE THE MONEY AND RUN went into waiting. Allen launched into another play. By August, he'd written the first draft of *Play It Again, Sam*, which was promising enough for producer David Merrick to announce he would open a new Woody Allen comedy on Broadway in early 1968. Adding to the excitement was this news: Allen was going to act the lead onstage. "It's a neurotic love story in which I play me," he told the *New York Times*.

As always keeping a full schedule, Allen took stand-up engagements near and far. He performed at the Americana and the Playboy Club in New York; the Westbury theater-in-the-round on Long Island; the Latin Casino in Cherry Hill, New Jersey; the Statler–Hilton Plaza in Miami, Florida; Mister Kelly's in Chicago (he helped reopen the club, which had closed after a fire); the hungry i in San Francisco; and Caesars Palace in Las Vegas.

He was always in search of a perfection he knew to be elusive—the perfect audience, for one thing, that might *get* him and his comedy. The first time he had played Las Vegas was in 1966 on a bill with the pop singer Petula Clark, whose number-one hit was "Downtown." Allen was easily recognizable, arriving at the airport dressed in the brown tweed sports jacket he always traveled in and wore for performances. He took a strange pride in wearing the same outfit onstage he also wore offstage. Allen was "very much un–Las Vegas," pop singer Clark remembered. "Petula was basically the star of the show," recollected Jim Murray, the MCA agent who arranged their booking. "It was a fantastic show. It did so much business you couldn't believe it."

That first Caesars Palace booking went over so well, Murray decided to split up the performers, maybe do twice the business. He brought Allen back as the headliner in August 1967 with *West Side Story* dancer-singer George Chakiris. "He [Allen] dies, no business at all," Murray recalled. "They had to move the potted plants around, so the room didn't look empty," Allen admitted. As for Chakiris, he remembered the forlorn Allen standing in the wings, anxiously waiting to go onstage. Chakiris couldn't stop chuckling at Allen's surreal humor—the jokes he told about "God Bless America" singer Kate Smith's failure to transform her career by taking on the role of Peter Pan, with the stage wires straining to elevate her obese, flailing body—but "Woody felt the audience wasn't getting him." Allen told Murray he couldn't forgive himself for his failure with the crowd, and he couldn't accept his $75,000 check. "Jim, I don't deserve to get paid," he said. "Tell your bosses." Murray informed the "crooked noses" and they said, "Absolutely not. He gets the check whether he wants it or not!"

It happened more than once. "I can make awful mistakes," Allen recollected, blaming himself, "[telling] stories about being divorced in front of a college crowd. . . ." One time, Charles Joffe liked to reminisce, Allen hosted a private event for Chevrolet dealers in New Jersey. And every joke bombed. "Not a single laugh," Joffe said. "Another time," Allen recalled, "I flew to DC to a religious college, and the father who handled this for the school was shocked by the small turnout." Again, Allen offered to cancel his fee. The priest said yes.

From time to time Rollins and Joffe thought Allen needed to reinvigorate his act, and to that end the management team offered up-and-coming comedy writers from their client list. One time Allen was presented with a young Canadian duo named Hart (Hart Pomerantz) and Lorne (Lorne Michaels), who were on the verge of recording their first comedy LP. When not communing with buddies like Mickey Rose or Marshall Brickman, however, Allen was wary of collaborators. Perhaps they wouldn't "get" him either. Anyway, his ideas raced ahead of the young writers. Hart and Lorne learned from Allen, but he didn't get much from them.

Over time he clung to certain attitudes in his comedy even when they were patently stale: like the jokes he peddled about his ex-wife Harlene Rosen. His ex-wife jokes persisted even after he married Louise Lasser. From the outset of his comedy career, he had used "the first Mrs. Allen," as he referred to her onstage, as a punching bag in his monologue, with many sarcastic quips that would hurt any woman's vanity. In his act he dubbed his ex-wife "Quasimodo" and "the Hunchback of Notre Dame." He said her long nose was convenient for paying his alimony "through the nose." His ex-wife had undergone six sex-change operations because "they couldn't come up with anything she liked." She cooked with Nazi recipes; her best dish—"Chicken Himmler." "The Museum of Natural History took her shoe and based on her measurement they reconstructed a dinosaur."

Friends and defenders insisted he told similar jokes about them. "He said the same kind of things about *everyone*," noted Judy Henske. "He said those things about himself." "You remember what he said about *my* cooking?" Lasser told Earl Wilson. "That he realized I wasn't much of a chef when he found a bone in the chocolate pudding." When Allen liked a certain joke, he brought it out in his act again and again, with slight variations, as he'd do in his films later on. When, for example, Louise (Janet Margolin) serves breakfast to Virgil Starkwell (Allen) in *Take the Money and Run*, the meal is burnt toast, coffee poured over tea bags, and thick-as-a-brick pancakes. When Zelig (Allen) is hypnotized by psychoanalyst Dr. Eudora Fletcher (Mia Farrow) and begins to speak the truth, he starts in on her cooking. "Please, no more pancakes," he begs.

Harlene hired a lawyer, who phoned Allen and told him to cease and desist. Allen admitted he had been warned. "Say, please don't print her name," he told journalists. "The thing is, when I use her name, she doesn't like it." Invariably, in print, Allen was extracomplimentary to "the first Mrs. Allen," even if he was wont to gild the lily by heaping related praise on himself. "I blossomed her" by putting her through college, he liked to say. Still, he couldn't let go of the ex-wife jokes and compulsively dissed the first Mrs. Woody in his act, once crossing the line by holding up a snapshot of Harlene and her sister on *The Tonight Show*. "I don't know why [I did]," Allen tried explaining to the *New York World Herald Tribune*. "I just wanted to show it, since I was talking about her." Harlene's lawyer phoned again, saying the incident really had "disturbed" her. Allen must stop.

The last straw for Harlene was the double insult of comedy at her expense that took place on a single night of broadcasting in March 1967. Allen mentioned "the ex-wife" on two different shows: First as a guest on *The Perry Como Show*, where he joked, "When I brought my first wife home, my parents liked her, but my dog died." Later that evening he sat in for Johnny Carson on *The Tonight Show* and, musing about predivorce settlements, gibed, "[My ex] got absolutely everything. In the event I remarry, and have children, she gets them."

Citing a long pattern of slander against her in Allen's monologues,

Harlene's lawyer filed a $1 million lawsuit against the comedian and the National Broadcasting Company—the home network of both *Perry Como* and *The Tonight Show*—for "holding her up to ridicule." Just as important, the lawsuit claimed Allen had not kept Harlene apprised of his steadily mounting income, and that he owed his ex-wife an estimated $8,000 in back alimony. "Poor," her lawyer, Jeremiah Gutman, described Harlene. "A struggling fine artist, painting in oils."

While insisting that an opportunistic lawyer had led "the first Mrs. Allen" astray, Allen doggedly fought Harlene's case in court for years. Allen hated to be told what to do, he hated to be told what was funny and what was not, and he insisted "the ex-wife" was a fictional creation just as "Woody Allen" was a fictional creation—not exactly him, not exactly her. Even after Harlene upped her damage claims to $2 million, the comedian still couldn't restrain himself from deriding the lawsuit and Harlene. "Wouldn't it be funny if I lost?" Allen cracked to *New York Post* columnist Leonard Lyons. "It would take me at least six weeks to pay it off."

As late as 1971, during a televised interview with David Frost, Allen again mocked his ex-wife Harlene's cooking, repeating the same language he had wielded against Louise Lasser ("I nearly choked to death on a bone in the chocolate pudding"); and in October of the same year he was still chuckling about the ongoing litigation on air with his friend Dick Cavett for Cavett's talk show, repeating the very anecdote from his act that had been cited as offensive in court papers. His ex-wife had been "violated" on a Manhattan street late one night, the comedian told Cavett. "Knowing my ex-wife," Allen jested, "it probably was not a moving violation. . . . If I ran into her on the street, we'd stop and chat and exchange blunt instruments."

In 1973, six years after the initial filing, Allen finally surrendered by paying a hefty out-of-court settlement. Allen "vowed to drop the jokes," Marion Meade reported, if Harlene "agreed not to discuss their marriage or the terms of the settlement." Even then Allen could not turn off the spigot. Not only did he expressly mention Harlene's name in *Sleeper*'s family-flashback sequence but, in Meade's opinion, Allen made Harlene "the model for the archetypical castrator," and his template for the ex-wives of *Play It Again, Sam*, *Annie Hall*, *Manhattan*, and *Deconstructing Harry*. Lasser begged to differ: "I was the ex-wife he always depicted in his pictures," Lasser insisted in one interview. With one notable exception—Allen's eightieth birthday in 2015, when the first Mrs. Woody publicly wished her ex-husband well—Harlene kept her bargain of silence.

"THE SECOND MRS. WOODY" was constructively occupied by a supporting role in a new Broadway play in the fall of 1967. Louise Lasser was playing a wary adulteress of Henry Orient's (Don Ameche) in *Henry, Sweet Henry*, the stage musical version of *The World of Henry Orient*. Allen could drop his wife off at the Palace Theatre and stroll over to *Don't Drink the Water*, still going strong at the Morosco. He might have skipped his play's premiere, but he'd attend dozens of performances over the long run, giving notes afterward to actors.

Their joint "happily married" interviews at home were sometimes partly sunny with a chance of rain. *Life* magazine photographed the couple sharing the malted milks they whipped up in the kitchen to satisfy their mutual cravings. It was a prerequisite that Allen's wives and girlfriends share his sweet tooth. They tried to make it one big happy family when they trooped off to Brooklyn occasionally for dinner with the Konigsbergs. Lasser thought Allen's father was "a really sweet guy," and Nettie was "just so funny." Woody was permanently "Allan" to Nettie, but Martin was capable of proudly referring to him as "son." His younger sister, Letty, had graduated from Brooklyn College, become a schoolteacher, and married the principal of the Flatbush elementary school where she taught. Allen phoned Letty, whom he'd nicknamed Sugar, nearly every day. "They talk for hours," Martin reported. "Woody always tries out his comedy on his sister first."

In the front window of the lower Manhattan engraving shop Martin operated nowadays hung a poster for *Don't Drink the Water*. His father was known to buy extra tickets and hawk them to customers. Martin shared occasional long walks with his successful progeny, with Allen normally quiet and seemingly lost in thought. "They never said much to each other, but they were close in an unspoken sort of way," Lasser recalled. "On every walk we pass a bookstore," Martin recounted in one interview, "and he runs in and buys five, six at a time." Walks were Allen's daily habit, intertwined with work, as he ruminated on jokes and scripts. Lasser found it hard to coax Allen into a genuine holiday, however. "He was addicted to work,"

Lasser recalled. True, he was "a compulsive writer," Allen admitted. "I write every day. I feel this enormous guilt if I don't."

One notorious time Lasser somehow got Allen into his father's car, and she drove them to Gurney's Resort at Montauk in Long Island for what was intended as a romantic weekend getaway. "It rained nonstop," Lasser recollected, "but Woody got sunstroke. He's the only person I know who can get ill from the sun when it's pouring down with rain. When the sun finally did shine, though, I had the best of times jumping around on the beach in the sand like a little kid, but he was sitting inside with his typewriter, looking very glum."

Sometimes her mood swings sent Lasser to bed all day, and they would have to cancel all their plans. She was prone to depression, she admitted in interviews, and Allen had the thankless job of constantly trying to cheer her up. Often it was the other way around, Allen insisted. Lasser was "pretty, effervescent, brighter than I am, funnier than I am, intelligent and thoroughly original. She's the only person I ever met who can cheer me up," he told an interviewer. "[Louise] accepts me and at the same time manages to hold me at arms-length," Allen said. Almost two years into their marriage there was no escaping the fact their two-floor, six-room penthouse was randomly furnished and didn't feel lived in. "We're like two children running around in a castle," said Lasser. "Woody loves to decorate with antiques but we have hardly any time."

THE OPPOSITE SIDE of Woody Allen the worrywart and workhorse was the man who knew what gave him pleasure. Fitting pleasures into his compartmentalized daily life was as essential as arranging for his writing time, or his stand-up comedy dates and travel calendar. The pleasures made the work possible, and vice versa. When in Las Vegas, for example, Allen never felt comfortable in the hyped-up atmosphere, but he sought out Jimmy Grippo, a hypnotist and sleight-of-hand artist who was "magician in residence" at Caesars Palace, and spent his spare time hanging out with Grippo. He also haunted the gaming tables and did a little card-playing. He liked eavesdropping on the hustlers and jotting down their weird names and lingo. Allen wouldn't be gambling much longer in his life, however, because one day producer David Merrick, once a big poker player, casually made a remark about "what a time waster it was," and "it rang a bell, so I quit," Allen recalled.

Sports, especially basketball and baseball, never lost their allure. In July, Allen enjoyed the lifelong fantasy of playing shortstop at Yankee Stadium. He was among the "Mad Show All-Stars," a who's who of comedy that included Mel Brooks, Jerry Lewis, and Godfrey Cambridge, playing against City Hall people and politicians dubbed the "Lindsay Lancers." At that time many progressive New Yorkers and show business folk backed the liberal Republican mayor John Lindsay, and aside from celebrity appearances for Lindsay, Allen was occasionally asked to write a few jokes for the mayor's speeches. The exhibition game was held as a benefit for slum children and as a warm-up for the "All-Star Celebrity Softball Game" in November in Los Angeles, pitting entertainers against professional baseballers, for broadcast on NBC. On that night of all-star softball Allen batted against Los Angeles Dodgers pitcher Don Drysdale and flied out, to his embarrassment. But in the outfield, he caught "a high fly ball" off Willie Mays, who was among his paragons. (In his stand-up routine and films, he'd vary a joke he made about iron-man Mays, renowned for his stamina, saying he often thought of the athlete during sex to prolong his lovemaking.) Ralph Kiner, from the announcer's booth, said, "Hey, Woody Allen's got good motion." "That meant as much to me as winning the Academy Award," Allen reminisced years later.

Allen was an abrupt quitter of certain habits as he grew older; no longer did he smoke cigarettes, or cigars. Mostly, these days, when he played baseball, it was in the outfield for a softball team—"A game I never loved"—in the Broadway Show League. One day, a younger player told him he'd be happy to lend a hand if any play was too difficult for the older guy. "Are you kidding me?" Allen retorted. "Any ball hit to the outfield I can chase down, autograph, and then catch." A short time later Allen flubbed a line drive "I would've caught behind my back in my earlier days" and, feeling intensely humiliated, he dropped his glove, walked off, and never played again. Baseball would endure in scenes and references in Woody Allen films, however.

Love of sports was one connection to Palomar Pictures, a new subsidiary of the American Broadcasting Company (ABC), which showed an interest in *Take the Money and Run*. Palomar's maiden production, *For Love of Ivy* with Sidney Poitier, had just finished filming, and the head of Palomar,

Edgar J. Scherick, was lining up future projects. Scherick was an ex–advertising agent who had specialized in sports placements on TV before helping to set up the first national baseball telecasts. In the early 1960s he pioneered *The Wide World of Sports* for ABC and then became vice president of programming, a mover and shaker behind hit small-screen shows such as *Peyton Place*, *Batman*, *Bewitched*, and *The Hollywood Palace* before quitting to run Palomar.

Scherick was in his forties, but freethinking and avowedly hip. Meeting with the producer, Allen inevitably discussed baseball with Scherick. Scherick liked Allen's pitch: the fast-and-cheap approach he planned for directing his first movie and the "no star cast" he promised to assemble, echoing the joke credits of *What's Up, Tiger Lily?* Scherick floated a one-picture deal with a $2 million budget. Allen said he'd take less money up front for autonomy in other areas including final cut. "When someone like Woody Allen talks over lunch about something like *Take the Money and Run*," Scherick told journalists, "you have to make a decision right there and then." Palomar agreed to produce Woody Allen's directorial debut, partnering on the screen comedy with Cinerama, a small firm—not the widescreen-format company—which would handle the distribution.

Rollins-Joffe oversaw the contractual details, with Charles Joffe guaranteed his producing credit. But Palomar wanted a seasoned professional to watch over the nitty-gritty on a daily basis, and Scherick paid a substantial sum to Universal Marion to borrow producer Sidney Glazier and his associate Jack Grossberg, who both had worked with Mel Brooks on *The Producers*, Brooks's maiden directing effort. "Here's, as they say, the beauty part," Allen said later, "though it wasn't in my contract," Palomar "trusted me to have artistic control and never once bothered me for a second." All the terms were in place by early December. Later that month Allen hosted *The Year 1967 in Review* television special for the *Kraft Music Hall*, with actress Liza Minnelli, soul singer Aretha Franklin, and right-wing pundit William F. Buckley Jr. among his guests. "I think he'll offer good contrast to me," Allen said of Buckley. His and Minnelli's takeoff on the slow-motion fusillade of death that climaxed *Bonnie and Clyde*, the year's most talked-about movie, "bordered on brilliance," *Variety* wrote.

Mr. and Mrs. Woody did not preside over their usual New Year's Eve shebang, however, because December 31, 1967, was the closing night of *Henry,*

Sweet Henry. Louise Lasser gave her last performance in the Broadway musical, which had been playing to shrinking crowds and hemorrhaging losses for its backers.

ALLEN CUT BACK on his comedy dates and spent much of his time in the first half of 1968 polishing the script for *Play It Again, Sam* while making plans for shooting *Take the Money and Run* in San Francisco. New York City had been the setting for *Money* in early drafts, but red tape and prohibitive costs forced Allen to shift to Chicago as his second choice, before finally settling on San Francisco as the best option. He departed for the West Coast in early April. Allen had grown increasingly comfortable with San Francisco and its audiences, and indeed, during the months of preproduction, he'd record the third album of his comedy routines at Eugene's, a pop-up club in the cabaret venue that was also home to The Committee.* Named for Minnesota senator Eugene McCarthy, Eugene's was one of a string of clubs that were springing up in major cities to support the peace candidate's presidential campaign. Even the cocktail waitresses were said to be moonlighting political activists.

Scouting the locations and finalizing the cast and crew were the initial testing ground for the first-time director. But the onetime high school underachiever and proudly diffident college dropout had been, all along, a keen student of motion pictures and of moviemaking techniques. Allen was fully primed and champing at the bit.

Apart from the announcer who narrates the story and his various interview subjects, the script's only other lead was the Pollyannaish laundress who falls for the lovelorn Virgil Starkwell, overlooking his glaring faults. "After fifteen minutes I wanted to marry her," explains Starkwell. "After thirty minutes I'd completely given up the idea of snatching her purse." That role—Allen's love interest in the comedy—had been expressly written for Louise Lasser and was named "Louise." But Allen's wife took another acting job in *Is the Real You Really You?*, a stage farce produced by David Merrick, which was having a pre-Broadway trial run in Fort Lauderdale. Consequently, Allen met Janet Margolin for lunch at the Russian Tea Room

* Considering the ongoing litigation between Allen and Harlene Rosen, there'd be no mention of "the ex-wife" on *The Third Woody Allen Album*, his third and final comedy recording.

to see if Margolin was right to play "Louise." A native New Yorker and graduate of the High School of Performing Arts, Margolin had scored an impressive big-screen debut in *David and Lisa* in 1962, playing a teenager with a split personality. Since then, however, her career had stalled. But she was game for comedy, and Allen liked her dreamy brunette look.

Lunching with Margolin was an exception to the rule. From the beginning of his directing career, Allen was known for spending as little time as possible with the actors whom he vetted for roles in his films. "I cast quickly," Allen told the *New York Times* in 1971. "I see actors only for a minute. Not that much is required. What interests me is the look." He added, "Also, I don't have the patience to get into acting discussions."

The German-born Marcel Hillaire, who would play Fritz the Director (i.e., Fritz Lang), and Lonny Chapman, as Jack the Convict, were among the handful of established performers in the cast. Deep-voiced Jackson Beck, whose credits stretched back to the 1930s and *The Adventures of Superman* on radio, narrated the film. It was Beck who had immortally intoned: "Is it a bird? Is it a plane? No, it's Superman!" As he'd do repeatedly in the future, Allen handed out small parts to amateurs, including his friend Minnow Moskowitz and longtime Brooklyn chums, who were invited to San Francisco for walk-ons and who mostly didn't make the final cut. When her play flopped in Florida, Lasser turned up among the final "mock" interviewees. "Everyone thought he was such a schlemiel, and it turned out he's a criminal," Lasser informs the camera. The amateurs got paid less than professionals and were a mark of Allen's knack from the outset for "making do."

Palomar and Rollins-Joffe had talked Allen out of black-and-white photography, which was considered commercially iffy. But he'd return to that idée fixe and in the future shoot films in black and white with impunity, more often than any other major American filmmaker of his era. He made a stab at hiring Italian cinematographer Carlo Di Palma, who had shot *Red Desert* and *Blow-Up* for Michelangelo Antonioni, but Allen would also have to wait awhile before luring Di Palma from Rome. Instead, largely because he was going to be working fast and loose, Allen chose first-time cameraman Fouad Said, who'd invented the Cinemobile vehicle, which contained sound, lighting, and camera equipment, and sprouted a crane for overhead shots.

He hired fellow New Yorker Marvin Hamlisch, who had written pop music hits but only one motion picture score to date, to compose the main theme and incidental music. Rollins and Joffe thought Allen needed a resourceful stand-in for his own scenes, and they urged the hiring of comedian and actor Howard Storm—a Rollins-Joffe client. Storm, whose build was similar to Allen's, knew the director from Upstairs-at-the-Duplex days. His presence allowed Allen to stage the action and frame the shots with Storm during camera rehearsals. If Allen liked Storm's emendations during the run-throughs, he could absorb them into his own performance.

Allen and Edgar Scherick had only one major disagreement—over the choice of editor. Allen did not wish to have a "creative editor" in the editing room; "All he wanted was a mechanic to put the film together as he decreed," the head of Palomar recalled. Scherick let Allen have his way, and the director engaged James T. Heckert, a native of California and veteran Hollywood cutter steeped in television shows and low-budget fare.

WHEN ALLEN FIRST arrived in the Bay Area, he told local columnist Herb Caen, who knew him from the hungry i, his script "has absolutely nothing to do with San Francisco," in "Mr. Everything's" words. "The setting is a Midwestern city, something like Gary, Indiana . . . [but] who wants to spend five months in Gary, Indiana?" One big reason Allen gravitated to San Francisco was the local jazz scene that would keep him happy at night and on weekends. During the two months of scouting, final casting, and other preparations for *Money*, he began wandering onto club stages with his clarinet, performing the traditional New Orleans music he loved for the first time with trombonist Turk Murphy's band at Earthquake McGoon's on Clay Street. Allen had become a regular at the club, a magnet for celebrities, on previous Bay Area trips. McGoon's had a Magic Cellar with magic acts, so Allen could kill two birds with one visit. He met Howard Cosell at McGoon's, shook his hand, and promised "the archetypal American sportscaster," in Allen's words, a part in his next picture.

Allen evinced an inferiority complex around professional musicians, and at McGoon's, as he tried to blend in and look inconspicuous, he'd peter out in the choruses, roll his eyes, and bow his head in front of the crowds. Murphy urged him not to be so apologetic. "I wish he'd stop worrying so much," the jazzman told local journalists. In gratitude Allen would give Murphy national exposure on *The Tonight Show* when substituting for Johnny Carson, and he'd join Murphy's band whenever he passed through San Fran in the years ahead.

As everything coalesced for the mid-June start date, Allen organized tutorials for the cast and crew of certain movies he loved that would help explain the "abstract feelings" that fueled his directorial vision. The company gathered to watch *Blow-Up* with Carlo Di Palma's color photography, and Claude Lelouch's *Live for Life* "for general sex education," reported the *New York Times*, itemizing the screenings.* The troupe was also treated to Mervyn LeRoy's *I Am a Fugitive from a Chain Gang*, because Virgil Starkwell, like Paul Muni in the 1932 classic Warner Bros. picture, would be doing some hard time on a chain gang. (Allen's chain-gang scenes wound up, in the end, quoting more from the recent *Cool Hand Luke*, from 1967.) The company also screened the Oscar-winning *Eleanor Roosevelt Story*, for its "documentary quality," according to the *Times*, and also because Sidney Glazier, a *Take the Money and Run* producer, had supervised the 1965 documentary about the first lady.

Allen had seen all these pictures and many more, which is why he called the first take on the first morning of principal photography with an "unshakeable confidence in himself," as assistant director Walter Hill recalled. The novice filmmaker impressed everyone with his composure, beginning with a complicated scene without the benefit of any "notes to self," or storyboards. The scene involved a hundred extras and took place on location at San Quentin State Prison. Hill, who had just finished similar assistant-director duties on *Bullitt*, which was also lensed in the Bay Area, nursed higher ambitions, and he wanted to learn from the directors he worked with. So he asked Allen about his formal education and training. Allen said he had no formal education or training, and the only person he had spoken to about directing was Arthur Penn in New York, because he regarded *Bonnie and Clyde* as "one of the best American movies" of all time. "I asked him to tell me what I should be looking out for, and he told me how he had looked at many vintage photographs of small Texas towns and banks and framed his shots based on them," Allen said. As ever, Allen did not think ahead very much to the staging of scenes; he liked to arrive on the set and

* *Live for Life* was also among the classic-film send-ups Allen wrote into *Rifkin's Festival*, made fifty years later in Spain.

go with the flow—his instincts. He and Penn did discuss the big shootout at the end of his script, in which Starkwell dies in a slow-motion hail of bullets à la *Bonnie and Clyde*. But Allen also had given that scene a dry run in the *Bonnie and Clyde* parody on his year-end TV special.

Allen didn't lean on storyboards, as so many directors did. "I've just watched a lot of movies in my life," he told Hill, "a *lot*." Movies had taught him to pay attention to the look of people, to costumes and decor, the colors in scenes. Allen wore "*Elvira Madigan* yellow" for the escape sequence for *Take the Money and Run*, Judy Stone wrote in the *New York Times*, adding, "It sounds funny, but he is actually concerned with every touch of color."

Allen picked the shots, angles, and camera moves from the how-to manual in his head. "I remember admiring his courage," said Hill, who'd go on to write and direct *The Warriors*, *The Long Riders*, *48 Hrs.*, and other lauded films. Allen seemed equally at ease with the daredevil photography, dangling precariously from a helicopter for high overheads, and the more intimate camerawork for romantic scenes he played with costar Janet Margolin. "I'm having the time of my life," the actress told interviewers. "We improvise every scene."

It always seemed paradoxical that Allen, who wrote the script, encouraged his casts of actors to improvise. But that is the way he worked best onstage performing his stand-up comedy, and he liked departing from his own pages. As time went on in his career many actors would come to regard his screenplays as sacrosanct, but that never was his intention and not all actors were improvisational creatures. Allen told Howard Storm to let him know if Storm could improve on any gag in the scenes, and "I wrote ten and he used two of them." Storm stood behind the camera alongside Allen for every shot, taking notes for himself. Like Hill, Storm was teaching himself how to direct, even as Allen himself was learning about camerawork and lighting techniques.

When Allen himself acted in a scene, he was not shy about the cast and crew watching him. Often, they had to choke back their laughter. Virgil Starkwell, from his point of view, was merely an extension of the neurotic-nebbish persona he had developed as a comedian. That profession, that persona, beckoned to him one weekend during the filming, even though Allen had plans to relax by watching Ingmar Bergman films. An urgent phone call summoned him to Las Vegas to stand by as a substitute for Milton Berle.

Berle had broken his leg, and the veteran comic wasn't sure if he could go onstage as scheduled at Caesars Palace. Allen was always dutiful in such situations, and he flew to the rescue, arriving to learn Berle had decided to perform his act from a wheelchair. Berle thanked Allen from the stage, calling on him to stand up amid the tremendous crowd in the cavernous Circus Maximus, "pale, suffering, muttering, 'This is the most embarrassing moment of my life.' "

The commanding side of Allen showed poise on the set, finishing scenes in a few takes, which helped avoid overtime costs. "Woody was not a guy racked by indecision," recalled Hill. "He was very pleasant throughout, by the way. Shy would be the operative word. He was not gregarious on the set. One thing about being a comedian is everyone expects you to be funny all the time. But he would make amusing remarks. . . ."

One early crisis demonstrated his confidence. Fouad Said was not meeting expectations. While his Cinemobile with lightweight, advanced equipment was a godsend, Said himself was not up to the demands of photographing a feature film. Allen saw the problem right away in early dailies. It was a tough call for a first-time director, but he quickly replaced the cameraman with Lester Shorr, a fellow Brooklynite with credits mainly in television and inconsequential features. But Shorr also had shot documentaries and worked on other Bay Area productions. Allen would prove shrewd and exacting about cameramen throughout his career, and he'd fire the great ones—Haskell Wexler on *Anything Else* early in the 2002 filming—along with lesser lights.

Personally, he remained wary and enigmatic. He usually ate alone, sparsely, at lunch. At least once a week Allen spent the lunch break in a phone booth, speaking to his New York analyst. Recognized everywhere, during filming he introduced the custom of a pseudonym, asking friends and associates to address him as Max whenever he ventured out in public. Partly to alleviate the stress, he daily practiced the clarinet.

GOOD NEWS CAME before he left San Francisco: *Play It Again, Sam* had been optioned by Arthur P. Jacobs, the producer of *Dr. Dolittle* and *Planet of the Apes*, for a projected 20th Century–Fox screen adaptation of his pending, second Broadway play. The stage cast had not yet been finalized, and *Sam* was not even scheduled to open until mid-February 1969. But the studio had paid $350,000 for the rights, with escalating clauses that might raise Allen's earnings to $1 million, and moreover, the contract called for Allen to star in the screen version.

Along with this announcement came news that producer David Merrick was planning an evening of one-acts called "Sex, God and Death," which included the new Woody Allen playlet *Death Knocks*, an existential farce with elements cribbed from Ingmar Bergman. *Death Knocks* would be combined with one-acts from David Mamet and Elaine May. The trio of one-acts was being audience-tested that summer in the Berkshires.

When he returned to New York in August, Allen plunged into the editing of *Take the Money and Run* while keeping a chock-a-block schedule of auditions and rehearsals for *Play It Again, Sam*. Not all filmmakers worked side by side with their editors, but Allen was as much a fussbudget about his footage as he was about everything else in his life. Reviewing and assembling the scenes he had captured in San Francisco, the director worked closely with editor James Heckert for most of the day, all day every day, except Saturdays and Sundays, which were off-limits to him according to Editors Guild rules. As he spliced a Woody Allen film for the first time—again learning on the job—he welcomed Howard Storm into the editing room to learn alongside him.

Invariably, Allen's directing let him down, and from the beginning he made expeditious decisions during editing. Heckert "was accustomed to the Hollywood system in which cutters are expected to follow orders and was therefore not inclined to raise objections or offer unsolicited solutions," Ralph Rosenblum recalled sympathetically. Allen had "little patience with his own material" and when scenes did not click, he "immediately removed anything that seemed inadequate. . . . The result was a picture that was too short, with too few jokes, and with enough dead spots to convince an untrained viewer that the entire work was rather flat or mediocre."

The rough cut assembled by Heckert had all these problems. Worse—a rookie mistake—the rough assemblage was shown to people without finished music, sound effects, or beginning and end title sequences. When Palomar executives, Jack Rollins, Charles Joffe, and groups of friends saw this first cut late in 1968, they were taken aback. At one screening a worried Palomar official turned to Mickey Rose and demanded to know, "Are all the reels like this?" The picture "wasn't particularly funny," Storm recalled. "We were all in shock." Allen tried a different tactic, recruiting complete strangers for showings, including soldiers from a nearby midtown USO, but all the early screenings proved equally "demoralizing." The audiences would watch "this thing with no titles, no explanation, no sound effects, no music or anything, and we would die with it," Allen remembered.

With some budget money that had been set aside for reshooting—standard operating procedure on this and future Woody Allen movies—the director returned to the West Coast, photographing fresh scenes in the Bay Area with a pickup crew and Walter Hill as his assistant. He added the new footage and Marvin Hamlisch's music to a reworked cut, yet the result still disappointed everyone. *Play It Again, Sam* had begun to take over his life. It was obvious to everyone, including Allen himself, that the editing crisis needed expert intervention.

Ralph Rosenblum was the man for the job, as he had been for *The Laughmakers* years earlier. Associate producer Jack Grossberg, who had been on David Susskind's staff in *Laughmakers* days, phoned Rosenblum in early January, just as the editor was "putting the finishing touches" on the movie of Philip Roth's novel *Goodbye, Columbus*. Grossberg asked Rosenblum to stop by the Forty-Third Street screening room and take a look at Allen's troubled first directorial effort. "No audience had yet been found that would laugh at the picture," said Rosenblum. Palomar "was on the verge of deciding not to release it." Allen himself was "despondent."

Watching the latest cut of *Take the Money and Run*, Rosenblum was treated to "a very unusual experience, a film that seemed to be flying all over the place, with highs as high as the Marx Brothers and lows as low as a slapped-together home movie." The movie, "very primitively shot—which really didn't matter as long as the gags worked," was too "frenetic and formless . . . even as I was enjoying it, I began to feel that it was going on forever. The whole thing was put together in a strange, inept way, with little rhythm and a very bad sense of continuity." The comedy ended dismally with Starkwell/Allen "gunned down by the police in a hideous death scene reminiscent of *Bonnie and Clyde*. The last shot in the movie has the camera pulling away from Starkwell's blood-drenched, bullet-ridden body. It was very chilling." This was to be capped by a glimpse of Janet Margolin mourning at Starkwell's open grave, with Starkwell/Allen's voice hissing from the coffin, "Psst! It's me. Get me out!"

When the lights went on in the screening room, Rosenblum felt "tremendous anxiety" emanating from the roomful of managers and producers waiting for his opinion. The editor was swarmed by the "imploring faces" of Rollins, Joffe, and Grossberg. Joffe asked: "Can you fix the film?" Rosenblum asked to read the script, discovering "it contained a wealth of jokes, many of them very funny, that I had not seen in the film." Grossberg assured Rosenblum "all of this material had been photographed, as well as a considerable bunch of jokes that Woody had improvised or invented while shooting." After agreeing to a fee and the screen credit of "editorial consultant," Rosenblum still required Allen's endorsement. Rollins and Joffe seemed to think "their young ward was a delicate orchid who might wither if approached incautiously." Rosenblum met the managers at the corner of Seventy-Second Street and Madison Avenue, from where he was led to a seafood restaurant.

Sitting alone at a corner table was Allen, glumly picking at his food. He "didn't put on airs." He was "very serious and very soft-spoken," so soft-spoken Rosenblum "had to lean forward to hear him, for in a gesture of involuntary modesty he put his hand in front of his mouth, whenever he was eating." Rosenblum liked Allen instantly, however, sensing they were kindred spirits, both "perennially joyless, pessimistic about our chances of happiness and easily sucked into low spirits." The neophyte filmmaker said he was on the verge of leaving New York for a few months, going on the road for previews of *Play It Again, Sam*. He'd have all the cans of footage delivered to Rosenblum's cutting room. "He made no effort to control what I would do with it in his absence."

Just like that, Allen surrendered *Take the Money and Run* to Rosenblum, who began exploring the two hundred boxes of celluloid that arrived at his office. Much of the footage was "so original, so charming, so funny in absolutely unexpected ways" that it made his chore "one of the most pleasurable in my years of editing." The editor discovered "many discarded jokes" that were "every bit as good as those I'd seen in the film. Invariably, they had flaws, flaws that could easily be cleaned up or worked around or finessed." While discarding valuable jokes, Allen had clung to "maudlin patches" revolving around Starkwell's romance with Louise, or his failures, creating solemn "dead spots" that evinced his "enduring need to communicate emotional anguish," in Rosenblum's words, his "obsessive desire to keep a strain of seriousness running through the film."

With Allen concentrating on *Play It Again, Sam*, Rosenblum began reconstructing *Take the Money and Run*. "I put back some scenes, extended or recut others, juggled the material to create a rhythm, which in some cases meant moving whole scenes from one part of the film to another, and trimming almost everything to quicken the pace." The editor tied the "haphazardly plotted" story more closely together with Jackson Beck's voice-over narration and the interview scenes with Starkwell. He incorporated more of Starkwell's parents and interviews with the people who meet him on the lam. "Transitional devices" bolstered the script continuity, and Rosenblum asked for a different and less grim—easing up on the *Bonnie and Clyde*—ending. Back in New York by early February for the opening of *Sam*, Allen agreed to most of the suggestions and supplied solutions without delay. He'd "go into a corner and emerge a few hours later with everything that was needed on scraps of paper," Rosenblum recalled.

Marvin Hamlisch's score was part of the problem, and part of the solution. Hamlisch's "collaboration with Woody, as important as it was for the picture, was not easy for Marvin, whose expressiveness turned melodramatic alongside Allen's unswerving calm," Rosenblum recalled. When Hamlisch, at one recording session, played for the first time his ballad for the title sequence, Allen's blank reaction—"What was *that*?"—upset the composer. "When Allen left the room," Rosenblum said, "Marvin lay down on the floor and wept."

Hamlisch tried a variation of the score where he simply played the piano. When Allen gave that version the thumbs-down, Hamlisch rerecorded the music with a full orchestra. "I still didn't like it," Allen recalled. The first-time director had requested "down notes" to heighten the pathos of scenes, mournful music that Rosenblum described as "Chaplinesque," and that Allen, in retrospect, agreed evoked "the worst side of Chaplin." For one key scene, where Starkwell, living in a rundown hotel, prepares for a date with his new girlfriend, Rosenblum replaced Hamlisch's melancholy track with a snatch of upbeat Eubie Blake ragtime. "The sequence was heavy and oppressive and unfunny," Rosenblum said. "Without changing a frame, just changing the music, the thing became funny." Time and again, Rosenblum asked for buoyant music to highlight the comedic aspects, and Hamlisch responded quickly with "the kind of music we needed in order to transform the tone of a scene."

Similarly, the "half dozen endings" Allen had shot were all "sentimental, weakly amusing, or sad," the editor recalled. The ending was simply too downbeat. The film needed uplift, and an ending that circled back to the beginning and rounded off the story. This, Rosenblum wrote, was "a demand that I would repeat on three of our next four films together." Allen responded by writing and shooting several new scenes, forming an inspired final sequence that mixed televised accounts of Starkwell's arrest with snippet interviews with his acquaintances, Louise Lasser included. The audience would be given one last glimpse of Starkwell in his prison cell, being interviewed and brooding on his criminal escapades. Returning to a joke from earlier in the picture, Starkwell asks the interviewer, as he busily whittles a bar of soap into a gun, "Do you know if it's raining out?"

Rosenblum's input saved the picture, and "Woody's spirits took a definite upturn." Working closely together on *Take the Money and Run* and five more Woody Allen films through *Interiors*, Rosenblum taught Allen invaluable postproduction strategies. Above all, he taught him that editing was the last stage of writing and rewriting.

ADDING TO THE stress he was under, by the time Allen first met with Ralph Rosenblum to discuss the reediting of *Take the Money and Run*, he and Louise Lasser had agreed to separate. As his career continued to boom, hers couldn't seem to lift off the ground. The play she had tested in Florida was not going to make it to Broadway. Her marriage to Allen was not working out. Nor was her career. Was she a comedian, a singer, an actress, or what, exactly? Lasser had managed to carve a foothold in television commercials, but she was always being held back by her chronic laryngitis, weight swings, manic depression, and days spent in bed. The couple loved each other and even discussed having a child together, but parenthood was not the answer. "He wanted me to have little girls," Lasser recalled, "and that was his big dream . . . but I was never able to be there for him." At times Allen desperately wished to save the marriage. Other times he frantically sought an exit. They avoided discussing their issues because talk led to tensions. Avoiding conflict was ingrained with Allen. "He keeps shooting billiards," Lasser plaintively told one interviewer. "It's sort of hard to talk to him that way."

Uncoupling was the ultimate conflict avoidance. Agreeing to an amicable separation, Lasser found a new place nearby on East Seventy-First. Allen made plans to move out of their home, whose design and decoration were never consummated. Dick Cavett and his wife would take over the apartment, and Allen found another penthouse duplex in a nearby luxury building on Fifth Avenue near East Seventy-Fourth. Having a comedian in the building worried the management, however, so Allen got a reference from a new friend, Mary Bancroft, a well-established neighborhood resident, who belonged to a family that once owned Dow Jones & Company. The two had struck up a conversation at the foot of a stairway at one of Norman Mailer's parties. Still beautiful in her sixties, Bancroft was a former World War II intelligence agent turned novelist and memoirist.

Allen's bid was accepted. "I paid a song for it [the apartment]," he told Peter Biskind years later, "it was like $600,000." Allen temporarily moved into a hotel while architects and builders toiled on renovations.

He met other interesting women too, thanks to *Play It Again, Sam*. Toward the end of the summer of 1968, he and David Merrick agreed on the man to direct Allen's second play. Joseph Hardy had staged the acclaimed *You're a Good Man, Charlie Brown* in a Greenwich Village theater in 1967. He had a reputation for working well with performers, and he also had a college connection to an actress being touted for the female lead.

Allen's contract for his second Broadway play acknowledged the success of *Don't Drink the Water* by giving the playwright—now lead actor too—the upper hand in casting, design, and staging decisions. The new balance was symbolized by Allen's comment at *Play It Again, Sam*'s Washington, DC, tryout, when the overbearing Merrick, elegantly dressed as usual in a blue suit, tried once too often to tell Allen what was funny. Allen interrupted. "David, I've made over a million dollars in my life by not listening to men in blue suits." Allen had mixed feelings about Merrick, who had good and bad qualities, but the power had shifted in their relationship.

With *Play It Again, Sam*, for the first time, Allen had written a script that blended his fictional persona with genuine elements of his life. The lead character he was playing is a writer in love with movies—just like Allen. The character, a film critic who goes by Allen's own birth name—Allan Felix (the Felix in honor of Felix the Cat)—is, like Allen, the forsaken survivor of a messy divorce. He is a romantic idealist and a perpetual loser with women whose lust will never be satisfied. Unlike *Don't Drink the Water*—and even

Take the Money and Run—this merging of public persona and private self was akin to Allen the comedian finding himself onstage.

The film critic boasts an imaginary muse in Humphrey Bogart, the tough-guy icon of Warner Bros. studio, whose tagline—paraphrased from *Casablanca*, the 1943 classic starring Bogart and Ingrid Bergman—gives Allen's play its title. Ghostly manifestations of Bogart and the critic's disapproving ex-wife haunt Allan, who stumbles into infidelity with his best friend's wife. For this part Allan sought a promising young newcomer.

Allen always had to feel the actors embodied the main characters as he had imagined them, and as a first-time stage actor it was even more crucial for him to feel compatible with the people cast as his best friend and his best friend's wife—his romantic crush. As soon as casting began in earnest in the fall of 1968, Allen contacted Anthony Roberts from *Don't Drink the Water* and asked him to play Dick, the best friend. But Linda, Dick's wife, with whom Allan/Allen trysts, loomed as an even more consequential role. The actress had to be competent, but she also had to evince sex appeal for Allen. In scripts and in life, he liked his romances to be kismet.

He met Diane Keaton for the first time at auditions. She underwent several callbacks. At first Allen saw the actress as a "rube," "a real hayseed," "a coat-check girl," as he said later, if half in jest. But Keaton was a coat-check girl to remember, with "an absolutely spectacularly imaginative combination of clothes," Allen recalled, "you know, a football jersey and a skirt . . . and combat boots and, you know, *oven mittens*." He had seen the actress onstage in *Hair*, although the rock-and-roll musical was not his sort of thing. He saw every Broadway play of note, and Allen and Roberts had gone to *Hair*, in which Keaton was notorious as the member of the ensemble who refused to doff her clothes in the all-nude finale. Clothed or not, Keaton could sing, and she had briefly taken over the lead from Lynn Kellogg, belting out the showstopper, "Good Morning Starshine."

Hair was Keaton's only major credit since moving to New York from California, where she was born in 1946 and where her beautiful mother was once crowned "Mrs. Los Angeles." As Diane Hall she had sung in the Methodist choir growing up, and she'd been a standout in talent shows and school plays, including as Maria in a campus production of *The Sound of Music*, before quitting Orange Coast College. In New York she'd studied acting with Sanford Meisner and dance with Martha Graham and, in time, changed her surname to Keaton. By the fall of 1968 when she auditioned for *Play It Again*, the newcomer was twenty-two years old—almost eleven years younger than Allen—living in a studio walk-up on West Eighty-Second, with her bathtub in the kitchen.

Keaton was also at least one or two inches taller than her prospective leading man—"Most of it is legs," as one *New York Times* reporter later observed. She was preternaturally skinny, with clear blue eyes, high cheekbones, and sandy reddish hair tumbling to her shoulders. She gave off a tall vibe. Director Joseph Hardy and Keaton had in common Orange Coast College and its resident drama mentor Lucien Scott. Keaton would be great in the part, Professor Scott told Hardy, and Hardy told Allen and David Merrick the same thing. The respected acting coach Meisner assured Merrick that Keaton was "just the best actress around," although Keaton said later Meisner had never seemed that enthusiastic about her when she took his classes.

Her height worried everyone, perhaps Allen too, perhaps not. Over time journalists would peg him as 5 feet, 5½ inches or 5 feet 6. His shortness was a vanity issue, which he kidded self-consciously in his comedy. It was vitally important, in *Annie Hall*, that singer Paul Simon, who plays the LA music producer who steals Keaton away from him, be a shorter man. "I wanted to lose the girl to a guy who was smaller than me," Allen said later. That same measuring stick was applied to his rivalry with Keaton's revered ex in *Manhattan*. When Allen meets the great man, he turns out to be stumpy Wallace Shawn. "I'm a detective," Allen lies in *Manhattan Murder Mystery*, on a dangerous mission with his wife—Keaton again. "They lowered the height requirement."

At one *Play It Again, Sam* audition Allen sprang onstage and walked around Keaton, "since one of the major concerns was to see whether or not I would be too tall for him. I was absolutely astonished to find that Woody was more frightened of me than I was of him," the actress recalled. Finally, Hardy took their measurements back-to-back. OK, maybe Keaton was a *little* taller, maybe they would always look a bit incongruous together—so what? Maybe that was better.

"The rehearsals are going okay," Keaton wrote her mother in California shortly after getting the part. "Woody Allen is cute and of course, very funny." The Halls were fans. "I was in love with him before I knew him,"

Keaton said later. "Our entire family used to gather around the TV set and watch him on Johnny Carson. He was even better looking in real life. He had a great body, and he was physically very graceful." She made no bones about it in interviews. "I've always thought he was kind of cute. . . . Gorgeous men always put me off."

Keaton herself was a singular combination of cute and gorgeous. "What did you do, grow up in a Norman Rockwell painting?" Alvy Singer asks in *Annie Hall*. She was Norman Rockwell crossed with Pippi Longstocking, all grown up and gone Southern California. Others had noticed her special qualities before: her charm and intelligence, her artistic soul. But casting Keaton as Linda in *Play It Again, Sam* is the best evidence of Allen's acumen for spotting talent. He could rightly claim to have discovered Keaton at a time when it seemed unlikely, if not impossible, that one day she'd be considered among the leading screen actresses of her generation.

To hear both tell it, they circled nervously during first rehearsals. Allen had been dating another actress, who auditioned for the part of Linda, was offered a smaller role, declined, and disappeared. And then there was that man who always seemed to be waiting for Keaton at the stage door—her manager, as it turned out.

By the time *Play It Again, Sam* opened in Washington, however—the first city on the tryout tour—the couple were eating together regularly and "we were lovers," Allen wrote in his memoir. "We remained lovers in Boston and back in New York." Allen might have waited until DC because of Louise Lasser . . . or Nettie Konigsberg. "Maybe it was the Freudian lifting of ambitions, or something," he joked in one interview, "being in a different city from the one where my mother lived." Soon enough, the three best friends in the script were three amigos offstage too—Allen, Keaton, and Tony Roberts—with the "Anthony" quickly vanishing after the run of *Play It Again, Sam*.

AS WAS ALWAYS the case with a Woody Allen play—and often as well, on his films—the script went through many iterations as *Play It Again, Sam* was tested in previews in Washington, DC, and Boston on the road to Broadway. Echoing Ralph Rosenblum and *Take the Money and Run*, director Joseph Hardy later gave interviews insisting there was no real third act or climax until he pushed Allen for revisions. The rewrites strengthened the entirety, and *Play It Again, Sam*'s tryout notices were better than those of *Don't Drink the Water*. Everyone commented favorably on the magical stage effects that turned Bogart and the ex-wife into ghostly beings.

Allen's acting ability had been a question mark. Could he pull off the memorization, the rigor of daily performances, and the different kind of performance skills that were called for than what he had done in the Charles K. Feldman pictures, or the jokey *Take the Money and Run*? He had to *become* Allan Felix, even if the divorced film critic was a Village-y character not too dissimilar from his stand-up comedy persona. The goal, Hardy told the press, was to transfer Allen's stand-up persona into Allan Felix, and see that persona "enlarged as an entity onstage." But the persona also had to deepen, and Allen had to take the character through an emotional arc. He couldn't just fall back on jokes. This was the challenge Allen had set for himself. "He tries," Hardy told journalists. "He takes direction . . . and he has taken ninety-five percent of my ideas with enthusiasm."

Then as later, Allen only ever spoke modestly about his acting expertise and his emotional depth in roles. "I can act realistically within a certain narrow range," he liked to say in interviews. "It's like Hope working with Crosby—Hope gives the correct response; it's not acting in the sense that Marlon Brando acts."

Opening night was February 13, 1968. Comedian Jack Benny, Allen's nemesis-turned-supporter Ed Sullivan, and actress Angela Lansbury were among the first-nighters at the Broadhurst Theatre. Keaton probably had the most stomach butterflies. But she and Allen had a teasing relationship on- and offstage. Her costars knocked on her dressing room with fretted brows. "Don't worry about your hands, you'll be alright," Allen and Tony Roberts reassured her. "What about my hands?" she demanded as they raced away. "Diane spent opening night maddeningly aware of her hands," Lee Guthrie wrote in her Woody Allen biography.

The critics were pleasantly surprised. Keaton got the best reviews, and she and Roberts would be Tony-nominated for their winning performances. Clive Barnes, who described the play as "slender but hilarious" in the *New York Times*, said the script might have fallen short, and "you wish Allen had aimed a little more accurately for a serious comedy of manners rather than just a situation farce." But the laughs were huge, and all the leads—including

Jerry Lacy as "Bogey"—were good. Allen himself "comes within striking distance of real success" as an actor, his "benignly frustrated presence" onstage a "joy forever,"* Barnes wrote.

Keaton's parents flew in from California for opening night. After the final curtain fell, everyone celebrated with champagne and cheesecake at Sardi's. At Sardi's "we were told that Woody Allen's new leading lady was his new heart interest too," her mother wrote in her journal. Curiously, according to Eric Lax, the man of the moment then visited estranged wife Lasser, staying overnight at her apartment, and "had his first report of the good reviews from a stranger on the street who congratulated him as he walked home the next morning."

ALLEN WOULD STAY close to Broadway and New York for the next seven months. His days were free, while his nights were occupied by *Play It Again, Sam*: eight shows a week, matinees on Wednesdays and Saturdays. He'd miss a few nights in early October because of illness, and he took an unauthorized day off for the October 15, 1969, national anti–Vietnam War moratorium, defying producer David Merrick and warnings from Actors' Equity that he would be penalized and fined. Allen canceled afternoon and evening shows to take a public stand against the war with other show business personalities at a mass rally of thousands of people held at Bryant Park in midtown Manhattan. Later in November, appearing alongside Pete Seeger and the cast of *Hair*, Allen would tell a few jokes at another antiwar protest in Times Square. With Allen there was often an asterisk to the "never, evers": he could drive a car if necessary; he visited the Hamptons on occasion; he contributed a fair amount politically. He'd gone, in his usual slow way, from supporting Lyndon Baines Johnson after Kennedy's assassination to disavowing LBJ and showing up at antiwar rallies and donating to peace organizations.

Allen told interviewers that acting on Broadway was a sheer pleasure for him. He could devote himself to writing in the morning, relax in the afternoons, then stroll to the theater for his nightly duties in front of an audience. "I didn't have to dress at all," Allen said. "I could leave home dressed in my

* Allen was the only one of the three amigos not to be Tony-nominated in his category: Best Performance by a Leading Actor.

normal clothes and walk right out onstage just as I was." According to columnists, his dressing room was stocked with Kierkegaard for reading, chocolate syrup for energy boosts, and honey for the sore throat that came with voice projection. "It was the easiest job in the world," Allen liked to say, calling for only "minimal acting" within "a little tiny range." Still, Tony Roberts, in interviews, said the boasting was deceptive. His friend suffered from obvious stage fright before many performances. One journalist observed Allen's warm-up regimen: the actor skipped an imaginary rope and shot fantasy basketballs in order to loosen up his nerves before going onstage.

At his side now day and night, Keaton resided with Allen at different times in all three apartments that spanned the run of *Play It Again, Sam*: the one Allen had occupied with Louise Lasser, the temporary hotel room, and his new Fifth Avenue penthouse duplex. Once in a while Keaton shadowed Allen at antiwar events, but most days she walked to the Broadhurst alongside him, talking and laughing. She was one of the world's great talkers, listeners, and laughers. "I was a good audience," Keaton wrote later. "I laughed in between the jokes. I think he liked that, even though he would always remind me I wouldn't know a joke if it hit me in the face."

The two interacted just as playfully onstage, with a chemistry as akin to Hope and Crosby as any Allen could dream of. Onstage he'd tease out his lines and timing, doing "a lot of let's just say unusual things onstage, things you wouldn't think a person of his stature would do," in Keaton's words, trying to force the actress into "breaking character" and exploding with laughter. Once, Keaton recalled, "in the middle of a scene he suddenly started impersonating James Earl Jones" in *The Great White Hope*, which was also current on Broadway. "I tried not to laugh but it was impossible." Allen usually broke character first. "Tony and I could mess up on a line and go on, but not Woody. And then you started laughing. The discipline some nights was really bad."

The transition from husband to boyfriend had been messy with Allen once before, when he and Harlene called it quits, which overlapped with his amorous pursuit of Louise Lasser. There would be another such lag before the public heard of his romance with Keaton. Backstage in the spring, Earl Wilson buttonholed Keaton, inquiring about her offstage relationship with Allen. The actress was tight-lipped. "Woody in this show is the loser in life," she said, to which Wilson added a knowing postscript, "But only, evidently, in this play." A few columns later Wilson interviewed Allen and asked him about the widespread rumors his marriage to Lasser was faltering. Allen admitted he and Lasser were amicably separated but insisted that divorce was "not imminent." Still, he did not explicitly confirm his affair with Keaton, which her parents had learned about on opening night.

By summer, the two were living in the penthouse duplex, although Keaton kept her small apartment on West Eighty-Second. With her innate good taste, the actress helped Allen finalize his interiors and furnishings. The eleven rooms in two adjoining apartments, positioned on the top two floors of a massive building on Fifth Avenue adjacent to Central Park, spoke to how far Allen had traveled from Flatbush in Brooklyn to fortune and fame as a comedian on the Upper East Side of Manhattan. Once again Olga San Giuliano was hired for the interior decoration, and when San Giuliano proposed, Keaton weighed in, although Allen was the decider. Allen was "a knowledgeable, serious man, without flash, but with a fantastically correct eye," San Giuliano said.

Reflecting Allen's evolved fastidiousness, the designer organized an "undecorated look" that combined, in the living room, for example, accordion-pleated, floor-to-ceiling solar glass windows, which highlighted a wraparound view of Central Park landscape and a "main conversation grouping" of furniture: two country sofas, lounge chairs, and English tavern chairs facing an American Colonial mantel crowned by a Picasso lithograph.

The dining room boasted a fifteenth-century French butcher's table with custom chairs. A Welsh dresser displaying English china was flanked by wing chairs. In the library were motifs of upholstery fabric, a banquette covered in a Hamadan carpet, Spanish chairs lined with nailheads, a coffee table, and working desk.

Allen's bedroom suite included a breakfast table and pair of Swiss tavern chairs. Printed linen draperies matched the canopy spread, the floors were stenciled, and the walls covered with white linen. Outside the upper floor sprawled a terrace, modest garden, and small pond. Allen typically did the bulk of his writing, first in longhand in the master bedroom, sprawled across his English four-poster bed, before moving to the typewriter. The bedroom he hid out in as a boy, safe from the world, was now, as an adult, the sacred room of his imagination.

••

WHILE STARRING ON Broadway, Allen kept up promotional appearances on *The Tonight Show*, *The Merv Griffin Show*, *The Dick Cavett Show*, and Hugh Hefner's *Playboy After Dark*. He even opened the fall season for CBS with his first and only television special, timed to coincide with the release of *Take the Money and Run*. Marvin Hamlisch composed the music for the special as he had done for Allen's directorial debut, and the costars included actress Candice Bergen; the pop group the 5th Dimension, whose hits included the *Hair* anthem "Aquarius/Let the Sunshine In"; and evangelist Billy Graham, whom Allen had chatted up at the White House in 1965. In one sketch Allen and Bergen shed their clothes while nervously auditioning for a nude scene. In their loosely scripted segment, Allen lightly skewered Reverend Graham, his approach as sly as it had been with conservative pundit William F. Buckley Jr. on *The Year 1967 in Review* for *Kraft Music Hall*. A gadfly, never a firebrand, Allen told Graham he'd be willing to attend one of his Bible rallies if the preacher would buy a ticket to *Take the Money and Run*. Reviewers gave Allen's one and only TV special a standing ovation. "An astonishing tour de force, with plenty of farce along the tour, and always with taste, style, and abrasive witticisms," said *Variety*. Yet somehow characteristic of his amorphous fan base, and as a portent of his TV future, *The Woody Allen Special* ranked number 150 of 176 specials in the Nielsen ratings from 1969 to 1970.

When the reediting of *Take the Money and Run* was finally done, the postproduction completed, Diane Keaton was the first of the first to be invited to the insiders' screening. "She said it was good and funny and not to be so worried," Allen recalled in *Apropos of Nothing*, "and she's been my North Star, go-to person ever since." For decades to come, Keaton would be among the select few who previewed each new Woody Allen picture.

One year after he had wrapped the initial photography, Allen's first movie as writer, director, and star opened in mid-August at the 68th Street Playhouse, on the corner of Sixty-Eighth and Third in his Upper East Side neighborhood, where he believed there was a natural constituency for his kind of urban, Jewish, sophisticated slapstick. The extra time and care paid off, and all these years later *Money* stands up as a little sparkler. It mows down every movie cliché in its path inside of a brisk running time—eighty-five minutes—setting the length standard for every future Woody Allen picture. If any single joke flags, the next one comes along fast and furious.

If the script was patchy and the direction serviceable, Allen was in his element as multiple-loser Virgil Starkwell, a cello player in a marching band in his youth, who grows up to become a bank robber so inept he misspells a crucial word in his holdup note. ("I'm pointing a gub at you.") He is a fugitive from justice, but not a man bad enough to qualify for the Ten Most Wanted. "It's very unfair voting," Louise/Janet Margolin complains, "it's who you know." And oh, is he sex deprived! The first of many psychiatrists in Allen pictures muses about Starkwell's cello as a possible sublimation of his torso and phallus fixations. When the psychiatrist asks Starkwell if sex is dirty, his answer is the movie's best line: "It is if you do it right." Starkwell can't be reformed, even by Louise, his appealing sweetie. He is an incorrigible lowlife and numbskull and is mystified by Louise's announcement that he will be a new father come Christmas. "All I needed was a tie," he says.

The leading New York critics offered "nothing but raves," *Variety* reported. "Five favorable" notices were submitted by Vincent Canby in the *New York Times*, Kathleen Carroll in the *Daily News*, Joseph Morgenstern in *Newsweek*, Stanley Newman in *Cue*, and Archer Winsten in the *Post*. Canby, from the first an unabashed Allen enthusiast, applauded *Take the Money and Run* as "the cinematic equivalent" of Allen's "best nightclub monologues." *Variety* added this cautionary note: "All but Miss Carroll [said] film ran out of steam before end."

Not all the critics agreed, of course, and also from the first, Woody Allen movies were a battleground of violent opinions. The raves often provoked adverse reactions from those who recoiled from what they regarded as exorbitant praise. Chief among the recoilers was Pauline Kael—"Witty, biting, highly opinionated," according to her *Encyclopaedia Britannica* entry—a Californian just beginning to hoist her flag at the *New Yorker*, where she was destined to become the high priestess of a ministry of critics including young acolytes sprinkled around the US. Dubbed "Paulettes," they earnestly parroted her opinions. Kael wrote of Allen's film that what "the press loved" was merely "a limply good-natured little nothing of a comedy, soft as sneakers."

After so many positive reviews the US box office proved a letdown. The marketing and release strategy Allen oversaw set a pattern for the future. *Take the Money and Run* had opened on the Upper East Side near where Allen lived, so the movie could attract positive reviews from important New

York critics, and on the Upper East Side Allen's first film broke many house records, playing to capacity crowds. Yet Cinerama struggled to find welcoming theaters outside New York City, and *Take the Money and Run* was forced into brief runs at independent and art-house venues across America. The one- or two-week bookings in cities that didn't boast specialty venues were not impactful: "fair" in Cleveland; "mild" in Kansas City; "thin" in Portland, in *Variety* parlance.

Palomar had only a limited budget for publicity and advertising. Allen penned an amusing self-interview for the *Los Angeles Times*, with a ready-made blurb as its title: " 'Take the Money and Run' Steals Your Heart Away." Such pieces were a painless exercise for him and a clever promotional tool—like the diary he kept for *What's New Pussycat?* He'd write self-reviews and -interviews intermittently in the years ahead, all the way up through *Vicky Cristina Barcelona*—a surprising number of short pieces that have never been collected.

Take the Money and Run stalled at number eight on *Variety*'s chart. A few months after its initial release, Allen's debut feature could be found in only one US city—New York—albeit in thirty-five theaters scattered around New York and its boroughs. Allen was forever after convinced the most reliable audience for a cosmopolitan, Jewish, New York–based, low-budget filmmaker was close to home. It became an arguable truism that "Woody Allen's movies have always been 'too Jewish' for mainstream American audiences," as Jack Mathews wrote in *Newsday* over twenty years later, when trying to explain the low grosses of *Husbands and Wives* in 1992. Whenever critics or audiences rejected a Woody Allen picture, there was often "more than a whiff of anti-Semitism" involved, Mathews argued, stating baldly what many people recognized as one of the main obstacles for the broad dissemination of Allen's pictures in America. Jack Rollins and Charles Joffe had a long-range goal, however: build on the US figures overseas, showcase Allen at foreign film festivals, and maximize international bookings to augment the earnings. Allen's Palomar deal—indeed, it would be true of all his future contracts—gave the filmmaker financial incentives outside the North American market.

When the Writers Guild of America nominated *Take the Money and Run* for Best Comedy Written Directly for the Screen in 1969, Allen's personal managers were probably prouder than their client. This was Allen's second

Guild nomination after a similar one for *What's New Pussycat?* But the honored nominee did not attend the Guild's annual award festivities, nor would he show up for any of the many Guild occasions to follow. Allen's script lost in its category to Paul Mazursky and Larry Tucker's for *Bob & Carol & Ted & Alice*.

Regardless, Allen had Diane Keaton on his arm; *Play It Again, Sam* remained a hot ticket; and *Take the Money and Run* was, if nothing else, a succès d'estime. Nineteen sixty-nine had been another very good year.

Chapter 5

1970

Clockwork

Woody as the Modern Chaplin (with Keaton)—and Declarations of Independence, Personally and Professionally

One night in mid-January of the new year, Allen acted on the Broadway stage for the last time. Bob Denver stepped into the Allan Felix role in *Play It Again, Sam*. Maybe Allen had seen Denver in *The Many Lives of Dobie Gillis* back in the 1950s, a hip television series with up-and-comer Warren Beatty in a recurrent role, not the dopier *Gilligan's Island*. He approved Denver's casting. "Wow," thought Denver. "I get to meet Woody Allen." Denver knocked on the star's dressing room on the last night. "He mumbled a hello and was out the door."

A month or two later, Allen and Louise Lasser flew to Mexico for the divorce both always described as mutual and agreeable. So mutual and agreeable they made a stopover in San Antonio and slept in the same hotel room the night before catching their connecting flight to Juarez. "We had a good time," Lasser remembered. "We had a lot of what now appear contradictions like that. Because at the time we were still drawn together."

"I didn't get much" in the divorce settlement, the actress later asserted, although Lasser hailed from affluence and probably did not suffer financially. Lasser's "father, a mensch to the end, brokered a split that was fair to both of us, and we parted great friends," Allen defended the settlement in *Apropos of Nothing*.

The divergence between Woody Allen's public and private selves was complete. With his new leading lady Diane Keaton, Allen could continue to play the nervous nelly on screen while developing as an assured, decisive director offscreen. The increasingly emboldened Allen produced consistent, quality comedy through these years as an actor and director, all of the activity and momentum building to the comedy costarring Keaton that would win multiple Oscars and make his name—and filmmaking—known around the world.

Diane Keaton and Tony Roberts left the *Play It Again, Sam* cast around the same time. During the run of the play, Keaton filled a small role in the screen adaptation of a stage comedy called *Lovers and Other Strangers*, but the appealing film got lost amid the shuffle when it was released. Otherwise, when trying to capitalize on her Tony-nominated role on Broadway, almost universally praised by critics, Keaton encountered stone walls. Going up for other Broadway, television, or movie roles, she was often dismissed as too kooky. Reduced to underarm deodorant commercials and thankless parts in TV crime series, Keaton grew discouraged.

Keaton had a terrible secret that hindered her success, adding to the insecurity she always felt about her looks and talent. She was bulimic, and she purged herself three times daily after enormous meals: a steak, potatoes, cheesecake. Everyone, Allen included, marveled at her ability "to really pack it in," while staying so thin. "She ate like Primo Carnera," wrote Allen. "I never saw a person outside a logging camp tuck it away like that." Even though they shared living space in various dwellings for much of 1969 and 1970, "Woody didn't have a clue what I was up to in the privacy of his bathroom," Keaton recalled in *Then Again*. "Ever vigilant and always on the lookout, I made sure he never caught me [vomiting]." Allen agreed; he wore blinders. "Who knew she was bulimic?" he wrote in *Apropos of Nothing*. "I didn't till I read it in her memoir decades later."

Allen commiserated over his girlfriend's failed auditions, he encouraged her pipe dreams of singing, and he praised her promising hobby of photography. He bore "the brunt of my constant need for support and encouragement after *Play It Again, Sam* closed," Keaton recalled. However, Allen insisted in interviews, Keaton gave him equal reinforcement. "She's been a crutch to me in many ways," he said. She wasn't so sure. Neurotic himself, Allen "loved neurotic girls," Keaton wrote. Although she worked hard to make Allen see her as "something more than a gal pal," he was always so busy, all day every day, "nothing much was required of me."

While at the same time they reinforced and bolstered each other, they had a uniquely taunting, and one-upping kind of friendship. The couple "shared a love of torturing each other with our failures," Keaton said. "He could sling out the insults, but so could I. We thrived on demeaning each other. His insights into my character were dead on, and—duh!—hilarious. This bond remains the core of our friendship and, for me, love."

Yet Allen knew enough about Keaton's vulnerabilities to suggest she begin appointments with an Upper East Side analyst to discuss her problems and her lack of self-esteem. And soon after both had left the cast of *Play It Again, Sam*, Keaton moved out of Allen's duplex and into her own new apartment, which the comedian helped her pick out, not far away near Seventy-Third and Third. Although "he was the only one who would live with me while walking on eggshells, as he claimed I forced him to do," a long-term relationship or marriage was not in the cards. "I don't feel that way about him and me," Keaton flatly told the press. "I just like him a lot." While they remained "lovers intermittently," Allen said, "gradually, we sort of cooled down and drifted apart more." Keaton never said much in her interviews or books about their love life, except "the demands of bulimia outshone the power of my desire for Woody." She guarded the privacy of her affairs with famous boyfriends.

As a close friend, however, Keaton stayed in Allen's life, and the New York public saw them out and about frequently. Together they attended Bergman and Buñuel screenings, art gallery and museum exhibitions, stage and screen premieres, New York Knicks basketball games, and the occasional rustic weekend on the Atlantic coast. Sometimes Tony Roberts was an add-on. He and Keaton bonded over their mutual tolerance of Allen and their amusement at his shortcomings. One weekend the three amigos took a beach house at Fire Island. Allen arrived with "the largest piece of luggage I have ever seen," Roberts recalled, "a giant black doctor's valise . . . [with] enough antibiotics and antacids to open a small drugstore. He even brought a remedy for snakebite."

Keaton and Roberts coaxed the reluctant Allen down to the beach after their friend wasted "the better part of the day reading the *Times* on the living room sofa, where he had spent the night." Thereupon he made an "inspired entrance into the Atlantic Ocean. He strode into the surf wearing his white skullcap for protection against scalp burn, then dove and flailed frantically as Keaton and I held our sides with laughter. . . . He tolerated the sun and the sand for a full day and a half before he fled by seaplane back to his Manhattan apartment."

Louise Lasser, now Allen's ex-wife, was still living close by and sometimes she joined the couple for dinners or excursions. In later interviews, Lasser insisted she and Allen had enjoyed an intense physical attraction in their relationship, while he and Keaton did not. "It wasn't like with me," Lasser explained. "He has a great sexual appetite, and she [Keaton] had one too, but for some reason he didn't have it for her." At times during their prolonged separation, divorce, and postdivorce period, during which time the comedian was romantically involved with Keaton, the second ex–Mrs. Allen felt confused and conflicted over where she now stood in Allen's life. "He carried on insisting that he was really attracted to me and that I was the one he wanted to have sex with," said Lasser. "He kept me dangling, but I'm happy he did because otherwise I would have flipped."

On the flight home from their Mexican divorce, Allen patted Lasser's arm and told her something he believed would boost her spirits. He had recently dashed off three full screenplays, according to *Variety*. Now and in the future, Allen would usually have three disparate scripts ready to go at any given juncture, according to Eric Lax. Allen kept a file folder marked "Best Three Ideas Currently." One of his three new film scripts was a comedy Allen intended to direct in the near future, and in it was a plum role he had tailored for Lasser.

UNITED ARTISTS HAD been in on the ground floor of the Woody Allen boom thanks to producer Charles K. Feldman and his multipicture deal with the comedian. After Feldman's death UA balked at backing Allen's first stab at directing a movie and allowed *Take the Money and Run* to slip through its fingers. Palomar Pictures had behaved well. "They were nice, enlightened men and they treated me the way an artist wants to be treated," but the fledgling film company had faltered when it came to distribution. Meanwhile, UA realized its stupidity.

One day in October 1969, at a John Lindsay rally in Madison Square

Garden, Charles Joffe ran into David Picker, who had begun in publicity and advertising and rose up to become the chief operating officer of UA. Allen was among the entertainers at the benefit raising funds for the reelection campaign of the liberal Republican mayor. Picker asked Joffe how Allen was doing and what he would have to offer to lure him back to UA. "Two million budget, total control after you approve the story idea, and a three-film contract," said Joffe.

Picker was the highest-ranking creative executive of the smallest of the major Hollywood studios, which prided itself on having an East Coast orientation and, despite having West Coast offices, saw itself, alone among the majors, as a New York entity. UA's proud tradition of nurturing independent filmmaking began with the establishment of the studio by Charles Chaplin, Mary Pickford, Douglas Fairbanks, and D. W. Griffith in 1919, partly to guarantee the creative freedoms of the four founders but, equally important, to ensure the artists received their deserved share of revenue. UA's revered elder statesman was Arthur B. Krim, who along with longtime partner Robert S. Benjamin, both still on the company board, took over the struggling UA in 1956, after the originators had left it behind. Although Krim had guided the studio through the 1950s and '60s—roller-coaster years of peaks and valleys—he left the creative sifting and winnowing to specialists like Picker.

Still a neighbor of Allen's on the Upper East Side, Krim nurtured a friendship with the comedian. A Democratic Party fundraiser and power broker, Krim helped bring Allen into political circles after President Kennedy's assassination, encouraging his early support, with appearances and donations, for Lyndon Baines Johnson, for whom Krim served as an adviser. Krim remained close to subsequent Democratic presidents. Like Alvy Singer—who in *Annie Hall* tells his first wife, "Lyndon Johnson is a politician. You know the ethics those guys have . . . it's like—uh, a notch underneath child molesters"—Allen had long since disowned LBJ. But he remained a dependable supporter of liberal political candidates and the charitable causes dear to Krim.

Picker was personable and energetic, twenty years younger than Krim, and he oversaw the negotiations with Jack Rollins, Charles Joffe, and Sam Cohn, who'd once been a lawyer for General Artists, the agency that booked Allen's earliest stand-up shows outside New York. Nowadays Cohn was

Allen's talent representative at Creative Management Associates, known by its acronym: CMA. Over time, through mergers and acquisitions, CMA would metamorphose into International Creative Management, or ICM. Cohn pretended powerlessness with Allen: "Gentlemen, I'm just the messenger here," he'd say apologetically. Rollins and Joffe played good cop/bad cop. Cohn had an aversion to Hollywood, but not Joffe, who was increasingly based in the American movie capital but bounced from coast to coast like a hard rubber ball during negotiations, upping the ante.

Allen liked to *like* his business partners, and he liked the UA team—Picker, Benjamin, Krim. He agreed to $350,000 for writing, directing, and starring in his next three movies for UA, for which the studio pledged $2 million budgets each. The Rollins-Joffe agency would earn a floor salary of $125,000 per picture. Bonuses were built into the contract, with budget overages to be subtracted from Allen's and Rollins-Joffe's set fees. The director stood to earn 50 percent of net profits, with a share apportioned to Rollins-Joffe.* If Allen received the go-ahead on a story—not necessarily a script—and stayed within the agreed budget, he could work without interference and with final cut. "Allen would tell me a story and if I liked the idea, it was a 'go,'" Picker said.

No one in the history of Hollywood had ever boasted such an arrangement with a major studio. No one except Chaplin, Pickford, Fairbanks, and Griffith long ago—with Chaplin making the most of it—and Orson Welles, for whom RKO had structured similar precedents for masterminding *Citizen Kane*. Picker swallowed hard. The Rollins-Joffe proposition "struck me as arrogant," he recalled. But with Krim's encouragement, Picker said yes. By mid-December the contract could be announced at an elaborate Museum of Modern Art press conference "replete with 'gag' releases," as *Variety* reported, "carefully rehearsed questions and answers between Allen and one of his press agents, and meant, generally, to provide a laugh for the assembled press." The first of the three United Artists–Woody Allen productions would be shot in 1970 and released in 1971.

* However, as Eric Lax cautioned in his official Allen biography, studio accounting methods were notoriously mysterious, and it was standard operating policy for a major studio to obscure any net profits on ledgers for films for which there were profit participants outside the studio itself. "It is unlikely, for instance," Lax wrote, "that *Take the Money and Run* will ever technically be in the black."

Soon after the publicity bash, Allen and Picker met to green-light his first UA project. Allen had his three scripts ready. He pitched his preference, the one called "The Jazz Baby." "The movie is about a jazz clarinetist, a brilliant musician, maybe a genius, but whose personal life is a catastrophe," Allen explained. Allen himself would play the brilliant, self-destructive clarinetist, or maybe the character would be a jazz guitarist—Allen was happy to take guitar lessons—either way, the story would revolve around, as Picker recalled the pitch, "the women in the musician's life, his addictions, his lack of character—he talked for about five minutes, and as I listened, I couldn't believe my ears. I had just made a unique deal with a great comic talent, and he wanted to make a serious, dark biopic of some bastard musician who's not worth spending ten minutes with."

Picker nodded. Very interesting, he said politely. "Jazz Baby" might well be a film UA could get behind, but couldn't Allen launch his new contract with an out-and-out comedy? Allen's face sagged. "I'll get back to you soon," he muttered, before racing out the door. "I wasn't sure I'd ever hear from him again," Picker said. A few days later Cohn phoned with another idea about "the perfect, neurotic nebbish trying to get the girl by fighting with revolutionaries in a fictional banana republic." Cohn had him at the title: *Bananas*. Approved!

ALTHOUGH MGM'S DESIRE to turn Richard Powell's *Don Quixote, U.S.A.* into the first movie directed by Woody Allen came to naught in 1967, Allen and Mickey Rose had read the novel and absconded with Powell's premise: an idealistic Bostonian, disillusioned by a failed romance, joins the Peace Corps and gets posted to a fictional banana republic, where he becomes embroiled in the ongoing revolution. Because Allen "did not want to be sued," the director asked United Artists to option the screen rights to Powell's novel for *Bananas*. Later, after Arthur Krim saw *Bananas*, and realized the picture "bore no resemblance" to the book for which he had paid a substantial sum, "he wanted to sue me for fraud," in Allen's words, and had to be dissuaded by David Picker.

Although Allen recalled "using zero from the book," he and Rose expropriated more than just the premise. In fact, their script preserved the major characters and plot ingredients of Powell's story. In Powell's novel the setting is a fictional Caribbean nation called San Marco, whose principal export is bananas; in Allen and Rose's script the nation is San Marcos (plural), somewhere in South America. The noble Peace Corps volunteer of the novel has his name changed from Arthur Peabody Goodpasture to Fielding Mellish. The Bostonian becomes a spurned New Yorker in the movie, a sad sack whose vacation to San Marcos—the plural South American one—plunges him into revolutionary monkey business. In both the novel and script there is a dictatorial generalissimo, who has led a coup overthrowing El Presidente, and a raffish comandante of jungle rebels trying to topple the generalissimo. In both works, the jungle rebels kidnap and adopt the tourist, and sweep to victory, and when the comandante goes power-mad the American replaces him as the new El Presidente.

In Allen and Rose's hands, however, the modest, grounded satire of *Don Quixote, U.S.A.* became surreal, nonsensical farce. Playing to Allen's strengths, their script allowed room for plenty of physical slapstick, with one daft scene introducing Mellish as the product tester of treacherous desk-exercise equipment. There was bent psychoanalysis, including Allen's first Ingmar Bergmanesque dream sequence depicting a crucified Mellish, borne aloft by priests, losing his car parking space to a rival martyr. There were montages of guerrilla life, with Mellish learning the dangerous lifestyle of a revolutionary and lovemaking à la Che—with the distaff rebel enjoying a manly smoke afterward. There were jabs at United Jewish Appeal and the Vatican, with a priest peddling New Testament cigarettes: "I smoke 'em," the priest exhales, jabbing his thumb skyward, "He smokes 'em!" There were shout-outs to *Potemkin*, *Inherit the Wind*, the Marx Brothers, Kierkegaard, and *Wide World of Sports*.

Even with preproduction planning in full swing, in February Allen found time for a profitable stand-up engagement at Caesars Palace in Las Vegas. Diane Keaton was waiting in the wings for him every night as he stepped off stage. Then he made a quick trip to Europe with Charles Joffe to map out a foreign release strategy for *Take the Money and Run*. Reluctantly, he agreed to tour Europe the next summer, promoting his first picture in overseas markets.

In April, Allen and Keaton visited New Orleans for the Jazz and Heritage Festival, an annual celebration of music and culture with multiple jazz concerts. Allen sat in "with a group of veteran New Orleans jazzmen led by trumpeter Punch Miller," wrote John S. Wilson in the *New York Times*, "who later admitted he didn't know who Woody Allen was but that his clarinet playing was in the authentic New Orleans tradition."

In early May, after New York casting and decision-making, Allen and his team departed for Puerto Rico, where they would shoot the "San Marcos" exteriors. Jack Grossberg, who had handled the location logistics and proved an asset on *Take the Money and Run*, was promoted to producer. Again, Howard Storm would serve as assistant director and Allen's stand-in. Marvin Hamlisch returned as composer. Ralph Rosenblum would function not only as the editor but as associate producer of the film. Cameraman Andrew M. Costikyan was a Hollywood outsider Allen knew from Chicago, where Costikyan had shot documentaries, commercials, and low-budget features.

In New York, Allen worked with casting director Marion Dougherty and her associate Juliet Taylor. He had already introduced the habit, when casting, of focusing on "the look" and "vibe" of actors, meeting them quickly, studying their faces to see if they conformed to the image he had in his mind for the characters, and interacting with them stingily. He sought people who personified the characters he had written. In Puerto Rico, with the help of local casting agent Vicky Hernández, he rounded up amateurs and professionals. The better-known Spanish-speaking cast members would include Mexican-born Carlos Montalbán, familiar from Savarin Coffee commercials, who plays the generalissimo; onetime bathing-suit model Naty Abascal, from Seville, Spain, as Mellish's terse guerrilla fling; and among the Puerto Ricans, Jacobo Morales as Esposito, the rebel chieftain.

Like the actors who came before him and many hundreds to follow over the years, Morales suffered through an uncomfortably brief interview with the director in which Morales was greeted with "reserved politeness." Allen barely said nice-to-meet-you, told Morales nothing about the role he was up for, didn't even ask the actor to read any dialogue from a script. Dismissed with a few words, Morales left with "slightly bewildered" disappointment, only to be chased down in the parking lot by an assistant who handed him pages and told him the part was his. The Puerto Rican arrived on the set having memorized his scenes. "What impressed me most about Woody," Morales said, "was his calmness, his ability to give precise and simple instructions. And his willingness to take the opinions of others into account."

One day, as Allen blocked a scene with guerrillas sitting on a rocky beach, Morales suggested the actors try their lines standing up. Allen, after thinking it over, agreed. Another time, filming a different scene, Allen said he didn't care for the dialogue he had written and suggested Morales improvise. "Yikes, improvise!" thought the actor with his lines memorized, "and in English." Then Morales got carried away, making "irrelevant" changes. Allen interrupted him sharply: "Let's go back on script!"*

The San Marcos scenes depicting the nation's capital and jungle surroundings would all be shot in Puerto Rico, including the inspired opening of *Bananas* outside the presidential palace, where El Presidente has just been assassinated. Allen crafted this funny scene expressly for Howard Cosell, making good on his vow to insert the sportscaster into the movie as a surreal version of himself. Cosell would play the rat-a-tat "color man" during the "live on-the-spot assassination," who entreats "one last word [from the victim] before he expires."

If Allen worked efficiently and less expensively than most directors, he also accumulated mounds of extra footage of jokes and scenes he'd inevitably forgo during editing. "If he thought he needed one hundred and fifty jokes in an hour and a half, he wrote and photographed three hundred," Ralph Rosenblum recalled. The footage that never made it into *Bananas* included a scene "in which government troops disguised as a rumba band were cha-cha-ing through the jungle to launch a surprise attack on the rebels," wrote Rosenblum, and a "technically complicated" sequence involving "three fighter planes loaded with phony explosives" that dump their load on a "sleazy South American comic" pretending to be Bob Hope and entertaining the guerrillas, all part of an elaborate ruse. "Sensational on the set," both sequences were dropped from the final cut. "Because Woody's comedies are based on a continuous stream of jokes and skits," said Rosenblum, "a larger than usual portion of our editing work entails a search for the moments that work and a careful weeding out of the ones that do not."

The triple-threat writer, director, and star stayed at the Sheraton in Old San Juan, sharing a suite with Diane Keaton, who did not have a part in the

* Although he had considerable experience before acting in *Bananas*, Morales, like Walter Hill and Howard Storm before him on *Take the Money and Run*, would take inspiration from Allen and emerge as a filmmaker—becoming one of Puerto Rico's distinguished stage and screen directors.

film. During his spare time and on weekends, he labored on the script for a new stage play. Corresponding with his friend Mary Bancroft in New York, Allen said he had "two-thirds" of it finished and missed the city, "despite all its problems . . . the best city in the world." Puerto Rico, alternatively, he found "unusually wretched."

Although Louise Lasser appeared only in the New York scenes of *Bananas*, she was invited to visit Puerto Rico and check out the operations. Crossing paths with Keaton, Lasser felt she was competing with the new girlfriend for her ex-husband's attention. Allen couldn't stop talking about how much he adored the woman who'd helped doom their marriage. "Diane is America's greatest actress," Allen crowed. "Diane is the greatest companion I ever had." He was "awful to me and flaunted Keaton," Lasser recalled. On the other hand, she understood why Allen might prefer Keaton. "There's *disturbed* disturbed, and there's *cheerfully* disturbed," Lasser recognized. "I was always *disturbed* disturbed. Whereas Keaton was *cheerfully* disturbed for him."

After Puerto Rico, Allen finished up in New York with filming that included other elaborate sequences destined for the cutting-room floor. One highlight was set at Columbia University, where El Presidente Mellish/Allen delivers a speech exhorting the campus crowd to revolution. Black radicals denounce him as a "honky," however, and El Presidente barely survives a bomb assassination attempt, emerging from the rubble of the blast in sooty blackface. The black radicals then mistakenly embrace Mellish as a soul brother. "It was one of those things that never made the transition from paper to the screen," Rosenblum recalled dryly.

Lasser was playing the role of Mellish's politically conscious girlfriend Nancy, a philosophy major in college—like a certain previous Allen sweetheart named Harlene. Nancy finds something strangely missing from their romance. True, Mellish is short, ugly, and bad in bed, but it isn't *that*—it's something she just can't put her finger on. During the editing, the right ending for the film proved elusive again. Allen and Rosenblum found the bookend by returning to Mellish's problematic love life and bringing back color commentator Howard Cosell. Mellish has married Nancy and will now make love to her "live," à la the *Wide World of Sports*—or the assassination of El Presidente earlier in the movie. Mic in hand, Cosell reappears to voice the blow-by-blow of Mellish's triumphant return to Nancy's bed.

Their lovemaking is a torrid tussle resulting in a "cut eye," in boxing vernacular. "I've never seen action like this!" Cosell drawls. "He's not the worst I've had—not the best—but not the worst," Nancy/Lasser avows in a postcoital interview with Cosell, as the credits begin.

Lasser was never more bewitching than in the role that Allen fashioned for her as a postdivorce mea culpa. Her daffy comic touch and sweet chemistry with Allen would be on fond display in some of the film's most fluid scenes. One way in which *Bananas* outshone *Take the Money and Run* was in the improved love story. One can't read Allen's memoir without feeling his passion for Lasser and the anguish in their relationship. Although Allen left Lasser behind in his career, he also brought her along in ways. Her mother, the suicidal interior decorator; the suffocating WASP family with painful secrets; the perfectly ordered home that ticks like a time bomb—Lasser's life story was embedded in many Woody Allen scripts. Above all, perhaps—coinciding with the settlement of Harlene's lawsuit—he abandoned the "ugly girl" jokes forever. Drawn to beautiful neurotic women in private life, increasingly he'd write parts for actresses who evinced beautiful faces and shapely bodies, but the female characters were "ugly girls" inside—promiscuous, tortured, imploding. Like Lasser.

THE POSTPRODUCTION CONSUMED the second half of 1970, with Allen arriving at the Manhattan mixing studio daily at exactly 8:58 a.m., according to Ralph Rosenblum, eschewing "the morning ritual of coffee and conversation" with the "room full of sound engineers, sound editors, and assistants in the mix." Allen dove into work, avoiding any small talk or friendly handshakes. "Those he gives—watery handshakes, no grip in them at all—seem to be moments of torture during which he won't know what to do with his eyes." The director avoided snacks and took "paltry lunches," often "no more than a glass of club soda." Allen probably would have preferred to edit *Bananas* "for twelve hours a day, seven days a week," Rosenberg said, "with nothing but short, carefully timed meal breaks until the job was done. Socializing, schmoozing, kibitzing are anathema to him."

On camera, however, Allen was comfortable schmoozing with Dick Cavett, and even while editing he gave high-paying stand-up performances at Caesars Palace in Las Vegas and the Playboy Club in New York. He squeezed in a repeat role as a fanciful expert on history and science for the Saturday morning "educational" children's series *Hot Dog*, produced by old Tamiment friend Frank Buxton. And in October the clarinetist made his "professional debut," in the words of the *New York Times*, leading a seven-piece jazz band at Barney Google's on East Eighty-Sixth, with Marshall Brickman, currently the head writer for Cavett, on banjo and bass.

For a month at Christmastime, while Keaton was away in California, Lasser moved in with Allen. His annual income had risen above $1 million for the first time in 1970, and with that money he installed his parents close by in an Upper East Side co-op, while also acquiring a winter getaway for Martin and Nettie Konigsberg near Miami Beach. His mother retired from her bookkeeping. His sister, now Mrs. Letty Aronson, and her husband, both of them public school educators, lived with their family nearby on the Upper East Side too.

Also at Christmastime, the completed *Bananas* was screened for privileged parties. "Afraid that viewers might not respond freely if they knew he was present," Rosenblum said, "Woody hid under the control console, a desk-like structure in back of the Movielab screening room, while I gave the rough-cut speech. He emerged when the lights went out, stayed to hear the reaction, and then disappeared again just before the film ended."

The public had to wait until late April for the second Woody Allen comedy, with its opening credits punctuated by rifle shots and Marvin Hamlisch's Latin-infused music. Continuing what was already the release pattern of his pictures, *Bananas* was given premieres at the Coronet on Fifty-Ninth and Third in New York, and two weeks later at the Fine Arts in Westwood in Los Angeles, followed by a gradual national distribution, counting on good reviews and word-of-mouth. In time *Bananas* would be shown simultaneously in thirty US theaters, many more than was the case with *Take the Money and Run*, and in June the movie peaked at number three at the box office.

Critics chuckled at the nutty presidential palace dinner with a string orchestra playing invisible instruments; at Mellish's deli takeout order to feed the hungry jungle guerrillas ("Cole slaw for nine hundred!"); at the comandante cum dictator declaring, in his inaugural address, the banana republic would henceforth be re-branded as Sweden and all citizens were expected to change their underwear every half hour; at the New York courtroom climax, with a Black Power mama, purporting to be a disguised J. Edgar Hoover, testifying against Mellish. Mellish interrogates himself, angrily denouncing his unjust arrest as "a travesty of a mockery of a sham." The reviewers did not always praise Allen's directing, although he had made strides and the picture was intelligently varied in its staging and composition—perhaps because they were laughing too hard. Meanwhile, Allen the actor made the most of his protuberant nose, big eyeglasses, rubbery face. *Bananas* was "the wildest piece of comic insanity since Harpo, Groucho, and Chico climbed Mount Dumont," said *Newsweek*.

UA prodded Allen to travel and publicize the movie, dishing out interviews at a junket whose location was switched from Houston to New Orleans, so Allen could mingle at the Jazz and Heritage Festival for the second year in a row. This time he played clarinet with several bands at the festival: his own seven-piece unit from New York; Turk Murphy's Jazz Band from San Francisco; and the Galvanized Washboard Band from New Haven, Connecticut. Howard Cosell had brought Allen to the Galvanized Washboard Band's Thursday night shows at the Red Coach Grill in New Haven. Allen sat in and Cosell made "learned comments about each tune we played," recalled tuba player Art Hovey. Turk Murphy and the Galvanized Band both were booked for festival performances.

Most mornings when in New Orleans, Allen set the alarm for 6 a.m. and jumped up to prowl the streets "absorbing jazz history." He played his clarinet in the afternoons with the Galvanized Washboard Band in the basement Economy Hall Club of the Royal Sonesta Hotel. At night he was likely to be found listening to the Preservation Hall Jazz Band, whose dynamic clarinetist, Albert Burbank, was among his musician idols. The Galvanized Washboard Band, with Allen sitting in, joined in the event's climactic concert, which featured the eighty-four-year-old trombonist Kid Ory, who was headlining the festival's tribute to ailing jazzman Louis Armstrong.

The publicity minitour was capped by Allen's *Tonight Show* appearance with Diane Keaton. Allen and Keaton made sure to mention *Play It Again, Sam*, which was due to be filmed later that year in San Francisco. The late-night talk show with Johnny Carson was a kind of national coming-out for the couple—ironically, considering they no longer cohabited, and their relationship, although warm, was increasingly platonic.

••

BANANAS QUICKLY OUTPACED the success of *Take the Money and Run* and, eventually, in terms of revenue, Allen's second comedy as director would rank among *Variety*'s Top 25 highest-grossing films of 1971. Excitement about Allen built more gradually in Europe. *What's New Pussycat?*—not really a Woody Allen film, per se—had struck gold in France and Italy, but neither *Take the Money and Run* nor *Bananas* attracted wide bookings in France outside Paris. The farsighted Jack Rollins and Charles Joffe pushed Allen to make foreign promotional appearances and send his films to international festivals for the added cachet. Almost two years after *Take the Money and Run* was first shown in the US, Allen flew to Paris on behalf of 20th Century–Fox, which was among the studio entities that divided up the foreign territories for distribution of Allen's first and second screen comedies as director. He visited Stockholm, Vienna, Amsterdam, and ultimately the Taormina Film Festival on the island of Sicily, screening *Take the Money and Run* for Italian cinephiles.

His attitude toward publicity could be grudging, and more than once that stance yielded sour interviews defeating their intended constructive purposes. But Allen was also conscientious about self-advertising. Joffe hovered behind Allen at the Hotel George V in Paris for his first sit-down with Mary Blume, an *International Herald Tribune* correspondent. In the early days Joffe often sat in on the press encounters and gave notes to Allen for betterment afterward—as he used to do to hone the comedian's stand-up performances.

Allen told Blume he was not looking forward to his European travels and especially not the Taormina stop in Sicily. "I hate resorts," Allen explained. "I hate the heat. I hate film festivals." Almost immediately regretting his bluntness, Allen added, "I'll do whatever I'm supposed to do. I don't know what it is, and I don't care as long as they get me back." During the *Herald Tribune* interview Allen announced his next movie project—which had thus far escaped mention in the trade papers—that is, his next film as director following the job of "acting only" in *Play It Again, Sam*. Allen said he planned to make a free-flowing adaptation of Dr. David Reuben's best-selling *Everything You Always Wanted to Know About Sex* But Were Afraid to Ask*. Blume asked, "Is sex funny to Americans?" Allen answered, "They'll laugh twice as hard because of the repression."

Allen approved an itinerary of places he wished to visit. In Stockholm, where he could revel in the milieu of Ingmar Bergman, *Take the Money and Run* had disappointed everyone locally by not doing the "expected business," in *Variety* argot. However, Allen laid the groundwork for *Bananas* and won the Swedish press over—as he usually did—with his humor and humility. In Vienna, where *Take the Money and Run* had performed surprisingly well—even better, according to *Variety*, in neighboring Hungary—Allen did likewise. He made a pilgrimage to the Sigmund Freud Museum, housed in the onetime apartment of the father of psychoanalysis, whose influence over Allen rivaled Bergman, Groucho Marx, Bob Hope, and whoever was next in ranking.

The Rollins-Joffe agency had lobbied hard for Taormina and, in the last week of July, Allen found the hilltop town on the eastern coast of Sicily arid and dusty. Worse, he discovered *Take the Money and Run* had been entered in some kind of "Festival of the Nations" subcategory of competition. Although his movie went over well—winning a festival laurel, along with two other US-produced pictures, John Erman's *Making It* and the rock documentary *Mad Dogs & Englishmen*—Allen hated the idea of any contest, and he vowed to avoid festivals for the foreseeable future. In the next decades, Woody Allen films would be dispatched to a handful of the most prestigious European festivals, but always assigned a noncompetitive status and without Woody Allen himself attending. He'd remember ancient Taormina when he got around to making *Mighty Aphrodite*, however.

Mainly to please the Rollins-Joffe agency, upon returning to New York Allen changed planes and embarked on a whirlwind trip to another resort destination—Tahoe City, Nevada. He was slowing down as a comedian, with less frequent appearances, but he had agreed to a week of stand-up. His personal management team had invested in the new Kings Castle Hotel gambling casino and resort on the shore of Lake Tahoe, and Rollins-Joffe had enterprisingly booked their client list into the resort lounge to inaugurate its first summer of operation. Through Rollins-Joffe, Allen had many small investments, including shares in Kings Castle. Yet he was not keen on the western trip. Driving from the airport on a forbidding road toward Kings Castle, the limo driver stopped the car and told Allen "we were at the most beautiful place in America," the comedian recalled. "All those mountains and lakes. I couldn't wait to get out of there and feel concrete underneath my soles."

Quietly tagging along was Diane Keaton, still not a well-known face in the motion picture industry, nor any kind of celebrity to the larger public. However, Keaton had just finished her scenes in the movie that would catapult her to fame: as the WASP girlfriend of Michael Corleone, portrayed by Al Pacino, in *The Godfather*. Keaton knew Pacino from early acting classes, but during the production they had reconnected and when making the *Godfather* sequels they'd kindle an affair more intense and long-lasting than her romance with Allen.

Allen delivered his monologue at two late shows nightly at Kings Castle. Between sets one evening, shortly after finishing "a romantic dinner with my girlfriend," as he told Craig Modderno, a young journalist following the comedian around, Allen pivoted toward his responsibilities onstage. "I just don't want to be funny anymore," he confessed wistfully to Modderno. "I don't want to do this tonight." Allen showed the journalist "a trick of the trade," a gold watch he pulled from his pocket toward the end of his act. "When I open the watch before I do the punch line," he explained, "I can see how much time I still have onstage." If the show was running fast, Allen said, he'd add a few jokes after pulling out the gold watch, taking his final exit on the last punch line. Allen seemed downhearted. "You'll be fine," Modderno encouraged him, almost physically nudging Allen onstage before the expectant audience. "He didn't want to," Modderno recalled. "While he had a young Diane Keaton up in his hotel room, that wasn't the reason. He was really doing it for Jack and Charlie."

After returning with Keaton to New York, Allen saw or spoke to the actress on the phone nearly every day as the two prepared to leave for San Francisco and *Play It Again, Sam*. He also launched into the first draft of *Everything You Always Wanted to Know About Sex**. This time he'd work alone in adapting the book, without *Take the Money and Run* and *Bananas* collaborator Mickey Rose. Rose had moved to Hollywood with television offers, and it was a major parting of the ways for the onetime high school chums, who never again would share a script credit. Keaton was more Allen's sounding-board nowadays, and the actress helped get the ball rolling on *Everything You Always Wanted to Know About Sex** one night when, together in bed, the couple watched Dr. David Reuben on *The Tonight Show*. Johnny Carson asked the author if sex was dirty, and Dr. Reuben answered with Allen's line from *Take the Money and Run*: "It is if you do it right."

Carson followed up by observing that probably the only person in the world who could successfully turn Dr. Reuben's bestseller into a movie was Woody Allen.

Allen was hooked. United Artists picked up the rights from actor Elliott Gould and producer Jack Brodsky, who had taken an early option on Dr. Reuben's sex manual when it was first published in 1969. The book had sold one hundred million copies worldwide, but Gould and Brodsky couldn't figure out how to make it into a movie. Mainly Allen laid claim to the title and subject matter of sex—the *terroir* of his comedy. He said in many interviews he never met Dr. Reuben, nor did he read the book, although—as with *Don Quixote, U.S.A.*—he turned the pages. The film's chapter titles derived from the book's question-and-answer format. For the first and last time in his career Allen adapted another person's work, nonfiction to boot.

As Allen wrote, his screenplay became a surreal parody of Reuben's book that bore no resemblance to the bestseller. He divided the script into eight vignettes—think of each as a "little souffle," or "minimovie." There was the tale of a medieval court jester who gets his hand stuck in a queen's chastity belt; one about the Armenian herdsman, enamored of a sexy sheep, whose infatuation is transferred to a Jackson Heights medical practitioner; an Italian subtitled lampoon of Antonioni with a horny Italian husband and his frigid signora, whose erogenous zones are activated only in public spaces; a portrait of a respectable suburbanite who is a secret cross-dresser; a rabbi confessing his peccadilloes on a "What's My Perversion?" television quiz show; two black widow spiders and their mating habits; a mad scientist who incubates a giant, terroristic breast; and the misadventures of a sperm brigade. Besides directing, Allen planned to star in five of the eight vignettes, each of them introduced by a provocative title-card question, such as "What Happens During Ejaculation?"

IN EARLY OCTOBER, Allen flew to San Francisco, taking along with him the working draft of *Everything You Always Wanted to Know About Sex**. *Play It Again, Sam* would be his second movie to be shot in the Bay Area. In addition to pairing him onscreen for the first time with Diane Keaton, who arrived separately from Los Angeles, the production reunited Allen with the other Broadway stars—Tony Roberts as his best friend, and Jerry Lacy as Bogart. Susan Anspach, who'd made a splash as Jack Nicholson's lover in *Five Easy Pieces*, was fourth-billed as Allan Felix's ex-wife, who dumps the couch potato in favor of a road trip with an Aryan biker.

The stage version took place in New York, but America's largest metropolis promised only "headaches, [problems with] permits, rival unions badgering a producer, small irritations like scouting for locations and people on the street interrupting shooting," in the words of Herbert Ross, the film's director. *Sam*'s modest production budget could be better managed in the Bay Area, where, incidentally, Allen was popular because of club appearances, and *Take the Money and Run* and *Bananas* still drew moviegoers in second-run theaters.

20th Century–Fox, the studio that originally optioned the Broadway play, had swapped the property out to Paramount because, as Peter Bart wrote in his book *Infamous Players*, "Allen's ambitions were not only to star in the adaptation but also to direct it." Richard Zanuck, the president of 20th–Fox, was ambivalent about Allen as either the star or director, according to Bart. "They didn't want me in it until *Bananas* started doing well," recalled Allen. Bart, who was working as a low-level Paramount executive, said he and Robert Evans, the head of the studio, were "very fond" of Herb Ross, a one-time dancer and choreographer who'd helmed the big-budget *Goodbye, Mr. Chips*, *The Owl and the Pussycat*, and *T. R. Baskin*—the last, in 1971, for Paramount. "I thought that Woody was making pictures for a relatively small audience," wrote Bart. "Herb Ross was making them for a much wider audience." After trading the rights to *Emperor of the North Pole* for *Play It Again, Sam*, Bart informed "Woody's very protective handlers" that "Ross's work was more accessible and that he would bring a wider audience to the film. Woody reluctantly agreed." 20th–Fox producer Arthur P. Jacobs followed the project to the new studio.

Paramount did not want a Woody Allen–ish free-form comedy. The studio wanted the proven Broadway hit faithfully transferred to the screen. To that end, most key scenes were carried over intact from the stage play, with only a few embellishments that could be called cinematic. The biggest change, in Allen's adaptation, was a climactic taxi race to the airport that would furnish action and strike a parallel with the ending of *Casablanca*. Location managers found a San Francisco corollary for what had been the main stage set—Allan's Greenwich Village apartment—and exteriors that were counterparts to the Manhattan parks and museums. One memorable scene in the movie would be Allan's encounter with a comely art-lover staring thoughtfully at a Jackson Pollock painting hanging in a gallery of the San Francisco Museum of Art. Nancy (Keaton) has urged Allan (Allen) to be more proactive in his hapless love life. When Allan asks the pretty art-lover what she discerns in the abstract painting, she exhales with a blast of despair and existentialism. Allan presses on with his cause: "What are you doing Saturday night?" She: "Committing suicide." He follows up, undeterred: "Then how about Friday?"

Allen worked happily under director Ross, and reprised scenes with Keaton, Roberts, and Lacy that repeated much the same dialogue they'd memorized during the Broadway run. He and Keaton went out nights, one time dining in Chinatown with Barbra Streisand, whom Allen knew well from the nightclub circuit and who was in the Bay Area making *What's Up Doc?* On another night, with Keaton again in tow, Allen played clarinet with Turk Murphy's band at Earthquake McGoon's. Tennessee Ernie Ford jumped up to croon a few tunes.

The company finished the San Francisco work in November, and the principals shifted to Los Angeles for interiors on Paramount soundstages. This was probably the Thanksgiving when Allen met the entire Hall family, sitting around a table with a giant turkey as the centerpiece. The fabled Grammy Hall (prejudiced against Jews as well as other ethnic groups and minorities) was there. So was Keaton's mother, Dorothy; her father, Jack; her young brother, Randy; and her two younger sisters Robin and Dorrie, both as fetching and eccentric as oldest sibling Diane. Then after the last scene was shot for *Play It Again, Sam*, Allen saw Keaton off at the airport, just as Allan Felix does with Linda in the film; then the entertainer lingered in Los Angeles, where he planned to shoot the bulk of *Everything You Always Wanted to Know About Sex** at MGM shortly after the new year.

"A fact that people don't realize is that when Keaton and I began working together in the series of films I wrote for her," Allen said in his memoir, "we had not been romantically involved for several years." Call it about two years they were romantically together during *Play It Again, Sam*—the play through to the film. In Los Angeles, Allen met with West Coast Creative Management Associates liaison Sue Mengers. Mengers wanted to host a dinner with Allen as her star guest. Knowing Allen and Keaton were no longer a couple—Allen told Mengers and anyone who privately inquired—she was determined to play matchmaker for a new girlfriend.

Born in Germany to a Jewish family that fled Hitler, Mengers was raised in the Bronx and started out in New York talent agencies as a secretary, the lowest rung of the ladder, before climbing up at CMA to become a hard-charging dealmaker for the likes of Steve McQueen, Paul Newman, Robert Redford, Barbra Streisand, and the most sought-after New York–based filmmakers such as Mike Nichols and Sidney Lumet. In 1969 Mengers moved to Hollywood to head up the West Coast offices of CMA, soon to merge with International Famous Artists and become ICM, where apart from continuing as a powerhouse agent she thrived as a fabulous party-giver, a.k.a. "Capital S" or "Hostess Sue." Sam Cohn, Allen's ICM agent based in New York, had known Mengers when she was an MCA receptionist, and Cohn always closed the big deals for Allen. But Mengers "would not hesitate to pitch an actor or actress to me who was wrong for my project," Allen told Mengers biographer Brian Kellow. "She epitomized the kind of Hollywood agent's mentality and ethics and scruples, and I had no interest in dealing with her on business. Everything she ever said to me about my films was always that I was a genius. She only said, 'Oh, this film is so great, you're so brilliant, and so-and-so would love to meet you.' "

Still, Allen got a kick out of Mengers. "Boy, was she funny," *Vanity Fair* editor Graydon Carter said at the time of her death in 2011. Allen, the reluctant laugher, chuckled whenever Mengers was around. He also liked her boyfriend—later to be husband—handsome Belgian director Jean-Claude Tramont. In the 1970s and 1980s, Allen often socialized with Mengers, or with her and Tramont, in Hollywood, New York, and Paris.

Mengers contrived to sit unmarried "sparklies"—her word for celebrities—next to each other at her dinner parties. One of her quirks was feeding items about her matchmaking, "sparklie" parties, and social outings to Joyce Haber, a *Los Angeles Times* columnist who was syndicated nationally. Mengers let Haber know she was contriving a dinner date with Allen and Tuesday Weld, another one of her clients, at her house on Bel Air Road. A gorgeous blonde who'd started out as a child performer, Weld had matured into a respectable dramatic actress. "Woody is going to pick you up," Mengers told Weld. "I was on one of my exercise sprees," Weld recalled, "and he came in his limo to pick me up and I said, 'Let's walk up there to

Bel Air.' He said, 'Walk? Are you kidding?' He had the chauffeur follow us for forty-five minutes. You don't walk in Bel Air."

Woody + Weld would not work out beyond their first date, but Mengers wouldn't give up. She loved having Allen as a guest attraction whenever he passed through Hollywood, as he'd frequently do in the years ahead. She tried to match him with other "sparklies" among her friends and clients. One time his matchup was Carol Lynley, another nubile blonde who'd started out as a child model; on another occasion it was the pre-*Superman* Margot Kidder. Mengers prided herself on her A-list—Barbra Streisand seemed omnipresent—and crossing paths with Allen at one of her shindigs was waifish *Rosemary's Baby* actress Mia Farrow. "We were introduced," Allen recalled, "made some polite small talk, the earth didn't move, and we went our separate ways."

WHILE ALLEN WAS in Hollywood, Random House published *Getting Even*, his first volume of "little souffles"—seventeen pieces, ten originally seen in the *New Yorker*, with a few new ones especially for the book, including *Death Knocks*, his one-act spoof of *The Seventh Seal* with an aging dress manufacturer playing gin rummy with Death. Returning to New York, Allen found himself with extra time and energy to burn. The West Coast filming of *Everything You Always Wanted to Know About Sex** would not begin until January. After he spoke to Jack Rollins and Charles Joffe, the management team delegated Sam Cohn to contact National Educational Television (NET), the public broadcasting organization that operated New York's WNET. NET executive Julius Kuney was surprised to receive a phone call from Cohn with this message: Woody Allen had a few weeks of "free time" on his schedule. He'd like to create a special for public television. Allen would accept scale ($135) for his acting, and he'd throw in his writing and directing for free. Would public TV care for a television special that would say "a few things about the current occupants of the White House"?

Yes! Kuney hurried to a meeting with Allen, Cohn, Rollins, and Joffe at the Rollins-Joffe offices on West Fifty-Seventh Street. What Allen had in mind "was a central character who was a White House insider," Kuney recalled, "an oversexed power broker named Harvey Wallinger, someone the president counted on for his every move. Woody would play the role himself, and it didn't take too much imagination to identify the role-model as Henry Kissinger." Speaking in the "softest of tones," Allen had a few questions for the NET official. "Are we talking about an hour?" Yes, Kuney improvised. "I'll try and get the script to you as quickly as I can," Allen said.

About ten days passed, Kuney recalled, before "a completely articulated script" arrived by courier, "deceptively simple, but yes—funny." The script bore the title "Men of Crisis," with the subtitle "The Harvey Wallinger Story," implying the special was but one episode of an ongoing series. (Another of the "men" to be profiled in a future episode teased onscreen was Israeli prime minister Golda Meir.) Loosely modeled on the *March of Time*–style newsreel Allen loved, the mock-documentary was packed with "barbed staccato scenes" showing Wallinger (played by Allen) reminiscing about Richard Nixon—the good old days of the Kennedy-Nixon debates, Nixon's loss in the California governor's race in 1962, his 1968 campaign victory over Democratic candidate Senator Hubert Humphrey, and the president's current tenure and misdeeds in the White House. Vice President Spiro Agnew, Secretary of Defense Melvin Laird, Attorney General John Mitchell and his wife, Martha, were among the contemporary figures who would be represented by actual footage or imitators. In the case of Nixon, it was both: Nixon ringer Richard M. Dixon would play the thirty-seventh president.

Marion Dougherty helped line up the many unbilled players who agreed to small parts, including two actresses who were not very hard to persuade and who, like everyone else, were willing to work for scale: Diane Keaton plays the current Mrs. Harvey Wallinger, and Louise Lasser is the previous Mrs. Wallinger, reminiscing about a relationship "something less than the wonderful first experience every girl should have." This would be the one and only time the two girlfriend-actresses were in the same Woody Allen production—a television show.

Over ten days at Christmastime, Allen shot the mockumentary, "most of it on the campus of Columbia University, during a series of cold winter days," Kuney recalled. "We were trying to replicate the look and feel of Washington, and we generally found it. We even staged a McCarthy-like hearing in the moot courts" of the law school. Although overtly political, much of the comedy was absurdist. "We decided to bomb Laos for a very strategic reason," explains Wallinger at one point. "We did not like the way it was spelled." The real footage mixed in with the fake reality was heroically scrounged from archival sources by NET staffer Dell Byrne, who'd return as a stock researcher for *Zelig*. Her detective work found a clip of Senator Humphrey, for example, in doctoral robes for an honorary degree, stumbling across a stage, and even better, giving the finger to the camera. She also found a shot of Agnew playing a clumsy game of doubles and conking his partner with his serve. "When Woody saw it," Kuney said, "he roared, one of the few times I ever saw him laugh aloud."

The editing was rushed because the PBS special had to be in the can by the end of December when Allen was due to depart for California. There was no time for remedial filming, and the promised hour of airtime got "honed down to 50 minutes, 40 minutes, and finally 25 very comedic minutes," as Allen discarded "whole scenes without the slightest compunction." Kuney began to grow concerned about the brevity of the show, but Allen, "amiable as a pussycat," volunteered to stop by affiliate KCET in Los Angeles and "fill in the remaining minutes of the hour by discussing some of his ideas about comedy and satire." PBS could promote the whole package—the mockumentary followed by the Allen interview—as "The Politics of Woody Allen."

After Allen left for California, Kuney submitted the special to the oversight board of the new Corporation for Public Broadcasting (CPB), which recently had taken over administration of NET and PBS. Public television was "notoriously conservative," Kuney recalled, and most affiliates avoided the type of satire that made fun of Boy Scouts, Harvard Law School, Catholic nuns, and sexual prudishness, as Allen typically did—and as he did in *The Harvey Wallinger Story* too. "I like sex, but it must be American sex," Wallinger/Allen tells the camera. "I don't like un-American sex." The Nixon administration put pressure, "inferred and direct," on PBS and the major networks to stay away from criticism of the government. As a later lawsuit revealed, Clay Whitehead, director of the White House Office of Telecommunications Policy, and presidential adviser Patrick Buchanan led the charge to kill controversial shows. *Wallinger* was a hot potato for the CPB board.

Among the sticking points was the moment when a nun, Sister Mary Elizabeth Smith, recalls the divorced Wallinger as one of DC's most exciting bachelors: "He's an unbelievable swinger, a freak." The footage of

Humphrey holding up his middle finger also bothered the public television overseers, as did the scene where Wallinger discloses that "Dick is out of the country a lot and sometimes Pat [Nixon] calls up and asks me to come over, but I say no." The CPB board asked Allen to delete those scenes, but he said no. One week before the February 21 air date CPB canceled the much-ballyhooed special because of "problems with equal time, personal attack, the fairness doctrine, and the subjective issue of good taste," according to a spokesman. "Woody stopped taking my phone calls the moment" the decision was made, Kuney recalled. "We brought it to public television," executive producer Charles Joffe told the *New York Times* when the news broke, "because we thought there, we would have complete freedom. But we don't intend to make a big issue of it."

The controversy lingered in the press. Sophisticated in style, breezily witty in content, a rough blueprint for the future *Zelig*, *The Harvey Wallinger Story* never made it on the air. Allen's public television special was shelved and forgotten, and the banned original was archived at New York's Museum of Broadcasting, now the Paley Center for Media, until copies began to resurface at retrospectives and on the Internet in 1997.

THE PREPARATIONS FOR *Everything You Always Wanted to Know About Sex** were more daunting than for Allen's previous comedies because it was as though he was planning eight different movies with separate casts and visual demands. Allen intended to use the anthology format to experiment visually. His camerawork, lighting, and scenic design had been effective but crude for *Take the Money and Run* and *Bananas*. The episodes of his third picture would allow him to adopt a more consciously artistic style. Almost as though he were a young copyist studying the art on the walls at the Prado, he could practice the aesthetic of masters by imitating them.

Once again, he had decided to shoot the comedy in eight parts in Hollywood because of regulations and logistical costs that might impede him in New York. Despite the distraction of *The Harvey Wallinger Story*, he kept to schedule, calling the first take on the second picture in his United Artists contract on the Monday morning after New Year's weekend. Allen kept to his one-movie-annually bargain "like clockwork," UA official David Picker marveled.

Jack Brodsky was on the job as producer. Behind the camera was the skilled, Los Angeles–based cinematographer David M. Walsh, whose offbeat credits included *I Walk the Line* (1970) and *Evel Knievel* (1971). Production designer Dale Hennesy, who had just finished *Dirty Harry* with Clint Eastwood, but whose earlier sci-fi *Fantastic Voyage* (1966) would come in handy for sequences like "What Happens During Ejaculation?", was the unsung hero of *Sex**, formulating a dissimilar look for all eight segments. Ralph Rosenblum, who'd begun his career assisting the pioneering documentarist Robert Flaherty, had committed to a documentary project, so Brooklynite Eric Albertson, who'd also worked on *The Harvey Wallinger Story*, was hired to edit *Everything You Always Wanted to Know About Sex**.

Walsh and Hennesy gave further proof of Allen's developing visual sophistication. "This is the first picture where I cared about anything but the jokes," Allen told *Cinema* magazine after the filming. "Well, maybe not. In the very first picture I did I cared about some things other than the jokes too. I cared about the shots, the compositions, and I found that when I got down to editing it, nothing mattered at all except the jokes."

And as a hint of his move away from traditional Hollywood soundtracks, Allen hired Mississippi-born jazz guitarist Mundell Lowe, a composer and orchestrator for movies and television. The first thing Allen and Lowe discussed was underscoring the opening credits with Irving Aaronson and His Commanders's version of "Let's Misbehave" from 1927. The song would be played over close-ups of a milling herd of bunnies—as in "breed like . . ." or "fuck like bunnies." Original music was recorded after the photography in New York, with Belgian jazz artist Toots Thielemans on the harmonica solos. The director left Lowe alone, "just sat in the control room and smiled and enjoyed the music." Lowe found Allen "a dear man but a weird little dude."

Assisted by casting director Marion Dougherty, Allen edged away from his "no stars" philosophy and toward marquee names, including celebrities playing "themselves." Frizzy-haired Gene Wilder, on the verge of big stardom—*Young Frankenstein* was still on the horizon—would play the sheep-lover in "What Is Sodomy?" John Carradine, a lantern-jawed face familiar from countless Golden Age movies, was cast as the deranged scientist whose sex research creates a monstrous mammary. Classically trained Lynn Redgrave, from the famous theatrical clan, would portray the medieval queen whose chastity belt stymies a lecherous court jester, played by Allen. Shakespearean Anthony Quayle was her king. Tony Randall, from Broadway and television—Allen knew him from *Hooray for Love* in 1960—and fast-rising Burt Reynolds were lab scientists playing it straight in the Kubrick-like NASA sperm-mission sequence, with Allen as the cowardly sperm. A versatile character actor Allen always had liked, even before *Don't Drink the Water*, Lou Jacobi was rewarded with the lead in one of the mini-movies, playing the middle-age Babbitt who secretly disports in women's wear.

Because, as the director said in interviews, Diane Keaton did not want to make it seem as though she appeared only in Woody Allen pictures—*The Godfather* had not yet been released—he bypassed Keaton in favor of former wife Louise Lasser. In the Italian-subtitled "Why Do Some Women Have Trouble Reaching Orgasm?" Lasser would play Allen's frigid newlywed, who gets turned on only in public venues, and she would also portray his insect partner in "What Makes a Man Homosexual?" which involved black widow spiders demonstrating their mating ritual. As filmed, their in flagrante delicto concluded with the female of the species devouring the male—Allen, of course—who was also glimpsed, at the end of the vignette, as a wispy scientist of indeterminate sexuality voyeuristically observing the copulating insects through a microscope.

The marquee names would be supported by an East Coast contingent of New Yorkers, including Allen friends, who were fitted to fleeting parts. The lesser-knowns saved a little money in the budget and also gave Woody Allen films their singular flavor. The Canadian actress Erin Fleming was Groucho Marx's companion, and she was also "The Girl" who is the intended sperm recipient in "What Happens During Ejaculation?" Jack Barry, Regis Philbin, Robert Q. Lewis, Pamela Mason, and Toni Holt were actual regulars on television game shows, and they'd form the panel of the scratchy black-and-white "What's My Perversion?" The guest star of "What's My Perversion?" is a naughty rabbi who savors being flagellated as his bored wife devours pork chops, and he'd be played by Baruch Lumet, the father of Allen's New York filmmaking colleague Sidney Lumet.

The January and February filming went by with scant press attention. Allen put a lid on the usual publicity, the first sign of the ultrasecrecy that would safeguard future "Untitled Woody Allen Projects." One reason to keep the press away from the set was that there were outlandish special effects written into a number of scenes, which caused unpredictable headaches and delays. For that reason, and because special effects drove up costs, Allen generally avoided gizmos and trick effects. One day, when photographing the breast-amok sequence in Agoura Hills, the huge artificial breast on a moving flatbed did not function properly for the cameras. An exasperated Allen grabbed his clarinet and walked off, plunking down on the grass and tootling away to becalm himself until the crew sorted matters out. Allen needed his clarinet and daily phone talks with his New York analyst, who around this time—another switch—became Dr. Kathryn Prescott, his first female psychiatrist. The crew had "trouble getting him to come back and get on camera so they could get the shot," recalled Mundell Lowe.

At the same time, because *Everything You Always Wanted to Know About Sex** was entirely "made in Hollywood," and Allen was working outside his usual comfort zone with famous non–New Yorkers, the filming occasioned the first accounts of a man who chose to say little or nothing to most actors, even if, on set, they harbored questions about their lines or their performances. "He said three things to me while we were shooting," recalled Wilder. " 'You know where to get tea and coffee?' and 'You know where to get lunch?' and 'Shall I see you tomorrow?' Oh, and there was one other thing—'If you don't like any of the lines, change them.' " Wilder's acting in *Everything You Always Wanted to Know About Sex** was nonetheless almost universally praised.

Returning to New York in March, Allen plunged into the editing of his latest film. *The Godfather* opened in theaters that same month—it was the American movie event of the year, if not the decade—proving a box office triumph and an instant contender for Oscars. The better-known actors overshadowed Diane Keaton in her drab role, but she had signed up for the sequels and *The Godfather* made her a rising star. One positive side effect of Keaton's breakthrough in *The Godfather* was that it paved the way for *Play It Again, Sam*, released in May.

While *Play It Again, Sam* looks relatively staid nowadays compared to the more demented comedy of *Take the Money and Run* and *Bananas*, it holds up as a traditional romantic comedy, albeit with a Woody Allen–ish unhappy ending that replicated *Casablanca*'s. The cleverness of the *Casablanca* conceit, the agile performances—with Allen and Keaton cute and funny together—and the professional gloss won over most reviewers. "A marvelous movie," the Allen-friendly Judith Crist declared on the *Today Show*, worth "a million laughs." Richard Schickel, writing in *Life*, agreed: "I laughed inordinately." Vincent Canby in the *New York Times* untypically complained about the occasional "nastinesses" of the script* and found *Play It Again, Sam* to be "the least anarchic of Allen's films" thus far. If Allen had directed the film, Canby added, he would have given it more verve.

Allen was already in the habit of leaving behind work that was done, and *Play It Again, Sam* was someone else's film anyway. He was busy with the postproduction of *Everything You Always Wanted to Know About Sex**. Indecisively, he kept shuffling the order of the eight minimovies. The spider-mating was still in the version screened late in the spring at Judith Crist's "Woody Allen Weekend" in Tarrytown on the Hudson River, where Allen was accompanied by Eric Lax, taking notes for his future books. Journalist Lea Lane was among the audience at the screening, and she thought the spider-mating comedy fell flat. "Better to leave it out," she wrote. "We attendees all agreed." Allen reluctantly cut the segment.

As was stipulated by his agreement with UA, only a few officials had read Allen's screenplay and most people in the company knew next to nothing about his adaptation of the sex-manual bestseller. The executive corps gathered for the first screening with Jack Rollins, Charles Joffe, and the usual sprinkling of Allen's friends and supporters. "I had never seen anything quite like it," recalled David Picker, "nor had anyone else. Certainly not Arthur Krim." Krim had initially recoiled from *Bananas*, because the movie departed so greatly from the *Don Quixote, U.S.A.* book, and also because he was "very

---

* Among those "nastinesses" was Linda (Keaton) musing about the pleasures of rape, dialogue that would be cited in future MeToo briefs against Allen when, in the aftermath of his breakup with Mia Farrow, his work was combed over for transgressions against women. The scene, performed as bantering comedy, was straight from the play, which ran for a year on Broadway at the height of the Women's Liberation Movement without any known protests against the lines:

LINDA: I think if anyone ever tried to rape me, I'd pretend to go along with it and then right in the middle pick up the nearest heavy object and let him have it.

(BOGART and ALLAN look troubled)

Unless of course I was enjoying it.

(Both men brighten)

ALLAN: They say it's the secret desire of every woman.

LINDA: Well, I guess it depends on who does the raping.

much concerned," in Eric Pleskow's words, "about the irreverence vis-à-vis certain religions" that was manifested in Allen's first UA comedy—the pokes at United Jewish Appeal, a favorite Krim charity. After Krim watched *Everything You Always Wanted to Know About Sex**, recalled Picker, UA's senior figure was even more appalled by certain sequences, "particularly the ['What Happens During Ejaculation?'] episode where all the actors [including Allen] are dressed in white, playing sperm cells." Krim asked Picker "to tell Woody to cut the scene. I refused," recalled Picker. It reached the filmmaker's ears that Krim regarded the sperm sequence as "kiddie porn." The sperm brigade stayed in *Sex**, but Krim's negative reaction rattled Allen's confidence in his future with UA. Allen later wrote Picker: "Thanks for having faith in me."

The Motion Picture Association of America's (MPAA) restrictive R rating, the first for a Woody Allen movie, also bothered UA, though it meant zilch to Allen. He kidded it in interviews: "R for Rabelaisian." The director detested and ignored the ratings system now and for the rest of his career. Still, it was another gulp for UA.

Critics didn't much care for the movie either, when Allen's third big-screen comedy was released in August, a fast six months after the filming had wrapped. The director had kept the running length under ninety minutes by deleting the least effective episode—the spider-mating tango—but he couldn't fix the other sketch-length chapters, which were of a piece, by eliminating the worst jokes in the same way he winnowed lesser scenes from *Take the Money and Run* and *Bananas*. Charles Champlin in the *Los Angeles Times* detected "a stale, sour raunchiness" in the picture. "I just didn't think it was funny," Archer Winsten wrote in the *New York Post*.

The performances were uneven; Louise Lasser was wasted. The four vignettes anchored by Allen were the best, most critics agreed. Auteurist Andrew Sarris said only one chapter—Allen as the cowardly sperm—was "brilliant," while the other six fell "in the disappointing range between tasteless and tedium." Stanley Kauffmann, in the *New York Times*, found the sperm brigade funny too, but the rest "truly depressing" yawns or sniggers. The box-office-minded *Variety* wrote: "The episodes on sex perverts [i.e., quiz show] and sexual clinics [John Carradine's segment with zombie boy scouts poised to rape Heather MacRae] may strike some viewers as tasteless, but the greater number are likely to find them the high points of this disappointing feature."

Allen had been right about one thing: repressed Americans loved the sex comedy. UA shrewdly waited for *Play It Again, Sam*, only a modest hit, to clear theaters before releasing the second Woody Allen picture of the year. *Everything You Always Wanted to Know About Sex** broke house records at small theaters across the nation, including the "class" houses of the Little Carnegie and the Coronet in New York. The weaker but more titillating people pleaser proved "magnum cum laude" (per *Variety*) out of the gate. *Everything You Always Wanted to Know About Sex**'s teasing title and bestseller link drew crowds until the picture surpassed Allen's previous movies in grosses and wound up, in *Variety*'s ranking, as the tenth-highest exhibitor's rental of 1972.

Allen had consolidated his growing stature as a director even if, in retrospect, he assessed *Everything You Always Wanted to Know About Sex** as "unworthy" of him. "While it had some funny things in it," Allen said later, "it was not my finest moment." Dr. David Reuben, author of the book, was perhaps its most astute critic, assessing the hit movie as "a sexual tragedy. Every episode in the picture was a chronicle of failure, which was the converse of everything in the book."

ALLEN BROUGHT DIANE KEATON along for Jerry Lewis's show at Brown's in the Catskills at the end of the summer. There were no hard feelings between Lewis and Allen. Comedians were a special category of human beings for Allen. There was much to admire about the hardworking Lewis who, like Allen, killed himself for laughs.

By summer's end, Allen had finished a draft script of the next Woody Allen project, crafting his first lead role for Keaton. But *Sleeper* would not go before the cameras for another nine months, and other decisions weighed on him. Allen felt he had reached a crossroads in his career as a comedian. He'd keep a three-week engagement at Caesars Palace in Las Vegas in October, paired with onetime Rollins-Joffe client Harry Belafonte. However, his stand-up gigs, nowadays for substantial pay at deluxe hotels, along with the occasional charitable or political benefits, had been stretching fewer and further in between. Allen would spend New Year's Eve 1972 at the Deauville Star Theatre in Miami on a bill with songstress Edie Adams. He doled out interviews in his hotel room, strewn with script pages. The small black case containing his clarinet was conspicuous.

Allen gave little hint he was winding down his stand-up career. He said he was always jittery before spieling his monologue. ("Onstage," *Miami Herald* entertainment editor John Huddy reported, Allen "seems to reek of anxiety.") Performing in new places "always takes me a while to get adjusted, to get oriented," he explained. Stand-up was fun, the hardest thing was "the pressure" for laughs. When it worked, when the applause and laughter came, he felt more alive than when he did anything else. Making movies took more time and effort but was "overwhelmingly the most rewarding." Asked if he was concerned that, one day, the fame-bubble would burst and live audiences would stop being entertained and stop laughing at his jokes, Allen answered without hesitation: "I worry [more] about what will happen if I die before getting the chance to complete any of the ten thousand ideas and projects I have in my head."

That New Year's Eve in Miami would be his last paid stand-up show, and he'd never make a fourth comedy LP. He had become a household name in comedy, but he believed—and always said—his success was modest and mixed. His humor was an acquired taste. Not enough people acquired it. "I was all over the press, really making it, yet interestingly never drawing," Allen wrote in his memoir. "Club owners would book me eagerly. The only problem was not a lot of people came to see me." All his recordings, praised by critics, "sold weakly," he added. "I would plug the albums on TV, on radio, in press interviews. Still, very modest sales."

Sometimes in years ahead he would wax nostalgic about his time as a stand-up comedian and muse about making a comeback. Jokes from his old monologues often cropped up in Woody Allen films, sometimes versions of the same joke in several different movies. There are variations of "My parents stayed together for forty years, but that was out of spite" in more than one of his pictures, and as John Leonard pointed out, reviewing *Side Effects* for the *New York Times*, Allen liked that riff "so much he uses it in two stories" in the collection.

He'd resort to veteran stand-up comics for reliable casting in many films; reliable because the comics would toy with their scenes and tinker with the dialogue Allen had written for them. The profession would be referenced here and there in his pictures, notably in the deli scenes of *Broadway Danny Rose*. Allen himself would play a stand-up comedian once, in *Annie Hall*, but he never treated the profession at length, procedurally or autobiographically, as for example Martin Scorsese tried to do with *The King of Comedy* starring Robert De Niro. For that matter, there is no Woody Allen movie set in the gambling and hotel capitals of Miami or Las Vegas, where he logged time. Atlantic City, in *Celebrity*, offered the gambling, but not the stand-up.

By early 1973 Allen was all but done with television as well. Once he had been everywhere on TV, trying anything: singing with a dog, dancing in top hat and tails, boxing a kangaroo. After his eponymous 1969 special, however, he began his withdrawal from the commercial networks. The *Tonight Show* and Dick Cavett appearances tapered off. Nor, with another asterisk for *Celebrity* and *Hannah and Her Sisters*, did he make any picture—nothing truly autobiographical—about the small-screen medium he knew well and said he despised.

QUITTING STAND-UP COMEDY was indicative of deeper concerns. His next project, *Sleeper*, would be Allen's third and last picture for United Artists in his current contract. The studio's hesitation over *Everything You Always Wanted to Know About Sex** gave him pause, and nowadays other studios, knowing the UA contract was short-lived, wooed him. Some offered starring vehicles that would be directed by other people; others were, like *Sex**, invitations to Allen to adapt established properties, starring and directing. Allen couldn't decide whether he was principally a writer, director, and star of Woody Allen films—or whether he might write, direct, or star *only* in his or someone else's movie, depending on circumstances. Must he always do all three at once?

Allen respected Sidney Glazier, who helped produce *Take the Money and Run* and now tried to coax him into a project based on Alan Abel's *The Great American Hoax*, which would tell the story of the prank organization Abel founded called SINA, or Society for Indecency to Naked Animals. Allen also liked and trusted director Herbert Ross and was open to partnering again with him, perhaps starring in the dark romantic comedy Ross was planning based on an Arnold Schulman script called "Alimony." Allen believed Ross "really and truly enhanced" *Play It Again, Sam*, "made it funnier" with his script suggestions, his staging, deepening the characters and enhancing the performances, including Allen's, which had not been a hallmark of either *Take the Money and Run* or *Bananas.* Allen had learned from Ross. Their talks went far enough for Warner Bros. to announce "Alimony," with Ross directing and Allen as the star, for 1973, after his UA contract was up.

What he was drawn to most, however, was a murder mystery being developed by 20th Century–Fox with writer Reginald Rose and producer Martin Poll. The story of "Death Is No Excuse"—a working title Allen hated unequivocally, so it was fast abandoned—involved illicit lovers, one a married woman, whose cuckolded husband is slain. Hollywood publicist John Dooley had crafted a promising treatment, and Rose, a scenarist Allen admired, wanted to collaborate with Allen on the full screenplay. A towering figure of the Golden Age of "live" television, Rose had won Emmys for his original dramatic teleplays for *Studio One* and *The Defenders* and was Oscar-nominated for his most famous credit, *Twelve Angry Men*, the 1957 Hollywood version of one of his "live" TV dramas. Producer Poll had important credits, including the Oscar-nominated *The Lion in Winter.*

As well as cowriting, Allen would star in and perhaps direct the murder mystery. Corresponding eagerly with Rose, Allen shared confidences about the crossroads he was facing in his career. He said he was tired of making merely amusing comedies. Personally, Allen told Rose, he'd prefer to make serious, important dramas with human lost-soul stories. United Artists had temporized over the first such project he had proposed, "The Jazz Baby," a rejection that still stung. Nobody wanted to see Allen act in or direct a drama, it seemed.

Jack Rollins and Charles Joffe kept telling Allen to be patient and wait for the right moment in his career to strike out in a radical direction. Anyway, the partners couldn't agree between themselves. Rollins thought a funny Woody Allen film ought to be all-out funny—"Funny-funny"—while a serious Woody Allen film should be an all-out drama—a "drama-drama," or ultra-drama. Joffe thought Allen could make a drama sprinkled with comedy: a comedic drama, or dramatic comedy. Allen himself was uncertain of the right balance. The murder mystery Rose was pushing sounded like it might be the forward path to a suspense spiced with laughs. That is what Allen brooded about as 1972 came to an end, and as he plunged into preproduction on *Sleeper*—his most daring comedy yet, costarring the actress and onetime girlfriend who would follow him down the mingled comedy-drama path, and cowritten by the friend who in time would help Allen find the perfect mixture.

MARSHALL BRICKMAN LIVED in an Upper West Side apartment just across Central Park from Allen. Residing nearby and playing weekly in their old-time-jazz band, Allen drew closer to the musician turned writer whom he'd first met in a Greenwich Village club ten years before. Boyhood pal Mickey Rose had been the right partner for cowriting the joke-laden *Take the Money and Run* and *Bananas*. Brickman was more cerebral. His humor was inflected with history, science, politics. He was a funny talker and good listener, whose comedy writing and show business acumen had been honed working for Johnny Carson and mutual friend Dick Cavett.

The collaborators had made a false start in the late 1960s, writing "The Filmmaker," a script about a jaded documentarist with a sideline in pornography. The documentarist is saddled with a frigid fiancée. He meets a schizophrenic woman while filming in a mental institution, falls in love with the warm-hearted schizoid, and leaves his fiancée at the altar. "The Filmmaker" never crystallized, however, and their script was jettisoned.

Allen and Brickman began talking about another story during their customary long walks in the afternoons, often broken up with a sweet stop at Häagen-Dazs. They concocted a Rip van Winkle kind of tale about a Greenwich Village nebbish named Miles Monroe—his last name in honor of New York Knicks guard Earl "The Pearl" Monroe—to be played by Allen. A Happy Carrot health food restaurant proprietor by day and a jazz band clarinetist at night, Miles undergoes a minor ulcer operation that ends badly. Doctors are forced to cryogenically freeze his body for two hundred years. The nebbish wakes up in a dystopian future in which America has become a police state ruled by a Great Leader. Robots—domestics and dogs—abound. Sex and drugs have been futurized. Just think of it: Miles/Allen hasn't had sex for two hundred years—"204 if you count my marriage." A renowned poetess with the inspired name of Luna, as full of herself as her Rod McKuen–influenced poetry is dopey, first enslaves Miles, when he is in robot guise, then frees him to join, *Bananas*-like, an underground revolt brewing against the Great Leader. The "Rebels Are We" song from *Bananas* is reprised.

At first, Allen and Brickman envisioned a two-part epic—complete with intermission—the first half to depict the tribulations of Miles in contemporary New York, with part two tracking his adjustments to the autocratic future. But the projected epic with intermission was unwieldy, and their focus narrowed to part two only. Uncharacteristically for Allen, the friends wrote together "line by line in a room," recalled Brickman. They filled their futuristic comedy with silent-era pratfalls, bizarre machines, and all the topical and obscure allusions now expected from a Woody Allen movie: mentions of Walter Keane, the supposed painter of big-eyed children,* and Albert Shanker, president of New York's United Federation of Teachers; glimpses of Billy Graham and Howard Cosell. There would even be a brief spoof of *A Streetcar Named Desire* with Allen as Blanche DuBois and Diane Keaton dead-on as Brando. The collaboration yielded Allen's most disciplined narrative yet, his "most coherently incoherent" script, as Charles Champlin later described *Sleeper* in the *Los Angeles Times*.

After the screenplay was completed, Allen spent the first months of 1973 in preproduction and casting. Here with *Sleeper*, as with his other films, the director demonstrated the same knack for choosing personnel for behind the camera as he did when picking leads and supporting players. Further advancing the development of Allen's aesthetic, for the first time the director employed a talented couturier, Joel Schumacher, for the modernistic wardrobe that would complement the visionary production design of Dale Hennesy, who had proven his futuristic eye with *Everything You Always Wanted to Know About Sex**. Other returning team veterans included cameraman David M. Walsh, supervising editor Ralph Rosenblum, and producer Jack Grossberg.

The casting, after the flawed experimentation of *Everything You Always Wanted to Know About Sex**, reverted to "no stars," with the hunky WASP John Beck, whose experience was mainly in television, third-billed as Erno, the rebel leader who is Miles's rival for Luna's affections. Comedians Myron Cohen and Jackie Mason would voice the Jewish-tailor robots who bicker over Miles's fittings. The only substantial role other than Allen's—the only other main character on constant view—was Luna, the renowned poetess

* Miles Monroe has apparently gone into his deep sleep before the revelation that Keane's wife, Margaret, whom he had divorced, was the true artist behind the widely reproduced series of paintings of big-eyed children. Tim Burton's 2014 film *Big Eyes* tells the story.

of greeting cards. After joining the subversives, Luna rescues/kidnaps Miles for the dangerous deed of assassinating the Great Leader. They learn that only the leader's nose has survived an explosion, and they must pose as cloning surgeons to carry out their mission. From the outset Luna had been conceived as a showcase for Keaton.

Allen began directing *Sleeper* in late April. The fourth Woody Allen movie would prove his most logistically demanding to date, with the cast and crew initially hopscotching among multiple locations in western states. The camerawork began in Colorado to take advantage of the gleaming avant-garde buildings set amid majestic natural backdrops that Allen had noticed in *Architectural Digest*. He'd use the UFO-shaped Sculptured House, designed by Charles Deaton, which is perched on a high point of Genesee Mountain near Denver as the home of Luna (it is also the home of the Orgasmatron). I. M. Pei's National Center for Atmospheric Research building, which was located along the Flatirons in Boulder, served as the picture's robot-repair laboratory. After Colorado, Allen also shot a handful of scenes in Monterey, California, and in the Mojave Desert, before moving into leased space at Culver Studios, David O. Selznick's onetime domain in Culver City.

Culver City is a small suburb south of Hollywood, encircled by Los Angeles, and Allen's office on the studio lot was situated in a cottage that was Clark Gable's during the making of *Gone with the Wind*. At night the writer, director, and star of *Sleeper* went home to Beverly Hills, although not to the mansion he originally had rented. On his first night in leased splendor, Allen woke up to the sound of birds fluttering noisily around the trees that beautified the grounds outside his bedroom. With a BB gun he had picked up on his travels for some reason, he shot at the birds, but it was dark outside, and he couldn't tell if he hit any of his targets. When he went back to bed, the birds resumed their infernal noise. In the middle of the night Allen got up and checked into the Beverly Wilshire Hotel. He didn't blame the BB gun, which he kept as a prize possession. Later, in New York, living in his penthouse, he aimed at the "filthy, dirty pigeons" on his patio overlook. "Rats with wings," Sandy Bates calls them in *Stardust Memories*, although the epithet was not original to Allen.

Allen told this anecdote to Jean vanden Heuvel, when he met the writer at one of Sue Mengers's parties during the filming. Vanden Heuvel was the chic daughter of Jules C. Stein, the founder of the Music Corporation of America (MCA), the forerunner of Universal Studios. Her sister was the New York socialite Susan Stein. As a young woman, Jean had moved to New York and married the man who gave her a new last name—William vanden Heuvel, then a special assistant to Robert Kennedy. Now she was divorced. Vanden Heuvel had carved out a career as a writer specializing in oral histories, often working in collaboration with George Plimpton. She had interviewed William Faulkner for the *Paris Review* and reputedly took him as a lover. Vanden Heuvel was developing a book about the ill-fated Warhol superstar Edie Sedgwick, which she would publish in 1982 under the byline Jean Stein. Despite this pedigree, meeting the "sparklie" Woody Allen at Mengers's soiree, vanden Heuvel was intimidated and desperately tried to make conversation. "I asked Woody if he liked California," vanden Heuvel recalled. "He seemed annoyed by the question but answered it. He said he hates it in California. He said it with such vehemence that it sounded like he thought he was in a torture chamber."

Indeed, *Sleeper* tortured Allen. There were problems with misbehaving robots, malfunctioning props, complicated stunts, "in some cases the failures . . . so repeated—wires and towropes snapping or flying into the frame," as Ralph Rosenblum recalled, "that after innumerable takes he moved on and left perfection to the editing." Rebuilding sets and remaking props added to the mounting takes and protracted filming. Above all, Allen felt dissatisfied with "his own performance," which fell below "his exacting standards," said Rosenblum.

His solace was Diane Keaton. Allen had not directed *Play It Again, Sam*, and now, with this script and his staging, he devised a "grand entrance" for his leading lady, an idea left over from his grounding in the theater. He devised the entrance so Keaton looked comical, covered with "green stuff on her face," yet eye-catching from the first. Outtakes show Allen collapsing in laughter as the star played his scenes with the actress who was his friend, especially the one in which the rebels, desperate to jog the sleeper's dazed memory, re-create a Sunday dinner in Flatbush circa 1962, with Keaton as Nettie and with exaggerated Brooklyn Jewish mannerisms.

The filming problems spurred overages that superseded the ironclad $2 million ceiling stipulated by United Artists. By the time editor Rosenblum arrived in Hollywood in August, Allen "was several weeks into fifty-one days of additional photography, which had already consumed the $350,000 fee he was due as coauthor, actor and director." *Sleeper* would prove the rare Woody Allen picture to exceed its specified budget, ultimately costing some $3.1 million. For comparison's sake, however, most major studio productions, in 1973, entailed far greater expense. *The Sting* ate up an $8 million budget, for example, while another Oscar winner, *The Exorcist*, cost $12 million. Rosenblum's presence on the West Coast was early and unusual in that Allen typically did not prefer to piece together footage until after photography was completed. But UA had him committed to a Christmas release with a "firm deadline [that] could be broken only at serious cost to the company, the director, and the relationship between the two," in Rosenblum's words. Grossberg had prevailed upon Allen to give Rosenblum a head start. With an outward show of calm, Allen met with Rosenblum and grudgingly consented to let him begin. Rosenblum saw how Allen "was beginning to show signs of impatience" with his team, including Grossberg. *Sleeper* would mark the end of his fruitful association with the producer.

"As often happens with Woody's films," Rosenblum recalled, "we rejected some of the most impressive material, frequently causing more pain to me than to the author himself." This, for *Sleeper*, included a Mojave Desert dream sequence with humans as chess pieces, and with Allen as a white pawn about to be sacrificed to a malicious black knight, who has just proven his mettle by bashing another pawn with a mace and chain and then stabbing his sword through the pawn's body. "You're next," croaks the knight, as the panicked Allen flees across the chessboard, knocking over the chess pieces and pausing to feel up the black queen before racing off into the desert, with the black knight pursuing. The desert sequence was magnificent, "one of the finest pieces of cinema Woody has ever created," but "it failed to fit the needs of *Sleeper*'s plot and comic pace." Out!

Returning to New York in September, Allen and Rosenblum and their team continued to whittle away at the surplus footage. "Keeping with practiced routine," in Rosenblum's words, the editor objected to Allen's planned ending, which was "a corny visual gag." Dutifully the filmmaker returned to Hollywood, stealing Keaton away from *The Godfather: Part II* for a one-day Sunday shoot, in which the actress had to "switch back into her role as the light-headed Luna on her day off," as Rosenblum recalled. Allen filmed new dialogue, lightly romantic badinage that would provide a better fade-out.

The rough cut of *Sleeper* was two hours and twenty minutes; the final length, one hour and twenty-nine minutes. The concise length of Allen's film was a fixation. "Each movie has a certain amount of time the audience can give to it," Allen informed Eric Lax. "A scene may be funny where it is, but if the movie is too long overall, you lose the audience at the conclusion."

For the eventual soundtrack Allen had a surprise in store. He flew to New Orleans and played clarinet with the Preservation Hall Jazz Band, recording traditional jazz and Dixieland for the background score. "Considering he is white, Jewish, from Brooklyn and half the age of the rest of the band—who are black, Baptist and from New Orleans," wrote Lax, covering the recording session for the *New York Times*, "his playing is given high marks by jazz cognoscenti." Later, Allen would record additional tunes with his New York combo, which now went under the moniker of the New Orleans Funeral and Rag Time Orchestra. The movie's music was exhilarating, perfectly complementing *Sleeper*, but don't go searching for the usual soundtrack album made available for sale to fans of a movie. Allen was against that kind of product merchandising, on principle. His near total switchover to traditional jazz, classical music, and opera on his soundtracks, along with, frequently, standards from the American songbook usually dating to pre-1953, the year of his high school graduation—music sometimes newly interpreted because of rights and costs—began with *Sleeper*. Allen possessed an exhaustive knowledge of the music of yesteryear. He had all the variant recordings in his private library. This way he could score films with music he loved, without hiring a composer and risking displeasure.

Allen's old-music, no-soundtrack policy drove United Artists crazy. During the 1970s and '80s, almost every Hollywood movie boasted a soundtrack led by a catchy theme song, whose vocalizing was assigned to an established pop star, with hopes the single and LP would become chartbusters. Hit movie theme songs and soundtracks added substantially to profits. But Allen in his career would approve very little soundtrack merchandising. It was just one more pill the maverick UA agreed to swallow to produce Woody Allen films.

HOWEVER, ALLEN WAS uncertain of his future with United Artists after *Sleeper*—the last in his three-picture deal with the studio. That is why he agreed to go ahead with what 20th Century–Fox trumpeted, in full-page *Variety* advertisements, as "A Woody Allen Film" for 1974, in collaboration with Reginald Rose. Allen made a solemn promise to 20th–Fox officials—"Partially written and partially oral," according to later court records—to collaborate with Rose on the script, and direct and star in the murder mystery, which had a new working title: "Kill the Critics." "Kill the Critics" was meant to follow *Sleeper.* Jack Rollins, Charles Joffe, and producer Martin Poll were attached to the putative agreement, which detailed billing, salaries, and start-up payments to all the named parties for travel and preproduction. The month that *Sleeper* wrapped up filming in Hollywood, 20th–Fox opened offices on its Century City lot for Hackenbush Productions, Allen's California business entity.

The 20th–Fox agreement gave Allen increased power and control over his filmmaking. He was guaranteed "final cut" of "Kill the Critics," for example, and approval of all "still" photographs taken for publicity purposes. He alone would decide any censorship issues raised by the MPAA. Hackenbush Productions was guaranteed a percentage of all gross receipts. Allen's main salary and perks were not yet cemented in contract language, though, and Allen took less money up front for the project than the producers—just a token sum.

20th–Fox paid $50,000 to Rose for an outline and first draft in consultation with Allen. Their collaboration would be largely epistolary and by telephone, since Rose lived in London, but the contract acknowledged Allen as the senior creative force, empowered as the star and director over the older veteran.

Their script talks began early in August, as *Sleeper* was still filming, with Allen residing at the Beverly Wilshire Hotel and taking French lessons on weekends for another project he hoped to shoot in Europe in 1974. Considering his reputation as a serious, biting dramatist, Rose submitted an initial story outline that surprised Allen with its many comedic digressions. Moreover, the comedy was not very funny. Rose posited Allen as a New York independent filmmaker who couldn't get his boldest opus yet into theaters. "Kill the Critics" referenced the murder victim, a harsh critic of the filmmaker's uncommercial oeuvre. The outline even posited a few scenes to be set at the Cannes Film Festival, which took Allen, not a festival fan, aback. Everything about the outline was unrealistic—"Too zany" and "too superficial," Allen complained to Rose as politely as possible—while insisting that he was "crazy" about the story overall and his concerns were "minor, and I mean minor."

Allen's series of multipage, single-spaced letters to Rose, typed on Beverly Wilshire Hotel stationery, asked for more drama and reality, less "zany" comedy in "Kill the Critics." In his correspondence with Rose, which continued for several months, Allen carried on an internal debate about the amount of comedy he might inject into a drama, and vice versa. He said he wanted to move toward more realistic filmmaking, but not neorealism in the Italian sense of the word. Maybe a naturalism. He also wanted to lend seriousness to his persona and find a balance between the comedic and dramatic in characters he played. Still, he wanted to avoid on-the-nose autobiography.

Allen picked at the small gambits and larger problems in the outline. He pointed out the clunky plotting and clichés. He said he was uncomfortable with the lead female character that, in Rose's story, his character was supposed to take to bed and fall in love with. "I feel we have all seen the 'girl under our noses' who is the absent-minded genius and is never appreciated until one day he steps back and realizes he loves her. I like women who attempt suicide a lot and can't have orgasms," Allen wrote Rose, "if the film's tone is to be real."

He scoffed at the film-director occupation Rose had devised for his lead character, with the character's big dream—a Cannes prize—as "totally unmeaningful to a mass audience." He mentioned parenthetically how much he disliked the character's name: Lionel. "It's announcing that we want to be funny with a guy named Lionel—not that his name must be utterly colorless, but Lionel is broad to me and suggests a little comic-prissiness." Allen never forgot a name he liked, nor one that he disliked. "Lionel, no son of mine is going to be named Lionel!" the father (Michael Tucker) in *Radio Days* declares, when sifting names for his wife's expected baby.

Any character he played in a picture, Allen cautioned Rose, ought to be "fictional naturally, but close to me in real life in certain ways." Rose, in an effort to tailor the story to the goofy side of Allen's comedic persona—fumbling with women and bumbling with devices as he'd done in *Take the Money and Run*, *Bananas*, and *Everything You Always Wanted to Know About Sex**—had fashioned the starring role as "more meek and milk-toasty than I am," in Allen's words, i.e., too much the fumbler and bumbler. Allen said his character ought to be more real, more adult; his character could be cynical or depressed, and perhaps he should be working at a trivial job to pay for therapy sessions. But it was essential his character demonstrate an "intelligence." Allen himself might not be "dynamite, but I'm also not a cretin," the star protested. Allen wanted Rose to appreciate the darker side of his persona: "I am not Julie Andrews but rather a nasty, wisecracking, sex-obsessed coward."

Allen insisted on more plausibility in Rose's plot. He told Rose he had been toying, with Marshall Brickman, on a similar murder mystery script that juggled comedy and drama. Allen proceeded, in his August 1973 correspondence with Rose, to relate the future story line of *Manhattan Murder Mystery* in some detail. "I live in New York with my wife," Allen narrated. "We are a modern, sophisticated (wisecracking?) couple, perhaps I work at an ad agency, she for Time Inc. Or whatever. It's Elaine's, East Hampton, P.J. Clarke's, the Thalia, apt. on East 74th St. in high rise, watching late movies on TV every night and two analysts.

"While at the incinerator, my wife meets a woman down the hall in bathrobe. They chat. . . ." An ambulance arrives a few weeks later. The wife has died of purported natural causes. The couple pay a condolence call on the husband. She glimpses vials of medicine not normally prescribed for heart problems. On and on . . . two single-spaced pages of meticulous plotting that would be reincarnated twenty years later.

Rose took the criticism like a champ, saying he would get back to work on a draft that would incorporate Allen's ideas and improve on the plausibility and his persona. Charles Joffe was concerned Rose might overdo the realistic tone and slight the comedy. You can always add the "funny" later, Joffe told Allen. Allen wasn't so sure. How much "funny" should there be in a movie intended partly as a serious murder mystery? Allen tried reassuring Rose. He flattered him, saying he had decided to partner with the older man because Rose could write "a terrific mystery" and "a much more serious script than I usually do because you can do that kind of thing and I can't."

Rose's first full draft arrived in New York in late October. Allen's character was now reconceived as a struggling children's book author with a day job as a floor clerk at F.A.O. Schwarz. The clerk meets cute with a married lady, who is shopping for toys for her young child. Although the clerk already has a neurotic girlfriend—attesting he is not a loser with women—he strikes up a friendship with the married lady. The two go for the customary walks in Central Park and pay visits to museums. Soon they launch into an affair. Then her husband—no longer a film critic, he was now an insurance salesman—is murdered under incriminating circumstances.

Allen reacted badly. He told Rose he detected "major problems" in the draft, owing to the fact the story was neither dramatic nor comedic enough to suit his needs. Mainly, the script was "too light," he complained, "too unreal almost, sometimes, silly." He wanted his romantic relationship in the story to be "between two, real, decent but troubled people," not the superficial, comedic types Rose had devised. "Either a film should be exclusively something for me (like one is for Groucho) or if it is a departure, it should be very far off." This "kept falling in the middle," and "as it stands now" the script would make "an amusing comedy . . . a solid picture," something like *A Touch of Class*, a romantic comedy Allen said he'd seen recently, which he found "very safe, uninspired, we've seen it before—always good because the formula is proven." Rose's script as it stood would be perfect for Gene Wilder, or Dustin Hoffman—the latter, among his paragons—but not Woody Allen.

"Charlie, Jack, and myself are groping," he wrote Rose sympathetically, while savaging the draft, "trying to break out of the usual type film I do, yet do it so it works. I don't think this type of thing is the answer."

Rose phoned Allen, and they spoke at length on several occasions. Undiscouraged, Rose vowed to go to work on heavy revisions, absorb the fault-finding and make the drastic changes Allen wanted to satisfy his qualms. At this point there was still optimism about the now untitled project, and Rollins-Joffe paid Rose an extra sum under the table for another draft above what was called for in his original 20th–Fox agreement.

But when Allen kept saying he didn't want to go "halfway" on a comedy or drama, and that the murder mystery had to be more dramatic and realistic, Rose dug in his heels. Rose brought up the Chaplin comparison, which he couldn't have known would make Allen squirm. "You've established a character as instantly recognizable, in its way as Chaplin's was in his," Rose wrote Allen, when submitting his revised draft in early December. "You've created that character brilliantly and audiences fall into fits laughing, even audiences which don't truly understand the sophisticated jokes and can't truly adapt to the wild situations. This character now exists so solidly that, in my estimation, the only way to begin to move it into another direction, even if only to see how it tastes, is to go 'halfway.' " Rose had kept some cuteness and contrivances in the new draft, and he aimed stubbornly for what he called a "halfway situation," a credible but amusing comedy-drama that he believed could be the transitional picture in Allen's career and lead to "something more serious in the future."

By the time Rose's revised draft arrived from London in December, however, the 20th–Fox murder mystery was already dead in the water. The main reason was Allen had lost confidence in Rose, while his own thoughts—and internal creative decision-making—raced ahead of his flailing collaborator. Rollins-Joffe intermediaries delivered the bad news: Allen no longer felt beholden to the project. It wasn't just the "halfway situation" Rose insisted upon writing. It was also because another project with serious overtones had suddenly emerged to compete with the 20th–Fox picture: a comedy-drama about 1950s blacklisting in television.

AFTER MONTHS OF equivocation, Allen began to act decisively, making moves that were partly prompted by United Artists finally waking up with a start. UA had been sending mixed signals to "Mr. Everything." In addition to the early consternation Allen had faced from the studio over *Everything You Always Wanted to Know About Sex**, Allen and studio officials went through a separate dustup in the fall over UA's attempt to sell *Bananas* to ABC for prime-time viewing, incorporating censorship cuts into the home broadcast that were mandated by the network. Allen rejected the cuts, UA was forced to rip up ABC's lucrative offer, and Allen decisively won the battle of *Bananas*. Implicitly, he won control over future TV sales of all his films.

Meanwhile, *Everything You Always Wanted to Know About Sex** had proved a resounding hit. After early screenings of *Sleeper*, studio officials predicted even greater success for the futuristic Woody Allen comedy.

In July, David Picker quit as head of the studio to set up his own autonomous unit producing films for UA. Picker's replacement, UA's new president and chief executive officer, was Eric Pleskow, a native Austrian and longtime foreign specialist for the company. Pleskow was even more gung-ho than Picker about Allen's future importance to UA, and he courted him assiduously, believing the next big Woody Allen frontier was the global market.

Arthur Krim, the senior UA figure who had waffled over *Bananas* and *Everything You Always Wanted to Know About Sex**, also swung hard back into Allen's corner. Krim regretted his earlier qualms and doubts. He crucially sided with Allen over the planned television censorship of *Bananas.* Although Pleskow was now the creative head of the studio—as Picker had been before him—the major UA decisions involving Allen would always go through Krim. With Krim and Pleskow united behind him, Allen's position was strengthened.

"After I left UA," Picker recalled, Krim "became the man Woody trusted most during his most fruitful years." Krim was "my biggest fan, my artistic sponsor, my personal friend," Allen corroborated in his memoir. More than that, some people thought Krim's relationship with Allen had a father-son quality, and even more so after Krim got married late in life to Mathilde Galland, a celebrated scientist and civil rights and AIDS activist. Getting on in years, the Krims remained a childless couple. Allen kept up friendships with both husband and wife, and reliably supported their charities and causes. In years to come, Allen would submit his scripts to Krim with another copy for Lehman Katz, the company's budget estimator. If Krim approved the script, which he always did, and Katz okayed the budget, Allen got the green light. No other filmmaker boasted the same freedoms and privileges from the studio. Why? "Woody's special," Krim, a militant for Allen, told people.

Setting their cap, UA officials offered Allen a four-picture contract, covering one a year for four years. The new contract, according to *Variety*, not only gave Allen veto power over television deals, it gave him a consensual clause over home video rights, whose future excited everyone in the entertainment business. Allen was empowered to supervise the packaging and content of his films for the home viewing market. He would take pride in being the only major American filmmaker of his generation to eschew the "extras"—deleted footage, director's cuts and commentary, interviews with the actors and director—these and other rote "bonuses" in VHS, Beta, LaserDisc, DVD, Blu-ray, and other home viewing iterations. "Extras" boosted sales and profits, according to conventional wisdom. Allen didn't care. His home editions *never* had such "extras."

His new UA contract even gave Allen a say in how his movies were shown on airplanes during overseas flights—i.e., no editing—because truncated airplane versions were among his pet peeves. Airplane sales were important auxiliary sources of revenue for studios and filmmakers, but UA made these and other concessions to Rollins-Joffe and Sam Cohn—always with Allen overseeing the fine print—including the filmmaker's right to approve any titles for his movies that had to be reworded for foreign consumption. While UA officials refused to confirm the industry scuttlebutt that Allen stood to earn 50 percent of all domestic monies after breakeven, Allen was believed to have carved out a share of the grosses and additional overseas allotments, which varied in value from territory to territory. Overall, *Variety* reported, Allen's new UA deal greatly "improved" upon the old one. "Most important element of Allen's new pact is that he had increased his artistic autonomy."

One key concession to "his artistic autonomy" was the studio's guarantee that he could direct one future picture without appearing on camera—a Woody Allen film without Woody Allen—which would not be a comedy. The contract stipulated Allen would write, direct, and star in three of the four movies, but the fourth—a serious drama—he'd write and direct only. Allen had decided he didn't need Reginald Rose for the realistic direction he wanted to pursue, nor for the drama-drama that the writer-director had been slowly building up to in his thinking. Internally at UA, the four were known as "Woody Allen #1," "#2," "#3," and "#4."

UA MADE ANOTHER rare concession: The contract was not "exclusive." Allen could appear in films for other studios if he was not writing, directing, and starring. His freedom as an actor was nonnegotiable, and it accommodated the prospect of "Alimony" (the Herbert Ross dark romantic comedy), the Reginald Rose murder mystery (although hopes were fast fading for that possibility), and above all the script that came to Allen in the fall of 1974, eclipsing the others. This script depicted the New York television world during the anticommunist hysteria of the 1950s. Walter Bernstein and Martin Ritt, a once blacklisted writer and director, both New Yorkers, won Allen over with their pitch that *The Front* was going to be a serious film about a serious subject—with laughs.

Soon, "Alimony" evaporated. When Allen then pulled out of the Reginald

Rose project, 20th Century–Fox sued, but Rollins-Joffe, bullish on their clients' rights, countersued. The litigation dragged on for years. From Rollins and Joffe, who first sued on his behalf over *What's Up, Tiger Lily?*, Allen learned to go to court at the proverbial drop of a hat. "Suit-happy," Mia Farrow once described him to his face. *Litigious*, he corrected her.

Sleeper, Allen's fourth comedy as writer, director, and star, went to theaters at Christmas. 'Terrific," rhapsodized Vincent Canby in the *New York Times*. "The comedy of the year," Judith Crist agreed in *New York*. "*Sleeper* establishes Woody Allen as the best comic actor and director in America," declared Roger Ebert in the *Chicago Sun-Times*. "The reviews were good," Allen wrote in *Apropos of Nothing*, adding (one of his never-ever exaggerations), "although it would be the last time I'd ever read a review or anything about myself."

Audiences concurred with the critics and swarmed to the riotous comedy, which was "loaded with throwaway literacy and broad slapstick," in the words of *Variety*, everything from Keystone Kops–like speeded-up action sequences to Allen slipping on a banana peel the size of a canoe. The futurisms—twinkle-toed robots, the Orb that delivers the ultimate high, and the Orgasmatron that is better than sex with an actual human being—were inspired. The strange gadgets, the individual whirlybirds and inflated hydro-vac suits, were as tacky as they were priceless. A Marx Brothers knockoff in many ways, *Sleeper* gave Allen the opportunity to come as close as he'd ever come to evoking the leering, cowardly Groucho, right down to replicating the mirror routine from *Duck Soup*. (For this film Allen also had Harpo's hair.) Keaton was his perfect sidekick, a thick-witted Chico, and beneath it all the picture worked as a screwball romantic comedy. The relationship between Luna (Keaton) and Miles (Allen) is flirtatious and coitus interruptus until their nose-assassination mission is accomplished. And then, from the Sunday reshoot ending, there is one of those teasing close-outs they did so well. Luna/Keaton asks the cynical Miles/Allen if he truly believes in anything, which prompts this final line from him: "Sex and death—two things that come once in a lifetime. But at least after death, you're not nauseous."

Miles/Allen leans in for the kiss. . . .

The box office returns stayed healthy for months until *Sleeper* wound up as the sixteenth-highest-grossing US movie of 1973. Overseas, especially in

France and Italy, the picture also proved a hit. Allen's first three UA movies had cost roughly $8.7 million to produce, grossed $36 million domestically and internationally, and returned immediate profits of at least $10 million. That was terrific money for the 1970s. When BuzzFeed, in 2013, tallied the grosses of every Woody Allen picture, adjusting the money for inflation, *Sleeper* stood tall at number five, with only three among Allen's top ten *not* released in the 1970s. Five of the ten (including *Sleeper*) were the downright UA comedies from the first half of the decade; the other four were *Bananas* (number eight), *Love and Death* (number six), *Everything You Always Wanted to Know About Sex** (number four), and *Annie Hall* (number one). UA, which profitably reissued *Sleeper* and Allen's other most popular comedies several times in the 1970s, had made "one of the happiest and smartest gambles in recent movie history," in the words of Steven Bach, a studio official who joined UA coinciding with Allen's new pact.

ALLEN ARRANGED TO visit Los Angeles to consult with Charles Joffe and UA officials around Valentine's Day in 1973, and with Sue Mengers's husband out of town he was the superagent's date for the evening at a closed-circuit telecast of the Muhammad Ali–Joe Bugner fight at the Playboy Mansion, hosted by Hugh Hefner. "Bunnies" and celebrities frolicked together in the Jacuzzi, some wearing skimpy swimsuits, others in the buff.

Returning to New York, Allen still made noises in interviews about a planned evening of one-acts called "Sex, God and Death" for producer David Merrick—but it was always "tentative," according to the *New York Times*, and would never eventuate on Broadway. The one-acts were not commercial enough for Merrick. Whatever play Allen had been scribbling on in Puerto Rico was set aside on his stack of scripts for the future.

Allen continued to pen his "little souffles" for the *New Yorker*. And every Monday he played clarinet with his jazz band, with Marshall Brickman on banjo, their gig now anchored at Michael's Pub on East Fifty-Fifth near Third Avenue. Onward, like the finest expensive Swiss watch, Allen ticked, although he took what seemed for him an inordinate amount of time in the first half of 1974 polishing the script for the next Woody Allen project. Diane Keaton, no longer his lover, was still his muse for stories and scripts. "She reads everything I do, and she's a great, natural, un-besmirched reservoir of judgment on it," Allen told interviewers. "She gives me an ingenuous, direct response, simple, unhostile and unpretentious." Keaton broadened his aesthetic imagination with her "utterly spectacular visual sense. I see many things today through her eyes, textures and forms I would never have seen without her. She showed me the beauty of faces of old people. I'd never been sensitive to that before. And there's a certain warmth and poignance associated with young women that I never would have seen without her. She's increased my affection, feeling, and understanding for women."

Whenever Keaton was in New York, they were spotted frequenting the places Allen itemized, in his correspondence with Reginald Rose, as typical haunts for a character he might portray in a film: like the restaurant Elaine's on the Upper East Side, which hosted glitterati from high society and the arts, with regulars that included Jacqueline Onassis, Tennessee Williams, Rudolf Nureyev, and Frank Sinatra; the regulars gave nourishment to paparazzi waiting outside, and perhaps it was better nourishment than was obtained by the clientele. "I often told Elaine," Allen wrote later, "that her food would have been turned down by the lost party on the Donner Pass." He and Keaton could be spotted at New York Knicks games; that season the Knicks made the playoffs, and tickets for the hoi polloi were scarce, but Allen had become a pricey season subscriber. The two went to movies, concerts, museums, and were glimpsed at a number of dance recitals. Keaton, who had benefited from dance lessons, encouraged Allen to enroll in Martha Graham's studio, and he stretched and twirled in Graham's classes. Less conspicuously, he and friend Dick Cavett took tap dancing tutorials.

During the summer Allen and Keaton flew to California. Allen met with Charles Joffe and turned up at another Sue Mengers dinner party, this time with Cher, Mike Nichols and his wife Annabel Davis-Goff, Herb Ross and his wife Nora Kaye, and producer David Geffen among the "sparklies." Keaton lingered in Hollywood when Allen returned to New York. He was flying to France in mid-August, to begin casting, preproduction, and location scouting for his fifth movie as the writer-director-star. His former girlfriend and favorite actress Keaton was among the small handful of people who knew what the script was about. The full screenplay was never passed out anymore. The cast got "sides," just pages, or scenes—another holdover stage tradition. Allen had grown obsessively secretive about his scripts, right down to the titles of them, if he had one, which were withheld from the press in favor of the pro forma "Woody Allen Project." "Woody doesn't want to give the plot away," Joffe told the *New York Times*, as if anyone could possibly steal the plot of *Love and Death*.

The script for *Love and Death* was, in a nutshell, a zany spoof of Tolstoy and *War and Peace* set in the era of Napoleon Bonaparte and Czar Alexander I of Russia. Allen was playing Boris, the cowardly scion of a respected family, whose obsession with death dates from hanging himself on a cross as a boy. Hopelessly in love with his clueless, twice-removed cousin Sonia (Keaton)—she wants profound conversation, he prefers superficial sex—Boris is thrust into meaningless wars, where he evades death on the battlefield and in pistol duels with amorous rivals. Eventually Boris and Sonia marry, survive lows—Sonia's cooking, Boris's failed suicides—and end up, much as in *Bananas* and *Sleeper*, plotting to assassinate Napoleon. The script reveled in familiar Woody Allen influences: Ingmar Bergman's recurring visions of Death, Groucho Marx's dialogue and slip-step staging, the either-or philosophy of Kierkegaard. But there were also many shadow influences for his enthusiasts to unravel, a searching quality, epic scope, and sweeping if fictionalized historical re-creation.

All the photography was planned for the fall of 1974 and the ensuing winter, budgeted at Allen's usual bargain-basement prices, amid Paris and Budapest locations, the latter pretending to be Saint Petersburg and Moscow, with the French countryside providing dachas and battleground landscapes. Martin Poll transitioned from the ill-fated Reginald Rose project to being the producer of *Love and Death*. For his cinematographer, Allen picked Ghislain Cloquet, the French cameraman of Jacques Demy and Robert Bresson films, and probably equally important to Allen, Arthur Penn's *Mickey One* starring Warren Beatty. His production designer, Willy Holt, was American-born though long a Parisian, who'd been Oscar-nominated for *Is Paris Burning?* Allen remembered costumer Gladys de Segonzac from *What's New Pussycat?* Again, Ralph Rosenblum would be his editor, and on his first trip to Paris Rosenblum listened to the director's ideas for scoring the picture wholly with the music of Igor Stravinsky. The editor thought that would be "too overpowering" and suggested one of his own favorite composers, Sergei Prokofiev, with a particularly generous sampling from the witty *Lieutenant Kijé* suite. Allen thought it over. The eventual *Love and Death* score would be entirely Prokofiev.

His parents, Nettie and Martin Konigsberg—often the targets of his barbed comedy—at their 1930 wedding; the errant kid genius with Letty, the younger sister he doted on. His first wife, Harlene Rosen, loved, divorced, and sued him. Born Allan Stewart Konigsberg, the creature renamed Woody Allen was concocted in his imagination and shape-shifted with the years.

Team writing for TV shows in 1958–59. *Left to right*: Mel Brooks (standing atop a desk to shout his ideas), Allen, Mel Tolkin, and Sid Caesar, the reigning king of television comedy. Woody the stand-up comedian: With single-minded determination and ambition, he evolved from a whispering scribe to a knock-kneed monologuist, whose braininess and neuroses brought stardom.

Woody, seen here as a guest on longtime friend Dick Cavett's show, became ubiquitous on television in the 1960s. Fame made him catnip to women, including his second wife, Louise Lasser, whom Allen left behind, but not before showcasing her memorably in *Bananas*. He also carried a torch for the bluesy folksinger Judy Henske, whose debut LP preceded his. Broadway beckoned, but so did Hollywood, and Allen was photographed for publicity purposes with an animal he privately loathed, perched on his beloved typewriter, for *What's New Pussycat?*.

Woody, displaying his pecs for Polly Bergen on *The Andy Williams Show*, would try anything for a laugh. But over the first half of the 1970s, he would complete his transition to movies, going from unconventional, hilarious leading man to serious filmmaker. Woody and (girlfriend and discovery) Diane Keaton famously spoofed *Casablanca* in *Play It Again, Sam*, the film version of his stage hit. In *Sleeper*, another feature with Keaton, he woke up in a future made extra-pleasurable by the Orb and the Orgasmatron.

His writing partner on the early hit comedies was his high school pal Mickey Rose. Frequent costars Diane Keaton and Tony Roberts, shown in *Annie Hall*, shared a three amigos–style camaraderie with him on- and offscreen. Marshall Brickman (on banjo for an early-1970s iteration of Woody's jazz band) came from a folkie background to serve as an important collaborator on several of his most beloved films, including *Sleeper*, *Annie Hall*, *Manhattan*, and later *Manhattan Murder Mystery*.

Courtesy of the LBJ Presidential Library, National Archives

The press, the public, and the social and political aristocracy embraced the budding great man. In 1968, he shook the hands of President Lyndon Baines Johnson and Lady Bird, who found him amusing. With Keaton making a threesome, Woody escorted another First Lady, Betty Ford—who also found him touching and funny—to a Martha Graham benefit in 1975. As Woody's literary career blossomed, he hobnobbed with litterateurs and was hailed as a fellow surrealist by Gabriel García Márquez.

Photographer unknown; courtesy of the Harry Ransom Center, University of Texas–Austin

In *Annie Hall*, Woody Allen's most acclaimed and popular picture, Alvy and Annie (Diane Keaton) arrive late for *Face to Face*, the new offering from Woody's idol Ingmar Bergman, so they switch to *The Sorrow and the Pity*, a four-and-a-half-hour documentary about Nazi-occupied France.

Seen on the set during filming, star-director Woody jokes with Keaton, Helen Ludlam (playing Grammy Hall), and Colleen Dewhurst (Mom Hall). The divergence between Woody Allen's public and private selves was complete. Peaking as a nervous nelly onscreen, offstage he was a confident ladies' man and master filmmaker.

Photographs by Brian Hamill for United Artists

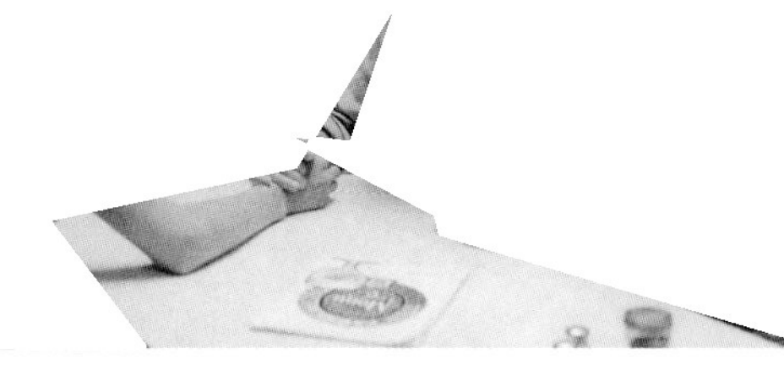

Photographs by Brian Hamill for United Artists

Personal managers Jack Rollins and Charles Joffe fulfilled their long-term promise to turn Woody Allen into a household name, and the duo (Joffe in front) accepted the Oscar for Best Picture for *Annie Hall*, with presenter Jack Nicholson smiling in the background. Disdaining the Academy Awards, the emboldened Allen was already busy with the bleak ultra-drama *Interiors*, Chekhov's *Three Sisters* by another name, with (*left to right*) Diane Keaton, Kristin Griffith, and Mary Beth Hurt. Next up was another signature work: the more comedic, more controversial *Manhattan*, with Woody and teenage lover Mariel Hemingway. Behind the camera is Gordon Willis, who helped sharpen Woody's visual approach.

Woody ushered in the 1980s with a series of great or near-great films. *Stardust Memories* was an ambitious homage to Fellini that for many critics was problematic. Moviemaker Sandy Bates's (Allen) crush on Daisy (Jessica Harper) echoed their offscreen romance, among the many real-life parallels in the film. *Zelig*, about a chameleonic man who becomes a populist celebrity, was a feat of cinematic trickery, while fans of the laugh-a-minute Woody were treated to the screwball comedy *Broadway Danny Rose*—both costarring Mia Farrow.

Photographs by Brian Hamill for United Artists (Stardust Memories) *and Orion Pictures* (Broadway Danny Rose)

Longtime Chicago friend and rising *Saturday Night Live* producer Jean Doumanian was a frequent traveling partner to Paris in the early 1980s, sometimes joined by Mia. Allen directed but did not appear in *The Purple Rose of Cairo*, a bittersweet romantic fantasy that revolved around Woody's love for old movies, with Jeff Daniels (in a dual role) and Mia at her finest. *Hannah and Her Sisters*—with Woody seen here directing Mia, Barbara Hershey, and Dianne Wiest—was one of his most perfectly realized blends of comedy and drama, his biggest hit of the 1980s and the recipient of seven Oscar nominations.

Purple Rose *and* Hannah *photographs by Brian Hamill for Orion Pictures*

Photograph by Brian Hamill for Orion Pictures

Photograph by Brian Hamill for Touchstone Pictures

Family portrait on the set of *Hannah and Her Sisters*: Mia; her mother, actress Maureen O'Sullivan, who plays the matriarch in the film; with (*front row*) Fletcher and (*back row*) Moses and Daisy Previn. Mia's children frequently played bit roles in Allen's pictures. The three disparate filmmakers of the *New York Stories* anthology: Woody with Francis Ford Coppola and Martin Scorsese.

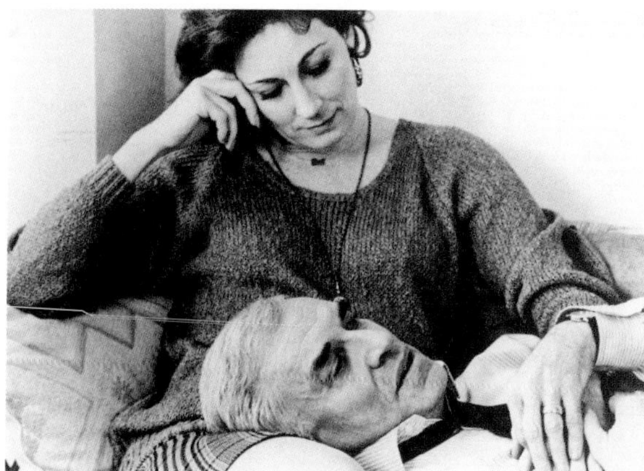

Radio Days *and* Crimes and Misdemeanors *photographs by Brian Hamill for Orion Pictures*

The semi-autobiographical, nostalgic *Radio Days* focused in part on a large dysfunctional Konigsberg-type family in the radio-crazy 1930s, with (*front row*) William Magerman, Seth Green as the Woody-kid, Leah Carrey, and (*rear, left to right*) Michael Tucker, Julie Kavner, Dianne Wiest, Joy Newman, Renée Lippin, and Josh Mostel. Anjelica Huston and Martin Landau were the star-crossed lovers of *Crimes and Misdemeanors*, a gripping story that earned a Best Supporting Actor nomination for Landau and Best Director and Script nods for Allen. In the late 1980s, Woody and Mia, seen here with Dylan (back to camera) and her younger brother Satchel (the future Ronan), struggled amid a deteriorating personal relationship. Dylan's adoption, and the surprise pregnancy bringing Satchel, accelerated their breakup.

Photograph © Jane Read Martin/Zuma Wire

Photograph by Brian Hamill for Orion Pictures

The extended Previn-Farrow–Woody Allen "family" tried to revive their togetherness on European vacations. The brood is photographed abroad here (Soon-Yi stands tall next to Mia) by Allen's personal assistant Jane Read Martin, later to marry his third important writing partner, Douglas McGrath. Amid the Mia–Soon-Yi–Dylan brouhaha, Diane Keaton reunited with her *Annie Hall* costar in the critic- and crowd-pleasing crime comedy *Manhattan Murder Mystery*. Woody doubters, however, had begun to stay away in droves.

As critics predicted his demise, Woody bounced back. The period gangster romp *Bullets over Broadway*—with Woody seen here directing his alter ego John Cusack—was nominated for seven Oscars and won Best Supporting Actress for Dianne Wiest. Woody and Soon-Yi Previn, touring Europe with his jazz band, were captured snuggling in a Venice gondola. The couple returned to Venice to be married in 1997. Labor-of-love jazz pseudo-biopic *Sweet and Lowdown*, with Sean Penn and Woody directing only, was a succès d'estime. Woody (photographed on the sidelines during the filming of the acclaimed *Match Point*) was often a solitary figure at work, saying little, keeping his own counsel, tootling his clarinet during breaks, playing chess games with himself.

Photograph by Brian Hamill for Sweetland Pictures

Photograph by John Clifford for Sweetland Pictures

Conquering critics and audiences, *Vicky Cristina Barcelona*, a romantic comedy about a volatile ménage à trois, with (*left to right*) Javier Bardem, Penélope Cruz, and Scarlett Johansson, was one of his most adventurous, free-spirited, nouvelle vague–influenced films. Continuing to make pictures overseas with abandon, Allen is seen here on the set with Owen Wilson for *Midnight in Paris*, a magical and beguiling work in his oeuvre that won over critics and audiences around the world. *Blue Jasmine* (with actresses Cate Blanchett and Sally Hawkins joining Woody for the Paris premiere) was the Tennessee Williams ultra-drama he'd aspired to master throughout his career.

Photograph © Lionel Guericolas/ Visual Press via Zuma Press

The Woody family: daughters Manzie Tio (*left*), Bechet, and Soon-Yi flank Allen on the red carpet at the 2023 Venice Film Festival for the world premiere of *Coup de chance*; Woody and his sister, Letty Aronson, who became his militant defender after the bust-up with Mia and produced "Woody Allen projects" for the next thirty years; Woody dances with Death in the final scene of *Love and Death*.

There were many pleasures for filmaholics in the European casting, which included Howard Vernon from the cinema of Henri-Georges Clouzot and Jean-Pierre Melville, and Olga Georges-Picot from Alain Resnais films. The handful of Americans included television character actor Harold Gould, who'd be razor-sharp as Boris's jealous rival—dueling over a countess—James Tolkan as a crisp Napoleon (the same height as Allen), and winsome Jessica Harper as Sonia's promiscuous cousin. Her attitude: "I never want to marry. . . . I just want to get divorced." *Love and Death* was Juliet Taylor's first Woody Allen movie as casting director. After serving as Marion Dougherty's assistant, Taylor would share Allen's confidences for the next forty years.

Keaton did not arrive in Paris until the cameras were ready to whir. Writing to the actress in California, Allen assured her *Love and Death* would be "easier" to make than *Sleeper*, which was "pure torture" with its futuristic props and special effects. He said he expected their scenes together to be "brisk and lively." Allen also wrote Keaton daily "throughout the filming," even on the days when both had scenes together. The letters were addressed to her pet name: "Worm." He treated her as his "endearing oaf" throughout the production, she later said.

Still, it was a toss-up whether the problem-plagued *Sleeper* was a greater ordeal than the arduous *Love and Death*. By all accounts this experience was Allen's most brutal as a filmmaker with frigid weather, hundreds of extras for scenes, and the constant shifting of locations amid time and budget constraints. Allen was often dissatisfied, and several times insisted on refilming in rented chateaus after the crew had moved on. It was "an endless feat of acrobatics," production designer Holt recalled. Although Allen practiced his French, communications with the multilingual cast and crew had to be translated, and Keaton spoke only English. Allen sprained his back and suffered the flu. Keaton struggled with a stomach bug. When the Plaza Athénée wasn't a hospital ward, it was like a hideout for outlaws. Visiting his suite to discuss plans for *The Front*, Walter Bernstein noticed Allen had covered the windows to block out sunlight. "Every day we would have the exact same meal in the hotel," Keaton said. "Woody would have fish, and I would have chicken. No wine."

They found mutual consolation in work. Their shared scenes were among the best in the script, which they nonetheless embroidered freely. Off- and on-camera, their special brand of repartee flourished. "The long, tangled philosophical, ontological, cosmological, phenomenological (in other words, funny) exchanges" in *Love and Death*, as Paul D. Zimmerman later observed in *Newsweek*, were "their way of saying 'I love you.'"

The postproduction went faster and easier. In the first weekend of June 1975, close to 150 journalists and critics from around the US were the beneficiaries of a United Artists junket that brought them to the Sutton Theatre in New York for the national premiere of *Love and Death*, followed by a press conference with the director himself. The studio probably did not need a lavish publicity liftoff for a picture of such exuberant comedy, so many sidesplitting scenes, all manner of looniness that could possibly be squeezed into a Woody Allen picture—a sex-hygiene play for soldiers; a village idiots' convention; hawkers strolling amid the crash of cannons selling Red Hots, blinis, and beer; errant quotations from Saint Thomas Aquinas, Plato, Tolstoy. "The funniest of my early funny ones," Allen once said, a rare time when he stooped to praising himself. Even Boris dying at the end was funny—one of the only two times Allen has played a character who succumbs in a movie. After an angel of God lies to him, Boris is executed for assassinating—not Napoleon—Napoleon's stand-in. Boris/Allen capers offscreen with Martha Graham agility, dancing with Death—quoting (in a humorous vein) from Ingmar Bergman's 1957 masterpiece, *The Seventh Seal*, which Allen adored.* Cue the credits.

Most critics heaped compliments on *Love and Death* and, following UA and Allen's standard operating procedure, the film was booked first in New York before it went national, rising to number five at the box office by the end of summer. Yet the popularity of a Woody Allen movie was always relative, and over time there were fewer and fewer refuges for "his audience" outside New York. While twenty-five smallish theaters in twelve cities showed *Love and Death*, *Jaws*, America's number-one movie, played in 106 of the largest in 19 cities. Overseas, *Love and Death* also elicited encomiums and drew crowds, contributing to its robust profits. UA, thanks to a half dozen titles, many of which also did well abroad, notched a year of record revenue in 1975.

---

* *The Seventh Seal* was the only Bergman picture on Allen's personal list of the ten best films of all time, which he contributed to the 2012 *Sight & Sound* poll rounding up the votes of nearly 850 film critics, scholars, archivists, programmers, and directors.

••

THAT SUMMER, *Without Feathers*, Allen's second volume of "little souffles," arrived in bookstores. Its title quoted from the opening of Emily Dickinson's poem " 'Hope' Is the Thing with Feathers." Allen and Marshall Brickman had been taking more long walks and discussing story possibilities for the next film. One thing they knew they wanted to do was craft a great lead role for Diane Keaton. While nursing a sideline as a club singer, the actress was suddenly in demand. Keaton had squeezed in the making of *The Godfather: Part II* between *Sleeper* and *Love and Death*, and then spent the spring in Hollywood, appearing with Elliott Gould in a romantic comedy directed by Norman Panama, a onetime Bob Hope writer. She would work again later in the year with Gould, Michael Caine, and James Caan in *Harry and Walter Go to New York*, which was to be shot in Ohio and California.

While their love life, such as it ever was, no longer existed, the couple remained soulmates. They kept in touch with regular phone calls and saw each other whenever their schedules overlapped in New York City or Hollywood. "We were quite a couple, one more hidden than the other," Keaton recalled wryly. "We both wore hats in public, and he always held my hand or, rather, gripped it without letting go. People were to be avoided."

When Allen, at Keaton's urging, took movement classes at the Martha Graham studio, he hadn't dared to introduce himself to the modernist choreographer whom he ranked as "a genius of the theater." "Impossible!" declared Graham, when an assistant informed her the famous Woody Allen was in her studio, wearing a leotard and dance belt. "He was doing some turns, he was doing splits, then running across the floor."

In early June Allen took a phone call from the White House, asking him to escort President Gerald Ford's wife—First Lady Betty Ford—to a Manhattan benefit for the Graham dance troupe, which was on the calendar for late in the month. The first lady, in younger days, also had studied dance and movement with Graham. Allen said Graham's greatness reminded him of Ingmar Bergman's, because her "best works express the psychology of women." As a matter of fact, two years earlier, he told the press, he had whipped up a script called "Dreams and Furies," which amounted to a kind of homage to Graham and loomed as a possible "highly stylized comedy [that] comes straight out of her [Graham]; it is mythological and lustful, Oedipal and funny." That script idea, one of the many he kept in his arsenal, went on the back burner owing to "problems."

Now he agreed to be the first lady's "date" for the Uris Theatre gala, with Keaton, who was in town, discreetly making three. Allen wore a tuxedo, black tie, and high-topped sneakers. He told Eric Lax it was an outfit devised for the maximum attention it would attract to aid the benefit. The president's wife was arrayed in purple chiffon, and Keaton sported tennis shoes to match Allen's. During the intermission, Allen took the stage with other notables for brief remarks, then after the event he and Keaton slipped away as fast as they could to talk and chuckle over iced coffee. Betty Ford was the second first lady to find herself captivated by the comedian. "He said he'd given up dancing because he was so sensitive about the way he looked in leotards," Mrs. Ford recalled of the occasion. (Ike/Allen would say pretty much the same thing in *Manhattan*.) "Very funny man, but very, very shy." The dance benefit raised $200,000; Allen contributed $5,000.

There was never a dramatic rupture between Allen and Keaton. They had never been together romantically as a couple, in any conventional sense. However, the romance "broke up two years before we shot *Annie Hall*," Keaton wrote in her memoir, which roughly dates their strict parting of the ways to May 1974, between the filming of *Sleeper* and the filming of *Love and Death*. Keaton's career was now in overdrive. The actress fielded many offers from Hollywood, whereas Allen always insisted that acting offers for him—apart from his own pictures—were few and far between. The end of their love affair was a natural occurrence, but it helped spur Allen into thinking about their onetime romance as the kind of dramatic comedy he had always wished to make as a movie. Their love story, fictionalized, could be "a deeper comedy . . . a more human film," not all-out funny-funny, but the story of a romance that might end more realistically, sadly, in a rueful breakup.

FIRST, *THE FRONT.* Allen had grown increasingly nervous about the job as he second-guessed his involvement in a film about the blacklist. Maybe audiences wouldn't take him seriously as an actor. His limited acting skills might not shoulder the weight of the subject. He had never acted in a role he hadn't written for himself.

As a young publicity and comedy writer, Allen had been largely oblivious to the persecution of purported members of the US Communist Party in show business that began, in 1947, with a secret House Committee on Un-American Activities (HUAC) inquiry in Hollywood in the spring, followed by public hearings in Washington, DC, in the fall, targeting screen personnel. The blackballing, which spread to all fields of entertainment, including radio, television, and theater, lasted into the 1960s. "I had a general awareness of [Senator] Joseph McCarthy," Allen once recalled, "but I wasn't aware of the implications of McCarthyism at all. I recall that neighbors of mine in Flatbush went to a Paul Robeson concert and got stoned by a mob and had their car smashed. When I heard about that, I considered it for a minute and then I turned on the ball game."*

Backstage at the hungry i, when Allen was performing stand-up comedy in San Francisco in the early 1960s, he had been wised up by Alvah Bessie, one of the Hollywood Ten who had stood up to HUAC in 1947 and ultimately served jail sentences for contempt of Congress. Allen had stayed in touch with Bessie, corresponded sympathetically with him, and encouraged the "spec" scripts Bessie wrote, hoping for the Hollywood comeback that never eventuated. Starting out on the lowest rungs of show business, Allen was also oblivious to the fact one of the "friendly" witnesses—the despised onetime communists who informed on their former comrades to elude the blacklist—was playwright Abe Burrows, his distant cousin who'd been so helpful with tips and connections early in his career. Bessie gladly would have socked Burrows on the jaw. Victor Navasky, in his book *Naming Names*, dubbed Burrows one of the "comic informers . . . who made clear that while he may have looked like a Communist and talked like a Communist and hung around with Communists, and others were justified in thinking him a Communist, 'In my own heart, I didn't believe it.'" In his testimony before HUAC in 1952, Burrows affirmed the identities of a handful of communists he'd been friendly with in show business, while his wife, former radio actress Carin Kinzel, was more obliging, naming upward of two dozen people in an executive session. Allen stayed in touch with Burrows, who still lived in New York, not far from where he lived.

---

* Allen is referring to Ku Klux Klan–backed riots protesting a planned concert appearance by the left-wing actor and singer Paul Robeson as a benefit for the Civil Rights Congress. The events took place in Peekskill, New York, in Westchester County, in late August and early September 1949. A mob attacked concertgoers, throwing rocks and injuring people, and the initial concert date had to be postponed and then rescheduled under heavy police protection.

Writer Walter Bernstein and director Martin Ritt, the creative team behind *The Front*, were friends and artistic collaborators dating back to their shared blacklist-era experiences. They struck a deal with David Begelman, who had been Ritt's agent at Creative Management Associates, or CMA, before becoming the head of Columbia Pictures in 1973. Begelman was willing "to stick out his neck and take a chance," in Ritt's words, and bankroll a movie treating the ticklish subject of the show business blacklist. They hoped to get Dustin Hoffman, Al Pacino, or Warren Beatty to play Howard Prince, the small-time bookie in Bernstein's script who acts as a "front," or alias, for his boyhood friend, who has been blacklisted as a writer. HUAC mistakes Prince for a communist and threatens him with a subpoena. Prince must decide whether to betray his friend—and also his idealistic girlfriend—or suffer the committee's punishment.

One day Ritt had another thought: "The kid, that funny kid . . . Woody Allen." Begelman got the script to Sam Cohn, a former colleague when both were agents at CMA. Jack Rollins and Charles Joffe, who were attuned to the politics of the blacklist, joined the chorus of people urging Allen to commit to the project.

In the end what it came down to—as was often the case with Allen—was the stretch of open time he had on his schedule while he waited for Diane Keaton to become available for the next Woody Allen picture. The money was frosting on the cake. *Variety* guessed Allen's up-front fee to be "almost certainly in the $1,000,000 or more area," but he'd get "ten percent of the gross receipts in excess of $3,500,000 until breakeven plus $2,000,000 and 12.5% of the gross receipts thereafter." Since *Take the Money and Run* Allen's comedies had grown steadily in popularity, and there were dreams of a box office hit as well as Oscar nods for *The Front*.

Bernstein and Ritt were "nice guys," Allen thought, when he first heard their ideas for *The Front*. When Allen hemmed and hawed, however, the nice guys proved just as tough and stubborn, batting away Allen's eleventh-hour equivocations—"Hey guys, how about a real actor like Peter Falk instead of me?" In the end they had to virtually drag Allen before the cameras in New York studios and to locations in September and October.

If Bernstein and Ritt ever considered any ditzy Diane Keaton flavoring in the romantic-comedic side of their serious movie, they banished that thought with their casting, as Allen's girlfriend, of the refined Andrea Marcovicci, best known as a soap opera actress and singer. She'd play the high-minded television producer who doesn't know Prince is a fraud and thinks he is a brilliant writer, and whose unwavering social conscience will impinge on their love story. The Falstaffian Zero Mostel, who had bounced back from blacklisting to stardom on Broadway, winning three Tonys, and in films—Mel Brooks's *The Producers*—would portray the larger-than-life entertainer Hecky Brown, who'd do anything to escape the HUAC inquisition, right down to committing suicide. The rest of the ensemble would be sprinkled with blacklist survivors. Among the supporting cast was earnest Michael Murphy, best known for Robert Altman films, who'd play the friend who needs a "front." Like other actors who depicted his best friends onscreen, Murphy became Allen's friend off-camera too.

Prince was a born loser in the script, a character at times so close to Allen's established persona it was as though Bernstein had written it for him from the outset. When his producer girlfriend tells Prince she is a swimming enthusiast, Prince gives her a Woody Allen riposte, "Swimming isn't a sport; it's what you do to keep from drowning." But Bernstein and Ritt went a long way around the barn to avoid many of Allen's trademark traits: the fumbling-and-bumbling comedy, the lecherousness and ineptitude with women, highbrow allusions, or mock philosophical digressions. There would be no dreams, visions, or comic flashbacks to his loser boyhood. There'd be no padding of scenes with interviews, voice-over, or dialogue spoken directly to the camera. The script was sacred to them, and there would be no improvisation, or reshooting with dialogue changes.

Mostly, Allen let the script be, but he squirmed under the rules. He did ask Bernstein to excise a Jewish mother from one scene, and he also contributed "a couple of jokes," Bernstein recalled. Bernstein had struggled to incorporate a certain amount of humor into Prince's showdown with HUAC, a climactic scene where Prince defies his interrogators by refusing to give names. The scene was decidedly weak. Allen suggested Ritt set the cameras up for another stab at it and let him wing it. "He was hilarious," remembered Bernstein. "Only it had nothing to do with the picture. It was like ten minutes of stand-up comedy. Reluctantly, we couldn't use it."

Ritt had been a conscientious actor in his salad days before the blacklist shut him down and he turned to directing. He was known for a sensitive touch with players, and Ritt drew a compelling performance out of Allen.

"Whether he would acknowledge it or not, Woody got a great deal from Marty in terms of his acting," Bernstein said. Yet Allen couldn't shake off his directorial impulses. The star was "never disrespectful" during filming, Marcovicci told Marion Meade, "but I sensed it was very hard for him to table his thoughts."

Hecky Brown was the pivotal character guiding the story into tragedy. Allen's unease with Mostel, flamboyant on- and offstage, added to their edginess in scenes together. Mostel, for example, was known to announce his farts. "Woody shrinks when anybody touches him," said Bernstein. "He was always polite to Zero, but it was clear he didn't want to be around him. In the film, you can read it in his body language."

Attending dailies, Allen behaved badly by openly finding fault with everything. He felt perfectly at home conducting himself in similar fashion when directing his own movies. "He drove Marty crazy by criticizing things in front of everyone, and finally Marty had to ask him to stay away because he was hurting people's feelings," Bernstein said. Astonished, Allen told Bernstein he couldn't fathom why people wasted time praising all the "good stuff" in rushes, rather than focusing on the "problems" he diagnosed. "It never occurred to him that people needed recognition for a job well done," Meade wrote. "Woody is never deliberately cruel," Bernstein explained, "but there's a certain lack of tact, to say the least. He's one of the most insensitive sensitive people I know."

Uncharitably, in *Apropos of Nothing*, Allen claimed he and Bernstein had a print of the picture delivered to them in New York, where they struggled—behind Ritt's back, Allen implies—to improve the film. The two "recut it and trimmed it. We did the best we could. It helped, but it was never the movie it should have been."

ON NOVEMBER 30, 1975, as the photography wound down, Allen turned forty. No longer the Kid, in nickname or years, he gave a birthday interview to the *New York Times*, announcing, "I want to do more risky films, less conventional ones, films I'm not secure with. I only just learned how to make films. The first few times I was just noodling around. I'm going to aim higher, and I want to push the audience with me." He said the next Woody Allen picture would be about "real people, real problems." On New Year's Eve, he celebrated by hosting another spectacular party at his penthouse with litterateurs such as Norman Mailer and Random House editor Bob Loomis, the editor of Allen's books, sharing the bubbly with sports figures like Walt Frazier and show business acquaintance Peter Falk and old friend Dick Cavett.

By the first day of 1976, he and Marshall Brickman were deep into the script of the next "Woody Allen Film"—the only title offered to the trade papers. Initially they debated different stories and brainstormed disparate ideas on alternate days, Brickman recalled. Somehow Allen had found time in Paris, while filming *Love and Death*, to write, in longhand, the draft of a novel, whose leading female character was distinctly Keatonish. The novel had the elements of a murder mystery. For a while he and Brickman discussed a period mystery with Allen and Keaton, which would be set in Boston around the turn of the century. After a lot of talk, the night before he planned to start writing, Allen decided against it, mindful that he had re-created historical periods in his past two pictures, *Love and Death* and *The Front*. The friends switched to discussing a contemporary murder mystery much like the one Allen had mused about in correspondence with Reginald Rose.

The comedic murder mystery was going to revolve around the death of a philosophy professor, who may or may not have committed suicide. A married couple turned amateur sleuths think the professor might have been murdered. Going back to the novel he had toyed with in Paris, Allen transplanted a couple from the novel, not unlike Alvy Singer and Annie Hall, into the murder mystery. One scene in the novel even had the couple, neighbors of the suicide/murder victim, meeting cute at a movie theater, with the male character's "obsessional thing of not wanting to go in after the movie had started," as Caryn James later wrote in the *New York Times*. Left behind as the script evolved, the suicidal professor would resurface later in *Crimes and Misdemeanors*.

Originally, they wrote the Annie Hall character as a neurotic New York journalist. However, as the story developed, Allen and Brickman began to incorporate more and more of Keaton's actual traits. Like Keaton, Annie would be depicted, professionally, as a combination of aspiring (but floundering) actress, photographer, and singer. As the script began to narrow on Alvy and Annie—and their relationship—they dropped the murder mystery angle. And Annie acquired the last name Hall, Keaton's real-life birth surname.

The script was always meant to be more about Alvy, Allen's character. "Woody wanted to take a risk and do something different," Brickman recalled. Over a period of weeks and months the writers crafted a loose-knit story about a stand-up comic "who lived in New York and was forty years old and was examining his life," in Brickman's words. There were "several strands" of the script, not just Alvy's "relationship with a young woman" named Annie Hall. "Another was a concern with the banality of the life that we all live, and a third an obsession with proving himself and testing himself to find out what kind of character he had," Brickman explained. Their script explored Alvy's midlife crisis as well as the Alvy-Annie love story, from Alvy's first encounter with Annie through to their ensuing romance, conflicts, and breakup. The drafts evolved into a romantic comedy, but a kind of antiromantic comedy without the standard happy ending.

Striking a humorous refrain in their script was the fact Annie hails from a euphonious-sounding place called Chippewa Falls, Wisconsin, which was of course the actual hometown of Allen's onetime girlfriend, folk singer Judy Henske. It was one of the ways in which "Annie Hall" was not entirely inspired by Keaton, or realistic; the character was a fictional mélange. Allen never had paid a visit to Henske's home in Chippewa Falls, much less anywhere else in Wisconsin, but he had sat down to a few family dinners with the Halls—including one Thanksgiving feast with Grammy in attendance. Thanksgiving in California became the Easter celebration of the Halls in Chippewa Falls. "A nice ham this year, Mom," Annie's mother compliments Grammy, a perfect throwaway line. Speaking generally, Allen seemed inauthentic when writing dialogue for west of the Hudson, and throughout *Annie Hall* Keaton would speak—nothing like a Wisconsinite—more like the Southern California gal she was.

True, on an early date Allen and Keaton did go see Marcel Ophuls's seminal 1969 documentary about the Holocaust, *The Sorrow and the Pity*, which ran over four hours and which Allen unreservedly admired. True, Grammy Hall had an anti-Semitic streak among her biases, which Allen himself had observed up close and personal. The film's colorfully exaggerated Halls, however, were "a generic, WASP family," in Keaton's view, not "remotely identifiable" with her true family. Her mother, who liked *Annie Hall*, thought Grammy Hall was nothing more than a "sight gag," and that Allen had vulgarized Keaton's brother Randy—"A sensitive person with a unique personality," in her words—for the eerily haunted character played by Christopher Walken.

Unlike Keaton, Annie Hall likes to relax by getting high before and after lovemaking, much to Alvy's dismay. Alvy and Annie's disappointing sex life contributes to their alienation—as it might have done with Allen and Keaton. Allen and Brickman wrote dialogue mimicking Keaton's own peculiar vernacular, including her cornball expletives like "La-dee-da!" Yet often there was no "clear provenance" for the famous dialogue, not even the "La-dee-da!" as the *New York Times* later recounted. Keaton said it was in the script. Allen told the *Times* Keaton came up with it. "He thinks I came up with it?" was her reaction. "I'm going to use that, then. If he said it, he's got to be right. How could I be right?" ("I did grope for words," she conceded in her memoir.)

The original script, decidedly more interested in Alvy than Annie, jumped in and out of Alvy's mind with ornate fantasy sequences, akin to Allen's earlier broad comedies. Alvy being a stand-up comic was an autobiographical touch, although Alvy would be seen only in passing onstage. The University of Wisconsin was as much Brickman as Henske, and Alvy's biggest stand-up scene supposedly takes place at the UW in Madison, where Brickman (and Henske) attended college. It was shot at New York University with $10-a-day student extras. Allen warmed them up: "I need a laugh from you people that sounds like it was laughed in Wisconsin."

Another quasi-autobiographical touch was Alvy's clumsy handling of lobsters. Allen had long made jokes about shellfish clashing with his Jewish roots. In *Annie Hall* he wins Annie over by physically tussling with lobsters, and then he repeats his clumsiness to less happy effect on a post-Annie girlfriend later in the film.

Also like Allen, Alvy doesn't know very much about smoking dope or snorting cocaine, a social defect that supplied good comedy at intervals in the script. Yet it was Brickman who was the veteran druggie. He had dropped mescaline with old bandmate John Phillips of the Mamas and Papas back in 1969, when Brickman lived at Gene Autry's Continental Hotel on the Sunset Strip and wrote for *The Tonight Show*. The Southern California milieu that provides the crucial last act—and the music business—Brickman knew better than Allen.

"After months of conversation and agonizing," Brickman said, Allen wrote a first draft "very quick," in a few days, maybe four or five. "Xeroxed, gave it to me, and I spent a couple of days making changes, and we'd shovel it back and forth before we felt reasonably confident." Later, it would be impossible to pinpoint the origin of many specific ideas, character traits, dialogue highlights, and key scenes, partly because the three principals—including Keaton, who did no writing, but was a veritable equal—were circumspect about making claims for the *Annie Hall* script. But that was also because the lines were truly blurred. "All I can say," Brickman said of all the scripts he wrote with Allen, "is that when you collaborate, you are both responsible for everything."

THE FRONT HELPED make filmmaking in New York easier and less expensive than it had been for a decade. Martin Ritt had publicly excoriated New York's Office of Motion Pictures and Television for letting high union costs and location fees hamper productions, adding an average of 40 percent to what the filming would cost in Los Angeles. Director Ritt blamed the city for being "less than fully responsive in specific production needs." His complaints and those of other New York filmmakers finally resulted in sweeping changes in the municipal office, addressing the coastal disparities and mediating problems with unions and neighborhoods. This was another one of Allen's takeaways from *The Front*, and for the first time he planned to shoot a Woody Allen movie largely in and around New York. He hired Robert Greenhut, the line manager who had resolved municipal issues during the making of *The Front*, and Greenhut would stay on the team as a producer for twenty years.

Casting director Juliet Taylor helped line up the numerous speaking parts. Along with Allen and Keaton, the faces from previous Woody Allen films included third-billed Tony Roberts as Rob, Alvy's best friend dating from schoolyard days, whose ambition to move to Hollywood and make big money in television echoes the career path trod by Mickey Rose. Alvy and Rob inexplicably call each other "Max," which was another borrowing from real life. Allen had told Roberts to call him "Max" in public, and Roberts responded with, "OK, but you have to call me Max too." "Max" was a recurring name for characters in Allen movies, including many times when Roberts played other roles in his films, when his characters were often named variations of "Max."

Frizzy-haired Carol Kane was cast as Alvy's sweet first spouse, an Adlai Stevenson volunteer who tires of Alvy's endless neuroses. Janet Margolin from *Take the Money and Run* would show a more astringent side as another ex-wife. Shelley Duvall from Robert Altman films would depict a *Rolling Stone* byliner who prattles on about the "transplendence" of Bob Dylan. She is Alvy's date at a Maharishi Mahesh Yogi event, and later they go to bed, underwhelmingly. Paul Simon, half of Simon & Garfunkel, was the hip music producer who connives Annie away from Alvy and New York. Christopher Walken would prove a standout in his scenes as Annie's dysfunctional younger brother, who gives the couple a scary car ride to the Chippewa Falls airport.

Eleven-year-old Brooke Shields and sixteen-year-old Stacey Nelkin were among Alvy's boyhood crushes in flashbacks. Dick Cavett, in television footage, and Truman Capote as "winner of the Truman Capote lookalike contest" were among the celebrities who turn up as themselves; it would become a thing in Woody Allen films. When Allen failed to lure either Luis Buñuel or Federico Fellini into the standing-in-line-at-the-movies scene, heavy thinker Marshall McLuhan—Keaton's suggestion—substituted, proving a different kind of funny. Allen's acquaintances in the cast included John Doumanian, now divorced from Jean but still in the circle, making the first of many appearances in his movies as the cokehead whose stash Alvy sneezes away; and Walter Bernstein, writer of *The Front* and an Allen near-lookalike, as Annie's date, when Alvy runs into them outside a *Sorrow and the Pity* revival. Alvy's date in the scene, uncredited, is Sigourney Weaver in her screen debut.

Allen took chances on new people behind the camera too. His first-time art director was Melvin B. Bornstein from Chicago, who went by the snappier Mel Bourne. Until then, Bourne, who had launched his career on the *Howdy Doody* children's television show, mostly art-directed commercials, forgettable TV, and obscure independent features. Quick and endlessly resourceful on the modest budgets he was always forced to accept, Bourne would stick around for eight years and stabilize the visual design of seven major Woody Allen pictures.

Allen went more out on a limb with Gordon Willis, who was reputed to be as prickly as he was consummate as a cameraman. Willis had just completed *The Godfather: Part II*—with Diane Keaton among the cast—and *All the President's Men*. Both were the kind of somber, low-lit dramas for which Willis was best known. His sobriquet was "The Prince of Darkness." Could the Dark Prince adapt to Woody Allen and comedies?

"I had heard how difficult he was, angry, all sorts of awful things," Allen recalled. He advised Robert Greenhut, "Let's sign a contract, but let's make the budget so that if we fire Gordie we can get another cameraman." But he and Willis communed like twins separated at birth. They had much in common. Both boasted tireless work ethics and studiously avoided any "fooling around" during filming. Both despised cinematic clichés. Willis told Allen he needn't worry about his darkness penchant. It didn't matter how dark a scene was lit, or how far away the jokes were from the camera; if the scene was funny the audience would laugh. "He was rigid, hard on his crew, short-tempered, but I never had a cross word with him," Allen said.

If Allen was rarely intimate with actors whom he didn't count as personal friends, i.e., most of them, he needed to feel attuned to his cameramen. Willis would collaborate on the distinctive look of this Woody Allen film, and seven more to follow over the next decade, some of Allen's most visually arresting work. More than any other single person Willis was responsible for "my maturity in films," Allen later said. As Keaton noted in her memoir, Willis took Allen under his wing for camera tricks and techniques and taught him the value of an encompassing tone and visual design. Willis indoctrinated Allen in the master shot, showing him how to choreograph the staging and camera movement for a master that "could be used to deliver the variety and impact an audience needed without cutting to close-ups," in Keaton's words. Allen switched to relying principally on masters—not the long, medium, and close-up combination dictated by Hollywood norms. Eschewing close-ups except within the master became emblematic of Allen's style, starting with *Annie Hall*.

He and Willis "went over every single shot before every movie" they collaborated on, Allen recalled, a rare and not always comfortable means of work-sharing for him. The two agreed to shoot the New York sequences in gray and twilight tones, the Los Angeles scenes in sunshine and glare, the dreams and flashbacks as golden memories. While this was not the first time Allen coordinated scenes with the weather, this approach would become a mania with him in the future: minimizing the sun and reveling in grayness and muted hues and rain and drizzle. His visual style, in effect, became more personal. In his real life, he had the same preferences.

While notoriously dogmatic, Willis also loved innovation, and Allen confronted him with unusual demands, including special effects and split-screen sequences. One scene would show Annie's phantom rising from bed to ruefully observe her passionless lovemaking with Alvy. Another sequence showed Alvy and Annie on a split screen, making diametrically opposite complaints about their sex lives to their respective therapists. Willis made a bold suggestion—why not shoot both therapy vignettes "live," and then frame them together on a divided stage?

Like Allen—who demanded it of his production team—the prickly cameraman also prided himself on adapting to surprises and conditions. Weather always affected shooting plans, and Allen learned from Willis it was OK to delay a shot for hours to avoid the harsh sunlight and wait for the gray clouds to arrive. Locations changed plans too. Scouting was an important stage of preproduction, and one maxim of Allen's, related to scouting, was "If we had to start shooting tomorrow, we'd go with this location, but let's keep looking. . . ." In the original script, Alvy Singer as a boy lived in Flatbush, where Allen hailed from in real life, but the director didn't want to use his actual boyhood house—too on the nose—and he wasn't thrilled about the boyhood house the location managers picked out. On their way to scout Coney Island sites one day, Mel Bourne told Allen, "I know you like Fellini. . . . I want to show you something that out-Fellinis Fellini." Bourne led the director to a frame house in the shadow of an abandoned roller coaster on Coney Island. Allen loved amusement parks, and roller coasters proliferate in his films. Just like that he switched Alvy's boyhood from Flatbush to Coney Island, necessitating a scramble by Bourne, Willis, everyone. Allen's team learned to embrace the scramble.

BEFORE FILMING BEGAN in the second week of May, Allen and Keaton discussed their scenes, and he suggested one final means of marrying the actress to the character she was playing. Allen told her to "wear what you want to wear." Keaton was taken by surprise. No director ever told her that before. She selected khaki pants, a vest, a tie, and a man's slouchy bolero, an outfit Keaton herself might wear in real life, finally *becoming* Annie

Hall and, after the film's release, igniting an antifashion trend of women adopting the Diane Keaton look. One of the first scenes to be shot was Alvy and Annie in the beach house kitchen, trying to corral live lobsters into a boiling pot. Allen and Keaton were so comfortable together they laughed uncontrollably as they quick-stepped and bantered around the scuttling lobsters. The natural lighting and impromptu staging were the exact opposite of what Gordon Willis was renowned for. Dancing behind the actors with a handheld camera, the cameraman gleefully captured the cramped comedy, which became an endearing highlight of the film.

The hard work of the production was the many flashbacks to Alvy's boyhood and the elaborate fantasy sequences that were almost always sans Keaton, with Allen directing himself as Alvy. These included a black-and-white *Invasion of the Body Snatchers* spoof about black people moving into Jewish neighborhoods; a German-subtitled visit to a Nazi headquarters; an interlude with Alvy and his *Rolling Stone* date (Shelley Duvall) frolicking in the Garden of Eden as they discuss "sex, anatomy, and the female orgasm with God"; Satan giving Alvy, Annie, and Rob an elevator tour of hell, with Richard Nixon on the basement level; and, most important, because it allowed him to take the floor at Madison Square Garden with his basketball heroes, a fantasy hoops game pitting the Knicks (Earl "The Pearl" Monroe, Walt Frazier, Bill Bradley, etc.) against great intellectuals and philosophers including Nietzsche, Kierkegaard, and Alvy Singer.

When Allen, Keaton, and Tony Roberts were in scenes together, it was old home week for the three amigos. Their performances were behavioral extensions of their off-camera camaraderie. Allen's directions to Keaton were "the same" as those he had given her on previous productions, the actress wrote later. "Loosen up the dialogue. Forget the marks. Move around like a real person. Don't make too much of the words." The filming was "effortless," Keaton recalled. Never again would Allen behave so nonchalantly. "During breaks," the actress reminisced in her memoir, "Woody would carry around a pack of Camels, take one out of his shirt pocket à la George Raft, flip it into his mouth, blow smoke rings, and never inhale. No one had any serious expectations. We were just having a good time. . . . As always, Woody concerned himself with worries about the script. Was it too much like an episode of *The Mary Tyler Moore Show*? I told him he was nuts. Relax!"

At night, after a long day of work, the three often dined together at Elaine's, arguing, and trying to top one another's jokes. Probably only Keaton and Roberts had read the whole script and knew what the film was "about." The other cast members with their "sides" knew less than most United Artists officials. After finishing in New York, Allen shot a few Los Angeles exteriors. The photography, except for later reshooting, which Allen and the budget anticipated, was completed by summer's end, and Allen shifted into postproduction.

THE FRONT WAS released in October, and Allen returned to the West Coast to meet with journalists flown in from around the country and quartered at the Beverly Wilshire. He'd make only "comedies of significance" in the future, he declared. "I don't want to do films that reinforce middle-class values, and that aren't threatening." His acting in *The Front* was "adequate," he said. "I know I'm not guilty of overacting, which is for me fine. I was reasonably believable, not embarrassing. But I wasn't moved by it. It wasn't like watching Al Pacino. . . ."

The reviews were uneven. Some critics liked the film; others were disappointed by a chronicle of the blacklist era that was not what they wished it to be. Vincent Canby and Andrew Sarris both deployed the same pejorative: "oversimplification." The memberships of both the Academy of Motion Picture Arts and Sciences and the Writers Guild of America disagreed, nominating Walter Bernstein's script among the finest of 1976. Columbia tried hard to peddle the "serious comedy" to exhibitors and audiences, but the studio couldn't figure out how to position *The Front* "correctly, no matter how hard the studio tried," according to the *New York Times*. "Bitter despair, suicide, and the film's two comic stars [Allen and Zero Mostel] were a blend that dismayed audiences." One of the year's notorious box office duds, *The Front* broke Allen's winning streak.

"I would like to make another picture that deals more seriously with that time and that subject," Allen said later, when *The Front* had come and gone a flop. "It might have a chance to be a better film." Walter Bernstein said Allen wrote a treatment for another "serious comedy" about the blacklist, which he himself intended to direct, before thinking better of the idea and squirrelling it away. Although *The Front* would look better and better over time, ten years would pass before Allen emoted for another director, working purely as a thespian.

STILL, HIS WORK ethic was incredible. He never took vacations. If he traveled, there were meetings, interviews, or appearances lined up for him. Allen wrote every day, and if he had the slightest writer's block, he bulled through it. He worked weekends too—like George S. Kaufman—when union people could not. He invented work for the weekends, even while he was making his pinnacle picture about Alvy Singer and Annie Hall.

Earlier in 1976, the cartoonist Stuart Hample, who had known Allen dating back to his scrounging days at Upstairs-at-the-Duplex, proposed a comic strip with Woody Allen as the lead character—the Woody Allen persona, that is, familiar to people from stand-up, stage, and screen. Rollins-Joffe liked the idea; Allen liked Hample, and he had always said his persona was akin to a cartoon version of himself. He and Hample began meeting on Saturdays to map out the strip. Hample drew Allen with a big nose and round glasses, framing what Tom Shales described as his "poached-egg eyes," going through life playing chess and seeing psychiatrists, and cracking wise about sex, death, and Kierkegaard. This was not your typical American comic strip.

Weekend work often complemented the weekday work, and the meetings with Hample gave Allen the idea for the cartoon takeoff on *Snow White* he'd integrate into his current project with Diane Keaton, now in postproduction. The cartoon insert would be executed by the former Walt Disney and Mr. Magoo animator Chris K. Ishii, and the takeoff would show Alvy nursing a crush on a Wicked Witch, voiced by Keaton.

"Inside Woody Allen" debuted in October, depicting Allen as a young nightclub comic who jokes about angst and women. The entertainer saw the comic-strip Woody Allen as another extension of his persona, and as he had done in his correspondence with Reginald Rose, he carefully delineated that persona for Hample. The comic-strip Woody Allen should be presented to the public as a credible human character with flaws and quirks, not as any kind of comically pathetic schmuck. "Please don't make me so masochistic. I'm not in life. Trying and failing is funny. Masochism is not," Allen explained to Hample. "The key is developing *people*," he told the cartoonist.

"They must have desires—goals—so we are interested in them . . . [and] you must be daring. The strip can probably exist on the level of 'cute' little jokes each day, but if you really want to involve the readers, it needs more substance." The strip, Allen insisted, should "risk being more offensive. I always believe that if I love a thing, ninety percent of the time there will be some people out there who also like it."

If Allen didn't like Hample's ideas for any specific strip, often it was because they seemed *too* Woody Allen–ish. He said he got tired of the constant wisecracking about therapy, relationships, God, and death. Wouldn't other people too? Allen asked for "more strips I'm not in. My folks. My lovers," Hample recalled.

As time went on "the anxious [newspaper] syndicate honchos demanded more gags and subjects accessible to the largest possible readership," Hample remembered. "Woody's response was that an artist has to follow his own intuition, rather than obey some huckster driven by readership surveys." When certain editors complained about explicit references to God and Death in the strip—suggesting Death be renamed "Fate"—Allen told Hample, "Better to call him Death. A character named Death can be quite funny. You have to take some chances. It'll be more alive if you use Death. Besides, you don't just want another strip that succeeds, do you?" When a sales director told the cartoonist a major California newspaper was backing away from the strip because it "dealt with too much rejection, disappointment, and sometimes even God," Allen told Hample, "I take that as a compliment. What's the worst that can happen? So, they'll cancel the strip."

Some papers did. But at one time or another, "Inside Woody Allen" appeared in two hundred publications in sixty countries. Throughout its eight-year run, Allen liaised closely with Hample on the strip, mostly on weekends and by phone.

Chapter 6

1977

Mr. Secretive

Ingmar Bergman or Boffo Box Office?—Love, Marriage, or Something De-Lovely in Between?

Variety had a new nickname for him: "Mr. Secretive." Nobody knew what the new Woody Allen film starring Diane Keaton was about. Nobody knew the title. The script was said to be some sort of realistic departure. Few could have predicted its runaway success would place Allen in a quandary, calcifying his established lovelorn persona in anarchic comedies even as, in his private behavior, he was increasingly freewheeling and attuned to the sybaritic culture of the 1970s. Even as Allen felt empowered to leave behind those surreal laugh-fests where the loser gets the girl, the new realistic romantic comedy would complicate and confuse his public image going forward.

The first version of the picture Allen and editor Ralph Rosenblum screened for Marshall Brickman, Jack Rollins, Charles Joffe, and a handful of guests in late 1976 featured a "very long" opening monologue, "repeatedly broken by cuts to scenes that amplified Woody's grievances and hang-ups," Rosenblum recalled. "It was loaded with some of the freest, funniest, most sophisticated material Woody had ever created." This opening monologue was intercut with an extended flashback to Alvy Singer's youth, the black-and-white science fiction spoof, haunting encounters with the grown-up versions of boyhood girlfriends, and "snatches of Woody on the Dick Cavett and Ed Sullivan shows." After "about thirteen or fourteen minutes" of monologue the film moved to the street scene—shot from an impossible distance away by rule-breaker Gordon Willis—introducing grown-up Alvy and his friend Rob (Tony Roberts), with Alvy grumping about anti-Semitism. "I was having lunch with some guys at NBC, and I said, 'Did you eat yet or what?' And Tom Christie said, 'No, d'Jew?'"

Then this first version jumped to Annie Hall's tardy rendezvous with Alvy at *Face to Face*, Ingmar Bergman's latest opus in 1976. Alvy is upset about having missed the beginning of the Bergman picture, and instead he and Annie rush to see *The Sorrow and the Pity*, where Alvy, standing in line, has his close encounter with Marshall McLuhan. Flashbacks introduced Alvy's first wife and more glimpses of his boyhood, with Alvy's "voluptuous cousin Doris" displaying her comic books about Hitler. The German-subtitled visit to a Nazi headquarters leads into the Alvy-Annie lobsters-at-the-beach-house scene. The first cut, two hours and twenty minutes long, focused heavily on Alvy, dwelling on "issues that were just touched in passing in the version that we know," Rosenblum recalled. "From an anxiety about proving himself and being tested to a distaste for intellectuals and an envy of athletes, Woody seemed intent on covering every issue of his adult life."

Most people, Brickman included, were distressed by what they saw. "It was like the first draft of a novel," said Brickman, "like the raw material from which a film could be assembled, from which two or three films could possibly be assembled." Annie Hall did not fully emerge as a character in the story until the second half, and even then the Alvy-Annie romance, Rosenblum recalled, merely provided "a taking-off point for innumerable flights into the past, into fantasy, into current dramatic action" exploring Allen's "personal themes."

Both Allen and Rosenblum felt discouraged. "It was clear to Woody and me that the film started moving whenever present-tense material with him and Keaton dominated the screen, and so we began cutting in the direction of that relationship," Rosenblum said. They started by slashing the flashbacks and fantasies. They said goodbye to the long opening "visual monologue"; many boyhood scenes, including Alvy being confronted on the boardwalk by a gang of young bullies; the *Invasion of the Body Snatchers* takeoff, the Garden of Eden sex colloquy, the elevator to hell, the Madison Square Garden basketball game, and the Times Square wraparound ticker with the message: "What are you doing, Alvy? Go to California. It's okay. She loves you."

Minor characters shrank or vanished. Scenes involving Alvy's previous marriages were abbreviated. The pacing of the film quickened, and the balance shifted toward Annie Hall when Keaton's scenes survived much of the cutting, although even the Wisconsin visit and Hall family Easter were trimmed. After they had assembled a fresh cut of the movie, Brickman was among the second round of watchers, and "with so much of his original material removed," in Rosenblum's words, the writer experienced a different kind of shock. Brickman felt as though his "flesh had been ripped off," he told Rosenblum. However, "a legitimate film was emerging." Allen also had a "mixed feeling" about the revamped version, Rosenblum said. He was especially sorry to lose the "surrealistic stuff," in Allen's words. "I didn't sit down with Marshall Brickman and say, 'We're going to write a picture about a relationship.' I mean the whole concept of the picture changed as we were cutting it."

Moving "the material around into logical and dramatically appropriate positions" was time-consuming, Rosenblum recalled, "and when we were unable to force a juxtaposition, Woody again had to shoot new scenes," including the coke-sneezing gag—which was later rewarded with big laughs in theaters—and a freshly devised ending. "As usual Woody was in a terrible quandary about how to end the film," said Rosenblum. Allen had shot several possible endings, including one of Alvy's awkward chance encounter with "Annie, repatriated in New York, dragging her new boyfriend [Walter Bernstein] to see *The Sorrow and the Pity*," but as with *Take the Money and Run* and *Bananas*, Rosenblum encouraged Allen to return "to the beginning of the film for a clue about how to end"—i.e., Alvy's stand-up monologue from the stage, reminiscing about Annie.

Allen jotted some lines down in a taxi on the way to the studio to record the voice-over for the ending, falling back on an old Groucho Marx joke about not wanting to belong to any club that would have him as a member, with Allen's addition—"That's the key joke of my adult life in terms of my relationships"—seeing it as membership in a club of losers at love. Giving the voice-over another twist the next day, again scribbling lines while riding in a taxi, Allen winged the film's capper: "It was great seeing Annie again. I . . . I realized what a terrific person she was, and . . . and how much fun it was just knowing her; and I . . . I, I thought of that old joke, y'know . . . this guy goes to a psychiatrist and says, 'Doc, uh, my brother's crazy; he thinks he's a chicken.' And, uh, the doctor says, 'Well, why don't you turn him in?' The guy says, 'I would, but I need the eggs.' Well, I guess that's pretty much now how I feel about relationships; y'know, they're totally irrational, and crazy, and absurd . . . but, uh, I guess we keep goin' through it because most of us . . . need the eggs."

Rosenblum asked Allen to read those very last lines against "the image of him and Keaton on the screen saying goodbye," then a montage of fond images from the Alvy-Annie romance, underscored by Annie singing "Seems Like Old Times"; the voice-over, the song, and the flashback montage gave the picture its bittersweet ending.

All along Allen had a secret title for the film he disclosed to few people—"Anhedonia"—a condition Alvy suffers from, which the dictionary defines as "a psychological condition characterized by an inability to experience pleasure in normally pleasurable acts." This was another personal grace note: Allen liked to describe himself as an "anhedonic," testing the vocabulary of friends and interviewers with the uncommon word. Although Arthur Krim supposedly walked over to a window in his high-rise office and threatened to jump out if the title remained "Anhedonia," United Artists dutifully prepared "Anhedonia" advertising and publicity while Allen sifted alternatives. Briefly, in-house, the title was "Annie and Alvy," and then finally, around Valentine's Day, 1977, six weeks before its scheduled premiere at the Los Angeles International Film Exposition (Filmex), a studio press release announced the inescapable decision. The movie the studio had promoted for months as "the new Woody Allen film" would have the "girl character's name": *Annie Hall*.

ANNIE HALL WAS unveiled at the noncompetitive Filmex festival in Los Angeles in late March. The Hall family were guests of honor at the event, but Allen, in Los Angeles for publicity interviews and meetings with United Artists executives, skipped the occasion. Accompanied by Sue Mengers, the star-director of the movie of the moment attended a dinner party at the Bistro Garden in honor of Gore Vidal, who was leaving to summer in Europe.

UA opened the picture in April, first at seven Manhattan locations including the Baronet, the Little Carnegie, and Thirty-Fourth Street East. After superlative New York reviews the film was dispatched to seventy-five theaters in sixteen American cities with plans to grow that number. *Annie Hall* quickly rocketed to number one at the box office. In the US and around the world the sixth Woody Allen movie became a genuine phenomenon. The long lines of moviegoers included many people waiting to see it for a second or third time. The quotable dialogue—"Don't knock masturbation . . . it's sex with someone I love!"—entered the popular idiom. Women started dressing like Annie Hall. The US Postal Service could have sold a postage stamp with the hand-holding Annie and Alvy.

Critics formed a wave. Judith Crist in *Saturday Review* hailed "Allen's most satisfying creation and our most gratifying comedic experience in recent years." Andrew Sarris in the *Village Voice* said *Annie Hall* was "the most brilliant Woody Allen movie to date." Joseph McBride, in *Variety*, pointed out resemblances to Ingmar Bergman and *Scenes from a Marriage*, both in content and visual style with flashbacks, split screen, "and other devices not typical to comedies." Vincent Canby, a onetime *Variety* byliner who read the trades, followed with a *New York Times* piece headlined "Woody Allen Is the American Ingmar Bergman—No Kidding." Canby also mentioned *Scenes from a Marriage* and described Diane Keaton as Allen's Liv Ullmann. Comparing Allen to Bergman became a commonplace for journalists from coast to coast. The glowing reviews ushered Allen "onto a higher artistic plateau," according to *Variety*, while also "drawing the masses."

Critics understandably viewed the script—with Keaton as the girlfriend of a stand-up comedian—as quasi-autobiographical. That was part of *Annie Hall*'s cachet, and seeing the picture that way deepened the critics' view of Allen as a filmmaker. Not only had he edged into a realism and naturalism, he had expressed himself in terms more personal than ever before. Charles Champlin in the *Los Angeles Times* praised Allen's work as his "best" to date as well as his "most autobiographical." Richard Schickel, writing for *Time*, said *Annie Hall* was "at least as poignant as it is funny and may be the most autobiographical film ever made by a major comic."

Nobody among the many thousands of people who had listened to Allen's stand-up routines thought his monologues were strictly autobiographical, unless they believed he had taken up moose hunting and brought his trophy moose to a costume party and then strapped the moose and a Jewish couple to the top of his car. The same could be easily said of his first five comedies—*Take the Money and Run*, *Bananas*, *Everything You Always*

*Wanted to Know About Sex**, *Sleeper*, and *Love and Death*. Those movies were not soul-baring.

The idea that Allen and Alvy Singer were indivisible bothered the writer, director, and star more as acclaim for *Annie Hall* mounted. After all, his and Marshall Brickman's original script had been even *more* personal and autobiographical. The way the picture evolved was serendipitous. The anhedonic director was made uncomfortable by the outpouring, and in interviews Allen tried to explain away the mass acceptance and applause by insisting *Annie Hall* was "a very middle-class picture," whose popularity was owed to its adherence to "middle-class values," which was a way of saying the movie was safe, pleasant, and basically unthreatening. The film did not reflect Allen's higher goals of attacking middle-class values. It certainly was not confessional.

He could have made "Annie Hall II" and dined out forever on the money. Instead at the precise juncture when he had maximized the audience for his comic persona, permanently cementing the image he had been building up in his stand-up and early movies, Allen braked, swerved, and reversed direction. What one scholar dubbed the "Bob Hope phase" of his career, what Allen himself once described as his "court jester phase," in which he routinely portrayed cowards and bumblers, embodying and satirizing life's also-rans, this chapter was over. Allen was determined to modify this idea of himself, now imprinted in the minds of critics and fans, an idea for which he alone was responsible. Just when he had made more people laugh than ever before—and dab away tears—Allen was determined to make the artistic ultra-drama that was his creative Moby Dick.

To that end, soon after signing off on the final cut of *Annie Hall*, "Mr. Secretive" paid a quiet visit to UA offices to meet with higher-ups. Not sounding at all like Alvy Singer, Allen asked for the go-ahead on an Ibsen/Strindberg/Bergman–type drama-drama about three sisters in a maladjusted family whose matriarch, an interior designer, is a suicidal depressive. For the first time, thanks to a contract that guaranteed this privilege, Allen would write and direct the film without appearing onscreen. Arthur Krim swallowed hard. "You've earned it," the studio elder told Allen. Around the UA office, people dubbed Allen, only half-jokingly, "Ingmar Allen."

Krim's decision was all the braver considering that the new ultra-drama might be the last Woody Allen picture he ever approved. Even as *Annie Hall* went into release, chairman of the board Krim, his longtime partner Robert Benjamin, and chief operating officer Eric Pleskow were locked in a struggle with San Francisco–based Transamerica, the holding conglomerate that controlled UA stock. Transamerica executives were increasingly made restive by UA's occasional X-rated releases, including *Midnight Cowboy* and *Last Tango in Paris*, and by studio go-aheads on artistic films that strained for profits. Transamerica wanted to reverse a trend of losses by tightening its authority over studio decision-making—decisions exactly like the one that would allow Allen to direct an ultra-drama without any hint of comedy. In late 1977, the executive triumvirate announced their resignations. Other key UA figures, including Mike Medavoy, the former talent agent and vice president of production on the West Coast, and publicity director Lloyd Leipzig, soon joined their exodus.

Krim and his team had produced every Woody Allen film since *Take the Money and Run*. According to the Hollywood rumor mill, the departing leadership might form a new studio, and perhaps Allen would join their enterprise at some point. However, after he made *Interiors*, Allen still owed #3 and #4 to UA and Transamerica.

The tremors that uprooted the Krim team were an augury of the earthquakes that were just beginning to roil and reshape the movie industry. During the first half of the 1970s, the custodians of a few major studios, along with UA, had capitalized on the breakdown of old Hollywood traditions and methods, and revitalized the American cinema by giving first-time opportunities to many younger, maverick directors, who were hailed collectively as "The Movie Brats," "The New Hollywood," or "The Hollywood Renaissance." By the early 1980s, this generation of filmmakers, including Allen, had begun to face growing obstacles as megacorporations took over the major studios, one by one. The conglomerates would reassert the old, moneymaking imperatives. Star vehicles, genre pictures, blockbusters, and sequels were the future of the new corporate Hollywood, and there would be fewer chances for low-budget, independent, free-spirited filmmaking. There would be fewer *Annie Hall*s.

THE CENTRAL MISUNDERSTANDING about *Annie Hall* was that the film was somehow the true story of Allen's romance with Diane Keaton, when really it was a pastiche of the reality—not all of it Keatonish—with imagined or exaggerated embellishments. Allen had left Keaton behind romantically years before. Though not all Keatons: In *Apropos of Nothing* Allen disclosed his "brief romance" with the actress's "beautiful sister" Robin and "a little fling" with "her other beautiful sister, Dory."* Keaton was apparently OK about this, although in *Then Again*, she complained "it drove her nuts" when Warren Beatty referred to Robin as her "pretty, sexy sister."

If people had known about Keaton's sisters at the time, certainly that would have mitigated any autobiographical interpretation of *Annie Hall*. As Allen made clear in interviews and in his correspondence with Reginald Rose, one thing he was anxious to refine about the public's perception of him was the belief, fostered by his comic persona, that he was hapless with women. He was not any kind of fool at love like Alvy Singer, even if repeatedly—even after *Annie Hall*—he played the loser-at-love type, which he knew to be more credible and appealing to audiences. Perhaps playing a conqueror of women would be too close to the truth.

Nowadays Allen was a confirmed bachelor who didn't mind being left home alone when the end credits rolled. Out of experience and temperament, Allen preferred living alone. He didn't think he'd ever marry for the third time. The pent-up sexuality he had always expressed in his writing, comedy, and motion pictures had been unleashed after two divorces, and as he grew increasingly rich and famous, he had his choice of women. The young comedy writer who once had trouble picking up girls was now hit upon by women everywhere he went. Eric Lax's first book—*On Being Funny: Woody Allen and Comedy*, published two years before *Annie Hall* in 1975—exulted in its anecdotes about the women who threw themselves at Allen. Other accounts in books, newspapers, and magazines confirmed how often Allen was approached and handed a note by a "not unattractive woman," in Lax's words, reading, "If you're who I think you are, I've always wanted to fuck you to death."

Some movie critics found Allen to be the avatar of a modern, less idealized Hollywood masculinity—compared, say, to tough guy Clint Eastwood, who was racking up the hits and plaudits simultaneously in the 1970s. Allen was a novelty on the screen, not the hoary cliché, a man who didn't solve

* In *Then Again* Keaton spells her sister's name as "Dorrie," as it is spelled for the *Stardust Memories* character played by Charlotte Rampling. Allen, in *Apropos of Nothing*, spells it "Dory."

problems with his fists or a gun. Feminists were more exacting. They hadn't forgotten Allen's long affiliation with *Playboy*, which included nude-women pictorials framed by his humorous prose and layouts with actresses from Woody Allen movies including China Lee (*What's Up, Tiger Lily?*) and Naty Abascal (*Bananas*). They remembered the trademark riffs in his stand-up routine about breasts, orgasms, and masturbation, not to mention all the "ugly girl" and ex-wife jokes. Again and again (it was one of his tropes), Allen had put himself in publicity stills and movie scenes with scantily clad women; in *Sleeper*, he's "Miss Montana" in the swimsuit competition of the Miss America beauty pageant. These photographs and scenes were invariably jokes, with Allen looking like a naughty boy with his hand caught in a candy jar, and mostly these tropes went away after *Annie Hall*. But it was too late for long memories.

The critic and journalist Vivian Gornick, who had related to Allen's anxiety at the Bitter End in 1964, evolved into a radical feminist and essayist. In 1976 Gornick visited Allen for the left-bohemian *Village Voice*, and while deciding the star was "much better-looking offscreen than onscreen" she also found him deficient as a male exemplar. Even a mild-mannered comedy like *Play It Again, Sam*, which Gornick had sat through, left her "angry and somewhat repelled" to feel as "though I'd been watching Woody Allen try to get laid for twenty years now." She rebuked Allen to his Zelig face: "You create out of a woman a foil who ultimately is an object of ridicule. Don't you see that? Don't you get enough flak from enough women so that you see that?"

"I don't think of it as girl-chasing," Allen replied ("with dignity," Gornick wrote). "People are lonely, they have difficulties with women, sex is a great area of human concern. I'm trying to show a guy caught up in all that." As a comic, Allen explained, "you're always offending someone." Then he added—perhaps he shouldn't have—"Jews are offended by my rabbi jokes. In the sixties everyone offended the blacks. Now, it's women."

Another feminist, Lee Guthrie, announced she had written the first major biography of Allen for Drake Publishers, and her book would investigate his love life as well as the depiction of women in his comedy and movies. Allen had tried to win Gornick over—in vain. But he went to court against Guthrie, filing a suit joined by Lax, who first had interviewed Allen for the *New York Times* in 1972 and would interview him again for the *Times* on multiple occasions over the years. They claimed Guthrie's book would pose an "unfair competition with his [Allen's] own biographical plans," according to press accounts, and would excessively draw from *On Being Funny*, the 1975 tome that was the first of the four books Lax ultimately wrote about Allen with his cooperation.

Guthrie was intimidated into softening her approach and, according to *Variety*, the out-of-court settlement forced Drake to "cease further publication" and "recall and destroy all existing copies." Allen could trust Lax to pay sympathetic attention to his comedy, his filmmaking, and his attractiveness to women while steering clear of unpleasantness in his personal relationships. First wife Harlene Rosen was covered sparsely in *On Being Funny*, without any mention of her lawsuit; and Lax's authorized biography, coming fifteen years later, painted a rosy portrait of his relationships with Keaton and Mia Farrow while leaving out all the women in between.

Allen preferred to be "Mr. Secretive" about his love life and his intimate friendships with women, some of whom—like Louise Lasser or Diane Keaton—influenced the female characters he created in his scripts. The public Woody Allen was separate from the private Woody Allen, even if the public Woody Allen told people quite a bit about the private Woody Allen in interviews, in his comedy, and in the characters he wrote for himself to play in movies. The public and private intertwined, sometimes with thin, blurred lines. Some secrets about the secretive Woody Allen were in the open. He could just as easily be known as "Mr. Open Secret."

More so than ever after *Annie Hall*, the paparazzi stalked America's Ingmar Bergman as he daily traversed Manhattan streets from his penthouse duplex to his offices on West Fifty-Seventh. Nightly, during the summer of 1977, the shutterbugs often caught him at Elaine's near the corner of Second Avenue and East Eighty-Eighth, where he held reserved table number eight, and was frequently joined by some combination of Tony Roberts, Michael Murphy, Diane Keaton, Louise Lasser, and/or Jean Doumanian. After obtaining a divorce from her recording-industry husband, Doumanian had made her way professionally in Manhattan, trading on her friendship with Allen. She worked for publicist Bobby Zarem at the preeminent Rogers & Cowan agency, then as a talent coordinator for Dick Cavett in the early 1970s. After also vetting talent for Howard Cosell's short-lived television variety show in 1975–76, Doumanian had moved to the production staff of *Saturday Night Live*.

At night, the paparazzi snapped Allen, slouched down, in the back seat of his chauffeur-driven, cream-colored Rolls-Royce as his vehicle crisscrossed Central Park headed to restaurants or shows. Often there were other people in the car, sometimes a beautiful woman. Who was she? She might be Doumanian, whose relationship with Allen always seemed platonic, or perhaps Keaton, another "gal pal," in her phrase. Since Allen was often glimpsed with women the columnists could not easily identify, the director was frequently asked, in interviews, if there was any special lady in his life, a line of interrogation that always made him fidget and stammer. Allen reluctantly answered to an "active bachelor life" while saying he had not sustained a relationship with any woman for more than a few months after he had stopped living with Keaton in 1971.

The time was long past when he was attracted solely to Village types, or when, as Allen approached the day of his first marriage, he required a sex tutorial from a Brooklyn guy-pal. If Allen was a shrinking violet as a young comedy writer, he had made up for lost time with growing confidence and celebrity. From Harlene Rosen and Judy Henske to Louise Lasser and Diane Keaton suggests an eclectic and free-spirited range.

He found "willowy lingerie models beautiful and sexy" too, Allen acknowledged in *Apropos of Nothing*. He'd also spent a fair amount of time as Hugh Hefner's guest at Playboy events in New York, Chicago, Los Angeles, and London. "It was an open house [in Chicago] nearly twenty-four hours, hung with Picassos and full of celebrities, sports figures, sexy women. The sexy women were the whole draw. Believe me, it wasn't the Picassos," he said. Allen confessed "over the years I have had brief dalliances with centerfolds," adding pointedly, as if to bolster his Don Juan credentials, "but it never came about from going to Hefner's mansion."

If Allen had learned to live happily without a marital partner, the famous man also hated going out at night alone without a "date," and the dates, as was his wont, were sometimes long flirtations with ambiguous goals.

Pamela Des Barres was a nubile blonde flower child and rock-and-roll gadabout who boasted of her affairs with illustrious members of the Rolling Stones, Led Zeppelin, and the Byrds. She later wrote a frank and lively memoir about that part of her life called *I'm with the Band: Confessions of a Groupie*. Des Barres, who lived in Los Angeles and briefly acted professionally in motion pictures, bumped into Allen one night at Elaine's, where many such Allen first encounters happened. They exchanged pleasantries and "the following night I found myself sitting at his dining-room table, eating duck jubilee and spinach salad" whipped up by his cook.

After dinner, they "shot off to see *The Exorcist*, which was full of sensationalist bullshit, but he made it hilarious," Des Barres wrote. When Linda Blair peed on the floor in a scene, Woody barked, "You can't take kids anywhere!" before slinking down and pulling his hat over his face. When Blair growled, "Your mother sucks cocks in hell!" Woody shouted, "You raise 'em, you try to bring 'em up right, and look what happens!"

Another time Allen escorted Des Barres to the Continental Baths, a gay bathhouse and sex club in the basement of the Ansonia Hotel, where she wanted to see her friend, the singer and comedian Judith Cohen—they had acted together in the movie *Arizona Slim*—perform in the cabaret. Allen would remember Cohen, and later cast her as "the friend of Sandy's sister" in *Stardust Memories*. "When people noticed him [at the Baths], he became even more noticeable by slouching, yanking his hat down over his ears, and turning red."

Whenever Allen and Des Barres stopped in bars, he cringed if the bartenders recognized him. One night they met Dick Cavett for drinks and dinner at Sardi's. "When he [Allen] had to go to the bathroom, he asked me if I saw anyone watching him. He studied every table, making sure all the patrons were involved in their conversations or plates of food before he put his fishing hat on and scuttled through, so conspicuously inconspicuous that all heads turned." Wherever the two went, an endless stream of people came up to him, asking for an autograph, and "every time it happened, he looked like the world was coming to an end."

Des Barres was the kiss-and-tell type, but she couldn't follow through where Allen was concerned. "I really like Woody," she wrote in her diary. "He's so cuddlable and kind and sweet." He promised they'd go to Disneyland together when he visited California, but that never came to pass. Instead, they became pen pals. When Des Barres came to New York a few years later, she let Allen know she was engaged to be married. "He wasn't amused," she wrote. "We had dinner and I never saw him again, except in the movies." Among the disparate groupies Des Barres may have inspired in Woody Allen films, there is a memorable though not very nubile example in

Stardust Memories and more of a Des Barres type who frolics with Kenneth Branagh and Leonardo DiCaprio in *Celebrity.*

THERE WERE MANY platonic relationships that may have been long flirtations that did not go on quite long enough. Allen had several dates with writer Jean vanden Heuvel, whom he first encountered at a Sue Mengers Hollywood party. Although they moved in somewhat different circles in New York, and vanden Heuvel was the mother of two children, they crossed paths at parties—one time, for example, at fashion designer Diane von Fürstenberg's, where power brokers like Henry Kissinger were chatting up sexy supermodels. Apropos of the gaudy decor and elite guest list, Allen told vanden Heuvel he thought the party was quite the "high-class degenerate scene."

One night, on a date with Allen in 1977, they went to *The Nutcracker* at the Metropolitan Opera. While stuck in traffic on the way to Lincoln Center, sitting with Allen in the back seat of his cream-colored Rolls-Royce, vanden Heuvel had an uncomfortable close-up of just how jumpy Allen got when venturing out in public. Were his clothes OK? he asked. She reassured him, although as far as she could tell he was wearing his usual checkered shirt and khakis with nondescript jacket—and sneakers—for what was a black-tie event. He was tense about arriving late. The photographers would spot him immediately, he worried; certainly they would, in the Alvy Singer–like outfit he was wearing, vanden Heuvel thought. If he entered the theater after the ballet had begun, everyone would stir and recognize Woody Allen. On and on he voiced such concerns.

The air conditioner was on full blast as they sat in stalled traffic. Making conversation, vanden Heuvel asked Allen about his driver—who was he, what was his life story? It was the same driver who'd been with him for four or five years on retainer, Allen said, and all he knew about him was his first name. It was sweltering outside, and vanden Heuvel commented on the car's nice and cold air-conditioning. Allen told her one year before he had been similarly stuck in Lincoln Center traffic. At the time, he owned a black Cadillac limousine. Allen was out with a date for the evening, and the air-conditioning was on high because it was hot outside then too. Suddenly, the air-conditioning failed. Allen was shaken, convinced his date had been ruined, and the next morning he called his accountant and ordered him to sell the black limo. That's why he now had a white one.

The couple attended fetes honoring author James Jones and *New Yorker* cartoonist Saul Steinberg, both of whom they admired. Vanden Heuvel got the invite to the celebration of Jones's latest novel ("Jean vanden Heuvel & Guest"), and it was she who was closely acquainted with Steinberg, even though Allen was a *New Yorker* confrere. For the Steinberg occasion, an exhibition preview at the Whitney Museum, again Allen dressed in his customary garb, fretting that black-tie people would take offense. As always, he also worried about the general public, and the inevitable scrum of photographers, telling vanden Heuvel, as his limousine neared the Whitney, "Don't worry, I'm going to act strange for a few minutes." Jumping out and walking toward the entrance, he dodged and weaved behind the elegantly dressed vanden Heuvel, a bit like an agile hockey player, she thought, avoiding the flashing lights of cameras and batting away hands outstretched with pieces of paper, "Sorry, I never sign autographs." Newspaper photos the next day showed him "cowering in her wake," as the *New York Times* recounted, with Allen resembling "a cross between bewildered Martian exiled to earth and a pale elf."

Inside the gala Allen was also discomfited. The slow museum elevator was "like being in Auschwitz," the claustrophobic comedian cracked. Allen couldn't forget the people left standing outside, without tickets. They evoked disgruntled revolutionaries, he told vanden Heuvel. He had a recurring fear of someone stepping out from an angry mob and tossing mace in his eyes. "Off with their heads for those inside," he quipped. She steered him toward Steinberg, introducing them. Allen told Steinberg his cartoons and illustrations, adorning the walls, were beautiful. "Yes, so beautiful," Steinberg murmured. "Woody is amazed and amused at the way Saul accepted his compliment," vanden Heuvel recalled, "and wishes he could take compliments with such self-assurance."

Curiously, after the reception, Allen strolled assuredly out with vanden Heuvel to meet a small knot of paparazzi still waiting. He no longer ducked and bobbed. One camera-clutcher asked politely if he could snap Allen's photo. "Now he agrees," vanden Heuvel recalled, "but in an almost regal way." Allen also spoke with the paparazzi for a few minutes before nudging her back into his limousine to head to Elaine's, where they were to meet the

Jann Wenners for late-night drinks and spaghetti. Allen had avoided food at the event. He was a night owl who liked to eat late at favorite places, even if he wasn't very hungry, and he drank next to nothing. Or, if he had filming duties the next day, he'd suddenly excuse himself. There seemed little "in-between" with him.

Vanden Heuvel took notes for a possible profile or book about Allen. She liked him enormously. She didn't pretend to understand him. Was he a walking contradiction, a paradox? friends questioned her. You tell me! she responded. "How much is the invented Woody Allen, and how much is the real Woody Allen?" vanden Heuvel asked herself in her notes. "Is it all a performance?" She went around and around with such questions.

ANOTHER "VERY INTERESTING friend" of Allen's was the dark-haired, vivacious, intellectually stimulating Mary Bancroft, the former World War II spy thirty years older than the filmmaker. Living in Switzerland during the war, Bancroft served as an effective intelligence agent for the OSS under Allen Dulles, with whom she enjoyed a long affair. Psychologist Carl Jung had treated Bancroft for sneezing and asthma, and she'd become a lifelong Jung champion and authority. Back in America after the war, Bancroft metamorphosed into a successful author of memoirs and fiction. The *Encyclopedia of World Biography* would list Allen among her several famous "male consorts," although probably he was more of an occasional and epistolary kindred spirit. Bancroft was full of advice and always urging Allen to make a Kafkaesque movie "in black and white, with the serious you wandering through it while actually coming across as hilarious," in her words. "We had lots of nice times together until she passed away," Allen wrote in *Apropos of Nothing*. Besides sending letters to each other, the two friends took walks and visited museums, and he always sent Bancroft flowers on her birthday. She had a cameo role in *Stardust Memories*, until he cut it. The absurdist *Shadows and Fog* owes more than a little to her encouragement. If their thirty-year friendship was purely platonic, in his memoir Allen didn't say.

Some flirtations didn't last beyond first dates. Eleven-year-old Brooke Shields had a brief scene in *Annie Hall* as "the focus of young Alvy's obsession . . . a sexy pilgrim in a flashback of a Thanksgiving-themed school play." Allen spoke almost not at all to the young girl, but he did ask her mother, Teri Shields, a model and actress, out to dinner. "I think it was only one night and it was just dinner," Shields wrote in a memoir of her mother. "She explained that Woody was too neurotic and was in too much therapy for her liking." Teri and Brooke liked to joke the date gone wrong was probably why Brooke's scene was ultimately lopped from the movie.

"OF THE MANY women I have been involved with over the decades," Allen wrote somewhat defensively in his autobiography, "almost none were much younger than I was"—note the "almost." In fact, he had a "barely legal" phase in the mid-1970s, when—for a little historical context—the rich, the famous, the fast-living, the hedonistic, and the sexually promiscuous reigned over the New York social scene. Suddenly, everything once forbidden was permissible: piercings and tattoos; cocaine and deadlier drugs; public, group, and all manner of sexual experimentation. The nightlife was more sinful than the Rev. Billy Graham could possibly have imagined.

Allen was in his early forties. Teenage girls fluttered around him in public, sometimes coming up to him at Elaine's, other times finding him at Michael's Pub, pleading for autographs and blowing kisses. John Simon, in his vitriolic putdown of *Stardust Memories*, referred to Michael's Pub as "Woody's real-life Deer Park," an allusion to Norman Mailer's 1955 novel that depicted a metaphorical playground of Hollywood depravity. Many New Yorkers knew about Allen's "occasional predilection for younger women, including one female in her teens," according to a 1980 *New York Times* profile of the director. This was *his* predilection, even if in *Annie Hall* Allen gave that socially unacceptable penchant to Rob (Tony Roberts), who is bedding twin sixteen-year-olds in Hollywood. "Can you imagine the mathematical possibilities?" Rob boasts. Alvy disapproves.

There were several "younger women" in Allen's real life, and at least two of the girls were sixteen when he first met them, still high school age. The odd case of Nancy Jo Sales was fated to be nonphysical. She was thirteen years old, in high school in Coral Gables, Florida, when she began penning letters to Allen, around the time he was filming *Interiors*. She wrote him about "how unhappy I was, how bored and full of yearning to do something *meaningful*" in life. He wrote back. "I don't know how he found the time—and can't say why he had the inclination," she later reflected. A man who set aside time every day for letter-writing, Allen kept up their correspondence with warm-hearted letters, saying "when I was thirteen I couldn't dress myself" but here she was grappling with "life's deepest philosophical problems, i.e., existential boredom." He encouraged her to read Proust and Kierkegaard and recommended prep schools and colleges, including one she ultimately attended.

Sales met Allen only once, when on a shopping excursion to Manhattan. After she left a note with his doorman, he phoned her hotel. Perhaps he was taken aback when she arrived with her stepmother and an "ultra–Palm Beach female acquaintance who had recently had a nose job." Her stepmother and the nose-job friend hijacked the conversation while Allen, who looked, behind his trademark glasses, "translucent," as Sales recalled, "like a corpse or an angel," sitting "Indian-style in an armchair, much like a thirteen-year-old, nodding politely, trying to catch my eye." Her adult companions chattered away embarrassingly. Before long "it was time to go, and I looked into his eyes only at the end of our meeting. 'Goodbye,' they said sadly." Allen gave Sales moral support at a crucial time in her life ("Your kind of mind and feeling is a prize to have even though you will have to pay a price for it") yet she never heard from him again. Recalling her friendship with Allen for *New York* magazine at the height of the Allen-Farrow custody case and Dylan Farrow child-abuse allegations in 1993, Sales said she preferred to view their brief connection as "more a cause for celebration than suspicion."

A more significant sweetheart was Stacey Nelkin, who was a Stuyvesant High School student when she met Allen. Casting director Juliet Taylor brought Nelkin in for *Annie Hall*, where she played the small role of Alvy's luscious older cousin Doris in a flashback scene—a comic twist on the beloved cousin he'd shared a room with in boyhood. A buxom brunette, Nelkin sucked seductively on a lollipop in her single scene. "She had to be pretty, and she had to be sexy for the jokes to work," Allen recalled, and Nelkin was "a beautiful, bright, charming young woman who caused Marshall [Brickman] and myself to spin around each other like electrons." In the fall, after the principal photography was finished, Allen invited Nelkin to hear his jazz band on a Monday night at Michael's Pub, by which time the young actress had turned seventeen. Her mother ("also quite charming") accompanied Nelkin and seemed to promote the relationship between her high-school-age daughter and the film director. Nelkin's *Annie Hall* scene was also scuttled, Nelkin thought, to keep their subsequent affair secret.

Nelkin was not a dippy groupie like the one portrayed by Amy Wright in *Stardust Memories*, who wears Sandy Bates's face on her T-shirt and sneaks into his hotel room with a hash brownie. The groupie's husband has driven her to the hotel for a freebie with Bates, played by Allen. When Bates protests sex with her would be empty sex, she delivers the line—"Empty sex is better than no sex, right?"—which could be marketed on a Woody Allen T-shirt. Nelkin was "sharp and educated," Allen wrote in his memoir, not any sort of witless fan.

Around the same time, while editing *Annie Hall* in the fall of 1976, Allen met another sixteen-year-old at Elaine's. Babi Christina Engelhardt was dining with fashion photographer Andrew Unangst. Catching Allen's eye, the blonde looker dropped a note at his table, along with her phone number: "Since you've signed enough autographs, here's mine!" A high school dropout who aspired to be a model and actress, Engelhardt was born on December 4, 1959, according to IMDb.com, and was probably seventeen by the time Allen, who turned forty-one on December 1, invited her to his place, "quizzing her on the meaning of life, challenging her to a chess match, inviting her to watch a basketball game in his TV room, making out with her," according to a 2018 account in the *Hollywood Reporter*. Anyway, "The Great Man," as "she considered him then, and still considers him now," never asked Engelhardt her age, and their affair "operated under two key unspoken rules. . . . There would be zero discussions about his work, and—owing to the celebrity's presumed necessity for privacy—they could meet only at his place. By her count, on more than a hundred subsequent occasions, she'd visit him at his apartment at 930 Fifth Ave., where she'd invariably make her way to an upstairs bedroom facing Central Park."

About a year after they began their affair, Allen started to bring other "beautiful young ladies" into his bedroom for occasional threesomes, Engelhardt claimed in the *Reporter* interview. One may well have been Nelkin, who told radio talk-show host Howard Stern she too was involved in threesomes with Allen—always with wholesome girls, never prostitutes, Nelkin added. In the spirit of the times the adventurous young women did not mind the threesomes. Engelhardt had "experimented with bisexuality" and found such experiences "interesting—a seventies exploration."

Allen's affair with Nelkin ended after two years when she moved to California to pursue acting. In horror films and comedies, Nelkin developed a cult following as a vivacious presence, and later she became a "relationship expert" with a website and her own YouTube channel. Nelkin remained in touch with Allen, and he would cast his former lover in fleeting parts in several Woody Allen pictures, including *Bullets over Broadway*. In the last scene of that 1994 movie, Broadway playwright David Shayne (John Cusack) is outside on a street at night arguing with the bohemian playwright Sheldon Flender (Rob Reiner), who is framed in his upstairs window with Shayne's girlfriend (Mary-Louise Parker). Flender brags about how good he is in bed. "Hey, I slept with Flender!" exclaims Nelkin, poking her head out of a neighboring window. "He's just OK!"

Nelkin and Engelhardt both believed they helped inspire the Tracy character in *Manhattan*. Engelhardt's affair with Allen continued for eight years, she claimed. Allen does not mention her in his memoir.

MANHATTAN WOULD BE written after the filming of *Interiors*, just as Allen wrote *Interiors* after finishing *Annie Hall*. He was in preproduction for the ultra-drama, the first film he'd direct without appearing on camera—the first to be shot entirely in New York studios and environs—when, on August 19, 1977, Allen learned of the death of his friend and comedy hero, Groucho Marx, who had passed away at age eighty-six in Los Angeles. Two months later the writer-director embarked on the least comical and least Groucho-like picture he'd ever make.

The three sisters at the heart of *Interiors* were nothing like the Keaton siblings except for their number. Diane Keaton was playing Renata, the oldest, most successful of the trio, a character who is the antithesis of Luna in *Sleeper*. A serious, elliptical poet, Renata takes little joy in her accomplishments. Her novelist-husband (Richard Jordan) views himself as a failure who has not lived up to his promise, and he drinks to excess. The youngest sister, Joey (Marybeth Hurt), is a thwarted photographer and actress who lives with a political filmmaker (Sam Waterston). Middle sister Flyn (Kristin Griffith) is a successful actress squandering her talent and beauty in television pabulum. The three sisters, who inevitably evoke Chekhov, must cope with the mounting mental fragility of their mother (Geraldine Page), an interior decorator whose husband (E. G. Marshall), a wealthy lawyer, abruptly announces their separation at a family breakfast. Nearly everyone is miserable, tortured. The story ends in an ocean suicide rather like *A Star Is Born*—another George Cukor film.

It was Keaton who suggested the casting of Page as the unstable mother. A bravura actress in her mid-fifties, acclaimed for roles on Broadway and in motion pictures, Page had been nominated for six previous Academy Awards without winning. She arrived eagerly for her interview with Allen, thinking she might be auditioning for a modest part like the one her friend Colleen Dewhurst had played in *Annie Hall* as Annie's Wisconsin mother, which had melted away in the editing. Allen took time in their meeting to let Page know Eve, her character, was important. Just as *Interiors* would be the first of many Woody Allen movies to fixate on sisters, Eve was the first of many women in his post–*Annie Hall* work to be depicted as psychologically adrift and self-destructive. The ruined lives of these characters were often linked to their careers in interior design or the arts.

Maureen Stapleton was another actor's actor, twice Oscar-nominated. She'd play Pearl, the only positive character in *Interiors*, "an outgoing, warm-hearted Jewish widow," in her words. The estranged father meets the aptly named Pearl on a Greek cruise, falling in love with her and bringing her home to meet his daughters. Pearl injects vitality into the third act. Stapleton was costumed by Joel Schumacher in bright reds and prints to contrast with the browns and beiges that suffuse the film. Pearl signals disaster for Eve, and Joey finds her father's girlfriend a "vulgarian" after she performs magic tricks and dances to Fats Waller and Jelly Roll Morton in their household. It's the only music in a movie given over to hushed silences, wind, and waves.

Knowing he was "in over my head with two of our country's greatest actresses, my first venture away from comedy," the writer-director invited the two actresses over to his apartment to discuss their characters and read through the script. A mistake: a rehearsal was "something I hadn't done before, and I have never done since. . . . I'm not a patient person when it comes to rehearsal demands. That's why, over the years, I shoot long masters and don't cover. I can't sit through doing scenes over and over. I like to do it, go home, and watch basketball."

Allen offered drinks to Page and Stapleton, and soon enough they were slurring their words and behaving rudely to him and each other. Later, on the set, Allen manifested a rare "combination of control and freedom for all" that was helpful, Page said later. But "when Woody gave her [Page] direction," Keaton countered in her reminiscences, "she smiled, nodded her head politely, then completely disregarded everything he said."

The elaborate preproduction included the renovation of an oceanside mansion in Southampton, which Allen chose for the family's weekend getaway house after rejecting dozens of similar estates. Carpenters, painters, and set dressers slaved to accommodate the muted tones and stark furnishings the director ordered up. "This blue has to go," a location manager told one owner whose property was leased for a scene, "Woody doesn't like blue." "It was very important for me to understand what Woody was driving at in the character of Eve [Page]," production designer Mel Bourne told the *New York Times*. "Everything in the film had to be imbued with her personality. Woody told me that she was a very austere woman, a purist, and an extremist, in whose work there was no room for embellishment. Her influence had to be felt in her family's beach house, her New York apartment, her husband's office, and in the homes of her three daughters. Everything had to be spare and exquisite." The filming was "the trial of the age to me," Bourne said later. "That [*Interiors*] was the worst. He'd [Allen] change entire sets suddenly, because he'd last-minute decided he just didn't like them."

Perhaps the Prince of Darkness was more at home with this ultra-drama, with its meticulously planned staging and composition and somber colors. Sometimes Gordon Willis shot day-for-night, including the "beach walk with Renata [Keaton] and Flyn [Griffith]," according to John Baxter, "lit and framed to recall an etching by Emil Nolde, whose work Allen had admired ever since he bought one of his watercolors" in London.

Wearing his army field jacket, corduroys, a flannel shirt, and battered gray hat, carrying thermoses of malted milks brought from home, Allen arrived and departed from the filming accompanied by Keaton, whose discomfort with her role would force her into a grim, strained performance. "Miscast as a brilliant writer in the vein of [former film critic turned novelist] Renata Adler," she later wrote, "I smoked cigarettes and knotted my brow in an effort to seem intelligent. The words Woody wrote didn't fit on the lips of my experience."

Allen was "antisocial" and "not exactly a bundle of laughs" on the set, according to Stapleton, but the actress was determined to lure the filmmaker into a bar for a drink some night after the work wrapped—perhaps he might lighten up. To everyone's surprise, the brassy Stapleton landed her quarry, and she and Allen did duck inside a bar for "a few beers" and loose conversation. "He didn't talk much and didn't give you a lot of things to work on or with [on the set]," Stapleton recalled, "but he sort of sensed if something was not right. He knew exactly what he wanted and had a perfect eye and ear for getting the desired results." Allen would give a tip of his hat to Stapleton in *Apropos of Nothing* as "one of the nicest and truly funniest women I've ever met."

After thc photography was done for the day and dailies watched, many nights Allen and Keaton returned together to Manhattan for a late dinner at Elaine's. On Mondays, he'd still blow his clarinet at Michael's Pub. The filming and refilming stretched for months. Editor Ralph Rosenblum remembered all during the editing and postproduction Allen underwent "great anxieties as a result of the dangerous new terrain he was treading."

BY THE TIME of Alvy and Annie's Oscar date, the *Interiors* filming had been completed and the editing was in high gear. The anhedonic director took scant pleasure in the five Academy Award nominations for *Annie Hall*: Best Picture, Director, Screenplay, Actress, Actor. Always maneuvering behind Allen's back, the United Artists executive team had asked producer Freddie Fields to forgo any Best Actress campaign for Diane Keaton in *Looking for Mr. Goodbar*, which was also released in 1977; her performance in *Goodbar* might conceivably take votes away from her in the same Best Actress category. Fields, who'd been a talent agency colleague of Mike Medavoy's, facilitated the favor, which bolstered the odds for Keaton's lead in *Annie Hall*. UA publicist Lloyd Leipzig managed to slot the picture on the Z Channel, a top-quality Los Angeles cable system that abided by Allen's no-editing edict, and *Annie Hall* was beamed into Oscar-voting living rooms.

Allen was proud of Keaton, and he didn't mind if the actress and his personal management team and his cowriter Marshall Brickman disported at the triumphant April 3, 1978, Academy Awards ceremony, picking up the Oscar trophies for Best Picture, Director, Screenplay, and Actress. "*Annie*

Hall was a wonderful experience," Keaton told the star-filled auditorium and worldwide television audience with brief remarks that pointedly praised the other Best Actress nominees sitting amid the audience—Anne Bancroft, Jane Fonda, Marsha Mason, Shirley MacLaine. "I just want to say thanks to Woody and thank you [all] very much."

Allen, who vied for Best Actor, was the only nomination *Annie Hall* didn't win. Although the vast majority of the Motion Picture Academy dwelled in the Los Angeles area, many were former East Coasters who didn't mind his gibes at Southern California in *Annie Hall* and other movies down the years. "I don't want to live in a city where the only cultural advantage is you can make a right turn on a red light," Alvy tells Annie in the movie's ringing dig at El Lay.* Probably older Academy voters were conflicted by the prospect of giving the acting prize to a comedian. The Academy would reward Woody Allen pictures with numerous nominations in the years ahead, but never again would Allen go up for another acting Oscar. He should have won for Alvy Singer. He was robbed by Richard Dreyfuss, who won for Neil Simon's *The Goodbye Girl*, a lesser job in a less fondly remembered picture.

Regardless, Allen had long before made it clear what he thought of Oscars and similar door prizes. Taking Groucho Marx's maxim to heart—"I would never want to belong to any club that would have someone like me for a member," which he had quoted in *Annie Hall*—Allen was invited and refused to join the Motion Picture Academy "about sixteen times," according to a 2008 account in the *New York Times*. On the occasion of *Annie Hall*'s conquest, he pointedly absented himself, playing his clarinet that Monday night at his weekly Michael's Pub gig. Without apparent curiosity, he even avoided the telecast, an annual event watched by tens of millions of people around the world. After playing for a packed audience at Michael's Pub he headed home, turned off his phone, and read a little of *Conversations with Carl Jung* before nodding off to sleep. Throughout Academy Award history, only a handful of nominees have intentionally skipped the momentous occasion. For most contenders, the Oscars are a glorious opportunity for partying and self-advertisement. This was largely why, as Adam Gopnik wrote

* "His Los Angeles barbs were famous and much quoted," onetime UA executive Steven Bach wrote in his memoir, "but they were mostly innocuous skewer gags, not toothless but without venom . . . [mirroring] an attitude curiously fashionable with a large percentage of the California Academy membership."

later in the *New Yorker*, many people saw Allen's deliberate no-show as "a unique act of integrity."

The next morning Allen woke up. As he was warming his croissant and drinking his orange juice, he unfolded the *New York Times* and saw *Annie Hall*'s Oscar bonanza emblazoned on the front page. "I was very surprised," the director told Gene Shalit later that year. "*Very* surprised. I couldn't believe it." Allen turned on his phone, it started to ring and ring, and it didn't stop all day. One phone call emanated from United Artists, whose sales officials wanted to refresh the *Annie Hall* advertising with posters displaying images of the four winning Oscar statuettes. Absolutely not, Allen said. "Those ads embarrass me," he explained to Shalit. "I don't want people to see *Annie Hall* because it won awards. I want them to see it because they'll have a good time seeing it." Under pressure from UA and Rollins-Joffe, Allen relented a little. The studio could tout the Oscars in publicity or advertising in any part of the US that was at least one hundred and fifty miles from New York City.

Truthfully, *Annie Hall* didn't need any bolstering in New York. Yet UA's post-Oscar campaign in other parts of the US spurred the antiromantic comedy to a second, higher summit of success. *Annie Hall* became the first Woody Allen film to attract crowds in, for example, Peoria, Illinois—as in the old vaudeville query, "Yes, but will it play in Peoria?" His previous pictures had been "art house" anathema in such places. "Before the awards, *Annie Hall* had not been a blockbuster," wrote Steven Bach. Now "middle America responded to Woody's New York anxiety." One year after its first release, *Annie Hall* shot up into the top ten again, lingering for months. Also, "for the first time," said Bach, "a foreign public seemed to get the jokes and rhythms, giving a lift to *Annie Hall*'s worldwide receipts and making possible foreign reissues of his earlier films."

Fifty years on, *Annie Hall* still tops the list of Allen's greatest hits, earning $38.3 million in domestic grosses—roughly $180 million adjusted for today's ticket prices and inflation—before adding in home video, repeat television airings, and international receipts. The Oscar-winning antiromantic comedy racked up record box office for Allen in Europe and Asia and gave him a foothold in hitherto unconquered markets in Latin America.

"I'm told that *Annie Hall* was the lowest-earning Academy Award movie in history," Allen always insisted. Or "I'd trade that Oscar for one more second of life," as the comedian and film director Sandy Bates (Allen) avers in

Stardust Memories. Allen said much the same in many interviews. Months after the Oscars, Allen told Shalit he didn't have the foggiest notion where his golden trophies reposed and didn't care. Charles Joffe must have been reading the clippings because Norma Lee Clark phoned to say they sat in the Rollins-Joffe office. "Well, I'm certainly not going to put Oscars in my house!" Allen told Clark, promptly remanding the sacred objects to his father and mother for their mantelpiece. "It's my father who polishes [them]," he said, years hence.*

IF WOODY ALLEN was famous before *Annie Hall*, he was a thousand times more famous afterward. Dating back to a 1966 interview, Allen voiced "a fear of being shot by a girl or a psychotic fan who imagines some connection between us." Nothing could be worse than a psychotic "connection" between himself and an obsessed fan, with an imagined idea of who he was—an idea he himself was constantly fine-tuning, never happy with, in films or in real life. Circulating widely in New York, amid cameras clicking at parties thronged by the wealthy and powerful, Allen was now more than ever a nervous, enigmatic figure, whose lifelong refusal to conform to conventional mores now encompassed his disdain for and fears about the magnitude of his celebrity in America.

His paradoxes fascinated the press and public as well as his closest friends. While Allen insisted that he ought never to be mistaken for Alvy Singer, he continued to walk around wearing his "standard uniform," as journalists liked to describe it, of a plaid shirt, corduroys, fatigue jacket, and fisherman's hat. That was akin to what Alvy might also wear, and was, in fact, often the costume Allen wore home from filming. Both the costume and his daily wardrobe were usually—no matter how much they looked off-the-rack—Ralph Lauren.

The famous face tried for anonymity at public events, while standing out in the crowd in his "disguise hat" and the same costume as his characters. The loser with women who was a playboy offscreen. The farceur who brooded about God and death. The comedian whose jokes gave people pleasure and made them chuckle and smile, while he himself was

* While in interviews Allen often referred to one Oscar, there must have been two—one for Direction; one for cowriting the Best Screenplay.

anhedonic and might chuckle but rarely guffawed. The supreme director and star of silly comedies who aspired to be an artist of profound searching tragedies like Ingmar Bergman. Jewish but not Jewish. Intellectual but not intellectual. As much Upper East Side as Brooklynese or Greenwich Village.

Some people were more irritated than intrigued by the incongruities, which had begun to fuel a backlash against Allen and his movies, later to become a veritable tsunami. Some people scoffed at Allen's hat disguise, his extreme introverted personality, and thought his social wariness was part of an elaborate charade. Along with heightened fame and success, *Annie Hall* also hardened this skepticism of the comedian and film director.

The comic strip artist Jules Feiffer had known Allen in passing from his stand-up days in small Village clubs. Allen "didn't strike me as particularly shy" at the time, Feiffer noted. "The more he became an 'auteur,' the more reticent he became. His shyness, however, had an idiosyncratic twist. Woody hid away from people . . . but he hid conspicuously, like at the head table at Elaine's." One night after *Annie Hall* struck paydirt, Feiffer stepped into an elevator with Allen and other worthies on their way to a party hosted by socialite Susan Stein—Jean vanden Heuvel's sister. Feiffer noticed how Allen both attracted and repelled the paparazzi who swarmed the hoist, shouting, "Just one Woody! Drop the hat!" Allen stood at the front of the packed elevator as the door tried to close. The shutterbugs pushed the door open, and it closed, opened, and closed. Allen's hat shielded his face. Feiffer finally barked, "Woody, let them take your picture, or get the fuck off the elevator!" Allen doffed his hat, cameras clicked, the door shut, and silence reigned as the elevator ascended.

Orson Welles's *Citizen Kane* was often praised by Allen as the only American movie to rank with foreign masterpieces. In private conversations tape-recorded for posterity and a later book, Welles told director Henry Jaglom how much he "hated Woody Allen physically"—one of the many digs Allen suffered for his looks. Welles had met the comedian in Paris during the making of *What's New Pussycat?* but "I can hardly bear to talk to him. He has the Chaplin disease. That particular combination of arrogance and timidity sets my teeth on edge. . . . He acts shy, but he's not. He's scared. He hates himself, and he loves himself, a very tense situation."

••

UNITED ARTISTS EXECUTIVES saw *Interiors* first. The outgoing Eric Pleskow gave Allen "a sick gentlemanly smile," David Evanier reported in *Woody: The Biography*. "A bore," Steven Bach later wrote, "I just hated it."

Still, the studio kept the faith with Allen, releasing *Interiors* in August 1978, launching exclusive premieres at the Baronet on the Upper East Side and at the Regent in Westwood in Los Angeles, where the ultra-drama was expected to attract glowing blurbs to accompany it into the wilds. No question the performers were impeccable, and so were the costumes, settings, the whole wintry aesthetic—the camera glides and the static compositions—the latter evoking Ingmar Bergman, even if Eve, the matriarchal character portrayed by Geraldine Page, leaned more toward Tennessee Williams. *Interiors* was austere and studied, but in a way the picture was splendid, and the director and his effort deserved high marks in the road-less-traveled department.

Many major critics could not get over the turnabout, however. Not a few recognized *Interiors* as Bergmanesque, yet lacking the Swedish filmmaker's undeniable mastery—"Something missing from my work," as Sam Waterston, as Renata's husband, says of his failed fiction. "The risk doesn't pay off," Jack Kroll wrote in *Newsweek*. *Variety*, and Andrew Sarris in the *Village Voice*, were merely polite. Vincent Canby, Allen's booster, saluted the performances, savored the picture's "isolated moments" of greatness, and praised the director's courage. But "I haven't any real idea what the film is up to," Canby hedged in the *New York Times*. Canby's disappointed reviews were always respectful, though. The *Times* critic, along with Jack Rollins and Arthur Krim, were three people "without whose support I never would have had the film career I had," Allen wrote in *Apropos of Nothing*, while adding incongruously about Canby: "I never read him on my films."

Louise Lasser had an intensely personal reaction to *Interiors*. She thought Eve (Geraldine Page) was obviously derived from her mother, and the father's sudden taking-of-leave was also eerily reminiscent. Upset, she phoned Allen. "That movie is about my family!" He listened patiently to his ex-wife's griping, while insisting other people told him the same thing: they recognized *their* family in the film. "In any case, I don't think you got my mother right," Lasser finished. "Really?" Allen pivoted. "I thought I was pretty spot-on."

Even if Allen had his own qualms about *Interiors*—writing in his memoir he should have brought the positive Pearl (Maureen Stapleton) into the story earlier in the ultra-drama—the movie found fans and an audience. The film ended up on many critics' year-end "best" lists. Allen's script was nominated for another Writers Guild Award and there'd be five Oscar nominations: Mel Bourne and Daniel Robert (for Art Decoration/Set Decoration), Maureen Stapleton (Best Supporting Actress), Geraldine Page (Best Actress), and Allen for Screenplay and Direction.* The box office was boosted by the better reviews, the curiosity factor, and the spill-over goodwill from *Annie Hall*. *Interiors* amassed $10.5 million in the US—some $45.7 million in today's terms—ranking it number ten on Allen's all-time list. Overseas, the picture also performed remarkably well.

ONE PERSON WHO really didn't think *Interiors* was very Bergmanesque was Ingmar himself. As *Interiors* played in theaters, the Swedish filmmaker paid a rare visit to New York to oversee the English-language dubbing of *Autumn Sonata*, his latest costarring Ingrid Bergman and Liv Ullmann. Ullmann had lived in New York in the mid-1970s, while appearing in a short run of *A Doll's House* on Broadway. Allen went to see the Ibsen revival, and afterward honored Ullmann by hanging her photograph in his apartment. "Woody was kind of courting me," Ullmann recalled, "probably to get to know Ingmar." The Swedish actress had been Bergman's muse in several masterworks, and they were lovers for years. Bergman fathered her daughter, born in 1966.

Bergman's fifth wife, Ingrid, whom he married in 1971, accompanied the auteur of auteurs to New York. Ingrid was Ullmann's despised rival for Bergman's affections—the woman who had stolen him away from her. This context framed Bergman's invitation to Allen and Ullmann to come dine with him and Ingrid in their hotel suite. "Woody Allen came to get me, and he was so excited he was shivering and talking, talking," Ullmann recalled. "Ingmar opened the door and said welcome. That's all he said. And the two of them looked at each other. Two geniuses met. We sat at the table—and this is the honest to God truth, Ingrid was sitting there, I was sitting there, Ingmar there, and Woody Allen there—and they did not talk. They just

---

* *Interiors* lost in all its Oscar categories, however.

looked at each other, almost lovingly. Ingrid, for once, was allowed to talk at the table, so she talked to me about meatballs. . . ." On the way home together Allen told Ullmann, "Thank you! He is an incredible man!" ("I couldn't believe it," Ullmann thought.) Bergman phoned with similar gush: "Thank you, Liv, what an incredible meeting!"

Rare for Allen, he bristled when asked about Ullmann's account of this momentous meeting of mutual admirers by an interviewer for the *Guardian* at a National Film Theatre event in London in 2001. "I wish she [Ullmann] was here now," Allen said, "because it's completely wrong. . . . I found him to be completely down-to-earth, totally conversational, [he] spoke to me about things which I'll tell you about, not at all the dark, foreboding genius that you might think. He was as sweet and friendly and down-to-earth as you can imagine.

"He said he had the same problems with films as I had—that he'd open a film and the producers would call him and predict how much money it was going to make and then twenty-four hours later reality sets in and we both realize that our films aren't going to make $20 million or $20 even. And he spoke to me about his insecurities as a director—about having these dreams where he comes on to the set and can't speak. He spoke about things that were bread-and-butter and totally down-to-earth and not at all like a great, mystical genius like I had built him up to be."

Allen arranged a screening of *Interiors* for Bergman. The Swedish filmmaker didn't see the ultra-drama as an imitation of his work, although it was certainly "a very European film," he told the *Los Angeles Times*. Bergman said Allen explained about the difficulty he had getting a quality actor to play the father of the three sisters. Allen first tried for Denholm Elliott, tracking him down by phone where Elliott was on vacation in Ibiza and asking the British thespian to recite "Hickory, Dickory, Dock" via long-distance to appraise his American accent. Elliott didn't work out, but Allen would remember him in the future. Other name actors said no before E. G. Marshall finally said yes. "Either the part was too small, or the money was too small," Bergman reported. "It is all right in the end for Woody; no one could be better than Marshall." Marshall's wrenching final encounter with Page, which takes place in the Saint Ignatius Loyola Catholic Church, flickering with candles, is a highlight of the picture. Bergman particularly admired the quieter scene where, at a breakfast, Marshall announces his leave of absence from the family. "Never to return! An extraordinary scene," noted Bergman.

Later, after catching up with *Autumn Sonata*, Allen told Eric Lax, "Although I was not, never had been, nor could ever be in the same universe as him [Bergman] as an artist or a filmmaker, of those two films, *Interiors* is in my view the better one." Regardless, the two geniuses stayed in touch, by phone and letters.

"The next film will be funny!" the clockwork writer-director promised interviewers and United Artists. Yet the *Manhattan* script, which was ready for filming before *Interiors* left theaters, was "in no way really autobiographical," Allen always insisted. The key word for nitpickers is "really." "I wrote that with Marshall Brickman," he'd say in interviews, pointing out Brickman "made up half of it." Brickman surely played his customary role of intelligent sounding-board—doing exactly what he had done with Allen as the coscenarist of *Sleeper* and *Annie Hall*. But after winning an Oscar for *Annie Hall*, Brickman signed a contract to write and direct his own motion pictures and, partly because he didn't have the advantage of Woody Allen in his casts, writer-director Brickman would never make a movie akin to—or as exciting as—*Sleeper*, *Annie Hall*, or *Manhattan*.

Together early in 1978, they had begun to develop the story line for *Manhattan*, which would revolve around Isaac Davis, a.k.a. Ike, a writer for a trendy television comedy show, reminiscent of *Saturday Night Live*, who quits his high-paying TV post after growing disgusted with censorship and other compromises. Ike takes up his lifelong quest to write a high-minded novel. His novel romanticizes Manhattan, but in the mundane world the writer finds himself torn between his good-hearted high school lover and a neurotic pseudointellectual who is trapped in an affair with his married best friend. Ike undergoes psychoanalysis; he has problems with ex-wives as well as girlfriends; and he whines about Allen's usual bugaboos such as mosquitoes. The script would reference Allen's favorite foreign films and New York restaurants, including Elaine's, the Russian Tea Room, Zabar's, and "the crab at Sam Wo's." Toward the end of *Manhattan*, Ike offers up a list of the revered athletes, musicians, artists, and works of art that make his life worth living—for Woody Allen as much as for Ike. It is hard to see how anything in that litany of treasures comes purely from Brickman.

Yet Brickman knew Stacey Nelkin, and both he and Allen, as affirmed in *Apropos of Nothing*, thought the aspiring actress was hot. Developing the script, Allen later wrote, "we called the character Mariel Hemingway played Tracy instead of Stacey in a burst of creative justice." Nelkin was a teenager when Allen met her; Tracy would also be a teenager. One scene would have Ike/Allen sending Tracy home after making love to her, cautioning his young lover not to miss high school the next day. "Allen was seen with her [Nelkin] at Elaine's, where he carried her schoolbooks—a detail that would surface" in *Manhattan*, David Evanier related in *Woody*. "I know the picture did her [Nelkin] justice, as we have remained friends," Allen said later.

Cognizant of Nelkin and other young girlfriends in Allen's life, the writers debated just how old Tracy should be. An early script draft, archived in Woody Allen's papers at Princeton University, described Tracy as perhaps as young as sixteen. In another archived draft, according to the *Hollywood Reporter*, "her age is typed as 'seventeen,' then crossed out and corrected by hand to add another year." But for most of the movie Tracy would be seventeen. The film's famous climax has Tracy leaving New York after graduating from high school and telling Ike/Allen, "Guess what? I turned eighteen the other day. . . . I'm legal, but I'm still a kid."*

The screenplay for *Manhattan* was not really a comedy, per se. Neither was it a drama. Charles Joffe, for one, saw *Manhattan* as the realization "of a twenty-year ongoing discussion, a serious film that's a drama with comedy rather than a comedy with drama." The script achieved the hybrid Allen had been groping toward for years—a comedy-drama, but also a sly hybrid of fiction and autobiography that marked some of his best work.

Diane Keaton had to be persuaded to play Mary Wilke, the freelancer of book reviews and movie novelizations, with a Radcliffe pedigree and a "losing personality," as Ike initially describes her—"Winner of the Zelda Fitzgerald Emotional Maturity Award." It is hate at first sight when Ike meets Mary and learns she has nominated Ingmar Bergman to her fantasy

* When Tracy says "I'm legal, but . . ." she is referring to the "age of consent" between adults, meaning the legal age at which an individual—usually girls in criminal cases involving older men—can legally consent to sexual activity. The "age of consent" varies from state to state in the US and is fluid with changes to laws. In New York the age of consent was, in 1977, and is still today, seventeen. A person is deemed incapable of consent when he or she is less than seventeen years old, according to New York penal laws. Perhaps it was simply good characterization for Tracy to declare her eighteenth birthday, but Tracy obviously consents to sex with Ike in the story and was actually "legal" all along, according to the statutes.

"Academy of the Overrated." Like the teenage Tracy, Mary was inspired by another mutual acquaintance of Allen and Brickman's, the journalist and author Susan Braudy, who hailed from Philadelphia.* " 'No, I'm from Philadelphia, we never talk about things like that in public,' " wrote Julian Fox in *Woody: Movies from Manhattan*, "comes to the screen all but verbatim" from Braudy.

Keaton saw herself as incompatible with the role of a brittle pseudointellectual. Also, she was spiraling out of Allen's orbit. She had joined Warren Beatty's. After Beatty met with her to discuss a role in *Heaven Can Wait*, and Keaton instead accepted the schoolteacher-gone-wild role, with nude scenes, in *Looking for Mr. Goodbar*, her friendship with Beatty grew. As *Goodbar* was filmed in Los Angeles in late 1977, Keaton and Beatty began "hanging out." Back in New York, "I was still Woody's sidekick. I can't explain why we continued to click. Maybe, as with an old couch, we were comfortable with each other. We still enjoyed sitting in Oldies Row at the entrance to Central Park, making observations on the parade of humanity passing by. We still had fun . . . and we still kept planning future projects, but things had changed. He was suddenly the comic genius. I was getting more opportunities." *Manhattan* would be Keaton's last Woody Allen film for a decade.

Allen cast Michael Murphy from *The Front* as the university professor Yale, who is having an illicit affair with Mary. Tony Roberts could have played the part, another interchangeable best friend of Allen's onscreen, but Murphy would evince more guilt and shame when bequeathing his inamorata to Ike. Meryl Streep had begun to display her greatness in supporting roles in *Julia* and *The Deer Hunter*, receiving her first Oscar nomination for the latter, but she would nail the supporting character of Ike's angry ex-wife Jill, a lesbian, and one of two former spouses to whom he pays alimony. Their marriage has produced a boy (played by Damion Scheller), now being raised by Jill and her lover (Karen Ludwig). It's the first time Allen played a father onscreen—another step in the maturing persona that had nothing to do with his real life. Ike and his son, whom he refers to as "the kid"—the character is nameless in the film—bond when Ike buys expensive F.A.O. Schwarz toys for the boy, or plays football with him in divorced-father/son leagues. Meanwhile, Jill is finishing a tell-all feminist memoir about her

* Braudy had interviewed Brickman at length, in 1977, for the *New York Times*.

lousy marriage. "There are a few disgusting little moments that I regret" about their life together, Ike confesses. Among the tidbits in Jill's forthcoming memoir, which is titled *Marriage, Divorce, and Selfhood*, are the threesomes contrived by her ex-husband. This detail was a more authentic update of Allen's persona, and the first inclusion of threesomes in one of his films; it wouldn't be the last.

Anne Byrne, who was married to Dustin Hoffman in real life, filled the colorless character of the "wonderful" wife Yale betrays. Budding playwright Wallace Shawn, the son of longtime *New Yorker* editor William Shawn, was recruited for his first role in a Woody Allen movie. Casting director Juliet Taylor spotted Shawn in a Public Theater staging of Machiavelli's satire *The Mandrake*, which Shawn had translated for the production, and Shawn was recruited for the part of Mary's ex-husband Jeremiah, her mentor and an "oversexed, brilliant kind of animal," in Mary's words. The portrait doesn't quite match his physical appearance, which was not unlike Allen's, as Ike discovers when he and Mary cross paths with Jeremiah and Ike sizes him up contemptuously as "this little homunculus." Many small or fleeting parts were sprinkled with notable New Yorkers such as feminist US congresswoman Bella Abzug and up-and-comers like Karen Allen and Tisa Farrow—the latter, the youngest (born 1951) of a brood of seven parented by Australian-born Hollywood director John Farrow and actress Maureen O'Sullivan. A willowy looker, Tisa had a last name that bore future implications.

The pivotal character around whom the story turns dramatically was Tracy, a senior at the elite Dalton School on East Eighty-Ninth when she is taken to bed by the middle-age Ike. Only after Ike drops Tracy for Mary does he realize Tracy is his heart's desire. He regrets abandoning Tracy. The young actress playing Tracy had to win the audience over and make them forget that other film in which Diane Keaton was the ideal girl lost to Allen.

Ernest Hemingway's granddaughter Mariel Hemingway had started her career with a small role in *Lipstick*, a rape-revenge drama, portraying the little sister of older sibling Margaux, followed by a credible telefilm in which she played a teenager choosing motherhood over abortion. One day the phone rang in the Hemingway home in Ketchum, Idaho, and Mariel's mother answered. Woody Allen was calling. "I had no idea who he was," Hemingway recalled. "He'd written a part for me in his new fall project—as yet untitled—and I'd have to wait to read it until I met with him. He said he wrote the part after seeing me with Margaux in *Lipstick*."

Hastening with her mother to New York, Hemingway kept an appointment with Allen, who "was very sweet and seemed almost as shy as I was. He made me feel welcome and important and tongue-tied." Handed the *Manhattan* script, Hemingway holed up in her hotel room and was taken aback to read her character's racy scenes. "Half of the sexy stuff was over my head, but I didn't want to admit it," she said. The young actress met with Allen again in a darkened theater, reading her scenes aloud, red-faced, giggling, with "my soon-to-be-branded 'Minnie Mouse' voice." She got the part. Tall at 5 feet, 11 inches ("If I stood up straight, I had a solid half foot on Woody"), still baby-faced, Hemingway would turn seventeen during the filming in the fall of 1978.

Once in a while someone got the full script, and occasionally Allen showered his attention on a player. For this film it was Hemingway, whom the director took under his wing, showing her *his* Manhattan the way Ike unveils the city to Tracy. Hemingway was staying with her paternal grandmother Mary Welsh Hemingway, the widow of the famous author, and her mother also paid visits to the set, but Mary Welsh Hemingway was fighting cancer and bouts of depression. The cast and crew became a surrogate family, offering Hemingway respite from her own dysfunctional family. Allen became a surrogate father. Since Hemingway was "far from the sexually astute teenager" depicted in the *Manhattan* script, in her words, the off-camera closeness with Allen helped prepare her for the kissing and postcoital scenes, discreetly staged, which were her first. So, for that matter, was eating Chinese takeout in bed; when Allen filmed that scene, Hemingway substituted granola.

"I spent all my free time with him [Allen]," Hemingway recalled. He escorted the teenager to museums and galleries, they sat together on his favorite Central Park benches, and the filmmaker was always "warm and funny," while "at the same time he treated me as an equal," the actress recalled. After shooting the first Ike-Tracy scene at Elaine's one morning, Allen lingered for a long lunch with Hemingway at his favorite wateringhole.

Their talks often circled around to France. Hemingway once took a trip with her father through France, and of course her father's father had a storied connection to the French capital. "We should go to Paris, just you and me," Allen teased her. It is not so unusual, in stage or motion picture circles, for a leading man, following the script of a love story, to become smitten with his leading lady. Yet Allen's "initial jokes about taking me to Paris kept resurfacing," and Hemingway began to worry about the true intent of his comments, and "maybe he wasn't joking," she was left wondering. "Our relationship was platonic, but I started to see that he had a kind of crush on me, though I dismissed it as the kind of thing that seemed to happen any time middle-aged men got around young women. And I encouraged the conversations and the walks because they validated me."

Perhaps because of Hemingway, Allen seemed more buoyant than usual during the filming. "Woody kept his set loose and fun," Hemingway recalled. "He would go to lunch with some of the cast and the crew members who were close to him, and we would sit and order food or whatever while everyone told jokes."

Oddly, Hemingway noticed, Allen did not seem as loose and fun around Keaton. "Woody was hard on her in terms of what he wanted out of her as an actress," Hemingway recalled. "She was forever reshooting her scenes until he was satisfied. He wanted a quality of pretentiousness [in her character] that didn't come naturally to her. She never complained, though. They seemed to understand each other's shorthand."

TOGETHER WITH CAMERAMAN Gordon Willis, Allen made decisions that were consciously artistic, beginning with, for the first time, painterly black-and-white photography and an opening montage of scenery and sights that would end with Fourth of July fireworks over Central Park—a montage that could have been billed to New York's Chamber of Commerce. The static compositions, including an iconic image of Allen and Keaton sitting on a park bench as the sun rises over the East River, would be interspersed with his prototypical master shots of walking, talking, and running on New York streets and long daring sequences like the one of Ike and Mary flirting their way through the stygian blackness of the Hayden Planetarium—catnip to the Prince of Darkness.

"He was as tough and romantic as the city he loved," Ike says in chapter 1 of the novel he is writing during *Manhattan*. *Annie Hall* had been the first Woody Allen picture to proclaim his affection for New York, and now *Manhattan* would consummate that love affair. Allen's choice of George

Gershwin's *Rhapsody in Blue*, performed by the New York Philharmonic under the opening, with its apotheosis timed to culminate with the explosion of fireworks, idealized the cityscape. Other orchestrated Gershwin music would be sounded throughout the picture. "I was shooting scenes deliberately to put [to] music that I knew beforehand," Allen said later. "I played those records every single day as soon as I got up in the morning. I played them on the way to work and listened to them over and over." *Manhattan* cemented the practice of incorporating music from his personal collection of recordings into the movies he was making. "This way I don't bother myself with anyone," Allen told the French journal *Positif*. "I take George Gershwin or Beethoven, I edit it into the film, and it works perfectly."

There was a lot to mix and match during postproduction, and after working on six Woody Allen projects editor Ralph Rosenblum was no longer on the job. After completing *Interiors*, Rosenblum had shaken hands with the director and moved on in his career to become, principally, a director of documentaries and television shows. But probably it was not entirely coincidental that Rosenblum also had completed his memoir, *When the Shooting Stops . . . the Cutting Begins*, which took an uncommon degree of credit for salvaging Allen's early comedies while offering a candid portrait of the director at work. Allen hated the "critical remarks about his foibles," according to Marion Meade, and also that Rosenblum had described outtakes with comedy setups that might be pilfered by others. It was an occupational hazard of comedians to fear the theft of jokes and ideas, and Allen's secrecy about his scripts extended to his outtakes and shelved ideas. On the other hand, there was the time Howard Storm overheard Jack Rollins telling Allen about an entertainer who'd usurped some of Allen's material. Rollins argued they should sue. "Oh, Jack," Allen demurred, "I'll just write some new jokes."

After perusing the galleys an annoyed Allen withdrew his offer to write an introduction to Rosenblum's book, according to Meade. *When the Shooting Stops . . . the Cutting Begins* would be published a few months after *Manhattan* was released. The editor credited for *Manhattan* was a new one, Susan E. Morse, who had been well trained as Rosenblum's assistant. In her midtwenties, hardworking and equable, Morse took over the position for Allen for the next two decades, bringing the same expertise and belief in editing as the "final draft."

Allen and Morse were "a little bit wary" of the *Rhapsody in Blue* overture, which "focused attention on the style as well as content of the photography," in Morse's words, and for months they debated the running time of the movie, with or without the overture. Again, major scenes were forfeited, including a Nazi rally Allen had laboriously staged in Englewood, New Jersey, which was dropped not only for its length but because it was "strident and depressive," Steven Bach wrote. Only a brief reference to Nazis marching in New Jersey would survive into the final cut. The Nazi march is mentioned at the Museum of Modern Art ERA fundraiser, where Ike runs into Dennis (played by Michael O'Donoghue from *Saturday Night Live*) and Mary (Keaton), who is Dennis's date. Their awkward conversation veers from Nazis and Charles Manson to Theodor Reik and orgasms. When a nearby listener—Tisa Farrow—volunteers that she finally achieved an orgasm, but her doctor told her it was the wrong kind, Ike declares: "I've never had the wrong kind . . . my worst one was right on the money."

BINGEING ON BOB HOPE movies after work and on the weekends to fashion a documentary tribute to Hope for a planned public gala in May, Allen applied the final postproduction touches to *Manhattan* in the first months of 1979. Whether it was the questionable May-September romance in the script, or something else was bothering him, the writer-director was more than normally dissatisfied. He proposed to Rollins-Joffe, he claimed in later interviews, destroying the negative in exchange for making the next Woody Allen films free of charge to United Artists.

In fact, the filmmaker was committed to only one more UA movie, "Woody Allen #4," under his renegotiated 1976 contract with the studio. After that, what? All Hollywood was on tenterhooks.

In early 1978, the former UA leadership team—Arthur Krim, Robert Benjamin, Eric Pleskow, Mike Medavoy, and William Bernstein—launched Orion Pictures as a joint venture with Warner Bros., which would handle the distribution of future Orion productions and support an initial line of bank credit. Because of the "debt of faith and the longevity of the relationship" between Allen and the new Orion entity, in the words of Steven Bach, "hardly anyone in the industry (certainly few who remained at UA) thought there was any way to prevent" him from jumping to Orion after he fulfilled his fourth picture. The exception was Andy Albeck, a UA official who'd served under Krim for thirty years but hadn't left the studio, taking over the presidency.

Albeck tried wooing Jack Rollins and Charles Joffe, but the management team played poker with all the best cards and sad faces. Repeatedly, Rollins told Albeck, "You know, Arthur [Krim] is like a father to Woody. . . ." Joffe, on the West Coast, asked for Rollins-Joffe agency backscratching. UA offered scripts and development deals to Rollins-Joffe clients, but nothing seemed to get produced, and the backscratching wasn't enough to turn the tide. Not unimportant to matters, Rollins-Joffe had been "profoundly offended" by Albeck, "not merely because he wasn't Arthur Krim (that too)," said Bach. Albeck was invited to the Comedy Store on the Sunset Strip in early 1978 to see Rollins-Joffe's prize new client Robin Williams. "They had dropped a zillion-dollar plum cake in Albeck's lap," and Albeck didn't laugh once. Albeck "didn't know talent when it was exploding in front of those windowpane eyeglasses of his, and this blindness weighed heavily against us all."

Knowing he was in the doghouse, Albeck turned the "Keeping of Woody" over to Bach, his chief lieutenant, who felt "ludicrously ill equipped." Even if on paper he seemed to have the right credentials—Bach had started his career in the early 1970s at Palomar Pictures, the company that bankrolled *Take the Money and Run*—he couldn't muster any rapport with Allen. He was neither Jewish, nor a New Yorker. "I was a white-bread Gentile, born and reared where the buffalo and precious little else roam"—Pocatello, Idaho. Moreover, Bach had made a singular error, after a "single reading" of the *Manhattan* script—"While one of Woody's assistants waited outside my office door to make sure no copies were made"—which Allen may have heard about. The studio official compiled a list of the artistic and literary allusions he regarded as "too esoteric for a general audience." Strindberg, Mahler, Jung, Dinesen, Fitzgerald (Scott and Zelda), Kafka, Cézanne, Flaubert, Mozart, Nabokov, Whitman, Coward, Böll, Brecht, and O'Neill—all in the script, all on Bach's list. "When it comes to relationships with women, I'm the winner of the August Strindberg Award" was a joke "unlikely to roll them in the aisles of Des Moines," thought Bach, who was only trying to do what UA always tried to do: grow Allen's audience. With the list of erudite allusions in his pocket, Bach visited Michael's Pub in the company of Joffe one Monday evening, waiting for Allen to step down from the stage. They had a brief and pleasant but strained encounter. Bach couldn't figure out how to bring up the subject of his "esoteric" list, so he stayed mum. Who knows what Allen, a vaunted mind reader, suspected? Later, the studio official would have cause to feel "ridiculous" about his list. When he and other UA officials saw a *Manhattan* preview, Bach left the Sixth Avenue screening room grinning, and humming Gershwin, feeling "pure unambiguous pleasure." *Manhattan* epitomized "all the reasons I had always wanted to live in New York . . . all the reasons I had wanted to be in the movie business." Maybe losing Allen was a foregone conclusion, but Bach was going to give his best effort to keeping him.

THERE WOULD BE a curious postscript to the Ike-Tracy romance that transpires onscreen in *Manhattan*. When the filming ended, seventeen-year-old Mariel Hemingway felt "distraught" about the prospect of returning to schoolbooks and her family in Idaho. "I couldn't bear it," she said later. "I wanted the talk about art, music, and Bergman movies to continue." She invited Allen to Ketchum, Idaho. To her astonishment, he accepted. "One of the cardinal rules of my life is: Never be anyone's houseguest," Allen explained in *Apropos of Nothing*. "But Mariel was so charming and so pretty and it was the whole Hemingway myth that was so enticing."

In her 2001 memoir Hemingway left out revealing details of Allen's visit to Ketchum, but she decided to tell the complete version of events in *Out Came the Sun: Overcoming the Legacy of Mental Illness, Addiction, and Suicide in My Family*, her 2015 follow-up, which was published in the wake of Dylan Farrow's renewed accusations against the director in *Vanity Fair* and the *New York Times*. Hemingway wrote she was excited to host Allen in Ketchum, but she fretted about the Paris trip he repeatedly had mentioned without making it clear if he was kidding. She told her parents about the feelers, "hoping they would squash [the idea] immediately. Instead, they were impressed and even a little enthusiastic." She upped the "threat level . . . I told them that I didn't know what the arrangements were going to be, that I wasn't sure if I was even going to have my own room. Woody hadn't said that. He hadn't even hinted it. But I wanted them to put their foot down. They didn't. They kept lightly encouraging me."

Taking a break from *Manhattan* editing, Allen flew by private jet to a small airport in Hailey, Idaho, arriving on a "bitingly cold" day in November 1978, with grays cloaking the mountains, lakes, and forests. "Oh my God," he said, stepping off the plane, feeling, he later wrote, "like I was landing on the moon." After a forty-minute drive to Ketchum, Allen was led to a guest room in the Hemingway home. Mariel's father, Jack, the only child from Ernest Hemingway's first marriage to Elizabeth Hadley Richardson, proposed a mountain hike. Allen dubiously assented. The family's slobbering Labradors accompanied Allen, Hemingway, and her father as they climbed, the latter pointing out birds and praising the country life. Allen fell behind, recalled the actress. "He was at altitude 6,500 feet, just off the plane from New York, and he was winded and then some."

Jack led the mountaineers to the top of a peak. Fog rolled in, then "a massive snowfall," and Hemingway "apologized to Woody, and we turned and went right back down again" through "high, snowy sagebrush" and gathering darkness. "Wet and miserable," Allen showered and changed his clothes. The family, including Mariel's sisters Margaux and Muffet, sat down to roast pheasant with tarte tatin. Allen told "fascinating stories," proffered "witty observations," and everyone got along nicely. "Woody was making a great show about how much he liked the food" when Jack mentioned he had shot the pheasant that very morning. "Woody's whole face fell." Yet he bounced back for "a long conversation about fly-fishing with my father."

Going to bed that night Hemingway tossed and turned, dismayed to think her parents were not going to bail her out of the Paris dilemma and panicking over the dangling proposition. She tiptoed downstairs to the guest room and roused Allen "from what was probably the deepest sleep of his life," in her words. "I'm not going to get my own room, am I?" Hemingway demanded. Allen was "terribly flustered, not quite awake, not quite in focus, feeling around for his glasses." Listen, she said, "I just want you to know I can't go to Paris with you. . . ."

The next morning, Allen woke up, "clearly disconcerted," and summoned his plane to return and retrieve him. Hemingway drove the filmmaker back to the Hadley airport. The young actress behaved with Allen "as cordially and casually as I could. Deep down, I was really sad. I loved him as a friend. He had made me feel important in ways that I hadn't, up to that point, felt. But I also knew that it was an impossible situation."

Allen told an alternative version in *Apropos of Nothing*. The real reason he had left so quickly, he wrote, was that he'd been "hit with a crushing piece of news" in Ketchum, which "I tried being a little soldier about but couldn't. It was announced that I would have my own bedroom, but I would be sharing a bathroom with her father." Allen hadn't shared a bathroom "with a male since I was twenty, marooned in Hollywood" in NBC's Comedy Development Program. He said little about the Paris invitation in his memoir, except to imply the offer was innocently intended. Hemingway's panic was "unbeknownst to me" until Allen read her 2015 book.

In her earlier memoir Hemingway wrote that, after the Ketchum misunderstanding, they "slowly lost track of each other over the years." She gilded the lily in 2015. "Woody didn't abandon me," Hemingway wrote in *Out Came the Sun*. "He was more careful, but we continued to talk through the years," with Allen sometimes showing her scripts, or early cuts of his movies. He'd cast her sister Margaux in a future Woody Allen film, and play tennis with Muffet. He did like sisters. Also, he gave Mariel a small part in *Deconstructing Harry* after "she told me close to filming she wanted to work, and it was all I had open. As usual she came through."

MANHATTAN GOT INTO its first kerfuffle with the Motion Picture Association of America (MPAA) ratings board, which gave an R rating to the movie, partly because of the f-word in dialogue, but also because chairman Richard Heffner was reported to have been offended by the sexual relationship between a forty-two-year-old man and a seventeen-year-old high school girl. UA fought hard behind the scenes against the R, believing the rating would hamper bookings across Middle America. The MPAA board convened a second vote, and *Manhattan* lost again.

Allen didn't care enough to stick around. He vacated New York promptly after the first screening for the studio and insiders, flying to Paris—not on a vacation, but to cast his next picture. Having failed to persuade Mariel Hemingway to accompany him, Allen traveled with Jean Doumanian and her boyfriend Jacqui Safra, a Brazilian financier headquartered in New York, who was descended from the Syrian-Swiss-Jewish Safra banking family and related to Edmond J. Safra, a Lebanese-born principal with Brazilian citizenship in an international series of holding companies of banks spread out across Europe, the Middle East, South America, and the US. Marion Meade described Jacqui Safra as "a beefy, swarthy man with a taste for the high life," who kept a "glamorous East Side apartment" where he almost never stayed and which he used mainly for parties.

Allen skipped the festive premiere of *Manhattan* at the Ziegfeld in the third week of April. After the screening, buses took invited audience members to a black-tie party at the Whitney Museum of Art, which is spotlighted in the picture. The Who's Who attendees of New York show business and the arts included Gloria Vanderbilt, Kurt Vonnegut, Neil Simon, Arthur Schlesinger Jr., Lillian Hellman, Dick Cavett, and Martha Graham; plus Bill Murray, Dan Aykroyd, and Gilda Radner from *Saturday Night Live*. Michael Murphy and Mariel Hemingway mingled with the cognoscenti, and Paul Simon and Maureen Stapleton represented the casts of previous Woody Allen movies. Hemingway would also escort the picture to the Cannes Film Festival later in May, where *Manhattan* would be unveiled—as always with Allen and film festivals—out of competition.

Allen lingered in Paris and was absent from the Film Society of Lincoln Center tribute to Bob Hope in early May. His truancy was noted by master of ceremonies Dick Cavett, who explained his friend "breaks out in a rash" if confronted with public extravaganzas. Diane Keaton along with Michael Murphy and Anne Byrne from *Manhattan* were in the audience enjoying the seventy-minute *My Favorite Comedian*, assembled and narrated by Allen. "It's great to have your past spring up in front of your eyes," cracked the seventy-six-year-old Hope, who had first met Allen in Hollywood when he was an aspiring comedy writer just out of his teens, "especially when it's done by Woody Allen, because he's a near genius. Not a whole genius, but a *near* genius."

Sensing a propitious moment, the new UA team switched from its standard slow dispersal of Woody Allen films to opening *Manhattan* in thirty theaters in New York, Los Angeles, and Toronto. The outpouring of moviegoers was spurred by the most adoring reviews of Allen's career, especially from those critics—the most influential—headquartered in the city to which the picture was his unabashed valentine. Allen was the pride of the metropolis. His Horatio Alger story, with origins in Flatbush, included an early chapter set in Manhattan, where he first found widespread fame as a stand-up comedian. Now he had reached the pinnacle of his career with

New York–centric films. Even more than *Annie Hall*, his face was the poster boy for "I ❤ New York."

Manhattan has "materialized out of the void as the one truly great American film of the '70s," Andrew Sarris proclaimed in the *Village Voice*. "An inspired, brilliant movie," Gene Shalit declared on NBC's *Today* show. "Moviemaking genius," exclaimed Kathleen Carroll in the New York *Daily News*. His "funniest, most serious, best film," rhapsodized Vincent Canby in the *New York Times*. "A masterpiece," agreed Richard Schickel in *Time*. Schickel intelligently appraised Allen's mature style as a director. "He lets long scenes play without break," Schickel wrote. "The camera often just sits on its haunches and stares, without even a close-up or a reverse angle intruding. Variation comes from movement within the frame; sometimes, in fact, the actor moves right out of it, keeps talking off-camera, and then reappears. When a director trusts his material that much, he encourages the audience to trust it as well." One of Allen's early admirers, Schickel was also among the longest-lasting. Allen, in his memoir, reciprocated, calling Schickel "a lovely man and a bright critic."

There were a handful of sharp-tongued *Manhattan* foes, however, adding to the counterforce of doubting Thomases that had been heating up on a slow boil ever since *Annie Hall* met similar critical adulation. The reviewers who wrote on daily or weekly deadlines were perhaps Allen's most steadfast exponents. National print and broadcast critics like Judith Crist, who had pioneered reviewing on the *Today* show and now wrote for *New York* and *TV Guide*, or Gene Shalit, who had succeeded Crist on the *Today* show, reached a greater number of people than the more literary critics whose essays would ultimately be collected in books. Among the short list of critics Allen thanked by name in his memoir were Crist and Shalit, whose "enthusiasm went a long way to getting me off the ground." The deadline critics had to write about nearly every movie that came along, and they greeted each new Woody Allen film as a break from the awful run of the mill. The more literary critics often reacted to new Allen movies with as much horror for the acclamation as dislike for the film itself.

"The chief impediment of *Manhattan* is the hype," wrote Stanley Kauffmann in *The New Republic*. "It's as if the media has been braiding laurel wreaths in advance, hoping for a minimal excuse to hail Woody Allen." Kauffmann pooh-poohed Allen's own performance, which "has his recently acquired negative virtue of avoiding physical comedy." The acerbic John Simon, holding forth in *National Review*, complained that "the majority of reviewers and audiences have hailed *Manhattan*, even more than *Annie Hall*, as a masterwork." Simon found *Annie Hall* "drearily inept," while *Manhattan* amounted to "unappetizingly smug self-exaltation." Even Diane Keaton disappointed Simon; her acting in *Manhattan* was reduced to "mugging" and "blithering."

Leonard Quart, a New York cinema studies professor, wrote a widely circulated piece bemoaning the premature "canonization of Woody Allen," arguing that "something [is] lacking [in *Manhattan*], since there are emotional levels that Allen can't communicate." The prominent Western novelist Larry McMurtry, who'd win the Pulitzer Prize for *Lonesome Dove* some years later, sniffed at "Woody Allen, Neighborhood Filmmaker" in *American Film*, the American Film Institute magazine, rating *Manhattan* as "more parochial and less appealing" than *Annie Hall*.

Hailing Allen as America's Ingmar Bergman got the attention of deep-think essayist Joan Didion, a California social critic transplanted to New York, who collected her thoughts about *Annie Hall*, *Interiors*, and *Manhattan* for the *New York Review of Books*, a longform erudite magazine to which Allen subscribed. He read the semimonthly religiously when it arrived "or else it piles up and becomes a matter of guilt." All three Woody Allen pictures, regarded as "serious" by his devotees—with the "serious" in quotes—evinced a "peculiar and hermetic self-regard," Didion wrote, with "the false and desperate knowingness of the smartest kid in the class." The "insider" references in *Manhattan* to "Jack and Anjelica" (i.e., Nicholson and Huston) or "Harvey" (Shapiro, the *New York Times Book Review* editor) were "nothing with which large numbers of people would want to identify." The adult characters in Woody Allen movies were "faux adults," while Tracy was nothing but an "adolescent fantasy" flaunting "perfect skin, perfect wisdom, perfect sex, and no visible family."

Didion particularly scorned Ike/Allen's recitation of life's indubitable pleasures, a list from *Manhattan*'s penultimate sequence, which was his personal list of Groucho Marx, Willie Mays, the second movement of Mozart's Jupiter Symphony, Louis Armstrong's "Potato Head Blues," Swedish movies, Flaubert's *Sentimental Education*, Marlon Brando, Frank Sinatra, Cézanne's apples and pears, and "the crab at Sam Wo's." These pleasures were abjectly passive and amounted to "the ultimate consumer's report," scoffed Didion. Is any attack on a filmmaker more personal than one ridiculing his favorite pastimes and private enjoyments?

Years later, reflecting on *Manhattan*, Allen admitted some criticisms of the movie were justified. For example, he received a letter from a woman who rebuked him for having left off Ike's young son—the nameless "kid" being raised by his lesbian ex-wife—from his list of experiences that made life worthwhile. Allen disregarded the letter at the time, but with hindsight he sided with Didion on this point at least: In some ways his list was hermetic self-regard. "Now it seems like an unthinkable mistake," said Allen, after becoming a father with children. "Once you have a child it is so powerful an experience it's impossible not to delight in it."

"Tracy's face . . ." was the last item on Ike/Allen's list and the only fictional one. Thinking of his former teenager lover stops Ike cold and sends him racing—literally sprinting up the sidewalks of New York, one of those cinematic moments that Allen specialized in—toward the story's denouement. The last scene, Tracy's painful, perhaps forever farewell to Ike, was among the most powerfully dramatic he ever crafted. For many critics, it validated the film. The compulsion to reevaluate Ike and Tracy would come later for most people.

Neither Allen nor Marshall Brickman seems to have considered the addition of any brief scene that might have mitigated the film's most problematic aspect: Ike's relationship with the underage Tracy. Tracy's parents could have opened the door to Ike's knocking and slammed it in his face. Behind the closed door a muffled argument could be heard before a rebellious Tracy slips out to keep her date with a flustered Ike. None of the characters of *Manhattan* express the slightest disapproval of the liaison between a middle-age man and a teenage girl—certainly not Tracy's "invisible" parents. As Mariel Hemingway, Stacey Nelkin, and Babi Christina Engelhardt well knew, parents proved little hindrance to Allen's real-life young-girl liaisons either.

Joan Didion was one of the few prominent commentators to object to the Tracy character in *Manhattan*, but she was not alone. Pauline Kael also took umbrage, although she held her fire because she had taken a year off from reviewing. Then there was Meryl Streep, so good in the movie as Ike's lesbian ex-wife, who gave an eyebrow-raising interview to *Ladies' Home*

Journal several months after the release of *Manhattan*. "I only worked on the film for three days, and I didn't get to know Woody," Streep said. "Who gets to know Woody? He's very much of a womanizer, very self-involved. On a certain level, the film [*Manhattan*] offends me because it's about all these people whose sole concern is discussing their emotional states or their neuroses."

Despite a cautionary note from "Berg" in *Variety*, tucked away at the end of his rave review, that Ike/Allen's relationship with a teenager "might turn off a few," *Manhattan* proved extraordinarily popular across Middle America, eventually ranking as Allen's second-biggest US hit of all time—second only to *Annie Hall*—with North American grosses of $48.3 million, or about $193 million in today's money. Foreign tickets doubled this sum.

The movie won the BAFTA for Best Picture of the year from the British Film Academy, and the Best Foreign Film César from the French equivalent, the Académie des Arts et Techniques du Cinéma. The New York Film Critics Circle and National Society of Film Critics named Allen Best Director. His script (with Marshall Brickman) earned another Writers Guild nomination, and the Directors Guild of America gave Allen his first Best Director nomination. *Manhattan* was also Oscar-nominated for Best Screenplay and Supporting Actress (Hemingway).

EXPECTATIONS WERE RAISED for the next Woody Allen project, which was destined to become his most misunderstood work. If he was America's Bergman, he was also America's Fellini, and this time he'd go whole-hog Fellini. "A Woody Allen Film," the only title "Mr. Secretive" offered to the press, went into production in the fall of 1979. Allen wrote the script alone; Marshall Brickman was off making his own movies now. Allen's story revolved around the creative angst of a onetime comedian named Sandy Bates (Allen). Bates has become a film director, acclaimed for his silly comedies, so when he tries to shift toward arty tragedies that explore the meaninglessness of existence he butts up against the resistance of fans and handlers. One of Bates's close friends has just died; he is recovering from a broken romance; and studio officials have recoiled at the bleak ending to his latest movie, which is mired in postproduction. For escape and publicity's sake, Bates accepts an invitation to a weekend festival of his oeuvre at a New Jersey seaside resort, the Stardust Hotel, hosted by "an important film critic," who stands in for Judith Crist. Crist's 1973 "Weekend with Woody Allen" at Tarrytown House on the Hudson River inspired the premise, and the hotel weekend lent the film its eventual title: *Stardust Memories.* Allen had been particularly "depressed" at Tarrytown, having just rewatched Bergman's *The Seventh Seal* and *Cries and Whispers.* "I see his films and I wonder what I'm doing," he told Eric Lax.

During the weekend at the Stardust Hotel Bates is mobbed by "a legion of the maladjusted, the pimply, the obese, the grasping, the senile, and the insane," in John Baxter's words. They—his fans—assail Bates with dumb questions, autograph demands, inane scripts, and scholarly studies ("a definitive study of Gummo Marx"), along with their pleadings for his involvement in sundry causes. The weekend triggers a kaleidoscopic journey into his mind, his past, his failed relationships with women, his ambivalence toward fame, his friction with his producers, his abiding neuroses. All the while Bates is chauffeured around in a cream-colored Rolls-Royce like the one Allen possessed in real life. Both the Rolls-Royce and its chauffeur figure into the plot twists. "What do you think was the significance of the Rolls-Royce?" asks an earnest questioner at the Stardust Hotel, having spotted the director's limo in his films. "I think it represents his car," Bates replies.

As clever, dazzling, and personally resonant as anything he'd ever write, the script was a burlesque of and homage to Federico Fellini's *8½*, which Allen would list among the ten greatest films of all time for the decennial *Sight and Sound* poll in 2012. Allen reimagined key turns from Fellini's 1963 masterpiece, with Mussorgsky's "Night on Bald Mountain" and snippets of Italian to echo the original, while re-creating the *8½* story in his own fictional universe, overlapping as well as savagely satirizing the life of a real filmmaker akin to Woody Allen.

The bold, sprawling script was peopled with an "enormous" cast of disparate characters, as Charles Champlin later wrote in the *Los Angeles Times*, calling for "more mug shots than in a high school annual."

First, there were a trio of leading ladies. Foremost among them is Charlotte Rampling as Dorrie, a beautiful actress whom Bates has picked up on one of his sets, where she is discovered reading Schopenhauer. Dorrie's story, told in flashbacks, encompasses her self-destruction, memorably photographed in rapid, disturbing jump cuts as she stares fixedly into a mirror.

Bates's description of Dorrie's psychological disorder—"She could be very fine and funny and bright and wonderful two days a month, the other twenty-eight she was lost"—was something Allen was known to say, with variations, about the funny and bright but maladjusted Louise Lasser.

Rampling had shot to fame as the Holocaust survivor embroiled in a sadomasochistic sexual relationship with a former concentration camp officer in Liliana Cavani's *The Night Porter* in 1974. The formidable British actress did not undergo the usual five awkward minutes with Allen. The other way around: when in Paris, the director spoke several times with the actress to win her over. "He's always liked Charlotte's looks," said costar Jessica Harper. "After he saw her in *Farewell My Lovely*, he was quite smitten with her." And it wasn't just her beauty: In one of his Nancy Jo Sales letters, Allen named Rampling as one of his ideal dinner party guests, seated alongside Tolstoy and Kafka. Her personality "reeks from neurosis," Allen wrote Sales.

Then there is Isobel, the good-hearted mistress Bates is in danger of squandering. She leaves her husband and shows up, children in tow, at the Stardust Hotel, forcing Bates to make a decision about their future together. Probably Allen's idea for the mistress to be a Frenchwoman originated during his May 1979 sojourn in Paris, where some of the writing and casting were done. Marie-Christine Barrault was known for her Oscar-nominated Best Actress role in the 1975 romantic comedy *Cousin, Cousine*, but she was also the star of André Delvaux's World War II drama *Femme entre chien et loup*, which happened to be in Paris cinemas during Allen's stay. Allen met with Delvaux while in Paris, and his colleague sang Barrault's praises. A revered figure in the Belgian national cinema, Delvaux asked for and received Allen's cooperation for the first full documentary about him, *To Woody Allen from Europe with Love*—more proof of the American's growing mystique abroad.

Allen formed a kinship with Barrault. The location work would take place mainly in New Jersey, where the Great Auditorium of the Ocean Grove Camp Meeting Association, a Methodist community located on the Jersey shore south of Asbury, stood in for the Stardust Hotel. Because Barrault was living temporarily in New York during the production, Allen offered the actress rides back and forth in his limousine, always tensing up as the automobile entered the east-west vehicular tunnels he abhorred, turning on music, "holding my hand and listening to Telemann," Barrault recalled. "A few days later, he wrote a scene in which the two of us were in an elevator, which was slow in reaching its destination, so he was panicking, and I was trying to calm him down."

The elevator scene would be discarded during editing. Still, in the same way Allen took Mariel Hemingway under his wing during the filming of *Manhattan*—the actress playing the woman he was in love with in the story—the relationship he developed with Barrault helped to enrich her characterization in the story. During filming rewrites, Isobel/Barrault acquired leftist politics, for example, partly owing to Allen's mistaken impression Barrault had been active in the May '68 riots in Paris (a side effect of her introducing the onetime Left Bank radical Daniel Cohn-Bendit to the director). Allen's closeness with Barrault would also influence the unusually tender ending to the movie-within-a-movie Bates has been finishing under duress—which, at the end of *Stardust Memories*, he premieres for the Stardust Hotel fans and all the billed players we (the actual audience) have been watching in the ongoing picture—mingling, in *8½* fashion, the new Sandy Bates movie and the Woody Allen film enveloping it.

Allen formed a different attachment to Harper, the ingenue from *Love and Death* now grown alluring. Her announced small role in *Annie Hall* may or may not have been shot, but she isn't in that movie. Harper was playing Daisy, the third female lead, a classical violinist, whose lesbian fling, weight phobia, and "lost feeling" reminds Bates of Dorrie. "I'm fascinating but I'm trouble," Dorrie says—like all women in Woody Allen films.

Making a strong impression in her first billed appearance was another young beauty, twenty-one-year-old Sharon Stone, who "looked sixteen and had this voice and this attitude" at her audition. The Felliniesque opening to *Stardust Memories* is a sequence from Bates's movie-within-a-movie, in which he is seen boarding a train that is crowded with strange, haunting faces—casting director Juliet Taylor's finest hour—headed for certain doom. Bates spots a beautiful woman (Stone), draped in a boa scarf, in the window of another train across the tracks. Partying with other passengers, the laughing beauty is obviously bound for a more fun destination. She blows Bates a kiss, planting her lips on the glass. "I gave it my best shot to melt the sucker," Stone said. Bates can't escape from his train, whose terminus is the municipal dump, which is the same, it turns out, for Stone and her revelers.

Tony Roberts had his usual role as Bates's smooth actor-pal "Tony," known for his appearances in all of Bates's comedies. Allen sent the *Stardust Memories* script to Judith Crist, whose friendship he had nursed for a decade, asking the critic if she might play the role—based on her—of the weekend festival host. Crist, daunted by the challenge, declined. "But promise me," Allen said, "that you'll do a little bit." Helen Hanft played the Crist part, while Crist herself has one line in the film. Playing other bits were other acquaintances, among them *Women's Wear Daily* arts editor Howard Kissel and William Zinsser, a journalist who had profiled Allen for the *Saturday Evening Post* in 1963. Along with a bit role for Andy Albeck, the United Artists honcho desperately trying to re-sign Allen to UA, Jack Rollins made his thespian debut as an impatient producer—not his last acting in a Woody Allen film—while Louise Lasser, uncredited, played Bates's beleaguered secretary. This time was her last.

ALLEN HAD DEVELOPED a visual strategy that gave his actors freedom and opportunity. He never rehearsed, and he preferred minimal blocking. He arrived on the set without preplanned camera moves. He favored long, relatively static master shots with the actors moving in and out of the frame, the camera sometimes trailing them. He shot as few takes as possible, but many, many takes if something bothered him. He rarely planned, or later instituted, any cuts within the lengthy master shots. He always closely watched the performers during the filming, and even when the camera was positioned at a distance, it seemed as though the camera was perched on his shoulder—with Allen studying the scene at eye level. Low angles, or overhead shots, were rare. At first, as video monitors became popular among American directors in the 1970s, he avoided the new technology. (Later he'd find video monitors another means of people avoidance.) His intuitive approach often forced reshooting or created problems that persisted into the final cut, but he didn't believe in overpolishing and, as with his stand-up comedy, loose logic and ragged ends were OK.

After initially shooting most scenes, "there are three variations that follow," Allen told Stig Björkman. "It either needs a little finessing; it's way off and I have to direct them [the actors] to make it right; or they get it and it's never as good again." His actors were always encouraged to tinker with their dialogue and absorb lines into their own vernacular. Some actors felt duty-bound to the screenplay. If he really had to nudge an actor, Allen might say, "Let me see these lines, maybe I made a mistake in the script." He'd read a little aloud, "presumably to myself but so they can hear it. And I'll play it for them so they can get the idea without my telling them to play it that way, then if they still don't get it"—here he laughed—"I think seriously about firing them."

Gordon Willis was still Allen's cameraman, and he would match Gianni Di Venanzo, Fellini's cinematographer for *8½*, with gorgeous black-and-white photography, often achieved, for the exteriors, by waiting hours for the sky and clouds to cooperate. Rare for him, by all accounts Allen strived for more of a perfectionism on *Stardust Memories*. Editor Susan E. Morse, production designer Mel Bourne, and costumer Santo Loquasto, working on his first Woody Allen movie of many to come, anchored the behind-the-camera unit. The music was arranged for the first time by Dick Hyman, a jazz pianist and composer who'd performed with Charlie Parker in the 1950s. Hyman would stick with Allen for thirty years, organize his vintage scores, compose the bridges and incidental music, and perform standards with his own band when certain rights proved expensive or elusive. The quintessential Woody Allen score for *Stardust Memories* would feature Glenn Miller, Sidney Bechet, Django Reinhardt, and the Original Dixieland Jass Band, along with a chorus line of Italian nuns, in one scene, tap-dancing to "Sweet Georgia Brown." Louis Armstrong's "Stardust" is showcased: Bates plays the recording on a sunny Sunday morning after a spring walk, with Dorrie (Rampling) lying on the floor lazily turning the pages of a newspaper, now and then lovingly glancing up toward him. The affecting moment is reminiscent of the *Manhattan* scene where Ike/Allen cites the Armstrong recording of "Potato Head Blues" as among the joys of living.

III

Scenes from a Non-Marriage

Chapter 7

1980

The Second Golden Age

In Which Outright Masterpieces (and a Few Stinkers) Are Made

One night in the late fall, after the day's work on *Stardust Memories*, Allen went to dinner at Elaine's and crossed paths with an actress he'd met in passing years earlier at a Sue Mengers get-together in Hollywood.

Mia Farrow had written the comedian and film director a "fan note" after seeing *Manhattan*, the precise contents of which Farrow did not disclose in her memoir. Allen described the note in *Apropos of Nothing*: "It ended with a sentence I do remember, and it was, 'Quite simply, I love you.'" The actress was dining at Elaine's after giving her nightly performance in *Romantic Comedy*, a new Broadway play by Bernard Slade, in which Farrow portrayed a prudish New England schoolteacher who becomes the writing partner of an arrogant New York playwright. Over the years, she falls in love with her collaborator. Anthony Perkins starred as the arrogant playwright. Allen never said whether he had gone to see *Romantic Comedy*, but he must have because a) Allen saw everything on Broadway; and b) the play was directed by Joseph Hardy from *Play It Again, Sam*.

Actor Michael Caine with his wife, Shakira, whom Farrow was meeting at Elaine's, noticed Allen at his usual table. Caine brought Farrow over to reintroduce them. Allen mentioned her fan note, saying, "It made my day." ("Without smiling," Farrow wrote in her memoir. But "I was stunned that he remembered.") Over dinner with the Caines, the actress confessed she had saved the photograph of Allen that graced the cover of the April 22,

1979, *New York Times Magazine*—a soulful shot of Allen standing on his penthouse balcony with the trees of grand Central Park falling away in the background. "Because there was something so interesting and appealing in his face or expression, I thought I might want to look at it again." Caine darted back to Allen's table to relay this compliment. Not long after, Allen invited Farrow to his New Year's Eve party.

If Allen avoided Lincoln Center galas, he did like to throw the occasional jamboree of his own devise, and for this New Year's he rented out Harkness House, the neo–French Renaissance building in his neighborhood that housed a ballet academy. With Jean Doumanian and Joel Schumacher, his favorite member of the behind-the-camera team to socialize with after hours—Schumacher told good stories and made him chuckle—Allen supervised the planning. Schumacher "knew the best people for flowers, music, lighting, all the stuff that makes a great party," and Doumanian watched over the font of the printed invitations, selected the disco bands, and ordered the hyacinths, wine, champagne, and alcohol, the oyster bar and catered caviar, shellfish, and filet mignon, all to be followed by a basement breakfast served at 4 a.m. Allen's cohost for the extravagant affair, which would usher in the new decade of the 1980s, was actress Jessica Harper from *Stardust Memories*.

Nineteen seventy-nine had been another very good year. The seventies would go down as Allen's miracle decade. His New Year's guest list of several hundred was "amazing in its diversity," one invitee, Charles Champlin, wrote in the *Los Angeles Times*, "and remarkable as evidence of the number of circles one life can touch." The merrymakers included Rolling Stone Mick Jagger with model Jerry Hall and ex-wife Bianca, too; Ruth Gordon and Garson Kanin, Kurt Vonnegut and his wife, photographer Jill Krementz; Robert De Niro, fattened up for *Raging Bull*; and Meryl Streep, making the scene, perhaps, because as Helen Gurley Brown once said, Allen's New Year's party was "a hard ticket; if you were invited, you went"; other actors including Lauren Bacall, Robin Williams and Liza Minnelli; radio comedians Bob and Ray; Bob Fosse, Arthur Krim, Howard Cosell, Tom Brokaw, Ted Sorensen, Gloria Vanderbilt, Lillian Hellman, Norman Mailer, and Arthur Miller; former New York Knicks players Walt Frazier and Earl "The Pearl" Monroe; and a contingent from the *New Yorker* including Roger Angell and Pauline Kael.* Allen had scribbled on Kael's invitation that "even if she didn't like most of the people there, she'd have him to talk to for laughs," according to her biographer. Reel- and real-life Allen friends Michael Murphy and Tony Roberts chatted in one room. Maureen Stapleton from *Interiors* mingled with Marie-Christine Barrault from *Stardust Memories*. Allen, in tux and tennies, and Harper circulated among the guests, smiling and whispering. They were said to be having a romance, but who knew? They were Mr. and Mrs. Secretive about it.

Allen's was "the last great party of the seventies," Marion Meade wrote, the "best" of several parties Andy Warhol and his retinue attended on the night the 1970s expired, with "wall-to-wall famous people," as Warhol wrote in his diary. "Mia Farrow is so charming and such a beauty," Warhol noted. (He also confessed to his diary: "I can't stand Woody Allen movies.") Farrow, who attended with her younger sister Stephanie, her Broadway costar Anthony Perkins and his wife, actress Berry Berenson, left alone "before midnight." The next day Farrow sent Allen a gift—Lewis Thomas's *The Medusa and the Snail*, a National Book Award winner that took jellyfish and snails as pretexts for essays about genius, life, and death—"With a note of thanks."

AFTER THE NEW YEAR'S partying was over, the *Stardust Memories* filmmaking resumed. Allen hoped to finish the bulk of the shoot by spring, when he planned a break from the grind for what was becoming an annual respite in Paris. The filming, refilming, and postproduction of the Felliniesque seriocomic drama would occupy most of the first half of 1980.

William Zinsser, who had two brief scenes in *Stardust Memories*, was an eyewitness to Allen's painstaking directorial methods. Zinsser's sneakers ran into Allen's sneakers on a Manhattan street one day, and Allen recognized the onetime journalist from ten years before. They greeted each other, and Allen took a long pensive look at Zinsser before parting. A week later

---

* One of the many small pieces of writing Allen churned out, "A Fan's Notes on Earl Monroe," documenting his admiration for and brief encounters with his "favorite basketball player," ran in the November 1977 issue of *Sport* magazine.

Zinsser got a call from Juliet Taylor asking him to come in for the role of the Catholic priest who is a passenger on the "ugly" train in the *Stardust* prologue. The priest rejects Bates/Allen's pleas to help him disembark and join the other train of beautiful people on a parallel track.

Zinsser showed up for the filming to be costumed in black robes and clerical collar. He said hello to Allen, who was inspecting the interior of the train for the sequence. "Do I look spiritual enough?" Zinsser asked. No, Allen said, frowning. Zinsser, these days a Yale professor, was wearing horn-rims that were more Ivy League WASP than Catholic priest. Allen summoned a prop woman with a box of eyewear and picked through them, choosing a chrome pair with "wide side pieces" that were exactly the "ugly" type of glasses that might be worn by "a blue-collar parish priest from Queens," Zinsser later wrote. Over and over Allen shot the scene, "all six seconds of it," spending all morning fussing with "lights and angles and sound." Knowing Zinsser was an amateur, Allen advised him to "show no emotion when he approached me as a supplicant. It was the best possible directing advice for someone who has no idea how to act and would ruin a scene by trying to."

Not by any means was Zinsser done. A few months later the phone rang, and he was ordered back for refilming of the last part of the sequence where both trains arrive at the municipal dump, their passengers "discharged to wander over acres of garbage." Allen had tried shooting this scene in the fall at a New Jersey dump site, but cold weather condensed everyone's breath into cloud puffs. The reshoot was planned for the city dump adjacent to Jamaica Bay, near Kennedy Airport, "the biggest dump in the world," in Zinsser's words.

On the appointed day Zinsser hopped on a bus in lower Manhattan, filled with "ugly" extras who were being driven across the East River to a senior citizens' center in outer Queens, where Zinsser and the others were to be costumed: same priest's habit and collar, same chrome glasses. Then they were bused to the dump, "a vast range of hills made entirely of garbage," with flocks of seagulls wheeling overhead. Visiting the site on the Sunday before, seeing the garbage "piled in a configuration that pleased his artistic eye," Allen had approved the site. "But Allen had forgotten that garbage doesn't hold still. Monday's picturesque formations had been compacted under new truckloads of trash, and the panorama that greeted him on Monday wouldn't do."

Production managers summoned fresh garbage. "Allen turned into Toscanini, conducting each driver to where he wanted the load dumped, until at last a high wall of garbage had risen not far from where we were standing," Zinsser said. "Woody was satisfied." For hours Allen photographed the extras walking around the garbage. "The skies were gray, and the sporadic sun reflected off the garbage unevenly. Allen and [Gordon] Willis wanted to make sure that whatever sequences they shot would match one another in quality of light and density of seagull." Satisfaction was elusive. A lunch break was called, after which the "unthinkable" occurred: the seagulls flew away. "We needed new gulls so that the afternoon scenes would match the morning scenes." A fleet of sanitation trucks arrived with more garbage to attract more screaming gulls. So it went, all day.

AROUND THE TIME Mia Farrow ran into Allen at Elaine's she was profiled in *People* magazine. The headline—"Mia Farrow Has Her First Broadway Hit, Loses Her Second Husband, and Adopts Her Seventh Child"—brought readers up to date on the onetime household name who had faded from gossip columns by the late 1970s.

"Mia" was the mangled childhood pronunciation of her given name: Maria de Lourdes Villiers Farrow. Born in 1945, she had been raised as a princess in a fractured Hollywood fairy tale. Her mother was the delicate beauty Maureen O'Sullivan, Irish-born and immortalized onscreen as the sexy Jane of the jungle in several Tarzan pictures, which starred Johnny Weissmuller in the 1930s. In 1936, O'Sullivan married the hard-drinking, womanizing, Australian-born director John Villiers Farrow, notorious in Hollywood as a bully and a sadist on movie sets. He inspired fear at home too: In her 2023 book *The Farrows of Hollywood: Their Dark Side of Paradise*, author Marilyn Moss documented Farrow's physical and verbal abuse of his children growing up, which scarred them.

Farrow's debauched lifestyle was intertwined with a fanatical Catholicism that extended to his writing books about saints and popes. Ava Gardner, who admitted to a fling with the married director on location in Utah while they were making the Western *Ride, Vaquero!*, saw Farrow as "a mean and lecherous character," in the words of Gardner biographer Lee Server, "cruel in equal measure to the horses and to the whores he flew in from Los Angeles."

O'Sullivan was also a devout Catholic, which may explain the seven children even though husband and wife were known to sleep in separate beds. Mia was the oldest daughter of four girls; though stricken with polio at age nine she had overcome the disease with the drive and willpower that belied her appearance—slender, fragile, angelic—a butterfly, but an iron butterfly. Farrow would be perfect casting for Peter Pan, and she did impersonate the flying boy once, opposite Danny Kaye as Captain Hook, in a *Hallmark Hall of Fame* special. The Farrows "were all beautiful," actress Rosalind Russell once said. "You didn't know which one to look at first." But Mia was fated to become the most famous of the children, and arguably the most beautiful.

The oldest Farrow offspring was a boy, Michael, who died first in an October 1958 midair crash of two planes over the San Fernando Valley, one of which was piloted by his flying instructor. The beloved Michael was nineteen. Only thirteen at the time, Mia assumed leadership of the lost children. In 2009, "another brother [Patrick] committed suicide with a gun," Allen later wrote, tallying the Farrow family's sibling misfortunes. "The third brother [John Charles] was convicted of molesting boys and sentenced to prison [in 2013]."

Michael's early death did little to calm the inner demons of her father—twice Oscar-nominated, once for writing, once for direction. John Farrow died of a massive heart attack at age fifty-eight in 1963. Mia was just seventeen.

"I don't want to be just 'one of the Farrows,' third from the top and fifth from the bottom," the young Mia later told Hollywood columnist Hedda Hopper. Convent-educated in London, she learned to admire missionaries and briefly contemplated becoming a nun. After her father's death, however, Farrow moved to New York City, where her mother was appearing in the Broadway comedy *Never Too Late* and where Farrow chummed around with artist Salvador Dalí. Inevitably entering the family trade, Farrow took acting classes and won her first small stage parts in New York, then bigger roles at home in Hollywood in television and motion pictures.

Her breakthrough came as the virginal (if nubile and illicit) daughter of the bookstore owner on *Peyton Place*, which debuted on ABC in the fall of 1964. The hit series was produced by 20th Century–Fox, and one day Farrow wandered over to the soundstage where *Von Ryan's Express* was being lensed on the lot, hoping to catch the eye of Frank Sinatra, which was not hard because Farrow, with striking long blonde hair and electric-blue eyes, was costumed in a sheer nightgown. Meeting Sinatra's gaze, she was filled with "a column of light," she said later. Soon after, Sinatra sent his private plane to fly her and her Angora cat to his Palm Springs home.

Ol' Blue Eyes had cast a spell on Young Blue Eyes ever since she was a little girl, meeting the actor and singer when Sinatra and her father dined together at Romanoff's. In 1964 Mia was nineteen, Sinatra was going on forty-nine. Less than two years later the couple were joined in matrimony in Las Vegas, his third marriage, with one more to come. "At his age, he should marry me!" Maureen O'Sullivan was jauntily quoted in the press. Ava Gardner, Sinatra's second wife, trumped O'Sullivan: "Ha! I always knew he would end up with a boy!" A raucous two-year union ensued, rife with alcoholism and violence on Sinatra's part, keeping the paparazzi busy.

From Farrow's point of view, theirs was an undying love. She always insisted Sinatra was good to her, and the sentence about the singer's abuse of Farrow "allegedly" going "beyond the verbal and the emotional," in Kristi Groteke's *Mia & Woody: Love and Betrayal*—a book written with Farrow's initial cooperation and confidences—angered her. Groteke and her cowriter Marjorie Rosen, a *People* magazine staffer and author of *Popcorn Venus*, a feminist film history, documented their allegation with an account of Farrow's 1967 hospitalization with an eyewitness, producer David Susskind, who attested Farrow had been "badly beaten."

"Sometimes I missed [Sinatra] more than was appropriate" during her second marriage to André Previn, Farrow wrote in her memoir, "which André knew, because I told him everything." The singer was possessive of Farrow, however, and partly because he was jealous whenever they were apart, in 1967 Sinatra demanded the actress walk off the set of *Rosemary's Baby* and join him in *The Detective*, which he was starring in and filming simultaneously in New York. In the horror picture being directed by Roman Polanski, the actress was playing the title role of a young housewife anointed by Satan to give birth to his son. Sinatra tried threatening Farrow, then he tried threatening producer Robert Evans, but when neither threat worked he delegated a flunky lawyer to serve divorce papers on Farrow while the Polanski production was still underway. In *Rosemary's Baby* and in lesser pictures Farrow proved an adept actress, "despite her fey, California ways,"

Polanski remembered, "as professional as her pedigree." Mia's other most famous role was as Daisy Buchanan, the lifelong love of Jay Gatsby (Robert Redford), in the glossy 1974 version of F. Scott Fitzgerald's magnum opus *The Great Gatsby*.

While still married to Sinatra, Farrow had already met the boyishly handsome Previn, a Berlin-born composer and conductor who wrote music for Hollywood movies and whom the actress also had encountered first in the company of her father when she was a little girl. Their paths crossed again at a boring party in London in the winter of 1967, where Previn was guest-conducting the symphony and Farrow was acting in *A Dandy in Aspic*. They ditched the party in favor of a cozy dinner at a restaurant. Previn was married to songwriter Dory Previn, but his wife, terrified of flying, was home in Los Angeles, swallowing pills and spending time in sanitariums. When Farrow returned to Hollywood for *Rosemary's Baby*, she befriended Dory.

Early in life Mia inherited her father's ability to perform gymnastically on the parallel bars of Catholicism and hedonism. In the last years of the 1960s the self-professed loner thrived in the limelight. Between Sinatra ("My *first* husband," as she liked to refer to him) and Previn there were many famous lovers according to the columnists, including singer Eddie Fisher, director Mike Nichols, actor Peter Sellers, and pop musician Papa John Phillips. There were marijuana, LSD, flower-child, and anti–Vietnam War causes; a London court summons for "boisterous" nightclub behavior; and a pilgrimage to India with her younger sister Prudence, a yoga instructor, where Mia sat at the feet of the Maharishi, intersecting with the Beatles in their sitar period. While meditating with the Maharishi, Prudence inspired the Lennon-McCartney song "Dear Prudence." John Lennon insisted Mia left the Maharishi's compound after the guru made sexual advances on the actress.

"The skin was translucent," Dory Previn acidly described Mia, "as though she were still wrapped in the gauze of her placenta." Dory suffered a series of breakdowns as Mia drew closer to her husband, who was leaving movie soundtracks behind in favor of a new life as a globe-trotting orchestra conductor. Previn created an updated *Peter and the Wolf* for the Houston Symphony with Farrow narrating the music. Their obvious affair embarrassed the local citizenry, however, and Previn left Houston under a cloud, accepting the lead baton of the London Symphony Orchestra. In early 1969, the couple set up housekeeping in England. By May the actress was pregnant. Previn wrote to his ailing wife, Dory, hospitalized in the US, asking for a divorce.

The divorce was a foregone conclusion, but not before twins Matthew and Sascha Previn were born in February 1970. Farrow and Previn were formally married six months later. Dory wrote a famous song about Mia's proactive role in corrupting her marriage, called "Beware of Young Girls," which was on her first LP as a singer-songwriter, *On My Way to Where*, in 1970. Farrow hated "Beware of Young Girls," which warned of a wolf in sheep's clothing, "wistful and pale of twenty-four," who was welcomed into her house and admired her wedding ring, but who betrayed her friendship with "a dark and different plan." It was a "tasteless" song, Farrow told the press, but she knew the song and album, which included another tune, "With My Daddy in the Attic," referencing an incestuous fantasy between a little girl and her clarinet-playing father in the attic.

And he'll play
His clarinet
When I despair
With my
Daddy in the attic

Mia appeared to settle down in her marriage to Previn. She gave birth to another biological son, Fletcher, in 1974, and in the early 1970s the couple adopted the Vietnamese orphans Kym Lark, whom she renamed "Lark Song," and then "Summer Song," who became "Daisy," from a Catholic orphanage in South Korea, and finally a girl, Soon-Yi, from another South Korean home for waifs. Previn, who had visited Korea and been struck by the plight of orphans, often said it was his idea to adopt children, but Farrow took the idea and upped the ante to "many children." The family lived on a 250-year-old estate in Surrey dubbed "The Haven," although Previn traveled incessantly and kept up his womanizing. Farrow walked in on her friend Heather Sneddon, the daughter of a Foreign Office mandarin, giving Previn a foot massage in 1978, and she separated from Previn.

Farrow's career as an actress was sacrificed as she mothered five young children. Her most recent credit, by the time she returned to live in New York and star on Broadway in *Romantic Comedy*, was an unfortunate remake of the 1937 John Ford movie *The Hurricane*, directed by Swedish filmmaker Jan Troell, which was noteworthy mainly for Troell's borrowing of Ingmar Bergman's cameraman Sven Nykvist. Farrow reportedly romanced Nykvist on Bora Bora locations while *Hurricane* was being shot, and earlier in 1979 she wrote Previn from the South Pacific, demanding a divorce. Previn would marry Heather Sneddon, his fourth wife, in 1982.*

PREOCCUPIED WITH *STARDUST MEMORIES*, Allen was not in the market for a girlfriend and for weeks he ignored the smoke signals Mia Farrow was sending to him—solicitous notes and gifts. It was true he was happily involved with the "sexy, bright, and talented" Jessica Harper, one of *Stardust*'s three leading ladies. "It was a casual thing," Allen said later. "We were not in love or committed to each other. Jessica was adorable but she liked snorkeling." That was OK for Harper, but as Larry Lipton (Allen) explains in *Manhattan Murder Mystery*, Allen was apprehensive of a pastime in which the goal was to dive down and stare into the eyes of brightly colored fish.

Farrow lived with her mother in a spacious apartment in the Langham, a luxury building on Central Park West between Seventy-Third and Seventy-Fourth, which was almost "directly opposite" Allen's duplex on the Upper East Side and, like his penthouse, boasted park and skyline views. The Langham apartment had been in the Farrow family since the 1960s. One day in early April the phone rang in the Farrow abode, and the voice on the other end introduced herself as Allen's secretary, Norma Lee Clark. She asked the actress about her availability for lunch with Allen in the week following, April 17 at 1 p.m. "The day after Jean-Paul Sartre died," Allen would dryly recall, noting the calendar date.† Arrangements were made for the two to rendezvous at Lutèce, a French shrine to haute cuisine on East Fiftieth that Zagat's ranked among the finest—and priciest—in the US.

Farrow recalled exactly what she wore: "a skirt and an Irish sweater, with sensible shoes, leggings, and socks. It was a brisk, windy day." The maître d'

---

* Previn and Heather Sneddon would divorce in 1999, and Previn would marry a fifth wife and divorce her too before his death in 2019.

† Allen recalled the date a tad inexactly: Sartre died on April 15, 1980.

led the actress to the table where Allen waited, "wide-eyed behind black-rimmed glasses . . . handsomely dressed in an unrumpled tweed jacket and tie." He thought she looked "like a zillion dollars." Having studied the object of her desire, Farrow knew his birth name—Allan Stewart Konigsberg—so she wasn't sure how to address him. "I would be pleased if you would call me Woody," he said. But the director could never bring himself to say the "awkward" name "Mia," she insisted in her memoir *What Falls Away*. "Sometimes I heard him refer to me by my name when he couldn't make the point with 'she' or 'her,' but he never directly called me Mia." He had no trouble in his memoir, frequently referring to "Mia."

The wine was Château Mouton Rothschild. The conversation revolved around Mozart, "Mahler's slow movements," Schubert, "the Heifetz recording of the Korngold," Christianity, Jefferson, "Walter Kaufmann as a guide through existentialism from Dostoyevsky to Sartre," Yeats's poetry, Farrow's children, "my lifelong passionate albeit imaginary relationship with James Agee, who died before I could meet him but whose wife had actually been named Mia." He mentioned his jazz idols: clarinetists Sidney Bechet and Johnny Dodds and pianist Jelly Roll Morton. She had never heard of these musical giants, "but I couldn't wait." After months of work the director had just finished the principal photography for *Stardust Memories*, Allen told her, and was embarking on a trip to Paris, his favorite city in the world after New York. They talked easily and continued talking as his chauffeur drove her home in his Rolls-Royce. "Floodgates opened" that day, Farrow wrote later.

Allen recalled how flattered he was by the attention of "a beautiful movie star" who couldn't have been "nicer, sweeter," and it was only later he learned her "family was rife with extremely ominous behavior that swelled in the years I knew her." The Konigsbergs were a family tree of "no violence, divorce, no suicide, no drugs or alcohol," while the Farrows boasted "drinking and major drug problems with siblings, criminal records, suicide, institution for mental troubles . . . every single Farrow cursed with flaws . . . except, it seemed, for Mia. I was amazed how she would grow up tiptoeing through that minefield of craziness and come out charming, productive, likable, and unscathed. But she hadn't been unscathed, and I should've been more alert."

••

OFF TO PARIS went Allen with Jean Doumanian and Jacqui Safra, who had just played his first cameo for Allen in *Stardust Memories* as the overweight, heart-attack-prone, stationary-bike exerciser married to Sandy Bates's sister (Anne De Salvo), whose character is a frenetic version of Allen's sister Letty. (Safra is billed as J. E. Beaucaire, the Bob Hope character in *Monsieur Beaucaire.*) Doumanian was poised to become the producer of *Saturday Night Live*, taking over from Lorne Michaels, although that was still an industry secret. As always, the week of fine dining and sightseeing included time set aside for Allen to write and meet with foreign business partners and cinephiles.

Yet Mia Farrow had captivated him, and over the summer he and Jessica Harper parted pleasantly. She would never spark another Woody Allen film with her sweet presence. Once again, the week Allen returned to New York, his secretary phoned Farrow to arrange their dinner date for a future Sunday, when there would be no scheduled performances of *Romantic Comedy*. The Sunday date went as well as the lunch at Lutèce, and Allen became a stage-door-Johnny at Saturday matinees, taking Farrow out for meals between shows. The couple began leaving small notes and gifts for each other with their respective doormen. From him: favorite recordings (Bach, the second movement of Stravinsky's Concerto in D for Strings, the Apollo Suite) and poetry (E. E. Cummings, as recited in *Hannah and Her Sisters*). They strolled around upper Manhattan on nights and weekends. Together they went to museums, the opera, the symphony, dance recitals, movie premieres.

Among Allen's regular dinner partners were gossip columnist Liz Smith and his onetime costume designer Joel Schumacher, who, in younger days, shared an apartment with Smith. Smith had inherited the inside gossip on Allen from Earl Wilson, who'd retired, and she broke the scoop of the Allen-Farrow romance at the end of May, noting the couple had been spotted dining at the Chinoiserie hideaway Pearl's, and on another night at the more populist Trader Vic's. "They were seen hand-holding while skipping down Fifth Avenue," another columnist reported. The *Daily News* weighed in with an account of Allen and Farrow "cooing, cuddling, and hugging" at Knicks games, where the director maintained his four VIP season tickets behind the scorer's table.

"He showed me the New York he loved," Farrow recalled. "High on a clock tower with a heart-stopping view, he took two wineglasses and a bottle of Château Margaux out of a paper bag. It was as if I had stepped into a Woody Allen movie . . . [only] he was more serious, less humorous, far more confident than in his films."

This was the slow waltz he'd often danced with girlfriends, but behind the idealized image of the courtship were misunderstandings between the couple from the get-go. On one early date in late spring, Allen and Farrow went to see the Australian film *My Brilliant Career*. Farrow turned to Allen during the movie and declared, "I want to have your baby." Like his cousin Abe Burrows, Allen blinked behind his glasses. Like his characters in his movies, he had long since ceased to believe in true love, marriage, or family. "I was taken aback but fielded it like a graceful shortstop," he reported in *Apropos of Nothing*. "I recall changing the subject to lawn mowers and put it all down to overdramatizing. After all, she was an actress and given to playing scenes."

Farrow's version of the event: After a slight cough signaling his discomfort, Allen glanced away. "Well, I don't know. I would have to think about it," Allen muttered. Farrow knew this "meant he would discuss it with his therapist," the actress recalled. "No decisions were ever made without her. He didn't even buy sheets without talking to her. I know that part of several sessions went into his switch from polyester-satin to cotton."

A few weeks later the lovers—Allen preferred the term "dating"—were supping at Pearl's when Farrow "suddenly suggested we get married," Allen related in his memoir. "The suggestion caught me mid–egg roll, and I thought maybe she didn't have her contact lenses in and was mistaking me for someone else. When I realized she was serious, I told her beside the fact we had only been dating a very short while, I saw marriage as an unnecessary ritual. I had been married twice, as had she, and I learned over the years if a relationship works, it works, but a binding piece of paper doesn't help to reinforce one's love nor rectify a situation."

Farrow was "visibly annoyed hearing my cop-out," Allen noticed, and the actress "withdrew the offer petulantly and made some remark about me spoiling things, by which I imagined she meant, we met, dated, liked one another, and suddenly I was unwilling to progress. Her idea of progress was to run out and marry."

Over the summer the couple found their equilibrium. In stages Allen introduced Farrow to his close circle at Elaine's, which included Marshall Brickman, Tony Roberts, Michael Murphy, Louise Lasser, and—less often nowadays as she increasingly spent time in Hollywood—Diane Keaton. Jean Doumanian joined Allen and Farrow frequently to make three of them for dinner—"Several times a week for a dozen years," Farrow recalled. But the actress "never became comfortable" with Allen's old Chicago friend. "The whole package was intimidating: her breezy, seamless confidence, well-timed remarks, chic all-black wardrobe, perfectly styled black hair, dark eyes, and thin lips on a chalk white face. Her show business anecdotes were the latest, her other interests were exercise, health food, massages, and acupuncture. I didn't know what to talk to her about."

Sometimes they socialized with Farrow's friends, a group that trended older: pianist Vladimir Horowitz and his wife Wanda Toscanini Horowitz; or Garson Kanin and his wife Ruth Gordon, the latter the rare couple that overlapped as friends of both Farrow and Allen. Kanin wrote *Born Yesterday*, the American stage play Allen treasured above all romantic comedies. Gordon, who was often her husband's cowriter on classic movie scripts of the 1940s and '50s, had played Farrow's oddball neighbor in league with the devil in *Rosemary's Baby*.

For six months it was always Norma Lee Clark who phoned to set up their dates. At the end of the summer, however, Farrow had to undergo an operation for peritonitis complications, and she took a hiatus from *Romantic Comedy*. She convalesced in a house on Martha's Vineyard, which the Farrow family kept for summers. Now Allen picked up the phone, calling her several times a day. Returning to New York and resuming their love story, Farrow decided it was time for Allen to meet her seven children. She was "acutely aware" the middle-aged entertainer "had lived his forty-five years entirely without children. . . . As he put it, 'I have *zero* interest in kids.'"

He met them "on an Indian-summer afternoon in late September 1980" when, "dripping chocolate ice cream cones," Mia and the Farrow-Previn kids returned "from the playground, just entering the lobby of our building." Allen was waiting to rendezvous with the actress. "Seven small faces stared up at him" for the first time: the four adoptees—three adopted by Farrow and André Previn, and the fourth adopted solely by Farrow after her divorce from Previn—and the three children naturally born to Farrow during her marriage to Previn.

The most recent foundling, staring up from his stroller, was two and a half years old and handicapped by cerebral palsy. Farrow had named the boy, rescued from a Korean Catholic children's home, Misha (Russian for Farrow's dead brother Michael) Amadeus (his birthdate coincided with Mozart's) Farrow. He was the only one of the children who did not carry the last name of Previn. Summer Song, the Vietnamese orphan now nicknamed Daisy, and Fletcher Previn, the biological son from the Previn marriage, were six years old. Lark Song (known as Lark) Previn, also from Vietnam, was seven. The twins Matthew and Sascha Previn, born to Farrow before her marriage to Previn in 1970, were ten. No one was ever quite sure of the birth year of the last orphan Farrow and Previn mutually adopted, one year before their divorce. Soon-Yi Previn was—best guess—nine or ten. The age of Korean orphans was notoriously elusive.* Allen said the children were "very cute," and "before spring [1981] arrived we were all staying at his place on Friday and Saturday nights."

STARDUST MEMORIES WAS unveiled to the Rollins-Joffe office, United Artists officials, and close Allen family and friends in the late summer of 1981. Waiting afterward for the director to arrive for a celebratory dinner at Elaine's, Steven Bach felt uneasy. "He's a genius!" exclaimed director Mike Nichols, among the insiders at the screening. "Woody has made his own Fellini film and a parody of *8½* at the same time." UA vice president Anthea Sylbert made a wisecrack: "Are you sure he hasn't made a Diane Arbus film?" Bach stayed as silent as the onetime list of *Manhattan* notes in his pocket. "Woody's most unguarded and autobiographical movie had soured in execution," was his private opinion. "Woody as a filmmaker, artist

---

* Soon-Yi Previn's precise age would become disputed during the 1992–93 controversies and court case. In her memoir Farrow maintained Soon-Yi was two or three years younger than her reported age, writing that in the fall of 1980 Soon-Yi was "seven going on eight (her age was finally determined through the standard method of x-raying her wrists)." Yet in 2016, as Daphne Merkin wrote authoritatively in *New York* magazine, "a document signed by both Mia and André Previn . . . has her date of birth as October 8, 1970."

in angst, simultaneously rejecting and exploiting celebrity, sending up pretentious critics, satirizing gaga fans . . . [the script was] fresh and funny and frank, but the gags turned grotesque" onscreen. Ironically, Andy Albeck, in his cameo as a studio boss, Bach wrote, "called the shot with ominous clarity in his single (Allen-authored) line: 'He's not funny anymore!' "

Among Allen's circle of trust were other key personalities who were taken aback by the dark Felliniesque comedy. His longtime friend and personal manager Charles Joffe walked out of the first preview "questioning everything," as Joffe later admitted to the *New York Times*. "I wondered if I had contributed over the past twenty years, more to this man's happiness or to his unhappiness. I didn't think he had shown enough joy. . . ." Joffe aired his qualms with his family—his wife and children—all of whom knew Allen through the years. Then "I talked to Woody himself, for hours. He said to me, 'Does that really seem like the way I feel?' "

An audience that doesn't get the joke is a funnyman's worst nightmare. Unnerved by the reactions of friends and associates, once again Allen fled to Paris to escape the reviews when *Stardust Memories* was released in October. The new picture was a knife's-edge satire of his profession and of Allen's own persona, a cool film without the warmth of *Annie Hall*, and its stylized black-and-white photography made it colder. Instead of charming dingbat Diane Keaton and the romantic spirit of *Annie Hall*, *Stardust* had pill-popping, suicidal Charlotte Rampling, hallucinations about the assassination of a celebrity, and a motley army of fans that included young groupies trying to jump in bed with their idol and a platoon of space creatures pleading for a return to silly comedies. "We enjoy your films," the alien leader intones in a vibrato, "particularly the early funny ones."

Fellini's *8½* also was an unsettling film but somehow the Italian maestro capped his masterpiece in upbeat fashion by reassembling the cast for a finale with Marcello Mastroianni as the ringmaster of an imagined circus parade. Allen tried for similar uplift at the end with feats of levitation, a fleet of hot-air balloons, and a reconciliation with his French mistress in the unsatisfying movie-within-a-movie Sandy Bates (Allen) is finishing under stress. But when the *Stardust Memories* cast gathers to watch Bates's latest movie at the Stardust Hotel weekend's last screening—just as audiences once watched a cut of *Everything You Always Wanted to Know About Sex** at Judith Crist's retreat—they are nonplussed. Charlotte Rampling and Jessica Harper, now as their actress-selves and no longer in character as Dorrie and Daisy, exit the auditorium whispering about what a bad kisser Bates/Allen was during their scenes. After a beat, Bates/Allen returns to the empty theater alone to pick up his forgotten sunglasses. He stares up at the blank screen, waiting for the answer to an unspoken question. Nothing. The filmmaker leaves the theater disappointed in himself for having failed and compromised.

Stardust Memories was unfunny, many prominent reviewers wrote, and worse, the film was sour autobiography. They accused Allen of hiding behind Sandy Bates, with "only the merest wisp of pretext that he is playing a character," in the words of Pauline Kael. The picture not only seemed to renounce his earlier comedies, but also to rebuke the critics who had thrown their weight behind the jokier works. The anti–Woody Allen camp, which had resented the Charles Chaplin and/or Ingmar Bergman comparisons and refused to join the *Annie Hall* or *Manhattan* delirium, had been festering and swelling. Now their voices rose to a crescendo.

Sometimes this camp lectured Allen on his leading-man attributes, and other times on his Jewishness, both of which they saw as deficient. When assessing *Manhattan*, John Simon had described Wallace Shawn as "perhaps the only actor in New York who looks worse than Woody Allen." Now, for *Stardust*, he again insulted Allen's physical appearance ("small, Jewish, and ugly"), sneered at his relationship on- and off-camera with the lovely Jessica Harper, and excoriated *Stardust* as "self-serving" and "self-loathing" without "self-irony."

His "parasitism" of Fellini, with a little Bergman mixed in, Stanley Kauffmann wrote in *The New Republic*, "made me angry." Kauffmann had complained of *Annie Hall* that Allen's "hypersensitivity about being Jewish seems more his problem at the moment than his society's." *Stardust* continued in the same vein, Kauffmann wrote, with Allen "trying to equate the world with his own view of himself, smearing dat ole debil Jewish self-hate all over everyone." Allen's writing and directing were sometimes OK, but "the viewer must decide personally whether it's credible," Kauffmann wrote, that so many beautiful women "want Allen as a lover."

The blast of invective targeting Allen personally, or what some critics saw as his smug "persona," was especially harsh, it seemed, when coming from prior supporters who had kowtowed to *Annie Hall* and *Manhattan* and even, grudgingly, *Interiors*. The previously sympathetic Andrew Sarris, from the

Village Voice, found *Stardust* "tortured," "a failed parody," "a patchwork quilt full of unfinished patterns" and "the most mean-spirited and misanthropic film I have seen in years and years." Roger Ebert in the *Chicago Sun-Times* described the new Allen picture as a cheap facsimile of *8½* "without the depth" or "personal involvement" of a Fellini. "What a pity, and what a waste," lamented Joy Gould Boyum in the *Wall Street Journal*.

Among the misunderstanders, and arguably the most vicious of those hitherto disposed to Allen, was Kael, who was not only a leading voice among New York colleagues but a national figure who cast a long shadow over the entire critical profession. The beginning of the end for Kael had been *Annie Hall*, which unlike most critics she had found "somewhat disappointing." Still, her assessment of *Annie Hall* as "the neurotic's version of *Abie's Irish Rose*" might have amused Allen, and that opinion did not put Kael much at odds with his own second-guessing. Penelope Gilliatt had offered the "official" *New Yorker* opinion of *Interiors* while Kael was on sabbatical, grouping Allen's work with Bergman, Chekhov, and *King Lear*. *Interiors* was "majestic," Gilliatt wrote, "as true a tragedy as any that has come out of America." That only seemed to goad Kael, who took a dim view of Allen's ultra-drama. Writing later, Kael scoffed at *Interiors* as a Jewish movie masquerading as a WASP movie, and little more than "a handbook of art-film mannerisms." As for *Manhattan*, which Gilliatt loved, prompting her to hail Allen as "one of our most majestically comic citizens," Kael also diverged from her colleague, writing belatedly about the applauded work as a "wet mixture" of Bergman and Chaplin. "What man in his forties but Woody Allen could pass off a predilection for teenagers as a quest for true values?" she asked.

According to biographer Brian Kellow, Kael believed Allen as a filmmaker "had been in decline for a while," and she had been saving her pent-up fury for *Stardust Memories*, issuing "the most annihilating piece of criticism she had done for some time," in Kellow's words. Kael described *Stardust* as an "obsessional pastiche" with few redeeming qualities; even Gordon Willis's acclaimed black-and-white cinematography was "bleached-out. . . . The Jewish self-hatred that spills out in this movie could be a great subject, but all it does is spill out." Allen "degrades the people who respond to his work and presents himself as their victim," her review continued. "He is not just the victim here, he's the torturer. (A friend of mine called the picture *Sullivan's Travels Meets the PLO.*)" Accusing Allen of a "horrible betrayal" of his fans and the critics who formed his friendliest cadre, Kael said that at least "the scenes are short, but there is not a single one that I was sorry to see end. *Stardust Memories* isn't a movie, or even a filmed essay; it's nothing. You see right through it to the man."

The personal attack from Kael and others stung. Allen had befriended Kael early in the 1970s and "frequently wrote to the influential critic when he happened to be in California filming," according to Kellow. Allen had praised Kael's advocacy for Robert Altman's risk-taking body of work and sent her the scripts of some of his early comedies for her feedback. In return, up to this time, Kael had given Allen's movies sensible or encouraging notices. Allen was not afraid to disagree with Kael in person, nor in letters, but he "cultivated her strenuously, going so far as to take her side after Peter Bogdanovich's rebuttal" to Kael's controversial "Raising Kane" in *Esquire*, which took up the cause of Herman J. Mankiewicz, the overlooked cowriter of *Citizen Kane*, and made the case that Mankiewicz had written the celebrated script almost entirely by himself. Ironically, Kael's piece tore down Orson Welles, one of Allen's idols. Allen advised Kael not to respond to Bogdanovich.

A few discerning critics saw *Stardust Memories* for the brave and bravura picture it was. Vincent Canby praised "a marvelous film, sometimes breathtaking . . . his most mysterious . . . [and] his funniest." "Ruthlessly honest," Charles Champlin wrote of *Stardust* in the *Los Angeles Times*, "a brilliant, uncomfortable work." But for the first time a surfeit of brutal reviews hurt a Woody Allen film. UA sucked it up, pouring money into promotion, and eventually *Stardust* "found its audience," Steven Bach wrote, "though it was a commercial disappointment after the triumph of *Manhattan*." Its failure with audiences has been exaggerated. *Stardust* wound up number eleven among Allen's films in domestic earnings, but the box office dip was an early signal the bloom was off the rose.

There would be no Oscar nominations nor any major critics' organization awards, just the usual Writers Guild nomination, Allen's seventh, for Best Original Screenplay. For decades in interviews, Allen would cite *Stardust Memories* among his favorite pictures, one of the few that had lived up to his imagined possibilities for it. Apart from the fact he would have preferred Dustin Hoffman rather than himself in the lead role, the director told Michel Ciment and Yann Tobin in 1995, "It's one of my films I like best.

I would remake it without changing anything." Strong words from someone who often functioned as his own most miserly critic.

A REVIEWER ONCE wrote that Allen's audience left him by degrees, but, as he himself reflected many years later, "The truth is, I left my audience. The backlash really started when I did *Stardust Memories*. People were outraged. I still think that's one of the best films I've ever made. I was just trying to make what I wanted, not what people wanted me to make." His films would continue to be "review dependent," as he put it, meaning his movies were fragile creatures that might be helped by good reviews but were always wounded by vitriol. After *Stardust Memories* he stopped reading those critics who seemed to go out of their way to attack him. But he still wrote complimentary notes to a few that he liked, and personally selected the best snippets for advertising.

He was polite to his critical foes whenever they met socially. Allen had known John Simon since his Broadway years, for example. "You're very forgiving," Simon told Allen once, after getting a warm hello from him. "The truth was I always liked John and while I assumed he meant he had panned me in reviews, I wouldn't have read them, and it never would have impeded my enjoying his company." Yet Allen had gone out of his way to be friendly with Pauline Kael before *Stardust Memories*, and her barbs struck deepest. Their friendship "froze solid," wrote Brian Kellow. Allen got her with a zinger. "She had everything a great critic should have," he wrote in *Apropos of Nothing*, "an encyclopedic knowledge of movies, passion, great writing style, but not taste."

To be fair, while pans might negatively affect the box office of his films, Allen was just as turned off by exorbitant praise. Dining out with Liz Smith and Joel Schumacher, he enjoyed listening to their escapades from the past when they were roommates. One night the columnist switched the conversation to how much she admired his camerawork and light directorial touch with actors in an early Woody Allen comedy she loved. He curtly interrupted her. "Now look," he admonished Smith, "your comments are nice, but a total waste of time. I already know what I did in that movie. It is behind me. What I need from you is 'input' that has nothing to do with me. I am wide-open for other stimuli, for what's happening, what's going on now. Tell me things I don't know. Talk about yourself, your life. Do some of those tales when you and Joel were living together and how you did all those bad 'little kid' things to get attention. But don't talk about me and my past work. . . ."

"As a result of *Stardust Memories*," Marion Meade wrote, "the press began gunning for him." The truth was some percentage of the press and critics had always gunned for him, dating back to his stand-up comedy days, when he offended prudes and moralists. Already many had stored up grievances against his serious films and, like those aliens, pined for the sillier entertainments of yore. There were those who thought Allen too effete or "New York–centric," too Bergmanesque or Felliniesque, too self-absorbed, too narcissistic. For some he was too Jewish, for others he was never the right kind of Jewish, or Jewish enough. There were feminists who didn't care for the onscreen persona that others perceived as a shift away from the traditional Hollywood model of masculinity. Many resented his Upper East Side affluence. Especially in New York, the press corps could speak of Allen and his films with familiar contempt, not only because they had made a study of him but because many of them knew Allen personally, and they took his peculiarities, his shifts in style and content, personally.

AS *STARDUST MEMORIES* faded out in theaters, Random House issued *Side Effects*, Allen's third volume of short pieces that saw original placement in the *New Yorker* and other publications. It cannot have been entirely coincidental that for the foreseeable future Allen would retreat from the *New Yorker*, Pauline Kael's high perch. He said he was going on a fiction hiatus. Allen didn't want to spend all his spare time accruing "little souffles."

The creeping revisionism toward his work affected book critics too. John Leonard complained *Side Effects* was a collection of "sketches, or routines, or riffs, or anxiety attacks" more than actual stories. "The odd effect of reading these stories in a single sitting," Leonard wrote in the *New York Times*, "is to feel that not only have anxiety and schizophrenia been made cute, but so also have Kafka and high culture. There is no threat." Yet *Side Effects* became another bestseller on the "nonfiction" list, where his fanciful essays were categorized.

Among Allen's distractions in the fall of 1980 was the change of leadership at *Saturday Night Live*, whose ratings had plummeted. Guiding light Lorne Michaels had burned out and quit. Yet Michaels, along with many people, were surprised when the network upgraded Jean Doumanian, a talent coordinator and associate producer on the *Live* staff, to producer of the comedy and variety series. Many among the regular cast and writers reacted in protest, and some resigned. Fast on the draw, Doumanian hired a stable of younger stand-ups including Joe Piscopo and Eddie Murphy, whom some people credit Doumanian with discovering, promising new writers like Douglas McGrath, and a fresh staff that included Allen's younger sister, Letty Aronson, who in her early thirties had been bitten by the show business bug. Aronson had long listened to her brother's jokes and read his scripts, commenting privately for his benefit. Now Letty left her schoolteaching career behind to join the late-night comedy series as a researcher, according to some accounts, or uncredited sketch writer, per others.

Many people believed Allen to be a whisperer behind Doumanian's promotion, even though the departing Michaels was an old acquaintance—dating back to when, as a Rollins-Joffe comic, Michaels had tried writing jokes for Allen's stand-up act—who had been a fixture at Allen's New Year's parties. The Doumanian regime was announced in June, and Allen, Doumanian, and Letty Aronson spent the summer brainstorming ways to resuscitate the ailing show. When the revamped *Live* returned in the fall, Allen habitually phoned Doumanian several times a day, according to accounts, telling whoever answered, "It's Mo Golden calling"—one of his aliases—although everyone knew Mo was Woody. According to scuttlebutt, Allen proffered ideas for casting and sketches for the revue format that echoed shows he'd cut his teeth on as a comedy writer in the 1950s and left behind in his career. But on the record with James Andrew Miller and Tom Shales for their definitive oral history, *Live from New York*, Doumanian insisted, "Woody Allen was not involved in the show in any way. I say that unequivocally."

"The influence of Allen caused endless speculation," Sally Bedell wrote in *TV Guide*. Loyal *Saturday Night Live* followers pointed to an uptick in "the cheap jokes about Jews, drugs, and homosexuality," Bedell reported, which might have worked better in more experienced hands. Doumanian clashed repeatedly with the writers and performers over what was, or wasn't, funny. Her peremptory management style led to the staff and the press giving her an array of scornful nicknames, among them "Ayatollah Doumanian" and

"Jean Dobermanpinscher." She and Allen's sister would not last the season; both of them were sent packing in March 1981.

Doumanian's contract was settled by a seven-figure check, according to the grapevine. In addition to helping his best friend and sister, Allen had enjoyed a refresher course in television to inform the character he'd devise for himself in *Hannah and Her Sisters*, who works as the producer of a modish TV series suspiciously similar to *Saturday Night Live*.

STEVEN BACH CLUNG to hopes of keeping Allen at United Artists, although he was not buoyed by the fate of *Stardust Memories*. Bach met dutifully with Allen at the Russian Tea Room, which was situated conveniently close to the Rollins-Joffe offices on West Fifty-Seventh. Bach and the current UA management had tried to outbid Orion on every contract incentive imaginable. Bach reminded Allen the UA package was competitive with Orion's, and said the company would continue to uphold his artistic independence, if he would remain with the studio that had produced all his films since *Bananas*. "Aside from Pauline Kael's head," Bach told Allen with a wink, "I can't think of anything more we can offer." Cracking a slight smile, Allen replied he did not want to disappoint anyone, but the Orion founders—the former UA leadership—were like his family.* In the end he and Bach agreed to "friendly goodbyes," and soon after the lunch Allen announced he was switching to Orion, signing a multipicture contract, exclusive this time, for three pictures over five years. He'd direct and star in two and direct the third without acting in it. Allen was guaranteed 15 percent of the gross receipts, with a portion set aside for Rollins-Joffe and a ration for producer Robert Greenhut. Allen's autonomy remained intact. After delivering a "one- or two-page summary of the plot" to Krim, and receiving budget approval, then as before with UA, Allen was free to "go off and make the movie," in the words of Orion cofounder Mike Medavoy, who himself admitted to having "very little, if anything to do with Woody other than serving as a cheerleader for his work."

"You need someone like Woody Allen to help define your company as

* However, the Orion family had lost one of its founding fathers, company cochairman and former United Artists cochairman Robert Benjamin, who died in October 1980, between the release of *Stardust Memories* and the re-signing of Allen to Orion.

an artistic haven," explained Medavoy in his memoir *You're Only as Good as Your Next One*, "and to gain the respect of other filmmakers to get to the bigger, more commercial movies." This was an increasingly isolated viewpoint in Hollywood, even if Orion saw itself, as UA had, as more of a New York studio with Allen's "unique voice" in the American cinema epitomizing that of "a distinctive New Yorker," in the words of Medavoy. "Arthur [Krim] and Eric [Pleskow] had a predilection for New York over Los Angeles, in both their personal and professional lives."

Although it was little remarked upon at the time, Orion's loan guarantee and production partnership with Warner Bros., which boasted the worldwide sales and distribution operation the new Orion operation lacked, bound the New York–oriented company to certain old-fashioned Hollywood prerogatives. In the late 1970s, the Warner Bros. studio had been taken over by the Kinney Corporation, which made its fortune in shoe stores, parking lots, and funeral homes. The venerable Warner Bros. had become increasingly corporatized under the aegis of Warner Communications, which added entertainment subsidiaries such as video games and Six Flags theme parks to its substantial growing share of the music recording, television, and motion picture market.

Frank Wells, the chairman and CEO of Warners, "didn't like the fact that Woody's films weren't consistent moneymakers," said Medavoy, nor the laissez-faire manner in which Allen was allowed to operate creatively. For the time being Orion and Rollins-Joffe would run interference for Allen, insulating him from tensions between Orion's liberal philosophy of filmmaking and the more dollar-driven view of Warner Communications.

THE CLOCKWORK WRITER didn't lose time. By year's end, when the new Orion pact kicked in, Allen had already completed a new Broadway play and the first two scripts for his three Orion-contracted pictures.

The stage play would come first in the spring of 1981. It so happened Allen served on the directorate of the Vivian Beaumont Theater, a dormant, problem-plagued playhouse that was considered a Broadway venue, even though it was located a mile from Times Square amid the Lincoln Center for the Performing Arts, near the intersection of Columbus Avenue and Broadway. As part of a concerted campaign to revitalize the Vivian

Beaumont, Allen submitted *The Floating Light Bulb*, his first theatrical work since *Play It Again, Sam* a decade earlier.

Set in the Canarsie area of Brooklyn in 1945, Allen's new play was a drama, dotted with laughs, which concerned a debt-ridden Jewish couple and their two sons. The oldest son is a stammering sixteen-year-old who hides out in his bedroom compulsively practicing a light bulb magic trick. Complications develop when his mother, a onetime dancer, alerts a talent scout to the budding teenage magician. The World War II era, Brooklyn milieu, Jewish types, and bedroom magic sprang from Allen's roots, and the overlap between the play and his boyhood were reinforced by the casting of Brian Backer, a twenty-four-year-old with a hangdog resemblance to Allen, as the teen magician. The playwright deflected any close similarities, however. "People keep thinking my films are autobiographical too," Allen told the press during rehearsals, "when in fact they're not."

Allen considered directing the play himself before handing the assignment to Ulu Grosbard—partly because his new Orion contract had set movie wheels in motion. Grosbard had a couple of good films starring Dustin Hoffman to his credit, but he worked more often on Broadway, where he was known for staging heavyweight dramas by David Mamet and Arthur Miller. He and Allen were acquainted dating back to 1962, when Grosbard worked on *The Laughmakers*. Liaising closely with Allen, Grosbard assembled a first-rate cast led by Bea Arthur and Danny Aiello as the mismatched parents. Aiello had crossed paths with Allen earlier on *The Front* and he also had played a small part in *Annie Hall* that was excised from the final picture. Jack Weston would be the Broadway Danny Rose–type talent scout whose dog-act impersonation was a highlight of Allen's script.

As with his earlier Broadway plays, Allen was involved in all the casting and staging decisions, with Santo Loquasto from his screen team taking charge of the atmospheric tenement scenery and costume design. But Allen let Grosbard do the talking, and during run-throughs the playwright slunk down in a dark back row, methodically turning the pages of the *New York Times*, holding the newspaper up to shield his face from the actors. "Occasionally," Aiello recollected, "the actors on the stage, myself included, would see him lower the newspaper slightly, peer briefly at us over the top of it, then duck down and go back to his reading."

Allen gave his input to Grosbard, who relayed anything important. "He never talked to the actors," Grosbard recalled. "He was absolutely ruthless with his own stuff. If a line wasn't working, I'd have to stop him from cutting it out. If he wasn't satisfied with something he'd walk into another room at the rehearsal hall and come back with four alternatives." At times Allen sent little encouraging notes to certain actors in their dressing rooms on "scraps of paper" or "odd brown-paper-bag stationery." His opening-night note to Aiello read: "Danny—Good Luck. . . . I think you're a great actor—now if we can only get you to believe it. Woody."

"I see it as very much a modest little play," Allen told journalists, "hopefully amusing and engrossing." He was characteristically AWOL when the play opened on April 27, having absconded to Paris again with Jean Doumanian and Jacqui Safra. Doumanian had just been fired from *Saturday Night Live*, which dampened everyone's spirits. "I was nervous," Allen told the press upon returning to New York. "Not nervous about the play, but nervous about being away from home. I just walked the [Paris] streets and couldn't really enjoy myself."

Disappointed reviewers pointed out *The Floating Light Bulb* could have benefited from more Allen comedy. The *New York Times*'s Frank Rich thought his script was "overly beholden to the early Tennessee Williams," and a "conventional, modest and at times pedestrian family drama," with magic clumsily used as "a metaphor for life's illusions." The name Woody Allen kept the production alive for sixty-five performances, however, and the show business community honored Backer—the Allen lookalike playing the teenage magician—with a Tony Award as Best Featured Actor of the season. But the famous playwright and the young actor "had very little contact," Backer admitted in interviews. "The only time we talked was when I was rehearsing the magic. It was kind of disappointing. He's very shy. I can't really say after working with him that I know him."

IT WAS STANDARD operating practice for Allen to bounce ideas off friends and rehearse the stories he was writing on walks with people, and just as standard to craft roles in his scripts for the girlfriends in his life. One day on a stroll with Mia Farrow, Allen said there was a part for her in his first Orion project. "A wild banshee jumped into my mouth and said loudly that

I wasn't much of an actress," Farrow recalled. Allen, taken aback, countered: "In the past, actresses who have worked with me have tended to come off very well." He said she was a "wonderful actress. . . . It will only be great. . . . And fun: We'll get to be together all the time and we'll grow even closer. You will do the best work of your life. Your kids will be proud of you, and I will be proud of you. . . ."

The first Golden Age of Woody Allen pictures—the Diane Keaton era—was over and done with. Allen's second Golden Age would begin with Farrow's pivotal role in a lighthearted period comedy, and Allen launched the new decade of Woody and Mia in June 1981 with the filming of—working title—"Summer Nights." That same week *The Floating Light Bulb* played its last on Broadway, and there would be some overlap in Allen's new script, which took his boyhood love for magic into the adult realm of the metaphysical.

"Summer Nights" bore similarities to Ingmar Bergman's *Smiles of a Summer Night*, but there was also a dash of Shakespeare in the script, set in 1905, which gathered six people for a wedding in the upstate New York country retreat of a stockbroker and inventor named Andrew (Allen). The host, not groom, of the wedding party, Andrew suffers from a "bad sex life" with his otherwise charming, beautiful wife (Mary Steenburgen). The prospective husband-to-be is a pompous philosophy professor (José Ferrer), while his bride is the freethinking Ariel (Mia Farrow), a diplomat's daughter raised by nuns, who has a reputation as a libertine for possibly making love to "writers, bankers, poets, the entire infield of the Chicago White Sox." The only other guests are Andrew's best friend Maxwell (Tony Roberts), a "medical Casanova," who has "never lost a patient, but he got a few of them pregnant," and his lusty nurse (Julie Hagerty), a last-minute add-on for the occasion.

The Elysian exteriors were staged at Kykuit, the vast John D. Rockefeller estate in Mount Pleasant near Tarrytown on the Hudson. Allen and Farrow shared a camper, as would become their custom on locations for most of the films they made together. "Our days were spent waiting for moments of perfect light," Farrow recalled in her memoir. Her divorced younger sister Stephanie—born 1949 and known as Steffi—pleaded with the actress for a job as her stand-in. Allen grudgingly consented, while grousing "he wouldn't have *his* sister on the set no matter what," Farrow recalled. Still, it worried the actress to have the sister Allen always referred to as her "pretty sister" hanging around "with me playing a role, and tons of people being so attentive to me." Farrow had to spend a lot of prep time in the trailer, "my torso compressed into a killer corset," her hair "tightly wrapped around cone-shaped curlers." Staring out the window, she noticed Steffi, "adorable in her jeans and baseball cap and straight hair, lounging in the tall grass, strolling under the trees, talking and laughing with Woody."

Her responsibilities in front of the camera were stressful. "Woody, now my director, was a stranger to me," Farrow recalled. "His icy sternness pushed my apprehension toward raw fear. . . . This seemingly straightforward material was beyond my capabilities." She gobbled Tagamet for the ulcer she developed. One day, "dispirited and humiliated," Farrow told Allen he might be better off with her as his production assistant on his next movie rather than as an actress. Eyeing her dubiously, Allen said, "It's hard work being an assistant." Later, discussing Farrow's unease with Eric Lax, Allen explained: "I tend to be maybe a little abrupt sometimes. So, I calmed her, but I was not completely sympathetic, because I didn't realize the dimensions, the gravity. I knew she'd be wonderful in it [the role]. It never occurred to me that she'd disappoint me."

Allen was nothing if not democratic when putting actors through ordeals, asking Ferrer for so many takes on the simple reading of one line—for the scene where Ferrer and nurse Hagerty get down to their lovemaking—the veteran actor exploded: "No, now I can't do it! You've turned me into a mass of terrors." It is possible he had not forgiven the actor for beating Brando to the Best Actor Oscar in 1950, or was subconsciously punishing him.

Be that as it may, Allen moved through this and other comedic scenes so briskly the photography was done by August. He had the music in mind. With only six characters and a straightforward story, the editing was not going to be any trouble. Allen had months to go before the scheduled release of the movie, and in his back pocket he had, all ready, the second script in his Orion contract. He thought he might save a little money by shooting scenes for the second movie in the same locations—i.e., the Rockefeller estate—where he'd be reshooting parts of "Summer Nights." Not only Orion, but much of Hollywood was taken aback by the announcement Allen would initiate filming of his second movie in the Orion deal before the end of the year.

"For the purposes of clarity," according to *Variety*, Orion's publicity department was giving the second picture the label of "Woody Allen's 1981 Untitled No. 2" to differentiate it from the just-completed "Summer Nights," or "No. 1." "Practice of shooting back-to-back pictures is a rarity these days," *Variety* commented.

ALLEN HAD BEEN completely won over by Farrow as an actress, and there would be a bigger role for her in "No. 2."

Andrew/Allen and Ariel/Farrow made love in one scene of the wrapped "Summer Nights," but their coupling is furtive and takes place off-camera; it is an unsatisfactory experience for both in the story. "At least we bulled our way through!" says the disappointed Ariel. More symbolic of their relationship were the long tracking shots Allen supervised of the couple traversing the woods, flirting and bantering as they walked, just as happened during the long walks they took daily nowadays through Central Park and on Manhattan streets.

As was true when he was romantically paired with Diane Keaton in earlier Woody Allen films, he and Farrow were never great onscreen lovers. There were never any nude scenes, few kissing scenes, little bedroom activity together. Offscreen, the Allen-Farrow romance was progressing, but not without tensions and wrinkles. For one thing, Farrow possessed a jealous streak, and she suspected Allen of nursing a crush on younger sister Steffi, her stand-in during the filming of "Summer Nights." When Allen planned for them a brief escape to Europe after the wrap, he suggested they bring Steffi along. "It seemed so out of character" for Allen, Farrow thought. Still, off the three jetted to Rome and Paris, with Farrow warily eyeing Steffi. Later, she discovered photographs of Steffi in Allen's apartment, she wrote in her memoir, and wondered if they had had an affair.

Soon enough, Farrow made the acquaintance of at least one of Allen's several inspirations for Tracy in *Manhattan*—his secret paramour Babi Christina Engelhardt. According to Engelhardt, Farrow was brought into a "handful" of the threesomes she experienced with Allen. Afterward, Engelhardt and Farrow sometimes smoked joints together, while Allen abstained. "To this day, I've never had a puff of marijuana," he insisted in his memoir. The women bonded over their mutual love for animals and other shared appetites. "When Mia was there, we'd talk about astrology and Woody was forced to listen," Engelhardt mused. "I was little more than a plaything," Engelhardt said, and in time she bid Allen adieu. Engelhardt's name is not mentioned in *What Falls Away*, Farrow's memoir, much less any threesomes. Nor is her relationship with Farrow mentioned in the 2021 *Allen v. Farrow* documentary in which Engelhardt is interviewed and pointedly avoids condemning Allen.

Farrow evidently accepted the threesomes, along with other stipulations Allen made in their relationship. After Maureen O'Sullivan became engaged to her second husband, James Cushing, and moved out of the family apartment at the Langham, Farrow took over the six rooms and enlarged the space for her children, annexing an adjacent unit. Allen visited the Langham regularly, but he found endless excuses for not staying overnight. He liked to sleep alone in his own bed. "I like to sleep with the air-conditioning on, while she [Farrow] doesn't like air-conditioning." Or he had to get an early morning start on the next day's work; or he didn't cotton to the shower and bathroom. Perhaps another turn-off was Farrow's bedroom, "strikingly nunlike," in the words of Kristi Groteke, who later became a nanny and confidante of Farrow's over two years of intermittent employment, with plain white walls and a "simple wooden crucifix" above the headboard. Too, Allen found it difficult to accept the household menagerie, which included a fluid number of pet dogs and cats, chinchillas, hamsters, gerbils, and mice in hutches, fish in aquariums, a canary, parakeets, and talking parrots. The furred and feathered creatures were anathema to Allen, and he "never ate our food or used our plates or utensils because of the cats, who had been known to jump onto the table. He couldn't stand the cats." The couple would never permanently cohabit at the Langham or anywhere, and not once did Allen sleep over at the Langham during his years with Farrow.

Farrow tried to inveigle Allen into visiting her family's retreat on Martha's Vineyard, but that didn't work out very well either. Martha's Vineyard was too far from New York, and the director couldn't make the round trip comfortably without an overnight stay. So Farrow sold her island house and purchased a two-story wooden Colonial within driving distance of New York on a sixty-acre spread with a pond near the quaint hamlet of Bridgewater in Litchfield County, Connecticut. The actress dubbed her new summer home "Frog Hollow."

Allen temporized about visiting Frog Hollow too. On top of his loathing of crickets and deer, Allen found fault with the bathroom shower. "The drain is in the middle," he told Farrow. ("Shaking his head dismissively, as if I should have known," Farrow wrote.) Side drains, Allen believed, acted more efficiently in washing away all the germs. And there was another reason why Allen needed his special kind of shower. "This sounds silly," he told Eric Lax, "but I'll be working, and I'll want to get into the shower for a creative stint. I'll stand there in the steaming water for thirty or forty minutes, just plotting a story and thinking out ideas." The actress preferred a bathtub for long, luxurious soakings, and she didn't care about showers. But the actress tried to please Allen by installing "Woody's Bathroom" with new fixtures and a corner drain. He didn't much like "Woody's Bathroom" either, though, and visited Frog Hollow reluctantly, and only infrequently overnight.

Curiously, the to-do surrounding the Frog Hollow acquisition seemed to arouse Allen's competitive instincts, and he added another paradox to his personality. In 1981, out of the blue, he began conducting a search for an ideal weekend home of his own, which like Frog Hollow ought to be located near the last thing in the world he had shown any previous interest in: a body of water. Allen showed realty agency brochures to Farrow, but the actress was discouraged from further involvement. "When he went to see them, he took Jean [Doumanian], not me. It was as disturbing and mysterious as the drain." Allen fixated on Southampton, the southern Long Island fiefdom he knew well as a weekend destination for well-off New Yorkers—it crops up, mockingly, in many Woody Allen movies. Allen convinced himself he could be a Southampton country gentleman although, outdoors in Frog Hollow, he wandered around in netting and a beekeeper's helmet.

Regardless, in late 1981 the famous filmmaker shelled out $3 million for the oceanside mansion known to the local populace as the Ark, a beach property once belonging to Fred Gershon, the partner of Bee Gees producer Robert Stigwood in his Stigwood Group, which came replete with sauna and Jacuzzi, two adornments Allen could be expected to shun. The weekend haven offered stunning views of the Atlantic with sea breezes. Inexplicably, the first thing Allen did was have the tall beach grass mown, which had given the estate its distinctive privacy. Allen organized architects, construction, and landscape crews, consulting with Doumanian over the colors, interior design, and furniture. "The creativity of doing the house was fun," Allen recollected. It took a year before, in the summer of 1982, the reconstruction transformed the Ark into something "just drop-dead beautiful . . . a mansion facing the waves," Farrow recalled, "with many cavernous rooms impeccably furnished with pale-pine antiques, all in shades of white except for the Laura Ashley curtains in the bathrooms and a brand-new restaurant-style kitchen. Every appliance, towel, plate, and billiard ball was in place."

Allen and Farrow had their own private housewarming when the house was ready. Allen "didn't have a sense of foreboding at first." The couple walked hand-in-hand on the beach, then Allen "went in the house and went out of the house and went in the house and went out of the house." He was beginning to get a queasy feeling. At night in bed, amid "the dead black of nowhere," with no place to go, no nearby Elaine's, with the incessant crashing of waves and blowing of wind driving him "nuts"—Allen realized he'd much rather hear shouting, sirens, traffic. In his mind echoed "the admonishing voice of my mother when I was a child, saying, 'You know you don't like the country. You *never* liked the country. You don't like to be away from the *city*.' "

The couple woke up the next morning, ate breakfast, and Allen phoned his accountant: "Sell the house." Although Farrow tried to talk him out of it ("You've just got to tough out the first couple of nights"), in the end the actress was "perfectly supportive" of Allen's decision to vacate. Farrow's ability to absorb and accept his peccadilloes would strengthen their bond as, personally and professionally, the two began to merge their lives.

DESPITE ALLEN'S USUAL quota of reshooting, "Summer Nights" was a relatively simple job of work. The all-consuming project was the second Allen-Farrow partnership—"Woody Allen's 1981 Untitled No. 2"—which was a story known, at different stages, as "The Changing Man," "The Cat's Pajamas," and finally *Zelig*.

Allen had crafted the script in the same pseudodocumentary format he had experimented with in *Take the Money and Run* and *The Harvey Wallinger Story*. The script unfolded as a mockumentary which traced the life of a fictional celebrity from the 1920s and '30s named Leonard Zelig, whose celebrity would be explored in fake newsreels, "expert" interviews, snapshots, and home movies, all juxtaposed with a faux–Warner Bros. programmer from the 1930s melodramatically re-creating Zelig's supposed real-life tale. Zelig is an "odd little man" who mingles with everyone from F. Scott Fitzgerald and Charles Chaplin to Pope Pius XI and Adolf Hitler. He has the singular capacity, which he is unable to control, of altering his personality and even his physical features to conform with disparate or hostile environments. Zelig is the "ultimate conformist," psychologist Bruno Bettelheim explains in one of the staged interviews, blending in anywhere because (as Zelig says) "I want to be liked." In a black nightclub Zelig's skin darkens, and he joins the jazz band. Socializing with fat people, his weight balloons. Renowned as "the human chameleon," Zelig becomes a symbol to America whose import is debated by pundits, politicians, religious figures. A psychiatrist at odds with the medical establishment (Farrow) treats his disorder in unorthodox fashion. Her quest to discover Zelig's genuine self leads to true love.

Ultimately *Zelig*'s message is Allen's personal motto: "Be your own man." His script wittily invested Zelig with trademark Woody Allen–isms—the character hates mosquitoes and would rather watch a baseball game than finish reading *Moby-Dick*—while commenting seriously on social conformity within the far-fetchery.

While the patchwork-quilt nature of *Zelig* would make the postproduction more demanding than any Woody Allen film ever, the actual filming was straightforward, Allen said in later interviews. "Of all the films we made," Farrow wrote, "the atmosphere on this set was the most relaxed." Partly that is because the two leads—Allen as Zelig, Farrow as Dr. Eudora Nesbitt Fletcher—showed up for work, sweetly holding hands.

Many performers played lesser roles, and these included Farrow's sister Steffi, this time on camera as Dr. Fletcher's sister. Allen's circle of friends and colleagues also supplied bits, including John Doumanian as a Greek waiter in the scene where Zelig "turns Greek," and *Love and Death* production designer Willy Holt as the German chancellor standing on the podium next to Adolf Hitler and Zelig at a Nazi rally. The voice-over announcers included Dwight Weist, who was known as the "Man of 1,000 Voices" for his impersonations on the *March of Time* series; Ed O'Herlihy, a broadcast personality Allen first met on Sid Caesar's show in the late 1950s; and British thespian Patrick Horgan, who did the heaviest lifting as the BBC-style narrator of the story.

Along with Bettelheim, the real-life notables sitting for mock interviews included essayist Susan Sontag, novelist Saul Bellow, and jazz singer Bricktop, reminiscing about Cole Porter's friendship with Zelig and the times when Zelig visited her Paris nightclub in the 1920s. The mock interviews would be scattered throughout the movie in the manner of *Reds*, Warren Beatty's epic about the Soviet revolution, costarring Diane Keaton, which was just arriving in theaters as *Zelig* was filmed. Allen tried but failed to lure Greta Garbo for one of the fake interviews and had to settle for Lillian Gish. Sadly, the first lady of the silent screen did not make the final cut, "because I didn't like the way it [the interview] came out," in Allen's words. As ruthless as ever about cutting scenes that hurt the whole, if Allen could lop his basketball hero Earl "The Pearl" Monroe out of *Annie Hall* he could also remove the immortal Lillian Gish from *Zelig*. Dating from October 1981, when principal photography began, a year and a half would elapse before *Zelig* was ready for release in mid-July 1983.

MEANWHILE, CRITICS AND audiences got to see *A Midsummer Night's Sex Comedy* in the summer of 1982.

For months there had been no announcement of a final title, much less any synopsis, and the reviewers were ill-prepared for a picture as unlike as any could possibly be from *Stardust Memories*, its controversial predecessor. *Midsummer* was as ethereal and quixotic as any Woody Allen film before or since—an improbable ode to nature and the transcendental, playfully infused with his signature musings on love, sex, and death. There were allusions to Bergman, the Bard, and Jean Renoir's *A Day in the Country*, and there was familiar nostalgia for Paris—"In the rain!" sighs Ariel/Mia. There was ravishing imagery of ladybugs and butterflies, fly-fishing and bird-watching, games of archery and badminton, even a sexually arousing chess match. An *E.T.*-like flying bicycle has a moment, as do affecting snatches of lieder and an ironic rendition of the Lord's Prayer. The casting was fortuitous: José Ferrer could sing the Schubert and Schumann, and Farrow and Mary Steenburgen both played a little piano. The interwoven story strands were improbably tied together at the finis by an all-seeing Spirit

Ball that transmits otherworldly visions—a device not unlike the floating light bulb from Allen's recent play—or, for that matter, the shiny orb passed around for the perfect "high" in *Sleeper.*

A suicide is averted. Cupid's arrows go astray—literally—and infidelity proves fatal under a beautiful summer moon. The soul of a sexually fulfilled deceased cynic rises to join other departed spirits in the enchanted woods. Allen had flirted with the phantasmal in *Annie Hall*, but *A Midsummer Night's Sex Comedy* represented the first flowering of the tendency in his work that Richard Schickel hailed as "magic realism."

Rare for him, Andrew/Allen is neither a particularly urban nor Jewish character. Even his vintage spectacles were a departure. Gordon Willis's photography was stylized and luminous. Santo Loquasto's splendid costumes aided the pretense. Allen as a nature lover was always a pretense: When his flying bicycle crashes into the river, Allen played the scene "soaked," but the germaphobe insisted that the water he was drenched with be Evian. Perhaps *Midsummer* was a folly, perhaps it was talky, its humor strained. Yet the film tried for magic.

A "limp bit of piffle," Sheila Benson pooh-poohed *Midsummer* in the *Los Angeles Times*, while the *New York Times* headline of Janet Maslin's dismissive review accused Allen of "shunning mastery." Some critics attacked Farrow, comparing her performance to Diane Keaton's in earlier Allen comedies, stupidly suggesting the current girlfriend had been "encouraged to mimic" Annie Hall. The more farsighted takeaway was that Allen's trust in Farrow as an actress—their chemistry together—had provided her with a grand entry into his oeuvre.

Warner Bros. had big eyes, dispatching *Midsummer* to five hundred theaters, supported by the first national television advertising for a Woody Allen picture. The studio even packaged an all-classical LP of the Mendelssohn-heavy score. Yet the $9 million domestic gross was Allen's lowest since *Take the Money and Run*. Aljean Harmetz, in her annual wrap-up of the national box office for the *New York Times*, grouped the movie among the "unexpected losers" of 1982. Over the course of Allen's career, different movie studios "tried big openings, small openings, sophisticated ads, rotten commercial ads, trumpeting my name, downplaying my name, opening different times of year, pushing some big stars in the cast," Allen wrote later. "All to no avail."

However, the experience of *Stardust Memories* had liberated Allen from both critical and box office exigencies. His Orion contract emboldened him, and his close relationship with Farrow energized his creativity.

Somehow, he managed to squeeze in a campaign for the Seibu department store chain, which was headquartered in Tokyo. He earned a reported $1 million for a campaign of clever sketches capitalizing on the fact that "Woody Allen" was hardly a household name in Japan. It was his first advertising in a decade, and the pocket money it brought to Allen helped redress the box-office failure of *A Midsummer Night's Sex Comedy*.

FOR SEVERAL MONTHS in late 1981 and early '82, while filming the *Zelig* mockumentary, Allen kangaroo-hopped around New York and New Jersey locations. He elaborately staged the baseball games, Nazi gatherings, San Simeon parties, and ticker-tape parades at which Zelig is spotted. His nimble behind-the-camera unit of cameraman Gordon Willis, production designer Mel Bourne, costume designer Santo Loquasto, and editor Susan E. Morse all segued straight from *A Midsummer Night's Sex Comedy*. Dick Hyman's services were not required for the all-classical-music soundtrack of *A Midsummer Night's Sex Comedy*, but Allen asked Hyman to organize a period jazz score for *Zelig*. Some of the established music had to be rerecorded by Hyman's band, and Hyman also wrote original tunes including "Doin' the Chameleon" which, in the movie, italicizes the Zelig dance fad.

Photographing the entire picture in black and white, Willis used 1920s newsreel camera lenses with fresh mounts to mimic the look of silent-era footage. Much of Willis's handiwork, which had been so immaculate for recent Woody Allen movies, was intentionally made to look scratchy in the style of *The Harvey Wallinger Story*. "We had our assistants going into the bathroom and holding the film under the shower, and then walking on it to get the effects we wanted," Allen said. "We'd all drag the film on the floor and stomp on it."

The time-consuming postproduction involved researching and sorting through mountains of newsreel and archival clips before optically inserting Zelig/Allen into the historical make-believe. "It's by far the most work I've ever had to do on a film," Allen told the *Los Angeles Times*. The fabricated image of Zelig/Allen had to precisely match the yesteryear *verité*. Zelig was shown mingling with dozens of famous people: F. Scott Fitzgerald takes note of him at a big garden party; Al Capone shares a beer with him at a Chicago speakeasy. "Our pride and joy," Morse said of the toughest editing match: Zelig on deck, the next batter up after Babe Ruth.

"We looked at endless reels of footage of Babe Ruth until we found something that had enough space in the frame to matte in Woody," Morse recalled. "The problem is baseball just isn't filmed that way. Finally, we found a space in one shot where someone could conceivably be in the on-deck circle. But the camera was moving. So, we had to steady the image by blowing up the frame and finding that part that we wanted within the entire span of the panning being done by the camera. By using an optical printer, we could overlay one piece of film over the next. . . . Woody was photographed in front of a blue screen, and then aged for contrast and grain structure, until he looked the same in the shot as Babe Ruth did. But there were shadows in the shot, and we had to animate those shadows crossing over Woody. We spent about five months on this one shot, which is used only twice, about six seconds each time. But it was worth it, because it's the first time you see Woody as Zelig."

Throughout the first months of 1982 Allen rewrote and reshot while working with his loyal team on the editing, sound, and music. He liked to jokingly describe *Zelig* as his "hobby film, because I kept coming back to it," adding, "We had to remember that we didn't want to over-press and make it *too* good. The challenge was to make it realistic." Still, even when dabbling in realism, Allen remained essentially a fantasist and fabulist.

WHILE HE EDITED one film, Allen always toyed with ideas for the next. "We tried to meet at some point during the day for a walk, and of course for dinner," recalled Mia Farrow. "Without fail, no matter what else was happening, he called me four or five times a day." The director and actress were a matched pair, a familiar, reassuring sight in public, talking as they walked in the park and along upper Manhattan streets. About the same height in heels, Farrow stood an inch or so shorter than Allen. Their clothing made similar antifashion statements, Allen with his persona wardrobe, Farrow typically dressed in what she called "dead people's clothes," used or well-worn garments. The couple appeared, in fact, "as vastly underdressed ragpickers," in the words of columnist Liz Smith, "no matter the occasion. They seemed afraid of being touched, talked to, or stared at by the great unwashed. Yet they went around town in a white Rolls so as not to be noticeable."

One night in 1982, as they headed to Elaine's for a late-night repast, the couple "stopped off en route" to view the body of jazz pianist Thelonious Monk, who had died and been put on display at a funeral home. "The first and only dead body I ever saw," Allen recalled. Farrow felt like an intruder. Allen didn't forget such experiences, and for *Alice*, which he shaped for the actress in 1990, he'd link Monk's music with her eponymous character, and in 1996's *Everyone Says I Love You* his script would pay a singing-dancing visit to a famous New York funeral parlor.

The restaurant wasn't always Elaine's, and another night they dined at Rao's on East 114th, a southern Italian oasis beloved by New Yorkers. Observing the proprietress, Annie Rao, as she bustled around, Farrow commented that one day she'd like to play a pure extrovert like Rao—"A fabulous character," in Allen's words, "with her stacked-up blonde hairdo and dangling cigarette, her New York style of talking, her roast peppers. Oh, and her ever-present sunglasses." Her remark got Allen to thinking. Farrow's ambition to depict "a tough, Brooklyn-Italian broad," in Farrow's words, coincided with his own actorly interest in returning to low comedy and portraying "a streety guy, an uneducated loser, a small-time hustler" on the fringe of show business.

He was inspired to write a script with the best role yet for Farrow. Two months after the release of *A Midsummer Night's Sex Comedy*, eight months before the first insider screenings of *Zelig*, Allen called action on his third movie in the Orion contract, whose title was confidently announced *before* filming: *Broadway Danny Rose*. "There were days," Farrow said, "when [in the same week] we shot scenes from two or three different films."

For the first time in a Woody Allen picture, portraying Tina Vitale in *Broadway Danny Rose*, Farrow could boast a bona-fide starring part. She had been folded into the ensemble of *A Midsummer Night's Sex Comedy*, and her role in *Zelig*, while substantial, was undemanding. This was a promotion from the boss. Yet knowing the boss, by now Farrow also knew "rehearsals, apart from a couple of perfunctory, disjointed camera run-throughs during which Woody paid little or no attention to the actors, were nonexistent." So she went to work building her performance through externals. The actress gained ten pounds on milkshakes, lowered her voice, and spent hours repeatedly watching *Raging Bull* for her lower-class diction. Farrow drew much of her "look and attitude" from Mrs. Rao, but the actress also borrowed details from the spouse of Jilly Rizzo, another New York Italian restaurateur, who was an inseparable crony of Frank Sinatra's. Other embellishments came from makeup designer Fern Buchner and hair designer Romaine Greene and Allen's new costume designer, Jeffrey Kurland, who had been Santo Loquasto's assistant on *Stardust Memories* and *Zelig*. They fitted Farrow with large false breasts ("removable") and "tight sexy clothes, stiletto heels, and big hair." Looking the part before playing the part, Farrow also donned dark sunglasses to hide her pale-blue eyes and project "toughness."

Allen's script revolved around the small-time talent manager Danny Rose (Allen), who is an elaboration of the Jack Weston character in *The Floating Light Bulb*. Danny is introduced pitching his oddball roster to the manager of Weinstein's Majestic Bungalow Colony, the Poconos hotel where Allen, as a teenager, performed magic tricks. It's a roster of cheap novelty acts, featuring everything from blind xylophonists to parrots that can peck out "September Song" on the piano. Danny bolsters his clients with aphorisms: "Star. Smile. Strong."

Danny's list of clients includes a once suave crooner from the 1950s, Lou Canova, who dreams of a comeback. Married-man Canova is besotted with Tina/Farrow, a New Jersey interior decorator—she'd love to redo Danny's place in "African Jungle"—who happens to be the widow of a "juice man" for the mob. Reluctantly agreeing to "beard" for Canova on the night of his big comeback opportunity, a booking at the Waldorf Hotel, Danny attaches himself to Tina and follows her to a pool party, where she ends her dalliance with an Italian lowlife. The disconsolate Italian attempts suicide by ingesting iodine. His aggrieved family peg Danny as the scumbag rival for Tina's affections, who has triggered the botched suicide, and they pronounce a vendetta on him. Danny and Tina go on the lam, dodging underworld killers. Their adventures become a shaggy-dog love story, which is told by a veteran comic regaling a group of Catskills funnymen noshing at the Carnegie Deli.

The masterstroke of casting was over-the-hill crooner Nick Apollo Forte as Lou Canova. After considering Danny Aiello or Robert De Niro—the latter proving elusive now and the other times Allen pursued him—casting director Juliet Taylor discovered Forte's face on an album cover in a used record store. The overweight nightclub journeyman and part-time tuna fisherman was in his mid-forties and had never acted professionally. But Forte could ring the bell of authenticity, and he could also sing his own songs in the movie.

Allen had idolized Milton Berle when he was a kid during Berle's heyday as television's biggest star. He had met Berle in Times Square and again in Hollywood when trying to write comedy for NBC stars in 1955. Allen had lost a weekend during the filming of *Take the Money and Run*, standing by as a substitute for the ailing comic at Caesars Palace in Las Vegas. Now he wrote Berle into the script as "himself," mulling Lou Canova as an opening act. Here again was Howard Cosell, also "himself," sitting next to Berle at the tryout.

The noshers at the Carnegie Deli were "themselves" too, people who had crisscrossed Allen's life and career. One day Howard Storm, the assistant director and stand-in on Allen's earliest comedy films, jumped on a Los Angeles plane bound for New York and found himself sitting next to comedian Sandy Baron, both hired for roles in Allen's latest project, neither with any idea what the script was about, or what roles they might be playing. (Baron would end up playing The Baron, who is the narrator of the shaggy-dog story; Storm is one of the deli show business veterans.) Morty Gunty, whom Allen first saw onstage at Midwood High School; Corbett Monica, for whom Allen had written jokes in the 1950s; comics Will Jordan and Jackie Gayle; and Allen's manager Jack Rollins were also in the deli gang. Their loosely scripted scenes framed and flashed back on the saga of Jewish Danny and Italian Tina. Broadway loved the fact Allen also convinced Gerald Schoenfeld, the all-powerful head of the Shubert Organization, to act a small part for union scale. Schoenfeld looked right for the role, and he performed competently as the big-time agent-in-waiting who snatches Lou Canova away from Danny.

With Gordon Willis again behind the camera, Allen shot for three months in the fall of 1982, making his third picture in black-and-white in five years. He himself acted in nearly every scene of the comedy. Then the retakes continued "for more than a year," Farrow wrote, "right up until the month [the movie] was released."

••

WATCHING FILMS TOGETHER was one of their weekend pastimes. Allen and Farrow would repair to the screening room in the production offices he had established in the mid-1970s on Park Avenue, where they had their pick of new releases and foreign classics such as *Bicycle Thieves*, which was among the titles Allen rewatched annually and "every bit as great as Frank [Sinatra] had told me," Farrow said. The last scene of Vittorio De Sica's tragedy inevitably provoked "Woody to shed a tear, although it's possible that his stye was itching." The persistent stye—in his memoir Allen said it was "chalazions," or little eyelid bumps—stumped his multifarious doctors. A Chinese herbalist whom Jean Doumanian knew "produced a cat's whisker and stuck it into Woody's tear ducts," Farrow recalled, which caused "no effect at all." Allen, amused by the experience, wrote the Chinese herbalist into a future script.

Personally as well as professionally, the couple had fallen into a rhythm. They still resided separately, Allen at his Upper East Side address, Farrow at the Langham across Central Park on the Upper West Side, but they slept together many weekend nights at Allen's penthouse duplex. Nowadays her seven kids tagged along to Allen's place, bringing games and friends for sleepovers. Farrow hung her robe on a bathroom peg and had her own shelf for toiletries next to a space still marked for Diane Keaton, "which I never presumed to touch, in the cabinet above the sink." The couple "settled into a steady, secure, and satisfying relationship," she believed.

Their close but separate relationship was public grist. "You've got to realize," Allen explained to critic Roger Ebert at the Russian Tea Room in the summer of 1982, "a relationship is always better if you don't actually have to live with another person." Living apart, a relationship becomes a "constant courtship," the comedian and film director said. "It's ever so much easier to get along with somebody if you aren't always having to go to bed with them, when you're tuckered out, and get up with them, when you're still sleepy."

Their main shared space was Allen's domicile—his kingdom. When the actress and her children paid their scheduled visits, he was "the king in our midst," wrote Farrow in her memoir, "who knew everything, whose concerns were greater than most, a *superior* person. His opinions were the final word. And he could cut you quicker than you could open your mouth. We admired him and we were afraid of him." Farrow worked as hard as she could to involve Allen with her kids, even going so far as to change Misha's name. "Because Woody said Misha was 'a wimp's name,' we changed it to Moses after the basketball star Moses Malone," she explained. No, "Moses" was Farrow's idea, Allen insisted in his memoir, which she came up with after witnessing his excitement one night, at Madison Square Garden, watching the fierce Philadelphia 76ers center defend the basket against the Knicks. "Never comfortable with the children," Farrow said, "in his way, he [Allen] tried."

He did try. A few years into the 1980s, for example, Allen traded in his cream-colored Rolls-Royce for another, black stretch limousine big enough for all the Farrow-Previn brood. If her children were not in school, they were welcome on his sets. Farrow turned their shared dressing rooms and campers "into playrooms with colorful posters on the walls, a little table and chairs, pots of clay, stacks of paper, glue, blocks, pens, scissors, puzzles, books, and cassettes." The actress played with the kids during breaks while Allen wrote. Sometimes the youngsters played alone, and he and she brought out a chessboard. "But mostly he made phone calls. Lots of phone calls. He had a California lawyer on retainer, and it seemed that he was always trying to sue somebody."

One or more children often went out with them to dinner. The Russian Tea Room was an all-family hangout and birthday-party tradition. Although Allen kept a French cook on salary, the paterfamilias dined out most nights except Mondays, when his jazz band performed. He "decided which restaurant, and what time," said Farrow, "and who would join us, and the topics of discussion, and when to leave. Invariably he paid the check."

On weekend mornings, if they woke up at Allen's apartment, he and she would take a long walk before separating for the day. Farrow whisked her children home for pancakes at the Langham. "Woody wanted to be alone to exercise, see his analyst, write, and practice his clarinet." The children had an endless variety of tutors, they had play dates with other kiddies, and they had excursions to parks and museums with their mother.

Some weekend afternoons, Allen brought a contingent from the Farrow-Previn household to his Park Avenue offices, where he presented a children's film festival of golden oldies he'd curated and hoped they would like. "While they polished off deep bowls full of candy left for them by Woody's assistant," Farrow recalled, "they watched the movies of Bob Hope, Jerry Lewis, Abbott and Costello, Chaplin, Cary Grant, Frank Capra, John Ford, and every science-fiction and kids' classic right up to the latest Disney and Spielberg."

Sometimes on Sundays there would be an all-family supper at the Langham: usually Chinese takeout, which was sacred sustenance for the director. But if Allen coped admirably with the von Trapp–like family parading into his home, he couldn't stand the Farrow pets jumping on the table or eating leftovers off the floor at the Langham. The paper plates, Styrofoam cups, and plastic utensils were another reason to love Chinese food.

Repeatedly, Allen made it clear he was interested only in writing and directing movies, while for Farrow the importance of motherhood rivaled that of being an actress. Motherhood was integral to her identity. "What would you think about us having a baby?" Farrow had asked the filmmaker, too early in their affair. Children, marriage, or some formal commitment between them persevered as an issue. Farrow clung to it as an issue.

Still, Allen had failed twice at marriage, and he never let go of the example of his own parents' unhappy union. "I never saw anyone treat another person the way he behaved with his parents," Farrow wrote. They almost "never" saw his sister, Letty, Farrow said, who lived nearby. "He spoke to her on the phone; he loved her, and he helped her financially, but he avoided her company. He described her as 'pushy,' and as an example he told me about her unwelcome and futile efforts to involve him with her children when they were younger."

In *A Midsummer Night's Sex Comedy* Tony Roberts plays the character who speaks for Allen, when he proclaims, "Marriage is the death of hope." A marriage certificate is just "a piece of paper," Allen told Farrow. "Our relationship had to be truer, purer, more responsible, more committed, *better*, because it stood solely on the quality of its own trust and love. Ours, surely was the highest form of marriage. He was never kinder or more reassuring than in those moments of my insecurity. 'Do I not behave as if we are married?' he would ask."

WARNER COMMUNICATIONS, WHICH had been disappointed by the blasé box office for *A Midsummer Night's Sex Comedy*, reverted to the United Artists model for *Zelig*. The studio premiered the film at prestigious New York and Los Angeles venues in the midsummer of 1983, before trumpeting the positive reviews for broader release. While a few major critics faulted Allen's pseudodocumentary about the human chameleon ("A masterly piece of filmmaking," Gene Siskel hedged his bets in the *Chicago Tribune*, while at the same time "obvious, repetitious and all-too-precious"), the one-of-a-kind picture generated an "unbridled enthusiasm" (Andrew Sarris, the *Village Voice*) among most reviewers. The mockumentary was a nonpareil; the mosaic construction was masterly; the comedy was almost as enjoyable as the conceit was admirable. And it was the closest Allen ever came to Kurosawa in the sense that, like *Rashomon*, the word "Zelig" triumphantly entered the lexicon and dictionary. Overall, the notices were the most sublime for a Woody Allen picture since *Manhattan*. "A jam-packed powerhouse of filmmaking wit, wisdom, hilarity and technology," Vincent Canby exclaimed in the *New York Times*. "It is *Citizen Kane* miraculously transformed into a side-splitting comedy."

Sarris wondered presciently if *Zelig* was "a comedy for the cognoscenti," and if the new Woody Allen comedy might be "really too good and too imaginative for the pabulum-craving masses." At its height, Warners managed to cram *Zelig* into one hundred theaters, mostly in big cities and college towns, and the movie briefly cracked the top ten. *Zelig* initially played strong overseas, but ultimately the rentals and grosses fell below that of *A Midsummer Night's Sex Comedy*. Allen's pictures were always "a break-even proposition in the long run," Mike Medavoy explained. "We never made a lot, but we never lost a lot." However, Warners wasn't interested in the long run. The larger, corporatized studio took a traditional Hollywood point of view toward Allen. His continued insistence on making pictures in black-and-white was a form of commercial suicide. Mia Farrow as his leading lady—compared to, say, Diane Keaton—added nothing to turnstile expectations. Allen's opposition to soundtracks, television, and home video extras—going against all Hollywood norms—added to the financial pitfalls. Frank Wells, the top man at Warners, believed "a thinly financed company like Orion shouldn't make movies that we knew might not make money," according to Medavoy. "To us, it was first about making good movies and then letting the money follow." For Wells, "any downside came out of the executives' profit pool."

Even before closing the books on *Zelig*, Warners had "signaled an end to the presumption of cordial relations" with Orion, Medavoy wrote later. Reading the handwriting on the wall, in early 1983 Orion had gone in search of a new financial partner and found one in the Home Box Office (HBO) cable television network. Then Orion acquired Filmways, a company known for its TV programming, but which also had long produced and distributed movies. Nowadays Filmways had lucrative prospects in the burgeoning fields of video and cable. Warners and Orion parted ways. It was "poetic justice," Medavoy said, that "the two movies Woody made" for Orion-Warners—*A Midsummer Night's Sex Comedy* and *Zelig*—didn't make "a dime" for Warners.

Coming so soon after the harsh reaction to *Stardust Memories*, the "cool reception" *Zelig* received from certain critics, in Medavoy's words, gave Allen a renewed determination to ignore those who faulted his movies. Allen read the *New York Times* daily and still tracked Canby's print reviews, and he and Farrow continued to dine "with the major critics of *Time* and *Newsweek*," she recalled. "But Woody reserved special contempt for film critics on television," and enjoyed mocking the high-profile duo he dubbed "the Chicago morons"—Gene Siskel at the *Tribune*, Roger Ebert at the *Sun-Times*. The latter, echoing Siskel, had unforgivably described *Zelig* as "antiseptic experimentation." "Everyone around us knew not to mention reviews in our presence," recalled Farrow. "Woody advised me not to read them. 'Just keep your head down and do good work.' "

Yet *Zelig*'s failure with audiences took Allen aback, according to Medavoy. Knowing his first two Orion–Warner Bros. productions had faltered at the box office and believing he owed a debt of gratitude to Arthur Krim and the former United Artists team, Allen made a rare "commercial" promise to the Orion leadership, Medavoy said. In the future, the director vowed, "instead of trying to mix comedy and drama in the same film," he would alternate "between comedies and dramas." While this pledge would never gain any clear long-term traction, the director—despite all protestations to the contrary—made small continual adjustments to Woody Allen pictures that were intended to address critical cavils, box office issues, and producers' concerns.

SERENDIPITOUSLY, *BROADWAY DANNY ROSE* was the first Woody Allen movie under the new Orion-Filmways banner. Deliberately fashioned as Allen's purest comedy in years, it went to American theaters in January 1984.

Allen's Danny Rose character was a sort of Damon Runyon version of

Allen's longtime persona, an idealistic loser working hard in a checkered profession. If Allen was born to this loser-role, Farrow proved astonishing as Tina Vitale, playing against her customary doe-eyed innocence. And first-timer Nick Apollo Forte made his every scene watchable as the dull-witted, golden-throated singer with a Cutty Sark and girlfriend problem. The swimming pool party with goombahs, the shootout, and near death in a warehouse filled with Macy's parade balloons (Danny and Tina with squeaky voices from inhaling the helium), the Thanksgiving frozen-turkey banquet hosted by Danny for his peculiar variety acts—all were inspired sequences.

The love story crept up on audiences. Tina initially embarrasses Danny, but the mob contract forces them into an alliance, and as fugitives they draw closer. At a crucial moment she betrays him. Regretting her actions, for the second time in the story Tina consults a fortuneteller, as also happens in *Bicycle Thieves*—Allen's favorite Vittorio De Sica film. Tina shows up at Danny's Thanksgiving celebration with a surprise apology, reprising a wisdom from Danny's uncle: "Acceptance, forgiveness, and love." Danny hesitates before one of those sidewalk running scenes Allen loved, which echoes the ending of *Manhattan*. The camera finds Danny catching up with Tina outside the Carnegie Deli. They talk and reconcile, with their interaction captured from across the street without discernible dialogue. Inside the deli, as the credits begin, the Catskills voices resume.

All along in his deliberative manner, Allen had been nudging Farrow toward center stage. Her brassy impersonation thrilled critics. "Woody Allen is the best thing that ever happened to Mia Farrow," crowed Rex Reed in the *New York Post*. Even the "Chicago morons" agreed: "The film's best performance," said Gene Siskel of Farrow, "reminding us that she is a genuine actress and not just an item in a gossip column." Roger Ebert echoed: "The real treasure among the performances." The Motion Picture Academy overlooked Farrow in film after Woody Allen film in the 1980s and '90s, but she should have been a Best Actress contender for Tina Vitale. Instead, Allen earned more Oscar nominations: Director and Screenplay. And the Writers Guild short-listed his script among the year's best—his tenth nomination. He won for the second time. *Annie Hall* was the first.

••

ALLEN SIGNED A three-picture extension of his Orion deal after *Broadway Danny Rose*, although the contract acknowledged that times were changing for him and American film. The contract left his up-front salary alone, and Allen only asked for a modest raise in his production budgets, because all costs were steadily rising. He continued to nibble away at the monies from the home video boom and to increase his percentages of foreign and ancillary revenue. "I do better now in Milan than in Moline [Illinois]," Allen boasted to Charles Champlin. Again paradoxically, some of his demands manifestly subtracted from his overall earnings. For example, Allen became the first US director to bar any distribution of his films in apartheid South Africa, even though *Annie Hall* had done whopping business in Johannesburg. Only Orion would allow such an exclusion. Over and over in unusual ways, Allen made it plain that money was secondary to his filmmaking, his beliefs, his principles.

Orion, following the United Artists model, positioned itself as different from the other Hollywood studios with a lineup that balanced artistic filmmaking with a few hoped-for moneymakers, gambling that maybe a few of the artistic movies would also generate profits. Yet Allen was an endangered species as the film industry in the 1980s embraced special effects, action franchises, and blockbusters. Multiplexes and mammoth theaters with hundreds of seats gobbled up the smaller houses. *Broadway Danny Rose* was booked into 582 theaters across the hinterlands, but only a fraction were specialty houses—Allen's niche—with their number declining.

What no one yet realized was that Orion—as much as Allen—was endangered. For the time being, the studio believed in Allen, even as he tested Orion when he informed officials of his first project under the new contract extension. A period picture, a mix of color and black and white, drama and comedy, starring Mia Farrow. A film without Woody Allen in the cast. He'd write and direct only for the first time since *Interiors*.

His contract extension retained the unusual clause allowing Allen to go over budget, if necessary, with the overages remitted out of his earnings. To Allen's credit he didn't flinch at this sacrifice, even when it came to the expense of replacing a leading man. The most famous instance of this took place early in the filming of the new project, *The Purple Rose of Cairo*, which initially starred, besides Farrow, the fast-rising Michael Keaton.

The Depression-era comedy-drama was launched without hype in

December 1983, beginning with the wholesale transformation of the Hudson River hamlet of Piermont, New York, into a New Jersey town in the 1930s. The Main Street theater was renamed the Jewel to conform with Allen's script, and its marquee was emblazoned with "The Purple Rose of Cairo"—the film's title, but also the title of the film-within-the-film.

Allen's script was his deepest dive yet into magical realism. Its antecedents included Buster Keaton's 1924 silent comedy *Sherlock Jr.*, in which Keaton, a projectionist, falls asleep and dreams of being a detective in the movie unspooling onscreen. Allen, because he was diffident about Keaton, pooh-poohed this influence. However, his script also had roots in "The Kugelmass Episode," one of his "little souffles" in the *New Yorker*, in which a magician transports a lovelorn professor named Kugelmass into Philip Roth's *Portnoy's Complaint* and Gustave Flaubert's *Madame Bovary*—Kugelmass makes love to Emma and brings her to New York.

In Allen's screen story, Cecilia (Farrow) is a café waitress in small-town America. Cecilia is trapped in poverty and an abusive marriage; her only solace is the weekly attractions at the Jewel. Cecilia's violence-prone, unemployed husband is cheating on her, and she is fired from her hash-house job for daydreaming. As, for the fifth time, a tearful Cecilia sits in the theater audience watching an RKO programmer called "The Purple Rose of Cairo," the dashing Egyptologist Tom Baxter, a hammy secondary character in the movie, notices her rapt presence. Tom begins to address Cecilia from the screen. Bored by his one-dimensional life, a fiction that monotonously repeats itself, Tom bursts out of the screen to escape from the theater with Cecilia on his arm.

The star-struck Cecilia takes Tom, in his pith helmet and breeches, on a whirlwind tour of podunky, hard-times America, a reality the fictional screen hero doesn't quite fathom, accustomed as he is, in his carefully written and censored Hollywood existence, to stage money, gentlemanly fighting (groin kicks forbidden), and smooching without sex. "Where's the fadeout?" Tom wails. "You can't make love without fading out!"

Meanwhile, the other "Purple Rose" actors are left floundering on the screen, trapped in their fantasy Manhattan. The cast gripes about Tom's irresponsible dereliction of duty while drifting aimlessly off script. Some audience members faint from the shock; other people rush to buy tickets. The press swarms. The unnerved owner of the Jewel phones RKO studios in Hollywood, alerting the producer of "Purple Rose of Cairo" to the disturbing phenomenon. The RKO producer and his entourage, including Gil Shepherd, the actor who plays the role of Tom Baxter, descend on the town to deflect the growing bad publicity and resolve the crisis.

Gil meets Cecilia, who brings him to face-to-face with Tom, his reel-life counterpart. "This is disconcerting," deadpans Tom, who is full of "cheerful bravado," while Gil, more self-absorbed, is drawn into a rivalry with Tom over Cecilia's affections. Tom escorts Cecilia back to the theater and into the film-within-a-film, reenergizing the aimless "Purple Rose of Cairo" with the cast newcomer. The screen-world nightclubs and champagne are exciting for Cecilia, even if, after eagerly sipping the sparkling wine, she notes it really is ginger ale in flute glasses. Gil wins her over by inviting Cecilia to Hollywood. A defeated Tom returns to the screen.

Tom Baxter and Gil Shepherd were written as dual parts for the same performer. Allen wanted Michael Keaton, who had just broken away from television sitcoms in the big-screen comedies *Night Shift* and *Mr. Mom*. But the director was forced to pay Keaton an unusually high salary for a Woody Allen film: $250,000.

Danny Aiello from *The Floating Light Bulb* was also in the cast as Cecilia's obstreperous husband. Allen again created a part for Mia's sister Steffi as Cecilia's sister, a fellow waitress, and he also found a small role for Mariel Hemingway's sister Margaux, although her scene would be ultimately eliminated from the picture. The onscreen "Purple Rose" ensemble, which sends up Hollywood cliché types, included the oft-stuffy Edward Herrmann, Irish character actor Milo O'Shea, former MGM musical star Van Johnson, Australian John Wood, and the imperious, multiple-Tony-winning Zoe Caldwell. Also, appearing in her first Woody Allen movie was Dianne Wiest, who'd make a vivid impression as the "working girl" who brings Tom to the local whorehouse.

Ten days into the filming, however, Allen decided Keaton's mannerisms were too contemporary. "I'd look at the dailies, and he was fine, but you got no sense of a 1930s movie star from him; he just was too hip." Through intermediaries Keaton was fired, and Allen scrapped all his completed scenes. Allen put out feelers to Kevin Kline before calling in Jeff Daniels, a strapping guy with a lopsided grin. Daniels had just finished his breakout role in *Terms of Endearment*, which would become one of the big hits of 1983. Meeting with Allen, Daniels was handed a few pages to read. He wasn't told he was up for a double lead. Later, when acting in his scenes, the director offered "no discussions about characters, motivations, and backgrounds," Daniels recollected. "It's as if he has a feather in his hand and he blows it, and it goes off in a dozen directions. That gives you the freedom to do twelve things—so it's alive and spontaneous; there isn't a right or wrong way."

That was more typical than not on a Woody Allen set. "Woody never raised his voice," Farrow recalled. "Actors knew not to expect discussion, explanations, encouragements, enthusiasm, or compliments. Criticism was quiet, quick, and cutting. I told people that if he said 'okay' or fine after a scene, that meant it really went well. As long as he didn't interrupt the scene, or say anything negative, it meant that he was pleased." Allen didn't waste time on rehearsals, so Farrow sometimes coached the actors. "I'd ask them if they wanted to run lines or something. They almost always did. I did too, because it was all the rehearsal we were likely to get."

The abrupt firing of Keaton cast a temporary pall over the production before wintry weather added more time and expense. For months the photography wore on, mostly in New York and New Jersey, with the interiors of the Jewel fabricated inside the Midwood, Allen's old neighborhood theater in Flatbush—once owned by his grandfather. Brief exteriors were lensed in Los Angeles. "Fully half of *Purple Rose* was rewritten and reshot after editing," according to Farrow. Yet as was true of Keaton's pay-or-play deal, when costs rose above projections Allen personally absorbed the loss. His quick, often brusque direction "left no margin for error," Farrow thought. "That is one reason that so many reshoots were necessary. The other reason is because, as we shot scenes, problems with the scripts were revealed, or Woody simply saw ways to rewrite and improve it."

The work spilled over into the first half of 1984, but if any picture validated Allen's singular creative process—the sometimes torturous, protracted path that involved revising and rewriting as he filmed—it was *The Purple Rose of Cairo*, only the second movie he had directed without appearing onscreen. Released in March 1985, *Purple Rose* was almost uniformly greeted as "a miniature masterpiece" in the words of Richard Schickel, writing in *Time*, rewarding both as entertainment and as a meditation on the lines between artifice and reality.

The production elements were again first-class. Gordon Willis's burnished color photography of the small-town milieu was juxtaposed with his faultless imitation of black-and-white "B" pictures from the 1930s. The marvelous set pieces included an atmospheric deserted fairgrounds that serves as a hideout for Tom Baxter; a humorous Catholic Church scene, where Cecilia tries to explain crucifixes to Tom; and a visit to the first warm and fuzzy brothel in Allen's oeuvre. The nightclub sequences were expertly mounted, with the chorus numbers offering the same break from the film-within-a-film as song and dancing did in the Golden Age, and the maître d' improvising tap steps when he realizes the script has been ditched. The ukulele duet between Cecilia and Gil is simply but beautifully staged: Farrow mimes the playing of "Alabamy Bound" (Allen jazz band regular Cynthia Sayer did the actual strumming), and the cute scene builds to rhapsody as Cecilia and Gil segue into "I Love My Baby, My Baby Loves Me," with an elderly music store owner (Loretta Tupper) joining in on piano.

All the actors were at the top of their game. Jeff Daniels was sweet and goofy.* Farrow seemed imbued with "a magic glow"—as Gil describes the beleaguered Cecilia—and the actress was never as tender and vulnerable in a Woody Allen picture. "Of the movies I have been in, *Purple Rose of Cairo* is one of my favorites," Farrow wrote in her memoir. Once more an Allen script was cited among the year's finest by the Motion Picture Academy and the Writers Guild of America. *Purple Rose of Cairo* took Best Script and Picture at the annual British Film Academy (BAFTA) awards and garnered the French César for Best Foreign Film of 1985.

Still, *Purple Rose of Cairo* grossed only $10.6 million domestically, roughly the same revenue—with less profit, considering inflation—as *Broadway Danny Rose*. It's been rumored that Orion pleaded with Allen to change the unhappy ending to the movie, but that seems improbable, and of course Allen wouldn't have wavered. As the ending stands, Cecilia/Farrow, abandoned by both versions of Jeff Daniels and doomed to life with her bullying husband, slinks back to the new offering at the Jewel. Watching the musical that has been booked to follow "Purple Rose of Cairo," she forgets her despair—as Allen so often did in his life—in the bliss of Fred Astaire and Ginger Rogers dancing "Cheek to Cheek" in *Top Hat*. That Irving Berlin chestnut is also heard beneath the opening credits. Allen often said the film's bittersweet final moments were essential to his vision and just as often cited

* It should go without saying that Michael Keaton recovered his footing and, like Jeff Daniels, went on to a major career.

Purple Rose of Cairo among the rare Woody Allen pictures that turned out almost exactly as he had wished.

NEVER, IN A Woody Allen film, would Allen play a happy husband with children, or a grandfather, say, dandling a baby. A keen student of his own range, he knew that such a role was not credible for him—or for his persona. Yet critics noticed a sentimentalism and contentment seeping into the pictures Allen made with Farrow, and he would come closest to suggesting a happy family man in prospect in his next project.

As the director walked and talked with the actress during the postproduction of *The Purple Rose of Cairo*, which overlapped the making of *Hannah and Her Sisters*, Farrow insistently brought up her desire for them to get married. Allen wouldn't let go of the sour attitude he had about marriage, influenced by the unhappy example of his parents. Farrow didn't give up. She wanted to have his baby. They could have a baby, and she'd do all the child-rearing. She wore him down. After talking things over with his therapist, "eventually, with the understanding that I would be responsible for the baby in every way," Farrow said, "he (they) agreed."

Then it was a surprise to both of them that Farrow didn't get pregnant right away. Weeks, then months passed. They wondered if Allen was infertile. It had to be Allen because Farrow had the track record.

For the first time, writing the script of *Hannah and Her Sisters*, Allen inserted elements of both his and Farrow's shared private lives into the storyline. He borrowed from Farrow's sisters and her family relationships, and floated in the fictional framework personal issues he and she had recently been dealing with. *Hannah* was stimulated, he said in interviews, by his rereading of *Anna Karenina* in the summer of 1983. He decided it would be "fun to do a movie" about a group of family members whose love stories are entangled, as in the Leo Tolstoy novel. Once again, as with *Interiors*, three female siblings would anchor the story. "I always thought it would be interesting to do a story about a man who had fallen in love with his wife's sister," explained the man who had dated Diane Keaton's sisters and perhaps Farrow's too. Allen would take a less mannered approach than with *Interiors*, however. The sisters would be more appealing if flawed, and there would be more laughs.

Over the first half of 1984, as Allen wrote, Hannah became the center of a dysfunctional family portrait, whose story would take place largely amid the upper Manhattan milieu he and Farrow inhabited. Hannah is an actress, the oldest, most stable of three sisters, happily married (she thinks) to her second husband Elliot, a financial consultant. Hannah's ex-husband is Mickey—the role earmarked as Allen's—a successful television producer whose hypochondria compels him to quit his job and ponder suicide. Elliot covets Hannah's ravishing sister Lee—so ravishing that, before the camera introduces her with a sweep of her face, the movie offers this title card: "God, she's beautiful!" Lee is a recovering alcoholic living uneasily with Frederick, an angry artist. Holly, the youngest sister, is a would-be actress, whose auditions are like her relationships with men—humiliating flops. Smart and charming but a troubled soul, Holly scrounges money from Hannah for cocaine.

The mother and father of the three sisters are show business troupers who were once "almost famous," and whose feelings for each other have been eaten away by advancing age and their years of rocky marriage. Friends of the family also weave in and out of the story. The script would rearrange many of Allen's standard tropes into a fresh jigsaw: his preoccupations with analysis and neurotic women; his passions for New York architecture, opera, classical music, poetry, and the Marx Brothers; his certainty that death is always looming.

In its character relationships (a large family presided over by theatrical parents) and bookend structure (the beginning and ending of the script framed by holiday celebrations) *Hannah and Her Sisters* evoked Ingmar Bergman's *Scenes from a Marriage* as much as Tolstoy, although the first sentence of *Anna Karenina* echoes one of the picture's main themes: "Happy families are all alike; every unhappy family is unhappy in its own way." And one of the Woody Allen–ish chapter headings was borrowed not from *Anna Karenina* but from Tolstoy's *My Confession*: "The only absolute knowledge attainable by man is that life is meaningless."

When she read Allen's finished screenplay, Farrow was taken aback by scenes that so obviously reflected many aspects of her family and their life. Allen had made no secret of his fascination with Mia's less successful, less-well-known younger sisters, and of Mia's relationship with them. The three he knew best all lived in New York. Tisa had appeared in *Manhattan*, while

Prudence, nowadays a Transcendental Meditation teacher, had worked in the art department for *The Purple Rose of Cairo*. Steffi, who was Farrow's stand-in in *A Midsummer Night's Sex Comedy* and played featured roles in *Zelig* and *The Purple Rose of Cairo*, had traveled with the couple. There seemed constant friction among the sisters, and even though Steffi, whom Farrow suspected of having a fling with the director, lived close by, "Mia never sees her," nanny Kristi Groteke wrote in her book, because "Steffi didn't like Woody, and the strength of her dislike for him affected the sisters' relationship."

Tying the script even closer to the Farrows was the fact seventy-three-year-old Maureen O'Sullivan, absent from important movies for a decade, was a shoo-in to play Norma, the show business warhorse and matriarch.

"Some of *Hannah* was drawn from my family," Farrow explained to Eric Lax for his authorized biography in 1992, "and I guess other sisters Woody has known, like Diane Keaton and her sisters. It's kind of nice. No one was upset in my family anyway." However, in Farrow's subsequent memoir, published five years after her acrimonious breakup with Allen, the actress revised this sanguine version of events. This time Farrow recalled her mother's "stunned, chill reaction to the script . . . enabled me to see how he [Allen] had taken many of the personal circumstances and themes of our lives, and, it seemed, had distorted them into cartoonish characterizations." With "a small sick feeling," Farrow recounted in her memoir, she realized Elliot's crush on Lee, in the screen story, "had openly and clearly spelled out his [Allen's] feelings for my sister [Steffi]."

Farrow wasn't just discomfited by the way the script drew on her sisters and her family relationships. Allen's script tacitly explored the difficulties she and Allen were having getting pregnant and their conflict over children. In one flashback, married-couple Hannah (Farrow) and Mickey (Allen) are depicted as being unable to conceive because, doctors believe, Mickey is infertile. The couple convince Mickey's producer friend Max to become their sperm donor. The children, born in vitro, are twin boys to whom Mickey is dutifully attentive following his divorce from Hannah, showering them with birthday gifts of baseball mitts and footballs. The twins belong to Hannah's extended brood, which includes several adopted Asian children—who would be played in the film by her own real-life children Moses, Daisy, Fletcher, and Soon-Yi—glimpsed at the children's table in the holiday scenes. (This upheld a long Farrow tradition, for Mia as a child had been given cameos in her father's movies.) In one final echo of Allen and Farrow's offscreen lives, at the height of Elliot's secret affair with Lee, Hannah tells her husband she'd like to get pregnant, and Elliot's reaction is akin to Allen's whenever Farrow brought up the subject. "I don't think it's a very good idea," Elliot snaps. "It's the last thing in the world we need right now."

For once, Farrow claimed in her memoir—it goes unmentioned in the Lax book—she dared to criticize an Allen script as "wordy," with characters that "seemed indulgent and dissolute in predictable ways." Allen "didn't disagree and tried to switch over" to an alternative script he had in the hopper, "but preproduction was already in progress, and we had to proceed." Allen doesn't mention this speed bump in *Apropos of Nothing*.

Allen gave Farrow the option of which sister to play, although he pressed for Hannah, the "most talented daughter," whom her siblings describe as "disgustingly perfect." The writer-director had intentionally crafted Hannah as "a romanticized perception of Mia," but her character was "the more complex and enigmatic" of the sisters, Allen argued, "whose stillness and internal strength he likened to the quality Al Pacino projected in *The Godfather*," she recalled. When Farrow finally consented to play Hannah and let the production team take over her apartment at the Langham, standing in for Hannah's household in the story, the convergence was complete.

ALSO, MORE THAN in previous films Allen's role—that of Mickey—was subordinated to the sisters. He'd be tucked into the ensemble. Yet Mickey also evinced autobiographical touches, which with Allen were always mixed with imagined details and exaggerations that preserved the fundamentally fictional nature of the characters he played. For example, Mickey's fear of a brain tumor in *Hannah and Her Sisters* came from an actual scary incident in Allen's life. It so happened, one day during the postproduction of *Zelig*, that Allen experienced sudden hearing loss. His doctors suspected an acoustic neuroma might be pressing on the auditory nerves of one ear. A brain scan was ordered to check for a possible brain tumor. Allen approached the scan with dread.

All Allen's friends knew he rushed to see physicians at the slightest twinge. The director "had a doctor for every single part of his body" and carried around a list of his doctors' home phone numbers and "a silver box of pills for any conceivable ailment," Farrow attested. "If he felt the least bit unwell, he would take his temperature at ten-minute intervals. He kept his own thermometer at my apartment." Every time a new Woody Allen picture was set to be unveiled, he held a special "doctors' screening," and the room was "always full."

In real life, Allen's brain scan turned out fine, but he had suffered from an anxiety and foreboding more crippling than usual, and consequently he turned Mickey into a man whose suspected hearing loss gives him a foretaste of death, and whose negative test results transform his outlook on life. Mickey quits his TV niche and flirts, hilariously, with a conversion to Catholicism, because it was a religion "so filled with beauty and ritual," as Allen later explained in an interview. "I got all that from Mia. When she was a little girl, she used to pray with her arms outstretched so it would be more uncomfortable." Coming to his senses about Catholicism, Mickey instead is drawn to suicide, but he bungles his attempt. In a daze, Mickey wanders into a theater showing *Duck Soup*. Entranced by the Marx Brothers cavorting onscreen, he undergoes a life-affirming rebirth.

A subtext of Mickey's father character is that he himself is unable to conceive a child. This was only the second time Allen played a father—a divorced father—yet there would be a few surprises at the end of the film, including his character unexpectedly finding happiness in a second marriage to none other than his ex-wife's sister.

Mickey's subplot runs on a parallel track with the main story of the three sisters, and it is a kind of amusing sideshow leavening the more painful drama in the script. But whenever Allen borrowed from his own reality or someone else's, the ingenuity and enduring power of his greatest scripts stemmed from his ability to blend and absorb the borrowings into something of his own unique creation, while deeply identifying with many of the characters and story elements. "There's something of me in all these people," Allen told interviewers about *Interiors*, especially the distraught mother played by Geraldine Page, but Diane Keaton's character too ("Renata speaks for me, without question!"). He said he related deeply to Cecilia in *The Purple Rose of Cairo*. Now Allen embodied several of the characters in *Hannah and Her Sisters*—not just Mickey.

Hannah has the practical-minded line that summarized Allen's philosophy of life. "My true gift is luck," Hannah tells her mother. Elliot, the self-loathing male lead and narrator of parts of *Hannah*, also speaks for Allen: "For all my accomplishment and wisdom, I can't fathom my own heart." Allen is also the haughty Frederick, who'd rather skip family togetherness and commune with his dark paintings. Of course, Allen is every bit the handsome architect who offers a Cook's tour of landmarks—less poeticized than *Manhattan*'s—to Holly and her friend April. And Allen is finally Holly, who triumphs over her misery and redeems herself as—of all things—the writer of a movie script Hannah abhors because it too closely mirrors the intimacies of her frayed marriage to Elliot. "I just took the essence and blew it up with drama," Holly defends herself: Allen's credo.

ALLEN CAST MICHAEL CAINE, who had guided Mia Farrow to his table at Elaine's, in the role of Elliot, Hannah's restless husband. Casting director Juliet Taylor and West Coast gal pal Sue Mengers—Caine's agent—convinced Allen to pay Caine's asking price, which was more than customary for a Woody Allen film. For the beautiful Lee, whom Elliot furtively pursues, Allen picked the inarguably gorgeous Barbara Hershey. Holly was the loser sister, and for this role Allen returned to Dianne Wiest, who'd stood out in *The Purple Rose of Cairo*. The terrible date Mickey (Allen) has with Holly—a grunge-rock stop at CBGB's, which he abhors, followed by listening to Bobby Short's cabaret jazz at the Café Carlyle, which she equally detests—heightens the surprise of them ending up in each other's arms.

Playing Hannah's father, problematically married in the story to "a boozy old flirt with a filthy mouth," as Norma (Maureen O'Sullivan) describes herself, was Lloyd Nolan, a durable Hollywood veteran Allen brought back for one last curtain call. (Nolan died shortly after the filming ended.) Allen cast Max von Sydow, forever linked to Ingmar Bergman masterworks, as the tortured painter Frederick, who prefers to stay home and brood, even if it means watching "a very dull TV show about Auschwitz." Daniel Stern would portray a pop music hitmaker shopping for an extra-large work of art for the walls of his Southampton beach house. Carrie Fisher from *Star Wars* was April, who competes with her friend Holly for acting jobs and men. Tony Roberts went uncredited as Mickey's friend and sperm donor, who goes by the familiar name "Max." Also uncredited was Sam Waterston, who gives Holly and April the great-buildings tour and pits them as rivals to be his girlfriend. Actors with initial appearances in a Woody Allen film included a young John Turturro ("Hey, who changed my sketch about the PLO?"), a pre-*Seinfeld* Julia Louis-Dreyfus, and Julie Kavner as Mickey's TV colleague.

In addition to Ingmar Bergman, *Hannah and Her Sisters* would be indebted to Italian cinema in the person of Carlo Di Palma, who had shot *Blow-Up*—one of Allen's favorite Antonioni pictures—and who succeeded Gordon Willis after ten years and eight Woody Allen films. Willis had "started losing his eyesight," Allen said later. "Nice deal, human existence. Full of delightful ironies." The change augured a naturalistic shift in Allen's aesthetic. Willis had been very specific, organized, everything thought out. Di Palma was more laissez-faire. For the foreseeable future Allen would still rely heavily on master shots, but with a visual strategy less composed and less dependent on lighting effects, which resulted in a more fluid as well as cheaper and quicker mise-en-scène. Di Palma preferred "to light a whole general area," for example, allowing Allen to shoot without camera rehearsals. "Go where you want," Allen began telling actors, "just walk wherever you want. Walk into the darkness, walk into the light, just play the scene as you feel it . . . just do whatever interests you."

Actors accustomed to having their every movement and gesture mapped out in advance, with explicit direction, received even less than the usual from Allen on *Hannah and Her Sisters*. When filming began in October 1984, the cast had to be on their toes. It was a welcome change for some. Maureen O'Sullivan contrasted Allen with Golden Age maestro George Cukor, who had directed her in *David Copperfield* in 1935. "George had a preconceived idea and he made you do his concept of what he wanted," she told the *New York Times*. "I liked working with Woody more because I felt he would, in his gentle way, find out in you what you could do and just let you do it. . . . With lots of directors, you ask silly questions like 'Shall I hold a glass here?' or 'Shall I sit down here?' But with Woody, you just do it. If he wants you not to do it, he'll tell you."

Others were forced into adjustments. "I was always told to save my best work for close-ups," Caine remembered, "because he doesn't cut away to close-ups at all—the only close-ups you get organically come out of the master." The solemn atmosphere on Allen's set surprised the actor. When Caine tried injecting a little lightness into some dialogue, Allen vetoed the actor's line readings. It was all "a bit like working in church," Caine explained. "The rehearsal and the take become indistinguishable. He just keeps shooting and shooting it."

When the underrated actress Barbara Hershey walked into Allen's office to meet the director for the first time, he boosted her spirits by saying "he had already decided on me." Hershey arrived on the set "with lots of wonderful ideas that Woody didn't like, and I had to just let go of them," Hershey explained later. For one thing, "he wanted me to wear *no* makeup. I've never done a film with no makeup before. . . . He wanted me dressing very down, and I wanted to wear funny clothes like Dianne Wiest. But then I realized what he was after—that he wanted a simplicity from me, which is not the easiest thing to do, by the way. As an actor you want to elaborate, you want to act, and to retreat from that and be very simple is something that he had to teach me."

Working together privately, Hershey and Max von Sydow meticulously rehearsed the fierce argument between their characters leading to their breakup. The performers tried to explore the emotional nuances of the scene, only to be told by Allen, when he shot it, to speed up everything they were doing. "I realized," Hershey recalled, "what's the point of doing a Woody Allen movie unless you're going to do it *his* way, unless you're going to see where *he* takes you. And as soon as I gave myself to him as an actor, it was great. I relaxed."

As usual, Allen revised the script as he shot. There were more emendations during the refilming too. The initial rough cut of *Hannah and Her Sisters* had Elliot still in love with Lee but resigned to his life with Hannah, but it felt wrong. Allen cut extraneous scenes—Tony Roberts at an art gallery, for example. He softened Hannah with a scene where she confesses her fragilities. Caine and Hershey's several episodes of lovemaking were tightened, and deleted entirely was a violent incident at the second Thanksgiving where Lee stabs Elliot in the hand with a scissors. Then Allen added a third Thanksgiving to round out the story with a miracle ending—considering Mickey's bouts with infertility—his marriage to Holly, her announcement of being pregnant.

••

OFFSCREEN, FARROW WAS not as fortunate as Holly, the character Dianne Wiest played in *Hannah and Her Sisters*. Although Allen was now more or less willing to father a baby, Farrow's biological clock kept ticking, and she crept closer to the age of forty—February 9, 1985—while mysteriously unable to attain a pregnancy.

Their agreement to conceive a child together had led to more discussions of marriage, "eight or nine sentences was all, repeating what had been said before," in Farrow's words. The actress voiced her fears: She hated when Allen lost his temper, like the time she asked him whether the conservative pundit William F. Buckley Jr. lived in a certain building in his neighborhood. Allen knew Buckley's home well—Buckley had appeared on his TV special in 1967—and he had pointed out the place before. He exploded. "The attack that followed, which was more stunningly awful than I had ever weathered in my life," she wrote, "did not cease until I was sobbing on the sidewalk, vaporized in front of a house that presumably was not William Buckley's."

Then there was "another time, when I didn't know the name of a certain kind of pasta; and again, when I was off in my estimate of the weather by only four degrees; and when I asked about a dream he'd had the previous night, when he had mumbled the words 'Dolly Parton.' Each of these times he had become so enraged, and his attacks were devastating. He always apologized afterward, but still I was afraid it might happen again."

No explosions, never again, Allen promised, but he offered no marriage pledges either. He spent most of his free time with Farrow and her brood anyway, so they discussed finding a place that would be big enough for him, her, the whole Farrow-Previn family, to which one day they still intended to add their own newborn. The actress proposed sharing her apartment at the Langham, which was a larger space than Allen's. "But it wasn't nearly big enough, he said, and it wasn't on the East Side." This spurred talk of replacing Frog Hollow with a bigger weekend and summer place Allen could share equally with the Farrow-Previns. The director hired "a woman whose only job was to check out the best available places on the shores of the Hamptons, Montauk, Maine, Nantucket, Martha's Vineyard, Block Island, Fisher Island, Rhode Island, and Cape Cod. He was nervous about flying in small planes, so whenever we went to look at a house, he chartered the biggest aircraft that the seaside airport could handle." The quixotic quest "ended with less than a whimper" one day at a small airport. Allen abruptly canceled the plane waiting for him to board and the home search concluded, once and for all.

All along Farrow tried to promote Allen's closer connections with her children. For a while she thought Fletcher—whose name is also her character's last name in *Zelig*—was the child Allen liked best. That would please her, because Fletcher was Farrow's "uniquely favored child," Allen believed, the one who really "called the shots" with his mother. Indeed, the actress evinced "an unnatural closeness" with Fletcher, Allen thought. Stepping into his limousine, she'd get on the phone with Fletcher only minutes after leaving him, or she'd insist upon bringing the boy along on their dinner dates early in their relationship, laying him "down to sleep under the table at Elaine's, while all the adults eat, drink, talk till midnight." One time, Allen suggested taking a quick trip to Paris. "Only if we can bring Fletcher," Farrow said, according to Allen. "But won't the other kids resent the obvious favoritism?" he asked. Farrow wouldn't relent. So Allen went, instead, with Jean Doumanian.

Sometimes on Saturday mornings, Allen took Fletcher and one or more of the kids to Times Square to roam the district he'd loved as a boy. "In Grand Central Station he showed them how you can whisper from one corner of the great station and be heard in the opposite corner," said Farrow. "He purchased elaborate 'effects' at the magic shop that they would perform for the rest of us; and he took Fletcher up on his terrace to shoot pigeon eggs with his BB gun—Woody waged war on pigeons because they messed up his terrace." Fletcher's part in *Hannah and Her Sisters* had been minuscule. The boy was promised a bigger role in Allen's next film.

Farrow worried most about Allen's relationship with Moses, the youngest boy, formerly called Misha. Of all her adoptees, Moses was the only child without a father. He was the only one with the last name Farrow. Moses had limped badly as a boy, until physical therapy gradually worked wonders. Moses was shy and sensitive; he yearned for a father. One day Moses asked Allen if *he* was his father, and Allen, taken aback, replied, "Sure kid," seeming "amused by the awkwardness of the request or the predicament he unexpectedly found himself in," according to Farrow. Whenever the director visited Frog Hollow, he'd "sometimes" play chess, basketball, or catch with Moses, "but never for longer than five or ten minutes. Fifteen tops. He didn't want to break a sweat," Farrow claimed. Later, however, Moses disputed his mother's portrait of Allen's presence in his life, writing he was "thrilled" when the filmmaker officially became his father "since he had already taken on that role in my life. We played catch and chess, fished and shot hoops." Incidentally, most of the Farrow children played chess; most took weekly lessons from a grand master who presided over lessons at Allen's apartment.

Even as Allen was portraying an infertile writer in *Hannah and Her Sisters*, in real life, over the course of 1984 and '85, he and Farrow lost all hope of conceiving. Farrow's solution was simple: Adopt another child—her eighth child—fifth orphan. Adoption was "not appealing" to Allen, Farrow conceded in her memoir. She tirelessly lobbied him, however, assuring Allen "the child would be entirely my responsibility." Privately, the actress hoped another adoption would help Allen better appreciate all the children in her family, "who were as dear as any on earth and who one by one had given up trying to win his heart; given all this, I don't know how I still hoped that he would love this [adopted] child, that she would be the one to open his heart, and that through her, he would learn to love without suspicion." Farrow prayed the new adoptee would unite the family.

Gradually Allen's resistance broke down. Eschewing her usual international channels, the actress began searching for an American-born orphan, preferably a blue-eyed blonde girl, "the kind of child, he [Allen] said, he would be most inclined to view positively, although, he was careful to add, it was certainly no guarantee."

Was he kidding about little blonde girls? Unclear. Like many male comedians Allen had made standard jokes about little girls with blonde hair dating back at least to 1967, when *Playboy* asked if he aspired to become the father of children, and Allen answered yes, "Eight or twelve little blonde girls. I love blonde girls." He also told Louise Lasser if the couple had a child, he would prefer a girl—"Five girls." When, later, a journalist asked if Allen was looking forward to becoming an uncle to his sister Letty's first child, he said yes, assuming it's a girl. "I like little girls overwhelmingly better than little boys." Small and big things in life were destined to disappoint him, though. Letty's first baby was a boy, to whom he became "Uncle Woody."

Regardless, they proceeded. Farrow handled all the adoption details. Later, Allen could decide whether he wanted to share in formal parenthood, or merely help out with the child-rearing. But if he co-adopted the new orphan, then perhaps Allen might also agree to adopt Moses, Farrow hinted, giving the boy a father, which Moses dearly wanted. Sometimes it seemed that was all Farrow could talk about: mothering, children, having a baby, adopting another child for her and Allen to love. One day, as the couple walked through Central Park, Farrow, "in a swell of excitement and against my better judgment," in her words, "began babbling" about the pending adoption. "Look, I don't care about the baby," Allen snapped. "What I care about is my work."

Yet Farrow kept at it, and in the midsummer of 1985 she traveled with her daughter Soon-Yi to "a state in the Midwest," according to her memoir. (Allen, in interviews, said "Texas.") They returned cradling a blonde, blue-eyed baby girl, American-born. "I was in on it from the beginning," Allen said later. "I was there when she got off the plane." Naming the little blonde girl would be the first act of their informally shared parentage. Farrow collected books and kept index cards and file folders of baby names. Naming her children was a sacred task for her, even if she was wont to change many of the names later. After deliberation, Farrow christened the baby Dylan (for Dylan Thomas) O'Sullivan (her mother) Farrow. The "Allen" would come later, if at all.

Chapter 8

1985

Sleepwalking into a Mess

A Folie à Deux (or Trois)—The Fictional and Real Collide—into a Ravel of Narratives

As Woody Allen and Mia Farrow took their long walks in the fall of 1985, he was completing postproduction of *Hannah and Her Sisters* while preparing *Radio Days*. "Baby Dylan [was] nestled snugly in the pouch on my chest, so quiet and small he barely noticed her," Farrow wrote. "In preparation for my role of Sally the cigarette girl [in *Radio Days*], I took daily singing lessons with my new daughter in my arms." The cute baby quickly won Allen over. He began showing up early mornings at the Langham, setting his alarm for daybreak so he could watch the baby wake up. "I got a great thrill out of pushing the baby cart and taking walks with her," he said later in court.

The family's optimism was reborn, while at the same time its center of gravity shifted. With a baby to care for, the Farrow-Previns returned full-time to the Langham and stopped shuttling across Central Park. Weekends at Woody's were over. It was also "increasingly rare," in Allen's words, for Farrow to accompany him to Elaine's for late-night dinners; she preferred early suppers at home. Gone too were the romantic days of yore when the director and his leading lady supposedly waved towels at each other from their balconies across the park, if that ever happened—it is a half-mile distance—although Allen's vaunted telescope might have helped.

Allen was obliged to visit the Langham whenever he wanted to see Dylan, so he got into the fresh habit of spending about an hour every morning and every night at Farrow's apartment, as the actress estimated in her memoir. Fine by him: "Mia is surrounded by kids and pets," Allen told the *New York Times* in 1987. "I live by myself across the park. I don't have to be there when the diapers are changed, or anything awful happens."

Because of Dylan the couple briefly resurrected the pipe dream of cohabiting as a couple with the family. They browsed available penthouses and mansions on the Upper East Side, finding "the house of our dreams on Seventy-Third Street," Farrow recollected, every room filled with sunlight, built on two lots, with a large garden and an outdoor playground area for the kids. "We will be the *Meet Me in St. Louis* family," the actress thought. Allen submitted a multimillion-dollar bid, "then, while we were dreaming, the owner changed his mind." Gradually, the air went out of the *Meet Me in St. Louis* balloon. "We went on looking and working and living our lives," remembered Farrow, "in all the same ways with one small but growing difference, baby Dylan."

But the warmth and togetherness of the Woody-Mia years were about to dissipate, and later each would have their own story of the slow-burn breakup that eventually embroiled friends and family, their studio, and the public.

Allen turned fifty on December 1, 1985—the year Farrow turned forty—the golden year in which *The Purple Rose of Cairo* (released in 1985), *Hannah and Her Sisters* (postproduction), and the filming of *Radio Days* intertwined. *Radio Days* had gone quietly before the cameras in the fall. A lavish New Year's Eve party on a New York rooftop crowned the screen story, and on the last day of 1985 Allen broke from directing and took lunch with Gene Siskel at a Chinese restaurant. "This may be my last New Year's Eve," Allen told Siskel at lunch. "I think I've outgrown it." After the interview, Allen brought Siskel to Julia Richman High School, where he was shooting classroom scenes for *Radio Days*. At 4:30 p.m., cake and champagne were wheeled out for the cast and crew. Later that night, Allen told Siskel, he had a dinner date with Mia Farrow and Diane Keaton—both in the cast—and the three had promised to stop by a New Year's Eve party. "If I had my way," Allen said, "I wouldn't go out." Siskel believed he had just spent time with "a happy man," whose forthcoming *Hannah and Her Sisters* loomed as a "life-affirming work" that attested to his growing mastery of the medium.

Hannah was dispatched to theaters in February 1986. The broken family that clings together regardless of difficulties, secrets, and angst—a bedrock theme in Allen's life's work—was never treated as sympathetically. The three troubled sisters were affecting. The drama was charged, at times the scenes were meditative, and the amount of laughter, most of it in the hands of Mickey/Allen, was just about right. The performances—the cast listed alphabetically, an Allen trademark—were consummate. Ending with a warm glow on a Thanksgiving, the most widely celebrated of American holidays, the latest Woody Allen film proved an instant triumph.

Apart from the occasional rotten tomato—"Agreeably skillful" was the best Pauline Kael could muster in the *New Yorker*, "half human"—the reviews were effusive. *Hannah and Her Sisters* "sets new standards for Mr. Allen as well as for all American movie makers," wrote the faithful Vincent Canby in the *New York Times*. *Hannah* "just may be a perfect movie," seconded Sheila Benson in the *Los Angeles Times*. "Woody Allen: You're the Top" was Andrew Sarris's Cole Porter–ish headline in the *Village Voice*. (Porter along with Rodgers and Hart, Bach, Puccini, and Count Basie were on the soundtrack.) Seventy-eight out of a hundred US critics would rank *Hannah* among their year-end top ten, making it the consensus "Best Film of 1986" (number two was *A Room with a View* on sixty-one lists). "The usual fever of adjectives—terrific, titanic, transcendent—sounds puny," Peter Travers enthused in *People*. "One of Allen's great films," *Variety* chorused, "the answer to the prayers of Allen fans."

Orion saw its faith and patience rewarded. *Hannah and Her Sisters* would become the first Woody Allen picture of the 1980s to lodge in the box office top ten for weeks on end. Shown at its peak on seven hundred US screens, the film ultimately grossed $40 million in North America ($109.7 million adjusted for today's money) to stand as Allen's third most remunerative of all time. The overseas earnings were his highest of the decade.

The New York and Los Angeles film reviewer organizations and the National Society of Film Critics cited *Hannah* as the best movie of 1987. The Writers Guild gave Allen its award for Best Screenplay ("Written Directly for the Screen"), and the Academy of Motion Picture Arts and Sciences bestowed seven Oscar nominations on the film: Best Editing (Susan E. Morse); Art Direction–Set Decoration (Stuart Wurtzel and Carol Joffe); Original Screenplay; Actress in a Supporting Role (Dianne Wiest); Actor in a Supporting Role (Michael Caine); Director (Allen); and Picture. Wiest, Caine, and Allen (for the script) were the winners.

In fact, prodded into action by the awards momentum for *Hannah*, the Writers Guild also bestowed its highest honor on Allen—the lifetime Laurel Award for Screenwriting Achievement—a plaque that was given only once annually to the likes of Ben Hecht, Billy Wilder, John Huston, and Preston Sturges. In absentia as usual, Allen delegated Jack Rollins to accept the Laurel on his behalf. Rollins said the award would be "greatly cherished," because "Woody always told me that what's good and bad in a picture resides in the script."

Of course, Allen didn't really care about the coveted Guild plaque, and the outpouring for *Hannah and Her Sisters* only deepened his customary suspicion of acclaim. At 107 minutes, the longest running time he had allowed to date, was *Hannah and Her Sisters* too long-winded? Was the script, tinged with autobiography, too close to home? Were the laughs too generously sprinkled? Was the upbeat ending hopelessly unrealistic?

He had struggled for an ending, finally deciding Hannah and her sisters would find rare happiness in a Woody Allen film. Hannah remains ignorant of her husband's philandering, but Elliot has gotten over his infatuation with Lee. What probably really stuck in Allen's craw—although he himself wrote and filmed it—is what happens to his character. Mickey marries Holly and learns she is expecting. Frank Capra couldn't have shot a more heartwarming (third) Thanksgiving. As the patriarch (Lloyd Nolan) teases out Rodgers and Hart's "Isn't It Romantic?" on the piano, an overjoyed Mickey muses, "The heart is a very, very resilient little muscle."

Probably, looking back, Allen sided more with Kael. He gave interviews after *Hannah and Her Sisters* had proved so successful, insisting its popularity was indebted to "middlebrow" compromises. *Hannah* was "a living-room picture," he told *Rolling Stone*, with nothing in it that might offend home viewers. "I feel I haven't gone deeply enough," Allen told the *New York Times*. The crankiest critics agreed. The ending was too sentimental, Chaplinesque, the whole story a "schmaltzy piece of uplift," complained the acid-tongued James Wolcott.

ALLEN WAS COLLEGIAL with other film directors, especially New Yorkers like Mike Nichols and Martin Scorsese, and he cosigned many petitions having to do with threats to directors over their legal or creative rights. But he had a special soft spot for the famous Frenchman who visited him early in 1987, as *Hannah and Her Sisters* reaped rewards.

When nouvelle vague filmmaker Jean-Luc Godard, one of Allen's many French admirers, asked him to appear in his free-associative version of *King Lear*, Allen said an automatic yes out of respect for Godard's one-of-a-kind career. He had not acted for another director for ten years since *The Front*. Whether Allen had his palms greased with "ten thousand dollars—in exchange, we don't use his name," as Godard later insisted, or the American emoted as a "favor," with "no money involved," in Allen's words, depends on who you believe.

Godard's *King Lear* was born out of an agreement Norman Mailer scribbled on a napkin at the Cannes Film Festival in 1985, with Allen always envisioned as among an all-star lineup in the French auteur's take on Shakespeare. Mailer reneged on writing the script, as per the napkin contract, but he did pop up in the eventual ensemble ("playing himself"). Others in the variegated roster included the avant-garde theater director Peter Sellars (William Shakespeare Junior the Fifth, a descendant of the Bard), Burgess Meredith (Learo), Molly Ringwald (Cordelia), and Godard himself (a character named Professor Pluggy). Allen's role, filmed in New York, was barely noticeable. Godard and crew dropped by the building as Allen was finishing *Radio Days* and photographed the American filmmaker at his editing console, intoning Shakespeare's sixtieth sonnet and pretending to snip celluloid with the tools of a tailor. Addressed by Godard on camera as "Mr. Allen," he was costumed in a Picasso T-shirt. Allen felt like "a fool," he confessed to Ringwald when she stopped by Michael's Pub to hear about his cameo before embarking for Switzerland, where the bulk of *King Lear* was to be shot, "although his character was referred to as the Editor. He told me he hoped I would have a better experience."

Allen was inconspicuous in the final product, one of Godard's more abstruse exercises in cinema, which is saying a lot. But the ease and pleasure of working with another director, one he admired, whetted Allen's appetite for more acting in the future—sometimes for fast money, or simply because he liked the people.*

---

* An obscure prelude to *King Lear* was Godard's twenty-six-minute film *Meetin' WA*, which

••

ALLEN WOULD PROFESS lasting pride in *Radio Days*, which was every bit as warm and sentimental as *Hannah and Her Sisters*. But if *Hannah* was quasi-autobiographical, much of it was poached from Mia Farrow, while *Radio Days* was entirely his story, and Allen spent months shooting the picture in late 1985 and the first half of 1986.

More nostalgic than forward-looking, *Radio Days* arose out of Allen's desire to write "a light film . . . that was the opposite of *Hannah*, something cartoony, full of music and bravura energy," with the picaresque scenes revolving around "memories of songs of my childhood." However, as Allen cautioned in interviews, "it really isn't my childhood exactly . . . there are many aspects of my childhood" in the movie but they were "put in for fun."

His roulette-wheel script spun around the radio dial, often landing, outside the world of broadcasting, on a cigarette girl whose ambitions are hampered by a Betty Boop squawk, and frequently returning to a Rockaway Beach family of aunts, uncles, cousins, grandparents, a mother and father, and a boy named Joe—an Allan Stewart Konigsberg sort of Joe—whose parents bicker over who punishes him best. There would be Nazi submarines lurking offshore; a group of little Peeping Toms that ogle an eyeful; communist neighbors who play their radio loudly on Yom Kippur; stops at Coney Island, Sardi's, and Radio City Music Hall, where *The Philadelphia Story* casts a hypnotic glow on the screen; urgent World War II bulletins; and closer to home, national broadcasts describing the race against time to rescue a little girl who has tumbled into a water well.* The grand finale had a snowfall and Allen's stock company reunited on a nightclub rooftop to ring in the New Year of 1944, a festive ending to another—atypical for Allen—feel-good movie. Big-band music would glue the disparate vignettes together, along with satirized jingles and programming, all the shows and

---

consisted of Godard interviewing Allen about his career for twenty-six minutes, assisted by New York film scholar Annette Insdorf. The Godard short was made "as a substitute for the traditional press conference with the director following the premiere of *Hannah and Her Sisters* at the Cannes Film Festival" in 1986, according to Wikipedia. "Knowledge of Godard's life and work," Wikipedia notes, "illuminate what might otherwise be an opaque encounter as one in which Godard was disappointed by his interview subject."

* Allen cheated on the World War II time frame by re-creating an actual 1949 incident in which three-year-old Kathy Fiscus fell into an abandoned water well in San Marino, California. Her plight was covered by "live" national radio broadcasts. Despite an outpouring of public sympathy and a massive life-saving effort, the rescue failed, and Fiscus's body was brought lifeless to the surface.

products fabricated because licensing the originals would have been cost-prohibitive. The snippets and songs from shows reinforced the theme of how radio, in the good old days, united Americans around a common campfire.

It helped for Allen to have Farrow in reserve as sure-bet casting for the cigarette girl transformed by brushes with heels, gangsters, and diction tutors into a radio gossip columnist. The boy portraying Joe had to evince the scrawny look and mischievous vibe of young Woody, and the *New York Times* ran a feature about the preteen talent hunt that had become de rigueur for his growing-up flashbacks since *Take the Money and Run*. Thirteen-year-old Seth Green was picked for Joe, and twelve-year-old Fletcher Previn skipped the cattle calls to play one of his partners in crime, pilfering from Jewish charity funds to save up for a Masked Avenger Secret Compartment Ring.

The ensemble was one of those all-hands-on-deck rosters that only Allen (or Robert Altman) could have collected under one tent. The deadpan radio broadcasters included Guy LeBow, a former Brooklyn bowling announcer, as the sportscaster who recounts a young pitching whiz who has lost an eye, an arm, and a leg in accidents, yet still manages to hurl blinding strikeouts. Wallace Shawn returned as the unlikely body and voice of "The Master Avenger," the radio superhero idolized by boys. Allen simulated his own family and relatives with Josh Mostel (Zero's son) as Uncle Abe, and Dianne Wiest as Joe's charmingly lovelorn Aunt Bea. Julie Kavner and Michael Tucker were Joe's argumentative mother and father, who optimistically welcome the boy's sole sibling—baby sister Ellen—into the world late in 1943. This valentine to Ellen "Letty" Aronson was, like Allen's every other public gesture toward his younger sister, the opposite of what Farrow claimed in her memoir; and the infant was played by none other than Dylan Farrow, not yet one year old. The family interiors, constructed at the Kaufman Astoria Studios in Queens, were modeled after Allen's boyhood home in Flatbush.

Communist neighbor Larry David appeared in his first Woody Allen picture. Danny Aiello, Jeff Daniels, and Tony Roberts turned up in small roles and made their way into the finale, as does, luminously, Diane Keaton, warbling Cole Porter's "You'd Be So Nice to Come Home To" at the New Year's Eve celebration. Jacqui Safra (as J. R. Beaucaire) can be glimpsed as a French-accented diction student. The vast ensemble was sprinkled with many Allen friends and acquaintances who were pro forma casting. Allen, as the grown-up Joe, narrates—an old writing device that suited the purpose. (Rockaway Beach is "stormy and rain-swept," his disembodied voice explains, because he remembers it that way "at its most beautiful.") Santo Loquasto's production design was spectacular on a shoestring; Carlo Di Palma's cinematography was radiant; Dick Hyman's Golden Age of Radio score, a browse of Allen's record collection, was a music lover's delight.

After two years of writing, filming, and postproduction, *Radio Days* was released in late January 1987, marking another pinnacle in Allen's career, another high point of his years of fruitful collaboration with Farrow. After the stellar run of *A Midsummer Night's Sex Comedy*, *Zelig*, *Broadway Danny Rose*, *The Purple Rose of Cairo*, and *Hannah and Her Sisters*—five motion pictures as different from one another as Woody Allen films could possibly be—*Radio Days* was Baked Alaska following the banquet years. Allen often pointed to George S. Kaufman as a comedy-writing exemplar, and he never got closer to Kaufman (and Hart) than in the New Year's Eve family conga line in *Radio Days* that could have been sneaked into *You Can't Take It with You*.

It might seem curmudgeonly for critics to carp, yet some did—"Aimless nostalgia," Paul Attanasio wrote in the *Washington Post*, which "you peel and peel away at it only to find, in the end, nothing"—which helps explain why Allen threw up his hands over movie reviews. Most of the critics were deeply pleasured, with Vincent Canby comparing Allen to Proust, and Richard Schickel saying *Radio Days* was positively Chekhovian. Peter Travers in *People* hailed "the richly romantic, poetic work of a mature artist at his peak."

Only one director had two pictures on Allen's list of the ten greatest films ever made: Fellini for *8½* and the memoiristic *Amarcord*.* The Bergmanesque *Hannah and Her Sisters* had added to his mystique, and now *Radio Days* was rightly seen as Allen's *Amarcord*. His quasi-autobiographical comedy performed as well as could be expected in the US; and overseas his reputation continued to build with critics and audiences. *Radio Days* would be nominated for two Oscars—Best Art Direction/Set Decoration and Best Original Screenplay—and for the thirteenth time the Writers Guild selected a Woody Allen script as being among the year's finest.

---

* Allen's list for the decennial *Sight and Sound* poll in 2012.

••

PERHAPS FAVORITE SON Fletcher Previn felt deputized by his mother. Coming home one day from the *Radio Days* set, he whispered about an actress behaving "affectionate in the extreme" with Allen, in Farrow's words. It was Dianne Wiest—one of Allen's favorite actresses—but suspicions ran freely in the Farrow household. Fletcher also told his mother he shivered in the cold of filming and wasn't fed properly. And Fletcher was "deeply upset," one day at dailies, to notice his mother playing a cigarette girl who seduces a guy, with the guy "all over me."

In 1987, as the calendar pages flew by, there was a change of domestic weather in Allen's life—rolling thunder and lightning flashes on the horizon. Farrow was a supermother who wanted Allen to become the superfather of her family. But Allen the novice father began to worry her as much as Allen the nonfather. Once indifferent to adoption, Allen began to behave so ardently toward baby Dylan that he neglected her other children, from Farrow's point of view. Maybe Fletcher was worried he was losing ground to cute little Dylan in Allen's eyes, but he was not the only member of the Farrow family to feel shortchanged. At the same time Allen was behaving less attentively to Farrow herself and, as Dylan's therapist Dr. Susan Coates later testified in court, the actress saw herself as competing with her adopted daughter for Allen's focus and affection.

Boasting his own key to the Langham, Allen "would creep up in the morning and lay beside her bed and wait for her to wake up," Farrow claimed in her memoir—written after their court case and the sex-abuse accusations. At night, according to the actress, Allen would materialize at dinnertime and head straight for the little blonde girl. "With his mouth wide open, bigger than a grin, his eyebrows high over the black frames of his glasses, it was a face unaccustomed to its own expression—an expression so asymmetrical, large, unguarded, hungry, and foreign, that I would blink to make the strangeness pass, as he scooped Dylan out of her high-chair and carried her off into another room." She thought he rudely ignored the other children—and her.

Later, countering his mother's alarmist version of Allen's morning visits, Moses Farrow described the numerous times when Allen arrived around 6:30 a.m., letting himself in the door and "bringing two newspapers and a bunch of muffins. I would wake before the others, and so he and I would sit at the kitchen table together for breakfast. While he read the *New York*

Times, I'd grab the *Post* and go straight to the comics and word puzzles. We'd spend this peaceful time together before waking Dylan. He'd make her a couple of slices of toast with cinnamon or honey and be there as she ate her breakfast. He hardly seemed like a monster to me."

Allen cooed over baby Dylan whenever the nanny brought her to the set of *Radio Days*, and he cooed over her some more during the filming of the small-ensemble, Chekhovian ultra-drama he launched before the cameras in the latter months of 1986. Unlike *Radio Days*, which had been a sprawling jigsaw of an operation, the Chekhovian ultra-drama looked on paper to be a simple proposition. Yet after Allen finished all the filming, he hated the footage so much he tried shooting the picture all over again a second time in the first half of 1987.

Allen had written a somber script, again without any acting role for himself. Keying off his fruitless quest for a country home, the story revolved around the Vermont summer retreat of an unstable family. Diane and Lane, a mother and daughter, are the main characters. Diane, a once-famous actress, is a vodka-swilling "tough cookie." Her backstory involves a scandal, the source of mother-daughter friction, which Allen cribbed from actual headlines dating back to his days as a TV writer. On April 4, 1958, Cheryl Crane, the teenage daughter of actress Lana Turner, killed her mother's gangster-boyfriend Johnny Stompanato during a domestic altercation. Or maybe Turner killed Stompanato—that is one theory—and let her daughter take the rap. Lane, the daughter in Allen's screenplay, has never recovered from a similarly lurid incident in the past, which involved her mother and a murky crime. One of Allen's hapless women dreaming of life as an artist, Lane is trying to sell the family's country house. Her girlfriend is visiting from New York. One neighbor is a widowed professor. Another is a handsome Madison Avenue man struggling to write a novel. Summer is ending.

Originally Allen intended to honor Farrow's wishes by shooting the picture at Frog Hollow, until he thought better of that idea and opted to work entirely on Kaufman Astoria soundstages with Santo Loquasto's artificial interiors. There'd be no exteriors, with the outside world glimpsed only through windows and doors.

Allen shot the first version of this ultra-drama with an ensemble led by Maureen O'Sullivan as Diane and Farrow, her own daughter, as Lane. The initial cast also featured Dianne Wiest, Denholm Elliott, Charles Durning, and Christopher Walken, the latter playing the would-be Madison Avenue novelist. After a few weeks of photography, however, Allen decided he and Walken, who had stolen his handful of *Annie Hall* scenes, "couldn't get copacetic on what to do." Walken was swapped out in favor of actor-playwright Sam Shepard, and the neighbor-novelist's scenes were reshot. After completing the filming and watching all the footage, however, Allen felt a sense of failure. He decided to scrap the first version and start over. He told Orion he was going to reshoot from scratch with a few cast changes. The costs could be deducted from his salary and earnings. What other American filmmaker would dare such a thing? What other studio would say yes?

Allen started over in the spring of 1987, rewriting wholesale as he filmed. Allen kept Farrow and Wiest in their original roles, as Lane and her friend visiting from New York; but he shook up the rest of the cast. Durning had another commitment, and Elliott was switched from Diane's boyfriend to the widowed professor with a crush on Lane. Jack Warden became the mother's boyfriend. Sam Waterston, who'd been reliable in previous Woody Allen movies, became the third actor to play the Madison Avenue novelist. Most important, partly because the new round of filming caused conflicts in scheduling, Allen cast a new Diane—substituting New York stage diva Elaine Stritch for Maureen O'Sullivan—a decision that went down hard in the Farrow clan.

O'Sullivan was "miscast," wrote Marion Meade. "Spoiled and selfish in real life, she bore similarities to the character but failed to project those unpleasant qualities in her performance." The actress resolved the awkward situation by bowing out "with a sudden diplomatic attack of pneumonia," according to John Baxter.

A miracle then occurred, as Allen was finishing the second version of the ultra-drama. Liz Smith had the late April scoop: Allen, fifty-one, and Farrow, forty-two, were expecting in December. Norma Lee Clark in the Rollins-Joffe office issued a confirmation: "Mr. Allen and Miss Farrow are both pleasantly surprised by the news."

Indeed, the actress was taken aback. "I'd given up thinking it was possible for Woody and me to have a child," Farrow recalled. Months earlier, in fact, they had discussed adopting yet another orphan as a playmate for Dylan. "Surely another baby will dilute this intensity [between Allen and Dylan]," Farrow thought.

Once again the director disappointed Farrow, however. She didn't think he seemed very excited about her pregnancy, and Farrow's own "first elation" about the child growing inside her turned to anxiety. Allen's "strange" behavior toward Dylan hadn't eased up; if anything, the filmmaker had become "more extreme" in his affections. "When I tried to talk to him about it, he got so angry," Farrow later wrote. "He had grown remote since our first years together, and cruel; not all the time, but so often he made me feel stupid and worthless." The actress toyed with ending their relationship but had "lost confidence in my ability to survive without him."

One day, while in the midst of the second filming of the country-house ultra-drama, the pregnant actress confronted Allen in her dressing room, saying "everything I felt." He acted "surprised and angry," Farrow said later. "I said that I couldn't continue and that I needed some distance from him. But he didn't go away. He would not go. It was so strange." After the filming, "he kept right on coming over to my apartment every single day," morning and night. "He came to Frog Hollow, too, even overnight," the actress wrote in her memoir. "I didn't know what to do. We politely ignored each other while he followed Dylan around. And then, after some weeks of this, I lost my resolve, the line blurred, and we were together again. I needed him and I loved him."

Regardless, Farrow felt optimistic when Allen suggested taking a European vacation with her and the children in the summer ahead. It would be their first time traveling as a family. For months Allen had struggled with the ultra-drama he had insisted on filming twice, and the work "had taken its toll on all of us. It was understandable. Having a baby was the last thing on his mind." Still, his "lack of enthusiasm was depressing."

ALLEN ALWAYS HAD preoccupations. In May, with the ultra-drama finally in the can and in postproduction, Allen trooped off to Washington, DC, as part of a show business delegation that included actress Ginger Rogers and fellow directors Milos Forman and Sydney Pollack. Cable television pioneer Ted Turner wanted to "colorize" the black-and-white libraries of MGM, Warner Bros., and RKO. With the gravitas he possessed as the American filmmaker who shot most frequently in black and white, not just as a one-time stunt, Allen testified against the "colorization" trend before a congressional hearing. It was "sinful" to colorize classic movies like *The Maltese Falcon* and *It's a Wonderful Life*, Allen said.* "No one should be able to alter an artist's work in any way whatsoever, for any reason," he wrote in a *New York Times* op-ed, "without the artist's consent."

In June, as promised, Allen and the Farrow-Previns flew to Europe, touring by van and limousine to "Paris, Stockholm, Helsinki, Venice, London, Luxembourg—we were averaging almost a country a day," Farrow recalled. Their entourage comprised nearly a dozen people, including Allen's new personal assistant Jane Read Martin, who had started out as a gofer on *Saturday Night Live* during Jean Doumanian's reign and who nowadays liaised daily with Allen, from inside his house and on the set during productions, on matters personal and professional. She organized the flights, hotel and restaurant bookings, vehicle drivers, the mail and faxes.

In Stockholm Allen phoned Ingmar Bergman, who was sequestered on the island of Faro, where Bergman lived, to say hello. They brought each other up to date. The mutual admirers held "a two-hour conversation on the phone, and again it was the same kind of thing [as their first meeting in 1978]. We talked about our fears. I talked about my fears, and he talked about his, but I'm me and he's Bergman, so it was very funny to me. I hear that on his set he's very touchy and warm and holds you, and I found that to be the case at dinner [in 1978]."

Allen was a "restless traveler, so we kept moving," Farrow remembered. One day, driving from Paris to Mont Saint-Michel, the director "took one look" at the unsatisfactory hotel that had been booked for them, "checked the rooms, ate an omelet, and we drove *all the way back*. We would have stayed overnight but there was something wrong with the bathroom." Wherever the travelers alighted, Allen was booked into his own separate suite, partly to "write in the separate room he kept," in Farrow's words, "and for the bathroom."

In Paris they celebrated Dylan Farrow's second birthday. ("Parisians are a lot nicer if you're with Woody Allen," Farrow mused.) The little blonde girl was now the star of the family. "At eighteen months she could sing a

* The latter, Frank Capra's Christmas classic, Allen listed in *Apropos of Nothing* as being among the widely popular films he just didn't like. *Some Like It Hot*, *Bringing Up Baby*, *An Affair to Remember*, *Vertigo*, and *To Be or Not to Be* were other classic movie "icons that surprisingly didn't mean as much to me as to the general public."

dozen songs and speak her mind clearly," her mother boasted. "At work and at home she was doted on." Still, Farrow worried about the doter-in-chief. The film director, a first-time midlife father, smothered Dylan with kisses, he tickled and read to her, while slighting her other children, as Farrow saw it. The adopted child intended to bring the actress and her other children closer to Allen was, in fact, disuniting the family.

On the night of Dylan's birthday party in Paris, Farrow "gathered all my courage" and told Allen "what I'd been thinking for many months and could no longer remain silent about: that I was worried about his behavior with Dylan," as she later wrote. "I told him that he'd been looking at the little girl in a sexual way. He stared at her whenever she was naked, and he was all over her, all the time fondling her, not giving her any breathing room." Later, testifying under oath in court, Farrow said when she described Allen's "sexual way" with Dylan, the actress conceded "sexual" was "not the name I used at the time. 'Inappropriate' is the word I used."

If this accusatory conversation took place within earshot of the kids on the trip, it isn't mentioned in her memoir. "All that happened," Farrow recalled, "was that he got very angry." Later, passing through London on their way back to New York, Allen gave an interview to the BBC in which he said he was delighted by Farrow's pregnancy and was looking forward to becoming a biological father. "I hope it's a she," Allen told the BBC. "That would be very important for me." He and the family returned to the States with Allen clutching a new script he had finished on the trip with a pivotal role he had written for Farrow, playing a pregnant woman.

Amniocentesis told them the developing fetus was a boy. "A more perceptive person would have noticed Woody's interest slip from zero to minus," Farrow wrote. Later court testimony would reveal the couple had stopped sleeping together regularly, not long after her pregnancy was diagnosed. "As my body expanded, I felt fat, undesirable, and exhausted," Farrow explained. "Woody seemed put off by my condition; he never touched my stomach, or felt the baby kick, or tried to hear his heartbeat. In fact, he scarcely mentioned the baby."

As was frequently the case, Allen's version of events starkly contradicted hers. "Mia turned to me" early in her pregnancy, Allen wrote in *Apropos of Nothing*, "and said that she would not be sleeping at my house ever again, that I should not get too close to the upcoming baby, as she had questions about our relationship continuing. The key she had given me to her apartment years ago, she now wanted back. Though I grasped that over the past years our relationship had become more serviceable than all-consuming, still, this came as a sudden shock." From that day forward, the actress became "cooler and indifferent" to him. "My theory," the filmmaker wrote dryly in his memoir, "is that I served my purpose knocking her up and had become irrelevant."

ON THE EVIDENCE of the two pictures that followed *Radio Days*—*September* and *Another Woman*, the latter, the script with Farrow as a pregnant woman—Allen was, for the first time in his career, floundering creatively. Although he had shot the ultra-drama twice, he took a long time to decide what to call the picture that was so obviously influenced by two Scandinavians he held in high regard—Ibsen and Ingmar Bergman. Not until August, after postproduction, did the title become *September*, as in "In a few days, it'll be September. . . ."

The release of *September* was set for Christmas, overlapping with the making of *Another Woman*. For the first time, Allen worked on *Another Woman* with Sven Nykvist, the Swedish wizard of photography closely associated with Bergman masterpieces of the 1960s and '70s. Gena Rowlands starred as a philosophy professor on book sabbatical. In leased space for writing, she overhears through a vent the confessions of Farrow, a pregnant woman speaking with a therapist in an adjacent office. The professor becomes fixated on Farrow, whose voiced thoughts of suicide trigger a reexamination of her own unhappy life. Flashbacks and dreams reveal her mistakes: her unfairly maligned brother; her sympathetic first husband; the abortion she now regrets; the novelist whose flirtations she spurned. The professor realizes her own "self-deception," and while reading the tear-stained last lines of "Archaic Torso of Apollo" in her mother's volume of Rilke she vows to alter her life.

Any synopsis would make the film sound intriguing. Along with Farrow and Rowlands, the formidable ensemble included Harris Yulin as Rowlands's brother, Philip Bosco as her first husband, Gene Hackman as the spurned novelist, John Houseman as the professor's cold intellectual father, Sandy Dennis as her onetime friend who denounces her in a drunken tirade, Martha Plimpton as her teenage stepdaughter, and Ian Holm as her husband, a serial adulterer. Klimt, Erik Satie, and an evocative Greek mask added spicing and thematics.

A few days before his fifty-second birthday Allen took a break from the filming to give an interview to Roger Ebert, promoting the upcoming release of *September.* Ebert asked the director about his impending fatherhood. Farrow was heavily pregnant—like the character she was playing, much of it voice-over work, in *Another Woman*—and her due date was in late December. What Allen told the *Chicago Sun-Times* critic was probably not what the actress wanted to read. "My feeling about the baby is very complicated," Allen explained to Ebert. "You know, Mia and I adopted a baby, Dylan, before she got pregnant. And there is absolutely no difference in the love I will feel for the new child and the love I feel for Dylan. In fact, I love Dylan so much that I would be pleasantly surprised if I love the baby we are having together as much as the one we adopted."

"We adopted" was a fanciful description of the elusive reality. Once the filmmaker accepted Dylan into his life, he had gone into overdrive trying to formalize his role as the girl's father, but there were obstacles. "He wanted to adopt her, to be her legal father, but his lawyers didn't know if it would be possible since we weren't married," Farrow recalled. "They were trying to figure out a way. I just listened. And privately, I worried."

Farrow's delivery date neared. Lamaze techniques involved a time commitment, and that was the excuse Allen used to get out of serving as her childbirth coach. Best friend Casey Pascal, a Frog Hollow neighbor who had known Farrow since they were teenagers in a Catholic boarding school in England, shared the Lamaze classes. "Like Mia," said nanny Kristi Groteke, Pascal was "a mother with a capital M" and "the single person" Farrow "completely trusted." A week before Christmas, Farrow went into the hospital for a caesarean. To her surprise, Allen volunteered to be in the delivery room, "with the provision that if it got too disgusting, he wouldn't stay. . . . He was by my side even when the epidural wore off while they were cutting me open."

Their nine-pound, four-ounce baby was born on Saturday morning, December 19. Leslee Dart, the head of the New York office of the high-powered show business publicity firm PMK and one of a circle of women who nowadays managed Allen's professional affairs, oversaw the press release. The angle was Allen boasting of "two productions" in the same week: the theatrical debut of *September* and the birth of his son. "The baby is fine, the baby is fine," the filmmaker was quoted, "the only problem is he looks like Edward G. Robinson"—a throwback joke that many comedians entering fatherhood had cracked for decades. In *Mighty Aphrodite* it's the same joke about Lenny Weinrib's (Allen) adopted baby, only with "Broderick Crawford" as the punch line.

Oddly, Farrow didn't fill in the father's name on the hospital birth certificate. Later, she claimed she gave Allen an official form to fill out and he never returned it. Allen said she was simply "not being truthful"; he never saw any form. "Why exclude me after all that heartfelt nonsense about wanting to have my child? Was he really not mine? Clearly I was being escorted out of the picture long before our dramatic break-up."

Equally important was the blank space for the baby's name. Both parents wanted the name to have a special connotation. Farrow deferred to Allen, and the boy was named Satchel O'Sullivan Farrow, with his forename in honor of Negro League right-hander Leroy "Satchel" Paige, who in 1948 became the first black American to pitch in a World Series. "It was better than Ingmar," Farrow later wrote, "which was his [Allen's] first choice."

Satchel came home from the hospital screaming. Nursing was the only thing that calmed him. Doctors explained Satchel was colicky: "high needs," with an "immature nervous system." Farrow became preoccupied with the newborn and his "nocturnal" habits. At the same time the mother was nursing the youngest member of the family Farrow had older children who were applying to Yale. The baby exhausted everyone. Little Dylan, who'd been looking forward to a baby brother, got tired of the screaming and wailed, "Throw him away!"

Once more, the actress found herself competing for Allen's attention—not over newborn Satchel—still with Dylan. After the colicky baby finally dozed off, his mother had a special nighttime reading and snuggling-in-bed ritual with the little blonde girl, and it was also at night after the day of filming that Allen carved out his own alone time with Dylan. "Now I could barely stand up," Farrow remembered, "and Woody kept taking her off to other rooms. He rarely came in to see me and he hardly glanced at the new baby. He never held or touched him, and he didn't seem to like nursing him. He seemed stern—or was it angry? He made me cry."

Allen had a different perspective. Farrow seemed "unnaturally obsessed" with the new baby, he said later. Satchel swiftly "usurped" Fletcher as her golden child. He even eclipsed Dylan. Farrow would grab her breast pump and lock herself in the bedroom with the baby, according to Allen. "She told me that there were native tribes in Africa or South America who breastfed their kids until seven or eight years old and that she had every intention of doing that with Satchel," Allen said. "When I'd go over there to have dinner with the kids, she would take Satchel into her bedroom and close the door." Breastfeeding became a curious subplot of their estrangement. Later, Allen's friends helped Denis Hamill with a New York *Daily News* article claiming—"Incorrectly," as Maureen Orth insisted in *Vanity Fair*, without providing clarification of the details—"Mia breastfed Satchel until he was three and a half and even had a special harness constructed to do so over Allen's objections."

Tensions between them always simmered below the surface. One day, after a doctor had diagnosed Farrow with anemia, Allen brought the actress a gift package of steaks to replenish her deficient blood cells. She thanked Allen, but added, "You've done these nice things for me, but you're so cold." The director exploded at Farrow (according to her). "That's a lie, that's an out-and-out lie!" More and more they walked on eggshells.

THE WEEK OF Satchel's birth, *September* arrived in US theaters, as "lifeless" as the novel Sam Waterston is writing in the film. Perhaps the desolate ultra-drama was well photographed, but it was staged claustrophobically, all indoors, à la the Golden Age of "live" television. The actors tried their darndest. Elaine Stritch and Jack Warden stood out. The rest were stuck with dialogue that spoke the subtext. (Lane/Mia: "I'm so wounded!") The script pined for Paris; mentioned Kurosawa, Art Tatum, and Ben Webster; offered a Ouija board reading, grumbling about mosquitoes, and loose talk about the futility of existence. But the reviews were tepid, bookings hard to come by. Big theater chains were merging, multiplexes booming, and even in Boston—where Woody Allen films were usually greeted with open arms—*September* had to scrounge for exhibitors. In most parts of the world *September* went straight to video, the first of Allen's movies to suffer that worst of fates.

The same was nearly as true of *Another Woman*, released the next year, also unmerrily at Christmastime. Clocking in at one hour and twenty-three minutes, *Another Woman* had a similarly muted color scheme with Bernie Leighton's same tinkling piano on the soundtrack. The professor/pregnant woman story was more tantalizing, however. Some critics praised the picture, though most didn't think much of it. Over time *September* has gained a following among feminist cinephiles. It would be Allen's last attempt at an ultra-drama for twenty years.

September and *Another Woman* would rank as the least profitable pictures Allen ever made for Orion: numbers forty-two and forty, respectively, on BuzzFeed's list of forty-four titles comprising "The Box-Office Gross of Every Woody Allen Film Adjusted for Inflation" from 2013. In 1987, the year both *Radio Days* and *September* were released, the number-one American movie was *Three Men and a Baby*, a remake of a French comedy, which grossed $167 million domestically. In those days a movie had to amass upwards of $60 million to enter the top ten in the US: *September* grossed less than half a million. *September* and *Another Woman* were the first Woody Allen films since *A Midsummer Night's Sex Comedy* to come and go without Oscar or Writers Guild nominations.

This downward box office spiral contributed to Allen's mounting professional crisis. The motion picture industry had changed drastically since the 1970s, and it had become increasingly rare for the major studios to invest in independent or artistic filmmaking. Orion badly needed modest hits every year, to absorb the costs of its less commercial slate, pay off loans, and balance the books. Although Orion had developed successful television properties and its home video division was doing OK, the studio did not have a single movie in the top ten in 1987. "No company has had as many kudos and awards," chairman Arthur Krim boasted at a studio conference, but many of the Orion award winners, including the Woody Allen movies, barely eked out a profit.

Orion was in danger of going under. A new financial partner and cash infusion were sorely needed. In 1986, Viacom, which owned the fast-rising, fee-oriented Showtime cable system, purchased a 15 percent stake in the studio, then pressed for a more active role in financial decisions, exactly the sort of move that had forced the United Artists team to quit UA and establish Orion in 1978. Longtime Krim ally John Kluge, the billionaire owner of Metromedia, a radio and television empire that Kluge had just sold to

Rupert Murdoch, stepped up to buy 6.5 percent of common shares in Orion, providing a cash infusion and leverage against Viacom. Kluge was awarded a seat on the board alongside another Metromedia official. However, Viacom was absorbed by the National Amusements exhibition chain, whose boss was Sumner Redstone, and Viacom's new parent company, Vestron, maneuvered to become the single largest stockholder in Orion. Redstone pushed for a "friendly takeover" of the studio. Kluge vied with Redstone for control, increasing his stock to 70 percent by late 1988.

Although Kluge finally got the upper hand, the outlook for spoils looked problematic. Again in 1988, the year of *Another Woman*, the US box office top ten did not include a single Orion title. The studio's most popular films were *Bull Durham* (number fifteen), *Colors* (number eighteen) and *Throw Momma from the Train* (number thirty-seven). They were not enough to pay off the deepening debt and reverse the slump. Krim, who was still chairman of Orion, still Allen's standard-bearer, would turn eighty in 1990. No longer was he involved on a daily basis. Kluge, a businessman who never pretended to be a movie producer, was in his midseventies. Orion's precious operating model, which had privileged independent filmmaking and nurtured Allen, was on the verge of extinction.

IN SOME WAYS new fatherhood creatively rejuvenated Allen. Producer Robert Greenhut had listened to the director muse about "a lot of juicy ideas that just couldn't be expanded into feature films," and Greenhut had the brainstorm of teaming Allen with two other major American directors for an anthology picture consisting of three "minimovies." Martin Scorsese and Francis Coppola, the latter cowriting his script with daughter Sofia, would direct the other two installments. With the ink barely dry on an agreement, Allen dashed off a script for his contribution to *New York Stories* and launched the photography in early April with his current team of cameraman Sven Nykvist, editor Susan E. Morse, production designer Santo Loquasto, and costumer Jeffrey Kurland. The press knew few details, though columnists reported Allen would throw off the doom and gloom of *September* and *Another Woman* and craft his first undiluted comedy since *Broadway Danny Rose*.

Orion's fragile future made Allen keenly aware his days with the little-studio-that-could were numbered. A side benefit of *New York Stories* was his "minimovie" amounted to only one-third of a Woody Allen movie, freeing Rollins-Joffe to sell the project to the highest bidder. Touchstone Pictures, a division of the mushrooming Walt Disney empire, stepped up to wholly finance and distribute *New York Stories*. It would be the first Woody Allen film since *Take the Money and Run* to be produced without a United Artists or Orion label.

Working fast, Allen finished his contribution, titled "Oedipus Wrecks," and sent it off to editing in May, just in time to fly with the family to Europe for a second time in the summer of 1988. Eric Lax, who interviewed Allen contemporaneously, supplied a detailed account of this trip in his biography. There were pilgrimages to *Peer Gynt* composer Edvard Grieg's house in Bergen and the Edvard Munch Museum in Oslo, Norway; pauses in Copenhagen and Stockholm, with still no second meeting with Ingmar Bergman; brief traipsing around Helsinki, a portal to the Soviet Union, where the sojourning family spent all of twenty-four hours, because "although Woody found Leningrad as beautiful a city as any in the world, he liked nothing about the Hotel Pribaltiyskaya"; and touchdowns in Vienna, Lake Como, Venice, Rome, Paris, and London.

Whenever they traveled, Allen always talked about the next script he was writing, and which part—if any—might be right for Farrow. After *September* and the birth of Satchel, however, the actress began to muse about quitting the acting profession and devoting herself full time to motherhood and social activism. She initiated a game with Allen—they played it together, a folie à deux—insisting she didn't want any part whatsoever in his next picture, whatever that might be. So he wouldn't write a part for her. Invariably, when the time came, Farrow asked, "What is my role?" or complained about being left out. Allen would go through a brief, intense period of creating or enlarging a part for her. It happened often enough that his producers put in a gap of several weeks between preproduction planning and the start of filming—a "nothing time"—for Allen to rewrite for Farrow.

Farrow did not report in her memoir any friction on the 1988 vacation, no memorable quarrels about Dylan. Satchel, the youngest in the family, had begun to settle down a little, and Allen had responded to Farrow's criticisms, agreeing to moderate his behavior. The actress was getting her sleep. Satchel was "a blessing: an affectionate, thoroughly rewarding little boy, and a silver-haired blue-eyed replica of my [deceased] brother Mike. He began to speak at seven months and was astoundingly articulate well before his first birthday." The only rub was that Allen seemed "indifferent, at best" to his biological offspring, in Farrow's opinion. "Not entirely in jest, he referred to [Satchel] as 'the little bastard,' or 'the completely superfluous little bastard,'" Farrow said, "to which the child responded with equal measures of indifference and hostility."

Perhaps, considering future events, "the little bastard" was a prescient joke. Allen always made constructive use of his time when in Europe. He wrote on hotel stationery, sitting at hotel desks, jotting in elevators. He returned to New York in August with a bulging draft of the tentatively titled "Brothers"—as in, *enough* with the sisters—tucked into "the breast pocket of his rumpled black linen jacket," according to Farrow. There was no clear part for her in the draft, however, because she had told him she didn't wish to act anymore. As usual she changed her mind, and he rewrote the script to pad a role for her in the "nothing time" during preproduction.

IN TIME "BROTHERS" would become *Crimes and Misdemeanors*, another drama leavened with a modicum of comedy, this time without the contrivances that had marred *Hannah and Her Sisters* from Allen's point of view. For a writer-director who was primarily comedic, absurdist, surrealistic, rarely if ever purely realistic in his stories, this would be a more true-to-life departure. For entertainment as well as the realism there would be a gripping murder at the center of the script. The killing—the first serious killing in a Woody Allen picture, and treated seriously, as he'd told Reginald Rose it should be done—furnished the springboard and narrative drive. The murderer's escape from justice would give Allen the excuse to step further outside his customary comedic paradigm, meditating on what, in *September*, he had defined as the "haphazard, morally neutral, and unimaginably violent" universe.

In Allen's script ophthalmologist Judah Rosenthal is a pillar of society whom audiences first meet at a public testimonial. Judah can't figure out how to end his secret fling with a flight attendant, who angrily threatens to disclose their affair to his wife. Judah's brother, who does "dirty work" for the mob, is willing to kill the mistress. The ophthalmologist guiltily confesses his adultery to Ben, the family rabbi, who is one of Judah's patients, slowly going blind. The rabbi urges him to tell his wife about his affair and have faith in her forgiveness. Although a man of science, Judah was raised religiously; still, he disregard's Ben's advice and, as well, the teachings of his own father, a rabbi, who is seen delivering mealtime homilies to his family in flashbacks. "The eyes of God are on us always," the rabbi father says, an admonition that adds to the script's thematic layering: a villainous ophthalmologist, a wise rabbi losing his sight, the eyes of the moviegoers.

As with *Hannah and Her Sisters*, Allen was playing a secondary character who lightens the movie. He is Cliff Stern, an independent, serious-minded filmmaker completing a documentary about a brilliant philosophy professor who believes in love at first sight, among other maverick views. Cliff feels increasingly alienated from his wife, who has two prominent brothers, one of whom is the kind and thoughtful rabbi Ben (Sam Waterston), while the other is Lester, a rich, smarmy producer of "sub-mental" television sitcoms. At his sister's behest, the obnoxious Lester hires the perpetually underachieving Cliff to direct a hagiographic documentary about his creative genius. While following Lester around, Cliff falls for Halley, a charming production associate—Halley was the character Allen bulked up for Mia Farrow—who is liaising with Lester on behalf of the TV network. Lester, who can beat Cliff at the game of quoting Emily Dickinson, becomes Cliff's rival for the affections of Halley. The jealous Cliff sabotages his plum assignment by capturing Lester at his worst and intercutting Mussolini with the TV producer in his documentary. Cliff loses his job—and Halley.

The screwed-up lives of the ophthalmologist and independent filmmaker are separate story threads, which barely intersect. The two men, both facing ethical dilemmas, barely know each other. They have only one sustained revelatory conversation in the final sequence, a wedding reception for the blind rabbi's daughter.

The script was another Woody Allen bouillabaisse, but with market-fresh ingredients as well as pantry staples. The profound philosopher surprises the documentarist by going "out the window." The charming network associate chooses pompous Lester over the brainy Cliff. The ophthalmologist gets away with murder.

The story would be enlivened with clips from vintage Hollywood movies that supply a witty cross-commentary on the plot—Betty Hutton singing

"Murder, He Says," for example, from *Happy Go Lucky*, made in 1943, the heyday of Allen's boyhood moviegoing. Cliff steals afternoons at the Bleecker Street Cinema with his teenage niece, to whom he inappropriately confesses his stale marriage. Her mother—Cliff's sister—has become lovelorn and clueless, after her husband's death; she roams the "Personals" column, meeting loser men whose turn-ons include defecating on her. Halley begins to supplant the niece for Cliff's movie matinees, they share Milk Duds, and she stays late in his editing room to watch the only print he owns: *Singin' in the Rain*.

The filming began in October 1988. Allen cast Martin Landau, who had a long, respected career, as Judah, the true lead, although first he had considered him to play the ophthalmologist's killer brother. For the latter he gravitated to Jerry Orbach, whose onetime dominance in stage musicals was eclipsed by his late-career surge in dramatic roles in movies and on television. Anjelica Huston, whom Allen had been watching since the late 1970s—she's mentioned in the *Manhattan* script—had come of age with a Best Supporting Actress Oscar for *Prizzi's Honor*. She'd portray the vindictive mistress. Alan Alda, whom Allen had known since his abortive stab at a sitcom in the 1960s, would portray Lester, the glib producer, Cliff's brother-in-law. Although Cliff/Allen has many bright one-liners (he loves Lester "like a brother—David Greenglass!"), Alda would make Lester just as funny. Sam Waterston would appear in his fourth Woody Allen picture as the kindly rabbi.

New York University professor Martin S. Bergmann, an authority on Freud and the history of psychoanalysis, would lend his dignity as the putative subject of Cliff's documentary in progress. The sprinkling of famous New Yorkers and Allen acquaintances in party scenes and bits included Nora Ephron, Wanda Toscanini Horowitz, former United Artists official David Picker, who delivered the opening tribute to the ophthalmologist but had to be replaced, for scheduling reasons, during reshooting; and three-year-old Dylan O'Sullivan Farrow, glimpsed among the children at the wedding reception finale. Claire Bloom (Judah's wife), Joanna Gleason (Cliff's wife), and Daryl Hannah (a Lester groupie) were among the large supporting cast.

The events of the past year pushed Allen deep into a groove. He worked intently with his usual team—with Sven Nykvist still as his cameraman—to stage the many diverse scenes, rewriting as he shot. There were exteriors on Long Island as well as in Manhattan, and Allen mounted virtuoso sequences without dialogue—the offstage murder of the flight attendant, followed by Judah's frantic cleanup of blood—scored with Schubert.

As he was wont to do, Allen had written a gracious letter to Anjelica Huston, explaining not all that much about the story of the picture but saying she "might respond to the character of Dolores, the needy flight attendant, whose constant demands" seal her doom. After the actress was cast, receiving her "sides" but not the full script, Huston telephoned Allen's office and asked to meet with the director. A few hours later Allen rang her back, stammering, "I heard you wanted to speak with me." She thought they might get together for "a drink, or tea, or something." After a long pause, Allen asked, Why? "Well, I thought it might be a good idea," Huston replied. Allen said he had a cold. "When did you want to have this tea—this drink?" Well, perhaps on Thursday, she suggested ("casting it out like a fly on a dry river"). OK, Allen said, adding but what if he still had his cold on Thursday? Whether sick, shy, or too busy to make nice with the daughter of John Huston, a third-generation member of the Huston dynasty, "the drink never happened," Huston wrote in her memoir.

Huston experienced approximately the same give-and-take from Allen for her first scene, which took place in her character's apartment. The location was "a nondescript glass high-rise in the East Thirties in Manhattan." It was the scene where "Dolores [Huston] threatens and cajoles Judah [Landau] and tosses down tranquilizers with alcohol," in her words. After getting costumed and made up, the actress walked upstairs from her trailer "into the bright hot lights and the bodies crowded into a small apartment, through cables and standing arcs and equipment. . . . Sven and Woody were wearing identical blue wool caps and neutral-colored parkas, like climbers on the Matterhorn. It was 150 degrees when Marty and I started the scene. Woody indicated that I should stalk from room to room, and I did my best, swallowing pills while desperately trying to remember my lines as I stumbled into doorways and lurched over cables and standing arc lights. Woody kept shooting. He asked if I could pronounce the word 'been' as 'bin,' which for some reason I found harder than speaking Russian. After his initial direction he never said another word, but we shot quite a few takes, and soon there was a deep frustration between Marty's character and mine, and I believe that was what Woody was looking for."

Is it surprising the scene is so electric in the movie? Like many actors who worked with Allen over the years, no matter how hard Huston tried to hit her marks, she felt his incurable dissatisfaction. Often on a film there was "one scene that Woody was never happy with." With Huston and *Crimes and Misdemeanors* it was the scene that "moved from a diner to a car wash to a Chinese restaurant, and every time we reshot it, I tried harder to make it good. I think that's probably what was wrong with it—you could see the effort."

Eric Lax said *Crimes and Misdemeanors* became the "most rewritten and reshot of his movies to date." Farrow recalled "the usual problems with the script," she later wrote, "especially the section involving Woody and me. He rewrote and reshot all of our scenes and at least a third of the rest of the movie." Was Allen, in a sense, struggling to rethink Farrow's entrenched status in his films, as he also reconfigured her place in his life?

ALTHOUGH ALLEN ROUTINELY referred in interviews to Dylan as his adopted child, his lawyers had made little progress in their attempts to secure a formal adoption. "The fact that we weren't married seemed to be an insurmountable obstacle for the court," Farrow wrote. "Quietly I was relieved and hoped the issue would disappear." The actress remained concerned about Allen's intense relationship with Dylan and "his insistence that there was nothing unusual about it." Raising the issue always created "specific tensions between us."

Yet their en famille summers in Europe had "brought Woody closer to the older kids," Farrow believed. Allen had become more conversational with Daisy, Farrow thought, and even with teenage Soon-Yi, who previously had behaved "a tad sullen" with the director, in Allen's view. Born in Seoul to an "extremely poor" birth mother, at age five Soon-Yi had run away from home and begun living on the streets, picking through garbage for food. Soon-Yi's mother had been a prostitute who beat her, according to Farrow, who said when the girl was rescued from the streets Soon-Yi suffered from "rickets, malnutrition—even her fingernails had fallen off, she had lice and sores everywhere." A mother with a penchant for videotaping her children on family occasions, Farrow once asked Soon-Yi to make a recording of her recollections of these horrors, but Soon-Yi, insisting she did not harbor those memories, refused. Police sent Soon-Yi to a Seoul orphanage, where she was among a group of children presented on a stage to prospective parents, including an emissary from the Friends of Children agency seeking an adoptee for Farrow and André Previn. "She'd twirled around and leaped off the stage," Daphne Merkin wrote in 2018 for *New York* magazine, "while the other children just bowed and walked off." Farrow returned to pick up the six-year-old girl in May 1977, "camera in hand," wrote Merkin.

Soon-Yi first lived with the Previns in Surrey, England, during which time Farrow briefly renamed the Korean adoptee "Gigi," the title of a 1958 film musical, set in Paris, for which her husband had composed the score. When Farrow and Previn got divorced in 1979, the actress took Soon-Yi and her other children back with her to the US, where she had landed her starring role on Broadway. Farrow and her family initially lived in Martha's Vineyard, then moved into the apartment with her mother at the Langham on Central Park West.

Allen was just another boyfriend of her mother's when, at age ten, Soon-Yi first encountered him. At the time, the young girl was attending the Ethical Culture School; at American schools she was always as much as two years older than fellow students because of her lag in education. She shared a bedroom with Lark and Daisy, her slightly younger adopted sisters. "Woody wasn't interested in meeting us children," she recalled. "The feeling was mutual; we weren't interested in meeting him." She regarded him as "her mother's lollipop."

As time went on, however, Allen began noticing Soon-Yi and stopping by her room, commiserating as she struggled with his own boyhood bête noire: homework. Later, the "little learning disability" she had, in Soon-Yi's words, gave the Farrow-Previns an excuse to publicly belittle her intelligence. "Mia drummed it into me to be ashamed about it," Soon-Yi said in 2018. "It comes out in spelling, and I had to work much harder in school. But I was driven and interested, and I wish I'd had a tutor." Her mother wrote "words on my arm, which was humiliating, so I'd always wear long-sleeved shirts," Soon-Yi said. "She would also tip me upside down, holding me by my feet, to get the blood to drain to my head. Because she thought—or she read it, God knows where she came up with the notion—that blood going to my head would make me smarter or something."

"Specifically at Mia's request," according to nanny Kristi Groteke, a confidante of Farrow's, Allen began taking "long walks" with the teenage girl "to help her feel more comfortable around men." Gradually, Soon-Yi warmed to Allen, and vice versa. "Without complaint," in Farrow's words, the filmmaker attended Soon-Yi's sweet sixteen party in October 1986, and the next year he and Farrow took her with a small group of her friends to the Russian Tea Room for her seventeenth birthday, before dropping the girls off at the Broadway musical *Phantom of the Opera*. Soon-Yi was slow to blossom. But the teenager was becoming noticeably pretty as her braces came off, and she finished her sophomore classes at the all-girls Catholic Marymount School in 1989.

NEW YORK STORIES, released in March 1989, proved Allen's funny bone was alive and pulsating. His rip-roaring installment, "Oedipus Wrecks," concerned a lawyer named Sheldon Mills (Allen), who nurses unresolved issues with his ultimate Jewish mother (Mae Questel). Sheldon's mother disapproves of his fiancée Lisa (Farrow), because she is a blonde shiksa and a divorced mother with three children from a previous marriage. (They include three of Farrow's actual children, with Dylan O'Sullivan Farrow again among the cast.) After confessing to his analyst (Marvin Chatinover) that he loves his mother "but I wish she would disappear," Sheldon takes his mother, Lisa, and Lisa's children to a magic show, where his mother is "volunteered" for the Great Chinese Box illusion and vanishes into thin air. Sheldon feels liberated. Never has he been "so relaxed and uninhibited in bed," he tells his analyst. Then his mother reappears as a gigantic apparition in the sky hovering over the Chrysler Tower, squawking loudly to all New York about Sheldon's boyhood bed-wetting.

Sheldon's analyst recommends Treva (Julie Kavner), a clairvoyant who might investigate and solve the mystery of his sky-mother. A pianist, a ballerina, and Genghis Khan's laundress in previous lives, in the present day Treva is a fraud whose tarot cards, spell-casting, and voodoo dolls fail to pacify Sheldon's mother. Yet Treva is also a mensch who can cook a sublime boiled chicken. Lisa breaks up with Sheldon; your mother is "also saying things about me!" Lisa tells Sheldon, who has noticed only his own humiliation. Then Sheldon has a brainstorm. He introduces his new fiancée, Treva, to his mother in the sky, and Mother approves, returning to earth in his living room and turning the pages of a family album, kvetching to Treva as the screen fades.

Farrow's part was bland, but Allen, the flamboyant Kavner, and the overblown Questel were priceless. Questel was a real find: a voice-over artist, she'd done some singing for *Radio Days* and was the voice of Betty Boop in the 1930s. The magician (real-life comedian-magician George Schindler), small parts (another Larry David appearance), and cameos by New York broadcasters and Mayor Ed Koch added to the tomfoolery.

Most critics thought the forty-minute "Oedipus Wrecks"—which had pride of place as the closing segment of *New York Stories*—salvaged a dream project whose high expectations were undercut by lesser works from Martin Scorsese ("Life Lessons") and Francis Coppola ("Life without Zoe"). By this time only Scorsese rivaled Allen, among film directors devoted to their cityscape, as Mr. New York. "Your New York is alien to me," Scorsese once said to Allen, albeit admiringly. Scorsese painted a grittier, turbulent, violent New York.

But Allen's romantic vision of New York had come under increasingly hostile scrutiny by the time of "Oedipus Wrecks." Oft-quoted and widely accepted was Joe Klein's observation, in *GQ*, that "Woody Allen's New York City—the city of his movies—has peculiar geography. It ends at Ninety-Sixth Street, where Harlem begins. It extends south to SoHo, but not as far as Wall Street. It allows, grudgingly, for one outer borough, Brooklyn. In fact, there are only two crucial neighborhoods in his New York: Times Square and the quiet, elegant Upper East Side." Never mind that, in the 1980s, *Stardust Memories*, *Zelig*, *Broadway Danny Rose*, and *The Purple Rose of Cairo* were as much New Jersey as New York stories, if exteriors count for anything, and *September*, even though it was filmed on a New York soundstage, supposedly takes place in New England.

Ever since Allen had left superficial comedies behind, his New York had also been a city of white people.* Critics repeatedly pointed out the paucity of substantial roles for black performers in his post–*Annie Hall* work. Only a handful of black characters were glimpsed in scenes, and these were mainly the stereotypical household servants in *Manhattan* and *Hannah and Her Sisters*, the latter film pocked by "a silent black maid gliding in to light

* At the same time, although it was little remarked upon, Scorsese's New York films were also dominated by white actors in speaking roles.

the dinner candles," in James Wolcott's words. When the Motion Picture Project, a New York activist group protesting the lack of minority employment on the screen and behind the camera, picketed *Hannah and Her Sisters* during filming, Allen agreed to hire four black production assistants. Yet time and again the director responded feebly to complaints about the scarcity of black characters in his scripts, or the lack of any actors of color being cast in major roles. Perhaps Juliet Taylor was equally to blame. "I always cast the person who fits the part most believably in my mind's eye," Allen stubbornly defended himself in *Apropos of Nothing*, insensitively pointing out he had participated in the March on Washington in 1963, donated to the ACLU to support the Voting Rights Act, and even named several of his children "after African American heroes."

AGAIN, IN THE summer of 1989, the patchwork Farrow-Previn-Allen family headed for Europe. "To avoid the unpleasantness of airports, Woody chartered a private jet for the entire trip," Mia Farrow recalled. "Fresh guacamole and chips were on the table when we boarded the plane at Teterboro Airport in New Jersey. The seats were huge and cushiony, the enchiladas (our food of choice for the flight) were tops; there were dozens of movies to choose from. You couldn't help feeling guilty at the luxury of it, but it sure was an easy way to travel. You come and go whenever you want (the crew stays in a hotel). Customs people come right on board to stamp passports."

The rest of the trip was a blur to Farrow. But Venice, Rome, and Paris were usually on the itinerary, as these cities were Allen touchstones. People in Italy and France flocked to Woody Allen movies, and he gave interviews on his summer vacations to promote upcoming releases in places where the foreign openings typically lagged a few months behind the US. As always, Allen maintained separate hotel rooms and carved out time in the mornings for writing. Returning to New York, Allen carried a draft of *Alice*, a script he wrote expressly to counter Farrow's ambivalence about acting anymore. Its story flattered her Catholicism, her veneration of missionaries, her social conscience.

Allen also usually brought home a bag of souvenirs for his mother and father, his sister, and his sister's family. Nowadays Martin and Nettie Konigsberg spent their winters in Florida in the Miami area condominium their prosperous son had arranged for them, but the couple, in their eighties, resided during most of the rest of the year in a nearby Upper East Side apartment, whose purchase and upkeep was also borne by Allen. Allen, the actress, and her children would visit "every few weeks or so in a ritual that did not vary," according to Farrow. "Woody would ring their doorbell and then cover the peephole. They always opened it anyway. From the time we walked in until we left a half hour later, he did not address them directly, or sit down or stop moving."

Nowadays Martin, eight years older than his spouse of six decades, was virtually deaf and watched television with the volume up to the max. Nettie doled out chocolate-chip cookies and made deprecating comments about her famous son. According to Farrow, Nettie watched "with amazement tinged with disapproval" as her son, in his midfifties, crawled and clambered after four-year-old Dylan. "It's too much," Nettie muttered, according to Farrow, "it's not good for her." Allen overheard. "Twist her nose off!" he told Dylan. "She's the wicked witch. Go on, twist it off." Perhaps this was another little joke Farrow didn't get. Allen's mother, hard of hearing, asked, "What'd he say?" Nothing, Farrow would reply, sadly shaking her head. "I told myself he'd never really played with a child before, he just didn't know how. Surely, he would relax in time."

The father of Sheldon (Allen) in *New York Stories* is long deceased in the backstory. Sheldon's mother is half alive, half dead, a monster who floats in the heavens above Manhattan, which is why she is such a crazy-fun character. The boy actors playing Allen as a kid growing up, and the boyhood flashbacks that were a constant in Woody Allen films since his debut as a writer-director, had gradually evanesced from his work. Perhaps now Allen had finally gotten Nettie out of his system too. The closing image of "Oedipus Wrecks" shows Sheldon/Allen breathing a rueful smile as he watches his incorrigible mother bond with Treva/Kavner. The scene suggests a kind of closure. It was also the last time he'd write a scene for anyone playing his mother.

IN MID-OCTOBER *CRIMES and Misdemeanors* opened to laudatory reviews. "Woody has assumed the status of a master," Janet Maslin declared in the *New York Times*. Referring to the religious themes, Catholic priest Andrew

Greeley, a sociologist and author, hailed Allen as "America's most theological filmmaker." The national release yielded his best box office since *Hannah and Her Sisters*, which was a more touching film with a stronger dose of comedy. *Crimes and Misdemeanors* was difficult, disturbing. Still, its $18 million gross in the US would rank it at number nine on Allen's all-time list of moneymakers. *Hannah*, with $40 million, was number three.

Martin Landau deserved his Academy Award nomination for Best Supporting Actor for a riveting performance as the self-absorbed ophthalmologist: an embezzler, an adulterer, ultimately complicit in murder. The veteran actor, enjoying a late-career boom, would lose the Oscar race this time but win five years later for *Ed Wood*. Anjelica Huston, Alan Alda, Sam Waterston, Jerry Orbach, Claire Bloom, and Joanna Gleason were in top form. Farrow, whom Allen loses to Alda, gave the challenging picture its "warm center," *Variety* noted. "The structural and stylistic conceit," *Variety*'s review continued, "is that when Landau is onscreen the film is dead serious, even solemn (harking back to Allen's controversial series of Ingmar Bergmanesque pictures starting with *Interiors*), while Allen's own appearance onscreen signals hilarious satire and priceless one-liners."

The hard truths of *Crimes and Misdemeanors* were more powerful because they seemed personal to Allen. "My heart says one thing, my mind says another" is Cliff's lifelong quandary about women. And Allen treated Judaism in the film more seriously than in any other film he made, without any of the sarcasm to be expected from someone who had left religion behind and who, like Judah, no longer believed in a God. A killer escaping punishment was the opposite of a Hollywood happy ending, as Judah points out to Cliff at the final wedding reception, but the tough-minded ending of *Crimes and Misdemeanors* was tempered by the moving last sequence in the picture. As the blind rabbi, Ben, twirls his daughter around the dance floor at her wedding, a montage of images reminiscent of the ending to *Annie Hall* reprises highlights from the movie and concludes with Judah's father, in a voice-over, reasserting his optimism for the human race owing to its capacity for love.

Along with *New York Stories*, released earlier in 1989, *Crimes and Misdemeanors* crowned Allen's second decade of uncommon range and depth. Aside from the nod to Landau for Best Supporting Actor, the Motion Picture Academy also gave the film Best Picture and Screenplay nominations.

(It lost in all its Oscar categories.) The Directors Guild nominated Allen as Best Director for the fourth time. The Writers Guild cited it as the Best Original Screenplay of 1989. Allen's fourth Writers Guild win equaled Billy Wilder's total, and his fourteen nominations surpassed Wilder, who had long held the guild record. Farrow, stingy with praise for Woody Allen films in her memoir, said she never watched *Another Woman* or *New York Stories*. "All I remember about making them is wanting to go home." *Crimes and Misdemeanors*, she wrote, was "chilling but brilliant."

ALLEN WAS ALREADY busy shooting *Alice*, the script he had hatched on his summer European vacation. Part screwball comedy, the *Alice* story concerned an Upper East Side convent-educated wife and mother who undergoes a midlife crisis and sheds her affluence to follow the self-sacrificing example of Mother Teresa. Mia Farrow had long idolized Mother Teresa and loved to tell the anecdote about taking her children to see the world premiere of a documentary about the world-famous Catholic nun, which was held at the United Nations in 1985. The family stood in line afterward to meet the missionary, later canonized by the Church for her charitable work among the poor and afflicted in India. "God bless you," Mother Teresa had greeted the actress and her gaggle of children. "She was the embodiment of everything I had tried to teach them [the children] about true success," Farrow recalled, "and what one person with conviction and courage can accomplish."

In the story Allen wrote, Alice grows alienated from her cold husband and self-absorbed lifestyle. She suffers mysterious back pains and heartaches and visits a Chinese herbalist and acupuncturist, whose hypnosis, concoctions, and opium send her spiraling through a looking glass of transformations. Spell-cast into a femme fatale, Alice initiates an affair with a handsome studio musician who picks up his child at her daughter's elementary school. Another potion from the Chinese medicine man grants her temporary invisibility and allows her to discover secrets about her musician boyfriend and her womanizing husband. Her attempts to launch herself into a career as a television writer fail, despite the help of a wisecracking Muse. The ghost of a dead lover flies her into the past, where she gains insights into her troubles—the flashbacks are like therapy sessions—and she is prodded into action. Alice's love affair goes bust, she tells off her cheating husband, and escapes to Calcutta, where she reinvents herself in imitation of Mother Teresa's supposedly selfless Catholicism.

The Mother Teresa ending demonstrated how far down the rabbit hole of Catholicism Allen had plunged with Farrow. Some people, including Christopher Hitchens in his scathing book *The Missionary Position*, saw the renowned missionary as a reactionary on social issues, whose work among the poor was often counteracted by her religious zealotry. But "Mother Teresa has been a major icon" in Farrow's life, Allen proudly told Roger Ebert. "She was raised Catholic, and it was always interesting to me to hear about it. I've always been interested in the aesthetics of Catholicism. It's such a lovely religion to an outsider from an aesthetic point of view."

Allen cast William Hurt as Alice's duplicitous husband, and Joe Mantegna as the divorced dad with whom she becomes enamored. Veteran American-born Chinese actor Keye Luke—"Number One Son" in the Charlie Chan series of the 1930s—was the wise old diagnostician with as much screen time as anyone except Farrow. His character was modeled after the herbalist who had failed to cure Allen's eye-stye problems. Alec Baldwin was the deceased flame taking Farrow on a magic carpet ride, and Bernadette Peters was her writerly Muse. The crack ensemble included Cybill Shepherd, Julie Kavner, Blythe Danner, Gwen Verdon, Patrick O'Neal, James Toback as a literary professor with designs on Farrow, and Australian actress Judy Davis making a dynamic entrance into Allen's oeuvre as Mantegna's whip-smart ex-wife who can't control her feral sex appeal.

With the exception of Sven Nykvist, who had left the fold in favor of the returning Carlo Di Palma, Allen's behind-the-camera team was intact. "Again, we reshot at least half of the movie as we went along, and, predictably, after the rough cut there were more reshoots," wrote Farrow. "The ending was a problem."

MEANWHILE, ALLEN HAD taken Soon-Yi, who was in her late teens, more under his wing. She was the only one of the Farrow-Previn children who shared his consuming interest in sports. "When he [Allen] sat in the library watching baseball, basketball, and football on television, Soon-Yi sat quietly beside him as he explained the games," Farrow recalled. "Her brothers and sisters began to tease her, saying she had a crush on him." In early 1990 Allen began taking Lark, Moses, and Soon-Yi to New York Knicks games. The first photograph of Allen sitting with the nineteen-year-old at a Knicks game, seeming to hold her hand, was published in January 1990. The hand-holding image was really Allen leaning over to speak to Soon-Yi about the game, he later protested. "Despite that famous photo, in which it looks like we're holding hands," Allen wrote, "I never took her hand."

At the time, Soon-Yi also insisted later, her relationship with Allen was platonic. "At that first basketball game I turned out to be more interesting and amusing than he thought I'd be. Mia was always pounding into him what a loser I was." The director began to invite Soon-Yi over to his screening room and show her his favorite foreign movies. Unbeknownst to the family, they slipped off together to other matinees. Soon-Yi stole away, "some Saturdays, some Sundays," according to Farrow's court testimony, "all dressed up as if it was nighttime, tight miniskirt, a lot of makeup . . . and say she was going to meet this friend at Bloomingdale's."

At this juncture Farrow was more preoccupied with Allen's "behavior with Dylan," which was "getting worse." The word she now adopted was "obsessed." According to Farrow, Allen "whispered her awake, he caressed her, and entwined his body around her as she watched television, as she played on the floor, as she ate, as she slept. He brought her into bed when he was wearing only his underpants. Twice I made him take his thumb out of her mouth." The thumb-sucking really bothered Farrow. She was fixated on the subject. "At exactly what point does it become child abuse? What kind of person puts his thumb in a little girl's mouth to suck on?" She asked a family therapist to caution Allen. Still, Farrow caught him doing it on occasion, she said later. He insisted it happened only a few times. She exaggerated, Allen said. Many fathers did the same thing.

"Most of the time Dylan was a bright, chatty little girl, brimming with opinions and observations," Farrow said. When Allen showed up, according to the actress, her daughter acted strangely. "She withdrew, her talk became sketchy and hard to follow, and instead of answering her questions she looked around the room. When he became more insistent, she hummed, talked like a baby, barked like a dog, sang, did anything to deflect his attentions; and this only made him more insistent. When she couldn't say good-night, when she wouldn't even look at him, he pinned her shoulders to the bed and demanded a response while her head thrashed back and forth." C'mon, just give her a kiss and go, Farrow would say, angering Allen. "If there was a problem he insisted that it lay with me, in my misinterpretation of his very normal paternal affection."

Dylan—Satchel too—would end up in therapy sessions, with Farrow and Allen also in the room for parental counseling. Nearly all the Farrow-Previns were in therapy, separately or together in different groupings, with the fees absorbed by the director, who had convinced Farrow of the benefits of analysis for everyone, children too. As the *Washington Post* discovered in its digging, even Farrow's bichon frise had a $150-per-hour "animal behaviorist." Allen paid for all the therapists, as he paid for all the children's tutors. Nanny Groteke estimated the therapy sessions alone cost Allen $1,750 weekly, plus expenses for the limousines bearing the doctors back and forth from Manhattan locations and, at different times, from New York to Connecticut.

Satchel had preceded older sister Dylan into therapy by several months in 1990. Two and a half years old, Satchel was still breastfeeding when he started his sessions with a child therapist in June. Apart from being a colicky, nocturnal child averse to his father, Satchel was believed to be exhibiting "gender problems," in Allen's words, "always identifying with the females on videotapes that were shown to him. Always saying he wanted to be Cinderella, Snow White. Wanted to wear women's clothes. And it alarmed Mia and myself."

Allen, in his later court testimony, blamed the gender problems on Farrow, saying she was smothering their son with affection and attention, the same way she accused him of behaving with Dylan. "Mia flew into a rage on the few occasions I said that," Allen stated. "She said it was not her fault, that it was probably genetic in some way. I, of course, think that Satchel had to be affected by the fact that he was constantly surrounded by females [including his sisters and nannies]. . . . For at least some of the time, Mia functioned as both mother and father."

One day a psychologist, who was "helping another child in the family," Farrow wrote in *What Falls Away*, noticed "only one brief greeting between Woody and Dylan" and expressed concern about their relationship. In her memoir Farrow did not name Dr. Susan Coates, a gender-identity specialist, nor the "child" then her patient—Satchel—whom Dr. Coates treated from

1990 to 1992, typically seeing the boy along with one or both parents, since his problems were their problems, and perhaps they were at the root of his problems. Now Dr. Coates began to see Dylan with the couple, helping Allen "understand that his behavior with the five-year-old was 'inappropriate' and had to be modified," in Farrow's words. Later in court, Coates said Allen's attitude was "inappropriately intense because it excluded everybody else, and it placed a demand on a child for a kind of acknowledgment that I felt should not be placed on a child." Farrow's memoir quotes this line from Dr. Coates, without mentioning her ensuing conclusion: "I did not see it [his relationship with Dylan] as sexual. . . ."

Yet the Coates sessions, which treated "the overall wooing quality of Woody's approaches, his own neediness expressing itself to Dylan," in Farrow's words, evinced positive results. "Many of the things that had so disturbed me seemed to improve. She made him stop putting his hands under Dylan's covers, stop putting his face in her lap, stop the constant caressing, stop hunting Dylan down, stop having her suck on his thumb."

Still, Dylan's psychology was considered so complex she was also remanded to Dr. Nancy Schultz, a family therapist who convened separate sessions with the little blonde girl. Dr. Schultz later testified she was asked to treat Dylan because the youngster lived "in her own fantasy world." She "had serious problems telling the difference between reality and fantasy," Allen said. Allen and/or Farrow also attended the Schultz sessions.

ORION PICTURES WAS teetering on the verge of collapse, and not simply because the US earnings and profits of Woody Allen pictures had continued their steady decline. Allen felt the pressure and the economic pinch.

By average-citizen standards Allen was wealthy, yet he maintained a high cost of living, and with all the family therapy sessions, child tutors, and European private-plane splurges, he suffered the occasional human twinges of financial anxiety. After talking it over with Jack Rollins and Charles Joffe late in 1989, Allen told his ICM agent, Sam Cohn, he wanted a "payday," a Hollywood term meaning an easy and lucrative acting job.

A divorce comedy by Roger L. Simon and Paul Mazursky, with Mazursky pegged to direct, had crossed Cohn's desk. Another Jewish filmmaker from Brooklyn—with that background as integral to Mazursky's films as it was to Allen's—Mazursky had tried coaxing Allen into previous projects. Mazursky's sophisticated run of pictures in the 1970s and '80s compared favorably to Allen's, and his recent *Enemies, A Love Story*, based on a novel by Isaac Bashevis Singer, its script cowritten by Mazursky and Simon, had yielded a Best Supporting Actress nomination for Anjelica Huston in the role that immediately followed *Crimes and Misdemeanors*.

The prospective *Scenes from a Mall* was entirely an ICM package. The script already had a commitment from Meryl Streep, who was also represented by Cohn and ICM. When Simon and Mazursky went into a meeting at the Walt Disney Studios, which was producing the film, the discussion of likely costars revolved around leading men such as Harrison Ford and Jack Nicholson. The partners were taken aback when Jeffrey Katzenberg, the chairman of the studio, who along with Michael Eisner ran the Disney operation, asked, "What about Woody?" A baby boomer and unabashed Allen fan, Katzenberg first had met Allen at a Sue Mengers dinner party and they stayed in touch. He had loved "Oedipus Wrecks" from *New York Stories*, which was underwritten by Disney's Touchstone division. "Katzenberg said he had been speaking with Woody," Simon said, "and, given this script with Paul directing, he might do it. We should go home and think it over."

Mazursky and Simon engaged in only a minimum of mulling, however, before agreeing to "the most important active filmmaker in world cinema, the auteur of auteurs," in Simon's words, "the king of the Jews." ("We'd call him that on the set, although not to his face, of course.") They did worry about "Woody always being Woody no matter who he played," in this case a man long married to a wife played by Meryl Streep, the supreme actress of her era. Their marriage would fall apart during a mall shopping spree, with mutual confessions of infidelity reducing them to tears. Had Allen ever wept in a movie before? No. The scene might require "an actual trained performer who could act roles." Who were they kidding? Both "wanted Woody with a fever."

Faster than you could say hold your horses, Meryl Streep, whose commitment had been penciled in, changed her mind. "She wouldn't do the movie with Woody." Mazursky and Simon had "avoided the obvious fact that Meryl, having worked with Allen on *Manhattan*, knew that Woody couldn't act," Simon recalled. "To his credit, Allen said as much to Paul in response to the script. He wasn't a real actor. He couldn't cry. He could just be himself." Just as quickly, however, Bette Midler, who had starred in Mazursky's huge hit *Down and Out in Beverly Hills* in 1986, agreed to portray Allen's wife. Disney preferred Midler anyway, "someone more commercial, funnier" than Streep, in Simon's words, a better match with Allen. And Allen liked the idea of Midler, whose talent he respected and whom he knew, from his growing interest in astrology, shared his birthday—December 1, albeit in 1945—making her a decade younger than the man who would play her husband.

The leads got $5 million each, "quite a munificent sum for that time," Simon recalled, "even for Hollywood." Still, Allen made a few unusual stipulations. The story had been specifically situated inside the Beverly Center, the eight-story, block-size indoor shopping mall between San Vicente and La Cienega Boulevards at the conjunction of West Hollywood and Beverly Hills. Allen didn't care to stay in Los Angeles for more than a few days, however, so this mandated the mocking up of another mall in Stamford, Connecticut, near Frog Hollow to resemble the Beverly Center, with the mall's interiors replicated on a Queens soundstage, "at ridiculous expense," according to Simon. "Woody also demanded to be ferried back and forth to California in the Disney jet with his then significant other Mia Farrow and a number of their adopted children."

Not that Allen was the type of guy likely to be spotted at any mall. "I don't know that I've ever been on a shopping mall," he told interviewer William E. Geist for *Rolling Stone* in 1987. "You said '*on* a shopping mall.' Shopping malls are enclosed, you know," Geist explained. "Oh, are they?" replied Allen. "Then I've never been in one, no. Then what am I thinking of? When I visit Mia in Connecticut, sometimes she'll go to buy something, and I'll be in the car with her, and I'll get off, and that's where I think I've been in a mall."

"And you don't get *off* a car either. You get out of a car," Geist pointed out.

"OK," Allen said.

The project's biggest incongruity was probably not the mall. It was Allen as a samurai-ponytailed Beverly Hills sports attorney long married to and in love with Midler who, "unflatteringly costumed," in Simon's words, "looked like somebody's Jewish aunt from Great Neck—the very thing Woody had been fleeing his entire life."

Still, everyone went to work with smiley faces. Except for brief shenanigans for Jean-Luc Godard, Allen had not truly emoted for another director since *The Front*, and his wary attitude about being controlled by someone else's script and direction had not evolved much in the intervening time. Allen the actor certainly knew his lines, but he intimidated Mazursky, and he failed to strike up any rapport, romantic or comedic, with costar Midler. A "cold fish," Simon said of Allen. "With the exception of production photographer Brian Hamill [Allen's own longtime unit still photographer], whose presence on the film was another Woody requirement, Allen rarely, if ever, talked casually to anybody on the set. He never palled around with the crew or the other actors, as most stars do to some degree. He didn't talk to me and he barely talked to Paul Mazursky when I was around. Nor did he work very hard. He'd shoot a couple of takes, then quickly say something like 'You got it?' to Paul and make a move to walk off. No matter what, he was gone to his trailer by four."

Simon suspected Allen's "quick departures" were prompted by the presence of Soon-Yi waiting in the trailer. The nineteen-year-old was an extra in the movie. As a young girl Soon-Yi had aspired to be a psychologist, according to Farrow. More recently she had voiced aspirations of becoming a model or actress. Although Farrow had already put her children on camera in several movies, she tried dissuading Soon-Yi. "I asked Woody to please not encourage her," Farrow said. "But his casting director was already sending her on auditions."

To be fair, Farrow was often waiting in Allen's trailer too. After the East Coast filming in June and July, the actress with some of her children, including Soon-Yi, flew with Allen on the Disney jet to Los Angeles for establishing shots inside and outside the Beverly Center. The trip was a tribulation for Allen, who complained incessantly about California. The couple alleviated their tensions during off-hours, according to the *Los Angeles Times*, with an actual shopping spree at the Beverly Center, where they dropped "about $500 worth of loot" at stores like F.A.O. Schwarz, buying Flik Flak watches to help toddlers like Satchel learn to tell time.

Again, watching Allen like a hawk around five-year-old Dylan, Farrow didn't pay as much attention to Allen with Soon-Yi. Allen's behavior with the little blonde girl had improved markedly, Farrow still believed (she later wrote), although he continued to cross lines. One day later that summer, her mother, Maureen O'Sullivan, her sister Tisa, and the film director happened to be visiting Frog Hollow on the same day. "Woody started rubbing some sunscreen on Dylan's shoulders," Farrow wrote in her memoir, quoting Tisa. "Then he got to her bottom and there he took his time. It was a momentary thing, but it was so *glaringly* inappropriate."

The summer of 1990 was also when Allen was stricken with a mysterious illness. He was "without energy, exhausted all the time. Throughout the workday, at every opportunity, he would lie down," Farrow wrote in her memoir. "His doctors thought he might have Lyme disease or chronic fatigue syndrome. There was talk about Epstein-Barr. . . . He went days without shaving or washing his hair." Late that summer, after completing *Scenes from a Mall*, the clockwork artist nonetheless completed the script for the next Woody Allen picture.

THE NEW SCRIPT was based on Allen's one-act play *Death*, which had been included among the pieces in his first anthology, *Without Feathers*, published fifteen years earlier. After *Death* became a perennial for little theater groups, it was published separately as a stage play and disappeared from future editions of *Without Feathers*.

Allen rewrote and expanded *Death* into the Kafkaesque *Shadows and Fog*, which was the type of dark farce his longtime friend Mary Bancroft had been urging upon him for years. He set the screen story entirely at night in a nameless central European town in the early 1920s, with the plot revolving around a milquetoast clerk named Kleinman. Kleinman is dragged from his sleep by a mob of vigilantes pursuing a mysterious serial killer preying on the town. Eventually, the mob turns on Kleinman, targeting him as their chief suspect. Allen bolstered the original one-act with bordello goings-on, pivotal scenes in a Catholic church, and the activities of members of a traveling circus troupe, whose addled magician would give the picture a *poof!* ending.

Planning the production, Allen made the expensive decision to evoke the German Expressionist silent-era masterpieces of Fritz Lang, F. W. Murnau, and G. W. Pabst by artificially simulating the streets and buildings of an imaginary European town of the 1920s. Santo Loquasto was tasked with designing and erecting "the biggest set ever made at the Kaufman Astoria Studios," in Allen's words. Only once before, for the ill-fated *September*, had Allen worked entirely indoors on soundstages. Moreover, Carlo Di Palma would shoot the movie in black and white, deploying a new high-contrast stock that would explore indeterminate shades of gray.

The cameras rolled in mid-November. Allen was Kleinman, and Mia Farrow was the circus sword-swallower, whose devotion to a morose clown (John Malkovich) is taxed by his refusal to get married. "I want to have a baby!" the sword-swallower begs the clown, which is a line from many Hollywood movies, but which also echoed Allen's real-life conversations with Farrow. People didn't yet suspect any breach between the filmmaker and his leading lady, but some did think it odd when Farrow said, "It's your turn to pick up the kids!" before angrily stalking off the set some days. Allen was known to call a break and jump into his limo or, if it was late in the day, set up an elaborate shot and rush away for the errand before shooting the scene the next day.

Allen also cast two-time Oscar-nominee Madeline Kahn as the Bear Lady of the circus troupe; Donald Pleasance as the town's deranged coroner; Lily Tomlin, Jodie Foster, and Kathy Bates as a contingent of cuddly prostitutes; and Madonna, John Cusack, Julie Kavner, Wallace Shawn, Kate Nelligan, Fred Gwynne, and Kenneth Mars in various supporting roles. On paper, the many known quantities seemed a good augury.

But *Shadows and Fog* was a problem-plagued project from the outset. A brief IATSE strike, which affected all American filming underway, drove up the production budget; so did Allen's perfectionist reshoots. Soon the picture was in the ledgers at $20 million, which was Allen's highest expenditure ever up to that time. Later, Allen said he "knew" the Kafkaesque comedy "was destined for commercial doom" even as he was shooting it.

Meanwhile, *Alice* bowed at Christmas. The new Woody Allen movie was a "charming piffle," Peter Rainer generously wrote in the *Los Angeles Times*, and again the script drew an Academy Award nomination—*Alice*'s only Oscar recognition. The film was neither fish nor fowl, however, and the convoluted story was too abstruse for the masses. As happened with *September* and *Another Woman*, poor word-of-mouth hurt bookings. In a year in which the number-one movie, *Ghost*, grossed half a billion dollars worldwide, *Alice* brought in $7.3 million.

TODDLER SATCHEL AND little Dylan kept their appointments with therapists and tutors. Allen took Soon-Yi to Knicks games and brought her to

Michael's Pub to hear his jazz band on Monday nights. He drew closer, more confidential, conspiratorial with Farrow's daughter. In her senior year Soon-Yi left behind her *Little House on the Prairie* wardrobe and began to wear very fitted clothing, her sister Daisy said later. Soon-Yi and Lark finished high school in June. "Woody surprised us all by showing up at Soon-Yi's graduation," Farrow wrote.

Later that month Lark (age eighteen) and Daisy (sixteen) were arrested for attempting to shoplift $342 of lacy lingerie from a G. Fox & Co. store at the Danbury Mall. As part of their probation agreement, they were left behind when, in late June, Allen and the Farrow-Previns flew by private jet to Europe for the fourth time in five years. Stopping first in Rome, Allen finished four of the five commercials he had agreed to create for the Italian supermarket chain La Coop Nordemilia. He had gotten a head start with Carlo Di Palma behind the camera in New York. Comedian Roberto Benigni was among the well-known Italian players who leaped at the chance to be directed by Allen in supermarket advertising. According to the business press, Allen took the job because he liked the idea of the grocery cooperative, and his spots did not have to promote specific food items. But the advertisements were also another form of payday: Allen was going to earn a reported $5 million.

Then it was on to Shannon Airport in Ireland, where the family embarked on a sentimental journey across the homeland of Farrow's mother, Maureen O'Sullivan, who had been born in Boyle, County Roscommon, eighty years before in 1911. With two chauffeur-driven limousines transporting four or five Farrow children, a nanny, and an assistant to Allen, the party did not travel lightly. They caravaned down the western Atlantic Coast, visiting Cong, Kenmare and Connemara, Limerick City in Munster, and seaside Rossnowlagh in County Donegal. The entourage took over multiple suites and entire floors of ancient castles repurposed as hotels. At one stopover, Allen tipped Guinness with the locals. The gray, rainy weather, he told the Irish press, was very nice and conformed to his aesthetic vision. Soon-Yi, among the group, was not identified in most accounts.

In her memoir Farrow reported no tension with Allen on this trip either. The main friction was between Allen and Satchel, who "acted out" around his father. "In vain," Farrow insisted later, she tried to "promote a better relationship between Woody and Satchel. When Woody took Dylan off into other rooms, I would mime, 'Take Satchel too.' When he brought Dylan a present, I asked that he bring one for Satchel, and for Moses too. I pointed out Satchel's many accomplishments and interests and I suggested ways that Woody might become involved" with the toddler, who was then three years of age going on four. The director, later defending himself, said he "overcompensated" with little Dylan because the actress was "always breastfeeding Satchel."

After three weeks the private jet flew the family to Switzerland. The vacation ended in Paris, the city that never lost its siren call for Allen, where they stayed under false names at the Ritz. Allen met with European journalists and the head of the Cannes Film Festival, Gilles Jacob, who implored him to send another Woody Allen film to Cannes—as he'd last done with *Hannah and Her Sisters* and *Radio Days*—and this time come along himself as an honored guest, or head of the jury. ("We invite him every year," Jacob said.) Mornings and in spare time, as always, Allen wrote as he traveled, returning to the US with his next script—*Husbands and Wives*—a savage comedy about romantic illusions, broken marriages, and older men's infidelities with young women.

Allen doesn't mention the European family trips in his memoir. The opposite: Reciting a litany of complaints against Farrow, he wrote, "No intimacy, not much dining together, *no traveling* [author's emphasis] . . ."

PERHAPS THE IRISH sojourn was a sop to Farrow, or Allen's beau geste. He and his leading lady, arm-in-arm, looked surprisingly sanguine in the press coverage, giving no hint that this was the calm before the apocalypse. In later testimony Farrow would say their romance had evaporated and their sex life had become nonexistent by mid-1991. "Maybe I'd made a mistake having him in the room during my caesarean," she told Kristi Groteke.

One of Farrow's solutions, astonishingly, was to push for adopting another child with special needs. The actress had a bottomless hole inside of her, Farrow told Groteke, which needed filling up with orphans. It took awhile to convince Allen, and during the Irish vacation he acceded to another adoption—sort of. Allen, "who had begun to believe that Ms. Farrow was growing more remote from him and that she might discontinue his access to Dylan," according to the *Allen v. Farrow* court judgment, "said that he would not take 'a lousy attitude towards it [another orphan]' if, in return, Ms. Farrow would sponsor his adoption of Dylan and Moses."

The court language compressed the actual sequence of events. Farrow had begun her campaign for another Asian orphan in the spring of 1991, displaying photographs of a six-year-old Vietnamese boy who was unable to walk for mysterious medical reasons, and who could be seen in snapshots with a blind girl a few years older than him. The girl had lost her eyesight due to a childhood ailment. "Woody commented on how pretty she was," according to Farrow, "and said, 'If it's not a big deal, why don't you see if you can get the girl too?' " While Allen was writing *Husbands and Wives* on the European trip, Farrow was finalizing the adoption details.

When they returned, in late August, Soon-Yi packed off to Drew University in Madison, New Jersey, a small, private, liberal arts college on a forested campus, situated about twenty-five miles west of Manhattan. Farrow, in September, flew to Vietnam, taking along almost-four-year-old Satchel with best friend Casey Pascal and Pascal's husband. "Woody was adamant that Dylan, now six, should not be taken out of school," the actress recalled. "But he was very supportive about the trip and about the new kids. He even tried to coax a film studio to provide a jet for the trip, and when that fell through, he offered to help me pay for it." Lark, Sascha, Fletcher, and Daisy would band together to help watch over six-year-old Dylan; Soon-Yi, living in a dormitory at Drew, promised to visit Manhattan on weekends; and Farrow hired extra babysitters with a therapist on call.

In Hanoi, lugging a suitcase full of toys for the orphans, Farrow met the six-year-old boy she called Sanjay, who "even given the incalculable deprivations of his circumstances," in her words, "did not appear to be functioning normally." The girl, eleven-year-old Nguyen Thi Tam—Tam for short—had been moved to an institution for the blind. Tam recoiled when Farrow offered her a stuffed bear, believing it to be a real bear. Satchel, with his blue eyes and shoulder-length white-blond hair, resembling a little girl as much as a boy, was a magnet in public. "Everybody wanted to touch his hair," Farrow said. It seemed a good omen when one morning, for the second time in her life, the actress encountered Mother Teresa, who was enjoying breakfast at the Hanoi Government Guest House, where both were staying. "God bless you," said the missionary, remembering her.

Even though the six-year-old Vietnamese boy appeared to be suffering from "profound retardation and degenerative illnesses" that robbed him of normal physical activity, Farrow consulted with experts and spoke to Allen and then filled out the final paperwork that would bring him to the US. Tam was slated to arrive in the US later, after the New Year. Sanjay arrived in mid-October, but his afflictions consumed Farrow and the household. The Vietnamese boy was diagnosed with "a rare type of cerebral palsy," Farrow remembered, and the six-year-old screamed nonstop "so after only five traumatic, heartbreaking days in our home, he left to join his forever family," in Farrow's words. Another willing adoptive family had been arranged as a backup.

All of a sudden then, the obstacles to Allen adopting Dylan evaporated. Farrow's version of events: "He and his lawyers had a new idea, one they hoped would be effective: if he were to adopt Moses, the only other child in the family who had no father, his petition would be much stronger." Farrow insisted adopting Moses was Allen's way to "piggyback Dylan's adoption." Allen's version was that his adoption of Moses was more Farrow's idea than his. Either way the actress endorsed the scheme. "Although Woody's behavior with Dylan was not yet on course, I believed he would continue to work on it in good faith." Farrow made the film director promise he wouldn't take Dylan for sleepovers at his house if the actress wasn't also staying overnight "and that if, God forbid, our relationship should ever falter, that he would never seek custody." Both adoptions were going to be made official before Christmas, right around Satchel's fourth birthday on December 19.

BY THEN, THE Allen-Farrow love story was loveless. Their relationship had proven a fruitful partnership, however unconventional, of mutual affection and shared professional interests, lasting more than a decade. Still, the absence of sworn betrothal, and the conflicts over adoptions and children—especially over Dylan and Satchel—had killed the romance, such as it ever existed. It seems reasonable to argue Farrow knew as little about conventional motherhood, and she was as intolerant of anything outside her own way of family life, as Allen was ignorant of conventional fatherhood and blind to his own faults. As Dr. Susan Coates testified later, "The amount of non-agreement between them was so great that it led me to ask why they were together."

Their sex life had declined rapidly, all parties agree, following the surprise announcement of Farrow's pregnancy in the spring of 1987. All the time they were together, Allen had enjoyed assignations with other women, according to Kristi Groteke, who later wore a device fitted on her by an "electronics Einstein" friendly with Farrow, and secretly recorded his limousine driver for courtroom use. The driver, declining to name any names, told her the filmmaker "had plenty of affairs during his twelve years with Mia," presumably even more toward the end of the time, when they were no longer sleeping together. Groteke was mystified as to whether the actress herself had any sex drive. "I wonder if it [sex] was ever really important to her," Groteke wrote.

In the fall of 1991, Allen had more excuses than usual to avoid sleeping with Farrow. He felt fatigued all the time and worried about Lyme disease, which he thought he might have contracted that summer in Frog Hollow. Or, possibly, it was some sort of chronic fatigue syndrome. He also suspected the possibility of HIV, according to Farrow, because (she said) Allen told the actress he had patronized prostitutes in the past. She wondered. "We've been together for nearly a dozen years," Farrow reminded him. But the incubation period for HIV, the sexually spread epidemic whose AIDS syndrome swept the world in the early 1980s, was lengthy and indeterminate, Allen said. Farrow urged Allen to get tested and he did, according to Farrow, with the negative results reported back around December 1, his fifty-sixth birthday. Still, they did not return to the same bed.

THE ARTISTIC AND box office sputtering of recent Woody Allen movies, especially *September*, *Another Woman*, and *Alice*, were inextricably bound up with his private life and the actress for whom they were meant as showcases. *Shadows and Fog*—also with Farrow, but for the first time in several years with Allen costarring—loomed as another disaster for Orion Pictures. Eric Pleskow's heart sank at the early screening for insiders. Despite nineteen Oscar nominations for its 1991 slate of films, Orion paradoxically faced overall losses so persistent and debt so bottomless the studio had halted all production months earlier. Despite those auguries, in August Arthur Krim and Pleskow extended Allen's exclusive contract for three more Orion films.

Mike Medavoy had departed Orion. With the handwriting on the wall, in 1990 Medavoy jumped to TriStar Pictures, a Sony division soon to merge with Columbia Pictures. Acutely aware of Orion's burgeoning problems, in the fall Allen asked studio officials for assurances Orion could fully finance his next project, *Husbands and Wives*, the planned follow-up to *Shadows and Fog*. For the first time, Krim and Pleskow had to say no to Woody Allen. They candidly advised him to look elsewhere—another studio—for the production budget. *Husbands and Wives* was not any kind of Disney/Touchstone film (ultimately it got an R rating), so Jeffrey Katzenberg was out of the running. Medavoy and TriStar stepped up, taking over the project with an option, if Orion continued to falter, of picking up the remaining films in his contract. Medavoy vowed to safeguard his independence as much as possible with autonomy and the same protections Allen counted on from Orion.

With Krim facing health issues, the commander of the sinking ship was Pleskow. In fact, Orion had a bunch of completed films in its vaults, which the company couldn't afford to distribute because distribution costs typically doubled the investment. Majority stockholder John Kluge desperately sought a buyer for the moribund studio, which had to borrow funds just to release *Shadows and Fog*. In more ways than one, Pleskow knew, at its very first screening, *Shadows and Fog* knelled the end of an era. Orion filed for bankruptcy in December.

Husbands and Wives therefore began filming in early November as a TriStar production. Allen's script followed the frayed marriages of two couples. One of the couples is Gabe (Allen) and Judy (Farrow), who have been together for ten years but are drifting apart. She works for an art magazine. Gabe is the reputable writer of "sad funny" short stories, who makes ends meet by teaching creative writing to college students. Judy yearns to be a poet and wants to get pregnant while she still can. Gabe thinks it's "cruel to bring life into this terrible world." The spark in their marriage has dimmed. Nowadays they "do it less and less," Judy complains.

Dining with Gabe and Judy at a Chinese restaurant, their long-married friends Jack (Sydney Pollack) and Sally (Judy Davis) announce a surprise: they are amicably separating. "People grow apart," explains Jack. The oversexed Jack takes up with a young aerobics instructor (Lysette Anthony), who is into tofu and crystals. Sally tries dating Michael (Liam Neeson), Judy's handsome and likeable office colleague. Allen had been following Neeson ever since *The Good Mother*, which starred Diane Keaton. The actor's strapping physical presence, towering over everyone else in the cast, prompted John Lahr to describe him as "a sequoia of sex."

Sally is a cold, cerebral Radcliffe grad; her thesis mounted an attack on fascist Bauhaus design, and she is obsessed with interior decoration. Hilariously, she divides men into hedgehogs and foxes, but Sally herself can't reach an orgasm, even with the good-hearted Michael.* Judy develops her own crush on Michael, while Gabe is drawn to a "gifted pupil" in his writing course. Her name is Rain, a variation of the first name of Austrian poet and writer Rainer Maria Rilke, most recently quoted in *Another Woman*. "I was born in a hurricane!" Rain boasts. Gabe keeps his flirtation secret from Judy. He and Rain take long, confiding walks. "Your approbation means more to me than anything," Rain tells Gabe admiringly. He wants Rain to read his novel in progress.

Although Allen and Farrow were impersonating a couple akin to themselves—Gabe and Judy have been married for as long as the director and actress were together—the casting, as with *Hannah and Her Sisters*, was Farrow's to decide. According to her own publicist, John Springer, Farrow "decided not to take the Judy Davis role, though she could have. She played the part she did because she felt it was more complex and demanding."

Twenty-one-year-old British-born Emily Lloyd, who had just finished emoting in Robert Redford's *A River Runs Through It*, started out playing the coquettish coed Rain, but Lloyd was battling mental health problems and Allen could not find the right rapport with her in their early scenes together, shot at Barnard College. The actress was thrown, Lloyd defended herself later, when one day "a union guy stormed on to the set to protest that Woody Allen didn't use black actors in his films." And "it didn't help that, for the scenes he didn't appear in, Woody would bark directions through a Tannoy loudspeaker system," she said. When Allen did speak to Lloyd, he showed little empathy. "He thought I spent too long on the setups, whereas he worked quickly and wanted scenes shot rapidly with an air of spontaneity." After several weeks Lloyd was abruptly let go.

Then Allen hired eighteen-year-old Juliette Lewis, who had just given her breakout performance, for which she would be Oscar-nominated, in

---

* This was an in-joke reference to British philosopher Isaiah Berlin's famous essay "The Hedgehog and the Fox," which divided thinkers and writers into two categories: hedgehogs, who see the world through the lens of a single idea; and foxes, who draw on diverse life experiences. Mia Farrow was a reader of Berlin and carried around *The Crooked Timber of Humanity* during the filming of *Husbands and Wives*.

Martin Scorsese's remake of *Cape Fear*. Allen proceeded to reshoot all the Gabe-Rain scenes with Lewis, who brought her special quality of edgy sexuality to the coed character.

Allen saw *Husbands and Wives*, in embryo, as unusually graphic for him, with frank language and explicit sexual situations. Again, he would give a rare nod to realism, as he had done with *Crimes and Misdemeanors*. But the jittery, documentary-like visual style he planned diverged far from the Italian neorealist masters. He'd incorporate handheld camerawork. There would be little camera rehearsal, and he'd favor prolonged takes without interruption, with Carlo Di Palma hovering over the shoulders of actors and constantly moving around and darting in for jarring close-ups that captured painful intimacies like minefield explosions. "Pick up the camera, forget about the dolly, just handhold the thing and get what you can," Allen described the new style to Stig Björkman. "When I first made films," he said, "you tend to . . . do a lot of coverage and protect yourself in many ways. And then, as time goes on, you get more and more knowledgeable and experienced and you drop all that, and you let your instincts operate more freely and you don't worry so much about the niceties."

Poker-faced as he guided scenes in the fall of 1991, it appeared the director was never looser, more relaxed. Filming the new way was cheaper, faster, more volatile, and creative. "It's the first time in years," Allen told Björkman, "that I came in under budget." Editor Susan E. Morse would add staccato cuts within scenes, similar to how Charlotte Rampling's mental breakdown was visualized in *Stardust Memories*. The fictional narrative would be interspersed with interviews with the actors in character, the questioning and voice-over narration assigned to costumer Jeffrey Kurland, who had supplanted Joel Schumacher—now busy in Hollywood as a director of big-budget blockbusters—as the person on the backstage team Allen saw most often after hours.

"THERE'S NO CORRELATION [to the situation with Mia in the content and style of *Husbands and Wives*]," Allen later told Eric Lax. "I was experimenting. I felt that with the documentary style it should be open, sexually and cinematically."

At nights and on weekends, though, Allen was up to secrets and lies eerily akin to Gabe's. Having initially bonded with Soon-Yi Previn over homework and the Knicks, he and Mia Farrow's daughter found common ground in griping about the actress, who was always calibrating and criticizing Allen's fatherhood and, according to Soon-Yi, similarly criticizing and calibrating her. Farrow had Catholic hang-ups about fathers physically touching their daughters, with a long list of dos and don'ts concerning Dylan. Meanwhile Allen thought she locked the door to her room for hours, lying nude in bed with Satchel, breastfeeding the little boy. Satchel still behaved negatively with his father, which Allen blamed on Farrow's overmothering of him.

Soon-Yi had an even harsher opinion of her mother, Allen was astonished to learn. "She and Mia didn't get along, and life at their home was quite different when I was not present," he said he was told. Later, much of what Soon-Yi said about her upbringing would be disputed by Farrow, and by some—though not all—of the Farrow-Previns. Soon-Yi described their relationship as "oil and water." Farrow repeatedly told her she was "hopelessly backward," Soon-Yi said, and slapped and spanked her when she rebelled against house rules.

Soon-Yi backed her statements up with painful anecdotes. According to Soon-Yi, the adopted older sisters were deputized, more often than the biological children, as "domestics" with grocery shopping, cooking, and cleaning chores. Farrow eschewed traditional maternal duties, and as Soon-Yi approached puberty her mother didn't pass on any makeup skills, "never taught me how to use a tampon, and my babysitter got me my first bra." Not once during girlhood, according to Soon-Yi, did Farrow "take her to a movie, a show, a museum, or even a walk in Central Park." She did not have a single pleasant memory of her upbringing, Soon-Yi insisted.

Soon-Yi also had prickly relationships with certain siblings, and she admitted detesting Fletcher, her mother's biological favorite. The actress drummed it into Allen's head too, he wrote later, that "Fletcher at four had a better brain than Soon-Yi at nine." If Fletcher was her mother's pet, as nanny Kristi Groteke confirmed, "Soon-Yi was her most frequent scapegoat," as Moses Farrow corroborated in 2018. "My sister had an independent streak and, of all of us, was the least intimidated by Mia. . . . For all of us, life under my mother's roof was impossible if you didn't do exactly what you were told, no matter how questionable the demand."

Listening sympathetically to Soon-Yi, Allen could not help but recall the early red flags in his relationship with Farrow, who up to this time had been his leading lady in fourteen Woody Allen pictures—who'd been his girlfriend for over a decade, who was the mother of his son, Satchel, and, also, his soon-to-be-adopted children Dylan and Moses. Allen recalled Farrow's premature determination to get married and bear his child. The actress always had favored Fletcher over the other children, Allen believed. Was Farrow's supermother image a sort of elaborate guise? Had Farrow always been, from the first with Allen, like the character the filmmaker had pegged for her in *Husbands and Wives*—a "passive-aggressive" pusher of her own agenda?

Over the two years that Allen kept increasing company with Soon-Yi, the young woman's confidences and confessions helped transform his view of Farrow, even as his estrangement from the actress deepened. Allen found the daughter Farrow had maligned (according to them) uncommonly bright and companionable. "I began to realize [Soon-Yi] was not an empty young woman as Mia had painted her but quite an intelligent, feeling, perceptive one," Allen wrote in *Apropos of Nothing*. "It was the start of a friendship that would slowly grow over time and climax with the preposterous realization that we cared a great deal about each other."

Allen was devoted to long, slow flirtations with women that might or might not build to a fruition. Allen had already demonstrated, repeatedly in real life and fictions—with the Tracy types he had dated before writing *Manhattan* as the perfect example—that he saw high-school-age women, as young as seventeen (the age of legal consent), as fair game.

Living in a dormitory at Drew University, Soon-Yi kept in close touch with Allen, with (as court records would attest) many dozens of phone calls between them. Away from home and alone for the first time, Soon-Yi felt like one of those "lost souls" that populate Woody Allen films. She had trouble adjusting to college. She asked Allen's advice about classes, changing her major, even switching to another school. On weekends, Soon-Yi visited New York and saw Allen. Those visits continued secretly when Farrow returned from Southeast Asia.

One weekend, during the making of *Husbands and Wives*, Allen set up a screening of *The Seventh Seal* for Soon-Yi in the green-walled screening room of the Park Avenue building where he maintained his offices, the Ingmar Bergman film he loved above all, which he had seen and reseen many times over the years. To "a young, attractive girl in from college," he wrote in *Apropos of Nothing*, "what could be more enjoyable than seeing a black-and-white film set in medieval Scandinavia dealing with the plague, death, and the emptiness of life?" Finally, on that Saturday, in a scene straight out of a Woody Allen movie, he yielded to the temptation and kissed the college girl. "I was wondering when you were going to make a move," Soon-Yi responded.

He was "sleepwalking into a mess," as Gabe/Allen puts it in *Husbands and Wives*. Or, like an ostrich with his "head in the sand," as Sidney J. Munsinger (Allen) explains himself in his later TV series *Crisis in Six Scenes*. Allen had always existed in a bubble, compartmentalizing his films and his life. He was like the callous father played by Gunnar Björnstrand in another Bergman masterpiece, *Through a Glass Darkly*, who explains his self-absorption thusly: "One draws a magic circle around oneself to keep everything out that doesn't fit one's secret games."

He and Soon-Yi were protected by a magic circle. Allen was oblivious to anything but his attraction to the college student. Their love affair began "the next time she came in from college," Allen later wrote. "We spent a few afternoons walking and talking, delighting in each other's company and, of course, going to bed."

One of those afternoons the couple did something else. Someone "who didn't know I had no interest in cameras," in his words, had given Allen the gift of a Polaroid instant camera. "The idea arose that we do some erotic photographs if I could figure out how to work the goddamned camera. Turned out she [Soon-Yi] could work it, and erotic photos they were, shots well calculated to boost one's blood up to two twelve Fahrenheit."

HOLIDAY SCENES IN Hollywood movies appeal to a wide demographic, with such scenes often providing a touching uplift. A surprising number of Woody Allen films honor these holiday conventions—often Thanksgiving (*Hannah and Her Sisters*), but Christmas too (there is a Beverly Hills Christmas in *Annie Hall* and Christmas even provides a grace note at the end of *Interiors*). In Allen's work the holiday scenes afforded the filmmaker, wary of expressing emotions on- or offscreen, an opportunity to end his pictures on notes of tenderness and humanity. Naturally Allen himself "disliked

Christmas and did not celebrate it himself," said Mia Farrow, "except for one year, when he put up a bare tree for us in his apartment with a black bat at the top."

The 1991 holiday season should have been a merry one for Allen. December was a milestone in several ways: Allen turned fifty-six, and his AIDS test came back negative (if Farrow is to be believed); and then one week before Christmas, his adoption of Moses and Dylan became final. "As far as I know," said his lawyer Paul Martin Weltz, "it's a first," i.e., the first adoption by an unmarried couple legalized by the State of New York.

Beneath the surface portrait of a happy family in Woody Allen films, however, there were adversarial parents and wounded children. Allen and the Farrow-Previns got together for Christmas 1991 at the Langham, an occasion made festive by Yuletide music spilling from the stereo and the bowls of fruit punch Farrow set out on tables. Still, Allen and Farrow "got on each other's nerves," the actress recalled, in part because the director could not stand the ceaseless Christmas carols and pointedly pressed his own apple drink from the juicer.

Christmas came and went, and so did New Year's. There would be a lot of dispute later about when exactly Allen first slept with Soon-Yi, but the date of the Polaroids was Sunday, January 12, 1992. "Mastermind that I was," Allen recalled, "I sequestered the photos in a drawer—but as it turned out, not all the provocative little snapshots. A number of them I had brilliantly put on my fireplace mantel. . . ."

On Monday, January 13, Farrow brought "one of the children," as she narrated in *What Falls Away*, over to Allen's apartment for his weekly session with a psychiatrist. The child was Satchel, who had turned four before Christmas. The previous night—the night of the day Allen took nude Polaroids of Soon-Yi—Allen and Farrow had sat in her apartment having a familiar conversation, musing about moving to Paris, the beloved city of their summer vacations. Allen argued that it would make an exciting change for the family, especially Soon-Yi, who might enroll in a French art academy.

Allen was supposed to rendezvous with Farrow at his apartment on January 13 because he and she usually joined Satchel's therapy sessions. He phoned to say he would be late. She had brought along her Isaiah Berlin book. Rummaging around, Farrow entered the den and, reaching for a tissue on the mantel, she spied a bunch of color Polaroid snapshots tucked under the tissue box. "Grabbing them up, the actress stared aghast at a half-dozen photographs of Soon-Yi, reclining nude on a sofa, her legs spread. Allen must have "subconsciously" left the nude Polaroids in a spot where she was bound to find them, Farrow later decided. "He wanted to destroy me," the actress theorized, speaking to nanny Kristi Groteke. "Not only did he want me to know that they were having an affair, but he also wanted me to see it for myself in an ugly, obscene disgusting way."

Allen disputed any ulterior motive in his memoir. "Did I leave the photos exposed to bring the enervated relationship with Mia to a head on purpose? Was it my way of causing a breakup without really realizing it? It was not. It was simply a blunder by a klutz. Sometimes, a cigar is just a blunder by a klutz." Yet Soon-Yi, in *New York* magazine years later, said *maybe* there was "something Freudian" in his lapse.

Shocked and disgusted, Farrow phoned Allen's office. "I found the pictures!" the actress gasped. "Get away from us!" She phoned Soon-Yi, who hung up on her. Confiscating the Polaroids, she rushed home with Satchel, telling Sascha, one of her twenty-one-year-old twins, "Woody's been fucking Soon-Yi! Call André!"—Previn. She barged into Soon-Yi's room, shouting, "*What have you done?*" Allen materialized, pushing into her bedroom where Farrow had retreated. "Sobbing, I tried with all my strength to push him out." She couldn't stop shaking.

"I'm in love with Soon-Yi," Allen said at first (according to Farrow). "I would marry her. . . ."

"Then take her," Farrow replied after a dazed moment of incomprehension, "and get out!"

"No, no," Allen backpedaled agitatedly (according to Farrow). "That's just something I thought of to say in the car coming over here. It's not what I feel. I don't want that. . . ."

Allen stayed at the Langham for hours, trying to calm Farrow down. Suspended between "rage and disbelief and horror," she wept, begging him to leave. "He talked nonstop," saying "everything I had ever wanted to hear during our dozen years." Allen insisted, according to the actress, that he loved only Farrow. The couple could "use this as a springboard into a deeper relationship . . . we have to try and put all of it behind us." The children listened furtively, with "little Satchel crouching under the sink; he must have heard everything."

In truth, Allen didn't know what he wanted at that terrible moment. He hadn't thought it through. As astonishing as it seems, Allen said he had not weighed the consequences of sleeping with his girlfriend's daughter, his children's sister. "Of course I understand her [Farrow's] shock, her dismay, her rage, everything," he explained in *Apropos of Nothing*. "Soon-Yi and I thought we could have our little fling, keep it secret, since Soon-Yi wasn't living at home and I lived alone like a bachelor. I thought it would be a nice experience, and probably Soon-Yi would eventually meet some guy at college and enter a more conventional relationship."

Horrified and infuriated, Farrow scarcely knew what she wanted either. According to Allen, at the family dinner that night the actress informed her assembled children Allen had "raped" Soon-Yi. In the middle of the dinner that very same rapist strolled in and sat down next to Dylan "as if nothing had happened," Farrow recalled. "He said hi to everybody and started chatting." The older kids, including fourteen-year-old Moses, Allen's newly adopted son, pointedly picked up their dinner plates and left the room. Allen pursued Farrow into the living room where she fled, for "another hour of him talking and talking and me crying." Finally, he left.

Farrow couldn't calm down. She didn't want to calm down. She memorialized her pain and anger by writing a letter to her children, which began, "An atrocity has been committed against our family. . . ." She phoned friends and associates and told them the filmmaker had "raped her underage, retarded daughter," according to Allen. The distraught mother "locked Soon-Yi in her bedroom, hit her and kicked her, and she and André cut off her college tuition. . . . [Farrow] then phoned me in the middle of the night several times to tell me Soon-Yi was awash in guilt and thinking of committing suicide. She's a good actress, and . . . it's unnerving."

The next days and weeks were hell. Experiencing panic attacks, Farrow took antidepressants. She suffered sleepless nights, "filled with rage and tears." Some nights she phoned Allen, screaming at him: Evil, devil, Satan! Other nights Allen phoned her, "ten or twenty times or more and I'd hang up," Farrow recalled.

But they had to communicate civilly. They had too much unfinished business. First there were the children, especially Farrow and Allen's three children. Farrow announced she didn't want Allen in her apartment ever again, nor would she permit the children to visit his place. Was it now or later that Allen understood his parenthood was endangered? That he may have traded Satchel and Dylan—Moses too—for Soon-Yi?

The actress sent her babysitter over to the director's screening room, demanding his keys to the Langham. She changed her locks and phone number, but she'd done that a few times before when the couple had blow-ups and it never lasted very long. Allen just showed up at her place anyway, "harassing her" and refusing to leave, according to nanny Kristi Groteke, whose stream of information came from Farrow, making threats and cursing "at her in a manner totally at odds with his public image." The only thing the couple could agree on, right away, was the children—their mutual three children and all the other Farrow-Previn children—should be signed up for extra therapy "to deal with the trauma," in Farrow's words. "Woody encouraged this and paid for it."

The unfinished business included *Shadows and Fog*, which was finally being given its release in March; the last thing that problematic picture needed was bad publicity. Then there was the next Woody Allen project, for which Farrow had signed an advance contract as the leading lady. And there were a few remaining Gabe and Judy scenes to be filmed for *Husbands and Wives*. The *New York Times* published this final schedule:

January 6: "In the shooting schedule, one scene carries the description: 'Judy and Gabe have no plans to break up. She'd like another child. They're stuck with each other.' "

January 14: "The shooting schedule calls for a scene with this description: 'Gabe is attracted to women who are trouble.' "

January 15: "The shooting schedule calls for a scene in Gabe and Judy's apartment at night with this description: 'They reminisce about things they did. Judy says it's over.' "

The handful of Gabe and Judy scenes "were put off for ten days," Farrow remembered. "I don't know how I went back and filmed them. Woody's behavior to me on the set was gentle, apologetic, and caring."

Chapter 9

1992

The Great Unpleasantness

The Controlmeister Loses Control—Mia Wins Bigly—The Public Is No Wiser

Three weeks earlier, Mia Farrow had signed papers making Allen the adoptive father of six-year-old Dylan and fourteen-year-old Moses. But her discovery of the director's love affair with Soon-Yi—and the upsetting nude Polaroids—changed everything for her. Apart from calling into question Allen's character and her future as an actress in his movies, the director's affair with Soon-Yi ramped up Farrow's established distrust of Allen's behavior toward Dylan, whom he had been showering with attention since infancy. "I no longer believed he could control himself. I no longer believed he was dealing with his problems responsibly. I was no longer sure that his 'inappropriate' and 'intense' behavior was not sexual." Farrow phoned Paul Martin Weltz, the lawyer who arranged Allen's adoption of Moses and Dylan, insisting the director "had deceived me, deceived him, deceived the judge, and deceived the children." Weltz said he was sympathetic, but he didn't know what he could do about the situation. Reaching out to a prominent New York divorce lawyer, Eleanor B. Alter, Farrow asked Alter to work on some type of shared custody agreement and, if possible, undo the adoption. Undoing adoptions was complicated, Alter advised her, but she began talking to Allen's lawyers about custody issues.

Allen was eager to buy time, anxious to keep secret the fact he had slept with Farrow's daughter, his children's older sister, which would make him look, to the public, like some sort of gum-chewing hillbilly in an X-rated cartoon. Ironically, Allen had devoted multiple court actions to protecting his image and brand: attacking a record company for exploiting his likeness on the soundtrack LP for *What's Up, Tiger Lily?*; trying to suppress the first unflattering biography written about him; even, once, suing a home entertainment chain for deploying a Woody Allen "lookalike" in its advertising to promote its video rentals. Now the man who had always so compulsively tweaked his image and persona stood on the brink of blowing up his life and career.

He was "terrified that the public would find out and desperate to get the Polaroids back," Farrow wrote later. *Vanity Fair* writer Maureen Orth may have been among the people with whom Farrow shared those Polaroids. In her later article for the magazine, Orth wrote as though she was staring aghast at the Polaroids: "Each managed to contain both her daughter's face and vagina. . . . [Mia] later told others, 'I felt I was looking straight into the face of pure evil.' " Curiously, in this tell-all era, even now when everything seems available on the Internet, the nude Polaroids, secreted in Farrow's lawyer's office, are the primary visual document in the tangled drama never to have been made public. Farrow always used a loaded word to describe them, a word usually defined in the eye of the beholder: "pornographic." Allen said they were erotic keepsakes between lovers.

The film director's vulnerable position was heightened by Farrow's physical custody of the children, which he had heretofore always accepted. "Visitation and custody of my children," Allen explained in *Apropos of Nothing*, "was a real issue, and on a lawyer's advice I had to be very careful till that issue was resolved."

Fourteen-year-old Moses played his cards without lawyers. After he learned about Allen and Soon-Yi, the teenager recoiled from the filmmaker and announced he no longer wished to have visits from his father. Allen had clear paternity rights with four-year-old Satchel, so Dylan was his crucial concern. As a peacekeeping measure, Farrow's lawyers persuaded Allen to agree to temporarily waive his "custodial rights" of Moses and Dylan, if Farrow were to predecease him, in exchange for daily one-hour supervised visits with Satchel and Dylan on several days of every week. "On February 3 we both signed a document to that effect," Farrow recalled. "I attached a statement, which I showed only to Woody, articulating my concerns about his behavior and my reasons for believing he would be an inappropriate custodial parent; and as proof I included photographs of the Polaroids he'd taken of Soon-Yi." The signed documents and statement were given to Allen's business manager, but not the originals of the Polaroids, which the actress continued to hold hostage.

On that same day, "unbeknownst to me," Farrow wrote in *What Falls Away*, "Woody signed a second document in which he stated that he had no intention of abiding by the agreement we had just signed." Farrow was not apprised of Allen's notarized revocation until six months later, when their custody struggle shifted to the courts. Allen said his lawyers advised him the quit-claim he signed with Farrow possessed no legal force anyway.

The estranged couple managed to patch things up for Farrow's birthday on February 9, dining out for sentimental reasons at Rao's, the Italian restaurant that sparked *Broadway Danny Rose*. Allen gifted Farrow with leather-bound volumes of Emily Dickinson. Hostilities flared anew on Valentine's Day, however. In her kitchen at the Langham Allen presented the actress with "a red satin box filled with chocolates and an embroidered antique heart," according to Orth. Inside the elaborate Victorian valentine Farrow handed to him was a snapshot of her and her children affixed to a red-paper heart. Needles were stabbed into the hearts of the children in the photo, however, with the largest one stuck into Farrow's. (The needles were "toothpicks," according to Orth; nanny Kristi Groteke described them as "real skewers" with a "real knife" piercing Farrow's image.) "My child you used and pierced my heart a hundred times and deep," the actress wrote on her card. She "crossed out the words 'love and joy' imprinted on the Valentine and substituted 'pain,'" according to Groteke.

During the child-custody hearing months later, lawyer Eleanor B. Alter defended the actress's morbid Valentine card: "I think it shows just how anguished she was. . . . I think it shows a woman who felt betrayal so deeply. To be honest, I've had the same feeling myself." In her subsequent courtroom appearance on Allen's behalf, however, Dr. Susan Coates, Satchel's therapist, testified that after learning of the Valentine's Day incident from the director she told Allen she feared for his safety—a warning that worried the filmmaker.

Later in February, the newest member of the family, eleven-year-old Tam, arrived from overseas. The orphan, who had gone blind in childhood, was plunged into the agitated Farrow-Previn household. The actress had spent only minutes with the girl in Vietnam before agreeing to her adoption. Farrow "immediately cut Soon-Yi's face out of a framed photograph that hung on the wall, replacing it with Tam's," according to Groteke, although the actress "guiltily" removed the mutilated photo from sight a few days later.

Curiously, Farrow had finalized arrangements for yet another adoptee: an inner-city African American infant with various medical issues, invariably described as "a black crack baby," in Groteke's words. The first hurdle would be weaning the baby from his addiction. The boy named Isaiah, Farrow's sixth orphan and twelfth child, arrived soon after Tam. According to Orth, Allen "went to the airport with Mia when Isaiah joined the family." Baby Isaiah would replace the Vietnamese orphan with a rare cerebral palsy, whom Farrow had sent away in the fall; or perhaps—time would tell—the new adoptee would replace the sullied Soon-Yi.

Soon Yi had gone back to Drew University, with Allen assuming her tuition and costs after her father André Previn, hearing of her affair with the film director, angrily cut her off. When speaking with Farrow, Allen tried to steer the conversation away from Soon-Yi, but he kept in constant communication with the college girl and Soon-Yi continued to sneak back to New York and visit Allen furtively. Soon-Yi "didn't come home anymore, and she didn't phone me," Farrow said. "To be perfectly honest I wasn't ready to have her back." The actress phoned Soon-Yi on occasion, asking her to promise to stay away from Allen. The college girl hung up.

All the while, during the first half of 1992, Allen worked on the postproduction of *Husbands and Wives* with editor Susan E. Morse. In March, *Shadows and Fog* received underwhelming reviews. The German Expressionist sets and striking photography, the Kurt Weill–Bertolt Brecht score, augmented by vintage Jack Hylton and his Orchestra recordings, were praiseworthy. But the expanded one-act had been stretched thin, and Allen's usual philosophical asides rang hollow. His familiarity with prostitutes, real or imagined, yielded odd brothel scenes with unnaturally happy hookers chuckling over men's fascination with "the little furry animal between our legs." The glittering ensemble barely registered. Fred Gwynne survived with one line in the final cut, and Kate Nelligan was seen only fleetingly in silhouette. Madonna was squandered. The director had tried to get Madeline Kahn into a Woody Allen picture for a decade, but like Lillian Gish,

Michael Keaton, Christopher Walken, and Sam Shepard before her, he didn't hesitate to eliminate the Bear Lady altogether.

In America the sparse audience turnout for *Shadows and Fog* made *September* look like a runaway hit. "A noble misfire," Peter Travers wrote sympathetically in *Rolling Stone*, discerning virtues in the "experimental" work, while finding the script and direction uninspired, with any laughs few and far between.

AMONG THE OUTSTANDING problems the couple had was the little matter of Farrow's participation in the next Woody Allen project. The director planned to dust off "The Couple Next Door," the comedic murder mystery involving a married team of amateur sleuths he had kept in reserve since the early 1970s. Allen and Marshall Brickman had sketched a draft before jettisoning the comedic murder mystery in favor of *Annie Hall*. Farrow had a rare pay-or-play deal for her fifteenth acting appearance for Allen, meaning her salary was guaranteed by the producers as long as she remained healthy and willing to play her part. The pay-or-play clause was itself proof of Farrow's rare status in Allen's movies. Although later characterized as "grossly underpaid for many years" by attorney Alan Dershowitz, the $300,000–350,000 (the sum fluctuated in accounts) Farrow now earned for each film was big money in Allen's tightly calculated world, where actors' salaries had peaked with Michael Keaton's $250,000 for dual roles in *Purple Rose of Cairo*—a disaster for the bottom line in that instance.

In conversations with Kristi Groteke, Farrow made the unverifiable claim she had turned down major roles in several Hollywood productions at Allen's behest, including portraying the mother in the 1991 remake of *Father of the Bride*. Another Allen alumna, Diane Keaton, ultimately played that part. Allen argued "there was no point in my doing other movies unless the director was Ingmar Bergman," according to Farrow. The filmmaker "worried that if she appeared elsewhere, it would make his own movies less exclusive," wrote Groteke. "He let her know that whatever she was being offered was only because of her affiliation with him."

In the first weeks following Farrow's discovery of the Polaroids, the couple mingled furious arguments, bouts of shouting, sobbing, and threats, with hoarse pledges to reconcile and vague talk of their next film project together. Twice the alienated couple repaired to a suite at the Carlyle Hotel, at Farrow's insistence according to Allen, trying to rekindle their sex life. The director's mood was dampened by Farrow's jittery behavior; he worried Farrow was going to threaten suicide, maybe jump out the window, a possibility that terrified him, as he later testified to courtroom chuckles, until Allen realized the hotel room's thick glass windows did not open. "I was placating her," he explained, "on the advice of doctors and lawyers."

Allen collected the advice of therapists too. At Farrow's insistence, he squeezed in extra sessions with several different therapists "and sometimes had appointments twice a day, including Sunday," she later claimed.

The paparazzi still followed the celebrity couple around, and hints of their rupture inevitably leaked into the tabloids. In early March, the New York *Daily News* published a *fumetti*-like panel of a series of photographs "showing Woody Allen and Mia Farrow in what looks like a dispute on a Manhattan street. What readers apparently see is Allen squawking at the actress, then comforting her, a low shot of Farrow wiping tears from her eyes and an exit shot of Farrow entering a building as Allen watches from the bottom of a stoop."

Wire services transmitted the *Daily News* account to dozens of US newspapers. National columnists followed up with hearsay of Allen's infatuation with *Husbands and Wives* actress Judy Davis. The rumors spread: The director and actress were "breaking up, mostly at her instigation." Allen publicly denied the gossip, telling columnist Liz Smith he and Farrow were still very much "together," despite "logistical problems" in their relationship. Allen asked Farrow "to issue a joint press release," she wrote in her memoir, "saying there was nothing to the rumors, that everything was fine, and that we were looking forward" to launching the next Woody Allen film in September. Farrow told Allen she "wouldn't say anything, period, but I wasn't going to lie about it."

The Farrow home was in a constant state of pain and uproar. Fourteen-year-old Moses still refused to meet with Allen, and Farrow permitted Allen to see Dylan and Satchel only if the actress or a third party was present in her apartment to supervise the visit. After Dylan told her therapist Dr. Nancy Schultz she overheard Soon-Yi threatening to kill herself, when Farrow first confronted her daughter over the affair, the therapist insisted Dylan "be told what was going on" because all the shouting and weeping had already traumatized the little blonde girl, and "although I'd asked the older children not to discuss the matter within earshot of the younger ones, obviously they too were upset and needed to talk. When the little kids were supposed to be asleep, we had found them listening outside closed doors," in Farrow's words. Together, the therapist and the actress spoke to Dylan. "Daddy became sort of like a boyfriend to Soon-Yi," Farrow told the six-year-old. "That was wrong because daddies are supposed to be daddies. But he is sorry, and he's getting help, and we promise you it will never happen again." Dylan played with her dolls on the floor during the entire conversation and "never looked up," Farrow wrote. Later, the six-year-old blonde girl relayed this account of Allen's affair with Soon-Yi to four-year-old Satchel, using much the same words, according to Farrow's memoir.

Allen tried to preserve the fragile peace while at the same time he, in his deliberative fashion, also tried to figure out what was the best possible path forward. The filmmaker feared Farrow's power over him and was keenly aware of the tightening influence she wielded over access to his three children. He was frustrated by their short-term agreement, which now restricted his time with his children to one hour every afternoon whenever Farrow was in New York, and overnight once a week when the family was in Frog Hollow. Their lawyers sparred over the subclauses of a permanent custody settlement contract that would be less punitive for Allen.

Farrow hurled a gauntlet in early March. She gathered her family at the Church of the Blessed Sacrament on West Seventy-First between Columbus and Amsterdam Avenues for a group christening of all her children who had not yet been baptized, and all of Casey Pascal's children as well. Farrow's youthful Catholicism had resurged with a vengeance. As she later testified, Allen's affair with Soon-Yi "underlined for me the importance of maintaining your moral roots and having a spiritual life." Matthew, who was employed, was the only one of the older children not present, most of whom already had been baptized. Tam, Isaiah, Satchel, Moses, Dylan, and Soon-Yi, who arrived from Drew University in jeans, had holy water poured over their heads by the priest and were pronounced Catholic. Dianne Wiest, also the mother of adopted children, was named the godmother of Isaiah and held him during the sacramental ceremony that, according to Catholic doctrine, absolved them from original sin and welcomed them into the faith. "Considering everything, it was a happy occasion," Pascal said. The occasion was most unhappy for Allen, however, who was Jewish. Although he had long since ceased to practice the religion of his birth, he was startled to learn his children were now Catholic. Of course, he was not invited to the church, nor to the ensuing celebration at the Langham.

Allen's attitude hardened. He began to lose patience. He was someone who worked all week and weekends when he had a goal. He was always impatient to resolve issues. Why didn't Farrow just forgive, forget, and move on? "By early spring Woody was no longer saying how sorry he was," Farrow wrote, "or that he couldn't live without me, or that he was the most trustworthy person on earth. Now he was saying, 'If we don't get back together, then I'm free to date Soon-Yi, or anybody I want.'" Farrow said it would be "psychological incest" for him to be with Soon-Yi. "This is crazy! I can't be your mother-in-law!" She found "a brilliant Jesuit priest" willing to enlighten Allen as to "the moral dimensions of the situation." Allen said, No, thank you.

Now, whenever Allen visited "he was tough and entirely unrepentant," Farrow said. "If I got angry or cried, he threatened to put me in a mental hospital and have the children taken away." In April, depressed and sleepless, Farrow began threatening suicide again. She sent a message to Allen, slipped into his apartment, phoned to say she was on the verge of self-murder, then stood "by the edge of the terrace and looked down. But I couldn't jump. All I could do was think of the children." Allen raced home "and he was very sympathetic."

Summer arrived, with Farrow arranging a job for Soon-Yi as a counselor at Camp Med-O-Lark, a camp for the arts in Washington, Maine, which would put hundreds of miles between her and Allen. After a few weeks, however, Farrow got a call from the camp director telling her Soon-Yi had been fired after receiving numerous phone calls, more than half a dozen a day, from a mysterious "Mr. George Simon." The incessant phone calls interfered with her responsibilities. The college girl had left the camp. Farrow didn't know where she went. Allen admitted he was "Mr. Simon" but insisted he didn't know where Soon-Yi had gone either. Farrow begged him to leave the college girl alone. "Well, I'd like to do this for you," Allen said, according to Farrow. "I will promise to leave Soon-Yi alone, if you will give me the pictures. Or we can burn them together if you like." It may be Allen wanted the Polaroids as much to protect Soon-Yi's decency as to prop up his own fading hopes to keep the incident a secret. The actress "did not, would not, give them to him," Farrow proudly wrote.

Farrow and most of her children decamped to Frog Hollow for the summer months. Allen remained in New York most of the time, although his tactic was to phone "ten times a day," according to Farrow, asking after Satchel, Dylan, and Moses. His voice on the phone was no more welcome than his once or twice weekly in-person visits to Frog Hollow. However, Farrow also made phone calls, Allen claimed, including "an infamous, chilling call" to Letty Aronson, telling Allen's sister, "He took my daughter, now I'll take his. . . ." In "another vituperative call," the actress supposedly told Allen, "I have something planned for you." According to Allen, "I joked that placing a bomb under the hood of my car was not an appropriate response. She said, 'It's worse.' "

Nanny Groteke was instructed to regard Allen as The Enemy. When the disgraced father arrived for his regulated visits, chauffeur-driven in his limousine, "he would usually be carrying, along with his bag of toys for the kids, a big, barbecued chicken. It is such a New York thing to do. But Woody did it for survival, not style." Allen often "brought his own dinner" to Frog Hollow, explained Groteke, because "he feared Mia might poison him." The actress, Groteke thought, seemed every bit as terrified Allen might murder her, perhaps put a "hit" on her just like the ophthalmologist does to get rid of his bothersome mistress in *Crimes and Misdemeanors*.

In addition to what she told her children, Farrow told many friends Allen had "sexually abused one of the kids," recounted Groteke. "Later that summer, Mia would come to use the word 'molest' on the advice of a child psychiatrist." The actress warned everyone at Frog Hollow to watch Allen, so that he could not "molest" another child of hers: little Dylan. The nanny was "puzzled by the vigilance with which Mia herself had been watching for signs of molestation. It sometimes seemed as if she were *willing* the incident to happen."

Keep a very close eye on The Enemy when he's with Dylan, Farrow cautioned Groteke. "I want you to follow him around and be very careful, because I'm suspicious of his behavior when he's with her." Farrow's "hysteria and terror were contagious," Groteke wrote. When Allen visited, "we all look at him like he's crazy, a monster. As he slowly turns his head in our direction, a little half-smile on his face, he tries to make eye contact with us—any of us. He wants everything to be normal again. Which it is not. How could it ever be?"

Groteke felt, however, as though she was "spying on my boss," since her salary was essentially paid by Allen, and "I didn't know any reason to be suspicious, nor did I really believe that Woody was capable of doing anything salacious." Groteke did observe Dylan fleeing from Allen's embrace on occasion, shrieking, "Hide me, hide me!" At least once the little blonde girl locked herself in the bathroom to escape her father.

Trying to grapple with the actress's mindset—hearing the new "molest" word from Farrow herself—Allen recalled Farrow family gossip. Her three ill-fated brothers "had been sexually aggressive with the beautiful Farrow sisters growing up," he claimed in *Apropos of Nothing*. This scuttlebutt closely echoed Moses Farrow's recollection: "Mia told me that she was the victim of attempted molestation within her own family."

In this hothouse atmosphere Dylan, a "shy and dreamy girl with a fragile emotional nature," in the words of Groteke, was going to turn seven years of age on July 11. The director attended the big family birthday party at Frog Hollow, along with the Pascals and their three children. Farrow warned Allen not to monopolize the birthday girl, nor ignore her other children in attendance, who included Satchel and Moses. But Allen was "all over the little girl," recalled Groteke. The Pascals became offended and left early. Later, Allen and Farrow argued about it. With a red crayon the actress scrawled a note, "unsuccessfully," according to Groteke, trying to shove it under the door of the guest bedroom, where Allen, banished from Farrow's room, slept. Instead, she tacked it to the main bathroom door for everyone including Dylan to see: "CHILD MOLESTER AT BIRTHDAY PARTY, MOLDED THEN ABUSED ONE SISTER. NOW FOCUSED ON YOUNGEST SISTER FAMILY DISGUSTED."

A few weeks "after the looney note, still prior to any allegation," in Allen's words, Farrow phoned Dr. Susan Coates, who later in court affirmed this is what the actress told her: "Somebody has to find a way to stop him." Dr. Coates "warned me about it," Allen said. Farrow phoned Dr. Coates repeatedly, the therapist attested, calling Allen "satanic and evil" in one breath, then asking the therapist, "Do you think I should marry him?"

Farrow was "understandably furious," Moses Farrow said later. For months she told her family Allen was "evil," "a monster," "the devil." Soon-Yi was "dead to us." "This was the constant refrain," said Moses, "whether or not Woody was around." Repeating and practicing the words they should use to refer to Allen were part of a familiar household regimen of "coaching, drilling, script, and rehearsing—in essence, brainwashing," said Moses. Four-year-old "super-intelligent" (Groteke's word) Satchel listened and learned. "My sister is fucking my father!" the boy blurted to nannies, according to Moses. "Rape," "molest," and "fucking" were now part of the family vernacular.

One reason Allen zeroed in on Dylan, while visiting Frog Hollow, was his time with his young daughter was tightly enforced while any time he managed to spend with Satchel was inevitably strained. He stayed overnight only to extend his time with the children. The director and actress tried to preserve their habit of "endless walks" through the surrounding fields, "Woody all covered up and buttoned down, Mia with her natural-color straw hat protecting her fair skin," Groteke wrote, but nowadays they shouted and gesticulated angrily as they walked. Groteke thought it odd how much time the couple still spent together and was "touched by the desperate lengths" Farrow seemed prepared to go "to forgive Woody" and somehow take him back.

Curiously, "even with Mia's agony over Soon-Yi and the demands of her newest kids," in Groteke's words, Farrow moved ahead with her decision to foster yet another "crack addicted baby," and take care of the needy infant until her natural mother had recovered her health. Farrow and Groteke sat on the beach "like two little girls playing house, and we would make up lists of baby names we liked." The two decided on "Tunisia." When Farrow informed Dylan and Satchel about "Tunisia," however, the two youngsters "told their mother that they didn't want any baby whom they would have to give back; they wanted one they could grow up with." So the actress set the wheels in motion for another *full* adoption, which would add another child to her brood.

The shifting number of children at Frog Hollow was augmented by many other individuals coming and going. All the children had visiting psychiatrists. Satchel and Dylan had French tutors, Fletcher had a German tutor, Vietnamese specialists helped Tam keep up her native language, and there were "social workers doing home studies for the adoption agencies, and music teachers (for Tam, who plays the piano)," wrote Groteke.

••

AUGUST 4 WAS going to be a momentous day no matter what. It would be the last time Allen visited Frog Hollow before August 6, the day he and Farrow were due to sign the torturously negotiated custody settlement that would define their rights and responsibilities for the three children whose parentage they shared. According to published accounts, the settlement contract would ensure Allen's access to his children and guarantee Farrow's continued appearances in his movies. The negotiated settlement would also bind Farrow to secrecy over Allen's liaison with Soon-Yi. "Most importantly," Farrow later wrote, the agreement, which has never been made public, "ensured that his contact with the children would be supervised. And it did not entitle him to spend the night at our [New York] home." Farrow said she wanted to end Allen's overnight stays at Frog Hollow but had left that issue up in the air. "I didn't press the point, because I feared he would try to have that privilege written into the settlement contract."

Farrow dreaded August 6 as her surrender to the man who had "raped" her daughter and posed a "molestation" threat to Dylan, even though at the same time she was still planning to star in his next picture and perhaps get around to marrying him one of these days. Allen saw the August 6 signing as his first victory in the long battle to regain control and involvement in the upbringing of Satchel and Dylan, giving him a second chance with Moses, and allowing him breathing room in his ongoing clandestine relationship with Soon-Yi.

August 4, a Tuesday, was "a warm, sunny day" at Frog Hollow, Moses recalled. The actress and Casey Pascal went shopping at a nearby mall to avoid Allen's presence as much as possible, taking with them the new adoptees Tam and baby Isaiah. Moses stayed home with Dylan, Satchel, and Pascal's three children. Monica Thompson, the family's senior nanny for seven years, who had helped raise the older children, was not working on August 4, because Thompson was on vacation. College girl Kristi Groteke was filling in for the day, although there was also a separate babysitter for Pascal's children, and the family's French tutor, Sophie Bergé, was present—a "full house," in Moses's words, with Allen due to arrive for his normal scheduled visit.

The older Farrow siblings always "left the house to stay with friends" when Allen came from New York, Farrow recalled. "It was hard for us to have him there." Since the actress "had put all of us on notice not to let him out of our sight," fourteen-year-old Moses, the oldest male child at home and therefore the proverbial "man of the house," took "Mia's warnings very seriously." Moses closely observed his adoptive father on August 4, and "deliberately made sure to note everyone's coming and coming." The youth had mixed emotions about surveilling his father, but he knew "to go against her [Farrow's] wishes would bring horrible repercussions."

Dylan often came down with "headaches and stomach aches" when Allen visited, according to Farrow, curling up in the hammock, or lingering in the bathroom. Yet the little girl seemed perfectly fine with her mother gone on August 4. Everybody watched *Who Framed Roger Rabbit* in the TV room. "Woody would leave the room on occasion," Moses said, "but never with Dylan. He would wander into another room to make a phone call, read the paper, use the bathroom, or step outside to get some air and walk around the large pond on the property."

After *Roger Rabbit* the group broke up. Some people went outside. The little blonde girl was scampering around in a white sundress. A brief period of time ensued during which, according to overlapping accounts, no one was quite sure where Dylan and her father had disappeared to. "Under my lapsed vigilance," wrote Groteke in her introduction to *Mia & Woody: Love and Betrayal*, "Woody spent *between ten and twenty minutes* [author's emphasis] alone with his adopted daughter." Later in the book's text, however, Groteke unaccountably changed this estimate to "fifteen to twenty minutes," adding five minutes to the possible time frame of Allen's Dylan alone-time and subtly privileging the longer estimate. Farrow, in her memoir, reinforced the substitution of "twenty," quoting Groteke as supposedly saying "for *about twenty minutes* [author's emphasis] they were missing." "Every day," Groteke explained in *Mia & Woody*, "there were periods of five or ten minutes when I could not locate them. It usually had nothing to do with guarding them against Woody." As the story was repeated, however, the time span kept stretching beyond the narrow estimate of ten minutes. Court findings would later eliminate the short possibility of "ten" minutes altogether, and echo Groteke by describing "a period of fifteen or twenty minutes."

Later, Dylan said during this interval of lost time her father herded her into a small attic off her mother's bedroom. "An unfinished crawl space, under steeply angled gable roof, with exposed nails and floorboards, billows of fiberglass insulation, filled with mousetraps and droppings and stinking of mothballs, and crammed with trunks full of hand-me-down clothes and my mother's old wardrobes," is how Moses described it.

Farrow and Pascal returned from shopping with Tam and Isaiah. The other children greeted them. "It was momentarily jarring when Sophie pointed out that Dylan had no underpants on under her sundress since, at seven, she was extremely modest," Farrow recalled. "They're wet," the girl explained to her mother, who guessed the wetness was from wading in the lake. "I asked Kristie to please put some underpants on Dylan."

Dylan was usually a modest girl, Farrow said later. Why wasn't she wearing underwear? "Nobody has ever been able to explain" this "at best, odd" fact, mused nanny Groteke, although "maybe the answer to this is less sinister than it seems. Maybe Dylan's panties had been wet or soiled from playing at the beach [at the lake], and she had just chucked them under a bed or into the laundry."

But at this juncture, Moses recalled, there were "no complaints by the nannies, and nothing odd about Dylan's behavior." Groteke agreed: "Nothing seemed ominous that evening" either. The director and his frequent leading lady dined out at a restaurant in nearby Bridgewater, although whenever they dined together "invariably I left the table in tears," Farrow said. *Husbands and Wives* was in the pipeline for a December release, so Allen talked "nonstop" about their upcoming film project, according to Farrow. *Manhattan Murder Mystery* had become the frontrunning title for the married-sleuths script that had been so long in gestation. The next Woody Allen production would begin shooting in September. Farrow was still in line to play Allen's wife in the picture, and the pending settlement contract clinched that job. "Talk is sparse," was Allen's version of the dinner, "but civil. Nothing brilliant from me, no Joan Crawford moments from her." By now, however, it was clear Allen was trying to ease their separation, personally and professionally. The actress was conflicted about both eventualities. "The [dinner] atmosphere is, shall we say," Allen wrote in *Apropos of Nothing*, "frosty."

Returning to Frog Hollow, Allen went up to the children's room to read a bedtime story to Dylan and Satchel, as was his wont. Also sharing the room was Tam, who had only ever experienced the family's hostility toward Allen. Tam "hated" the evil ogre Allen because he virtually ignored her, according to both Groteke and Farrow. Tam interrupted the bedtime story with "screaming," distracting Dylan and Satchel, who stared "worriedly" at their distressed sister. Farrow asked Allen to hurry up and finish. "He glared at me and continued." When the bedtime story was over, Farrow kissed the kids goodnight and stepped into the hallway, where Allen waited, "livid," the actress recalled. "Just look what you've done," the filmmaker upbraided her (according to Farrow). "You'd better shape up, or there's no way you're going to be in this movie." She started weeping and demanded to know "Why is everything always my fault?" as he headed downstairs to the guest room.

Before he left in the morning, Allen sat on the living room floor with Dylan and Satchel, who marked toys from the F.A.O. Schwarz catalogue they wanted their father to bring on his next visit. "It was a cheerful, playful atmosphere," Moses said. "They had laughingly managed to check off virtually every toy in the catalogue." His chauffeur picked up Allen, and Moses congratulated himself on a job well done on behalf of his mother.

LATER THAT SAME day, Wednesday, August 5, Casey Pascal phoned Farrow to say her babysitter Allison Stickland had "seen something at my house that had bothered her" the day before, during Allen's visit. "Prompted by Mia to be hypervigilant," in Allen's words, Stickland had peeked into the TV room, where Dylan was "sitting on the couch, staring straight ahead with a blank expression." Her father was kneeling in front of the little girl with his face in her lap, according to Stickland, who was "shocked" because the situation looked "intimate, something you'd say, 'Oops, excuse me,' if both had been adults." Allen had been "told by the therapist not to do precisely that thing," according to Farrow. Allen, in later court statements, said Stickland was mistaken, and he "certainly didn't do anything improper" in the TV room. According to his testimony, "there were no seats for me, so I sat on the floor and might have leaned my head back on the sofa on Dylan's lap for a moment."

No one else in the "room full of people watching TV midafternoon," in Allen's words, was able to corroborate the babysitter's account, which Stickland also reiterated in court. The only other eyewitness who was present on that day, later giving his own account, was Moses. "Really?" Moses said in 2018. "With all of us in there? And if she had witnessed that, why wouldn't she have said something immediately to our nanny?"

This was the spark that ignited the conflagration, although later—after being superseded by the attic charges—it became an almost forgotten footnote to the day. The lurid implications of Dylan mysteriously running around without underwear gained in salaciousness with the image of her father's head plunged into her lap.

Remembering that Dylan, whose molestation Farrow feared and predicted, "had not been wearing underpants" the day before, the actress went to the little girl. "Did Woody have his face in your lap yesterday?" Yes, answered the seven-year-old. According to Farrow, she had just finished videotaping Isaiah, so she turned the camera lens around on her daughter and asked her what her father did. "Dylan went on to say that he was breathing into her, into her legs. She told me he was holding her around the waist and that when she tried to get up, he 'secretly put one hand here'—she pointed—'and touched my privates, and I do not like that one bit.' "

Later in the afternoon, after he had "*touched my privates*" [author's emphasis] in the TV room, her father took her upstairs into the attic space, Dylan told Farrow, and again "touched her private parts with his finger," the actress recalled. Dylan said Allen told her, "Don't move. I have to do this. If you stay still, we can go to Paris. . . ." According to Farrow's memoir, Dylan said Allen smothered her with kisses, and the little girl "got soaked all over the whole body. I had to do what he said. I'm a kid, I have to do whatever the grown-ups say. . . . It hurt, it hurt when he pushed his finger in. . . . He said the only way for me to be in the movie [he was making] is to do this. I don't want to be in his movie. Do I have to be in his movie? He just kept poking it in.*"

Over the "next twenty-four hours," according to Farrow, "whenever she [Dylan] brought it up, in fits and starts, I switched on the camera" to make a videotape recording of Dylan's accusations. Part of the time Dylan was shown naked (in the bathtub) or wearing only underwear. This video recording would become one of the most disputed elements of the child-abuse case. Later, in court, some expert witnesses for Allen's side characterized Farrow's recorded questioning of the child as leading to conclusions: "Did he make you take off your underwear? . . . How did he touch you? . . . Did he use his finger? . . . Did he stick the whole finger in?"

When senior nanny Monica Thompson returned early from vacation,

* In the courtroom, Mia Farrow testified, somewhat differently, Allen "inserted a finger partially," rather than "he just kept poking it in."

reporting back to work on August 5, Moses brought Thompson up to date on what Dylan had been claiming. Nanny Kristi Groteke says that when she arrived later, Thompson told her, "I don't think anything happened. I think Mia is exaggerating. She's trying to make you feel bad for not staying with Dylan the entire day." Both Thompson and Moses later said they witnessed Farrow's videotaping of Dylan, agreeing it took the actress more than twenty-four hours to complete the recording—more like two or three days. Thompson supplied an affidavit to support Allen's custody claim in court, testifying, "I recall Ms. Farrow saying to Dylan at that time, 'Dylan, what did Daddy do . . . and what did he do next?' Dylan appeared not to be interested, and Ms. Farrow would stop taping for a while and then continue." Allen's attorneys also cited other household sources to allege Farrow rewarded their young daughter with small treats and encouragements, "toys and ice cream," as the taping evolved over several days.

The several days help explain the discontinuity, the jumps in time, in the videotape recording. "There was a splice," remembered Groteke, "that cut out some tape inadvertently capturing Dylan's private parts, and which, Mia felt, was 'inappropriate to show.' The tape had undeniably, however, been stopped and restarted several times. I suppose it's possible that in the interim Mia *could have* told her daughter what to say. Some viewers have watched and said that it looks rehearsed, as if Dylan is acting. . . . [However] I was with Mia several times while she actually tried to get Dylan to recant her story, and each time the child would refuse."

According to Eric Lax, who included an interview with Moses, along with the observations of sex-crime professionals in his book *Start to Finish: Woody Allen and the Art of Moviemaking*, the tape recording was composed of "eleven segments [that were] shot at different times in different places, one nude in a bathtub, others showing her [Dylan] topless." Lax did not cite a source for this detailed breakdown of the second key visual document in the case, which in 2017, when *Start to Finish* was published, had not been made public.

Groteke was one of the few people to describe the videotape contemporaneously. Farrow insisted both nannies watch the recording. Groteke was treated to the videotape "all by myself" in Farrow's bedroom:

> It is chilling. It begins with Dylan sitting on Mia's bed. Mia, holding the video camera, is not in the picture, but we hear her asking Dylan

questions like, "Where did Daddy take you?" And Dylan answers, "He took me to the attic." Mia asks several more questions while Dylan sits on the bed. Then the scene shifts to the lake. Now we see Dylan lying in one of the lounge chairs by the water. Mia asks her questions like, "Where did he touch you?" And Dylan, whose legs are slightly open, says, "He touched me here, and he touched me here, and he touched me here." Each time she says this, she points to her genital areas. During this scene, Dylan seems manic and distracted and there are many interruptions. She gets up from her chair often. Occasionally, too, Tam runs into the picture to play, blocking Dylan from view. Finally, one distraction too many. Mia stops the tape.

When she starts it again, Dylan tells her that she wishes that André were her daddy. "Mommy, it hurts there, it hurts there," she says and holds her genital area. Mia pauses, she sounds very upset, and Dylan says something about Woody putting his finger inside her. Dylan says again, "It hurts." Toward the end of the tape Dylan repeats her claim that Woody has taken her to the attic and has told her that if she doesn't move, if she lies very still, he will take her to Paris and put her in his next movie. Then she says, a serious expression on her face, "I don't want to be in the movie, and I don't want to go to Paris." The tape closes as Dylan looks at Mia and asks, "Mommy, did your daddy do this to you?"

LATER IN THE day of August 5, Farrow phoned her lawyer Eleanor B. Alter, who told her to immediately take Dylan to a local pediatrician, Dr. Vadakkekara Kavirajan, whose offices were in nearby New Milford. What else Alter discussed with Farrow, who had a looming deadline on the joint custody agreement, is not known. Alter must have realized the accusation was a police matter. Farrow and Dylan went to see Dr. Kavirajan, where Dylan avowed her father "had put his face in her lap and had touched her, but when she was asked where she wouldn't talk anymore." The doctor told Farrow to come back with Dylan the next day for another visit. When they got in the car to go home, the little girl explained, "I just don't like talking to strangers about my private parts."

Dylan's primary therapist, Dr. Nancy Schultz, happened to be on summer vacation in Europe. Farrow phoned Dr. Susan Coates, who also saw Dylan, and "who'd been working with Woody for almost two years about his behavior [with Dylan]. As soon as I told her what Allison [Stickland] had seen him doing, she interrupted, 'He's not supposed to do that.'" Because of laws governing child-abuse accusations, Dr. Coates said she would have to report the purported incident to authorities, "but first she was going to tell Woody," according to Farrow, in part because Dr. Coates wanted to confront Allen with the news in person at their forthcoming session. "Let's hope it is her fantasy," Dr. Coates told Farrow, Groteke related in her book. The actress pleaded with Dr. Coates not to inform Allen because she feared the director's wrath.

Later that same day, Allen kept a previously scheduled appointment with Dr. Coates, "who I was conferring with to try and navigate the waters and do what was best for the kids. She broke the news to me that I was being accused of molestation and she had to report it. It was the law." He was "dumbfounded" and couldn't believe his ears. "I thought the whole notion was preposterous," he recalled. "I said no problem, report it. Coates would testify that unlike actual predators I made no attempt to dissuade her from reporting it. That was because I hadn't done anything and assumed no sane person would take the idea of me molesting anybody seriously."

Farrow and Dylan returned to the pediatrician on August 6, the day when she and Allen were supposed to affix their signatures to the laboriously mediated child-custody agreement. Before this second visit, Farrow told Dylan, according to nanny Groteke, "If you tell the truth, it will help Daddy. . . . He forgot to act like a daddy." This time Dylan told the pediatrician Allen had touched her private parts, and "that evening, when I put her in the bath," added Farrow, "she wouldn't sit down. In the bath she said her vagina hurt." The doctor told Farrow he was obligated to report the case to authorities, an inevitability Farrow already knew about from Dr. Coates and her attorney. In her subsequent affidavit, nanny Thompson said Farrow returned from Dylan's second visit to the pediatrician in a surprisingly lighthearted mood, telling Thompson, "Everything is all set. . . ." (according to Thompson's testimony) and "There, now I've got him!" (according to Allen). She said it "with relish," the film director later testified, embroidering this anecdote.

At home, according to her memoir, the actress reflected solemnly on the magnitude of the ominous wheels now set in motion. Her mood was broken by Allen phoning. They had a tense conversation. The director was outraged by the child-abuse accusation and infuriated to learn the custody agreement was again up in the air. Allen said his lawyers would fight back. Farrow begged him to give her two weeks to investigate Dylan's claims. "I will not hold off!" Allen shouted. "This is absurd, and I can't believe you're accusing me of this."

Farrow continued her personal investigation regardless. On August 9, according to Groteke, "a purely external physical examination [by Dr. Kavirajan] showed no evidence of sexual abuse; even so, Dylan was so reluctant to have it done that she had to be sedated." A few days later, Farrow, accompanied by Groteke, brought her young daughter to Saint Luke's Roosevelt Hospital in Manhattan, where the actress had the seven-year-old slotted for an internal gynecological exam under the aegis of New York City's Child Welfare Administration. "Mia was so convinced of the abuse," remembered nanny Groteke, "that she seemed anxious and eager for this delicate internal exam to take place. Yet again Dylan flipped out, crying and insisting she didn't want it done. Frankly, Mia would have gone against her daughter's wishes, and she actually begged the doctors to sedate the little girl. . . . Well, St. Luke's refused to knock Dylan out against her will, which is too bad in one sense, since Mia felt certain that the tests would have offered closure, for better or worse."

After Dr. Kavirajan notified Connecticut state police, investigators contacted Farrow, asking her to arrange for the seven-year-old to meet with child welfare officials, preparatory to opening an official inquiry. "The interviewing caseworker determined that there was cause to believe that sexual abuse might have occurred," Farrow wrote in *What Falls Away*. Dr. Coates "belatedly"—Farrow's word, because Coates hesitated for a week, hoping to meet with Dylan and question the child—informed New York City's Child Welfare services "Mr. Allen had put a finger in her [Dylan's] vagina." The city agency launched a parallel investigation.

Allen and Farrow engaged in a flurry of heated telephone conversations. "Is there any way out?" Farrow quotes him saying, "I just want to be friends." She told him she thought he was crazy. "Where were you when everybody looked all over the house? If you weren't in the attic, where were you?" Farrow asked him "maybe twenty times," as she recalled. "He stumbled and stuttered, but he wouldn't answer my question."

Lawyers trying to act as peacemakers convened a meeting. Harvard Law School professor, author, and frequent talk-show guest Alan Dershowitz, who often defended celebrity clients, was engaged to represent Farrow's interests. Allen had been "a hero of mine," Dershowitz said later, but after taking the case and examining his behavior he began to regard the comedian and film director as a "sleazebag." "A source familiar with the meeting," according to a *Newsday* account, said Dershowitz threatened Allen with incremental pressures. Dershowitz reputedly asked for a "lump sum annuity" of $8 million to underwrite Farrow's household. The lawyer also asked for an additional lump sum of $2.5 million for the loss of Farrow's position as Allen's frequent leading lady, a sum that would cover the five to ten years of Woody Allen films she was bound to forfeit. The film director saw the payoffs as hush money. The deal was, according to Allen, "if I submitted to their demands, they would not press the allegations, and that they would make my children unavailable to the authorities."

Dershowitz denounced Allen's version of events as "absolutely untrue," and said the $8 million sum was "an attempt by both sides to come up with a figure that would reflect what had already been offered" in child support and upkeep. He and his cocounsel David Levett issued a joint statement describing the lump sums as the aggregate "costs of support, education and medical expenses [that] were advanced for mutual discussion."

Allen was even more furious after the lawyers' meeting. He had his back against the wall. Farrow had not yet made any public statements, but he knew he was about to be criminally investigated for the supposed sexual abuse of Dylan and, quite apart from any effect this might have on his reputation and career, the terrible child-abuse accusation would doom his ability to claim parental privileges over Dylan in the future. The whole thing, in his view, was a crazy stab at forestalling the custody settlement and further curtailing his parental rights.

The filmmaker decided to act preemptively with a chess move either he, or his lawyers—or both—mistakenly believed would checkmate Farrow, who was reputedly as averse to publicity, particularly negative publicity, as Allen. On August 14, only one week after the proposed settlement deadline passed, Allen's lawyers filed suit for custody of Satchel, Dylan, and Moses, charging Farrow "has been, and presently is, emotionally disturbed and is under constant heavy medication. . . . I believe that The Children are in great fear of the Respondent by reason of her emotional instability and abusive conduct." The hastily drawn petition said Allen had been "falsely accused of sexually abusing Dylan and Satchel"—thereby himself making the first public disclosure of the charges—"A total fabrication from start to finish," he claimed, then, and invariably later.

The filing was the opening shot that ricocheted around the world. The court papers, which did not mention Soon-Yi, revealed the breakup of the celebrity couple and the child-abuse accusations. "The documents speak for themselves," Allen's publicist Leslee Dart told reporters in famous last words. "Mr. Allen has never discussed his private life in public and does not wish to begin doing so now. The last thing he wants is media attention." Regardless, overnight, Allen recalled, he found himself "at the center of a cosmic explosion."

THE STARTLING HEADLINES swept across European capitals, where Allen's films were popular, and rippled in the media of major metropolises in Africa, Asia, and Latin America. Although the Allen-Farrow breakup and scandal was covered by newspapers and magazines across the US, the story was seismic in Los Angeles and New York, the former the heart of the American motion picture industry of which Allen was a brand name of excellence, and the latter the hometown that held him dearest. The Allen-Farrow relationship "has been something of a New York institution," noted the *New York Times*, which could just as easily have said "something of a show business" or "national institution." "A pall has fallen on the city and on Woody Allen and upon many people who love him," Pete Hamill wrote in the *New York Post*. "I'm floored," Eric Lax was quoted. Lax's authorized *Woody Allen: A Biography*, which Allen himself had penciled up in manuscript form, had been published two years earlier. He had portrayed Allen and Farrow as a happy couple, and the contemplative dust jacket photo of the director was taken by the leading lady of so many of his films. "I saw him three weeks ago," Lax told the press ruefully, "and he was on his way up to the country to see her."

The Farrow family swiftly struck back, with the first public denunciation—and first insinuations about Allen's affair with Soon-Yi—coming from Maureen O'Sullivan, via her longtime publicist John Springer, who was also Farrow's press agent. The lawsuit was "a cheap shot from a desperate and evil man," said the eighty-one-year-old actress, who had praised Allen's directing skills when appearing in *Hannah and Her Sisters* and who was a grandmother to Mia's children, adopted and biological. Farrow was "a wonderful girl and the best mother [and] . . . those kids would be dead or prostitutes if not for her," O'Sullivan said. "It has been tragic to watch what she has gone through in the last seven months," Mia's mother said, adding, "the truth of the story will soon be made public." Farrow's siblings chimed in, with Tisa echoing that Allen was "an evil, evil man."

Not to be outdone, Allen's nonagenarian parents also spoke to the press. Martin Konigsberg, probably as yet unaware of his son's amorous relationship with Soon-Yi, told Reuters that perhaps "her [Farrow's] mother put her up to all this. . . . It's a frame-up, if you ask me." As for Nettie, Allen's mother, still residing with her husband of sixty years in an apartment near their famous son, "She doesn't seem upset," Martin averred.

Over the weekend New York newspapers frantically chased the story. On Monday, August 17, came the first unsourced accounts of Allen's affair with Soon-Yi. "Woody Loves Mia's Daughter" was the *New York Post* headline. Leslee Dart urged Allen to issue a public statement in his own defense, and he rushed out a proclamation of his love for Soon-Yi. "Regarding my love for Soon-Yi—it's real and happily true," Allen declared. "She's a lovely, intelligent, sensitive woman who has and continues to turn my life around in a wonderfully positive way." The press release insisted Allen's love for Soon-Yi had nothing to do with the custody lawsuit ("totally separate issues"), and the statement did not mention the police and agency investigations in Connecticut and New York, which unfortunately for Allen broke into headlines later that same day, with confirmation from the Connecticut police they were looking into little Dylan's sex-abuse claims.

Frank Maco, the state's attorney for the Litchfield District, which encompassed Frog Hollow, was supervising the Connecticut side of the investigation. As part of his remit, Maco, who alone would make any decision on criminal charges because there was no grand jury process in Connecticut, told the press he had referred the matter to Yale–New Haven Hospital's respected Child Sexual Abuse Clinic, which would interview Allen, Farrow, Dylan, and other principals, then submit an expert opinion as part of the evidence-gathering.

That Monday night the embattled film director reported to Michael's Pub for his weekly gig and played his clarinet with his old-time jazz band, as he'd continue to do without fail over the grueling months ahead.

On Tuesday, however, Allen called a press conference. This was the classic gambit, encouraged by his publicist, which might help him "get out in front of the story!" Wearing his standard oxford cloth shirt and khakis, looking "haggard and distressed," as the *Los Angeles Times* reported, Allen took the podium in a ballroom packed with journalists at the Plaza Hotel. He began by reminding the press how much he had "assiduously avoided publicity" over the years—an outlandish canard for someone who had given hundreds of interviews, unless he meant, previously, he had assiduously avoided discussing his love life with journalists. Yet now the film director faced terrible innuendos and untruths and was forced to speak out. Always someone more comfortable with reading words he had typed out beforehand on paper, Allen spoke from a two-page declaration. "Except for clearing his throat and saying 'um' a couple of times as he stepped up to the microphone," recounted the *New York Times*, he "uttered only one sentence that was not in his prepared text."

Allen's statement maintained there was no basis to the child-molestation charges. He condemned Farrow for engaging in the "unconscionable and gruesomely damaging manipulation of innocent children for vindictive and self-serving purposes." The actress also had privately accused him of "sexually abusing" Satchel, Allen noted, which was one of the interesting early assertions in the case that was hastily abandoned. This specific red herring apparently arose out of comments made by Farrow to Allen on a phone call, or by Farrow to one of Dylan's therapists. The Satchel-abuse allegation "has quietly vanished, I suppose, because its substance was too insane even for the instigator to stay with," Allen told the press. He reiterated his love for Soon-Yi and said the abuse accusations were "totally separate" issues connected only by Farrow's vindictive actions. "The one thing I have been guilty of," proclaimed Allen, "is falling in love with Miss Farrow's adult daughter at the end of our own years together, and, painful as that might be, I and certainly the children do not deserve this form of retribution." The only winging-it by the onetime stand-up comedian known for improvisational skills—the single sentence alluded to by the *Times*—was a weak joke Allen lobbed to reporters as he rushed out of the room to avoid shouted questions. "My one public appearance in years, and it's all straight lines," Allen muttered.

Although the lawsuit forced Farrow "from the privacy she so treasures," in publicist John Springer's words, the actress would prove the more convincing performer in the public spotlight and, long term, more astute in handling the press. Although Farrow's family later made a big point of excoriating Allen's high-powered publicity machine, John Springer Associates was a veteran show business firm that represented Hollywood stars harking back to Gary Cooper and Marilyn Monroe, and whose current top-of-the-line client list included Lincoln Center, the Alvin Ailey dance troupe, and many Broadway shows. Springer had started out at Rogers & Cowan, a giant of publicity in the entertainment business, where Leslee Dart, incidentally, also got her feet wet.

Farrow's allies were not shy about backing her. One Hollywood friend leaked her correspondence, in which the actress said Allen had "spoiled and mutilated" his better self. Farrow had many like-minded "seconds," in the phrase of the *New York Times*—"Seconds" as in a colonial-era pistol duel—"Children, close friends and well-paid publicity agents—calling reporters, releasing private letters and trying to see that her side of the story is told." One of Farrow's attorneys was more famous than Allen's and more conspicuous. Alan Dershowitz appeared on *CBS This Morning* and NBC's *Today* show, scoffing at mention of possible abuse of Satchel, which he insisted was never a formal claim, and ridiculing Allen's suggestion the $8 million annuity was a bargaining chip in the dispute. Legendarily, the actress had accepted only a favorite rocking chair as her alimony in the Frank Sinatra divorce. "Ms. Farrow has never been interested in money," declared Dershowitz.

Farrow proved more elusive than Allen, even though reporters swarmed to Frog Hollow. Her children were also among her proxies. Fourteen-year-old Moses Farrow walked to the end of the Frog Hollow driveway to meet with the gathered journalists and paparazzi one day, reading from a letter repudiating his father. "That person is capable of doing it to anybody," Moses's letter read in part. "People like that should be locked up." Twenty-five years later the grown-up Moses, then almost forty and a professional therapist, told Eric Lax: "I was showing loyalty to my mother. Mia already established with us that 'you have to be with me or you're against me,'" adding,

"That public denouncement of my father remains the biggest regret of my life."

The other Farrow-Previn children—always excepting Soon-Yi—joined in. The family's attempt to smear Soon-Yi's intelligence, which was briefly adopted by the media as a truism, infuriated Allen and Soon-Yi above all. Tisa Farrow told *Newsweek* the twenty-one-year-old object of Allen's affections, her niece, "has a double-digit IQ. It's not like she's a drooling idiot, but she's very naive and very immature." Farrow called Letty Aronson, according to the director's staunchly supportive sister, and said Allen had raped a "retarded girl." (Farrow offered subsequent testimony, denying she had ever described Soon-Yi as "retarded.") Fletcher Previn gave an interview to WWOR-TV, Channel 9 in New York, saying he believed Soon-Yi could be as young as seventeen, and his sister was "easily led." Lark and Daisy Farrow visited the *New York Post* offices, searching for scuttlebutt about the whereabouts of their sister, who had put distance between her and her family and was quietly enrolled in a summer session at Rider College in New Jersey. While at the *Post*, nineteen-year-old Lark, three years younger than Soon-Yi, let the paper know her sister was "emotionally immature for her age."

The Farrow camp not only made a concerted attempt to slur her intelligence, *People* reported the whispering that Soon-Yi "may still be a teenager" and Dershowitz proclaimed, "Woody has made her twenty-one for his purposes." By the time the case went to court, however, the underage strategy was also largely abandoned.

WAR WAS DECLARED: Allen versus Farrow. The skirmishes would take place in the press as much as the courtroom. A one-time joke-writer for a public relations firm, who had spent his career honing his image and persona, Allen should have been press-savvy, but he was clumsy. Over time, Farrow was the adept.

The videotaped recording of Dylan was always the stealth lethal weapon in Farrow's arsenal. Soon after Allen's press conference, a copy of the videotape of the seven-year-old girl being interviewed by her mother was mysteriously messengered over to a New York Fox television affiliate, Channel 5, and marked to the attention of morning show anchor Rosanna Scotto, whose children attended the same private Brearley School as Dylan. Fox producers viewed the videotape preparatory to scheduling it for broadcast. The lawyers for both "feuding parents" halted the airing, according to Farrow spokesman John Springer. Allen's publicist Leslee Dart pointed out the tape could only have come either from Farrow's attorneys, or someone connected with the Farrow household, since the actress was the only person known to have possession of it. "The tape seemed to support Farrow's allegations of abuse," a Fox spokesman said. "The child seemed nervous and visibly shaken."

The film director also had "seconds" besides his family. Restaurateur Elaine Kaufman, talk-show host and old friend Dick Cavett ("If Woody Allen is a child molester, I will publicly kiss Pat Buchanan"), longtime costume designer Jeffrey Kurland, and Allen's veteran casting director Juliet Taylor (who said it was she who "introduced Soon-Yi to the Flick [modeling] Agency at the request of Mia") were among the people who went on the record defending Allen. Diane Keaton gave a statement to Liz Smith decrying the allegations as "absurd. . . . There's no way in the world Woody would ever abuse anyone, much less his seven-year-old daughter. To be falsely accused is horrible and as his close friend of many years I really feel for him."

After the first week of potshots, Farrow and Allen spoke by phone on the weekend, trying to broker a white flag. "Can we stop this grotesque publicity circus?" the actress asked (according to Allen). "You have hired a lawyer," he replied (according to him), "you're parading relatives and the kids on television, you leaked this videotape of Dylan unconscionably. . . ." Farrow begged (according to Allen), "Can't we negotiate this?"

"Sure," the filmmaker responded (according to him). "First, you must clear my name unequivocally. And if you do that and we can agree to give Dylan some real therapy to get over the dreadful scars of this thing, and I am part supervisor of that therapy, then OK, we can talk and see if there's a way of toning things down."

The answer was no. Repeatedly over the coming months, Allen offered to settle the child-custody issues out of court, if the actress would withdraw what he regarded as the spurious accusations he had sexually abused Dylan. "Woody wanted to, she didn't," wrote nanny Kristi Groteke. "By going forward with these child-abuse allegations, she has created a situation in which, for perhaps the only time in their relationship, she has power."

Farrow's obduracy redoubled Allen's fury and determination to fight but it didn't necessarily clear his thinking. Coached by Leslee Dart, in the last week of August he went on a one-man crusade, giving three-hour interviews to *Time*, *Newsweek* and the *Los Angeles Times*, and speaking to numerous other media outlets.

"In light-years I wouldn't go into an attic. . . ." Allen told *Time*. "And I would not molest my daughter." In *Newsweek* he used the never-word: "I have never been in an attic." Not always at his finest when being interviewed, the director did himself few favors when trying to explain his love for Soon-Yi. The nude photo-taking was "a lark of the moment," he said to *Time*. "I am not Soon-Yi's father or stepfather," Allen explained clunkily. "The only thing unusual is that she's Mia's daughter. But she's an *adopted* daughter and a grown woman. I could have met her at a party or something. . . . I didn't feel any great moral dilemmas whatsoever."

The platitude concluding the *Time* Q and A might as well be etched on his tombstone, in part because it was notoriously recycled in so much of the press coverage: "The heart wants what it wants. . . . There's no logic to these things. You meet someone and you fall in love and that's that." Perhaps Allen was making a half-kidding reference to Emily Dickinson, and her line: "The heart wants what it wants—or else it does not care." One of his favorite poets, Dickinson was also invoked in the forthcoming *Husbands and Wives*. (Gabe: "My heart does not know from logic.") Compelled to pretty things up, Allen painted his love for Soon-Yi poetically. He couldn't very well say—equally true—that the little head had been thinking for the big head. But if quoting a favorite line of poetry was a joke, it landed with a thud. Like a comedian who believes in his joke, even if the audience refuses to laugh, Allen would make "the heart wants . . ." an insistent motif of future films.

Worse was when he was politely asked if Soon-Yi was "mentally handicapped." No! Allen barked. "Am I going to spend time with a mental deficient?" Soon-Yi, giving interviews to the same newsweeklies, proved she could speak capably for herself. The college student was unaccustomed to being mocked publicly by *Saturday Night Live*, *Mad TV*, and Howard Stern, on top of the insults being hurled in her direction by her own family, and she was incensed. "I think Mia would have been just as angry if he [Allen] had taken up with another actress or his secretary," Soon-Yi told *Newsweek*. Skeptics pointed out Soon-Yi's words closely echoed Allen's own but, after all, they slept together and presumably conversed. "I don't think you can raise eleven (and soon she will have thirteen) children with sufficient love and care," Farrow's by now permanently disenfranchised daughter continued. "Take it from one who's lived through it—it can't be done. Some of us got neglected, some got smothered. Anyhow, there's problems. . . . I'm not a retarded little underage flower, who was raped, molested and spoiled by some evil stepfather—not by a long shot. . . . I admit it's offbeat, but let's not get hysterical. The real tragedy here is that, because of Mia's vindictiveness, the children must suffer."

Farrow's publicist John Springer insisted his client did not care to air her grievances in the press, but the actress also squeezed in interviews for *Newsweek*, the *New York Times*, and the *Post*. "I just feel if I didn't have any lawyers at all," she told the *Times* (presciently, as events turned out), "and no one said a word, that if I just showed up in court with all my children there, that they would speak most eloquently for themselves."

Two of the children spoke eloquently enough to Dr. Nancy Schultz who, upon returning from Europe, visited Frog Hollow in late August. She arrived as a marked woman in Allen's limousine driven by his chauffeur, which is how, in the past, she always had been ferried from New York to Connecticut for the scheduled sessions. (Inside the family, the children's therapy appointments were "known surrealistically as 'playtimes,'" wrote Groteke.) This time Dylan and Satchel had fun scissoring Dr. Schultz's dress, pouring glue on her hair, and telling her to get out of the house and don't come back. She left, never to return. Shortly after that visit, Farrow fired Dr. Schultz and also discharged Dr. Susan Coates, because, according to her lawyers, she felt Coates sided reflexively with Allen. Dr. Coates could continue to see Satchel or Allen—not both—Farrow informed the therapist. Dr. Coates replied that sessions with Satchel would be useless without Allen.

Over the next "traumatic year, one marked by endless interviews with policemen, social workers, doctors and, most especially psychiatrists," in Groteke's words, the actress kept therapists away from Dylan. The Connecticut police reportedly advised against the little blonde girl seeing one. This was added to Allen's persistent complaints in the intermittent talks between his lawyers and Farrow's: Get Dylan back into therapy.

Also eventually quitting was Monica Thompson. The nanny was suspected of "spying for Woody," Groteke wrote. Farrow believed Thompson was capable of conspiring with Allen to kidnap the children. His mother "was pressuring her [Thompson] to take her side and support the accusation," according to Moses Farrow. Ostensibly, all three—the therapists and Thompson—were dismissed because Allen paid their salaries. In fact, he paid for all the nannies, tutors, and therapists out of the annual household fund he provided for Farrow, who managed the money, the hiring, and supervised the staff and professionals. In that sense, Allen even contributed to the children's regular allowances, which, in one of the household's peculiarities, Farrow distributed by check.

August 24—nearly three weeks since the fateful day of August 4, and ten days after Allen filed his custody lawsuit and the world first learned about his rupture with Farrow, his relationship with Soon-Yi, and the child-abuse accusations—was the day of opening motions in *Allen v. Farrow*. Events had moved so quickly. Already the battlefield reeked of smoke and charred flesh. Justice Phyllis Gangel-Jacob filled in for Justice Elliott Wilk, who had been randomly assigned to the case by the New York State Supreme Court but was on vacation.

Allen's lawyers began by submitting the results of a lie detector test the movie director had taken and passed "with flying colors," in Allen's words, which was administered by a polygraph expert for the Federal Bureau of Investigation paid by his legal team. Farrow did not take any lie detector test, then or later.

Alter brought out a manila envelope with the nude Polaroids, offering it to Justice Gangel-Jacob so she could see the Polaroids were not "modeling photographs," as Allen had characterized them in *Time*. "They are pornographic. They indicate the mental instability of the man in question," said Alter. The judge declined to peruse them.

Trying to clamp down on the public hysteria—"Eleven days of attacks, counterattacks, and character assassination," in the words of *Newsday*—after a brief open-court session in the State Supreme Court building, Justice Gangel-Jacob ordered the sullen couple into her fifth-floor chambers for a three-hour meeting. Allen had not seen his children in three weeks. He asked to be allowed three hours with his children twice weekly, and one full day every weekend, and his lawyers requested a third party be present so Farrow could not fabricate new claims of impropriety. Justice Gangel-Jacob instructed the attorneys on both sides to work out a visitation schedule with Satchel and Moses while temporarily excluding Dylan. "In their private meeting with the judge," reported the *Los Angeles Times*, the couple were "believed to have discussed the visitation rights question and possibly an agreement by Farrow to drop the child-abuse charge in return for Allen's withdrawing the custody petition." Justice Gangel-Jacob instructed Farrow to keep her minor children in the US until the custody was resolved, but declined to confiscate the family passports, as Allen's lawyers urged. Both sides agreed to halt the open warfare and "voluntarily agreed and represented to Justice Gangel-Jacob that they would make no further statements to anyone, including the press," said Allen's publicist Leslee Dart—more famous last words.

DURING THE WEEK of opening motions in the child-custody case, an anxious TriStar delegation flew to New York to meet with Allen. Head of production Mike Medavoy had seen a preview of *Husbands and Wives* earlier in the month and declared the picture "one of Woody's best." That was before Medavoy received a phone call from the director with the disturbing news about the lawsuit, Allen's breakup with Mia Farrow, his relationship with Soon-Yi, and the child-abuse claims. Medavoy instantly realized *Husbands and Wives* was doomed.

With Medavoy on the plane was Alan Levine, chief of TriStar's parent company, Sony. The Sony and TriStar executives worried that Allen's various unsavory controversies would drive filmgoers away from a movie in which the studio had invested $15 million before advertising and distribution. It wasn't just the crisis of a single film; it was the issue of Allen's future with the company. His three-picture deal with Orion was "pay or play," and TriStar had taken over the contract with the terms intact. TriStar president Jon Dolgen wanted to buy out Allen's other two films. Levine, who also had seen the *Husbands and Wives* preview, fretted about the parallels between Allen's real-life affair with Soon-Yi, and Gabe/Allen's flirtations with the college girl Rain (Juliette Lewis) in the screen story. "Personally, I felt we had an obligation to Woody," Medavoy wrote in his memoir. "Frankly, I liked and trusted Woody and didn't believe he was ever capable of molesting a young child."

During the long flight from Los Angeles, Levine outlined "the various scenarios to me and I nervously expressed my dislike for all of them," Medavoy recalled. Medavoy couldn't help but reflect, as Allen welcomed the studio officials into his screening room, on the happier days he had spent with the director in the past. "Woody looked as if he was in a trance," said Medavoy. "He had been beaten up daily in the *New York Post* and the New York *Daily News*, and it seemed painfully obvious that the entire situation was weighing heavily on him."

Looking Allen squarely in the eyes, Levine, "in a highly clinical manner and without revealing any emotion one way or another," asked about the scandals. "For about half an hour Woody openly and honestly explained that his relationship with Soon-Yi had been going on for quite some time. They were both adults, he pointed out, and he was in love with her. He detailed the tensions between him and Mia over the kids, and he surmised that discovering his affair with Soon-Yi had led Mia to bring the child molestation charges against him. He insisted that those charges were false." After he finished speaking, the filmmaker slumped in his chair.

Levine asked about the Connecticut investigation. Allen explained "the first in a series of decisions would be handed down after the first of the year." Levine and Medavoy exchanged a meaningful glance. The TriStar officials decided on the spot to move up the release date of *Husbands and Wives* so the picture would be out of theaters by the time of any possible adverse ruling. Looking relieved, Allen said the speeded-up timing would be fine with him. Levine asked what the director intended to do about *Manhattan Murder Mystery*, the second Woody Allen production meant for TriStar, which had Farrow on the books as costar and was due to start shooting soon. Farrow had kept a costume-fitting appointment with Jeffrey Kurland to force Allen to fire the actress, columnist Liz Smith reported, and make good on her "pay-or-play" contract. Allen said he had just replaced Farrow with Diane Keaton. The words "Diane Keaton" brought slight reassuring smiles to the corporate faces.

"Can you be funny?" Levine asked Allen, only half kidding.

"Yeah, sure," said Allen, sounding anything but funny.

The studio rushed the trailers for *Husbands and Wives* into theaters. The public, especially in New York, had been reading the headlines, and they were already the public most schooled in his films. Now Allen was hoist on the petard of his own persona, which had always blurred a fictional Woody

Allen with autobiographical realities. The trailer audiences were said to erupt with laughter at the snippet where Judy (Farrow) asks Gabe (Allen) if he is ever attracted to other women, and Gabe replies, "Like, who?" With scant promotion, TriStar block-released the movie in late September, just as Allen launched the principal photography of *Manhattan Murder Mystery*. Originally meant to premiere in eight cities, *Husbands and Wives* was dumped onto 865 US screens, "the most for any of Woody's previous films," according to Medavoy. However, the picture grossed only $10 million domestically, doing "mediocre business" because "women, Woody's once faithful audience, no longer trusted him," Medavoy said. Later, Allen sniffed at the supposedly "mediocre" grosses and told interviewers *Husbands and Wives* made "no more or less than my movies usually do."

Medavoy was right about one thing. *Husbands and Wives* was "major Woody," in the words of Todd McCarthy in *Variety*, arguably the closest the director had yet come to the elusive ultra-bleak drama that was, at times, scathingly funny. Much of the humor came from Judy Davis, playing a ball-buster as impossible as she is sympathetic, wreaking havoc on her own life. Director Sydney Pollack, moonlighting as an actor for Allen, his character making all the wrong decisions, was nearly as edgy, Liam Neeson held his own, and Juliette Lewis was a scene-stealer as the precocious co-ed with a penchant for father figures. The nouvelle vague style was thrilling, and the script was replete, for the first time in a Woody Allen film, with f-word dialogue. While *Husbands and Wives* was arguably Allen's least composed work, with many moments of ugly behavior, there were also scenes of dazzling cinematic beauty—Gabe and Rain, at her birthday party, for example, sharing a kiss in her parents' kitchen, which has been plunged into darkness by a storm, with thunder booming outside and lightning flashing.

Along with many embedded Woody Allen-isms—Yeats, *Wild Strawberries*, Kurosawa's *Ran*, Russian novelists—his provocative script displayed roundness and wild swerves and poignant depths. Excerpts from Gabe's comic fiction—whose only manuscript copy Rain loses in a taxi—add irony and layers. Allen's sparse but elegant soundtrack was varied, boasting snatches of Irving Berlin, Cole Porter, Wes Montgomery, Gerry Mulligan, Mahler's Ninth, and Kern and Hammerstein's "Making Whoopee" (again with Bernie Leighton on the piano).

Many reviews were laudatory: "One of his most accomplished ever,"

Kenneth Turan pronounced in the *Los Angeles Times*. Vincent Canby, summarizing the director's estimable career in his last *New York Times* review of any Woody Allen picture—headlined "Fact? Fiction? It Doesn't Matter"—wrote: "The entire Allen canon . . . represents a kind of personal cinema for which there is no precedent in modern American movies."

Yet *Husbands and Wives* also marked a distinct upsurge of the critical queasiness over similarities between Allen and the characters he played—his persona, the hang-ups shared by his reel and real selves—the "parallels that range from intriguing to uncanny," in the words of William Grimes, also writing in the *Times*. Among the intersections of fiction and reality: The "sexually carnivorous" love of Gabe/Allen's past, glimpsed in flashback, is a self-destructive knockoff of Louise Lasser. Gabe/Allen muses about moving to Paris, with Judy/Farrow seeing such idle talk as just another "flirtation technique." Gabe admits a lifelong attraction to "kamikaze women," who crash their planes into him, etc. Little of this was new to his work, but because of what was going on in the real world of Woody Allen, the many self-references stood out like raisins in rice.

Not as remarked upon were the meaningful creative divergences from Allen's reality. Gabe has "never cheated on Judy," and Judy is the character who ends up happily with the man of her dreams. Gabe quits Rain after a single kiss, and he is the character left alone and lonely at the end, struggling with his next book, which he predicts will be "less confessional." In a voice-over Gabe confesses, "I blew it." To the extent *Husbands and Wives* is autobiographical, the film was also an auto-critique. As is the case with most of his starring vehicles, Gabe/Allen is a deeply flawed human being who can be counted on to flub life's big decisions. Gabe's failings strengthen the picture, which remains powerful right down to Allen's final tossed-off line of dialogue. As he squirms under Jeffrey Kurland's mockumentary questioning, Gabe/Allen asks, "Can I go when this is over?"

A NOISY FACTION of critics began to develop second thoughts about Allen and his entire body of work, finding the sins of his private life inexactly mirrored in his films. The press took sides. Public figures weighed in.

As Harvey Wallinger might say, Allen had engaged in "un-American sex." Throughout the fall the filmmaker found himself condemned as a loathsome human being by media pundits, politicians, and even a few religious figures, including Jewish leaders such as Rabbi Martin Siegel of Long Island, who in *Newsday* called for "economic reprisals" against Allen for having inflicted "a moral damage to the community." Allen was publicly excoriated by such pillars of traditional morality as Newt Gingrich, the Republican congressman from Georgia, and the currently serving US attorney general William Barr. Gingrich, knowing Allen to have been a Democratic Party stalwart, assailed the director amid the ongoing national presidential campaign of 1992, describing Allen's love affair with Soon-Yi as "a weird situation [that] fits the Democratic Party platform perfectly. Woody Allen had non-incest with his non-daughter because they were a non-family." Barr, addressing a conference of conservative Roman Catholics in Washington, DC, similarly castigated Allen's romance with college-age Soon-Yi, saying their relationship amounted to a "pithy summary" of America's cultural morass. The attorney general seized on Allen's "the heart wants what the heart wants" credo as "the guiding principle behind our moral decline—the rallying cry of the long binge that began in the mid-1960s."

The tabloid press and national weeklies tended to line up more sympathetically with Farrow. The fair-minded *New York Times*, which had been the fount of Allen worship—the *Times* that was "a New York, Jewish, Communist, left-wing, homosexual newspaper," as Harvey Wallinger describes it in Allen's suppressed PBS mockumentary from 1971, "and that's just the sports section"—tried to stay above it all, at least at first. Within the staff of newspapers or media outlets, there was just as often disagreement, and camps for Mia or Woody.

Female reporters, columnists, and reviewers were more likely to take offense at a man who has fallen in love with his girlfriend's daughter and they were also more likely to believe Allen might be a child predator. Prominent New York female journalists such as Carole Agus of *Newsday*, Rosanna Scotto of the Fox 5 television channel, and *New York Post* columnist Andrea Peyser aligned openly with Farrow. The *Post*'s widely read gossip columnist Cindy Adams estimated her incoming mail ran ten to one against Allen, with readers' insults ranging "from calling him a nerd and a turd to gentler phraseology of bum, scum, crumb, and creep. Also, pig." Onetime Allen friend Liz Smith, covering the charges and countercharges column by column, also took "Mia's side of things" in what she deemed "The Great

Unpleasantness." (Years later, however, Smith wrote in her memoir, "I haven't wavered in my critical admiration for Woody's talent, his genius, his offbeat films.")

Allen's press defenders were mostly, though not exclusively, men. Often, they were personally acquainted with Allen, as many New York journalists were. These included the Hamills: Denis at the New York *Daily News* and his famous older sibling Pete at the *Post*, brothers of Allen's longtime unit photographer Brian Hamill. The Hamills were "particularly vicious" Farrow attackers, Maureen Orth would charge in *Vanity Fair*.

One woman who remained steadfastly by Allen's side was Diane Keaton, who had jumped into her role in *Manhattan Murder Mystery* on a moment's notice, calming TriStar and, to some extent, shaken Woody Allen fans. "It was crazy," Keaton wrote in *Then Again*. "Outside, the press circled Woody's trailer. A day didn't go by without microphones in his face." In her face too: "What's *your* take on the custody battle with Mia?"

The new Woody Allen project began filming in September. In the screen story Allen was playing Larry Lipton with Keaton as his wife Carol. The Liptons are a long-married couple who return from a *Double Indemnity* revival to discover a nice neighbor in their building has died suddenly of a heart attack. Oddly, her widower doesn't seem very upset. According to Eric Lax, Allen originally had written the role of Carol in a straightforward vein for Farrow, while his character, the budding detective Larry, was tailored more for Allen's comedic skills. Allen quickly switched things around for Keaton, so she could play "the more buoyant, fanatical half of the partnership," a middle-age Nancy Drew, with Allen as the "straight man, a solemn spoilsport."

Larry/Allen is a HarperCollins editor. Carol/Keaton is thinking of opening a restaurant. The two have a mutual friend, Ted, a playwright, who carries a long-standing torch for Carol. "The well-named Marcia Fox," in Roger Ebert's words, is a sexy author under Larry's imprint. Stirred by Carol's (more than Larry's) suspicions of homicide, Ted and Marcia Fox and other friends of Larry and Carol sift the clues and set an elaborate trap to catch their prime suspect. It all ends backstage at a revival theater, for which Allen wrote a visual climax evoking a celebrated sequence from Orson Welles's *The Lady from Shanghai*. Although Marcia Fox flirts with Larry and Ted flirts with Carol, solving the mystery breathes new life into Larry and Carol's moldering marriage.

To portray Ted, Allen went for one of his old reliables, Alan Alda, while bringing back Anjelica Huston, who had also proven her mettle in *Crimes and Misdemeanors* as the foxy Marcia. Casting director Juliet Taylor steered Allen to Jerry Adler for the dull-on-the-surface businessman who manages a vintage movie house and whose wife suspiciously drops dead. Part of the Adler family show business dynasty, which dated back to the Yiddish theater, Adler was better known as a stage manager and director before turning actor. Filling in the small parts were Ron Rifkin, who had been Rain's analyst and spurned lover in *Husbands and Wives*, Joy Behar as a friend of Larry and Carol's, Zach Braff in his screen debut as Larry and Carol's grown son, and repeat cameo players like John Doumanian. The behind-the-camera team was the same as for *Husbands and Wives*.

Although this was Keaton's eighth Woody Allen picture, it had been ten years since she last had acted in scenes with her friend, and the "totally terrified" actress consulted her New York thespian coach Marilyn Fried, who'd also been Mia Farrow's coach. Allen started by staging a scene between Keaton and Alda, and at first Keaton felt tentative and panicked. Allen kept shooting in his "totally honest, totally straight, nonsentimental way" until the actress felt more at ease, and soon the two found themselves slipping into old patterns. "He responds to me the way he always responds to me," Keaton said, "which is like I'm a complete idiot. It's like an old marriage, or like I'm a kid sister." In no time "it felt like *Annie Hall* days," she later wrote, "only looser, if that was possible. Carlo Di Palma shot the movie handheld. Entire scenes were completed in one take. We were in make-up at seven a.m. and wrapped at two-thirty in the afternoon. I couldn't believe how easy it was."

Keaton's loyalty never wavered. Allen "has great balls," she told John Lahr a few years later, praising Allen's integrity as a director and his courage under duress. "He's got balls to the floor." Allen spent the workday of his fifty-seventh birthday with his all-time favorite leading lady, filming final takes for *Manhattan Murder Mystery*. Keaton's personality buoyed him. "It was great therapy for me," Allen said later, "a great palliative." During the shoot he'd poke his head into "the hair and make-up trailer to tease Diane about her hair and her big photograph books, all diligently marked with yellow Post-it paper," recalled Huston, who noticed a freer spirit than the man who had guided her in *Crimes and Misdemeanors*. "Around Diane, he was open and accessible."

The set was "oddly free of anxiety, introspection, and pain," Huston remembered. However, outside the bubble the press stood ready to swarm, and a few people, spotting Allen at various locations during filming, hurled epithets. Between takes the filmmaker held daily phone conferences with his lawyers as the abuse investigations and custody case moved forward. Allen was "being hassled by the rabble as he shoots his new movie on New York streets," the wire services reported. "He's been pelted with shouts of 'child molester.' One verbal assault came as he was setting up a scene with Diane Keaton behind Fifth Avenue's Public Library."

Allen, who was never more in the zone than when directing, insisted he never heard or witnessed any of these supposed public outbursts. "Not true at all," the filmmaker told Denis Hamill. "There wasn't a single nasty incident during the shooting. And not on the way to Elaine's, the Knicks games, in Michael's Pub." On the set, Allen—Keaton's costar, director, and friend—"never brought up personal problems while working," she said.

IN THE MEANTIME, Farrow's legal team filed a separate claim in New York Surrogate's Court, seeking to nullify Allen's December 1991 adoption of Dylan and Moses because he had perpetrated a "fraud and deceit" by romancing Soon-Yi during the paperwork stages. There would be a series of skirmishes in the Surrogate's Court, which would entertain much the same testimony as voiced in State Supreme Court, but Judge Renee Roth kept a low profile, never admitted the press or public, and tried not to get ahead of other proceedings.

Taking over Supreme Court preliminaries after his vacation, in November Justice Elliott Wilk rejected Farrow's motion that Allen's suit for sole custody be postponed, pending outcome of the adoption case. When Justice Wilk tried to allow radio and television in court for the trial, however—"Whatever interest the children had in maintaining any anonymity is gone," the judge insisted—lawyers for both Farrow and Allen united and objected. An administrative court overruled Wilk. Reporters would be permitted in court, not broadcasters.

On numerous occasions in the fall, the Yale–New Haven Hospital team separately interviewed Farrow, Allen, Dylan, and nanny Kristi Groteke. On three separate occasions in January and February, the specialists met for hours with Allen and Farrow together. Allen traveled to Connecticut to be questioned by police detectives. New York's child welfare agency also assigned a caseworker to the sexual abuse investigation.

It was Farrow who broke the fragile press truce. Her family, friends, and allies cooperated with Maureen Orth for a high-profile cover story in the November 1992 *Vanity Fair*, New York's widely read glossy magazine anchored by celebrity coverage, which was pre-released to newspapers in early October. Orth and Farrow always maintained they never met, and that the actress herself wasn't involved. Orth's cocktail of reportage and innuendo included interviews with a few people in Allen's corner, not necessarily to their advantage, such as Jane Read Martin and Allen's sister, Letty Aronson, who told Orth when it was all over Allen would be regarded forever as a "giant in the industry" while Farrow would still be "a second-rate actress, a bad mother, a completely dishonest person . . . operating completely out of vindictiveness." Orth's article baldly stated what was later contradicted in testimony by psychologist Dr. Susan Coates: that Dylan had been in therapy for years, not "for an inability to distinguish fantasy from reality," Orth wrote, but for "separation anxiety" issues including "shyness," and because Dylan "didn't want to be left by her parents at nursery school." Orth exaggerated Farrow's professional victimhood—"All she reportedly earned from Allen was a modest $200,000 per film"—to insinuate Allen's guilt and reach the conclusion that the movie director was a "chilling figure of power, a potentate of reel life who doesn't seem to have to play by the rules." Orth also embraced the subtheme of Soon-Yi's subpar intelligence. "Soon-Yi does not know half these words, what they mean," Orth quoted someone "close" to the family. Allen threatened to sue *Vanity Fair*, but his lawyers didn't see the benefit, and their hands were full.

In late October Farrow also welcomed the British magazine *Hello!* into the Langham for a candid sit-down that was a scoop as pictorial as it was textual. Farrow told *Hello!* her ex-boyfriend always had displayed certain "sociopathic tendencies," but what was worse, which infuriated Allen, the actress allowed "photos to be taken of her and her children in their never-before-seen apartment on Central Park West," Liz Smith reported.

Vanity Fair and *Hello!* drove Allen into the arms of broadcast correspondent Steve Kroft, who interviewed him about his controversies for *60 Minutes* in late November. The top-rated, Sunday-night, CBS News magazine show had profiled Allen several times dating back to 1974. On this occasion four-year-old Satchel arrived for a negotiated visit with his father, accompanied by a family babysitter, just as the CBS crew was setting up their cameras inside Allen's apartment. Allen scurried down to the lobby to send Satchel back home. Farrow, declaring it was all a setup to get the boy on camera with his father, suspended any future visits. *60 Minutes* issued a public statement to the effect that no one on its production team had so much as glimpsed the boy.

Perhaps for these reasons Allen was by turns introspective and vitriolic on *60 Minutes*. Allen took Kroft out on his balcony and ruefully pointed across Central Park to where Farrow and his alienated children dwelled. He told the Valentine's Day story and also the red-crayon "Child Molester" anecdote. On camera, for the first time Allen claimed that Farrow had told him more than once, by phone and in person, "I have something very nasty planned for you," and "You took my daughter and I'm going to take yours." Farrow "threatened to have me killed and to kill me," he told Kroft, "and then to stick my eyes out, to put my eyes out, to blind me, because she became obsessed with Greek tragedy and felt that this—that that would be a fitting, you know, vengeance."

Asked when he had intended to tell Farrow he was sleeping with her daughter, Allen replied, "I never thought about it." Allen and Soon-Yi had an "adult" relationship, he said. "Those people that feel—they want to feel that it's questionable, or not to their taste, or she's too young for me, or she's Mia's daughter, or whatever they want to think, I'll take that heat. That does not mean that I should be charged with child molestation."

Allen vigorously denied sexually abusing Dylan, using the same language echoed in many later interviews. "Be logical about this," the filmmaker told Kroft. "I'm fifty-seven. Isn't it illogical that I'm going to, at the height of a very bitter, acrimonious custody fight, drive up to Connecticut . . . and suddenly on visitation, pick this moment in my life to become a child molester? . . . If I wanted to be a child molester, I had many opportunities."

Kroft concluded the Allen-friendly segment by attesting, "Reports we were shown seem to support his contention that he's not a child molester." Now Farrow was incensed. Carly Simon watched the telecast with her friend Mia and told Fox 5 the director was "a desperate man" who "probably feels as if an indictment is coming down." "Let him have *60 Minutes*," the *Daily News* quoted Farrow, "I have [Fox] Channel Five News."

Other "close friends and confidantes" stepped up to whisper in the ear of *Newsday*'s Carole Agus for her on-site depiction of Thanksgiving 1992 at Frog Hollow. The first Thanksgiving "in twelve years celebrated without Woody Allen," Agus wrote, was "nothing like the famous scenes in *Hannah and Her Sisters*," as the Farrow-Previn family struggled to come together and be positive. "Dylan did not give thanks. She sat at the table and said nothing." The article furnished the first details of Allen's purported child abuse (Dylan: "He kissed me all over"); told of his HIV/AIDS fears; cited, without identifying, his teenager romances before *Manhattan*; and lingered on Allen's dread of showers without special drains. A Farrow friend was quoted: "Sometimes she says, 'I hope Dylan's wrong, I hope Dylan's wrong, I don't want to believe this. There's a piece of me that still loves him.'"

Partly because of this fresh fusillade of media jousting, another court hearing was convened in mid-December. Justice Elliott Wilk again "pleaded with the warring parties not to take their already highly public case to news organizations," the *New York Times* recounted. Justice Wilk heard a panoply of motions from lawyers representing the opposing sides, encompassing issues large and small, right down to whether the disgraced father should be allowed to give Christmas and birthday gifts to his three children (the answer was yes). The overwrought hearing was characterized by "anger and mistrust," according to the *Times*. "Lawyers for the two sides repeatedly interrupted each other, accused each other or each other's clients of dishonesty, and, unwilling or unable to compromise directly, appeared determined to litigate every detail of the dispute."

Farrow's lawyers asked the court to force Allen to pay her mounting legal bills of $300,000. Statements were submitted attesting Allen possessed assets of over $16 million, while Farrow's wealth was estimated at $3.8 million. Farrow's lawyers insisted Allen was worth at least $20 million and complained the actress had still not been remunerated to the tune of $350,000 for the "pay or play" *Manhattan Murder Mystery*. Allen's lawyers pointed out Farrow had just signed a book deal with Doubleday, purportedly for $3 million, which was not reflected in her stated assets. "Lawyers on both sides accused each other's clients of lying on statements of their net worth," reported the *Times*.

In the words of Harvey I. Sladkus, one of Allen's lawyers, Farrow had been "systematically and intentionally trying to drive a wedge between Mr. Allen and the three children" since August 4. The film director had not glimpsed Dylan since that day; Farrow now blocked visits with Satchel, whom Allen had not seen for nearly a month; and Moses refused to meet with his father. Allen had telephoned Moses, but any good intentions he might have had for easing their standoff were offset by him asking to see the youth's therapy records. Hanging up on his father, Moses consulted with his mother, who "was afraid that the court would subpoena the records," wrote Kristi Groteke, "and discover Moses telling his therapist that she didn't pay enough attention to him." Farrow checked in with Moses's psychiatrist, who said he would strive to keep the records confidential.

Recently, Allen had made an attempt to see Dylan by visiting the Brearley School on the Upper East Side. The filmmaker claimed he was trying to set up a parent-teacher conference. A principal stopped him, phoning Farrow. The actress believed Allen was visiting the school partly to pump Dylan for dirt about her. Farrow asked for and got a court order restraining Allen from visiting the school and soliciting information from educators. Justice Wilk also rejected Allen's request for a court-appointed psychiatrist for his daughter and court guardians to superintend the welfare of all his three children. He advised Farrow's lawyers to work out a visitation plan with Satchel, but he declined to set binding terms. "I will defer to Ms. Farrow's judgment," the judge said. Justice Wilk said he would revisit the question of visitations with Dylan at future hearings.

If the film director wasn't allowed to see Dylan, shouldn't his lawyers at least have an opportunity to see the videotape of his daughter's abuse claims? Channel 5 had been slipped a copy, and Allen's lawyers believed Farrow had shown it to celebrity friends such as Carly Simon and George Plimpton. Allen's lawyers argued they were "probably the only people who haven't seen that tape." Perhaps it was a pyrrhic victory, but the court ordered Farrow's lawyers to furnish a copy. Allen's side later insisted that the tape was doctored, and it is unclear whether Allen himself ever watched it. He never directly commented on the recording.

Farrow did not attend this hearing, but Allen sat "quiet and expressionless" throughout, afterward speaking briefly to a throng of reporters. "Emotionally, I just want to see my children," the filmmaker said.

••

LIKE A FEARLESS point guard driving toward the hoop—say, Walt Frazier—nothing short of a hail of bullets could be expected to break Allen's stride. Bullets and a neophyte Broadway dramatist were the subject of the surprisingly playful script the writer-director launched in earnest during the postproduction of *Manhattan Murder Mystery*. He took on a new writing partner for the first time since his collaboration with Marshall Brickman fifteen years before, perhaps because "he needed a distraction on the level of the Olympic Games," in the words of Douglas McGrath, and "his personal resources were being tested." A native Texan twenty-some years younger than Allen, balding and puppyish, as Marion Meade described him, McGrath was a *Saturday Night Live* sketch writer during Jean Doumanian's tenure. His girlfriend was Allen's former assistant Jane Read Martin. A multitalent, known for penning short fiction and humorous essays as well as scripts, McGrath had just finished the scenario for an unfortunate remake of *Born Yesterday*, the Garson Kanin stage comedy prized by Allen, with contemporary stars Don Johnson, John Goodman, and Melanie Griffith.

The new collaborators warmed up, some days, by making lists of favorite movies. Allen's all-time comedies, "if you take out the Marx Brothers and W. C. Fields," were Ernst Lubitsch's *Trouble in Paradise* and *The Shop Around the Corner* and George Cukor's *Born Yesterday*, the classic one "with Judy Holliday," Allen told McGrath with his Zelig face. ("He was polite enough not to add 'not the inane version you had a hand in,'" said McGrath.) His favorite Woody Allen pictures, as of then, were the ones whose scripts he felt he had most successfully brought to fruition: *Stardust Memories*, *Zelig*, *The Purple Rose of Cairo*, *Husbands and Wives*.

Allen wanted to follow *Manhattan Murder Mystery* with another comedy. Something fun to direct (without himself acting), and for audiences to enjoy. Allen let McGrath choose from "several ideas of mine, all of them good," including the stories of future films *Small Time Crooks*, *The Curse of the Jade Scorpion*, and *Hollywood Ending*. "Which one of these strikes you as most fun to work on?" he asked. "The one where the gangster turns out to be the playwright," said McGrath. Allen raised an eyebrow. "Really? Because that is last on my list. . . ."

They talked and acted out scenes as they sequenced the plot and fleshed out characters. "Acted in the loosest sense," McGrath recalled. "Woody stood and gave a very animated performance of one [scene], while I listened.

After he finished, I said, 'I think there's just something familiar about it.' He immediately slumped and said, 'I know, I know.' The great thing about it is he wanted to fix it. He didn't want me to puff him up."

As he had done with Brickman and Mickey Rose before him, Allen and McGrath "chatted, planned structure, then he went off and I wrote the script" for *Bullets over Broadway*, Allen said. McGrath was impressed by Allen's focus and his ability to compartmentalize with all the chaos erupting in his personal life.

"One day we were in the living room in our familiar positions," McGrath remembered, with the film director "pacing back and forth coming up with good ideas, me slouched on the couch, hoping he'd keep it up. He [Allen] was telling us the movie. This was a standard way to begin. We would describe the movie to each other as far as we had it and then would try to see what the next scene should be. He began by raising his arms in a sort of Zorba the Greek–like attitude and snapping his fingers as if to signal the start of a show. Then he began: 'It's the Roaring Twenties, and here's this playwright who thinks of himself as a great artist—' "

A ringing phone interrupted. Allen lifted a finger to signal a pause and took the call. "He spoke in low tones," McGrath continued his account, "saying things like 'a long history of mental problems . . . tried every drug known to man . . . private detectives.' Then he hung up and turned back to me. He caught his breath, smiled, lifted his arms, and snapped his fingers: 'OK, Roaring Twenties, playwright, great artist, and he goes to a producer seeking a production of the play, but he wants to direct it himself to protect his artistic integ—' "

Again, ringing. Again, Allen took the call. "Intensely claustrophobic," he hissed into the phone. "Two red eyes at the window . . . sent her child to the *Post* . . . hairs in a glassine envelope." Hanging up for the third time, Allen "just smiled sheepishly" before saying, "OK, let's get back to work on our little comic bauble!"

Writing was an oasis from the great unpleasantness. So were Knicks games and his Michael's gigs. The big difference between yesteryear and nowadays was mostly at night. Temporarily, he went to Elaine's less frequently. His habit of jumping into his limousine for a movie premiere or a Broadway show was suspended. No one among his close friends and family was certain what the future portended for Allen and Soon-Yi. But he and the college girl, who turned twenty-two during the filming of *Manhattan Murder Mystery*, stayed home most nights, going out on his rooftop terrace to escape the "crucible of intense terror tactics" and "get our fresh air for the day," he recalled. Sometimes the couple found themselves "laughing that it seemed like the entire world was against us. Downstairs we couldn't go out of the house because there were television trucks and paparazzi all over," Allen recalled. "We were housebound sometimes for a week. You know, it was quite romantic. . . ."

Christmas 1992 passed, then New Year's. *Bullets over Broadway* progressed, and the editing of *Manhattan Murder Mystery* went smoothly. Stuck for an ending, Allen reshot a discarded joke plucked from the middle of the script for a coda with Larry (Allen) and Carol (Diane Keaton) returning home after the *Lady from Shanghai*–style climax. Larry is still complaining about Ted (Alan Alda) coming on to his wife. "Take away his elevator shoes and his fake suntan and capped teeth and what do you have?" Larry asks. Carol: "You!"

Early in 1993 Allen and Soon-Yi began to venture out for late-night dinners at Felidia's and Le Cirque where "the mistress of a famous man," as Marion Meade wrote, cattily building her case against Soon-Yi, "was observed eating with her fingers." (The premier French restaurant would compete as a setting with Elaine's in future Woody Allen movies.) Unfazed as yet by his scandals, Hollywood rewarded *Husbands and Wives* with major Academy Award nominations: Judy Davis for Best Supporting Actress, Allen for Original Screenplay—his twelfth script nomination, tying him for the record in Oscar-writing nods with Billy Wilder. The always respectful Writers Guild also included his screenplay on the list of nominees for the best of 1992, a year that tolled the bitter end of the Allen-Farrow partnership, private and public, which had defined the American cinema for a decade.

FARROW WAS HARDLY idle, and in the months ahead she'd flaunt several new boyfriends as though to contest Kristi Groteke's portrait of her as diffident about her sex life. One companion was William Goldman, a screenwriter famous for *Butch Cassidy and the Sundance Kid* and other intelligent box office hits. Farrow also accepted her initial screen roles outside of Allen's sphere of influence to prove herself anew as an actress. Her first substantial part came courtesy of former flame Mike Nichols, a Frog Hollow neighbor, whom Allen in *What Falls Away* bitingly described as being Farrow's "frequent fantasy" of an old boyfriend she'd like to recapture. Nichols cast Farrow as Jack Nicholson's wife in *Wolf*, which Nichols was due to helm in Hollywood starting in the spring.

The actress renamed Dylan "Eliza" and Satchel "Harmon," names she insisted they picked for themselves. Eliza Doolittle was the character Julie Andrews played in the 1964 film version of *My Fair Lady*, which Dylan loved and whose soundtrack had been arranged and conducted by Farrow's second husband André Previn. Five-year-old Satchel selected his name from Farrow's Filofax list of cognomens the actress kept handy for adoptees, according to nanny Groteke. When Allen caught wind of Satchel's new name, he did his best to ignore this additional affront to his parentage, and many people were confused by the changing names. The new names couldn't really be mentioned in court in the custody proceedings because it might sound a little odd to the judge and press, so "Eliza" and "Harmon" were quietly tabled after a few months, and "Dylan" and "Satchel" temporarily restored.

At another preliminary hearing in January, Justice Elliott Wilk again scolded both sides for venting their animosities in the press. The informal agreement over Satchel had broken down, Allen had not seen the boy, and he still pushed to visit Dylan. Moses continued to ignore his father's solicitations. Farrow's lawyer Eleanor B. Alter submitted a new affidavit by the actress that went over like a stink bomb. Dylan had revealed something hitherto unmentioned during her late December interview with Connecticut police, which took place with Farrow present: Dylan said on a visit to Allen's apartment in the late summer or early autumn of 1991, when she was six years old, she surprised Allen and Soon-Yi in bed in his room "doing compliments" and "making snoring noises," according to Farrow; or, as the actress quoted Dylan more explicitly in her memoir, "putting his penis into Soon-Yi's vagina."

This stunning allegation, which dated their lovemaking several months earlier than previously suspected, made Allen's hoped-for visits with Dylan "unthinkable," Justice Wilk declared, before the court had rendered any verdict in the custody case. Allen raged in the hallway after the hearing, denying having sex with Soon-Yi at such an early juncture, a date that would have jeopardized his fight to defend his adoptions of Dylan and Moses in New York Surrogate's Court, insisting the notion was "too insane to even think about." Farrow's lawyers said she would agree to restart Satchel's visits with Allen—and Dylan's psychotherapy, which she had curtailed after August 4—if Allen would consent to temporarily suspend his demands to see Dylan. Allen did consent, and the judge ordered that Satchel's visits to his father resume.

Regardless of Justice Wilk's admonitions, the New York press swirled with rumors stoked by the antagonists. The city's inquiry into the child-abuse charges was tainted by a mystery surrounding Child Welfare Administration caseworker Paul Williams, who, according to Williams, was ordered by superiors to dumb down his examination and declare the charges "unfounded." However, according to Elkan Abramowitz, who had taken over as Allen's primary lawyer, Williams "acted in a rude fashion and appeared to be biased" against Allen in his investigation. An irate Allen walked out of one meeting with the city worker. After he kept digging, Williams was transferred to other cases. One angle Williams was pursuing was whether, during his youth, Allen ever had engaged in sexual relations with his sister, Letty. The question must have emanated from Farrow's side—"Mia's myrmidons," as Allen, with his love for arcane words, labeled them in his memoir—how else would Williams know he had a sister with whom he was close? Williams wanted to try that question on Allen's longtime analyst, Dr. Kathryn Prescott, but Dr. Prescott recoiled at the idea, which was inconceivable in her view, and through lawyers she later submitted a two-page affidavit to the court, stating she knew of no hint of any such transgression in Allen's boyhood. Dr. Prescott ended communications with Williams.

The city investigation had been slowed down if not altogether stymied, according to speculation in the press, by Allen's legal team's connections to current New York mayor David Dinkins. Mayor Dinkins felt beholden to Allen, according to this press theory, because Allen had stumped for then candidate Dinkins at a celebrity fundraiser in 1989. "Moreover," as the *Village Voice* elaborated, "as one of the last filmmakers to use city locations for his movies, Allen is a major taxpayer and icon for New York." High-ranking municipal officials also had colluded with Allen's lawyers, according to the *Voice* and other press outlets, to keep his name secreted in grand jury records as someone who in the past had used a prostitution service to arrange sex with teenage girls. The grand jury gossip was vehemently denied by Allen's lawyers, who said the reports were "outrageously false" and the name in records referred to *another* man named Woody Allen. Although widely disseminated, the gossip was never substantiated. Still, the teen-prostitute insinuation left a lingering odor.

The effort to link him with other unwilling teenage girls—his sister, anyone—reportedly led the Farrow side to approach actress Stacey Nelkin, at least according to Allen. Farrow might have known Nelkin from threesomes with Allen in the early 1980s; after all, Farrow had joined the Babi Christina Engelhardt threesomes, according to Engelhardt. When asked if she would testify against Allen, however, his former lover declined. "I wasn't underage when I dated Woody," Nelkin told author Tim Carroll for his book. "It was a two-year relationship, and it wasn't just about the bedroom. It was a very moral relationship. There were a lot of wonderful things about it."

As Douglas McGrath overheard in the phone conversations between Allen and his subordinates, lawyers for both sides employed dubious detectives and snoops. Both sides used smear-and-destroy tactics. Allen's lawyers compiled a dossier attesting to Farrow's mental instability, complete with a list of her antidepressants. Farrow was convinced that Allen, early on, made surreptitious visits to her bathroom to make notes on her vials, and had her house and apartment bugged. Both sides did bug and secretly tape-record the other, with some of those secret tape recordings later heard in court and some leaked to newspapers. Allen taped a fifteen-minute call with Farrow's longtime housekeeper in which the cleaning woman made disparaging remarks about Farrow's competency as a mother. Farrow stealthily taped several phone calls between her and Allen in which she mocked his aging sexual prowess and commented bitterly on his attraction to teenaged girls. Leaked to columnist Cindy Adams after the court case ended, one recording featured the actress reminding "the man who had been her lover for twelve years exactly what she had to do to coax him to performance capability." The court would never hear Kristi Groteke's clandestine recording of the film director's limousine driver, however, which failed in its mission of discovering the identity of his lovers and was disclosed only in her book.

All the while the Connecticut investigation into Dylan's charges proceeded quietly under the supervision of state's attorney Frank Maco, while the Yale–New Haven Hospital child-abuse specialists conducted their interviews and compiled findings. On March 17, Allen and Farrow were notified that the hospital team had completed its report and wanted to see them. They traveled separately to the hospital on Thursday, March 18.

The hospital team of experts included a pediatrician, a nurse, and two social workers. Over a period of weeks, dating back to September, members of the team had "repeatedly interviewed" Allen, Farrow, Dylan, and nanny Groteke, and watched and rewatched the notorious videotape recording of Dylan's assertions. Briefing Allen and Farrow for two hours, the team cited "important inconsistencies" in the little girl's version of events, and "a rehearsed quality" to her tales. Later, after being aired in the courtroom, it would be revealed the team described Dylan as "an intelligent, verbal seven-year-old whose storytelling was quite elaborate and fantasy-like at times," according to the official report. "She appeared confused about what to relate to the interviewers and was very controlling of what she would say. In her statements and her play she elaborated interrelated themes. She was upset by the loss of her father and Soon-Yi, and worried that her father might take her from her mother's care. She felt protective of and worried for her mother. Dylan was very much attuned to her mother's pain, and her mother reinforced Dylan's losses and her negative view of her father." In her sessions with the hospital team, the little blonde girl explained that her negative feelings about her father—the person she referred to nowadays, curiously, only as "Woody Allen"—began after witnessing her mother suffer such unhappiness over discovery of the Soon-Yi affair. "I'm like, why me? . . . Why do I have to solve this problem?" Dylan was quoted.

Among the wrinkles: one day Dylan retracted her sex-abuse story, and later that day, after lunch with her mother, she retracted her retraction. "She told us initially that she hadn't been touched in the vaginal area," Dr. John M. Leventhal, head of the Yale team, said later in a sworn statement. "She then told us that she had, then she told us that she hadn't." Dr. Leventhal added, "It's quite possible—as a matter of fact, we think it is medically probable—that she stuck to that story over time because of the intense relationship she had with her mother."

In her book Groteke wrote that Farrow reassured Dylan before some visits to the medical experts by telling her, "If you don't want Daddy to be your Daddy anymore, he doesn't have to be." The little blonde girl told the hospital team, "I love my mother and I hate my dad."

The team of experts considered "three hypotheses to explain Dylan's statements. First, that Dylan's statements were true, and that Mr. Allen had sexually abused her; second, that Dylan's statements were not true, but were made up by an emotionally vulnerable child who was caught up in a disturbed family and who was responding to the stresses in the family; and third, that Dylan was coached or influenced by her mother, Ms. Farrow." Regardless, they decided: "It is our expert opinion that Dylan was not sexually abused by Mr. Allen."

The hospital experts told all this to Allen and Farrow. The director closely watched his former lead actress as she reacted to the briefing. "You would think any mother would be relieved that a three-member panel, two of them women, found that her daughter had *not* been molested," he reflected later. "But so deep is her venom that she actually sees this as a loss." Farrow was "bitter" about the team's conclusions, even though "she knows I never molested Dylan," Allen told Denis Hamill back at his apartment later that night—shortly after taking a congratulatory phone call from Diane Keaton—as news of the Yale team's findings sped across the media.

For the time being, both sides in the dispute "agreed that the report would not be made public because a child's privacy was at stake," as Allen's publicist Leslee Dart announced. But after the team completed its briefing, Allen wrote in his memoir, Farrow angrily "stormed out" and, leaving the hospital, the actress gave this statement to journalists that had gathered outside: "I just want to say I will always stand by my children." Without going into details, Farrow's lawyer Eleanor B. Alter denounced the conclusions as "incomplete and inaccurate," adding that "what actually happened will be determined after many witnesses testify under oath in a court of law." It became central to Farrow's argument, in later interviews and in *What Falls Away*, that "the [lead] pediatrician who wrote the report [Dr. Leventhal] never even met Dylan. The report was widely criticized."

Allen also faced the press corps, estimated at eighty people, who were gathered on hospital steps. He looked "very much at his ease," wrote Carole Agus in *Newsday*. "Here was the man," she added, rather inaccurately, "who refused to be interviewed when he won Best Picture for *Annie Hall*. Here was the man who pilloried his own fans, portraying them as hideous sycophants in *Stardust Memories*. Then sex abuse reared its head and, for the first time in his life, Woody Allen called a press conference." The *New York Times* saw things differently. Although Allen said the Yale–New Haven report had vindicated him, the comedian and film director appeared "grim," wrote the *Times*. "I believe this will turn everything around," the comedian and director told the press.

In fact, the full report was not made public: there was a two-page summary, easily found online nowadays, but also a longer, detailed exegesis. Farrow's side quickly leaked highlights to Carole Agus at *Newsday*, focusing on excerpts—some apparently from the long form—that reflected poorly on Allen. *Newsday*, in next-day coverage, said the lengthier report concluded Dylan may have been "confused" about the "sexualized overtone" of Allen's affections toward her. The father needed to "establish appropriate boundaries" between himself and his children, and Allen was urged to seek "continuous psychotherapy" to address his "disturbed relationships" with Satchel and Dylan. However, the excerpts also recommended Farrow submit to therapy.

Asked for his reaction to the hospital team report, Connecticut state's attorney Maco said he would give the findings "due consideration," balancing the experts with other factors. But Maco also tipped his sympathy for the actress. "There has been no evidence presented in the state police investigation that suggests that Ms. Farrow acted in any way other than that of a concerned mother," the prosecutor declared. "The evidence does not show Ms. Farrow to be the prime instigator in bringing to light the alleged incidents."

Allen's lawyers FedExed a copy of the Yale hospital team report to the New York Surrogate's Court and, separately, to Justice Elliott Wilk, who was presiding over his custody case in the State Supreme Court. In the latter instance, Justice Wilk had already scheduled another hearing for the morning of Friday, March 19, the very next day. On that morning, Justice Wilk surprised both sides by ordering the trial to begin in the afternoon, forcing Farrow to choose between the custody case and her pending role in *Wolf*, the Mike Nichols movie slated to begin rehearsals two weeks hence in Hollywood. Reluctantly, the actress resigned from *Wolf*.

DRAGGING FARROW THROUGH a court proceeding was meant to force her to drop the abuse claims Allen considered spurious and to accept their long-delayed coparenting settlement. Allen and his lawyers had hoped for a settlement without going to trial. Now to win the trial, the film director had to prove the actress an unfit mother. The quixotic if not implausible corollary of this legal strategy would be to prove Allen the better single parent.

"The executive producer of the Woody/Mia miniseries," as Carole Agus of *Newsday* dubbed him, Justice Elliott Wilk was Brooklyn-born, in his early fifties, a trim, handsome marathon runner who did not like to wear judicial robes. Once a lawyer for Vista, the national public service program addressing poverty, and the radical National Lawyers Guild—he defended Attica inmates after the 1971 uprising—after his election to the Civil Court in 1977, Wilk forged a reputation as a staunch liberal jurist. Although a photograph of Cuban revolutionary Che Guevara hung in his office, he was "a traditionalist," according to *Newsday*, "in matrimonial cases." If ever a Woody Allen fan, Wilk would be hard-pressed to find fathers attentive to their children in the director's movies, right down to the latest, *Husbands and Wives*, in which the daughter of Judy (Farrow), and the children of Sally (Judy Davis) and Jack (Sydney Pollack), are mentioned in dialogue and then never heard of again. Justice Wilk "seemed to relish confrontations with the rich and powerful," the *New York Times* later said in his obituary.

Farrow's lawyer was Eleanor B. Alter, with the "B" for the former chief judge of the New York Court of Appeals, Charles D. Breitel, her father. A high-priced family law and divorce specialist for wealthy clients and celebrities—later she'd handle the Billy Joel–Christie Brinkley divorce—Alter was proud of her abrasive reputation. "Lots of people will tell you I'm a bitch," she once boasted to the *Times*. "A dogged but often incomprehensible questioner," Alter was otherwise described by William Grimes, who enlivened the custody case with his observations in the *Times*, as someone who seems "to have trouble constructing any sentence more complicated than subject-object-verb." Farrow made hay, in her memoir, out of Allen being represented by "six different law firms, led by a criminal attorney," as compared to her single-female-lawyer defense, but Alter was a full partner in Rosenman & Colin, a premier trust and real estate firm with hundreds of lawyers and offices in three states. Alter worked with a team of paralegals, associates, and a family law partner.

Allen's point man was Elkan Abramowitz, one of New York's leading white-collar trial attorneys, who was known for representing prominent people embroiled in high-stakes crises. The onetime chief of the Criminal Division in the US Attorney's Office for the Southern District of New York, in 1979 Abramowitz joined Martin, Obermaier & Morvillo, known for its regulatory and business litigation, eventually becoming a named partner. A tall (6 feet, 3 inches) man with a booming voice, Abramowitz was a "super-decent, upright family man" who never would have defended Allen if he didn't believe in him, wrote Liz Smith. Abramowitz was "a deliberate worker," reported Grimes, "the kind of lawyer who, if a witness recalls picking up a fork, will ask him with what hand, and then, how many tines?" Behind his deceptive plodding he was a superb oral advocate.

Print and broadcast media from around the world descended on the wood-paneled Courtroom 341 of the State Supreme Court at 31 Chambers Street off Foley Square, with some journalists missing the first afternoon because of the rush scheduling and limited seating. There were correspondents from London, Paris, Rome, and other major foreign outposts where Woody Allen films were distributed. Wire services filled in the gaps. In New York alone, the *Times*, *Daily News*, *Post*, *Newsday*, and numerous radio and television outlets followed the twists and turns of the story, often as lead or front-page news. The metropolitan area media spoke to millions daily—the New Yorkers who were the target audience for Allen's New York–centric films.

The rich and powerful filmmaker was the first "self-assured" (according to *Newsday*) witness, "relaxed, one arm draped over the back of his chair," giving answers "that were lengthy, conversational, even funny" (according to the *Times*). "With the good news from New Haven still ringing in his ears," Marion Meade wrote, "he had every reason to feel confident." Most days in the courtroom Allen sported the spectacles, tweed jacket, and khakis his characters wore in Woody Allen films. His Zelig face only infrequently betrayed irritation or anger, yet from the beginning he gave off bad vibes to Justice Wilk. "He and I did not like each other and neither tried to hide it, which was not to my advantage in a battle where he is the decider," Allen later reflected.

As Allen testified during the first afternoon, Farrow watched from close by, separated from her former significant other by a few chairs and an empty table. At times the actress was stone-faced and other times she wept. Inside her purse she clutched a lifeline: the heavy wooden rosary beads with a silver cross once belonging to her father, the Hollywood director John Farrow. During recesses, she smoked Marlboros in the hallway.

Allen ran through his version of life with the actress: how, early on, she'd asked to bear his children; how initially, after Dylan's adoption, he didn't care very much about the baby, until he realized "she's pretty cute, and I started feeling paternal for her"; how his boundless affection for Dylan was exaggerated by Farrow as a weird kind of lust; how after Farrow became pregnant with Satchel in 1987 she told him, "Don't get too close to him, I don't think this relationship is going any place"; how—the single revelation of the day—regardless of the strain in their relationship, after earning more than usual from Italian commercials and *Scenes from a Mall*, Allen bestowed a $1 million gift on Farrow in 1991; and how, not long after that—a few days before Christmas, more or less, because he never pinpointed the date—Allen embarked on his love affair with Soon-Yi Previn.

The filmmaker told Justice Wilk and reporters and the few spectators who had managed to squeeze into the courtroom that he had initiated his romance with Soon-Yi in late 1991, believing their affair would be "just a short thing and completely private." After Farrow discovered the nude Polaroids, however, the actress had concocted the sexual abuse incident as a means of manipulating the child-custody disagreements, exploiting their three mutual children—Satchel, Dylan, and Moses—"In the most shameless, degrading way as pawns."

Justice Wilk asked Allen pointedly if he ever had considered the effect that learning of his affair with Soon-Yi would have on the other Farrow-Previn children—all of them—but especially his three children, her siblings.

"I felt nobody in the world would have any idea," Allen replied.

"Wasn't that enough," pressed Wilk, "that you would know that you were sleeping with your children's sister?"

"I didn't see it that way," said Allen. "I'm sorry."

He vigorously denied sexually molesting Dylan. "It's unfathomable," the film director said. "It's unconscionable. It's disgusting. It's unappealing. It's not in my history, or something I would ever do."

Allen and his attorneys and Farrow and her attorneys left the courtroom, avoiding the sea of reporters. The consensus was that Allen had won the day. Over the weekend, Allen later revealed, he phoned the actress, asking her to "shake hands" and end their dispute civilly. "But it's been fourteen months, and her rage has not abated."

On Monday morning Allen returned to the stand, defending the nude Soon-Yi Polaroids from tenacious probing by Farrow's attorney. Entering the half-dozen snapshots into evidence, Eleanor B. Alter asked Allen if he had ever told Soon-Yi it was wrong to have photographed her in the nude. "We were two adults," answered Allen. "We don't think that way." Alter extracted details: The Polaroids were Soon-Yi's idea, Allen (and Soon-Yi) always maintained. While the comedian and filmmaker "bumbled" with the unfamiliar camera, he explained (the word evoking the early, silly Woody Allen comedies), Soon-Yi removed her clothes. Then Allen's directorial instincts kicked in. "I posed her on the sofa. I said, 'Lay back and give me your most erotic poses. Let yourself go.' " The Polaroids were "erotic, provocative," Allen insisted, not in any way pornographic.

Still, Allen expressed remorse for "some of his other actions," according to press accounts. His personal relationship with Farrow had become "joyless, sexless," the film director explained, and "rightly or wrongly" that was partly why he had drifted into an affair with her daughter. "I did love her [Soon-Yi]," Allen protested. "I do love her." He accused Farrow "of behaving worse still" by trumping up the child-abuse charges. "I screwed up," Allen conceded. "I caused this thing to happen. OK, but don't seek vengeance on me through the kids."

Throughout the second day of Allen's testimony, the actress stared impassively at him, but she no longer shed tears. Occasionally Farrow rolled her eyes and shook her head at his testimony. She also took notes.

By all accounts the third and final day of his testimony, when Alter and Justice Wilk really let loose on him, was the worst for the filmmaker, who until now had not showed the full stress and strain of doing what he loathed—airing his dirty laundry in public. His stand-up comedy, which always had been largely rehearsed, made it on the averages; as an actor Allen was known to improvise, but always from a well-constructed script under circumstances he controlled. Not so on the third day, which started with Alter reading aloud from Moses Farrow's impassioned condemnation of his father. You could have heard a proverbial pin drop in the courtroom, journalists noted. "Mom is a great mother, and she always finds the time and patience to play with us," Moses's letter stated. "All you did is spoil the little ones, Dylan and Satchel. Everyone knows not to have an affair with your son's sister, including that sister, but you have a special way to get that sister to think that that is OK." The letter continued: "You can't force me to live with you. . . . You have done a horrible, unforgivable, needy, ugly stupid thing." Moses concluded brutally: "I hope you get so humiliated you commit suicide."

Under Alter's terse questioning, Allen admitted Moses's letter seemed authentic. Maybe Moses typed it, he added, but the sentence "You probably think Mom is telling me to say these things, like before," evidenced Farrow's hand in the writing, as did words like "needy." "Needy is Mia's favorite word," Allen noted. Previously relaxed and self-assured, during the day's cross-examination "he spoke quietly, sometimes mumbling, often asked that questions be repeated and at times searched in vain for a way to phrase his answers." Allen couldn't "remember details and had to refer to printed transcripts, taking off his glasses," the *New York Times* said, "bringing his nose in contact with the paper, looking remarkably like a befuddled old man."

Alter got Allen to acknowledge sleeping with Farrow at least twice in early 1992, not long after the Polaroids discovery. This was hitherto undisclosed news. Allen haltingly explained he was trying to placate Farrow, who insisted on sleeping with him, and that he hoped to win her over to a "coparenting" agreement best for the children. "Was having an affair with their sister the best thing for the children?" Alter riposted.

Once more, Allen suffered the worst nightmare of a comedian who'd like to forget the jokes that bombed. Alter noted the director had repeatedly referred to Satchel, his own son, as a "little bastard." Allen insisted this was misunderstood in context, admitting perhaps he had made such remarks on occasion—like the time Satchel deliberately poked Dylan in the eye—but usually it was out of the boy's personal earshot. The phrase was all a jest anyway because, after all, according to Webster's—as Rodney Dangerfield might say—Satchel was, in fact, born out of wedlock. Any Allen gag he himself chuckled at, regardless of audiences, tended to crop up in his pictures once or twice and, for example, there'd be mention of "little bastard" children later in *Café Society*.

His own words, more than once, boomeranged. Asked about the family summer vacations in Europe, the director said, "The purpose of my going was to be with my three children. The other children did not interest me.

I did not speak with them. I played with my own children and primarily worked on my film scripts."

According to Carole Agus, whose perspective was underlined by "The Big Director Is a Small Father" headline of her *Newsday* account, Alter reduced Allen to "a father who was two inches tall" after a barrage of questions about his children: Did the good father know the names of their friends, what grades were on their report cards, who were their teachers and doctors, did he ever take the children for a haircut, or give them their baths? The answers were almost always no. "He thought his son Moses had an interest in baseball," Agus wrote acidly. "He'd never taken him to a game. Alter piled on the questions and Woody got smaller with every one."

Speaking "in a quiet voice, a gentle voice," Justice Wilk took over in the afternoon, his persistent questions settling "on the courtroom like bombs," Agus wrote. There was "a claim of some misbehavior with respect to Dylan," Wilk began. "Do you believe that Miss Farrow brainwashed Dylan with respect to that accusation?"

"I do believe she brainwashed Dylan."

"When did you think and how did you think she did that?"

"Mia encouraged all the children to say the worst things about me. That I was a rapist. That I was a molester. . . . Over a period of time, she kept promulgating the idea to her [Dylan] over and over again."

It was not a good sign that Justice Wilk had trouble with the whole brainwashing concept, which Allen's testimony had relentlessly advanced in the previous days and which was central to his child-abuse defense. "My question is," Wilk continued, "if she [Farrow] was told on the 4th [of August] that something happened, by their babysitter, when did she have time to brainwash the child . . . ? From the time she was told, until she alerted whomever she alerted for the first time that you had done this . . . ? What I don't understand is how you think she brainwashed her before August 4th, to say that you had done something on August 4th . . . ?"

Justice Wilk switched subjects to that of Soon-Yi, whose romance with Allen seemed to bother the judge more than the child-abuse allegations—perhaps because he knew the validation of the abuse allegations belonged to another jurisdiction. "The other thing that occurs to me," Justice Wilk continued, "involves your relationship with Soon-Yi. In the letter that was read from Moses, you refer to her not having had any friends besides you. . . ."

"To the best of my knowledge that is correct."

What would Soon-Yi's support system be if Allen broke off their affair? Wilk wondered. The college girl couldn't find comfort with friends, not having any, or with her family. "It would not have been an issue," Allen said in a worst moment. "My thought was I would be the one abandoned. I don't see it the other way around."

Asked repeatedly why he was qualified to be the primary custodian of his children, Allen replied complacently he was the better financial provider who could afford their creature comforts and educational expenses, and "their day-to-day behavior will be done in consultation with their therapist." His implacable insistence that "if [the children] are with me, they will have a better life" sounded like cold logic to Wilk. "The Judge had held a mirror up to Woody Allen," Agus wrote in *Newsday*, "and had shown him his soul."

Elkan Abramowitz valiantly tried to regain ground, with Allen's attorney eliciting a more roseate version of Allen's relationship with Dylan and details of Farrow's "needy" and "hostile" behavior. Under Abramowitz's redirect, the movie director rallied, "sometimes impressively," according to the *Times*. By the end of the third day, however, Allen no longer looked rich, powerful, or self-assured. He looked pale and hunched. Later, after the court adjourned, in the hallway Abramowitz defended his client's flat affect, his oft-hesitant testimony. "That's the way he talks," Allen's lawyer explained to the press. "I think you could tell he was very, very sincere." Alter snorted: "I don't think Woody Allen cares about anyone. I think he's incapable."

ON THE FOURTH day the star witness was Mia Farrow. Elkan Abramowitz had "tried to portray her as a woman so wounded by Mr. Allen's affair" with her daughter, in the words of the *New York Times*, "she would stop at nothing to strike back." Accoutered in "a pleated teal skirt, a navy blazer and a white shirt buttoned to the throat," the actress gave more the impression of a "gentle flower," or "a Roman Catholic schoolgirl, the kind who earns straight A's for deportment and penmanship." Marion Meade described "her mane of fluffy hair, curly in girlish corkscrews." The actress spoke calmly, slowly, choosing words carefully, for the first time publicly relating her wrenching story from finding the Polaroids through to Frog Hollow on August 4.

Farrow said Dylan told her the August 4 molestation began with her father's head in her lap and his hand under her bottom, something Farrow had witnessed several times before ("his head in her stomach or crotch"). "He was breathing into her legs and holding her around the waist," the actress testified Dylan told her. "She said he put his hand underneath her and touched her." Later, Dylan said, her father led her up to the attic.

After relating what Dylan said transpired in the attic—Allen's supposed whispers about a part for her in his next movie, the two of them going to Paris together, him poking his finger into the little girl's vagina—the actress surprised the court by raising a "second claim of sexual abuse," in the words of the *Los Angeles Times*, another alleged incident at Frog Hollow not previously mentioned. During the summer of 1991, when her daughter was then age six, Farrow said, Dylan recalled her father slipping his hand under her shorts when he was boosting the little blonde girl up on the ladder of her bunk bed. Although the Yale hospital team had interviewed Dylan nine times, the girl had neglected, before now, to remember this incident. Farrow said she only recently had learned about this from Dylan, some ten days before the hospital report was issued.

Farrow explained why the videotape she made of Dylan's accusations had stops and starts. She turned the machine on whenever Dylan was in the mood to talk, Farrow said. She had videotaped her little blonde daughter because "I wanted this documented, because it had happened before." She recounted Dylan's several doctor visits, including the physical examination by a local pediatrician in which nothing amiss could be detected.

Farrow said she had worried about Allen's behavior with Dylan ever since her daughter was two and a half or three years old. Whenever the little girl visited Allen's apartment, "they would always end up in his bed playing, but the quality of the playing would arouse her [Dylan]. She would grab him." Sometimes Allen was lying in bed in his underwear, Farrow asserted, and at least once, the girl grabbed at his genitals. There was an uncommon urgency to Allen's fixation on Dylan, the actress repeated. There was "this very needy quality."

She admitted posting the red-crayon "Child Molester" note outside the Frog Hollow bathroom, for all to see, prophetically warning of Allen's future misdeeds. But Abramowitz could not rattle the actress during his interrogation, when he asked her to compare Soon-Yi's age to her own tender years when she had wooed and married Frank Sinatra, whom she had met as a little girl. Switching to husband number two, André Previn, whom the actress also knew in girlhood, Abramowitz inquired, "Did you become pregnant by Mr. Previn while he was still married?" Farrow replied evenly: "He was estranged from his wife." Asked if she was aware of Dory Previn's song "Beware of Young Girls," Farrow answered, "I know that it referred to me."

Farrow disputed the implication in Allen's testimony that they hardly ever made love after Satchel's birth but confessed that by 1991, their life together was "sexually and romantically diminished." The courtroom went silent as she described Allen's affections cooling toward her. "He would do little things for me, bring little things to me, tokens, and that stopped. I was hurt and perplexed that that had gone from our relationship."

There were other surprising tidbits, accusations thrown around, and humiliating intimacies about their personal and professional lives. At one time, Farrow confessed in court, she wondered if Allen was dabbling in homosexuality, one of the long list of sexual peccadilloes she suspected the director of at one time or other. Yet the actress lost her composure only twice, according to reportage, first when Abramowitz recited from the declarations she had made on Dylan and Moses's adoption papers. Allen "is far more of a father" to Dylan "than most natural fathers are," Farrow had attested. Quietly but with banked emotion, the actress said she had signed the papers, page after voluminous page, penned by lawyers, without careful reading. When admitting she punched and kicked Soon-Yi after the college girl admitted sleeping with Allen "all her senior year, on Saturdays and Sundays"—although this hearsay and timeline were vigorously contested by Allen's lawyers—the actress openly wept. "I'm not proud of it," Farrow said. Soon-Yi saw a doctor after the scuffle, added Abramowitz.

Most reporters described a long, grueling day of testimony, at times tedious, with intriguing inferences by Abramowitz that never quite climaxed, and Farrow, overall, spellbinding on the stand. "Her affect was studied," Andrea Peyser of the *New York Post* told Marion Meade. "It sure played well with the judge, though."

Yet Farrow needed a solid script and firm direction as much as Allen did, and the actress lapsed on her second day when she was again called to the stand by Abramowitz as a hostile witness. Allen's attorney picked up the pace, clashing with Farrow and her lawyer, cutting off her slow replies. This time Farrow was more sullen and hostile, and "her clipped answers lay somewhere between cool and icy," according to the *Times*.

One account described this as "the day of the broken legs," because Allen's feeble joke about his "bastard" children found its cousin in Abramowitz asking about rumors that Farrow's first ex-husband Sinatra—or was it perhaps her second ex-spouse, André Previn?—offered to punish Allen by breaking his legs. Which of the husbands was it? Abramowitz wondered. Eleanor B. Alter hastened to object, and Justice Wilk blocked Farrow from answering. "It was a joke," she finished irritably. It was Sinatra, Farrow wrote in her memoir.

Farrow confessed she once told Dr. Susan Coates that Allen might abuse Satchel, or any of her children. She was "hysterical" at the time, she explained, and no longer believed in that possibility where Satchel was concerned. When Abramowitz inquired if she would ever allow their children to see Allen again, her answer came "sternly," according to accounts. "I would hope I could empower them to make the decision whether to see him." When Allen's lawyer followed up by asking whether the children would be allowed to love their father, Farrow replied with pursed lips, "If they want to, they may." Under persistent questioning, the actress said there had been no discussion of any exchange of money "to keep the allegations quiet," in Abramowitz's words.

Alter countered Abramowitz in her friendly redirect of the actress, bringing out more odd details of Allen's wary visits to Frog Hollow, including his endlessly bruited-about qualms about shower drains. Farrow dwelled on the showering "in some detail, [as part of] a catalogue of unforgivable sins, but it was this that seemed to stop her cold for a moment," reported the *Times*, "the weirdness of it striking her for the first time."

Farrow's major goal was to secure custody of Dylan, Satchel, and Moses, and if Allen began his affair with Soon-Yi before he signed adoption papers it would taint his claims to fatherhood of Dylan and Moses. (Satchel, as time would tell, was another matter.) Allen insisted, in interviews and testimony, he had sex with Soon-Yi for the first time just a few days before Christmas 1991—*after* the adoption papers were signed. Yet in his memoir Allen wrote, somewhat differently, the affair "began the next time she [Soon-Yi] came in from college," after their kiss at the *Seventh Seal* screening. Alan Dershowitz guessed the date to be December 1, 1991, Allen's fifty-sixth birthday. In her testimony Farrow said she believed the affair began during Soon-Yi's senior year in high school because of clues she had gleaned in retrospect. That was the time when, in hindsight, Farrow recalled a "dramatic change" in Soon-Yi's attitude, in her words, "the new laugh of superiority, the smugness, and the coldness to other kids." Still another reason for her belief, she testified, was what Dylan had told her about her visit to Allen's place in the summer or autumn of 1991 and catching Allen and Soon-Yi in bed.

Farrow juxtaposed Allen's fawning devotion to Dylan with the little blonde girl's discomfiture with her father, Dylan's sometimes screaming fits when her father visited, locking herself in the bathroom. The actress testified Allen behaved violently toward Dylan on at least one occasion, and that he posed a danger to Satchel and Moses too. To stories of Farrow slapping and striking Soon-Yi now was added Allen's similar trespasses: He once shoved Dylan's face into a plate of hot spaghetti, he threatened to kick in Moses's teeth, and to break Satchel's "fucking leg." "Absolutely untrue," Allen defended himself. Perhaps "I'll kick your teeth in . . ." was another bad joke that was less funny in the courtroom. The plate of hot spaghetti, the teeth-kicking, and "the leg-breaking seemed to lend thematic unity to the day's testimony," William Grimes dryly reported in the *Times*.

The "day of the broken legs" was Friday, March 26. The actress was announced for additional redirect on Monday, but her lawyers had second thoughts and Farrow stood down. Allen never addressed the courtroom again, but Farrow returned to the stand in late April "for less than five minutes," according to *Newsday*, "to clarify several puzzling statements Dylan made to researchers at the Yale–New Haven Medical Center."

So far, the case was a melodrama stingy on comedy, all very tangled and murky. The audience—the US and the whole world—was left wanting. "What is the truth?" plaintively asked *Newsweek*. "Shadows and fog," declared *Time*. "Movies have resolutions. The Woody-Mia affair is only a confusing series of scenes." One thing Farrow said in her testimony may have been the most on target: "There were so many untruths, so many versions of what was going on, so many contradictions. A person could go crazy just trying to keep track."

••

THERE ENSUED ANOTHER four weeks of similar mudslide in which experts disputed sexperts, longtime nannies vied with fleeting sitters, therapists tried to explain the inexplicable, and lawyers fiercely butted heads with lawyers.

The attention of the press waxed and waned. The New York press—the media of the city celebrated in Woody Allen movies—were the most fascinated and appalled. *Ms.* magazine founder Gloria Steinem showed up outside the courtroom to voice her "concern about child abuse," telling the press, "The mother is often turned into the jealous or vindictive woman and is often disbelieved." Steinem had met with city social worker Paul Williams, who investigated the child-abuse charges and, as she later told the *Allen v. Farrow* documentarists, she found Williams to be credible, deciding "people with power were able to get the [city] case removed." Many New York pundits thought Allen victimized women—lumping Farrow together with her daughters Soon-Yi and Dylan—while others simply found him immoral. In his memoir Allen mentioned Steinem, whom he had "really admired," and an even more outspoken left-liberal detractor, Pulitzer Prize–winning *New York Post* columnist Murray Kempton, among the journalists whose nonsupport most disappointed him. Kempton, who led the Allen-is-immoral faction, said the film director was "a hateful creature" who had instigated the "concourse in sin" with Soon-Yi.

The headlines summed up the remainder of the trial: "Allen and Farrow Mute as Others Debate Their Judgment and Actions" (March 31, 1993, *New York Times*); "Shrink Raps: Doc Knocks Woody & Mia as Parents" (March 31, *Newsday*); " 'Crazy Mia' or 'Woody No-Goody'?: The Question in the Allen-Farrow Mess" (April 7, *Washington Post*); "Clash of the Nannies: At Woody-Mia Trial, More Finger-Pointing" (April 7, *Washington Post*); "Is She Vengeful? Is He a Moral Tumbleweed? Are Woody and Mia Both Right?" (April 12, *People*); perhaps everyone's favorite—"Dershowitz Testimony Turns into 3-Hour Shouting Match" (April 17, *New York Times*). Last, but not least: "Judge Admits He's Baffled" (April 28, *Newsday*).

Among those weighing in on Allen's side was Dr. Kathryn Prescott, the director's psychiatrist since 1972, whose two-page affidavit affirmed in part "there has never been any suggestion that Mr. Allen was suffering from a sexual perversion/deviant behavior."

The Yale–New Haven Hospital team report was picked apart by specialists recruited by Farrow's lawyers: they pointed out that Allen was accompanied to his interviews by his lawyers; the lead pediatrician Dr. John Leventhal never personally interviewed Dylan—only the social workers interviewed the little girl—while Leventhal interviewed Allen and Farrow multiple times; the Yale team had destroyed their notes on the girl (as was their standard custom); and if Dylan's claims at times seemed inconsistent, her attestations were not entirely inconsistent, and there was an overall consistency to them, etc.

On the stand, or in depositions, the Farrow squad (nanny Groteke, French tutor Sophie Bergé, city caseworker Paul Williams) vied against the Allen gang (Jane Read Martin, Monica Thompson, the children's dismissed therapists). Thompson said in testimony that the actress slapped Moses one day when the boy could not find the family dog leash. (The grown-up Moses, in 2014, would confirm this anecdote and supply details.) Martin, buttressing Allen's assertion that Farrow handled her biological children in a more humane fashion than she treated her adopted kids, said the actress ordered Lark around like "a scullery maid." Groteke's equivocal testimony was similar to what the nanny later wrote in her book, which attempted to be judicious and which, like many of the experts called to testify in the courtroom, struggled to arrive at a conclusive determination. In their effort to answer thorny questions, the loyalists and experts, no matter how they were aligned, often hedged bets and crossed sides, saying it was very hard if not impossible to divide the blame and know the facts.

Dr. Susan Coates was on the stand for three days, partly in closed session and ostensibly on Allen's behalf, saying tests on Dylan indicated the little blonde girl could "be taken over by fantasy with minimal stimuli." Farrow's lawyer nibbled away at the therapist, extracting minor concessions. Yes, Allen put Farrow down at times, but "I think they each put down the other." Dr. Coates admitted that Allen lied during some of their sessions; he had dissembled about the high number of phone calls he had placed to Soon-Yi over the summer, for example. But Dr. Coates refused to adopt Farrow's terminology and label the film director "evil," a word she did not care for. She said only that Allen showed "extreme bad judgment" in his affair with Soon-Yi. When pressed by Justice Wilk as to which parent, in her opinion, should be rewarded with custody, considering where the matter stood, Dr. Coates replied: "I really feel that, from where I sit now, I wouldn't know what to do."

Dr. Nancy Schultz, also summoned to the courtroom by Allen's lawyers, said she did not believe Allen had sexually abused Dylan and that he should have some visiting rights unless abuse was proven without doubt.

A little lost in the shuffle was Letty Aronson, who had stood in her older brother's shadow, his number-one fan, all her life. In her "brief but spirited" testimony, according to the *Times*, Aronson said Allen doted on his children, performed magic tricks for them, played games with them. She gave his fatherhood "a rave review," reported the *Times*, saying he was just as good an uncle to her three children, whose education tuitions he paid to the tune of $60,000 annually. Aronson thought her brother's relationship with Soon-Yi was "inappropriate, the way it happened," while adding, "What he did wasn't right and was socially unacceptable. What she has done is terribly wrong, but more socially acceptable." Aronson said, "If Mia hadn't rubbed their noses in it [the affair], it didn't have to have such a deleterious effect." Farrow had pitted the children against their father, Aronson told the court, and nowadays Satchel greeted Allen at his scheduled visits with: "My mommy says I can't love you. My mommy says you're bad." When Allen kissed him, the boy would say, "Mommy says I have to wipe these kisses off." Jane Read Martin added her observations: Satchel, arriving at Allen's place, would declare, "I don't want to be here," before getting down to fun and games with his father. The boy habitually asked, "Why do you keep Soon-Yi from coming to our house? Why don't you give Mommy money?"

Probably the most devastating series of testimonies were never reported. These interrogatories and affidavits were restricted to closed sessions, from which everyone except lawyers, plaintiffs, and witnesses were barred. "We get kicked out, the press and public," one journalist noted, "at intervals at this trial." For example, one day in court the videotape recording of Dylan was screened for the privileged few. Other important closed-door sessions were noted briefly in nanny Groteke's book *Mia & Woody*: the court appearance of Soon-Yi and depositions by Farrow-Previn children. Dated April 16, 1993, Groteke's seemingly contemporaneous journal excerpt from her book recounts: "Mia told me that in court Soon-Yi was reprimanded by the judge for possible perjury. Mia felt that Soon-Yi had been coached not only by Elkan [Abramowitz], but by Woody, and so she misled the judge when she described, under oath, the family's home life. After Judge Wilk listened to the other children's (sealed) testimony, he took her [Soon-Yi] aside—and took her to task." Interestingly, Farrow would have been foresworn to keep secret any details of her children's testimony, including Soon-Yi's. Groteke, when later writing her book, was under no such obligation. The press was banished from the courtroom during Soon-Yi's testimony; therefore her attestations were not reported, and the judge's supposed chiding cannot be confirmed.

Quite apart from suggesting that Justice Wilk had taken an instinctual dislike to Soon-Yi, the significance of this passage is that if Farrow's children gave testimony adverse to Allen—the list would exclude the youngest, Isaiah, and perhaps the most recent adoptee, Tam, but not necessarily the superbright, talkative Satchel, who could write or chatter above his age—the judge would have had six or eight kids on record *against* Allen's paternal qualifications. Moses had already testified in damning epistolary fashion. Dylan had told her story on videotape. The only child who had spoken out in Allen's favor was Soon-Yi, with whom he was sleeping.

Justice Wilk had already frowned over Allen's pitch for himself as the best imaginable parent and his blindness to any damage caused to the family by sleeping with his children's sister. Perhaps above all, Allen hurt his case by repeatedly insinuating his romance was acceptable because, after all, Soon-Yi was *adopted*. Outside of relatives and former staff, Allen's defense made only slight inroads on the issue of whether he might qualify as the superior parent. Notably, one Brearley School staff member, "the second wife of one of Woody's longtime colleagues," according to Marion Meade, testified Allen had been a diligent father who showed up at all of the parent-teacher conferences.

The lengthy trial ended not with a whimper but with a bang on May 4, "much as it began," in the words of the *Times*, "with angry charges and countercharges." Allen and Farrow sat quietly, without speaking to the court or looking at each other, as Eleanor B. Alter, in a sarcastic closing, told Justice Wilk that Allen had "no concept of how to behave like a responsible, decent human being, let alone a father," and asked that his current visitation schedule—now twice weekly with Satchel, with no contact at all with Dylan—be continued. Elkan Abramowitz said Farrow's rage over Allen's relationship with Soon-Yi may have been justified, but the actress had "distorted" her rage into manufactured sex-abuse charges and deployed her children as "soldiers and pawns in a negative publicity barrage" against Allen.

Abramowitz conceded: "I don't think he'll ever recover from the damage to his reputation. There will always be a segment of the public that thinks he did it [molested Dylan]."

Banging his gavel to end the stormy proceedings, Justice Wilk said he would need at least a month to contemplate his decision. Yet was the judge truly "baffled," as Wilk stated in court? Or did Wilk inherently favor the glamorous movie star, "a wonderful, beautiful mother who adopted disabled children," as Allen himself wrote self-mockingly in *Apropos of Nothing*, over her "slimy" director-boyfriend, "a roué who seduced her daughter thirty-five years younger than him, and exploited the poor college student for pornographic photos"?

IV

The Great Rectification Campaign

Chapter 10

1993

The Tears of a Clown

Showing Creative Resilience, Rehabbing Privately and Publicly

The die was cast, and the next month would be a nail-biter while Allen waited for the court decision. The director put his shoulder to the wheel on the postproduction of *Manhattan Murder Mystery* and finished the script for his next film project. He watched his beloved Knicks lose to the Chicago Bulls in the Eastern Conference Finals and found time to lay down tracks with a thirteen-piece New York Jazz Ensemble led by banjo player Eddy Davis, whose band Allen had first sat in with in Chicago in 1965. *The Bunk Project* album, recorded at Harkness House, was released in the month of May.

Allen's commercials for the Italian supermarket chain La Coop Nordemilia were also unveiled. The Catholic Church in Italy had condemned Allen, following the Soon-Yi revelations and Dylan Farrow abuse accusations, and the last of his five spots was canceled. The other four were shown on Italian television. Stefano Hatfield, writing in the British-based magazine *Campaign*, said the advertisements were sheer "joys, containing all the surreal and pithy wit one would expect of the Manhattan master." The two 45-second and two 60-second commercials bore "traces of many Allen movies," wrote Hatfield, with familiar Woody Allen characters, music stylings, and setups involving sex, food, shrinks, spaceships, art galleries, and silicone implants. The grocery chain got its money's worth because the commercials were excerpted on many Italian news programs.

In her court testimony Allen's sister, Letty Aronson, had hinted at major behind-the-scenes developments. Aronson had moved from *Saturday Night Live* to New York's Museum of Broadcasting, where as a museum executive Aronson had organized a 1989 retrospective of Allen's television work—his writing and appearances. In court, however, Aronson newly introduced herself as the "vice president of a production company."

That production company was headed by Jean Doumanian and her deep-pocketed boyfriend Jacqui Safra, who had launched themselves as motion picture producers early in 1991 with shared financing of two Swedish films, both indebted to Allen and Ingmar Bergman connections. Cameraman Sven Nykvist, who wrote and directed a handful of movies, first told Doumanian the story of *The Ox* on a Woody Allen set. Produced by Doumanian and Safra, *The Ox*, directed by Nykvist and starring Liv Ullmann, would become Sweden's official entry and nominee for the Best Foreign Language Film Oscar in 1992. Allen attended its January 1992 premiere in New York, the day before the Polaroids were discovered. The second Doumanian-Safra production, in 1993, was *Sunday's Children*, directed by Daniel Bergman, one of the auteur's children, from a script by his father. It mainly played festivals. Early in 1993, Allen's sister had quietly joined their company, Sweetland Films, as a VP.

One night during the trial the four people had gone to dinner, with Allen down in the dumps. They finalized a discussion that had been going on for months behind the scenes of the court case. Doumanian and Safra, the latter with his access to lines of bank credit, would take over Allen's TriStar contract and produce his next three pictures. Sweetland would not have access to a studio advertising and distribution apparatus, unlike United Artists, Orion, and TriStar, but the new company would guarantee Allen's production budgets and sell the distribution rights to the highest bidders. Much of the initial financing would come from foreign investors—Safra's specialty—which would help secure the up-front production costs. Overseas, Sweetland would cede advantages to France, Italy, and Germany, Allen's best foreign markets in that order. Sweetland alone would control the North American rights and monies. To release Woody Allen pictures in the US, Sweetland would partner with Hollywood studios willing to invest in the productions on the back end.

Over the next six months lawyers drew up a thirty-five-page contract for three film partnerships between Sweetland and Moses Productions—named for Allen's disaffected son. The first was stipulated as *Bullets over Broadway*, the script Allen had written with Douglas McGrath, which had been previously earmarked as part of the TriStar pact. *Bullets* was a "period comedy" with a bigger budget than usual for Allen, and he was going to direct it without acting in the picture. But Allen agreed to star in the next two movies—the first two made expressly for Sweetland. Allen's services would be contractually "exclusive" to Sweetland. He'd receive a "fixed compensation" of $1.5 million for *Bullets*—less money because he wasn't appearing onscreen—and $2.5 million for the second and third pictures. Moses Productions would draw annual operating expenses, and Allen stood to earn 50 percent of the "adjusted gross proceeds" from the Sweetland movies after production and distribution costs were deducted. Most important, all three films would be cross-collateralized, their combined losses subtracted from total profits, because the higher-budgeted *Bullets* hurt Safra's chances to recoup his investment. Allen agreed to a "special accommodation" for joint-accounting purposes to enable *Bullets*.

Except for provisions defining the running length and budget overruns, the contract guaranteed the creative autonomy the filmmaker always had enjoyed. The "aggregate budgeted costs" of the three pictures was projected at $52 million, with the expensive *Bullets over Broadway* given a $20 million ceiling while the other two movies were divided equally into budgets of no more than $16 million each. The trade press would report this as a 25 percent hike in Allen's previous budget outlays. Under her contract Allen's sister would be credited for the first time, on *Bullets over Broadway*, as a co–executive producer. As ever, longtime personal managers Jack Rollins and Charles Joffe would also be listed as producers and be compensated under Allen's aegis.

The truth was that Rollins and Joffe, the former nearing age ninety, nowadays did little on Woody Allen productions other than rubber-stamp his decisions and tinker with his contracts. The personal managers never spoke publicly about his Soon-Yi romance, or the child-abuse allegations. Allen continued to pay their long-cemented percentages out of his share, even though they protested they no longer did much to earn their money.

Sweetland appealed to Allen in prospect as a mom-and-pop operation, he told interviewers. While Mike Medavoy was unhappy to learn he was losing a filmmaker whose work he always had cherished, he accepted the news as the wisest course of action, relieving TriStar of future controversy. Regardless, Allen had read the tea leaves. Medavoy was not long for the world of TriStar; he would quit the company and become an independent producer in January 1994. The Sweetland move was announced in midsummer 1994. The change would conclusively sever Allen's connections with the original farsighted United Artists–Orion–TriStar leadership that had sustained his career, produced his greatest commercial hits and artistic triumphs, and given Allen the quixotic independence that, more than anyone, allowed him to operate outside normal Hollywood parameters.

ON MONDAY, JUNE 7, Justice Elliott Wilk issued a blistering thirty-three-page decision. Justice Wilk described Allen as a "self-absorbed, untrustworthy, and insensitive" father, with "serious parental inadequacies," whose petition for custody was "frivolous." He ruled in favor of Satchel, Dylan, and Moses remaining in the custody of Mia Farrow, while restricting Allen's future access to his children. Farrow's "principal shortcoming" as a mother, Justice Wilk stated, was "her continued relationship with Mr. Allen." Still, the judge ordered an increase in four-year-old's Satchel's visits, from two to three two-hour sessions, or six hours weekly, always supervised. Allen was forbidden from seeing the almost eight-year-old Dylan for six months, after which time the judge recommended a review of the situation and a therapy-guided restart of visitation if the review was favorable. Allen was not permitted to have any contact with fifteen-year-old Moses until the teenager decided he wanted to see his father again. Regardless, Wilk wrote, "Mr. Allen's interactions with Moses appear to have been superficial." Adding to his misery, Allen was ordered to pay Farrow's court costs, roughly $1.2 million.

"Credible testimony" indicated Allen's "behavior towards Dylan was grossly inappropriate and that measures must be taken to protect her," Wilk ruled. "We will probably never know what occurred on August 4, 1992," the judge asserted—perhaps his least arguable point. However, Wilk was skeptical of the Yale–New Haven Hospital team report and leaned toward crediting the abuse claims. "The evidence suggests," he wrote, "that it is unlikely that he [Allen] could be successfully prosecuted for sexual abuse. I am less certain, however, than is the Yale–New Haven team, that the evidence proves conclusively that there was no sexual abuse."

Eleanor B. Alter phoned Farrow from the courthouse. New York social worker Paul Williams, Carole Agus of the New York *Daily News*, and Rosanna Scotto from Fox 5 were among the celebrants in the Madison Avenue offices of Rosenman & Colin. Arriving in a T-shirt and blue jeans, accompanied by nanny Kristi Groteke, Farrow carried an armful of children's books she had stopped to buy for Isaiah, Satchel, and Dylan. As the press began to gather, she sent Groteke back to her apartment for a better wardrobe of skirt and jacket.

Clutching the court decision "as though she were holding a sacred tablet," in Agus's words, Farrow, to the cheers of surrounding well-wishers, "almost ceremonially" recited the passages condemning Allen. "Mr. Allen still fails to understand that what he did was wrong," the actress read. "It is evident that [Ms.] Farrow loves children and has devoted a significant portion of her emotional and material wealth to their upbringing."

Meeting cameras after her costume change—"Her hair was fluffed, her makeup flawless," Marion Meade reported—Farrow told the press her family's long public and private nightmare was over. "So many months of this torture, this ordeal, are now behind us. These were the worst days of my life. . . . I should have extracted myself from the relationship a lot earlier. He was cruel and cold and abusive. I shouldn't have taken that. That's my message to myself and all women." That night, the actress donned a black baby-doll dress by trendy fashion designer Betsey Johnson and dined out, hoisting champagne with her new beau William Goldman.

Wearing his best Zelig face, Allen met with reporters after Justice Wilk's verdict and said he was "delighted" by certain parts of the ruling, especially the possibility he might get to see Dylan after six months, if his fatherhood was positively reappraised. In his memoir Allen said the verdict was "a brutal blow to me, a cruel deprivation for Dylan, but the successful culmination of 'You took my daughter, now I'll take yours.' "

Elkan Abramowitz announced Allen would appeal Justice Wilk's decision. All parties were due in Surrogate's Court two days hence, Wednesday, where Alter would argue to overturn Allen's 1992 adoption of Dylan and Moses. In the intervening two days Allen again advanced an offer to drop any appeal of Wilk's decision if, in exchange, Farrow would cease her challenge to his adoptions. The actress replied in the negative, and Allen would lose his initial appeal of Wilk's ruling in the New York State Supreme Court's Appellate Division in May 1994, albeit with two of five judges dissenting; then again in 1995, when a state panel upheld Justice Wilk's 1993 ruling by declining to hear Allen's appeal, noting they were restricted to matters of law.

A less publicized outcome was Farrow gradually losing her attempt to overturn Allen's adoptions. The press was barred from the Surrogate's Court, but Farrow in her memoir said total victory eluded her grasp when Judge Renee Roth "sidestepped the issue of fraud and requested an additional hearing on the 'best interest of the children,'" in her words. "But I had already spent a half million dollars on the fraud hearing. Faced with a choice between higher education for my children and continuing the litigation, I let it go." Although the actress hinted at endless appeals, Allen remained and remains the father of Moses, Dylan, and Satchel—perhaps.

JUSTICE ELLIOTT WILK would stay involved in the ongoing child-custody disputes. Mia Farrow took steps calculated to thwart Allen's future attempts to redeem himself in the eyes of Satchel, Dylan, and Moses.

Dylan's sex-abuse accusations were still being investigated. Little noticed was Eleanor B. Alter's appearance on Charlie Rose's public television talk show on the night of Justice Wilk's ruling. Farrow's lawyer described Soon-Yi Previn as "probably the greatest victim in all of this," and predicted that the college student, banished from the Farrow family, "may never recover." Asked whether Allen had sexually abused Dylan, Alter responded carefully. "Whether the ultimate things that Dylan accuses him of actually happened," Alter averred, "or whether because of his behavior with her, and his behavior with her sister, some of which she witnessed, caused Dylan to project or fantasize, I don't know. . . . I don't think we're ever going to really know."

One of the many ironies of the custody case, taken together with Dylan's sex-abuse charges, is that many comedians joined the media pundits, film critics, religious leaders, and right-wing politicians who ridiculed Allen, helping to guarantee that, for many people, the facts were forever blurred. *The Simpsons* made him a punching bag. Beavis and Butt-Head began referring to their penises as "my Woody Allen." David Letterman and Jay Leno made repeated jokes at his expense on their late-night talk shows: "Mix Old Granddad with a Shirley Temple your wife ordered," Leno quipped. Bill Maher dubbed Allen "the white O. J. Simpson."

Satchel, the couple's only biological child, was the stealth victim. Although Farrow had thoroughly vanquished Allen—*Allen v. Farrow* was his Waterloo—the actress could not forget or forgive, and she refused to make peace with Allen, using her five-year-old son, whom he had a clear legal right to co-parent, as a cat's-paw in their ceaseless hostilities. Justice Wilk gave Farrow wide latitude as a mother, and Wilk did not expressly forbid the actress from taking Allen's children out of the US, as the first judge did in the case.

Consequently, when in August Farrow journeyed to Ireland to emote in her first new film project sans Woody Allen, the actress took along her youngest children, including Dylan and Satchel. She had snared a good part as one of the rivalrous women who survive their husbands in *Widows' Peak*, being shot in County Wicklow by English director John Irvin. While on location Farrow would enjoy a fling with a set designer, according to Kristi Groteke, still her confidante.

Allen was forewarned about the trip, and Farrow said he could visit Satchel in Ireland if he cared to travel that far for the privilege. But when, according to publicist Leslee Dart, Allen put Ireland on his schedule, the actress balked. Armed with a court order and accompanied by Soon-Yi, his sister, Letty Aronson, and her husband, Allen boarded a private jet to Dublin, where he held tearful press conferences leading to headlines like "Heartbroken Star" and "Woody's Anguish." He pleaded for his entitled time with Satchel—thrice weekly, according to Justice Wilk's recent stipulations. He told the press he couldn't even get Farrow on the phone. Several days passed, with Farrow explaining to journalists she was not stalling but was organizing the details.

Now eight years old, Dylan had reclaimed the name "Eliza." Allen would never see the little girl again. Satchel had renamed himself "Seamus." Farrow, in interviews, insisted this was because kids bullied him about his name, believing "Satchel" referred to luggage. When Allen finally got Satchel/Seamus for part of a day, a four-hour tour of the Dublin Zoo, the famous father and son were trailed by dozens of reporters and paparazzi.

Soon-Yi stayed hidden at the Shelbourne, the grand old hotel overlooking St. Stephen's Green in the city center. Farrow always insisted Soon-Yi be absent whenever Satchel visited his father, while Allen persistently pushed for Soon-Yi to be present so she might restore her sibling relationship with Satchel. Court decision after decision left the issue up to the mother. After Wilk's ruling, "as sure as death," Farrow wrote in her memoir, "Soon-Yi was gone from our lives. . . . I no longer want to see her, but for the rest of my life I will miss her."

After his zoo excursion with Satchel/Seamus, Allen and Soon-Yi vacationed on the Irish coast. The holiday was timed for the US release of *Manhattan Murder Mystery*. The director always liked to be away from America when one of his new pictures opened. The Irish press depicted him as a sad loser, sadder and even more of a loser than the characters he played in Woody Allen films. He certainly had lost big: financially, his reputation, all three of his children. The embarrassing intimacies of his love life with Farrow and Soon-Yi had been splashed across the world press. He was demolished in the courtroom. True or false, the child-abuse taint would never be washed away. For almost two years the star and film director had been pummeled in public, even if some of those wounds were self-inflicted. Later, Allen would threaten to make a movie about the whole brouhaha—his secret affair with Soon-Yi leading to the unwarranted sex-abuse claims and the disastrous custody case—but of course he'd never follow through. Although the public confused Allen with his sad-loser persona, as much as his life served as one springboard for his fictions, he was not that kind of confessional, soul-baring, purely autobiographical moviemaker.

THE COMEDIAN AND filmmaker Charles Chaplin had his US reentry permit lifted after he traveled to London for the premiere of *Limelight* in 1952. Exiled from America, Chaplin became the only director to be politically punished during the blacklist era by expulsion from the Screen Directors Guild. Professionally, in his films and with his little-man persona, Allen often had been compared to Chaplin, much to his discomfort. Now their life stories evinced personal similarities as well. In his heyday, Chaplin had a known penchant for wooing and sometimes marrying women much younger than him. He endured two paternity trials in the 1940s over his relationship with Joan Barry, an actress thirty years his junior. One ended in a deadlocked jury; the other found Chaplin to be the father of her child. Blood tests proving Chaplin was *not* the father did not alter the verdict, nor the public impression. Briefly, Chaplin faced deportation. It took several more years for puritans and reactionaries to hound him out of America. Chaplin was able to make only two more movies abroad in his twilight years.

As with Chaplin, Allen's most dismayed fans were usually women. Even prominent female writers who met with the filmmaker and tried to view him sympathetically were forced to concede many of their friends felt differently. "Women friends gave me an earful when I said I was writing about Woody Allen," said Erica Jong when profiling Allen for *Marie Claire* in 1998. "Words like 'pervert' were quick to come out of their mouths." The feminist film critic Molly Haskell, when interviewing Allen in 2000 for the *Guardian*, told the director face-to-face, "Some women I know won't go to your movies since the Soon-Yi episode. The French have a different attitude toward artists, feel they should be exonerated from all sorts of transgressions. As an American and a woman, I have very mixed feelings. We're closer to you and feel involved."

"But why would your girlfriends never see my movies?" Allen asked Haskell in apparent astonishment.

"Because they feel betrayed," she told him. "[Making] off with your girlfriend's daughter! A woman's worst nightmare. Also, they, we, had maybe romanticized your relationship, seen as idyllic you on one side of the park, she on the other, each with his/her own space."

"Why was that their dream of a good relationship? I would question that," Allen countered. "I would think there's something not quite kosher there. Why do they need to have that degree of separation?"

"You're right about that," Haskell agreed, adding, "There's also the sense of closeness we feel to you, one of us again. There's no distance."

"No distance," he repeated, after a moment adding, "I've always benefited from that and suffered from it."

As Allen fought comparisons to Chaplin, he also fought the public hysteria and vilifications that consumed Chaplin's final decades. The Great Woody Allen Rectification Campaign began with *Manhattan Murder Mystery*. The filmmaker would never call it that. His comedy and films had always scoffed at social improprieties. What he had done—falling in love with Soon-Yi—was a private matter that never should have exploded into the public, in his view. Dylan's abuse charges were a fantasy grown into a lie, Allen insisted. Yet in the same way that he always had adjusted his filmmaking, his persona, to criticisms and audience reaction, Allen now began to listen to his better instincts. His sister and Jean Doumanian were the chief promulgators of the great rectification campaign, knowing Allen had wounded himself and wanting him to rehabilitate his image.

After the sordid first half of 1993, the timing was good for the first Woody Allen comedy in a decade—with the exception of the "Oedipus Wrecks" "minimovie." Released in mid-August, *Manhattan Murder Mystery* was greeted with a sigh of almost universal collective relief from those movie critics remaining who had not declared the director an enemy of humanity. The new picture was not in the least Ingmar Bergmanesque, nor was it any kind of crazy mirror held up to his private life. Allen had just lost a championship match to an opponent who danced away from his blows like Muhammad Ali, or Peter Pan. But he would fight on. Life was a series of bouts, and terrible defeats happened. *Manhattan Murder Mystery* turned the page, threw off the onus, dug down anew.

The brash spirit of the new comedy was established in the opening credits, which featured an unbroken aerial shot of Allen's beloved Manhattan as Bobby Short sang an exuberant rendition of Cole Porter's "I Happen to Like New York." The camera descends to Madison Square Garden, where Larry (Allen) and Carol (Diane Keaton) are rooting for the New York Rangers—Larry more enthusiastically than Carol—she has agreed to the hockey game only if he'll go to next week's Wagner opera. From its upbeat opening, *Manhattan Murder Mystery* was a lark reminiscent of Allen's earlier, silly comedies, more W. S. Van Dyke than Orson Welles—even though the suspense builds to a sequence intercut with the mirror-shard climax from *The Lady from Shanghai*. It was nothing like the serious, realistic murder mystery Allen originally tried to get off the ground in the 1970s.

The logic was flimsy, the goings-on zany. Allen and Keaton are not only happily married, Allen at one point even cooks a tuna casserole. The screen couple have a grown son (Zach Braff), rare in previous Woody Allen pictures, who seems perfectly normal and is doing well in college. The script was sprinkled with only a soupçon of the customary Woody Allen–isms (he could find endless ways of teasing Paris into a story). He had fretted the picture might seem a breezy "airplane read," in his words, and that is pretty much how it turned out.

The unassuming goings-on were inordinately boosted by Keaton's charm. Although she and Allen did not share any romantic or lovemaking scenes, there were quite a few with the couple sprawled in their marital bed with the pillow talk recapturing their long-lost rapport. (There's nothing wrong with the crime-obsessed Carol/Keaton that "a little Prozac and a polo mallet wouldn't cure," Larry/Allen cracks.) In her *New York Times* profile of Keaton, in which the actress declined to say anything negative about Mia Farrow, Maureen Dowd itemized the ways in which Carol/Keaton evoked a premenopausal Annie Hall. Carol/Keaton's baggy, layered costumes. Her improvised, unintelligible lines of dialogue: "God, you know, I mean, anything, really, yeah, yeah." Her "physical tics run amok (she fiddles with her hair, rubs her nose, toys with her hands)."

Allen gave a playful performance, restraining his usual quirks and foibles. As proudly superficial as the film was entertaining, *Manhattan Murder Mystery* was welcomed by major critics as—if not the balm of Gilead—the best possible prescription for depressed Woody Allen fans. No less a skeptic than Pauline Kael found it "the most enjoyable movie he's made in years." OK, maybe it was "a frivolously entertaining movie mystery," noted David Denby defensively in *New York*, "it could be better. But some of it is pretty funny." Frank Rich in the *New York Times* hailed "a coherent movie, a funny movie, the most persistently lighthearted movie Woody Allen has made in years." "Effortlessly funny" agreed Desson Howe in the oft-anti-Woody *Washington Post*.

Nonetheless, most notices were mixed, and some reviewers reflexively juxtaposed their commentary on the picture with references to Allen's personal travails, a practice that would become de rigueur for more and more critics as time passed. The cold box office opinion was left to Todd McCarthy in *Variety*, who liked the movie, more or less (he assessed it as "thin but fun"), but warned "the commercial wild card, of course, remains whether the public and even longtime Allen fans have turned off the idea of seeing his films in the wake of recent events."

Although TriStar did all it could to promote Allen's final picture for the studio, *Manhattan Murder Mystery* performed "poorly" in movie houses, according to Mike Medavoy, ending with a US gross of $11 million (number twenty-one on BuzzFeed's list). In time many critics would highly rate the comedic murder mystery, and most moviegoers who bothered to go and see the film in 1993 enjoyed themselves. As of this writing, the last Woody Allen–Diane Keaton pairing on the screen scores a 7.3 out of 10 on IMDb.com's crowd rating system, with over 47,000 votes tallied. Not too bad: *Annie Hall*, with six times the votes, gets an 8.

AS *MANHATTAN MURDER MYSTERY* demonstrated weak "legs" in theaters, prosecutor Frank Maco, the state's attorney in Litchfield, Connecticut, issued a public statement on the Friday before the last weekend in September, announcing he was concluding his investigation into Dylan Farrow's sex-abuse claims without filing charges. In consultation with her mother, Maco said, he decided it would further traumatize Dylan to drag her into a courtroom. "This was no time for a damn-the-torpedoes prosecutorial approach," Maco said.

Still, Maco went out of his way to declare there was "probable cause" to believe Farrow's daughter had been molested by her father. For one thing, the Connecticut police had discovered hairs "microscopically similar to Woody's," according to Farrow in her memoir, in the attic crawl space where the sex-abuse allegedly took place. This factoid was not in Maco's 1993 public statement, but it was in Farrow's book, and it may have come from police files via Maco. "We found hair in the attic," conceded forensic specialist Dr. Henry Lee, chief of Connecticut's state crime laboratory, "but what does it prove? It doesn't necessarily prove guilt."

When Maco was asked, at the press conference, if he had enough evidence to wrest a guilty verdict from a jury, the prosecutor replied, "Arguably, I do." Although the Yale–New Haven Hospital team report found the little blonde girl had been under family duress and evinced problems separating fantasies from reality, Maco said his investigators learned nothing that "would lead me to question the credibility of the child."

Experts on legal ethics such as Stephen Gillers, a New York University law professor, denounced Maco's gambit. "You don't declare the man guilty and then say you're not going to prosecute, leaving him to defend himself in the press," Gillers told the *New York Times*. "It's a violation of Allen's constitutional rights."

Allen and his lawyers vigorously attacked Maco. At a swiftly called press conference at the Plaza Hotel, precisely where he'd launched his child-custody lawsuit one year earlier, a livid but controlled Allen read for half an hour from a prepared text. Once again, the director declined any questions from the assembled reporters, who had to settle for Elkan Abramowitz. Allen said he ought to be happy with the news that he would not be facing criminal charges, but he was too "disgusted" by what Dylan had been put through and angered by Maco's "McCarthyite tactic" of declaring him probably guilty until proven definitely innocent. Allen drew laughs from journalists when describing his cooperation with Connecticut police as a series of slapstick scenes involving the taking of fingerprints and hair samples—like outtakes from *Manhattan Murder Mystery.*

Yet his "long, torturous diatribe" against Maco and Farrow "occasionally seemed to follow its own internal logic," reported the *New York Times.* Allen branded Farrow a "vindictive" woman in cahoots with "a cowardly, dishonest, irresponsible state's attorney," whose "cheap scheming reeks of sleaze and deception." He said Maco and his unit were probably prejudiced against him because he was "a diehard New Yorker," whereas the actress was "a Connecticut local." Toward the end of the press conference, Allen addressed Dylan directly, speaking to television cameras. He apologized for being excluded from her eighth birthday party in July, and assured her "the dark forces will not prevail . . . I'm too tough for all of them put together and I will never abandon you to the bad guys." He switched abruptly to flattering Farrow, proposing they cease-fire for the sake of the children. "If the Arabs and Israel can do it, we can. I publicly apologize for hurting you. I know you can be forgiving and quite terrific at times. You're a first-rate actress and a beautiful woman."

Farrow's attorney Eleanor B. Alter, meeting with reporters the same day, praised Maco's wise decision and declared there would be no letup in the effort to delegitimize Allen's adoption of Dylan and Moses. "Mr. Allen's idea of peace is for us to give up," the attorney said. She cautioned parents whose children might be brought into contact with the film director in years ahead to "use the proper vigilance." Allen's relationship with Soon-Yi was "absolutely one of the most immoral things I can think of," Alter added, almost as an afterthought.

Incensed by Maco's "probable cause" remarks and by other actions of the prosecutor, which included sending an unsolicited copy of his official statement to the Surrogate's Court taking a second look at the adoptions of Dylan and Moses, Allen lodged a complaint with a legal oversight panel in Connecticut. He did not warm to Maco any more than to Justice Elliott Wilk, and in *Apropos of Nothing* branded the state's attorney "a clown" and "a sad schlemiel." There might have been some "canoodling between Maco and Mia," the filmmaker mused, because friendly sources fed him supposed tales of Farrow, bedecked and perfumed, publicly wining and dining the prosecutor, regaling Maco with her version of what a terrible father and likely molester he was.

The seven-member Connecticut Criminal Justice Commission took six weeks to examine Allen's complaint before unanimously deciding Maco had not violated the canon of legal ethics. While judges on the panel qualified their votes in comments to the press—with one judge saying Maco's "probable cause" remarks were "insensitive and inappropriate"—the prosecutor was cleared of formal wrongdoing. Reached for this book, Maco was asked if he could reveal his theory of Dylan's molestation: Was the crime a one-time, impulsive act of child abuse, a syndrome that is generally regarded as a lifetime pathology? Or what? Maco shouted down the phone: If he answered that question, he would be disbarred. When reminded he had retired in 2003 and no longer practiced law, Maco said no matter what he replied to the question, Woody Allen was bound to sue him.

THE OTHER SHOE dropped in early October, when New York State Department of Social Services officials informed Allen they had closed their parallel investigation into accusations he had molested Dylan in Frog Hollow on August 4, 1991. "No credible evidence was found that the child named in this report has been abused or maltreated," the agency letter stated. "This report has, therefore, been considered unfounded."

At work Allen was not an angry man. Work was always separated in his mind from whatever was going on in his private life. With his inner clock always ticking, he proceeded with the next Woody Allen project. In late September—on the Monday following Frank Maco's announcement—Allen launched the filming of *Bullets over Broadway*. Although *Bullets* was going to be his first picture for Sweetland Pictures—a.k.a. "a Jean Doumanian production"—the behind-the-camera unit were veterans of his regime: cinematographer Carlo Di Palma, production designer Santo Loquasto, editor Susan E. Morse, costume designer Jeffrey Kurland.

Allen and Douglas McGrath had composed a witty send-up of Warner Bros. crime movies and backstage musicals, set in the Roaring Twenties, which revolved around the lead-up to the Broadway premiere of a bleak tragedy by David Shayne, a "budding Chekhov" who insists upon the purity of his art until reality lowers the boom; gangsters and a diva past her prime force him into compromises. Allen was too old to play the earnest young playwright, whose lofty principles are played for laughs in the screen story. "I could have played it [the role] if I was younger," Allen wistfully told Stig Björkman. So he opted for John Cusack, whom Allen had enjoyed working with among the ensemble of *Shadows and Fog*. "He's not one of those actors who sound like they're acting," Allen described Cusack. "And he's got an intellectual quality, so he's believable as a writer."

Shayne's lead actress is Helen Sinclair, a grande dame ("I'm still a star! I never play frumps or virgins!"), who flirts with him and complicates life with his girlfriend. Shayne must accept financial backing from a mobster who conditions his largesse on a good part for his moll, a dimwitted chorine named Olive with grandiose thespian aspirations. A mob flunky named Cheech, appointed as Olive's bodyguard, proves a born dramaturge as well as stone-cold killer. There are side trips to Greenwich Village where a cynical unproduced playwright sneaks in Allen's philosophy of right and wrong: "Guilt is petit bourgeois. An artist creates his own moral universe."

The part of the scenery-chewing diva was written expressly for Dianne Wiest, who asked Allen to craft a substantial role for her after an absence from eight Woody Allen films following *Radio Days*. (Wiest had been busy raising two young children.) After reading the *Bullets over Broadway* script, however, Wiest didn't feel confident she was right for such a flamboyant role. Wiest equivocated: "I can't do this, you've got to get another actress. . . ." The director told Wiest, "Are you kidding? You're the greatest actress in the world." Keaton, Farrow, and Wiest were the same that way, Allen said. "They can't, they can't, they can't, but in the end, they're brilliant."

In Wiest's very first scene, which found Helen Sinclair in a speakeasy with David Shayne, ordering multiple martinis, she seemed off her game. "It's no good," Allen told the actress. Watching the dailies, Wiest had to agree she was awful, and she offered to resign from the cast. Allen suggested Wiest drop the pitch of her voice and adopt a throatier enunciation. "It helped her to play it in a more—I don't know what—a more pretentious voice," Allen later explained. Whenever Wiest's performance lapsed, Allen reminded her with one word: "Voice." Although the actress was hesitant to "camp it up," Allen insisted. "To show her what I wanted I came flouncing in and said, 'Oh God!' . . . and she said, 'Really? You want it that broad?' " Yes, he did.

Allen professed an unfamiliarity with actor-writer Chazz Palminteri, whose one-man stage show *A Bronx Tale* had been turned into a Robert De Niro–directed movie, as yet unreleased, before Juliet Taylor walked Palminteri in for the part of Cheech. Allen took one look at Palminteri's soulful Italian mug and nodded. Taylor helped round up the rest of the troupe: Jennifer Tilly, the vulgar moll who forgets the next line after "To be or not to be . . ."; Joe Viterelli, the beetle-browed gangster trying to boost his mistress's career; Mary-Louise Parker, the playwright's forsaken girlfriend; Jim Broadbent, The Leading Man Who Eats Too Much; Tracey Ullman, an antic supporting actress with a yapping dog; Rob Reiner, the bohemian playwright; Jack Warden, the beleaguered producer; Harvey Fierstein, the agent for the grande dame; Stacey Nelkin, popping her head out of a window in the last sequence; and assorted unbilled no-names like Allen's rabbit's-foot John Doumanian.

"Chazz, Tracey, Jennifer improvised," Allen told *Positif*, "because they like to do it. Others who feel less sure of themselves thank you for the opportunity you're offering them but prefer to remain faithful to the script." While much of the period detail would be faked on soundstages, including superb nightclub sequences filled with tap-dancing chorus girls, Allen recreated the Times Square of 1928 for the climactic scene where Shayne's portentously titled "God of Our Fathers" finally reaches its Broadway summit: filling streets with men in suspenders and homburgs, flappers in cloche hats and fur coats, Rolls-Royces and Model Ts, billboards for Eugene O'Neill's *Strange Interlude*. The photography was completed a few weeks before Christmas 1993.

Still, the $20 million budget—Allen's highest yet, slightly surpassing *Shadows and Fog*—had to accommodate the stylized sets, costumes, and large cast. And there would have to be cutbacks in the Doumanian years.

Fewer reshoots, for example. "No big problems on that picture [*Bullets*]," Allen told Eric Lax. "The one thing I reshot was the scene in MacDougal Alley [in Greenwich Village] at the end. I shot and moved the camera and moved the camera. And then I went home and thought, 'It's probably not going to work like that, I should just do it and cut it.' And I did that and after I had gotten the whole company together again, I went back to my original shot."

THE ANNUS HORRIBILIS of 1993 mercifully drew to a close. After all the controversy and setbacks, Allen made a concerted effort to lower his profile, giving few interviews while toiling on the postproduction of *Bullets over Broadway* and carpentering his next script from another idea taken from the list he'd shown Douglas McGrath.

The director continued to be preoccupied with Satchel and Dylan, and he continued to fail in the courts and with Mia Farrow. The six-month deadline for Allen possibly visiting Dylan was extended to March 1994 after Dylan's new psychiatrist reported that the little blonde girl continued to insist "Woody Allen touched my privates." In March, future visits were again postponed. Meanwhile Farrow prepared to abandon the Langham and move her family year-round from New York to Connecticut, planning to evacuate by early summer 1994, thereby creating permanent logistical problems for Allen because of the distance between Frog Hollow and Manhattan. He knew the family's departure would kill his relationship with Satchel, now Seamus, occasionally "Sean."

Allen fought the uprooting in court, once more losing to Justice Elliott Wilk. Allen filed for a review of the decision, citing the judge's "pattern of extreme bias," but the filmmaker would lose repeatedly to Wilk, whom Cindy Adams quoted as saying "I don't trust him [Allen]" in her *New York Post* column. Wilk might not have appreciated the crack Allen made in print, in 1994: "I went seeking Solomon," Allen told *New York*, "but I wound up with Roy Bean [the frontier 'hanging judge']." Maybe he would create a "funny and sad" mockumentary about the "bad judge," called "An Error in Judgment," he mused publicly. But "the fun for me is in the doing of the thing," Allen said, and what would be the fun in expending all that effort on Justice Wilk?

Eric Lax estimated Allen spent upwards of $7 million on court actions defending himself in two states against child-abuse claims, trying to gain custody of his children, and pressing for visitation rights with Dylan and Satchel. (The $7 million included his mandated tab of Mia Farrow's court costs.) Allen discussed his finances in more than one interview, laboriously explaining he was cumulatively wealthy because of all his movies, with the dividends accruing over time, but his annual income was erratic. "There have been many times over the years that I have given my whole salary back to the film company for five or ten days of extra shooting," the comedian and film director said. "I have at times worked the whole year for virtually no money."

FEELING THE PINCH, in April 1994 Allen squeezed in the making of his first telefilm as writer, director, and star—his first stab at anything for the smaller-sized screen since the ill-fated *Harvey Wallinger Story* twenty years earlier. The chief attraction of adapting his 1966 Broadway play *Don't Drink the Water* for ABC was surely the compensation, but perhaps it was also an opportunity to wipe away the memory of the first, big-screen version, which Allen had not directed and which he considered "a disaster, an embarrassment." He also savored playing the lead originally written for Lou Jacobi on Broadway and essayed by Jackie Gleason in the movie: Walter Hollander, the vacationing New Jersey caterer who is mistaken for a spy and is trapped with his family in an American embassy behind the Iron Curtain. Allen set it all up with his usual production designer, editor, and cameraman. *Don't Drink the Water* would anchor a three-telefilm deal Jean Doumanian negotiated with ABC.

Allen cast the familiar sitcom face Michael J. Fox, who had rocketed to fame on *Family Ties*, as the hapless diplomat in charge, with Julie Kavner playing his wife. One of his go-to actresses ("she never disappoints"), with her unconventional looks, Kavner had portrayed Allen's sister, girlfriend, wife, even the mother of his alter ego in *Radio Days*. Her name was usually forgotten when critics harped on his casting of young lovelies. The director picked Mayim Bialik, the star of NBC's *Blossom*, to play the young daughter who becomes enamored of the diplomat, and the reliably daffy Dom DeLuise as the priest-magician holed up in the embassy.

Allen shot his retooled script over two weeks on New York soundstages in April, with a hundred demonstrators for affirmative action crashing the set one day to provide a burst of excitement that perhaps, Godard-like, should have been incorporated into the final cut. Allen's revivification of his first Broadway hit proved surprisingly uninspired, when aired months later at Christmastime. It would be hard to say whether Allen's performance or the camerawork was more frenetic. As usual the director permitted only limited rehearsal time, while his visual approach, also per usual, was mostly "big master shots," in Allen's words. The camera darted around feverishly to catch up with actors trying to hit their marks. "Long uninterrupted takes with no cutaways forced cinematographer Carlo Di Palma to swim through and around the actors, swish-panning his handheld camera," Fox remembered. Allen's acting improvisations, while "gifted and hilarious," in Fox's words, unsettled him and other performers. "Since it was impossible to know what he was going to do next, it was futile to try to plan my own performance in advance. There were no close-ups, no pickups. Each actor had to go all out every time or feel the cold breeze of Carlo's camera swish-panning elsewhere."

The script improvements were minimal, and the comedy remained flimsy. "Allen has not updated this material, and many of the jokes feel like they come back from a different era," *Variety* pointed out. Doumanian may have entertained hopes of a robust foreign theatrical release, or perhaps strong home video sales; but neither was going to happen. Nor did the other telefilms in the Sweetland-ABC contract eventuate.

Still, Sweetland got a big shot in the arm in June, when Doumanian and Jacqui Safra sold the domestic and foreign distribution rights to *Bullets over Broadway* to Miramax, a young go-getter studio in the Orion mold and New York's leading independent production company. Recently acquired by Walt Disney Pictures, Miramax continued to operate autonomously. Producer Harvey Weinstein, one of two brothers, native New Yorkers and Jewish, who ran Miramax, bid on the new Woody Allen movie sight unseen, which was how Sweetland offered *Bullets over Broadway* to prospective coproducers, forcing Allen's financial partners to accept his long-established creative primacy. Weinstein did not care. When the producer finally saw *Bullets*, he loved the period picture, hailing Allen as "a comic genius." The Disney studio in Hollywood—from which Allen superfan Jeffrey Katzenberg had just departed to form DreamWorks—was "thrilled," Weinstein told the press. Miramax paid the rumored sum of $20 million, which was the picture's entire budget nut. But Miramax was known for "director-driven indie films," in the words of *Variety*, and an aggressive sales approach overseas, where art-house works often earned back in foreign revenue what was elusive in the US. Weinstein promptly began to recoup costs, selling *Bullets over Broadway*—sight unseen—to French distributors for the reported record sum of $4 million. Foreign markets, which Allen and Rollins-Joffe had foreseen as lucrative and had nursed from early days, would become increasingly vital as, for many reasons, Allen's customary New York and American base eroded.

FOR A TIME, after the child-custody case verdict, Soon-Yi took her own apartment, and the press speculated on whether the relationship between she and Allen was foundering. Nowadays the couple ventured out more in public, even if they were both wont to dress inconspicuously, avoid photographers, and ignore shouted questions. They frequented Manhattan's fine restaurants and attended stage shows of interest—one night, for example, sitting among the rapt audience for a magic performance by "Ricky Jay and his 52 Assistants."

The film director spent the summer of 1994 quietly preparing his next project and readying the release of *Bullets over Broadway*. *Manhattan Murder Mystery* was not the first Woody Allen film to make more money in Europe than the US, but its $11.3 million domestic gross was augmented by $7.5 million in France, $3 million in Italy, and another $1.5 million in Germany. Orion had launched his recent "Germanic" work—*September*, *Another Woman*, *Crimes and Misdemeanors*, *Shadows and Fog*—at the Berlin Film Festival. Yet all the major European festivals wanted Allen's films for premieres, even if they were always shown out of competition—and, as part of the Great Rectification Campaign, Allen began to shift the festival focus to Venice and Italy.

Manhattan Murder Mystery had been the first Woody Allen picture to have a Venice Film Festival premiere since *A Midsummer Night's Sex Comedy* in 1982. *Bullets over Broadway* was slated for Venice in September 1994, and for the next seven years, through 2001, Allen's European premieres would become an institutional highlight of the annual Italian event, second in world prestige to Cannes. Another departure was the announcement that *Bullets* would have its American premiere at the forthcoming 32nd New York Film Festival in October. The leading US festival had never before featured one of Allen's films and, coming after the child-custody case and dismissed abuse charges, the festival premiere was a significant gesture of reconciliation.

The festival's gala screening at the Ziegfeld was a benefit for AIDS research with the director himself in attendance—another first. "The movie's theme is that some people are born artists, and some are not," Allen told journalists, "and no matter how much you study and take on the trappings of an artist, it doesn't matter."

That and other tried-and-true Woody Allen motifs, familiar and comforting to his followers, were strewn throughout *Bullets over Broadway*, which continued to manifest the filmmaker's renewed lightness of spirit and confidence of tone. "Beneath the smooth comic professionalism," observed Janet Maslin, who had taken over the first-string chair—and Allen-admiring—from Vincent Canby in the *New York Times*, "lurked truly audacious thoughts about art, love and genius. This sly expert period piece," she wrote, combines "big laughs with real bite."

Allen's second movie following his vitriolic breakup with Mia Farrow unspooled as a bold romp with impeccable period gloss. Dianne Wiest as Helen Sinclair and Jennifer Tilly as Olive were hoots—Allen had instructed the latter to babble and improvise, keeping the other actors off-guard with her Billie Dawn–dimwit affect—and the other performers also fired on all cylinders. Although *Bullets* could be enjoyed without knowledge of prior Woody Allen movies, the mentions of Paris, Nietzsche, Freud, Strindberg, Cole Porter, etc., doubled the fun. Allen and Douglas McGrath's script mocked his pretensions—with Olive sneering at David Shayne's (John Cusack) tin-eared dialogue: "The heart obeys its own rules—hah!" Allen's personal grace notes included Helen Sinclair's favorite Central Park bench, and the party where Shayne crosses paths with George S. Kaufman, one youthful god whom Allen never met. "I'm not an artist," Shayne concludes ruefully at the end, returning to Pittsburgh, reconciled with his girlfriend. How many times had Allen told interviewers he wasn't either?

Reviewers found little to fault, with most of the second-guesses revolving around Cusack as "the Woody Allen surrogate," introducing this quibble for the first time in criticism of his movies. (It would have made less sense to score this point apropos of previous pictures Allen directed, without him appearing onscreen: *Interiors*, *September*, *Alice*, *Another Woman*, even *The Purple Rose of Cairo*.) "Is that Woody Cusack?" mused the *New York Times*, which also explored whether Cusack's girlfriend character was somehow a Mia Farrow allusion.

Unlike certain future Woody surrogates, Cusack did not physically resemble Allen in the slightest. The actor was tall (6 feet, 2 inches), darkly handsome, thirty years younger, and an Irish Catholic from the Midwest. Still, his dialogue sounded so much like "one of Mr. Allen's own trademark auto-neurotic monologues about love and art," Bob Morris wrote in the *Times*, covering the premiere, "the actor almost seems to be lip-synching."

Cusack gave interviews gamely trying to rebut this notion. He admitted he was "sort of depressed when I read a review that said, 'He does the Woody Allen to a T.' " The actor said he interpreted his David Shayne character as "in many ways, a typical Woody protagonist, a tortured intellectual struggling in a moral gray land." Cusack insisted he "tried to forget Woody and play my version of the fool." Yet it was futile to try too hard, Cusack added, because sometimes the director's guidance came in the form of acting out a specific bit of business to show how it should be done. "There is no better physical comedian than him," explained Cusack. "He would jump in and do the scene, and the whole crew would crack up. I would say, 'Woody, you can't do that to me. It's humiliating.' " Allen assured Cusack the crew laughed harder at him only because "I pay them."

Allen chimed in to disavow the Woody-surrogate theory, which would haunt his pictures unabatedly in the future. "Maybe now and then because I wrote it and I'm directing it, maybe a mannerism will creep in," Allen mused. "I probably would have played the whole thing much more broadly. I couldn't have done the part the way John did. My personal influences have been basically Groucho Marx and Bob Hope. John is an actor."

Cusack's performance was really a nonissue, and *Bullets over Broadway* was a different, spectacular Woody Allen film that, like *Manhattan Murder Mystery*, sublimated his persona and personal life, and should have played as well in Peoria as New York. The picture would go on to be nominated for eight Academy Awards, which included both Dianne Wiest and Jennifer

Tilly for Best Supporting Actress, Chazz Palminteri for Best Supporting Actor, and Allen for Best Director and Screenplay. Wiest was the only winner, but the eight nominations were more than for any of Allen's other movies. *Hannah and Her Sisters*, in second place, had received seven nominations.

BY LATE OCTOBER, as Allen gave interviews promoting *Bullets over Broadway*, he was thinking more about his next job: *Mighty Aphrodite*. He would shoot the new movie partly in New York and, as another sign of his continuing outreach, partly in Europe—for the first time in twenty years—moreover, in Sicily and at the Teatro Antico of Taormina, which Allen recalled as "an incredibly beautiful spot" from his 1971 visit to the island.

The screenplay had been long festering. Its origins dated back twenty years to the "Dreams and Furies" script Allen wrote that was influenced by Greek mythology and his adoration of Martha Graham. Now he updated the comedy so it was Oedipal and animated by Allen's feelings about fatherhood and adopted children. "Years ago," Allen noted in one interview, "I was looking at Dylan, and I thought, 'Gee, she's so bright and charming and funny, she must have come from good biological parents.' The idea went out of my head." Allen himself would star as a sportswriter searching for the birth mother of his preternaturally gifted adopted son—surely the mother must be a genius—discovering, to his dismay, the birth mother makes ends meet as a porno star and prostitute. "It's the third part I've written like that," Allen said, similar to Billie Dawn and the ill-bred characters of Tina Vitale (Mia Farrow) in *Broadway Danny Rose* and Olive Neal (Jennifer Tilly) in *Bullets over Broadway*. As the sportswriter tries to reform the vulgar birth mother, he and she draw steadily closer in friendship. "I try and try and try," Allen said of his character, "and she still remains kind of a dumb piece of sexy merchandise."

He rounded up an alphabetical lineup of accomplished players including F. Murray Abraham, Allen second-billed (although he was clearly the central character), Claire Bloom, Helena Bonham Carter, Olympia Dukakis, Michael Rapaport, Mira Sorvino, Donald Ogden Stiers, Jack Warden, and Peter Weller.

The sportswriter is married, in the story, to a rising star in the art gallery world, who is the mother of their adopted son. Finding the right actress to play his wife was the usual quest, and at first Allen considered different Americans, at one point asking Juliet Taylor, "What about Mia? She would be perfect." He could work with Farrow by compartmentalizing their past, he explained. Yet Taylor and other people on his team were horrified by the suggestion.

Allen had already begun to gravitate to European actors for certain roles in his pictures; the Europeans weren't prima donnas, they didn't dicker over money, and they approached their jobs like blue-collar workers carrying lunch pails. So he and Taylor traveled to London to interview British actresses, including Bonham-Carter, whom Allen remembered from the James Ivory and Ismail Merchant "bonnet pictures" *A Room with a View* and *Howards End*. He thought she was "beautiful" and "classy." He had inched toward change in his attitude about auditions too, nowadays allowing for "very short readings," in his words, "I mean a page, just to get a little suggestion." Bonham Carter won him over in a brief meeting by displaying a perfect American accent.

"His way of filming is different," the actress noted later. "He shoots it from just one angle. On most films you're waiting for the sun to come out. With Woody, you're waiting for it to go in. We spent a whole day on the beach and didn't shoot a thing, because he hates sunlight. He's utterly perverse. He doesn't talk very much. What he said to me all the time was, 'Just be real and be American.' " Bonham Carter tried to "be real" in their bedroom and kissing scenes as well, but Allen asked her to keep her lips "tight closed," and while one scene called for him to be lying in bed with his clothes off, he kept his shoes on under the sheets "in case of fire."

For a while the director also thought he wanted plummy British accents for the Greek chorus that echoes and comments on the plot as it unfolds. In London Allen met with several titled Englishmen before reverting to Pittsburgh-born F. Murray Abraham as the chorus leader. Abraham had Shakespearean gravitas (he had played Macbeth on Broadway) while his Brooklynese inflections made his declamations funnier. The same went for Jack Warden, appearing in his last Woody Allen film as Blind Tiresias, rattling a cup on the streets of Manhattan and pretending to be sightless.

More important than his wife was the bigger role of the porn actress/prostitute Linda, who is revealed to be the "genius" birth mother of the sportswriter's adopted son. Allen found the perfect actress by chance in

London also, even though she too was an American—Mira Sorvino. Sorvino had initially read for Allen in New York, where she arrived for her audition and spoke her first line from a "side"—"Hello, are you my three o'clock?"—without knowing anything more about the character, thinking perhaps she was a . . . therapist? When Sorvino, by chance, ended up in London at the same time as Allen, the actress asked to read for him again, this time turning up in a garish short skirt and high boots—exactly the type of costume Linda might wear in the comedy.

"You're going to need a voice, because not only is she cheap but she's stupid," Allen told Sorvino after awarding the part to her, and she responded by creating "a deliciously guileless bimbo falsetto," as the *Los Angeles Times* described it. "I had some uneasy moments about it [the voice] during shooting, though I didn't tell her," Allen admitted. The actress "brought a lightness" to the character, however, playing her "like such a cartoon." Sorvino exhibited "a number of needs," Allen grumbled, "she didn't want to be photographed from this side or that way, and I was happy to give in to all of them, because it made her happy. I didn't care if it was really a nuisance. She was worth it, and funny in her needs—her silly health-food candy bars. Very endearing."

Allen does not get enough credit for the lesser-knowns and wild cards he often gambled on for major roles in the many pictures he directed who, cast as finely delineated characters in his better scripts, responded with surprising and cathartic performances. The twenty-seven-year-old Sorvino would prove "genius" casting.

IN FEBRUARY 1995, the Fox network broadcast the four-hour *Love and Betrayal: The Mia Farrow Story*, a telefilm loosely based on nanny Kristi Groteke's book, with lookalikes Patsy Kensit playing Mia and Dennis Boutsikaris as Woody. Farrow reportedly had tried to stop the publication of Groteke's book, despite having assisted her former nanny with input, because of the intimacies it revealed. After the book was published in May 1994, the actress never spoke to Groteke again. As a television drama the subject was a legal minefield, and Allen made noises about suing Fox before washing his hands of the telefilm. Farrow was more determined, and her threats to take court action resulted in a détente behind the scenes. The solution was to focus sympathetically on the broad sweep of Farrow's life and leave off-camera Allen's supposed Dylan sexual abuse and the Soon-Yi romance. Partly because of this solution, and because Fox saw the audience for such fare as largely female, Farrow's character was virtuously drawn while Allen was depicted as an unscrupulous cad. Marion Meade reported the formerly antagonistic lawyers Eleanor B. Alter and Elkan Abramowitz, now friendly, watched the telefilm together. Not many Americans did; the TV show attracted remarkably low ratings. "People were really sick of Woody and Mia by then," Groteke's cowriter Marjorie Rosen told Meade.

Allen was busy editing *Mighty Aphrodite* while devoting himself to writing a new one-act play. Jean Doumanian wanted Sweetland to branch into stage productions, and she had formed a partnership with the established theatrical producer Julian Schlossberg, who intended to organize an evening of one-acts led by Allen's *Death Knocks*, which had never been performed in New York. Allen thought *Death Knocks* was outdated, however, so he quickly penned "Central Park West" to join another one-act from Elaine May, called "Hotline," and David Mamet's "An Interview." The trio would be collectively known as *Death Defying Acts*.

Allen's one-act concerned two neighboring married couples, both living in an Upper West Side apartment building, with farcically entangled love lives. There would be the usual surfeit of lies and lust, a female analyst scorned by her husband, a pretty Barnard College coed as part of the mix, and a wild gunshot finale.

The producers tapped the distinguished English national stage director Michael Blakemore to work closely with the three one-act playwrights from September 1994 through to the New York opening in March 1995, a span of time that overlapped the making of *Mighty Aphrodite*. Blakemore had recently conquered Broadway with *City of Angels*, the Tony-winning Best Musical of 1992, with a book by the one and only Larry Gelbart.

Part of the conceit of *Death Defying Acts* was that the lead actors would play several roles across the trio of one-acts. One of Blakemore's early close encounters with Allen was at the first round of auditions, which began in late September. Blakemore, with Allen and Elaine May, heard their pages read by actors ushered in by casting director Stuart Howard. "Good people showed up to read," Blakemore said, "but Woody ruled them out if they displayed the least sign of theatrical presentation. He seems to want a sort of open-ended movie acting, but this is hard to sustain over eight performances a week. The uncomfortable thing about the afternoon was that though I was nominally in charge—talking to the actors, telling them when to start and when to stop—there was no doubt where the true focus of the room was. Yet from Woody came not so much as a nod or a smile."

The candidates included Garry Shandling, the former stand-up comic known for creating, on cable television, the acclaimed *It's Garry Shandling's Show* and *The Larry Sanders Show*, but who was open to trying something different and acting "live" onstage. Shandling came recommended by May, who was "thinking in terms of names," Blakemore said. Shandling tried for a rapport with Allen by reminding him of a long-ago attributed remark—"That if he could choose to be a part of Warren Beatty's body, he'd like to be his fingertips," Blakemore recalled. "I didn't say that," Allen said tersely. "No, I never said that. I might have. But I didn't."

Everyone tried to recover from this "hiccup," as Blakemore described the gaffe, with ten minutes of casual conversation. After Shandling was escorted out of the room, however, Allen complained, "What are we doing, socializing?" Typically, when listening to the nervous actors, the filmmaker moonlighting as a playwright sat, with his Zelig face, doodling on the list of actors' names he'd been given, "writing tiny cryptic notes or drawing faces," Blakemore said. "During one of the less successful auditions I saw him write, in block capitals, HELP!"

Shandling dropped out after several frustrating callbacks. The leads in the one-acts were winnowed down to Tony winners Linda Lavin and Debra Monk and television veterans Gerry Becker and Paul Guilfoyle. Rehearsals began in January, and Allen began paying visits to the run-throughs as the out-of-town opening loomed at the Rich Forum Theatre in Stamford, Connecticut. One day, after watching progress silently from a back row, Allen slid next to Blakemore. "This [run-through] has been a real step backward," he told Blakemore. "It's so bad. I don't know where to begin. . . . They're all racing through it. Nobody seems to know what they're saying. Laugh after laugh is being missed." All along he had been making changes in the script. Now he needed to rewrite scenes for specific actors, Allen said, asking to speak to the ensemble before the Stamford opening.

"With some misgivings," Blakemore recounted, a few days later "I allow him to speak to the cast directly." Allen launched into a half hour of reproving notes aimed primarily at a single actress. "She's not slow enough, not malicious enough, not funny enough—the list of her shortcomings is endless." Afterward, in her dressing room, Blakemore tried to reassure the poor actress—"Woody is essentially on your side." But she was convinced she was about to be fired, her confidence was shattered, and the actress wept as Blakemore consoled her.

Later this actress became Allen's darling in the piece, and during the Stamford dates another actress became his goat. After ruthlessly critiquing the second lady Allen told Blakemore ominously, "We can always replace her." ("I feel a chill run through me," Blakemore wrote.) That was the pattern. Allen, sometimes, seemed pleased and praised the work of everyone, privately to Blakemore. Other times he declared the production "terrible," every other run-through "a great step backward," with "a million things wrong." Allen clearly couldn't stand the fact he wasn't the director, and he responded to the show "in precise manic-depressive cycles," said Blakemore, having "as much to do with the audiences as . . . with the various performances."

The Saturday of their first full house in Stamford was the night Allen, "relaxed and expectant," arrived arm in arm with Soon-Yi, "an attractive young woman who knows her own mind and is very different from the waiflike creature one thought one was seeing in photographs and on television." Also accompanying him were his sister, Letty, and her husband, Jean Doumanian, and Helena Bonham Carter, "whom I know from London," wrote Blakemore. She told him, "I'm in Woody's new film," to which Allen added, "She plays my wife," which Blakemore interpreted as "rather the way a small boy who knows what he wants might announce the proud ownership of a new train set."

The state of the work still in progress discouraged everyone. After the performance, Allen met privately with Blakemore in the greenroom while the cast cooled their heels anxiously outside. Since Allen was a wild card whenever he addressed the cast, sometimes overly harsh, lambasting everything from the performers and stage business to costumes, Blakemore asked him to channel his future criticisms through him, the director. The evening of one-acts would never be successful with "a demoralized company," Blakemore explained.

Tonight, however, Allen wanted to proffer "hundreds and hundreds" of notes. He and Blakemore talked for twenty minutes. The hour grew late, and Blakemore had to dismiss the exhausted company until the next day, when he relayed the notes as constructively as possible. Allen phoned him, "pushing to get his hands on the actors again. He's convinced a word from him will show them how it should be done." Every time Blakemore was able to get Allen to refocus on the writing, making script cuts and tweaks as the answer to problems, Allen switched to being the complete professional—pleasant, cooperative. Yet one week later, after attending another performance, Allen again handed Blakemore a fistful of notes, saying the actress who'd been bothering him was "ninety-nine percent better," but "the rest of it—I'm sorry to be a party pooper—is just terrible." Some notes were frantically scribbled: "Just awful." "*Still* shit." "PATHTIC" ("which I interpret to mean pathetic").

Blakemore was becoming "really quite angry." Producer Schlossberg acknowledged the awkward situation, phoning to defuse the tension: "Woody's excitability is probably related to the pressures he's under. He's trying to edit one film and write another. His father is ninety-four and ailing. There's been Mia Farrow to deal with; *Bullets over Broadway*, despite rave reviews, isn't doing business. And Woody has agreed to act again, something he doesn't enjoy doing except in his own films. He's doing *The Sunshine Boys* with Peter Falk for TV."

The rewriting challenges were what really enthused Allen, Blakemore realized. Allen suffered mood swings about the actors because he "has an exact reading in his head for every line in the play, and since he is foremost a performer, any departure from it drives him crazy. He also judges each performance as if it were the only one he's seen so that if an actor of whom he had previously approved is having an off night, he's suddenly the one who is ruining the show." Allen insisted Blakemore adopt a harder line with the performers. "You've got to tell them—really tell them!—how ghastly it is," he exhorted Blakemore. "You've got to be really tough with them!" Allen believed many of the problems persisted simply because Blakemore was such a softy.

At the five-hundred-seat Variety Arts Theatre near Union Square in the East Village, where the evening of one-acts was slated to premiere, the stage director gave Allen one last opportunity to meet with the company. Allen began graciously enough, praising actresses he had previously chastised, but "as he got into the swing of it and as, one by one, the rest of the cast were introduced into the discussion, he found more and more to object to. Eventually he was simply reading them the play line by line, and at a frantic pace. I sat there feeling a variety of things—initially some hurt pride, then irritation that he should assume I'd not been struggling for weeks with most of these problems. Then, as always, this gave way to a certain fascination with the man himself," Blakemore continued, musing. "He'd scheduled these two hours in what was doubtless a busy day and was giving himself over to the task with an almost fanatical zeal. I don't think I've ever met anyone so puritanically committed to his work, so consumed by it. It's as if his small frame were in the process of diminishing further in the heat of his activity, like a sculpture made of ice. It is wondrous to behold, but I'm not sure it is enviable."

The torture wasn't over. Allen handed over "cuts and alterations" in his parked limo after one late preview—"It was a bit like a tryst with a gangster"—and delivered more notes, even after press nights, despite the fact Blakemore had "frozen" the show. He sent "individual cast members envelopes full of changes. All are funny. A few are desperate." One actress, having been excoriated once too often, "refuses to open her envelope."

The critics fell hungrily upon Allen's playlet when *Death Defying Acts* opened in March. His was the longest of the three, taking up half of the evening after intermission, and his name attracted rote analogies to his private life. To some, the nubile twenty-one-year-old coed who goes from therapy sessions to her analyst's husband's bed smacked of Soon-Yi. His one-act was "riddled," wrote Jan Stuart in *Newsday*, "with jarring echoes of Allen's own May-September infidelity." Jeremy Gerard in *Variety* said his playlet was "self-serving and ugly."

Others saw his one-act differently. Vincent Canby, now the theater critic of the *New York Times* and still a wholesale Allen admirer, described Mamet's and May's playlets as protracted sketches. But Allen's was "a joy," Canby said, "fully developed," a "chef-d'oeuvre about the sexual bungles of the overarticulate."

Theater audiences agreed more with Canby, and *Death Defying Acts* ran for over a year in its small off-Broadway niche. Later, it occurred to Blakemore he had coaxed a genuine smile from Allen just twice during the entire ordeal. Once was the time when they were discussing a new ending that Allen was going to have to write, which enthused him. The other was at the first New York preview, when the show went better than any previous performance up to that time. Allen exclaimed, "That was really quite good!" That is when Blakemore got only his second brief "sighting of Woody's teeth," which were "just a glimpse of tiny teeth in the shadow of a smile."

Eric Lax asked Allen what he thought of Blakemore's journal excerpts, deconstructing Woody Allen, after their publication in the *New Yorker*. "Some of it was exaggerated in a comic way, but I don't think any of it was intended meanly," Allen answered. "I can't say that it was necessarily untrue. That's the way I work."

OVERLAPPING THE SAGA of *Death Defying Acts*, Allen had embarked on his second telefilm since his venomous and financially onerous split-up with Mia Farrow. One-acts were not very remunerative, but network television could be quite lucrative, and this was another payday. The producer, Robert Halmi, wanted marquee names for the second filmed version of Neil Simon's 1972 stage hit *The Sunshine Boys*, and he "threw a lot of money at Woody," according to the appointed director, John Erman—somewhere in the neighborhood of $2 million.

Simon updated his stage script for the Hallmark Hall of Fame special that was to be aired on CBS. Allen had remained friendly with Simon, whose older brother, Danny, had been a mentor to him, and with whom Allen had worked on Sid Caesar's show and other TV series in the 1950s. Simon's script revolved around a once-famous comedy team, Lewis and Clark, billed as "The Sunshine Boys," who have quit performing together because they don't get along offstage. Clark is struggling with health problems. His niece, a talent agent, attempts to reunite the team for a TV special. Allen would play Lewis, with Peter Falk as Clark. Others in the cast were Sarah Jessica Parker as the niece, Michael McKean, Liev Schreiber, and the unbilled Whoopi Goldberg in a cameo.

Erman, a replacement after the first director quit, suffered a worse ordeal than Michael Blakemore. Although Allen and Falk knew each other socially, the two had never worked together and evinced little in common; much like the comedy team they were depicting, they refused to harmonize. Starting out, Falk was fixated on playing Clark in as ancient a manner as possible—it would enhance the acting possibilities, he argued—so Falk made himself a septuagenarian in makeup and wardrobe. Allen insisted upon "looking fifty-five," as fit and trim as he was in real life. It was illogical for two people who were supposed to be contemporaries. Moody and quick to anger, Falk wouldn't budge. Allen shrugged off the issue. He was going to do it his way.

One day Erman tried for a little fellowship, visiting Allen in his cutting room where the filmmaker was putting the icing on *Mighty Aphrodite*. The TV director reminded Allen of the disparity: one actor who insisted upon resembling a decrepit old man, another who wanted to appear in his prime. "How would you handle this problem as a director?" Ermin asked Allen. "I'd fire one of us," Allen replied blandly. The conversation was over. Allen thus made it clear he was "a gun for hire," said Erman, "that he didn't really want a collaboration."

Allen hated rehearsals, which Falk loved. Allen refused to discuss the nuances of his characterization. Falk mused endlessly about his acting theories. The two stars barely spoke to each other except when they had dialogue in scenes together. Allen kept improvising, paraphrasing Simon's sacrosanct script. When Erman called him on it he'd say, "My writing is much better than Neil's. Why do I have to say exactly those words?" Falk liked multiple takes. Allen wanted to perform only one or two takes, and he'd complain if asked for more.

Allen was "the most uncommunicative person I've ever worked with," recalled Erman, an actor turned filmmaker, who boasted Directors Guild and Emmy awards and credits dating back to the early 1970s when one of his earliest directorial efforts was shown alongside *Take the Money and Run* at the Taormina Film Festival in Sicily. Making *The Sunshine Boys* was "the most unhappy experience of my life." The result did not please network executives either, and the expensive telefilm was not broadcast until Christmas 1997 after "spending a lot of time on the shelf," in the words of *Variety*, which noted the discrepancy between the two main characters and said the TV version was inferior to all the others, sluggish and humorless. "Allen does a terrific, if slightly exaggerated, imitation of Woody Allen now," conceded *Variety*. His old friend Neil Simon, agreeing with *Variety*, said he honestly thought Allen gave a "terrific" performance." "I never saw it [the telefilm]," said Allen—his usual policy. Hardly anyone did.

••

ALLEN CHANGED SLOWLY, personally and professionally. He always had reacted to influences and criticisms, even when insisting he was impervious to influences and criticisms. He continued to surprise as a writer and filmmaker, taking old and leftover ideas into bold new territory. The personal behavior he had difficulty modifying in private, the words he could not find within himself to speak in court, were transplanted into his characters in scripts and films, where he could say and do things in art he was unable to say or do in life.

Released in October 1995, *Mighty Aphrodite* had moments of brilliance and hilarity and was indicative of Allen's continuing evolution. The movie was hobbled by a slow beginning. Allen shot introductory scenes with sportswriter Lenny Weinrib (Allen), spotting future wife Amanda (Helena Bonham Carter) on the street and following her home to ask for a first date. But he jettisoned these for length. Instead, the picture begins with the couple already married and the usual proclamation—"Let's have a baby!"—followed by talk of adoption. He's against it; she's all "The world is full of needy kids!" and soon they are nestling an infant boy. The boy's name is debated: Should it be Groucho, Thelonious, Earl the Pearl, Django, or Shane? What goes best with Weinrib? They settle on Max—an Allen chestnut. The family scenes remind audiences only how little the filmmaker knew about real-world domesticity. However, in one of the picture's great ideas, a stentorian Greek chorus led by F. Murray Abraham interrupts the story, rooting for Lenny and letting the audience know Lenny is trying.

Art gallerist Amanda moves the family downtown where the action is—the first signal this Woody Allen Manhattan story will diverge from previous ones. Her come-hither investor Jerry Bender (Peter Weller) has a house in the Hamptons, which they visit. (Lenny vomits into the wind while sailing on choppy waters.) Meanwhile, Lenny dotes on Max, who has begun to evidence an unusually high IQ, and Lenny grows curious about Max's birth parents, one of whom must have been a veritable Einstein. Through devious means the sportswriter manages to ferret out the identity of the secret birth mother, learning, much to his disbelief, that she is a porn actress and hooker best known for her pseudonymous work as Judy Cum in "The Enchanted Pussy."

The film comes alive at the thirty-minute mark, when Mira Sorvino enters the story as this lowbrow of many noms de guerre, whom Lenny calls

Linda. Linda is her own interior decorator, and her apartment is adorned with clocks that simulate sex acts and gewgaws with penises. The porn star and hooker is statuesque, bosomy, all business about sex, and a little miffed Lenny doesn't care to partake of her services. Appalled to realize Linda is the mother of his precious son, Lenny has booked Linda without mentioning his ulterior motives, and he really just wants to talk. Yet like Billie Dawn in *Born Yesterday*, Linda has character and personality to spare, and also higher ambitions. A member of the Screen Extras Guild, Linda aspires to become a legitimate actress, and she displays her talent for Lenny, reading stridently from *The Philadelphia Story*. Yet Linda is complicated and bewitching, and she will emerge as a feminist figure as *Mighty Aphrodite* progresses.

The story becomes part *Born Yesterday* and part *Pygmalion* as Lenny, benevolently drawn to Linda, tries to dissuade her from porning and hooking. The right man might help her change and elevate her life. Lenny even offers his treasured courtside Knicks tickets to her threatening pimp. Still, he doesn't tell Linda about Max, to whom he remains an attentive father, while his alienated, ambitious wife slides into an affair with Jerry, the come-hither investor.

At one hour, just when the story needs another shot in the arm, Michael Rapaport enters as Kevin, a young boxer at the gym where Lenny hangs out. Kevin is dumber than a rock, so he is perfect for Linda. Lenny brings them together for a touching date at a restaurant, where Kevin asks Linda about her life's dream. She confides: "My dream is that someone would come along and think I'm special." The audience already knows who that someone is. The boxer busts Linda in the face when he learns she is a (retired) porn star, and Lenny arrives at her apartment, a wreck, having just been told by Amanda that she's leaving him. The two losers—for that is what Linda calls Lenny and how she now views herself—fall into each other's arms for one night of solace.

Allen rarely played as sincere and winning a character as Lenny Weinrib. And when directing himself in his *Aphrodite* scenes the actor was generous with Michael Rapaport and Mira Sorvino, unlike when he costarred with Peter Falk for another director. His camera spotlights their performances. His acting defers to theirs.

The Greek chorus flits in and out of the story, sometimes appearing in New York scenes and sometimes with Lenny and Amanda materializing for advice in the ancient Italian arena. Half the time the chorus sounds pretty much like Allen himself ("I see terrible danger and lawyers!"), and at crucial moments they speak the subtext ("He's playing God! It's hubris!"). No one has all the answers, not even Zeus, who is conveniently not at home when the Greek chorus phones in an emergency; they must leave a message on his answering machine.

The Greek mythology is cleverly interwoven, right down to a deus ex machina that involves a helicopter crashing down from the sky to introduce Linda's savior. Lenny and his wife reconcile. A year or two later Lenny and Linda meet by chance at F.A.O. Schwarz. She is pushing a baby—his, from their single night of passion—although she doesn't tell Lenny he's the father. Lenny has Max with him and introduces the boy, without telling Linda or his son that Linda is his birth mother. Each has the other's child, and it doesn't matter. The tender-hearted ending affirmed adoption and parenthood, however mixed up the genetic trail might be.

"Isn't life ironic?" the Greek chorus intones, before they break into a spectacular dance while singing (another great idea) one of the film's a cappella numbers, "When You're Smiling." The credits unspool.

MIRA SORVINO PICKED up a Best Supporting Actress Oscar. Allen himself was nominated for Best Script.

Although a few reviewers liked *Mighty Aphrodite* well enough ("Cheerful fluff," Janet Maslin described the film in the *New York Times*, though "witty, agile and handsomely made"), many critics sneered at the picture. Increasingly, a faction of Woody Allen skeptics would tie everything so closely into Allen's personal life, so literally, that their conclusions grew ridiculous. "It's a measure of the movie's obtuseness the two children have been cheerfully stripped of their birthright," Joe Morgenstern complained in the *Wall Street Journal*. Kenneth Turan in the *Los Angeles Times* said the unhoned script, "like a first draft"—later to be Oscar- and Writers Guild–nominated—relied too heavily on Allen "working in variations off his own situations and possibly even his own fantasies. One can't help, for instance, thinking of ex-love Mia Farrow in Allen's dismissive skewering of a woman who considers herself too busy to have children of their own." Turan added: "Allen's fascination with older men/younger women relationships" was "uncomfortable" to watch as Allen grew older, and "throwing in the venerable male fantasy of getting involved with an attractive prostitute adds to the off-putting taste."

The slings and arrows of critics mounting a noncourt case against him hurt Allen most in the US, where small, independent movies were being squeezed out of the market anyway in favor of studio franchised and prefabricated hits. Even *Bullets over Broadway*, which was light-years removed from any of his controversies, couldn't overcome its $20 million budget, earning $6 million less domestically than it cost to make. In 1995, *Mighty Aphrodite* competed for theaters and moviegoers against lavishly budgeted sequels in the *Die Hard* and *Batman* series—*Batman Forever*, directed by Joel Schumacher, on a $100 million budget—along with *Waterworld*, *GoldenEye*, and *Jumanji* in the top ten. *Aphrodite* brought in only $7.3 million domestically.

Overseas, however, Woody Allen pictures continued to show resilience. *Bullets over Broadway* doubled its US earnings. *Aphrodite* took in another $12.6 million, grossing $6 million in Italy alone, where the new Woody Allen comedy was screened at the Venice festival and officials bestowed on Allen (in absentia) the honorary Golden Lion for his lifetime of work, his name called out on a dais that included filmmakers Martin Scorsese and Alain Resnais, Italian actors Monica Vitti and Alberto Sordi, and composer Ennio Morricone.

ALLEN WAS STOICAL about his waning American box office. Like many writers he was primarily concerned with how much money he was going to be paid up front to finish a particular project, and on the back end he wanted to be protected if there were profits. Beyond that, Allen was skeptical of all box office figures, often repeating the anecdote about the day he and Ingmar Bergman fell to chuckling over how producers exaggerated box-office success during the initial days of a release, only to adopt long faces as the actual returns trickled in.

Continuing the burst of creativity that followed his courtroom and public relations debacles, by the time *Mighty Aphrodite* died out in the US Allen had finished more than half the photography of a new, especially ambitious project, his second in a row—for those hung up with his New

York–iness—set partly in Europe: Paris and Venice. Be that as it may, most of *Everyone Says I Love You* was shot "right in my neighborhood, where I live."

Allen's new script revolved around Steffi and her second husband, Bob, "limousine liberals" who live on the Upper East Side with a blended household that includes a daft grandfather, housekeepers and cooks, and a passel of kids from former marriages including college girl Skylar, a journalism major, who is in love with a preppie in her dad's law firm named Holden (as in Caulfield). Steffi is a bleeding-heart who invites a felon on parole to her birthday party, where the reprobate falls for Skylar and takes her on a crime spree. Steffi's ex-husband Joe is a novelist in Paris who regularly visits New York, preserving his friendship with Steffi. The two are the proud parents of the movie's narrator, teenage Djuna, as in Barnes—DJ for short. DJ sympathizes with her father's lifelong aching for true love and does something comedically that another character does dramatically in a Woody Allen film. DJ eavesdrops on the therapy sessions of Von, an art history professor, learning Von's romantic Achilles' heels. A well-prepped Joe contrives to meet Von while jogging in Venice.

How nice that Allen thought of Goldie Hawn, who was more often stuck in Hollywood fluff, for the lead role of Steffi, resurrecting, for the name of the character Hawn played, his onetime fondness for Mia Farrow's younger sister. The filmmaker returned one last time to the versatile Alan Alda for Steffi's husband, Bob. Allen picked Drew Barrymore for Skylar, Edward Norton as Holden, Tim Roth as the unreconstructed felon, and Natasha Lyonne as DJ, daughter of "original Dad" Joe. Natalie Portman would portray the daughter of "second Dad" Bob. Lukas Haas was cast as Scott, the sole Republican in the liberal family, with Liv Tyler as his girlfriend, and Tracey Ullman as Bob's former wife. Julia Roberts, Hollywood's most bankable actress after starring in the international smash hit *Pretty Woman* in 1990 (playing a prostitute in that picture, incidentally), agreed to the supporting role of Von at Woody Allen prices. Naturally, Joe was going to be played by Allen.

Alda, a repeat Allen player, offered one of the better explanations why the director, who minimally interacted with actors, consistently extracted great performances. "Woody throws you into the Mixmaster and turns on the switch," he told John Lahr. "One of the things that happen is that the actors are so without their usual props—without the usual acting tricks that they can rely on—that they reach out to each other onscreen in an extraordinary way. You see wonderful relating in his movies. People really look like they're talking to each other.

"The other reason they look like they're talking to each other," Alda continued, "is that they really are listening, because they don't know what the other one's gonna say. They know the gist of it, but he seems to deliberately write it in a formal, uncolloquial way and asks you to make it colloquial. Most of the time he'll say, 'That sounds too much like a joke. Mess it up a little bit so it doesn't sound so much like a joke.' "

Described only as a "comedy-musical" as Allen shot scenes, in the fall of 1995, the news leaked out that everyone in the cast was going to be singing 1920s and '30s songs by Cole Porter, Rodgers and Hart, and other worthies. The eventual title of *Everyone Says I Love You* was borrowed from a Bert Kalmar–Harry Ruby ditty that is heard in the Marx Brothers movie *Horse Feathers*—one of several Marx Brothers songs to be featured in the film's score. All the music would be arranged by the dependable Dick Hyman, who'd also orchestrated *Mighty Aphrodite*, from the Greek bouzouki numbers down to the a cappella choruses. Would Allen himself be crooning on camera? "I won't say," maestro Hyman told the press, keeping the secret, as curiosity built.

The dances would be handled by Argentina-born choreographer Graciela Daniele, who had trained in ballet in Buenos Aires and Paris before studying modern dance under Martha Graham and Merce Cunningham in New York. Daniele had led Ballet Hispánico and served as a director-in-residence at Lincoln Center. She had been the stealth factor of two previous Woody Allen movies, having choreographed the nightclub sequences for *Bullets over Broadway* and the expressive Greek chorus in *Mighty Aphrodite*. The filmmaker would stage the *Everyone Says I Love You* numbers in a throwback style. Although there was elaborate planning, choreography, and rehearsal, he photographed the dancers in full body—"Straight on, simple, proscenium and no cuts," in his words—as they executed their steps from start to finish in master shots, employing the bare minimum of takes. The song-and-dance filming was fast and easy. "I had a very good time making that film," Allen told Eric Lax.

••

COINCIDING WITH HIS sixtieth birthday and the release of *Mighty Aphrodite*, Allen gave an expansive interview to actual sportswriter Ira Berkow for the *New York Times*, using the occasion to talk less about filmmaking than to wax nostalgic about Willie Mays, Sugar Ray Robinson, and *New York Post* sports columnist Jimmy Cannon, whom he'd read devoutly in the 1950s. He said he was addicted to sports—any sports—on television. "I watch timber-cutting, and rodeos when they try to catch the Brahman bulls—I even know all the rules." He quoted memorable Cannon-isms ("the serene dependability of Stan Musial") and precisely recalled the column Cannon wrote about being at a New York apartment party late at night, where Frank Sinatra sang at the piano, then he walked home alone through "the melancholy of New York streets as the sun was coming up."

That "dream of Manhattan is harder for Allen to sustain today," Berkow wrote feelingly. "On the streets of his New York, he knows that he is viewed by some as everything from a dirty old man to a child molester."

There were no ground rules for the interview, no hovering publicist, as there never was anymore these days. Berkow brought up the subject of the child-abuse allegations and the custody case defeat. "I seriously considered whether I still wanted to entertain, to work hard at whatever gift I had to offer these people" who looked askance at him on New York streets, Allen ruefully admitted. "Then I told myself that not everyone was that way, that some still believed in me. And so I went on [making films]—it's also the way I earn my living."

Soon-Yi, now twenty-five, had graduated in English from Drew University and was pursuing a master's degree in childhood education from Teachers College at Columbia University. "We love each other. It's one of the best relationships I've ever had. Maybe the best," Allen said. She laughed at his jokes: no small thing.

Moses, finishing high school, still rejected his father. Allen had not seen Dylan, now ten, nor spoken to her since August 4, 1992. He was allotted six hours weekly with Satchel, Berkow wrote, those visits supervised by a social worker, not out of concern for the boy's physical safety, more because of Allen's "demonstrated inability to understand the impact his words and deeds have upon the emotional well-being of the children."

Although the tenuousness of his parenthood shed light on the affecting themes of *Mighty Aphrodite*, Berkow's piece did not say anything else about

Satchel, and in fact what Berkow reported was sadly out of date. Either Allen wasn't asked or didn't elaborate. At first, after Mia Farrow moved to Frog Hollow, Allen tried making trips and spiriting Satchel away to a mall or movie for his strictly apportioned and monitored time. It was "driving four hours to see him for three," in Allen's words. If their return was tardy the minutes were subtracted from his next visit. Satchel was expected to make the same round trip to New York via Allen's limo, although Farrow contested the logistics and came up with endless rescheduling excuses—this tutor, that doctor's appointment.

"As time passes," Allen wrote in his memoir, "the kid enters my apartment with the supervisor, carsick, belligerent, raging with ambivalence, having been taught I'm Moloch in Ralph Lauren corduroys. Then comes the stiff, unnatural mess of a supervised visit." More than once Satchel told his father, "I'm supposed to say I hate you," or worse, "I wish you were dead." On at least one occasion the boy arrived, having thrown up in Allen's limousine, and his custodian handed over the bag of vomit saying, "Mia wanted you to have this." Allen kept a bedroom ready for Satchel, dubbed "The Monster Room," because it was filled with large, expensive boy toys from F.A.O. Schwarz. Yet Farrow did not allow Satchel to bring home any of the toys, and he was never allowed to sleep over at Allen's place. Soon-Yi's presence was forbidden. Satchel's visits dwindled, then they were suspended. In late 1995, Satchel claimed Allen "physically abused him, an episode Woody vehemently denied," in Marion Meade's words, but the boy's therapist told Justice Elliott Wilk that he suffered from "nightmares and stomach aches" triggered by "memories" of his father. Justice Wilk rejected Allen's appeals, denied him all access to Dylan, and said the Connecticut visits with Satchel could resume only in the presence of the therapist. By the time of the *Times* interview, the director had not seen or spoken to his son in months.

AS THE PRINCIPAL photography for *Everyone Says I Love You* wound down, Allen, his sister, Letty Aronson, Jean Doumanian, and Jacqui Safra enjoyed another one of their "friendly" dinners, according to Doumanian's later testimony, and the filmmaker agreed to extend his contract with Sweetland for another four or five pictures, informally consenting to "just keep going on the same terms." How and when this discussion transpired, and what the actual agreement constituted, was later disputed and referred to in legal documents only as the "Dinner Table Conversation." According to Doumanian and her Sweetland partner, Safra, they and Allen, inevitably joined by his sister Letty, now a coproducer of Woody Allen pictures, dined together literally on "hundreds" of occasions during the Sweetland era. One famous time, in 1992, dining at Primola on Second Avenue, Doumanian began choking on bread, which gave Allen the opportunity to demonstrate one of his rare skills: He grabbed her around the waist, performed the Heimlich maneuver, and saved her.*

Allen's initial three-picture deal with Sweetland had concluded with *Everyone Says I Love You*. Although *Bullets over Broadway* cost so much that it hung like a pall over the books, everyone was still bullish on the future as Allen's popularity overseas continued to rise.

Allen's lawyer Irwin Tenenbaum and Sweetland's lawyer Barry Haldeman attempted to get the "Dinner Table Conversation" on paper, but it is difficult to say who tried the hardest. Legal missives flew back and forth without any contract getting physically drawn up and signed between Moses Productions and Sweetland, in part because Safra did not take Tenenbaum "seriously as far as [negotiating] anything because we had a direct line to Woody," according to later court records. For the time being the oral "Dinner Table Conversation" was sufficient, and the future would begin, optimistically enough and in unlikely fashion after the approaching new year, in March, with Allen's first jazz-band tour of Europe, which was being planned as a documentary feature.

ALLEN MADE HEADWAY on the postproduction of *Everyone Says I Love You*, but the unusually complicated sound and music would keep the "comedy-musical" from availability for the spring Cannes Film Festival—Cannes

* Allen reprised his Heimlich maneuver heroics in 2023 at a dinner at the Upper East Side Italian restaurant Caravaggio with Soon-Yi, lawyer Alan Dershowitz (apparently forgiven for publicly branding Allen a "sleazebag" during the *Allen v. Farrow* custody case), and the former New York City Council president Andrew Stein. The seventy-six-year-old Stein "turned red and struggled to breathe" while trying to chew and swallow, according to Page Six in the *New York Post*, when Allen, then eighty-seven, swung into action. "I am embarrassed to say it, but Woody actually saved my life," Stein was quoted.

badly wanted it—and Venice in the fall. His looming musical sojourn in Europe also slowed the pace.

Trying to buff her brother's image, Letty Aronson as much as Jean Doumanian promoted the jazz-band tour documentary as a means of bringing Allen out more, showing his positive side, doing something he loved—playing his clarinet and pleasing audiences. Let people see he wasn't a bogeyman. Aronson and Doumanian both would travel along on the ambitious twenty-three-day schedule of eighteen European cities in nations that were solid foreign markets for Woody Allen films. Doumanian's former husband, John, planned the tour.

The initial director of the project, Terry Zwigoff, was a roots music enthusiast whose first documentary, *Louie Bluie*, told the saga of a country blues musician named Howard "Louie Bluie" Armstrong. Zwigoff later made the acclaimed *Crumb* about underground cartoonist R. Crumb. Zwigoff met pleasantly with Allen, but he and Doumanian crossed swords when she told him Allen/Sweetland would probably insist on final cut, and Zwigoff quit over "money and control." In February, a few weeks before the monthlong European trip was due to start, Doumanian used *Saturday Night Live* connections to reach out to Barbara Kopple, who had won a Best Documentary Oscar for *Harlan County U.S.A.* in 1976 and made other provocative, socially conscientious documentaries in the years since. "I didn't think for more than ten minutes before I agreed!" Kopple recalled.

Meeting Allen for the first time in his Fifth Avenue apartment, the disparate filmmakers spoke for thirty minutes about "everything under the sun except the film and the tour," Kopple said. They talked "a lot about a mutual friend, a magician named David Blaine." They talked about movies: Allen had seen her documentaries and "knew I wasn't a trash filmmaker." She had seen only a few Woody Allen movies and had never read one of his books. As he walked her toward the door, Kopple asked, "Are you looking forward to doing this?" No, Allen said. "I don't want to go. . . . I never thought it would come [to pass]. It's mushroomed all out of proportion." She began to see the possibilities for a "fish-out-of-water" narrative about a celebrity forced out of his cocoon into the public spotlight. Kopple insisted on total access. Allen said fine. She thought: "It's going to be so much fun."

Kopple did not meet "the notorious Soon-Yi Previn," as Allen jokingly liked to refer to her, until the documentarist and her small crew arrived at the Teterboro, New Jersey, airport to fly by private plane to Spain with Doumanian, Aronson, Allen, Soon-Yi and her dog, "a silver-gray, sixty-pound slobbering Weimaraner named Jasmine," in Marion Meade's words, whose affections Allen recoils from in the film, saying "I'd rather be bitten by a dog than licked by one." "When he's in control of something like his movies," Kopple said later, "he's a man of steel. But when he's not in control, he's much more fragile. He needs Soon-Yi for these things." Kopple and her team turned their cameras on as the plane rose into the sky. Allen and Soon-Yi wore wireless mikes throughout the expedition that began in Madrid, stopped in Geneva, Turin, Vienna, Milan, Bologna, Rome, and Paris, then ended in London, with Kopple's cameras hovering over Allen's shoulders for sixteen- and eighteen-hour days. He never objected to what Kopple wanted to film and never halted the cameras.

The intrepid documentarist even invaded their hotel suites—always, with an extra private room or bathroom booked exclusively for Allen. She filmed the couple eating breakfast—prunes for Allen, before which he ritually swallowed his premeal "multivitamin, baby aspirin and antibiotic"—side-by-side on treadmills, swimming in their personal hotel pools, shopping for clarinets in Paris, hand-holding on walks as well as queasily riding on gondolas, with Allen experiencing "maximum tension" and "white knuckle" apprehension.

Sample breakfast table talk:

Soon-Yi: "The shower was excellent, wasn't it?"
Allen: "Yes, great pressure. The problem is it comes out over the drain. The drain's not in the corner, so you have to stand close to the drain. So, if you put a mat in there—because I can't stand on the marble—the water doesn't drain."

The six members of the touring band, led by Allen's old Chicago friend, banjoist Eddy Davis, traveled separately. Half the musicians were veterans of Allen's Monday night jazz shows, which had moved, after Michael's Pub closed its doors in 1996, to the Café Carlyle in the Carlyle Hotel on East Seventy-Sixth. The other half derived from the Bunk Project. Allen didn't seem to know all their names, which Soon-Yi pointed out, saying "you look like a crazy" when Allen addressed only Davis and ignored everyone else in the band during greenroom talks. "You should let them all know they're very good because it's nice to hear it," she chides him.

Soon-Yi often "steals the show," Dana Kennedy later wrote in the *New York Times* when the documentary, called *Wild Man Blues*—the title of a Louie Armstrong–Jelly Roll Morton song—was released in 1997. More than a few critics agreed with her observation. At one point Soon-Yi cheerfully admits to never having seen *Annie Hall* and says *Interiors* "drones on and on." "By turns bossy, maternal, nurturing and insulting, speaking with a hint of an unidentifiable accent even though she has been in the United States since the age of eight," Kennedy noted, "Ms. Previn has the Diane Keaton role in *Wild Man Blues*, but she's no ditzy Annie Hall."

Although he liked to boast he never took medicine, Allen traveled with a silver pillbox containing tablets of Compazine for anxiety, Librium (also anxiety), Excedrin for aches and pains, Zantac for heartburn, Donnazyme for digestive purposes, and Lomotil (possible diarrhea)—just in case. He winged a little French and Italian for audiences but apologized for his meager Spanish, saying "I didn't pay attention in school years ago." Often wearing a fearful expression, Allen posed for paparazzi and shook hands with fans. At one point in the subsequent film, Soon-Yi is seen prodding him out on the balcony of their hotel to acknowledge a crowd. Now and then, on the stages of sold-out auditoriums, Allen cracked a few jokes, which he almost never did at New York gigs. The standing ovations were thunderous. "He couldn't have been more happy," Kopple said later, because of "the presence of Soon-Yi Previn at his side, who gave him a youthfulness of spirit and behavior."

Although there were "no rules," Kopple did not interrogate Allen about the child-custody case or sex-abuse allegations. "That wasn't what I was after," the documentarist explained later. "I don't operate like a *Hard Copy* sort of journalist. I'm content to observe and record and let the life right in front of us unfold. If the touchy subjects came up, they would be pursued. But the instigation wouldn't come from us. Woody or Soon-Yi or Letty or someone who crossed their path during the tour would have to bring up the unpleasant stuff."

Allen's musicianship, which he himself deprecated at every opportunity, didn't always draw raves from the specialists. "The repertoire was of the kind you might run into on a Sunday lunchtime in an English pub," John

Fordham wrote of the London concert in the *Guardian*, "but at times the affectionate collectivity of the idiom lifted the music to a kind of eager, communicative grace that transcended preoccupation with the famously evasive figure in the check shirt and beige cords. Allen's clarinet sound rarely exhibits the liquid, sensuous qualities of the long-departed heroes of the instrument, and is querulous and shrill above the middle register, but occasionally embraces a mixture of heart-on-the-sleeve romanticism and blueness that rises above the general hum."

Soon-Yi never lost her poise, even when the couple returned home and paid their ritual visit to the Konigsbergs. Accompanied by his sister, Allen and Soon-Yi went to lunch at his parents' apartment, bringing a box of presents that included all the plaques and city keys bestowed upon them by European dignitaries. Martin Konigsberg, now ninety-five, silver-haired and dapper though deaf as a post, and Allen's mother Nettie, eighty-nine, resembling "an older, more animated version of Woody," in Marion Meade's words, proved they still had their faculties and sharp tongues. Nettie remembered that when Allen was young "the kid" had a "terrific brain," but "never pursued" the boyhood talent he had evinced for tap dancing, sports, and music. Allen repeated his claim that his mother used to smack him daily, and said it was a miracle he didn't grow up to be a dope fiend, or criminal. "I'm sorry, but you were brought up in a household that knew right from wrong," Nettie snaps. "Don't you think for a minute that you are what you are all by yourself." Martin chimes in: "You think you're a big shot."

"A lunch from hell," Allen cracks. Yet Soon-Yi never flinched, not even when Nettie says she still "doesn't think it's right" for her son to live with an "Asian girl." Nettie would have preferred a nice Jewish girl. Soon-Yi's reaction to this thinly disguised racism demonstrated her uncommon maturity and ability to survive. "Ms. Previn merely laughs out loud as if this is the funniest thing she ever heard," Kennedy noted in the *Times*.

EARLIER IN 1996, the Directors Guild of America had announced it would honor Allen with its highest accolade: the D. W. Griffith Award for Life Achievement. Previous beneficiaries of this peer tribute, considered rare because it was not bestowed every year, included John Ford, Alfred Hitchcock, Frank Capra, Orson Welles, George Cukor, John Huston, Ingmar Bergman,

Akira Kurosawa, and Robert Altman. "I was very, very surprised and amazed," Allen greeted the news. "I thought that maybe they were giving it out for quantity this year." He was also happy to have prearranged his convenient absence from the event, as he was busy playing his clarinet in Europe. "I have this policy that I never accept any award, the bestowing of which is contingent upon my presence," the director told Stig Björkman. "I always think in those situations that I am undeserving and that off the top of my head I could think of a dozen people that should get the award sooner than I should."

Actress Mira Sorvino accepted the high honor in his stead at the March banquet of the East Coast branch. "I recently turned sixty years old," Allen told the audience from Europe in brief videotaped remarks. "Practically a third of my life is over. I hope in the rest of my life I can live up to the honor you've bestowed on me."

As usual, the winner gave the trophy to his parents. It's "around here somewhere" in their apartment, he explains in *Wild Man Blues*. He just didn't care for awards. A few years later, the *New York Times* discovered Allen had received France's Commandeur des Arts et des Lettres in 1989, which was the senior grade of a Knight Commander, "topping [Maurice] Chevalier and [his ranking of] *Oficier*," according to the *Times*. When not handed over personally, the decree, signed by Culture Minister Jack Lang, was usually pouched to a French embassy for delivery. Something went amiss. The *Times* learned of the honor in 1998, and it was the first Allen heard of it. "Thank you for uncovering this utterly esoteric piece of information," he told the *Times*.

Tick-tock: The clarinetist went back to filmmaking. Allen spent the bulk of the summer putting the gloss on the final form of *Everyone Says I Love You*, which involved entirely eliminating Liv Tyler and Tracey Ullman and trimming songs and dances to get the length down to one hour and forty-one minutes. "I had to cut it," Allen said of Ullman's musical number. "It was a pity, because she was great." Also left on the scrap heap was a "wonderful number" with Alan Alda and Goldie Hawn, getting ready to meet their prospective in-laws; and a flashback to Grandpa (Patrick Cranshaw) in spryer days, cutting a rug with his wife in a twenties speakeasy.

"When I actually make the cut," Allen told Eric Lax, "to me, it's like removing a tumor. I mean, I find it a mercy-killing. . . . I don't save anything for the DVDs. Once I've thrown away a scene, it's gone."

The director also was deep into the planning of his next project, tentatively titled "The Meanest Man in the World," with a script that—no matter how much Allen staunchly insisted it didn't—reinvented Ingmar Bergman's classic *Wild Strawberries*. Allen's story involved a celebrated author with the parodic name of Harry Block, who is suffering from the syndrome of writer's block. His upstate alma mater, which tossed him out in college days, wants to honor him with the kind of life achievement ceremony Woody Allen took extreme measures to avoid in real life. Experts at the college specialize in "deconstructing" Harry's famous fiction, and in flashbacks and fantasies the "deconstruction" reveals how Harry has strip-mined his private life for his stories, earning the undying enmity of former girlfriends, ex-wives, and family members. The script mingled Harry's insalubrious real life with exaggerated characters and situations from his short fiction and novels. The mingling of reality and fiction long had been in "my psychic repertoire," in Allen's words, with *The Purple Rose of Cairo* and "The Kugelmass Episode" among the prime examples. The only people in his real life that dirty Harry can convince to join him at the college life achievement ceremony are a hypochondriacal pal, a black prostitute, and his young son, whom Harry abducts from school because his ex-wife won't change his visitation schedule.

Time went by with Allen failing to lure a marquee name to play Harry Block. "I first went to Robert De Niro," the director recalled. "I went to Dustin Hoffman. I went to Elliott Gould. I went to Albert Brooks. I spoke to Dennis Hopper. I couldn't get anyone to do it for one reason or another. One person wasn't available, one person wanted too much money, somebody else didn't want to play it because he thought he was too young."

Sometimes, nowadays, Soon-Yi accompanied Allen when he had a meet and greet with prospects, softening the casting calls with her smiles and nudging. Juliet Taylor also worked on Allen to loosen up the chitchat. "I saw you on *Cheers*," Allen told Kirstie Alley, a star on the long-running NBC sitcom. "He said it with his New York accent, 'Cheeas,'" she recalled. Alley was up for one of Harry's ex-wives in "The Meanest Man in the World," but she had no idea what the movie was about. After receiving her "sides," she guessed she was playing a psychiatrist. Alley dared to phone Allen's office, telling him, "I know this is going to sound weird, but I hate psychiatry and shrinks." After a pause, Allen said, "Yeah, who doesn't?" She asked if she could play her character "wackier than she's written" and improvise. "Sure, yeah [a lengthy pause], as long as it's funny."

With his lead still vacant, Allen collected an array of talent—new and seasoned—few filmmakers could boast of gathering under one umbrella: alphabetically Caroline Aaron, Kirstie Alley, Bob Balaban, Richard Benjamin, Eric Bogosian, Billy Crystal, Judy Davis, Hazelle Goodman, Mariel Hemingway, Amy Irving, Julie Kavner, Eric Lloyd, Julia Louis-Dreyfus, Tobey Maguire, Demi Moore, Elisabeth Shue, Stanley Tucci, Robin Williams.

Allen had his usual cameraman Carlo Di Palma, production designer Santo Loquasto, and editor Susan E. Morse. Jeffrey Kurland's last costume design for a Woody Allen picture had been *Everyone Says I Love You*, and Kurland would be succeeded, now and for many future films, by Suzy Benzinger, who had created the costumes for the TV version of *Don't Drink the Water*. But with two weeks before the start of photography in October, Allen still didn't have a marquee name for Harry Block. To everyone who told him he was obviously the prototype, Allen stubbornly replied he had written the part with someone more like the novelist Philip Roth in mind.

Roth too was a philanderer who, like Harry Block, once underwent a breakdown. Later, people would wonder about the comparisons between Harry Block and Roth. Was Allen's script some kind of an ad hominem attack on Roth, who was said to be romantically entwined with Mia Farrow? No, the script was written long before Farrow and Roth got together, and Allen took many creative liberties, he pointed out. Besides, Allen idolized Roth (Gabe/Allen's last name in *Husbands and Wives* is "Roth.") "He is a dazzling writer, a brilliant, brilliant writer, a genius," Allen said. "Thinking of his insights and his work, I can't mention mine in the same breath."

Finally, Allen, yielding to pragmatism, relented: OK, he'd play Harry Block. He fretted that the autobiographical implications would distract audiences and critics. Still, Allen was indeed perfect for the part, and Jean Doumanian couldn't have been happier. Despite the troubles that had tarred his career, his producers still believed Woody Allen comedies did much better at the box office when Allen starred in them.

EVERYONE SAYS I LOVE YOU was released in December, and it proved one of Allen's sunniest works, a glorious musical of the kind Camp Tamiment used to stage where everybody in the cast sings and dances, and nobody cares how good they are because everyone onstage and in the audience is having so much fun. As far back as *Annie Hall*, Allen had the brainstorm for characters bursting into song rather than speaking dialogue for a scene or two, but Marshall Brickman had frowned over that suggestion, and it went into the box of future ideas.

Whether *Everyone Says I Love You* should be categorized as a musical or quasi-musical—people debated it—the slight script was merely a pretext for Allen to showcase some of his favorite music from the American songbook, certain famous and beloved songs, others obscure, cobbled together in the style of the vintage musicals that always had been a guilty pleasure, for Allen, on stage and screen. The Fred Astaire musicals didn't have such great "books" either. "I don't even think of it [*Everyone Says*] as a musical but as a comedy where the characters sing and dance," Allen said. Maybe some of the actors sang like amateurs; so what? "The people in the music department were saying, 'They can't sing!' and the distributors were saying, 'They can't sing!' and I kept saying, 'Yes, I know, that's the point. If they can sing as well as they could in the shower, as well as you and I could sing, that's the idea. I don't want Edward Norton to start singing and sound like Pavarotti.' "

Drew Barrymore was the only performer who copped a plea, insisting she was tone-deaf, and her voice was "outside the limits of human tolerance," in Allen's words. Barrymore was dubbed by a friend of Soon-Yi's, the vocalist Olivia Hayman, who'd be rewarded with bits in future Allen movies. The actor playing Joe, Allen himself, took the dare, ruefully singing a stanza of "I'm Through with Love." Not an earthshaking moment in screen annals, although it is rather sweet and plucky and no worse than Clint Eastwood's rumblings on his soundtracks. "I'm Through with Love" and other songs recur during the musical in various guises; later, a brief hip-hop version with "an obscene first line" proudly written by Dick Hyman is chanted by black rappers.

What an optimistic paean to love and life *Everyone Says* is, once you have accepted the Upper East Side privileges, the elite academies the kids attend, Itzhak Perlman performing at Steffi's fundraisers, and the family's annual Christmas vacations at the Ritz in Paris. (Allen was originally going to call the picture "Christmas at the Ritz.") Carlo Di Palma reinvented *Manhattan* in color with exquisite imagery of the changing seasons—spring blossoms, the blazing summer, fall hues, and winter snow blanketing Central Park. The story pays visits to Zabar's, the Hamptons, Harry Winston, Le Cirque, and the Frank E. Campbell Funeral Chapel.

Yves Saint Laurent mannequins in shop windows stir balletically. The clerks at Harry Winston break into time steps. Homeless people lift their voices. Cripples throw off their crutches and perform backflips, while doctors waltz with their nurses. The small moments—Alan Alda, the son of a man who played Gershwin in a Hollywood biopic, playing the piano and crooning a birthday song to Steffi/Hawn—are as lovingly staged as the big numbers—dead Grandpa and ghosts in the funeral parlor delivering a rollicking "Enjoy Yourself, It's Later Than You Think." The music is wonderfully integrated; Graciela Daniele's choreography is exceptional.

Allen, for whom many films were personal wish-fulfillment, finally moves to Paris in *Everyone Says I Love You*. The Venice scenes are pivotal, but the Paris ending is—literally—magical. Bob/Alda has a bad cold or flu, and broken-hearted Joe (Von has ditched him) becomes ex-wife Steffi's date for a Christmas Eve masquerade ball at the Cinémathèque Française. The chorus of Groucho lookalikes—another Marx Brothers homage among many that date as far back as Tamiment with Allen—perform a French version of "Hooray for Captain Spaulding!" that is nothing less than spectacular. Allen and Hawn, wearing Groucho moustaches, slide into Marxian mannerisms and steal away to a fondly remembered place from their courtship down along the Seine under the Pont de la Tournelle, where the once-marrieds enjoy an otherworldly pas de deux, luminously moonlit and photographed by Di Palma. Their duet evokes a similar dream dance on the Seine performed by Leslie Caron and Gene Kelly in *An American in Paris*. Hawn, once a Las Vegas showgirl, shows she still has all the right moves, even though, rare for Allen, the dance is choreographed with the aid of special effects. Wearing high heels and a black cocktail dress, her strawberry blonde hair streaming around her in an aureole, Hawn levitates and soars through the air like a wondrous kite connected to a string tugged by the gracefully twirling Allen. All is love, even for DJ (Natasha Lyonne), who gets the last shot in the joyous movie, dancing at the ball with a French Harpo.

Many critics got it. "It would take a heart of stone to resist this movie," Roger Ebert enthused in the *Chicago Sun-Times*. "A burst of exhilaration that rarely touches the ground," Peter Travers wrote in *Rolling Stone*. For others, the ersatz musical was tainted by the name Woody Allen. "A sluggish, sputtering tune fest performed almost entirely by the vocally challenged," complained Rita Kempley in the *Washington Post*. Foster Hirsch, in *Love, Sex, Death, and the Meaning of Life: The Films of Woody Allen*, pilloried the well-intentioned entertainment as "a desecration of the kind of American musical of the past that Allen venerates."

For some the problem was the everyday singing. For others, such as Kenneth Turan in the *Los Angeles Times*, it was "the notion that Allen has concocted some of his recent scenarios . . . merely to play love scenes with the most glamorous actresses he can corral." His *Times* colleague Kristine McKenna wrote a follow-up condemning Allen's "weird romantic proclivities" in movie after movie, notably his character's involvements with actresses like Roberts that explored "erotic relationships between very young women and very old men."

"Thirty-two years younger," McKenna added disapprovingly. Leaving aside the question of whether Allen was "very old" when, at sixty-one, he made *Everyone Says I Love You*, McKenna might have missed the joke that Joe is so good in bed only because DJ has fed him secrets about Von's erogenous zones. Eavesdropping on therapy sessions, which Turan called an "unpalatable twist" that privileged Allen's character in the script, would have been a perfectly acceptable story line in a Hollywood romantic comedy of the 1930s, albeit with Production Code adjustments for the time period. The older man/younger woman setup was also as ancient as Aeschylus. In classic Hollywood love stories, you'd find, among numerous examples, Fred Astaire, then 58, dancing with Audrey Hepburn (28) in *Funny Face*; Clark Gable (61), appearing in his last screen role, romantically aligned with Marilyn Monroe (34); 54-year-old Cary Grant sniffing around Sophia Loren (24) in *Houseboat*. Always yoked to side-of-the-mouth mention of his relationship with Soon-Yi—and sly allusions to the sex-abuse claims—this critical knock against Allen, as he continued to age, was added to critics' growing objections to his films.

MIRAMAX PRODUCER HARVEY Weinstein "hated" *Everyone Says I Love You*, according to Allen. Weinstein, who saw Allen's musical only after it had been completed, asked the director to take the word "motherfucker" out of the rap version of "I'm Through with Love," so the movie might obtain a G rating and open at Radio City Music Hall. Allen declined, *Everyone Says* was rated R, and the musical continued the downward spiral of US earnings for his pictures, stalling at $9.5 million, less than *Mighty Aphrodite. Everyone Says I Love You* had to make up the difference overseas, where it pulled in another $20 million in foreign receipts, becoming—after the subtraction of $22 million for negative costs—the most profitable Allen/Sweetland film in adjusted proceeds. Yet as his foreign earnings continued to rise, so did the costs, while US oases for his movies continued to dry up.

Allen and Jean Doumanian found fault with certain Miramax decisions. "Sources close to Allen say he was unhappy that Miramax did not use its clout to keep his latest, *Everyone Says I Love You*, on screens longer," *Variety* reported. Consequently, Sweetland decided to switch to Fine Line Features, a specialty division of New Line Cinema, itself an autonomous subsidiary of Warner Bros., for the handling of *Wild Man Blues*, the forthcoming documentary, and for *Deconstructing Harry*—the ultimate title for "The Meanest Man in the World," currently in postproduction. Fine Line was Miramax's chief rival as a distributor of independent films.

As decided by "dinner table" conversations, Allen would write and direct his next two projects for Sweetland after *Deconstructing Harry* without appearing on the screen. He'd also write, direct, and star in a third film. After riffling his files, Allen launched two scripts: the first, a black comedy about fame, which would shape up as more of an ensemble picture, without his appearing on screen; while for the other film not starring Woody Allen, he'd return to "The Jazz Baby," his shelved project from the late 1960s, with plans to reconfigure that script for a Hollywood personality.

One day a few years back a Hollywood visitor had stopped by Allen's editing suite in New York. Another maverick in the film industry, Sean Penn was transitioning into directing, and he wanted to discuss methods and strategies. Allen had seen Penn in a few roles. He thought Penn played "quite a likeable character" in *Racing for the Moon* and had been "fascinating" as the drug-addicted lawyer in Brian De Palma's *Carlito's Way*.* Chiefly

* In the fame-themed black comedy Allen was writing he'd also give a shout-out to *The Falcon and the Snowman*, which stars Sean Penn.

an explosive dramatic actor, Penn was sometimes "wonderfully funny," Allen thought. He had liked Penn in person too, finding the star "tortured," much like himself, "someone who was interested in the artistic side of filmmaking, no bullshit . . . he wanted to take the tough route and try to make really good, interesting films."

Allen quietly made inquiries about the mercurial thespian, checking with other New York filmmakers he knew about how temperamental Penn was. The "Jazz Baby" rewrite began to evolve into *Sweet and Lowdown*.

Simultaneous with the final editing of *Deconstructing Harry*, Allen put the finishing touches on his darkly comic script about fame, which grew into a caustic commentary on the fashion goddesses, sports superstars, fleeting public figures, and television and movie personalities that dominate American popular culture. "You could learn a lot about a society," as one character explains, "by whom it chooses to celebrate." Allen's sprawling script revolved around a freelance travel and entertainment writer who is a frustrated novelist. The writer divorces his neurotic schoolteacher wife; both undergo midlife crises. The writer enjoys chance sexual encounters with a Hollywood bombshell and a supermodel who, like some who came before her in Woody Allen films, is "polymorphously perverse." The writer also betrays a sensible girlfriend for a waitress-cum-actress, who becomes the obscure object of his desire. A young, pumped-up movie star takes the writer on a coke, gambling, and group-sex binge in a casino city. Meanwhile, his ex-wife miraculously transforms herself into a glib broadcaster, although she can't manage to shed her sexual hang-ups. The freelance writer ultimately gets no satisfaction—creatively or sexually. The skywritten HELP! would flash across the screen as the first and last image of the picture. The title of Allen's script spelled out its obvious subject matter: *Celebrity*.

Allen was ready to take *Celebrity* before the cameras in New York locations in September 1997 with a cast that featured (alphabetically, as usual) Hank Azaria, Kenneth Branagh, Judy Davis, Leonardo DiCaprio, Melanie Griffith, Famke Jannsen, Michael Lerner, Joe Mantegna, Bebe Neuwirth, Winona Ryder, and Charlize Theron. Branagh was playing the central character, the divorced and emotionally adrift freelance writer Lee Simon.

THERE WAS GROWING financial anxiety in the air, and Allen's services were no longer contractually "exclusive" to Sweetland, especially if he didn't appear on camera and simply lent his voice to a role. Over the summer of 1997 Allen devoted the spare time he could always find in his crowded schedule to "voicing" the lead in a $42 million animated feature. *Antz*, which became one of his least likely, biggest-ever paydays, was the joint project of the computer animation company Pacific Data Images (PDI) and the boutique Hollywood studio DreamWorks SKG, which had been founded in 1994 by three high-profile partners—the S for Steven Spielberg, the K for former Disney executive Jeffrey Katzenberg, and the G for music mogul David Geffen.

From its earliest glimmers as a film, Zak Penn, cowriter of the original story, entertained the hope that a certain famous comedian might "voice" the hero of *Antz*. Penn "grew up on the Upper East Side block where Woody Allen lived," wrote Nicole Laporte in *The Men Who Would Be King*, and "was a devoted fan of the filmmaker." Katzenberg, another devoted fan who had championed Allen for *Scenes from a Mall* when he was at Disney, pitched the possibility to Allen over drinks one day in New York, and from that day forward the *Antz* script was expressly tailored for the comic to play Z, a wisecracking slave ant in a totalitarian ant world with an unhappy childhood and love life, regular therapy appointments, and a thing about bullies. Z accidentally survives a termite war and becomes the unlikely conquering hero of an uprising against slavery, conformity, and despotism. When the animators brought the final screenplay to Allen for approval, "he was amazed at how much it sounded like him," producer Patty Wooten said. "Somebody knows me very well," Allen commented.

They knew him well enough to create a scene with Z belting out a snippet of "Almost Like Being in Love," the Lerner and Loewe classic from *Brigadoon*. Allen was already in the mood for singing after *Everyone Says I Love You*, and his "voice" performance in *Antz* is full-throated and amusing. Sharon Stone, Sylvester Stallone, Gene Hackman, and Dan Ackroyd, alumni of past and future Woody Allen pictures, were among the other voice artists for *Antz*, released in October 1998 and swiftly grossing more than $90 million in the US.

FINE LINE FEATURES tried an old strategy intended to bolster Allen's waning US box office returns, and *Deconstructing Harry* was given a limited release at Christmas 1997, before going national after the New Year.

Although the contrarian in him insisted he never had wanted to play Harry Block, who was in many ways unlike the real Woody Allen—Harry guzzles tequila while popping antidepressants, for example—Harry was also an obvious alter ego, and the new movie was like a wild ride in a brakeless car with Allen gripping the wheel. The director ushered in an arresting visual style in the opening sequence, which entailed jump-cut variations of the same vignette, swiftly repeated a half dozen times: Harry's irate ex-girlfriend Lucy (Judy Davis) bursts into his apartment. A gun is in her purse, and she intends to shoot Harry for viciously caricaturing her in his fiction. Allen wrote the quick editing—reminiscent of how Charlotte Rampling is treated in *Stardust Memories*—into his script. "Sometimes, if I am dealing with a very neurotic character," he later explained, "I like to cut neurotically, I like the cuts to be atonal or asymmetrical and not balanced." The jump cuts occur only in Harry's reality, not during the fictional interludes, because fiction is "an existence entirely controlled by art."

What unfolds is a masterpiece of construction, as Harry's reality collides with his imagination, his fictional creations enacting scenes from his books and short stories that he has drawn and distorted from his personal life for literary purposes. The fictive characters turn up in Harry's real world to lecture him about his shortcomings. The fiction-within-fiction sketches are hilarious: the family picnic with blind Grandma wandering into the pantry, where Julia Louis-Dreyfus is getting down and dirty with Richard Benjamin; the Hollywood star (Robin Williams) condemned to soft-focus; the elderly wife who discovers her husband is an ax murderer (he has devoured his previous family); an elevator to hell, left over from *Annie Hall*, which descends the levels of depravity. (Floor 7—The Media: "Sorry, that floor is all filled up.") Hell's basement is replete with bare-breasted women, S&M activity, the man who invented aluminum siding, Harry's father (who has been condemned to Hades for behaving "unconscionably to his son"), and Billy Crystal as the devilish Larry, who has stolen Harry's girlfriend. Harry and Larry, both professional writers, are old acquaintances with shared memories, however, and they kibitz fondly about their threesomes with the blonde WASP Sherman sisters.

The juddering editing style was one break from the past, and Allen's bust-up with Mia Farrow had also liberated his comedy. *Harry* boasted sexual circumstances and frank language that would have been unheard of in previous Woody Allen films. "You fucked-up fuck! . . . fuck you!" screams Harry's first wife, Joan (played by the improvising Kirstie Alley). An analyst, Joan holds sessions with her patients in their home, but a flashback reveals Harry has slept with a few of her clients, including one who is young enough to be his daughter. "Who else do I meet but your patients?" the incorrigible Harry/Allen pleads. Harry is a chronic philanderer, and as he sneaks off to an assignation with Lucy (Davis), his second wife Jane's (Amy Irving) sexier sister, he switches over to a beguiling young fan of his books, whom he meets by chance in the elevator going up. Her name is Fay Sexton, as in Sexy Fay, and she is sweetly portrayed by Elisabeth Shue. Oh, and Harry is addicted to prostitutes, he tells his analyst. Thank God for the hooker named Cookie, played by Trinidad-born Hazelle Goodman, whom Harry hires to "tie me up, hit me, give me a blow job." Cookie agrees to accompany Harry to the "honoring day" at his upstate alma mater as long as he pays her day rate.* Goodman's performance is so terrific—her hooker as memorable as Mira Sorvino's in *Mighty Aphrodite*—the actress almost makes up for a quarter century of lily-white casting in much of the rest of Allen's oeuvre.

A-list and future-name actors show up in scene after breakneck scene. Watch for young Tobey Maguire as the lascivious boy-Harry, who has an unwanted encounter with the Grim Reaper, returning from *Love and Death*. There is also Harry's once-beloved sister (Caroline Aaron), who has gone piously kosher. Harry pays her a rare visit on the way to the ceremony, and they argue about God and Judaism. She calls him a self-hating Jew. "I may hate myself," Harry replies, with one of the film's great one-liners, "but not because I'm Jewish." Harry's friend Richard (Bob Balaban), whose doctor has just pronounced him in perfect health, tags along for the ride and suffers a fatal heart attack in the back seat. The fourth passenger is Harry's young son Hilly (Eric Lloyd), whom Harry has sort of "kidnapped." He wrests the boy from the arms of a school mom (Mariel Hemingway), "an aggressive,

* With Allen's love for naming, the alma mater is called "Adair College" in *Deconstructing Harry*, a nod to the poet Virginia Hamilton Adair, a frequent contributor to the *New York Review of Books* and the *New Yorker*. Scarlett Johansson in *Scoop* introduces herself as an Adair journalism student, and "Adair College" is where Joaquin Phoenix hails from in *Irrational Man*.

tight-ass, busybody cunt," in Harry's opinion, who has overheard Harry and Hilly talk about the boy giving his penis the nickname of "John Dillinger." The abduction is a necessary evil because ex-wife Joan/Kirstie Alley won't change Hilly's strict visitation schedule for the boy to witness his father's honoring day. Hilly, Harry finally realizes, is the one pure good thing in his life. Father and son pay a visit to F.A.O. Schwarz, where Harry tells the boy he can buy any toy his heart desires, and on the road to the college everyone—Harry, Hilly, Cookie, Richard—stop at a roadside fair to ride the carousel and Ferris wheel.

Deconstructing Harry reweaves favorite, familiar Allen ideas into an ingenious new quilt—wives, sisters, children of divorce with errant fathers, carousels, Judaism, black holes, Kafka, Samuel Beckett, therapists crazier than their clients, the sand and bugs of the Hamptons, the miraculous 1951 Giants. So many real and imaginary persons berate Harry, he screws up so pervasively, he decides he is probably the fourth-worst man in the world after, you know, Hitler, Goebbels, and Goering. Yet his nagging problem is not the women in his life, it's the depression he is suffering from because, for the first time, after spending his next book's advance, Harry is "blocked."

In the end, however, the honoring ceremony doesn't happen, because the police arrest Harry for absconding with Hilly as he arrives on campus. Cookie too: nabbed not for hooking, but for her marijuana pouch. Harry lands in jail, where he meets the ghost of dearly departed Richard, who tells him the only lesson death has taught him is "to be alive is to be happy." Bailed out by Larry (Crystal) and Fay (Shue), who rush over from their wedding, Harry goes home in a daze. Suddenly he has an inspiration. Harry fantasizes the honoring ceremony taking place regardless, with all his friends and family, the real and imaginary people, the entire cast gathered for another *Stardust Memories*–type curtain call. Harry is revealed as "a character who's too neurotic to function in life, who can only function in art." Sitting down at his manual typewriter, on fire with ideas, Harry begins to type furiously. "His writing, in more ways than one," says the voice-over, "saved his life."

Those lines came straight from the heart. "Artistic creation was a savior" in his life too, the filmmaker told *Positif* interviewers. "As a matter of fact," Allen elaborated, "this is a character I feel within myself."

The rawness, the confessional tone, and the thin line between Harry

Block and Woody Allen—Hilly was roughly the same age as Satchel—divided critics more than any of his movies since *Stardust Memories*, a previous quasi-autobiographical transgression some reviewers cited. They saw *Harry* as a sloppy remix of his long-standing idées fixes—Bergman and Fellini through the prism of Woody Allen. Among the prominent thumbs-downs was Gene Siskel in the *Chicago Tribune*. "The laughs are few," he wrote. "What is offensive, at least to me, is a vicious, self-hating parade of Jewish characters, mostly women." Andrew Sarris, now at the *Observer*, said "what follows the credits are some of the coarsest and sourest scenes of badgerings and betrayals since the lacerating cruelties of *Stardust Memories*." The *New York Times*, less and less in Allen's corner, published the opinions of female commentors who scolded the age-disparity between old Allen (sixty-three) and his young love interest Shue (thirty-four). A leading feminist film critic, Molly Haskell (married to Sarris, incidentally), dismissed *Harry* as "one long diatribe against women, wives and Jews." Op-ed columnist Maureen Dowd, a nonfilm critic who had interviewed Allen for features, embarked on a series of *Times* columns excoriating Allen—her op-eds would win a Pulitzer in 1999—calling *Harry* an "infomercial with bad info," demonstrating Allen's "creepy obsession" with "younger and younger" babes in movies. She also squeezed in mention of Soon-Yi.

Many were affronted by Cookie the hooker. Marion Meade described *Bullets over Broadway*, *Mighty Aphrodite*, and *Deconstructing Harry* as Allen's "Hooker-Fellatio Trilogy," even though the trilogy was preceded by *The Purple Rose of Cairo* and *Shadows and Fog* and the hooker trend would continue with many subsequent Woody Allen pictures including *Celebrity*, *Sweet and Lowdown*, *To Rome with Love*, *Café Society*, and so on. Maybe Allen just liked writing such parts and thought he was good at turning prostitutes into comical and likeable characters. Why do all the prostitutes say, "Beats the hell out of waitressing!" Harry/Allen asks.

A few established critics were won over to the film's greatness, however, recognizing that *Harry* danced on a pin. The brutal comedy worked because of its self-referential honesty. "A genuine masterpiece," Rex Reed exclaimed in the *Observer*. "Self-flagellating and fearless," declared Kenneth Turan in the *Los Angeles Times*, who had not admired recent Woody Allen pictures. "His best, funniest, and angriest film in years," agreed Janet Maslin, the

Times first-stringer, who along with a handful of reviewers named Allen's twenty-eighth feature to their Ten Best lists for 1997. The Motion Picture Academy gave Allen another Best Screenplay nomination.

Although it was an irrelevancy to the filmmaker, the MPAA's R rating didn't improve the box office in the US, which bottomed out at $8.1 million, less than half of the movie's production costs. It remained for foreign nations, where critics and audiences were less censorious, to add $17.6 million and nudge *Deconstructing Harry* into the black.

ALTHOUGH SHE HAD kept a low public profile for a couple of years, one of Allen's real-life exes—never quite wife—published her autobiography earlier in 1997. Mia Farrow's *What Falls Away* treated the actress's entire life story, with only the final third of the memoir covering her relationship with Allen and its devastating climax.

Farrow's life had continued to take twists and turns. Following the verdict that gave her custody of Satchel, Dylan, and Moses, the actress adopted a boy, a paraplegic child from India whom she named Thaddeus. Farrow gave the boy the middle name "Wilk," as in the surname of a judge who had continued to rule in her favor. Then she adopted another onetime African American crack baby, born Kaeli-Shea and called Quincy; and, in 1995, a three-year-old blind Vietnamese orphan she named Frankie-Minh, as in Ol' Blue Eyes. Refueling her Catholicism with family retreats to a Connecticut abbey of Benedictine nuns, Farrow was by now, at age fifty, the mother of fourteen children, although she wasn't on speaking terms with at least one of her kids.

A new celebrity had entered her romantic life—Philip Roth, the author of *Portnoy's Complaint* and other notable fiction often focused on Jewishness—who was a Connecticut neighbor. "She met Roth at our house when we were having a dinner for [then president of the Czech Republic] Vaclav Havel," Rose Styron, the widow of author William Styron, told *Vanity Fair.* "She came all dressed in leather, looking gorgeous, and they both fell for her. She had affairs with both." Roth only recently had divorced his third wife, British actress Claire Bloom, who appears in the Woody Allen films *Crimes and Misdemeanors* and *Mighty Aphrodite*. Bloom did not say very much about Allen's directing style in *Leaving a Doll's*

House, her memoir published the year before Farrow's, but she did air her ex-husband's health problems and depression, his promiscuity, and verbal abuse. Both Farrow and Roth, Marion Meade assured readers of her book, "despised Woody Allen."

Farrow made the publicity rounds for *What Falls Away*, a book that "likely benefited from the extensive editorial assistance of several people," Meade wrote. She appeared on Jay Leno's *The Tonight Show* where "during a commercial break," in Meade's words, "Dylan was seen backstage in the greenroom munching potato chips with her mother and Satchel. This rare glimpse of Woody's kids," whom Allen himself had not seen since 1992 in Dylan's case, and 1995 in Satchel's, revealed the little blonde girl, now twelve, to have grown into "a gawky, preadolescent girl, while Satch was still blond and adorable, a nine-year-old boy who resembled his mother."

Their estranged sister Soon-Yi Previn was now twenty-seven. A man, sixty-two years of age, pledging his troth to such a much younger woman was precisely the age-inappropriate scenario scorned by the critics averse to *Everyone Says I Love You* and *Deconstructing Harry*, but that is what happened at Christmastime in Venice, Italy, in 1997. On the afternoon of a "cold dark day" at the Palazzo Cavalli, as Allen recalled, he and Soon-Yi exchanged vows at a private ceremony with only his sister, Letty Aronson, one of Letty's children, and the wife of Italian cameraman Carlo Di Palma in attendance. Venice mayor Massimo Cacciari officiated. The couple had wanted "a quiet, secret wedding," in Allen's words, so they sneaked out of their Gritti Palace suite and arrived at city hall from separate directions. But the press was on the alert. "After the wedding," the *New York Times* reported, "the happy couple were hounded down the serpentine streets of the city by paparazzi and television crews," before they landed at Harry's Bar for truffles, scampi, and prosecco. On to Paris for a honeymoon at the Ritz, with the trip as usual timed to coincide with publicity for the French premiere of *Deconstructing Harry*.

Almost every year since 1993 the couple had taken an end-of-year vacation in Venice, "a town we both loved," in Allen's words. Venice had been spotlighted in *Everyone Says I Love You*, and its film festival in recent years had become the go-to launching pad for European premieres of Woody Allen films. Why get married (the third time, incidentally, his parents were not among the witnesses)? "Not for romantic reasons but strictly financial,"

Allen wrote later. "I adored Soon-Yi and knew I was much older and could drop dead at a moment's notice. If I did, I wanted her to be legally protected to get all I owned automatically with no hitches."

Allen's marriage to Soon-Yi suggested another comparison to Charles Chaplin, who married for the fourth time to Oona O'Neill in 1943, at the height of the Joan Barry scandal. Chaplin was fifty-four; O'Neill, the daughter of Eugene O'Neill—one of Allen's playwriting avatars—was eighteen. Despite being blacklisted and exiled from America, which cast a shadow over his final years, the couple bore eleven children and stayed happily married until Chaplin's death in 1977.

John Springer, the spokesman for Mia Farrow, said only that "of course Mia wouldn't dignify this event with a comment." Nor did the actress care to discuss the milestone with Dylan or Satchel, often referred to nowadays in press accounts as Eliza and Seamus. Allen had tried writing "sweet, affectionate, brief letters" to Dylan, "asking how she was doing." The letters were "intercepted" by Seamus, who replied in "curt, evasive" fashion, beginning with "I told Dylan about your letter, and she is not interested." Allen wrote his son directly, asking, "Do you always open your sister's mail and read it?" Seamus replied, "if I really wanted to help out, I should send money," according to Allen, "[though] I already was supporting them generously by law."

Details of the blonde girl's life after that fateful day of August 4, 1992, were elusive. By Christmas 1997, however, the preteen was being groomed by tutors for early admission to Bard College, a private liberal arts college in a Dutchess County hamlet overlooking the Hudson River. "I was terrified of being touched by men," Dylan said later. "I developed an eating disorder. I began cutting myself." Every time Dylan noticed her father's image—once on a T-shirt worn by a Bard classmate—she relived the trauma of her alleged abuse.

Age ten by the time Allen married Soon-Yi, Seamus had been skipping grades and taking courses from the Center for Talented Youth, part of a Johns Hopkins University network, and soon he would become the youngest student ever admitted to Simon's Rock college in Great Barrington, Massachusetts, a unit of Bard, which offered college credits to prodigies. When, two years later, reporters contacted Allen and asked for his reaction to news of his "genius" son taking college courses, Allen said, "This is the first I'm hearing of it."

That was 1999. Farrow's new lawyer William Beslow told wire services Seamus was "positively phobic" about his famous filmmaking father and would never have anything to do with Allen. "He sees Woody less as his father," Beslow explained, "and more as the man who was having an affair with his sister Soon-Yi."

JEAN DOUMANIAN PUSHED for drastic changes behind the scenes to reduce operating costs and improve the income flow for Sweetland Pictures. There would be many ways Woody Allen films changed gradually and definitively, though not all of them were cost-related. The spot appearances of famous New Yorkers that had helped bestow a unique texture on his films began to melt away after the child-custody courtroom defeat, notably with the VIP-free *Manhattan Murder Mystery* and then all but ending with *Celebrity*. The huge number of speaking parts and extras that also gave a density to pictures such as *Stardust Memories* or *Radio Days* were now a thing of the past. (There would still be many nonfamous Allen friends and professional family popping up in small parts, however.) Probably most important, the director would not have the same luxury of reshooting scenes, much less an entire movie. "As the years have gone on, I've done less and less reshoots," the director explained to Eric Lax a few years later. "One, I haven't had the money. But it was more than that. I reshoot as I go along. If I don't like the dailies on Thursday, I reshoot on Friday. I don't wait to the end of shooting like I used to."

Listening to Doumanian, his sister, Letty, and Diane Keaton, in early summer Allen dropped the agent who had represented him for thirty years—Sam Cohn of International Creative Management—who had hated visiting Los Angeles and wasn't proactive about getting acting jobs for Allen in other people's movies. Allen switched from ICM to the William Morris Agency and the Los Angeles–based John Burnham, head of the motion picture department, who had been Keaton's agent for fifteen years. Allen wanted more payday opportunities such as *Scenes from a Mall* and *Antz*—the moonlighting that had worked out best for him financially.

Also, by early summer, word had leaked to the press that Allen had asked long-standing key creative personnel from his production unit to accept pay cuts. "I took a substantial reduction in what I was getting," the film director told the *New York Times*. "A number of people who worked for years at certain prices couldn't afford to stay on. These are good friends. They just couldn't afford to work for this kind of money."

Among the departures was Robert Greenhut, the producer of Woody Allen movies dating back to *Annie Hall*. The veteran was asked to take a 60 percent decrease in pay, according to accounts. He was considered expendable now that Letty Aronson and others made Sweetland top-heavy with producers. "It was a wonderful situation," Greenhut graciously told the press. "I was glad to be part of it. I wish them luck." He was less diplomatic, speaking to Marion Meade, who informed him Doumanian said she could watch the costs better. The news "gets my dander up," Greenhut said. Doumanian hired Richard Brick, formerly the New York film commissioner, whose producing style was "noisy and confrontational" compared to Greenhut's, according to the *Times*, but who was meant to snap the whip. Allen's longtime assistant director Thomas Reilly also left.

Deconstructing Harry was the last Woody Allen picture to be shot by the Italian cameraman Carlo Di Palma, who'd begun to experience poor health, and *Celebrity* was the last for Swedish cinematographer Sven Nykvist and editor Susan E. Morse, once Ralph Rosenblum's assistant, who'd been at Allen's side since *Manhattan*.

All the changes were expected "to ensure the money goes on the screen," which was Allen's philosophy, Doumanian told the press. "Over the years, I haven't made very much money with my films," Allen insisted in interviews. "It's always been a struggle to break even. In the US they rarely break even. I've always depended on Europe to supplement my grosses, so I have a chance of breaking even or making a little money."

Up and down the line veteran personnel were replaced by new, younger people whose lesser credentials translated into lower salaries. Allen's productions had always eschewed the "fun money" found in most Hollywood budgets: there were never any end-of-filming or holiday parties, no "wrap" gifts for actors or the crew, no per diems for the stars, and few dined with Allen, seeing him pick up the check. Hollywood names like Goldie Hawn in *Everyone Says I Love You*, Demi Moore in *Deconstructing Harry*, and Melanie Griffith and Leonardo DiCaprio in *Celebrity* were paid as much as $10,000 weekly in the past; now they accepted "about $5,000 a week," according to the *Times*. The exigent measures had reached the point where free coffee was eliminated on the set of *Mighty Aphrodite*, until the crew complained vociferously, and the free coffee vats were reinstated.

"Those who remained with Woody and agreed to work for scale, sometimes at half their regular compensation, usually had personal reasons," Marion Meade wrote. "Circumspect in public, they grumped among themselves. Unwilling to place the blame on Woody himself, his associates reserved their hostility for Jean Doumanian and Letty Aronson. Jean was smart but abrasive; Letty was known for her temper."

Not only trimming salaries and daily frills, Doumanian set in motion plans for a public auction of surplus props, set dressings, and costumes from past Woody Allen pictures, along with thousands of books, movie posters, scripts, and scene stills. The proceeds of the auction, which was carried out later in 1999, were targeted to benefit breast cancer research and AIDS foundations, but the sale also reduced inventory and storage fees.

While his movies were being downsized, Allen also modified his private lifestyle while turning a surprising profit in that area. He quietly launched plans to vacate his longtime Fifth Avenue penthouse duplex with wraparound windows on East Seventy-Fourth for a family-style, five-story Victorian townhouse on East Ninety-Second in the Carnegie Hill district. Realtors sold the former for a reported $14 million, giving Allen a substantial profit on the $600,000 he had paid in the early 1970s. "I made more money in real estate than I've ever made from movies," he told Peter Biskind. The comedian and director plunked down $17 million for the new place, and he and new wife Soon-Yi moved into leased Fifth Avenue space while the townhouse was being renovated.

THE GLOWING NEWLYWEDS came to view one of the earliest rough cuts of *Wild Man Blues*, acting like "two kids" in the screening room, Barbara Kopple recalled. "They sat, she surrounded in his arms, he was leaning over her and they giggled like crazy nonstop locked in their intimate cocoon." The first cut was nine hours; Allen and Soon-Yi watched the three-and-a-half-hour version of the jazz-band documentary. "Very entertaining," Allen enthused. "How are you going to edit it down?" That's my problem, Kopple answered. "I'm glad!" chirped Allen, before the couple darted out of the room. Allen saw the Kopple film as "a home movie about the trip."

Kopple regretted having to lose a few precious scenes: the one with the couple taking a break from the tour and attending Fashion Week in Milan, where Soon-Yi "was jealous to see all these great-looking models"; another of the director lunching with haute designer Gianni Versace. But she whittled the footage down to an hour and forty-five minutes for its April 1998 release. Apart from Soon-Yi and Allen's parents, the documentary boasted rare glimpses of Letty Aronson and "always on the edge of the shot, though never identified," in John Baxter's words, "hovers an impassive, black-dressed Jean Doumanian, Mrs. Danvers to the last."

Typical of its genre, the Kopple documentary was shown only in niche theaters and aroused more critical than audience intrigue. It didn't take much to offend some reviewers, who now always had Mia Farrow, Dylan, and Soon-Yi lurking in their minds. Amy Taubin in the *Village Voice* scathingly panned the mild-mannered, deferential documentary as a PR "snooze." David Edelstein, writing for *Slate*, described *Wild Man Blues* as "depressing" spin control. "The only Woody Allen film not directed by Woody Allen," sniffed *Newsweek*.

Many other critics enjoyed the music and praised *Wild Man Blues*, while puzzling over whether they had just been treated to a penetrating, unadorned cinema vérité portrait of Allen, or was it all just the consummate masquerade of his persona? "The most talked about segment," in *Los Angeles Times* byliner Kenneth Turan's phrase, was the last ten minutes of Allen's awkward homecoming visit to his parents. "We see that in marrying Previn," Taubin noted, "Allen has married his mother (they're similarly self-involved and uninterested in him as an artist)." This was a common observation in the negative and positive reviews. But wasn't the picture really the ultimate *Pygmalion* story in reverse, with Soon-Yi the real-life Eliza Doolittle schooling Henry Higgins?

ALLEN FINISHED A novel he'd been writing, off and on for years, over the slow summer. "Finished it like a dedicated drone," he recalled. Allen showed it to one friend who told him "it had a lot of good things in it, but it wasn't really good enough." Roger Angell of the *New Yorker* and Vincent Canby of the *New York Times* also read the manuscript and offered notes. "They were very kind to me and very helpful, but I could see that I just didn't pull it off." Deep into his drawer it went. "I didn't want to have a novel out there that would be regarded as the work of a celebrity. I didn't want it looked down upon or embraced because it had a celebrity name."

That summer Allen took his new bride on a hand-holding tour of old Brooklyn haunts. They got out of his chauffeur-driven Mercedes on Avenue L near Wingate Park, walking nostalgically up and down the blocks where the Konigsberg family had lived fifty years before. Allen spotted shops in the area, now predominantly Hasidic, that he knew from boyhood. "I love it, love going back," he said. "It's a wonderful old neighborhood, and I will always be from there." Still, Allen never attended a high school reunion. Kenneth Branagh has an awkward time at his in *Celebrity*. "I'm sure it would be very depressing," the director told Stig Björkman.

Sweet and Lowdown began photography on the last day of summer. Partly for budget reasons the movie, set in the 1920s and '30s, was shot mostly in the New York area, with many of the Chicago, road-trip, and Hollywood scenes credibly mocked up "within thirty blocks of my house," as Allen boasted to Björkman. Allen's first-time editor was Alisa Lepselter, who had been an assistant editor on pictures directed by Jonathan Demme, Francis Coppola, Martin Scorsese, and Nora Ephron, and who would stay in Allen's employ for the next twenty years. Allen's latest cinematographer was Zhao Fei, who was known for masterful work on many Chinese pictures made by the so-called Fifth Generation, including Zhang Yimou's chef d'oeuvre *Raise the Red Lantern*. Allen shrugged over Zhao's sole drawback, which was the cameraman's minimal English.

Sean Penn starred as the self-destructive (fictional) jazz guitarist Emmet Ray, whose talent reputation is second only to Django Reinhardt. To play opposite Penn, Allen picked twenty-year-old Samantha Morton, after watching the 1997 British film *Under the Skin* and being struck by the newcomer's intensity and raw sexuality. Hattie, her dissimilar character in *Sweet and Lowdown*, is a simpleminded mute. Allen had tried writing Hattie as deaf—so she couldn't hear Ray's music—yet that ploy presented complications. One of the few directions Allen gave Morton was that Hattie should be played "like Harpo Marx." "Who's Harpo Marx?" the young actress inquired. He recommended a few Marx Brothers comedies and told her Hattie should be "very loveable," someone "who personified all the sweet things that Emmet was not." Morton was "used to everybody having a chat on the set about how they're going to approach this today," the actress recalled. "But Woody would be quite monosyllabic at times about what he required, and you just have to not take any of the stuff personally. I just had my lip buttoned the whole time, anyway, playing Hattie . . . but Sean handled him really well."

Also in the cast were Uma Thurman in a showy supporting role, playing a onetime Chicago debutante infatuated with Ray and his music, and Anthony LaPaglia as the underworld thug who tries to steal her away.

Allen asked Penn to take some guitar lessons. Penn was sent to Howard Alden, whom *Jazz Times* called "maybe the best guitarist of his generation," and who was going to dub Penn's solos for the picture. Penn was "an incredibly great observationist," Alden recalled, and "picked up mannerisms from me that I didn't even know I had." By the time the star arrived on the set he had perfected what the movie's publicity described as Django Reinhardt's "hyper-dexterous fingering" style, so Penn could mime the guitar-playing for closeups. Emmet Ray's Hot Quintet was modeled after Reinhardt's legendary Quintette du Hot Club de France—minus Stéphane Grappelli and his violin. The musicians who mimed during filming also doubled as actors (Allen's banjo friend Eddy Davis can be glimpsed on the upright bass). The stellar unit rounded up for the soundtrack included guitarist Bucky Pizzarelli, bassist Kelly Friesen, drummer Ted Somers, and clarinetist Ken Peplowski.

Penn was always superserious about his acting and steeped himself in his characters. One time Allen called cut on a scene they were filming and said to the lead actor, "Sean, do you know what was wrong with that take?" A long pause. "*Everything* . . ." Yet the director had to speak to the star only "two or three times," Allen explained later, because "ninety-eight percent of it was just hiring Sean and getting out of his way."

Shortly after filming began Penn had to fly to the West Coast to the bedside of his ailing father, the actor and director Leo Penn, who died on September 5. Penn returned immediately after his father's death and reported straight to work on the set. "When you're with Sean, you see that he's very sensitive and that he suffers all the time," Allen reflected, almost as though he were musing about himself. "So, obviously, the suffering of his father's death, it was nothing new to him in a certain sense. He's wounded by the appropriately tragic and awful mess that everybody's in in life, the difficulty of that. He's not a light-hearted, happy-go-lucky individual who just bounces along. He thinks about the world, and it causes him a correct amount of suffering: suffering that you see in great artists who find the world a very difficult place to make excuses for."

The two ended up as good friends, with Allen agreeing to act a small role in one of Penn's future vehicles.* Central to nearly every scene in *Sweet and Lowdown*, Penn eschewed any star perks and accepted alphabetical billing, fifth from the top of the roll call. Somehow, however—it's all a bit mysterious—the budget crept up to $29.5 million, making the faux-biopic of the jazzman Sweetland's most expensive Woody Allen picture.

CELEBRITY, WHICH AGAIN debuted at the Venice Film Festival and opened the New York Film Festival, went into release at Thanksgiving. Barbara Kopple had shown audiences a flawed mortal in *Wild Man Blues*, and arguably her documentary was the superior work. Despite stunning black-and-white visuals by Sven Nykvist, and a cast studded with current and tomorrow's stars, *Celebrity* was a disappointment, leaving many people cold.

The two leads, Kenneth Branagh and Judy Davis, were capable and watchable, yet stuck with characters that never quite sprang to life from an ambitious though muddled script. Asked about his approach with Davis, Allen once said he barely knew the actress, they had not "exchanged a hundred words in our lifetime," and Davis was "a truly great actress—intimidatingly great for me." His secret was to avoid giving her direction.

Davis portrayed Robin Simon, the overwrought schoolteacher who gets divorced from her skirt-chasing husband, Branagh. She is a sensitive soul who can quote Tennessee Williams, yet she lucks into a new career as a slick television host. Robin can't escape her uptight Catholicism, and certain sex acts will always be sinful for her—perhaps this was a dig at Mia Farrow. Her one hysterical scene comes when she visits a call girl for fellatio lessons because, among other reasons, mental images of the crucifixion always distract her during oral sex. Bebe Neuwirth, in a brief role, is a standout as the blowjob expert who nearly chokes herself to death on the demonstration prop: a banana. Allen shot and later cut more than one such sex lesson, including a scene with a group of hooker instructors. Davis is never very

* The future Sean Penn project costarring Allen never happened, in large part because the motion picture, a comedy with Penn as an antimarriage guru that was being planned for the early 2000s, got embroiled in a lawsuit, having nothing to do with Allen.

sympathetic in the picture, but she is the most redeeming character in the story, and she enunciates a key Allen precept: "It's luck . . . when it comes to love, it's luck."

At intervals Neuwirth and other winning players enter the unruly narrative to inject the film with vitality. Charlize Theron is the supermodel who is a walking-talking Orgasmatron. ("She's so hot," Allen told his friend Denis Hamill, "that if she was in this room, your buttons would melt.") Leonardo DiCaprio is every bit on fire, playing the testosterone-charged movie star on a coke-gambling-groupie binge in Atlantic City, "ad-libbing all over the place," to Allen's satisfaction. (It was the pre-*Titanic* DiCaprio, whom Allen had just seen in the ensemble drama *Marvin's Room*, with Diane Keaton among the cast.) Lee Simon's spurned girlfriend, Famke Janssen, takes the greatest imaginable revenge on the "asshole" writer. Marquee name Melanie Griffith is the lead of "The Liquidator," the film-within-the-film, who has a blowjob scene of her own. "Very beautiful, very sexy and very gifted," Allen said of Griffith. The director had spotted her early in her career in Arthur Penn's *Night Moves*, loved her in Mike Nichols's *Working Girl* and, regardless of comparisons to Judy Holliday, was impressed by her in the recent *Born Yesterday* remake scripted by Douglas McGrath.

Others in the billed cast included Joe Mantegna, returning as another likeable Joe wooing Davis, and Winona Ryder as the lost soul/kamikaze girlfriend, with Hank Azaria, Allison Janney, Debra Messing, and Gretchen Moll at their best. It would be the last Woody Allen sightseeing tour of New York celebritydom, with cameos by *Fear of Flying* novelist Erica Jong; Joey Buttafuoco, whose underage mistress, "the Long Island Lolita," shot his wife in the face; Tony-nominated Broadway star Robert Cuccioli, who sings "The Impossible Dream" at Lee's high school reunion; New York Knicks power forward Anthony Mason; avant-garde stage director André Gregory; Rao's restaurateur Frank Pelligrino (he also appears in *Broadway Danny Rose* and *Manhattan Murder Mystery*); and the one and thankfully only Donald Trump, who interrupts his power lunch to boast about his plans to tear down Saint Patrick's Cathedral for a new building emblazoned with his name.

Vanessa Redgrave's scenes were deleted wholesale—"Obviously it had nothing to do with the acting," said Allen. And so was an extended sequence positioned toward the end of the picture, where Lee visits an old classmate he'd met at his high school reunion. The classmate confesses he and his wife have been depressed over "the growing loss of humanity" in the world. They've made a suicide pact. His wife is lying dead elsewhere in the apartment. Now the classmate questions his vow to kill himself. What should he do? Allen shot the scene but "I just couldn't get it right," Allen told Stig Björkman. "But that is a scene I do plan on doing at some point, either in another film, or as part of a stage thing, or somehow. I am not going to throw it away because I think that is a good scene." Also because, he might have added, he never threw anything away forever.

Celebrity possessed a weak center in Branagh, the Belfast-born, London-trained Shakespearean whom Allen cast as Lee Simon, the celebrity-chasing, bed-hopping writer. Branagh was known for trying anything, and Allen viewed him as "a regular guy, a street person, a bar person." Many critics saw Branagh as a pale Woody Allen imitation, however. Not only was Branagh playing a writer—like Allen, struggling with a novel—but there were other personal echoes in his backstory (like Allen, Lee/Branagh was a high school runner). And Branagh deployed "all the ellipses, fluttering hands, and nervous tension" of Allen's persona, Denis Hamill pointed out in the New York *Daily News*. "One of the most colossal casting faux pas in memory," Todd McCarthy pointed out in *Variety*.

Allen told Hamill that when he sent the full script to Branagh he enclosed an admiring letter that included these cautionary words. "This part is not me," Allen explained to the British actor. "If I was younger, I would definitely not play it. When I was writing the thing, before I thought of you, I had someone like Alec Baldwin in mind. I think he would have been great doing it, but he was not available, and I want to be completely upfront about this. But this is definitely no way me. It requires a younger and more attractive person than me. Even when I was younger, I wasn't attractive enough to play this part. I need someone who's got more flair."

"No way me," but Allen himself said later he had to pull Branagh aside during the filming and warn the actor, "It seems to me you are doing me." Branagh said not to worry, but then the actor continued on in the same vein. Out of respect for Branagh's choices—"What's the smartest thing to do here? Do I try to force him into a different mold, or do I go with his take on the character?"—the director "just sort of threw in the towel."

Branagh was forced to defend himself when doing publicity interviews.

"The situations the character finds himself in are unquestionably, to my eye anyway, the kinds of things you'd expect Woody to be doing," the actor explained to one journalist. "And the way it [the script] was written, I found it impossible to play it without the kind of energy he has. It wasn't funny, unless you were desperately, physically kind of jumpy."

His character, like much of the film, was shallow, and ultimately more downbeat than funny. Lee is a freelancer yet he owns a high-priced Aston Martin—which he crashes, without apparent repercussions—and he can afford to lose $6,000 at Atlantic City tables. If he has a fussy editor demanding deadlines, or financial crises, they are not in the movie, and Lee rarely does any actual writing for all his supposed magazine articles, his three early promising novels, and the proverbial "spec" screenplay called "Heist." In real life, Allen was moving into a $17 million townhouse, and this side of him shows up in his pictures as a detachment from or ignorance of the financial reality of ordinary lives. His characters lived mainly in his imagination, and his lack of interest in research or authenticity outside his imagination sometimes walled the fictions off from believability.

Wild Man Blues brought in a mere $25,000 domestically while the US grosses for *Celebrity* stalled at $8.3 million. While both would recoup their budgets with modest profits after foreign sales, the auguries were not improving, and Jean Doumanian was happy to know that the director's next picture—the script he was finishing as he edited *Sweet and Lowdown*—would be a return to loose-knit comedy starring the sillier Woody Allen.

WITH UNSTEADY EARNINGS from his recent pictures and his personal expenses mounting, in late winter Allen flew with Soon-Yi to Hollywood, where his new William Morris agent John Burnham had arranged a three-week acting gig for $5 million. Allen agreed to star in a small, independent black comedy called *Picking Up the Pieces*, which had been packaged by the agency for Kushner-Locke Company, an HBO and syndicated television entity that was trying to expand its product line and launch an international distribution arm. The entire production coin was $10 million, so Kushner-Locke gambled that Allen's half of the budget would be offset by his marquee value overseas.

Picking Up the Pieces had begun its long trek to the screen a decade before with a screenplay by Bill Wilson, who imagined an offbeat religious satire, set in Mexico, which revolved around a dismembered hand discovered in the desert. The hand is hailed as a relic of the Virgin Mary by a provincial village envisioning a fortune in tourism from the press coverage. After the script had taken a Rip van Winkle nap in the William Morris offices, Mexico City–born Alfonso Arau, best known for acting in *Three Amigos!* and directing *Like Water for Chocolate*, took over the project, thinking Woody Allen might play the Brooklyn butcher who murders his sexpot wife only to mislay her chopped-off hand. He flew to New York to meet the famous comedian and filmmaker. "Why do you want to direct me?" Allen asked. Arau explained he had a background in comedy, had studied physical theater and mime with Etienne Decroux and Jacques Lecoq in Paris, and was steeped in the traditions of the Italian commedia dell'arte. He saw Allen, Arau said, as a one-man commedia dell'arte, playing the same role throughout his lifetime. Although *Picking Up the Pieces* was supposed to take place in Mexico, Arau intended to stage most of the exteriors on a standing Mexican-village set near Vasquez Rocks Park in northern Los Angeles County. Arau asked: Although Allen was notoriously averse to Hollywood, would he be willing to shoot all his scenes in California? Surprising everyone, Allen said yes. This was the new Allen-for-hire, shorn of previous apprehensions about being stuck with someone else's script and being controlled by another director. It helped when Arau assured Allen that he could improvise to his heart's extent.

Although Allen's salary was lopsided, other well-known names—most of them William Morris clients—jumped into the project, accepting Screen Actors Guild scale for the privilege of appearing in an ersatz Woody Allen comedy. In a finger-snap the list included Sharon Stone, Cheech Marin, David Schwimmer, Kiefer Sutherland, Andy Dick, Fran Drescher, Joseph Gordon-Levitt, Elliott Gould, Eddie Griffin, and Lou Diamond Phillips.

There was a pre-filming party at Sue Mengers's house with Barbra Streisand among the circulating guests. Soon-Yi hovered protectively at Allen's side. The star of *Picking Up the Pieces* arrived on time at the various locations every day, knew his lines, and was courteous to everyone, although he hung out mostly in his trailer, where he played chess with a pal from Brooklyn who had tagged along, or Kiefer Sutherland. On every production Allen usually found someone among the cast or crew to play chess with during the

long intervals of waiting. If not, as when in London for the filming of *Match Point*, he played chess with himself between takes.

The original script as well as budget took hammer blows. Wilson swiftly doctored pages to accommodate Allen's age and speech cadences, resurrecting a few scraps from previous Woody Allen pictures. Allen told Wilson he would act only—"I will not write anything"—but he ad-libbed if in the mood. Wilson recalled one great ad-lib, when the butcher (Allen), stewing about his duplicitous wife (Sharon Stone), mutters, "Her diaphragm needs call waiting. . . ." Another time, they were running lines, and something bothered Allen. "The scene is one line too long," he told Wilson. "Let's do it again and you tell me which one." They ran the dialogue again. "I said I thought it was the second to last line in the scene," recalled Wilson. "He smiled. We took it out." In fact, Arau, who reckoned himself Allen's "number-one fan," and saw his star as a "genius," was disappointed Allen didn't improvise more. "Sometimes after he said his lines," Arau said, "I would ask him, 'Woody, here, after this line, please improvise' and then I spoiled several takes because I couldn't contain my laughter."

Another Italian was behind the camera—Vittorio Storaro, who had lensed Bernardo Bertolucci's *Last Tango in Paris*, Warren Beatty's *Reds*, and Francis Coppola's *Apocalypse Now* as well as Coppola's segment of *New York Stories*. Allen went out of his way to befriend Storaro. That may have been half the appeal of the job. Yet unlike what transpired backstage during *The Front* or *Scenes from a Mall*, Allen had relaxed into being a gun for hire, and he was pleasant and professional throughout the shoot. Soon-Yi was his omnipresent smiling ally, and the two even attended the Chasen's wrap party, with everyone agog at his presence and Allen lingering.

His central performance is splendidly lunatic. The strange thing about *Picking Up the Pieces* is that, as demented as the script was, the movie turned out almost completely unfunny. The producers could not find a US distributor, and the laughless comedy went straight to video. Few overseas theaters wanted the picture. Mexico banned it outright as sacrilegious. Screenwriter Wilson thought the balance was thrown during editing, which heavily favored Allen, although that was hardly the only problem. Arguing against the postproduction decisions of Arau and the producers, Wilson wrote Allen during the editing stages, asking for his support as a fellow writer. "I never see the movies I'm in," Allen replied from New

York, apologizing for his delayed letter because "I've been moving" and "it's [been] a radical change" in his life. "I've never seen any of them, even my own I don't see after the last day of editing. So, I can't comment to the [*Picking Up the Pieces*] producers on how I feel about it. I can say that my sympathies always are with the writer and any request the author makes to re-edit or re-shoot, I'm all for. I always feel the author knows best what he wanted up on the screen."

However, Allen had such a good time making *Picking Up the Pieces* that he began to accept many other small parts and cameos in films by his friends—and, just as remarkably, sometimes waving off the nominal paycheck.

Chapter 11

1999

The Soon-Yi Era

Woody Keeps a-Goin'—and Tries Something New—Family Life

Radical changes were indeed afoot. Woody Allen was about to do something he'd avoided his whole life: settle down as a family man. In late April 1999 newspaper tipsters reported a baby made three in the Allen household. Allen and Soon-Yi were pushing a stroller around the Upper East Side. Soon-Yi knew a thing or two about adoptions, and soon after returning from Hollywood the couple finalized arrangements for taking custody of a five-month-old girl, whom they named Bechet (in honor of jazz musician Sidney Bechet) Dumaine (a street in the French Quarter where the original New Orleans Jazz Museum had been located) Allen.

Mia Farrow, who had "no comment" when asked about Allen's marriage to Soon-Yi in 1998, had a visceral reaction to news her daughter and ex-boyfriend were the newly adoptive parents of a baby. "I don't know how the courts permitted this," Farrow told the *Atlanta Journal-Constitution*. "I guess if you have enough celebrity, you can snow anybody." The actress, visiting Atlanta to give a public talk about special-needs adoptions, said she felt "frightened" for baby Bechet, having to grow up with "an old pedophile" as her father. Farrow's words were telegraphed across America by the wire services, keeping alive the child-abuse allegations against Allen and spurring headlines such as "Grandma Mia Farrow Won't Be Dropping In." Typically, as when the *Journal-Constitution* later recapped the story and wrongly identified Soon-Yi, the corrections ("She is not his stepdaughter, but is the daughter of Mia Farrow, who was Allen's companion") did not circulate as widely.

Movie critics sometimes made the same conflation: Roger Ebert's positive review of *Mighty Aphrodite* referred to the risk-taking subject matter of the script from a man "whose recent life has sometimes seemed drawn from Greek tragedy, especially as it applies to those who would kill their wives and marry their daughters—or, because we are more prudent in the twentieth century, divorce their wives and date their adopted daughters." Deborah Hornblow, commenting on *The Curse of the Jade Scorpion* for the *Los Angeles Times* in 2001, mused that watching Allen in the comedy made audiences queasy because "he divorced Mia Farrow and married his stepdaughter." Yet Allen and Farrow were never married, nor was Soon-Yi his stepdaughter, as the *Times* corrected a day later. No wonder "people think I fell in love with my daughter," Allen said in interviews.

The summer was spent in moving and new parenting and postproduction toil on *Sweet and Lowdown*. The trickiest work involved the picture's soundtrack, which called for an intricate combination of standards from the 1930s, with some of the music freshly recorded and other songs preexisting, including several Django Reinhardt recordings. The originals had to be blended with the contemporary versions, with all the music orchestrated by Dick Hyman. Personal Allen favorites were reprised from his earlier movies, such as Duke Ellington's "Caravan," used in *Alice*, or "I'll See You in My Dreams" from *Stardust Memories*, while obscure one-offs were plucked from Allen's voluminous library of recordings. The earliest tune in the soundtrack dated from 1861; the latest was composed in 1937. The music for this picture would prove a jazz buff's bonanza, with the tracks, in addition to Reinhardt's, featuring Ted Lewis and His Orchestra, Coleman Hawkins, Benny Goodman, Jack Teagarden, Glenn Miller, Sidney Bechet and Noble Sissle's Swingsters, Red Nichols and His Five Pennies, Bunny Berigan and His Orchestra, Henry Busse and His Orchestra, and Bix Beiderbecke and His Gang.

Looking forward to the seasonal change in light and colors, the director launched the filming of his next project in the fall. Known by the tentative title "Once in the Life," the story came from "an old idea of mine that was lying around for years," a "trivial" comedy, in Allen's words, which was just the sort of Woody Allen movie Jean Doumanian had all but gone down on her knees and begged for. Triggered, Allen always insisted, by a newspaper item about a robbery, his script followed a lowlife married couple, Ray (Allen) and Frenchy (Tracey Ullman), whose abortive bank heist leads to forging a chocolate chip cookie empire. Never mind comparisons to Mario Monicelli's classic Italian comedy *Big Deal on Madonna Street*, Allen said his script was more inspired by the marriage between Jackie Gleason and Audrey Meadows in *The Honeymooners*, which the man who normally scorned situation comedies described as "the greatest television sitcom of all time."*

In time the project's title became *Small Time Crooks*. Along with Ullman ("A massive comic talent, limitless in her ability," in the director's words), the ensemble included Woody Allen alumni Michael Rapaport and Elaine Stritch, with English smoothie Hugh Grant, *Saturday Night Live* comedian Jon Lovitz, and longtime Allen acquaintance Elaine May among the newbies to his work. "I named the character May when I wrote it," Allen said later, "and Elaine was the first choice." He had tried to coax May into his first picture, *Take the Money and Run*, and then others over the years. Their paths often crossed, but May, who wrote and directed her own acclaimed movies, was "evasive." Sharing the experience of *Death Defying Acts* brought them closer.

Steve Kroft, the *60 Minutes* correspondent who sympathetically profiled Allen at the height of the child custody/abuse tempest, was rewarded with a sequence replicating the format of the CBS television show, in which Ray and Frenchy are interviewed about their cookie empire. *Bullets over Broadway* co-scenarist Douglas McGrath also played a bit part; McGrath had become a semi-regular in Woody Allen films, appearing in *Bullets over Broadway* and *Celebrity*; McGrath was also one of the mock experts on Emmet Ray in *Sweet and Lowdown*.

Since Allen and McGrath were seeing so much of each other, why shouldn't Allen play a role in McGrath's new movie, which was being shot concurrently?† The looser Woody Allen didn't demand $5 million from his

---

* Mel Gussow wrote a piece for the *New York Times*, following the release of *Small Time Crooks*, also pointing out resemblances in the story to the short-lived 1941 Broadway play *The Night before Christmas*, written by Allen hero S. J. Perelman and his wife Laura.

† Allen performed a few other (unbilled) acting favors around this time. For Stanley Tucci, part of the *Deconstructing Harry* cast, he acted a big—and funny—scene as a director presiding over auditions in Tucci's *The Imposters*, with Tucci and Oliver Platt as an out-of-work Depression-era comedy team. Allen also can be glimpsed in fellow New York filmmaker James

friend McGrath, but the nonsalary may be the reason why his name is conspicuously absent from the billed credits of *Company Man*, which was co-written and -directed by McGrath with collaborator Peter Askin.

Most sources indicate Allen plays only a cameo in *Company Man*, but that is probably because the comedy was barely released in the US in March 2001, and not very many Woody Allen fans can boast of having seen the picture. The plot—a wimpy teacher becomes an unlikely recruit in a plot to assassinate Fidel Castro—makes *Company Man* sound like a loose remake of *Bananas*. In addition to McGrath as the wimpy spy (Roger Ebert described his performance as "a low-rent cross between Jack Lemmon and Wally Cox"), the motley cast included Sigourney Weaver, John Turturro, Anthony LaPaglia, Denis Leary, Alan Cumming, and Ryan Phillippe. Once again donning his actor's hat, Allen was gung-ho as the CIA's deranged point man in Havana, and he lights up a surprising number of scenes. Neither as good as *Bananas*, nor as bad as *Picking Up the Pieces*, *Company Man—numero tres* of Allen's informal Hispanic Trilogy—should be requisite viewing for his completists.

SWEET AND LOWDOWN was perversely offered to US moviegoers in December following screenings in September at the Venice Film Festival in Europe and Telluride in Colorado. Although Allen had been drawn to Sean Penn for his comedic as well as dramatic capabilities, the laughs were scattered, and the tone was resolutely bleak. Maybe Allen stepped in as one of the "expert" commentators to supply his reliable light touch and maybe he did so to satisfy Sweetland's preference to have him listed among the cast. The interviews seemed like comic padding this time—the last time Allen would deploy the mockumentary conceit for one of his films.

Samantha Morton was a godsend as Hattie, the mute girlfriend of wild-man guitarist Emmet Ray (Sean Penn). Taken to bed and under his wing by the jazzman, Hattie makes the story in part another one of Allen's *Pygmalion* tales. Morton's sweetness, her soulfulness, elevates the first half of the story, which includes a backstage visit to Hollywood in the 1930s, where Ray, to his utter frustration, must play guitar anonymously

---

Ivory's *A Soldier's Daughter Never Cries*, which fictionalized the family life of novelist James Jones.

in a background jazz band for a short subject, while his simpleminded mute girlfriend is "discovered" for her cute looks and easy charm and is rewarded with a love scene in a major studio production where she doesn't have to speak.

Hattie finds Ray's music divine. Most viewers did too. When Ray abandons her because she crimps his style, Hattie disappears for most of the second half of the film. Uma Thurman enters, doing her best to lend conviction to the character of a former Chicago debutante who marries Ray and takes notes on him for a book she intends to write. Anthony LaPaglia plays another Cheech in minor key. The "alternative" Ray anecdotes proffered by interviewees are a useful script stratagem that leads to the picture's only glimpse of the "real" Django Reinhardt, the foremost guitar player in the universe, whose first-place ranking awes and rankles Ray.

The most poignant scene in *Sweet and Lowdown* is the final chance encounter between Ray and Hattie, which occurs on an Atlantic City boardwalk in the shadow of a roller coaster—a hallmark Woody Allen setting. Ray is trapped in a downward spiral, but Hattie, making do as a laundress, tells him—scribbling on a piece of paper—she is happily married with a child. Ray has let the only good thing in his life slip through his fingers.

With a thin rapier moustache, Penn looked the part of a dead-end Dapper Dan. The star dug deep for his portrayal of this heel, part-time pimp, gambler, kleptomaniac, alcoholic, born loser, impossible man, whose idea of fun is to watch locomotives roar by while drunk, and shoot rats at municipal dumps. Ray's only salvation is music. The character is another Harry Block who harms everyone including himself. Only his art redeems him. The last scene shows Ray abusing a girl he has picked up, scaring her away, then bashing his guitar to bits in the woods. The musician screams as he crumples fetally: "I made a mistake!" Loosely appropriated from Fellini's ending of *La Strada*, where Anthony Quinn is reduced to sobbing on a beach, it made for a fadeout similar to the "HELP!" sky-written at the close of *Celebrity*. Merry Christmas, America.

SAMANTHA MORTON (BEST Supporting Actress) and Sean Penn (Best Actor) picked up Oscar nominations. Over the years, twelve actresses were nominated for Academy Awards in Woody Allen movies. Penn was the fourth actor nominated for his performance in an Allen film, although Penn and Morton both lost in their categories.

Sweet and Lowdown was an honorable flop with audiences at a time when Sweetland badly needed a box office boost. Court records show the film starring Sean Penn took in $2.5 million in the US and $14.6 million overseas for a net loss of $14.5 million. *Small Time Crooks*, which had been shot for half the budget of *Sweet and Lowdown*, was going to be the fifth Sweetland/Allen production since the unwritten "Dinner Table Conversation," and the next project, *The Curse of the Jade Scorpion*, loomed as another silly comedy with Allen playing the lead. But Sweetland was suddenly faced with cash-flow problems. According to reporting in the *Los Angeles Times*, Safra had spent "a reported half-billion dollars" to purchase the *Encyclopaedia Britannica* in 1995, and over four years he had drained his resources trying to expand the reference books online. As Allen was editing *Small Time Crooks* and preparing to shoot *The Curse of the Jade Scorpion*, Doumanian phoned him to bow out of the marketing of the former film and give "her longtime friend forty-eight hours to find new financing" for the latter. Sweetland had produced its last Woody Allen project.

Riding to the rescue shortly after the new year was DreamWorks SKG, which had enjoyed the experience of *Antz* with Allen, and where superfan Jeffrey Katzenberg was still the K. DreamWorks would take over the distribution of *Small Time Crooks*, as well as produce three future Woody Allen pictures, in exchange for their US rights. Allen believed his movies would do better with DreamWorks anyway, because the boutique Hollywood studio was run by the savviest people in the film industry. Now Letty Aronson, who had apprenticed behind the scenes for Sweetland on her brother's eight most recent productions, took over as his top-listed producer.

DreamWorks SKG partnered with the German company VCL Film & Media AG, which kicked in $50 million for the foreign rights and licensing to *Small Time Crooks* and the three Woody Allen titles to follow. Renaming his business entity Gravier Productions—Gravier was another street in New Orleans—Allen stood to "earn a considerably higher fee and also will own his films, as he did at Orion," according to Eric Lax.

DreamWorks liked *Small Time Crooks* and wanted more throwback comedies with Allen as their star. "I know that they [DreamWorks] prefer funny films to a deadly serious film," Allen told Lax, "and for me to act in many of them. I don't mind that at all." For the time being Allen and Doumanian remained close friends. *Death Defying Acts* had whetted Doumanian's appetite for the theater world, and after a period of adjustment she shifted into producing off-Broadway and Broadway shows. Allen and Soon-Yi attended her opening nights. Allen still phoned her daily, and they continued to dine out together. Doumanian could be spotted courtside with Allen at Knicks games, "as elegant as the day he met her," in the words of one local columnist, "lipstick-lean in size four Saint Laurent, her storied cheekbones casting a long shadow under the halogen lights."

ALLEN AND SOON-YI celebrated the New Year of 2000 and the coming New Millennium by vacationing in Venice and Paris, as always mixing business with pleasure. These days the couple mused about moving to Italy rather than France, and Allen contemplated buying a fifteenth-century palazzo on the Grand Canal. They roamed abroad for several weeks at the end of every year. Soon-Yi liked traveling. Allen's young wife was "opening me up," he told John Lahr. She had "a salubrious effect" on him. "I'm willing to play more, or be more playful."

The cinema's most celebrated analysand, as one journalist dubbed him, quit therapy soon after his marriage to Soon-Yi. After more than thirty years on the couch, Allen had not been cured but he had learned all he could learn from psychiatrists. "On balance," he reflected at a 92nd Street Y event broadcast to Jewish community centers and psychoanalytic groups across America, "I would say it [analysis] has been helpful, but not as helpful as I had hoped, and helpful in a way they didn't intend. As a crutch, it helped me." One therapist, he recalled, told him he thought it would be exciting to examine Woody Allen, only to discover the reality was like being stuck in a room with a lawyer. "I feel I have wasted a lot of time talking about dreams," Allen added.

His own dreams disappointed him. Strangely, unlike some other filmmakers—Robert Altman, for example—Allen dreamed his share of comedy bits, but never an entire story that he developed into a script. Perhaps this was because Allen was a bad sleeper, a sufferer of night terrors and, trying to fall back asleep after a terrible dream, he was more likely to cogitate esoteric lists than jot mental notes toward a script. The lists often involved sports figures (a team of baseball all-stars whose specialty was singles), or ten-best categories of movies.

Like the ghost of the friend who visits Harry Block in jail in *Deconstructing Harry*, Allen had begun to savor the life he was living. Joe Morgenstern in the *Wall Street Journal* praised *Deconstructing Harry* for showing "great progress in his [Allen's] long-term public psychoanalysis," and the last movie released before the director's marriage to Soon-Yi and his announcement that he was finished with therapy would also be the last Woody Allen movie that could be mistaken for any sort of auto-critique. The edging toward naturalism and realism, the personal exploration of self that began with *Annie Hall*, all but ended with *Sweet and Lowdown*. When Allen starred in future movies, he would aim more to please, and his Rubik's Cube persona—once shifting and twisting in its coloration—was frozen into an engaging pattern. *Small Time Crooks* and the DreamWorks pictures inaugurated a neo-silly phase in his career. Even if he, or lead characters played by other actors, evinced any Woody Allen–ish traits, most future works would fall back on the more amiable of his established values and traits. Never again would his movies evidence the edgy autobiographical specificity of *Manhattan* or *Deconstructing Harry*. There'd be no fictionalized Soon-Yi in a Woody Allen picture. No child-molester character, actual or accused.

He and Soon-Yi adopted another baby in the spring, a newborn they named Manzie Tio for Sidney Bechet's drummer Manzie Johnson and clarinetist Lorenzo Tio, a New Orleans master whose students had included Bechet. Rare press visitors to their home described a household taken over by the children, their equipage, and toys. Once more Allen poured himself into fatherhood, and he became a crusader in the Carnegie Hill neighborhood, appearing before the Landmarks Preservation Commission and crafting a three-minute film that protested plans to top a Citibank branch at Madison Avenue and Ninety-First with a sixteen-story tower. "The first Woody Allen video" had "what Hollywood types would call extremely limited distribution," dryly noted the *New York Times*, "about a dozen copies" for the commission. For continuity with the rest of his career, there was even a Rodgers and Hart song.

Martin Konigsberg died at the age of one hundred early in 2001, and the death of Allen's mother Nettie followed one year later. Allen's second try at fatherhood forced him to reappraise the parents he had always underrated.

He had made a kind of peace with them. "For all the mistakes my parents made," Allen told the 92nd Street Y audience, "they loved me and took care of me. They wanted for me only those things that all other kids' parents want: They wanted me to not turn out to be a criminal, to go to school, to go to college, to amount to something." As Allen aged, he resembled his mother physically, he admitted, which meant his Zelig face was beginning to evoke the elderly Groucho Marx, only without a moustache. He was asked in an interview how his mother and father shaped his worldview. "I think—and my sister would agree—that I've inherited the worst of each parent. I have my father's hypochondria and lack of concentration. I have his amorality. I have everything bad that he had. Then I have my mother's surly, pill-like, complaining, whining attitude. The only positive thing you could say is that my mother instilled in me—probably at a greater cost than it was worth—an enormous sense of discipline, and a feeling that the highest achievement I'm capable of is not good enough."

DREAMWORKS WANTED HAPPY-ENDING comedies with Allen as their star: stories without the lust, angst, and surfeit of F-words epitomized by *Deconstructing Harry*. The studio liked PG ratings, and that's what it got with *Small Time Crooks*, *The Curse of the Jade Scorpion*, and *Hollywood Ending*. Practical-minded, Allen tried to please the S, K, and G. There was no wiggle room for him to reshoot and deduct costs from his salary or grosses. The drift away from elaborate master shots, which were time-consuming and costly, became pronounced. The director was more likely to cover dialogue with conventional medium shots, two-shots, and over-the-shoulders.

Small Time Crooks proved congenial enough, with Allen and his ensemble giving rambunctious performances in the unreal and uncompelling story about inept bank robbers turned chocolate chip cookie entrepreneurs. Accompanied by Soon-Yi and his daughter, Allen even hit the college circuit to promote the picture for DreamWorks, answering student questions at New York University, the University of Chicago, the University of California at Los Angeles, and Harvard University, raising his profile among the *Dumb and Dumber* generation. Critics like Kevin Thomas of the *Los Angeles Times*, who saw the movie as "delicious, giddy fun," were kind. "Allen received more praise than he had in recent years and the film was seen as a mini-comeback," Nicole LaPorte wrote in her book about DreamWorks. *Small Time Crooks* raked in $9.5 million in the US and $15.1 abroad, amassing a $6 million profit. Sweetland made more money from its investment in *Small Time Crooks* than any Woody Allen picture except *Everyone Says I Love You*, which had tremendous success overseas.

The Curse of the Jade Scorpion, the first genuine Woody Allen–DreamWorks production, upped the quotient of nonsense. Another evergreen from Allen's story file, whose genesis dated back to the late 1960s, this pastiche of film noir and screwball comedy was, he said, the kind of movie he once loved to get lost in as a boy. Allen's script involved a soft-boiled insurance investigator who is hypnotized by a shady nightclub swami into an infatuation with his antagonistic boss, played by Helen Hunt from television's *Mad About You*. Under a spell, he and she embark on a series of "inside job" jewel heists, becoming the chief suspects. Even the music is lackadaisical: the robberies are underscored by "In a Persian Market," recycled from "Oedipus Wrecks."

Charlize Theron returned with less vavoom as a Lauren Bacall knockoff. The 1940s period ornamentation was meticulous. But the repartee was belabored, Allen and Hunt evidenced minimal sexual chemistry, and all the goings-on were Golden Age–ish. "It may be the worst film I ever made," Allen confessed to Eric Lax, not blaming "the exceptionally talented cast"—just himself. Another actor was supposed to play the gumshoe but dropped out at the eleventh hour. Allen stepped in "on short notice," and "I went wrong in playing the lead."

Hollywood Ending, his third silly comedy in a row in 2003, had another preposterous if more Buñuellian concept—"An idea that had been around for years" in his desk drawer, long before briefly discussed with Marshall Brickman. The cast was precocious, and there were amusing gibes at Hollywood, France, the directing profession, and Allen himself. The story concerned a once-pretentious, washed-up filmmaker named Val (Allen), given one last chance for a comeback by his former wife (Téa Leoni), now a producer affianced to a Hollywood studio blockhead (Treat Williams). Nerve-wracked, Val goes psychosomatically blind and must pretend he can see to finish the shoot. His solicitous ex-wife furtively assists him. The comic fumbling and stumbling is heightened by the language barrier between Val and his Chinese-speaking cameraman, but it was no longer Zhao Fei behind the camera for Allen, nor was it Haskell Wexler, "one of the all-time great cinematographers," in Allen's words. Wexler had started work on the production but was cashiered by Allen after a week or two of filming, because "he always wanted to shoot a million angles." Allen kept telling Wexler, "I don't have the patience, we don't have the money, we need to move on." German veteran Wedigo von Schultzendorff stepped in seamlessly, and production designer Santo Loquasto supplied the overall sheen.

Miraculously, in the story, French cinephiles embrace Val's blindly directed movie as a masterpiece, and the *auteur*, reconciled with his ex-, flies off to a new life in Paris at the end. Leoni is a treat, Williams is oddly likeable as a studio stiff, and Allen's colleague, director Mark Rydell, makes for the world's most obsequious William Morris agent. Adding sparkle to their scenes were George Hamilton as a studio watchdog, and Debra Messing as Val's girlfriend, the standard neurotic actress. Allen the actor revived his Flatbush accent for the DreamWorks comedies, which was another sign of relaxation in his posttherapy, postmarriage persona.

Rare for Allen, he believed in the quality of *Hollywood Ending* after finishing the movie. Again, he toured college audiences, making "first-ever" trips to Canada and Texas, winding up in Georgia where, after answering questions at an Atlanta screening, he and Soon-Yi and their daughters took a side trip to Savannah and sampled "real Southern cooking," like cheese biscuits and fried chicken, "stuff which I later learned is fried in Crisco and sticks of butter." The director felt so good about the picture he finally accepted an invitation to Cannes, after years of pleading from festival organizers, planning his first appearance at the ritual spring extravaganza in 2002.

THE GREAT RECTIFICATION CAMPAIGN, which had begun under Sweetland Pictures and now continued with Allen's sister, Letty Aronson, at the helm, worked. Allen found creative breathing room and improved his public standing. His slouching toward a revised sense of self was epitomized by his March 2002 appearance—his one and only—at the Academy of Motion Picture Arts and Sciences annual awards ceremony. Six months earlier, on September 11, 2001, four coordinated al-Qaeda airplane attacks on US government and civilian targets had taken their worst human toll on New York, where two commercial flights hijacked by terrorists crashed into the north and south towers of the World Trade Center. The towers collapsed with a death toll of over 2,600 people, along with thousands of injuries. On the same day hundreds perished from a related plane crash into the Pentagon building in Washington, DC, and more died from casualties on an airliner that went down, as its passengers fought the hijackers, in Shanksville, Pennsylvania. Allen was due in Germany a few days later to promote the European opening of *The Curse of the Jade Scorpion*. When he followed through on his travel plans, flying overseas, Allen gave interviews to German, French, Italian, and British television, where he was often asked to comment on the tragedy and where he came off as one small symbol of Big Apple pluck.

For the Academy Awards show, fellow New York filmmaker Nora Ephron had crafted a tribute to the city, which consisted of memorable images from motion pictures shot on borough locations. Because the 9/11 attacks had delivered such an economic blow to New York, this documentary salute was intended to encourage Hollywood to return to the metropolis for future production work. Ephron had appeared as herself in two Woody Allen pictures: *Crimes and Misdemeanors* and *Husbands and Wives*. Laura Ziskin, producer of the global telecast, wanted Allen to introduce Ephron's short film onstage. She prevailed upon Jeffrey Katzenberg to relay the invitation.

Allen insisted upon secrecy, and at rehearsals Ephron herself introduced the New York tribute. "Not even the network knew," Ziskin recalled. "Woody arrived at 5 o'clock on Sunday and slipped in through the rear entrance and sat in my office until it was time for him to go on." A standing ovation greeted the star and filmmaker—the man universally recognized as synonymous with Manhattan—as he ambled onstage without a script or teleprompter. "Thank you very much," Allen began. "That makes up for the strip search. . . ." When the Academy contacted him a few weeks back, asking him to participate, "I thought they wanted their Oscars back." He gave brief interviews backstage ("I'd do anything for New York City") before bolting for his return flight. He had sacrificed his Monday night jazz band gig for the first time in memory.

The Oscar-telecast appearance was also excellent publicity for Allen's upcoming appearance at the 55th Cannes Film Festival, premiering *Hollywood Ending*, later that spring. Arm in arm with Soon-Yi, the film director strolled the red carpet for the first time, accompanied by cast members Treat Williams and Debra Messing, smiling as he waved to hundreds of screaming fans. When Allen entered the Lumiere Theater, "adoring Gallic colleagues saluted his arrival with a standing ovation" before the screening, reported *Variety*.

The US reviews for the new screen comedy were polite. "I liked the movie without loving it," Roger Ebert said in the *Chicago Sun-Times*. Yet *Hollywood Ending* has many partisans among Woody Allen fans, including himself. "It is a funny picture with a funny idea, executed funny," he told Eric Lax. "I was amusing in it." Despite Allen's best publicity efforts, however, Americans stayed away. *The Curse of the Jade Scorpion* fell below *Small Time Crooks* to $7.5 million in the US, and *Hollywood Ending* sank to $4.9 million. Foreign audiences continued to offset the domestic letdown, though, and *Hollywood Ending* did especially well in France.

But *Small Time Crooks*, *Curse of the Jade Scorpion*, and *Hollywood Ending* did little to improve Allen's standing with critics who more and more had their knives sharpened for him. To complaints against Allen that his pictures were too Jewish, not Jewish enough, or slurred Jews; that the actor was too ugly to kiss beautiful leading ladies, too old for young beauties, or obsessed with hookers; that his scripts were too autobiographical, or not honest enough about his life, could now be added the objection that his once vaunted comedic touch had grown toothless. While his producers wanted him to star in Woody Allen films, some critics had grown weary of his face, and David Thomson, writing in *Film Comment* in 1998, went so far as to posit "the self-destructiveness of Woody acting in his own movies," from his earliest comedies down through *Deconstructing Harry*. An admirer of some of Woody Allen's moviemaking as a director, but less so of Allen as a leading man, Thomson finished his widely read piece, "I'd shoot the actor, given half the chance."

Consequently, Allen's fourth picture for DreamWorks SKG, *Anything Else*, departed from the recent light-comedy mode. The script and subject matter were more mature; there would be lust and angst, and a PG-13 rating; and even though Allen played a crucial role onscreen, he was not the star and his name would be downplayed in the advertising.

Filmed in 2003, this dark romantic comedy combined one of Allen's longstanding ideas from the backlog—a self-destructive mentor, based on an old Tamiment friend—with "a certain amount" of material from the novel he had discarded after humbling criticisms. Trying to rope in the twentysomethings, his script centered on Jerry Falk, played by twentysomething Jason Biggs, who was neither Jewish (Allen never asked) nor particularly well-known outside the youth-market *American Pie* franchise. "I never saw *American Pie*," Allen later said. "I'm sure it's too stupid for words. When I was younger, my generation had no patience or interest in stupid films."

Falk/Biggs is a struggling comedy writer and wishful novelist, whose girlfriend Amanda, played by the unconventional Christina Ricci, is a neurotic, promiscuous, would-be actress—both characters variations on the long-entrenched types in Woody Allen pictures. Amanda's middle-age mother (Stockard Channing), whose pipe dream is to sing in nightclubs, moves in with the uneasy couple. Allen plays the mentor, David Dobel, a polymath schoolteacher and part-time comedy writer, who doles out obscure multisyllable words like "hebetudinous" and "tergiversate." Dobel, who is paranoid about anti-Semitism, among other fears, serves as Falk's life coach during long walks and talks. Danny DeVito, a Broadway Danny Rose type, has one great scene collapsing into a screaming heart attack, and Channing beguiles at the piano singing Peggy Lee's "There'll Be Another Spring."

In one of their interview sessions Douglas McGrath asked Allen which of his characters in movies might best sum up his own worldview. "In terms of just me personally, as a kind of wretched little complaining *vantz*," the filmmaker replied, "I think you would see that in *Anything Else*. There's a lot of me in there." But Allen also wrote himself into Falk/Biggs, whose boyhood memories include Cheerios and raisins for breakfast. Biggs, whose acting is earnest, might have been better off going for more of a "junior Woody," and he and Ricci become tiresome as the story goes on. Allen, regardless, said only good things about the actors in the cast (he was "crazy about Christina"), and maybe along with other post-1992 adjustments he had softened his attitude toward his own work. Allen thought *Anything Else* was underrated. So do many Allen aficionados.

While DreamWorks did not go as far as the fictional studio in *Hollywood Ending*—which values the "inciting" incident in a screenplay, demographic marketing, and preview cards—the real-life boutique studio tried a radical departure in selling *Anything Else*. Although Allen claimed first billing and inordinate screen time, the studio privileged Biggs and Ricci in the trailers, posters, and advertising. DreamWorks had released Allen's first three comedies during summer months, but *Anything Else* was sent first to Venice for its premiere in the late summer, before a fall release in the US. Allen added to the hoopla with his first personal appearance at the Italian film festival. The private caterpillar was becoming the public butterfly, as he once was in the 1960s.

Even so, *Anything Else* stagnated at $3.2 million in the US, and the fourth comedy of the "DreamWorks Quartet"—encompassing Sweetland's *Small Time Crooks*—performed the least well of the four in foreign territories. Perhaps the picture was most noteworthy for being the director's first collaboration with the Iranian-French cinematographer Darius Khondji, who had just finished *The Panic Room* for David Fincher, and who'd return to work with Allen several more times and bring luster to major Woody Allen movies to come.

THE BOOKEND TO the Sweetland years came suddenly and unexpectedly in the form of litigation. In April 2001, lawyers for Allen filed suit against Jean Doumanian, Jacqui Safra, and Sweetland Pictures in the New York State Supreme Court, a move that "shocked some of their friends but hardly surprised many of Mr. Allen's associates" who knew of trouble brewing behind the scenes, according to the *New York Times*. The suit alleged Sweetland had not provided a full financial accounting for the earnings of the eight pictures Doumanian and Safra had co-produced with Allen from 1993 to 2001, depriving him of his rightful share of adjusted proceeds.

Allen had wrestled with the possibility of filing a lawsuit for months, according to the *Times*, even as the filmmaker continued to dine out with Doumanian and Safra and plead with them to explain why he was not receiving more income from his movies. "Jacqui would say, 'Jean will take care of it,' while Jean would say, 'Don't call Jacqui. He's very busy with *Encyclopaedia Britannica*. I'll speak to him about it,'" Allen's sister, Letty Aronson, explained to the *Los Angeles Times*. "Woody's not good about pushing things with friends."

His patience ran out after, early in 2001, his business manager forced an audit of Sweetland accounting in Amsterdam, where the company had offices for banking and tax purposes. The audit suggested Allen's pictures had been bundled with lesser Sweetland investments, and that he might be owed substantial monies. Robert Greenhut, who also awaited payments that had not eventuated as the producer of the first four Woody Allen films for Sweetland dating back to 1993, told the *New York Times* there had been "heel-dragging" by the producers. "It's amazing that Woody has taken this long to say, 'Where are the dollars and cents?'" Greenhut was quoted. *Wild Man Blues* documentarist Barbara Kopple said she too failed to obtain a satisfactory result after fruitless letter-writing. "I'm owed money too," Kopple informed the *Los Angeles Times*.

It's just "a little business disagreement," Allen handwrote to Doumanian shortly after filing the lawsuit. "It nowhere says a tiny bad thing about you or Jacqui or Sweetland." He suggested the friends all go to dinner one more time and try to good-humoredly hash out their dispute. Their differences were akin to Hepburn and Tracy, married lawyers on opposing sides in the classic comedy *Adam's Rib*: "Lawyers by day, friends by night."

Doumanian did not think so. Stung by the court action, she and Sweetland countersued, retaining the powerful Hollywood attorney Bertram Fields, who told the press Sweetland had rescued Allen in the motion picture business at a time when he was drowning from his problems, his recent movies had incurred "significant losses," and now Allen was subjecting his longtime friends to unfair and "embarrassing" media exposure.

At the heart of the conflict was the unwritten "Dinner Table Conversation" of 1996. Doumanian and Safra insisted Allen had agreed to joint-account, or cross-collateralize, the five films Sweetland produced starting with *Deconstructing Harry* (a number that included *Wild Man Blues*), just as he had joint-accounted their first three coproductions in his 1993 contract, which offset the bigger-budgeted *Bullets over Broadway*. "This would mean with each subsequent film Moses [Allen's company] agreed to put the profits it had already earned from prior films at risk, with Moses's risk increasing with each film," in the words of Allen's lawyers in court attestations, a premise which "is not only unprecedented in the film industry but has no basis in fact." Every self-respecting auteur, much less one of Allen's stature, knew joint accounting to be a black hole. Yet Doumanian and Safra insisted Allen had orally committed to blanket joint accounting in their dinner-table talks.

When the case went to court in May and June 2002, Allen's lawyers claimed he had been cheated out of "at least $12 million" from the estimated grosses and profits of the five Sweetland/Allen movies produced after 1996, with some of the allegations of breach of contract reaching back to encompass the first three Sweetland/Allen pictures: *Bullets over Broadway*, *Mighty Aphrodite*, and *Everyone Says I Love You*. Peter Parcher, a lawyer for Doumanian and Safra, insisted the "bogus case [was] being orchestrated by Woody Allen's handlers," with business manager Stephen Tenenbaum as the point man. The testimony was spread over two weeks with less audience turnout in the courtroom than in 1992 and '93. Tenenbaum testified Allen had long ignored his advice to challenge Sweetland. Allen just wanted to make films. If one or two movies did poorly, "he said he wanted to make a third picture, and when it was done, he wanted to make a fourth picture."

The director himself took the stand for half an hour one day, taking a break from the shooting of *Anything Else* on Manhattan locations, and admitting he had signed the first joint-accounting arrangement "for less compensation than I was accustomed to getting," in his words, "because this was all done in good spirits" between friends. Allen insisted, however, he did not agree to joint accounting for the later work covered by the "Dinner Table Conversation." He believed accounting tricks had made his movies appear less successful.

Some days Allen sat in court looking "as painfully afflicted as one of his film personas," according to an account in the *New York Times*, alternately worn down and annoyed while listening to the witnesses. When the director signed a court artist's rendering of himself, he joked he did not recognize his own pathetic likeness.

Described by the press as Doumanian's companion of thirty years standing, Safra spent one day in court being interrogated, saying he had stepped up to bankroll Woody Allen films "because I was trying to help a friend in need" and now he felt betrayed and "it broke my heart" to learn his friend was suing Sweetland. It did not help Safra's cause that Allen's lawyers accused him and Doumanian of "diverting for their own use and enjoyment property held for the [joint] benefit of Sweetland and Moses," including the Aston Martin sports car driven by Kenneth Branagh in *Celebrity*—the one his freelance-writer character really couldn't afford. "Said Aston Martin now resides on the grounds of the California vineyard owned directly or indirectly by Safra."

Allen contrived his absence from court on the day Doumanian, his friend of forty years, gave her side of the "ugly and at times highly personal" case, according to the *Los Angeles Times*. The producer had choked back tears during the first week of testimony, but now her "cool, evasive" air on the stand did not endear her to the press. While the slender, frizzy-haired producer "looked fashionable in a black suit and pumps, she proved forgetful about details," reported the *Daily News*, sometimes sounding "like the star of *Dumber and Dumber*."

Just as he had done during Allen's testimony, Judge Ira Gammerman repeatedly interrupted Doumanian's digressive responses, correcting the producer. Doumanian insisted it was normal for *Celebrity* to have been sold to Italy as part of a $7.5 million package with three obscure Sweetland titles, including a period comedy directed by Jason Alexander called *Cherry Pink*, a.k.a. *Just Looking*—with only $4.5 million of the total credited to Allen's royalties account. Allen's lawyers alleged this was a prime example of block booking, which "increases the value of the less desirable films at the expense of the more desirable films," directly injuring Allen "by this parasitic borrowing of value." "Is it your testimony that those three movies dragged up the price of *Celebrity*?" asked Judge Gammerman incredulously. Yes, Doumanian replied, maintaining her composure.

The judge also looked askance when Doumanian explained why she had given herself a raise from $500,000 to $750,000 as producer of Woody Allen pictures that appeared, on paper, to be steadily losing money. This happened in 1997, Doumanian said, after she "spoke to Letty about it, and Letty said it was OK." Gammerman looked surprised and asked, "You, as president [of the company], asked the secretary [of the company] for a raise?" Her salary increase was concealed from Allen, according to his lawyers, when it was charged to the budget of his movies as "overhead" and not as a "producer's fee." Doumanian said she had mentioned the raise to Allen, although she didn't "tell him how much it was," nor that the raise would essentially be coming out of Allen's share of monies, according to the *New York Post*. Nor did Doumanian mention, until pressed by Allen's lawyer Michael Zweig, that she took an additional $500,000 in licensing fees per picture, "meaning her total pay for each of the last three films she did with Allen was $1.25 million, half his take," according to the *Post* account.

The back and forth, so many financial figures, was confusing. But Doumanian's problematic testimony prompted lawyers for both sides to huddle and agree to halt the proceedings. They carved out a settlement. Allen, in court for the dismissal, apologized to jurors. "I know it was no fun to sit there and listen to all this," he said. "It sure was dull." The nuances were withheld—an "undisclosed amount awarded to Woody," according to Eric Lax—but Doumanian was also ordered to cover Allen's $95,000 legal fees. Although the former partners shook hands in the courtroom, Doumanian no longer phoned Allen, nor did she join him for dinners. Doumanian extracted minor revenge by going back to court and winning permission, as producer of the films, to prune scenes from *Bullets over Broadway*, *Mighty Aphrodite*, *Everyone Says I Love You*, *Deconstructing Harry*, and *Sweet and Lowdown*, should they require censorship or shortening for airlines or television.

Doumanian's ex-husband John, who had introduced her to the comedian during his Chicago gigs, would endure in Allen's circle as the manager of his jazz band for concerts and tours, and John continued to make regular cameos in most Woody Allen movies up through 2017's *Wonder Wheel*. Letty Aronson was unmoved by the loss of her brother's longtime ally. Tenenbaum joined Aronson on the list of producers of future Woody Allen productions. A good guess is Soon-Yi also didn't much like Doumanian, who went on to an impressive career as a Broadway producer. Only Allen said plaintively, from time to time, how much he missed his old friend.

ALLEN RETURNED TO Europe in the fall to promote the opening of *Hollywood Ending*, making one stop in Italy, where the filmmaker made good on his longtime promise to Rome mayor Walter Veltroni, a onetime movie critic, and performed with his old-time jazz band in the city council chambers on the Capitoline Hill. The invited crowd of four hundred VIP guests included the actress Virna Lisi, fellow film directors Ettore Scola and Gillo Pontecorvo, composer Ennio Morricone, and Allen's own Italian-born cameraman Carlo Di Palma.

As regular as a metronome, Allen had launched the writing of *Melinda and Melinda* over the summer within days of calling the last take on *Anything Else*. "I'm truly not a workaholic as people have described me over the years," Allen protested in interviews. "I spend a lot of time recreating." Still, he did write seven days a week, most mornings, often sprawled on his bed and working in longhand on yellow legal pads after an early breakfast, leading into lunchtime. After lunch he would take long walks and shop and tend to other matters, but he was known to cheat in the afternoons with more writing when in the throes of an idea. Writing had long been a habit, a discipline, a compulsion, and most strangely of all, a means of enjoyment. Allen also refreshed himself by writing nonmovie projects, including a flurry of stage plays in the post-Sweetland years that were originally intended for Jean Doumanian before their rude parting. Although he no longer dashed off "little souffles" for the *New Yorker*, Allen whipped up other small essays on demand, including thoughtful pieces on towering figures that influenced him, like George S. Kaufman and Ingmar Bergman, for the *New York Times*.

In October 2003 came the first accounts of Allen toying with a memoir. A short proposal ("As few as ten pages," according to the *Times*) was circulated to Manhattan publishers and possible foreign buyers at the Frankfurt Book Fair, until the bidding reportedly froze at $3 million. Allen was said to have asked for at least $10 million for unbosoming himself. Publishers in America were hesitant, according to scuttlebutt, because they feared the controversy if they let Allen tell his side of the Mia Farrow story. Clouding the situation, journalists weighed in against the autobiographical tome as yet unwritten. "You should not write a book," Peter Bart wrote from his editor's perch at *Variety*. "You're too private, plus you're trapped inside your own head as your films continue to demonstrate." Maureen Dowd wrote another of her anti–Woody Allen columns ridiculing the notion that the director might receive millions of dollars for writing an autobiography, as many famous people, including Farrow, did. Allen was wallowing in the pig's trough of *Celebrity*, Dowd said in the *Times*.

ALLEN HAD AN itch to try directing one of his stage works, something he thought he should have done before with his playlet for *Death Defying Acts*—to avoid the crossing of swords, as happened, with Michael Blakemore. The Atlantic Theater Company, a 165-seat playhouse in Chelsea, was happy to give Allen the chance, in 2003, with *Writer's Block*, consisting of his new pair of one-acts. "Riverside Drive" was a three-character absurdist comedy set on the Upper West Side, which involved a deranged homeless man, a philandering writer, and the writer's wife. "Old Saybrook," with seven characters combusting over extramarital infractions, took place in the eponymous Connecticut town best known for Katharine Hepburn's beach home.

Allen drew his actors, as he often did these days, from hit television shows. "Riverside Drive" starred Paul Reiser—the other half, and creator, of *Mad About You*—as the philandering scribe. (As part of his splurge of acting cameos, Allen had done a "voice" appearance on the NBC comedy series toward the end of its seven-year run.) The cast of "Old Saybrook," whose centerpiece was a Santo Loquasto–designed living room with a mysterious door, included Grant Shaud from *Murphy Brown*, Jay Thomas from *Murphy Brown* and *Cheers*, and Bebe Neuwirth from *Cheers* and also *Celebrity*, where she had played the hooker who gives blowjob lessons.

Allen was still rusty about theater protocols, as he'd proven to be during *Death Defying Acts*. When actress Annabelle Gurwitch auditioned for "Old Saybrook," she was told not to shake hands with Allen, speak to him, or make eye contact. After being cast in a supporting role in the one-act, however, Gurwitch met with the director and found him "warm, funny and supportive." Yet, as the actress wrote in her memoir—called, for good reason, *Fired!*—the rehearsals were "very tense. . . . Everyone wanted to be funny for Woody. One cast member was so obsequious to Woody, it was as though he were performing a colonoscopy with his tongue. In fact, Woody seemed to really be making an effort to appear human, but he clearly hasn't spent much time developing his people skills. His rehearsal process was running the play over and over, with little to no feedback."

Allen asked for one-on-one meetings with each performer. Gurwitch volunteered to go first. Gone was the supportive warmth and humor. "He gave me line readings for each of my lines right down to which words to emphasize." One day Allen told her, "What you're doing is terrible, none of it good, all of it bad, don't ever do that again, even in another play." Stricken, the actress mumbled, "Well, don't hold back, Woody. . . ." Gurwitch tried to "soldier on," but on another day she says he told her, "You look retarded." Two weeks into rehearsal she got a letter from theater management saying she was sacked because "Woody needs to rethink the role."

Vincent Canby, Allen's venerable champion at the *New York Times*, had died in 2000. Bruce Weber, who took over some of the theater reviewing in the *Times*, brought a measured tone to his critique of the one-acts, describing "Riverside Drive" as "satisfying entertainment," and "Old Saybrook" as evincing moments of "a very funny, if conventional, sex farce." Weber was unaccountably followed by Alex Abramovich, who wrote a "think piece" for the *Times* re-reviewing the playlets and complaining that neither was very funny or original. "Mr. Allen stopped being delightful in 1992, when news of his own sexual indiscretions surfaced," Abramovich wrote. "He seemed to stop having new experiences and began cannibalizing his own work with a vengeance." *Variety* went further: While the "somewhat sour proceedings" contained "juicy laughs," the show represented Allen "in less than top form" with the first-time stage director seemingly "at a loss" for blocking in scenes that involved long dialogue exchanges between two actors, leaving "the rest of the characters stranded on stage."

UNABLE TO HALT the decline of his American box office, DreamWorks SKG temporarily parted company with Allen after *Anything Else*. Not for the first or last time did pundits predict Allen's long reign as a leading American film director was over. "Woody has all but run out of companies willing to distribute his films," reported *Variety* editor Peter Bart in August 2003, one of a series of Bart columns skeptically monitoring Allen. Bart, who liked to congratulate himself on keeping Allen from having directed the movie version of *Play It Again, Sam* back in the days when he was a Paramount functionary, was oddly ill informed for a man at the center of the motion picture industry. Even as Bart's malediction appeared in the widely read trade paper, Allen had found fresh footing and was planning a picture for the fall of 2003 with a new co-producing entity: Fox Searchlight, a division of 20th-Century Fox. Allen had been courted in a series of phone calls by Peter Rice, the Englishman in charge of the Fox specialty division. *Bend It Like Beckham*, which Allen raided for casting, was among Rice's worldwide hits. On the phone Allen told Rice a tale of two Melindas, one Melinda in a comedy, the other Melinda at the center of a drama—"An idea I always wanted to do." Rice loved what he heard. On the phone or in person with *simpatico* producers, Allen always performed a little, cracking self-deprecating jokes.

Hollywood and America in the 1970s had been more hospitable to his iconoclastic, artistic-minded style of filmmaking. Allen had enjoyed the early benefit of strong advocates at United Artists and Orion. But Arthur

Krim had passed away in 1994—ten years ago, now. His other UA and Orion protectors—David Picker, Eric Pleskow, Mike Medavoy—were either retired, or scrambling to promote their own independent production companies. Allen's once formidable managers, Jack Rollins and Charles H. Joffe, now elderly, no longer read his scripts before filming, nor did they have anything momentous to say about his projects. Although the filmmaker's budgets remained modest, nowadays the corporation-run studios prided themselves on banging out movies that cost hundreds of millions of dollars and were expected to gross a billion or more, worldwide.

Across America small vintage theaters and art houses had given way to chain multiplexes that were block-booked with the huge crowd-pleasers. Allen always said he was never quite sure who formed his audience, back in his heyday or later, but he knew there were certain venues where his limited success was guaranteed, especially in New York City. In *Annie Hall* Allen had dragged Diane Keaton to see *The Sorrow and the Pity* at the New Yorker Theater on Broadway near Eighty-Ninth, a storied venue long since razed in favor of a high-rise co-op. "You cannot imagine how thrilling it was," Dan Talbot, the owner of the New Yorker, once wrote in a letter to the *New York Times*, "to stand in line at the Beekman," another small theater operated by Don Rugoff on the Upper East Side, "waiting to see the new Woody Allen movie" in the 1970s. *Manhattan* had packed Woody Allen fans into the Coronet, the Baronet, the Little Carnegie, and the Walter Reade 34th Street East—all gone now. *Hannah and Her Sisters* had scored a hit at the Murray Hill Cinema, demolished in 2002, and the Beekman had closed, reopened, then closed again. In *Anything Else*, Jason Biggs takes Christina Ricci to see *The Exterminating Angel* at the Quad Cinema, a small-screen multiplex in Greenwich Village, which was one of only a handful of Manhattan revival houses still extant in 2003. References to revival houses and Luis Buñuel, which link *Annie Hall* with *Anything Else*, were increasingly dated and squandered on younger audiences.

A new generation of movie critics had come along as well, inevitably younger and less attuned to historical context and any appreciation of a director old enough to be their grandfather. The New York critics whose praise had elevated Allen's prestige were no longer as relevant. Social media and bloggers had entered the mix, and some of Allen's most influential backers had been long since retired, or had gone to their graves. The young newcomers had not grown up watching Allen on TV, didn't socialize with him at New York parties, certainly not after the Mia–Soon-Yi–Dylan uproar. They didn't often meet with and interview the comedian and filmmaker, as had many of the old-school critics—such as Judith Crist, Roger Ebert, and Charles Champlin.

Janet Maslin, who had begun to take over from Vincent Canby in 1977, the year of *Annie Hall*, proved astute and attuned to Allen's career for twenty-two years, before she retired from film criticism in 1999. A. O. Scott, a book critic for *Newsday*, was one of several groomed to replace Maslin, quickly rising to first-string status. Scott's first review of a Woody Allen picture was *The Curse of the Jade Scorpion*, which he described as "a charming trifle that flatters the good taste of everyone involved," while making the audience "still feel a bit cheated. His movies were once, to him and to some of us, more than a hobby." Eleven years old when *Annie Hall* was released, Scott was "alarmed" to find the onetime Alvy Singer, in *Anything Else*, "looking like my late grandfather every time I see him." From the outset of his *Times* reviewing career, Scott found "perpetual disappointment with his [Allen's] new films." Scott opened a fresh window of grievance against Allen—not aired against Altman or Spielberg, for instance—complaining he was "maddeningly prolific," churning out his clockwork pictures.

EVERY ONCE IN a while, in fact, Allen did skip a year. That was the case in 2004, at least technically in the US, when for the first time in decades a year passed without a Woody Allen film trying to find a slot in America's shrinking movie marketplace. His greening of Europe assumed greater importance, and he understood this better than anyone with all the instincts for self-preservation that had guided him in his long filmmaking career. By the time experts were predicting Hollywood was through with him, and film critics were calling him grandpa, Allen already had laid plans to move with Soon-Yi and his daughters to London for the summer of 2004 and shoot his first picture entirely on foreign soil since *Love and Death* thirty years before.

This remarkable development was made possible by his new producing team of Letty Aronson and Stephen Tenenbaum, which converted friendly overtures from BBC Films, the motion picture arm of the British Broadcasting Corporation, into Allen revising one of his available scripts into a

London story with a largely English cast and crew. When bidding on the London project rose, Fox Searchlight hesitated to overinvest in a second Woody Allen production. DreamWorks, which remained interested in Allen, stepped in, pledging the money that helped secure the financing in exchange for US rights. The Bank of Ireland was part of a foreign consortium that guaranteed the operating budget estimated at 9–12 million euros, which converted into roughly $15–18 million. This was in the ballpark of where Allen's recent film budgets had stabilized in the US.

"What we're doing," explained David Thompson, the head of BBC Films, "is backing a hunch that the combination of Woody Allen and the UK might be a real treat. If you're going to take a punt on anything, it might as well be someone with the track record of Woody Allen." Allen said he loved "the idea of spending the summer in London," adding he hoped to "live up to the high standards of the British movies I grew up with."

With several scripts oven-ready at any given moment, Allen had one idea that had been lying "around for years," in his words. He originally envisioned setting this yarn in the Hamptons, that stretch of affluent seaside hamlets on Long Island that Allen poked fun at in many pictures. With production costs steeply rising, the Hamptons story looked prohibitively expensive to shoot in New York. The BBC deal prompted Allen to rework the story for London. "I anglicized it myself," he later explained, "but I asked an [English] friend to point out where I made blunders. Occasionally [during filming] an actor would say, 'You'd really say "dodgy" and not "dicey" here,' or something." The subject matter was not announced. The English press described it only as "a high-society romantic comedy," referred to as "WASP-04," or "Woody Allen's Summer Project, 2004."

Rather than seeing him as an artist willing to take risks abroad, certain commentators, and some movie critics, treated the announcement as though Allen was betraying New York, or fleeing humiliation with his tail between his legs. His foreign admirers were to be pitied. "The relative unfamiliarity of European critics with New York City may be one reason they have generally been kinder to Mr. Allen's recent movies than have American critics," Stephen Holden opined in the *New York Times*, "who consider him sadly out of touch."

There was a lot to do before departing for England, including Allen selling his family's Carnegie Hill residence. He and Soon-Yi wanted to relocate to more family-oriented space after the summer. The newspapers reported the film director enjoyed giving personal tours of his Carnegie Hill home to prospective buyers, one of whom offered the record sum of $24.5 million, yielding a clear profit from the $17 million Allen had shelled out in 1997. Temporarily, Allen leased another Upper East Side address. Before heading overseas, he and Soon-Yi attended the late March opening of the Ben Hecht–Charles MacArthur play *Twentieth Century*, because Soon-Yi had nudged Allen back into the habit of attending Broadway shows; he had a soft spot for revivals; and Alec Baldwin, an actor who delighted him, led the cast.

Arriving in England, the filmmaker unveiled his cast. He and Juliet Taylor had long scouted talent in London and kept up with the national pool. *Titanic*'s Kate Winslet was announced to head an ensemble that also featured the Dublin-born, Cork-raised thespian Jonathan Rhys Meyers from *Bend It Like Beckham*; Matthew Goode, who'd been Inspector Lynley's brother in the popular BBC television series; Emily Mortimer, memorable as Hugh Grant's "Perfect Girl" in *Notting Hill*; the burly Scottish character actor Brian Cox; and Penelope Wilton, a seasoned pro of the English stage and screen. Within three weeks of the cameras turning in July, however, Winslet withdrew from the project, apologetically explaining she had decided to devote the summer to her young children and husband, director Sam Mendes. Allen responded with a gracious handwritten note: "Don't worry. Forget all about it. Family must come first." He vowed to make it up to Winslet in the future.

The crisis was averted serendipitously when Allen managed to snag Scarlett Johansson, a former child actress (*The Horse Whisperer*), now nineteen and being hailed as a rising star du jour for her performance in Sofia Coppola's *Lost in Translation*. Allen also had seen *Ghost World*, a 2001 black comedy with Johansson, directed by Terry Zwigoff, the man who almost helmed his jazz-tour documentary. The director thought the young actress was "very sexy, very pretty." The English personnel quota and tax requirements for "WASP-04" had already been satisfied, and thus Allen hastily rewrote Winslet's role for Johansson, who'd now have an American backstory in the London story. "It was not a problem," Allen said later. "It took about an hour."*

Allen, Soon-Yi, and their two daughters settled into a luxury mansion—location confidential—with a swimming pool for their exercise and lessons

* Johansson, born in Manhattan, would have qualified as "half-European," as she held Danish co-citizenship through her father.

for the children. Soon-Yi began taking the girls to parks and museums, while Allen focused on preproduction. He picked up cameraman Remi Adefarasin, a London native who had just finished *In Good Company* for Paul Weitz, and veteran production designer Jim Clay, whose many credits included *Love Actually*. The tried-and-true Santo Loquasto had bowed out of the London project owing to US obligations, and Allen's usual editor Alisa Lepselter would assemble the footage back in New York. Allen maintained offices at Ealing Studios, and he would shoot interiors at that studio complex in West London, where classic Alec Guinness comedies had been made that were part of his 1950s moviegoing diet.

Clay spent several weeks with Allen, taking him on guided tours of London, showing him the kind of neighborhoods, buildings, and scenery that might enhance the film. They wanted "to be careful not to make it look like a tourist movie," Clay explained later, while also including enough London landmarks that audiences wouldn't feel cheated. Clay took Allen to the Gherkin, a famous skyscraper in the financial district that could be utilized as a key backdrop in the picture, and other places that ranged from seedy Covent Garden hotels to grand country estates. Because Allen often liked to photograph lengthy walking-and-talking sequences in master shots, and that was not as possible in London, which did not boast New York's miles-long avenues, the walking-and-talking was transplanted to Saint James Park. Clay was "meticulous and imaginative—sometimes quite astonishingly," Allen remembered, "working in the same way Santo works, which is on a very limited budget."

The photography was launched in July, with the press describing an upbeat, almost ebullient Allen. He praised the cool and cloudy summer weather and the gray, overcast skies he had anticipated in London. "The flat light gives a color saturation to everything that's very rich and very beautiful for photography," Allen said. London's food improved on Manhattan's—"There are more terrific restaurants," he told the press—even the catering for cast and crew. (Allen was more wont to lunch on brown bread and salad, while a French chef serviced his household.) The streets were "more relaxed," whereas New York filmmaking was "very union-oriented and very regimented," making "WASP- 04" a throwback to the footloose days of *Take the Money and Run*.

"Here [in London] it's like student filmmaking in the best sense of the word," Allen explained to London journalists. "Everybody does everything. The stand-in directs traffic, the cameraman runs in front of the camera and stands in, I can move chairs. In New York, you have to have a formal break for an hour and ten minutes either side for traveling, here, you just grab a sandwich. Everybody is just interested in making the film. Brits take cultural life very seriously, so you get this enormous vitality and concentration on the project."

The actors received only the pages of their scenes, "the producers even less," according to press accounts. Trying to guess the top-secret screen story, columnists spotted Allen in a frayed green baseball cap guiding exteriors in Belgravia, Fulham Road, Whitehall, Notting Hill, and Saint James Park. Cast, crew, and director were also glimpsed at Covent Garden's Royal Opera House, the Saatchi Gallery, the Tate Modern, and for several days at the elite Queen's [tennis] Club in West Kensington, where white-cotton-shoed members volunteered as extras. Londoners, recognizing Allen, rushed past security to stammer praise before being led away. "People are so nice to me," Allen said. "If only everyone who is so keen to see me would go to see my movies." He eschewed interviews on the set but made an exception one day in July with the death in Rome of Carlo Di Palma, age seventy-nine, who had lensed twelve Woody Allen movies. "This is a very sad day," he broke away from filming to say. "Carlo is one of the great artists of the cinema and he was also a close friend."

The Queen's Club was a clue to the hush-hush story of the movie, which was not much of a comedy, as it turned out. Rather, it was a nail-biter about luck, fate, and social climbing with the aid of a certain racket sport—absent from recent Woody Allen films—serving as life's metaphor. "I remember watching a tennis match on television years ago," Allen explained subsequently, "and after one of those things where the ball bounced over or back after hitting the top of the net, the commentator saying, 'A favorable bound on two or three of those in a match and you have the match. It can make all the difference.' And I always remembered that."

While cameras and lights were being set up, Allen fixated on the *New York Times* sports section, his glasses up on his forehead, Brian Cox recalled. The actors were sworn to silence, although few knew the plot details anyway. Allen worked astonishingly fast. "I think he intimidates everybody, because he trusts you to do your job," Cox said. "He doesn't give you vast notes. I think he knows what he wants, but he doesn't declare that. Woody will say"—slipping into a decent impression—"'You know it would be nice if I could recognize some of my own words, but that's OK.' He's like Clint Eastwood; you're wrapping by one o'clock in the afternoon."

There was rarely any rehearsal, Rhys Meyers, who had the true lead in the picture, confirmed. "C'mon Johnny, let's shoot it," was Allen's most frequent direction to him. "If you do it wrong, he'll let you know. Woody would never compliment you on anything. The fact you're still on the job after three weeks is enough."

Johansson had to smoke fake cigarettes because of the multiple takes required for some of her scenes. "My character was neurotic," the actress later explained, "and Woody thinks smoking looks great on film." Several times Allen reshot her first appearance in the picture, where she is seen playing high-stakes Ping-Pong against all comers. Not because Johannson wasn't good at Ping-Pong—she was not and had to take lessons—but to make sure the actress had her grand entrance into his cinema. "I changed her hair," Allen told Eric Lax. "I changed her costume [she appears in a low-cut, tight white dress]. I changed the way I shot it; the cameraman [Remi Adefarasin] and I talked about it. It was very important for me to present the vision of her as I felt her in that character." Johansson recalled being "really nervous the first day I worked with him. I came to the set and the first couple of takes were just horrible." Soon the young actress was deep into the groove of her character, however. Johansson behaved in "no-nonsense" fashion throughout the shoot, in Allen's phrase, nailing her scenes. A laugher and kidder, the actress didn't take herself too seriously and made the hard work look easy.

"She can do no wrong, incapable of a bad moment," Allen said later. "She was just touched by God." He and Johansson developed an affinity, he took her around to favorite London shops, and soon he began to muse about making another movie with the young actress, maybe catering to her carefree side with a comedy.

Being Allen, his weekends were as chockablock as the production log, with family time interrupted by one weekend in Germany, where he met up with his jazz band for a concert, and another spin away to Spain and Monaco, where Allen played his clarinet with musicians for a Red Cross gala in the presence of Prince Albert.

He gave a lengthy interview to the *Observer* to promote the late summer opening of *Anything Else* in the UK. While declining to reveal anything about the still-untitled London project underway, Allen said writing the script for a film was always easy for him, while the directing was enervating. "Tonight, I'll go see the dailies, yesterday's work, and hopefully it will be good. I'll go home, play with the kids, my wife and I will go out to a nice restaurant for dinner, go to sleep." The London shoot was going well, Allen believed, but "I hope it's not just that the English voices are so beautiful to my ear that they cover a multitude of my sins." Maybe he'd make "a great movie" someday, but "I've resigned myself. I'm functioning within the parameters of my mediocrity."

Allen was asked if, approaching age seventy, he had any regrets about his life, and the comedian and director said he often reflected on the golden time he had spent in Paris in 1964, making *What's New Pussycat?* "In retrospect I regret not staying and living in Paris. Living in Paris was a very happy experience."

Asked point-blank if he brooded over the child-custody case and abuse allegations and the poisonous breakup with Mia Farrow that had tarred his image for many movie-lovers and adversely affected his career, he replied with the same Zelig face he always presented to such interrogatories. "I never give it any thought," Allen said. "It never meant anything to me. I just function, and the tabloids do their work, and it never had any direct bearing on my life. It didn't make my pictures better or worse. It didn't make me happy or unhappy."

"WASP-04" was the rare Woody Allen production that ended with small memento gifts for the lead actors, beautifully wrapped books hagiographically inscribed by the film director. (Rhys Meyers received a biography of Byron.) As the photography wound down, Allen and his family planned a stopover in Paris, then a short trip to Spain, where Allen would continue his personal minitour of European film festivals—Cannes in 2002, followed by Venice in 2003—making an early September appearance at the 52nd San Sebastian Film Festival, considered one of the world's most dazzling because it was a gastronomical as well as cinematic orgy. There Allen would present the world premiere of *Melinda and Melinda*, with cast members Radha Mitchell, Amanda Peet, Chloe Sevigny, and Chiwetel Ejiofor attending. Allen was honored with a retrospective and the lifetime achievement Donostia Award. The vow Allen took to skip awards in person in the US was broken in Europe.

Leading Spanish auteur Pedro Almodóvar bestowed the Donostia. "Two people have shaped my vision of New York," Almodóvar declared, "Superman for its skyline, and Woody Allen for the restaurants, cinemas." Allen improvised a brief acceptance speech. "I don't think I've been of much service to humanity," the director said. "I haven't come up with anything useful like a scientist or a doctor. But then I got to thinking my films are a great cure for insomnia—I hope you like this one [*Melinda and Melinda*]. If not, don't worry, I just finished filming another one last week." As he flew home, the press reported "he's even getting close to giving it a title."

AS THE FAMILY adjusted to a temporary leased home, Allen worked on postproduction of the London story, giving the film the title of *Match Point*, which in tennis refers to the crucial final point that wins the match for a player. He also plunged into writing his next screenplay, which was fashioned as a change of pace for Scarlett Johansson. Actually, Allen wrote three complete and entirely different scripts "in the last twelve weeks," he told Eric Lax, before marrying two ideas from the hopper: one involved a reporter who returns from the dead to pursue a scoop, and the other was about a businessman who tucks his mistress's murder into a serial killer's spree.

Undeterred by the harsh reviews for his stage effort the previous year, Allen also wrote and directed another play for the Chelsea-based Atlantic Theater Company. *A Second Hand Memory*, which Allen brought to audiences in November 2004, was a two-act, seven-character drama revolving around the travails of a 1950s Brooklyn family, focusing on the son who has failed in Hollywood and returns home to take over his father's jewelry business. Christopher Isherwood in the *Times* deplored the "gloomy clichés" of Allen's play, while *Variety* said the work was artificial, pallid, and hackneyed, once again deriding "Allen's unrefined skills as a stage director [with] the poorly planned blocking often leaving them [actors] stranded around Santo Loquasto's traditional, multi-location set." If such critics wished to dissuade Allen from future stage directing, they did.

Match Point was meanwhile put to bed, Christmas arrived, and along with the new year came numerous sightings of Mia Farrow and seventeen-year-old Seamus Farrow, who were making the interview rounds on television. The third act of Farrow's life found her following in the footsteps of her beloved Mother Teresa as a goodwill ambassador for UNICEF, striving to eradicate polio in the Third World. Then in late 2004, Farrow was drawn into activism by Nicholas Kristof's coverage in the *New York Times* of the ongoing refugee crisis and genocide in the Darfur region. The actress reached out to Kristof, whose columns "tore me apart and re-arranged me," asking to travel with him to refugee camps in Darfur, where tribes caught in the middle of the civil war were being subjected to ethnic cleansing. At first Kristof declined, but then he began running into Farrow on the ground in Darfur, as she made repeated trips to the region on behalf of UNICEF. They became friends, he praised her good deeds in his columns, and the two lent their names to fundraisers aiding Darfur victims.

After his mother helped arrange her son's appointment as a UNICEF youth ambassador, Seamus began accompanying Farrow on her African forays. He had graduated early from Bard College and was planning to enter Yale Law School in the fall of 2005, where he was poised to become one of its youngest law students in history. Mother and seventeen-year-old Seamus appeared side by side on programs such as Chris Matthews's *Hardball*, speaking about the Darfur situation. Separately or together, the Farrows were often asked about Allen and Soon-Yi. The actress also kept that part of her life story alive with her one-woman stage presentation, based on *What Falls Away*, which covered her time with Allen and told her version of their breakup and his romance with Soon-Yi, touching on the child-abuse accusations. Dylan had disappeared from public view, or mention.

In interviews Farrow repeated her astonishment that the filmmaker had qualified for adopting children—Bechet and Manzie. Her Catholic zeal to punish Allen's immorality burned just as brightly in her son. "He's my father, married to my sister, and that makes me his son and his brother-in-law," Seamus stated in an interview in early 2005, words that reverberated in print and broadcast media around the world. "That is such a moral transgression. I cannot see him. I cannot have a relationship with my father and be morally consistent."

MELINDA AND MELINDA was screened at the San Sebastian and Toronto film festivals in the fall, but the new Woody Allen movie still had not been released theatrically in the US as of early 2005. *Variety* had scouted the San

Sebastian premiere, hailing the picture as "a return to form after a trio of slighter works," but Fox Searchlight was forced to jockey for bookings, and it wasn't until March that *Melinda and Melinda* received a limited New York opening—one Manhattan theater, another in Brooklyn. Allen, in his public-mingling guise, attended the gala premiere party at Pastis, the Meatpacking District French eatery deployed as a setting in the picture.

Perhaps *Melinda and Melinda* was once intended as an evening of contrasting one-acts for the stage that Allen had reworked into a script for a film. His imaginative conceit opened on a group of diners at Pastis, among them two playwrights debating the merits of comedy versus tragedy. From which can be obtained the greater depth of human understanding? Or is everything in the eye of the beholder? This *Broadway Danny Rose*–type frame segued into parallel stories, shifting back and forth, one featuring a self-destructive Melinda who shows up at a dinner party of old college friends, the other with a light-hearted Melinda crashing a similar occasion.

Both halves were suffused with Woody Allen motifs—everything from Henry Higgins to ticks in the Hamptons—but there were also novelties in both, and characters and situations that were audacious and deeply felt. One character new to Allen's oeuvre was "Ellis Moonsong from Harlem USA," a gifted black pianist and opera composer who courts the tragical Melinda. The pianist-composer was indelibly played by Chiwetel Ejiofor from Stephen Frears's thriller *Dirty Pretty Things*. Foundering married couples appear in both stories—the tragic and comic—and in each half is an Aladdin's lamp. Moonsong, whose race is scarcely noted, is not the only character to speak for Allen when he rubs an enchanted lamp and praises the saving grace of magic.

Since the stories of the two Melindas are mere table talk, the halves don't necessarily have to cohere, and swift intercutting helps blur their lines. The comedic half of *Melinda*, despite Will Ferrell's best efforts as Hobie—an out-of-work actor who performs all his roles with a limp—is only ever mildly funny. Hobie/Ferrell has his best slapstick moment snooping outside the light-hearted Melinda's apartment. Hobie is hopelessly in love. Melinda is busy inside with a date. Sexy Barry White R&B oozes through the keyhole, throwing Hobie—and anyone else familiar with the usual Woody Allen soundtrack—for a loop. Apart from the magnetic Ejiofor and the fumbling-bumbling Ferrell, the capable ensemble includes Chloë Sevigny as a touchingly unfulfilled wife; the pre-famous Steve Carell as Hobie's best pal; trampolining, big-game-hunting dentist ("The Ernest Hemingway of the root canal set") Josh Brolin; Vinessa Shaw as a Republican *Playboy* pinup named Stacey (as in Nelkin) Fox (as in *Manhattan Murder Mystery*); and Wallace Shawn among the pontificators at Pastis.

Two Melindas meant a single actress had to perform double duty, much as Jeff Daniels did for *The Purple Rose of Cairo*. One Melinda was sweet and adorable; her pill-popping twin had a backstory involving murder and—shades of Louise Lasser—an Upper East Side mother, once "a gifted interior decorator," who has succumbed from suicide. As *Melinda and Melinda* unfolds, the tragic Melinda will also give self-murder a try.

To play both Melindas, Allen held out until the eleventh hour for Winona Ryder, who had come up aces in *Celebrity*, but Ryder was arrested in 2001 for shoplifting, she struggled with depression, and the completion bonding companies wouldn't insure the actress. (Allen also sought Robert Downey Jr. to play a role in the picture and had the same insurance obstacles.) Radha Mitchell was known mainly in Australia for the long-running soap opera *Neighbours*, but Allen noticed her in the recent *Man on Fire* and the just-finished *Finding Neverland*. Although her name meant little in America, the director cast Mitchell as the dual character that appears in nearly every scene of *Melinda and Melinda*. Allen "doesn't like to rehearse, and his direction is often fairly minimal," Mitchell said later. "A lot of people came to the set without any idea what the script was about and played it out rather blindly, trusting in him. I think that creates a certain kind of neurosis that he's an expert at depicting and continues to celebrate in his films." Up to the challenge, she made both Melindas watchable.

Still, it was nigh impossible to find *Melinda and Melinda* in theaters: its US gross was $3.8 million. Some prominent critics simply skipped the latest Woody Allen picture. Roger Ebert in the *Chicago Sun-Times* said *Melinda* was—a plaudit that cut both ways—"One of his best recent films." The *Los Angeles Times* handed *Melinda and Melinda* off to a third-stringer who described it as "strenuously twee" with Allen's trademark wit "calcified into pastiche and unintended self-parody." A. O. Scott said the double Melinda was "almost-good."

••

THE CRITICS HAD only a few months to rethink their death knell pronouncements before Allen unveiled *Match Point*—out of competition—at the 58th Cannes Film Festival in May, arriving in France with the look of a cat who has swallowed the canary, because he knew the power of his latest work. Accompanied by cast members Scarlett Johansson, Jonathan Rhys Meyers, and Emily Mortimer, Allen gave many interviews, because *Match Point* was going to be his first picture to be distributed in Europe before its US release. Hampered from delivering a full review of *Match Point* before its scheduled Christmas opening in America, from Cannes A. O. Scott in the *New York Times* wrote sparingly to say *Match Point* was the "surprise" of the festival, a "first-rate movie directed by Woody Allen . . . returning to form." In *Variety*, Todd McCarthy applauded "the most satisfying picture on the Croisette," which was more backhanded praise, because 2005 was widely regarded as a lousy year at Cannes, lacking "a great film or anything close to it." McCarthy kicked around some of the wild theories circulating at Cannes among the anti-Woody school of critics unable to comprehend the filmmaker they regarded as a fuddy-duddy, striking out in such a bold direction. "Critical reaction broke down strongly along national lines," McCarthy reported, "with most Americans liking [*Match Point*], the French loving it, and Brits blowing it off for reasons that seemed to begin with the ease with which the Scarlett Johansson character is able to rent a nice flat. Such was the general astonishment over the Woodman being able to make a film this good after so many stinkers that several rude 'explanations' began circulating: *Match Point* was an old script the English partners had lying around that Allen merely revised; Allen paid a 'front' to write it, then put his name on it; and/or Allen didn't actually direct it at all, a theory attributed to the fact that he has never before used a visual metaphor like the indelible one [a slow-motion tennis match point] that begins and climaxes this picture."

Cannes was a pit stop for Allen, who was bound for London, where he planned to spend another pleasant summer guiding his second BBC Films–sponsored project starring Johansson. This time the young actress was playing a college journalist on the trail of a psycho killer, with the handsome Australian versatilist Hugh Jackman and charismatic Ian McShane, recently a Western villain in television's *Deadwood*, representing the British Empire in the cast. Allen himself would essay "a low-grade American entertainer, which is perfect for me. That's what I am." DreamWorks, which was in the process of being sold to Viacom-owned Paramount, stepped away from producing another Woody Allen film after *Match Point*, and his second London story became the first almost entirely financed by foreign interests, with Focus Features, a subsidiary of Universal Pictures, pitching in for the US rights. The project's humble budget would fall well below that of *Match Point*.

Once more, Allen, Soon-Yi, and their daughters—six-year-old Bechet and five-year-old Manzie—took a six-bedroom in tony Belgravia with swimming pool, sauna, and a humongous garage for the cars belonging to their retinue, which included their au pair and French chef. Again, the family took excursions to Hyde Park and Legoland. "There's so much special to do here [in London] for the children," Soon-Yi told the press, "that I've managed not to duplicate anything special we did here last summer." The screen story, as before, was a secret. But unlike *Match Point* Allen's script was "a very light comedy," he said. It even had a title already—*Scoop*.

RETURNING TO NEW YORK, Allen had a rough cut of *Scoop* assembled by the end of September and, as he told Eric Lax, his spirits sank. The cut was a real "cold-shower moment." The first version was two hours and fourteen minutes. In the end, the running length would be reduced to ninety-one minutes. "There were scenes I wish I could reshoot," Allen said, but those were the good old days. "I wanted to do a comedy and enjoy myself, and what I wound up with, at the end, is a light comedy, a dessert," the director admitted. "When I finished *Scoop*," Allen continued, "I thought to myself, what a nuisance. I'm wasting my time with this little comedy, and I could be doing another piece of work like *Match Point*—another meaty thing. Why am I wasting my time with this? Now I wish I had come to this conclusion twenty-five years ago, but I didn't. And I don't know that I could have implemented it that easily because there was a fierce pressure on me from many people to do comedy."

On the brink of his seventieth birthday, Allen sat for multiple interviews to promote the upcoming US release of *Match Point*, the most thorough and compassionate of which was Peter Biskind's profile in November's *Vanity Fair*. It didn't matter to Allen that the magazine had been a persistent thorn in his side during all the Mia–Soon-Yi–Dylan commotion. Nor did he care when Scarlett Johansson gave an interview publicizing *Match Point* to another detractor, Cindy Adams of the *New York Post*. Because of the buzz building up for the new movie, the piece by Biskind, an Allen admirer, bore the tone of a valedictory, or victory lap.

Biskind spoke with Allen about how the critical ground had shifted against his movies, most notably at the *New York Times*, whose "culture pages had once functioned as virtual Allen house organ," in Biskind's words. Biskind pointed out the "extraordinary and venomous front-page piece" published by the *Times* three years earlier, bylined by "two *Times* reporters with no particular expertise in film," describing the "grand total of eight people" attending a matinee of *Hollywood Ending*, which was then still in its first month of release but had been relegated to "exactly one theater in Manhattan, a $4.95-a-ticket discount house in Times Square." (The matinee had to be canceled due to technical problems and patrons got their money back, the *Times* reported.*) The *Times* article had been timed to coincide with court activity in the Allen/Sweetland lawsuit, and focused on the court case, while declaring Allen's "long moment as a cultural icon may be over." Inside the *Times* some journalists were appalled. "I thought at the time 'This is outrageous,'" former first-string *Times* film critic Janet Maslin told Biskind. "It was an unusually spiteful and vindictive piece. . . . If Vincent Canby had been alive, he would have gone berserk." Roger Ebert, the Pulitzer Prize–winning Chicago-based film critic, was "offended" to the extent of writing a personal letter to the editor, published in the *Times*. Ebert said the article, which came replete with a chart to demonstrate the declining box office of Allen's movies, was specious. "Surely you don't equate box-office with quality?" Ebert asked. He cited Allen's high audience ratings on the Tomatometer on RottenTomatoes.com and his numerous Oscar nominations and wins. "Few directors do as well," Ebert wrote.

At times Allen thought critics "represent the lowest level of the culture," as grunge musician Scumbag X (Mark Webber), Val/Allen's alienated son from a previous marriage, tells his film director father in *Hollywood Ending*. (It's a funny, heartwarming scene, with Val breaking down and admitting, "I love you, Scumbag!") Long ago Allen had reconciled himself to critical affronts, and nowadays he truly no longer read his reviews, although he

* "Curse of the Jaded Audience: Woody Allen, in Art and Life," bylined by non-film critics Andy Newman and Corey Kilgannon, appeared in the June 5, 2002, *New York Times*.

caught their drift from people. "I've been around a long time," he explained in the *Vanity Fair* interview, demonstrating how perceptive he could be about his own work. "Some people may just get tired of me, which I can understand. I've tried to keep my films different over the years, but it's like they complain, 'We've eaten Chinese food every day this week.' I want to say, 'Well, yes, but you had a shrimp meal, and you had a pork meal, and you had a chicken meal.' They say, 'Yes, yes, but it's all Chinese food.' That's the way I feel about myself. I have a certain amount of obsessive themes, and a certain amount of things that I'm interested in, and no matter how different the film is, whether it's *Small Time Crooks* here or *Zelig* there, you find in the end that it's Chinese food. If you're not in the mood for my obsessions, then you may not be in the mood for my film. Now, hopefully, if I make enough films, some of them will come out fresh, but there's no guarantee. It's a crapshoot every time. . . . It could come out interesting or you might get the feeling that, 'God, I've heard this kvetch before.' "

Biskind's questions were probing, and Allen was dutifully responsive, with no question off-limits as usual and never, as once was the case, a nearby publicist. They discussed Allen's affluence, which "compared to my contemporaries, it's relatively nothing," Allen insisted. The film director was "not Hollywood wealthy. I've never taken advantage of the sell-out opportunities I've had," like making an "Annie Hall II"—which people still begged him to do. Asked if he ever saw his children—Seamus, now almost 18; Dylan, 20; or Moses, 27—Allen said no, "I feel terrible about it." Most mornings, Allen told Biskind, he ate much the same breakfast he enjoyed as a boy—Cheerios in skim milk with raisins and sliced bananas—seven slices—although you still could never be sure if he wasn't kidding. "I count them and recount them," Allen elaborated, "to make sure there's seven. Because my life has gone well with seven slices, and I don't want to tempt fate with six or eight."

How was family life going with Soon-Yi and his children? Biskind asked. "If somebody told me when I was younger, 'You're going to wind up married to a girl thirty-five years younger than you and a Korean, not in show business, not having any real interest in show business,' I would have said, 'You're completely crazy,' " Allen replied. "Because all the women that I went out with were basically my age. Two years younger. Ten years was the maximum. Now, here, it just works like magic. The very inequality of me being older and much more accomplished, much more experienced, takes away any real meaningful conflict. So, when there's disagreement, it's never an adversarial thing. I don't ever feel that I'm with a hostile or threatening person. It's got a more paternal feeling to it. I love to do things to make her happy. She loves to do things to make me happy. It just works out great. It was just completely fortuitous. One of the truly lucky things that happened to me in my life."

Leaving aside the fact Allen was known to have dated women *several* decades younger than the "ten years maximum," Biskind followed up. "There must be a Pygmalion-esque dimension to it [their relationship]? . . . The way Alvy [Singer] forced books on Annie Hall and dragged her to *The Sorrow and the Pity*?"

"No," the filmmaker said. "I do not mold Soon-Yi into anything. She's very self-possessed, and she runs the house and the kids and our life. She runs it better than I could ever run it because she's interested in it. She will check the accountant's statements, and she will deal with health issues, and she will structure the kids' lessons after school and their playdates. And I am free to work and have a great time with her and have a great time with the kids. As I say, it was like two people that you would have thought, 'Are you kidding? Forget it—it's the craziest thing in the world.' And just by sheer accident, it worked out just delightfully."

THE CAFÉ CARLYLE sold out on most Monday nights to neighborhood folks who liked the food and the music, but often celebrities stopped by—Cary Grant for example, back in the day of Michael's Pub; and nowadays younger famous people and fellow musicians such as, one Monday, the entire Coldplay band. The crowd usually included foreigners who had thronged there from all around the globe, eager to watch the clarinet player with his jazz band. They were not disappointed if the diminutive figure, who dressed a lot like he did in Woody Allen movies, his hair gone white with a bald spot on his crown, increasingly deaf, sang little, spoke rarely to the audience, and chiefly interacted with old friend Eddy Davis, "the fat man with the plaid shirt opening onto a buffalo neck, who accompanies him on the banjo," in the words of French intellectual Bernard-Henri Lévy. Steadfast admirers like Lévy basked in the presence of "this famous little man, the *schlemiel* with the physique of the eternal loser, heir to Keaton, Chaplin and Harold Lloyd." After his 2005 visit to the Carlyle, Lévy wrote: "Oh, the intense joy on his face, this countenance of an old, consumptive adolescent metamorphosed into a semi athlete, his air of absolute triumph, when he reaches the end of one of those solos and you don't know if that amazing breath comes from his mouth, his body movements, the force of his soul, or all three at once."

December 1, 2005, fell on a Thursday. How Allen and his family celebrated his birthday milestone is unknown because the paparazzi no longer chased the comedian, writer, director, and clarinet player, nor did the columnists write about him as frequently. Perhaps he and Soon-Yi spent a quiet night at home, but just as likely they went out for the steak Allen liked on rare occasions, dining at Ben & Jack's in Midtown, or Sparks on East Forty-Sixth, where mobster Paul Castellano was gunned down in 1985 and where Allen liked the table in the back, so it'd be harder to shoot him. "Cloquet hated reality but realized it was still the only place to get a good steak," from "The Condemned," one of Allen's "little souffles" in the *New Yorker*, was among his oft-quoted witticisms.

After premieres in New York and Los Angeles, which Allen attended, giving more interviews, *Match Point* opened on Christmas Day, by which time the septuagenarian was en route to Europe for his annual holiday with his family with stays in Venice and Paris. The itinerary was coordinated with his band's minitour of European venues. He'd thank England with a one-night stand in Brighton, not London, because "I'd done London last time. My wife was keen on Brighton. We can bring the kids, look around." Another concert took Allen to Spain, where in Barcelona the famous man was mobbed by the press and well-wishers, and where he signed a contract with MediaPro, an international multimedia production company with headquarters in the city, to direct a future Woody Allen picture in the capital of Catalonia in 2007, with a Spanish production team and actors.

Match Point proved nothing less than a sensation in the US, "the best movie he has made in more than a decade," as Jami Bernard wrote in the *New York Post*, "maybe stretching back to 1989's *Crimes and Misdemeanors*," which the new work echoed with its murderer going unpunished. Adagio-paced—one of his longest films at two hours and four minutes—the story of a failed Irish tennis pro, born to rags, who marries into privilege and position but then is nearly undone by a torrid affair with a volatile mistress, was the perfect Hitchcockian thriller no one had ever predicted from Woody Allen. His usual signposts were so muted they could have been missed by anyone not in the know: Dostoyevsky's *Crime and Punishment*, chess games, art galleries, grand opera. A mousey wife consulting fertility doctors and pleading with her husband ("I want you to make me pregnant!"), while the husband's lover, a would-be actress not getting callbacks, is fatally inseminated. The filmmaker made the transfer to England—garden estates, country churches, skeet shooting, bank holidays—seem effortless. The performances were sublime, especially Jonathan Rhys Meyers and Scarlett Johansson with their steamy lovemaking in cheap hotels or in the pouring rain, the latter demonstrating her full "thrill capacity."

Both Rhys Meyers and the upper-class Matthew Goode, whom he befriends as a tennis tutor, are opera buffs, and the contemplatively paced thriller was bolstered by a classic opera soundtrack that reinforced the story's motifs. The Donizetti, Verdi, Bizet, Gomes, and Rossini arias, with Enrico Caruso often heard from tinny century-old recordings, exerted a haunting effect. No other American director, except Robert Altman, would have dared such musical backing, although Allen had done much the same with Prokofiev, Mendelssohn, and George Gershwin. Critics routinely referred to *Match Point* as Allen's "return to form," even "a departure," but the director always had admired Hitchcock, and *Match Point* embodied Allen's lifetime of craft and was his homage to Hitchcockian suspense. Yet this was modernized suspense that rated coincidence above God and earthly justice: the way a tennis ball drops after it strikes the net; what happens to the essential clue of a ring when it strikes a guardrail and falls, not into the Thames as intended, but onto a footpath to await discovery. Hitchcock believed in the moral consequences of crime. Allen, a moral skeptic, believed in chance and luck.

Match Point entertained audiences around the world, earning above its budget in America, more than doubling its $23.2 million domestic gross in foreign territories, and in the end becoming one of only three movies from the post–Mia Farrow era among the top 15 (number 14) on the BuzzFeed list of Allen's all-time US box-office hits. Curiously, many London critics savaged the picture, rolling their eyes over everything from the touristy landmarks to the falsity of the posh English ("supremely clunky dialogue," according to Peter Preston in the *Guardian*). Entire nations disagreed with the British, however: *Match Point*'s categorization as a UK film won for it the Goya as Best European Film of 2005 in Madrid; and it was the ninth Woody Allen movie to be nominated for a French Cesar as Best Foreign Film (*Manhattan* and *The Purple Rose of Cairo* both won in their years of release). Allen's deft script was also nominated for an Oscar—the first nomination for a Woody Allen film since *Sweet and Lowdown*, and his first script in contention since *Deconstructing Harry*.

RETURNING TO THE US after the New Year, Allen's first order of business was to finalize the purchase of a Georgian-style town house at 118 East Seventieth, a building designed by Trowbridge and Livingston in 1900 ("with a spectacularly wide fanlight" among its distinguishing features, in the words of the *New York Times*), perched on "an exceptionally handsome block between Lexington and Park Avenues" locally dubbed "Millionaire's Row." (In fact, the building was situated on a favorite Allen block, where he had shot some scenes for *Annie Hall*.) Workmen would stream in and out for months, making renovations and preparing the place for Allen, Soon-Yi, and their family to move in after the director shot his next picture in France over the summer of 2006.

Allen had written a romantic time-travel comedy with a lead for Michelle Williams from *Brokeback Mountain*. The story concerned a young American tourist couple who travel to Paris and into the past, meeting artists and writers from the Paris of the 1920s—famous figures like Gertrude Stein. Allen was only a few weeks away from the photography, however, when the director developed qualms. Curiously, his sister, producer Letty Aronson, gave him pause when she argued that the younger generation of moviegoers didn't know or care who Gertrude Stein was. When French budget estimates kept escalating, Allen tabled the Paris time-travel script.

Remarkably, he had a backup prepared, another meaty drama that could be easily resituated in England, and the filmmaker was working so expeditiously at this time, so nimbly was he able to switch gears, he was up and running with *Cassandra's Dream* by midsummer in London. His script was partly indebted to *A Second Hand Memory*, Allen's most recent produced play, which had hinged on a mysterious character, a well-off Uncle Phil, upon whom the entire family pins their hopes and dreams. Although

Allen's plays, like some of his Tamiment sketches, might be flawed, there were often ideas that could be reworked, and he now reimagined Uncle Phil as the dark savior of a star-crossed family. With quick casting—Juliet Taylor liaised with London counterparts on *Match Point*, *Scoop*, and *Cassandra's Dream*—Allen cobbled together an estimable all-English ensemble.

The actors included Ewan McGregor, whom Allen had watched onstage in London, during his *Scoop* summer, playing Sky Masterson in *Guys and Dolls*; Colin Farrell, who had a sixty-second meeting with Allen: "That's the guy!"; two-time Oscar nominee Tom Wilkinson; Shakespeare-trained Sally Hawkins from Mike Leigh films; and Hayley Atwell, the least known, a television actress who was flown to New York to meet Allen after he viewed her audition tape. Maria Djurkovic, who had been the production designer for *Scoop*, was brought back for this very different assignment. Also returning was the highly regarded cameraman Vilmos Zsigmond, a Hungarian émigré who adapted well to commercial or maverick Hollywood directors and who had worked with Allen on *Melinda and Melinda*. "What separates the men from the boys is the lighting," Allen said, "and he's wonderful at lighting." Allen had it in the back of his mind to score the picture with Miles Davis.

Meanwhile the pleasantly distracting *Scoop* was released in the midsummer in the US, with critics and audiences nonplussed after the more rousing *Match Point*. The story concerned a college reporter, a prestidigitator, a serial killer, and a boat ride in the afterlife with Death at the helm. You couldn't watch the movie without appreciating the warm, jokey chemistry between Johansson as the college girl trying to follow a dead man's scoop, and Allen as her magician-partner in crime detection. (An American illusionist living in London, he goes by the stage name of Splendini.) *Match Point* had evoked comparisons to the George Stevens film *A Place in the Sun*, and *Scoop* would poke more fun at the same classic motion picture with references to one of its famous scenes, when Hugh Jackman goes on a romantic boating idyll with Johansson and tries to drown her. The murder attempt is feministly foiled: it turns out the college girl is a champion swimmer. *Scoop* was exactly the sort of baloney Allen's loudest critics warned him against but the kind of trivial comedy he returned to now and then these days, if only to prove he could do whatever he pleased.

One of the *New York Times*'s new, younger critics, Manohla Dargis, found the latest Woody Allen film to be "not especially funny yet oddly appealing." One peculiarity of this period in Allen's career, however, was that UK critics took particular offense at his London stories. As the director ticked off scenes for *Cassandra's Dream* in the summer of 2006, living with his family on upscale Old Church Street in Chelsea, screenings of *Scoop* were held for UK scribes. John Patterson in the *Guardian* complained about Allen landing on his London doorstep, making execrable pictures. "We have to settle for Woody Allen in his creatively bankrupt dotage," Patterson wrote, "looking for all the world as if he's on the lam from some morals charge back home, but who's welcomed like the risen ghost of Jean Renoir despite not having made a worthwhile movie in years (full disclosure: I would cheerfully burn the negative of *Match Point* if I could swing it)." Charles Nevin in the *Independent* also saw *Scoop* as decrepitude. "Much of the un-enthusiasm concentrates on Woody's age," Nevin said. "The incessant whine that was funny when he was in his thirties and trying to get laid, now sounds like the unmodulated hiss of air escaping from a tyre. . . . Being a loser in your seventies, even a loveable one—isn't funny." Following these venomous critiques, *Scoop* would never even be released officially in the UK.

It was a genuine occupational syndrome for comedians who starred in their own movies that their comedy routines became more familiar over time and less amusing as they aged. Those, like Allen, whose personas relied in part on slapstick and physical comedy, inevitably lost a step. The pantheon—from Buster Keaton and Charles Chaplin to the Marx Brothers and Bob Hope—made late-career vehicles that were either ignored or condemned by increasingly youthful audiences. If those reviewers who were blasé about Allen appearing in his latter-day comedies wanted to dissuade him from starring in any more of his films, they were successful. His starring roles in Woody Allen movies stretched fewer and further in between. After *Scoop*, there would be only one more.

AFTER THE SUMMER Allen and his family moved into the renovated townhouse on East Seventieth, a narrow six-story with separate living quarters for everyone, connected by flights of stairs and an elevator. The living room with floor-to-ceiling windows led to an outside garden. The townhouse was filled with "very personal bric-a-brac," according to visitor Daphne Merkin, among which were "drawings by Oskar Kokoschka and John Sloan in addition to a collection of Americana: an assortment of pewter jugs (a favorite of Allen's but not of Soon-Yi's), a cradle with quilts, a green leather spa chair from a sanitarium, and a bellows on the wall." East Seventieth was fated to be the last mailing address for a man who'd spent his boyhood and adult life as a habitual itinerant.

Allen plunged into the editing and postproduction of *Cassandra's Dream* while finishing the script for the project he'd agreed to direct the next summer in Barcelona. Having tested the waters earlier in the year with a rare appearance outside Manhattan with his band at the Rochester International Jazz Festival, Allen now agreed to an ambitious first-time US minitour of the "Eddy Davis New Orleans Jazz Band featuring Woody Allen," embarking, after his seventy-first birthday, on a circuit that began with cities in Southern and Northern California. The Los Angeles stop would reinforce his rapprochement with the city he had ridiculed in *Annie Hall*, and his concert sold out at Royce Hall at the University of California at Los Angeles, where the crowd was avid even though critics were grudging. "Despite the sometimes squawky quality of his tone," grumped Don Heckman in the *Los Angeles Times*, "the musical content of what he played was generally well-done." The Christmastime barnstorming would climax on New Year's Eve with a concert at West Palm Beach in Florida, a state where Allen had not performed publicly—as a comedian or musician—since New Year's Eve 1972.

Before and after the tour, during postproduction Allen reshaped *Cassandra's Dream* more than was the case with his previous two London projects. He cut entire characters and scenes. He decided against Miles Davis; nor did he want music from the repertoire, opera recordings (as with *Match Point*) or jazz and classical (as with *Scoop*). One of his team suggested approaching the minimalist composer Philip Glass, which worried Allen insofar as he had not engaged a musical outsider for over three decades and never had he employed one of Glass's preeminent stature. Yet Allen met Glass and liked him and surprised the composer by leaving him "completely alone to place the music in the film. He welcomed my suggestions as to the temper of the music as well." Sometimes he'd say, "No, that's a little too heavy," "That's a little too light," or "A little too much music," but Glass's brooding score, "riddled with apprehension," in Allen's words, would heighten the atmosphere of the picture.

While progressing on his Barcelona script, after the new year Allen met with two of Spain's most celebrated actors, Penélope Cruz and Javier Bardem, both of whom were also recognized names in America. Cruz had been Best Actress–nominated in 2006 for her dazzling performance in Pedro Almodóvar's *Volver*—a surreal comedy, Allen told her, he'd seen and enjoyed. (He watched all Almodóvar films.) Bardem would win a Best Actor Oscar for his role as the brutal hitman in the Coen brothers' *No Country for Old Men* in 2007. Visiting New York, Cruz phoned Allen's office and asked to meet him, telling Allen she keenly desired to be in the Barcelona project. In person, the raven-haired actress was "ravishing and more sexual than I had imagined," Allen said. Bardem followed suit and he too was cast in the picture, as yet without a completed script, or title.

So badly did the filmmaker wish to please the Spanish thespians, Allen went to the rare length of sending the full draft screenplay to both players before the filming, saying they should feel free to tweak his dialogue and emendate his scenes. He did the same with Scarlett Johansson, for whom he had written a pivotal third lead. He added, as a fourth principal, Rebecca Hall, the daughter of English stage, screen, and opera director Sir Peter Hall. Hall had publicly campaigned for a role in a Woody Allen movie while he was shooting *Match Point* and *Scoop* in London. "If Woody Allen is reading this, I want a part," Hall declared in one interview. "Please call my agent!" Allen needed only a "very, very short" meeting with the actress—"Full-lipped and long of limb," as the *Los Angeles Times* later described her. He asked Hall if she could do an American accent, she said yeah, and he said OK, you've got the part—goodbye. The American Patricia Clarkson was recruited for a supporting role.

Allen, his wife and daughters, and his team were due in Barcelona on June 1. Revamping something he'd once written about two college girls vacationing in San Francisco, Allen arrived with as freeform and jazzlike a script as any he'd ever written. The twisting story focused on two young Americans summering in Barcelona, therefore enabling all the postcard sights and tourist stops dyspeptic English critics had whined about suffering in *Match Point*. In the story the young Americans (Johansson and Hall) become entangled in *amor loco* with a libidinous, flamboyant painter (Bardem) and a tempestuous artist who is his recently divorced ex-wife (Cruz).

Allen began the weeks of preparation with excursions around Barcelona, steeping himself in the city, as Jim Clay had helped him do with London for *Match Point*, this time with production designer Alain Bainée, who frequently worked with the Catalan filmmaker Jaume Balagueró. The cameraman the director engaged for the "Barcelona Project," as it was known, was Javier Aguirresarobe, whose credits included Fernando Trueba's *The Girl of Your Dreams* starring Cruz. Alisa Lepselter once again would manage the editing back in New York.

Although Allen continued to fall back on bargain budgets compared to Hollywood's bloated productions, and MediaPro was underwriting the picture in a partnership with other Spanish film and television companies, the fact that 10 percent of the approximately $20 million budget came from tax set-asides from Barcelona and the region of Catalonia stirred blowback in the local media. Barcelona mayor Jordi Hereu supported the government investment, however, and predicted the "Barcelona Project" would become "a huge advertisement for the city that will be seen around the world." In time Mayor Hereu's words would prove prophetic.

The photography stretched through August, with Allen staging scenes with the backdrops of Gaudi's La Sagrada Familia, Casa Mila, and Park Güell, the Museu Nacional d'Art de Catalunya, the Basilica de Santa Maria del Mar, and similar landmarks across the country in Oviedo on the Atlantic Coast, where the story would also pay a visit. Perhaps Oviedo sneaked onto the screen because, in 2002, after being honored with Spain's Prince of Asturias prize, the town erected a bronze statue of Woody Allen. (The statue is not in the film.)

When Hall was cast as Vicky, the actress didn't realize her role was "the emotional heart and thematic spine of the film," as the *Los Angeles Times* later described Vicky—the first word of Allen's eventual title. On the set, Hall asked Allen, "What did you see in me that persuaded you to take this strange risk in giving me this really amazing part?" His response was "incredibly vague," Hall recalled. He didn't know; he couldn't say.

Johansson, playing Vicky's best friend Cristina—the second word of the title-to-be—developed an ease with Allen over their three collaborations. The other actors could only envy their close relationship. Johannson bestowed mocking nicknames on the director: Woodrow, or Your Woodness. As with Diane Keaton, Allen couldn't get the best of the actress. When he cracked wise, she had a snappy comeback. "We have the same humor,"

Johansson explained. "We badger each other. For instance, when someone asked, in front of him, how I'd describe him, he put in, 'The word genius can be used.' And I said, 'modest and humble.' I love him."

Bardem said later he "talked to Woody Allen like three times during the whole shoot. One day he was on the set and he said to me, 'Oh Javier, how are you?' He said hi to me like he was surprised I was on the set!" One early morning, Allen photographed the screaming street scene between Bardem and Cruz—one of their most ferocious scenes—and after just a single take Allen said fine, that's a wrap. The Spanish players were dumbfounded. "That cannot be it for me today!" Cruz protested. "I'm gonna go home and drive myself crazy, not having the opportunity to do other things." Huh, said Allen, "but I love what you guys did." He allowed two more takes.

Cruz, who lived in Madrid, said the director seemed at home in Barcelona and, ultimately, he knew the city "better than I did." The Spanish actress adapted to his singular methods. "Sometimes he watches through monitors," Cruz said, "and sometimes he's near the actors. It's true there are almost no rehearsals and very few takes but it doesn't matter—he has the whole movie in his head, the whole puzzle perfectly put together so you know you're working with one of the masters. You don't miss rehearsal time. He doesn't need you to get too methodic about it. I came to him with a thousand questions for [my character] Maria Elena, and he was patient and listened and said, 'You don't have to do that. We're going in the right direction but if that's the way you work, that's fine.' " The American director had "a clever strategy he uses to keep actors in [the present] because all of the time you feel as if you are running out of time. And don't his characters always feel like that?"

They must have done something right because Cruz would be Oscar-nominated for Best Supporting Actress for *Vicky Cristina Barcelona*, and she and Bardem also fell in love during filming and later got married.

The complicated production, involving exteriors on both coasts, was completed by the end of August. "Wrap party as usual a little sad," Allen wrote in a faux-diary of the filming experience he penned for the *New York Times*. "Slow danced with Scarlett Johannson. Broke her toe. Not my fault. When she dipped me back, I stepped on it. . . . Sentimental moment. Everyone in cast and crew chipped in and bought me a ballpoint pen."

••

HE RETURNED TO New York and postproduction during the day, Elaine's, La Cirque, and Knicks games at night, except for Mondays at the Cafe Carlyle. Indeed, Allen's jazz band roamed freely these days, performing at a Hugo Boss fashion event in October, and at Christmastime there'd be another foreign tour, with Allen and his family choosing fresh places to visit with the jazz band, such as Budapest and Athens. A new collection of short pieces, *Mere Anarchy*, was published in November, Allen donated signed drawings to a food pantry auction, and he cohosted a radio show playing jazz standards. Amateur magician that he'd always been, he had no difficulty keeping a number of plates spinning in the air while at the same time juggling multicolored balls.

As the filmmaker shaped *Vicky Cristina Barcelona* in the editing room, he also worked feverishly to complete a new script before a pending Writers Guild strike shut down most production from November to February. After four pictures abroad, the big news was the next project would mark his return to Manhattan locations—although there'd been a few New York moments in *Vicky Cristina Barcelona*. MediaPro CEO Jaume Roures spoke to the director about producing other Woody Allen films to come, but the arrangements were still in flux. Allen would launch the Manhattan project in the spring, not autumn, which was his known predilection. "Whatever [idea] I find in my drawer written on a matchbook is what I do," he told the New York *Daily News*.

Allen had signed off on *Cassandra's Dream* in the spring, after which the movie was submitted to the MPAA for imminent release and received a PG-13 rating. Allen hosted a sneak preview in Aviles near Oviedo in August, while shooting *Vicky Cristina Barcelona*, before attending the picture's official premiere at the Venice Film Festival in September, flanked by leads Ewan McGregor, Colin Farrell, and Hayley Atwell. Ray Bennett, covering Venice, slammed the new Woody Allen offering in the *Hollywood Reporter*, saying *Cassandra's Dream* was a misfire that wouldn't interest very many moviegoers, with "lazy plotting, poor characterization, dull scenes, and flat dialogue." Stung by this negative review, Harvey Weinstein, whose Weinstein Company had acquired the US rights, kept delaying its release until eventually, Allen liked to joke, the movie was assigned to the Witness Protection Program and sneaked into a handful of theaters in American cities in January. The low-key release, all-English cast, and obscure title—referring not only to Greek mythology, but to a racehorse, and to the good and bad dreams that haunt the characters—guaranteed failure for the movie in the US, where *Cassandra's Dream* grossed only $1 million. In the UK, where the *Independent* savaged McGregor's and Farrell's Cockney argot as "Dick Van Dyke–like London accents," the film did even worse.

The harsh assessments of the *Hollywood Reporter* and other outlets ("One of the worst films I've ever seen," declared Simon Hattenstone in the *Guardian*) were unfair. *Cassandra's Dream* was almost as gripping as *Match Point*, with hypnotic music and moody photography that framed the doom-and-gloom story of loser brothers who purchase a boat they can't afford, to sail away from their problems. McGregor as the "brains" of the brothers, and Farrell as the drinker and gambler, are compelling, and Sally Hawkins, as Farrell's spouse, makes a salt-of-the-earth impression in her first Woody Allen film. Just as striking are Hayley Atwell as McGregor's actress-girlfriend, kinky on- and offstage, and Tom Wilkinson as the "Uncle Howard" of dubious means who wants a whistleblower killed in exchange for assisting his nephews. The masterful scenes include the brothers' first botched attempt at murder, but Atwell and Wilkinson fade out of the story after providing initial excitement, and the film's stark ending—an allusion to Vittorio De Sica's *Shoeshine*—is abrupt. The brothers destroy each other as their boat spins adrift. Allen's third act lacked the emotional gut punch of the Italian neorealist classic. And the brother characters could have used that slight pinch of warmth his mother always wished from Allen.

Some US critics saw virtues in *Cassandra's Dream*, however. Even Manohla Dargis in the *New York Times* viewed Allen's "latest excursion to the dark side of human nature" as "good enough that you may wonder why he doesn't just stop making comedies." Still, Allen's third London story struggled for audiences overseas too. In Germany, *Cassandra's Dream* went straight to DVD. The movie was "treated far kinder by the French critics than elsewhere," *Variety* smirked, especially in Paris, where it played, upon its opening, to lines of moviegoers.

IN FEBRUARY, THE director cast the leads of "Woody Allen's Untitled Spring Project" (WAUSP): Larry David, who had graduated from small parts in *Radio Days* and "Oedipus Wrecks" to become cocreator of *Seinfeld* and the star of his own hit series *Curb Your Enthusiasm*; and Evan Rachel Wood, a young veteran of television and independent movies. The filming began in mid-April on the morning after the director attended a party at Elaine's with Soon-Yi and their daughter Bechet, celebrating the forty-fifth anniversary of his favorite restaurant, which he did not visit as often nowadays, not in real life, nor in his films. One of the last times was *Celebrity*, where Elaine's hosts a book launch, and a comedian does a cockeyed imitation of Jack Nicholson at a seder.

Tellingly, *Cassandra's Dream*—neither the picture, nor its financial fate—did not deflate the enthusiasm of Sony Classic Pictures, which had swooped in to sign Allen for "WAUSP" and his next six film projects, extending into 2015. Sony Classics copresidents Michael Barker and Tom Bernard had been instrumental in organizing the earlier United Artists and Orion classics divisions. When Orion went under in 1992, Barker and Bernard created Sony's specialty branch. Like Arthur Krim before them, the Sony executives had a farsighted appreciation for Woody Allen. "A very artistic-minded outfit," in Allen's words, Sony Classics invested prudently in his budgets in return for US rights, and the leadership maintained a hands-off attitude toward the filmmaker.

Once upon a time Allen had envisioned the "WAUSP" script as a vehicle for Zero Mostel after *The Front*, but he had filed the story away after Mostel's death in 1977. His script, revised for David, concerned a misanthropic onetime physicist who squanders his brainpower giving chess lessons to children. When a free-spirited runaway from Mississippi (Wood) enters his life, the grouchy genius falls for the girl and has his life transformed by a "barely legal love interest," in the words of *New York Post* columnists trying to keep tabs on Allen's first Manhattan project since *Melinda and Melinda*. Patricia Clarkson from *Vicky Cristina Barcelona* and Ed Begley Jr. were the runaway's estranged parents, embroiled in their own midlife crises, with Henry Cavill as an actor with a crush on her. In time *Whatever Works*, a colloquialism muttered by Rebecca Hall in *Vicky Cristina Barcelona*, became the title, aptly summing up Allen's free-and-loose approach to filmmaking these days.

One night during the filming Allen and Dick Cavett went to see Mort Sahl at B.B. King Blues Club in Times Square, where the nonagenarian was still delivering his comedy act. Old friends like Cavett and longtime idols like Sahl were to be cherished. When Cavett was hospitalized for depression in the 1980s, Allen, overcoming his anxiety about hospitals, was among his most diligent visitors. Allen tried, whenever visiting California, to check in on Sahl and see how the grand old crank was doing. Allen's circle, his generation, were aging. Ingmar Bergman, the pen pal whose masterworks Allen never tired of rewatching, had died in 2007. His venerable manager Charles H. Joffe would die at seventy-eight in July 2008, and Joffe's name would show up for the last time onscreen for *Whatever Works*. Allen's longtime agent Sam Cohn passed away in May 2009.

Once Mr. Elusive, nowadays Allen seemed to be an addict of major European film festivals. In late May, after calling the last takes on *Whatever Works*, he attended the unveiling of *Vicky Cristina Barcelona* at Cannes, accompanied by Soon-Yi and joined on the rostrum by Penélope Cruz and Rebecca Hall. The new Woody Allen picture would enjoy a separate Spanish premiere at the San Sebastian Film Festival in the fall, again with Allen in attendance and giving interviews alongside Javier Bardem. By then the Weinstein Company had already released *Vicky Cristina Barcelona* in the US, where the sophisticated variation on a romantic comedy proved a late summer smash, easily making up its budget with US grosses of $23.2 million—number seventeen on the BuzzFeed list.

Bardem was magnetic as the womanizing Juan Antonio who attempts to seduce the summering Americans, passionate Cristina (Scarlett Johansson) and sensible Vicky (Hall), pushing for a threesome in bed, but succeeding only with one girl at a time. Entering the story midway, Maria Elena (Cruz), his fiery, suicidal ex-wife, herself a tortured artist, lights up the movie like a comet. Maria Elena hates/loves Cristina, who has moved in with Juan Antonio, but soon the three wild hearts become entangled. Cristina begins to fret about her life and decamps to France. Meanwhile Vicky forges a bourgeois future with new husband Doug (Chris Messina), while pining for Juan Antonio. Vicky gets one last chance with him, and Maria Elena turns up with a gun.

Vicky Cristina Barcelona was one of the most worldly, free-flowing, humanistic Woody Allen films. Like a child's toy kaleidoscope, the script takes bits of familiar colored glass and spins them into new configurations. The women are neurotic and dangerous, the marriages fraudulent; there are Spanish shrinks and Chinese restaurants, Hitchcock movies in the afternoon, and dialogue remaindered from previous Woody Allen movies. ("The heart was more puzzling than ever.") Allen would earn another deserved Best Script nomination from the Writers Guild—his fifteenth. Underlying the romance and comedy was a serious theme of contempt for the "appropriate police" who try to dictate the mores of love and sex. The scenes whiz by with breathtaking views of Oviedo and Barcelona. Patricia Clarkson as Vicky's American cousin, herself drifting into adultery, and Juan Antonio's aged father Julio (Josep Maria Domènech), who refuses to publish his angry poetry, lend ballast to the main storyline. The recurring title song by Giulia y los Tellarini, a Barcelona indie band, was the highlight of an eclectic all-Spanish soundtrack, including classical and flamenco. With Allen incorporating, at times, slow motion, split screen, bicycle shots, dissolves, lingering close-ups, and subtitles, the technique and the subject matter were nouvelle vague. "In style," Allen said later, "*Vicky Cristina* is almost more of a French movie."

The four personable leads won most critics over, and the write-ups improved upon *Match Point*'s. Some US reviewers, liking *Barcelona* more than they had guessed, felt obliged to remind readers of the director's "long string of uncertain or downright disappointing films," in the words of Joe Morgenstern of the *Wall Street Journal*, before acknowledging the "sunny, summery romantic comedy," which was perhaps as good as it was because "he isn't in it." Many, seduced by *Barcelona*, found something to excoriate in the narration by Christopher Evan Welch—a performer from *Writer's Block*—that evoked a writer reading his picaresque tale aloud. The voice-over could have been done by Allen, but perhaps the director handed it off to another performer because Morgenstern and other critics kept warning him against acting in his own films anymore.

AFTER A LOW-KEY summer in New York, Allen headed to the West Coast where he had been asked to stage Puccini's *Gianni Schicchi* for the Los Angeles Opera in September. "I have no idea what I'm doing," he drolly informed the *Los Angeles Times*, "but incompetence has never prevented me from plunging in with enthusiasm." Puccini's only comedy, *Gianni Schicchi* was part of a triptych of one-act operas being organized by fellow film director William Friedkin. Santo Loquasto accompanied Allen to design the costumes and sets. "Brilliantly sung and acted down to the most minor character," observed *Times* music critic Mark Swed. "Allen—Woody, that is—manages to be both irreverent and absolutely true to the music and the spirit of the work." Curiously, Allen's few experiments in opera attracted better reviews than his stage directing in New York, or his public clarinet-playing when touring with his band. In fact, the Los Angeles Opera was so universally praised that Allen and *Gianni Schicchi* were booked for the Spoleto festival in Italy in June 2009.

The year 2008 ended with his seventy-third birthday followed by the family's annual overseas holiday, never without visits to London, Paris, and Rome; publicity interviews and meetings with foreign producers; and nowadays always coordinated with his New Orleans Jazz Band for a few concerts in European cities. In Warsaw on the penultimate day of 2008, Allen tootled his clarinet before a sold-out crowd of three thousand.

Soon-Yi was also on the plane with her husband when, for the fourth time in six years, Allen departed for another summer in London, where he'd preside over a cast boasting Anthony Hopkins, Naomi Watts, Gemma Jones, Antonio Banderas, Lucy Punch, Freida Pinto from *Slumdog Millionaire,* and—the sole American among the leads—Josh Brolin. Brolin had worked for all of four days in *Melinda and Melinda*, but after watching him in Oliver Stone's *W.*, a darkly comedic biopic of President George W. Bush, Allen sent the actor an admiring email: "I don't know if you remember me from *Melinda and Melinda*. I was the director. . . ." Brolin, who surely remembered, framed the email. "I don't know to this day whether Woody was serious or not." Allen offered Brolin the pivotal role of a first-time novelist struggling with his second book, as a chasm widens in his marriage. The blocked novelist becomes transfixed by a sexy woman in stages of undress, seen voyeuristically through her window across the street. "My first suggestion was that my character be in a wheelchair," recalled Brolin, referencing Jimmy Stewart in *Rear Window*. "Woody's response to me was simply no."

Allen was still busy in London when Sony Classics released his New York placeholder in mid-June. *Whatever Works* begins haltingly with a lengthy monologue by Larry David, speaking directly to the camera, which establishes Boris, his character, as a soured genius whose jaundiced view of existence has been worsened by divorce and a failed suicide attempt. The mood improves with the arrival of the homeless Melody, an oddball fugitive from Mississippi, irresistibly portrayed by Evan Rachel Wood. A onetime beauty contestant, Melody becomes a stripling Pygmalion to Boris's dyspeptic Henry Higgins. He instructs her to avoid clichés and use bigger words, takes her New York sightseeing, buys her the best knishes, and lectures on the "vast, black, unspeakably violent universe." Warmth and humor emerge, along with quotations from Fred Astaire and *Touch of Evil*. When Melody's parents arrive—also with great names: Marietta (Patricia Clarkson) and John Celestine (Ed Begley Jr.)—all expectations go out the window. Boris does too, literally. The imaginative plotting provides love partners for everyone on New Year's, with a champagne toast to "the irrational heart."

The way ideas persisted and bridged different Woody Allen films, Boris/David walks with a clumsy limp, in the same manner that Will Ferrell boasts of essaying all his college leads in *Melinda and Melinda*. Patricia Clarkson gets the surprisingly fulfilling threesome she was deprived of in *Vicky Cristina Barcelona*. Viagra has a cameo in *Whatever Works*, and it would crop up again in *You Will Meet a Tall Dark Stranger*. What most critics missed when critiquing Larry David as a stand-in for Allen—it was also true of the character played by Josh Brolin in *You Will Meet a Tall Dark Stranger*—is how Boris/David savagely caricatures Allen, mocking his bleak philosophy of life, his crankiness, his weird personal hang-ups. (Boris, while compulsively washing his hands, repetitively sings "Happy Birthday!" to himself.) There is weak comedy, but also wonderful scenes, including a long meetup between Melody's father and a "gay" at a bar—he is Christopher Evan Welch, the narrator of *Vicky Cristina Barcelona*—which attest to *Whatever Work's* overall magnanimous spirit.

Newspapers made bad puns with headlines of the negative reviews: " 'Whatever' Doesn't Work" (*Los Angeles Times*); "Kvetch Your Enthusiasm" (*New York Times*); and "A One-Note Larry David Curbs Any Enthusiasm for Allen's Works" (*Wall Street Journal*). Yet audiences were never going to flock to a Woody Allen film starring Larry David, an un-movie star if there ever was one. The American flop of *Whatever Works*—number thirty-five on the BuzzFeed All-Time List—was followed by low figures overseas. Still, Allen was undaunted.

RETURNING FROM LONDON, Allen plunged into editing and postproduction while revising the script for his next film. Over the upcoming summer he planned to shoot the time-travel romantic comedy he'd abandoned in 2005, revolving around an American couple vacationing in Paris. His story hearkened back to "How I Became a Comedian," the 1971 humor piece he wrote for newspapers, and a script he once dashed off on "spec" for Cary Grant, who came to hear Allen's jazz band in New York, behaving like "the biggest fan in the world," in Allen's words. Fast-talking Hollywood agent Swifty Lazar whispered in Allen's ear, telling him the retired sex symbol was open to a comeback. "So, I cooked up this film where a car pulls up on Sutton Place in Manhattan and Cary Grant is in it and he takes me to a party and all of a sudden we're in 1920s New York." But Grant said no: "I'm retired." Garson Kanin belatedly warned Allen: "Don't ever believe anything Swifty Lazar says."

Allen's script idea became viable again after the French government began offering tax-relief incentives to foreign filmmakers to recoup their production costs, and now, with financing from MediaPro and other European backers, Allen could afford to film his story in Paris. Visiting the French capital at the end of 2009, amid his annual European jaunt, he and Soon-Yi were invited to *petit dejeuner* with French president Nicolas Sarkozy and his wife, the fashion model and singer Carla Bruni-Sarkozy. Struck by Bruni's beauty and elegance, on impulse the film director asked France's first lady if she would consider playing a small part in his Paris project. Soon enough, Owen Wilson, the blond slacker with a cabbage nose, who was a fixture in Wes Anderson indie features and the star of comedy megahits such as *Meet the Parents* and *The Wedding Crashers*, was announced as the film's star, with Rachel McAdams, also from *Wedding Crashers*, as his fiancée.

Wilson's role was originally written for "an Eastern intellectual, who would have been more Ivy League," Allen recalled. "If I was younger, I would have played it—not that I'm intellectual, but I look intellectual. And I couldn't find anybody who was really right who was available and Eastern. And then I was talking with Juliet Taylor, and Owen's name came up." Allen saw Wilson, a native Texan, as most audiences did—"A blond, beachcombing guy with a surfboard." Hastily reworking the role for a "West Coast character," Allen sent the revised script to Wilson, assuring him the dialogue was not sacred. Wilson didn't "nail every preposition exactly," the actor admitted later. "I never had to give him any direction, he knew just what to do," Allen said.

Allen still wrote seven days a week, usually mornings, longhand, often lying in his bed. His staff later typed up his pages. "I don't own a computer, have no idea how to work one, don't have a word processor and have zero interest in technology," the filmmaker told Dave Itzkoff for the *New York Times*. Between script projects, Allen said, his favorite pastime was sipping a beer while watching football games on television. "I take my kids to school in the morning," Allen stated. "I go for walks with my wife, play with my jazz band. Then there's the obligation of the treadmill and the weights to keep in shape so I don't get more decrepit than I am."

While preparing the time-travel romantic comedy, in the spring he also worked "monstrously hard" on recording the audiobooks of what were now four volumes of "little souffles," previously published from 1971 to 2007. "I hated every second of it," Allen said, "regretted that I had agreed to it, and after reading one or two stories each day, found myself exhausted." In June he and his family relocated to Paris, preparing his forty-first feature in as many years. Paris was where he first acted in a script he wrote, "What's New Pussycat?," in 1965. It would always be his second favorite place in the world. He never stopped musing about moving to Paris, even if New York remained first in his heart. A constant refrain in his conversations, Paris seemed omnipresent in his movies, referenced by dialogue, often a sentimental touchstone for his characters. For him as for many in the world, Paris was the center of sophistication. Nowadays it was the city that most loved him and Woody Allen films.

Once again Allen engaged the Iranian-born cinematographer Darius Khondji, who had lensed *Anything Else*. But this was a special milieu for Allen, and Khondji had orders to bathe Paris in a warm glow. The Paris-based production designer was Anne Seibel. Allen's script eschewed any title during the filming, as usual, and only a few insiders knew the story line. The fact that Hemingway, the Fitzgeralds, Gertrude Stein, Josephine Baker, Picasso, Matisse, Degas, Gauguin, Salvador Dalí, and Luis Buñuel were characters in the story leaked to the press and tipped the fact there would be fantastical time-travel and magic besides romance and laughs.

Although Allen was more steeped in Paris than in the environs of London or Barcelona, first came the scouting, and the photography did not begin until July. Bystanders spotted the famous American auteur presiding over actors in scenes at Shakespeare and Company, Notre Dame, the Church of Saint-Étienne-du-Mont, the Paris Opera House, the Arc de Triomphe, Versailles, the Louvre, the Monet gardens in Giverny, and the Saint-Denis flea market. The Musée Rodin was rented for a day. In his seventies, the director worked faster than ever, with little or no rehearsal for the actors and as few takes as possible, before knocking off early if he had amassed his daily quota. On weekends, he, Soon-Yi, and their daughters revisited some of the same touristy sites that cropped up on the daily production log. To fall asleep at night, Allen read thick Tolstoy and Mailer novels, he told *Times*-man Dave Itzkoff via email, "things that had slipped through the cracks over the years."

Allen sent *You Will Meet a Tall Dark Stranger* ahead to Cannes for its world premiere in May, where *Variety*'s Justin Chang set the bar low with his review, grumbling that the new movie was only "fitfully amusing." Perhaps that was because *Stranger* was not much of a comedy; the seriocomic story followed several marriages in shambles, with the husbands, wives, and ex-spouses seeking answers to their life crises. Other US critics carped about the familiar Woody Allen elements when Sony Classics released *You Will Meet a Tall Dark Stranger* in September: the proverbial tortured novelist (Josh Brolin); the migraine-prone wife (Naomi Watts) who seems unable to conceive a child; the older man (Anthony Hopkins) chasing a call-girl gold digger (Lucy Punch); and "the metaphysical pessimism that constitutes Mr. Allen's annual greeting-card message to the human race," in the words of A. O. Scott in the *New York Times*. These critics, if they could go back in time like Owen Wilson, might have told Alfred Hitchcock to lay off the serial killers and sexy blondes, and Ernst Lubitsch—enough with the ménages à trois! Allen's stories, repeated with creative variation in film after film, were the signposts of his imagination, and his artistic compulsions were akin to Hitchcock's or Lubitsch's.

What also may have unsettled critics was *You Will Meet a Tall Dark Stranger*'s openminded attitude toward fortune-telling, reincarnation, and occult communications—which are woven into the plot. Allen did not play those scenes for laughs either. After early preoccupations with Judaism, Catholicism, and God, in the post–Mia Farrow era Woody Allen's films, while still on a first-name basis with Death, were increasingly comfortable with the magical and supernatural. "We need some delusions to keep us going," Allen explained in interviews.

Another unseen storyteller (Zak Orth) glibly narrated *When You Meet a Tall Dark Stranger*, connecting the dots between the intertwined stories. Although Gemma Jones as Naomi Watts's unhappy, intrusive mother, who has been cashiered by Hopkins, her husband of forty years, gets too much screen time in her spiritual quest, the actors were all good, and the disparate scenes were handsomely photographed by Vilmos Zsigmond. The film's ending—still sometimes an Achilles' Heel for Allen—comes too fast. A higher budget and a little re-shooting, as in the good old days, might have eased the problem. *Stranger*'s limited release never got bigger in the US, where so many American critics had written off Allen, telling him he was stale, and if he happened to surprise them with a good picture, then he had "returned to form" and made his first decent picture "in years."

TURNING SEVENTY-FIVE ON December 1 in 2010, Allen worked daily to put the postproduction icing on the Paris time-travel romantic comedy, for which he had long since decided on the unannounced title of *Midnight in Paris*. He would have the movie ready for the Cannes festival in May, cheerfully greeting the world's press, as cameras flashed, posing with French actress Léa Seydoux, who plays Owen Wilson's modern-day infatuation. "I consider myself a hugely lucky filmmaker," he told journalists. "I've never considered myself an artist. I've aspired to be one, but I've never felt that I have the depth or substance or the gift to be an artist." If Kurosawa, Buñuel, Fellini, and Ingmar Bergman were artists, Allen said, "then it's clear as a bell that I'm not an artist."

From Cannes, Allen decamped to Rome, where he had a $25 million budget from Italy's Medusa Film, and a script in preproduction that would raise a similar "declaration of love" to the Eternal City. For the first time in six years Allen himself would perform as an actor amid an international cast that featured Penélope Cruz, Judy Davis, Alec Baldwin, Jesse Eisenberg, and Roberto Benigni. After scouting, the Italian casting, and a welcoming ceremony from the mayor, he called action on "Bop Decameron"—the working title—in July.

The director had to adjust to the dry heat and the bright glare of summer in Rome. He and cameraman Darius Khondji commissioned a Milanese company to create helium-filled balloon-mattresses that could be floated overhead to cut the harsh sunlight. Although there was one rainy scene, Khondji's photography would again be suffused with mellow light and hues. "With Woody," Khondji said, "the best parallel is music. If you play in turn with him and get his rhythm, he will give you all the freedom to improvise as you tell his story."

With the filmmaker absent from the US, *Midnight in Paris* was shrewdly timed for a summer release. Before the scroll of main credits with the customary alphabetical cast listing—the same white Windsor Light Condensed font over a black background Allen had been using since *Annie Hall*—a series of shimmering images of streets and scenery revealed Paris from dawn to dusk, sun-dappled and rain-spattered, underscored by the full three-minute recording of Sidney Bechet's haunting "Si tu vois ma mère." Audiences were thus guided into Allen's love affair with the City of Light, which he shares with Gil (Owen Wilson), the story's protagonist.

Gil is a hack Hollywood scenarist, vacationing with his bride-to-be (Rachel McAdams) and her parents—a Tea Party businessman and his interior-decorator wife—dreaming of a time when he might give up his big studio paychecks, Beverly Hills mansion, and swimming pool, for a novelist's garret in Paris. When their holiday is taken over by his fiancée's onetime boyfriend (Michael Sheen), a know-it all who guides them to palaces and museums, discoursing knowledgeably on art, history, and wine, Gil sulks off to explore the Paris at night he idealizes. Lost in back alleys, he is picked up by a chauffeur-driven 1920s Peugeot and transported back in time to the era of *A Moveable Feast*, to a party for Jean Cocteau where Cole Porter performs "Let's Do It!" and he meets F. Scott and Zelda Fitzgerald; then to the Polidor in the Sixth Arrondissement, where Ernest Hemingway sits waiting at a table. Affable but intimidating, speaking in bullet points, Hemingway offers to show Gil's novel to the discriminating Gertrude Stein, if he'll bring along the manuscript the next day.

This was the setup for which Allen had waited a lifetime, celebrating so many of his perpetual enthusiasms while giving flesh and blood to all the fabulous personalities he might have wished to meet in the bohemian artist and literary circles of Paris in the 1920s. His script is larded with personal touches, and the nuances circle back to his boyhood (Sidney Bechet) and many earlier Woody Allen movies including *Zelig* (watch for Bricktop) and *Manhattan* (Mariel Hemingway's grandfather). Allen was never more in command of the commingling of comedy and romance. Gil has a nostalgic love for the past, which is false and sentimental, as well as a palpable love for the Paris of today—and the Parisian women of today—that will impact his future.

Allen's casting was never better, and the actors who parade by as the famous folk were especially on target: Corey Stoll as an indelible Hemingway, faintly mocking himself; Kathy Bates, an all-wise Gertrude Stein; Adrien Brody, a grandiloquent Salvador Dalí; Tom Hiddleston and Alison Pill as the ill-destined Fitzgeralds. So many dead luminaries pop up, a cheat sheet could have been passed out with the tickets. Some of them are there only to deliver quick in-jokes, as when Gil suggests the surrealistic plot of a future film, *The Exterminating Angel*, to a thoroughly befuddled Luis Buñuel (Adrian de Van). "I don't get it!" Buñuel exclaims. Carla Bruni is surprisingly winning in her turn as a Musée Rodin docent, correcting the know-it-all in one scene, and in another, answering Gil's Woody Allen–ish question: Can a man love two women at the same time? Marion Cotillard is luminous as the muse who has slept her way through Modigliani, Braque, and Picasso, and now has her eye on Gil. "Now" is fluid, and there is a side trip to Maxim's in the belle époque, which Cotillard prefers to the Golden Age of the 1920s. In the end nostalgia is both celebrated and criticized as fuzzy and sentimental.

It is hard to imagine *Midnight* without Wilson. Despite playing, with a glazed look, a "lost soul" who makes Woody Allen–ish side-of-the-mouth comments about living in "a cold, violent, meaningless universe," the khaki-clad, tousle-haired actor brought his likability, painful sincerity, and dogged optimism to the film.

Critics couldn't do much to hurt this good-hearted valentine to Paris. Some tried to find fault with Wilson as a "Woody Allen in quotes and beach blond drag," as Karina Longworth wrote in the *Village Voice*. His "best film in more than a decade" (David Edelstein, *New York* magazine) was still more backhanded praise. "Here's a sentence I never thought I'd write again," Kenneth Turan began his review in the *Los Angeles Times*, "Woody Allen has made a wonderful new picture." A. O. Scott in the *New York Times* conceded, however, that "Mr. Allen has gracefully evaded the trap built by his grouchy admirers and unkind critics—I'm not alone in fitting both descriptions—who complain when he repeats himself and also when he experiments. Not for the first time, but for the first time in a while, he has found a credible blend of whimsy and wisdom."

Many simply saluted the happy experience. Roger Ebert, who over time had emerged as one of Allen's most ardent defenders in the *Chicago Sun-Times*, put it best: "There is nothing to dislike about it. Either you connect with it or not. I'm wearying of movies that are for 'everybody'—which means nobody in particular." The millions of people who flocked to see *Midnight in Paris* didn't care if the surprisingly popular picture was Allen repeating himself or experimenting—of course it was both—and many did not care who directed the movie. Certainly, the vast majority did not worry if Owen Wilson was any kind of Woody Allen replicate. While his once faithful, now fickle audience was undeniably aging, *Midnight in Paris* ultimately was booked on over one thousand screens in the US, a record for Allen, and the time-travel romance was seen by millions of young moviegoers for whom Woody Allen as a comedian, actor, filmmaker, or social phenomenon was not the slightest factor. *Midnight in Paris* is "playing in theaters that have never played a Woody Allen film before," crowed Sony Classics cochairman Michael Barker. "It's getting big numbers in the theaters in Idaho and Montana, in Mississippi and Alabama."

The year 2011 in the American cinema was led by mega-money sequels—with *Harry Potter 2* earning $1.3 billion worldwide and *Kung Fu 2*, *Cars 2*, *Pirates of the Caribbean 4*, and *Mission Impossible 2* also crowding the Top Ten, earning similar hundreds of millions. But *Midnight in Paris* was the most enjoyable adult movie of the summer, earning $56.8 million in US grosses and triple that overseas. A success on anyone's terms, much less Allen's, alone among his post-1992 works *Midnight in Paris* is the only film to rank among his Top Ten at the box-office.

AUTUMN WAS TAKEN up with Allen's new one-act, which was part of another triptych of playlets being produced by Julian Schlossberg. The first-time stage director of the one-acts—Allen's "Honeymoon Hotel," preceded by shorter works from Elaine May and Ethan Coen—was John Turturro, the actor whose career had quickened since his small part in *Hannah and Her Sisters* and with whom Allen had reconnected during the making of *Company Man*. The farcical "Honeymoon Hotel" revolved around members of "a Long Island wedding gone spectacularly wrong," in the words of Charles Isherwood in the *New York Times*, who gather for recriminations at a tacky love motel. The show premiered on Broadway in late October 2011 with a cast that included Steve Guttenberg, Grant Shaud, Mark-Linn Baker, and Julie Kavner, the last the veteran of many Woody Allen films. Some critics loved the Allen contribution (Isherwood: "short and unruly but very funny"), and the one-acts known collectively as *Relatively Speaking* ran for three months at the Brooks Atkinson Theater.

In mid-November, *Woody Allen: A Documentary* was presented as an American Masters special, a PBS series that was like a kind of Good Housekeeping seal of approval. *Curb Your Enthusiasm* director-producer Robert B. Weide supervised the three and a half hours of footage, photographs, and interviews, with part one rooted in Allen's boyhood up to *Stardust Memories*. A second evening squeezed his subsequent thirty-one features into ninety minutes. The documentary skirted the court cases and controversies of the early 1990s, and the interviews came from "within the bubble," as *New York Times* TV critic Mike Hale observed. Soon-Yi was not interviewed, much less Mia Farrow, but Allen (interviewed) and friends (Diane Keaton et al.) helped make for respectable programming that emphatically reappraised his life and career. Its "bubble" approach was no different from other American Masters installments on living artists, from whom cooperation was negotiated.

At year's end hitherto doomsaying movie critics delivered their roundups, with many including *Midnight in Paris* among the best works of 2011. The Directors Guild nominated Allen as Best Director and the Writers Guild gave his script another best nomination in the "original" category. *Midnight in Paris* earned four major Academy Award nominations: Best Picture, Director, Screenplay, and Art Direction (jointly listed as Anne Seibel for production design and Hélène Dubreuil for set decoration). Allen easily won at the Writers Guild, and his script also took Best Original Screenplay during the Oscar telecast of 2012. Presenter Angelina Jolie accepted on behalf of the truant scribe, who was spending the night with his jazz band at the Café Carlyle in New York.

Chapter 12

2012

Stuff Happens

Another Few Masterpieces—The Farrow Family Stirs—Woody Brushes Off a Controversy or Two—and Adopts the Mantle of an Elder Statesman of Film

Asked by one journalist to identify his greatest vice, Allen answered, "Laziness." But the man who, every day, wrote and wrote, and who had made a movie annually for going on fifty years, couldn't stop. "I do the movies just for myself, like an institutionalized person who basket-weaves," Allen explained in one interview. "Busy fingers are happy fingers. I don't care about the films. I don't care if they're flushed down the toilet after I die."

Occasionally an interviewer dared to ask whether his pictures would be improved if Allen spent more time on the writing and filming of them. "They wouldn't be better," Allen told the *Los Angeles Times*. "I have thought about that, yes, but they wouldn't be. When I've had time to do something, it doesn't come out better. There's no correlation between the time spent and how it comes out. It's really about the luck of a good idea."

During postproduction the Rome project acquired the ebullient title of *To Rome with Love*, and Sony Classics, trying to mimic the summer success of *Midnight in Paris*, opened the latest Woody Allen movie in July, following its premiere in the titular city in April. Allen's arrival on the red carpet of New York's Paris Theatre, arm in arm with Soon-Yi, was treated as the homecoming of a prodigal son. "It's always a pleasure coming home," Allen told the press. "I always feel alive here." He hated the sultry Manhattan summer, however. "It was cooler in Rome." Along with Soon-Yi, Penélope Cruz, Greta Gerwig, and comedian Chris Rock—not in the film, alas—Allen attended the premiere and after-party at the Park Avenue Italian restaurant Casa Lever.

Unfortunately, *To Rome with Love* proved no "Midnight in Rome." Allen later said the pressure to create an Italian follow-up to *Midnight in Paris*, which had struck such a worldwide nerve with audiences, might have made him overcompensate with the multiple stories quilted into an omnibus that was overstuffed with characters and incident. It was surrealism (not unlike *Midnight in Paris*) jumbled with farce (sex farce à la *What's New Pussycat?*), underscored by Italian music that ranged from the grandest opera to the cheesiest pop.

Alec Baldwin plays a vacationing architect who bumps into young-American-in-Trastevere Jesse Eisenberg and becomes his mentor. Overused by a director obviously relishing his performance, Baldwin shadows Eisenberg wherever he goes, becoming his love whisperer. Much like other Woody Allen protagonists, Eisenberg is torn between two cuties, the responsible Greta Gerwig and the "polymorphously perverse" Ellen Page, the latter as a smart, talented actress temporarily between boyfriends, perhaps because she is hopelessly neurotic. "It's like filling an inside straight," Baldwin tells Eisenberg. "Even her name is hot—Monica!"

Again, astutely deploying vacationing Americans as characters, Allen's camera visits postcard places, such as the Fontana di Trevi and Frank Gehry's Vitra Design Museum. The many Italian players (half the episodes are entirely subtitled in Italian) enliven their scenes: the known quantities include Roberto Benigni as an ordinary man who wakes up to a celebrity makeover, and Antonio Albanese as a testosterone-charged Italian matinee idol. But the young romantic couple (Alessandro Tiberi and Allessandra Mastronardi) are also appealing—hopelessly in love, while not immune to adulterous temptations.

Penélope Cruz, marking the return of happy hookers in Allen's oeuvre, alone is worth the price of admission, but so is Allen acting a major role in one of his own movies for the last time, not playing a loser at love, but happily married to none other than Judy Davis—and a proud parent besides. "I would have played that [Jesse Eisenberg] part if I was younger," he said ruefully in one interview. "I am too old now, is the problem. I like to get the girl.

Now, I can't play that part, so I am reduced to the father of the fiancée. . . . It's a sad, terrible pill to swallow."

Allen plays Jerry, a retired music recording company A&R man with a sideline as a visionary opera director—think *Rigoletto* with everyone onstage dressed as white mice. Davis is Phyllis, a psychiatrist who zings her husband with Freudian insights. They are in Rome for the wedding of their daughter (the engaging Alison Pill, the Zelda Fitzgerald of *Midnight in Paris*) to a handsome Italian lawyer with left-wing sympathies (Flavio Parenti). Allen's passion for opera is incorporated into the story: the lawyer's father, a mortician, sings glorious arias in the shower, and Jerry decides to "discover" the father. But on dry land the aria singer can never quite deliver the same exciting quality. Jerry has a brainstorm, and the show goes on. While the shower joke, like a few others, is done to death, at times it is very funny, and the Italian tenor Fabio Armiliato is game for the folderol.

"Stuff happens," Alec Baldwin says at the end of *To Rome with Love*, explaining why the architect surrendered his youthful artistic idealism for more financially remunerative work. Nothing serious is going on in this sunny picture, as Allen floats the usual debates between anonymity and celebrity, adultery versus monogamy. But a lot of stuff *does* happen, and much of it is entertaining. Roger Ebert said three of the four interwoven stories were "funny and charming." (The one that became "tiresome," Ebert wrote, was the one with Benigni and his overnight fame.) "If they cannot all be great Woody, it's churlish to complain if they're only good Woody," wrote Ebert in the last review he'd write of a Woody Allen picture. (The Chicago-based critic would pass away in 2013.) "A few critics have said unkind things about his age, which strikes me as bad manners. . . . Is his timing still skilled? Is he still funny? Aren't we happy to have another picture?"

By now in his career, it should have become clear that Woody Allen marched to his own drummer, not straight ahead to sequels, more thrilling thrillers, louder or sillier laughs, or anything else demanded of him by the wits and half-wits, critics or producers. He was a zigger and zagger, a circler-arounder. Allen made movies the way he used to write those Tamiment sketches in the 1950s, following his personal compass, not brooding or seeking perfection, but taking what had almost worked once before and reworking it for the next show.

The reviews were mixed (the movie's "limitations," A. O. Scott wrote in the *New York Times*, were "inseparable from its delights"), and consequently there was a big drop in the *Midnight in Paris* grosses in North America (from $57 to $17 million) and France as well ($14.5 to $4 million). Yet despite the drubbing Italian critics gave to Allen's ode to the Eternal City, *To Rome with Love* proved a colossal hit with moviegoers in Italy and in other nations where Allen's popularity had not yet peaked—his best openings yet in Portugal and Poland, high numbers in Russia and Israel—eventually grossing $65 million worldwide. Not too shabby.

AFTER A TIGHTLY packed spring and early summer of festivals, premieres, and preproduction, in August Allen—much like the protagonist in the first scene of the script he was carrying—boarded a plane for the West Coast. He would orchestrate some scenes later in New York, but first he'd photograph *Blue Jasmine* exteriors in San Francisco, where back in his scrounging days Allen had performed stand-up at the hungry i and sat in with Turk Murphy, now deceased, at Earthquake McGoon's, long since closed. The Golden City was a lucky city for him. Allen had gotten his feet wet on Bay Area locations filming *Take the Money and Run* and *Play It Again, Sam.*

The star of *Blue Jasmine* was Australian actress Cate Blanchett, acclaimed on stage and screen, and winner of a Best Supporting Actress Oscar for her impersonation of Katharine Hepburn in Martin Scorsese's *The Aviator*. Allen telephoned Blanchett in Sydney, where she lived, asking politely if the actress would read a screenplay he'd written with her in mind for the lead, and Blanchett was "gobsmacked" by the honor. After reading Allen's script, Blanchett phoned Allen directly. "It was a really short call. You could count the seconds. 'See you in San Francisco. Thank you.'" The other *Blue Jasmine* cast members included Sally Hawkins and Alec Baldwin, whom the director knew he could count on; Bobby Cannavale, who'd won an Emmy as Will's dim-cop boyfriend on *Will and Grace* and cut a violent swath as a bootlegger in *Boardwalk Empire*; the well-traveled supporting player (Coen brothers, Martin Scorsese, *Boardwalk Empire*) Michael Stuhlbarg; the boyish-looking Peter Sarsgaard; and the stand-up comedians Andrew Dice Clay and Louis C.K. Allen's backstage personnel included *Vicky Cristina Barcelona* cameraman Javier Aguirresarobe, his longtime New York production designer Santo Loquasto, and costume designer Suzy Benzinger—who'd been missing in action from the European productions—along with Alisa Lepselter, Allen's editor of three decades standing.

The title could easily have been "A Streetcar Named F-Line" because the *Blue Jasmine* script explored ideas and themes conspicuous in Tennessee Williams's enduring stage play, which had been Allen's holy grail dating back to the 1950s. As was his wont, Allen, in interviews, adamantly rejected any comparisons to *A Streetcar Named Desire*, insisting "The story [of *Jasmine*] was inspired by an actual incident that my wife told me about that mirrors the story almost exactly." Be that as it may, "the allusions" to *Streetcar*, as Manohla Dargis later wrote in the *New York Times*, are "copious and obvious," ranging "from the French connection that links Blanche [DuBois from *Streetcar*] and Jasmine's names to Mr. Allen's staging of a violent skirmish," to the "blue piano" and jasmine scent mentioned in *Streetcar*, and the New Orleans jazz dominating the musical score.

Allen's masterstroke was updating *Streetcar* and blending it with his own reveries, making "Jasmine French" (the pseudonym of Blanchett's character) the ex-wife of a man like New York financial wheeler-dealer Bernie Madoff, who was convicted of fraud and imprisoned in 2009. (Perhaps this was the "actual incident" Soon-Yi mentioned.) Jasmine's past is a tragic muddle; her husband has hung himself in prison after she betrayed him to police—her revenge for his philandering—and her stepson despises her. On her way to visit her blue-collar sister Ginger (Hawkins) in San Francisco—both adopted into the same family yet from different parents—the elegantly dressed Jasmine is broke, her privileged life in the Hamptons and Upper East Side gone forever. She has become delusional and talks to herself, fellow passengers recoiling, as her flight lands.

The comparisons to *Streetcar* also included Blanchett having starred in a celebrated revival of the Tennessee Williams play at the Brooklyn Academy of Music in 2009, directed by Liv Ullmann. (Allen insisted he had never seen that 2009 revival either.) Aside from this grounding, Blanchett spent time on the Upper East Side, people-watching. The actress also screened Robert B. Weide's documentary about Allen, and along with Hawkins, trained with a vocal coach to hone her American accent. Other performers cautioned Blanchett, "You don't get anything back from Allen," but she found her equilibrium with the director working initially on the San Francisco locations and, later, for the New York and studio scenes. "I felt him simultaneously fascinated by the work," the actress reflected, "and utterly disinterested. And I found that really refreshing because there's no preciousness. The danger, because we all revered him so much, is that we can cover ourselves in cotton wool and make our offerings precious. And I think it's his background in stand-up comedy, but, with him, it works, or it doesn't work. And if it doesn't work, he'll tell you. And if it works, we're moving on. When I realized he was never going to be entirely happy, I stopped trying to please him and just started doing the work."

ALLEN FINISHED *BLUE JASMINE* in New York in October; then came the editing, sound mix, scoring, optical effects, color corrections, and other postproduction stages many filmmakers left to their subordinates. Allen always closely involved himself. According to Ben Hoyle, he also devoted time to a script he planned to shoot in the South of France over the upcoming summer of 2014. And Allen acted in his last picture, to date, for another director.

Back in the spring, Allen had agreed to emote in the independent production John Turturro was preparing called *Fading Gigolo*. Lead roles in other people's movies rarely came his way, and it was this offer from someone he had befriended earlier in his career, not the low money, that convinced him to star in Turturro's fourth feature as a writer-director. Allen had stalled, critiquing various script drafts, before giving in to Turturro's determined wish that he would portray the broke antiquarian book dealer who, in the story, becomes the world's most unlikely (wait for it) pimp, hawking the services of a shy, flower shop attendant, played by Turturro. The shy florist blossoms into a high-priced call boy, and among his "Johns" are beauties Sofía Vergara and Sharon Stone, the latter setting some sort of record for odd appearances in Allen-affiliated films.

Allen would essay his role for Turturro in November and December, amid the final postproduction of *Blue Jasmine* and planning for the next summer's *Magic in the Moonlight*. December marked his birthday and Christmas, which Allen had learned to accept and enjoy because Soon-Yi did. They stayed in New York for New Year's Eve, their annual travel to Paris postponed until spring, and raised a glass to 2013 at Le Cirque.

After signing off on *Blue Jasmine*, there was time again for Knicks games, off-Broadway plays such as *Old Jews Telling Jokes*—Sam Hoffman and Eric

Spiegelman's adaptation of their web series with jokes and anecdotes about the trajectory of Jewish American experiences—Lincoln Center ballet, the annual amfAR black-tie gala during Fashion Week, and bundled-up walks along Park Avenue with his wife and daughters. There was even a little time for nonmovie projects. Allen squeezed out an essay on "Hypochondria" for the *New York Times*. ("What worries me most is winding up a vegetable—any vegetable, and that includes corn, which under happier circumstances I rather like.") And he finally got down to brass tacks on the Broadway show that was intended to cap his theatrical momentum of the past decade. Allen had long procrastinated about adapting his and Douglas McGrath's script for *Bullets over Broadway* into a stage musical, and now he'd have to do the job without friend McGrath, who was toiling on a Broadway show based on Carole King's songbook. The Carole King musical was due to open on Broadway in early 2014, around the same time as the projected *Bullets over Broadway*.

His sister, Letty Aronson, and stage producer Julian Schlossberg—and Jean Doumanian before them—had for years pestered Allen about the potential for turning *Bullets over Broadway* into a stage musical. The main thing the original movie lacked was music, except for fleeting nightclub scenes, and in early 2000 Marvin Hamlisch, who had composed the scores for Allen's first two pictures, *Take the Money and Run* and *Bananas*, and *Rent* lyricist Craig Carnelia began fooling around with songs. The Doumanian lawsuit crimped their progress, then Allen couldn't find the necessary window of set-aside time, until finally he became diffident about having original music.

Before Allen flew to San Francisco for *Blue Jasmine* the long-dormant idea for a *Bullets over Broadway* musical had been infused with fresh energy by Susan Stroman, the former choreographer turned five-time Tony-winning director, who in 2001 guided Mel Brooks's *The Producers*—and later, *Young Frankenstein*—to unparalleled success for a movie retooled as a Broadway musical: a record fifteen Tony nominations (twelve wins), sell-out crowds, a seven-year run. Allen had faltered as a stage director. He needed someone to feel good about, who came highly recommended. "People who knew her told me she was a pleasure to work with, very creative, and had a wonderful sense of humor," he told John Lahr. "She had worked very well with Mel."

Stroman had never met Woody Allen before the producers phoned her in April 2012. In middle age, with all the bounce of the chorus girl she once was and looking like one too with "blond hair, a round open face, high cheekbones and a ring-a-ding smile," in Lahr's words, the stage director instantly communed with Allen over his decision to turn *Bullets* into a jukebox musical, utilizing only "existing music" from the 1920s. Stroman knew the American songbook as well as Allen, and they enjoyed trading favorites, narrowing the tunes, discussing the script, batting around cast and staging ideas. They often convened, in the fall of 2012 and spring of 2013, on the fifth floor of Allen's townhouse. "We would take the stairs, because he won't go in the elevator," said Stroman. "We worked in the children's playroom. We sat on children's chairs at a low children's table."

With Stroman came some of the same team that had crafted the Mel Brooks Broadway musicals, including orchestrator Doug Besterman and costume designer William Ivey Long. Stroman herself would choreograph the dances, as she always did with her musicals. The man whose production design had enhanced the 1995 movie, Santo Loquasto, was also around to preside over the stage show's scenic design; while a comfort factor on Woody Allen films, Loquasto had never allowed the Broadway half of his career to flag. The casting would begin in June, with workshop scenes in October after Allen returned from France, and run-throughs planned for January 2014.

THE FAMILY'S BRIEF Paris trip in the spring allowed Allen to meet with the French producers of his upcoming summer project. While he was away from the US, his high school buddy and onetime collaborator Mickey Rose died of cancer in Beverly Hills, at age seventy-seven. Rose had stayed busy in television as a staff writer of *The Smothers Brothers Show*, *The Dean Martin Show*, and (most prolifically) *The Tonight Show* with Johnny Carson, while directing one big-screen comedy, *Student Bodies*, in 1981, which has a cult following. "No more malteds" was the inexorable meaning of death, his lifelong friend, three years older than Allen, once said.

Back in New York the film director called in Emma Stone, the former child actress, now twenty-seven. Stone had just broken out as the love interest of the titular superhero in *The Amazing Spider-Man* and was in New

York to repeat her role in the sequel. Stone's mother timed their meeting on her cell phone, and it took all of four minutes for Allen to know that the fresh-scrubbed, apple-cheeked actress, more of a seeming ingenue than Scarlett Johansson, was perfect for what he had in mind for the South of France story. Allen kept his Mondays at the Café Carlyle until June and his slated departure abroad. One of the last things he did before leaving was preside over a staged reading for investors in *Bullets over Broadway*, and announce the lead casting of Zach Braff, who'd portrayed his son in *Manhattan Murder Mystery* before going on to star on television in the hit series *Scrubs*. Braff would play the quixotic playwright David Shayne, the role filled by John Cusack in the movie.

The *Magic in the Moonlight* producing team continued to enforce Allen's artistic independence on production budgets that were pennywise according to any Hollywood metric. There were roughly a dozen *Moonlight* producers: seven credited on the screen, another five noted on IMDb.com. As a group they covered all the chapters of the filmmaker's life and career and reflected his managerial and financial acumen. There were six French producers to watch over the Gallic needs and interests. Allen's once-upon-a-time personal manager Jack Rollins, nearing a hundred years of age and no longer involved on any actual basis, was still listed as executive producer. Allen's sister, Letty Aronson, and his onetime accountant Stephen Tenenbaum were the lead Americans. Coproducer Helen Robin spanned the United Artists and Orion years, during which time she had risen up as an assistant under Robert Greenhut. Edward Walson, the president and owner of a New Jersey based cable company, first invested in Allen's play *Relatively Speaking* and graduated to producer on *Blue Jasmine*. There were always new names, including quiet Americans, and one new investor was Ronald L. Chez of the Merriman Capital bank in Chicago, who knew Allen in passing and phoned his office out of the blue one day to say how much he loved his films and would like to be involved. Chez's $9 million chit secured half the production coin, and the investment banker promised $20 million over the next three Woody Allen movies. Sony Classics, run by people who began their careers at United Artists and Orion, paid for the North American rights, while the French, who still led the world in admiration for Allen, took the French and international prerogatives.

The cast that Allen assembled in the South of France was a mix of British and Americans, with the contingent of the former embodied by Colin Firth, middle-aged but still dapper; Simon McBurney, known for *Tinker Tailor Soldier Spy*; Eileen Atkins, a veteran who had cocreated *Upstairs, Downstairs* and memorably appeared in Robert Altman's *Gosford Park*, among many stage and screen credits; and Australian Jacki Weaver, who would be Oscar-nominated for her role in *Silver Linings Playbook* in 2013. The young Americans included Stone and Hamish Linklater, the dog-faced costar of Julia Louis-Dreyfus's TV series *The New Adventures of Old Christine*. The reputable Marcia Gay Harden, who'd won an Academy Award for *Pollock*, assumed a supporting role. French players filled smaller parts, but the French were prevalent behind the camera.

Allen had written a script that evoked the long-ago, otherworldly *A Midsummer Night's Sex Comedy*. A metaphysical romantic comedy, set in 1928, his screen story was partly located on a sprawling country estate in southern France, with its intrigues revolving around a London magician who poses as a Chinese conjuror onstage (his best trick: vanishing a live elephant). The London magic man takes on the challenge of debunking a young American clairvoyant, whose communications with the spirit world have the aim of bilking the dowager of a coal-rich Pittsburgh family living in the French countryside. Cameraman Darius Khondji was back for his fourth Woody Allen picture. Allen had production designer Anne Seibel and costumer Sonia Grande from previous European ventures. The score would mix Stravinsky, Ravel, and Beethoven with the American songbook and vintage Berlin cabaret from modern German singer Ute Lemper.

"Open, funny, warm and bright," as actress Parker Posey later described her, Stone had a nervous energy and youthful spirit that were contagious. The press described the actress as Allen's "new muse," which was going too far but, like his previous muses Diane Keaton and Scarlett Johansson, Stone's exuberance, gibes, and bantering with Allen made the filming a blithe experience for everyone. Allen was still photographing the scenes in France when, in mid-July, the past year's *Blue Jasmine* starring Cate Blanchett premiered in New York.

THE NEUROTIC UPPER EAST SIDER awash in Stoli Martinis; the skunk husband up to his neck in women and financial chicanery; interior decorating delusions; a French au pair who spoils fond memories of Paris; adoptive sisters and treacherous mothers; acute anxiety and fear of doctors; a perfect terrace for a telescope—this was again Woody's world, endlessly refurbished in films. Jasmine French—real name: Jeannette—was the cousin once removed of Geraldine Page in *Interiors*, but this story was more Tennessee Williams than Ingmar Bergman, and allowed Allen to finally achieve the power and depth he long had sought in an ultra-drama.

The casting and performances were unerring. Grocery clerk Sally Hawkins, who'd be Oscar-nominated, and grease-monkey boyfriend Bobby Cannavale sympathetically embodied the working class. Andrew Dice Clay, whose heyday was the 1990s, made a startling impression as Hawkins's justly embittered first husband, cheated out of his lottery winnings by Alec Baldwin. Baldwin's duplicitous role was oddly colorless. Preying dentist Michael Stuhlbarg and hoodwinked suitor Peter Sarsgaard ably delivered unenviable parts. Cate Blanchett dominated: imploding and exploding, quivering with fragility and arrogance, the villain of her own self-destruction, as was the case with so many female characters in other Woody Allen films. The director was as comfortably at home in San Francisco—"The city is so beautiful, so European," Jasmine rhapsodizes—as he had been in London, Barcelona, Rome, and Paris. From its final image the movie could be understood as the backstory of a Chanel-dressed homeless woman, her clothes soiled and torn, muttering aloud to herself on a park bench.

Many critics embraced *Jasmine* as one of Allen's most riveting triumphs. "A brilliantly effective star vehicle," wrote the oft-equivocal Joe Morgenstern in the *Wall Street Journal*, "the filmmaker's strongest work in years." Anne Hornaday, even more of an Allen skeptic, echoed in the *Washington Post*: "To say that *Blue Jasmine* marks some kind of return to 'serious' form is unforgivably condescending, because his work has been so remarkably diverse and entertaining, even with one or two misfires. Still, this one feels different." Manohla Dargis in the *New York Times* hailed "his most sustained, satisfying and resonant film since *Match Point*."

Male and female journalists praised Jasmine French as the latest in a long line of "strong and memorable women" in Woody Allen pictures, as Dave Itzkoff wrote in the *New York Times*, "as much a hallmark of his movies as the venerable Windsor font in their credits." There was a surfeit of feature articles about Blanchett's wardrobe—"I see her in Chanel," Allen, always attentive to costume and accessories, had instructed Suzy Benzinger—her Vuitton luggage, the Birkin bag she carries like a shield. *Jasmine* drew favorable attention from musicologists too. "Blue Moon," which Jasmine remembers ruefully from her first date with her louse husband, was a 1934 Rodgers and Hart tune revivified by Zambian-born, Grammy-winning pianist Conal Fowkes, who'd been working with Allen since *Midnight in Paris*. The song was "guaranteed to stick in your mind long after summer ends," Ben Brantley wrote in the *Times*. There was also rowdy New Orleans jazz from Louis Armstrong, King Oliver, Jimmie Noone, Mezz Mezzrow, Sidney Bechet, Lizzie Miles, and Trixie Smith.

Audiences responded. On the strength of the publicity and reviews, by August *Jasmine* was being shown in fifty US theaters and packing in people desperate for something beyond comic-book movies. Another Woody Allen movie was the grown-up hit of the American summer. Eventually *Blue Jasmine* would gross $33.4 million in North America and several times that around the globe. It appeared on many critics' best lists and received nominations and year-end awards from groups and organizations nationally and internationally.

THE GREAT RECTIFICATION CAMPAIGN had not worked on the Farrow family, and they were stirring. Allen's run of successes—*Match Point*, *Midnight in Paris*, and especially the woman-centered *Blue Jasmine*—galled them.

Maureen Orth returned, in the November 2013 *Vanity Fair*, with a feature that circled back to check in with Mia Farrow twenty years after the scandals and controversies of the early 1990s. Mounting acclaim for *Blue Jasmine* was not on the actress's mind, however, Orth insisted in her piece titled "Momma Mia!," which was advanced to the press in October. Farrow said she "did not know what I was talking about" when Orth mentioned the recent Woody Allen picture. Orth herself drew simplistic parallels between *Jasmine* and what happened between Allen and Farrow. "*Blue Jasmine* is about two very different adopted sisters," she wrote. "Jasmine (Cate Blanchett) has changed her name (as a number of Mia's children have). A scene in which Jasmine's rich and crooked husband (Alec Baldwin) confesses his infidelity with a teenage au pair is played out in their New York apartment, and Jasmine freaks out. After Mia reacted to the news of Soon-Yi, Allen's circle sought to characterize her as a vengeful female, drinking and popping pills, as Cate Blanchett does. . . ."

The pretext for "Momma Mia!" was the high honor Farrow and her twenty-five-year-old son Ronan, formerly Satchel/Seamus/Sean, were due to receive for their social activism. This was the annual Richard C. Holbrooke Award for Social Justice given by Blue Card, an organization that assisted Holocaust survivors. Although "her focus is no longer on acting"—her last film had been Todd Solondz's *Dark Horse* in 2011—and the sixty-eight-year-old actress was "far removed from the media circus," in Orth's words, she boasted 233,000 followers on Twitter.

In "Momma Mia!" Orth recapped Farrow's life story, dwelling on Frank Sinatra, described as the great love of the actress's life, before moving on to André Previn, Woody Allen, Soon-Yi, Ronan, and Dylan. The journalist spoke to eight of Farrow's fourteen children and many of her friends, who painted her as a complicated heroine: "a little bit Joan of Arc," second husband Previn was quoted, "it was a bit much; if you went over there, all you discussed was Africa." One of the children was thirty-nine-year-old Fletcher Previn, "his mother's protector," in Orth's words, who lived next door to Farrow in Connecticut. A computer geek since a teenager, who had grown up to be an IBM information officer, Fletcher had "painstakingly photoshopped Woody Allen out of every single family photo and edited him out of family videos," according to Orth. Fletcher said proudly of this anti-*Zelig*-like achievement: "We can look at them and be reminded of the good and not be reminded of the bad." Among the children not interviewed were Soon-Yi and, just as noticeably, thirty-five-year-old Moses Farrow, about whom there was only a short paragraph hinting that the filmmaker's adopted son no longer voted with the household majority: "He is a family therapist and a photographer. Separated from his wife and two children, Moses does not keep in touch with any of the others."

Buried in the recap were nuances and changes in the old story—retired Connecticut prosecutor Frank Maco admitting he should have referred to seven-year-old Dylan, in public statements, as a child "complainant" not as a "victim"—while in the main upholding Mia and Dylan's long-standing rendition. The Farrow narrative was supported by the first public interview ever with now twenty-eight-year-old Dylan, "a college graduate, married to an information-technology specialist who serves as her buffer," in Orth's words. "Before our conversation, which lasted four hours, I promised her I would not reveal where she lives or other identifying details. Quick-witted and extremely intelligent, she is writing and illustrating a five-hundred-page novel in the *Game of Thrones* genre."

Orth guided Dylan through a painful recitation of what she said had transpired in 1992, which was similar to Orth's previous account in *Vanity Fair*, again with slight revisions. Dylan now said the purported attic abuse was an "isolated" incident of sexual abuse in her relationship with her father. "A lot I don't remember, but what happened in the attic I remember," she told Orth. Dylan blamed herself for much of the Farrow-Previn travail and upheaval that followed her abuse allegations. The girl "became reclusive and plunged into severe depression. At one point she started cutting herself," and made "a half-hearted attempt at suicide," wrote Orth.

Jazz gave her the shivers, because Dylan recalled herself as a little girl sitting between Allen's legs ("I felt like a dog or something") when he played his clarinet on Mondays at the Carlyle. Her depression was "exacerbated" when Allen sent her a typed letter from London in 2004, during the filming of *Match Point*, wishing his daughter a happy nineteenth birthday and saying he yearned to meet her "anytime, anywhere and would send a helicopter to her," according to Orth, because—Dylan said—he "wanted to set the record straight about what your mother has told you. Love, your father." When, as a college senior, Dylan received "a large stuffed mail envelope" from Allen, with the "fake return name: Lehman," her depression was triggered anew. Inside was "a four-inch-thick explosion of pictures of me and him—pictures, pictures, pictures everywhere. Some had tack holes in them. There was never anybody else in the pictures." The photo package was "scary," Dylan said. ("None of them was inappropriate," Orth added, in case readers wondered.) Allen enclosed a letter, which said, according to Orth, "I thought you'd want some pictures of us, and I want you to know that I still think of you as my daughter and my daughters think of you as their sister. Soon-Yi misses you."

Ronan was minimally noted and quoted. "I am so proud of my family," Ronan told Orth, saying that growing up with siblings who suffered from cerebral palsy and blindness helped him understand societal "problems and needs." His limited input was curious because Ronan was generally regarded as the light of Farrow's life, and often they acted as one, as was the case the past June when he tweeted, "Happy father's day—or as they call it in my family, happy brother-in-law's day." To which Farrow, retweeting, added: "Boom."

He had been calling himself Ronan since 2007 when, not quite twenty, he began sharing bylines with his mother, often op-ed pieces that took liberal political stances. Following his graduation from Yale Law School, Farrow had joined President Obama's administration, working under diplomat Holbrooke and later for Secretary of State Hillary Clinton as a global youth adviser from 2009 to 2012. He left government for a Rhodes scholarship studying poverty in underdeveloped nations, writing a thesis he'd later turn into a book. Now nearing age twenty-six, Ronan had eased his way into journalism. He had grown tall and blond, resembling his mother in his Peter Pan looks. Since 2011 he had been romantically involved with the former Obama speechwriter Jon Lovett, a Long Island native, five years older than him, who'd turned podcaster and television producer.

How and why Ronan grew to be so tall (five feet, ten inches), when his parents were both short, became one of the side mysteries of his life story—like how often and for how many years he was breastfed as a boy. Ronan told interviewers he incurred a bone infection in the Sudan at age nineteen, which over the years had to be treated with multiple surgeries, crutches, and braces. Pro–Woody pundit Robert B. Weide, in his blog, enjoyed taunting Ronan with hearsay about Ronan resorting to the Ilizarov apparatus, which can stretch the bones in limbs. Weide theorized Ronan had undergone such painful treatment to extend his height and thus fulfill his mother's abiding ambition that he grow up with looks that evoked a tall, handsome media personality.

Ronan's height fueled other rumors. The single mind-boggling revelation to come out of Orth's *Vanity Fair* article had to do with his paternity. Farrow was going on and on about Sinatra ("He came back, over and over and over and over . . . I mean, we never really split up") when Orth mentioned a Liz Smith item from her column back in August 2012, wondering why Ronan had been visiting Nancy Sinatra Jr. in Los Angeles, which "has caused the anti–Woody Allen contingent to point out that such a connection gives heft to the ongoing theory that Ronan is not the son from [Mia's] relationship with Woody, but from her postdivorce romantics with the late

Sinatra himself," in Smith's words. Orth "asked Mia point-blank if Ronan was the son of Frank Sinatra," she wrote. "Possibly," Farrow replied. "No DNA tests have been done," Orth added coyly.

The Blue Card event at the Museum of Natural History fell during the same week that *Vanity Fair* was delivered to subscribers and newsstands, and roughly coincided with the announcement Ronan would host his own MSNBC show, *Ronan Farrow Daily*, starting in February. Ronan declined to comment on the Sinatra gossip at the Natural History Museum event, but he tweeted to his "nearly 140,000 followers," according to the *New York Times*: "Listen, we're all 'possibly' Frank Sinatra's son." True or not, the hook had been deeply set, and new MSNBC colleague Chris Matthews set the tone by referring to Ronan as "Young Blue Eyes."

ALLEN COULD ONLY have read *Vanity Fair* with wide brown eyes. His nonparticipation in "Momma Mia!" was explained briefly: "Woody Allen's lawyer Elkan Abramowitz says that Allen still denies the allegations of sexual abuse." The film director surely knew about the Frank Sinatra tease in Liz Smith's column—his old friend Liz, actually a pretty good journalist. Even so, he had to be taken aback by Mia Farrow's wink-wink to Sinatra as Ronan's father. The update on Dylan (her depression, attempted suicide, quailing when her father reached out to her) might have been sad, surprising news to him. Back from France and for weeks into the fall, Allen doled out interviews promoting *Blue Jasmine*, but made no public comments about his children: Moses, Ronan, Dylan.

Amid the postproduction for *Magic in the Moonlight* he penned the script for next year's project, which he was calling "The Boston Story" because the story was going to be set in Boston. Chiefly, he devoted himself to the *Bullets over Broadway* musical. Except for Zach Braff as David Shayne, the casting had not progressed very far—nor could it—while he was in France. While Allen still felt comfortable with director Susan Stroman, he was slow to make up his mind about who should play Helen Sinclair, the grande dame role that had won an Oscar for Dianne Wiest. He and Stroman met with stage divas Patti LuPone, Bernadette Peters, and Betty Buckley, but Allen, mumbling and averting his eyes, could not be nudged into taking a marquee name as box office insurance, something he never did for his movies. He held out for Marin Mazzie, who was younger and less of a Broadway goddess than the others, although highly regarded, a three-time Tony winner, the star of the *Kiss Me Kate* revival in 1999, which Allen had seen. Additional casting was also marshaled—Nick Cordero as Cheech, Heléne Yorke as Olive—as Allen reworked the script, and he and Stroman wrangled over songs.

When Allen put his foot down, as he did when choosing a nonsensical ditty about his favorite breakfast fruit—"Yes, We Have No Bananas!"—for the show's closing number, his word was law. Yet he had learned from previous stage collaborations to leave the directing to Stroman, and her buoyant personality won him over time and again. Stroman was irresistibly creative, and moreover, in the words of musical supervisor Glen Kelly, another holdover from the Mel Brooks musicals who was penning additional lyrics for *Bullets over Broadway*, she "rules by niceness." The twenty-odd songs ultimately included chestnuts like "Up a Lazy River," "I'm Sitting on Top of the World," and Cole Porter's "Let's Misbehave"—the latter also heard on the *Bullets over Broadway* movie score as well as under the opening and closing credits of *Everything You Always Wanted to Know About Sex**. These were combined with more esoteric borrowings from the Great Black American Songbook: Sidney Bechet, Jelly Roll Morton, the Original Dixieland Jass Band, Butterbeans and Susie, and Clarence Williams's Blue Five.

The Farrow family had set in motion a series of attacks against Allen, however, which would peak just as *Bullets over Broadway* rehearsals got underway. It so happened the previous September, following the release of *Blue Jasmine*, that the Hollywood Foreign Press Association had announced Allen as the recipient of its lifetime Cecil B. DeMille Award, to be bestowed on the filmmaker at the organization's January 12, 2014, annual awards dinner. "There is no one more worthy of this award than Woody Allen," organization president Theo Kingma declared in a press release. "His contribution to filmmaking has been phenomenal, and he is an international treasure." The Golden Globes, as the Hollywood Foreign Press Association awards dinner was colloquially known, had increased its activity and visibility in recent years, and the annual dinner event, which was broadcast internationally, was widely hyped as a run-up to and indicator of the Academy Awards.

Since no one expected Allen to materialize physically at the Golden Globes, *Magic in the Moonlight* star Emma Stone had been deputized to pay tribute to the absent master ("Woody's work has been changing the way we think about love, life, and the pursuit of neuroses for decades"), and the actress most identified with his heyday, Diane Keaton, agreed to accept the award. After a highlight reel, Keaton took the stage at the occasion, offering a toast to Allen and the "world's most captivating actresses" who had appeared in his movies, one of whom, Cate Blanchett, won the Golden Globe for Best Actress in a Drama (i.e., *Blue Jasmine*) during the evening. "They wanted to be in his films," Keaton said of herself and the other actresses in rambling remarks. "They wanted to because Woody's women can't be compartmentalized. They struggle, they love, they fall apart, they dominate, they're flawed. They are, in fact, the hallmark of Woody's work. But what's even more remarkable is absolutely nothing links these unforgettable characters from the fact that they came from the mind of Woody Allen." Keaton conceded Allen would have none of that, and if he was watching her speech, he'd probably say "get the hook and get her off the goddam stage," at which point the producers cut away from any more cursing. Keaton ended by goofily singing the Girl Scout song "Make New Friends," which she dedicated to her longtime friend.

Ronan Farrow was watching and waiting. After Keaton's comments he took to Twitter: "Missed the Woody Allen tribute—did they put the part where a woman publicly confirmed he molested her at age 7 before or after *Annie Hall*?" Ronan appended a link to the *Vanity Fair* piece. His mother, Mia, who had logged off her account as Keaton walked onstage, commented on her Twitter feed: "A woman has publicly detailed Woody Allen's molestation of her at age 7. Golden Globe tribute showed contempt for her & all abuse survivors."

By that late date there wasn't much the Farrow-Previns could do about the 2014 Oscar nominations, which were announced three days later on January 15. *Blue Jasmine* received three nods: Cate Blanchett for Best Actress, Sally Hawkins for Supporting Actress, Allen for Original Screenplay. Allen's script was also Writers Guild–nominated. Still, it wasn't too late to influence Oscar voters, and to that end Nicholas Kristof brought an "open letter" from Dylan Farrow to *New York Times* op-ed editor Trish Hall, asking to run it in the op-ed pages, one of the most coveted placements in American journalism. Kristof wrote a lot in his columns about child trafficking and abuses, so he had gravitas on the issue. Knowing Kristof's "famous friends" included Mia Farrow, Hall debated the decision ("The allegations were not new, but her piece was wrenching"), consulted with higher-ups, and ultimately rejected Dylan's letter "because, by definition, an op-ed does not give the other party a chance to comment. It seemed unfair to run an article alleging a crime without getting a reaction from Allen."

It took Kristof a few days to devise his solution, publishing the unedited "open letter" from Dylan on his *Times* blog on February 1, and on the next day, February 2, excerpting the letter along with his editorial commentary in his *Times* column: "Dylan Farrow's Story." Kristof's strategy "seemed fine to me," Hall later wrote. "It didn't have the same legal ramifications, because in his column, Nick could ask Allen for comment." "Full disclosure: I am a friend of her mother, Mia, and her brother Ronan," Kristof noted, parenthetically in his fourth paragraph, adding, "I reached out to Allen several days ago and he declined to comment on the record."

Thus Kristof, a two-time Pulitzer Prize winner, an essayist not known for his sophistication about film but for his political and moral rectitude—like Farrow a Christian but "not a particularly religious" one, in his words—elevated "Dylan's Story" into a national discussion. Describing Dylan as "a writer and artist," Kristof revealed she "is now married and living in Florida." Allen's adopted daughter had recently been diagnosed with posttraumatic stress disorder, Kristof wrote—a detail missing from "Momma Mia!"—and after hearing about the Golden Globes "she curled up in a ball on her bed hysterically." Dylan "got in touch with me," Kristof explained. People have "weighed in on all sides" of the "lively debate" about "whether it is appropriate to honor a man who is an artistic giant but also was accused years ago of child molestation," but "one person who hasn't been heard out is Dylan," Kristof wrote, neglecting to mention Maureen Orth's interview in *Vanity Fair.*

The newspaper version was sanitized. "I know it's 'he said, she said,'" Kristof quoted Dylan from his interview with her. "But to me, it's black and white because I was there." Dylan said she was coming forward now because "for so long Woody Allen's acceptance silenced me. It felt like a personal rebuke, like the awards and accolades were a way to tell me to shut up and go away." Yet "survivors of sexual abuse who have reached out to me" gave her heart and strength, and she was determined to fight "the message that Hollywood sends."

The blog version was more graphic with wrenching intimacies the staid

Times might have frowned upon publishing, quite apart from the journalistic ethics. "Why publish an account of an old case on my blog?" Kristof wrote, introducing Dylan's first-person narrative. "Partly because the Golden Globe lifetime achievement award to Allen ignited a debate about the propriety of the award. Partly because the root issue here isn't celebrity but sex abuse. And partly because countless people on all sides have written passionately about these events, but we haven't fully heard from the young woman who was at the heart of them. . . ."

Neither the blog nor print version added major revelations to the long courtroom and newspaper record, as the *Times* op-ed editor had determined. As in the *Vanity Fair* piece, Dylan recalled her earliest apprehensions and fears of Allen as a little girl, while embellishing some of what had been previously alleged. "I didn't like it when he would place his head in my naked lap and breathe in and out," she said, suggesting that what supposedly occurred in the television room at Frog Pond on August 4, 1992, happened more than once. (Her mother, in *What Falls Away*, said therapists had worked with Allen to stop him "putting his face in her [Dylan's] lap," without ever using the word "naked.") "There were experts willing to attack my credibility," Dylan wrote, before introducing a word into her account that was having a renewed vogue in the American idiom. "There were doctors willing to *gaslight* [author's emphasis] an abused child."* Not her mother Mia, "who found within herself a well of fortitude that saved us from the chaos a predator brought into our house."

Among the apparent new specifics in her "open letter" on Kristof's blog was twenty-eight-year-old Dylan's first public assertion that in the "dim, closet-like attic on the second floor of our house" back on that fateful August day in 1992, her father had instructed the little blonde girl to "lay on my stomach and play with my brother's electric train set. Then he sexually assaulted me. He talked to me while he did it, whispering that I was a good girl, that this was our secret, promising that we'd go to Paris and I'd be a star in his movies." Dylan wrote she would always remember "staring at that

* "Gaslighting" refers obliquely to a psychological thriller directed by Allen favorite George Cukor, *Gaslight* from 1944, based on Patrick Hamilton's stage play, in which a woman (played by Ingrid Bergman) descends into insanity after a series of incidents staged and manipulated by her devious, murderous husband (Charles Boyer). Brought back into vogue during the Trump presidency, "gaslighting" became loose usage for, according to *Merriam-Webster*, a person or group subjecting someone "to a series of experiences that have no rational explanation."

toy train, focusing on it as it traveled on tracks in a circle around the attic," adding "to this day, I find it difficult to look at toy trains."

This putative train set would become a stubborn point of contention. Moses Farrow, in 2018, disputed his sister, stating flatly there was no electric train set in the attic, no room for any such elaborate toy, and that Dylan, over time, had conflated her memories with another brother's toy train that was set up in a play shed outdoors at Frog Hollow. In *Allen v. Farrow*, the sensationalized 2021 documentary about the case, Dylan reprised the train set anecdote, and the documentarists produced a rough sketch of the attic, generated by the state police during their investigation, showing a train. But what kind of train set was it? Nanny Kristi Groteke, in her courtroom testimony, described the train as "big heavy, plastic green tracks and they fit into each other like puzzle pieces, and the train is a train car that is made for a child to sit on and ride." *American Masters* documentarist turned pro-Woody blogger Robert B. Weide supplied a photo of the sort of nonelectric, giant train in the attic that never went around and around on tracks, as Dylan had implied, like the train in Dory Previn's song "With My Daddy in the Attic," with a clarinet-playing father molesting his daughter.

In the second paragraph of the print version of his column, Kristof performed his journalistic duty, noting blandly: "Allen's defenders correctly note that he denies the allegations, has never been convicted and should be presumed innocent." Yet the columnist had engaged in textbook McCarthyism, another term from the past, stretching back to Senator Joseph McCarthy's 1950 claim that over two hundred Communist Party members held jobs at the State Department, a claim that helped to ignite the Red Scare in the US. *Merriam-Webster* defines McCarthyism as, in part, "the use of tactics involving personal attacks on individuals by means of widely publicized indiscriminate allegations especially on the basis of unsubstantiated charges."

Later in his piece, for the first time in the paper of record, Kristof opened the door to a generalized indictment of sex abusers, with the rote inclusion of Woody Allen's name. "Look, none of us can be certain what happened," the columnist wrote of the child-abuse claims. His column did not pretend to have investigated the allegations; Kristof referred to the incident as though all claims and counterclaims were common knowledge. "Shouldn't the standard to honor someone be that they are unimpeachably, well, honorable?" Kristof warned rhetorically. "The Golden Globes sided with Allen, in effect accusing Dylan either of lying or not mattering. That's the message that celebrities in film, music and sports too often send to abuse victims."

Dylan's "open letter" carried the same warning for Hollywood, with celebrities targeted by name. "What if it had been your child, Cate Blanchett? Louis C.K.? Alec Baldwin? What if it had been you, Emma Stone? Or you, Scarlett Johansson. You knew me when I was a little girl, Diane Keaton. Have you forgotten me?"

SUSAN STROMAN ARRIVED at the *Bullets over Broadway* rehearsals on Monday morning, February 3, keenly aware of Nicholas Kristof's *New York Times* column and Dylan Farrow's "open letter" on his blog, which had leaped and bounded across America in print, broadcast, and social media. The Broadway director convened the company to address "the situation," which existentially threatened the musical that was scheduled to open in early April. "We never go into the personal lives of those around us," Stroman said. "We don't know anything about personal lives—we only know about talent. We're here to put on a show, and we're here to talk only about the show." Later, Stroman told John Lahr she "never broached the subject" of Dylan with Allen. "We have no small talk. He's never asked me anything about my personal life, and I wouldn't ask him anything about his."

After Kristof's column, the *Times* was barraged with letters—some supporting Dylan, others defending Allen—and inside the newspaper there was also division and soul-searching. "To his credit, Mr. Kristof is clear [in the column] about where he's coming from," the *Times* public editor Margaret Sullivan equivocated in a follow-up dissection on the editorial pages. "He is a longtime friend of Mia Farrow's. But was that enough? Given the close relationship with the Farrows, complete fairness might not have been possible here, some readers said. In other words, disclosure was absolutely necessary, but still might not have been sufficient."

Allen had rebuffed Kristof because he knew of the columnist's closeness to the Farrows, and doubted his "complete fairness." Leslee Dart, still Allen's publicist, phoned the *Times*, insisting the filmmaker be allowed to write a response to Kristof in the Sunday editorial pages. "Polite discussions over timing, space, fact-checking, and the like ensued," recalled op-ed editor Trish Hall. The film director's chief demand, which the *Times* met, was to be granted an amount of space that was equal to Kristof's. Allen's piece arrived to the office longer than Kristof's, but the op-ed editor found it "powerfully written, in great detail." Hall told Allen she "had to run it by our lawyer, and then it would have to be fact-checked," two vettings Kristof's column might have evaded.

The *Times* published "Woody Allen Speaks Out" on Sunday, February 9. Much of it reiterated Allen's previous interviews and courtroom testimony in explaining why he believed he had been falsely accused of child molestation: his romance with Soon-Yi, which precipitated his breakup with Mia Farrow; the battle for child custody; the dreamed-up incident in the attic. He reminded readers of the Yale–New Haven Hospital Child Sexual Abuse Clinic findings ("Most likely a vulnerable, stressed-out seven-year-old was coached by her mother," in Allen's words); that he had lost the courtroom case ("Justice Wilk was quite rough on me and never approved of my relationship with Soon-Yi"); and that Farrow had been successful in her goal of permanently alienating him from his three children. Moses had been "very angry with me." Little Satchel "I didn't know well because Mia would never let me get close to him from the moment he was born." And Dylan, "whom I adored," Allen wrote, "[but] never saw again, nor was I able to speak to her, no matter how hard I tried."

The director revealed that after two decades of noncommunication, Moses, in his mid-thirties and nowadays a family therapist, had reconnected with his father and Soon-Yi "in a loving, productive way." Allen quoted the only other Farrow-Previn family member present at Frog Hollow on that summer day. "My mother drummed it into me to hate my father for tearing apart the family and sexually molesting my sister," Moses said. "Of course, Woody did not molest my sister. . . . She loved him and looked forward to seeing him when he would visit. She never hid from him until our mother succeeded in creating the atmosphere of fear and hate towards him."

Moses gave a few other interviews at this time, saying much the same to *People* and discussing the supposed electric train set with Eric Lax. The incriminating train set was among the "few little added creative flourishes that seem to have magically appeared" in the two decades since their "estrangement," Allen wrote.

"Not that I doubt Dylan hasn't come to believe she's been molested," Allen continued, "but if from the age of seven a vulnerable child is taught by a strong mother to hate her father because he is a monster who abused her, is it so inconceivable that after many years of this indoctrination the image of me Mia wanted to establish has taken root?" Proving he'd been following Farrow's interviews and tweets, which cast aspersions on his family life, Allen said that "despite what it looked like" his love for Soon-Yi was "authentic," and the couple had been "happily married for sixteen years with two great kids, both adopted." Pointedly, he added: "Incidentally, coming on the heels of the media circus and false accusations, Soon-Yi and I were extra carefully scrutinized by both the adoption agency and adoption courts, and everyone blessed our adoptions."

In his dry manner the film director even addressed "the Ronan situation," i.e., the paternity of his offspring, which had become an overnight staple of derisive commentary on all forms of media. "Is he my son or, as Mia suggests, Frank Sinatra's? Granted, he looks a lot like Frank with the blue eyes and facial features, but if so, what does this say? That all during the custody hearing Mia lied under oath and falsely represented Ronan as our son? Even if he is not Frank's, the possibility she raises that he could be, indicates she was secretly intimate with him during our years. Not to mention all the money I paid in child support. Was I supporting Frank's son? Again, I want to call attention to the integrity and honesty of a person who conducts her life like that."

Ending his *Times* contribution, Allen said: "No one wants to discourage abuse victims from speaking out, but one must bear in mind that sometimes there are people who are falsely accused and that is also a terribly destructive thing." He added, in parentheses: "This piece will be my final word on this matter, and no one will be responding on my behalf to any further comments on it by any party. Enough people have been hurt." True to his word, Allen said little more about Dylan or Ronan until his 2019 memoir. By then Allen still thought it a distinct possibility that Sinatra was the father of the person he always stubbornly called Satchel. Perhaps Farrow believed or wanted to believe Sinatra was Ronan's father, just as she and Dylan believed their abuse story.

"WOODY ALLEN SPEAKS OUT" did not put the hubbub to rest, however. Although Sinatra's widow, Barbara Sinatra, slammed Mia Farrow's paternity innuendo as "just a bunch of junk" after publication of the piece in *Vanity Fair*, and his daughter Tina said it was impossible for Sinatra to have impregnated Farrow because the crooner had undergone a vasectomy before 1987, the year of Ronan/Satchel's birth, Mia and Ronan never forcefully retracted the tease, and the insinuation never really went away. Although James Kaplan, in his deeply researched biography of Sinatra, concluded the singer was far away on the West Coast and in Hawaii, incapacitated and impotent following major abdominal surgery, during the probable period of Ronan/Satchel's inception, Kaplan could not account for every minute of Sinatra's time; and he did not investigate Farrow's travel during the same period. Wouldn't she have visited the great love of her life in his time of calamity?

Farrow issued a statement saying Moses had fabricated his version of life in her household, "perhaps to please Woody," noting gratuitously, "Moses has cut off his entire family including his ex-wife who was pregnant when he left." Dylan, also quoted on Moses, echoed her mother, saying: "My brother is dead to me."

The public-shaming strategy of the Farrows (and Nicholas Kristof) accelerated as the Academy Awards race heated up. "Dylan Farrow's Op-Ed Targets Woody Allen But Could Hurt Cate Blanchett More" proclaimed the headline of Steve Feinberg's *Hollywood Reporter* column. By the date of Dylan's "open letter," many votes had already been cast for the Best Actress of 2013, a competition that early on had been predicted by many people to be a lock for Blanchett. Yet the actress felt tremendous pressure to say something about "the situation" as she picked up the Golden Globe, the Screen Actors Guild, and the BAFTA Best Actress honors. Boris Kachka of *New York* magazine covered many of the events and parties that typically crowded the calendar leading up to the Academy Awards ceremony on March 2, including the low-profile Santa Barbara Film Festival one week before the Oscars, where Blanchett was named Outstanding Performer of the Year. Accepting her recognition in Santa Barbara, the *Blue Jasmine* actress "neglects to thank Woody," Kachka wrote pointedly. Blogger Jeffrey Wells, "committing the evening's lone act of journalism," in Kachka's words, caught up with Blanchett, asking her a question about the child abuse claims. "Um," responded Blanchett, struggling to maintain her dignity, "I mean it's obviously been a long and painful situation, and I hope they find some resolution and peace."

Regardless, Blanchett took home the Oscar—the only *Blue Jasmine* nominee to win. The actress gave a stirring speech upholding films with women at the center of their stories. "Audiences want to see them, and in fact, they earn money," Blanchett said from the podium. "I'm here accepting an award in an extraordinary screenplay by Woody Allen," Blanchett added. "Thank you so much, Woody, for casting me. I truly appreciate it." Typical of the blogosphere, BuzzFeed's Kate Aurthur characterized this as only a glancing reference to Allen and added in her online account: "Allen's name was met with what sounded like hesitant and tepid applause."

Allen's *Blue Jasmine* original screenplay lost to John Ridley's for *12 Years a Slave*. These were the last Oscar nominations or awards any Woody Allen movie would ever see. Over time, sixteen performances in Allen films, including his own in *Annie Hall*, were Oscar-nominated, with four women among the five winners. "The inescapable fact," wrote Steve Rose in the *Guardian*, is "Allen has given women better roles than pretty much any filmmaker of the modern era." Four Woody Allen movies were nominated for Best Picture Oscars, and seven were nominated for Best Direction. (Only *Annie Hall* won Best Picture and Director.) His scripts were Oscar-nominated a record sixteen times, with wins for *Annie Hall*, *Hannah and Her Sisters*, and *Midnight in Paris*.

Blue Jasmine was also the last Woody Allen script to contend for a Writers Guild award. (Spike Jonze won for *Her*.) Beginning with his first nomination for *What's New Pussycat?* his screenplays had been nominated twenty-one times, winning "best" five times. Billy Wilder, second with fifteen Guild nominations, ties him with five wins.

Allen's peer generation was aging out in the Motion Picture Academy and Writers Guild, and a younger constituency supported the Farrow-Previns. ("Young Women Speak Out on Allen: Some of the Most Aggrieved Reactions to Dylan Farrow's Letter about Him Are from Those Under 40" was the *Los Angeles Times* headline.) Movie audiences, film critics, and the Hollywood press were also aging out; print media was now increasingly irrelevant to short form readers, and tweeting and texting on various electronic platforms had become the news stream of choice for the trending under-thirty demographic. While it would be amusing to imagine the young, indefatigable, wisecracking Woody Allen fighting back on Twitter and Facebook, the older, set-in-his-ways, typewriting Allen did not rely on email or use a computer, and Instagram and apps were Greek to him.

The seventy-year-old Wallace Shawn, a repeat performer in Woody Allen films since *Manhattan*, was among the few actors who dared speak up against the anti-Woody tide. His op-ed in the *Los Angeles Times* began with a reference to age discrepancies: "When I was growing up, an allegation of sexual abuse made by a child against an adult would rarely be believed. Now everyone knows that abuse is common, and many more people are prepared to accept a story told by a child." Shawn concluded: "We don't have overwhelming evidence about what happened or didn't happen on the day in question. And yet when I turn on my computer, I hear a din of voices declaring unequivocally that Woody Allen committed a crime, a disgraceful, indefensible, sickening crime—I hear voices inciting hatred against him. Obviously if he did not in fact commit the crime, this is an appalling situation."* Young movie fans did not share the same context, the warm feeling for Allen's past body of work and probably never heard of *The Children's Hour* or *The Bad Seed*, much less the McMartin case, or the Scottsboro Boys.

ESPECIALLY IN THE blogosphere the noise seethed about *believing* Dylan, *disbelieving* Allen, and *punishing* the filmmaker in some way for actions for which he had never been charged, or convicted. Lena Dunham, creator of the hit television series *Girls*, was among the handful of celebrities to speak out publicly at this juncture, saying Allen's purported actions "disgusted" her, but that his work stood apart from his behavior. Actress Rosie O'Donnell, appearing on *The View* to promote her appearance on the TV show *The Fosters*, said she "totally believes" Dylan, a comment widely recirculated by other believers. O'Donnell admitted she was a good friend of Mia Farrow's, and host Barbara Walters briefly asserted Allen's innocence until such a time as he was proven guilty. The feminist author Roxane Gay, who wrote essays on race, gender, and cultural and political issues for many outlets, sided with Dylan's "open letter" and spoke for the younger female

* Seven years later, after starring in *Rifkin's Festival* for Allen, Wallace Shawn reiterated his support for the comedian and film director and explained "[why I] personally have concluded that Woody didn't commit the crime," in "Why I'm Still Willing to Work with Woody Allen" (The Wrap, November 10, 2021).

demographic and those who felt even Nicholas Kristof had gone too far in cautioning that Allen should be "presumed innocent." "[Kristof] wants it both ways," Gay wrote. "As the latest discourse about Woody Allen unfolds, I doubt anyone's minds will be changed. I know where I stand and why. I know I would rather stand where I stand and eventually be proven wrong than support Woody Allen and eventually be proven wrong. We believe what we believe, and it isn't the place of public intellectuals to adjudicate such a fraught matter, to boldly declare who is right and wrong."

"How do we respond when we learn that someone capable of creating great art is also capable of wrongdoing?" Gay wrote another time. "There has been talk of boycotting Woody Allen, of no longer contributing to any financial success or critical acclaim he might reap for his work. Is a boycott enough of a stand?"

ALLEN'S IMAGE WAS probably not improved by playing a pimp to John Turturro's male prostitute in *Fading Gigolo*, which was released in April to a small number of US art houses. Thoroughly ludicrous as a story, *Gigolo* was notable primarily for the ménage à trois scene—without Allen—Sofia Vergara, Sharon Stone, and writer-director-star Turturro, for whom the whole picture seemed a preening ego trip. Manohla Dargis, reviewing the film in the *New York Times*, found it "leaden whimsy," while allowing that Allen was "amusingly frenetic" in his sizeable role, enlivening "his every scene" in the last movie in which he'd appear as an actor onscreen.

Throughout the "open letter" hullabaloo he attended every *Bullets over Broadway* run-through and preview, fine-tuning and improving the dialogue and jokes, but perhaps he was rattled—he'd say not—his judgment affected. When "the situation" broke, advance sales, the bedrock of any Broadway musical, took a blow. The producers, including his sister, encouraged Allen to skip press events and leave the publicity to others.

Bullets over Broadway opened at the Saint James Theatre in mid-April to a critical consensus: the show was middling. Not even the dancing and singing was all that great, which had been expected of Stroman, perhaps because too many of the songs were old, overly familiar ones. "Forcing the funny," wrote Peter Marks in the *Washington Post*, *Bullets* was a "sledgehammering act of period-tune-driven desperation." Not as funny as it might be, Jesse Green agreed in *New York*, "Allen's book tries way too hard." The stage musical was "occasionally funny but mostly just loud," according to Ben Brantley in the *New York Times*, and "charm-free." Terry Teachout in the *Wall Street Journal* opined that Allen hadn't directed a funny movie since *Bullets over Broadway*, so the show represented a "belated return to form" that was "solidly entertaining in its unoriginal unchallenging way."

Broadway musicals needed strong reviews even more than independent pictures did. The prestige of a few Tony awards might have rescued *Bullets Over Broadway*. The voting took place after the Oscars, with the last rounds during previews and early performances. On April 29, the show pulled eight nominations: although *Bullets over Broadway* was shut out for Best Musical or Direction of a Musical, it garnered Tony nods for Best Book (Allen), Supporting Actor in a Musical (Nick Cordero), Scenic Design (Santo Loquasto), Costume Design (William Ivey Long), Orchestration (Doug Besterman), and Choreography (Susan Stroman). At the June 10 awards evening, however, the musical lost in all its categories, and *Bullets over Broadway* limped through 156 performances, closing on August 24. There would be a road-show company, but the stage musical version of Allen's Oscar-garlanded movie was, in part, a casualty of the "open letter."

SONY PICTURES RELEASED *Magic in the Moonlight* in mid-July, and the romantic comedy was still in theaters when *Bullets over Broadway* gave its last Broadway performance. Allen attended the New York premiere but suffered a recurrence of entrance anxiety at the door to the celebratory post-party and dove into his limousine. The new picture ran counter to expectations and, playing in hundreds of theaters, briefly held its own against the outpouring for *Guardians of the Galaxy*, *Teenage Ninja Mutant Turtles*, *Dawn of the Planet of the Apes*, and *The Expendables 3*. Along with winning lead performances—Colin Firth as the master magician from London, and Emma Stone as the faux-mentalist he is trying to debunk while falling for her charms—*Magic in the Moonlight* offered rapturous photography and clever plotting along with a few exquisite scenes, like the one with Firth and Stone hiding from a violent storm in a planetarium, where a giant telescope points toward a slivered moon, a black sky glittering with stars, and infinity beyond. Natural wonders are pitted against fake magic, thematically, but

Stone teaches the cynical illusionist, a confirmed atheist ("Why would God go to so much trouble if everything comes to nothing?"), to embrace the magical above the mundane—a persistent thread in Allen films.

Still, A. O. Scott in the *New York Times* found *Magic in the Moonlight* tedious, saying the "nearly thirty-year gap" between Stone and Firth left a "sour taste" in his mouth. "Even if it were possible to watch this movie without thinking about Mr. Allen's personal life—or to avoid arguments afterward about whether he is a creep, a monster or a misunderstood artist whose behavior has no bearing on his work," Scott wrote, "it would be hard to miss the complacency at its heart and the purely mechanical expediency of its execution." Other critics were more generous and managed to write reviews without reminding readers of the controversies recently reinvigorated in Allen's life. "A very lovely but loosely imagined lark," Betsey Sharkey wrote in the *Los Angeles Times*. "Think of it as a ninety-seven-minute seance that draws you in," Joe Morgenstern enthused in the *Wall Street Journal*, "spins you around, subverts your suppositions, levitates your spirits, and leaves you giddy with delight."

THE SCRIPT FOR the summer project was another Hitchcockian or Chabrol-esque story, but with a self-referential thread: the plot involved a disillusioned philosophy professor who decides he can help right the wrongs of the world by killing the biased magistrate in a nasty divorce case. This premise bore vestiges of "An Error in Judgment," the film project about Judge Elliot Wilk that Allen had once floated in the press. "The idea of a judge denying custody of children to a parent is personal to Woody," wrote Eric Lax, "and although it was not the impetus for his writing 'The Boston Story,' it is often on his mind." For budget reasons Rhode Island had to be substituted for Boston, and the fictional Braylin College of the story was, in real life, the Catholic Salve Regina University campus in Newport, which the production company leased for the summer. Allen's players included Joaquin Phoenix as the brooding visiting professor Abe Lucas, an expert on Heidegger and fascism, who is turned on by murder; Emma Stone as a precocious undergrad with a crush on the bad-boy prof; and Parker Posey as Abe's man-hungry faculty colleague. Behind the camera Allen had long-timers Darius Khondji, Santo Loquasto, Suzy Benzinger, and Alisa

Lepselter. Sony Classics was again in for the US penny, with the deep-pocketed Ronald L. Chez and Edward Walson—both listed as coproducers now—and foreign companies picking up the slack.

Soon-Yi and family accompanied the director to Rhode Island for the principal photography in August. He was tentatively calling the project "Crazy Abe," but that was a title no one else liked. Sixteen-year-old Bechet and fourteen-year-old Manzie kept busy at self-improvement summer camps, but both teenagers hung around the set and had onscreen cameos. Lax was also on location, covering the shoot for his fourth Woody Allen book.

A ritual early riser, Allen took to shooting exteriors from 7 to 9 a.m., before the summer sun blazed too brightly, while devoting most afternoons to interiors. (The film would boast only one of his signature rainy scenes.) There would be more outside opportunities from 6 to 8 p.m. "Takes longer because I need dark days," Allen explained to a columnist. "Sun affects color saturation. No shadows. Also, you set up for forty-five minutes, then the sun constantly moves. I need soft gray light, so actresses look gorgeous. Bright harsh light isn't nice on a face."

Emma Stone already knew the drill. "You can't ask questions about your character," the actress explained to the press, "because he'd be like, 'You know this is a movie, right?' " Some actresses had trouble not looking gorgeous. "Emma Stone radiates," Allen said later. "Charismatic. Terrific dramatic sense. She's warming."

Posey wrote a charming memoir describing her adjustments to the filmmaker, whom she first met—without luck—in casting calls for *Shadows and Fog* and the *Bullets over Broadway* movie. She and Allen's casting director Juliet Taylor ran into one another at a Kraków, Poland, film festival where both were judges, and Posey asked for another chance. Taylor got her four minutes with Allen. Posey knew she might play a professor and "dressed appropriately." The two made "small talk about this and that and about Kraków—about the salt mines he wouldn't be able to visit because of his claustrophobia." Allen told her the star of the movie would be Joaquin Phoenix, and she "gushed over Joaquin, calling him soulful and poetic, to which Woody simply said, 'Uh-oh.' "

Still, she got the job, followed by "sides" with the proverbial stamped title "WASP": "Woody Allen Summer Project." "The pages were terrific, and he'd captured my voice so distinctly that I wondered if he'd written the pages the night before specifically for my cadence." Arriving in Rhode Island for wardrobe and camera tests, Posey met Manzie ("She was spirited and lovely") and made more small talk with Allen ("We spoke quietly, as if talking would interfere with the world he was shaping—we spoke in church whispers") before being led in front of a camera, muttering "Wow, we're shooting a film," to which Allen said, "Well, this *is* a movie," Posey recalled, "at which I laughed, alone. I turned and walked to the mark in the back of the room, feeling like there was toilet paper on the bottom of my shoe, or that my skirt was tucked into my pantyhose."

Posey also met the other performers, including Phoenix and Stone, who understood her newcomer's nervousness. "Emma is savvy," Posey recalled, "and she and Woody had a great rapport, like school chums. They caught up between takes with casual witty banter, like Groucho Marx and Ethel Merman." Phoenix "had gained like thirty pounds for the part and we laughed about that," the actress wrote, "and about how Woody told him not to grow any facial hair or do anything weird when they talked on the phone about working together. Here's something else that's funny about Woody: his strong aversion to blue jeans. He asked [costumer] Suzy [Benzinger] what the students would be wearing, and she said blue jeans. 'No one wears blue jeans,' he said. 'Students wear blue jeans,' she responded. 'No, they don't,' and that went on until everyone was in khakis."

Posey, like some of the actors who came before her, was worried by the brusque remarks Allen made during her first scenes, which took place in a bar. ("There isn't much he can say that isn't funny, even if the joke's on you and it's not a joke.") "A big part of being an actor is falling into the projection that a director wants, or being in the director's subjectivity," the actress mused. " 'Rita [her character's name] is a lonely woman,' Woody repeated to me a few times," which Allen had not emphasized in the letter he sent to her describing the role. " 'Lonely woman' has a deeper weight to it than the 'unhappy marriage' he'd mentioned in the letter."

During "my coverage" in the bar scenes Posey felt so jittery she "did twenty takes" for the first time in her life. The director began giving the nervous actress "line readings, which is the biggest blow to an actor's ego. The hundred extras were there, though, to support my meltdown and to witness the greatest living film director's frustration at my performance. At one point he said I was a terrific actress and a complicated woman but that he didn't want to see any of that in his movie. I don't know what I felt in that moment—caught but liberated into unknown territory? I stared into the eyes of the focus puller, who was an arm's length away, and she smiled to assure me that anything and everything was right in the world—she even gave me a thumb's-up."

Somehow Posey finished to Allen's satisfaction, then the actress had another little scene to do in which she fantasized about her and Phoenix escaping to Europe, or "anywhere but here." She performed one take with sound problems, and another where she was meh, but Allen came over and told her the sound was bad again, so they would give the scene another try. "I told him I was good at looping, and he said he didn't like looping." He reminded her Rita was "a lonely woman" in "an unhappy marriage." She nodded. "No, smiling," he said. She nodded, smiling. "He moves his hands and fingers when he talks, like he's holding invisible space for you to figure out exactly what it is, to communicate some sensitivity, maybe. That's my interpretation anyway.

"Before he sat back down at the monitor, he shouted out, like an afterthought, 'Just make sure your voice doesn't get too soft, you don't want to sound too actressy.' . . . It took me aback, and I immediately stood up and took a deep breath like I was going to faint; and fake-stabbed myself in the stomach, letting out an '*ugh*'; and stuck my tongue out, like a dying possum. 'That was deliberate,' he said quickly, and with humor, and I took the fake knife out of my side and put it in the other side and laugh-screamed, 'Do it again!'

"And I knew that moment said we could work together."

THE TRIPLE WHAMMY of Maureen Orth's article in *Vanity Fair*, Nicholas Kristof's *New York Times* column, and Dylan Farrow's "open letter" on Kristof's blog inarguably damaged Allen's reputation, casting a shadow over the Oscars, where *Blue Jasmine* had lost traction. *Bullets over Broadway* had been wounded on Broadway. Increasingly wary of Allen, dismissive film critics hurt the hopes of *Magic in the Moonlight* in the US. But the long-term consequences were unclear. Allen's *Times* op-ed satisfied many people unwilling to cast guilty stones outside the courtroom. The Farrow family and friends' full-throated call to arms against Allen had been answered by only a handful of public figures. Perhaps the comedian and film director had weathered the storm.

Back from Rhode Island, the filmmaker was also back on the clock. By day he worked on the postproduction of "Crazy Abe" while also crafting the script for his next production. At night he was glimpsed at public events and dining out with Soon-Yi and his daughters. The early 2014 uproar seemed to dissipate, and perhaps there was a bounce in Allen's step because the onetime canny poker player had a hidden card in his deck that vouchsafed a winning hand. If not an ace, at least the card did start with the letter A: Amazon.com.

As he turned seventy-nine, Allen had received a vote of confidence from the multimedia technology giant that dominated e-commerce and was beginning to produce theatrical motion pictures and programming for television. Roy Price, the vice president of Amazon Studios, wanted to marry Allen's prestige to the company's emerging entertainment brand, and Price courted the director over a series of meetings in New York. The son of Frank Price, who had run Universal and Columbia Pictures in the 1970s and '80s, Price had launched his career as an executive at Disney during Jeffrey Katzenberg's reign, when Allen was a hallowed name. Amazon Studios had been dipping into TV waters with new adult-oriented series like *Transparent*, a dark comedy involving a transgender father. Now, talking up a Woody Allen TV miniseries, Price made a lucrative offer that guaranteed creative control to the director. Allen listened to all such offers as a matter of policy, and after a while he couldn't think of a reason to say no. Amazon Studios announced the first-ever Woody Allen cable television miniseries from a man who had often inveighed against the medium and who watched little on the small screen apart from news and sports, once boasting he'd never seen a single episode of the classic 1950s—constantly rerun—*I Love Lucy*. Amazon would stream his miniseries to their Prime Instant Video subscribers.

There was a stealth part of the deal, which was unknown to the press in January 2015. Price was also whispering to Allen about leaving Sony Classics and making his future movies under the Amazon Studios banner. Price made oral assurances that could not be put into contractual language, in effect that Amazon was willing to underwrite all future Woody Allen films and provide the director with a " 'home' for the rest of his career," according to a legal complaint later filed by Allen. Amazon would give him his customary autonomy and creative freedoms. The Internet giant would raise his production budgets. The whispering was irresistible.

"I don't know how I got into this," Allen told the press. "I have no ideas [for a TV series], and I'm not sure where to begin." He added, "My guess is that Roy Price will regret this." A refer on the front page of the *New York Times* led to Emily Steel's disclosure of the Amazon announcement, which did not mention the still-brewing motion picture component, noting Allen "is a polarizing figure," and even "though Dylan Farrow, in her letter, challenged actors to examine their willingness to work" with him, "he has remained a fixture in the film industry."

ALLEN'S DATEBOOK FOR the year he turned eighty was nearly as jammed as his incessant road days in the 1960s. The filmmaker would make an overseas trip to the Cannes Film Festival with a stop in London, and he'd fly to Moscow for a museum opening. He'd materialize in Washington, DC, and Los Angeles. He'd attend the NBA All-Star game, held in New York that year, as well as ballet performances, Broadway plays, and art auctions at Sotheby's. He was conspicuous at a private screening for a Linda McCartney documentary with Sir Paul in attendance, he graced the seventieth birthday party of billionaire businessman Richard LeFrak, and he was among the celebrities at the opening of David Geffen Hall at Lincoln Center. Allen often attended gala events nowadays because Soon-Yi and his daughters enjoyed them. Elaine's had closed in 2011 after the death of its proprietor, and the couple nowadays dined at newer places: Elio's, Sette Mezzo, Philippe's, Caravaggio.

Emma Stone and Parker Posey joined Allen in Cannes for the unveiling of *Irrational Man*, the final title of "Crazy Abe," which Allen borrowed from William Barrett's 1958 tome about existential philosophy. He and Soon-Yi were among the throng at Fiat heir Jean Pigozzi's annual pool party at his Villa Dorane on Cap d'Antibes. Allen was circumspect about his forthcoming Amazon cable series. "I thought it would be a cinch," the director told the foreign press dolefully. "But it's not. It's very, very hard. I'm not good at it. I don't watch any television. I don't know what I'm doing. I'm floundering. . . . I expect this to be a cosmic embarrassment."

The June flight to Moscow was arduous, even if the gratis ticket was first-class. The occasion was the opening of architect Rem Koolhaas's Garage Museum of Contemporary Art, which was the pet project of Russian oligarchs Roman Abramovich and Dasha Zhukova. Other Hollywood guests included *Star Wars* creator George Lucas, Leonardo DiCaprio, Salma Hayek, and producer Harvey Weinstein. Again, Allen had agreed to the exhaustive trip to please Soon-Yi and oldest daughter Bechet, who attended festivities at his side.

At times *Irrational Man*, which Sony Classics released in the US in mid-July, threatened to be gripping, but the pace of the suspense was leisurely. Emma Stone had a better part in the more fanciful *Magic in the Moonlight*. Joaquin Phoenix, on low simmer, was nonetheless compelling. (A reference to his potbellied character having lost his ideals in Darfur proved Allen had tracked Mia and Ronan Farrow's United Nations adventures.) Parker Posey's vulnerability shone through her eccentricities. Allen had begun to sneak past the 1950s for his music, and the recurrent "The 'In' Crowd" by the Ramsey Lewis Trio, from 1964, provided a jaunty undertow to a story otherwise dominated by despair, impotence, treachery, and murder. As ever, there was Emily Dickinson, Edna St. Vincent Millay, Hannah Arendt, and *Crime and Punishment* for intelligent thematics, and *Irrational Man* would be the last Allen movie with the scenery made luminous by Darius Khondji's camerawork. It was also the last with a coproducer credit for Jack Rollins, who passed away in June at age one hundred.

One thing it surely was not was "the Woodman's worst movie ever," as Lou Lumenick pilloried it in the *New York Post*. (Lumenick also had found *Magic in the Moonlight* "appalling.") "Worst movie ever" or "his movies keep getting worse" had become the new cliché for certain critics, with the New York reviewers, hyperaware of his private life and conscious of his desertion—betrayal—of Manhattan, often among the most offended parties. Yet Manohla Dargis wrote astutely, and not entirely unsympathetically, in the *New York Times* that "each new [Woody Allen] film registers as another chapter in a project that, in its scale and scope, and in the way in which it seems to speak to his personal life, has come to resemble a weird metafiction."

Sony Classics hurried *Irrational Man* into over nine hundred theaters, but the offbeat drama without very much comedy in it didn't have *Magic in the*

Moonlight appeal and stalled at $5 million in US grosses, a loss in the short term, probably to be later remedied by ancillary sales. As Eric Lax pointed out in *Start to Finish*, Sony Classics got its money's worth on the seven Woody Allen pictures produced by the division between 2009 and 2015, with total US grosses of "about $130 million, ranging from the $3.2 million for *You Will Meet a Tall Dark Stranger* (plus $31 million foreign) and $5.3 million for *Whatever Works* ($30 million foreign) to the $57 million for *Midnight in Paris* (another $95 million foreign) and $34 million for *Blue Jasmine* ($65 million foreign)." On average Allen's movies still did OK, if you didn't expect a half billion dollars in accrued tickets.

Playing the long game, the director was already behind the camera on his next project—"No title yet," he told the press. Only Allen's two young leads, Jesse Eisenberg and Kristen Stewart, knew the full contours of the script, which was going to be the first Woody Allen picture since *Annie Hall* to be half photographed in Los Angeles, with filming of the Los Angeles part of the story—including beach exteriors—to start in August.

Allen liked Eisenberg, famously spending fifteen minutes with the actor ("The longest in history," in Emma Stone's words) before casting him in *To Rome with Love*. Eisenberg and Stewart had worked well together as a pair in other pictures, and Stewart had become a major name suddenly because of *The Twilight Saga* series. In supporting roles were Parker Posey, who had won Allen over in *Irrational Man*; *Gossip Girl*'s Blake Lively; Corey Stoll, the Ernest Hemingway of *Midnight in Paris*; Elaine May's daughter, Jeannie Berlin; and Steve Carrell, whose career had soared since *Melinda and Melinda*, playing the role originally announced for Bruce Willis. Veteran Italian Vittorio Storaro, whom Allen befriended on *Picking Up the Pieces*, was the cameraman.

All the press knew was that Eisenberg was playing the director's shadow self, much as was the case in his previous Woody Allen picture. Stewart was filling the shoes of Scarlett Johansson and Emma Stone. And socks: "I needed someone who could play an adorable little secretary from Nebraska with white little socks on and little dresses," who could metamorphose into "a sophisticated beauty in cosmopolitan Manhattan," Allen later told journalists at Cannes. Stewart, who got along as smoothly with the filmmaker as her predecessor "muses," helped to translate Allen's "mansplaining": "The way he describes this lightness and this feminine nature, it does suggest that it's a little thoughtless. I think he has a tendency in interviews to say, 'It was an idea, and I had the idea, and I wrote the idea, and I hired the girl, and she did it.' But there's more going on. . . ."

On weekdays in August, Allen guided Los Angeles scenes for the 1930s romantic comedy-drama, whose milieu was divided between the screen colony of Hollywood and New York gangsterdom. One Saturday he appeared at the downtown Orpheum Theatre with his jazz band, patiently signing autographs after the show and telling people who had seen him play his clarinet before—three times in five years in Los Angeles—"You'll notice I have not improved." He squeezed in a jazz band minitour on weekends in San Francisco, Seattle, and Minneapolis, and finished the Los Angeles filming with a *Gianni Schicchi* revival at the Los Angeles Opera.

In September Allen bent to capturing the film's remaining scenes in New York locations and on Santo Loquasto sets in a Brooklyn studio. The first Woody Allen movie to be shot in New York since *Whatever Works* piqued the curiosity of columnists. Allen dressed the same as in the 1970s, they reported, and while at work, directing, he wore his "omnipresent wardrobe," as Cindy Adams observed in the *New York Post*, of "rumpled chinos, cotton shirt, same battered hat you can buy off a pushcart on Canal Street." The filmmaker and his cast and crew were spotted on the Upper West Side, outside the Church of Notre Dame, at the Brooklyn Public Library, in Chinatown, and in the Conservatory Gardens and on the Bow Bridge of Central Park.

Allen's unusual rapport with Eisenberg extended to oyster lunches at the Pearl Room in Bay Ridge near the Brooklyn studio. The main photography was completed by late October, with Allen telling the *Post* he was skipping the wrap party that was a new extra in the budget. "I'm going home," the near octogenarian said. "To bed. To watch the Cubs and the Mets." In a rare gesture of hospitality—probably because Soon-Yi liked Eisenberg too—Allen had the leading man over to his house for dinner the next night. Allen even told Eisenberg to bring his mother, a big fan, and he'd answer all her questions about his old movies—"The early, funny ones."

Allen's eightieth birthday rolled around on December 1. A few weeks later, arm in arm, he and Soon-Yi went to another party thrown by Jean Pigozzi at Pigozzi's West Sixty-Seventh townhouse—an extravagant Christmas party like the New Year's Eve ones Allen used to host—with every

A-lister in town, from Salman Rushdie to Kid Rock, in the crush. Then in early 2016 it was time to film his cable television miniseries.

The cast had been announced: for young folks the star was Miley Cyrus, the former Hannah Montana from the Disney Channel, who in her twenties had become a pop singer; for seniors, it was Allen and Elaine May, the only players to appear in all half dozen episodes. There would be a few returnees from other Woody Allen projects including Douglas McGrath and Michael Rapaport. The director would photograph most of the exteriors around affluent Briarcliff Manor in Westchester County, where Sidney J. Munsinger (Allen) and his wife Kay (May) live in a wooded house. But a few scenes would be shot in Greenwich Village, still pretty much the way it was in the 1960s, the era in which Woody Allen became a household name and the series was nostalgically set.

V

A Travesty of a Mockery of a Sham

Chapter 13

2016

Mr. Nothing

A Second Firestorm—MeToo Counts Woody Out—Once Celebrated, Now Canceled, Our Protagonist Finds Solace in Europe

By early 2016 the burgeoning movement to punish powerful men who had sexually abused women had gained a second wind from a flurry of legal actions involving prominent sexual-predator cases. And there would arise a fresh firestorm against Woody that would reflect a culmination of themes from his life and career—the disdain from those who disliked nonconformity, puritanical censure by an intolerant younger generation, and the perpetual inability many critics had demonstrated in trying to parse Allen's varying selves.

Some of the most notorious sexual-predator examples involved show business figures such as R&B and hip-hop singer R. Kelly, comedian Bill Cosby, and film director Roman Polanski. Allen had known Cosby from the time when both were young jokemeisters in small Greenwich Village clubs. Over time numerous women attested that Cosby had drugged and sexually assaulted them, some of the highly publicized incidents dating back to the mid-1960s. In December 2015, the growing outcry against Cosby built to civil suits and three counts of aggravated indecent assault lodged against the comedian in a Pennsylvania court. By January, it had become increasingly routine for the press and social media coverage to link Cosby with Allen—both of them comedians with career roots in the 1960s—pointing to a commonality about their cases without regard to any disparities. Even the *New York Times*, on its news pages, began to lump Allen in with Kelly, Cosby, and Polanski as entertainers whose "allegations of sexual misdeeds" had drawn "heightened cultural attention" from the social justice and empowerment movement that was dubbed "MeToo" by harassment survivor and activist Tarana Burke.

Allen had signed petitions supporting Polanski, who pled guilty to sexually assaulting a thirteen-year-old girl in Los Angeles in 1977, then after psychiatric sequestration and a disputed plea bargain fled to France in 1978. Arrested on an outstanding warrant in Switzerland in 2010, Polanski was eventually freed from jail but had been fighting Interpol limits on his travel and attempts to extradite him from France. (Polanski admitted to one crime, but multiple women accused him of others.) Allen was hardly alone among the international fraternity (by and large it was a fraternity) of directors supporting Polanski, with Martin Scorsese, Michael Mann, and Alexander Payne among the American contingent, although another petition-signer was Mia Farrow, the star of Polanski's *Rosemary's Baby*. As with Cosby, it was easy for news outlets to bracket Polanski with Allen—both filmmakers whose careers were tainted by sexual assault charges. In August 2015, for example, when a Polish court forestalled Polanski's extradition, a New York *Daily News* editorial lamented the decision and pointed to Allen among Polanski's "defenders . . . whose histories may help explain their points of view."

Among the press voices nowadays was a member of the Farrow-Previn clan, newly raised to journalistic prominence, who had his sights trained on Allen. As Ronan Farrow recounted in *Catch and Kill*, the family met one day "in the TV room at our home in Connecticut, with stacks of fading VHS tapes," to discuss their bête noire. The most militant person in the room was twenty-seven-year-old Dylan, who wanted to "revive her allegation of sexual assault against Woody Allen," as Ronan referred to his putative father. "I don't see why you can't just move on," Ronan told his sister. "You had that choice," Dylan retorted. "I didn't." Her younger brother assured her, "I support you. But you just—you have to stop," but their argument ended with Dylan hissing, "Fuck you!"

Ronan Farrow Daily had lasted about a year on MSNBC before the program was terminated in February 2015 because of a precipitous ratings decline. MSNBC announced Ronan was in line to host a series of prime-time specials, but the young television host had been sidelined since his show's cancellation into intermittent correspondent spots on the *Today* show, where he fed celebrity interviews and features to Matt Lauer and other anchors.

The upcoming world premiere of *Café Society* at the spring 2015 Cannes Film Festival, with the director and cast members scheduled to be present, coincided with an announcement by Amazon Studios that sent "shock waves through the indie film world," in the words of one trade paper. Sony Classics would no longer be producing Woody Allen films; his productions for the foreseeable future would be financed and released by Amazon. Sony had been caught flatfooted when the Internet giant climaxed its months of wooing Allen by outbidding the specialty division for the distribution rights to *Café Society* ("sight unseen"). Amazon paid $15 million up front for the US controls, while pledging another $20 million for advertising. Not only that, but Amazon would solely fund Allen's next four projects after *Café Society*, in exchange for all US rights. Each picture would be guaranteed a $25 million budget. Although the director had been holding the line against inflation with $18–$20 million budgets, this gave him a substantial cushion for above- and below-the-line costs. Amazon had not yet produced a single motion picture, but the company had set an internal goal of twelve a year, in the $5–$25 million range, "from top and up-and-coming creators." Allen, with favored-nations clauses, would lead the charge.

Keying off the Amazon bombshell, the *Hollywood Reporter* prepared a standard interview with Allen for its Cannes bumper issue, which was always sent to print before the festival and shipped to France ahead of its publication date for promotional purposes. The interview focused on *Café Society*, but staff writer Stephen Galloway also noted the "accusations that Allen abused [his] own seven-year-old daughter Dylan," which "were dismissed after an investigation, but the battle still rages, with a grown-up Dylan reasserting the claims two years ago in the *New York Times*." Ronan, who spent a lot of time in Los Angeles (his longtime companion, Jon Lovett, lived in Los Angeles, and Hollywood was also Ronan's beat nowadays), seized on this opportunity to make up for lost time with his sister. He publicly inveighed against what he described, in *Catch and Kill*, as the *Reporter*'s laudatory profile of Allen (it wasn't), which made only "glancing mention" of Dylan's sex-abuse claims. The *Reporter*, which had respectably covered Dylan's revived accusations in 2014, faced "intense criticism" for going easy on Allen, Ronan claimed in *Catch and Kill*, although Galloway said that intensity came mainly from Farrow himself, who tweeted his ire to editor Janice Min—"Love you, Janice, but what's next, a Bill Cosby cover?" He retweeted the *Reporter* profile to his thousands of followers. Min, who was friendly with Ronan, spoke to him by phone and said, "If you feel so strongly about it, why don't you write a piece?"

Although Ronan "made no claim to be an impartial arbiter of my sister's story," as he wrote in *Catch and Kill*, "I decided to interview my sister about what happened in detail, for the first time. And I dove into the court records and any other documents I could find." Within a few days, this interview and deep-dive research yielded a "guest column" in the *Reporter*, published on May 11:* "My Father, Woody Allen, and the Danger of Questions Unasked." Ronan introduced his "guest column" with four paragraphs tying his own botched attempt to ask a Cosby biographer about the "rape and sexual abuse" charges against the entertainer on *Ronan Farrow Daily*, to "the press's grudging evolution" on Cosby, and connections "some reporters have drawn" to "a painful chapter in my own family's history." He said the true story of what happened had been suppressed by "Allen's powerful publicist," whose emails "featured talking points ready-made for print and air, complete with validators" in the form of links "first to blogs, then to stories at high-profile outlets repeating the talking points."

As an example of the uphill battle his sister faced, Ronan revealed that the *Los Angeles Times* initially had declined to publish her "open letter." The *New York Times* gave it only "936 words online, embedded in an article with careful caveats." Thankfully, "Nicholas Kristof, the Pulitzer Prize–winning reporter and advocate for victims of sexual abuse, put it on his blog." (Ronan didn't mention his or his family's friendship with Kristof.) The *Times* awarded Dylan's "alleged attacker twice the space—and prime position in the print edition, with no caveats or surrounding context." Perhaps, Ronan said, he had "succumbed" too long to the pressure "to distance myself from my painfully public family history" because he "wanted my work to stand on its own."

He had been reflecting on what happened. "I believe my sister," Ronan

* So fast did Ronan Farrow do his deep-dive research and writing, in fact, his May 11 "guest column" predated the official publication date (May 13) of the *Hollywood Reporter*'s special Cannes issue with Allen's interview that had been shipped overseas in advance.

declared in the "guest column." "This was always true as a brother who trusted her, and, even at five years old, was troubled by my father's strange behavior around her: climbing into her bed in the middle of the night, forcing her to suck his thumb—behavior that had prompted him to enter into therapy focused on his inappropriate conduct with children prior to the allegations."

The issue of thumb-sucking, with its obvious sexual implications, was among the curious story points of the child-abuse allegations that, like Ronan's breastfeeding or leg surgeries, refused to go away. The thumb-sucking was often mentioned by the Farrow family, and just as often disputed by Allen—"Even in its most innocuous form, this story is pure fabrication," the film director said. The 2021 HBO documentary *Allen v. Farrow* would showcase nonfamily members, albeit Farrow family friends, who claimed to have witnessed Allen offering his thumb to Dylan for sucking. Whether the supposed thumb-sucking acts were "forced" or happened "*in the middle of the night*" appears to have been Ronan's fresh embroidery, exclusive to the *Hollywood Reporter*. In her courtroom testimony, Mia Farrow said she once saw Dylan grab her father's thumb and stick it in her mouth, and another time she witnessed Allen putting the little girl's thumb in his mouth: In *What Falls Away* the actress wrote: "*Twice* [author's emphasis] I made him take his thumb out of her mouth."

Ronan, in his "guest column," revealed that he had objected to the trade paper's reference to Dylan's sex-abuse charges as having been "dropped." Henceforth the paper would use the terminology "not pursued." "The correction points to what makes Allen, Cosby, and other powerful men so difficult to cover," Ronan wrote. "The allegations were never backed by a criminal conviction. This is important. It should always be noted. But it is not an excuse for the press to silence victims, to never interrogate allegations." The "facts are persuasive and well-documented," Ronan insisted, and had been "meticulously reported by journalist Maureen Orth in *Vanity Fair.*" Galloway's interview was a "sterling example of how not to talk about sexual assault."

To fight "this culture of impunity and silence," Ronan, like his sister before him, named a few actors, trying to shame them into speaking out against Allen, saying each time "one of her [Dylan's] heroes like Louis C.K. or a star her age, like Miley Cyrus," acted in a picture directed by Allen,

Dylan suffered anew. Ronan roll-called Kristen Stewart, Jesse Eisenberg, Steve Carrell, and Blake Lively, the ensemble leads of *Café Society*, adding that those performers needn't overly worry, "they can trust that the press won't ask them the tough questions."

PERHAPS IT WAS a subtlety that Ronan Farrow, a rising journalist, had raised the ante by taking the family crusade to a trade paper that was also at the heart of the Hollywood blacklist. As was true of McCarthyism in the 1950s, now if people—public figures, or journalists—didn't support Dylan Farrow, they could be seen as akin to communist sympathizers. The masterstroke of Ronan's "guest column" in the *Hollywood Reporter* was timing its publication for the day before *Café Society* held its world premiere at the Cannes Film Festival. Critics and journalists had gathered from around the globe at the most important festival in filmdom. Amid terror threats and bomb sweeps, Allen, in tuxedo and dress shoes, with Soon-Yi and accompanied by Jesse Eisenberg and Kristen Stewart, walked the red carpet. Master of ceremonies Laurent Lafitte, a French comedian who had a movie in competition at Cannes, greeted the director amid the hoopla with a joke that seemed to reference Ronan's "guest column," which already had the press abuzz. "It's very nice that you've been shooting so many movies in Europe, even if you are not being convicted for rape in the US." Lafitte later explained he was making a joke about Roman Polanski and "American puritanism" that he had scripted three weeks before.

Manohla Dargis, in the *New York Times*, wrote that by the day after the premiere "talk about the movie [*Café Society*] and its merits had given way to an increasingly loud hum" about Ronan's "guest column." In her festival report, Dargis offered an extended pan of the new Woody Allen film as a "middling entertainment," when it had long been *Times* policy to hold reviews until the US opening, even going so far as to find fault with Vittorio Storaro's lush pictorialism: "Its thin-sharp-edged digital look . . . neither period-appropriate nor realistic," with the colors more "urine-hued than sun-kissed." (The *Times* later followed up with another article that said *Café Society* had been greeted by "mixed but generally positive reviews" from the Cannes audience.)

At a *Café Society* press luncheon on the day after the premiere, Allen was asked about Lafitte and said, "I'm completely in favor of comedians making any jokes they want." He also insisted he hadn't read his son's "guest column" in the *Hollywood Reporter*. "My comment is that I've said everything that I have to say about that silly situation in the *New York Times*," Allen said. "I have so moved on that I never think about it. I work, I do my movies, and hope that people like them." Margaret Sullivan, who had been public editor at the *Times* when Dylan Farrow's "open letter" was excerpted by Nicholas Kristof, now filled a similar position at the *Washington Post*, and she wrote about what Ronan's "guest column" portended for the future. The press had an obligation to "make reference to these troubling chapters" in lengthy pieces about the filmmaker's life "even if it means losing access to Allen," Sullivan wrote. She gave as an example of the retribution the press might have to face: "The *Hollywood Reporter* was banned from a Cannes lunch after it published Ronan Farrow's article."*

Shortly after the "guest column" appeared, comedian Sarah Silverman tweeted: "My comedy hero Woody Allen and his untouchable PR machine and our not wanting it to be true. But it is." Susan Sarandon, in Cannes to receive a twenty-fifth anniversary award for *Thelma and Louise* and to promote the animated *Spark*, in which she voiced a nanny robot, jumped on the bandwagon. "I think he sexually assaulted a child, and I don't think that's right," she declared at a festival event. Silverman was famous for her acid-tongued comedy, and Sarandon was an Oscar winner—albeit the actress had never emoted in a Woody Allen film—and an avowed leftist theoretically not given to blacklisting. Their words indicting Allen crackled across the wires and Internet.

It was to be Allen's last appearance at Cannes, which organizers had begged him for years to honor with a visit, where fans screamed his name, the festival he had grown to love—that loved him back—above all.

IN ANY OTHER context *Café Society* would have been greeted as an elegantly crafted if antediluvian jewel from an old master, who flaunted his age in his voice-over narration. Think of it as *Bullets over Broadway* crossed

* Indeed, Amazon Studios publicists and Leslee Dart felt blindsided by the "guest column" and took their minor revenge, such as it was, by excluding the *Hollywood Reporter* from the *Café Society* press luncheon.

with *Radio Days*. Allen's first visit to Hollywood as a young comedy writer in 1956 was transplanted to the 1930s. Early scenes were set at the motel where he'd stayed—called Ali Baba in the movie—on the same corner of Yucca and Grace, replete with a novice's mistake with a hooker and the jazz recordings Allen and his first wife, Harlene Rosen, had listened to for sanity. New York family moments, mean streets, and pulsating nightclubs were intercut with Hollywood pool parties, wheeling and dealing, and a tenderhearted romance that was not going to end well.

Jeannie Berlin is Rose, the consummate reimagining of Nettie, the mother of three children in the story. The youngest is the protagonist, "Bobby Dorfman from the Bronx" (Jesse Eisenberg). Middle daughter Evelyn (Sari Lennick) is married to a communist intellectual (Stephen Kunken). The third, oldest, most successful, and favorite son Ben (Corey Stoll) is a killer who has poured money into a Manhattan nitery patronized by slick millionaires, high-class models, corrupt politicians, and gangland cronies. Stoll knocks it out of the park as he had done with his Hemingway impersonation in *Midnight in Paris*, and after an arrest, conviction, and electric-chair sentencing, the disarming gangster is converted to Catholicism by the prison priest. "First a murderer, then he becomes a Christian!" Rose wails. "What did I do to deserve this?" Rose and Marty (Ken Stott), her religious skeptic of a husband, argue riotously about the afterlife denied to Jews, with Rose lapsing into Yiddish.

The Los Angeles part of the picture is tinged with nostalgia for old Hollywood—Grauman's Chinese Theatre, the Brown Derby, the showcase homes of the stars—all the places Allen had visited on foot in 1956 and that were nowadays ancient history, or transmogrified. Rose sends wide-eyed Bobby to California, hoping her agent brother Uncle Phil (Steve Carell) will help him get a start in life. (Ben slips him the phone numbers of LA hookers.) Uncle Phil is a top dealmaker ("Joel McCrea will be perfect to play the lead!"), cheating on his wife in a torrid affair with his fetching young secretary, Vonnie (Kristen Stewart). Phil delegates Vonnie to show Bobby around town, and he falls hard for her, not realizing she belongs to Uncle Phil.

The bicoastal stories coil and entwine. If Jesse Eisenberg never quite musters any romantic appeal, Kristen Stewart has oomph to spare, and there are understated performances from Parker Posey as a New York fashion maven and Blake Lively as Bobby's second-choice wife. Sumptuously designed, the film is intricately plotted, with deft scenes, and reflective as well as ringing dialogue. "Life is a comedy written by a sadistic comedy writer," says narrator Allen. The script never lets the audience know what year it is precisely, but it might be 1935, the year of Woody Allen's birth, judging by the matinee Vonnie and Bobby sneak off to see; and *Café Society* concludes, as other Allen pictures do, with cross-cutting New Year's Eve parties on opposite coasts. The true lovers are married to other people and wonder wistfully what might have been. The communist intellectual resignedly toasts the future, musing about life as "a bewildering journey leading where? Why?"

Ronan Farrow's strategy of conflating his father with Bill Cosby and calling on journalists, including himself, to account for their sins exerted an obvious effect on film critics in New York, Allen's hometown, the media center of America. "A tired act and ready for retirement," wrote Robert Levin in *Newsday*. "Woody Allen has made forty-six films, of which I've seen forty-six, and I'm not sure which of us is more tired of him," Kyle Smith agreed in the *New York Post*. The headline of A. O. Scott's "official" review in the *New York Times* told readers that "*Café Society* Isn't Woody Allen's Worst Movie," but neither was it "much in the way of a return to form. It is, overall, an amusing little picture with some inspired moments" and "the hint, now and then, of an idea." Like some critics, Scott was as pained by recovered Allen tropes (the prostitute) as by jokes that appeared to echo his real-life problems—like the one about "Errol Flynn's sexual interest in underage girls. It's hard to say if Mr. Allen is testing the audience's tolerance or trolling our sensitivities, or for that matter if he's just blithely carrying on as he always has, oblivious to changing mores or the vicissitudes of his own reputation."

Even if the movie reviewers of 2016 did not boast the same prestige as Vincent Canby, Pauline Kael, or Andrew Sarris, it was hard to overcome such invective in New York, Allen's base US audience. *Café Society* earned only $11 million in the US (the *Times* would describe the film as a "modest" hit). Elsewhere in the world, with better reviews, *Café Society* added $32 million. But seeds of doubt and worry had been planted at Amazon.

THE DIRECTOR WAS as usual immersed in preparations for his next film, the first "Untitled Woody Allen Project" to be entirely bankrolled by

Amazon Studios and the first since *Whatever Works* to be shot entirely in New York environs. By late September, Allen was on locations in Coney Island and the Rockaways in Queens, with a buffet cast that included English actress Juno Temple, Jim Belushi (the late John Belushi's younger brother, well known for his long-running television sitcom *What About Jim?*), singer and actor Justin Timberlake, and another English thespian, Kate Winslet—in the case of the latter, with Allen keeping the promise he'd made when Winslet dropped out of *Match Point* to tailor another script for her talents.

The script revolved around Ginny (Winslet), a migraine-prone, tippling clam house waitress who shares a ramshackle home in the shadow of the Wonder Wheel on Coney Island with Humpty (Belushi), a carousel operator and abusive alcoholic. Ginny has a young firebug son from her first marriage (Jack Gore). Carolina (Temple), Humpty's estranged wayward daughter, arrives to hide out on the boardwalk from her hoodlum husband; she is a "marked woman" who has cooperated with police against her spouse. Timberlake is Mickey Rubin, an ex-swabbie who lifeguards in the summers while pursuing his master's degree in European drama at NYU. Mickey narrates the story as it unfolds before the audience's eyes; the lifeguard views the fatally flawed Ginny and her unhappy life as the kind of Eugene O'Neill tragedy he dreams of writing. He falls for Ginny, then falls for Carolina. All except for Mickey the lifeguard—intelligent, sensitive, devil-may-care—are lost souls. All are doomed. The year is 1950, which the audience knows because *Winchester '73* is on the marquee of the boardwalk theater.

Of course, the full script was off-limits to all but a handful. Allen's team behind the camera was the same as that of *Café Society*, with the exception of casting director Juliet Taylor, who had retired and passed her brief on to longtime associate Patricia DiCerto. *New York Post* columnist Cindy Adams caught up with the man in the rumpled hat as he directed crowd scenes on a freshly "dressed" Coney Island—it was the cold, rainy off-season and not usually bustling—and guessed there was a lifeguard and a burger joint in the story. As lunchtime neared, the columnist suggested they grab one of those famous Coney Island hot dogs. The director demurred ("If I eat one, I'll have guilt and be up all night") but he found Adams a wiener with sauerkraut. "The movie's set in the fifties, and we're re-creating the Parachute Jump," Allen told Adams. "Even sunny beaches. It's no longer my job to have to run around and find that anywhere. Today we live in the future. While I'm here, some nerd wearing glasses in an office with a computer turns dials and creates sunny beaches.

"We're filming in the Bronx and all over the city," he continued. "I've taken 6,355 steps today. I checked. And notice I keep standing. The longer you stand, the longer you live." Turning reflective, Allen said: "I like dramatic, romantic movies with passion and some laughs. Today it's all car crashes. I like that old-time stuff. I remember the days with beat cops. I remember when milk went to eleven cents, my mother said: 'Impossible. Used to be two cents.' " Proudly old-fashioned, Allen pointed out bicyclists whizzing past and "went off" on them for a moment, Adams wrote. "Please. They're not for a sane metropolis. New York's a walking city."

ALLEN WAS BEAVERING away on Coney Island when his much-ballyhooed Amazon miniseries, *Crisis in Six Scenes*, debuted on cable. In small ways the show was a departure, with newsreel and a blast of Jefferson Airplane's "Volunteers" inaugurating the first episode, which whisked viewers back to the late 1960s, where Allen's whimsical story began. Lennie (Miley Cyrus) is a gun-toting revolutionary fugitive who bursts into the suburban home of therapist Kay (Elaine May) and novelist turned sitcom writer Sidney J. Munsinger (Allen), becoming their unwanted house guest (her mother knew Kay's mother). Among the funny ideas is Kay's octogenarian woman's book club that, under radical influence, evolves from Kafka to Frantz Fanon.

This would be Allen's very last acting job to date, and he hogs the television miniseries with lines and bits reprised from more youthful incarnations, from his inept handling of gadgets to his pro forma hypochondriacal visits to a doctor. The plot is not in any particular hurry, most scenes are long and talky, and the still fit and trim (despite deafness) octogenarian Allen doesn't play "elderly" any more than he did for the television remake of *The Sunshine Boys*. Elaine May was even older (eighty-something), and he and she flee police and leap across rooftops. (It sounds better than it is.) Part *Manhattan Murder Mystery*, part *Bananas*, the series sprinkled priceless one-liners with strong performances, including from Cyrus. Anyone with the patience to stick around for the last episode would be rewarded in the form of Michael Rapaport as a dumb state trooper who pulls over Munsinger/Allen's car (the militant is hiding in his trunk) and begs for his autograph, mistaking S. J. Munsinger for J. D. Salinger.

"Instantly forgettable," wrote Mike Hale in the *New York Times*. "A blazing disappointment," Verne Gay said in *Newsday*. "Passably mediocre," added Hank Stuever in the *Washington Post*. But the West Coast reviews were, as was becoming oddly customary, more tolerant: "This isn't Allen at his wittiest or wildest—his career is almost by definition a thing of peaks and valleys," Robert Lloyd opined in the *Los Angeles Times*, "and he can be satisfying and frustrating within a single film. But he has a voice, and he has not yet lost it. Anyone susceptible to that sensibility will find many familiar pleasures here."

Regardless, young viewers stayed away, everyone agreed with Allen that television was not his forte, and Amazon saw the failed series as another augury.

AFTER EIGHTY-NINE YEARS in business, the Carnegie Deli announced its main Carnegie Hall branch, which was on display in *Broadway Danny Rose*, would close at the end of 2016. In November, after completing all the scenes for the new picture, which he was going to call *Wonder Wheel*, Allen and Soon-Yi, with Douglas McGrath and his wife, Jane Read Martin, Allen's assistant in *Broadway Danny Rose* days and now a children's book author, celebrated with a sentimental last visit to the delicatessen. They dined on stuffed derma, gefilte fish, and rugelach and ordered two Woody Allens to go—the humongous corned beef–and–pastrami sandwich named in his honor.

Probably the filmmaker and his friends enjoyed an empty laugh when the Democratic Party candidate Hillary Clinton returned his quiet donation to her 2016 presidential campaign. Her staff feared a backlash if the front-runner was mentioned in the same breath as Allen. Donald Trump, who'd performed a self-mocking cameo in *Celebrity*, defeated Clinton in the election, and Allen's decades of Democratic Party giving ended ignominiously.

Allen and Soon-Yi stayed in New York for Christmas and New Year's. William Morris agent John Burnham occasionally visited; he and Allen were friendlier than Allen ever had been with his longtime talent representative

Sam Cohn, and they'd sneak off to Saturday matinees, with Soon-Yi tagging along.

In the spring of 2017, as Allen tended to the postproduction of *Wonder Wheel*, he also labored on the script for his second Amazon Studios project, which he planned to shoot later in the year. And as he had for decades, he played with his jazz band on Monday nights. Allen and Soon-Yi also attended Knicks games, art exhibits, and performances, plays on Broadway and off.

The comedian and film director made a secret trip to Los Angeles in the first week of June, walking out onstage at the close of the 45th American Film Institute Life Achievement Award ceremonics at the Dolby Theatre. Dressed in a formal tuxedo, Allen was greeted by a standing ovation that for several minutes delayed his remarks to a star-filled crowd and a special audience of one—Diane Keaton—teary-eyed and beaming from the audience. Allen said he and Keaton were old friends who knew each other from way back. "I don't know how to describe her to you, actually," he went on, slipping into old rhythms of the stand-up comic he once had been. "You're probably familiar with the fictional movie character Eve Harrington. This is not to suggest that Diane, when I met her, was ruthlessly ambitious. But she did make an interesting Freudian slip when we started going out. She meant to refer to me as a talented young director, but instead she called me a stepping-stone. So that was a red flag."

Although Allen knew Keaton well, he said reading her memoirs had enlightened him. He hadn't realized, when treating her to high-priced dinners in the 1970s, that she was bulimic—he only knew she'd proclaim her love for him and then throw up. He could have saved a lot of money by taking her to a Pizza Hut.

The zingers continued as laughter exploded, with the loudest shrieking coming from Keaton. "Her beauty is not conventional," Allen said. "I mean pleasing to the eye. She dresses as you know to hide her sexuality and always has and has done a great job because it's never emerged over the years. . . . I always used to say that Keaton dressed like the woman in *A Streetcar Named Desire* who comes to take Blanche to the institution. . . . She's a beautiful girl," he went on, "and she's never succumbed to any face work or anything. She's very uncompromising. She prefers to look old." Glancing around the theater, where fellow presenters Warren Beatty and Al Pacino were seated,

Allen noted Keaton had been "involved romantically with a half dozen of the most gifted, charismatic, attractive men in Hollywood, and it's very interesting because every one of them has dumped her."

Allen turned serious before summoning the actress to the stage to receive her Life Achievement accolade. "From the minute I met her," he finished, "she was a great, great inspiration to me. Much of what I've accomplished in my life, I owe for sure to her. I've seen life through her eyes. This is a woman who is great at everything she does—actress, writer, photographer, fellatrix"*—a rare word that was left out of the subsequent AFI press release quoting him, and which had audience members turning to each other and mouthing *what?*—"and director."

It was six minutes of a perfect monologue that proved Allen could do the old soft-shoe anytime he really wanted to. The celebrity turnout, which included presenters Meryl Streep, Morgan Freeman, Sidney Poitier, Jane Fonda, Steve Martin—and scattered Woody Allen alumni such as Emma Stone and Dianne Wiest—were convulsed throughout his speech. No one could have guessed it might have been Woody Allen's swan song in Hollywood.

Coinciding with the summer break at the Carlyle in July, Allen embarked on a two-week jazz band tour of Europe, with dates in London, Lisbon, Antibes, Girona (Spain), and Copenhagen, ending with a performance in Hamburg. At the Elbphilharmonie in Hamburg, two topless female activists briefly disrupted the concert, storming the stage and shouting, "Stop the culture of silence!" The topless activists, who belonged to the women's rights collective Femen, which opposed patriarchy, said they wanted to draw attention to Dylan Farrow's sexual abuse allegations. The women were removed by security personnel, and the concert resumed without another hitch. Allen, who had perfected a blinkered existence, said later that he hardly noticed the incident and afterward issued a press statement, calling the protests "silly" and declining further comment.

THAT SUMMER, TWENTY-NINE-YEAR-OLD Ronan Farrow was quietly—and not so quietly—chasing the great white whale that was Harvey Weinstein, a goal other journalists were competing for, culminating in shock

* Merriam-Webster defines *fellatrix* as "a woman who performs fellatio."

waves affecting all of show business, including the touring clarinetist. Farrow had been languishing in his role as a show-biz features correspondent for *The Today Show* ("Ronan Farrow Goes from Anchor's Desk to Cubicle" was the snarky headline of the *New York Post*'s Page Six) before his 2016 "guest column" in the *Hollywood Reporter*. He leveraged the column condemning his father and the complicit media into a plum assignment to investigate the Hollywood casting couch for MSNBC.

Soon enough Ronan began to narrow his sights on Weinstein, the powerful independent producer who for years was rumored to be a serial womanizer and abuser, who paid attorneys and women for their silence and who, it so happens, produced several Woody Allen films. Working for months with a collaborator, by mid-summer 2017 Farrow thought he had nailed the Weinstein story, but from the point of view of network higher-ups his research was weakened by the reluctance of victims to go on camera about their experiences. Ronan pushed to go on air. MSNBC balked, for reasons detailed in his book *Catch and Kill*, which, in brief, involved network officials with their own dubious, womanizing pasts, who were susceptible to Weinstein's pressures to kill the investigation.

After Ronan interviewed Ken Auletta, a media critic who once had adversely profiled Weinstein for the *New Yorker*, and confided in him about the obstacles he was encountering at MSNBC, Auletta introduced the journalist to *New Yorker* editor David Remnick, who met with Ronan in late August and immediately perceived the "building blocks" of a breakthrough article, "the groundwork of a major scoop." Ronan told MSNBC he had decided to write up his investigation for the *New Yorker*. All along, two *New York Times* journalists were working on a parallel research track. Jodi Kantor and Megan Twohey had the same problem as Ronan, trying to convince Weinstein victims to go on the record and risk the producer's punitive tactics: smear campaigns and career destruction. When he learned from Nicholas Kristof about the rival *Times* investigation, Ronan raced furiously with *New Yorker* editorial support to outpace Kantor and Twohey and beat them to the punch.

The synchronous timing couldn't have been worse for *Wonder Wheel*, which had been selected for the Closing Night slot at the 55th New York Film Festival on October 15. The world premiere of the latest Woody Allen film would take place at Alice Tully Hall, with its public release slated to follow on December 1, coinciding with the director's eighty-second birthday. "I'm not quite sure what I expected when I sat down to watch *Wonder Wheel*, but when the lights came up I was speechless," said New York Film Festival director Kent Jones, in the late-summer press release announcement about the closing night selection. "There are elements in the film that will certainly be familiar to anyone who knows Woody Allen's work, but here he holds them up to a completely new light. I mean that literally and figuratively, because Allen and Vittorio Storaro use light and color in a way that is stunning in and of itself but also integral to the mounting emotional power of the film. And at the center of it all is Kate Winslet's absolutely remarkable performance—precious few actors are that talented, or fearless."

Allen himself had not RSVPed for the premiere, as he was already, by late September, deep into shooting his next Amazon Studios production—title pending—with former child actress (and younger sister of Dakota Fanning) Elle Fanning; Timothée Chalamet, who had a 2017 breakthrough in the Italian romantic drama *Call Me by Your Name*; Liev Schreiber, currently riding high on television as the eponymous *Ray Donovan*; the twice-Oscar-nominated Jude Law; Diego Luna from *Y Tu Mama También*; and Rebecca Hall, last seen as Vicky in *Vicky Cristina Barcelona*. New York columnists who tracked the two young stars, Fanning and Chalamet, as the cast and crew popped up in various city locales, reported there seemed to be an awful lot of rainy scenes.

Allen was aware of the Weinstein situation building to a climax, if for no other reason than because the producer, feeling increasingly cornered, reached out to the director one day as he steered scenes for the rainy movie in Central Park. "He wanted to know if Allen would intercede on his behalf. Allen shut down the idea," Ronan wrote in *Catch and Kill*. "Jeez, I'm so sorry," he quotes Allen. "Good luck." ("But he did have knowledge that Weinstein would later put to use," Ronan went on, working in mention of Dylan. "Weinstein's credit card receipts show his purchase of a book of interviews with Allen, written by a die-hard fan of his, documenting all of the arguments Allen and his army of private investigators and publicists had come up with to smear the credibility of my sister, the district attorney, and a judge who had suggested she was telling the truth.")*

---

* The Weinstein phone call is not sourced in the otherwise copious "notes" for *Catch and Kill*. Nor is the book Weinstein purchased identified. The "die-hard fan" to which Farrow refers could only have been Eric Lax. His *Conversations with Woody Allen* was reprinted and

Twohey and Kantor won the reporting race with their October 5 front-page story in the *New York Times*, the first of two documented examinations of Weinstein's long history of sexually predatory practices. (This was one week before the New York Film Festival premiere of *Wonder Wheel*.) The immediate outcry forced the Miramax board to fire Weinstein on October 9. Farrow's eight-thousand-word article expanding on Weinstein's misdeeds and revolving around the testimony of thirteen abused women, a number of whom identified themselves publicly for the first time in his reporting, was made available on October 10 (with an October 23 *New Yorker* cover date). Listing the many motion pictures produced by Weinstein as part of his backstory, Farrow did not mention his father or any Woody Allen film, probably because *New Yorker* editors advised against opening another can of worms. (Nor did Twohey and Kantor mention Allen.)

Yet another shoe dropped almost simultaneously on the West Coast—a few days later—with equally injurious ramifications for Allen. Rumors had swirled for months around Roy Price, the president of Amazon Studios, who had forged the Internet giant's unique contract with Allen to make the cable series *Crisis in Six Scenes* and *Wonder Wheel*—the first of four Allen projects Amazon had pledged to fully produce. Price had faced an internal investigation over sexual harassment claims, and on October 12 the producer making those claims against Price seized on the Weinstein revelations to go public. Isa Dick Hackett, the daughter of science fiction author Philip K. Dick, who had helped produce several Amazon series, including the Dick property *The Man in the High Castle*, alleged the executive had made lewd "dick" comments in her presence and pressured her for sex. Dick's public statement forced Amazon to immediately suspend Price, and the studio president resigned a few days later on October 16. Price was Allen's main booster inside the company, and in fact Allen's jazz band had tentatively agreed to play for his planned New York wedding, which was called off by his fiancée as Price's problems mounted.

Red-carpet festivities for the New York Film Festival showing of *Wonder*

---

updated in 2017. But Lax politely skirted the Dylan Farrow accusations in *Conversations with Woody Allen*. Or was it Lax's *Start to Finish*, also published in 2017, that covers the filming of *Irrational Man* and is more reportorial in form, rather than a book-length extended interview with Allen? *Start to Finish* featured Moses Farrow's account of what happened in 1992–93 and his recollections about growing up in the family. But Ronan's older brother's name was not mentioned once in *Catch and Kill*.

Wheel were summarily canceled because the Weinstein and Price headlines had resurrected the spotlight on Allen's own controversial past, according to *Variety*, and "cast members likely would have faced multiple questions about allegations by Allen's daughter Dylan Farrow." The lead actress, Kate Winslet, was already "under fire," reported *Variety*, for defending Allen and Roman Polanski (who'd directed her in his 2011 film *Carnage*) in publicity interviews, saying, "I didn't know Woody and I don't know anything about that family. As the actor in the film, you just have to step away and say, I don't know anything, really, and whether any of it is true or false. Having thought it all through, you put it to one side and just work with the person. Woody Allen is an incredible director. So is Roman Polanski. I had an extraordinary working experience with both of those men, and that's the truth."

Especially considering his son's byline on the *New Yorker* exposé, the BBC asked the film director, doing an interview timed to coincide with the premiere of *Wonder Wheel*, about his onetime ties to Weinstein. Allen said the numerous sexual abuse accusations against Weinstein were "tragic for the poor women involved, sad for Harvey that his life is so messed up" but, having absorbed the lessons of a blacklist from Alvah Bessie and *The Front*, the director also warned against the "witch-hunt atmosphere, a Salem atmosphere" that seemed to be mushrooming, merging with the social justice and empowerment movement dubbed "MeToo" by the harassment survivor and activist Tarana Burke. Allen told the BBC he had no prior knowledge of Weinstein's crimes. "No one ever came to me or told me horror stories with any real seriousness," Allen said. "And they wouldn't, because you are not interested in it. You are interested in making your movie." (Many other show business personalities who had worked with Miramax, including actress Meryl Streep, also issued statements saying they were horrified by the producer's behavior, about which they never suspected the reality.) Allen's interview raced across the wires and Internet, with journalists, bloggers, and tweeters rising up in arms over his words of seeming sympathy for Weinstein. Allen was forced to clarify his remarks, telling *Variety* he thought he had made it clear he believed Weinstein to be "a sad sick man."

REGARDLESS, THE "WEINSTEIN effect," as *Variety* termed it, swept across the screen world, indeed across America and much of the Western world, like a pick-your-"disaster metaphor—tsunami, hurricane, avalanche, landslide," in the words of the *New York Times*, all of which "seem to be in endless rotation" to describe the national reckoning that was the MeToo movement. Within the next two months MeToo cut like a scythe through all fields and professions with a special appetite for show business and media figures. Political journalist Mark Helprin, Fox broadcaster Bill O'Reilly, actor Kevin Spacey, writer-director James Toback, director-producer Brett Rattner, comedian Louis C.K., talk show host Charlie Rose, US senator Al Franken, *Prairie Home Companion*'s Garrison Keillor, playwright Israel Horwitz, cofounder of Pixar John Lasseter, actor Jeffrey Tambor, and *Today Show* anchor Matt Lauer were among the prominent figures who went down, many admitting trespasses and retiring from public view, some pushing back, most never to reclaim their careers. The Internet swiftly became "a clearinghouse for complaints," according to the *New York Times*, with a "whisper network" of websites and back channels where women—famous and ordinary—shared their MeToo stories.

More than ever, Woody Allen's name was now rotely added to the company of powerful men who had gotten away with sexual harassment and abuse. Tens of millions of Americans heard Allen's name repeatedly associated with egregious MeToo offenses, often in patently misinformed statements, as when actress Ellen Pompeo, who played the title character on *Grey's Anatomy*, the most-watched prime-time drama on network television, tweeted "he married his daughter. . . . Kind of hard not to see who this fool is."

Now it was no longer cool to caution—as Nicholas Kristof once had done in his column—that Allen had never been charged or convicted, and that he vehemently denied the claims. There was no longer a "lively debate," in Kristof's words. Now it was settled argument.

The Salem witch trials angle was gleefully embraced by some women, including *Times* guest columnist Lindy West: "Yes, this is a witch hunt. . . . So, Mr. Allen, et al., I know you hate gossip and rumor mills but unfortunately they're the only recourse we have. . . . The witches are coming but not for your life. We're coming for your legacy."

Now it also became acceptable to add Soon-Yi's name to the shaming. A New York *Daily News* columnist, invoking the MeToo Movement, asserted that Soon-Yi had been complicit with Dylan's ordeal. The columnist,

Linda Stasi, addressed her directly: "You, too, are a victim—but one of your own making," wrote Stasi. "At 47, you still haven't figured that out. You still denounce your mother as the horror while you sleep with the enemy, who happens to be your mother's former lover." Stasi added: "In fact, your husband has continued to this day to make movies about underage girls and older men—taking it so far that there is reportedly a perverse sex scene" in the movie Allen just finished, "in which a 44-year-old man (Jude Law) has sex with a 15-year-old girl (Elle Fanning)." Not to split hairs, but Law was forty-five years old when this was written, and Fanning, twenty-one years old, was playing a college student who does not have sex with Law in the screen story. In fact, her character doesn't have sex with anyone in the film, which was one of its running jokes.

DYLAN FARROW, WHO'D be repeatedly cited in *Catch and Kill* as her brother's muse and conscience during his investigative quest, emerged anew with a second "open letter" published in the *Los Angeles Times* in early December, declaring "we are in the midst of a revolution"—the MeToo revolution—which, thus far, in her opinion, unforgivably had "spared" Woody Allen. Reiterating that her father sexually abused her in the attic of her Frog Hollow home when she was seven years old, Dylan said the "simple facts" of her case had been muddied by "Allen's public relations team and his lawyers" into an "allegation . . . still too complicated, too difficult" for many to process, making it easier for Hollywood and the public to ignore. "In this deliberately created fog," Dylan wrote, "A-list actors agree to appear in Allen's films and journalists tend to avoid the subject." As before, she called out actresses by name, including Greta Gerwig from *To Rome with Love*, Blake Lively from *Café Society*, and Kate Winslet, the star of *Wonder Wheel*, which was due to open nationally in the days ahead.

Subsequently, Dylan gave a spate of other interviews, including an appearance on *CBS This Morning*, in which she sharpened her language from 1992. "As a seven-year-old I would say, I would have said he touched my private parts," Dylan said. "As a thirty-two-year-old, he touched my labia and my vulva with his finger."

Amid this atmosphere, in early December, *Wonder Wheel* was dispatched to nearly six hundred US theaters, where it quickly sank like a stone. It was pretty much the film Kent Jones had described: rapturous scenic design and photography, a *Blue Jasmine* relocated to Coney Island, Tennessee Williams crossed with Eugene O'Neill, and menacing hoodlums in a script that kidded its own pretensions, the echoes from Allen's real life reimagined as an uncomfortable fiction. Another lapidary work from the old gem-cutter. There were terrific performances from Juno Temple (the wayward daughter trying to start a new life), James Belushi (brave casting as a working stiff always on the edge of belligerence and violence), Justin Timberlake (a jaunty lifeguard living the melodrama he will later write as a play), and above all Kate Winslet as a falling-apart woman consumed by fantasies and jealousies. In any other year Winslet would have been a shoo-in Oscar nominee, and perhaps that was the subtext of her later harsh reversal against Allen. The bewitching film affirmed (out of the lifeguard's mouth) Allen's stubborn adage: "The heart has its own hieroglyphics."

The reviews were not uniformly scathing. "Good, not great," wrote Mick LaSalle in the *San Francisco Chronicle*, but by now many film critics could find ingenious ways to mention Dylan Farrow in their takedowns. "One of his [Allen's] more unfortunate contributions to cinema," Manohla Dargis wrote in the *New York Times*, adding, "The allegations as well as discomfort about his marriage to Soon-Yi have hovered over him." The film "clunks and groans," wrote Michael Phillips in the *Chicago Tribune*. "In code, *Wonder Wheel* dances along the edge of the writer-director's off-screen life, namely the allegations by Dylan Farrow, Allen's adopted daughter, of sexual molestation, and Allen's controversial marriage to Soon-Yi Previn, the adopted daughter of Allen's then-partner Mia Farrow." *Wonder Wheel* was "a Coney Island dog," the *Boston Globe* headlined, "an embarrassment," in the opinion of critic Ty Burr, noting that as the romance burgeoned between Mickey (Timberlake) and the stepdaughter (Temple) of Ginny (Winslet), a plot turn that sends Ginny off the deep end, "it's impossible not to wonder what scores Allen might be trying to settle here."

THROUGHOUT DECEMBER AND January, *Wonder Wheel* shed venues and maxed out at about $14.5 million in US grosses; another $14.5 million would be earned overseas, with the best earnings coming from France, Italy, and Spain.

The picture's dismal box-office fate in America was aggravated by the sudden traffic jam of actors and actresses from previous Woody Allen movies who began to denounce their former director, following Dylan's second "open letter" in the *Los Angeles Times*. Some issued tweets, or posted on Instagram. Others were asked Allen gotcha questions by journalists. Michael Caine, Ellen Page, Chloé Sevigny, Freida Pinto, Hayley Atwell, Marion Cotillard, Greta Gerwig, Colin Firth, Rachel Brosnahan, Evan Rachel Wood, and David Krumholtz (who gives Justin Timberlake philosophical advice about his love life over a chess game in *Wonder Wheel*) were among the many players offering up public statements to the effect that they hadn't known very much about the Dylan Farrow case when they acted in their Allen films and now wished they hadn't taken the jobs.

Mira Sorvino, who'd won a Best Supporting Actress Oscar for *Mighty Aphrodite*, penned a much-quoted "open letter" to Dylan online for the Huffington Post. "I confess at the time I worked for Woody Allen I was a naive young actress," Sorvino explained. "I swallowed the media's portrayal of your abuse allegations against your father as an outgrowth of a twisted custody battle . . . for which I am terribly sorry. For this I also owe an apology to Mia." Peter Sarsgaard answered a curt "no" when a reporter asked if he'd ever again act for Allen, before adding: "I would continue to watch Woody Allen movies." Placing a curse on the next, already completed and forthcoming Amazon–Woody Allen production, now titled *A Rainy Day in New York*, cast members Griffin Newman (a one-scene role), Rebecca Hall, and Timothée Chalamet repudiated their involvement. Hall said she had contributed her acting salary to Time's Up, a Hollywood organization for women of color embroiled in abuse situations, while Chalamet announced he was donating his wages to several charities, including Time's Up.

"He swore to my sister," Allen claimed of Chalamet in *Apropos of Nothing*, "he needed to do that as he was up for an Oscar for *Call Me By Your Name*, and he and his agent felt he had a better chance of winning if he denounced me." Chalamet's largesse and similar actions by other performers who had been in Allen pictures were not "as heroic a gesture as it seems," the film director added wryly, "as we can only afford to pay the union minimum, and my guess is that if we paid more usual movie money, which often runs quite high, the actors might have righteously declared they'd never work with me again but would possibly leave out the part about donating their salary."

"Woody Allen's Actors Are Turning Against Him, and It's About Time" was the headline of contributing editor Angie Han's mid-January piece on the Mashable digital media website, which boasted over six million Twitter followers and nearly four million Facebook watchers. "Major stars who have yet to comment on their work with Woody Allen," Han wrote in a postscript to her list of anti–Woody Allen stars, embracing the name-shaming tactic of the Farrow clan, "include Justin Timberlake, Emma Stone, Owen Wilson, Tom Hiddleston, Larry David, Selena Gomez, Joaquin Phoenix, Scarlett Johansson, Jude Law, Meryl Streep, Steve Carell, Kristen Stewart, Colin Farrell, Blake Lively, Cate Blanchett, Rachel McAdams, and Hugh Jackman."

A few on the Mashable list, including Phoenix and Gomez, would surrender to the intense pressure over time. Sometimes the actorly condemnations of Allen were full-throated, yet just as often they were terse or tortured. The steady drip, drip, drip eventually claimed John Turturro, who had acted in several Woody Allen pictures and who was the writer-director of *Fading Gigolo*, and in 2019, *Wonder Wheel*'s Kate Winslet—both of whom you might think owed Allen unusual debts of gratitude. Director Spike Lee, who once defended Allen's artistic right to make his Upper East Side films populated mainly by white people, and who had interviewed Allen in convivial fashion for a book about their mutual love of basketball, said something vaguely supportive of his New York directorial colleague, then he swiftly backtracked when social media pounced.

Dylan Farrow kept up the intimidation. In early January, Blake Lively tweeted her support of Time's Up, with the actress saying she stood with "women in every industry who are subjected to indignities and offensive behavior." Dylan replied on Twitter, "You worked with my abuser, @blakelively. Am I a woman who matters too?"* Dylan also scoffed at the *New York Times* tweet that announced, "Cate Blanchett, a vocal campaigner against

* It took Mia Farrow a few years to weigh in against the show business name-shaming of her children Dylan and Ronan, or perhaps it was simply good publicity for her 2024 return to Broadway, costarring in a play with Patti LuPone. Reflecting on the memorable Woody Allen films she made, the actress told John Dickerson on the CBS Sunday Morning show, "I completely understand if an actor decides to work with him [Woody]. I'm not one who says, 'Oh, he shouldn't . . .'"

sexual harassment, will lead this year's Cannes jury." Dylan fired back, "Can one be a 'vocal campaigner against sexual harassment' and a vocal supporter of Woody Allen? Seems a tad oxymoronic."

ONCE THE FILMMAKER had been hailed by the motion picture industry as "Mr. Everything." Now the anti–Woody Allen crowd wanted to "cancel" his existence—turn him into a "Mr. Nothing." It was no longer enough to repudiate Allen's latest release. His detractors wanted to erase Allen's entire career, all his films.

The *New York Times* was at the top of the pecking order of film criticism and when, in quick succession in early 2018, Manohla Dargis and A. O. Scott offered post-Dylan reappraisals of Allen's cinematic legacy, it was akin to twin thunderbolts hurled by Hera and Zeus. "I've liked and loved some of Mr. Allen's movies, and loathed others," Dargis explained in her film wrap-up of 2017, "but I've always put the allegations against him aside because he wasn't charged and I wanted to review the work, not the man. Even so, Mr. Allen's movies can be hard to take if you're a woman. He has written great female characters—given humanity by brilliant performers—but too many are ditzes, shrews, and dewy young things gaga over uncomfortably older men and Allen stand-ins. *Wonder Wheel* manifests some of his worst tendencies; the sexism is overt, and his blurring of life and art is repellent. In my review, I cited his marriage to Ms. Previn and Dylan Farrow's allegations, a history I've seen as a malignant cloud. I had never referred to that history before because I hadn't seen it in the work. Now I did."

Scott trailed his colleague with his famous—infamous to some—"My Woody Allen Problem" on January 31, in which the critic, like many in the growing anti-Woody camp, found as much fault with himself as with the director and his oeuvre. "I've seen all of his movies, and I think he's guilty," declared Scott, while referencing his discomfort at the "rape" joke in *Play It Again, Sam* and "the preoccupation with very young women" in many Allen films, particularly *Manhattan*. "What I find most ethically troubling about Mr. Allen's work at present is the extent to which I and so many of my colleagues have ignored or minimized its uglier aspects."*

* Revised opinions of Allen's films became common in the *Times*. Scott was soon followed by third-stringer Glenn Kenny who, when handicapping Sally Hawkins's chances for an Oscar

There ensued a frenzy of combing through Allen's past work—plays, motion pictures, and published short pieces—seeking evidence of infractions against women. Evidence there was, obvious (*Manhattan*, older guy/younger leading lady age disparities, prostitute characters) as well as subjective. Vicki Marquette, on Media.com, found "No Surprise Here: Woody Allen Joked About Sexual Coercion in a 1971 *Playboy*," referring to his tongue-in-cheek annotation of a nude layout of *Bananas* costar Natividad (Naty) Abascal. "Before Naty signed her movie contract, I told her about the sexual obligation that was a part of the job of any actress who worked with me," Allen wrote, offending Marquette fifty years later. "I still recall what she said. It was 'Yucch!'"

Richard Morgan's plunge into the fifty-six-box archive of "drafts and scribblings" in Allen's archives in the Firestone Library of Princeton University gave grist to Scott and many journalists and bloggers weighing in at this crucial juncture. A New York freelancer who had previously written for the *Post* about having been date-raped, Morgan published his negative findings in the *Washington Post* in early January, asserting that Allen's writings over the decades were "filled with misogynist and lecherous musings," in Morgan's words, "an insistent, vivid obsession with young women and girls." Often referencing past works that had gone unproduced or unpublished, some undated, with others harking back to the 1960s that had cowriters like Marshall Brickman—including a deconstruction of "The Filmmaker"—Morgan bemoaned the many Allen jokes about women's legs, breasts, or asses, even if they were patent satire or deliberate parody, to argue that the title of every Woody Allen project ought to be "A Woman Gets Objectified by a Man." Did Allen ever truly write great parts for actresses? Only "sort of," argued Morgan, because Allen used Oscars as bait for "[Diane] Keaton and the others the way Harvey Weinstein used Meryl Streep"—i.e., for respectability. The freelancer name-shamed Miley Cyrus, Selena Gomez, and Kate Winslet as trapped by "an Oscar lure shiny enough to blind aspiring acolytes to his darkness, though some of them recognized that darkness and decided to participate anyway."

Nicholas Kristof approvingly cited Morgan's blanket condemnation of Allen's life's work when he chimed in with his second influential column

---

for *The Shape of Water*, flippantly cited her previous role in *Blue Jasmine*—a film nominated for three Academy Awards including Best Original Screenplay—as "a not very good movie featuring a lot of acting."

supporting Dylan Farrow in early February. "I'm a friend of Dylan and her family, so I'm not an unbiased observer," Kristof noted this time, but "over the years I have reviewed the evidence, and *on balance* [author's emphasis] it persuades me." Once again, the columnist interviewed Dylan, touting "the need to listen to victims" and linking her cause to abused gymnasts, Harvey Weinstein's victims, the perversions of the Catholic Church, and "the innumerable girls and boys suffering anonymously at the hands of abusive coaches, relatives, family friends or bosses." Dylan found it "incredibly healing" that certain actors had renounced Allen, or were donating to sex-abuse organizations, she told Kristof. The columnist wondered "if there was any chance that this was a false memory, that she had been brainwashed," and Dylan "flatly" said, "No, I think it's more logical almost that the people who accuse me of being brainwashed are brainwashed themselves by the celebrity, the glamour, the fantasy, the pull they have to Woody Allen, their hero on a pedestal." This time Kristof did not include any cautionary note about Allen's presumed or avowed innocence.

The stamp of approval by *Times* grandees Dargis, Scott, and Kristof validated the MeToo backlash against Allen in lesser outposts. *Hollywood Reporter* critic Miriam Bale publicly vowed never to review another Woody Allen movie. Allen was snipped out of a documentary about, of all things, the Carlyle Hotel. The Goodspeed Opera House in East Haddam, Connecticut, dropped a slated revival of *Bullets over Broadway* "in light of the current dialogue on sexual harassment and misconduct." Twelve thousand students signed a petition, organized by Savannah Lyon, a twenty-three-year-old theater major, to shut down a Woody Allen film course at the University of California in San Diego. "They [who offer this course] do not care that Woody Allen is on his way out of Hollywood," her petition read. "They do not care that the class is less than one-third full, making it an unpopular class that has no reason to be taught. They do not care that there are thousands of other directors who could teach the same film basics that they use Woody Allen to teach, directors who haven't raped seven-year-old girls."

When Ronan Farrow won a Pulitzer in 2018, sharing the prize for Public Affairs Reporting with the two *New York Times* journalists whose Harvey Weinstein investigation preceded his into print, the award gave another endorsement from on high to the anti-Woody momentum. Allen's putative son became an in-demand public speaker, making joint appearances with

MeToo galvanizer Tarana Burke. Repeatedly, Ronan tweeted in support of his sister and against his father. The director, and all past and present Woody Allen films, were condemned amid a blizzard of negative media.

CAFÉ SOCIETY, CRISIS in Six Scenes, *Wonder Wheel*—three strikes, and Allen was out. Amazon Studios had invested $25 million in *A Rainy Day in New York*, which was all but foredoomed after star Timothée Chalamet and Rebecca Hall, who plays a supporting role in the film, publicly disavowed Allen. MeToo had sent Roy Price, Allen's ally inside the Amazon operation, packing. "Increasingly shaky" is how the *Hollywood Reporter* described Allen's deal with the Internet giant. Although his contract called for two more pictures after *Rainy Day*, "internally," wrote the *Reporter*, "the consensus is that Amazon will have no choice but to sever ties with the director, even if that means a hefty payout." Amazon CEO Jeff Bezos announced the reorganization of his film division to produce more mainstream movies. Former NBC Entertainment president Jennifer Salke was named to succeed Price. Behind the scenes, company lawyers for the Internet giant drafted a suit against Allen.

Although he still played jazz on Mondays, Allen became less conspicuous at public events, parties, and restaurants. For weeks, he declined interviews. The filmmaker stuck to the silence he had vowed on the subject of Dylan Farrow, except for once, referring to the furor when speaking to the Argentinian television show *Periodismo para Todos*, to publicize the South American release of *Wonder Wheel*. Allen said he resented the child-abuse accusations against him as being associated with MeToo, when "I should be the poster boy for the MeToo Movement," in his words, after working with "hundreds of actresses and not a single one—big ones, famous ones, ones starting out—have ever, ever suggested any kind of impropriety." Amazon lawyers took note, and later argued in court papers that Allen's interview had "sabotaged" his future box office prospects.

As the Argentinian interview fanned more adverse press, the comedian and film director revived the notion of an autobiography, taking out notes for the memoir he first outlined and tried to sell in 2003. He was intent on writing his own testament, once and for all: his life story, his version of what happened between him and Mia Farrow—and supposedly with Dylan—a version of events that had never varied, but that he no longer reiterated in interviews.

During the mass bombardment of Allen, a few prominent people spoke up resolutely in his defense, including members of the press corps. Op-ed columnist Bret Stephens in the *New York Times*, for example, implicitly rebuked his colleague Nicholas Kristof by questioning the smear campaign: "Shouldn't the weight of available evidence, to say nothing of the presumption of innocence, extend to the court of public opinion too?" A number of movie critics professed skepticism about Dylan's accusations, as did celebrities from other fields, including bestselling author Stephen King, but supporters or skeptics had to be careful with their words.

Many famous people with Allen connections were asked not once but every time they stepped in front of a microphone or met with a journalist. Poor octogenarian Michael Caine first blasted Allen; then, in a second interview, reneged on his words, saying the evidence against the director amounted to "hearsay." He was given a third chance by *Rolling Stone*. "If he had a trial and someone proved he had done something, I wouldn't do it [act in another Woody Allen film]," Caine explained. Every time a person associated with Allen spoke out, he or she tempted their own firing squad. "Woody Allen is my friend and I continue to believe him," Diane Keaton tweeted on January 29, 2018, attaching a YouTube link to Allen's *60 Minutes* interview from 1992. To which the writer-director Judd Apatow tweeted: "I see a man who wanted what he wanted and didn't care that he was having an affair with a 19 year old* when he was 54 who was also his daughter's sister. He also took nude photos of this child who he had known since she was nine and left them out for his family to see. Narcissism."

Among Allen's vocal defenders, the majority were older entertainers, often Jewish, long-standing friends and people who had been involved in more than one Woody Allen production. This group included Wallace Shawn, Alec Baldwin, Jeff Goldblum, Nick Nolte, Scarlett Johansson ("He maintains his innocence, and I believe him"), Anjelica Huston (in interviews the actress said she'd work with Allen again "in a second"), Alan Alda ("I'm not qualified to judge him"), Javier Bardem ("I don't agree with the public lynching that he's

* Soon-Yi's age was often blurred by Allen detractors, as it had been initially, by the Farrow-Previn family, in the 1993 court skirmishes. But the college student was twenty-one at the time her affair with Allen was discovered. Bloggers like Princess Weekes for the *Mary Sue* pointed out Apatow's comparative "silence" on the alleged sexual misconduct of his friend—and frequent costar of Apatow screen comedies—actor James Franco.

been receiving"), and many other performers, who pointedly held their fire—including, standing against her costars in *A Rainy Day in New York*, Tony- and Emmy-winning actress Cherry Jones, who portrayed a pivotal character in the new film. Asked if she would work with Allen again, Jones said: "There are those who are comfortable in their certainty. I am not. I don't know the truth. When we condemn by instinct our democracy is on a slippery slope."

Members of Allen's family finally let their voices be heard, including, again, Moses Farrow; his nineteen-year-old daughter Bechet, speaking publicly for the first time; and Soon-Yi, in her first substantial interview since 1992.

Following the months of public vilification of his father, Moses posted a blog essay titled "A Son Speaks Out" on May 23, 2018. Prefacing his comments with "I'm a very private person and not at all interested in public attention," Moses, now forty, retold the story of August 4, 1992, from his point of view as "the oldest child at the house that summer day," elaborating on his previous accounts, insisting nothing out of the ordinary occurred. Moses spoke of "a deep and persistent darkness within the Farrow family," originating with Mia's upbringing and her alcoholic father, and the fact, which he said he learned from her conversations with him, that Mia herself "was the victim of attempted molestation within her own family." When Allen's romance with Soon-Yi began, Moses wrote, "it was unorthodox, uncomfortable, disruptive to our family and it hurt my mother terribly. But the relationship itself was not nearly as devastating to our family as my mother's insistence on making this betrayal the center of all our lives from then on." Moses said Mia's image as a supermother warranted deeper scrutiny. She "had good intentions in adopting children with disabilities from the direst of circumstances, but the reality inside our walls was very different." In part Moses blamed his mother for the untimely deaths of three siblings: Tam, struggling with depression, who overdosed on drugs at age seventeen, "a situation exacerbated by my mother refusing to get her help"; twenty-seven-year-old Thaddeus "shooting himself in his car less than ten minutes from my mother's house"; and Lark's death in poverty at thirty-five, from AIDS-related causes.*

* Three years passed before, in 2021, following the broadcast of the *Allen v. Farrow* documentary, Farrow tweeted her response to Moses, regarding the three deaths. "Few families are perfect," the actress wrote, rejecting the blame cast by Moses. "These are unspeakable tragedies," she wrote. "Any other speculation about their deaths is to dishonor their lives and the lives of their children and loved ones."

Moses said "the fatal dysfunction within my childhood home had nothing to do with Woody. . . . Life under my mother's roof was impossible if you didn't do exactly as you were told." Conflicted by what happened at Frog Hollow, Moses reported, he had wanted to "reach out to Woody" after earning his master's. His mother forbade him to have contact with "that monster." After disobeying Mia, he was excommunicated.

Dylan and Ronan swiftly blasted their older brother on Twitter, the latter saying Moses's version of life in the Farrow household was part of the orchestrated "smear campaign" to discredit his sister and "extraordinary" mother.

Bechet Allen, then a college student at Bard, spoke out publicly for the first time with a brief statement on Facebook. "I never wanted to involve myself in the social media debates involving my father," Allen and Soon-Yi's oldest adopted daughter declared, "but there comes a point when I realize that I can either continue pretending that none of this is going on, or stand up for him. . . . He has been nothing but supportive and loving."

In late summer Soon-Yi submitted to a lengthy sit-down with novelist and cultural critic Daphne Merkin, an Upper East Side neighbor and acquaintance of Allen's dating back several decades, which was published in *New York* magazine. Allen's forty-seven-year-old wife sided with Moses in telling a story "strikingly different from what's put forth by Mia and Dylan as well as their son and brother Ronan Farrow," harshly assessing Mia as a mother who tried to create "a fairy-tale version of reality" while treating Soon-Yi and her adopted sisters as "domestics." Soon-Yi insisted "there was a hierarchy" in the Farrow-Previn family, with Fletcher as the "golden child. Mia always valued intelligence and also looks, blond hair and blue eyes." Asked repeatedly if she had "any positive recollections of her years with Mia," Soon-Yi said, "It seems hard to imagine, but I really can't come up with one." Although Soon-Yi avoided commenting on Dylan's charges per se, Merkin quoted Dylan's reaction to Soon-Yi's remarks: "This [version of events] only serves to revictimize me. Thanks to my mother, I grew up in a wonderful home." One could read Soon-Yi's words and Moses's blog and believe that, decades earlier, alternative realities coexisted inside the Farrow-Previn home, and that some of Mia's fourteen children might regard her as a saintly mother, while others might have found her impossible.

Perhaps it is unsurprising to learn that the Pulitzer Prize winner and other members of the Farrow family exerted pressure on *New York* editors, in the days before publication, trying to worry the magazine into dumping the article. "I wasn't used to this level of fear . . . fear of Ronan, of being sued, of the power of Mia and Ronan, simply culturally, their power on Twitter," Merkin told the *New York Post* several years later.

Just as there was a small army of anti-Woody bloggers, entire websites sprang up to support Allen and praise his pictures, or to debunk Dylan's claims, pointing out discrepancies, inconsistencies, and elisions in her various accounts, and those of Ronan, which were repeated by journalists or spread on social media. One of Allen's most persistent and knowledgeable Internet guardians was Robert B. Weide, director of the American Masters documentary about Allen and an Emmy winner for producing and directing the *Curb Your Enthusiasm* series starring Larry David (another Allen loyalist who didn't shrink from praising him). Weide wrote a series of protracted examinations of the 1992 incident, rebutting the Farrow accounts, and offering Ronan $100,000 cash to the charity of his choice if the journalist could produce "a shred of 'evidence'" for "his provably false claims" against Allen. Although there are ways they could take him to court, the Farrows have never filed a civil suit to press Dylan's claims. Repeatedly, Weide has dared the Farrows to file civil charges against the filmmaker in Connecticut and "sue him for every penny he's got," in Weide's words. "The statute of limitations won't expire until Dylan turns forty-eight," Weide wrote. "Ronan could even be her lawyer!" he added.

"The day is coming when every actor who has denounced #WoodyAllen will be as proud of their decision as those who named names during the McCarthy hearings," Weide warned in a tweet.

IN LATE SPRING, without any public fanfare, Ajay Patel, an associate general counsel for Amazon Studios, sent an email to Allen's legal representatives, saying the company's contract with him had been terminated. The deal had become "impracticable," according to the studio in later court filings, because of "supervening events, including renewed allegations against Mr. Allen, his own controversial comments, and the increasing refusal of top talent to work with or be associated with him in any way, all of which have frustrated the purpose of the agreement."

Plans for the summer opening of *A Rainy Day in New York* were halted.

The US rights to the movie were embargoed by Amazon. Perhaps, or so it seemed at the time, no American would ever see the film except for Allen's small circle of family and friends, which he sometimes claimed was his principal target audience anyway. Spending a quiet summer with his wife and daughters, Allen kept writing—another film script—yet mainly devoting himself to his memoir. There were no Monday nights at the Café Carlyle, which always went dark over the summer. There would be no European vacation, not at Christmas or New Year's. Turning eighty-three, the filmmaker whose name was synonymous with New York City, and who was acclaimed as America's Bergman and Fellini, faced a grim future.

He even hit a wall after he finished his autobiography. A few publishers were offered the full manuscript in early 2019, and according to press accounts only a small handful of top New York editors agreed to read the book. To a person, those who examined the manuscript said the first half, which mainly concerned Allen's early life and career, was lively and colorful, while the second half, beginning in time when Allen met Mia Farrow, was like finding yourself seated next to a crazy man at a dinner party who does nothing but rant about his ex-wife. Allen offered the work for a nominal advance, but he had a few strict stipulations, among them: "No editing." The handful of editors who seriously considered the book went behind closed doors for their readings, while a William Morris agent waited outside to whisk the manuscript away after they were done. Regardless, it wasn't the "no editing" that depressed the bidding. "Publishers are skittish about working with authors accused of sexual misconduct," according to the *New York Times*, "for pragmatic reasons as well as ethical ones. Authors facing harassment allegations have been dropped by their agents, their finished books pulped, literary rewards revoked, and their books pulled from the shelves. Boycotts by readers and book-sellers often snowball. . . ."

"Woody Allen Is Shunned Even Further" read a breathless *Times* headline.

Every time another serial abuser fell to the MeToo movement, it seemed, an easy connection could be made to Allen, and probably worst of all was the New York financier Jeffrey Epstein, whose involvement in the trafficking of underage girls, while eluding justice, stirred headlines early in 2019. Epstein also resided on the Upper East Side, and there was no evidence he and Allen shared anything other than a neighborly and social acquaintance except for the fact that Allen and Soon-Yi had made the mistake of accepting invitations to numerous soirees and dinner parties at Epstein's townhouse, where other public figures and celebrities were also invariably present. Some occasions were more in the nature of salons, sometimes scientific, sometimes cultural, Allen told the sympathetic interviewer Roger Friedman in 2024. "One evening he had an evening of all comedians," Allen said. "And one evening he had an evening of all magicians."

The *Wall Street Journal* subsequently elaborated on the relationship between Allen and Epstein, reporting that Epstein wished to accompany Allen on visits to famous artist studios or auction houses; and, most improbably, that at one point Epstein tried to convince the film director to give lessons on editing to a select group of guests, using Alfred Hitchcock's *Psycho* as his guide. There is no evidence these extracurricular activities took place. An Allen spokesman said "there were always other guests" at any Epstein gathering he and Soon-Yi attended.

For example, the publicist Peggy Seagal included Allen and Soon-Yi on her A-list for the dinner party in honor of Prince Andrew of England that she organized at Epstein's place in 2011. Prince Andrew was later alleged to have participated in Epstein's sex trafficking circle. Other guests that night included comedian Chelsea Handler and the broadcasters Katie Couric and George Stephanopoulos, but the name Woody Allen stuck out. Handler, Couric, and Stephanopoulos did not make Maureen Dowd's honor roll of "monsters"—Allen, Epstein, Bill Cosby, R. Kelly, film director Bryan Singer—whom she tagged in her February 17, 2019, column, decrying how their "celebrity supersedes criminality." Getting into the spirit a short time later, a *New York Times* editorial enumerated the famous "friends and acquaintances" of the despised Epstein: "Prince Andrew, Bill Clinton, Kevin Spacey, Woody Allen, and Donald Trump."

Still, you could punch and kick that guy Woody Allen, pour bullets into him and light gasoline on his body, only to be amazed when a wraith wearing a jester's hat and a weary old man's grin stepped from the ashes of the pyre. Allen could have rested on his laurels; he surely had enough money to scrape by, even with two daughters in college. Maybe what stopped him is that Allen hated to be told what to do, to be bullied, told what is funny and what is not, to be compelled to conform to other people's idea of his persona, his comedy, his films, his life.

He refused to behave like a corpse. In February 2019 Allen countersued

Amazon Studios with a $68 million lawsuit submitted in New York federal court. Amazon's rescindment of his contract referenced "a 25-year-old baseless allegation against Mr. Allen," according to the filing, charges which Allen had consistently denied. "That allegation was already well known to Amazon (and the public) before Amazon entered into four separate deals with Mr. Allen," the lawsuit asserted. "There simply was no legitimate ground for Amazon to renege on its promises." Amazon cited, in counterfilings, Allen's BBC interview ("a witch-hunt atmosphere, a Salem atmosphere"), in which "Mr. Allen seemed to express sympathy for Harvey Weinstein," the *New York Times* reported.

Simultaneous with the lawsuit came news of another Allen-hurled gauntlet. He announced he would be directing the next Woody Allen film in the summer of 2019, to be shot entirely in and around San Sebastian, Spain, revolving around the annual film festival there. Allen had the script in hand and his team had already scouted the locations. The cast for "WASP19" would be spearheaded by Wallace Shawn, whose frequent appearances in Allen pictures dated back to *Manhattan*, and the idiosyncratic American actress Gina Gershon, best known for portraying a bisexual stripper in *Showgirls*. Important roles had been carved out for French actor Louis Garrel from Bernardo Bertolucci's *The Dreamers*, and Viennese-born actor Christoph Waltz, a two-time Oscar winner for Quentin Tarantino movies. The script would revolve around a husband and wife who discover extramarital temptations during the annual festival extravaganza. Allen's sister and other producers—it was now pretty much a family operation with several Aronsons by birth or marriage strewn among the credits—had renewed ties with Jaume Roures and MediaPro in Barcelona while picking up support from Wildside, a London-based division of the Fremantle company, which produced television and films for Italy. "We have a ten-year relationship with Mr. Allen," MediaPro announced in a press release, "and, like all projects we produce, we judge the creator by its work."

In July, Allen would kick off the busy summer with an eight-city tour of Europe, playing his trusty clarinet with the Eddy Davis New Orleans Jazz Band. All the concerts were sold out in advance with at least three shows—performances in Barcelona, Madrid, Bilbao—scheduled in Spain before Basque Country filming.

••

IN LATE JUNE Allen arrived, with Soon-Yi and his daughters, in San Sebastian. The first order of business was a press conference revealing *Rifkin's Festival* as the title of the film-to-be, and introducing the Spanish additions to the cast—Elena Anaya from Pedro Almodóvar films, Sergi López from *Pan's Labyrinth*. Allen told journalists he wanted to make the picture in San Sebastian because Barcelona was too hot and sunny in the summers, and he wanted a novel Spanish setting for his new film. He was happy to spend family time in a city he had loved since bringing *Melinda and Melinda* to the San Sebastian Film Festival in 2004. He batted away questions about his troubles in America. "My philosophy, since I started many years ago in show business," he said, "is that no matter what happens is to keep focused on my work." Asked when he might stop making films, Allen replied, "I don't think of retiring. I'll probably die in the midst of setting a film shot one day on the set, making a movie."

Allen was joined at the publicity launch by Gina Gershon and Elena Anaya, the two leading ladies, both of whom were asked if, before accepting their roles, they had considered the controversies swirling around Allen. Anaya said unflinchingly, "I'm responsible for the projects I choose," while Gershon explained, "It's a wild time in America. While I think there's a lot of good coming out of these different movements, I also feel that it's really important people take a look at every single situation and make up their own minds." In addition to Wallace Shawn as the titular Rifkin, the Americans who journeyed to San Sebastian for small roles in *Rifkin's Festival* included Richard Kind, another *Mad About You* alumnus; Steve Guttenberg, who'd appeared in Allen's play *Relatively Speaking*; and Allen friend and regular Douglas McGrath.

Although Allen again had Alain Bainée as his production designer, the scouting was simplified by the story taking place largely within the geographic confines of the festival: San Sebastian's famous hotels, screening venues, and the crescent-shaped La Concha Beach, with sightings of the monumental Comb of the Wind sculptures on Ondarretta Beach and several Old Town scenes. There'd also be a visit to the fishing hamlet of Orio.

Allen's script concerned a retired film studies professor (Shawn) who attends the annual festival with his wife (Gershon), a high-powered New York publicist, whose clients include a pretentious French director (Garrel) accepting festival laurels. As his wife dallies with the Frenchman, the retired professor dreams at night of *Citizen Kane* and the European masterworks he used to show in his classes, putting himself and his fears into his reimagined film classics. A hypochondriac and would-be novelist—just like you know who—the professor daydreams about the pretty Spanish doctor (Anaya), who can't seem to find anything wrong with him but who takes him on an idyllic tour of San Sebastian. Their happy day ends with an automobile breakdown near her home, where they discover her husband (López), another wild and crazy painter, frolicking with his nude model.

The words everyone used to describe the two months of filming were "low-key" and "amiable." Allen and Vittorio Storaro closely conferred on the lighting for the unavoidably bright daytime exteriors in which they tried to temper the glare. Allen had a genial relationship with Shawn, who was playing a rare lead, appearing in nearly every scene. The retired film professor was in many ways like other Allen stand-ins—"A walking smorgasbord of neuroses," as the script describes him. Allen told one interviewer he was nostalgic for acting in a movie, but he felt he was just too old to play the part. He was already stretching matters with Shawn, in his late seventies, as the husband of Gershon, in her fifties, while chasing the fantasy of Anaya, in her forties.

Wearing his familiar battered hat to ward off the sun, Allen moved from setup to setup with as few takes as possible. On good days he was willing to shut down and send everyone home in the midafternoon, perhaps to join one of his family's sightseeing excursions. The cast pleased him. "The actors are almost never the problem," he told one journalist. "They are almost always good professionals. The errors are usually in the writing. The stories don't always work." Allen confessed to filming scenes too quickly, because directing was the least enjoyable part of the process for him. The writing and editing were "what I really like," Allen said, "two things I can do in my house and in my office, without schedules, alone, even without leaving my room."

In fact, Allen slashed a week—which meant savings on a week of costs—from the production schedule, allowing for extra family time and leisurely stops in Paris and London on his way back to New York by Labor Day weekend.

••

A RAINY DAY in New York had its world premiere outside the US in September at the 45th Deauville American Film Festival, a yearly event in the Normandy region of France devoted to new and neglected works of the US cinema. European distribution groups followed Deauville with a theatrical release in the host country, then Italy, Spain, Mexico, and Russia. The romantic comedy drew international filmgoers for months, even after COVID-19 became a pandemic and shut down most of the world's theaters. Ironically, when South Korea experienced a dip in coronavirus infections and a surge of attendance in May 2020, *A Rainy Day in New York* briefly reigned at number one in global box office.

The US impediments began to crumble in November when Allen and Amazon Studios mutually agreed to settle their litigation. The details were kept confidential, but one can safely guess that the director collected tens of millions of dollars for *not* making the two Woody Allen films that were left unfulfilled in his contract. Amazon could write off the loss as less risky than producing the movies and daring the wrath of a MeToo lynch mob. Allen got *Rainy Day* back for his purposes, and now it was up to his team to find an American distributor for the movie, which would take months. However, with more than a pinch of irony, *Rainy Day* was not so objectionable that Amazon couldn't quietly program the picture on its cable channel in 2021.

In the meantime, Allen found plenty to do, what with the postproduction of *Rifkin's Festival* and the final emendations and galleys for his memoir, *Apropos of Nothing*, which he had quietly peddled to Grand Central Publishing. Formerly Warner Books, Grand Central was now an imprint of the publishing giant Hachette Book Group. Grand Central didn't announce the acquisition until the first week of March 2020, setting an April 7 publication date. Publisher Ben Sevier had secured world rights for hardcover print, e-book, and audiobook editions. The author himself, while not especially caring for the rigors of the job, had recorded the twelve-hour unabridged audiobook.

Grand Central's imminent publication date gave Dylan and Ronan Farrow only a brief window of opportunity to react. Having failed thus far to stop the director from making any more films, now they wanted to keep their father—he was still their father—from writing his life story or, more accurately, getting it published. Dylan tweeted that the publication announcement was "deeply upsetting," and she and her brother Ronan had never been contacted by any "fact-checkers to verify the information in this 'memoir,' demonstrating an egregious abdication of Hachette's most basic responsibility." Ronan was especially piqued because *Catch and Kill*, his account of his Pulitzer Prize–winning bringdown of Harvey Weinstein, with side commentary on Allen, had been issued in 2019 by Little, Brown, another Hachette Book Group imprint, selling a fast, remarkable 160,000 copies in hardcover. Ronan sent an outraged email to Hachette CEO Michael Pietsch: "Your policy of editorial independence among your imprints does not relieve you of your moral and professional obligations as the publisher of *Catch and Kill*, and as the leader of a company being asked to assist in efforts by abusive men to whitewash their crimes." Ronan couldn't "in good conscience work with you anymore. Imagine this were your sister."

Grand Central's publication announcement made news on a Monday. On Wednesday Ronan cut ties with Little, Brown. On Thursday, dozens of Little, Brown and other Hachette staff members, roughly 75 to 100 in total, staged a walkout to demand the withdrawal of the memoir, that the publisher publicly apologize for his errors in judgment, and that the staff be granted the right to protest future planned books of which they disapproved. Although Pietsch, in initial interviews, declared "we do not allow anyone's publishing program [within Hachette] to interfere with anyone else's," on Friday he declared Hachette would not publish the book and that he would revert the rights to Allen. By Sunday, Allen had struck a quick deal with the independent Skyhorse publishing company which, under its Arcade imprint, was distributed worldwide by Simon & Schuster. Jeannette Seaver, an editor at Skyhorse, whose potpourri list of titles included many conspiracy books about the Kennedy assassination, said the company was acquiring *Apropos of Nothing* on its merits but also in the firm belief that the comedian and filmmaker's autobiography should not be banned.

This "ferocious backlash" against publishing *Apropos of Nothing*, in the phrase of the *New York Times*, was praised as MeToo vigilance by some, denounced as rank censorship by others. "No matter how deep his [Ronan's] anger," the *New York Post* editorialized, "it's obscene for a journalist to be silencing anyone." Bret Stephens wrote another *Times* op-ed in which the columnist said he was on the panel that had voted to give Ronan the Pulitzer, but that he also voted (metaphorically) "in favor of [Allen's] publication, both as a matter of principle and public interest." Suzanne Nossel, the president of PEN America, an organization to which the household-name comedian and film director belonged and had always supported generously with appearances and donations, released a series of statements defending the protest rights of publishing employees while concluding, somewhat oddly: "As a defender of free speech and the availability of a wide breadth of books and ideas, we also fervently hope that the outcome does not lead publishers to shy away from manuscripts that editors think are worthwhile, but that are about, or even by, people who may be considered contemptible."

With its camera-ready galleys, *Apropos of Nothing* could be rapidly issued in late March with Diane Keaton's affectionate back-jacket photograph of the author slumped on a sofa. Reviewers, on full alert, flogged the reminiscence mercilessly. "Disgusting, tone-deaf, ridiculous," wrote pop culture journalist Maureen Callahan in the *New York Post*, saying Allen's book was among the most "bitter, self-pitying, horrifically un-putdownable memoirs since *Mein Kampf*." The eye-popping headline of *Washington Post* gender columnist Monica Hesse's review was "If You've Run Out of Toilet Paper [because of the coronavirus pandemic] Woody Allen's Memoir Is Also Made of Paper." Hesse went on to describe the filmmaker's tome as "boring, vindictive, and self-indulgent." *USA Today*'s books editor, Barbara VanDenburgh, a "rabid cinephile and bibliophile" according to her bio on the paper's website, found the memoir "devoid of feeling, introspection, and accountability." Mark Harris, whose Vulture.com review also came with a snappy headline ("I Read This Book So You Don't Have To"), wrote that the "appalling and antediluvian perspective" of the memoir "is not just a blind spot or an age spot; it reeks of an iron-willed determination to resist time, counterargument and any self-interrogation whatsoever."

To be sure, there were appreciative readers such as Larry David (who found it pretty, pretty good) and Peter Biskind, who reviewed the book for the *Los Angeles Times*, with full knowledge that "agreeing to write this review felt like signing up for a lifetime of social distancing. . . . If you're one hundred percent convinced that he [Allen] molested his daughter, this book is not for you. But for those of us who admire that career and can still muster an interest in it, this memoir is for the most part a pleasure to read and entertaining company." Although Andrea Peyser, who had covered the child-custody case for the *New York Post*, did not profess to love *Apropos of*

Nothing, she too decried the "scorched-earth campaign" aimed at negating the book or blackening Allen's name beyond recognition. "Most of us who experienced the spectacle" of the child-custody trial, Peyser recalled in a counter-opinion piece for the *New York Post*, "believe that Mia helped emotionally cripple Dylan and alienated her from her father. . . . Now, the mob, acting on faulty information, has issued its verdict."

Perhaps Allen had waited too long to write the book: because he was in his eighties, his memory was faulty, his writing was at times tired and repetitious, and as a writer he never had been known for nonfiction or introspection. Too long because his loathing for Mia Farrow, which had been given new life by Dylan Farrow's "open letters," had built to a white fury. The counterslam against Mia dominated the book, which needed an editor for many reasons. Yet many things for which the book was pilloried—Allen's Damon Runyon voice, the many times he described actresses or women with synonyms for "gorgeous"—were also Allen cracking wise and provoking the Pavlovian response. The first third about his boyhood and early show business years was quite good and, for better or worse, after attempts to censor him failed, Woody Allen had finally written his life story.

The memoir entered the top ten of bestselling nonfiction in its first weeks, but with bad publicity and reviews, *Apropos of Nothing* sold only about twenty thousand hardcover copies in the US. As of this writing, however, American readers give it four and a half out of five stars from nearly five thousand respondents on—what else?—Amazon.com. Allen's memoir quickly made up the difference with foreign editions in France (where, as *Soit dit en passant*, it was published by a Hachette subsidiary), Spain, Germany, Italy, the Netherlands, Sweden, Japan, and counting.

OVERSEAS THE NEWSPAPERS were more open to allotting generous space to Allen, and he gave numerous interviews to promote the widening release of *A Rainy Day in New York* and the foreign editions of his memoir. "You can ask me anything," he'd say at the outset of interviews, preferring to talk about movies, but inevitably drawn into the early 1990s scandals encompassing his affair with Soon-Yi and Dylan's sex-abuse claims.

"I assume that for the rest of my life a large number of people will think I was a predator," Allen would say phlegmatically. (He gave it the

Brooklynese: "pred-a-tah.") "Anything I say sounds self-serving and defensive, so it's best if I just go my way and work." How did he feel about the mostly young actors from Woody Allen films who publicly damned him? "It's silly," he said. "The actors have no idea of the facts and they latch on to some self-serving, public, safe position. Who in the world is not against child molestation? That's how actors are, and [denouncing me] became the fashionable thing to do, like everybody suddenly eating kale."

His version of what happened—or didn't happen—in 1992 scarcely varied from what he had said publicly two decades before. The film director repeatedly stated he thought Dylan believed everything she said, which was the lasting effect of the voodoo spell cast on the girl by her mother. Yet he never uttered an unkind or personally critical word about his daughter, who in her mid-thirties published her first book in the second half of 2020, a 384-page young adult (grades seven to nine) fiction called *Hush*, the first of a planned sword-and-sorcery trilogy.

Thirty-two-year-old Ronan Farrow, in 2019, disclosed his engagement to comedian and podcaster Jon Lovett, his longtime companion. In May 2020 the *New York Times* published an examination of the Pulitzer Prize winner's work titled "Is Ronan Farrow Too Good to Be True?," which questioned the ethics of his reporting for a *New Yorker* piece, and the factual basis of portions of *Catch and Kill*. Farrow "delivers narratives that are irresistibly cinematic—with unmistakable heroes and villains—and often omits the complicating facts and inconvenient details that may make them less dramatic," wrote *Times* media critic Ben Smith.

His maybe-son rankled Allen more than his adopted daughter. "I found him [Ronan] to not be an honest journalist in relation to me at all, but I write that off, because you know, I understand he's loyal to his mother," the film director told the *Telegraph*, a London newspaper. "Now people are beginning to realize that it isn't just in relation to me that his journalism has been kind of shoddy, and I'm not sure his credibility is going to last."

The *Telegraph* said Allen's tone, when discussing his antagonistic son and daughter, was "extreme nonchalance," and his interviewers were astonished, time and again, by Allen's refusal to weep, confess heartache, or fulminate extravagantly as he had done in his memoir. "I'm angry that I was deprived of seeing my children grow up and I'm angry at what's been done to Dylan and Ronan," the director conceded, speaking to the *Guardian*. "I haven't spoken a word to the children in over twenty-five years and they've been raised to think the worst of me. So sure, I was angry about that. But, professionally, I haven't suffered at all." This stoicism could only have enraged the Farrow-Previns.

WOODY ALLEN DEVOTEES—HATERS too—finally got an opportunity to see *A Rainy Day in New York*, when the 2019 film was released in the fall of 2020, thanks to a limited partnership between Signature Productions, the UK distributor, and MPI Media Group, a small Illinois company. The pandemic release date meant the picture could be shown to only the most intrepid moviegoers in a smattering of theaters before going to DVD in the same year.

What a beguiling work the embattled picture turned out to be. The college girl assigned to interview a tortured American screen artist is one of Allen's artificial constructs, a fantasy without any pretense to reality, much like the rest of the script and the vast body of his filmography. Ashleigh is a southwestern belle, whose name is not spelled, she points out, like that other Ashley in *Gone with the Wind*. The tortured American director, his angst-ridden British scenarist, and the handsome Spanish icon cross the path of Ashleigh, a college-girl reporter played by Elle Fanning, and take turns falling in love with her. Ashleigh/Elle conquers most people with her smile and bounce.

As the aptly named Gatsby, her aimless, rich boyfriend with a poker habit, Timothée Chalamet is more problematic as he slowly adjusts to playing "the Woody role"—so retro-Woody that Gatsby smokes with a cigarette holder, lives for vinyl and old movies, and admires the long-dead sports columnist Jimmy Cannon—as if anyone his age could possibly know who Cannon was. But Chalamet also delivers a seductive performance, increasingly woeful, sitting down at the piano to sing a lilting "Everything Happens to Me" after his girlfriend goes AWOL. For a sweet bonus there is Selena Gomez—Gatsby's ex–high school girlfriend's younger sister, who also has a great name: Chan—sneaking up in the story as the more New York–y girl after Gatsby's heart.

Liev Schreiber as the tortured American filmmaker, Jude Law as the beleaguered scriptwriter, and Diego Luna as the Spanish Don Juan hit their best marks, and Cherry Jones stands out as Gatsby's suffocating Upper East Side mother, who commands her son's presence at her "big fall bullshit blow-out" party. Deserted by Ashleigh, who is off having her own piquant adventures, Gatsby picks up a high-class call girl at (where else?) the Carlyle. His mother smells hooker when he waltzes in the door with his escort, and Jones has a sensational moment in which she teaches a life lesson and puts paid to all the gripes about prostitutes in Woody Allen films.

There is scattered hilarity. (Gatsby's brother's fiancée has the world's worst laugh, which can kill an erection.) The rain-drenched photography is wondrous. The picture is Allen's final (to date) paean to Manhattan, not simply the museums and uptown society, but also Greenwich Village: Gatsby passes by the Minetta Tavern, where Eugene O'Neill used to drink for inspiration; and Cafe Wha?, where Allen performed early stand-up gigs. *Rainy Day* is also another of Allen's odes to Central Park, carriage rides, and favorite spots like the Delacorte Clock near the Children's Zoo, where a final rendezvous echoes *An Affair to Remember*.

Not every US critic berated *A Rainy Day in New York* as much as A. O. Scott did, in his *New York Times* review, mentioning the Dylan Farrow accusations in the second paragraph. Scott sniffed at Allen's "latest cocktail of Great American Songbook excerpts, luxurious interiors, dated cultural allusions and casual misogyny." There were thoughtful notices from less elevated perches, including from Peter Tonguette in the *Washington Examiner*, who admired the movie as "brightly written, charmingly acted, and imaginatively directed." And guess what? Amid the coronavirus horrors, with hardly any theaters open for business, critics mattered less than ever to Allen, and *Rainy Day* had already accumulated upward of $21 million in the world.

AROUND THE SAME time, Allen offered the initial glimpse of *Rifkin's Festival* to Spanish cinephiles. Bucking the trend everywhere else, the 68th San Sebastian Film Festival went on as planned as a physical event, and *Rifkin's Festival* had its world premiere in the Spanish coastal city, where it had been filmed, on September 18, 2020. Allen stayed safely distant in New York. His forty-ninth film as writer and director was greeted as a modest autumnal work by an American master. Perhaps the *New York Times* published such a long, empathetic dispatch, bylined by *Variety*'s Jessica Kiang, because at the time it seemed unlikely the picture would ever be shown in the US.* Unlike recent *Times* notices, Kiang failed to reference Allen's real-life controversies in her review. She wrote appreciatively of the light script, the photography, the performances—with Wallace Shawn as Mort Rifkin, "one of the more endearingly self-effacing of Allen avatars"—and the mini-masterpiece send-ups dreamed by Rifkin, with himself inserted. "Some of these black-and-white interludes are overworked," Kiang wrote, "a few are pretentious-puncturing fun." Among the latter was a mini–*Seventh Seal* with Christoph Waltz as the Grim Reaper, who'd been a recurring character in Allen films for decades. "Life is meaningless, not empty," Death chides Rifkin. "Don't confuse the two." "As thin on real meaning as it is," Kiang wrote, "*Rifkin's Festival*, viewed charitably, is actually quite full—of a rueful acknowledgment of the lateness of the hour, and the silliness of an old man applying old-man's values to a world that's getting younger around him by the day."

"THERE ARE MANY injustices in the world far worse," Allen would say, when asked how the court case and child-abuse accusations had affected his career. In New York, during the coronavirus summer of 2020, the museums, shops, restaurants, movie theaters, athletic games, and shows shuttered. The death toll mounted nationally, and among the hundreds of thousands of casualties, in April, was Eddy Davis, Allen's longtime friend from Chicago, the banjoist and leader of his jazz band, who died at age seventy-nine of COVID-19 complications. Would Allen ever again play his clarinet before an audience? He still practiced in private, playing along to Bunk Johnson or Albert Burbank recordings, as he once did from vinyl LPs, but nowadays the music was loaded onto electronic devices with earbuds.

Weirdly optimistic despite everything, Allen kept some hours at his editing and screening complex near his Park Avenue residence, where he had maintained offices since the 1970s. He wrote a new play and several film scripts. Wearing face masks, daily the film director and his wife took their arm-in-arm strolls on city streets past dark stores, or they wended through Central Park, pausing at favorite benches, statuary, and ponds.

---

* *Rifkin's Festival* would not, in fact, get a limited release in America until a year and a half later in late January 2022.

Sometimes their daughters accompanied them. Twenty-three-year-old Bechet and twenty-year-old Manzie were unscathed by the atmosphere of controversy, the filmmaker insisted in interviews. The whole brouhaha was "a total non-issue in their lives. That is because none of us make a big deal out of it."

Strangers sometimes recognized the old man in a crumpled hat and said hello, with Allen cringing, Soon-Yi polite and friendly, both edging away. He told friends he felt confident New York would recover from the pandemic and be a great city again one day. "There's no way to convey how I feel when I come down those steps in the morning from my bedroom, go to the front door to fetch the *New York Times*, and outside there in all seasons is my beautiful street," he said to Eric Lax. "It's New York, it's Manhattan, it's right out my door. I live there: I actually own a piece of Manhattan. I can't tell you what a thrill it is. I could stand there for five minutes and just look—the trees, the people passing, it's Manhattan and I'm just on the other side of the door."

On December 1, 2020, Woody Allen turned eighty-five, a milestone privately celebrated. Perhaps Moses Farrow turned up with other family and friends. Ironically, for someone who had made the fear of death a constant refrain in his work, the director was relatively healthy. His parents had lived long. His hearing was lousy, he was stooped, he had a droop in his left eye, but he was alive and well, still writing, playing his clarinet, using the treadmill, and taking outside walks, with plans to make another motion picture if the pandemic ever lifted.

The Farrows had one more card to play with a long-brewing HBO documentary that began airing in February 2021. *Allen v. Farrow* would once and for all prove Allen a child-sex fiend. A trial by documentary would be the courtroom hearing Dylan never got. And a shrewd, convincing documentary *Allen v. Farrow* was, if you left out every possible mitigating factor and counterargument and anything negative about Mia Farrow, and allowed the Farrow-Previn family, their friends, and friendly experts on their side to inveigh against Allen without fear of contradiction. Not a single person who supported Allen's side of events in the custody or child-abuse allegations appeared onscreen. A perfect documentary for the fake-news Trump age, its "findings" were cheered along onscreen by Pulitzer Prize winners Nicholas Kristof and Ronan Farrow.

It was also a trial by filmography, which was now au courant in social media and among repentant critics. The onscreen commentators broadly attacked Allen's movies, especially his "age-gap" films, without noting any examples to the contrary, or even the best Woody Allen pictures starring Mia Farrow.

Lending publicity to the documentary, Dylan Farrow, now thirty-six, appeared on *The Drew Barrymore Show*, a syndicated talk show advertising itself as "optimism TV." In an emotional moment Barrymore hugged Dylan and apologized for acting—she did no singing—in the 1996 musical *Everyone Says I Love You*, because, at the time, "there was no higher career calling card than to work with Woody Allen," in her words. Barrymore had grown to realize she "was one of the people who was basically gaslit into not looking at the narrative beyond what I was being told." The actress burst into tears, a recurrent highlight of her show. "I'm trying not to cry right now," Dylan responded. "It's so meaningful because it's so easy for me to say, 'Of course you shouldn't work with him. He's a jerk. He's a monster.' I just find it incredibly brave and incredibly generous that you would say to me that my story and what I went through was important enough to reconsider that."

Allen and Soon-Yi reacted to the *Allen v. Farrow* cable television series with a terse public statement, issued through his sister and producer, Letty Aronson, denouncing the documentary as "a hatchet job riddled with falsehoods," while taking note of HBO's "standing production deal and business relationship with Ronan Farrow."

STILL, BENEATH THE condemnation and censure there remained a wide range of opinion about Allen and his films, as a poll of 104 US film critics, scholars, and entertainment journalists, conducted for this book, conclusively affirmed. The results in the poll attest that Allen's legacy as a filmmaker has been compromised by his controversies, as much by the post-2014 assault on his reputation as, twenty years earlier, by his affair with Soon-Yi, the child custody battle, and the original abuse charges. Still, the debate over whether art can be separated from the artist has been fostered in large part by people outside the critical profession and the movie industry, who, in Woody Allen's case, never really cared about the art or artist. When reviewers and professors are surveyed, the vast majority still think highly of his films and are unconvinced of his guilt or innocence.

The bulk of the votes in this poll were collected in 2020–2021, with many tallied after the broadcast of the *Allen v. Farrow* documentary. The respondents were voluntary, and some people, when initially contacted by the author, opted out of participation because of the hostile climate surrounding the filmmaker and his oeuvre. More than one admitted a wariness of expressing any sort of approval of Woody Allen. The majority of people in the poll were longtime critics or scholars, including a percentage who could boast of having written about Allen's earliest screen comedies in real time dating back to the 1970s. An effort was made to balance the sampling in terms of age, race, gender, and geographic representation (half the 104 respondents are men and the other half women). The participants were asked which Allen movies they held in the highest esteem; whether they believed the comedian and film director was guilty of Dylan Farrow's claims; and how their opinions of Allen and his work might have been permanently affected by the scandals and allegations, the press coverage, and social media climate.

Only 21 of the 104 specialists, with a preponderance of 15 women among those 21, said they believed Allen was "guilty" of a sex-abuse crime. A higher number, 27 including 12 women, said they thought Allen was "not guilty." "He's a weirdo, for sure," explained one female critic, requesting anonymity. "But I have serious doubts about the 'evidence' provided." The rest—56 of the 104, over half—said they remained "undecided" about his guilt.* Less than half said their perspective on Allen's pictures had been negatively affected by the sex-abuse claims, but most felt his legacy had nonetheless been irreparably tarnished. "He's permanently damaged his reputation and his obsession pervades his filmmaking," stated Rita Kempley of the *Washington Post*, "whether he, or a surrogate, portrays the horny old goat who is a babe magnet for no logical reason."

More than a few pointed to a key work, *Manhattan*, as "well-nigh impossible to watch" today, in the words of former *Philadelphia Inquirer* critic Carrie Rickey. Regardless, *Manhattan* racked up 46 votes to rank third among

* A handful of poll participants refused to cast their vote on the "guilt" question. "The issue doesn't interest me in the slightest," one respondent wrote when asked if Dylan Farrow's charges should be believed, and another reviewer said, "Why ask a film critic?"

the Woody Allen movies that film critics and scholars held in the highest regard, or as one of someone's favorites among his filmography. Almost half that total came from women (21), with even scattered votes for *Manhattan* coming from a few women who saw Allen as "guilty," but nonetheless love that problematic film.

Annie Hall was by far the top vote-getter with eighty-four critics or scholars choosing Allen's most famous and popular movie as his most enduring achievement. The tightest race was for second place—a dead heat between *Hannah and Her Sisters* and *Crimes and Misdemeanors*—two of his most successful comedy-drama admixtures from the 1980s. Since the respondents were randomly chosen and contacted for participation in the poll, and several dozen people declined or did not reply to the queries, number two could have gone either way.

The top ten vote-getters (actually thirteen films, including ties) were as follows:

1. *Annie Hall* (84 votes)
2. *Crimes and Misdemeanors* (54); *Hannah and Her Sisters* (54)
3. *Manhattan* (46)
4. *Purple Rose of Cairo* (26)
5. *Midnight in Paris* (24)
6. *Zelig* (21)
7. *Broadway Danny Rose* (20)
8. *Radio Days* (18); *Match Point* (18)
9. *Vicky Cristina Barcelona* (13); *Blue Jasmine* (13)
10. *Bullets over Broadway* (12)

Woody Allen haters were welcome in the poll, and a small number of participants said they had sworn never to watch or review another Allen picture. Simonie Wilson, a reviewer for a Missouri weekly, said she did not hold a single Woody Allen movie in favorable regard. "I am not interested in how well Hitler painted," Wilson explained by email, invoking the name of a genocidalist and the author of *Mein Kampf*, much as one reviewer did of Allen's memoir. "Just because we knew Allen for his artistic prowess before his personal atrocities does not mean the calculation is any different."

Many who participated in the poll complained about Allen's prolificacy and his diminished creativity in the post-2000s. "His overall legacy has been seriously weakened by the sheer volume of his output, and by how many so-so movies have come down the lane since the turn of the century," commented David Ansen, formerly a *Newsweek* critic. Yet *Midnight in Paris*, *Match Point*, *Vicky Cristina Barcelona*, and *Blue Jasmine* easily cleared the top ten, with the post-1992–93 films *Husbands and Wives* (11 votes) and *Manhattan Murder Mystery* (10) just missing the cut. In fact, every decade except for the 1960s is represented by Allen movies in the top ten, and the remarkable number of 39 pictures were cited as being among his five best by at least one poll participant. The early, silly comedies *Take the Money and Run*, *Bananas*, *Sleeper*, and *Love and Death* received numerous votes, threatening to sneak into the top ten. There were random votes for *What's New Pussycat?*, *What's Up, Tiger Lily?*, and *Play It Again, Sam*—not Woody Allen films, per se—for *New York Stories*, *Alice*, *Another Woman*, *Shadows and Fog*, *Mighty Aphrodite*, *Everyone Says I Love You*, *Celebrity*, *Hollywood Ending*, *Scoop*, and *You Will Meet a Tall Dark Stranger.*

It's easier, in fact, to mention the omissions. They include *Interiors*, the Bergmanesque ultra-drama nominated for five Oscars in 1978, which did not elicit a single vote as someone's "best" or favorite. All the others passed over by the voters can be found among his post-2000 credits: *Small Time Crooks*, *The Curse of the Jade Scorpion*, *Anything Else*, *Melinda and Melinda*, *Whatever Works*, *To Rome with Love*, *Magic in the Moonlight*, *Irrational Man*, *Café Society*, *A Rainy Day in New York*, and *Rifkin's Festival.*

"He's written some of the funniest lines I know of in films," the redoubtable Stanley Kauffmann told Marion Meade for her book. "He's not a major artist but a notable and unique figure who will be remembered by the history books as an object of study and scrutiny . . . probably the future will think more highly of him."

"Inevitably the Soon-Yi scandal colors the films and our perceptions of them," said Molly Haskell, the pioneering feminist author of *From Reverence to Rape: The Treatment of Women in the Movies*, "especially when the Allen protagonist's fondness for young girls becomes all too apparent. It's disturbing and always will be. But (unlike some I know) I haven't blackballed his films or downgrade[d] my preferences accordingly."

"Artists and critics who view his work clearheadedly and in context will always see him as a unique filmmaker with a dozen standout achievements," said Michael Sragow, a critic who has written for *Rolling Stone* and the *New Yorker*, "and as a cultural figure who shook up Hollywood models of masculinity."

"I'm afraid his legacy has been negatively affected," stated Stony Brook film studies professor and author E. Ann Kaplan, "although he will surely always be seen as an inventive, creative, completely original director, who made a number of very good films, made us laugh and cry, and whose love of jazz is somehow redeeming. His specifically Jewish humor is an attraction too and he offers diverse studies of an atypical American manhood. If he's somewhat of a misogynist, how many American men of this age aren't?"

"My position is that even if the accusations against him were proved true, it's always a bad idea to judge art by what you think of the private life of an artist," argued James Naremore, an emeritus Indiana University in Bloomington professor and author of many books about the cinema. "Allen's early stand-up comedy was brilliant, and he remains a talented comic writer. As a filmmaker I think he has weaknesses and limitations, but his art should be defended against judgments that have nothing to do with what he puts onscreen.

STAYING FOCUSED THROUGHOUT the pandemic, Allen worked on a new collection of short pieces, a play he was writing, and the next movie he planned to direct—his fiftieth. As usual, Allen had several scripts prepared, and he sifted among them, eventually choosing a story set in Paris that he might film entirely with a French cast in the French language. He could cobble together the financing and distribution in Europe and leave the US for later. He, an American director making a French film, would culminate a lifetime of Francophilia and be a dream come true.

OK, he only knew "a few words" of French. "We hired somebody to translate it [the script]," Allen explained later, "and he or she, I don't even know, translated it. And then when we gave it to the actors, the actors said, no, no, they never talk like this. And then the actors put it in their own words."

So it came to pass. In late September 2022, Allen called action on a capable all-French cast that included Lou de Laâge, Melvil Poupaud, Niels Schneider, Valérie Lemercier, Sara Martins, and Elsa Zylberstein. Again, the estimable Vittorio Storaro was his cameraman. The plot was rumored to evoke *Match Point*, but the film-in-the-making was known only as "WASP 2022" (i.e., "Woody Allen Summer Project 2022") in the French handbills closing off parks and streets.

Soon-Yi was by his side on the Paris locations, and the eighty-six-year-old filmmaker looked surprisingly fit, wearing his usual slouch hat and a puffy jacket in the unseasonably warm weather. He was energetic and good-humored, even signing autographs for onlookers. The crew was small, the budget humble; there was no waiting for gray weather—it would be a sunshiny film. And there'd be no reshoots as in the flush days of yore. "I used to be able to do reshoots the next day," the director later told Sam Wasson. "It was me and Diane Keaton, me and Mia Farrow. It was easy to make a phone call. Now you can't just say, 'I want to shoot a whole other ending.' I would have to fly over to France, make sure the actors were available."

The filming was nearly done when, in early November, Allen lost his friend and writing partner, a bit player in many of his post-1992 films, Douglas McGrath. McGrath's career included nominations for a Tony, an Emmy, and an Oscar for *Bullets over Broadway*. There'd be no more malteds for McGrath, who died of a heart attack, while at his office in New York.

During postproduction, the picture was given a title that also referenced a *Match Point* motif —one of Allen's persistent motifs—*Coup de chance*, meaning "Stroke of Luck." The fiftieth Woody Allen film was ready in time for the September 2023 Venice Film Festival, where the filmmaker, accompanied by his wife and two daughters, was rapturously greeted on the red carpet and applauded after the premiere with a standing ovation that lasted several minutes.

The story was revealed as an upper-middle-class murder-for-hire thriller, with an unscrupulous wheeler-dealer killing off his wife's bohemian paramour. The tone was more lighthearted than *Match Point*, but the plotting was canny, the pace brisk, the dialogue sharp, and the French ensemble in good form. Autumn in Paris was never more lovingly photographed.

The headline of the review in *Variety* proclaimed it "His Best Movie Since 'Blue Jasmine' (or Maybe 'Match Point')." "As a culture," veteran critic

Owen Gleiberman enthused in the trade paper read by all of Hollywood, "I wouldn't be surprised if we found ourselves debating whether the time has come to give Woody Allen, as a filmmaker, another *coup de chance*."

Many of the early critiques were equally favorable, but the European rollout had the usual Woody glitches, such as the dozen or so topless women from Italian feminist collectives, wearing tape across their chests, who protested the Venice premiere in front of the Palazzo del Cinema venue, chanting in support of victims of rape and sexual abuse. Later, Allen again put his foot in his mouth, when interviewed by the Spanish outlet *El Mundo*, defending then-embattled Spanish soccer chief Luis Rubiales for force-kissing Women's World Cup winner Jenni Hermoso after the August final. Rubiales didn't deserve to lose his job for "just a kiss," volunteered Allen, who had not previously revealed himself a soccer aficionado. "The kiss on the soccer player was wrong," said Allen, "but he did not burn down a school. He has the duty to apologize and go ahead. . . . They didn't hide, nor did he kiss her in a dark alley."

The reconfigured Woody Allen and his New Orleans Jazz Band performed for the first time since COVID to boost the European openings, touring to sellout crowds in Italy, France, Portugal, and Spain. Conal Fowkes, who had been frequently heard on the soundtrack of Allen's pictures over the preceding fifteen years, including *Midnight in Paris*, *Blue Jasmine*, and most recently *A Rainy Day in New York*, played piano and led the musicians in the band. New York–based jazz guitarist and banjoist Josh Dunn was the newest member, replacing the deceased Eddy Davis. (Fowkes was absent from the *Coup de chance* soundtrack, however, which leaned heavily on cornetist Nat Adderley in the lineup of vintage jazz from Allen's collection, featuring the Modern Jazz Quintet, Art Farmer, Donald Byrd, Hank Jones, and Adderley's combos.)

After Venice, the reviews in Europe settled into a mixture—even in Paris, where *Coup de chance* opened robustly before tapering off. As of this writing, Rotten Tomatoes gives the film a high 82 percent rating, averaging eighty-two reviews, with an audience score of 79 percent. The turnout was solid in France, Italy, Spain, and Russia, though, adding up to $7.6 million in international monies.

America would have to wait another seven months before, in the first week of April 2024, the same Illinois-based MPI Media Group that handled

A Rainy Day in New York and *Rifkin's Festival* scrounged a limited theatrical release in the US: thirteen theaters in seven cities. The world of American film had changed, much less the world of Woody. Arthouse theaters were a rare species, and furthermore, millions had lost the moviegoing habit during the COVID years.

Domestic critics pounced on the movie, its breezy style and familiar themes—life is a black farce, the heart is ruthless, luck and coincidence prevail. The references to Gatsby and *Anna Karenina*, with French sprinklings of Jean Anouilh and Mallarmé; the jaunty jazz; the single roses exchanged between doomed lovers. All this, once celebrated, now denigrated.

Variety had hailed the achievement. Its trade rival, *Hollywood Reporter*—the outpost for Ronan Farrow's denunciation of his father—declined to review the new Woody Allen film. Robert Abele, in the *Los Angeles Times*, said the French-language film (released with English subtitles) might be a first for Allen, but there was another "ignominious first" to be noted, "the first film he's made since the explosive 2021 docuseries *Allen v. Farrow* deepened for many the credibility of the child sexual-abuse allegations against Allen." Admitting the film boasted a certain appeal, on balance it showed "an artist slackening into repetition and mild inconsequence." Los Angeles–based Justin Chang, on National Public Radio, also sniffed that "nothing about *Coup de chance* is terribly surprising," unless it be the lavish Marklin train set owned by the film's cad, Melvil Poupaud, which reminded him of another very different train set in the Dylan saga.

There were outliers, including Rex Reed, who had been reviewing since *Take the Money and Run* and, now at the *New York Observer,* declared Allen's career had been "unfairly derailed" and the "endlessly mesmerizing" *Coup de chance* restored "the masterful filmmaker to his deserved position as one of the screen's most profound storytellers." In Boston, once an Allen stronghold, the film played briefly at a single theater in the suburb of Arlington. Columnist Alex Beam went on behalf of the *Boston Globe* and saw a "strikingly beautiful [film] . . . at its heart a cutting, Stephen Sondheim–like comedy, not so gently mocking" the lives of its characters. Decrying Allen's radioactivity, Beam wrote: "Catch the movie on the big screen, if you can. It's also streaming on Amazon. There is an 88-year-old genius among us, and he won't be here forever."

••

THE KID GENIUS, or not, will turn ninety in 2025—God willing—a god he doesn't believe in.

Mia Farrow will turn eighty. Dylan Farrow, in 2022, published a second novel in her *Hush* young-adult fantasy series. While continuing to write investigative articles for the *New Yorker* and produce HBO documentaries, Ronan Farrow also appeared as a guest host of *The View* and a judge on *Ru Paul's Drag Race*. He separated from his longtime partner, podcast host Jon Lovett.

Unfortunately for the Farrow-Previns and their allies, barring a deathbed confession of lying either by Allen or Dylan Farrow, likely there will never be proof positive of any crime or guilt. Despite the anti-Allen hysteria, which echoes the show business witch hunt during the McCarthy era as depicted in *The Front*, due process and presumption of innocence are on Allen's side.

For now, he is "canceled," but "someone asked me about cancel culture," Allen told the blogger Roger Friedman, "and I said, 'If you're going to be canceled, this is a culture that you want to be canceled from. Because who wants to be part of this culture?' " Friedman noted, as Allen said this, he was "surrounded by the emblems (remnants?) of a previous culture": great authors on the bookshelves; DVDs (*The Godfather, Reds, Annie Hall*—three with Diane Keaton) on the coffee table.

The Farrow-Previns were quiet during the workup and release of *Coup de chance*, but it is doubtful the family will be deterred in their quest to punish Allen. There are many suicides, botched and otherwise, in Woody Allen movies. Do the Farrow-Previns want Allen to jump out of a window as the persecuted Hecky Brown (Zero Mostel) does in *The Front*? Or does the family hope for his being jailed as a pervert? His bankruptcy? When the director goes abroad to make another film, or play his clarinet in European concerts, if they could somehow get his passport revoked while he was away from American soil, that would complete the Chaplin analogy; perhaps then the Farrows would be satisfied with the jerk, the monster, at a far, safe distance.

Their task of revenge and supposed justice is Sisyphean. So, in another sense, is Allen's mission to use his time left on earth constructively—as his mother used to say—and creatively.

He gave a handful of interviews in his East Seventieth Street haven to promote *Coup de chance*, including to Friedman, an Allen supporter on his Showbiz 411 website, and film book author Wasson, who is also a writer at large for Air Mail and "a longstanding member of Woody Allen's unofficial fan club." The filmmaker's words sounded weary and stoical. His wife Soon-Yi was not present for the interviews. His grown daughters Bechet and Manzie, Friedman reported, were off in France working behind the scenes on the television show *Emily in Paris*.

Nowadays, social media reigned among young Americans; predisposed to epic-scale and superhero movies, if young people bothered with movies at all, they were indifferent to Allen's "handmade product," in his words. In golden days *Annie Hall* would have played in more than a dozen theaters in Manhattan alone. "All the romance of filmmaking is gone," Allen lamented.

Nonetheless *Coup de chance* was "probably not Woody's final film," Friedman wrote. Rumors abounded that he might make his next picture in Italy, entirely in Italian—a bookend to *Coup de chance*. He had "at least two screenplays that could be fixed up quickly," Friedman reported. (Duly noted: in golden days it used to be three.) But Allen was on the fence about directing his fifty-first. "I don't want to have to go out to raise money," he explained. "I find that a pain in the neck. But if someone shows up and calls in and says we want to back the film, then I would seriously consider it. I would probably not have the willpower to say no, because I have so many ideas.

"What I really need is, you know, like a Medici," he told Friedman sardonically. "Somebody to feel that they want to patronize an artist and they've mistaken me for one."

Wasson asked Allen about what he does in his spare time. Did he still find pleasure in watching old footage of Mort Sahl, the stand-up comedy idol from his youth, who died in 2021?

"I do," Allen admitted. "I go on my phone. I get the thing, whatever you call it, the . . ."

"YouTube?"

"YouTube on the phone. I still think he was the best thing I ever saw in terms of stand-up, bar none." Then, Wasson wrote, Allen added with a twinkle, "Sometimes I feel I'd like to do stand-up material again."

What about television? If he watches television, Allen said, he first tunes in to Turner Classics to see if anything is airing he might like to see; for example, he'd hate to miss a rerun of *A Streetcar Named Desire*. He's selective about TV and never saw the hit comedy series (perpetually rerun) *The Office*. He was familiar with the show's format, however, and boasted mildly,

"I think I was the first to do the documentary style [with] *Take the Money and Run*."

Mostly he gravitates to sports on the small screen. "It's pointless," he admitted, "and yet whether the Dodgers win or the Yankees win has as much meaning as anything out there."

Did Isaac's list of sublime pleasures from *Manhattan*—*8½*, Louis Armstrong, Groucho Marx, etc.—still apply and make life worth living? "Well, there are oases of pleasure in life," he told Wasson, "but they are oases in a sea of sadness. At the end, it ends, and then what do you got?"

Friedman asked if he could see Allen's office, and the comedian and filmmaker led him to an upper floor, "where he's set up with a tiny desk," Friedman wrote. "On the desk is his famous, small portable manual Olympia typewriter. He's had it for decades and never switched to, say, an IBM Selectric and certainly not a computer." A stack of yellow-lined legal paper pads was piled on one side for Allen to pencil notes on and write his first drafts in longhand.

Among other things, he was working on another novel, Allen revealed. He had failed once or twice before, trying long-form fiction. "Yeah, I want to see if I can do it," Allen said (not kiddingly, wrote Friedman). "I don't know if I can do it. . . . I'll throw it away if I can't do it."

Friedman asked if he could take a photo of Allen at his desk, and the answer was sure. "I am now in an altered state," the journalist wrote. "This would be like Paul McCartney showing off his original Hofner bass." Friedman got his picture, and they went downstairs and said their goodbyes.

Whereupon the aging kid genius probably went back upstairs to his office and started typing.

Sources and Acknowledgments

Why write a biography of Woody Allen, and why now? When I began my work of research and interviews, in early 2019, Allen's career seemed at a terminal ebb. College students had signed petitions against teaching his best pictures of yesteryear in film studies courses, and his newest ones were cinema non grata in US theaters. His trial by media, conviction by social media, and condemnation and blacklisting seemed a fait accompli.

Allen's acrimonious breakup with actress Mia Farrow; his intimate relationship with Mia's daughter Soon-Yi Previn, which later blossomed into marriage; and the disputed child-abuse allegations involving Dylan Farrow that originated during the Allen-Farrow child-custody struggle in 1992–93 had been refreshed by the MeToo movement in 2014. The past controversies and accusations were given a second life, with the campaign against Allen led by his estranged, adopted daughter Dylan and his natural-born son Ronan Farrow. In Trump-era vernacular, Allen became a casualty of the "cancel culture." To borrow another term from the Stalin era, the once beloved comedian and most acclaimed American filmmaker of his time was now a "nonperson," which is how Stalin dealt with his political enemies in the Soviet Union of the 1930s and 1940s, purging them from party rolls and from histories, and in many cases worse, banishing them to work camps, or ordering their executions.

The subjects of my other film biographies were not strangers to unorthodox or criminal behavior. Fritz Lang possibly murdered his first wife. Nicholas Ray's teenage son went to bed with his wife, actress Gloria Grahame—who was his stepmother—and later the son and stepmother married. The great and only Oscar Micheaux was a plagiarist. Jack Nicholson will never know who his father really was because his mother slept around. At least twice in his life Clint Eastwood stepped out on the women with whom he shared an address, and fathered a "secret" family with fleeting girlfriends. Alfred Hitchcock may or may not have sexually harassed Tippi Hedren. I am long past dividing ordinary people, much less famous movie people, into sinner or saint categories. As a biographer I am interested in the personality, the character, the values, and behavior of my subjects—encompassing their faults as well as their admirable qualities—but I try not to adopt a moral high ground. I endeavor to understand how their lives influence the patterns and themes of their motion pictures.

The honest answer as to why I write any specific book is that, for me, it is a job of work, and one book follows another contractually, sometimes logically, sometimes in mysterious ways. A small part of my past book, *Mel Brooks: Funny Man* from 2019, depicted Allen and his shared time collaborating with Brooks in Sid Caesar's vaunted writers' room during the 1959 television season. From that seed my editor proposed a new book about Allen. Writing about another comedian turned film director seemed a natural segue, and perhaps I had a predisposition to Allen, dating from college, when I and a friend—Gerald Peary, who voted in this book's poll of critics and scholars—ran a campus film society we called Tar and Feathers at the University of Wisconsin in Madison. We often booked *Take the Money and Run* and *Bananas* for showings, and reliably these early Woody Allen comedies drew packed crowds. The guys counting the money laughed as hard as anyone during the repeat viewings. In the intervening decades I managed to keep up with most of Allen's movies, which was no small feat considering his prolificacy. Some of them I loved. Some left me unmoved. I am not one of the people who really liked *Manhattan*, because of the Tracy/Mariel Hemingway relationship that I thought was superficially drawn, but also, perhaps, because my orientation is midwestern and Wisconsin-ish. I am not as enamored of New York City as the film is unabashedly. But the only filmmaker on par with Allen in the American cinema of the 1970s and '80s was the equally maverick and protean Robert Altman, about whom I also wrote a biography, in 1989, at a time when his reputation was similarly mixed and mired. Altman's triumphant third act surprised people, including me. Nor would I count Allen out until the fat nonbinary person sings.

The hubbub and tumult surrounding Allen and his continued active filmmaking have rendered the early Allen biographies, some of them quite good, nonetheless outdated. David Evanier's more recent *Woody*, also good and valuable, does not purport to be a traditional biography. Eric Lax's four books about the comedian and film director are substantial, but they are, for some, tainted by Allen's close oversight. Allen's strict compartmentalization of his private life was reflected in Lax's *Woody Allen: A Biography*, which Allen read and emendated before it was published in 1991. That book painted a happily-ever-after portrait of Allen's decade-long personal and professional relationship with Mia Farrow. One year later came the headlines about Allen's romance with Soon-Yi, his custody fight with Farrow, and seven-year-old Dylan's sexual abuse claims.

I set out to write a "warts and all" biography of Allen, as the saying goes, reporting on his life from birth and childhood through to his years as a comedy writer, stand-up comedian, and director of widely praised movies. I wanted to explore the films and his cinematic legacy and balance the achievement with the private life. I realized there would be a high degree of difficulty in writing fairly and accurately about the events of 1991–93, but such challenges always whet my appetite for the work. I planned to go where the facts, research, and interviews led, which is what I have always done in my books, whose subjects, as I say, have led lives every bit as messy. I faced a situation I have never experienced during work on previous biographies, especially with subjects who were alive and active as I conducted my research—Brooks and Altman, Nicholson and Eastwood. Typically, people who know the famous person you are writing about ask to go off the record with certain anecdotes, details, or opinions that are either especially intimate, or negative. These friends and acquaintances often fear reprisal from the celebrity subject. I like to hear the intimacies, although I'd always prefer they be on the record. Anonymity can be suspect. On this book, I had the opposite experience. I never contacted so many people who had only positive things to say about Woody Allen but who didn't want to be quoted or identified because they did not want to be documented on the record in his favor. They worried about their own MeToo repercussions.

People were painfully torn when I asked to interview them. One example may suffice. Through an intermediary, a mutual friend, I made contact via email with Chazz Palminteri, the unforgettable Cheech of *Bullets over Broadway*. Palminteri was planning to bring his one-man show to Milwaukee, where I live. I don't get many opportunities to do my book interviews close to home, and I try to take advantage of those that pop up. I phoned Palminteri to arrange a time to interview him, theoretically during his show's Milwaukee stint. Palminteri said he didn't care to be interviewed, however, because the actor didn't want to say anything that could possibly hurt Allen, who had been helpful to him in his career and who was a good guy and who was still his friend. What exactly did I want to ask him? Palminteri wondered. I said I would ask him only about how Allen directed him, what tips or guidance might have shaped his Oscar-nominated performance. That was tame, but it worried Palminteri. He wanted to know who else I was speaking to, what other people had said. He wanted to know what kind of book I meant to write, how I would treat Allen. I couldn't satisfy him with my answer that I was writing a truthful biography encompassing Allen's personal life and his public career. The onset of the COVID pandemic was another unusual factor that shaped the book, and it curtailed Palminteri's Milwaukee appearance. He stopped taking my calls and dodged the interview. Others had similar trepidations.

The national community of film reviewers and scholars also presented obstacles, when I began contacting and polling people for a brief section in the final chapter of this book about the critical consensus on Woody Allen and his films today. Critics in the profession whom I had known for decades begged off. "I wouldn't touch that poll with a ten-foot pole!" one female critic told me. Some were happy to cooperate and tell me why they didn't cotton to Allen or his movies anymore. Others admitted to still loving some of his pictures, but they didn't want to risk naming their favorites and associating their names with his. Eventually, 104 critics and scholars got involved, prominent names whom I knew personally after fifty years in the field, as well as many youngbloods from websites and blogs. I am thankful to those who accepted my invitation, voted in the poll, and gave me their opinions about Allen and his films. There was disagreement, factions, and surprising consensus.

I am grateful to the many sources who spoke to me on the condition they would not be identified, as well as to those who went on the record. I am especially indebted to the librarians and archivists who filled my numerous long-distance requests for documents, when their services were closed to the general public during the first wave of the COVID epidemic, which hampered travel and research. Not one of them, not even the Princeton librarians in charge of Allen's papers, asked me what I was writing, or what I thought of Woody Allen, *Annie Hall*, or anything. From the many published memoirs, newspaper accounts, and court papers, I found much of the story was waiting to be sifted and winnowed. Allen himself was copiously on the record.

Time and again fellow writers, critics, and journalists assisted me, even when they disagreed with my views on this or that re: Woody Allen. My University College Cork friend Gwenda Young, no great Woody Allen fan, helped me with Irish research and many tips; my dear coconspirator John Baxter, in Paris, didn't hold it against me that I was writing a book on one of his previous subjects; he generously fielded my queries and volunteered connections and sources. Paul Nagle, in California, kept up a flurry of links and suggestions and read an early draft of the book with a special eye to the sections about the business side of moviemaking. Michael Elias was also a painstaking reader of an early draft, kindly pointing out idiotic mistakes of fact and language, including the real bonehead stuff that finds a way to sneak into every manuscript despite best intentions. Another big tip of the Hatlo hat to Joseph McBride, without whom this book would never have come to life. I don't always agree with my old Wisconsin friend, an elder statesman of film studies whose biographies and critical works are models in the profession, but I try to meet him halfway on his criticisms. I hope he—and you, the readers—will enjoy the final form, which is deeply indebted to his advice. All its faults are mine.

The enthusiasm of my HarperCollins editor, Jonathan Jao, got the ball rolling, and his discreet suggestions and pencil work immeasurably enhanced the final product. His team guided the initial legal review and copyediting. Hannah Long succeeded him with her own editing suggestions and supervised the final design and production. My agent, Gloria Loomis, and her associate Julia Masnik were, as always, staunchly supportive of my work. Gloria's husband, Walter Bernstein, was the screenwriter of *The Front*, which is how Gloria and I got to know each other, through Hollywood blacklist circles, over thirty years ago now. Walter died at age 101 in early 2021, while I was laboring on this book. A strong, intelligent film, *The Front* now appears prescient in speaking to the witch-hunt atmosphere surrounding Woody Allen's alleged crimes—an atmosphere of fear that has made Allen a social pariah in America. Walter started out his writing career as a correspondent for *Yank* during World War II, and I know he valued fact-based reportage as well as higher truths. I miss Walter, and I will miss what he might have had to say about my book, because although he was a famously nice guy, and truly so, he was also tough and honest. I have tried to write a factual and truthful book.

Collegial Advice and Assistance

Thanks to the many friends and colleagues who gave advice and assistance, including John Baxter, Dan Bessie, Gianni Bozzacchi, Yannick Dehée, Joseph Harriss, John Haynes, Laurent Herbiet, Susan King, Christine Leteux, Justin Levine, Vincent LoBrutto, Glenn Lovell, Ken Mate, Paul Nagle, David Pollock, Santiago Rubín de Celis, Peter Rainer, Christina Rice, David Rensin, Alan K. Rode, Carlos Ruiz, Nat Segaloff, Michael Sragow, Jeffrey Spivak, Bertrand Tavernier, Joey Tayler, Matt Tyrnauer, William B. Winburn, Chris Yogerst, Cathleen Young, Gwenda Young, and Francesco Zippel.

Terry Gilliam answered my queries about *Help!* I was assisted in my archival researches by Mac B. Gill in Iowa; Bill Fagelson in Austin, Texas; and Andy Chen and Larissa Guimaraes at Princeton University. Dating back to my Hitchcock biography, Mary Troath has helped me out with my London research. Gwenda Young pointed me to many items from Irish and European newspapers. Sky McGilligan did yeoman service in New York City libraries and courts and on the Internet.

Without the reference librarians and the Interlibrary Loan Department of Marquette University, where I teach film courses, this book could not have been written. Again and again, the library staff, especially Rose Trupiano and Nia Schudson, answered queries, checked facts, and tracked down rare books and publications.

Correspondence and Queries

The people who were willing to go on the record, either in correspondence or interviews, include Alfonso Arau, George Chakiris, John Erman, Judy Henske, Walter Hill, Jacobo Morales, Paul Nagle, Paul Pumpian, Roger L. Simon, Louise Sorel, Howard Storm, and Bill Wilson. I interviewed Walter Bernstein and Martin Ritt long before this book was contracted. Many other people spoke or corresponded with me off the record.

Film Critics and Scholars Who Voted in the Poll

Thank you to the following people, alphabetically listed as in the cast of a Woody Allen movie, for proving there is a community of film critics and scholars in the US who can unite on at least one matter involving Allen and his pictures—a poll. I am listing only their names as it would take up too much space to identify them more extensively by including all of their affiliations and publications. The majority can be found on Wikipedia. The others are easily searchable on the Internet. Thank you one and all for your opinions and your participation:

Beth Accomando; Sarah Knight Adamson; Steven Adler; John Anderson; David Ansen; Julia Bader; Jeanine Basinger; Gayle Bass; Marjorie Baumgarten; Sheila Benson; Amy Biancolli; Peter Biskind; Michael Blowen; David Bordwell; Anne Brodie; Robert W. Butler; Duane Byrge; Maria Elena de las Carreras; Mike Clark; Laura Clifford; Robin Clifford; Rebecca Daniel; A. A. Dowd; Duane Dudek; David Edelstein; David Ehrenstein; David Elliott; Jason Evans; Felicia Feaster; Kathy Fennessy; Sara Michelle Fetters; Jill Franks; Frank Gabrenya; Colleen Glenn; Molly Haskell; J. Hoberman; Andrew Horton; Dan Hudak; Annette Insdorf; Harlan Jacobson; Kent Jones; Brett Ashley Kaplan; E. Ann Kaplan; Rita Kempley; Christina Lane; Joanna Langfield; Will Leitch; Shawn Levy; Amy Longsdorf; Glenn Lovell; Cynthia Lucia; Lou Lumenick; Karen Martin; Philip Martin; Joseph McBride; Todd McCarthy; Patrick McGavin; Michael McKinney; Priscilla Meyer; Marcianne Miller; M. V. Moorhead; Dustin Morrow; Howie Movshovitz; Steve Murray; James Naremore; April Neale; Farran Nehme; Mary P. Nichols; Monica Osborne; Gerald Peary; Peter Rainer; Joanna Rapf; Rex Reed; Carrie Rickey; Eleanor Ringel; Rene Rodriguez; Jonathan Rosenbaum; Robert Roten; Candice W. Russell; Julie Salamon; Alissa Simon; Jeff Simon; Michelle Solomon; Nick Spake; Michael Sragow; Susan Stark; David Sterritt; Lisa Szefel; Kevin Thomas; David Thomson; Anne Thompson; Kristin Thompson; Gene Triplett; Ken Turan; Paula M. Uruburu; Steve Warren; Max Weiss; Stephen Whitty; Alison Willmore; Simonie Wilson; Susan Wloszczyna; Dianah Wynter; Stephanie Zacharek; and Pamela Zoslov.

A number of the veteran journalists and film scholars have passed away after casting their votes, and they did not live to see this book published. I suppose this too is a sign of the changing climate of film criticism. I would like to pay special tribute to the memory of Sheila Benson of the *Los Angeles Times*. Via telephone, emails, and old-fashioned letter-writing, I enjoyed decades of friendship with Benson, who died in 2022. With invariable good humor, she helped, encouraged, and improved my books.

Archives and Organizations

Research Services, Boston Public Library (Boston, Massachusetts); Diana Bowers-Smith and Michelle Montalbano, Reference Librarians, Brooklyn Public Library; Michael McCurdy, Witkin State Law Library, California State Library; Sharon Gissy, "Ask a Librarian," Chicago Public Library; Nadine Kramarz, Reference Librarian, Fort Myers Regional Library (Fort Myers, Florida); Jennifer Fauxsmith, Research Librarian, Schlesinger Library on the History of Women in America, Radcliffe Institute, Harvard University (the Mary Bancroft papers); Sarah Cunningham, Audiovisual Archivist, LBJ Presidential Library (Austin, Texas); Chamisa Redmond, Reference Specialist, Library of Congress (Lucy Kroll papers); Eileen Pollis, Long Beach Public Library (New York); Carey Stumm, Archivist, National Archives and Research Administration at New York City; George Fuller, Selective Service Registration Records, National Archives and Research Administration at St. Louis; Misty Flores, Museum of Fine Arts, Houston (Texas); Matthew J. Boylan, Senior Reference Librarian, New York Public Library; John Calhoun, Nailah Holmes, New York Public Library (Joe Layton, Max Liebman, and Abe Burrows papers); Jeremy Megraw, Billy Rose Theatre Division (including the Buddy Hackett papers), New York Public Library; Tal Nadan, Brooke Russell Astor Reading Room for Rare Books and Manuscripts, Steven Schwarzman Building, New York Public Library (the Jean Stein papers); Danielle Marie Nista, Shannon O'Neill, Michael Koncewicz, Elizabeth Lewis, Tamiment Library (including Tamiment documents and the Tamiment Oral History Collection), New York University; Rebecca Jewett and Orville Martin, Thompson Library Special Collections (the Earl Wilson papers), Ohio State University (Columbus, Ohio); Emma Sarconi, Reference, Special Collections (the Woody Allen papers), Princeton University (Princeton, New Jersey); Adele Heagney, St. Louis Room, St. Louis Public Library (St. Louis, Missouri); Nathan Coy, Sound Archives Librarian, San Francisco Traditional Jazz Sound Collection (Turk Murphy files), Stanford University; Robert L. Cagle and Paula Carns, University Library, University of Illinois at Urbana Champaign; Laura E. Michelson, Special Collections (the Marion Meade papers), University of Iowa Libraries (Iowa City); Molly Haigh, Special Collections (Larry Gelbart papers), Charles E. Young Research Library, University of California at Los Angeles; John R. Waggener and Clarissa Anderson Nord, Special Collections (including the Mimi Benzell collection and the Alan Handley papers in the Robert Wynn Collection), American Heritage Center, University of Wyoming (Laramie); Mary Huelsbeck, Wisconsin Center for Film and Theater Research (including the Alvah Bessie, National Broadcasting Corporation Records 1921–1976 and Reginald Rose papers), University of Wisconsin, Madison; Hilary Swett, Archivist, Writers Guild Foundation (Los Angeles).

Photographs and Permissions

PHOTOGRAPHS: Andy Sharlein, Allied Digital Photo; eMoviePoster.com; Chris Galbreath and Historic Images; Jerry Ohlinger's Movie Material Store; LBJ Presidential Library; Movie Market; Photofest; Silver Screen Mementos; IMS Vintage Photos (The Netherlands); Florence Comber, Zuma Press; and the author's collection. Special thanks to Brian Hamill for his courtesies.

PERMISSIONS: Michael Blakemore permitted extensive quotation from his reminiscence about Allen and *Death Defying Acts* as long as I referred readers to the entire "Death Defying Director," from the May 26, 1996 *New Yorker.* Tamiment Oral History Collection and Records courtesy of the Tamiment Library and Robert F. Wagner Labor Archives, New York University. Mary Bancroft (1862–1997) papers courtesy of her collection at the Schlesinger Library, Radcliffe Institute, Harvard University, Cambridge, Massachusetts.

Key Texts

Woody Allen's memoir *Apropos of Nothing* (Arcade, 2020) was essential. Also indispensable, for select chapters, was Mia Farrow's *What Falls Away* (Doubleday, 1997) and Diane Keaton's *Then Again* (Random House, 2011). Four books by Eric Lax were vital reading: *On Being Funny: Woody Allen and Comedy* (Charterhouse, 1975); *Woody Allen: A Biography* (Knopf, 1991); *Conversations with Woody Allen: His Films, the Movies, and Moviemaking* (Knopf, 2009 updated edition); *Start to Finish: Woody Allen and the Art of Moviemaking* (Knopf, 2017). Earlier Allen biographies were requisite: Lee Guthrie, *Woody Allen: A Biography* (Drake, 1978); Gerald McKnight, *Woody Allen: Joking Aside* (W. H. Allen, 1982); Tim Carroll, *Woody and His Women* (Little, Brown, 1993); John Baxter, *Woody Allen: A Biography* (HarperCollins UK, 1998); Marion Meade, *The Unruly Life of Woody Allen* (Scribner, 2000);

and David Evanier, *Woody: The Biography* (St. Martin's Press, 2015). Also well thumbed and often cited: Stig Björkman, *Woody Allen on Woody Allen* (Grove Press, 1993 revised edition); Kristi Groteke with Marjorie Rosen, *Mia & Woody: Love and Betrayal* (Carroll & Graf, 1994); Adam Harvey, *The Soundtracks of Woody Allen: A Complete Guide to the Songs and Music in Every Film, 1969–2005* (McFarland, 2007); and Robert E. Kapsis, ed., *Woody Allen: Interviews* (University Press of Mississippi, 2016 updated edition).

Notes

People identified by name in the text are quoted from my interviews with them, from emails or paper correspondence, or from previously published or archival sources. If the source is clear in context, there is no citation. In all chapters unless otherwise stated, Allen is quoted from *Apropos of Nothing*. Mia Farrow is usually quoted from *What Falls Away*. Diane Keaton is often cited from *Then Again*. When memoirs conflict with contemporaneous or other sources I point out the discrepancy, but I harbor the quaint notion that when famous people write their autobiographies one should pay attention to their carefully chosen words, which is a form of sworn testimony. I draw primarily from Eric Lax's authorized *Woody Allen: A Biography* while noting the material drawn from Lax's other three books about Allen here and there. I list box-office grosses and rankings from Peter Lauria, "The Box Office Gross of Every Woody Allen Movie Adjusted for Inflation," BuzzFeed (August 2, 2013). But box-office grosses, profits, and budgets have been compared with other books and Internet data. The ballpark figures and rankings are best guesses based on available sources.

Chapter 1: 1935: *Prep Day*

The colonoscopy prep day anecdote is from Allen's remarks at the American Film Institute Life Achievement Award event honoring Diane Keaton in 2017. "Unbelievably charismatic" (Ingmar Bergman) from "Bergman Admits Nazi Past," BBC News, September 7, 1999. "An attractive young woman" from *The Unruly Life of Woody Allen*. "Running in and out of rooms" from Tim Carroll, *Woody and His Women*. "Lower-lower-middle-class" from John Lahr, "The Imperfectionist," *New Yorker* (December 9, 1996). "An intense sense of failure" from JoAnne Stang, "Verbal Cartoons," *New York Times* (November 3, 1963). "A paradise" from Lax, *Conversations with Woody Allen*. The oft-quoted "genetic dissatisfaction" from Jon Winokur, *Encyclopedia Neurotica* (Macmillan, 2006). "The world would have been poorer" from Robert B. Weide's *Woody Allen: A Documentary* (2011) in the American Masters series. "Backward and anti-Semitic" and "never a pleasurable experience" from William Geist, "Woody Allen: The *Rolling Stone* Interview," *Rolling Stone* (April 9, 1987). "Mean-looking, sorry" from *Woody Allen on Woody Allen* (*WA/WA*). "With other teachers" from *Woody and His Women*. "Although I never laughed" from "Verbal Cartoons." "Having a child" from Baxter, *Woody Allen: A Biography*. "I remember going to school" from Michael Kohn, "Woody Allen Comes Home," *Independent Voice* (Long Beach, New York) (June 10, 1982). "Roses are red / Violets are blue" from Joseph Berger, "Our Towns: Suburbanites Heed the Call of the City," *New York Times* (November 29, 1998). "By Letty's account" from Lax, *Start to Finish*. "From that moment on" from the Associated Press, "Bob Hope the Actor Honored in N.Y.," *Los Angeles Times* (May 9,

1979). "I've never cared" from Michel Ciment and Yann Tobin, "My Heroes Don't Come from Life, But from Their Mythology," *Positif* (February 1995), translated and reprinted in Kapsis, ed., *Woody Allen: Interviews*.

"Biggest regret" from Lax, *Woody Allen: A Biography*. "Timid" and "withdrawn" (Martin Konigsberg) from Guthrie, *Woody Allen: A Biography*. "You would see pirates" from *WA/WA*. "I had a vicious" (boxing), "a good shot" (basketball), and "I was a terrific hitter" (baseball) from Guthrie. "Always the lead-off" and "one of the first " from Leonard Probst, *Off Camera* (Stein and Day, 1975). Mickey Rose, Jerry Epstein, Elliot Mills, Jack Victor, Jack Freed, Alan Lapidus, Bryna Goldstein, and Sadie Goldstein are quoted from *Woody and His Women*, unless otherwise noted. "Allan was just OK" (Jerry Epstein) from Baxter. "Arky Vaughan once kicked me" from Joe Klein, "Woody on the Town," *Gentlemen's Quarterly* (February 1986). "Near a newsstand" from Spike Lee with Ralph Wiley, *Best Seat in the House: A Basketball Memoir* (Crown, 1997). "He would just sit in the living room" from the *American Masters* documentary. "Bullshit prayer" from *Apropos of Nothing*. "There was an awful lot" (Mickey Rose) from McKnight, *Woody Allen: Joking Aside*. "Sleazy projects" and "Never, ever" from William K. Zinsser, *Pop Goes America* (Harper & Row, 1966). "There was never a week" from Baxter. "I just sit down" and other extracts from the unbylined high school newspaper interview with WA in *Midwood Argus* (February 27, 1953). "It cost me $40" from the American Masters documentary. "I've thought about sex" from *Woody and His Women*. "I saw a hermaphrodite" from "Woody on the Town." "A great, great actor, no question" from *WA/WA*. "Because he was the dominant" from the interview with Jack Victor in *The Unruly Life of Woody Allen*. "I was just an adolescent" from *WA/WA*. "The best comedy play in America" from *Conversations*. "Cutting out paper dolls" from Tom Shales, "Woody: The First Fifty Years," *Esquire* (April 1987). "Terribly shy" (Mickey Rose) from Francine du Plessix Gray, "Woody Allen: America's Melancholy Funnyman," *Cosmopolitan* (September 1974). "To look like Bogart" (Elliot Mills) from Evanier, *Woody: The Biography*. "Always toted a gun," "a typical Jewish neighborhood cliché," and "He never let a thought" from Gene Siskel, "Woody's Folks: They Ought to Be in Pictures," *Chicago Tribune* (January 26, 1986). "Extremely naggy" and "When she had cataracts" (Jack Victor) from *The Unruly Life of Woody Allen*. "Hot temper" from the Jack Freed interview in *The Unruly Life of Woody Allen*. "Silly people in a grotesque way" from Helen Dudar, "Woody Allen: They Laughed When . . ." *New York Post* (December 22, 1963). "She gets up in the morning" from Paul Krassner's interview in the April 1965 *Realist*, republished in Krassner, *Impolite Interviews* (Seven Stories Press, 1999).

"Allan Konigsberg" is bylined in the May 1952 *Genii: The Conjurer's Magazine*. Epstein ("eventually he got fired") from *Woody: The Biography*. Marion Drayson from *Woody Allen: A Biography*. Elliot Mills ("It was an ongoing discussion") from his interview in *The Unruly Life of Woody Allen*. Earl Wilson from assorted clippings, notes, and writings in his archives. Warren Beatty from Rosemarie Jarski, ed., *The Funniest Thing You Never Said 2* (Ebury Press, 2010). Alan Lapidus from his interview in *The Unruly Life of Woody Allen*. Morris Purcell anecdote from *Woody Allen: Joking Aside*. "Very quiet and peaceful," etc. from Roger Ebert, "Woody Allen Pokes into Inspiration for 'Alice,' " *Chicago Sun-Times* (December 23, 1990). Dave Alber and Mike Merrick quoted from *Woody Allen: A Biography*. "Had heard so much" from *Woody Allen: A Biography*. "Like being paid to play baseball" from "The *Rolling Stone* Interview." "Always five to a page" from Jack Kroll, "Woody," *Newsweek* (April 24, 1978). "More mature than" and "poetic style" from *WA/WA*. "He was a startling musician" from Ralph J. Gleason, "On the Town," *San Francisco Chronicle* (October 15, 1965). "I never actually failed" from *Pop Goes America*. "I did not like elementary" from Guthrie. "Soft, nice" (Jack Victor) from *Woody: The Biography*. "Very big breasts" from "Woody Allen: America's Melancholy Funnyman."

"Jules Feiffer type of girl," "All I knew about was baseball," and "I found I liked" from Lax, *On Being Funny: Woody Allen and Comedy*. "I had to read to survive" from Emily Eakin, "Woody Allen, So Sorry He's Funny," *New York Times* (May 22, 2001). "The things those women read and liked" from *Woody Allen: A Biography*. Mike Merrick and Tad Danielewski from *Woody Allen: A Biography*. "Their combined salaries" from Terry Gross's 2009 National Public Radio interview in *Woody Allen: Interviews*. "'Mama Mia'" from NBC archives. "The last roll we propose" is Danielewski from NBC memoranda.

Chapter 2: 1955: The Woodman Cometh

Abe Burrows from *Honest, Abe: Is There Really No Business Like Show Business?* (Little, Brown, 1980) and from correspondence in his papers in the Billy Rose Theatre Division of the New York Public Library. Adolph Green from Enid Nemy, "Abe Burrows Is Extolled at Memorial Service," *New York Times* (May 21, 1985). Allen's first contracts are in the Burrows papers. Mort Sahl on the subject of WA from *Heartland* (Harcourt, 1976). "Blown away" from *Apropos of Nothing*. "Revolutionized the medium" from Gerald Nachman, *Seriously Funny: The Rebel Comedians of the 1950s and 1960s* (Back Stage Books, 2004). "I loved everything he did" from James Curtis, *Last Man Standing: Mort Sahl and the Birth of Modern Comedy* (University Press of Mississippi, 2017). Harvey Meltzer from *Woody and His Women*. Bob and Ray and WA from David Pollock, *Bob and Ray: Keener Than Most Persons: The Backstage Story of Bob Elliott and Ray Goulding* (Applause Books, 2013). Milt Rosen from *Woody Allen: A Biography*. Danny Simon's writing precepts from *Apropos of Nothing*. WA's letters home to Brooklyn friends from *Woody Allen: A Biography*, with exceptions noted. "I was theoretically" from *Woody Allen: A Biography*. "They are tremendous people" from Baxter. Footnote: "Prostitutes are interesting" from "All My Films Have a Connection with Magic." "Mount her like a young bull!" is WA quoted by Tamiment Playhouse folk singer/sketch writer Dick Davy in Phil Berger, *The Last Laugh: The World of the Stand-Up Comics* (Morrow, 1976). "Turned several shades of red" from *Woody and His Women*. "One of the many things" from *Woody: The Biography*.

Stanley records from NBC archives. "At home or late in hotel rooms" from WA's "I Appreciate George S. Kaufman," *New York Times* (October 24, 2004). "I couldn't stand my wife's friends" from *Apropos of Nothing*. "Gee Max, I didn't know" from interview with NBC executive Ross Donaldson in "TV-Radio Production Centres," *Variety* (October 30, 1968). "We didn't converse at all" and "Woody would listen" from the Max Liebman interview in *Woody Allen: Joking Aside*. Buddy Hackett from his interview in *The Unruly Life of Woody Allen*. "Too strong a personality and too wrong-headed" from *Woody Allen: A Biography*. "Rubs them out" from *Woody Allen and His Women*. WA on Danny Simon ("Very secretive") from *Woody Allen: A Biography*. "I was very unhappy" from Edwin Miller, "The Tallest Dwarf in the World," *Seventeen* (May 1966), reprinted in Miller, *Seventeen Interviews: Film Stars and Superstars* (Macmillan, 1970). "In, whine for fifty minutes" from "Woody Allen: America's Melancholy Funnyman." All Tamiment background and material from Martha Schmoyer LoMonaco, *Every Week, a Broadway Revue: The Tamiment Playhouse, 1921–1960* (Greenwood Press, 1992) and from the oral histories (many conducted by LoMonaco) on deposit among the Tamiment papers in Special Collections at the Tamiment Library of New York University. (Other sourced interviews with Tamiment veterans are noted.) Christopher Hewett from his interview in *Woody Allen: Joking Aside*. Moe Hack (and Paula Cohen) from their oral history and *Woody Allen: Joking Aside*. The summer playbills are among the Tamiment papers. WA's Tamiment sketches—including multiple drafts and versions ultimately staged—are in the *From A to Z* papers in the Carroll and Harris Masterson Collection in the Harry Ransom Library. "When he typed" (Len Maxwell) from *Woody Allen: A Biography*. "A very close-knit" (Jerry Bock) from LoMonaco.

"People joked" (Mary Rodgers) and "More like little kids" (Jane Connell) from their interviews in *The Unruly Life of Woody Allen*. WA on his Tamiment experience from LoMonaco's September 12, 1986, interview among the Tamiment oral histories. "Various hosts" from Kliph Nesteroff, "The Early Woody Allen: 1952–1971," "WFMU's Beware of the Blog," (February 14, 2010). There are various versions of the Gelbart anecdote about WA joining Sid Caesar's show; mine is from the dissertation by Jules A. Malarcher, "Tickets to His Head: Larry Gelbart (1928–) As Writer and Adaptor" (St. John's College, 1997), which draws on Gelbart interviews and predates his autobiography. "I'd run into the bathroom" from WA on the podcast "Maltin on Movies," January 28, 2022. Gelbart is quoted in this book from Malarcher and from Gelbart, *Laughing Matters: On Writing M*A*S*H, Tootsie, Oh God! And a Few Other Funny Things* (Random House, 1998). "A mass of hostilities" from Penelope Gilliatt's *New Yorker* profile of WA included in *Three-Quarter Face: Reports & Reflections* (Coward, McCann & Geoghegan, 1980). "We'd walk home together" from *Apropos of Nothing*. "Writing for Caesar" from "The Early Woody Allen: 1952–1971." Allen on the "joyful" Mel Brooks from *Off Camera*. "I went up to the door" from Gene Siskel, "Wide-Ranging Words from Woody on Marriage, Murders—and More," *Chicago Tribune* (June 12, 1981).

Marshall Barer from his Tamiment oral history. "Well, I've got to go back" is WA quoted by Dick Davy in *The Last Laugh*. "On reflection, I guess she just didn't" (Bob Dishy) and "Not everyone thought" (Hewett) from *Woody Allen: Joking Aside*. Pat Boone ("In his agitated, insistent way") from his interview in *The Unruly Life of Woody Allen*. "I'd slide down the wall laughing" from Stephen J. Abrahamson's 2010 interview with Boone in the Television Academy Foundation oral history archives. Sugar Ray Robinson anecdote from Ira Berkow, "In the Editing Room with Woody Allen: From Defense to Offense," *New York Times* (November 2, 1995). *From A to Z* production history from the Masterson collection. "A hard time for Woody" (Bob Dishy) from *Woody Allen: Joking Aside*. "Always unhappy, because" (Harvey Meltzer) from *Woody and His Women*. "Tried hard to please" (Jack Victor) from *Woody and His Women*. "Cheapening his gifts" (Harlene Rosen Allen) from *Seriously Funny*. The Superman comic strip exchange from *Apropos of Nothing*. Steven Bach is quoted throughout this book from *Final Cut: Dreams and Disaster in the Making of* Heaven's Gate (New American Library, 1987). Rollins from his interview in *Woody Allen: Joking Aside*; Rollins and Joffe from their interviews in *The Last Laugh*; also from Phil Berger, "The Business of Comedy," *New York Times* (June 9, 1985); and from *Woody Allen: A Biography*. "At eleven at night, I'd get in a cab" is from Cleveland Amory's interview with WA in the *Newark Evening News* (February 18, 1968). "To start with" (Rollins) from *Woody Allen: Joking Aside*. "He would recite his stuff" (Rollins) from John Lahr, "The Imperfectionist," *New Yorker* (December 9, 1996). "He was arrogant and hostile" (Joffe) from *Woody Allen: A Biography*. "He didn't know anything" (Rollins) from "The Early Woody Allen: 1952–1971." "You do lines" (Joffe) and "What are you doing" (Harlene Rosen Allen) from *Woody Allen: A Biography*. "It was unspeakably agonizing" from "The Tallest Dwarf in the World." "Do you fellas really think" from *Woody Allen: A Biography*. "The character was really assigned" from Dick Kleiner, "Woody Allen Started as Comedy Prodigy," *New York World–Telegram & Sun* (November 7, 1963). "Predazzled" and "I had the feeling" from Dick Cavett and Christopher Porterfield, *Cavett* (Harcourt Brace Jovanovich, 1974). "I was such a great fan of Mort Sahl's" from "The Early Woody Allen: 1952–1971." Hal Gurnee from Ron Simon's 2018 interview in the Television Academy Foundation oral history archives. "Where sex was fine" from *The Realist* interview. Garry Marshall from *My Happy Days in Hollywood: A Memoir* (Crown, 2012). Jay Landesman from *Rebel without Applause* (The Permanent Press, Sag Harbor, New York, 1987) and *Jaywalking* (Weidenfeld & Nicolson, 1993). Details about Lasser's sexual proclivities, here and in other chapters, come from Allen, writing in *Apropos of Nothing*. While Lasser gave many interviews substantiating her psychological struggles during the years of her relationship with and marriage to Allen, she did not comment extensively on their sex life.

Chapter 3: 1961: The Big Noise

"The big noise" from "Woody Allen: They Laughed When . . ." Max Gordon from *Live at the Village Vanguard* (St. Martin's Press, 1980). Vivian Gornick on Allen at the Bitter End from *Woody: The Biography*. "Long walks in the [Central] Park" (Lasser) from David M. Alpern, "Louise Went 'Bananas,'" *New York Times* (July 11, 1971). "A sort of Judy Garland–ish" (Jack Victor) from *Woody and His Women*. Coleman Jacoby anecdote from *Woody Allen: A Biography*. The *Open End* papers (with Allen's self-written bio) are in the David Susskind papers at the Wisconsin State Historical Society. "Nonfeasance" (Garry Moore) from Steve Allen, *Funny People* (Stein and Day, 1981). "I'd hand in sketches" from "Pushing Back," *Newsweek* (August 20, 1962). "I didn't blame them" from Paul O'Neill, "Woody," *Life* (April 28, 1967). "A relatively unknown comedian" from John S. Wilson, "Y.M.H.A. Presents 2d Jazz Concert: Allen, Comedian, Heard with Evans and Mann Groups," *New York Times* (March 19, 1962). Arthur Gelb's "Young Comic Rising in 'Village': Woody Allen Is at the Bitter End, a Coffeehouse" ran in the November 21, 1962, *New York Times*. *The Laughmakers* from papers in the Susskind collection, and from Ramsey Ess, "A Rare Look at Woody Allen's Unaired Pilot about an Improv Comedy Team," Vulture.com, December 14, 2012. "I didn't understand the concept" and "I began to get comedy ideas" from WA's interview in *Seriously Funny*. Abe Lastfogel anecdote from "The Early Woody Allen: 1952–1971." "Midway through his opening" (Don Asher) from *Seriously Funny*. WA's letter to Cavett from *Woody Allen: A Biography*.

Vicky Tiel from her interview in *Woody: The Biography*, her interview in *Woody and His Women*, and her memoir *It's All About the Dress: What I Learned in Forty Years About Men, Women, Sex, and Fashion* (St. Martin's Press, 2012). "She stood apart" from Mick Houghton, *Becoming Electra: The True Story of Jac Holzman's Visionary Record Label* (Jawbone, 2010). Bill Cosby anecdote from Judy Henske. "The Unmentionables" appeared in the October 1963 issue of *Help!* "*Fumetti* were the perfect training" from Terry Gilliam, *Gilliamesque: A Pre-Posthumous Memoir* (Canongate, 2015). Background on *Help!* and the fumetti from *James Warren: Empire of Monsters* by William Schelly (Fantagraphic Books, 2019). "Write something" (Charles K. Feldman) from *Woody Allen: A Biography*. "I didn't have breathtaking" from Peter Biskind, *Star: How Warren Beatty Seduced America* (Simon & Schuster, 2010). "The kid's a genius . . ." from Robert Evans, *The Kid Stays in the Picture* (Phoenix, 2006). "I doubt if I was noticed" from the *Realist* interview. "His material was not going over" from Jesse Kornbluth, "Play It Alone, Brickman: Marshall Brickman, Woody Allen's Collaborator, Strikes a Blow for Brainy Humor in a Film All His Own," *New York Times* (February 24, 1980). "He did premise stuff" and "I would back into premises" from Kliph Nesteroff's interview with Marshall Brickman on the "Classic Television Showbiz" blog, classicshowbiz.blogspot.com (January 30, 2016). "An ophthalmologist," "the fact that you're going to die," and "such similar inflections" from Susan Braudy, "He's Woody Allen's Not-So-Silent Partner," *New York Times* (August 21, 1977). Allen Funt from Funt and Philip Reed, *Candidly, Allen Funt: A Million Smiles Later* (Barricade, 1994). "Idiot stuff" from Alfred Bester, "Conversations with Woody Allen," *Holiday* (May 1969).

"Worst crowd ever" from Guthrie. WA on Groucho Marx from *Apropos of Nothing*. "Gazed longingly at it as the sun set" from *Cavett*. "Typed on Corrasable Bond" from *Apropos of Nothing*. "I had named the lead female" from *Star*. WA's $50,000 donation to Mark Lane cited in Mel Hyman, *Burying the Lead: The Media and the JFK Assassination* (Trine Day, 2018). "After my late show" and "I sort of closed" from Michael Phillips, "Woody Allen in the Rearview

Mirror," *Chicago Tribune* (July 24, 2014). "With a five-minute bit" from "His Own Boswell," *Time* (February 15, 1963). "Judy Henske is one of the few" from *Conversations*. "Two of the ugliest" from *Woody and His Women*. *Don't Drink the Water* was announced in Sam Zolotow, "Richards Named to Musical Post," *New York Times* (June 26, 1964). "[Allen] would occasionally" is Clive Donner from Paul Sutton, *Six English Filmmakers* (Buffalo, 2014). "All the cues and format," "I don't have the faintest idea," and "I hate to say it, but" from Alan Patureau, "All the World's a Plank and Woody Walks It," *Newsday* (July 10, 1964).

Allen's correspondence with publicist Richard O'Brien from *Woody Allen: A Biography*. "The funniest script I ever read" (Warren Beatty) from *Woody and His Women*. Donner and Feldman's casting exchange from *Six English Filmmakers*. "Eyed one another carefully" from Allen's *Pussycat?* diary, written for publicity, from Ed Sikov, *Mr. Strangelove: A Biography of Peter Sellers* (Hachette, 2002). "Not nice" from Sian Phillips, *Public Places: The Autobiography* (Sceptre, 2002). I also drew on Roger Lewis, *The Life and Death of Peter Sellers* (Hal Leonard, 1997). "They used to give me rewrites . . ." from John Kobal, "The Kobal Tapes" from 1964, *Films and Filming* (December 1985). "Crucifying" from *Woody Allen: A Biography*. "Every museum and cathedral" from Guthrie. "Black stockings, blonde braids" from a WA letter to Richard O'Brien, quoted in *Woody Allen: A Biography*. WA's correspondence with theatrical producer Max Gordon from Gordon's papers in Special Collections at Princeton University. Norma Lee Clark from Tony Schwartz, "The Conflicting Life and Art of Woody Allen," *New York Times* (October 19, 1980). Vicky Tiel's twenty-first birthday from *It's All About the Dress* and her interview in *Woody and His Women*. "I'll never forgive her" (Paula Lasser) from *The Unruly Life of Woody Allen*. "I opened by saying" is from a WA letter to Richard O'Brien quoted in *Woody Allen: A Biography*. "What were they talking about?" from "President and Rafters Rock at Gala," *Washington Post* (January 20, 1965). Lady Bird Johnson from her January 18, 1965, audio diary, available online from the LBJ Presidential Library. Dorothy Kilgallen from "Comics in Bad Taste," *New York Journal–American* (January 19, 1965).

Chapter 4: 1965: The First Golden Age

"Mr. Everything" from "Chas K. Feldman's 15-Film Deal with United Artists; First Present Woody Allen as 'Mr. Everything,'" *Variety* (November 10, 1965). "Already, before a foot of film" from Ronald Bryden, "Success Rushing Up on Woody," reprinted from the London *Observer* in the *Washington Post* (March 14, 1965). "I like a big room" from John S. Wilson, "Woody Allen 'Copes' at the Royal Box," *New York Times* (January 22, 1966). "I hate all critics" from Marcia Seligson, "Portrait of a Man Reading," *Washington Post* (June 6, 1969). Whitney Bolton from "Woody Allen Admits He Wrote Script—But Not This Mishmash," *Morning Telegraph* (June 28, 1965). Studs Terkel's June 1, 1965, interview with WA is online at "Studs Terkel Radio Archive," WFMT, studsterkel.wfmt.com. WA also quoted here from the *Realist* interview. "A huge plus for me" and "was the big launching pad" from Guthrie. Early plans for "I'll Take the Money and Run" from A. H. Weiler, "On the Run toward the 'Money,'" *New York Times* (December 19, 1965). Lenny Bruce and Henry Saperstein from Donald Liebenson, "What's Up? 'Tiger Lily' Makes a Return," *Los Angeles Times* (January 16, 1998). Len Maxwell from *Woody Allen: A Biography*. "A word they invented" from Harold Mantell, "The Words and Ways of Woody Allen," *Media & Methods* (December 1977). *The Ed Sullivan Show* from *Woody Allen: A Biography* and from James Maguire, *Impresario: The Life and Times of Ed Sullivan* (Billboard Books, 2006). Allen-Lasser nuptials from Jack O'Brian, "Woody Allen's Wedding Was in Typical Style," *New York Times Herald*, syndicated in the *Washington Post* (February 7, 1966). "Woody Herman" anecdote and other Lasser material in this chapter from her interview in *Woody and His Women*, unless otherwise noted. "I guess it was not" from

Marilyn Cole Lownes, "If I Can Make It There," London *Sunday Times* (October 15, 2005). "Of course doing a bit" from Stephen Watts, "An 007 Movie without Connery? Get Headquarters!" *New York Times* (May 22, 1966). Val Guest from the Baxter biography and from Guest's memoir *So You Want to Be in Pictures* (Trafalgar Square, 2001). "Dangerously derivative" from Michiko Kakutani, 'Woody Allen, The Art of Humor," *Paris Review* (Fall 1995). Roger Angell from *Woody Allen: A Biography*. "How I Became a Comedian," which Allen dashed off during appearances at Mister Kelly's, originally appeared in the Sunday Panorama section of the *Chicago Daily News* (August 3, 1968). WA's London reminiscences from "If I Can Make It There," with his reflections on Lasser during this period from *Apropos of Nothing*. "How would you like to be" from "The Early Woody Allen: 1952–1971." "I am a surprisingly bad player" from Mel Gussow, "Hey There, Woodycat Allen, How's the World Treating You?" *New York Times* (December 24, 1967). "Preposterously expensive" and "I like to wake up" from Mimi Benzell's radio show "Luncheon from Café Francais," WNBC (July 14, 1964). "Sparsely furnished" from Alfred Bester, "Conversation with Woody Allen," *Holiday* (May 1969).

"I wanted to show" and "Her part had never emerged" from Cecil Smith, "Woody Allen—A Legitimate Use of Farce," *Los Angeles Times* (October 26, 1966). "I adored him [Gleason]" from Jason Bailey, *The Ultimate Woody Allen Film Companion* (Voyageur Press, 2014). "A real terrible play" and "I was in the picture" from "The Words and Ways of Woody Allen." "A nice idea that" from Martin Mull, "An Afternoon with Woody Allen: Dueling Bananas," *Crawdaddy* (December 1972). "Woody later played the tapes" from "Hey There, Woodycat Allen." Jerry Lewis from clippings and from Shawn Levy, *King of Comedy: The Life and Art of Jerry Lewis* (St. Martin's Press, 1996). "It's a neurotic love story . . ." from A. H. Weiler, "Knight Time for Woody Allen," *New York Times* (March 12, 1967). Petula Clark from Sharon Verghis, "Star Chanteuse Turns on Glamour," *Sydney Morning Herald* (March 10, 2004). Jim Murray from Jean Stein, *West of Eden: An American Place* (Random House, 2016). "I can make awful mistakes" from "The Tallest Dwarf in the World." "Not a single laugh" (Charles Joffe) from *Woody Allen: A Biography*. "Another time, . . . I flew to DC" from Douglas McGrath, "If You Knew Woody Like I Know Woody," *New York* (October 17, 1994), reprinted in *Woody Allen: Interviews*. "You remember what he said" (Louise Lasser) from Earl Wilson, "It Happened One Night," *New York Post* (May 19, 1971). "Say, please don't" and "I don't know why" from Jack Nessel, "Woodywoodywoody, You've Got It Knocked," *New York World Journal Tribune* (December 18, 1966). Woody/Harlene lawsuit details from documents in the Marion Meade papers. "Poor . . . a struggling fine artist" (Jeremiah Gutman) from *Woody Allen: Joking Aside*. "Wouldn't it be funny . . . ?" from Baxter. "I was the ex-wife" (Lasser) from *Woody and His Women*.

"They talk for hours" and "On every walk" (Martin Konigsberg) from Guthrie. "He was addicted to work" and "It rained nonstop" (Lasser) from *Woody and His Women*. "A compulsive writer" from "Woody," Paul O'Neil, *Life* (April 28, 1967). "Pretty, effervescent" from Judy Stone, "Woody, This Is Your Dream Life," *New York Times* (September 22, 1968). "We're like two children" from the Louise Lasser interview by Beverley D. Wilson in "Wife Reveals 'Woody' as Intelligent and Serious Offstage," *Miami Herald* (April 2, 1968). "That meant as much to me" from Ira Berkow, "From Defense to Offense: In the Editing Room with Woody Allen," *New York Times* (November 2, 1995). Edgar J. Scherick from "Taking Chance on New Talent Is Essential, Stresses Ed Scherick," *Variety* (October 15, 1969) and from *Edgar Scherick* (Jeffrey Norton Audiobook on Cassette, 1977). "Here's, as they say, the beauty part" from *Apropos of Nothing*. "I think he'll offer good contrast" from Guthrie. "Has absolutely nothing to do" from Herb Caen's column, "Big Wide Wonderful Whirl," *San Francisco Chronicle* (April 11, 1968). "The archetypal American sportscaster" from "Names and Faces," *San Francisco*

Chronicle (October 17, 1971). "I wish he'd stop worrying" (Turk Murphy) from Herb Caen's column "Mister Nite Life," *San Francisco Chronicle* (November 6, 1972). "I cast quickly" and "Also, I don't have the patience" from Mel Gussow, "Woody Allen Says He's Still Incompetent," *New York Times* (June 9, 1971). The screenings for *Take the Money and Run* cast and crew, Janet Margolin interview, and the anecdote about Allen helping Milton Berle out in Las Vegas from "Woody, This Is Your Dream Life." I drew from my interview with Howard Storm and also his memoir *The Imperfect Storm: From Henry Street to Hollywood* (BearManor, 2019). "I asked him to tell me" from *Start to Finish*. Ralph Rosenblum is always quoted from his memoir *When the Shooting Stops . . . the Cutting Begins: A Film Editor's Story* (Viking, 1979). "He wanted me to have little girls" (Lasser) from *Woody and His Women*. "He keeps shooting" (Louise Lasser) from Earl Wilson, "Earl Wilson on Broadway," *New York Post* (November 18, 1967). "I paid a song for it" from Peter Biskind, "Reconstructing Woody," *Vanity Fair* (December 2005). Mary Bancroft is always quoted from notes and correspondence among her papers.

Diane Keaton is always quoted from *Then Again* (Random House, 2011), with exceptions noted. I also drew reliably on Deborah C. Mitchell's *Diane Keaton: Artist and Icon* (McFarland, 2001). "A real hayseed" from Natalie Gittelson, "The Faces of Diane Keaton," *McCall's* (November 1978). "Rube" and "A coat-check girl" from *Apropos of Nothing*. "An absolutely spectacularly" from Ben Fong-Torres, "The Life and Lurves of Diane Keaton," *Rolling Stone* (June 30, 1977). "Most of it is legs" from Joan Gage, "Woody Was as Scared of Me as I Was of Him," *New York Times* (May 28, 1972). "Just the best actress" (Sanford Meisner) from Jack Kroll, "Thoroughly Modern Diane," *Newsweek* (February 15, 1982). "I wanted to lose the girl" from Mal Karman, "Comedy Directors: Interviews with Woody Allen," *Millimeter* (October 1977). "Since one of the major concerns" from Guy Flatley, "The Applause You Hear Is for Diane Keaton," *Los Angeles Times* (May 12, 1974). Excerpts from Keaton's letters to her mother and her mother's journal from *Then Again*. "Maybe it was the Freudian" from Jonathan Moor, *Diane Keaton: The Story of the Real Annie Hall* (St. Martin's Press, 1989). Joseph Hardy from Richard J. H. Johnston, "You Name It, Woody Is Doing It," *New York Times* (February 14, 1969) and the transcript of his American Film Institute seminar (December 11, 1974). "I can act realistically" from Guthrie. "I didn't have to dress" from Kathleen Carroll, "Woody Allen Says Comedy Is No Laughing Matter," New York *Daily News* (January 6, 1974), included in *Woody Allen: Interviews*. "It was the easiest job" from *WA/WA*. Allen's Manhattan apartment is described in "Woody Allen's Penthouse," *Architectural Digest* (November–December 1972).

Chapter 5: 1970: Clockwork

Bob Denver from *Gilligan, Maynard & Me* (Citadel, 1993). Louise Lasser in this chapter quoted from *Woody and His Women*, unless otherwise noted. "We had a good time" (Lasser) from *Woody: The Biography*. "She's been a crutch to me" is Allen. "Shared a love of torturing" (Keaton) from *Then Again*. "He was the only" (Keaton) from Daphne Merkin, "Another Woman: Diane Keaton Is the American Film Actress Most in Control of Her Narrative," *New York Times* (October 23, 2005). "I don't feel that way" from "Woody Was as Scared of Me as I Was of Him." "Lovers intermittently" from "The Life and Lurves of Diane Keaton." Tony Roberts from his memoir *Do You Know Me?* (Tony Roberts, 2015). "They were nice" from David Remnick, "Comedy Isn't Funny," *Saturday Review* (June 1986). David Picker from *Must, Maybes, and Nevers: A Book About the Movies* (CreateSpace, 2013). "Replete with 'gag' releases" from "Woody Gags & Cameras amidst Art Galleries Pales MMA's Curators," *Variety* (December 17, 1969). "Did not want to be sued" from *Apropos of Nothing*. "With a group of" from John S. Wilson, "Is New Orleans Jazz Dying?" *New York Times* (May 16, 1971). "Diane is America's greatest" is WA from *Woody and His Women*. Allen and the New Haven band from Art Hovey,

"Early History of the Galvanized Jazz Band," GalvanizedJazz.com. "I hate resorts" from Mary Blume, "Woody Allen Imperfectionist," *International Herald Tribune* (July 10–11, 1971), reprinted in the *Los Angeles Times* (July 14, 1971). Craig Modderno from his May 16, 1967, piece in the *Contra Costa Times* ("An Inside Look at Woody Allen") and *Woody: The Biography*. Herbert Ross ("headaches, permits") from Guthrie. Peter Bart wrote about *Play It Again, Sam* in *Infamous Players: A Tale of Movies, the Mob (and Sex)* (Weinstein Books, 2011). "They didn't want me" from Robert Greenfield, "Seven Interviews with Woody Allen," *Rolling Stone* (September 30, 1971). Sue Mengers from columnist clippings and Brian Kellow, *Can I Go Now? The Life of Sue Mengers, Hollywood's First Superagent* (Viking, 2015). "Boy, was she" from Graydon Carter, Editor's Letter, "Everybody Came to Sue's," *Vanity Fair* (December 2011).

Julius (Jack) Kuney's reminiscences about *The Harvey Wallinger Story* from *Woody Allen, Bob Dylan and Me: A Memoir* (Trafford, 2006). "We brought it to public television" (Charles Joffe) from George Gent, "Woody Allen's Satire Program Withdrawn for Public TV Airing," *New York Times* (February 15, 1972). Allen gave an interview ("This is the first picture") during the filming of *Everything You Always Wanted to Know About Sex** to Robert Mundy and Stephen Mamber for the Winter 1972–73 *Cinema*. Mundell Lowe from Jim Carlton, *Conversations with Great Jazz and Studio Guitarists* (Mel Bay, 2009). Gene Wilder from *Kiss Me Like a Stranger: My Search for Love and Art* (St. Martin's Press, 2005). Lea Lane from "Judith Crist: Thanks for the Stardust Memories," Huffington Post (August 8, 2012). "While it had some funny things" from *Apropos of Nothing*. David Reuben's widely quoted comments ("a sexual tragedy)" from Vernon Scott's interview with Reuben for United Press International, which was recycled in numerous US newspapers, print, and broadcast outlets including "Dr. Reuben Raps Woody Allen's 'Sex' Movie," New York *Daily News* (October 16, 1972). John Huddy's interview with WA from "Woody Isn't So Nervous—Once He Gets 'Oriented,'" *Miami Herald* (December 30, 1972). "The pressure" from his interview with Larry Wilde in *The Great Comedians Talk about Comedy* (Citadel Press, 1968). "Really and truly enhanced" and "made it funnier" from Joyce Haber, "Woody Allen—The Total Comedian," *Miami Herald* (July 2, 1972). "Line by line in a room" (Brickman) from Tony Crawley, "Marshall Brickman: Simply Simon," *Films Illustrated* (November 1980). Jean vanden Heuvel (a.k.a. Jean Stein) is quoted from her papers at the New York Public Library. "Grand entrance" and "green stuff on her face" from *Woody Allen: A Biography*. Allen's correspondence with Reginald Rose, the synopses and drafts of their project, are in the Rose collection at the Wisconsin Center for Film and Theater Research. Additional background on the doomed Allen-Rose collaboration from the 1974 *20th Century–Fox Film Corporation v. Woody Allen, et al.*, court documents in the Superior Court records of Los Angeles. "Considering he is white" from Eric Lax, "What's Woody Allen Doing on the Music Page?" *New York Times* (December 2, 1973). "Most important element" from "Woody's Happy UA Deal Because His Pictures Make $; Respect His Fear of TV Surgery," *Variety* (November 7, 1973). "She reads everything" from Charles Champlin, "Woody: The Frown Behind the Smile," *Los Angeles Times* (January 29, 1978). "Utterly spectacular visual" from Jack Kroll, "Woody." "Woody doesn't want" (Charles Joffe) from A. H. Weiler, "News of the Screen," *New York Times* (October 13, 1974). Allen's letters to Keaton re: *Love and Death* from *Then Again*. "An endless feat" (Willy Holt) from Baxter. "The funniest of my early" from *Apropos of Nothing*. "We were quite a couple" from *Then Again*. Martha Graham from *Blood Memory: An Autobiography* (Doubleday, 1991). Betty Ford from her memoir (with Chris Chase) *Times of My Life* (HarperCollins, 1978). "A deeper comedy . . . a more human film" from *On Being Funny: Woody Allen and Comedy*. Origins of "Dreams and Furies" from Anna Kisselgoff, "Woody Allen to Escort Mrs. Ford at Dance Benefit," *New York Times* (June 17, 1975). *The Front* from my interviews with Martin Ritt and Walter Bernstein, along with interviews with Bernstein and Andrea Marcovicci from *The Unruly Life of Woody Allen*. "I had a general awareness of

Joseph McCarthy" from Guy Flatley, "Woody Allen: I Have No Yen to Play 'Hamlet,' " *New York Times* (October 3, 1976). Alvah Bessie from past interviews with Bessie, correspondence with his son, and related items in his papers in the Wisconsin Center for Film and Theater Research. Bessie blacklist anecdote ("How dare you") from "Guy Flatley, "Woody Allen: 'I Have No Yen to Play 'Hamlet,'" *New York Times* (October 3, 1976). Victor Navasky wrote about the HUAC testimony of Abe Burrows (and his "friendly" wife Carin Kinzel) in *Naming Names* (Viking, 1980). "Almost certainly in the $1,000,000" from Frank Segers, "Male Film Stars on Gravy Train," *Variety* (January 28, 1976). "I want to do more risky" from Mel Gussow, "Everything You Wanted to Know about Woody Allen at 40," *New York Times* (December 1, 1975).

Caryn James is quoted from "Auteur! Auteur!" *New York Times* (January 19, 1986). "Woody wanted to take a risk" and "Another was a concern with" from Brickman's interview in *When the Shooting Stops*. Keaton and the Hall family reaction to their portrait in *Annie Hall* from *Then Again* with additional detail from Keaton's subsequent *Brother & Sister* (Knopf, 2020). The origins of "La-dee-da" from Bruce Weber, "A Lifetime of Comedy? Well, La-dee-da; Diane Keaton Reflects on Keeping 'Em Laughing," *New York Times* (March 17, 2004). "I need a laugh from you" from "Woody Allen, in Making a Film, Pays for Laughs," *New York Times* (August 7, 1976). "After months of conversation" (Brickman) from "Marshall Brickman: Simply Simon." "All I can say" (Brickman) from "He's Woody Allen's Not-So-Silent Partner." "Less than fully responsive" (Martin Ritt) from Frank Segers, "Pictures: Irked by Ritt's Gotham Slam, Wood Offers Rosenthal Rebuttal," *Variety* (December 30, 1975). "I had heard how difficult" from Ira Halberstadt, "Scenes from a Mind: Woody Allen Is Nobody's Fool," *Take One* (November 1978), included in *Woody Allen: Interviews*. "He was rigid" from *Apropos of Nothing*. "My maturity in films" from *WA/WA*. Mel Bourne anecdote from Vincent LoBrutto, *By Design: Interviews with Film Production Designers* (Praeger, 1992). "Comedies of significance," "I don't want to do films," and "I know I'm not guilty" from Gregg Kilday, "Woody to Eschew Triviality," *Los Angeles Times* (October 9, 1976). "Correctly, no matter how hard" from Aljean Harmetz, "The Movies That Draw Hatred," *New York Times* (May 4, 1981). "I would like to make another" from Baxter. "Inside Woody Allen" from Stuart Hample's article "How I Turned Woody Allen into a Comic Strip" in the *Guardian* (October 18, 2009) and from Hample's book *Dread & Superficiality: Woody Allen as Comic Strip* (Abrams, 2009).

Chapter 6: 1977: Mr. Secretive

"Mr. Secretive" from "Pictures: Woody Allen's Latest Stars Self, Rampling in Living B & W Laffer," *Variety* (August 22, 1979). "It was like the first draft" from the Marshall Brickman interview in *When the Shooting Stops*. "Surrealistic stuff" and "I didn't sit down with" from WA quoted in *When the Shooting Stops*. "A very middle-class picture" from Ira Halberstadt, "Scenes from a Mind." "You've earned it" (Arthur Krim) from *WA/WA*. "Not unattractive woman" from *On Being Funny: Woody Allen and Comedy*. Vivian Gornick (and WA) from "Face It, Woody Allen, You're Not a Schlep Anymore," *Village Voice* (January 5, 1976). "Unfair competition" from "Legal Punchline for Woody Allen, His Bio Is Yanked," *Variety* (May 17, 1978). "Active bachelor life" from Gene Siskel, "Woody Talks about His Off-Screen Self," *Chicago Tribune* (September 25, 1978). Pamela Des Barres from *I'm with the Band: Confessions of a Groupie* (Beech Tree, 1987). Jean Stein (Jean vanden Heuvel) anecdotes and observations from notes and papers in her collection. "Cowering in her wake" from Enid Nemy, "A Snappy Gathering for Steinberg," *New York Times* (April 15, 1978). Teri Shields anecdote from Brooke Shields, *There Was a Little Girl* (Dutton, 2014). "Occasional predilection" from "The

Conflicting Life and Art of Woody Allen." Nancy Jo Sales from "Woody and Me," *New York* (April 5, 1993). Nelkin from *Apropos of Nothing*, her interview in *Woody and His Women*, and her appearance on *The Howard Stern Show*, April 7, 2011. Babi Christina Engelhardt from Gary Baum, "Woody Allen's Secret Teen Lover Speaks," *Hollywood Reporter* (December 17, 2018). Maureen Stapleton from (with Jane Scovell) *A Hell of a Life* (Simon & Schuster, 1995). "This blue has to go" from James Feron, "Enter Woody Allen, Dining-Room Left," *New York Times* (June 4, 1978). Mel Bourne from "Inside Woody Allen's 'Interiors,'" *New York Times* (November 8, 1978) and "The trial of the age" (Bourne) from *Woody Allen: Joking Aside*. Freddie Fields anecdote from his unpublished memoir, courtesy of David Rensin. Allen declined to join the Academy "about sixteen times" according to Michael Cieply, "Honor Just to Be Asked In, as Film Academy Tightens Its Ranks," *New York Times* (December 1, 2008). "A unique act of integrity" from Adam Gopnik, "The Imposter," *New Yorker* (October 25, 1993). "I was very surprised" and "Those ads embarrass me" from Gene Shalit, 'What's Happening," *Ladies Home Journal* (August 1978). "I'm told that *Annie Hall*" from Guy Flatley, "Woody Opens the Door to 'Interiors,'" *Los Angeles Times* (September 3, 1978). "It's my father who polishes" from Tom Shales, "Woody: The First Fifty Years," *Esquire* (April 1987).

"A fear of being shot" from "The Tallest Dwarf in the World." Jules Feiffer from his interview in the Baxter biography and his memoir *Backing into Forward* (Doubleday, 2009). Orson Welles from Peter Biskind, *My Lunches with Orson: Conversations Between Henry Jaglom and Orson Welles* (Metropolitan Books, 2013). "That movie is about" (Louise Lasser) from *Woody and His Women*. Liv Ullmann, Ingmar Bergman, and WA from Ullmann interview in Simon Hattenstone, "A Lifelong Liaison," *Guardian* (February 3, 2001). WA's version of his get-together with Bergman from Geoff Andrew's interview and transcript published as "The *Guardian* Interview with Woody Allen" (September 27, 2001). Bergman on *Interiors* from Charles Champlin, "Bergman: At Ease Among His Friends," *Los Angeles Times* (October 15, 1978). "In no way really autobiographical," etc., from Tomm Carroll, "Bullets over Broadway Danny Rose of Cairo: The Continuous Career of Woody Allen," *DGA Magazine* (May–June 1996). The *Hollywood Reporter* reported on the different drafts of *Manhattan* in "Woody Allen's Secret Teen Lover Speaks." "Of a twenty-year ongoing" (Charles Joffe) from Richard Schickel, "A Comic Genius: Woody Allen Comes of Age," *Time* (April 30, 1979). "No, I'm from Philadelphia" (Susan Braudy) from Julian Fox, *Woody: Movies from Manhattan* (Overlook Press, 1996). Mariel Hemingway, unless otherwise noted, is always quoted from her books *Finding My Balance* (Simon & Schuster, 2003) and *Out Came the Sun: Overcoming the Legacy of Mental Illness, Addiction, and Suicide in My Family* (Simon & Schuster, 2015). "I was shooting scenes" from Baxter. "This way I don't bother" from "My Heroes Don't Come from Life, But from Their Mythology." Susan E. Morse from Vincent LoBrutto, *Selected Takes: Film Editors on Editing* (Praeger, 1991). Steven Bach from *Final Cut*. "Breaks out in a rash" (Dick Cavett) and "It's great to have your past" (Bob Hope) from Judy Klemesrud, "Bob Hope Honored at Film Society Gala," *New York Times* (May 8, 1979). Joan Didion's "Letter from 'Manhattan'" appeared in the August 16, 1979, *New York Review of Books*. "Now it seems like an unthinkable" from *Conversations*. Meryl Streep spoke about WA and *Manhattan* in "Meryl Streep" by Diane de Dubovay, *Ladies Home Journal* (March 1980). "He's always liked Charlotte's looks" (Jessica Harper) from Joan Goodman and Mike Bygrave, "Sampling the Revamping of Charlotte Rampling," *Los Angeles Times* (November 16, 1980). Marie-Christine Barrault from her interview in Baxter and from her memoir *Ce long chemin pour arriver jusqu'à toi* (Éditions XO, 2010). "Looked sixteen" (Sharon Stone) from Michael Munn, *The Sharon Stone Story* (Robson Books, 1997), and "I gave it my best shot" (Stone) from *Woody: Movies from Manhattan*. Judith Crist on WA and *Stardust Memories* from Karen Herman's 2006 interview with Crist in the Television Academy Foundation oral history collection.

Chapter 7: 1980: The Second Golden Age

"Knew the best people" from *Apropos of Nothing*. Helen Gurley Brown from her interview in *The Unruly Life of Woody Allen*. Pauline Kael's party invitation from Brian Kellow, *Pauline Kael: A Life in the Dark* (Viking, 2011). Andy Warhol from Pat Hackett (ed.), *The Andy Warhol Diaries* (Grand Central Publishing, 1989). William Zinsser from "My Stardust Memories," *American Scholar* (August 2, 2010). "Mia Farrow Has Her First Broadway Hit" by Andrea Chambers ran in the December 17, 1979, *People*. *The Farrows of Hollywood: Their Dark Side of Paradise*, by Marilyn Ann Moss, was issued by Skyhorse Publishing in 2023. "A mean and lecherous character" is Lee Server characterizing Ava Gardner's view of John Farrow from *Ava Gardner: "Love Is Nothing"* (St. Martin's Press, 2007). The Farrows "were all beautiful" (Rosalind Russell) from Edward Z. Epstein and Joe Morella, *Mia: The Life of Mia Farrow* (Delacorte, 1991). "I don't want to be" (Mia Farrow) from Kitty Kelley, *His Way: The Unauthorized Biography of Frank Sinatra* (Bantam, 1986). "A column of light" from *What Falls Away*. "At his age" (Maureen O'Sullivan) from her Wikipedia entry. The oft-quoted "Ha! I always knew" (Ava Gardner) from *Ava Gardner: The Secret Conversations* (Simon & Schuster, 2013). "Despite her fey" from Roman Polanski, *Roman* (Morrow, 1984). "Boisterous" nightclub behavior and background on the André Previn–Mia Farrow relationship from Martin Bookspan and Ross Yockey, *André Previn: A Biography* (Doubleday, 1981). "The skin was translucent" from Dory Previn, *Bog-Trotter: An Autobiography with Lyrics* (Doubleday, 1980). The *Stardust Memories* unveiling and conversation at Elaine's from *Final Cut*. Footnote about Soon-Yi's true age from Daphne Merkin, "After Decades of Silence, Soon-Yi Speaks," *New York* (September 16, 2018). "Questioning everything" (Charles Joffe) from "The Conflicting Life and Art of Woody Allen." Pauline Kael from her writings and from Brian Kellow's biography. Steven Bach from *Final Cut*. "It's one of my films" from "My Heroes Don't Come from Life, But from Their Mythology." "The truth is, I left my audience" from Sean Mitchell, "Woody Allen: Still Walking in His Own Shadow," *Los Angeles Times* (March 15, 1992). John Simon anecdote from *Apropos of Nothing*. Liz Smith from her memoir *Natural Blonde* (Hachette, 2000).

Jean Doumanian's *Saturday Night Live* reign from Sally Bedell Smith, *Up the Tube: Prime-Time TV and the Silverman Years* (Viking, 1981), and James A. Miller and Tom Shales, *Live from New York: The Complete, Uncensored History of Saturday Night as Told by Its Stars, Writers and Guests* (Little, Brown, 2015). Mike Medavoy is always quoted, unless otherwise noted, from his autobiography (with Josh Young) *You're Only as Good as Your Next One: 100 Great Films, 100 Good Films, and 100 Films for Which I Should Be Shot* (Atria, 2003). Danny Aiello from his autobiography (with Gil Reavill) *Danny Aiello: I Only Know Who I Am When I Am Somebody Else: My Life on the Street, on the Stage, and in the Movies* (Gallery, 2014). Ulu Grosbard ("He never talked") from John Andrew Gallagher, *Film Directors on Directing* (Praeger, 1989). "People keep thinking" and "I see it" from Eleanor Blau, "Woody Talks—a Little—about a 'Light Bulb,'" *New York Times* (March 19, 1981). "I was nervous" from Gene Siskel, "Wide-Ranging Words from Woody on Marriage, Murders—and More," *Chicago Tribune* (June 1, 1981). "Had very little contact" (Brian Backer) from Nan Robertson, "New Face: Brian Backer, Winner of the Woody-Allen-Kindred Soul Contest," *New York Times* (May 22, 1981). "I tend to be maybe" from *Woody Allen: A Biography*. José Ferrer's outburst ("No, now I can't do it!") from *Conversations*. *Variety*'s announcement of back-to-back Allen films ("for the purposes of clarity") from "Woody Allen Begins His 2nd Film in 1981 for Orion: Untitled," *Variety* (October 12, 1981). Engelhardt from "Woody Allen's Secret Teen Lover Speaks." "I like to sleep with the" from *The Unruly Life of Woody Allen*. "This sounds silly" and "the dead black of nowhere" from *Conversations*. Lillian Gish anecdote from *WA/WA*. WA and Susan E. Morse on *Zelig* from Dale Pollock, "Allen's 'Zelig': Perfecting Imperfection," *Los Angeles Times* (July 26,

1983). "Vastly underdressed ragpickers" from *Natural Blonde*. "The first and only dead" from *Apropos of Nothing*.

"You've got to realize" from Roger Ebert, "Movies," *Chicago Sun-Times* (July 11, 1982). "I do better now" from Charles Champlin, "Woody Allen Goes Back to the Well," *Los Angeles Times* (February 15, 1981). "I'd look at the dailies" from *Conversations*. "No discussions about characters" (Jeff Daniels) and "a romanticized perception" (WA) from "Auteur! Auteur!" In this and other chapters I cite from the annual national "Ten Best" roundups Mark Rowland and I tallied for ten years beginning in 1981, originating in the *Los Angeles Times* but also published at different times in the *Washington Post*, the *Chicago Tribune*, and *American Film* magazine. "I always thought it would be" from Alexander Walker's interview with WA in Australia's *Cinema Papers* (July 1986), included in *Woody Allen: Interviews*. "So filled with beauty" from "Woody Allen Pokes into Inspiration for 'Alice.'" "There's something of me" from Jack Kroll, "Woody." "Renata speaks for me" from Ira Halberstadt, "Scenes from a Mind." "Started losing his eyesight" from *Apropos of Nothing*. "George had a preconceived" (Maureen O'Sullivan) from Maureen Dowd, "The Five Women of 'Hannah and Her Sisters,'" *New York Times* (February 2, 1986). Michael Caine from Maria Aitken (ed.), *Acting in Film: An Actor's Take on Moviemaking* (Applause Books, 1990). Barbara Hershey from Myra Forsberg, "Barbara Hershey: In Demand," *New York Times* (March 29, 1987). "Uniquely favored child" from *Apropos of Nothing*. "Thrilled" and "Since he had already taken on" from Moses Farrow, "A Son Speaks Out," Mosesfarrow.blog (May 23, 2018). "Eight or twelve" from "Playboy Interview: Woody Allen," *Playboy* (May 1967). "Five girls" from "Wife Reveals 'Woody' as Intelligent and Serious Offstage." "I was in on it" from Gene Siskel, "Woody Allen at 50: A Happier Man . . . Considering," *Chicago Tribune* (January 26, 1986).

Chapter 8: 1985: Sleepwalking into a Mess

"I got a great thrill" from *Allen v. Farrow* testimony quoted in *The Unruly Life of Woody Allen*. "Mia is surrounded by kids" from the Associated Press, "Woody Allen Talks of Films and Fatherhood on the BBC," *New York Times* (November 14, 1987). "This may be my last" from Gene Siskel, "Woody Allen at 50: A Happier Man . . . Considering," *Chicago Tribune* (January 26, 1986). "Greatly cherished" and "Woody always told me" (Jack Rollins) from "Allen Gains WGA Award for 'Hannah,'" *Variety* (April 1, 1987). It's become a commonplace that Allen referred to *Hannah and Her Sisters* as "middlebrow"; Farrow quotes this pejorative in *What Falls Away*. "A living-room picture" from "The *Rolling Stone* Interview." James Wolcott from *Critical Mass: Four Decades of Essays, Reviews, Hand Grenades, and Hurrahs* (Doubleday, 2013). WA and Godard's versions of making *King Lear* from Richard Brody, *Everything Is Cinema: The Working Life of Jean-Luc Godard* (Henry Holt, 2008). Molly Ringwald wrote about the making of *King Lear* and her conversation with Allen about Godard in "The King and I," *New Yorker* (December 19, 2022). The footnote from Wikipedia draws on an *Open Culture* entry and a *Senses of Cinema* interview with Tom Luddy. "A light film" from "Auteur! Auteur!" "Memories of songs" from *Conversations*. "Bringing two newspapers" from "A Son Speaks Out." WA and Christopher Walken "couldn't get copacetic" from Eric Lax, "For Woody Allen, 60 Days Hath 'September,'" *New York Times* (December 6, 1987). "Mr. Allen and Miss Farrow are" (Norma Lee Clark) from press statement carried by wire services on April 30, 1987. "No one should be able" from WA's "The Colorization of Films Insults Artists and Society," *New York Times* (June 28, 1987). Phone call with Ingmar Bergman from Stockholm from the *Guardian*/National Film Theatre transcript. "Sexual" was "not the name I used" (Farrow) from *Allen v. Farrow* testimony. "I hope it's a she" from "Woody Allen Talks of Films and Fatherhood on the BBC." "My feeling about the baby" from Roger Ebert, "Woody Allen and 'September,'"

Chicago Sun-Times (November 29, 1987). "Two productions" and "the baby is fine" from Associated Press, "Son Born to Mia Farrow and Woody Allen," *New York Times* (December 22, 1987).

"She told me that" from "After Decades of Silence, Soon-Yi Speaks." Denis Hamill discusses Mia Farrow's breastfeeding regimen in "Allen Pals: She Just Went Ballistic," New York *Daily News* (August 24, 1992). "No company has had" (Arthur Krim) from Richard Gold, "Orion's Krim Sees Fine Times Ahead, Despite Sharp Remarks During Shareholders Meeting," *Variety* (August 12, 1987). "A lot of juicy ideas" (Robert Greenhut) from "Woody Allen, Coppola, Scorsese Will Direct A 3-Part BV Release," *Variety* (March 30, 1988). Anjelica Huston is always quoted, unless otherwise noted, from *Watch Me: A Memoir* (Scribner, 2014). "She'd twirled around," "Woody wasn't interested" (Soon-Yi Previn), and Soon-Yi's backstory and learning disabilities from "After Decades of Silence, Soon-Yi Speaks." "Woody Allen's New York City" from "Woody on the Town." "Your New York is alien" (Martin Scorsese) from Lynn Hirschberg, "Two Hollywoods: The Directors," *New York Times* (November 16, 1997). "Some Saturdays, some Sundays" and "all dressed up . . ." from Farrow's courtroom testimony cited in Groteke. Farrow's bichon frise and the "animal behaviorist" from Paula Span, "The Poop on Mia's Pooch," *Washington Post* (April 10, 1993). "Gender problems" and "always identifying with the females" from Allen's courtroom testimony cited in Groteke. "Mia flew into a rage" (WA) from Groteke. "Inappropriately intense" is Dr. Susan Coates from courtroom testimony quoted by Jean Seligmann and Mary Talbot, "A Game for the Whole Family," *Newsweek* (April 12, 1993). Dr. Nancy Schultz ("in her own fantasy world") from Peter Marks, "Psychologist Testifies about Visitation Rights for Allen," *New York Times* (April 2, 1993). "Had serious problems" from *Apropos of Nothing*.

Roger L. Simon from my interview with him, and from his book *Blacklisting Myself: Memoir of a Hollywood Apostate in the Age of Terror* (Encounter Books, 2009). *Rolling Stone* exchanges from William E. Geist's 1987 interview with Allen. "About $500 worth of loot" from "Woody, Mia Do Scenes of a Toy Store," *Los Angeles Times* (September 21, 1990). "The biggest set ever" and "was destined for commercial doom" from *Apropos of Nothing*. "Mother Teresa has been" from "Woody Allen Pokes into Inspiration for 'Alice.'" "Overcompensated" and "always breastfeeding" (WA) from Groteke. "We invite him" (Gilles Jacob) from "Cannes Director Looks for Variety at 42nd Festival," *Variety* (May 10, 1989). "Who had begun to believe" from *Allen v. Farrow* court ruling. "Woody commented on" from *What Falls Away*. "The amount of non-agreement" (Dr. Susan Coates) from Peter Marks, "Reporter's Notebook: Therapists in Allen Case Often Seem Like Family," *New York Times* (April 4, 1993). "There's no correlation" and "I was experimenting" from *Conversations*. "Decided not to take" (John Springer) from Liz Smith, "Mia Answers Her Critics," *Newsday*, (September 22, 1992). Springer defended Farrow in Smith's column after *Husbands and Wives* was released, and Owen Gleiberman reviewed the picture in the September 18, 1992, *Entertainment Weekly*, saying Farrow looked "ghostly and haggard," perhaps because she was on antidepressants after learning of Allen's affair with her daughter. All but a handful of Farrow's scenes were completed before the Polaroids' discovery, however, and Springer insisted Farrow was not "using drugs of any kind." Emily Lloyd from her memoir *Wish I Was There* (Metro, 2013). "Pick up the camera" from *WA/WA*.

"Oil and water," "hopelessly backward," and "never taught me how" from "After Decades of Silence, Soon-Yi Speaks." "Soon-Yi was her most" from "A Son Speaks Out." "Who didn't know I had no interest" and "the idea arose" from *Apropos of Nothing*. "As far as I know" (Paul Martin Weltz) from Richard Corliss, "Adoption Fever," *Time* (September 7, 1992). "An atrocity has been committed" from *What Falls Away*. "Locked Soon-Yi in her bedroom" from *Apropos of Nothing*. The final days of shooting *Husbands and Wives* from William Grimes, "A

Chronology of a Film's Making and a Relationship's Unmaking," *New York Times* (August 31, 1992).

Chapter 9: 1992: The Great Unpleasantness

"Had deceived me" from *What Falls Away*. "I think it shows just how" (Eleanor B. Alter) from Dennis Duggan, "New York Diary: Outside the Door, It Was All Smiles," *Newsday* (November 19, 1992). "Grossly underpaid" (Alan Dershowitz) from Paula Span, "The Brawling Barristers," *Washington Post* (April 17, 1993). Accounts of Allen and Farrow squabbling publicly, first depicted in the March 10, 1992, New York *Daily News* series of photographs, quickly spread to newspapers and magazines around the US. "Underlined for me the importance" (Farrow's testimony) and "Considering everything" (Casey Pascal) from Groteke. "Infamous, chilling" from *Apropos of Nothing*. "He took my daughter" from "Woody Allen Speaks Out," *New York Times* (February 7, 2014). "I have something planned," "another vituperative call," and "I joked that placing a bomb" from *Apropos of Nothing*. Variants of the text of the bathroom note ("CHILD MOLESTER . . .") have been reported. One of the earliest, Groteke's version, is in all CAPS, for example, and omits the words "at birthday party." Meade's (which is quoted in this chapter) has "at birthday party" and spelling and grammatical errors. The court later acknowledged the existence of the bathroom note in its final opinion in *Allen v. Farrow*, with Judge Elliott Wilk, in noting, "After Mr. Allen retired to the guest room for the night, Ms. Farrow affixed to his bathroom door, a note which called Mr. Allen a child molester. The reference was to his affair with Soon-Yi." Judge Wilk oddly did not mention the "NOW FOCUSED ON YOUNGER SISTER" part. "Somebody has to find a way to stop him" (Dr. Susan Coates) from Samuel Maull, "Farrow's Attorney Cites Errors by Allen's Therapist," Associated Press (March 20, 1993). "Warned me" from *Apropos of Nothing*.

Unless otherwise noted, Moses Farrow is always quoted from "A Son Speaks Out." "There were no seats" from *Apropos of Nothing*. "Dylan went on to say" from *What Falls Away*. Monica Thompson's statement ("I don't think anything happened") from Groteke. "With relish" (WA) quoted in Groteke. The "Is there any way out?" exchange from *What Falls Away*. "Inserted a finger partially" (Farrow) from Richard Pérez-Peña, "Farrow Testifies That Daughter Accused Allen of Molestation," *New York Times* (March 26, 1993). "I recall Ms. Farrow saying" (Monica Thompson) from John J. Goldman, "Nanny Casts Doubt on Farrow Charges," *Los Angeles Times* (February 2, 1993). "Who'd been working with Woody" from *What Falls Away*. "Who I was conferring with" from *Apropos of Nothing*. "A hero of mine" from Paula Span, "Dershowitz: Woody Would Not Budge," *Washington Post* (April 16, 1993) and "sleazebag" from Span, "The Brawling Barristers," *Washington Post* (April 17, 1993). "If I submitted" (WA) and "costs of support, education" (Alan Dershowitz and David Levett) from James Barron, "Striking Back, Woody Allen Denies Child Sex-Abuse Allegations," *New York Times* (August 19, 1992). "An attempt by both" and "absolutely untrue" (Dershowitz) from "Attorney Disputes Allen," *Los Angeles Times* (August 20, 1992). "A total fabrication" from *Apropos of Nothing*. Leslee Dart's famous last words from Bruce Weber, "Woody Allen Files Child-Custody Lawsuit," *New York Times* (August 14, 1992). "At the center of a" from John J. Goldman, "Woody Allen Paints Fight as a 'Cosmic Explosion,'" *Los Angeles Times* (August 25, 1992).

The Allen-Farrow relationship "has been something of a . . ." from Jonathan Rabinovitz, "War! Mia Fights Back with (Gasp!) Publicity," *New York Times* (August 16, 1992). "A pall has fallen" from Pete Hamill, "Woody: The Inside Story," *New York Post* (August 21, 1992). "I saw him three weeks" (Eric Lax) from "Woody Allen Files Child-Custody Lawsuit." "A cheap shot from" (Maureen O'Sullivan) from "War! Mia Fights Back With (Gasp!) Publicity." Martin Konigsberg ("Her mother put her up," etc.) from Reuters news service, carried in the *New York*

Post and *Miami Herald* (August 27, 1992). "Regarding my love" from Bruce Weber, "Public Disclosures from the Private Life of Woody Allen," *New York Times* (August 18, 1992). "Haggard and distressed" from Jane Hall and Terry Pristin, "Woody Deals with Manhattan Nightmare," *Los Angeles Times* (August 19, 1992). "Except for clearing" and "The one thing I have been guilty of" from "Striking Back, Woody Allen Denies Child Sex-Abuse Allegation." "From the privacy she so" (John Springer) from Zachary Margulis, "Mia's Mama Mad, Calls Woody an 'Evil Man' for Custody Suit" (*Newsday*, August 16, 1992). "Spoiled and mutilated" from Associated Press, "Mia's Letter to Her Friend," *Newsday* (August 20, 1992). Farrow's "seconds" ("children, close friends") are discussed in James Barron, "Private Lives, Public Battleground," *New York Times* (August 24, 1992). "Ms. Farrow has never" (Dershowitz) from "Striking Back, Woody Allen Denies Child Sex-Abuse Allegation." Moses Farrow's open letter ("That person is capable of") recounted in "But She's Not Part of My Family," *Newsweek* (August 30, 1992). "I was showing loyalty" (Moses Farrow) from *Start to Finish*. "Has a double-digit IQ" (Tisa Farrow) from Jerry Adler, "Unhappily Ever After," *Newsweek* (August 31, 1992). That Farrow allegedly phoned Letty Aronson in February 1992 and said Allen had taken advantage of a "retarded girl" by raping Soon-Yi was reported in Jean Seligmann and Mary Talbot, "A Game for the Whole Family," *Newsweek* (April 12, 1993). "Easily led" (Fletcher Previn) from Dennis Duggan, "New York Diary: Few Seem to Be on Woody's Side," *Newsday* (August 20, 1992). "Emotionally immature" (Lark Previn) from *The Unruly Life of Woody Allen*. Whispers that Soon-Yi "may still be a teenager" and "Woody has made her twenty-one" (Dershowitz) from Tom Gliatto and Sue Carswell, "A Family Affair," *People* (August 31, 1992).

"Feuding parents" and "The tape seemed to support" (Fox spokesman) from Laurie Goodstein, "Tape Is Held to Contain Child's Recounting of Abuse," *Los Angeles Times* (August 20, 1992). "Introduced Soon-Yi" (Juliet Taylor) from Mitch Gelman, "Soon-Yi's Roommate: She's Still a Teenager," *Newsday* (August 28, 1992). "Absurd" (Diane Keaton) from Liz Smith's August 26, 1992, column in *Newsday*. "Can we stop this?" (Farrow) quoted by WA from Walter Isaacson, "The Heart Wants What It Wants," *Time* (August 31, 1992). "In light-years I wouldn't," "A lark of the moment," and "Am I going to spend" (all WA) also from "The Heart Wants What It Wants." "I think Mia would" (Soon-Yi) from "Soon-Yi Speaks: 'Let's Not Get Hysterical,'" *Newsweek* (August 31, 1992). "I just feel if" (Farrow) from "Private Lives, Public Battleground." "With flying colors" from Emily Sachar, "A Bitter Battle: He Decries Charge; She'll Show in Court," *Newsday* (August 25, 1992). "Modeling photographs" is Eleanor B. Alter's explication; what Allen told Walter Isaacson was: "Soon-Yi had talked about being a model and said to me would I take some pictures of her without her clothes on. At this time, we had an intimate relationship, so I said sure." "Eleven days of attacks" from Emily Sachar and Mitch Gelman, "Sounds of Silence from Woody, Mia," *Newsday* (August 27, 1992). "They are pornographic" (Alter) and "In their private meeting with" from David Treadwell, "Judge Won't Look at Nude Photos by Allen," *Los Angeles Times* (August 26, 1992). "Voluntarily agreed" (Leslee Dart) from Bruce Weber, "Allen and Farrow Meet with Judge in Chambers," *New York Times* (August 26, 1992). Mike Medavoy, here and elsewhere, from *You're Only as Good as Your Next One*. "No more or less" from Maureen Dowd, "Diane and Woody, Still a Fun Couple," *New York Times* (August 15, 1993). "Parallels that range" from "A Chronology of a Film's Making and a Relationship's Unmaking."

"Was pressuring her" (Moses Farrow) from "A Son Speaks Out." The rabbi's call for "economic reprisals" from Martin Siegel, "Woody's Crime and Punishment," *Newsday* (September 17, 1992). Newt Gingrich ("a weird situation") quoted from Molly Ivins's August 26, 1992, column in the *Washington Post*. "Pithy summary" and "the guiding principle" (William Barr) from David Johnston, "Justice Official Sees Weakening of Moral Fiber: Attorney General

Points to Woody Allen Case," *New York Times* (October 8, 1992). "From calling him a nerd" from Cindy Adams, "Woodenhead Allen," *New York Post* (August 28, 1992). "I haven't wavered" from *Natural Blonde*. "Gloria Steinem's "concern about child abuse" from Keith Greenberg, "Steinem Weighs in on Woody/Mia Trial," *USA Today* (March 31, 1993), and from the 2021 *Allen v. Farrow* documentary, in which Steinem is interviewed. Murray Kempton called Allen "a hateful creature" in "A Bastard in the Pejorative Sense," *Newsday* (March 24, 1993) and denounced his "concourse in sin" with Soon-Yi in "Woody Oblivious to Error," *Newsday* (June 10, 1993). "Has great balls" (Diane Keaton) from "The Imperfectionist." "It was great therapy" from "Diane and Woody, Still a Fun Couple." Keaton on filming *Manhattan Murder Mystery* from *Then Again* and from "Diane and Woody, Still a Fun Couple." Anjelica Huston from *Watch Me*. "Being hassled by the rabble" from wire reports, which appeared in the *Dallas Morning News* (October 29, 1992) and many other US publications. "Not true at all" from Denis Hamill, "How Woody Survived a Father's Nightmare," New York *Daily News* (March 21, 1993).

"Fraud and deceit" from "Outside the Door, It Was All Smiles." "Whatever interest the children had" (Wilk) from Linda Winer, "Allen-Farrow Soap Opera Coming to TV," *Newsday* (November 14, 1992). Maureen Orth in this chapter from "Momma Mia!" "Sociopathic tendencies" (Farrow speaking to *Hello!*) and "photos to be taken" from Liz Smith, "Mia Speaks, Woody Preps," in *Newsday* (October 27, 1992). The "Woody Allen episode" of *60 Minutes* aired on November 22, 1992; a transcript can be found at www.cbsnews.com/news/woody-allen-defends-himself-on-60-minutes-in-92. "Let him have *60 Minutes*" from New York *Daily News* (March 21, 1993), quoted in *The Unruly Life of Woody Allen*. Carole Agus reported on Thanksgiving at Frog Hollow in "Mia's Story: Confidantes Tell a Tale of Weird Woody Actions Even Before Very Public Custody Battle Began," *Newsday* (November 29, 1992). "Pleaded with the warring parties" and my account of the December custody case hearing, unless otherwise noted, from Richard Pérez-Peña, "Vitriol Is Order of the Day in Allen-Farrow Case," *New York Times* (December 16, 1992). 'I will defer to Ms. Farrow's judgment" (Wilk) from David Kocieniewski, "Allen 'Sneaks' into Court," *Newsday* (December 16, 1992). Douglas McGrath's account of his collaboration with WA on *Bullets over Broadway* from "If You Knew Woody Like I Know Woody." "Crucible of intense" and "laughing that it seemed" from "The Imperfectionist." Groteke's book discusses the process of finding new names for Dylan and Satchel, starting with Eliza and Harmon. "Doing compliments" and "making snoring noises" from Peter Marks, "Farrow Says Daughter Became Distraught over Allen's Relentless Attention," *New York Times* (March 27, 1993). "Putting his penis" from *What Falls Away*. "Too insane" (WA) from Hal Davis and Marianne Goldstein, "Dylan: I Watched as Daddy and Soon-Yi Had Sex," *New York Post* (January 13, 1993). "Unfounded" (Paul Williams) from James Bennet, "Agency's File Forces Inquiry in Allen Case," *New York Times* (February 11, 1993). "Moreover, . . . as one of the last" and background of scuttlebutt that WA used an escort service to procure underage girls from James Rosenthal, "The Favor Bank," *Village Voice* (March 2, 1993). Farrow's suspicions regarding Allen's list-making of her pills, and her fears about his "bugging" of her residences, from Groteke.

The Yale Hospital team report is located easily on many websites. Dr. John M. Leventhal's sworn statement ("She told us initially") from Richard Pérez-Peña, "Doctor Cites Inconsistencies in Dylan Farrow's Statement," *New York Times* (May 4, 1993). Allen on the Yale meeting from *Apropos of Nothing* and from "How Woody Survived a Father's Nightmare," Denis Hamill's interview with WA on the evening following the day of the Yale team report. "Agreed that the report would not" (Leslee Dart) from Richard Pérez-Peña, "Woody Allen Says Report Clears Him," *New York Times* (March 19, 1993). "I just want to say" (Farrow) and "incomplete and inaccurate" (Eleanor B. Alter) from "Woody Allen Says Report Clears Him." "Very much at his ease" and "Here was the man" from Carole Agus, "His Fiction, Our Reality," *Newsday* (March 19, 1993). "Grim" and "I believe this" from "Woody Allen Says Report Clears Him." "Establish appropriate boundaries" and "continuous psychotherapy" from Rob Polner, Wendy Lin, and Carole Agus, "Woody Says He's Cleared: Report: No Sign of Sex Abuse," *Newsday* (March 19, 1993). Frank Maco ("There has been no evidence") from Richard Pérez-Peña, "Woody Allen Tells of Affair as Custody Battle Begins," *New York Times* (March 20, 1993).

"A traditionalist" from David Kocieniewski, "No Nonsense Judge Was Witty Referee," *Newsday* (June 8, 1993). "Seemed to relish" from Douglas Martin, "Elliott Wilk, Judge and Dry Wit, Dies at 60," *New York Times* (July 3, 2002). "Lots of people will tell you" (Eleanor B. Alter) from Jan Hoffman, "Counsel to the Brokenhearted; For Lawyer, Bitter Divorces and Touch of Humor," *New York Times* (August 16, 1995). "A dogged but often" from William Grimes, "A Courtroom Drama; Woody Allen Finds Himself in New Role," *New York Times* (March 25, 1993). "Super-decent, upright" from Liz Smith, "Woody's New Lawyer," *Newsday* (November 24, 1992). "A deliberate worker" from William Grimes, "Farrow Tries to Avoid Role of a Woman Scorned," *New York Times* (March 26, 1993). "Self-assured" from William Bunch, "Woody on Stand: Custody Hearing Off to an Early Start," *Newsday* (March 20, 1993). "Relaxed, one arm draped" from a recap of the first day in court by Richard Pérez-Peña, "Son's Letter of Anguish Rivets Court in Allen Case," *New York Times* (March 24, 1993). "He and I did not like" from *Apropos of Nothing*. "She's pretty cute," "Just a short thing," and "It's unfathomable" from "Woody on Stand." "In the most shameless, degrading way as pawns," "joyless, sexless," "rightly or wrongly" and "It's been fourteen months" from the Associated Press wire service account (March 23, 1993). Exchange between Justice Wilk and WA from "Woody Allen Tells of Affair as Custody Battle Begins." "We were two adults," "erotic, provocative" and "some of his other actions" from Richard Pérez-Peña, "Nude Photographs Are Focus of Woody Allen's Testimony," *New York Times* (March 23, 1993). "I posed her on the sofa" from Patricia Cohen, "My Mistake, Woody: Affair with Soon-Yi an 'Error,'" *Newsday* (March 23, 1993). "I did love her" from John J. Goldman, "Allen Says He Told Farrow Lie to Calm Her," *Los Angeles Times* (March 23, 1993). "Of behaving worse still" and "I screwed up" from "Nude Photographs Are Focus of Woody Allen's Testimony." "Mom is a great mother" (Moses Farrow) from "Son's Letter of Anguish Rivets Court in Allen Case." "Needy is Mia's favorite word" (WA) from Patricia Cohen, "Woody's Kid: 'Drop Dead, Moses' Letter Rocks Courtroom," *Newsday* (March 24, 1993) and Farrow describes WA as "needy" in Patricia Cohen, "Mia's Turn to Testify: Tells Court of Dylan's Halting Words: 'Daddy Touched Me,'" *Newsday* (March 26, 1993). "Remember details and had to refer," "was having an affair . . . ?" (Judge Wilk) and "sometimes impressively" from "A Courtroom Drama." "Little bastard" exchange from "Woody's Kid: Drop Dead." "The purpose of my going" (WA) from courtroom testimony cited in Groteke. Carole Agus's "The Big Director Is a Small Father" appeared in the March 24, 1993, *Newsday*. Wilk's interrogation of WA ("I do believe she brainwashed Dylan" and "it would not have been an issue") from transcript included as part of "The Big Director Is a Small Father." "Their day-to-day behavior will be done" (WA) quoted in "Conclusions" section of Judge Wilk's ruling. "That's the way he talks" (Elkan Abramowitz) and "I don't think Woody Allen cares" (Eleanor B. Alter) from "Son's Letter of Anguish Rivets Court."

"Tried to portray her" from William Grimes, "Farrow Tries to Avoid Role of a Woman Scorned," *New York Times* (March 26, 1993). "He was breathing into" (Farrow) from Patricia Cohen, "Mia's Turn to Testify: Tells Court of Dylan's Halting Words: 'Daddy Touched Me,'" *Newsday* (March 26, 1993). "Second claim of sexual abuse" from John J. Goldman, "Farrow Tells of Offer to Break Allen's Legs," *Los Angeles Times* (March 27, 1993). "I wanted this documented," "They would always end up in his bed," and "I know that it referred" (Mia Farrow) as well as "Did you become pregnant" (Elkan Abramowitz) from Richard Pérez-Peña, "Farrow Testifies That Daughter Accused Allen of Molestation," *New York Times* (March 26, 1993). "He would do little things," "is far more of a father," "all her senior year," and "I'm not proud" (Farrow) from "Farrow Tries to Avoid Role of a Woman Scorned." "This very needy quality" (Mia Farrow) from Peter Marks, "Farrow Says Daughter Became Distraught Over Allen's Relentless Attention," *New York Times* (March 27, 1993). "Sexually and romantically diminished" is Farrow quoted in Groteke. "Her clipped answers" and "the day of the broken legs," along with "it was a joke," "I would hope I could empower" and "if they want to" (Farrow), from William Grimes, "Fear and Anger as Mia Farrow Is Cross-Examined," *New York Times* (March 27, 1993). "To keep the allegations quiet" (Abramowitz) from "Farrow Says Daughter Became Distraught Over Allen's Relentless Attention." "In some detail, a catalogue" and "the leg-breaking seemed to lend" from "Fear and Anger as Mia Farrow Is Cross-Examined." "The new laugh of superiority" from *What Falls Away*. "Fucking leg" and "absolutely untrue" (WA) quoted in Groteke. "For less than five minutes" from David Kocieniewski, "Woody-Mia: Shrinking Judgment," *Newsday* (April 27, 1993). "There were so many untruths" (Farrow) from Paula Span, " 'Crazy Mia' or 'Woody No-Goody'?: The Question in the Allen-Farrow Mess," *Washington Post* (March 30, 1993).

"The man who had been her lover" from Cindy Adams, "Woody Sex Tapes," *New York Post* (August 11, 1993). "There has never been" (Dr. Kathryn Prescott) from Patricia Hurtado, "Woody's 33 Years on the Couch; Allen's Not a Pervert, Says Longtime Therapist's Letter," *Newsday* (April 20, 1993). "A scullery maid" (Jane Read Martin) from David Kocieniewski, "Nanny Changes Her Tune about Mia, Says Farrow an Unfair Mother," *Newsday* (April 6, 1993). "Taken over by fantasy" (Dr. Susan Coates) from David Kocieniewski, " 'I Helped Her': Mia Cites Woody on Soon-Yi Affair," *Newsday* (March 30, 1993). "I think they each" and "I really feel" (Dr. Susan Coates) from David Kocieniewski, "Shrink Raps: Doc Knocks Woody & Mia as Parents," *Newsday* (March 31, 1993). "Extreme bad judgment" (Coates) from William Grimes, "Farrow's Lawyer Takes Aim at Doctor's Judgment," *New York Times* (March 31, 1993). "Brief but spirited" and Letty Aronson's testimony from Peter Marks, "Allen's Sister Says Farrow Sows Hatred in Children," *New York Times* (April 3, 1993). "We get kicked out" from Carole Agus, "Dr. Susan Coates, Shock Therapist," *Newsday* (March 30, 1993). "Much as it began" and last day in court from Peter Marks, "Allen-Farrow Trial Ends in a New Round of Old Charges," *New York Times* (May 5, 1993). "I don't think he'll ever recover" from Paula Span, "Courtroom Notebook," *Washington Post* (May 4, 1993). Abramowitz's summary ("soldiers and pawns") from Daniel Wise, "Accusations Fly in Summations at Allen-Farrow Custody Trial," *New York Law Journal* (May 5, 1993).

Chapter 10: 1993: The Tears of a Clown

Stefano Hatfield wrote about "Woody Allen's First Ads" in the April 24, 1992, *Campaign*. Sweetland contract and legal documents from New York court records. Justice Elliott Wilk's ruling, reported from various press accounts, can be found online on several websites, including woodyallenmoblynching.com/court-document-judgement. "As though she were holding," and Farrow's public statements after the court ruling, from Carole Agus, "He Wasn't Worthy to Be in a Family," *Newsday* (June 8, 1993). Allen was "delighted" according to Carole Agus, "He Wasn't Worthy to Be in a Family," *Newsday* (June 8, 1993). Eleanor B. Alter's June 7, 1993, appearance on *The Charlie Rose Show* can be found at CharlieRose.com. Erica Jong from "Woody, or Wouldn't He?" *Marie Claire* (December 1998). Molly Haskell from " 'My Bust-Up with Mia Would Have Made a Great Movie,' " *Guardian* (November 23, 2000). "Airplane read" from *Apropos of Nothing*. Diane Keaton and *Manhattan Murder Mystery* from *Then Again* and from "Diane and Woody, Still a Fun Couple."

Frank Maco's press conference and WA's public statement ("long, torturous diatribe," etc.) from Melinda Henneberger, "Connecticut Prosecutor Won't File Charges Against Woody Allen," *New York Times* (September 25, 1993). "Microscopically similar" from *What Falls Away*. "We found hair" (Dr. Henry Lee) from Andy Thibaut, "How Straight-Shooting State's Attorney Frank Maco Got Mixed Up in the Woody-Mia Mess," *Connecticut Magazine* (March 31, 1997). "You don't declare" (Stephen Gillers) and "Mr. Allen's idea of peace" (Eleanor B. Alter) also from "Connecticut Prosecutor Won't File Charges Against Woody Allen." "Probable cause" and "insensitive and inappropriate" from Randy Kennedy, "Woody Allen Fails to Beat a Prosecutor," *New York Times* (November 4, 1993). "No credible evidence" from Richard Pérez-Peña, "Agency Drops Abuse Inquiry in Allen Case," *New York Times* (October 26, 1993). "I could have played it" from *WA/WA*. "He's not one of those actors" from Ellen Pall, "John and Woody and Mary-Louise and Mia," *New York Times* (October 23, 1994). "Are you kidding?" (WA on Dianne Wiest in *Bullets over Broadway*) from *Conversations*. "It helped her" from Ellen Pall, "Hannah's Neurotic Sister? That Was Ages Ago," *New York Times* (October 9, 1994). "Camp it up" from *Conversations*. "Chazz, Tracey, Jennifer improvised" from "My Heroes Don't Come from Life, But from Their Mythology." "No big problems" from *Conversations*. "Woody Allen touched" (Dylan Farrow), "pattern of extreme bias" (WA on Justice Elliott Wilk), and "I don't trust him" (Wilk on WA) from Cindy Adams's column in the March 13, 1995, *New York Post*. "I went seeking Solomon" from "If You Knew Woody Like I Know Woody." "An Error in Judgment" from "The Imperfectionist."

"There have been many" from *WA/WA*. "A comic genius" and "thrilled" (Harvey Weinstein) from Claudia Eller, "Woody Hits Bull's-Eye at Miramax," *Los Angeles Times* (June 17, 1994). "A disaster, an embarrassment" and "big master shots" from *WA/WA*. Michael J. Fox from *Lucky Man: A Memoir* (Hachette, 2003). "The movie's theme" (WA) and "One of Mr. Allen's own trademark" from Bob Morris, "The Night: Glamorous Ancestors, Movie, Evening Wear," *New York Times* (October 16, 1994). "Is that Woody Cusack?" "sort of depressed," etc. (John Cusack), and "maybe now and then" (WA) from "John and Woody and Mary-Louise and Mia." "An incredibly beautiful spot" from *WA/WA*. "Years ago, . . . I was looking at Dylan" from Lesley White, "Primal Screen," London *Sunday Times Magazine* (February 11, 1996). "I try and try and try" and "What about Mia?" from *WA/WA*. "Bonnet pictures," etc. (re: Helena Bonham Carter) from *Conversations*. "Very short readings" and "I mean a page" from *WA/WA*. Bonham-Carter ("His way of filming is different") from Sean MacAulay, "Can't See the Woody for the Trees," London *Times* (December 6, 2002). WA on Mira Sorvino from Patrick Goldstein, "Making the Hollywood Honor Roll: Ivy Leaguer Mira Sorvino," *Los Angeles Times* (November 4, 1995) and from *WA/WA*. Paul Nagle, then a Fox Network executive, supplied background on the telefilm *Love and Betrayal: The Mia Farrow Story*. Michael Blakemore wrote about his experience with WA and *Death Defying Acts* in "Backstage Notes: Death Defying Director," *New Yorker* (May 26, 1996). "I never saw it" from *WA/WA*. "Some of it was exaggerated" from *Woody Allen: A Biography*. "Right in my neighborhood" from *WA/WA*. "Woody throws you into" (Alan Alda) from "The Imperfectionist." "I won't say" (Dick Hyman) from Nadine Brozan, "Chronicle," *New York Times* (July 8, 1996). "Straight on" and "I had a very good time" from *Conversations*. Ira Berkow's "In the Editing Room with Woody Allen: From Defense to Offense" appeared in the November 2, 1995, *New York Times*. Details about Satchel's visits to Allen from "Dylan Farrow's Molestation Claims Against Woody Allen Were Planted by Mia Farrow" by Denis Hamill, New York *Daily News* (February 4, 2014). "Bag of vomit" from "If You Knew Woody Like I Knew Woody."

Allen's Heimlich maneuvers from Emily Smith, "Page Six: Woody Allen Saves Pal's Life," *New York Post* (May 22, 2023). Background on the "Dinner Table Conversation" from *Allen v. Sweetland* court documents. "Money and control" (Terry Zwigoff) from John Clark, "The Woman Who Reeled in Elusive Woodman," *Los Angeles Times* (April 19, 1998). Barbara Kopple and WA from Michel Ciment, "Woody Captured on the Spot, without a Script," *Positif* (February 1998), and Gary Arnold, "Woody Allen's 'Wild' Concerts: Filmmaker Blows Own Horn on His European Jazz Tour," *Washington Times* (May 8, 1998), both included in *Barbara Kopple: Interviews* (University Press of Mississippi, 2015). "Multivitamin, baby aspirin" and sample breakfast-table talk from Dana Kennedy, "A Rare Tour of Woody Allen's Private Side," *New York Times* (April 19, 1998). "Maximum tension" and "white knuckle" from Joe Morgenstern's review of *Wild Man Blues* in the *Wall Street Journal* (April 24, 1998). WA on the D. W. Griffith Award from *DGA Magazine* (May–June 1996). "I have this policy" from *WA/WA*. WA's Commandeur des Arts et des Lettres from Alan Riding, "Dear Woody, Have We Got News for You," *New York Times* (March 29, 1998). "I had to cut" (WA) on Tracey Ullman's scenes, and Alan Alda and Goldie Hawn dancing "a wonderful number" in *Everyone Says I Love You*, from *WA/WA*. "When I actually make the cut" and "my psychic repertoire" from *WA/WA*. "I first went to Robert De Niro" from *Conversations*. Kirstie Alley from *The Art of Men: I Prefer Mine Al Dente* (Atria, 2012). "He [Philip Roth] is a dazzling writer" from *WA/WA*. WA lists his favorite musicals, with slightly different lists, in *WA/WA* and *Conversations*. "I don't even think of it" from *The Soundtracks of Woody Allen*. "The people in the music department" from *Conversations*. "Outside the limits" (Drew Barrymore) from Daniel Jeffreys, "A Passionate Man: Woody Allen Has Made His First Musical," *Independent* (UK) (October 24, 1996). Kristine McKenna wrote about "weird romantic proclivities" in Allen films in "This Old Dog's Tricks Are Getting Tiresome," *Los Angeles Times* (December 14, 1997).

WA and background on filming of *Sweet and Lowdown* from Richard T. Kelly, *Sean Penn: His Life and Times* (Canongate, 2004). *Antz* from Nicole Laporte, *The Men Who Would Be King: An Almost Epic Tale of Moguls, Movies, and a Company Called DreamWorks* (Houghton Mifflin, 2010) and David Chute, "It Was No Picnic for the Artists," *Los Angeles Times* (October 4, 1998). "Sometimes, if I am dealing" from *WA/WA*. "Artistic creation was a savior" from Michel Ciment and Franck Garbarz, "All My Films Have a Connection with Magic," *Positif* (February 1998), translated and included in *Woody Allen: Interviews*. Maureen Dowd wrote about *Deconstructing Harry* as "an infomercial with bad info" in "Liberties: Auteur as Spin Doctor," *New York Times* (October 1, 1995). "She met Roth" (Rose Styron) from Maureen Orth, "Momma Mia!", *Vanity Fair* (October 23, 2013). WA and Soon-Yi's Venice wedding and "of course Mia wouldn't" (John Springer) from Glenn Collins, "Mixed Reviews Greet Woody Allen Marriage," *New York Times* (December 25, 1997). "I was terrified" (Dylan Farrow) from Nicholas Kristof, "Dylan Farrow's Story," *New York Times* (February 1, 2014). "Genius" son and "This is the first" (WA) and attorney William Breslow on "Seamus Farrow" from Mitchell Fink and Laura Rubin, "Mia's Boy Genius: Woody Learns Son, 11, Is in College," New York *Daily News* (December 9, 1999). "As the years have gone" from *Conversations*. Budget cutbacks, reduced star salaries, new producer controls, and comments from Allen, Robert Greenhut, and Jean Doumanian from Bernard Weinraub, "Deconstructing His Film Crew: Woody's Long-time Staff Is Hit by Cost-Cutting Efforts," *New York Times* (June 1, 1998). "I made more money" from "Reconstructing Woody." "They sat, she surrounded" and "was jealous to see" (Barbara Kopple) from "Woody Captured on the Spot, without a Script." "Finished it like a dedicated drone" from Denis Hamill, " 'I'm Just Another Kid from Brooklyn': Woody Allen Talks about His New Movie 'Celebrity'—and His Life as One," New York *Daily News* (November 15, 1998). "They were very kind" from *Conversations*. "I didn't want to have a novel" from Simon Garfield, "Why I Love London," *Guardian* (August 8, 2004). "I love it, love going back" from

" 'I'm Just Another Kid from Brooklyn.' " "I'm sure it would be very depressing" (re: *Celebrity*) and "within thirty blocks" (re: *Sweet and Lowdown*) from *WA/WA*. Samantha Morton and Harpo Marx anecdote also from *WA/WA*. "Why Woody Plays It Straight," *London Evening Standard* (May 31, 2000). "Very loveable," etc. from *WA/WA*. WA on Sean Penn and Morton on WA and *Sweet and Lowdown* filming from *Sean Penn: His Life and Times*. Howard Alden from Jude Hibler, "Howard Alden—An Engaging Explorer," *20th Century Guitar* (December 1999), quoted in *The Soundtracks of Woody Allen*. WA on Judy Davis from *Conversations*. "She's so hot" (WA on Charlize Theron) from " 'I'm Just Another Kid from Brooklyn.'" "Ad-libbing all over the place" (WA on Leonardo DiCaprio) from *Conversations*. "Very beautiful, very sexy" (WA on Melanie Griffith) from *WA/WA*. WA on Vanessa Redgrave ("obviously it had nothing to do") from *Conversations*. "I just couldn't get it" and WA on Kenneth Branagh ("a regular guy") from *WA/WA*. WA's letter to Branagh and his strategy directing Branagh ("What's the smartest thing" and "just sort of threw in the towel") from " 'I'm Just Another Kid from Brooklyn.' " Branagh ("The situations") from Sean Mitchell, "Holiday Films: A Not-So-Proper Kenneth Branagh Has Some Fun," *New York Times* (November 15, 1998).

Chapter 11: 1999: The Soon-Yi Era

"I don't know how the courts" (Mia Farrow) from Richard L. Eldredge, "Farrow 'Frightened' for Allen Baby," *Atlanta Journal-Constitution* (May 10, 1999). The Atlanta newspaper correction was published August 31, 1999. "People think I fell in love" from "The Imperfectionist." "An old idea of mine," WA on Tracey Ullman, and "I named the character May" from *Conversations*. "The greatest television sitcom" from "If You Knew Woody Like I Know Woody." Mel Gussow's "Funny Coincidence: Woody Allen, Meet S. J. Perelman" appeared in the August 30, 2000, *New York Times*. Background of the Allen-Doumanian lawsuit, along with the quotes from Robert Greenhut and Barbara Kopple, from Rachel Abramowitz, "Small Films, Big Drama," *Los Angeles Times* (July 1, 2001). Also valuable was the Loeb & Loeb LLP study guide, "Everything You Always Wanted to Know about Litigating Oral Contract Cases: The Perils and Privileges of Representing Woody Allen" by Michael Zweig and Alyson Weiss, partners, and associate Christian Carbone, Litigation Department, promoting the expertise of the firm, which represented Allen, on such issues. This study guide contains court filings and complete transcripts of the testimony of Jacqui Safra, Jean Doumanian, and WA. "Earn a considerably higher" and "I know that they prefer" from *Conversations*. "Opening me up" from "The Imperfectionist." WA at the 92nd Street Y, speaking about analysis and his parents, from Sarah Boxer, "So Woody, Do You Feel Like Talking about It?" *New York Times* (November 11, 2002). The first "Woody Allen video" from James Barron, "Sequel to *Manhattan* is a Horror Film of Sorts," *New York Times* (March 12, 2000). Inheriting "the worst of each parent" from Douglas McGrath's Q and A with WA in *Interview* (September 2008), included in *Woody Allen: Interviews*. WA onstage and backstage at the 2002 Oscars from Richard Natale, "For First-Time Producer, Getting Allen Was Coup," *Los Angeles Times* (March 26, 2002). "It may be the worst" and "an idea that had been" from *Conversations*. Allen on Haskell Wexler from *Start to Finish*. "First-ever" trips to Canada, Texas, Atlanta, Savannah, etc. from Paul Lieberman, "Woody's Wish: His Life a 'Third' Over, Hopes Age and Humor Can Thrive Together," *Los Angeles Times* (May 15, 2002). "It is a funny picture" and "a certain amount" from *Conversations*. "I never saw *American Pie*" from Fiona Morrow, "Woody Allen: 'I Do Not Idolize the Young. They're Illiterate,' " *Independent* (July 17, 2013). "In terms of just me personally" from Douglas McGrath's 2008 Q and A with WA in *Interview*. WA on Christina Ricci from *Conversations*.

"Jacqui would say" (Letty Aronson) and "I'm owed money too" (Barbara Kopple) from "Small Films, Big Drama." "Heel-dragging" (Robert Greenhut) from Bernard Weinraub, "Friendship

Founders Over Suit by Woody Allen," *New York Times* (June 11, 2001). "At least $12 million" and "bogus case" (Peter Parcher) from Susan Saulny, "Woody Allen Goes to Court, But the Scenario Is Not a Comedy," *New York Times* (May 31, 2002). "He said he wanted to make" (Stephen Tenenbaum) from Susan Saulny, "Woody Allen Settles Suit against Longtime Producer," *New York Times* (June 12, 2002). "For less compensation" from Andy Newman, "Hollywood Accounting Cost Him $12 Million, Allen Hints," *New York Times* (June 4, 2002). "As painfully afflicted" from "Woody Allen Goes to Court." "Ugly and at times highly personal" from Anita M. Busch and Rachel Abramowitz, "Woody Allen's Suit against Former Partner Settled," *Los Angeles Times* (June 12, 2002). "Because I was trying" and "it broke my heart" (WA) from Mike Claffey and Dave Goldiner, "Judge Backhands Woody's Rival," New York *Daily News* (June 6, 2002). "Cool, evasive" and "looked fashionable" from Mike Claffey and Dave Goldiner, "Woody's Angel Turns Forgetful," New York *Daily News* (June 11, 2002). "Is it your testimony" (Judge Ira Gammerman) from "Woody's Angel Turns Forgetful." "Spoke to Letty" (Jean Doumanian), the exchange between Judge Gammerman and Doumanian, and "meaning her total pay" from Dareh Gregorian, "Woody's Legal Foe Hits Back," *New York Post* (June 11, 2002). "I know it was no fun" from Dareh Gregorian, "Woody's a Critic—Calls Trial a Sleeper as He Thanks the Jury," *New York Post* (June 13, 2002). "Undisclosed amount" from *Start to Finish*.

"I'm truly not a workaholic" from Joyce Wadler, "Boldface Names," *New York Times* (March 31, 2004). The backstory of WA's initially aborted memoir from David D. Kirkpatrick, "Woody Allen Seeking Bids on Memoir," *New York Times* (October 10, 2003) and Kirkpatrick, "Woody Allen Is Seeking Big Payout on Life Story," *New York Times* (October 17, 2003). "You should not write" from Peter Bart, "Woody's Misbegotten Memoir," *Variety* (November 3–9, 1993). Maureen Dowd on Allen writing his memoir from "Woody's Starbust Memories," *New York Times* (October 19, 2003). Annabelle Gurwitch from *Fired! Tales of the Canned, Canceled, Downsized, & Dismissed* (Touchstone, 2006). "Woody has all but run out" from Peter Bart, "Hollywood Hindsight," *Variety* (August 4–10, 2003). "An idea I always wanted" from *Conversations*. "You cannot imagine how thrilling" (Dan Talbot) from "Donald Rugoff: In Memory of a Wild Genius," Letter to the Editor, *New York Times* (May 21, 1989). A. O. Scott reviewed *The Curse of the Jade Scorpion* in the August 24, 2001, and *Anything Else* in the September 19, 2003, *New York Times*. "Perpetual disappointment" (Scott) from "Why We Won't Let Woody Grow Up," *New York Times* (March 13, 2005) and "maddeningly prolific" (Scott) from "The Best Films of the Year," *New York Times* (December 25, 2005). David Thompson ("What we're doing") from Xan Brooks, "The *Guardian* Profile: Woody Allen," *Guardian* (July 29, 2004). "The idea of spending" from "Winslet for Woody Allen Film in Britain," London *Times* (June 19, 2004). "Around for years" from *Start to Finish*. "I Anglicized it myself" from Emma Brockes, "Q: Is Life, Essentially, Comic or Tragic?" *Guardian* (December 20, 2005). "The relative unfamiliarity" from Stephen Holden, "Woody Switches Cities," *New York Times* (September 11, 2005). "A gracious handwritten note" from James Burleigh, "I Want to Spend More Time with My Family," *Independent* (September 8, 2004). "It was not a problem" from "Why I Love London." WA, Jim Clay, and *Match Point* from Peter Kelly, "From Brooklyn to Blackfriars," *Blueprint* (April 2005). "The flat light gives" from Dalya Alberge, "London Is Just Capital for Woody Allen's New Film," London *Times* (May 13, 2005). "There are more terrific," "more relaxed," and "very union-oriented," etc. (WA) from "If I Can Make It There." "The producers even less" and interview with Allen in London and comments re: Scarlett Johansson ("She can do no wrong," etc.) from "Why I Love London." "This is a very sad" from Jason Solomons, "Screen," *Observer* (July 18, 2004). "I remember watching a tennis match" from *Conversations*. Brian Cox from Leo Benedictus, "I'm the Elephant Man," *Guardian* (August 5, 2000) and Cox, *Putting the Rabbit in the Hat* (Grand Central Publishing, 2022). Jonathan Rhys Meyers from Sharon Waxman, "At

Home in Oliver's Macedonia and Woody's London, *New York Times* (November 6, 2005). "My character was neurotic" (Scarlett Johansson) from Cindy Adams, "It's a Love Match with Ms. Scarlett," *New York Post* (December 16, 2005). "I changed her hair" from *Conversations*. "Really nervous the first day" (Scarlett Johansson) from Mike Goodridge, "Scarlett Fever," *Mail on Sunday* (UK) (February 13, 2005). "Two people have shaped" (Pedro Almodóvar) and report from San Sebastian Film Festival from John Hopewell and Deborah Young, "Almodovar Fetes Allen," *Variety* (September 17, 2004).

"In the last twelve weeks" from *Conversations*. "Tore me apart and re-arranged me" (Mia Farrow) from her interview in *Reporter*, the 2010 HBO documentary about Nicholas Kristof. "He's my father, married" (Satchel/Seamus) from an interview given to *Saga* magazine, quoted by George Rush and Joanna Malloy in "Gossip," New York *Daily News* (January 25, 2005). Radha Mitchell from Scott Foundas, "On a Role," *Variety* (January 10, 2005). A. O. Scott wrote about *Match Point* as the "surprise" of the festival in "Before the Films Begin, a Dose of Cannes Pomp, *New York Times* (May 13, 2005). Todd McCarthy wrote about the reaction to *Match Point* at Cannes breaking down "along national lines" in "Gray, and Kind of Thinning," *Variety* (May 23–29, 2005). "A low-grade American" from Michael Fleming, "Woody Now High on Hugh," *Variety* (June 19, 2005). "There's so much special" (Soon-Yi Previn) from "If I Can Make It There." "A very light comedy" from Scott Foundas, "Still a Working Stiff," *LA Weekly* (December 15, 2005), included in *Woody Allen: Interviews*. "Cold-shower moment" and first impressions of *Scoop* from *Conversations*. Roger Ebert's "Letter to the Editor" appeared in the June 6, 2002, *New York Times*. Bernard-Henri Lévy on WA from *American Vertigo: Traveling America in the Footsteps of Tocqueville*, translated by Charlotte Mandell (Random House, 2006). "I'd done London" from John Bungey, "Woody's Blast from the Past," London *Times* (December 9, 2005).

"With a spectacularly wide fanlight" and other features of the new residence and surrounding neighborhood from Christopher Gray, "Along Millionaires' Row, at the Crest of Lenox Hill," *New York Times* (September 17, 2006). "What separates the men" from *Conversations*. "Very personal bric-a-brac" and the description of household interiors from "After Decades of Silence, Soon-Yi Speaks." Philip Glass from *Words without Music* (Liveright, 2015). WA on Glass from *Conversations*. "Ravishing and more sexual" (WA on Penélope Cruz) from Allen's "Excerpts from the Spanish Diary," *New York Times* (August 20, 2008). "If Woody Allen is reading" (Rebecca Hall) from Charlotte Cripps, "Rebecca Hall: My Art Belongs to Daddy," *Independent* (October 10, 2011). Hall and her experience with WA and *Vicky Cristina Barcelona* from Sandra Ballentine, "In America," *New York Times* (April 25, 2010) and Michael Ordona, "Rebecca Hall: Working with Woody Allen on 'Vicky Cristina Barcelona' Was a Dream Fulfilled for the British Actress," *Los Angeles Times* (August 4, 2008). "A huge advertisement" (Barcelona mayor Jordi Hereu) from Pascale Harter, "Catalans Help Pay for Woody Allen 'Love Letter,'" Reuters (July 29, 2007). "We have the same humor" (Scarlett Johansson) from "It's a Love Match with Ms. Scarlett." Javier Bardem from Emily Zemler, "The IMDb Files: Javier Bardem: An Actor Curious about What Drives the Villain," *Los Angeles Times* (June 11, 2017). Penélope Cruz from Lauren Mechling, "Weekend Journal: Just Asking Penelope Cruz," *Wall Street Journal* (August 8, 2008) and Robert Abele, "Contender Q. and A.: Passionate Embrace: Penelope Cruz stirred up 'Vicky Cristina Barcelona'—and Apparently Some Academy Voters," *Los Angeles Times* (February 4, 2009). "Wrap party" from "Excerpts from the Spanish Diary." "Whatever [idea] I find in my drawer" from George Rush and Joanna Rush Molloy, "A Pain in Spain for Woody Allen," New York *Daily News* (December 19, 2007). "A very artistic-minded" from *Start to Finish*. "In style, *Vicky Cristina*" from *Conversations*.

WA on directing *Gianni Schicchi* from Chris Pasles, "Woody Allen Is Taking an Operatic

Turn," *Los Angeles Times* (June 22, 2007). Josh Brolin on WA and *You Will Meet a Tall Dark Stranger* from Lynn Hirschberg, "Tough Enough," *New York Times* (March 10, 2010). Cary Grant (like "the biggest fan") and the origins of *Midnight in Paris* ("So, I cooked up this film") from Kenneth Turan, "Cannes Film Festival: Film Critic: No Longer Hiding Behind Comedy, Woody Allen Says Aging Has Freed Him," *Los Angeles Times* (May 2, 2016). WA on rewriting for Owen Wilson ("An Eastern intellectual") from Kent Jones, "The *Film Comment* Interview," *Film Comment* (May/June 2011), included in *Woody Allen: Interviews*. "Nail every preposition" from Todd Longwell, "'Midnight' One More Global Hit for Wilson," *Variety* (December 5–11, 2011). "I never had to give" from "The *Film Comment* Interview." I drew repeatedly from Dave Itzkoff, "Talk Therapy: Audiobooks by Woody Allen," *New York Times* (July 21, 2010), including WA's comments about audiobooks and computers. "We need some delusions" from Dave Itzkoff, "Woody Allen on Faith, Fortune Tellers, and New York," *New York Times* (September 15, 2010). "I consider myself" and WA's remarks at the Cannes Film Festival from Ben Hoyle, "I've Never Had Enough Depth, Says Allen," *London Times* (May 12, 2011). "Declaration of love" from Eric J. Lyman, "Woody Allen Confirms He'll Film Next Movie in Rome," *Hollywood Reporter* (March 7, 2011). "With Woody, . . . the best parallel" (Darius Khondji) from Elaine Sciolino, "Camera in Hand, Italian at Heart: The Cinematography of Darius Khondji," *New York Times* (July 15, 2012). Michael Barker from Patrick Goldstein, "The Big Picture: Sony Team Helps 'Paris' to Sizzle," *Los Angeles Times* (July 9, 2011).

Chapter 12: 2012: Stuff Happens

"Laziness" from Adam Higginbotham, "Woody Allen: Interview," *Telegraph* (June 22, 2010). "They wouldn't be better" from Mark Olsen, "Write, Shoot, Edit, Then Repeat" *Los Angeles Times* (September 21, 2010). "It's always a pleasure" from Mike Vilensky, "Coming Home to New York," *Wall Street Journal* (June 21, 2012). "I would have played that" from Rachel Dodes, "The Interview: Woody Allen," *Wall Street Journal* (June 15, 2012). Cate Blanchett (unless otherwise noted) from Glenn Whipp, "In Full Bloom: 'Blue Jasmine' Fulfilled Cate Blanchett's Long-Held Goal of Working in a Woody Allen-directed Film," *Los Angeles Times* (November 7, 2013). "The story [of *Jasmine*] was inspired" from Rachel Dodes, "Sally Hawkins Goes American in Woody Allen's 'Blue Jasmine,'" *Wall Street Journal* (July 18, 2013). Manohla Dargis compared *A Streetcar Named Desire* to *Blue Jasmine* in her July 25, 2013, *New York Times* review. WA's "Hypochondria: An Inside Look" appeared in the January 12, 2013, *New York Times*. WA, Susan Stroman, and behind the scenes of the *Bullets over Broadway* musical from John Lahr, "Joy Ride," *New Yorker* (March 31, 2014). Parker Posey from *Parker Posey: You're on an Airplane* (Blue Rider Press, 2018). Dave Itzkoff wrote about "strong and memorable women" in "Woody Allen's Distinctive Female Characters," *New York Times* (July 21, 2013). "Has caused the anti–Woody Allen" from Liz Smith's August 29, 2012, column in the *Chicago Tribune*. Ronan Farrow's "nearly 140,000 followers," etc., according to Michael Schulman, "Ronan Farrow: The Youngest Old Guy in the Room," *New York Times* (October 27, 2013). "Rules by niceness" (Glen Kelly) from "Joy Ride." "There is no one more worthy" (Theo Kingma) from September 14, 2013, press statement on GoldenGlobes.com.

Former op-ed editor Trish Hall wrote about the Nicholas Kristof column in *Writing to Persuade: How to Bring People Over to Your Side* (Liveright, 2019). Public editor Margaret Sullivan wrote about the issues in her op-ed "Beyond Blank Slates: Writers Under Fire," *New York Times* (February 9, 2014). Nicholas Kristof devoted his *Times* column to "Dylan Farrow's Story" on February 2, 2014. The entire text of "An Open Letter from Dylan Farrow" was published on kristof.blogs.nytimes.com, one day earlier, February 1, 2014. Moses Farrow from "Woody Allen Abuse Scandal: A Family Torn Apart," *People* (February 17, 2014) and *Start to Finish*.

"Just a bunch of junk" (Barbara Sinatra) from Susan King, "Working Hollywood," *Los Angeles Times* (June 6, 2014). James Kaplan investigated and dismissed Frank Sinatra's possible paternity of Ronan Farrow in *Sinatra: The Chairman* (Doubleday, 2015). "Perhaps to please Woody" and "Moses has cut off" from Sopan Deb, "New Book about Woody Allen Alleges Abusive Parenting by Mia Farrow," *New York Times* (September 29, 2017). Dylan Farrow may not have actually uttered the words "He's dead to me," but the Internet frequently quotes her as though she did. Boris Kachka's account of the Santa Barbara Film Festival, "For Their Consideration: In the Most Competitive Oscar Season Ever, a Cabal of Internet Oddsmakers Are Keeping Score," appeared in the February 24, 2014, *New York*. "The inescapable fact" from Steve Rose, "Woody Allen's Oscar-Winning Women: How Did His Direction Affect Them?" *Guardian* (February 26, 2018). "Young Women Speak Out" from the February 8, 2014, *Los Angeles Times*. Wallace Shawn from "The Woody Allen Case," *Los Angeles Times* (February 16, 2014). Lena Dunham ("disgusted") from Marc Maron's *WTF* podcast, as reported by many outlets including Ashley Lee, "Lena Dunham on Woody Allen," *Hollywood Reporter* (March 18, 2014). Rosie O'Donnell ("totally believes") from *The View*, as reported by many outlets, including Hilary Lewis, "Rosie O'Donnell Returns to 'The View,' Says She 'Totally Believes' Dylan Farrow," *Hollywood Reporter* (February 7, 2014). "[Kristof] wants it both ways" (Roxanne Gay) from "Compartmentalizing Woody Allen: What America Chooses Not to See," Salon.com (February 2, 2014). "How do we respond" (Gay) from "Woody Allen Is Just the Beginning: Why We Can't Hide from the Truth Anymore," Salon.com (February 11, 2014). I drew on *Start to Finish* and *Parker Posey: You're on an Airplane* for the filming of *Irrational Man*. "Takes longer because" and "Emma Stone radiates" from Cindy Adams, "Cloudy Days Sway Woody," *New York Post* (June 24, 2015). "You can't ask questions" (Emma Stone) from "Yes, I Did Say That!" Seth Abramovitch, *Hollywood Reporter* (July 3, 2015). "'Home' for the rest of his career" and other details of Allen's Amazon contract from court documents. "I don't know how" (WA) and "polarizing figure" from Emily Steel, "Amazon Signs Woody Allen to Write and Direct TV Series," *New York Times* (January 13, 2015). "I thought it would be a cinch" from "Woody Allen Uncomfortable with Standing Ovation," *Washington Post* (May 17, 2015). Emma Stone on WA's meeting with Jesse Eisenberg ("The longest in history") from *Start to Finish*. "I needed someone" (WA) and "The way he describes" (Kristen Stewart) from Rachel Donadio, "At Cannes, Women Turn Out in Force," *New York Times* (May 17, 2016). "You'll notice I have not improved" from Robert Spuhler, "Woody Allen and His New Orleans Jazz Band Pay Tribute to the Big Easy at L.A.'s Orpheum," *Los Angeles Daily News* (August 10, 2015). Cindy Adams reported on her "Day in the Park with Woody" (filming New York scenes for *Café Society*) in the October 26, 2015, *New York Post*.

Chapter 13: 2016: Mr. Nothing

Allen, R. Kelly, and Bill Cosby were linked together as entertainers whose "allegations of sexual misdeeds" had drawn "heightened cultural attention" in Joe Coscarelli, "A Pop-Punk Singer and the Blurred Line Between Digital Fan Mail and Trouble," *New York Times* (January 9, 2015). The editorial "Roman Polanski, the Sequel," conflating Allen with Polanski, appeared in the August 14, 2015, New York *Daily News*. Ronan Farrow is always quoted, unless otherwise noted, from *Catch and Kill: Lies, Spies, and a Conspiracy to Protect Predators* (Little, Brown, 2019). The Amazon announcement that sent "shock waves" and "sight unseen" from Tatiana Siegel, "Whoa, Woody! Amazon's $15M Bid Won Allen's Next Film," *Hollywood Reporter* (March 4, 2016). Stephen Galloway's "No, Woody Allen Won't Read This Interview" appeared in the May 13, 2016, *Hollywood Reporter*. Ronan Farrow's "guest column," "My Father: The Danger of Questions Unasked," appeared in the May 11, 2016, *Hollywood Reporter*.

(It is dated earlier in time because Galloway's appeared in a special issue sent ahead overseas to Cannes.) "Even in its most innocuous form" (WA) from Rick Worley, "The Rise and Fail of Ronan Farrow," ronanfarrowletter.wordpress.com (July 20, 2020). "It's very nice that you've" (Laurent Lafitte) from Frank Lovece, "Woody Allen: Ronan Farrow's Abuse Allegations Are 'Silly,'" *Newsday* (May 13, 2016). "American puritanism" (Lafitte) from Chris Gardner, "Laurent Lafitte on Woody Allen Rape Joke," *Hollywood Reporter* (May 12, 2016). Manohla Dargis wrote about Cannes and *Café Society* in "Even on Alert, It's Still Cannes," *New York Times* (May 12, 2016). "Mixed but generally positive" and "My comment is that" (WA) from Rachel Donadio, "Woody Allen on Abuse Allegations: 'I Have So Moved On,'" *New York Times* (May 12, 2016). "I'm completely in favor" (WA) and "I think he sexually assaulted" (Susan Sarandon) from Tory Maguire, "Susan Sarandon Has 'Nothing Good to Say' about Woody Allen," Huffington Post (May 16, 2016). Margaret Sullivan wrote about Dylan Farrow's "open letter" and "unasked questions" in "The Media Dug Deep on Brock Turner and Bill Cosby. What about Woody Allen?" in the *Washington Post* (June 19, 2016). Sarah Silverman from the May 11, 2016, tweet on her Twitter feed. "Cast members likely," Kate Winslet "under fire" and "I didn't know Woody" (Winslet) from Daniel Holloway, "Amazon, the Democrats and Fallout from the Harvey Weinstein Scandal," *Variety* (October 17, 2017). WA's BBC interview re: Harvey Weinstein from Jillian Capewell, "Woody Allen Says Harvey Weinstein Scandal Is 'Very Sad for Everyone Involved,'" Huffington Post (October 15, 2017). "A sad sick man" from Leo Barraclough, "Woody Allen Clarifies Weinstein Comments: 'He Is a Sad, Sick Man,'" *Variety* (October 15, 2017).

"Disaster metaphor" from Jessica Bennett, "The 'Click' Moment: How the Weinstein Scandal Unleashed a Tsunami," *New York Times* (November 5, 2017). "A clearinghouse for complaints" and the MeToo "whisper network" from Gabriela Herman, "Women's Whisper Network Raises Its Voice," *New York Times* (November 4, 2017). Lindy West from "Yes, This Is a Witch Hunt. I'm a Witch and I'm Hunting You," *New York Times* (October 17, 2017). Dylan's second "open letter," the op-ed "Why Has the #MeToo Revolution Spared Woody Allen?" appeared in the December 7, 2017, *Los Angeles Times*. "As a 7-year-old I would say" from Jyotsna Basotia, "Woody Allen and Dylan Farrow's Shocking Sexual Assault Allegations: 'He Touched my Labia and Vulva with his Finger,'" MEAWW.com (February 21, 2021). Linda Stasi from "You're a Victim: Soon-Yi, Recognize Woody As the Sicko He Is," New York *Daily News* (September 18, 2018). Ellen Pompeo from her January 5, 2018, tweet. Mira Sorvino's "Open Letter to Dylan Farrow" from Huffington Post (January 10, 2018). Peter Sarsgaard ("I would continue to watch") and other actors' comments from Angie Han, "Woody Allen's Actors Are Turning against Him," Mashable.com (January 17, 2018). Blake Lively's tweet ("women in every industry") and Dylan Farrow's Twitter reply ("You worked with my abuser") and Dylan's comments about Cate Blanchett from Jessica Sager, "Dylan Farrow Calls Out Cate Blanchett, Blake Lively for Hypocrisy," New York *Daily News* (January 5, 2018). Manohla Dargis's revised thoughts on WA ("I've liked and loved") from "Hollywood on the Brink," *New York Times* (January 3, 2018). Woody Allen's "I'll Put Your Name in Lights, Natividad Abascal" appeared in the April 1971 *Playboy*. Richard Morgan's "I Read Decades of Woody Allen's Private Notes. He's Obsessed with Teenage Girls" appeared in the *Washington Post* (January 4, 2018). Nicholas Kristof's second column about WA, "Woody Allen Meets #MeToo," appeared in the *New York Times* (February 3, 2018). Cancellation of *Bullets over Broadway* from Michael Paulson, "Goodspeed Cancels Woody Allen Musical," *New York Times* (January 25, 2018). Savannah Lyon and her initiative from Blake Bunch, "Petition to End 'Films of Woody Allen' Course," *La Jolla Village News* (February 23, 2018). "Increasingly shaky" from Tatiana Siegel, "Streamers Look Past Sundance for Their Own Blockbusters," *Hollywood Reporter* (January 31, 2018). WA's interview on Argentinian television from Benjamin Lee, "Woody Allen: 'I Should Be the Poster

Boy for the #MeToo Movement,'" *Guardian* (June 4, 2018). Bret Stephens wrote about "The Smearing of Woody Allen" in the February 9, 2018, *New York Times*. "I'm not qualified" (Alan Alda) from Benjamin Svetkey, "Alan Alda on 'M*A*S*H' Legacy and Why He'd Work with Woody Allen Again," *Hollywood Reporter* (January 25, 2019). "There are those" (Cherry Jones) from Melena Ryzik and Brooke Barnes, "Can Woody Allen Work in Hollywood Again?" *New York Times* (January 28, 2018). "I don't agree" (Javier Bardem) from Andrew Pulver, "Javier Bardem Condemns 'Public Lynching' of Woody Allen," *Guardian* (October 19, 2018). "If he had a trial" (Michael Caine) from David Browne, "The Last Word: Michael Caine on the First Time He Got High and the Role He Regrets," *Rolling Stone* (January 22, 2019). "In a second" (Anjelica Huston) from Andrew Goldman, "In Conversation: Anjelica Huston," Vulture.com (May 1, 2019). "Woody Allen is my" (Diane Keaton) from her January 29, 2018, tweet. "I see a man" (Judd Apatow) from his January 29, 2018, tweet. Robert B. Weide dared Ronan and Dylan Farrow to sue WA "for every penny he's got" in his March 7, 2021, "The Interview That Never Happened" blog on ronanfarrowletter.wordpress.com. "The day is coming" (Weide) from his January 16, 2018, tweet. Mia Farrow's response to Moses Farrow from Rachel Yang, "Mia Farrow Addresses 'Vicious Rumors' about Deaths of 3 of Her Adopted Children," April 1, 2021, EW.com. Bechet Allen ("I never wanted to involve myself") from Page Six, "Allen Defense," *New York Post* (May 30, 2018). "I wasn't used" (Daphne Merkin) from Jon Levine, "Ronan Farrow Tried to Kill *New York* Magazine Story on Woody Allen's Wife, Daphne Merkin Claims," *New York Post* (May 23, 2020).

Background and details of the *Allen v. Amazon* lawsuit from court documents easily found online at SDNYBlog.com. "Publishers are skittish" from Alexandra Alter and Cara Buckley, "Filmmaker Is Shunned Even Further," *New York Times* (May 2, 2019). The *New York Times* listed Allen among Jeffrey Epstein's "friends and acquaintances" in its editorial "The Cowardly Labor Secretary" (March 3, 2019). Allen's "dozens" of dinners and other activities with Epstein are detailed in Khadeeja Safdar and David Benoit, "Epstein Courted Notable Friends With Favors," *Wall Street Journal* (May 4, 2023). WA on Jeffrey Epstein's salons from Roger Friedman, "Exclusive: Woody Allen on Marriage, Kids, His Great Films, Influence on Movie Making, Writing a Novel, Epstein, and Not Retiring," on Friedman's website Showbiz411 .com, April 17, 2024. "Mr. Allen seemed to express" from Brooks Barnes, "Amazon Studios Counters Woody Allen's Lawsuit and Defends Severing of Ties," *New York Times* (April 3, 2019). "We have a ten-year relationship" (MediaPro) from "Woody Allen to Film New Movie in Spain," *Business Today* (February 23, 2019). "My philosophy, since I started" (WA) and "It's a wild time" (Gina Gershon) from Andrew Pulver, "Woody Allen: 'I Never Think of Retiring,'" *Guardian* (July 9, 2019). "I'm responsible for the projects" (Elena Anaya) from Elisabet Cabeza, "Woody Allen Launches New Film in San Sebastian," ScreenDaily.com (July 9, 2019). "The actors are almost never," etc. (WA) from translated Spanish media clippings about the filming of *Rifkin's Festival*. Dylan Farrow's public statement ("deeply upsetting," etc.) from James Crowley, "Dylan Farrow Says Publication of Woody Allen's Memoir Is 'Deeply Upsetting,' Says She Wasn't Contacted by Fact Checkers," *Newsweek* (March 3, 2020). Ronan Farrow ("Your policy of editorial independence," etc.) and Michael Pietsch ("We do not allow anyone's") from Jennifer Schuessler and John Williams, "'Imagine This Were Your Sister,' Ronan Farrow Tells Woody Allen's Publisher," *New York Times* (March 3, 2020). "Ferocious backlash" from Alexandra Alter and John Williams, "Woody Allen's Memoir Is Published," *New York Times* (March 23, 2020). "No matter how deep" from the editorial "Silencing Woody Allen Is an Abuse of Power by Ronan Farrow" in the *New York Post* (March 6, 2020). Bret Stephens wrote in favor of publication, in "Woody Allen Meets the Cancel Culture," *New York Times* (March 18, 2020). Suzanne Nossel's PEN America statement on the controversy from PEN.org (March 6, 2020). WA's "You can ask me," "I assume that for the rest," "I'm angry," "There are many injustices," and "a total non-issue" from Hadley Freeman, "'Do I Really Care?' Woody Allen Comes Out Fighting," *Guardian* (May 29, 2020). Ben Smith's "Is Ronan Farrow Too Good to Be True" appeared in the May 17, 2020, *New York Times*. "I found him [Ronan] to not be an honest" from Robbie Collin, "Woody Allen Interview: 'Ronan Farrow's Journalism Is Shoddy,'" *Telegraph* (May 29, 2020). "There's no way to convey" from *Start to Finish*.

All polled film critics quoted with permission. Stanley Kauffmann is cited from his interview in *The Unruly Life of Woody Allen*. Drew Barrymore and Dylan Farrow from Antonio Ferme, "Drew Barrymore Regrets Working with Woody Allen, Was 'Gaslit' into Dismissing Allegations," May 18, 2021, Variety.com. Allen and Spanish soccer chief Luis Rubiales from David Avere, "Woody Allen Defends Spanish Football Chief," *Daily Mail* (September 4, 2023). WA about *Coup de chance* and his post-*Coup* plans from Roger Friedman, "Exclusive: Woody Allen On Marriage, Kids, His Great Films, Influence on Movie Making, Writing a Novel, Epstein, and Not Retiring," and Sam Wasson, "All the Romance of Filmmaking is Gone," airmail.news, April 6, 2024.

Filmography

Only major works included. Only principal cast (billed before the title) and main crew are listed. Consult text and IMDb.com for all actors identified in the end credits, unbilled performers, and Allen's numerous television and documentary appearances.

1965

What's New Pussycat?
As writer and actor.

Prod: Charles K. Feldman. *Dir:* Clive Donner. *Sc:* Allen. *Ph:* Jean Badal. *Ed:* Fergus McDonell. *Art Dir:* Jacques Saulnier. *Cos:* Gladys de Segonzac. *Music:* Burt Bacharach/Hal David.

Cast: Allen, Peter Sellers, Peter O'Toole, Romy Schneider, Capucine, Paula Prentiss, Ursula Andress.

(Famous Artists Productions/United Artists, 108 min.)

It is a bad picture. It is like such a bad picture that one wonders if it is not good.
—Jean-Luc Godard, "Godard Est Godard," *New Yorker* (October 9, 1965)

1966

What's Up, Tiger Lily?
(Dubbed/edited from *Kokusai himitsu keisatsu: Kagi no kagi,* a 1964 Japanese film directed by Senkichi Taniguchi).

As director, associate producer, writer, actor.

Prod: Reuben Bercovich, Henry G. Saperstein. *Dir:* Allen. *Sc:* Allen with Frank Buxton, Louise Lasser, Julie Bennett, Len Maxwell, Mickey Rose, Bryna Wilson. *Ed:* Richard Krown. *Prod Conception:* Ben Shapiro. *Music:* The Lovin' Spoonful.

Japanese cast: Tatsuya Mihashi, Akiko Wakabayashi, Mie Hama, Tadao Nakamaru, Susumu Kurobe.

American cast: Allen with (voices) Frank Buxton, Louise Lasser, Julie Bennett, Len Maxwell, Mickey Rose, Bryna Wilson.

(American International Pictures, 80 min.)

Take one lousy imitation Japanese James Bond, give it to Woody Allen, who erases the soundtrack and substitutes his own wild dialogue, add a groovy Lovin' Spoonful score and you have What's Up, Tiger Lily?—the funniest spy spoof of them all.
—Kevin Thomas, *Los Angeles Times*

1967

Casino Royale
As writer (uncredited) and actor.

Prod: Jerry Bresler, Charles K. Feldman. *Dir:* John Huston, Ken Hughes, Val Guest, Joe McGrath, Robert Parrish. *Sc:* Wolf Mankowitz, John Law, Michael Sayers (based on the

Ian Fleming novel). *Ph:* Jack Hildyard. *Ed:* Bill Lenny. *Prod Des:* Michael Stringer. *Cos:* Julie Harris. *Music:* Burt Bacharach.

Cast: Allen, Peter Sellers, Ursula Andress, David Niven, Joanna Pettet, Orson Welles, Daliah Lavi, Deborah Kerr, William Holden, Charles Boyer, John Huston, George Raft, Jean-Paul Belmondo.

(Famous Artists Productions/Columbia, 137 min.)

Woody Allen's sex-hungry schlemiel persona may have already been standard expectation in 1967, but here, garbed in a Mao suit, he suggests the infantile psychosexual complexes behind the vengeful modern warlord. Allen detests the film and takes little pride in his creation of Dr. Noah, but his own Third World farce Bananas, and the futuristic totalitarian satire Sleeper, seem to spring from the still edgy political black comedy of his self-written role in Casino Royale.

—Robert von Dassanowsky, *Bright Lights*

1969

Don't Drink the Water

Playwright and uncredited script contribution (as R. S. Allen).

Prod: Charles H. Joffe. *Dir:* Howard Morris. *Sc:* R. S. Allen and Harvey Bullock. *Ph:* Harvey Genkins. *Ed:* Ralph Rosenblum. *Art Dir:* Robert Gundlach. *Cos:* Gene Coffin. *Music:* Pat Williams.

Cast: Jackie Gleason, Estelle Parsons, Ted Bessell, Joan Delaney, Michael Constantine, Howard St. John, Danny Meehan, Richard Libertini, Pierre Olaf, Avery Schreiber.

(Jack Rollins and Charles H. Joffe Productions/Joseph E. Levine Productions/ AVCO Embassy Pictures, 100 min.)

Never have I seen a film cut away so quickly from what it clearly means to present as hilarious ideas. It is as if the hilarity were all in the idea and not in the execution, and the director were anxious for you to get the idea but forget the mess of it he made in filming. This is artistic economy on the poverty level.

—Roger Greenspun, *New York Times*

1969

Take the Money and Run

As director, writer, actor.

Prod: Charles H. Joffe. *Dir:* Allen. *Sc:* Allen and Mickey Rose. *Ph:* Lester Shorr. *Ed Consultant:* Ralph Rosenblum. *Supervising Ed:* James T. Heckert. *Art Dir:* Fred Harpman. *Music:* Marvin Hamlisch.

Cast: Allen, Janet Margolin, Marcel Hillaire, Jacquelyn Hyde, Lonny Chapman, Jan Merlin, James Anderson, Jackson Beck (narrator), Howard Storm, Mark Gordon, Micil Murphy, Minnow Moskowitz, Nate Jacobson, Grace Bauer, Henry Leff, Ethel Sokolow, Louise Lasser.

(Jack Rollins and Charles H. Joffe Productions/Palomar Pictures International, 85 min.)

Woody piles on the gags; the immature humor and the forced humor being far outnumbered by comic gems . . . an audacious debut, but nothing to prepare us for Allen's later masterpieces.

—Danny Peary, *Guide for the Film Fanatic*

1971

Bananas

As director, writer, actor.

Prod: Jack Grossberg. *Dir:* Allen. *Sc:* Allen and Mickey Rose. *Ph:* Andrew M. Costikyan. *Assoc Prod and Ed:* Ralph Rosenblum. *Prod Des:* Ed Wittstein. *Cos:* Gene Coffin. *Music:* Marvin Hamlisch.

Cast: Allen, Louise Lasser, Carlos Montalbán, Natividad Abascal, Jacobo Morales, Miguel Suárez, David Ortiz, René Enríquez, Roger Grimsby, Don Dunphy, Martha Greenhouse, Dan Frazer, Stanley Ackerman, Charlotte Rae, Howard Cosell.

(Jack Rollins and Charles H. Joffe Productions/United Artists, 82 min.)

Bananas made me laugh uproariously, and it should do the same for you unless you are on some save-the-world kick. Be forewarned. I was one of the few people who roared over Where's Poppa? Be forewarned also that Allen hits you with about a dozen bad gags for every good one, but after awhile you can't tell the difference, and after awhile more you don't care that there is a difference.

—Andrew Sarris, *Village Voice*

1972

Men of Crisis: The Harvey Wallinger Story **(telefilm)**

As director, writer, actor.

Prod: Jack Kuney. *Dir and Sc:* Allen. *Ph:* Paul Goldsmith. *Ed:* Eric Albertson. *Art Dir:* Gene Rudolf. *Music:* John Q. Adams.

Cast: Allen, David Ackroyd, Wil Albert, Conrad Bain, Court Benson, Milo Boulton, Harold Chidhoff, Jean David, Jean De Baer, Richard M. Dixon, Abe Drazen, Dan Frazer, George Harris, Graham Jarvis, Mitchell Jason, Diane Keaton, Tom Lacy, Louise Lasser, Tom Rosqui, Lee Wallace, and Reed Hadley (narrator).

(Charles H. Joffe/Educational Broadcast Company, 26 min.)

It's cheeky and provocative, but not offensive, and is refreshingly contemporary in a Trumpian world in which news has splintered into prepackaged formats with more politically ideological stances. [Its] primary target is the Republican establishment, but there's a sense if a worthy/inept Democrat equivalent were in office, the barbs would be just as absurd.

—Mark R. Hasan, KQEK.com (Toronto)

1972

Play It Again, Sam

Playwright, writer, actor.

Prod: Arthur P. Jacobs. *Dir:* Herbert Ross. *Sc:* Allen. *Ph:* Owen Roizman. *Ed:* Marion Rothman. *Prod Des:* Ed Wittstein. *Cos:* Anna Hill Johnstone. *Music:* Billy Goldenberg.

Cast: Allen, Diane Keaton, Tony Roberts, Jerry Lacy, Susan Anspach, Jennifer Salt, Joy Bang, Viva, Suzanne Zenor, Diana Davila, Mari Fletcher.

(Arthur P. Jacobs/Rollins-Joffe Prods./Paramount Pictures, 85 min.)

Less the scattershot, multidirectional laugh explosion that was Bananas or Take the Money and Run. But what it loses in unbridled goofiness, it makes up in continuity and pacing. It also allows Allen a chance to act as well as cavort, to openly explore the sad sack side of his nature. His fluttering eyelids when confronted by a leather-jacket bully, his foot-in-mouth approach to conversation with women, are samples of skillful acting rather than comedic techniques. The laugh-getters in the script cover a broad enough spectrum to satisfy almost all audiences.

—Dick Lochte, *Los Angeles Free Press*

1972

Everything You Always Wanted to Know About Sex But Were Afraid to Ask*

As director, writer, actor.

Prod: Charles H. Joffe. *Dir and Sc:* Allen (based on David Reuben's book). *Ph:* David M. Walsh. *Supervising Ed:* James T. Heckert. *Prod Design:* Dale Hennesy. *Cos:* Arnold M. Lipin, G. Fern Weber. *Music:* Mundell Lowe.

Cast: Allen, John Carradine, Lou Jacobi, Louise Lasser, Anthony Quayle, Tony Randall, Lynn Redgrave, Burt Reynolds, Gene Wilder, Jack Barry, Elaine Giftos, Toni Holt, Robert Q. Lewis, Heather MacRae, Pamela Mason, Sidney Miller, Regis Philbin, Titos Vandis.

(Rollins-Joffe and Brodsky/Gould Prods./United Artists, 88 min.)

The best of his superb brewings and certainly the funniest sex comedy we've encountered to date. His mad genius rampant, saddled with only the title of the [David] Reuben book, Allen has brought forth a seven-episode scenario marked by seven questions, that, under his own rollicking directing, springs to pure hilarity on the screen, with wonderful actors to match Allen.

—Judith Crist, *New York*

1973

Sleeper

As director, writer, musician, actor.

Prod: Jack Grossberg. *Dir:* Allen. *Sc:* Allen and Marshall Brickman. *Ph:* David M. Walsh. *Ed:* Ralph Rosenblum. *Prod Des:* Dale Hennesy. *Cos:* Joel Schumacher. *Music:* Allen, the Preservation Hall Jazz Band, and the New Orleans Funeral Ragtime Orchestra.

Cast: Allen, Diane Keaton, John Beck, Mary Gregory, John McLiam, Bartlett Robinson, Don Keefer, Brian Avery, Chris Forbes, Peter Hobbs, Susan Miller, Spencer Milligan, Lou Picetti, Jessica Rains, Stanley Ross, Marya Small.

(Rollins-Joffe Prods./United Artists, 88 min.)

The simplest measure of Sleeper's success is perhaps the fact that one recalls it not by quoting Allen's one-liners but by trying to describe—inadequately—his beautifully built visual gags.

—Richard Schickel, *Life*

1975

Love and Death

As producer, director, writer, actor.

Ph: Charles H. Joffe. *Dir and Sc:* Allen. *Ph:* Ghislain Cloquet. *Ed:* Ralph Rosenblum. *Art Dir:* Willy Holt. *Cos:* Gladys de Segonzac. *Music:* Sergei Prokofiev.

Cast: Allen, Diane Keaton, Harold Gould, Olga Georges-Picot, Zvee Scooler, Despo Diamantidou, Sol L. Frieder, Jessica Harper, Lloyd Battista, Alfred Lutter III.

(Rollins-Joffe Prods./United Artists, 85 min.)

Just as Sleeper anticipates the romantic format and cinematic inventiveness of Annie Hall, Love and Death anticipates Annie Hall's greater depth and, further down the road, the moral conflicts in Manhattan and Stardust Memories. As the last and best of Allen's clearly nonbiographical comedies, it also stands a bit apart from the rest of his work—profoundly commenting on a world unencumbered by the specific personalities and New York situations of the upcoming films.

—Diane Jacobs, *. . . but we need the eggs: The Magic of Woody Allen*

1976

The Front

As actor only.

Prod and Dir: Martin Ritt. *Sc:* Walter Bernstein. *Ph:* Michael Chapman. *Ed:* Sidney Levin. *Art Dir:* Charles Bailey. *Cos:* Ruth Morley. *Music:* Dave Grusin.

Cast: Allen, Zero Mostel, Herschel Bernardi, Michael Murphy, Andrea Marcovicci, Remak Ramsay, Marvin Lichterman, Joshua Shelley, Lloyd Gough.

(Rollins-Joffe Prods./Persky-Bright Prods./Columbia, 95 min.)

Much of the critical frustration stemmed from disappointment that the first film about the blacklist was not angrier and darker. Yet, despite its comic veneer, [Martin] Ritt's film is sharply satiric and damning of the witch hunters. Like a Pinter play, [Walter] Bernstein's script offers comedy with an edge, comedy whose element of whimsical fun abruptly gives way to a mood of foreboding and death. It effectively embodies a chaotic, upside-down cosmos wherein people's lives are ruined by the mere mention of their names and it is not necessary for charges to be substantiated.

—Gabriel Miller, *The Films of Martin Ritt*

1977

Annie Hall

As director, writer, actor.

Prod: Charles H. Joffe. *Dir:* Allen. *Sc:* Allen and Marshall Brickman. *Ph:* Gordon Willis. *Ed:* Ralph Rosenblum. *Art Dir:* Mel Bourne. *Cos:* Ruth Morley.

Cast: Allen, Diane Keaton, Tony Roberts, Carol Kane, Paul Simon, Shelley Duvall, Janet Margolin, Christopher Walken, Colleen Dewhurst, Mordecai Lawner, Donald Symington, Joan Newman, John Glover, Jonathan Monk, Russell Horton, Christine Jones, Mary Boylan, Marshall McLuhan.

(Rollins-Joffe Prods./United Artists, 93 min.)

[Keaton] took me by surprise. . . . She blossomed into something more than just another kooky dame—she put the finishing touches on a type, the anti-goddess, the golden shiksa from the provinces who looks cool and together, who looks as if she must have a date on Saturday night, but has only to open her mouth or gulp or dart spastically sideways to reveal herself as the insecure bungler she is, as complete a social disaster in her own way as Allen's horny West Side intellectual is in his. A fit of misfits, a pair of compatible insecurities, they are the romantic couple of the seventies.

—Molly Haskell, Film Forum

1978

Interiors

As director and writer.

Prod: Charles H. Joffe. *Dir:* Allen. *Sc:* Allen. *Ph:* Gordon Willis.

Ed: Ralph Rosenblum. *Prod Des:* Mel Bourne. *Cos:* Joel Schumacher.
Cast: Kristin Griffith, Mary Beth Hurt, Richard Jordan, Diane Keaton, E. G. Marshall, Geraldine Page, Maureen Stapleton, Sam Waterston.
(Rollins-Joffe Prods./United Artists, black and white, 92 min.)

The work of an artist whose potential we thought had been fully and satisfyingly realized in other kinds of films; with this one Woody Allen gives us the enormous excitement of seeing gifts in use that we never suspected he possessed.

—Alexander Walker, *The Evening Standard* (London)

1979

Manhattan

As director, writer, actor.

Prod: Charles H. Joffe. *Dir:* Allen. *Sc:* Allen and Marshall Brickman.
Ph: Gordon Willis. *Ed:* Susan E. Morse. *Prod Des:* Mel Bourne. *Cos:* Albert Wolsky.
Music: George Gershwin.
Cast: Allen, Diane Keaton, Michael Murphy, Mariel Hemingway, Meryl Streep, Anne Byrne, Karen Ludwig, Michael O'Donoghue, Gary Weis, Kenny Vance, Tisa Farrow, Damion Scheller, Wallace Shawn, Helen Hanft, Bella Abzug, Victor Truro.
(Rollins-Joffe Prods./United Artists, black and white, 96 min.)

This is, for Manhattan, a rave. Woody comes out of the stilted, militantly serious Interiors a refreshed man. Interiors turns out, as some suspected it might, to be a picture of hidden value, specifically, a picture with therapeutic value for the filmmaker, if not for the mass audience that got to know and love him in Annie Hall. Manhattan restores to us the anxious boy-man with the pleading eyes, sets him on his home turf and lets him roam free. The city has never been more appealing, nor has Woody Allen.

—Susan Stark, *Detroit News*

1980

Stardust Memories

As director, writer, actor.

Prod: Robert Greenhut. *Dir and Sc:* Allen. *Ph:* Gordon Willis. *Ed:* Susan E. Morse.
Prod Des: Mel Bourne. *Cos:* Santo Loquasto.
Cast: Allen, Charlotte Rampling, Jessica Harper, Marie-Christine Barrault, Tony Roberts, Helene Hanft, Daniel Stern, John Rothman, Amy Wright, Anne De Salvo, Gabrielle Strasun, David Lipman, Bob Maroff, Joan Neuman, Leonardo Cimino, Eli Mintz, Robert Munk.
(Rollins-Joffe Prods./United Artists, black and white, 88 min.)

Apparently the least liked of Woody Allen's comedies, this romp through the adulation that greets Allen's alter ego as a successful filmmaker seems less self-indulgent than acidly self-indicting: of Allen-by-any-other-name's solemnity, overwrought aspirations, romantic acquisitiveness and much else. He shoots his adulators and assorted sycophants down with him, but he remains his own most riddled target, allowing himself only (as in Manhattan) a moment of revealing tenderness and a wistfulness for genuine love. . . .

A brilliant, uncomfortable work.

—Charles Champlin, *Los Angeles Times*

1983

A Midsummer Night's Sex Comedy

As director, writer, actor.

Prod: Robert Greenhut. *Dir and Sc:* Allen. *Ph:* Gordon Willis. *Ed:* Susan E. Morse.
Prod Des: Mel Bourne. *Cos:* Santo Loquasto. *Music:* Felix Mendelssohn.
Cast: Allen, Mia Farrow, José Ferrer, Julie Hagerty, Tony Roberts, Mary Steenburgen.
(Rollins-Joffe Prods./Orion/Warner Bros., 88 min.)

> *Smiles of a Summer Night, Woody-Allen style; a quirky, entertaining diversion about sexual byplay among three couples on a summer weekend in the country circa 1900. Appealing cast (including [Mia] Farrow, in her first film with Woody), exquisite Gordon Willis photography.*
> —Leonard Maltin, *Leonard Maltin's Movie Guide*

1983

Zelig

As director, writer, actor.

Prod: Robert Greenhut. *Dir and Sc:* Allen. *Ph:* Gordon Willis. *Ed:* Susan E. Morse.
Prod Des: Mel Bourne. *Cos:* Santo Loquasto. *Music:* Dick Hyman.
Cast: Allen, Mia Farrow, John Buckwalter, Patrick Horgan (narrator), Garrett Brown, Stephanie Farrow, Willy Holt, Sol Lomita, John Rothman, Deborah Rush, Marianne Tatum, Mary Louise Wilson.
Interviews (as themselves): Susan Sontag, Irving Howe, Saul Bellow, Bricktop, Dr. Bruno Bettelheim, Professor John Morton Blum.
(Rollins-Joffe Prods./Orion/Warner Bros., black and white, 79 min.)

> *A brilliant cinematic collage that is pure magic, and allows Woody to satirize all sorts of things, from nostalgia, psychoanalysis, and the American Dream to critics, himself, and much more. . . . His Zelig is a romantic who desperately wants the supreme cocktail of realism mixed with glory—the Great Gatsby as schlemiel.*
> —Jack Kroll, *Newsweek*

1984

Broadway Danny Rose

As director, writer, actor.

Prod: Robert Greenhut. *Dir and Sc:* Allen. *Ph:* Gordon Willis. *Ed:* Susan E. Morse.
Prod Des: Mel Bourne. *Cos:* Jeffrey Kurland. *Music:* Dick Hyman. *Songs:* Nick Apollo Forte.
Cast: Allen, Mia Farrow, Nick Apollo Forte, Paul Greco, Craig Vandenburgh, Frank Renzulli, Herb Reynolds, Olga Barbuto, Gerald Schoenfeld, Edwin Bordo, Sandy Richman, Peter Castellotti, Gina DeAngeles, Milton Berle.
The Comics: Corbett Monica, Will Jordan, Howard Storm, Jackie Gayle, Morty Gunty, Jack Rollins, Sandy Baron.
(Rollins-Joffe Prods./Orion, black and white, 84 min.)

> *A delightful comedy that sees Allen as a no-hope theatrical agent (his clients include balloon twisters, wineglass players and bird trainers, who all leave him when the big time beckons) who acts as beard for an adulterous, unmusical crooner on his books, and gets involved with a brassy Mafia widow (Farrow, unrecognizable). The jokes are firmly*

embedded in plot and characterization, and the film, shot by Gordon Willis in harsh black-and-white, looks terrific; but what makes it work so well is the unsentimental warmth pervading every frame.
—GA, *TimeOut*

1985

The Purple Rose of Cairo
As director and writer.

Prod: Robert Greenhut. *Dir and Sc:* Allen. *Ph:* Gordon Willis. *Ed:* Susan E. Morse.
Prod Des: Stuart Wurtzel. *Cos:* Jeffrey Kurland. *Original Music:* Dick Hyman.
Cast: Mia Farrow, Jeff Daniels, Danny Aiello, Dianne Wiest, Van Johnson, Zoe Caldwell, John Wood, Milo O'Shea, Deborah Rush, Irving Metzman, John Rothman, Stephanie Farrow, Alexander H. Cohen, Camille Saviola, Karen Akers, Michael Tucker, Annie Joe Edwards, Peter McRobbie, Juliana Donald, Edward Herrmann.
(Rollins-Joffe Prods./Orion, 82 min.)

He continues to be the most innovative and most prolific American director at work today, tackling big themes in a comic way. While we're laughing at the chaos on and off the screen in New Jersey in Purple Rose, we're also contemplating the role of movies in our lives. Is it the function of movies to be solely a diversion from life? That's the way the film industry is running these days, but The Purple Rose of Cairo, in a very tricky and funny way, seems to be arguing otherwise.
—Gene Siskel, *Chicago Tribune*

1986

Hannah and Her Sisters
As director, writer, actor.

Prod: Robert Greenhut. *Dir and Sc:* Allen. *Ph:* Carlo Di Palma. *Ed:* Susan E. Morse.
Prod Des: Stuart Wurtzel. *Cos:* Jeffrey Kurland.
Cast: Allen, Michael Caine, Mia Farrow, Carrie Fisher, Barbara Hershey, Lloyd Nolan, Maureen O'Sullivan, Daniel Stern, Max von Sydow, Dianne Wiest, and Sam Waterston (uncredited).
(Rollins-Joffe Prods./Orion, 107 min.)

A great film, the richest and most complex of Woody's creations, and also the most fluent. The movie has some of the breathtaking swiftness and decisiveness of Truffaut's work, the mix of rigor and casualness, the exhilarating leaps across boundaries and categories.
—David Denby, *New York*

1987

Radio Days
As director, writer, actor (voice).

Prod: Robert Greenhut. *Dir and Sc:* Allen. *Ph:* Carlo Di Palma. *Ed:* Susan E. Morse.
Prod Des: Santo Loquasto. *Cos:* Jeffrey Kurland. *Music:* Dick Hyman.
Cast: Danny Aiello, Jeff Daniels, Mia Farrow, Seth Green, Robert Joy, Julie Kavner, Diane Keaton, Julie Kurnitz, Renee Lippin, Kenneth Mars, Josh Mostel, Tony Roberts, Wallace Shawn, Michael Tucker, David Warrilow, Dianne Wiest.
(Rollins-Joffe Prods./Orion, 88 min.)

This is one of those quiet films that cuts America open to the eye, and leaves you longing for those old days (like [The Magnificent] Ambersons). It's a masterpiece, a one of a kind.
—David Thomson, *"Have You Seen . . . ?"*

1987

September
As director and writer.

Prod: Robert Greenhut. *Dir and Sc:* Allen. *Ph:* Carlo Di Palma. *Ed:* Susan E. Morse.
Prod Des: Santo Loquasto. *Cos:* Jeffrey Kurland.
Cast: Denholm Elliott, Mia Farrow, Elaine Stritch, Dianne Wiest, Sam Waterston, Jack Warden.
(Rollins-Joffe Prods./Orion, 83 min.)

Chamber drama about smart, unhappy people chewing over their misspent lives in the last days of a Vermont summer. Everyone makes good entrances and wistful exits, but Allen left out the middle—the stuffing that would make it all matter. Still, it's not a bore, due to the crack cast.
—David Elliott, *San Diego Union*

1988

Another Woman
As director and writer.

Prod: Robert Greenhut. *Dir and Sc:* Allen. *Ph:* Sven Nykvist. *Ed:* Susan E. Morse.
Prod Des: Santo Loquasto. *Cos:* Jeffrey Kurland.
Cast: Philip Bosco, Betty Buckley, Blythe Danner, Sandy Dennis, Mia Farrow, Gene Hackman, Ian Holm, John Houseman, Martha Plimpton, Gena Rowlands, David Ogden Stiers, Harris Yulin.
(Rollins-Joffe Prod./Orion, 84 min.)

Like [Ingmar] Bergman, Allen luxuriates in examining characters stranded at the crossroads of emotion and intellect. In a Bergman movie, they could also be stuck on a cold island in an empty universe. Allen's world is warmer, more sentimental; his island is Manhattan, where at every intersection the possibility of hailing a cab at least offers a form of escape.
—Brian D. Johnson, *MacLean's*

1989

New York Stories ("Oedipus Wrecks" segment)
As director, writer, actor.

Prod: Robert Greenhut. *Dir and Sc:* Allen. *Ph:* Sven Nykvist. *Ed:* Susan E. Morse.
Prod Des: Santo Loquasto
Cast: Allen, Mia Farrow, Julie Kavner, Mae Questel.
(Rollins-Joffe Prods./Touchstone, 123 min.—"Oedipus Wrecks," 40 min.)

Woody's recent forays into solemnity haven't dimmed his comic timing a bit, and his acting seems to have acquired new subtleties. One long take, in which he discovers his heart's true desire while gazing at a chicken leg, achieves Chaplinesque grace. The ultimate Jewish-mama joke, "Oedipus Wrecks" takes that tired old riff to cosmically humiliating heights.
—David Ansen, *Newsweek*

1989

Crimes and Misdemeanors

As director, writer, actor.

Prod: Robert Greenhut. *Dir and Sc:* Allen. *Ph:* Sven Nykvist. *Ed:* Susan E. Morse.
Prod Des: Santo Loquasto. *Cos:* Jeffrey Kurland.
Cast: Allen, Caroline Aaron, Alan Alda, Claire Bloom, Mia Farrow, Joanna Gleason, Anjelica Huston, Martin Landau, Jenny Nichols, Jerry Orbach, Sam Waterston.
(Rollins-Joffe Prods./Orion, 104 min.)

One of the most important films of its era, this tragicomedy of contemporary New York has an almost biblical gravitas. An eminent eye surgeon stands to lose everything over a sexual indiscretion. An ethical documentary filmmaker is commissioned to cover the life of a cynical opportunist. If Allen's protagonists have been stranded in a world of compromise, nothing in his oeuvre prepared us for this angry indictment of contemporary moral relativity.

—Richard Armstrong, *The Rough Guide to Film*

1990

Alice

As director and writer.

Prod: Robert Greenhut. *Dir and Sc:* Allen. *Ph:* Carlo Di Palma. *Ed:* Susan E. Morse.
Prod Des: Santo Loquasto. *Cos:* Jeffrey Kurland.
Cast: Alec Baldwin, Blythe Danner, Judy Davis, Mia Farrow, William Hurt, Keye Luke, Joe Mantegna, Bernadette Peters, Cybill Shepherd, Gwen Verdon.
(Rollins-Joffe Prods./Orion, 106 min.)

It doesn't pump itself up with Bergmanesque pretensions. Still, if it's piffle, it's charming piffle. It has some of the same, tiny companionable pleasures as his short episode for New York Stories. Allen probably regards these movies as interludes between his real "serious" work. But working in a minor, throwaway mode brings out his comic side. The weightlessness gives his jests a real lift.

—Peter Rainer, *Los Angeles Times*

1991

Scenes from a Mall

As actor only.

Prod: Pato Gutzman, Patrick McCormick. *Prod and Dir:* Paul Mazursky.
Sc: Mazursky and Roger L. Simon. *Ph:* Fred Murphy. *Ed:* Stuart Pappé. *Prod Des:* Pato Guzman.
Cos: Albert Wolsky. *Music:* Marc Shaiman.
Cast: Allen, Bette Midler, Bill Irwin, Paul Mazursky, Fabio Lanzoni.
(Touchstone Pictures, 89 min.)

Allen becomes everything he fears and loathes as Nick Fifer, an LA sports lawyer with a ponytail, a beeper, and a perpetually ringing car phone. He's still Annie Hall's Alvy Singer on the inside, though, and his tart, neurotic New Yorker's soul shows through the aging yuppie. That's probably for the best, since Scenes is another outsize California joke, better—as usual—when delivered by an elitist from the East Coast.

—Rita Kempley, *Washington Post*

1992

Shadows and Fog
As director, writer, actor.

Prod: Robert Greenhut. *Dir:* Allen. *Sc:* Allen. *Ph:* Carlo Di Palma. *Ed:* Susan E. Morse.
Prod Des: Santo Loquasto. *Cos:* Jeffrey Kurland.
Cast: Allen, Kathy Bates, John Cusack, Mia Farrow, Jodie Foster, Fred Gwynne, Julie Kavner, Madonna, John Malkovich, Kenneth Mars, Kate Nelligan, Donald Pleasence, Lily Tomlin.
(Rollins-Joffe Prods./Orion, black and white, 85 min.)

A black-and-white throwback to early Allen with the little man, almost Chaplinesque, trying to survive in a world with which he cannot cope. Even his name, Kleinman, translates from the German or Yiddish as "little man." It's a film with considerable charm, lots of one-liners and a message delivered in a slow, steady manner.
—Joe Pollack, *St. Louis Post-Dispatch*

1992

Husbands and Wives
As director, writer, actor.

Prod: Robert Greenhut. *Dir and Sc:* Allen. *Ph*: Carlo Di Palma. *Ed:* Susan E. Morse.
Prod Des: Santo Loquasto. *Cos:* Jeffrey Kurland.
Cast: Allen, Blythe Danner, Judy Davis, Mia Farrow, Juliette Lewis, Liam Neeson, Sydney Pollack, Lysette Anthony, Cristi Conaway, Timothy Jerome, Ron Rifkin, Jerry Zaks, and Jeffrey Kurland (interviewer).
(Rollins-Joffe Prods./TriStar Pictures, 108 min.)

Unlike the guarded and remarkably unperceptive Woody Allen defending his behavior in Time magazine, Woody Allen the director and writer reveals an intimate knowledge and awareness of neurosis and human frailty. Mr. Allen in Time may seem like a jerk, but the artist behind Husbands and Wives is anything but. Maybe it's because as a director and writer Mr. Allen doesn't feel compelled to justify the behavior of his characters, just to try to understand it.
—Julie Salamon, *Wall Street Journal*

1993

Manhattan Murder Mystery
As director, writer, actor.

Prod: Robert Greenhut. *Dir:* Allen. *Sc:* Allen and Marshall Brickman. *Ph:* Carlo Di Palma.
Ed: Susan E. Morse. *Prod Des:* Santo Loquasto. *Cos:* Jeffrey Kurland.
Cast: Allen, Alan Alda, Anjelica Huston, Diane Keaton, Jerry Adler, Joy Behar, Ron Rifkin.
(Rollins-Joffe Prods./TriStar Pictures, 107 min.)

A must-see . . . for me, it's ample cause for breaking out a magnum of champagne. While the movie is no masterpiece, it represents both a significant (albeit tentative) advance in Allen's work as art and an agreeable (if uneven) return to his practice of "simply" entertaining.
—Jonathan Rosenbaum, *Chicago Reader*

1994

Bullets over Broadway
As director and writer.

Prod: Robert Greenhut. *Dir:* Allen. *Sc:* Allen and Douglas McGrath. *Ph:* Carlo Di Palma. *Ed:* Susan E. Morse. *Prod Des:* Santo Loquasto. *Cos:* Jeffrey Kurland.
Cast: Jim Broadbent, John Cusack, Harvey Fierstein, Chazz Palminteri, Mary-Louise Parker, Rob Reiner, Jennifer Tilly, Tracey Ullman, Joe Viterelli, Jack Warden, Dianne Wiest.
(Sweetland Films/Miramax, 99 min.)

The last few years saw Woody dragged through perils of his own—the press ambush, the bull-ring of the courts—with such force that you expected him to disappear forever, to grub a hole in the sand and stay here. And if he did come back, people asked, what kind of pictures would he make? Ibsen on the Hudson? A new Oresteia, only less funny? But no, we get Manhattan Murder Mystery and Bullets over Broadway: airy, unimportant, very slightly mad movies, neither bulging with gags nor straining on tiptoe to grab moral philosophy off the top shelf. They are the best—in retrospect, the only—reply he could have made.
—Anthony Lane, *New Yorker*

1994

Don't Drink the Water **(telefilm)**
As director, writer (based on his play), actor.

Prod: Robert Greenhut. *Dir and Sc:* Allen. *Ph:* Carlo Di Palma. *Ed:* Susan E. Morse. *Prod Des:* Santo Loquasto. *Cos:* Suzy Benzinger.
Cast: Allen, Mayim Bialik, Dom DeLuise, Michael J. Fox, Edward Herrmann, Julie Kavner.
(Sweetland Films/ABC, 92 min.)

Mr. Allen sets the plot in motion and keeps it spinning wackily. The dexterity of the principal players is matched flawlessly by the supporting cast. . . . Allen does a perfect take on his patented Everyman as harried whiner with a Bronx-Brooklyn accent. Here's a trip to the past very much worth taking.
—John J. O'Connor, *New York Times*

1995

Mighty Aphrodite
As director, writer, actor.

Prod: Robert Greenhut. *Dir and Sc:* Allen. *Ph:* Carlo Di Palma. *Ed:* Susan E. Morse. *Prod Des:* Santo Loquasto. *Cos:* Jeffrey Kurland.
Cast: Allen, F. Murray Abraham, Claire Bloom, Helena Bonham Carter, Olympia Dukakis, Michael Rapaport, Mira Sorvino, David Ogden Stiers, Jack Warden, Peter Weller.
(Sweetland Films/Miramax, 95 min.)

Mighty Aphrodite is unabashedly a fable, Woody Allen's sweet-tempered tale of romantic rescue. The movie features, at regular intervals, a Greek chorus—I mean an honest-to-God chorus of masked, choreographed chanters who comment on the proceedings from a mountaintop theater. The loftiness of these solemn observers is, of course, a joke (their commentary is salted with quaint anachronisms like "schmuck"). More than that, it's a sign that Woody Allen's filmmaking hasn't quite lost its preciousness.
—Owen Gleiberman, *Entertainment Weekly*

1996

Everyone Says I Love You
As director, writer, actor.

Prod: Robert Greenhut. *Dir and Sc:* Allen. *Ph:* Carlo Di Palma. *Ed:* Susan E. Morse.
Prod Des: Santo Loquasto. *Cos:* Jeffrey Kurland. *Music:* Dick Hyman.
Cast: Allen, Alan Alda, Drew Barrymore, Lukas Haas, Goldie Hawn, Gaby Hoffman, Natasha Lyonne, Edward Norton, Natalie Portman, Julia Roberts, Tim Roth, David Ogden Stiers.
(Sweetland Films/Miramax, 101 min.)

It's difficult not to be impressed by what Allen has achieved with this film: successfully reviving the musical comedy in such a thoroughly delightful fashion. The production may be uneven, but it's still wonderful to behold, even at the end, when the structure frays around the edges. Of course, the real force that makes Everyone Says I Love You work is Allen himself. As actor, director, and writer, he once again shows that he's willing to take chances. And, in doing so, he gives us a movie that is recognizable as both "a Woody Allen film" and something refreshingly different.
—James Berardinelli, ReelThoughts, RealViews.com

1996

The Sunshine Boys **(telefilm)**
As actor only.

Prod and Dir: John Erman. *Sc:* Neil Simon, based on his play. *Ph:* Tony Imi. *Ed:* Jack Wheeler.
Prod Des: Ben Edwards. *Cos:* Helen P. Butler. *Music:* Irwin Fisch.
Cast: Allen, Peter Falk, Michael McKean, Liev Schreiber, Edie Falco, Sarah Jessica Parker, and Whoopi Goldberg (uncredited).
(Hallmark Entertainment/CBS, 120 min.)

Allen does good work as the more stable half of the duo. Too bad the usually reliable Falk, who has substantially more screen time, made the decision to play his part in a grumpy-old-man voice that sounds as if it could have been overdubbed by Adam Sandler on a particularly lazy day.
—Keith Phipps, The AV Club (of *The Onion*)

1997

Deconstructing Harry
As director, writer, actor.

Prod: Jean Doumanian. *Dir:* Allen. *Sc:* Allen. *Ph:* Carlo Di Palma. *Ed:* Susan E. Morse.
Prod Des: Santo Loquasto. *Cos:* Suzy Benzinger.
Cast: Allen, Caroline Aaron, Kirstie Alley, Bob Balaban, Richard Benjamin, Eric Bogosian, Billy Crystal, Judy Davis, Hazelle Goodman, Mariel Hemingway, Amy Irving, Julie Kavner, Eric Lloyd, Julia Louis-Dreyfus, Tobey Maguire, Demi Moore, Elisabeth Shue, Stanley Tucci, Robin Williams.
(Sweetland Films/Fine Line Features, 96 min.)

Tabloid hell catapulted Woody Allen into his best, funniest, and angriest film in years. Raw and bitter, tinged with unwelcome wisdom, it recognizes the power of art to deliver salvation even as it also sinks to settling scores. As a fiction writer whose prose is his lethal weapon, Mr. Allen wins no popularity contests here but delivers a structurally sophisticated, newly imaginative recapitulation of his own most personal work.
—Janet Maslin, *New York Times*

1998

Wild Man Blues **(documentary)**
As himself.

Prod: Jean Doumanian. *Dir*: Barbara Kopple. *Ph*: Tom Hurwitz. *Ed:* Lawrence Silk. (Sweetland/Fine Line, 105 min.)

An invariably positive and endearing portrait. No doubt Allen saw it as an opportunity to restore his image. Or perhaps music does, indeed, soothe the savage breast. Certainly, his pleasure in performing music is genuine. In its surprisingly entertaining concert footage, the film justifies Allen's twenty-five-year Monday-night ritual of playing the clarinet with his band. . . . Before often appreciative, sometimes bewildered crowds, he and his cohort find new wrinkles in old chestnuts like the title Louis Armstrong number, and Allen seems truly liberated, his foot tapping, his riffs with the other musicians exuberant and witty.

—Peter Keough, *Boston Phoenix*

1998

Celebrity

As director and writer.

Prod: Jean Doumanian. *Dir and Sc:* Allen. *Ph:* Sven Nykvist. *Ed:* Susan E. Morse.
Prod Des: Santo Loquasto. *Cos:* Suzy Benzinger.
Cast: Hank Azaria, Kenneth Branagh, Judy Davis, Leonardo DiCaprio, Melanie Griffith, Famke Janssen, Michael Lerner, Joe Mantegna, Bebe Neuwirth, Winona Ryder, Charlize Theron.
(Sweetland/Miramax, black and white, 114 min.)

Celebrity is one of Woody Allen's finest. This is a minority opinion—most critics I know are put off by the film's shallow ease with itself, or nettled by [Kenneth] Branagh's unsettling mimicry of Woody Allen, fluttering hands, Brooklyn nasalness and all. But I prefer Allen when he works in a minor key—Broadway Danny Rose, Radio Days—precisely because he's not trying to be profound, only true to firsthand observation. In this, Branagh's demon-possession by the Allen persona feels indispensable, a snarl of self-critical honesty.

—F. X. Feeney, *LA Weekly*

1998

Antz

As actor only (voice).

Dir: Eric Darnell, Tim Johnson. *Sc:* Todd Alcott, Chris Weitz, Paul Weitz.
Cast: Allen, Dan Aykroyd, Anne Bancroft, Jane Curtin, Danny Glover, Gene Hackman, Jennifer Lopez, John Mahoney, Paul Mazursky, Grant Shaud, Sylvester Stallone, Sharon Stone, Christopher Walken.
(Pacific Data Images/DreamWorks, 83 min.)

Antz, with its deadpan witticisms, its heart-stopping shifts of perspective, is completely entertaining, a kids' movie that will leave grown-ups quoting the best lines to one another. The script has been fashioned for Woody Allen's personality, and Woody delivers the lines with his own peculiarly incisive petulance. He's a drone who whines: As a voice coming out of an ant, he's even more like Woody than he is speaking in his own body.

—David Denby, *New York*

1999

Sweet and Lowdown

As director, writer, actor (interview subject).

Prod: Jean Doumanian. *Dir and Sc:* Allen. *Ph:* Zhao Fei. *Ed:* Alisa Lepselter.
Prod Des: Santo Loquasto. *Cos:* Laura Cunningham Bauer. *Music:* Dick Hyman.
Cast: Allen, Anthony LaPaglia, Brian Markinson, Gretchen Mol, Samantha Morton, Sean Penn, Uma Thurman, James Urbaniak, John Waters.
(Sweetland/Sony Pictures, 95 min.)

Following the shapeless agitation of Celebrity, Woody Allen's cogent return to form in Sweet and Lowdown proves that he is fascinated less by celebrity and the noisy now, than by obscurity and the sublime mysteries of the forgotten. . . . [The film is] as simple and affecting as the title suggests—a series of anecdotes framed with commentary by jazz experts. But through this structure, Allen examines the difficulty of truly fathoming artists of the past, either through their work or through the stories told about them. The hard evidence about Emmet is in his recordings, while the catalogue of anecdotes about him is open to variation. . . . All the stories are equally valid in this patchwork of fragments, and the Emmy Ray legend becomes all the more concrete the less the gaps are filled in.

—Jonathan Romney, *Sight and Sound* (UK)

2000

Small Time Crooks

As director, writer, actor.

Prod: Jean Doumanian. *Dir and Sc:* Allen. *Ph:* Zhao Fei. *Ed:* Alisa Lepselter.
Prod Des: Santo Loquasto. *Cos:* Suzanne McCabe.
Cast: Allen, Tony Darrow, Hugh Grant, George Grizzard, Jon Lovitz, Elaine May, Michael Rapaport, Elaine Stritch, Tracey Ullman.
(Sweetland/DreamWorks, 95 min.)

Over the years, many people have expressed nostalgia for the early Allen comedies such as Take the Money and Run and Bananas, both of which had an unpretentious tossed-off quality. Crooks isn't exactly a parallel because, for one thing, the eye-filling colors from cinematographer Zhao Fei (Sweet and Lowdown) don't come from two minutes of setup time. But it's just close enough for the hardest of hard-core Allen fans to invest a short time (95 minutes) for some small-time amusement.

—Mike Clark, *USA Today*

2000

Picking Up the Pieces

As actor only.

Prod: Paul L. Sandberg. *Dir:* Alfonso Arau. *Sc:* Bill Wilson. *Ph:* Vittorio Storaro.
Ed: Michael R. Miller. *Prod Des:* Denise Pizzini. *Cos:* Marilyn Matthews. *Music:* Ruy Folguera.
Cast: Allen, Sharon Stone, Maria Grazia Cucinotta, Cheech Marin, David Schwimmer, Kiefer Sutherland, Alfonso Arau, Enrique Castillo, Danny de la Paz, Andy Dick, Fran Drescher, Joseph Gordon-Levitt, Elliott Gould, Eddie Griffin, Lou Diamond Phillips.
(Kushner-Locke/Cinemax, 95 min.)

Allen emerges relatively unscathed, spending most of the film muttering third-rate Allenisms to himself and his dog before recounting each of Pieces's easy ironies in a film-closing voice-over for those not paying attention.

—Nathan Rabin, The AV Club (of *The Onion*)

2000

Company Man

As actor only (unbilled).

Prod: Guy East, Rick Leed, John Penotti, James W. Skotchdopole. *Dir:* Peter Askin, Douglas McGrath. *Sc*: Askin and McGrath. *Ph:* Russell Boyd. *Ed:* Camilla Toniolo. *Prod Des:* Jane Musky. *Cos:* Ruth Myers. *Music:* David Lawrence.

Cast: Allen, Douglas McGrath, Sigourney Weaver, Ryan Phillippe, Denis Leary, John Turturro, Alan Cumming, Anthony LaPaglia.

(Film Foundry Partners/GreeneStreet Films/Intermedia Films/SKE Films/Paramount Classics, 95 min.)

Allen's part in Company Man might be Bananas's Fielding Mellish plus thirty years. Here, he's having a blast and he doesn't even care that it's in the low-down dirtiest of shames.

—Wesley Morris, *San Francisco Chronicle*

2001

The Curse of the Jade Scorpion

As director, writer, actor.

Prod: Letty Aronson. *Dir and Sc:* Allen. *Ph:* Zhao Fei. *Ed:* Alisa Lepselter.

Prod Des: Santo Loquasto. *Cos*: Suzanne McCabe.

Cast: Allen, Dan Ackroyd, Helen Hunt, Brian Markinson, Wallace Shawn, David Ogden Stiers, Charlize Theron, Elizabeth Berkley, Peter Gerety, John Schuck.

(Gravier-Perdido/DreamWorks-VCL, 102 Mins.)

It's a real charmer from a director who feels that a knockabout romantic farce doesn't have to be mindless. . . . Allen, as writer, director, and star, shrewdly plays for giggles in the style of one of his idols, Bob Hope (please note that Hope was older than Allen and still cracking wise with blondes in films such as 1972's Cancel My Reservation).

—Peter Travers, *Rolling Stone*

2002

Hollywood Ending

As director, writer, actor.

Prod: Letty Aronson. *Dir and Sc:* Allen. *Ph:* Wedigo von Schultzendorff. *Ed:* Alisa Lepselter. *Prod Des:* Santo Loquasto. *Cos:* Melissa Toth.

Cast: Allen, George Hamilton, Téa Leoni, Debra Messing, Mark Rydell, Treat Williams, Peter Gerety, Erica Leerhsen, Jodie Markell, Isaac Mizrahi, Marian Seldes, Aaron Stanford, Tiffani Thiessen, Mark Webber.

(Gravier-Perdido/DreamWorks-VCL, 112 min.)

It's not a masterpiece like Annie Hall, but that's not the way to think about it. Instead, imagine if this were Allen's first movie. Audiences and critics would be floored by the sheer funniness of the one-liners: "To me the best part of masturbation is afterward—the cuddling time." They'd also be impressed by the screenplay's heart and humanity, by the economy of storytelling and by the delightful ensemble cast. This is an excellent comedy.

—Mick LaSalle, *San Francisco Chronicle*

2003

Anything Else

As director, writer, actor.

Prod: Letty Aronson. *Dir and Sc:* Allen. *Ph:* Darius Khondji. *Ed:* Alisa Lepselter. *Prod Des:* Santo Loquasto. *Cos:* Laura Jean Shannon.

Cast: Allen, Jason Biggs, Stockard Channing, Danny DeVito, Jimmy Fallon, Christina Ricci, Anthony Arkin, David Conrad, Adrian Grenier, William Hill, Erica Leerhsen, Fisher Stevens, Joseph Lyle Taylor.

(Gravier-Perdido/DreamWorks, 107 min.)

The movie avoids the usual pitfalls of comedies about young romance and gets jolts from the supporting work by Channing and DeVito. And Allen is inimitable as the worrywart who backs into every decision, protesting and moaning about the pitfalls and certain disappointment sure to lie ahead. At a time when so many American movies keep dialogue at a minimum so they can play better overseas, what a delight to listen to smart people whose conversation is like a kind of comic music.

—Roger Ebert, *Chicago Sun-Times*

2004

Melinda and Melinda

As director and writer.

Prod: Letty Aronson. *Dir and Sc:* Allen. *Ph:* Vilmos Zsigmond. *Ed:* Alisa Lepselter. *Prod Des:* Santo Loquasto. *Cos:* Judy Ruskin Howell.

Cast: Chiwetel Ejiofor, Will Ferrell, Jonny Lee Miller, Radha Mitchell, Amanda Peet, Chloë Sevigny, Wallace Shawn, David Aaron Baker, Arija Bareikis, Josh Brolin, Steve Carrell, Stephanie Roth Haberle, Shalom Harlow, Geoffrey Nauffts, Zak Orth, Larry Pine, Vinessa Shaw, Brooke Smith, Daniel Sunjata.

(Gravier/Fox Searchlight, 99 min.)

Happy proof that news of Allen's artistic death has been much exaggerated. . . . Like many of his films, it's about storytelling and how it is done. A bunch of friends are at dinner in a Manhattan bistro, mulling over the Janus-faced state of the human condition. Should we think of life as fundamentally tragic or inescapably comic? This is a question so close to the director's heart that it is as if he's hovering over the scene, arguing with the other side of his face—Allen the humorist in dispute with the one who brought us Interiors and Crimes and Misdemeanors.

—Sandra Hall, *Sydney Morning Herald* (Australia)

2005

Match Point

As director and writer.

Prod: Letty Aronson, Lucy Darwin, Gareth Wiley. *Dir and Sc:* Allen. *Ph:* Remi Adefarasin. *Ed:* Alisa Lepselter. *Prod Des:* Jim Clay. *Cos:* Jill Taylor.

Cast: Brian Cox, Matthew Goode, Scarlett Johansson, Emily Mortimer, Jonathan Rhys Meyers, Penelope Wilton, Ewen Bremner, James Nesbitt, Rupert Penry-Jones.

(Jada/BBC Films/Thema Prod. SA/DreamWorks, 124 min.)

Match Point is Woody Allen's best picture in more than a decade—an excellent character piece/social study that evolves into a suspense thriller with an O. Henry twist. Though there are clearly some parallels with Crimes and Misdemeanors and even Hannah and Her Sisters, Match Point doesn't mark the return of the "old" Woody Allen. The London air must have done something for the veteran filmmaker, because this is an entirely new voice. If his name weren't in the credits, critics would be raving about a stimulating newcomer with a distinctive style.

—Eleanor Ringel, *Atlanta Journal-Constitution*

2006

Scoop

As director, writer, actor.

Prod: Letty Aronson, Gareth Wiley. *Dir:* Allen. *Sc:* Allen. *Ph:* Remi Adefarasin. *Ed:* Alisa Lepselter. *Prod Des:* Maria Djurkovic. *Cos:* Jill Taylor.

Cast: Allen, Hugh Jackman, Scarlett Johansson, Ian McShane, Charles Dance, Romola Garai, Kevin R. McNally.

(Jelly Roll Prod./BBC Films/Ingenious/Focus Features, 96 min.)

It is something like Allen's exuberant last hurrah as a topflight tummler, but it's much more: a comedy about death, about an old man contemplating his own death—as well as a sombre view of an old man's relationship with a young person and the self-sacrifice it will demand of the man if the young person is going to get anything out of it. As such, it goes far beyond its comic effervescence to become deeply moving and just plain deep.

—Richard Brody, *New Yorker*

2007

Cassandra's Dream

As director and writer.

Prod: Letty Aronson, Stephen Tenenbaum, Gareth Wiley. *Dir:* Allen. *Sc:* Allen. *Ph:* Vilmos Zsigmond. *Ed:* Alisa Lepselter. *Prod Des:* Maria Djurkovic. *Cos:* Jill Taylor. *Music:* Philip Glass.

Cast: Hayley Atwell, Colin Farrell, Sally Hawkins, Ewan McGregor, Tom Wilkinson, John Benfield, Phil Davis, Clare Higgins.

(Iberville Prod./The Weinstein Company, 109 min.)

Allen's approach to his material is casual. No jokes, puns, or humorous asides. No heavy forays into grave, metaphysical exposition. It's a laid-back style that might disarm or annoy Allen fans, but aside from a rather harried ending, I found Cassandra's Dream to be a pleasure and a treat, the effect being not unlike the experience of sitting down with a decent crime novel; in this case, one in which we can put ourselves in the places of two regular guys suddenly faced with a life-altering decision. It's not Dostoyevsky, but neither is it a shopworn trifle. It is, if you will excuse the literary metaphor, a good read.

—Dan DiNicola, *Schenectady Daily Gazette* (New York)

2008

Vicky Cristina Barcelona

As director and writer.

Prod: Letty Aronson, Stephen Tenenbaum, Gareth Wiley. *Dir and Sc:* Allen. *Ph:* Javier Aguirresarobe. *Ed:* Alisa Lepselter. *Prod Des:* Alain Bainée. *Cos:* Sonia Grande.

Cast: Javier Bardem, Patricia Clarkson, Penélope Cruz, Kevin Dunn, Rebecca Hall, Scarlett Johansson, Chris Messina, Zak Orth, Carrie Preston, Pablo Schreiber, Josep Maria Domènech, and Christopher Evan Welch (narrator).
(Gravier-Dumaine/MediaPro/The Weinstein Company, 97 min.)

Rather than fault Allen for blatantly eschewing a realism that I don't think was ever on his agenda to begin with, I think there's something interesting about the falseness of it all—the unnecessary, didactic narration, the cliché personalities crashing into one another, and the very, very minor fissures that result. His point is taken: nothing ultimately, means anything, but in the moment, we forget that, and become convinced that inconsequential matters mean the world. Vicky Cristina Barcelona may be frivolous, but under the surface there's a serious pondering of how the most frivolous things can temporarily cloud brains and hold otherwise reasonable people hostage, of how even a momentary giving over to impulse can slip an unignorable pea under the mattress of the best-laid plans, of how sometimes functioning façades are shattered by a single slip of judgment over the course of a single night.
—Karina Longworth, *SpoutBlog*

2009

Whatever Works
As director and writer.

Prod: Letty Aronson, Stephen Tenenbaum. *Dir and Sc*: Allen. *Ph:* Harris Savides. *Ed:* Alisa Lepselter. *Prod Des:* Santo Loquasto. *Cos:* Suzy Benzinger.
Cast: Ed Begley Jr., Patricia Clarkson, Larry David, Conleth Hill, Michael McKean, Evan Rachel Wood, Henry Cavill, John Gallagher Jr., Jessica Hecht, Carolyn McCormick, Christopher Evan Welch.
(Gravier–Perdido–Wild Bunch/Sony Pictures Classics, 93 min.)

A very funny Woody Allen movie about things that many—all right, most—of Allen's movies are about: the fear of death, the vagaries of love, the transformative power of New York City, and the crucial role played by chance, luck, and magic in the human condition, which is not, in Allen's movies as on earth, an enviable state. Doomed, blind, groping through a deadpan, godless, amoral cosmos, lust-driven, fear-riddled witnesses to—and perpetrators of—every manner of betrayal on our merry way to eternal oblivion. Wonderful stuff, and I truly don't know why his movies don't sell more tickets. But that's me—I love schmaltz herring, too.
—Scott Raab, *Esquire*

2010

You Will Meet a Tall Dark Stranger
As director and writer.

Prod: Letty Aronson, Stephen Tenenbaum, Jaume Roures. *Dir and Sc:* Allen. *Ph:* Vilmos Zsigmond.
Ed: Alisa Lepselter. *Prod Des:* Jim Clay. *Cos:* Beatrix Aruna Pasztor.
Cast: Antonio Banderas, Josh Brolin, Anthony Hopkins, Gemma Jones, Freida Pinto, Lucy Punch, Naomi Watts.
(Gravier/Versátil Cinema/MediaPro/Sony Pictures Classics, 99 min.)

A low-key ensemble dramedy set in London, it has familiar late Allen flaws: it can be contrived, sometimes odd-sounding, like a New York script from his seventies/eighties heyday uncertainly translated into what the author imagines to be a modern British idiom. Yet it is also inventive, persistently diverting, speckled with ideas. Line by line, scene by scene, I always found something there to hold the attention. It is never boring.

—Peter Bradshaw, *The Guardian*

2011

Midnight in Paris

As director and writer.

Prod: Letty Aronson, Stephen Tenenbaum, Jaume Roures. *Dir and Sc:* Allen. *Ph:* Darius Khondji.

Ed: Alisa Lepselter. *Prod Des:* Anne Seibel. *Cos:* Sonia Grande.

Cast: Kathy Bates, Adrien Brody, Carla Bruni, Marion Cotillard, Rachel McAdams, Michael Sheen, Owen Wilson, Nina Arianda, Kurt Fuller, Tom Hiddleston, Mimi Kennedy, Alison Pill, Léa Seydoux, Corey Stoll.

(Gravier/Versátil Cinema/MediaPro/Sony Pictures Classics, 94 min.)

With its four-star cast, the postcard vision of Paris, the bright and shimmering photography of Darius Khondji and the music by Sidney Bechet that sets the pace for the film, Midnight in Paris turns out to be a funny, moving, intelligent film, imbued with a magic specific to the director with round glasses.

—Sabrina Piazzi, DvDFR.com (France)

2012

To Rome with Love

As director, writer, actor.

Prod: Letty Aronson, Stephen Tenenbaum, Giampaolo Letta, Faruk Alatan.

Dir and Sc: Allen. *Ph:* Darius Khondji. *Ed:* Alisa Lepselter. *Prod Des:* Anne Seibel.

Cos: Sonia Grande.

Cast: Allen, Alec Baldwin, Roberto Benigni, Penélope Cruz, Judy Davis, Greta Gerwig, Ellen Page, Antonio Albanese, Fabio Armiliato, Alessandra Mastronardi, Ornella Muti, Flavio Parenti, Alison Pill, Riccardo Scamarcio, Alessandro Tiberi.

(Gravier-Perdido/Medusa/Sony Pictures Classics, 112 min.)

Woody Allen's latest love letter to Europe doesn't have the charm of Midnight in Paris, or the sizzle of Vicky Cristina Barcelona, but there are worse places to spend your time than Rome. Silly and sentimental, the film follows natives and tourists, among them Roberto Benigni's suddenly famous office drone, Cruz's happy hooker, and Baldwin's wry architect, who gives life lessons to a young man (Jesse Eisenberg) not unlike himself. Since Rome is the Eternal City, Allen toys with time, the overlapping stories lasting days or just hours. The results are amusing, if sloppy.

—Alynda Wheat, *People*

2013

Blue Jasmine

As director and writer.

Prod: Letty Aronson, Stephen Tenenbaum, Edward Walson. *Dir and Sc:* Allen. *Ph:* Javier Aguirresarobe. *Ed:* Alisa Lepselter. *Prod Des:* Santo Loquasto. *Cos:* Suzy Benzinger.

Cast: Alec Baldwin, Cate Blanchett, Louis C.K., Bobby Cannavale, Andrew Dice Clay, Sally Hawkins, Peter Sarsgaard, Michael Stuhlbarg.

(Gravier-Perdido/Sony Pictures Classics, 98 min.)

Blue Jasmine is brilliant. It's brilliantly written, directed, and observed; it's brilliantly watchable, if not mesmerising; and brilliantly performed, particularly by Cate Blanchett, who will knock your socks off, and may knock them off so explosively there is every chance you will never retrieve them again. (They might be knocked off all the way to kingdom come, for example.) This is possibly a return to form, now I think about it, although whether it's a return to form from having been off-form or not off-form exactly, just sliding from form, and not yet halfway down, I really couldn't say. So many "forms." Hard to keep track.

—Deborah Ross, *The Spectator* (UK)

2014

Fading Gigolo

As actor only.

Prod: Jeffrey Kusama-Hinte, Bill Block, Paul Hanson. *Dir and Sc:* John Turturro.
Ph: Marco Pontecorvo. *Prod Des:* Lester Cohen. *Cos:* Donna Zakowska.
Cast: Allen, John Turturro, Vanessa Paradis, Liev Schreiber, Sharon Stone, Sofía Vergara, Tonya Pinkins, M'Barka Ben Taleb.
(Millennium Entertainment, 90 min.)

Fading Gigolo isn't without the odd perk. It gives us Woody Allen, in his frail body but with the energy of a thirty-year-old. He is unusually relaxed and has great chemistry with Turturro. The film is at its funniest outside of the weak plot. Watching the duo niggle and discuss their unconventional business venture makes for pleasant viewing.

—Hannah McHaffie, Unsung Films

Magic in the Moonlight

As director and writer.

Prod: Letty Aronson, Stephen Tenenbaum, Edward Walson. *Dir and Sc:* Allen. *Ph:* Darius Khondji. *Ed:* Alisa Lepselter. *Prod Des:* Anne Seibel. *Cos:* Sonia Grande.
Cast: Eileen Atkins, Colin Firth, Marcia Gay Harden, Hamish Linklater, Simon McBurney, Emma Stone, Jacki Weaver,
(Gravier-Perdido/Dippermouth/Sony Pictures Classics, 97 min.)

The central suggestion throughout Magic in the Moonlight is that letting go of pessimism and caution can bring happiness. Yet this notion is not forced upon us, nor does it teach us a lesson. [The film] offers philosophical ponderings, romantic declarations, and a plot twist to keep everyone guessing. Woody Allen succeeds in providing yet another endlessly enjoyable comedy, and while it may not win any awards, or be his best work, the sheer enchantment of it all makes this romantic comedy well worth a watch.

—Jen Grimble, *On: Yorkshire Magazine* (UK)

2015

Irrational Man

As director and writer.

Prod: Letty Aronson, Stephen Tenenbaum, Edward Walson. *Dir and Sc:* Allen. *Ph:* Darius Khondji.
Ed: Alisa Lepselter. *Prod Des:* Santo Loquasto. *Cos:* Suzy Benzinger.
Cast: Jamie Blackley, Joaquin Phoenix, Parker Posey, Emma Stone, Betsy Aidem, Ethan Phillips.
(Gravier-Perdido/Sony Pictures Classics, 95 min.)

I'm happy to report that Irrational Man is a delight (although, I should note, a good number of film critics disagree with my assessment). This new film finds Woody Allen working in the mode of Match Point and Crimes and Misdemeanors, previous films he's made about committing a perfect murder. Like those films, Irrational Man is a drama with comic underpinnings, in which existential ruminations abound. Since the protagonist Abe Lucas (Phoenix) is a college philosophy professor and author, the character's discussions of Kant and Kierkegaard make contextual sense, rather than seeming like academic asides.

—Marjorie Baumgarten, *Austin Chronicle*

2016

Café Society
As director, writer, and actor (voice).

Prod: Letty Aronson, Stephen Tenenbaum, Edward Walson. *Dir and Sc:* Allen. *Ph:* Vittorio Storaro. *Ed:* Alisa Lepselter. *Prod Des:* Santo Loquasto. *Cos:* Suzy Benzinger.
Cast: Allen, Jeannie Berlin, Steve Carrell, Jesse Eisenberg, Blake Lively, Parker Posey, Kristen Stewart, Corey Stoll, Ken Stott, Anna Camp, Stephen Kunken, Sari Lennick, Paul Schneider.
(Gravier-Perdido/Lionsgate/Amazon Studios, 96 min.)

Excelsior! In Café Society, Woody Allen returns to his favorite setting—the past—and emerges triumphant. He does that a lot, squeezing fabulous music, breathtaking scenery, and nostalgic charm out of Paris, Rome, London, Barcelona, and even Queens. But Hollywood is uncharted territory—a place that has always eluded, disoriented, challenged, and intimidated him. Until now. Romantic, bittersweet, and funny as hell, Café Society turns Hollywood inside out, rooting through the superficial tinsel to find the real tinsel. You go away gobsmacked, beaming and happy to be both.

—Rex Reed, *New York Observer*

2016

Crisis in Six Scenes **(cable television miniseries)**
As director, writer, actor.

Prod: Erika Aronson, Helen Robin. *Dir and Sc:* Allen. *Ph:* Eigil Bryld. *Ed:* Alisa Lepselter. *Prod Des:* Carl Sprague. *Cos:* Suzy Benzinger.
Cast: Allen, Elaine May, Miley Cyrus, John Magaro, Rachel Brosnahan, Joy Behar, Mary Boyer, Marylouise Burke, Margaret Goodman, Julie Halston, Sondra James, Margaret Ladd, Rebecca Schull, Mary Shultz, Barbara Singer, Lewis Black, Douglas McGrath, Tom Kemp, Michael Rapaport.
(Amazon Studios, six 23-minute episodes)

There is, of course, the slight stiffness and stodginess that's crept into Allen's filmmaking of late, a half-theatrically stilted, half-literary dustbin approach in which exposition is a little too plainly displayed and some zingers come wheezing to the punchline. But even when the writing gets a tad stale, the cast is so energetic and pleasantly amusing, it coasts along on comfortable charms and relaxed charisma. Allen is the quintessential Allen type, May is totally at ease playing the slightly frazzled upper-middle-class pseudo-intellectual (her comfort zone since her Nichols and May days), and Cyrus is just the right young, earnest, half-idealistic/half-cynical goof to send them spinning.

—Benjamin Kramer, The Voracious Filmgoer

2017

Wonder Wheel

As director and writer.

Prod: Letty Aronson, Erika Aronson, Edward Walson. *Dir and Sc:* Allen. *Ph:* Vittorio Storaro.

Ed: Alisa Lepselter. *Prod Des:* Santo Loquasto. *Cos:* Suzy Benzinger.

Cast: Jim Belushi, Juno Temple, Justin Timberlake, Kate Winslet, Max Casella, Jack Gore, David Krumholtz.

(Gravier-Perdido/Amazon Studios, 111 min.)

This film is worth watching for Vittorio Storaro's candy colored, sunlit orange photography and the period costumes alone. Woody Allen's crowded claustrophobic Coney Island and the wonder wheel become oppressive despite their beauty. Altogether there's something almost Sirkian and expressionist about the way this film is shot that matches Ginny's [Winslet] conception of herself as being in a melodrama.

—Bina007 Movie Reviews (Caterina Benincasa), www.bina007.com

2019

A Rainy Day in New York

As director and writer.

Prod: Letty Aronson, Erika Aronson. *Dir and Sc:* Allen. *Ph:* Vittorio Storaro. *Ed:* Alisa Lepselter. *Prod Des:* Santo Loquasto. *Cos:* Suzy Benzinger.

Cast: Timothée Chalamet, Elle Fanning, Selena Gomez, Jude Law, Diego Luna, Liev Schreiber, Annaleigh Ashford, Rebecca Hall, Cherry Jones, Will Rogers, Kelly Rohrbach.

(Gravier-Perdido/MPI Media Group, 93 min.)

Don't judge—just see this film. All his classic comedy of confusion touches are intact, as good as any of them, Annie Hall, Vicky Cristina Barcelona, Blue Jasmine, etc. It's charming throughout. Brilliant writing and casting.

—Oliver Stone on X

2020

Rifkin's Festival

As director and writer.

Prod: Erika Aronson, Letty Aronson, Jaume Roures. *Dir and Sc:* Allen. *Ph:* Vittorio Storaro.

Ed: Alisa Lepselter. *Prod Des:* Alain Bainée. *Cos:* Sonia Grande. *Music:* Stephane Wrembel.

Cast: Wallace Shawn, Elena Anaya, Michael Garvey, Gina Gershon, Louis Garrel, Christoph Waltz, Sergi Lopéz, Richard Kind, Steve Guttenberg, Douglas McGrath.

(Gravier-Perdido/Wildside/Orange/Televisió de Catalunya/MediaPro, 88 min.).

A trenchant, absurd, fantastically funny comedy that is on its face improbable but altogether winning. Almost from the very beginning of this story about an unhappy couple who travel to the very same San Sebastian Festival [where the film was premiered] you are laughing from down deep. And of course, all the big Woody themes are in place: Why are we here? What's the meaning of life? And what about death?

—Roger Friedman, Showbiz411.com

2023

Coup de chance
As director and writer.

Prod: Letty Aronson, Erika Aronson, Helen Robin, Raphaël Benoliel. *Dir and Sc:* Allen. *Ph:* Vittorio Storaro. *Ed:* Alisa Lepselter. *Prod Des:* Véronique Melery. *Cos:* Sonia Grande.
Cast: Lou de Laâge, Melville Poupaud, Niels Schneider, Elsa Zylberstein, Valérie Lemercier, Sara Martins, Bárbara Goenaga, Grégory Gadebois, William Nadylam, Arnaud Viard, Guillaume de Tonquédec, Yannick Choirat, Jeanne Bournaud, Anne Loiret, Emilie Incerti-Formentini, Philippe Uchan, Sâm Mirhosseini, Benoît Forgeard.
(Gravier/Perdido/Dippermouth/Petit Fleur, 93 min.)

How Allen continues to conduct his career is obviously his business alone. But if he were ever minded to collect his winnings and quit the table, his fiftieth feature might be a decent film to go out on. Coup de chance is variously funny and sad, energetic and easygoing; a stumbling but satisfying autumnal drama that wanders amid the fading light and the golden leaves. For good measure, Allen even throws in an ending which stirs the memory of the classic moose-hunting routine from his old 1960s standup days, a rueful, airy aside that serves to bring the man's career full circle.

—Xan Brooks, *The Guardian*

Index

About the Author

Patrick McGilligan is the author of *Funny Man: Mel Brooks*; *Young Orson: The Years of Luck and Genius on the Path to* Citizen Kane; *Alfred Hitchcock: A Life in Darkness and Light*; *Fritz Lang: The Nature of the Beast*; *George Cukor: A Double Life*; and biographies of Nicholas Ray, Robert Altman, Oscar Micheaux, Jack Nicholson, and Clint Eastwood, among other books. His books have been translated into a dozen foreign languages. He lives in Milwaukee, Wisconsin.